Wendell F. Combs 6-80

From: Springfield First F.W.B.

THE
BIBLE COMMENTARY

F. C. COOK, *Editor*

ABRIDGED AND EDITED
BY J. M. FULLER

EXODUS—RUTH

BAKER BOOK HOUSE
Grand Rapids, Michigan

Library of Congress Catalog Card Number: 55-11630

ISBN: 0-8010-0503-5

First printing, January 1953
Second printing, January 1957
Third printing, January 1959
Fourth printing, October 1960
Fifth printing, February 1962
Sixth printing, January 1964
Seventh printing, December 1965
Eighth printing, September 1967
Ninth printing, April 1969
Tenth printing, July 1970
Eleventh printing, October 1971
Twelfth printing, December 1973
Thirteenth printing, February 1975
Fourteenth printing, November 1976
Fifteenth printing, January 1977
Sixteenth printing, June 1978
Seventeenth printing, August 1979

PHOTOLITHOPRINTED BY CUSHING - MALLOY, INC.
ANN ARBOR, MICHIGAN, UNITED STATES OF AMERICA
1979

EXODUS.

INTRODUCTION.

1. THE book of Exodus consists of two distinct portions. The first (cc. i.—xix.) gives a detailed account of the circumstances under which the deliverance of the Israelites was accomplished. The second (cc. xx.—xl.) describes the giving of the law, and the institutions which completed the organization of the people as "a kingdom of priests, and an holy nation," xix. 6.

The name Exodus, *i. e.* "the going forth," assigned to it by the Alexandrian Jews, applies rather to the former portion than to the whole book.

The narrative is closely connected with that of Genesis, and shews not only that it was written by the same author, but that it formed part of one general plan. Still it is a distinct section; the first events which it relates are separated from the last chapter in Genesis by a considerable interval, and it presents the people of Israel under totally different circumstances. Its termination is marked with equal distinctness, winding up with the completion of the Tabernacle.

The book is divided into many smaller sections; each of which has the marks which throughout the Pentateuch indicate a subdivision. They are of different lengths, and were probably written on separate parchments or papyri, the longest not exceeding the dimensions of contemporary documents in Egypt. They were apparently thus arranged for the convenience of public reading.[1]

This general view of the structure of the book is what might have been expected.

2. Some of the most convincing evidences of the Mosaic authorship are supplied by the contents of this book.

One argument is drawn from the representation of the personal character and qualifications of Moses, a representation perfectly intelligible as proceeding from Moses himself.

What other men have seen in Moses is—the chief agent in the greatest work ever intrusted to man, an agent whose peculiar and unparalleled qualifications are admitted alike by those who accept and by those who deny the Divine interposition: what the writer himself sees in Moses is—a man whose only qualification is an involuntary and reluctant surrender to the will of God. The only rational account of the matter is, that we have Moses' own history of himself and of his work.

Another argument rests on external facts. The book of Exodus

[1] The narrative portion of the book (cc. i.—xix.) is composed of the following sections: An Introduction. i. 1-7.; (*a*) i. 8. & ii.; (*b*) iii. 1—vi. 1; (*c*) vi. 2-27; (*d*) vi. 28—xi. end; (*e*) xii. 1-42; (*f*) xii. 43—xiii. 16; (*g*) xiii. 17—xiv. end; (*h*) xv.; (*i*) xvi.—xix.

could not have been written by any man who had not passed many years in Egypt, and who had not also a thorough knowledge, such as could only be acquired by personal observation, of the Sinaitic Peninsula.

We have no probable alternative but to admit that the narrative in its substance came from Moses, or from a contemporary; and we can have little hesitation as to our choice between these alternatives, when we consider that none of the contemporaries of Moses had equal opportunities of observation, and that none were likely to have received the education and training which would have enabled them to record the events.

3. A weighty argument is drawn from the accounts of the miracles, by which Moses was expressly bidden to attest his mission, and by which he was enabled to accomplish the deliverance of his people.

We have throughout the miracles the characteristics of local colouring, of adaptation to the circumstances of the Israelites, and of repeated announcements followed by repeated postponements, which enabled and indeed compelled the Israelites to complete that organization of their nation, without which their departure might have been, as it has been often represented, a mere disorderly flight.

There are some who fear to compromise the miraculous character of events by admitting any operation of natural causes to a share of them. Yet the inspired writer does not fail to record that it was by the east wind that the Lord brought the locusts (Exod. x. 13) and sent back the sea (xiv. 21), and by the mighty strong west wind (x. 19) took back the plague that he had sent. Nor is the miracle at all lessened, because the winds of heaven were made God's messengers and instruments in the doing it. The miracles in Egypt were supernatural in their greatness, in their concentration upon one period, in their coming and going according to the phases of the conflict between the tyrant and the captive race, in their measured gradation from weak to strong, as each weaker wonder failed to break the stubborn heart. King and people so regarded them; they were accustomed perhaps to frogs and lice and locusts; but to such plagues, so intense, so threatened, accomplished, and withdrawn, as it were so disciplined to a will, they were not accustomed; and they rightly saw them as miraculous and divinely sent. And further it will be noticed that the phenomena that are put to this use are such as mark the country where this great history is laid. No Jewish writer, who had lived in Palestine alone, could have imagined a narrative so Egyptian in its marks. All evidence tends to prove that the history was written by some one well conversant with Egypt; and we shall look in vain for any one, other than Moses himself, who possessed this qualification for writing under divine guidance the history of the emancipation of the Israelites.

The narrative which records them, remarkable as it is for artlessness and simplicity, is moreover not one which could have been concocted from documents of different ages, constructed on different principles, and full of internal discrepancies and contradictions. It is the production of one mind, written by one man, and by one who had alone witnessed all the events which it records, who alone was at that time likely to possess the knowledge or ability required to write the account.

4. The portion of the book, which follows the account of the departure from Egypt, has characteristics marked with equal distinctness, and bearing with no less force upon the question of authorship. These chapters also are pervaded by a peculiar tone, a local colouring, an atmosphere so to speak of the desert, which has made itself felt by all those who have explored the country.

Modern travellers point out the following coincidences between the narrative and their own experiences. Absence of water where no sources now exist, abundance of water where fountains are still found, and indications of a far more copious supply in former ages; tracts, occupying the same time in the journey, in which food would not be found; and in some districts a natural production similar to manna, most abundant in rainy seasons (such as several notices shew the season of the Exodus to have been), but not sufficient for nourishment, nor fit for large consumption, without such modifications in character and quantity as are attributed in the narrative to a divine intervention. The late explorations of the Peninsula of Sinai have thrown much light upon the fact that the route taken by the Israelites was probably determined by conditions agreeing with incidental notices in the history; and when we come to the chapters in which the central event in the history of Israel, the delivery of God's law, is recorded, we find localities and scenery which travellers concur in declaring to be such as fully correspond to the exigencies of the narrative, and which in some accounts (remarkable at once for scientific accuracy and graphic power) are described in terms which shew they correspond, so far as mere outward accessories can correspond, to the grandeur of the manifestation.

5. A very valuable argument of the same evidential character is drawn from the account of the Tabernacle. In form, structure, and materials the tabernacle belongs altogether to the wilderness. The whole was a tent, not a fixed structure, such as would naturally have been set up, and in point of fact was very soon set up, in Palestine. The metals, bronze, silver and gold, were those which the Israelites knew, and doubtless brought with them from Egypt; the names of many of the materials and implements which they used, and the furniture and accessories of the tabernacle, the dress and ornaments of the priests, are Egyptian; and it is also certain that the arts required for the construction of the tabernacle, and for all its accessories, were precisely those for which the Egyptians had been remarkable for ages; such as artizans who had lived under the influence of Egyptian civilization would naturally have learned.

Two separate accounts of the erection of the Tabernacle are given. In the first Moses relates the instructions which he received, in the second he describes the accomplishment of the work. Nothing would be less in accordance with the natural order of a history written at a later period than this double account. It is however fully accounted for by the obvious hypothesis that each part of the narrative was written at the time, and on the occasion, to which it immediately refers.

6. The Chronology of Exodus involves two questions, the duration of the sojourn of the Israelites in Egypt, and the date of their departure. So far as regards the direct statements in the Hebrew text, the answers to both questions are positive and unambiguous. Exodus xii. 40 gives 430 years for the sojourn, Genesis xv. 13 gives 400 years for the whole, or the greater portion, of the same period. Again, the first book of Kings, (vi. 1), fixes the Exodus at 480 years before the building of the Temple in the fourth year of Solomon's reign. This would settle the date within a few years, about 1490 B.C.; a date which appears on the whole to be reconcileable with the facts of history, and to rest on higher authority than any other which has been proposed.

THE SECOND BOOK OF MOSES,

CALLED

EXODUS.

CHAP. 1. NOW [a] these *are* the names of the children of Israel, which
came into Egypt; every man and his household came with
2, 3 Jacob. Reuben, Simeon, Levi, and Judah, Issachar, Zebulun,
4, 5 and Benjamin, Dan, and Naphtali, Gad, and Asher. And all the
souls that came out of the [1]loins of Jacob were [b]seventy souls:
6 for Joseph was in Egypt *already*. ¶ And [c]Joseph died, and all
7 his brethren, and all that generation. [d]And the children of
Israel were fruitful, and increased abundantly, and multiplied,
and waxed exceeding mighty; and the land was filled with them.
8 ¶ Now there [e]arose up a new king over Egypt, which knew not
9 Joseph. And he said unto his people, Behold, [f]the people of
10 the children of Israel *are* more and mightier than we: [g]come on,
let us [h]deal wisely with them; lest they multiply, and it come to
pass, that, when there falleth out any war, they join also unto
our enemies, and fight against us, and *so* get them up out of the
11 land. Therefore they did set over them taskmasters [i]to afflict

[1] Heb. *thigh*.

[a] Gen. 46. 8. ch. 6. 14.
[b] Gen. 46. 26, 27. Deut. 10. 22.
[c] Gen. 50. 26. Acts 7. 15.
[d] Gen. 46. 3. Deut. 26. 5. Acts 7. 17.
[e] Acts 7. 18.
[f] Ps. 105. 24.
[g] Ps. 10. 2. & 83. 3, 4.
[h] Job 5. 13. Ps. 105. 25. Prov. 16. 25. Acts 7. 19.
[i] Gen. 15. 13. ch. 3. 7. Deut. 26. 6.

I. 1. *Now*] Literally "And," indicating a close connection with the preceding narrative. This chapter in fact contains a fulfilment of the predictions recorded in Gen. xlvi. 3, and in Gen. xv. 13.

every man and his household] It may be inferred from various notices that the total number of dependents was considerable, a point of importance in its bearings upon the history of the Exodus (cp. Gen. xiii. 6, xiv. 14).

5. *seventy*] See Gen. xlvi. 27. The object of the writer in this introductory statement is to give a complete list of the heads of separate families at the time of their settlement in Egypt. See note on Num. xxvi. 5.

7. In no province does the population increase so rapidly as in that occupied by the Israelites. See note on Gen. xlvii. 6. At present it has more flocks and herds than any province in Egypt, and more fishermen, though many villages are deserted. Until the accession of the new king, the relations between the Egyptians and the Israelites were undoubtedly friendly. The expressions used in this verse imply the lapse of a considerable period after the death of Joseph.

the land was filled with them] *i.e.* the district allotted to them (Gen. xlv. 10).

8. The expressions in this verse are peculiar, and emphatic. "A new king" is a phrase not found elsewhere. It is understood by most commentators to imply that he did not succeed his predecessor in natural order of descent and inheritance. He "arose up over Egypt," occupying the land, as it would seem, on different terms from the king whose place he took, either by usurpation or conquest. The fact that he knew not Joseph implies a complete separation from the traditions of Lower Egypt. At present the generality of Egyptian scholars identify this Pharaoh with Rameses II., but all the conditions of the narrative are fulfilled in the person of Amosis (or, Aahmes) I., the head of the 18th Dynasty. He was the descendant of the old Theban sovereigns, but his family was tributary to the Dynasty of the Shepherds, the Hyksos of Manetho, then ruling in the North of Egypt. Amosis married an Ethiopian princess, and in the third year of his reign captured Avaris, or Zoan, the capital of the Hyksos, and completed the expulsion of that race.

10. *any war*] The North Eastern frontier was infested by the neighbouring tribes, the Shasous of Egyptian monuments, and war was waged with Egypt by the confederated nations of Western Asia under the reigns of the successors of Amosis. These incursions were repulsed with extreme difficulty. In language, features, costume, and partly also in habits, the Israelites probably resembled those enemies of Egypt.

out of the land] The Pharaohs apprehended the loss of revenue and power, which would result from the withdrawal of a peaceful and industrious race.

11. *taskmasters*] The Egyptian "Chiefs of tributes." They were men of rank, superintendents of the public works, such as are often represented on Egyptian monuments, and carefully distinguished from the subordinate overseers. The Israelites were employed in forced labour, probably in de-

[k] ch. 2. 11. Ps. 81. 6.
[l] Gen. 47. 11.
[m] ch. 2. 23. & 3. 9. Num. 20. 15.
[n] Ps. 81. 6.
[o] Prov. 16. 6.
[p] Dan. 3. 16, 18. & 6. 13. Acts 5. 29.
[q] See Josh. 2. 4, &c.
[r] Prov. 11. 18. Eccles. 8. 12. Isai. 3. 10. Heb. 6. 10.
[s] See 1 Sam. 2. 25. 2 Sam. 7. 11, 13, 27, Ps. 127. 1.
[t] Acts 7. 19.
[a] ch. 6. 20. 1 Chr. 23. 13.
[b] Acts 7. 20. Heb. 11. 23.

them with their [k]burdens. And they built for Pharaoh treasure
12 cities, Pithom [l]and Raamses. [1]But the more they afflicted them,
the more they multiplied and grew. And they were grieved
13 because of the children of Israel. And the Egyptians made the
14 children of Israel to serve with rigour: and they [m]made their
lives bitter with hard bondage, [n]in morter, and in brick, and in
all manner of service in the field: all their service, wherein they
15 made them serve, *was* with rigour. ¶ And the king of Egypt
spake to the Hebrew midwives, of which the name of the one *was*
16 Shiphrah, and the name of the other Puah: and he said, When
ye do the office of a midwife to the Hebrew women, and see *them*
upon the stools; if it *be* a son, then ye shall kill him: but if it *be*
17 a daughter, then she shall live. But the midwives [o]feared God,
and did not [p]as the king of Egypt commanded them, but saved
18 the men children alive. And the king of Egypt called for the
midwives, and said unto them, Why have ye done this thing,
19 and have saved the men children alive? And [q]the midwives
said unto Pharaoh, Because the Hebrew women *are* not as the
Egyptian women; for they *are* lively, and are delivered ere
20 the midwives come in unto them. [r]Therefore God dealt well
with the midwives: and the people multiplied, and waxed very
21 mighty. And it came to pass, because the midwives feared God,
22 [s]that he made them houses. ¶ And Pharaoh charged all his
people, saying, [t]Every son that is born ye shall cast into the
river, and every daughter ye shall save alive.
CHAP. 2. AND there went [a]a man of the house of Levi, and took
2 *to wife* a daughter of Levi. And the woman conceived, and bare
a son: and [b]when she saw him that he *was* a goodly *child*, she

[1] Heb. *And as they afflicted them, so they multiplied, &c.*

tachments, but they were not reduced to slavery, properly speaking, nor treated as captives of war. Amosis had special need of such labourers, as proved by the inscriptions.

treasure cities] "Magazines," depots of ammunition and provisions (1 Kings ix. 19; 2 Chron. viii. 4 and xxxii. 28).

Pithom and Raamses] Both cities were situate on the canal dug or enlarged in the 12th Dynasty. The former is known to have existed under the 18th Dynasty: both were in existence in the beginning of the reign of Rameses II., by whom they were fortified and enlarged. The name "Pithom" means "House or temple of Tum," the Sun God of Heliopolis (see xiii. 20). The name of Raamses, or Rameses, is generally assumed to have been derived from Rameses II., the Sesostris of the Greeks, but it was previously known as the name of the district. See Genesis xlv. 10; xlvii. 11.

14. The use of brick, at all times common in Egypt, was especially so under the 18th Dynasty. An exact representation of the whole process of brickmaking is given in a small temple at Thebes, erected by Tóthmosis III., the fourth in descent from Amosis. Immense masses of brick are found at Belbeis, the modern capital of Sharkiya, *i.e.* Goshen, and in the adjoining district.

all manner of service in the field] Not merely agricultural labour, but probably the digging of canals and processes of irrigation which are peculiarly onerous and unhealthy.

15. *Hebrew midwives*] Or "midwives of the Hebrew women." This measure at once attested the inefficacy of the former measures, and was the direct cause of the event which issued in the deliverance of Israel, viz. the exposure of Moses. The women bear Egyptian names, and were probably Egyptians.

16. *upon the stools*] Literally "two stones." The word denotes a peculiar seat, such as is represented on monuments of the 18th Dynasty, and is still used by Egyptian midwives.

21. *made them houses*] *i.e.* they married Hebrews and became mothers in Israel. The expression is proverbial. See marg. reff.

22. The extreme cruelty of the measure does not involve improbability. Hatred of strangers was always a characteristic of the Egyptians (see Gen. xliii. 32), and was likely to be stronger than ever after the expulsion of an alien race.

II. **1.** *a man...a daughter of Levi*] Amram and Jochebed. See vi. 20.

2. *bare a son*] Not her firstborn; Aaron and Miriam were older than Moses. The object of the writer is simply to narrate the

3 hid him three months. And when she could not longer hide him,
she took for him an ark of bulrushes, and daubed it with slime
and with pitch, and put the child therein: and she laid *it* in the
4 flags by the river's brink. [c]And his sister stood afar off, to wit
5 what would be done to him. And the [d]daughter of Pharaoh
came down to wash *herself* at the river; and her maidens walked
along by the river's side; and when she saw the ark among the
6 flags, she sent her maid to fetch it. And when she had opened
it, she saw the child: and, behold, the babe wept. And she had
compassion on him, and said, This *is one* of the Hebrews' children.
7 Then said his sister to Pharaoh's daughter, Shall I go and call to
thee a nurse of the Hebrew women, that she may nurse the
8 child for thee? And Pharaoh's daughter said to her, Go. And
9 the maid went and called the child's mother. And Pharaoh's
daughter said unto her, Take this child away, and nurse it for
me, and I will give *thee* thy wages. And the woman took the
10 child, and nursed it. And the child grew, and she brought him
unto Pharaoh's daughter, and he became [e]her son. And she

[c] ch. 15. 20. Num. 26. 59.
[d] Acts 7. 21.
[e] Acts 7. 21.

events which led to the Exodus, and he omits to notice what had no direct bearing upon that object.

a goodly child] See marginal references. Probably Jochebed did not call in a midwife (i. 15), and she was of course cautious not to show herself to Egyptians. The hiding of the child is spoken of as an act of faith in Heb. xi. 23. It was done in the belief that God would watch over the child.

3. The ark was made of the papyrus which was commonly used by the Egyptians for light and swift boats. The species is no longer found in the Nile below Nubia. It is a strong rush, like the bamboo, about the thickness of a finger, three cornered, and attains the height of 10 to 15 feet. It is represented with great accuracy on the most ancient monuments of Egypt.

slime and pitch] The "slime" is probably the mud, of which bricks were usually made in Egypt, and which in this case was used to bind the stalks of the papyrus into a compact mass, and perhaps also to make the surface smooth for the infant. The pitch or bitumen, commonly used in Egypt, made the small vessel water-tight.

in the flags] This is another species of the papyrus, called tufi, or sufi (an exact equivalent of the Hebrew *suph*), which was less in size and height than the rush of which the ark was made.

5. The traditions which give a name to the daughter of Pharaoh are merely conjectural. Egyptian princesses held a very high and almost independent position under the ancient and middle empire, with a separate household and numerous officials. This was especially the case with the daughters of the first sovereigns of the 18th Dynasty.

Many facts concur in indicating that the residence of the daughter of Pharaoh and of the family of Moses, was at Zoan, Tanis, now San, the ancient Avaris (i. 8 note), on the Tanitic branch of the river, near the sea, where crocodiles are never found, and which was probably the western boundary of the district occupied by the Israelites. The field of Zoan was always associated by the Hebrews with the marvels which preceded the Exodus. See Ps. lxxviii. 43.

to wash] It is not customary at present for women of rank to bathe in the river, but it was a common practice in ancient Egypt. The habits of the princess, as well as her character, must have been well known to the mother of Moses, and probably decided her choice of the place.

6. *She had compassion on him*] The Egyptians regarded such tenderness as a condition of acceptance on the day of reckoning. In the presence of the Lord of truth each spirit had to answer, "I have not afflicted any man, I have not made any man weep, I have not withheld milk from the mouths of sucklings" ('Funeral Ritual'). There was special ground for mentioning the feeling, since it led the princess to save and adopt the child in spite of her father's commands.

10. *he became her son*] See marg. ref. His training and education was, humanly speaking, all but indispensable to the efficient accomplishment of his work as the predestined leader and instructor of his countrymen. Moses probably passed the early years of his life in Lower Egypt, where the princess resided. There may however be substantial grounds for the tradition in Josephus that he was engaged in a campaign against the Ethiopians, thus shewing himself, as St. Stephen says, "mighty in word and deed."

Moses] The Egyptian origin of this word is generally admitted. The name itself is not uncommon in ancient documents. The exact meaning is "son," but the verbal root of the word signifies "produce," "draw forth." The whole sentence in Egyptian

called his name [1]Moses: and she said, Because I drew him out
11 of the water. ¶ And it came to pass in those days, [f]when Moses
was grown, that he went out unto his brethren, and looked on
their [g]burdens: and he spied an Egyptian smiting an Hebrew, one
12 of his brethren. And he looked this way and that way, and when
he saw that *there was* no man, he [h]slew the Egyptian, and hid him
13 in the sand. And [i]when he went out the second day, behold, two
men of the Hebrews strove together: and he said to him that did
14 the wrong, Wherefore smitest thou thy fellow? And he said,
[k]Who made thee [2]a prince and a judge over us? intendest thou
to kill me, as thou killedst the Egyptian? And Moses feared, and
15 said, Surely this thing is known. Now when Pharaoh heard
this thing, he sought to slay Moses. But [l]Moses fled from the
face of Pharaoh, and dwelt in the land of Midian: and he sat
16 down by [m]a well. [n]Now the [3]priest of Midian had seven
daughters: [o]and they came and drew *water*, and filled the
17 troughs to water their father's flock. And the shepherds came
and drove them away: but Moses stood up and helped them, and
18 [p]watered their flock. And when they came to [q]Reuel their
19 father, he said, How *is it that* ye are come so soon to day? And
they said, An Egyptian delivered us out of the hand of the
shepherds, and also drew *water* enough for us, and watered the
20 flock. And he said unto his daughters, And where *is* he? Why

[f] Acts 7. 23, 24. Heb. 11. 24.
[g] ch. 1. 11.
[h] Acts 7. 24.
[i] Acts 7. 26.
[k] Acts 7. 27, 28.
[l] Acts 7. 29. Heb. 11. 27.
[m] Gen. 24. 11. & 29. 2.
[n] ch. 3. 1.
[o] 1 Sam. 9. 11.
[p] Gen. 29. 10.
[q] Num. 10. 29, called also *Jethro*, or, *Jether*, ch. 3. 1, &c.

[1] That is, *Drawn out*.
[2] Heb. *a man, a prince*, Gen. 13. 8.
[3] Or, *prince*, as Gen. 41. 45.

---

would exactly correspond to our Version. She called his name Moses, *i.e.* "son," or "brought forth," because she brought him forth out of the water.

11. *went out unto his brethren*] At the end of 40 years. The Egyptian princess had not concealed from him the fact of his belonging to the oppressed race, nor is it likely that she had debarred him from intercourse with his foster-mother and her family, whether or not she became aware of the true relationship.

an Egyptian] This man was probably one of the overseers of the workmen, natives under the chief superintendent (i. 11). They were armed with long heavy scourges, made of a tough pliant wood imported from Syria.

12. The slaying of the Egyptian is not to be justified, or attributed to a divine inspiration, but it is to be judged with reference to the provocation, the impetuosity of Moses' natural character, perhaps also to the habits developed by his training at the court of Pharaoh. The act involved a complete severance from the Egyptians, but, far from expediting, it delayed for many years the deliverance of the Irsraelites. Forty years of a very different training prepared Moses for the execution of that appointed work.

13. *thy fellow*] **Thy neighbour:** the reproof was that of a legislator who established moral obligations on a recognised principle. Hence in the following verse the offender is represented as feeling that the position claimed by Moses was that of a Judge. The act could only have been made known by the Hebrew on whose behalf Moses had committed it.

15. No Egyptian king would have left such an offence unpunished, but the position of Moses, as adopted son of a princess, made it necessary even for a despotic sovereign to take unusual precautions.

the land of Midian] The Midianites occupied an extensive district from the eastern coast of the Red Sea to the borders of Moab.

16. *the Priest of Midian*] Reuel (*v.* 18). His name, and the detailed notices in ch. xviii., prove that he was a priest of the one true God Who was known to the patriarchs especially under the name El. The great bulk of his tribe, certainly those who lived farther north and more closely in contact with the Hamites of Canaan, were already plunged in idolatry. The conduct of the shepherds (*v.* 17) may indicate that his person and office were lightly regarded by the idolatrous tribes in his immediate neighbourhood.

18. *Reuel*] Or, as in Num. x. 29, Raguel. The name means "friend of God." It appears to have been not uncommon among Hebrews and Edomites; *e.g.* Gen. xxxvi. 4, 10. If Reuel be identified with Jethro, a point open to grave objection (see iii. 1), then Reuel was his proper name, and Jether or Jethro, which means "excellency," was his official designation.

19. *An Egyptian*] They judged from his costume, or language.

is it *that* ye have left the man? Call him, that he may [r]eat bread. [r]Gen. 31.
21 And Moses was content to dwell with the man: and he gave 54. & 43. 25. [s]ch. 4. 25.
22 Moses [s]Zipporah his daughter. And she bare *him* a son, and he [t]ch. 18. 3.
called his name, [1][t]Gershom: for he said, I have been [u]a stranger [u]Acts 7. 29.
23 in a strange land. ¶ And it came to pass [x]in process of time, Heb. 11. 13. [x]ch. 7. 7.
that the king of Egypt died: and the children of Israel [y]sighed [y]Deut. 26. 7.
by reason of the bondage, and they cried, and [z]their cry came Ps. 12. 5. [z]ch. 3. 9.
24 up unto God by reason of the bondage. And God [a]heard their [a]ch. 6. 5.
groaning, and God [b]remembered his [c]covenant with Abraham, [b]Ps. 105. 42. [c]Gen. 15. 14.
25 with Isaac, and with Jacob. And God [d]looked upon the children & 46. 4.
of Israel, and God [2][e]had respect unto *them*. [d]ch. 4. 31.
Chap. 3. NOW Moses kept the flock of Jethro his father in law, [e]ch. 3. 7. [a]ch. 2. 16.
[a]the priest of Midian: and he led the flock to the backside of the [b]ch. 18. 5.
2 desert, and came to [b]the mountain of God, *even* to Horeb. And 1 Kin. 19. 8.

[1] That is, *A stranger here.* [2] Heb. *knew.*

---

21. Moses tells us nothing of what he may have learned from his father-in-law, but he must have found in him a man conversant with the traditions of the family of Abraham; nor is there any improbability in the supposition that, as hereditary priest, Reuel may have had written documents concerning their common ancestors.

22. *Gershom*] The first syllable "Ger" is common to Hebrew and Egyptian, and means "sojourner." The second syllable "Shom" answers exactly to the Coptic "Shemmo," which means "a foreign or strange land."

23. *in process of time*] Nearly forty years (Acts vii. 30). This verse marks the beginning of another section. We now enter at once upon the history of the Exodus.

their cry came up unto God] This statement, taken in connection with the two following verses, proves that the Israelites retained their faith in the God of their Fathers. The divine name God, Elohim, is chosen because it was that which the Israelites must have used in their cry for help, that under which the covenant had been ratified with the Patriarchs (cp. Jas. v. 4).

24. *remembered*] This means that God was moved by their prayers to give effect to the covenant, of which an essential condition was the faith and contrition involved in the act of supplication. The whole history of Israel is foreshadowed in these words: God heard, remembered, looked upon, and knew them. It evidently indicates the beginning of a crisis marked by a personal intervention of God.

III. This chapter marks the commencement of the series of events which immediately preceded the Exodus. Hitherto the narrative has been studiously brief, stating only what was necessary to be known as preparatory to those events; but from this point Moses dwells minutely on the details, and enables us to realize the circumstances of the catastrophe which in its immediate and remote consequences stands alone in the world's history

1. *Jethro his father-in-law*] Or "brother-in-law." The word in the Hebrew is a word signifying relative by marriage. When Moses arrived in Midian, Reuel was an elderly man (ii. 16); 40 years later (ii. 23 note), Reuel's son, Jethro, had probably succeeded him.

the backside] *i.e.* "to the west of the district." Among the Hebrews the East is before a man, the west behind him, the south and north on the right and left hand.

desert] Or **wilderness,** not a barren waste, but a district supplying pasturage. The district near Sherm, on the west of the gulf of Akabah, where Jethro may have resided, is described as barren and parched; on the west and east are rocky tracts, but to the north-west lies the district of Sinai, where the pasturage is good and water abundant. The Bedouins drive their flocks thither from the lowlands at the approach of summer. From this it may be inferred that the events here recorded took place at that season.

to Horeb] More exactly, **towards Horeb.** Moses came to the mountain of God, *i.e.* Sinai, on his way towards Horeb, a name given to the northern part of the Sinaitic range. Moses calls Sinai "mountain of God" by anticipation, with reference to the manifestation of God. There is no authority for assuming that the spot was previously held sacred (see *v.* 5); but it has been lately shewn that the whole Peninsula was regarded by the Egyptians as specially consecrated to the gods from a very early time.

2. *the angel of the* Lord] See note on Gen. xii. 7. What Moses saw was the flame of fire in the bush; what he recognized therein was an intimation of the Presence of God, Who maketh a flame of fire His angel. Cp. Ps. civ. 4. The words which Moses heard were those of God Himself, as all ancient and most modern divines have held, manifested in the Person of the Son.

of a bush] Literally **of the bush,** or "seneh," a word which ought perhaps to be retained as the proper name of a thorny

[c]the angel of the LORD appeared unto him in a flame of fire out
of the midst of a bush: and he looked, and, behold, the bush
3 burned with fire, and the bush *was* not consumed. And Moses
said, I will now turn aside, and see this [d]great sight, why the
4 bush is not burnt. And when the LORD saw that he turned aside
to see, God called [e]unto him out of the midst of the bush, and
5 said, Moses, Moses. And he said, Here *am* I. And he said,
Draw not nigh hither: [f]put off thy shoes from off thy feet, for the
6 place whereon thou standest *is* holy ground. Moreover he said,
[g]I *am* the God of thy father, the God of Abraham, the God of
Isaac, and the God of Jacob. And Moses hid his face; for [h]he
7 was afraid to look upon God. ¶ And the LORD said, [i]I have
surely seen the affliction of my people which *are* in Egypt, and
have heard their cry [k]by reason of their taskmasters; for [l]I know
8 their sorrows; and [m]I am come down to [n]deliver them out of
the hand of the Egyptians, and to bring them up out of that land
[o]unto a good land and a large, unto a land [p]flowing with milk and
honey; unto the place of [q]the Canaanites, and the Hittites, and
the Amorites, and the Perizzites, and the Hivites, and the Jebu-
9 sites. Now therefore, behold, [r]the cry of the children of Israel is
come unto me: and I have also seen [s]the oppression wherewith
10 the Egyptians oppress them. [t]Come now therefore, and I will
send thee unto Pharaoh, that thou mayest bring forth my people

[c] Isai. 63. 9. Acts 7. 30.
[d] Ps. 111. 2.
[e] Deut. 33. 16.
[f] ch. 19. 12. Josh. 5. 15. Acts 7. 33.
[g] Gen. 28. 13. Acts 7. 32.
[h] So 1 Kin. 19. 13. Isai. 6. 1, 5.
[i] ch. 2. 23. Neh. 9. 9. Ps. 106. 44. Acts 7. 34.
[k] ch. 1. 11.
[l] Gen. 18. 21.
[m] Gen. 11. 5. 7.
[n] ch. 6. 6, 8. & 12. 51.
[o] Deut. 1. 25. & 8. 7, 8, 9.
[p] ch. 13. 5.
[q] Gen. 15. 18.
[r] ch. 2. 23.
[s] ch. 1. 11.
[t] Ps. 105. 26. Mic. 6. 4.

---

shrub common in that district, a species of acacia.

4. *the* LORD *saw*] The interchange of the two divine names is to be observed; *Jehovah* saw, *God* called.

5. *put off thy shoes*] The reverence due to holy places thus rests on God's own command. The custom itself is well known from the observances of the Temple, it was almost universally adopted by the ancients, and is retained in the East.

holy ground] This passage is almost conclusive against the assumption that the place was previously a sanctuary. Moses knew nothing of its holiness after some 40 years spent on the Peninsula. It became holy by the Presence of God.

6. Our Saviour adduces this passage as a proof that the doctrine of the Resurrection was taught in the Old Testament (Matt. xxii. 32), and He calls this book the book of Moses (Mark xii. 26), two points to be borne in mind by readers of the Pentateuch.

7. *taskmasters*] Oppressors. A different word from that in i. 11.

I know] The expression implies personal feeling, tenderness, and compassion (cp. ii. 25. marg.).

8. The natural richness of Palestine, the variety and excellence of its productions, are attested by sacred (cp. Jer. xxxii. 22. Ez. xx. 6) and ancient writers, whose descriptions are strongly in contrast with those of later travellers. The expression "flowing with milk and honey" is used proverbially by Greek poets.

the Canaanites, &c.] This is the first passage in this book where the enumeration, so often repeated, of the nations then in possession of Palestine, is given. Moses was to learn at once the extent of the promise, and the greatness of the enterprise. In Egypt, the forces, situation, and character of these nations were then well known. Aahmes I. had invaded the south of Palestine in his pursuit of the Shasous; Tothmosis I. had traversed the whole land on his campaign in Syria and Mesopotamia; representations of Canaanites, and of the Cheta, identified by most Egyptologers with the Hittites, are common on monuments of the 18th and 19th Dynasties, and give a strong impression of their civilization, riches, and especially of their knowledge of the arts of war. In this passage, the more general designations come first—Canaanites probably includes all the races; the Hittites, who had great numbers of chariots (892 were taken from them by Tothmosis III. in one battle), occupied the plains; the Amorites were chiefly mountaineers, and, in Egyptian inscriptions, gave their name to the whole country; the name Perizzites probably denotes the dwellers in scattered villages, the half-nomad population; the Hivites, a comparatively unwarlike but influential people, held 4 cities in Palestine proper, but their main body dwelt in the north-western district, from Hermon to Hamath (see Josh. xi. 3, and Judg. iii. 3); the Jebusites at that time appear to have occupied Jerusalem and the adjoining district. Soon after their expulsion by Joshua, they seem to have recovered possession of part of Jerusalem, probably Mount Zion, and to have retained it until the time of David.

11 the children of Israel out of Egypt. ¶ And Moses said unto God,
[u] Who *am* I, that I should go unto Pharaoh, and that I should bring
12 forth the children of Israel out of Egypt? And he said, [x] Certainly I will be with thee; and this *shall be* a token unto thee, that
I have sent thee: When thou hast brought forth the people out
13 of Egypt, ye shall serve God upon this mountain. And Moses
said unto God, Behold, *when* I come unto the children of Israel,
and shall say unto them, The God of your fathers hath sent me
unto you; and they shall say to me, What *is* his name? what
14 shall I say unto them? ¶ And God said unto Moses, I AM THAT
I AM: And he said, Thus shalt thou say unto the children of
15 Israel, [y] I AM hath sent me unto you. And God said moreover unto Moses, Thus shalt thou say unto the children of Israel,
The LORD God of your fathers, the God of Abraham, the God of
Isaac, and the God of Jacob, hath sent me unto you: this *is* [z] my
16 name for ever, and this *is* my memorial unto all generations. Go,
and [a] gather the elders of Israel together, and say unto them, The
LORD God of your fathers, the God of Abraham, of Isaac, and of
Jacob, appeared unto me, saying, [b] I have surely visited you,
17 and *seen* that which is done to you in Egypt: and I have said, [c] I
will bring you up out of the affliction of Egypt unto the land of
the Canaanites, and the Hittites, and the Amorites, and the
Perizzites, and the Hivites, and the Jebusites, unto a land flow-
18 ing with milk and honey. And [d] they shall hearken to thy
voice: and [e] thou shalt come, thou and the elders of Israel, unto
the king of Egypt, and ye shall say unto him, The LORD God of
the Hebrews hath [f] met with us: and now let us go, we beseech
thee, three days' journey into the wilderness, that we may sacri-
19 fice to the LORD our God. And I am sure that the king of Egypt

[u] ch. 6. 12. 1 Sam. 18. 18. Isai. 6. 5, 8. Jer. 1. 6.
[x] Gen. 31. 3. Josh. 1. 5. Rom. 3. 18.
[y] ch. 6. 3. John 8. 58. 2 Cor. 1. 20. Heb. 13. 8. Rev. 1. 4.
[z] Ps. 135. 13. Hos. 12. 5.
[a] ch. 4. 29.
[b] ch. 2. 25. Luke 1. 68.
[c] Gen. 15. 14, 16. ver. 8.
[d] ch. 4. 31.
[e] ch. 5. 1, 3.
[f] Num. 23. 3, 4, 15, 16.

---

11. *Who am I*] These words indicate humility (cp. Num. xii. 3), not fear. He feared failure owing to incompetency, especially in the power of expression.

12. *a token unto thee*] Or **the sign**. The word means a declaration or promise of God, which rests absolutely on His word, and demands faith. The promise that God would have the people serve Him in that place was an assurance, if fully believed, that all intervening obstacles would be removed by His power.

13. *What is his name*] The meaning of this question is evidently: "By which name shall I tell them the promise is confirmed?" Each name of the Deity represented some aspect or manifestation of His attributes (cp. Intro. to Genesis, p. 8). What Moses needed was not a new name, but direction to use that name which would bear in itself a pledge of accomplishment. Moses was familiar with the Egyptian habit of choosing from the names of the gods that which bore specially upon the wants and circumstances of their worshippers, and this may have suggested the question which would be the first his own people would expect him to answer.

14. *I am that I am*] That is, "I am what I am." The words express absolute, and therefore unchanging and eternal Being. The name, which Moses was thus commissioned to use, was at once new and old; old in its connection with previous revelations; new in its full interpretation, and in its bearing upon the covenant of which Moses was the destined mediator.

15. *The* LORD *God*, &c.] Better, **Jehovah, God of your fathers, God of Abraham, God of Isaac, and God of Jacob.** It corresponds exactly to the preceding verse, the words **I am** and **Jehovah** being equivalent. This name met all the requirements of Moses, involving a twofold pledge of accomplishment; the pledges of ancient benefits and of a new manifestation.

name...memorial] The name signifies that by which God makes himself known, the memorial that by which His people worship Him.

18. *three days' journey*] *i.e.* A journey which would occupy three days in going and returning. This was a demand quite in accordance with Egyptian customs. The refusal of Pharaoh and the subsequent proceedings were revealed to Moses at once; but it is important to observe that the first request which Pharaoh rejected could have been granted without any damage to Egypt, or any risk of the Israelites passing the strongly fortified frontier.

19. *no, not*] See the marginal rendering. Others explain it to mean, Pharaoh will not let the people go even when severely smitten.

[g] ch. 5. 2. & 7. 4. [h] ch. 6. 6. & 7. 5. & 9. 15. [i] ch. 7. to ch. 13. Deut. 6. 22. Neh. 9. 10. Ps. 135. 9. Jer. 32. 20. Acts 7. 36. [k] ch. 12. 31. [l] ch. 11. 3. Gen. 3. 21. & reff. [m] ch. 11. 2. & 12. 35. [n] Job 27. 17. Prov. 13. 22. Ezek. 39. 10. [a] ver. 17, 20. [b] ch. 19. 9. [c] ch. 3. 15. [d] Num. 12. 10. 2 Kin. 5. 27. [e] Deut. 32. 39. 2 Kin. 5. 14. Matt. 8. 3.

20 [g]will not let you go, [1]no, not by a mighty hand. And I will
[h]stretch out my hand, and smite Egypt with [i]all my wonders
which I will do in the midst thereof: and [k]after that he will let
21 you go. And I [l]will give this people favour in the sight of the
Egyptians: and it shall come to pass, that, when ye go, ye shall
22 not go empty: [m]but every woman shall borrow of her neighbour, and of her that sojourneth in her house, jewels of silver,
and jewels of gold, and raiment: and ye shall put *them* upon
your sons, and upon your daughters; and [n]ye shall spoil [2]the
Egyptians.
CHAP. 4. AND Moses answered and said, But, behold, they will
not believe me, nor hearken unto my voice: for they will say,
2 The LORD hath not appeared unto thee. And the LORD said
unto him, What *is* that in thine hand? And he said, [a]A rod.
3 And he said, Cast it on the ground. And he cast it on the
ground, and it became a serpent; and Moses fled from before it.
4 And the LORD said unto Moses, Put forth thine hand, and take
it by the tail. And he put forth his hand, and caught it, and it
5 became a rod in his hand: that they may [b]believe that [c]the
LORD God of their fathers, the God of Abraham, the God of
6 Isaac, and the God of Jacob, hath appeared unto thee. ¶ And
the LORD said furthermore unto him, Put now thine hand into
thy bosom. And he put his hand into his bosom: and when he
7 took it out, behold, his hand *was* leprous [d]as snow. And he
said, Put thine hand into thy bosom again. And he put his
hand into his bosom again; and plucked it out of his bosom,
8 and, behold, [e]it was turned again as his *other* flesh. And it
shall come to pass, if they will not believe thee, neither hearken
to the voice of the first sign, that they will believe the voice of

[1] Or, *but by strong hand*. [2] Or, *Egypt*.

---

22. *shall borrow*] **shall ask.** The Egyptians had made the people serve "with rigour," and the Israelites when about to leave the country for ever were to ask or claim the jewels as a just, though very inadequate, remuneration for services which had made "their lives bitter." The Egyptians would doubtless have refused had not their feelings towards Moses (see xi. 3) and the people been changed, under God's influence, by calamities in which they recognized a divine interposition, which also they rightly attributed to the obstinacy of their own king (see x. 7). The Hebrew women were to make the demand, and were to make it of women, who would of course be specially moved to compliance by the loss of their children, the fear of a recurrence of calamity, perhaps also by a sense of the fitness of the request in connection with a religious festival.

jewels] Chiefly trinkets. These ornaments were actually applied to the purpose for which they were probably demanded, being employed in making the vessels of the sanctuary (cp. xxxv. 22).

sojourneth in her house] This indicates a degree of friendly and neighbourly intercourse, in accordance with several indirect notices, and was a natural result of long and peaceable sojourn in the district. The Egyptians did not all necessarily share the feelings of their new king.

IV. With this chapter begins the series of miracles which resulted in the deliverance of Israel. The first miracle was wrought to remove the first obstacle, viz. the reluctance of Moses, conscious of his own weakness, and of the enormous power with which he would have to contend.

2. *a rod*] The word seems to denote the long staff which on Egyptian monuments is borne by men in positions of authority. It was usually made of acacia wood.

3. *a serpent*] This miracle had a meaning which Moses could not mistake. The serpent was probably the basilisk or Uræus, the Cobra. This was the symbol of royal and divine power on the diadem of every Pharaoh. The conversion of the rod was not merely a portent, it was a sign, at once a pledge and representation of victory over the king and gods of Egypt.

6. *leprous*] The instantaneous production and cure of the most malignant and subtle disease known to the Israelites was a sign of their danger if they resisted the command, and of their deliverance if they obeyed it. The infliction and cure were always regarded as special proofs of a divine intervention.

9 the latter sign. And it shall come to pass, if they will not
believe also these two signs, neither hearken unto thy voice,
that thou shalt take of the water of the river, and pour *it* upon
the dry *land:* and [f]the water which thou takest out of the river — f ch. 7. 19.
10 [1]shall become blood upon the dry *land.* ¶ And Moses said unto
the LORD, O my Lord, I *am* not [2]eloquent, neither [3]heretofore,
nor since thou hast spoken unto thy servant: but [g]I *am* slow of — g ch. 6. 12.
11 speech, and of a slow tongue. And the LORD said unto him, — Jer. 1. 6.
[h]Who hath made man's mouth? Or who maketh the dumb, or — h Ps. 94. 9.
12 deaf, or the seeing, or the blind? Have not I the LORD? Now
therefore go, and I will be [i]with thy mouth, and teach thee — i Isai. 50. 4. Jer. 1. 9.
13 what thou shalt say. And he said, O my Lord, [k]send, I pray — Matt. 10. 19.
14 thee, by the hand *of him whom* thou [4]wilt send. And the anger — k See Jonah
of the LORD was kindled against Moses, and he said, *Is* not — 1. 3.
Aaron the Levite thy brother? I know that he can speak well.
And also, behold, [l]he cometh forth to meet thee: and when he — l ver. 27. 1 Sam. 10.
15 seeth thee, he will be glad in his heart. And [m]thou shalt speak — 2, 3, 5.
unto him, and [n]put words in his mouth: and I will be with thy — m ch. 7. 1.
mouth, and with his mouth, and [o]will teach you what ye shall — n Num. 22. 38.
16 do. And he shall be thy spokesman unto the people: and he — Deut. 18. 18.
shall be, *even* he shall be to thee instead of a mouth, and — Isai. 51. 16. Jer. 1. 9.
17 [p]thou shalt be to him instead of God. And thou shalt take — o Deut. 5. 31.
18 [q]this rod in thine hand, wherewith thou shalt do signs. ¶ And — p ch. 7. 1.
Moses went and returned to [5]Jethro his father in law, and said — & 18. 19. q ver. 2.
unto him, Let me go, I pray thee, and return unto my brethren
which *are* in Egypt, and see whether they be yet alive. And
19 Jethro said to Moses, Go in peace. ¶ And the LORD said unto
Moses in Midian, Go, return into Egypt: for [r]all the men are — r ch. 2. 15.
20 dead which sought thy life. And Moses took his wife and his — Matt. 2. 20.
sons, and set them upon an ass, and he returned to the land of

[1] Heb. *shall be and shall be.*
[2] Heb. *a man of words.*
[3] Heb. *since yesterday, nor since the third day.*
[4] Or, *shouldest.*
[5] Heb. *Jether.*

---

10. *eloquent*] See margin. The double expression "slow of speech (Ezek. iii. 5 marg.) and of a slow tongue" seems to imply a difficulty both in finding words and in giving them utterance, a very natural result of so long a period of a shepherd's life, passed in a foreign land.

since thou hast spoken] This expression seems to imply that some short time had intervened between this address and the first communication of the divine purpose to Moses.

12. Compare with this our Lord's promise to His Apostles; Matt. x. 19; Mark xiii. 11.

13. *And he said*] The reluctance of Moses is in accordance with the inner law of man's spiritual development, and specially with his own character; but under the circumstances it indicated a weakness of faith.

14. *anger*] The words of Moses (*v.* 13) indicated more than a consciousness of infirmity; somewhat of vehemence and stubbornness.

Aaron] This is the first mention of Aaron. The words "he can speak well," probably imply that Aaron had both the power and will to speak. Aaron is here called "the Levite," with reference, it may be, to the future consecration of this tribe.

he cometh forth] *i.e.* is on the eve of setting forth. Not that Aaron was already on the way, but that he had the intention of going to his brother, probably because the enemies of Moses were now dead. See *v.* 19.

15. *thou shalt speak*] Moses thus retains his position as "mediator;" the word comes to him first, he transmits it to his brother.

16. *instead of a mouth*] We may bear in mind Aaron's unbroken habitude of speaking Hebrew and his probable familiarity with Egyptian.

instead of God] The word "God" is used of persons who represent the Deity, as kings or judges, and it is understood in this sense here: "Thou shalt be to him a master."

20. *an ass*] Lit. "the ass," which according to Hebrew idiom means that he set them upon asses. This is the first notice of other sons besides Gershom.

the rod of God] The staff of Moses was consecrated by the miracle (*v.* 2) and became "the rod of God."

[s] ch. 17. 9. Num. 20. 8. [t] ch. 3. 20. [u] ch. 7. 13, &c. Deut. 2. 30. Josh. 11. 20. Isai. 63. 17. John 12. 40. Rom. 9. 18. [x] Hos. 11. 1. Rom. 9. 4. 2 Cor. 6. 18. [y] Jer. 31. 9. Jam. 1. 18. [z] ch. 11. 5. & 12. 29. [a] Num. 22. 22. [b] Gen. 17. 14. [c] Josh. 5. 2, 3. [d] ver. 14. [e] ch. 3. 1. [f] ver. 15, 16. [g] ver. 8, 9. [h] ch. 3. 16. [i] ver. 16. [k] ch. 3. 18. ver. 8, 9. [l] ch. 3. 16. [m] ch. 2. 25. & 3. 7. [n] Gen. 24. 26. ch. 12. 27. 1 Chr. 29. 20.

21 Egypt: and Moses took [s]the rod of God in his hand. And the
LORD said unto Moses, When thou goest to return into Egypt,
see that thou do all those [t]wonders before Pharaoh, which I
have put in thine hand: but [u]I will harden his heart, that he
22 shall not let the people go. And thou shalt say unto Pharaoh,
23 Thus saith the LORD, [x]Israel *is* my son, [y]*even* my firstborn: and
I say unto thee, Let my son go, that he may serve me: and if
thou refuse to let him go, behold, [z]I will slay thy son, *even* thy
24 firstborn. ¶And it came to pass by the way in the inn, that the
25 LORD [a]met him, and sought to [b]kill him. Then Zipporah took
[c]a sharp [1]stone, and cut off the foreskin of her son, and [2]cast *it*
at his feet, and said, Surely a bloody husband *art* thou to me.
26 So he let him go: then she said, A bloody husband *thou art*,
27 because of the circumcision. ¶And the LORD said to Aaron, Go
into the wilderness [d]to meet Moses. And he went, and met him
28 in [e]the mount of God, and kissed him. And Moses [f]told Aaron
all the words of the LORD who had sent him, and all the [g]signs
29 which he had commanded him. ¶And Moses and Aaron [h]went
and gathered together all the elders of the children of Israel:
30 [i]and Aaron spake all the words which the LORD had spoken unto
31 Moses, and did the signs in the sight of the people. And the
people [k]believed: and when they heard that the LORD had
[l]visited the children of Israel, and that he [m]had looked upon
their affliction, then [n]they bowed their heads and worshipped.
CHAP. 5. AND afterward Moses and Aaron went in, and told
Pharaoh, Thus saith the LORD God of Israel, Let my people go,

[1] Or, *knife*. [2] Heb. *made it touch*.

---

21. *I will harden*] Calamities which do not subdue the heart harden it. In the case of Pharaoh the hardening was at once a righteous judgment, and a natural result of a long series of oppressions and cruelties.

22. *my firstborn*] The expression would be perfectly intelligible to Pharaoh, whose official designation was "son of Ra." In numberless inscriptions the Pharaohs are styled "own sons" or "beloved sons" of the deity. It is here applied for the first time to Israel; and as we learn from *v.* 23, emphatically in antithesis to Pharaoh's own firstborn.

24. *in the inn*] Or "resting place." See Gen. xlii. 27 note.

met him, and sought to kill him] Moses was attacked by a sudden and dangerous illness, which he knew was inflicted by God. The word "sought to kill" implies that the sickness, whatever might be its nature, was one which threatened death had it not been averted by a timely act. Zipporah believed that the illness of Moses was due to his having neglected the duty of an Israelite, and to his not having circumcised his son; the delay was probably owing to her own not unnatural repugnance to a rite, which though practised by the Egyptians, was not adopted generally in the East, even by the descendants of Abraham and Keturah. Moses appears to have been utterly prostrate and unable to perform the rite himself.

25. *sharp stone*] Not "knife," as in the margin. Zipporah used a piece of flint, in accordance with the usage of the patriarchs. The Egyptians never used bronze or steel in the preparation of mummies because stone was regarded as a purer and more sacred material than metal.

cast it at his feet] Showing at once her abhorrence of the rite, and her feeling that by it she had saved her husband's life.

a bloody husband] Lit. "A husband of blood," or "bloods." The meaning is, the marriage bond between us is now sealed by blood. By performing the rite Zipporah had recovered her husband; his life was purchased for her by the blood of her child.

26. *So he let him go*] *i.e.* God withdrew His visitation from Moses.

Moses sent Zipporah and her children back to Jethro before he went to Egypt, xviii. 2. The journey would have been delayed had he waited for the healing of the child.

29. *all the elders*] The Israelites retained their own national organization; their affairs were administered by their own elders, who called a public assembly (*v.* 31) to hear the message brought by Moses and Aaron.

V. **1.** *Pharaoh*] This king, probably Tothmosis II., the great grandson of Aahmes (i. 8), the original persecutor of the Israelites, must have been resident at this time in a city, probably Tanis (ii. 5), of Lower Egypt, situate on the Nile.

the LORD *God*] **Jehovah God of Israel**

2 that they may hold [a]a feast unto me in the wilderness. And
Pharaoh said, [b]Who *is* the LORD, that I should obey his voice
to let Israel go? I know not the LORD, [c]neither will I let
3 Israel go. And they said, [d]The God of the Hebrews hath met
with us: let us go, we pray thee, three days' journey into the
desert, and sacrifice unto the LORD our God; lest he fall upon
4 us with pestilence, or with the sword. And the king of Egypt
said unto them, Wherefore do ye, Moses and Aaron, let the
5 people from their works? get you unto your [e]burdens. And
Pharaoh said, Behold, the people of the land now *are* [f]many,
6 and ye make them rest from their burdens. ¶ And Pharaoh
commanded the same day the [g]taskmasters of the people, and
7 their officers, saying, Ye shall no more give the people straw to
make brick, as heretofore: let them go and gather straw for
8 themselves. And the tale of the bricks, which they did make
heretofore, ye shall lay upon them; ye shall not diminish *ought*
thereof: for they *be* idle; therefore they cry, saying, Let us go
9 *and* sacrifice to our God. [1]Let there more work be laid upon the
men, that they may labour therein; and let them not regard
10 vain words. ¶ And the taskmasters of the people went out, and
their officers, and they spake to the people, saying, Thus saith
11 Pharaoh, I will not give you straw. Go ye, get you straw
where ye can find it: yet not ought of your work shall be
12 diminished. So the people were scattered abroad throughout
13 all the land of Egypt to gather stubble instead of straw. And
the taskmasters hasted *them*, saying, Fulfil your works, [2]*your*
14 daily tasks, as when there was straw. And the officers of the
children of Israel, which Pharaoh's taskmasters had set over
them, were beaten, *and* demanded, Wherefore have ye not fulfilled your task in making brick both yesterday and to day, as
15 heretofore? ¶ Then the officers of the children of Israel came
and cried unto Pharaoh, saying, Wherefore dealest thou thus
16 with thy servants? There is no straw given unto thy servants,
and they say to us, Make brick: and, behold, thy servants *are*
17 beaten; but the fault *is* in thine own people. But he said, Ye

[a] ch. 10. 9.
[b] 2 Kin. 18. 35. Job 21. 15.
[c] ch. 3. 19.
[d] ch. 3. 18.
[e] ch. 1. 11.
[f] ch. 1. 7, 9.
[g] ch. 3. 7.

[1] Heb. *Let the work be heavy upon the men.*

[2] Heb. *a matter of a day in his day.*

demanded the services of His people. The demand, according to the general views of the heathens, was just and natural; the Israelites could not offer the necessary sacrifices in the presence of Egyptians.

2. *I know not the* LORD] Either Pharaoh had not heard of Jehovah, or he did not recognize Him as a God.

3. *three days' journey*] See iii. 18 note.

with pestilence, or with the sword] This shews that the plague was well known to the ancient Egyptians. The reference to the sword is equally natural, since the Israelites occupied the eastern district, which was frequently disturbed by the neighbouring Shasous.

4. *let*] *i.e.* hinder.

6. *their officers*] Or **scribes**. Hebrews able to keep accounts in writing, appointed by the Egyptian superintendents, and responsible to them for the work; see *v.* 14. Subordinate officers are frequently represented on Egyptian monuments, giving in written accounts to their immediate superiors.

7. Some of the most ancient buildings in Egypt were constructed of bricks not burned, but dried in the sun; they were made of clay, or more commonly of mud, mixed with straw chopped into small pieces. An immense quantity of straw must have been wanted for the works on which the Israelites were engaged, and their labours must have been more than doubled by this requisition.

12. *stubble instead of straw*] Rather, **for the straw**: *i.e.* to be prepared as straw. This marks the season of the year, viz. early spring, after the barley or wheat harvest, towards the end of April. Their suffering must have been severe: at that season the pestilential sand-wind blows over Egypt some 50 days, hence its name Chamsin. (cp. Gen. xli. 6 note).

17. *Ye are idle*] The old Egyptian lan-

are idle, *ye are* idle: therefore ye say, Let us go *and* do sacrifice
18 to the LORD. Go therefore now, *and* work; for there shall no
straw be given you, yet shall ye deliver the tale of bricks.
19 And the officers of the children of Israel did see *that* they *were*
in evil *case*, after it was said, Ye shall not minish *ought* from
20 your bricks of your daily task. ¶ And they met Moses and
Aaron, who stood in the way, as they came forth from Pharaoh:
21 [h]and they said unto them, The LORD look upon you, and judge;
because ye have made our savour [1]to be abhorred in the eyes of
Pharaoh, and in the eyes of his servants, to put a sword in their
22 hand to slay us. ¶ And Moses returned unto the LORD, and
said, Lord, wherefore hast thou *so* evil entreated this people?
23 Why *is* it *that* thou hast sent me? For since I came to Pharaoh
to speak in thy name, he hath done evil to this people; [2]neither
hast thou delivered thy people at all.

CHAP. 6. THEN the LORD said unto Moses, Now shalt thou see what
I will do to Pharaoh: for [a]with a strong hand shall he let them
go, and with a strong hand [b]shall he drive them out of his land.
2 ¶ And God spake unto Moses, and said unto him, I *am* [3]the LORD:
3 and I appeared unto Abraham, unto Isaac, and unto Jacob, by
the name of [c]God Almighty, but by my name [d]JEHOVAH was
4 I not known to them. [e]And I have also established my covenant with them, [f]to give them the land of Canaan, the land of
5 their pilgrimage, wherein they were strangers. And [g]I have also
heard the groaning of the children of Israel, whom the Egyptians keep in bondage; and I have remembered my covenant.
6 Wherefore say unto the children of Israel, [h]I *am* the LORD, and
[i]I will bring you out from under the burdens of the Egyptians,
and I will rid you out of their bondage, and I will [k]redeem you
7 with a stretched out arm, and with great judgments: and I will
[l]take you to me for a people, and [m]I will be to you a God: and
ye shall know that I *am* the LORD your God, which bringeth you
8 out [n]from under the burdens of the Egyptians. And I will bring
you in unto the land, concerning the which I did [4][o]swear to give
it to Abraham, to Isaac, and to Jacob; and I will give it you

[h] ch. 6. 9.

[a] ch. 3. 19. [b] ch. 11. 1. & 12. 31, 33, 39. [c] Gen. 17. 1. & reff. [d] ch. 3. 14. Ps. 68. 4. & 83. 18. John 8. 58. Rev. 1. 4. [e] Gen. 15. 18. & 17. 4. [f] Gen. 17. 8. & 28. 4. [g] ch. 2. 24. [h] ver. 2, 8. [i] ch. 3. 17. Deut. 26. 8. Ps. 81. 6. [k] ch. 15. 13. Deut. 7. 8. 1 Chr. 17. 21. Neh. 1. 10. [l] Deut. 4. 20. & 14. 2. & 26. 18. 2 Sam. 7. 24. [m] ch. 29. 45. Deut. 29. 13. Rev. 21. 7. [n] ch. 5. 4, 5. Ps. 81. 6. [o] Gen. 15. 18. & reff.

[1] Heb. *to stink*, Gen. 34. 30. 1 Sam. 13. 4. & 27. 12. 2 Sam. 10. 6. 1 Chr. 19. 6.
[2] Heb. *delivering thou hast not delivered*.
[3] Or, *Jehovah*.
[4] Heb. *lift up my hand*. See Gen. 14. 22. Deut. 32. 40.

guage abounds in epithets which shew contempt for idleness. The charge was equally offensive and ingenious; one which would be readily believed by Egyptians who knew how much public and private labours were impeded by festivals and other religious ceremonies. Among the great sins which, according to Egyptian belief, involved condemnation in the final judgment, idleness is twice mentioned.

23. The earnestness of this remonstrance, and even its approach to irreverence, are quite in keeping with other notices of Moses' naturally impetuous character. See iii. 13.

VI. 2, 3. There appears to have been an interval of some months between the preceding events and this renewal of the promise to Moses. The oppression in the mean time was not merely driving the people to desperation, but preparing them by severe labour, varied by hasty wanderings in search of stubble, for the exertions and privations of the wilderness. Hence the formal and solemn character of the announcements in the whole chapter.

2. *I am the* LORD, &c.] The meaning seems to be this:—"I am Jehovah, and I appeared to Abraham, Isaac, and Jacob as El Shaddai, but as to my name Jehovah, I was not made known to them." In other words, the full import of that name was not disclosed to them. See iii. 14.

3. *God Almighty*] Rather, "**El Shaddai**," it is better to keep this as a proper name.

6. *with a stretched out arm*] The figure is common and quite intelligible; it may have struck Moses and the people the more forcibly since they were familiar with the hieroglyphic which represents might by two outstretched arms.

9 for an heritage: I *am* the LORD. And Moses spake so unto
the children of Israel: [p] but they hearkened not unto Moses for [p] ch. 5. 21.
10 [1] anguish of spirit, and for cruel bondage. ¶ And the LORD spake
11 unto Moses, saying, Go in, speak unto Pharaoh king of Egypt,
12 that he let the children of Israel go out of his land. And Moses
spake before the LORD, saying, Behold, the children of Israel
have [q] not hearkened unto me; how then shall Pharaoh hear [q] ver. 9.
13 me, [r] who *am* of uncircumcised lips? And the LORD spake unto [r] ver. 30.
Moses and unto Aaron, and gave them a charge unto the chil- ch. 4. 10. Jer. 1. 6.
dren of Israel, and unto Pharaoh king of Egypt, to bring the
14 children of Israel out of the land of Egypt. ¶ These *be* the
heads of their fathers' houses: [s] The sons of Reuben the first- [s] Gen. 46. 9.
born of Israel; Hanoch, and Pallu, Hezron, and Carmi: these 1 Chr. 5. 3. [t] Gen. 46. 10.
15 *be* the families of Reuben. [t] And the sons of Simeon; Jemuel, 1 Chr. 4. 24.
and Jamin, and Ohad, and Jachin, and Zohar, and Shaul the [u] Gen. 46. 11. Num. 3. 17.
son of a Canaanitish woman: these *are* the families of Simeon. 1 Chr. 6. 1,
16 ¶ And these *are* the names of [u] the sons of Levi according to their 16.
generations; Gershon, and Kohath, and Merari: and the years [x] 1 Chr. 6. 17. [y] Num. 26.
17 of the life of Levi *were* an hundred thirty and seven years. [x] The 57.
sons of Gershon; Libni, and Shimi, according to their families. 1 Chr. 6. 2, 18.
18 And [y] the sons of Kohath; Amram, and Izhar, and Hebron, [z] 1 Chr. 6. 19.
and Uzziel: and the years of the life of Kohath *were* an hun- & 23. 21.
19 dred thirty and three years. And [z] the sons of Merari; Mahali [a] ch. 2. 1, 2. [b] Num. 16. 1.
and Mushi: these *are* the families of Levi according to their 1 Chr. 6.
20 generations. And [a] Amram took him Jochebed his father's 37, 38.
sister to wife; and she bare him Aaron and Moses: and the [c] Lev. 10. 4. Num. 3. 30.
years of the life of Amram *were* an hundred and thirty and seven [d] Ruth 4.
21 years. And [b] the sons of Izhar; Korah, and Nepheg, and Zithri. 19, 20. 1 Chr. 2. 10.
22 And [c] the sons of Uzziel; Mishael, and Elzaphan, and Zithri. Matt. 1. 4.
23 And Aaron took him Elisheba, daughter of [d] Amminadab, sister [e] Lev. 10. 1. Num. 3. 2.
of Naashon, to wife; and she bare him [e] Nadab, and Abihu, 1 Chr. 6. 3.

[1] Heb. *shortness*, or, *straitness*.

---

9. *they hearkened not*] The contrast between the reception of this communication and that recorded in iv. 31 is accounted for by the change of circumstances. On the former occasion the people were comparatively at ease, accustomed to their lot, sufficiently afflicted to long for deliverance, and sufficiently free in spirit to hope for it.

for anguish] See the margin; out of breath, as it were, after their cruel disappointment, they were quite absorbed by their misery, unable and unwilling to attend to any fresh communication.

11. *go out of his land*] Moses is now bidden to demand not a permission for a three days' journey (iii. 18 note), which might be within the boundaries of Egypt, but for departure from the land.

12. *uncircumcised lips*] An uncircumcised ear is one that does not hear clearly; an uncircumcised heart one slow to receive and understand warnings; uncircumcised lips, such as cannot speak fluently. The recurrence of the hesitation of Moses is natural; great as was the former trial this was far more severe; yet his words as ever imply fear of failure, not of personal danger (see iii. 11).

13. *unto Moses and unto Aaron*] The final and formal charge to the two brothers is given, as might be expected, before the plagues are denounced. With this verse begins a new section of the history.

14. *These be the heads*] We have in the following verses, not a complete genealogy, but a summary account of the family of the two brothers. Moses records for the satisfaction of Hebrew readers, to whom genealogical questions were always interesting, the descent and position of the designated leaders of the nation. See *vv.* 26, 27.

20. *Amram*] This can scarcely be the same person who is mentioned in *v.* 18; but his descendant and representative in the generation immediately preceding that of Moses. The intervening links are omitted, as is the rule where they are not needed for some special purpose, and do not bear upon the history.

Jochebed] The name means "the glory of Jehovah," one clear instance of the use of the sacred name before the Exodus.

father's sister] This was within the prohibited degrees after the Law was given (Lev. xviii. 12) but not previously.

24 Eleazar, and Ithamar. And the [f]sons of Korah; Assir, and
Elkanah, and Abiasaph: these *are* the families of the Kor-
25 hites. And Eleazar Aaron's son took him *one* of the daughters
of Putiel to wife; and [g]she bare him Phinehas: these *are* the
heads of the fathers of the Levites according to their families.
26 ¶These *are* that Aaron and Moses, [h]to whom the LORD said, Bring
out the children of Israel from the land of Egypt according to
27 their [i]armies. These *are* they which [k]spake to Pharaoh king of
Egypt, [l]to bring out the children of Israel from Egypt: these
28 *are* that Moses and Aaron. ¶And it came to pass on the day
29 *when* the LORD spake unto Moses in the land of Egypt, that the
LORD spake unto Moses, saying, [m]I *am* the LORD, [n]speak thou
30 unto Pharaoh king of Egypt all that I say unto thee. And Moses
said before the LORD, Behold, [o]I *am* of uncircumcised lips, and
how shall Pharaoh hearken unto me?

CHAP. 7. AND the LORD said unto Moses, See, I have made thee [a]a
god to Pharaoh: And Aaron thy brother shall be [b]thy prophet.
2 Thou [c]shalt speak all that I command thee: and Aaron thy
brother shall speak unto Pharaoh, that he send the children of
3 Israel out of his land. And [d]I will harden Pharaoh's heart,
and [e]multiply my [f]signs and my wonders in the land of Egypt.
4 But Pharaoh shall not hearken unto you, [g]that I may lay my
hand upon Egypt, and bring forth mine armies, *and* my people
the children of Israel, out of the land of Egypt [h]by great judg-
5 ments. And the Egyptians [i]shall know that I *am* the LORD,
when I [k]stretch forth mine hand upon Egypt, and bring out the
6 children of Israel from among them. And Moses and Aaron
7 [l]did as the LORD commanded them, so did they. And Moses *was*
[m]fourscore years old, and Aaron fourscore and three years old,
8 when they spake unto Pharaoh. ¶And the LORD spake unto
9 Moses and unto Aaron, saying, When Pharaoh shall speak unto
you, saying, [n]Shew a miracle for you: then thou shalt say unto
Aaron, [o]Take thy rod, and cast *it* before Pharaoh, *and* it shall

[f] Num. 26. 11.
[g] Num. 25. 7, 11. Josh. 24. 33.
[h] ver. 13.
[i] ch. 12. 17. Num. 33. 1.
[k] ch. 5. 1, 3. & 7. 10.
[l] ch. 32. 7. & 33. 1. Ps. 77. 20.
[m] ver. 2.
[n] ver. 11. ch. 7. 2.
[o] ver. 12. ch. 4. 10.
[a] ch. 4. 16. Jer. 1. 10.
[b] ch. 4. 16.
[c] ch. 4. 15.
[d] ch. 4. 21.
[e] ch. 11. 9.
[f] ch. 4. 7.
[g] ch. 10. 1. & 11. 9.
[h] ch. 6. 6.
[i] ver. 17. ch. 8. 22. & 14. 4, 18. Ps. 9. 16.
[k] ch. 3. 20.
[l] ver. 2.
[m] Deut. 29. 5. & 34. 7. Acts 7. 23, 30.
[n] Isai. 7. 11. John 2. 18. & 6. 30.
[o] ch. 4. 2, 17.

26, 27. This emphatic repetition shews the reason for inserting the genealogy. The names of Moses and Aaron are given twice and in a different order; in the 26th verse probably to mark Aaron as the elder in the genealogy, and in the 27th to denote the leadership of Moses.

28. This and the following verses belong to the next chapter. They mark distinctly the beginning of a subdivision of the narrative.

30. See ver. 12.

VII. With this chapter begins the series of miracles wrought in Egypt. They are progressive. The first miracle is wrought to accredit the mission of the brothers; it is simply credential, and unaccompanied by any infliction. Then come signs which shew that the powers of nature are subject to the will of Jehovah, each plague being attended with grave consequences to the Egyptians, yet not inflicting severe loss or suffering; then in rapid succession come ruinous and devastating plagues, murrain, boils, hail and lightning, locusts, darkness, and lastly, the death of the firstborn. Each of the inflictions has a demonstrable connection with Egyptian customs and phenomena; each is directly aimed at some Egyptian superstition; all are marvellous, not, for the most part, as reversing, but as developing forces inherent in nature, and directing them to a special end. The effects correspond with these characteristics; the first miracles are neglected; the following plagues first alarm, and then for a season, subdue, the king, who does not give way until his firstborn is struck. Even that blow leaves him capable of a last effort, which completes his ruin, and the deliverance of the Israelites.

1. *I have made thee a god*] Or "appointed thee." See marg. reff. Moses will stand in this peculiar relation to Pharaoh, that God will address him by a prophet, *i.e.* by one appointed to speak in His name. The passage is an important one as illustrating the primary and essential characteristic of a prophet, he is the declarer of God's will and purpose.

3. *wonders*] A word used only of portents wrought to prove a divine interposition; they were the credentials of God's messengers.

9. *thy rod*] Apparently the rod before described (iv. 2), which Moses on this occasion gives to Aaron as his representative.

10 become a serpent. And Moses and Aaron went in unto Pharaoh,
and they did so [p]as the LORD had commanded: and Aaron cast [p] ver. 9.
down his rod before Pharaoh, and before his servants, and it
11 [q]became a serpent. Then Pharaoh also [r]called the wise men and [q] ch. 4. 3.
[s]the sorcerers: now the magicians of Egypt, they also [t]did in [r] Gen. 41. 8.
12 like manner with their enchantments. For they cast down every [s] 2 Tim. 3. 8. [t] ver. 22.
man his rod, and they became serpents: but Aaron's rod swal- ch. 8. 7, 18.
13 lowed up their rods. And he hardened Pharaoh's heart, that
14 he hearkened not unto them; [u]as the LORD had said. ¶ And the [u] ch. 4. 21.
LORD said unto Moses, [x]Pharaoh's heart *is* hardened, he re- ver. 4. [x] ch. 8. 15.
15 fuseth to let the people go. Get thee unto Pharaoh in the & 10. 1, 20,
morning; lo, he goeth out unto the water; and thou shalt stand 27.
by the river's brink against he come; and [y]the rod which was [y] ch. 4. 2, 3.
16 turned to a serpent shalt thou take in thine hand. And thou ver. 10.
shalt say unto him, [z]The LORD God of the Hebrews hath sent [z] ch. 3. 18.
me unto thee, saying, Let my people go, [a]that they may serve [a] ch. 3. 12,
me in the wilderness: and, behold, hitherto thou wouldest not 18.
17 hear. Thus saith the LORD, In this [b]thou shalt know that I *am* & 5. 1, 3. [b] ch. 5. 2.
the LORD: behold, I will smite with the rod that *is* in mine ver. 5.
hand upon the waters which *are* in the river, and [c]they shall be [c] ch. 4. 9.
18 turned [d]to blood. And the fish that *is* in the river shall die, and [d] Rev. 16.
the river shall stink; and the Egyptians shall [e]lothe to drink 4, 6. [e] ver. 24.

---

a serpent] A word different from that in iv. 3. Here a more general term, "Tannin," is employed, which in other passages includes all sea or river monsters, and is more specially applied to the crocodile as a symbol of Egypt. It occurs in the Egyptian ritual, nearly in the same form, "Tanem," as a synonym of the monster serpent which represents the principle of antagonism to light and life.

11. Three names for the magicians of Egypt are given in this verse. The "wise men" are men who know occult arts. The "sorcerers" are they who "mutter magic formulæ," especially when driving away crocodiles, snakes, asps, &c. It was natural that Pharaoh should have sent for such persons. The "magicians" are the "bearers of sacred words," scribes and interpreters of hieroglyphic writings. Books containing magic formulæ belonged exclusively to the king; no one was permitted to consult them but the priests and wise men, who formed a council or college, and were called in by the Pharaoh on all occasions of difficulty.

The names of the two principal magicians, Jannes and Jambres, who "withstood Moses," are preserved by St. Paul, 2 Tim. iii. 8. Both names are Egyptian.

enchantments] The original expression implies a deceptive appearance, an illusion, a juggler's trick, not an actual putting forth of magic power. Pharaoh may or may not have believed in a real transformation; but in either case he would naturally consider that if the portent wrought by Aaron differed from that of the magicians, it was a difference of degree only, implying merely superiority in a common art. The miracle which followed (*v.* 12) was sufficient to convince him had he been open to conviction. It was a miracle which shewed the truth and power of Jehovah in contrast with that of others.

13. *And he hardened*] Or **Pharaoh's heart was hardened.** See iv. 21.

15. *he goeth out unto the water*] The Nile was worshipped under various names and symbols; at Memphis especially, as Hapi, *i.e.* Apis, the sacred bull, or living representation of Osiris, of whom the river was regarded as the embodiment or manifestation. If, as is probable, the king went to offer his devotions, the miracle would have peculiar force and suitableness. It was also the season of the yearly overflowing, about the middle of June; and the daily rise of the water was accurately recorded, under the personal superintendence of the king. In early inscriptions the Nilometer is the symbol of stability and providential care.

17. *turned to blood*] This miracle would bear a certain resemblance to natural phenomena, and therefore be one which Pharaoh might see with amazement and dismay, yet without complete conviction. It is well known that before the rise the water of the Nile is green and unfit to drink. About the 25th of June it becomes clear, and then yellow, and gradually reddish like ochre; an effect due to the presence of microscopic cryptogams and infusoria. The supernatural character of the visitation was attested by the suddenness of the change, by its immediate connection with the words and act of Moses, and by its effects. It killed the fishes, and made the water unfit for use, neither of which results follows the annual discoloration.

18. *shall lothe*] The water of the Nile has

19 of the water of the river. ¶And the LORD spake unto Moses,
Say unto Aaron, Take thy rod, and [f]stretch out thine hand
upon the waters of Egypt, upon their streams, upon their rivers,
and upon their ponds, and upon all their [1]pools of water, that
they may become blood; and *that* there may be blood throughout all the land of Egypt, both in *vessels of* wood, and in *vessels of*
20 stone. And Moses and Aaron did so, as the LORD commanded;
and he [g]lifted up the rod, and smote the waters that *were* in the
river, in the sight of Pharaoh, and in the sight of his servants;
and all the [h]waters that *were* in the river were turned to blood.
21 And the fish that *was* in the river died; and the river stank, and
the Egyptians [i]could not drink of the water of the river; and
22 there was blood throughout all the land of Egypt. [k]And the
magicians of Egypt did so with their enchantments: And
Pharaoh's heart was hardened, neither did he hearken unto them;
23 [l]as the LORD had said. And Pharaoh turned and went into
24 his house, neither did he set his heart to this also. And all the
Egyptians digged round about the river for water to drink; for
25 they could not drink of the water of the river. And seven days
were fulfilled, after that the LORD had smitten the river.

CHAP. 8. AND the LORD spake unto Moses, Go unto Pharaoh, and
say unto him, Thus saith the LORD, Let my people go, [a]that
2 they may serve me. And if thou [b]refuse to let *them* go, behold,
3 I will smite all thy borders with [c]frogs: and the river shall
bring forth frogs abundantly, which shall go up and come into
thine house, and into [d]thy bedchamber, and upon thy bed, and
into the house of thy servants, and upon thy people, and into
4 thine ovens, and into thy [2]kneadingtroughs: and the frogs shall
come up both on thee, and upon thy people, and upon all thy
5 servants. ¶And the LORD spake unto Moses, Say unto Aaron,
[e]Stretch forth thine hand with thy rod over the streams, over

[f] ch. 8. 5, 6, 16. & 9. 22. & 10. 12, 21. & 14. 21, 26.
[g] ch. 17. 5.
[h] Ps. 78. 44. & 105. 29.
[i] ver. 18.
[k] ver. 11.
[l] ver. 3.
[a] ch. 3. 12, 18.
[b] ch. 7. 14. & 9. 2.
[c] Rev. 16. 13.
[d] Ps. 105. 30.
[e] ch. 7. 19.

[1] Heb. *gathering of their waters.* [2] Or, *dough.*

---

always been regarded by the Egyptians as a blessing peculiar to their land. It is the only pure and wholesome water in their country, since the water in wells and cisterns is unwholesome, while rain water seldom falls, and fountains are extremely rare.

19. The *streams* mean the natural branches of the Nile in Lower Egypt. The word *rivers* should rather be *canals*; they were of great extent, running parallel to the Nile, and communicating with it by sluices, which were opened at the rise, and closed at the subsidence of the inundation. The word rendered *ponds* refers either to natural fountains, or more probably to cisterns or tanks found in every town and village. The *pools*, lit. "gathering of waters," were the reservoirs, always large and some of enormous extent, containing sufficient water to irrigate the country in the dry season.

in vessels of wood] The Nile water is kept in vessels and is purified for use by filtering, and by certain ingredients such as the paste of almonds.

21. *the fish*, &c.] The Egyptians subsisted to a great extent on the fish of the Nile, though salt-water fish was regarded as impure. A mortality among the fish was a plague much dreaded.

25. *seven days*] This marks the duration of the plague. The natural discoloration of the Nile water lasts generally much longer, about 20 days.

VIII. **2.** *with frogs*] Some months appear to have elapsed between this and the former plague, if the frogs made their appearance at the usual time, that is in September. The special species mentioned here is of Egyptian origin. This plague was, like the preceding, in general accordance with natural phenomena, but marvellous both for its extent and intensity, and for its direct connection with the words and acts of God's messengers. It had also apparently, like the other plagues, a direct bearing upon Egyptian superstitions. There was a female deity with a frog's head, and the frog was connected with the most ancient forms of nature-worship in Egypt.

3. *into thine house*] This appears to have been peculiar to the plague, as such. It was specially the visitation which would be felt by the scrupulously clean Egyptians.

kneadingtroughs] Not "dough," as in the margin. See xii. 34.

the rivers, and over the ponds, and cause frogs to come up upon
6 the land of Egypt. And Aaron stretched out his hand over the
waters of Egypt; and [f] the frogs came up, and covered the land
7 of Egypt. [g] And the magicians did so with their enchantments,
8 and brought up frogs upon the land of Egypt. ¶ Then Pharaoh
called for Moses and Aaron, and said, [h] Intreat the LORD, that
he may take away the frogs from me, and from my people; and
I will let the people go, that they may do sacrifice unto the
9 LORD. And Moses said unto Pharaoh, [1] Glory over me: [2] when
shall I intreat for thee, and for thy servants, and for thy people,
[3] to destroy the frogs from thee and thy houses, *that* they may
10 remain in the river only? And he said, [4] To morrow. And he
said, *Be it* according to thy word: that thou mayest know that
11 [i] *there is* none like unto the LORD our God. And the frogs shall
depart from thee, and from thy houses, and from thy servants,
12 and from thy people; they shall remain in the river only. ¶ And
Moses and Aaron went out from Pharaoh: and Moses [k] cried
unto the LORD because of the frogs which he had brought
13 against Pharaoh. And the LORD did according to the word of
Moses; and the frogs died out of the houses, out of the villages,
14 and out of the fields. And they gathered them together upon
15 heaps: and the land stank. But when Pharaoh saw that there
was [l] respite, [m] he hardened his heart, and hearkened not unto
16 them; as the LORD had said. ¶ And the LORD said unto Moses,
Say unto Aaron, Stretch out thy rod, and smite the dust of the
land, that it may become lice throughout all the land of Egypt.
17 And they did so; for Aaron stretched out his hand with his rod,
and smote the dust of the earth, and [n] it became lice in man,
and in beast; all the dust of the land became lice throughout
18 all the land of Egypt. And [o] the magicians did so with their
enchantments to bring forth lice, but they [p] could not: so there
19 were lice upon man, and upon beast. Then the magicians said
unto Pharaoh, This *is* [q] the finger of God: and Pharaoh's [r] heart
was hardened, and he hearkened not unto them; as the LORD

[f] Ps. 78. 45. & 105. 30.
[g] ch. 7. 11.
[h] ch. 9. 28. & 10. 17. Num. 21. 7. 1 Kin. 13. 6. Acts 8. 24.
[i] ch. 9. 14. Deut. 33. 26. 2 Sam. 7. 22. 1 Chr. 17. 20. Ps. 86. 8. Isai. 46. 9. Jer. 10. 6, 7.
[k] ver. 30. ch. 9. 33. & 10. 18. & 32. 11. Jam. 5. 16, 17, 18.
[l] Eccles. 8. 11.
[m] ch. 7. 14.
[n] Ps. 105. 31.
[o] ch. 7. 11.
[p] Luke 10. 18. 2 Tim. 3. 8, 9.
[q] 1 Sam. 6. 3, 9. Ps. 8. 3. Matt. 12. 28. Luke 11. 20.
[r] ver. 15.

[1] Or, *Have* this *honour over me, &c.*
[2] Or, *against when.* Heb. *to cut off.*
[4] Or, *against to-morrow.*

---

7. The magicians would seem to have been able to increase the plague, but not to remove it; hence Pharaoh's application to Moses, the first symptoms of yielding.

9. *Glory over me*] See the margin, "have honour over me," *i.e.* have the honour, or advantage over me, directing me when I shall entreat God for thee and thy servants.

when] Or **by when**; *i.e.* for what exact time. Pharaoh's answer in *v.* 10 refers to this, **by to-morrow**. The shortness of the time would, of course, be a test of the supernatural character of the transaction.

13. *villages*] Lit. inclosures, or courtyards.

16. It is observed by Hebrew commentators that the nine plagues are divided into three groups: distinct warnings are given of the first two plagues in each group; the third in each is inflicted without any previous notice; viz. the third, *lice,* the sixth, *boils,* the ninth, *darkness.*

the dust of the land] The two preceding plagues fell upon the Nile. This fell on the earth, which was worshipped in Egypt as the father of the gods. An especial sacredness was attached to the black fertile soil of the basin of the Nile, called Chemi, from which the ancient name of Egypt is supposed to be derived.

lice] The Hebrew word occurs only in connection with this plague. These insects are generally identified with mosquitos, a plague nowhere greater than in Egypt. They are most troublesome towards October, *i.e.* soon after the plague of frogs, and are dreaded not only for the pain and annoyance which they cause, but also because they are said to penetrate into the body through the nostrils and ears.

19. *the finger of God*] This expression is thoroughly Egyptian; it need not imply that the magicians recognised Jehovah as the God Who wrought the marvel. They may possibly have referred it to a god hostile to their own protectors.

[s] ch. 7. 15. [t] ver. 1. [u] ch. 9. 4, 6, 26. & 10. 23. & 11. 6, 7. & 12. 13. [x] Ps. 78. 45. & 105. 31. [y] Gen. 43. 32. & 46. 34. Deut. 7. 25, 26. & 12. 31. [z] ch. 3. 18. [a] ch. 3. 12. [b] ver. 8. ch. 9. 28. 1 Kin. 13. 6. [c] ver. 15. [d] ver. 12.

20 had said. ¶ And the LORD said unto Moses, [s]Rise up early in
the morning, and stand before Pharaoh; lo, he cometh forth to
the water; and say unto him, Thus saith the LORD, [t]Let my
21 people go, that they may serve me. Else, if thou wilt not let
my people go, behold, I will send [1]swarms *of flies* upon thee,
and upon thy servants, and upon thy people, and into thy
houses: and the houses of the Egyptians shall be full of
22 swarms *of flies*, and also the ground whereon they *are*. And
[u]I will sever in that day the land of Goshen, in which my
people dwell, that no swarms *of flies* shall be there; to the end
thou mayest know that I *am* the LORD in the midst of the earth.
23 And I will put [2]a division between my people and thy people:
24 [3]to morrow shall this sign be. And the LORD did so; and
[x]there came a grievous swarm *of flies* into the house of Pharaoh, and *into* his servants' houses, and into all the land of
Egypt: the land was [4]corrupted by reason of the swarm *of flies*.
25 ¶ And Pharaoh called for Moses and for Aaron, and said, Go ye,
26 sacrifice to your God in the land. And Moses said, It is not
meet so to do; for we shall sacrifice [y]the abomination of the
Egyptians to the LORD our God: lo, shall we sacrifice the
abomination of the Egyptians before their eyes, and will they
27 not stone us? We will go [z]three days' journey into the wilderness, and sacrifice to the LORD our God, as [a]he shall command
28 us. And Pharaoh said, I will let you go, that ye may sacrifice to
the LORD your God in the wilderness; only ye shall not go very
29 far away: [b]intreat for me. And Moses said, Behold, I go out
from thee, and I will intreat the LORD that the swarms *of flies*
may depart from Pharaoh, from his servants, and from his
people, to morrow: but let not Pharaoh [c]deal deceitfully any
more in not letting the people go to sacrifice to the LORD.
30 ¶ And Moses went out from Pharaoh, and [d]intreated the LORD.
31 And the LORD did according to the word of Moses; and he
removed the swarms *of flies* from Pharaoh, from his servants,

[1] Or, *a mixture of* noisome beasts, &c.
[2] Heb. *a redemption*.
[3] Or, *by to morrow*.
[4] Or, *destroyed*.

---

20. *cometh forth to the water*] See vii. 15 note. It is not improbable that on this occasion Pharaoh went to the Nile with a procession in order to open the solemn festival, which was held 120 days after the first rise, at the end of October or early in November. At that time the inundation is abating and the first traces of vegetation are seen on the deposit of fresh soil.

The plague now announced may be regarded as connected with the atmosphere, also an object of worship.

21. *swarms of flies*] Generally supposed to be the dog-fly, which at certain seasons is described as a far worse plague than mosquitos. Others however adopt the opinion that the insects were a species of beetle, which was reverenced by the Egyptians as a symbol of life, of reproductive or creative power. The sun-god, as creator, bore the name Chepera, and is represented in the form, or with the head, of a beetle.

22. *I will sever*, &c.] This severance constituted a specific difference between this and the preceding plagues. Pharaoh could not of course attribute the exemption of Goshen from a scourge, which fell on the valley of the Nile, to an Egyptian deity, certainly not to Chepera (see the last note), a special object of worship in Lower Egypt.

25. *to your God*] Pharaoh now admits the existence and power of the God Whom he had professed not to know; but, as Moses is careful to record, he recognises Him only as the national Deity of the Israelites.

in the land] *i.e.* in Egypt, not beyond the frontier.

26. *the abomination*] *i.e.* an animal which the Egyptians held it sacrilegious to slay. The ox, bull, or cow, is meant. The cow was never sacrificed in Egypt, being sacred to Isis, and from a very early age the ox was worshipped throughout Egypt, and more especially at Heliopolis and Memphis under various designations, Apis, Mnevis, Amen-Ehe, as the symbol or manifestation of their greatest deities, Osiris, Atum, Ptah, and Isis.

27. *three days' journey*] See iii. 18 note.

32 and from his people; there remained not one. And Pharaoh
[e]hardened his heart at this time also, neither would he let the [e] ver. 15.
people go. ch. 4. 21.
Chap. 9. THEN the Lord said unto Moses, [a]Go in unto Pharaoh, [a] ch. 8. 1.
and tell him, Thus saith the Lord God of the Hebrews, Let my
2 people go, that they may serve me. For if thou [b]refuse to let [b] ch. 8. 2.
3 *them* go, and wilt hold them still, Behold, the [c]hand of the [c] ch. 7. 4.
Lord is upon thy cattle which *is* in the field, upon the horses,
upon the asses, upon the camels, upon the oxen, and upon the
4 sheep: *there shall be* a very grievous murrain. And [d]the Lord [d] ch. 8. 22.
shall sever between the cattle of Israel and the cattle of Egypt:
and there shall nothing die of all *that is* the children's of Israel.
5 And the Lord appointed a set time, saying, To morrow the
6 Lord shall do this thing in the land. And the Lord did that
thing on the morrow, and [e]all the cattle of Egypt died: but of [e] Ps. 78. 50.
7 the cattle of the children of Israel died not one. And Pharaoh
sent, and, behold, there was not one of the cattle of the Israelites
dead. And [f]the heart of Pharaoh was hardened, and he did not [f] ch. 7. 14.
8 let the people go. ¶ And the Lord said unto Moses and unto & 8. 32.
Aaron, Take to you handfuls of ashes of the furnace, and let
Moses sprinkle it toward the heaven in the sight of Pharaoh.
9 And it shall become small dust in all the land of Egypt, and
shall be [g]a boil breaking forth *with* blains upon man, and upon [g] Rev. 16. 2.
10 beast, throughout all the land of Egypt. And they took ashes
of the furnace, and stood before Pharaoh; and Moses sprinkled
it up toward heaven; and it became [h]a boil breaking forth *with* [h] Deut. 28. 27.
11 blains upon man, and upon beast. And the [i]magicians could [i] ch. 8. 18, 19.
not stand before Moses because of the boils; for the boil was
12 upon the magicians, and upon all the Egyptians. And the 2 Tim. 3. 9.
Lord hardened the heart of Pharaoh, and he hearkened not
13 unto them; [k]as the Lord had spoken unto Moses. ¶ And the [k] ch. 4. 21.
Lord said unto Moses, [l]Rise up early in the morning, and stand [l] ch. 8. 20.
before Pharaoh, and say unto him, Thus saith the Lord God of
14 the Hebrews, Let my people go, that they may serve me. For I

IX. 3. *a very grievous murrain*] Or "pestilence;" but the word murrain, *i.e.* a great mortality, exactly expresses the meaning. This terrible visitation struck far more severely than the preceding, which had caused distress and suffering; it attacked the resources of the nation.

the camels] These animals are only twice mentioned, here and Gen. xii. 16, in connection with Egypt. Though camels are never represented on the monuments, they were known to the Egyptians, and were probably used on the frontier.

6. *all the cattle*] *i.e.* which were left in the field; cp. *vv.* 19—21.

7. *was hardened*] See iv. 21. Pharaoh probably attributed the exemption of the Israelites to natural causes. They were a pastoral race, well acquainted with all that appertained to the care of cattle; and dwelling in a healthy district probably far more than the rest of Lower Egypt.

8. This marks a distinct advance and change in the character of the visitations. Hitherto the Egyptians had not been attacked directly in their persons. It is the second plague which was not preceded by a demand and warning, probably on account of the peculiar hardness shewn by Pharaoh in reference to the murrain.

ashes of the furnace] The act was evidently symbolical: the ashes were to be sprinkled towards heaven, challenging, so to speak, the Egyptian deities. There may possibly be a reference to an Egyptian custom of scattering to the winds ashes of victims offered to Typhon.

9. *a boil*] Means probably a burning tumour or carbuncle breaking out in pustulous ulcers. The miracle consisting in the severity of the plague and its direct connection with the act of Moses.

11. This verse seems to imply that the magicians now formally gave way and confessed their defeat.

13—34. With the plague of hail begins the last series of plagues, which differ from the former both in their severity and their effects. Each produced a temporary, but real, change in Pharaoh's feelings.

14. *all my plagues*] This applies to all the plagues which follow; the effect of each was

will at this time send all my plagues upon thine heart, and
upon thy servants, and upon thy people; [m]that thou mayest
15 know that *there is* none like me in all the earth. For now I will
[n]stretch out my hand, that I may smite thee and thy people
16 with pestilence; and thou shalt be cut off from the earth. And
in very deed for [o]this *cause* have I [1]raised thee up, for to shew
in thee my power; and that my name may be declared through-
17 out all the earth. As yet exaltest thou thyself against my
18 people, that thou wilt not let them go? Behold, to morrow
about this time I will cause it to rain a very grievous hail, such
as hath not been in Egypt since the foundation thereof even
19 until now. Send therefore now, *and* gather thy cattle, and all
that thou hast in the field; *for upon* every man and beast which
shall be found in the field, and shall not be brought home, the
20 hail shall come down upon them, and they shall die. He
that feared the word of the LORD among the servants of Pha-
21 raoh made his servants and his cattle flee into the houses: and
he that [2]regarded not the word of the LORD left his servants
22 and his cattle in the field. ¶ And the LORD said unto Moses,
Stretch forth thine hand toward heaven, that there may be
[p]hail in all the land of Egypt, upon man, and upon beast, and
upon every herb of the field, throughout the land of Egypt.
23 And Moses stretched forth his rod toward heaven: and [q]the
LORD sent thunder and hail, and the fire ran along upon the
ground; and the LORD rained hail upon the land of Egypt.
24 So there was hail, and fire mingled with the hail, very grievous,
such as there was none like it in all the land of Egypt since it
25 became a nation. And the hail smote throughout all the land
of Egypt all that *was* in the field, both man and beast; and the
hail [r]smote every herb of the field, and brake every tree of the
26 field. [s]Only in the land of Goshen, where the children of Israel
27 *were*, was there no hail. ¶ And Pharaoh sent, and called for Moses
and Aaron, and said unto them, [t]I have sinned this time: [u]the
28 LORD *is* righteous, and I and my people *are* wicked. [x]Intreat
the LORD (for *it is* enough) that there be no *more* [3]mighty thunderings and hail; and I will let you go, and ye shall stay no
29 longer. And Moses said unto him, As soon as I am gone out of
the city, I will [y]spread abroad my hands unto the LORD; *and*

[m] ch. 8. 10.
[n] ch. 3. 20.
[o] Rom. 9. 17. See ch. 14. 17. Prov. 16. 4. 1 Pet. 2. 9.
[p] Rev. 16. 21.
[q] Josh. 10. 11. Ps. 18. 13. & 78. 47. & 105. 32. & 148. 8. Isai. 30. 30. Ezek. 38. 22. Rev. 8. 7.
[r] Ps. 105. 33.
[s] ch. 8. 22. & 9. 4, 6. & 10. 23. & 11. 7 & 12. 13. Isai. 32. 18, 19.
[t] ch. 10. 16.
[u] 2 Chr. 12. 6. Ps. 129. 4. & 145. 17. Lam. 1. 18. Dan. 9. 14.
[x] ch. 8. 8, 28. & 10. 17. Acts 8. 24.
[y] 1 Kin. 8. 22, 38. Ps. 143. 6. Isai. 1. 15.

[1] Heb. *made thee stand.* [2] Heb. *set not his heart unto*, ch. 7, 23. [3] Heb. *voices of God*, Ps. 29. 3, 4.

---

foreseen and foretold. The words "at this time" point to a rapid and continuous succession of blows. The plagues which precede appear to have been spread over a considerable time; the first message of Moses was delivered after the early harvest of the year before, when the Israelites could gather stubble, *i.e.* in May and April: the second mission, when the plagues began, was probably towards the end of June, and they went on at intervals until the winter; this plague was in February; see *v.* 31.

15. *For now*, &c.] Better, **For now indeed, had I stretched forth my hand and smitten thee and thy people with the pestilence, then hadst thou been cut off from the earth.** The next verse gives the reason why God had not thus inflicted a summary punishment once for all.

16. *have I raised thee up*] See the margin. God kept Pharaoh "standing", *i.e.* permitted him to live and hold out until His own purpose was accomplished.

18. *a very grievous hail*] The miracle consisted in the magnitude of the infliction and in its immediate connection with the act of Moses.

19. In Egypt the cattle are sent to pasture in the open country from January to April, when the grass is abundant. They are kept in stalls the rest of the year.

20. *the word of the* LORD] This gives the first indication that the warnings had a salutary effect upon the Egyptians.

27. *the* LORD] Thus for the first time Pharaoh explicitly recognizes Jehovah as God (cp. v. 2).

29. *the earth is the* LORD'S] This declara-

the thunder shall cease, neither shall there be any more hail;
30 that thou mayest know how that the [z]earth *is* the LORD's. But [z] Ps. 24. 1.
as for thee and thy servants, [a]I know that ye will not yet fear 1 Cor. 10. 26, 28.
31 the LORD God. ¶ And the flax and the barley was smitten: [a] Isai. 26. 10.
32 [b]for the barley *was* in the ear, and the flax *was* bolled. But [b] Ruth 1. 22.
the wheat and the rie were not smitten; for they *were* [1]not & 2. 23.
33 grown up. ¶ And Moses went out of the city from Pharaoh,
and [c]spread abroad his hands unto the LORD: and the thunders [c] ver. 29.
and hail ceased, and the rain was not poured upon the earth. ch. 8. 12.
34 And when Pharaoh saw that the rain and the hail and the thunders were ceased, he sinned yet more, and hardened his heart,
35 he and his servants. And [d]the heart of Pharaoh was hardened, [d] ch. 4. 21.
neither would he let the children of Israel go; as the LORD had
spoken [2]by Moses.

CHAP. 10. AND the LORD said unto Moses, Go in unto Pharaoh:
[a]for I have hardened his heart, and the heart of his servants, [a] ch. 4. 21. & 7. 14.
2 [b]that I might shew these my signs before him: and that [c]thou [b] ch. 7. 4.
mayest tell in the ears of thy son, and of thy son's son, what [c] Deut. 4. 9.
things I have wrought in Egypt, and my signs which I have Ps. 44. 1. & 71. 18.
done among them; that ye may know how that I *am* the LORD. & 78. 5, &c.
3 And Moses and Aaron came in unto Pharaoh, and said unto Joel 1. 3.
him, Thus saith the LORD God of the Hebrews, How long wilt [d] 1 Kin. 21. 29.
thou refuse to [d]humble thyself before me? Let my people go, that 2 Chr. 7. 14.
4 they may serve me. Else, if thou refuse to let my people go, & 34. 27.
5 behold, to morrow will I bring the [e]locusts into thy coast: and Job 42. 6. Jer. 13. 18.
they shall cover the [3]face of the earth, that one cannot be able to Jam. 4. 10.
see the earth: and [f]they shall eat the residue of that which is 1 Pet. 5. 6. [e] Prov. 30.
escaped, which remaineth unto you from the hail, and shall eat 27.
6 every tree which groweth for you out of the field: and they [g]shall Rev. 9. 3. [f] ch. 9. 32.
fill thy houses, and the houses of all thy servants, and the houses Joel 1. 4. & 2. 25.
[g] ch. 8. 3, 21.

[1] Heb. *hidden*, or, *dark*. [2] Heb. *by the hand of Moses*, ch. 4. 13. [3] Heb. *eye*, ver. 15.

---

tion has a direct reference to Egyptian superstition. Each God was held to have special power within a given district; Pharaoh had learned that Jehovah was *a* God, he was now to admit that His power extended over the whole earth. The unity and universality of the Divine power, though occasionally recognized in ancient Egyptian documents, were overlaid at a very early period by systems alternating between Polytheism and Pantheism.

31. *the flax was bolled*] *i.e.* in blossom. This marks the time. In the north of Egypt the barley ripens and flax blossoms about the middle of February, or at the latest early in March, and both are gathered in before April, when the wheat harvest begins. The cultivation of flax must have been of great importance; linen was preferred to any material, and exclusively used by the priests. It is frequently mentioned on Egyptian monuments.

32. *rie*] Rather **spelt,** the common food of the ancient Egyptians, now called *doora* by the natives, and the only grain represented on the sculptures: the name, however, occurs on the monuments very frequently in combination with other species.

34, 35. *hardened*] Different words in the Hebrew. In *v.* 34 the word means "made heavy," *i.e.* obtuse, incapable of forming a right judgment; in *v.* 35 it is stronger, and implies a stubborn resolution.

X. **4.** *the locusts*] The locust is less common in Egypt than in many eastern countries, yet it is well known, and dreaded as the most terrible of scourges. They come generally from the western deserts, but sometimes from the east and the south-east. No less than nine names are given to the locust in the Bible, of which the word here used is the most common; it signifies "multitudinous," and whenever it occurs reference is made to its terrible devastations.

5. *the face*] Lit., cover "the eye of the earth," alluding to the darkness which follows, when the whole atmosphere is filled on all sides and to a great height by an innumerable quantity of these insects.

shall eat every tree] Not only the leaves, but the branches and even the wood were attacked and devoured. The Egyptians were passionately fond of trees.

6. *fill thy houses*] The terraces, courts, and even the inner apartments are said to be filled in a moment by a locust storm. Cp. Joel ii. 9.

of all the Egyptians; which neither thy fathers, nor thy fathers'
fathers have seen, since the day that they were upon the earth
unto this day. And he turned himself and went out from Pharaoh.
7 ¶ And Pharaoh's servants said unto him, How long shall this man
h ch. 23. 33. be [h] a snare unto us? Let the men go, that they may serve the LORD
Josh. 23. 13. 1 Sam. 18. 8 their God: knowest thou not yet that Egypt is destroyed? And
21. Moses and Aaron were brought again unto Pharaoh: and he
Eccles. 7. said unto them, Go, serve the LORD your God: *but* [1] who *are*
26. 1 Cor. 7. 35. 9 they that shall go? And Moses said, we will go with our young
and with our old, with our sons and with our daughters, with
i ch. 5. 1. our flocks and with our herds will we go; for [i] we *must hold*
10 a feast unto the LORD. And he said unto them, Let the LORD
be so with you, as I will let you go, and your little ones: look *to*
11 *it;* for evil *is* before you. Not so: go now ye *that are* men, and
serve the LORD; for that ye did desire. And they were driven
12 out from Pharaoh's presence. ¶ And the LORD said unto Moses,
k ch. 7. 19. [k] Stretch out thine hand over the land of Egypt for the locusts, that
l ver. 4. 5. they may come up upon the land of Egypt, and [l] eat every herb
13 of the land, *even* all that the hail hath left. And Moses stretched
forth his rod over the land of Egypt, and the LORD brought an
east wind upon the land all that day, and all *that* night; *and*
14 when it was morning, the east wind brought the locusts. And
m Ps. 78. 46. & 105. 34. [m] the locusts went up over all the land of Egypt, and rested in
n Joel 2. 2. all the coasts of Egypt: very grievous *were they;* [n] before them
there were no such locusts as they, neither after them shall be
o ver. 5. 15 such. For they [o] covered the face of the whole earth, so that the
p Ps. 105. 34. land was darkened; and they [p] did eat every herb of the land,
and all the fruit of the trees which the hail had left: and there
remained not any green thing in the trees, or in the herbs of the
16 field, through all the land of Egypt. ¶ Then Pharaoh [2] called for
q ch. 9. 27. Moses and Aaron in haste; and he said, [q] I have sinned against
17 the LORD your God, and against you. Now therefore forgive, I
r ch. 9. 28. pray thee, my sin only this once, and [r] intreat the LORD your
1 Kin. 13. 6. 18 God, that he may take away from me this death only. And he
s ch. 8. 30. 19 [s] went out from Pharaoh, and intreated the LORD. And the
LORD turned a mighty strong west wind, which took away the
t Joel 2. 20. locusts, and [3] cast them [t] into the Red sea; there remained not

[1] Heb. *who, and who, &c.* [2] Heb. *hastened to call.* [3] Heb. *fastened.*

---

7. For the first time the officers of Pharaoh intervene before the scourge is inflicted, shewing at once their belief in the threat, and their special terror of the infliction. Pharaoh also for the first time takes measures to prevent the evil; he does not indeed send for Moses and Aaron, but he permits them to be brought into his presence.

let the men go] *i.e.* the men only, not all the people. See *v.* 8.

9. *with our young,* &c.] The demand was not contrary to Egyptian usage, as great festivals were kept by the whole population.

10. *evil is before you*] *i.e.* "your intentions are evil." Great as the possible infliction might be, Pharaoh held it to be a less evil than the loss of so large a population.

13. *an east wind*] See *v.* 4. Moses is careful to record the natural and usual cause of the evil, portentous as it was both in extent and in connexion with its denouncement.

14. *went up*] At a distance the locusts appear hanging, as it were, like a heavy cloud over the land; as they approach they seem to rise, and they fill the atmosphere overhead on their arrival.

over all the land] Travellers mention a cloud of locusts extending over 500 miles, and so compact while on the wing that it completely hid the sun. This passage describes a swarm unprecedented in extent.

17. *this death only*] Pliny calls locusts a pestilence brought on by divine wrath. Pharaoh now recognizes the justice of his servants' apprehensions, *v.* 7.

19. *west wind*] Literally "a sea wind," a wind blowing from the sea on the north-west of Egypt.

Red sea] The Hebrew has the "Sea of Suph": the exact meaning of which is dis-

20 one locust in all the coasts of Egypt. But the LORD [u]hardened
Pharaoh's heart, so that he would not let the children of Israel
21 go. ¶ And the LORD said unto Moses, [x]Stretch out thine hand
toward heaven, that there may be darkness over the land of
22 Egypt, [1]even darkness *which* may be felt. And Moses stretched
forth his hand toward heaven; and there was a [y]thick darkness
23 in all the land of Egypt three days: they saw not one another,
neither rose any from his place for three days: [z]but all the
24 children of Israel had light in their dwellings. ¶ And Pharaoh
called unto Moses, and [a]said, Go ye, serve the LORD; only let
your flocks and your herds be stayed: let your [b]little ones also go
25 with you. And Moses said, Thou must give [2]us also sacrifices
and burnt offerings, that we may sacrifice unto the LORD our
26 God. Our cattle also shall go with us; there shall not an hoof be
left behind; for thereof must we take to serve the LORD our God;
and we know not with what we must serve the LORD, until we
27 come thither. But the LORD [c]hardened Pharaoh's heart, and
28 he would not let them go. And Pharaoh said unto him, Get thee
from me, take heed to thyself, see my face no more; for in *that*
29 day thou seest my face thou shalt die. And Moses said, Thou
hast spoken well, [d]I will see thy face again no more.

CHAP. 11. AND the LORD said unto Moses, Yet will I bring one
plague *more* upon Pharaoh, and upon Egypt; afterwards he will
let you go hence: [a]when he shall let *you* go, he shall surely
2 thrust you out hence altogether. Speak now in the ears of the
people, and let every man borrow of his neighbour, and every
woman of her neighbour, [b]jewels of silver, and jewels of gold.

[u] ch. 4. 21. & 11. 10.
[x] ch. 9. 22.
[y] Ps. 105. 28.
[z] ch. 8. 22.
[a] ver. 8.
[b] ver. 10.
[c] ver. 20. ch. 4. 21. & 14. 4, 8.
[d] Heb. 11. 27.
[a] ch. 12. 31, 33, 39.
[b] ch. 3. 22. & 12. 35.

[1] Heb. *that* one *may feel darkness.*

[2] Heb. *into our hands.*

puted. Gesenius renders it "rush" or "sea-weed;" but it is probably an Egyptian word. A sea-weed resembling wood is thrown up abundantly on the shores of the Red Sea. The origin of the name "Red" Sea is uncertain: [naturalists have connected it with the presence of red infusoria, cp. vii. 17].

21. *darkness*] This infliction was specially calculated to affect the spirits of the Egyptians, whose chief object of worship was Ra, the Sun-god; and its suddenness and severity in connexion with the act of Moses mark it as a preternatural withdrawal of light. Yet it has an analogy in physical phenomena. After the vernal equinox the south-west wind from the desert blows some fifty days, not however continuously but at intervals, lasting generally some two or three days. It fills the atmosphere with dense masses of fine sand, bringing on a darkness far deeper than that of our worst fogs in winter. The consternation of Pharaoh proves that, familiar as he may have been with the phenomenon, no previous occurrence had prepared him for its intensity and duration, and that he recognized it as a supernatural visitation.

23. *had light in their dwellings*] The sand-storm, if such were the cause, may not have extended to the district of Goshen; but the expression clearly denotes a miraculous intervention, whether accomplished or not by natural agencies.

24. *your flocks and your herds*] Pharaoh still exacts what would of course be a complete security for their return: but the demand was wholly incompatible with the object assigned for the journey into the wilderness.

XI. **1.** *the* LORD *said*] Or "the Lord had said." The first three verses of this chapter are parenthetical. Before Moses relates the last warning given to Pharaoh, he feels it right to recall to his readers' minds the revelation and command which had been previously given to him by the Lord.

when he shall let you go, &c.] When at last he lets you depart with children, flocks, herds, and all your possessions, he will compel you to depart in haste. Moses was already aware that the last plague would be followed by an immediate departure, and, therefore, measures had probably been taken to prepare the Israelites for the journey. In fact on each occasion when Pharaoh relented for a season, immediate orders would of course be issued by Moses to the heads of the people, who were thus repeatedly brought into a state of more or less complete organization for the final movement.

2. *every man*] In iii. 22 women only were named; the command is more explicit when the time has come for its execution.

borrow] "ask." See iii. 22 note.

3 [c]And the LORD gave the people favour in the sight of the Egyptians. Moreover the man [d]Moses *was* very great in the land of
Egypt, in the sight of Pharaoh's servants, and in the sight of
4 the people. ¶ And Moses said, Thus saith the LORD, [e]About
5 midnight will I go out into the midst of Egypt: and [f]all the
firstborn in the land of Egypt shall die, from the firstborn of
Pharaoh that sitteth upon his throne, even unto the firstborn of
the maidservant that *is* behind the mill; and all the firstborn of
6 beasts. [g]And there shall be a great cry throughout all the land
of Egypt, such as there was none like it, nor shall be like it
7 any more. [h]But against any of the children of Israel [i]shall
not a dog move his tongue, against man or beast: that ye may
know how that the LORD doth put a difference between the Egypt-
8 ians and Israel. And [k]all these thy servants shall come down unto
me, and bow down themselves unto me, saying, Get thee out,
and all the people [1]that follow thee: and after that I will go
9 out. And he went out from Pharaoh in [2]a great anger. ¶ And
the LORD said unto Moses, [l]Pharaoh shall not hearken unto you;
10 that [m]my wonders may be multiplied in the land of Egypt. And
Moses and Aaron did all these wonders before Pharaoh: [n]and the
LORD hardened Pharaoh's heart, so that he would not let the
children of Israel go out of his land.

CHAP. 12. AND the LORD spake unto Moses and Aaron in the land
2 of Egypt, saying, [a]This month *shall be* unto you the beginning
3 of months: it *shall be* the first month of the year to you. ¶ Speak
ye unto all the congregation of Israel, saying, In the tenth *day*
of this month they shall take to them every man a [3]lamb, accord-

[c] ch. 3. 21. & 12. 36. Ps. 106. 46.
[d] 2 Sam. 7. 9. Esth. 9. 4.
[e] ch. 12. 12, 23, 29. Amos 5. 17.
[f] ch. 12. 12, 29. Amos 4. 10.
[g] ch. 12. 30. Amos 5. 17.
[h] ch. 8. 22.
[i] Josh. 10. 21.
[k] ch. 12. 33.
[l] ch. 3. 19. & 7. 4. & 10. 1.
[m] ch. 7. 3.
[n] ch. 10. 20, 27. Rom. 2. 5. & 9. 22.
[a] ch. 13. 4. Deut. 16. 1.

[1] Heb. *that is at thy feet.* So Judg. 4. 10. & 8. 5. 1 Kin. 20. 10. 2 Kin. 3. 9.
[2] Heb. *heat of anger.*
[3] Or, *kid.*

---

4. *And Moses said*] The following words must be read in immediate connexion with the last verse of the preceding chapter.

About midnight] This marks the hour, but not the day, on which the visitation would take place. There may have been, and probably was, an interval of some days, during which preparations might be made both for the celebration of the Passover, and the departure of the Israelites.

5. Two points are to be noticed: 1, The extent of the visitation: the whole land suffers in the persons of its firstborn, not merely for the guilt of the sovereign, but for the actual participation of the people in the crime of infanticide (i. 22). 2, The limitation: Pharaoh's command had been to slay all the male children of the Israelites, one child only in each Egyptian family was to die. If Tothmosis II. was the Pharaoh, the visitation fell with special severity on his family. He left no son, but was succeeded by his widow.

the mill] This consisted of two circular stones, one fixed in the ground, the other turned by a handle. The work of grinding was extremely laborious, and performed by women of the lowest rank.

firstborn of beasts] This visitation has a peculiar force in reference to the worship of beasts, which was universal in Egypt; each district having its own sacred animal, adored as a manifestation or representative of the local tutelary deity.

7. *shall not a dog move his tongue*] [A proverb expressive of freedom from alarm and immunity from assault.]

XII. **1.** This chapter was written some time after the Exodus, probably when Moses put together the portions of the book towards the end of his life. The statements that these instructions were given in the land of Egypt, and that they were given to Moses and Aaron, are important: the one marks the peculiar dignity of this ordinance, which was established before the Sinaitic code; the other marks the distinction between Moses and Aaron and all other prophets. They alone were prophets of the Law, *i.e.* no law was promulgated by any other prophets.

2. *This month*] Abib (xiii. 4). It was called by the later Hebrews Nisan, and corresponds nearly to our April. The Israelites are directed to take Abib henceforth as the beginning of the year; the year previously began with the month Tisri, when the harvest was gathered in; see xxiii. 16. The injunction touching Abib or Nisan referred only to religious rites; in other affairs they retained the old arrangement, even in the beginning of the Sabbatic year; see Levit. xxv. 9.

3. *a lamb*] The Hebrew word is general,

4 ing to the house of *their* fathers, a lamb for an house: and if the
household be too little for the lamb, let him and his neighbour
next unto his house take *it* according to the number of the souls;
every man according to his eating shall make your count for the
5 lamb. Your lamb shall be [b]without blemish, a male [1]of the
first year: ye shall take *it* out from the sheep, or from the
6 goats: and ye shall keep it up until the [c]fourteenth day of the
same month: and the whole assembly of the congregation of
7 Israel shall kill it [2]in the evening. And they shall take of the
blood, and strike *it* on the two side posts and on the upper door
8 post of the houses, wherein they shall eat it. And they shall
eat the flesh in that night, roast with fire, and [d]unleavened
9 bread; *and* with bitter *herbs* they shall eat it. Eat not of it raw,
nor sodden at all with water, but [e]roast *with* fire; his head with

[b] Lev. 22. 19, 20, 21. Mal. 1. 8, 14. Heb. 9. 14. 1 Pet. 1. 19.
[c] Lev. 23. 5. Num. 9. 3. & 28. 16. Deut. 16. 1, 6.
[d] ch. 34. 25. Num. 9. 11. Deut. 16. 3. 1 Cor. 5. 8.
[e] Deut. 16. 7

[1] Heb. *son of a year*, Lev. 23. 12.

[2] Heb. *between the two evenings*, ch. 16. 12.

---

meaning either a sheep or goat, male or female, and of any age; the age and sex are therefore specially defined in the following verse. The direction to select the lamb on the tenth day, the fourth day before it was offered, was intended to secure due care in the preparation for the great national festival. The custom certainly fell into desuetude at a later period, but probably not before the destruction of the Temple.

4. Tradition specifies ten as the least number; but the matter was probably left altogether to the discretion of the heads of families.

The last clause should be rendered:—"each man according to his eating ye shall count for the lamb."

5. *without blemish*] This is in accordance with the general rule (marg. ref.): although in this case there is a special reason, since the lamb was in place of the firstborn male in each household. The restriction to the first year is peculiar, and refers apparently to the condition of perfect innocence in the antitype, the Lamb of God.

6. *until the fourteenth day*] It should be observed that the offering of our Lord on the selfsame day is an important point in determining the typical character of the transaction. A remarkable passage in the Talmud says: "It was a famous and old opinion among the ancient Jews that the day of the new year which was the beginning of the Israelites' deliverance out of Egypt should in future time be the beginning of the redemption by the Messiah."

in the evening] The Hebrew has **between the two evenings**. The meaning of the expression is disputed. The most probable explanation is that it includes the time from afternoon, or early eventide, until sunset. This accords with the ancient custom of the Hebrews, who slew the paschal lamb immediately after the offering of the daily sacrifice, which on the day of the Passover took place a little earlier than usual, between two and three p.m. This would allow about two hours and a half for slaying and preparing all the lambs. It is clear that they would not wait until sunset, at which time the evening meal would take place. The slaying of the lamb thus coincides exactly with the death of our Saviour, at the ninth hour of the day (Matt. xxvii. 46).

7. *the upper door post*] Or **lintel**, *v.* 23. This direction was understood by the Hebrews to apply only to the first Passover: it was certainly not adopted in Palestine. The meaning of the sprinkling of blood is hardly open to question. It was a representation of the offering of the life, substituted for that of the firstborn in each house, as an expiatory and vicarious sacrifice.

8. *in that night*] The night is thus clearly distinguished from the evening when the lamb was slain. It was slain before sunset, on the 14th, and eaten after sunset, the beginning of the 15th.

with fire] Among various reasons given for this injunction the most probable and satisfactory seems to be the special sanctity attached to fire from the first institution of sacrifice (cp. Gen. iv. 4).

and unleavened bread] On account of the hasty departure, allowing no time for the process of leavening: but the meaning discerned by St. Paul, 1 Cor. v. 7, 8, and recognized by the Church in all ages, was assuredly implied, though not expressly declared in the original institution. Cp. our Lord's words, Matt. xvi. 6, 12, as to the symbolism of leaven.

bitter herbs] The word occurs only here and in Numbers ix. 11, in reference to herbs. The symbolical reference to the previous sufferings of the Israelites is generally admitted.

9. *raw*] *i.e.* "half-cooked."

sodden...with water] It was probably more common to seethe than to roast meat; hence the regrets expressed by the Israelites for the seething pots of Egypt.

the purtenance thereof] or **its intestines.** This verse directs that the lamb should be

[f] ch. 23. 18. & 34. 25.
[g] Deut. 16. 5.
[h] ch. 11. 4, 5. Amos 5. 17.
[i] Num. 33. 4.
[k] ch. 6. 2.
[l] ch. 13. 9.
[m] Lev. 23. 4, 5. 2 Kin. 23. 21.
[n] ver. 24, 43. ch. 13. 10.
[o] ch. 13. 6, 7. & 23. 15. & 34. 18, 25. Lev. 23. 5, 6. Num. 28. 17. Deut. 16. 3, 8. 1 Cor. 5. 7.

10 his legs, and with the purtenance thereof. [f]And ye shall let
nothing of it remain until the morning; and that which remaineth
11 of it until the morning ye shall burn with fire. And thus shall ye
eat it; *with* your loins girded, your shoes on your feet, and your
staff in your hand; and ye shall eat it in haste: [g]it *is* the LORD'S
12 passover. ¶ For I [h]will pass through the land of Egypt this night,
and will smite all the firstborn in the land of Egypt, both man and
beast; and [i]against all the [1]gods of Egypt I will execute judg-
13 ment: [k]I *am* the LORD. And the blood shall be to you for a token
upon the houses where ye *are*: and when I see the blood, I will
pass over you, and the plague shall not be upon you [2]to destroy
14 *you*, when I smite the land of Egypt. ¶ And this day shall be unto
you [l]for a memorial; and ye shall keep it a [m]feast to the LORD
throughout your generations; ye shall keep it a feast [n]by an ordi-
15 nance for ever. [o]Seven days shall ye eat unleavened bread;
even the first day ye shall put away leaven out of your houses:
for whosoever eateth leavened bread from the first day until the

[1] Or, *princes*, ch. 21. 6. & 22. 28. Ps. 82. 1, 6. John 10. 34, 35.
[2] Heb. *for a destruction*.

---

roasted and placed on the table whole. No bone was to be broken (see *v.* 46, and marg. reff). The bowels were taken out, washed and then replaced. The Talmud prescribes the form of the oven of earthenware, in which the lamb was roasted, open above and below with a grating for the fire. Lambs and sheep are roasted whole in Persia, nearly in the same manner.

This entire consumption of the lamb constitutes one marked difference between the Passover and all other sacrifices, in which either a part or the whole was burned, and thus offered directly to God. The whole substance of the sacrificed lamb was to enter into the substance of the people, the blood only excepted, which was sprinkled as a propitiatory and sacrificial offering. Another point of subordinate importance is noticed. The lamb was slain and the blood sprinkled by the head of each family: no separate priesthood as yet existed in Israel; its functions belonged from the beginning to the father of the family: when the priesthood was instituted the slaying of the lamb still devolved on the heads of families, though the blood was sprinkled on the altar by the priests; an act which essentially belonged to their office. The typical character of this part of the transaction is clear. Our Lord was offered and His blood shed as an expiatory and propitiatory sacrifice, but His whole Humanity is transfused spiritually and effectually into His Church, an effect which is at once symbolized and assured in Holy Communion, the Christian Passover.

10. This was afterwards a general law of sacrifices; at once preventing all possibility of profanity, and of superstitious abuse. The injunction is on both accounts justly applied by our Church to the Eucharist.

burn with fire] Not being consumed by man, it was thus offered, like other sacrifices (*v.* 8), to God.

11. These instructions are understood by the Jews to apply only to the first Passover, when they belonged to the occasion. There is no trace of their observance at any later time. Each of the directions marks preparation for a journey; the long flowing robes are girded round the loins; shoes or sandals, not worn in the house or at meals, were fastened on the feet; and the traveller's staff was taken in hand.

the LORD'S *passover*] The great and most significant name for the whole ordinance. The word Passover renders as nearly as possible the true meaning of the original, of which the primary sense is generally held to be "pass rapidly," like a bird with outstretched wings, but it undoubtedly includes the idea of sparing (*v.* 13). See Isaiah xxxi. 5, which combines the two great ideas involved in the word.

12. *I will pass through*] A word wholly distinct from that which means "pass over." The "passing through" was in judgment, the "passing over" in mercy.

against all the gods of Egypt] Cp. marg. ref. In smiting the firstborn of all living beings, man and beast, God smote the objects of Egyptian worship (cp. xii. 5).

14. *a memorial*] A commemorative and sacramental ordinance of perpetual obligation. As such it has ever been observed by the Hebrews. By the Christian it is spiritually observed; its full significance is recognized, and all that it foreshadowed is realized, in the Sacrament of Holy Communion.

15. *cut off*] The penalty inflicted on those who transgressed the command may be accounted for on the ground that it was an act of rebellion; but additional light is thrown upon it by the typical meaning assigned to leaven by our Lord, Matt. xvi. 6.

16 seventh day, [p]that soul shall be cut off from Israel. And in the
first day *there shall be* [q]an holy convocation, and in the seventh
day there shall be an holy convocation to you; no manner of
work shall be done in them, save *that* which every [1]man must
17 eat, that only may be done of you. And ye shall observe *the*
feast of unleavened bread; for [r]in this selfsame day have I
brought your armies out of the land of Egypt: therefore shall
ye observe this day in your generations by an ordinance for
18 ever. [s]In the first *month*, on the fourteenth day of the month at
even, ye shall eat unleavened bread, until the one and twentieth
19 day of the month at even. [t]Seven days shall there be no leaven
found in your houses: for whosoever eateth that which is leavened,
[u]even that soul shall be cut off from the congregation of Israel,
20 whether he be a stranger, or born in the land. Ye shall eat
nothing leavened; in all your habitations shall ye eat unleavened
21 bread. ¶ Then Moses called for all the elders of Israel, and
said unto them, [x]Draw out and take you a [2]lamb according to
22 your families, and kill the passover. [y]And ye shall take a
bunch of hyssop, and dip *it* in the blood that *is* in the bason, and
[z]strike the lintel and the two side posts with the blood that *is*
in the bason; and none of you shall go out at the door of his
23 house until the morning. [a]For the LORD will pass through to
smite the Egyptians; and when he seeth the blood upon the
lintel, and on the two side posts, the LORD will pass over the
door, and [b]will not suffer [c]the destroyer to come in unto your
24 houses to smite *you*. And ye shall observe this thing for an
25 ordinance to thee and to thy sons for ever. And it shall come to
pass, when ye be come to the land which the LORD will give
you, [d]according as he hath promised, that ye shall keep this
26 service. [e]And it shall come to pass, when your children shall
say unto you, What mean ye by this service? That ye shall
27 say, [f]It *is* the sacrifice of the LORD'S passover, who passed over
the houses of the children of Israel in Egypt, when he smote

[p] Gen. 17. 14, Num. 9. 13. [q] Lev. 23. 7, 8. Num. 28. 18, 25. [r] ch. 13. 3. [s] Lev. 23. 5. Num. 28. 16. [t] Ex. 23. 15. & 34. 18. Deut. 16. 3. 1 Cor. 5. 7, 8. [u] Num. 9. 13. [x] ver. 3. Num. 9. 4. Josh. 5. 10. 2 Kin. 23. 21. Ezra 6. 20. Matt. 26. 18, 19. Mark 14. 12—16. Luke 22. 7, &c. [y] Heb. 11. 28. [z] ver. 7. [a] ver. 12, 13. [b] Ezek. 9. 6. Rev. 7. 3. & 9. 4. [c] 2 Sam. 24. 16. 1 Cor. 10. 10. Heb. 11. 28. [d] ch. 3. 8, 17. [e] ch. 13. 8, 14. Deut. 32. 7. Josh. 4. 6. Ps. 78. 6. [f] ver. 11.

[1] Heb. *soul*. [2] Or, *kid*.

---

16. *an holy convocation*] An assembly called by proclamation for a religious solemnity. See Lev. xxiii. 2; Num. x. 2, 3. In the East the proclamation is made by the Muezzins from the minarets of the mosques.

save that, &c.] In this the observance of the festival differed from the Sabbath, when the preparation of food was prohibited. The same word for "work" is used here and in the 4th Commandment: it is very general, and includes all laborious occupation.

19. *born in the land*] A stranger or foreigner might be born in the land, but the word here used means "a native of the land," belonging to the country in virtue of descent, that descent being reckoned from Abraham, to whom Canaan was promised as a perpetual inheritance.

21. *Draw out*] *i.e.* draw the lamb from the fold and then take it to the house.

the passover] The word is here applied to the lamb; an important fact, marking the lamb as the sign and pledge of the exemption of the Israelites.

22. *a bunch of hyssop*] The species here designated does not appear to be the plant now bearing the name. It would seem to have been an aromatic plant, common in Palestine and near Mount Sinai, with a long straight stalk and leaves well adapted for the purpose of sprinkling.

bason] The rendering rests on good authority and gives a good sense: but the word means "threshold" in some other passages and in Egyptian, and is taken here in that sense by some Versions. If that rendering be correct it would imply that the lamb was slain on the threshold.

none...shall go out, &c.] There would be no safety outside the precincts protected by the blood of the lamb; a symbolism explained by the marg. reff.

27. *It is the sacrifice of the* LORD'S *passover*] or **This is the sacrifice of the Passover to Jehovah.** The most formal and exact designation of the festival is thus given: but "the Passover" may mean either the act of God's mercy in sparing the Israelites, or the lamb which is offered in

the Egyptians, and delivered our houses. And the people [g]bowed
28 the head and worshipped. And the children of Israel went
away, and [h]did as the LORD had commanded Moses and Aaron,
29 so did they. ¶ [i]And it came to pass, that at midnight [k]the LORD
smote all the firstborn in the land of Egypt, [l]from the firstborn of
Pharaoh that sat on his throne unto the firstborn of the captive
30 that *was* in the [1]dungeon; and all the firstborn of cattle. And
Pharaoh rose up in the night, he, and all his servants, and all
the Egyptians; and there was a [m]great cry in Egypt; for *there*
31 *was* not a house where *there was* not one dead. ¶ And [n]he called
for Moses and Aaron by night, and said, Rise up, *and* get you
forth from among my people, [o]both ye and the children of Israel;
32 and go, serve the LORD, as ye have said. [p]Also take your flocks
and your herds, as ye have said, and be gone; and [q]bless
33 me also. [r]And the Egyptians were urgent upon the people,
that they might send them out of the land in haste; for they
34 said, [s]We *be* all dead *men*. And the people took their dough
before it was leavened, their [2]kneadingtroughs being bound up
35 in their clothes upon their shoulders. And the children of Israel
did according to the word of Moses; and they borrowed of the
36 Egyptians [t]jewels of silver, and jewels of gold, and raiment: [u]and
the LORD gave the people favour in the sight of the Egyptians,
so that they lent unto them *such things as they required*. And [x]they
37 spoiled the Egyptians. ¶ And [y]the children of Israel journeyed
from [z]Rameses to Succoth, about [a]six hundred thousand on foot

[g] ch. 4. 31.
[h] Heb. 11. 28.
[i] ch. 11. 4.
[k] Num. 8. 17. & 33. 4. Ps. 78. 51. & 135. 8. & 136. 10.
[l] ch. 4. 23. & 11. 5.
[m] ch. 11. 6. Prov. 21. 13. Amos 5. 17. Jam. 2. 13.
[n] ch. 11. 1. Ps. 105. 38.
[o] ch. 10. 9.
[p] ch. 10. 26.
[q] Gen. 27. 34.
[r] ch. 11. 8.
[s] Gen. 20. 3.
[t] ch. 3. 22.
[u] ch. 3. 21.
[x] ch. 3. 22. Ps. 105. 37.
[y] Num. 33. 3, 5.
[z] Gen. 47. 11.
[a] Gen. 12. 2. & 46. 3. ch. 38. 26. Num. 1. 46. & 11. 21.

[1] Heb. *house of the pit*.
[2] Or, *dough*, ch. 8. 3.

---

sacrifice: more probably the latter, as in *v.* 21. This gives a clear sense to the expression "to Jehovah;" the Passover-lamb was a sacrifice offered to Jehovah by His ordinance.

29. This plague is distinctly attributed here and in *v.* 23 to the personal intervention of THE LORD; but it is to be observed that although the Lord Himself passed through to smite the Egyptians, He employed the agency of "the destroyer" (*v.* 23), in whom, in accordance with Heb. xi. 28, all the Ancient Versions, and most critics, recognize an Angel (cp. 2 Kings xix. 35; 2 Sam. xxiv. 16).

32. *bless me also*] No words could shew more strikingly the complete, though temporary, submission of Pharaoh.

34. *kneadingtroughs*] (Cp. marg. and Deut. xxviii. 5). The troughs were probably small wooden bowls in which the cakes when baked were preserved for use. The Hebrews used their outer garment, or mantle, in the same way as the Bedouins at present, who make a bag of the voluminous folds of their burnous. See Ruth. iii. 15; 2 Kings iv. 39.

35. *borrowed*] "Asked of." See iii. 22 note.

36. *lent*] Or **gave**. The word in the Hebrew means simply "granted their request." Whether the grant is made as a loan, or as a gift, depends in every instance upon the context. Here the word "spoiled" ought to be regarded as conclusive that the grant was a gift, a moderate remuneration for long service, and a compensation for cruel wrongs.

37. *Rameses*] See i. 11 note. Rameses was evidently the place of general rendezvous, well adapted for that purpose as the principal city of Goshen. The Israelites were probably settled in considerable numbers in and about it. Pharaoh with his army and court were at that time near the frontier, and Rameses, where a large garrison was kept, was probably the place where the last interview with Moses occurred. The first part of the journey appears to have followed the course of the ancient canal. The site of Succoth cannot be exactly determined, but it lay about half-way between Rameses and Etham (xiii. 20). The name Succoth (*i.e.* "tents" or "booths" in Hebrew), may have been given by the Israelites, but the same, or a similar word, occurs in Egyptian in connection with the district.

600,000] This includes all the males who could march. The total number of the Israelites should therefore be calculated from the males above twelve or fourteen, and would therefore amount to somewhat more than two millions. This is not an excessive population for Goshen, nor does it exceed a reasonable estimate of the increase of the Israelites, including their numerous dependants.

38 *that were* men, beside children. And [1]a mixed multitude went
up also with them; and flocks, and herds, *even* very much cattle.
39 And they baked unleavened cakes of the dough which they
brought forth out of Egypt, for it was not leavened; because
[b]they were thrust out of Egypt, and could not tarry, neither had [b] ch. 6. 1.
40 they prepared for themselves any victual. ¶ Now the sojourning & 11. 1. ver. 33.
of the children of Israel, who dwelt in Egypt, *was* [c]four hundred [c] Gen. 15. 13.
41 and thirty years. And it came to pass at the end of the four Acts 7. 6.
hundred and thirty years, even the selfsame day it came to pass, Gal. 3. 17.
that all [d]the hosts of the LORD went out from the land of Egypt. [d] ch. 7. 4.
42 It *is* [2][e]a night to be much observed unto the LORD for bringing ver. 51.
them out from the land of Egypt: this *is* that night of the LORD [e] See Deut. 16. 6.
to be observed of all the children of Israel in their generations.
43 ¶ And the LORD said unto Moses and Aaron, This *is* [f]the ordi- [f] Num. 9. 14.
44 nance of the passover: There shall no stranger eat thereof: but
every man's servant that is bought for money, when thou hast
45 [g]circumcised him, then shall he eat thereof. [h]A foreigner and [g] Gen. 17.
46 an hired servant shall not eat thereof. In one house shall it be 12, 13. [h] Lev. 22. 10.
eaten; thou shalt not carry forth ought of the flesh abroad out
47 of the house; [i]neither shall ye break a bone thereof. [k]All the [i] Num. 9. 12.
48 congregation of Israel shall [3]keep it. And [l]when a stranger John 19. 33, 36.
shall sojourn with thee, and will keep the passover to the LORD, [k] ver. 6.
let all his males be circumcised, and then let him come near and Num. 9. 13. [l] Num. 9. 14.
keep it; and he shall be as one that is born in the land: for no
49 uncircumcised person shall eat thereof. [m]One law shall be to [m] Num. 9. 14.
him that is homeborn, and unto the stranger that sojourneth & 15. 15, 16.
50 among you. Thus did all the children of Israel; as the LORD Gal. 3. 28.
51 commanded Moses and Aaron, so did they. ¶ [n]And it came to [n] ver. 41.
pass the selfsame day, *that* the LORD did bring the children of
Israel out of the land of Egypt [o]by their armies. [o] ch. 6. 26.

[1] Heb. *a great mixture.* Num. 11. 4.
[2] Heb. *a night of observations.*
[3] Heb. *do it.*

---

38. *a mixed multitude*] Probably remains of the old Semitic population, whether first brought into the district by the Hyksos or not is uncertain. As natural objects of suspicion and dislike to the Egyptians who had lately become masters of the country, they would be anxious to escape, the more especially after the calamities which preceded the Exodus.

very much cattle] This is an important fact, both as showing that the oppression of the Israelites had not extended to confiscation of their property, and as bearing upon the question of their maintenance in the Wilderness.

40. *who dwelt*] Read, **which they sojourned.** The obvious intention of Moses is to state the duration of the sojourn in Egypt.

43. *And the* LORD *said*] From this verse to xiii. 16 are instructions regarding the Passover. Such instructions were needed when the Israelites were joined by the "mixed multitude" of strangers; and they were probably given at Succoth, on the morning following the departure from Rameses.

no stranger] Lit. "son of a stranger." The term is general; it includes all who were aliens from Israel, until they were incorporated into the nation by circumcision.

44. *servant*] The circumcision of the slave, thus enjoined formally on the first day that Israel became a nation, in accordance with the law given to Abraham, (see marg. ref.) made him a true member of the family, equally entitled to all religious privileges. In the household of a priest the slave was even permitted to eat the consecrated food: Lev. xxii. 11.

45. *A foreigner*] or **sojourner:** one who resides in a country, not having a permanent home, nor being attached to an Israelitish household.

46. *In one house*] *i.e.* "in one company." Each lamb was to be entirely consumed by the members of one company, whether they belonged to the same household or not.

break a bone] The typical significance of this injunction is recognized by St. John, (see marg. ref.) It is not easy to assign any other satisfactory reason for it. This victim alone was exempt from the general law by which the limbs were ordered to be separated from the body.

[a] ver. 12, 13, 15. ch. 22. 29, 30. & 34. 19. Lev. 27. 26. Num. 3. 13. & 8. 16, 17. & 18. 15. Deut. 15. 19. Luke 2. 23.
[b] ch. 12. 42. Deut. 16. 3.
[c] ch. 6. 1.
[d] ch. 12. 8.
[e] ch. 23. 15. & 34. 18. Deut. 16. 1.
[f] ch. 3. 8.
[g] ch. 6. 8.
[h] ch. 12. 25.
[i] ch. 12. 15.
[k] ch. 12. 19.
[l] ver. 14. ch. 12. 26.
[m] See ver. 16. ch. 12. 14. Num. 15. 39. Deut. 6. 8. Prov. 1. 9. Isai. 49. 16. Jer. 22. 24. Matt. 23. 5.
[n] ch. 12. 14.
[o] ver. 2. Ezek. 44. 30.
[p] ch. 34. 20.

CHAP. 13. AND the LORD spake unto Moses, saying, [a]Sanctify
2 unto me all the firstborn, whatsoever openeth the womb among
the children of Israel, *both* of man and of beast: it *is* mine.
3 ¶ And Moses said unto the people, [b]Remember this day, in which
ye came out from Egypt, out of the house of [1]bondage; for [c]by
strength of hand the LORD brought you out from this *place:*
4 [d]there shall no leavened bread be eaten. [e]This day came ye
5 out in the month Abib. And it shall be when the LORD shall
[f]bring thee into the land of the Canaanites, and the Hittites,
and the Amorites, and the Hivites, and the Jebusites, which he
[g]sware unto thy fathers to give thee, a land flowing with milk
and honey, [h]that thou shalt keep this service in this month.
6 [i]Seven days thou shalt eat unleavened bread, and in the seventh
7 day *shall be* a feast to the LORD. Unleavened bread shall be
eaten seven days; and there shall [k]no leavened bread be seen
with thee, neither shall there be leaven seen with thee in all thy
8 quarters. And thou shalt [l]shew thy son in that day, saying,
This is done because of that *which* the LORD did unto me when I
9 came forth out of Egypt. And it shall be for [m]a sign unto thee
upon thine hand, and for a memorial between thine eyes, that
the LORD's law may be in thy mouth: for with a strong hand
10 hath the LORD brought thee out of Egypt. [n]Thou shalt therefore
11 keep this ordinance in his season from year to year. ¶ And it
shall be when the LORD shall bring thee into the land of the Ca-
12 naanites, as he sware unto thee and to thy fathers, and shall
give it thee, [o]that thou shalt [2]set apart unto the LORD all that
openeth the matrix, and every firstling that cometh of a beast
13 which thou hast; the males *shall be* the LORD's. And [p]every
firstling of an ass thou shalt redeem with a [3]lamb; and if thou

[1] Heb. *servants.* [2] Heb. *cause to pass over.* [3] Or, *kid.*

XIII. **2.** *Sanctify unto me*] The command is addressed to Moses. It was to declare the will of God that all firstborn were to be consecrated to Him, set apart from all other creatures. The command is expressly based upon the Passover. The firstborn exempt from the destruction became in a new and special sense the exclusive property of the Lord: the firstborn of man as His ministers, the firstborn of cattle as victims. In lieu of the firstborn of men the Levites were devoted to the temple services.

4. *Abib*] April. Cp. xii. 2. It is uncertain whether this name was ancient or given then for the first time. It is found only in the Pentateuch, six times as the name of the first month, twice in the sense of young wheat, hence its etymology, viz. the month when the wheat began to ripen. The name resembles the Egyptian Epiphi, and may possibly have been derived from it.

5. *the Canaanites*] Five nations only are named in this passage, whereas six are named in iii. 8, and ten in the original promise to Abraham, Gen. xv. 19–21. The first word Canaanite is generic, and includes all the Hamite races of Palestine.

9. Hebrew writers have generally regarded this as a formal injunction to write the precepts on slips of parchment, and to fasten them on the wrists and forehead; but other commentators are generally agreed that it is to be understood metaphorically. The words appear to be put into the mouths of the parents. They were to keep all the facts of the Passover constantly in mind, and, referring to a custom prevalent ages before Moses in Egypt, to have them present as though they were inscribed on papyrus or parchment fastened on the wrists, or on the face between the eyes. If, as may be inferred from Deut. vi. 7, 8, Moses adopted this custom, he would take care to warn the people against the Egyptian superstition of amulets. Modern Israelites generally allege this precept as a justification for the use of phylacteries.

13. *an ass*] The ass could not be offered in sacrifice, being an unclean animal:—possibly the only unclean animal domesticated among the Israelites at the time of the Exodus. This principle was extended to every unclean beast; see Num. xviii. 15.

thou shalt redeem] The lamb, or sheep, was given to the priest for the service of the Sanctuary.

firstborn of man] The price of redemption was fixed at five shekels of the Sanctuary: Num. iii. 47, where see note.

wilt not redeem it, then thou shalt break his neck: and all the
14 firstborn of man among thy children [q]shalt thou redeem. [r]And
it shall be when thy son asketh thee [1]in time to come, saying,
What *is* this? that thou shalt say unto him, [s]By strength of
hand the LORD brought us out from Egypt, from the house of
15 bondage: and it came to pass, when Pharaoh would hardly let
us go, that [t]the LORD slew all the firstborn in the land of Egypt,
both the firstborn of man, and the firstborn of beast: therefore
I sacrifice to the LORD all that openeth the matrix, being males;
16 but all the firstborn of my children I redeem. And it shall be
for [u]a token upon thine hand, and for frontlets between thine
eyes: for by strength of hand the LORD brought us forth out of
17 Egypt. ¶ And it came to pass, when Pharaoh had let the people
go, that God led them not *through* the way of the land of the
Philistines, although that *was* near; for God said, Lest peradventure the people [x]repent when they see war, and [y]they return
18 to Egypt: but God [z]led the people about, *through* the way of the
wilderness of the Red sea: and the children of Israel went up
19 [2]harnessed out of the land of Egypt. And Moses took the
bones of Joseph with him: for he had straitly sworn the children of Israel, saying, [a]God will surely visit you; and ye shall
20 carry up my bones away hence with you. And [b]they took
their journey from Succoth, and encamped in Etham, in the
21 edge of the wilderness. And [c]the LORD went before them by
day in a pillar of a cloud, to lead them the way; and by night
in a pillar of fire, to give them light; to go by day and night:
22 he took not away the pillar of the cloud by day, nor the pillar
of fire by night, *from* before the people.
CHAP. 14. AND the LORD spake unto Moses, saying, Speak unto
2 the children of Israel, [a]that they turn and encamp before [b]Pi-

[q] Num. 3. 46, 47. & 18. 15, 16.
[r] ch. 12. 26. Deut. 6. 20. Josh. 4. 6, 21.
[s] ver. 3.
[t] ch. 12. 29.
[u] ver. 9.
[x] ch. 14. 11, 12. Num. 14. 1—4.
[y] Deut. 17. 16.
[z] ch. 14. 2. Num. 33. 6, &c.
[a] Gen. 50.25. Josh. 24. 32. Acts 7. 16.
[b] Num. 33. 6.
[c] ch. 14. 19, 24. & 40. 38. Num. 9. 15. & 10. 34. & 14. 14. Deut. 1. 33. Neh. 9. 12, 19. Ps. 78. 14. & 99. 7. & 105. 39. Isai. 4. 5. 1 Cor. 10. 1.
[a] ch. 13. 18.
[b] Num. 33. 7.

[1] Heb. *to-morrow*.
[2] Or, *by five in a rank*.

18. *harnessed*] More probably, "marshalled" or "in orderly array." There is not the least indication that the Israelites had been disarmed by the Egyptians, and as occupying a frontier district frequently assailed by the nomads of the desert they would of necessity be accustomed to the use of arms. Cp. i. 10.

20. *Etham*] The house or "sanctuary of Tum" (the Sun God worshipped specially by that name in Lower Egypt), was in the immediate vicinity of Heliopolis, called by the Egyptians the fortress of Zar, or Zalu (*i.e.* of foreigners); the frontier city where the Pharaohs of the 18th dynasty reviewed their forces when about to enter upon a campaign on Syria. The name Pithom (see i. 11) has precisely the same meaning with Etham, and may possibly be identified with it.

21. *pillar of cloud*] The Lord Himself did for the Israelites by preternatural means that which armies were obliged to do for themselves by natural agents. The Persians and Greeks used fire and smoke as signals in their marches, and in a well-known papyrus, the commander of an Egyptian expedition is called "A flame in the darkness at the head of his soldiers." By this sign then of the pillar of cloud, the Lord showed Himself as their leader and general (xv. 3, 6).

XIV. **2.** *That they turn*] *i.e.* away from the wilderness, and go southwards, to the west of the Bitter Lakes, which completely separated them from the desert.

Pi-hahiroth] The place is generally identified with Ajrud, a fortress with a very large well of good water, situate at the foot of an elevation commanding the plain which extends to Suez, at a distance of four leagues. The journey from Etham might occupy two, or even three days.

Migdol] A tower, or fort, the *Maktal* of Egyptian monuments; it is probably to be identified with Bir Suweis, about two miles from Suez.

Baal-zephon] The name under which the Phœnicians, who had a settlement in Lower Egypt at a very ancient period, worshipped their chief Deity. There can be no doubt it was near Kolsum, or Suez. From the text it is clear that the encampment of the Israelites extended over the plain from Pi-hahiroth: their head-quarters being between Bir Suweis and the sea opposite to Baal-Zephon. At Ajrud the road branches off in two directions, one leading to the wilderness by a tract, now dry, but in the time of Moses probably impassable (see next note); the other leading to Suez, which was doubtless followed by the Israelites.

hahiroth, between [c]Migdol and the sea, over against Baal-
3 zephon: before it shall ye encamp by the sea. For Pharaoh
will say of the children of Israel, [d]They *are* entangled in the
4 land, the wilderness hath shut them in. And [e]I will harden
Pharaoh's heart, that he shall follow after them; and I [f]will
be honoured upon Pharaoh, and upon all his host; [g]that the
Egyptians may know that I *am* the LORD. And they did so.
5 ¶ And it was told the king of Egypt that the people fled: and
[h]the heart of Pharaoh and of his servants was turned against
the people, and they said, Why have we done this, that we
6 have let Israel go from serving us? And he made ready his
7 chariot, and took his people with him: and he took [i]six hundred
chosen chariots, and all the chariots of Egypt, and captains over
8 every one of them. And the LORD [k]hardened the heart of
Pharaoh king of Egypt, and he pursued after the children of
Israel: and [l]the children of Israel went out with an high hand.
9 But the [m]Egyptians pursued after them, all the horses *and* chariots of Pharaoh, and his horsemen, and his army, and overtook
them encamping by the sea, beside Pi-hahiroth, before Baal-
10 zephon. ¶ And when Pharaoh drew nigh, the children of Israel
lifted up their eyes, and, behold, the Egyptians marched after
them; and they were sore afraid: and the children of Israel
11 [n]cried out unto the LORD. [o]And they said unto Moses, Because
there were no graves in Egypt, hast thou taken us away to die in
the wilderness? Wherefore hast thou dealt thus with us, to carry
12 us forth out of Egypt? [p]*Is* not this the word that we did tell
thee in Egypt, saying, Let us alone, that we may serve the
Egyptians? For *it had been* better for us to serve the Egyptians,

[c] Jer. 44. 1.
[d] Ps. 71. 11.
[e] ch. 4. 21. & 7. 3.
[f] ch. 9. 16. ver. 17, 18. Rom. 9. 17, 22, 23.
[g] ch. 7. 5.
[h] Ps. 105. 25.
[i] ch. 15. 4.
[k] ver. 4.
[l] ch. 6. 1. & 13. 9. Num. 33. 3.
[m] ch. 15. 9. Josh. 24. 6.
[n] Josh. 24. 7. Neh. 9. 9. Ps. 34. 17. & 107. 6.
[o] Ps. 106. 7, 8.
[p] ch. 5. 21. & 6. 9.

---

3. *They are entangled,* &c.] The original intention of Moses was to go towards Palestine by the wilderness: when that purpose was changed by God's direction and they moved southwards, Pharaoh, on receiving information, was of course aware that they were completely shut in, since the waters of the Red Sea then extended to the Bitter Lakes. It is known that the Red Sea at some remote period extended considerably further towards the north than it does at present. In the time of Moses the water north of Kolsum joined the Bitter Lakes, though at present the constant accumulation of sand has covered the intervening space to the extent of 8000 to 10,000 yards.

5. *the people fled*] This was a natural inference from the change of direction, which indicated a determination to escape from Egypt. Up to the time when that information reached Pharaoh both he and his people understood that the Israelites would return after keeping a festival in the district adjoining Etham. From Etham the intelligence would be forwarded by the commander of the garrison to Rameses in less than a day, and the cavalry, a highly-disciplined force, would be ready for immediate departure.

7. *six hundred chosen chariots*] The Egyptian army comprised large numbers of chariots, each drawn by two horses, with two men, one bearing the shield and driving, the other fully armed. The horses were thoroughbred, renowned for strength and spirit. Chariots are first represented on the monuments of the 18th dynasty. By "all the chariots of Egypt" we are to understand all that were stationed in Lower Egypt, most of them probably at Rameses and other frontier garrisons near the headquarters of Pharaoh.

captains] The word (Shalishim, lit. third or thirtieth) may represent an Egyptian title. The king had about him a council of thirty, each of whom bore a title, Mapu, a "thirty man." The word occurs frequently in the books of Kings. David seems to have organized the Shalishim as a distinct corps (see 2 Sam. xxiii. 8 Heb.), retaining the old name, and adopting the Egyptian system.

9. *and his horsemen*] See *v.* 5.

11. *no graves in Egypt*] This bitter taunt was probably suggested by the vast extent of cemeteries in Egypt, which might not improperly be called the land of tombs.

12. *Let us alone*] This is a gross exaggeration, yet not without a semblance of truth: for although the Israelites welcomed the message of Moses at first, they gave way completely at the first serious trial. See the reference in margin. The whole passage foreshadows the conduct of the people in the wilderness.

13 than that we should die in the wilderness. And Moses said
unto the people, [q]Fear ye not, stand still, and see the salvation
of the LORD, which he will shew to you to day: [1]for the Egyptians whom ye have seen to day, ye shall see them again no more
14 for ever. [r]The LORD shall fight for you, and ye shall [s]hold your
15 peace. ¶ And the LORD said unto Moses, Wherefore criest thou
unto me? Speak unto the children of Israel, that they go for-
16 ward: but [t]lift thou up thy rod, and stretch out thine hand over
the sea, and divide it: and the children of Israel shall go on
17 dry *ground* through the midst of the sea. And I, behold, I will
[u]harden the hearts of the Egyptians, and they shall follow them:
and I will [x]get me honour upon Pharaoh, and upon all his host,
18 upon his chariots, and upon his horsemen. And the Egyptians
[y]shall know that I *am* the LORD, when I have gotten me honour
19 upon Pharaoh, upon his chariots, and upon his horsemen. ¶ And
the angel of God, [z]which went before the camp of Israel, removed and went behind them; and the pillar of the cloud went
20 from before their face, and stood behind them: and it came
between the camp of the Egyptians and the camp of Israel; and
[a]it was a cloud and darkness *to them*, but it gave light by night
to these: so that the one came not near the other all the night.
21 And Moses [b]stretched out his hand over the sea; and the
LORD caused the sea to go *back* by a strong east wind all that
night, and [c]made the sea dry *land*, and the waters were [d]divided.
22 And [e]the children of Israel went into the midst of the sea upon
the dry *ground:* and the waters *were* [f]a wall unto them on their
23 right hand, and on their left. ¶ And the Egyptians pursued,
and went in after them to the midst of the sea, *even* all Pharaoh's
24 horses, his chariots, and his horsemen. And it came to pass,
that in the morning watch [g]the LORD looked unto the host of
the Egyptians through the pillar of fire and of the cloud, and
25 troubled the host of the Egyptians, and took off their chariot
wheels, [2]that they drave them heavily: so that the Egyptians
said, Let us flee from the face of Israel; for the LORD [h]fighteth
26 for them against the Egyptians. And the LORD said unto Moses,
[i]Stretch out thine hand over the sea, that the waters may come
again upon the Egyptians, upon their chariots, and upon their
27 horsemen. And Moses stretched forth his hand over the sea, and

[q] 2 Chr. 20. 15, 17. Isai. 41. 10, 13, 14.
[r] ver. 25. Deut. 1. 30. Josh. 10. 14, 42. 2 Chr. 20. 29. Neh. 4. 20. Isai. 31. 4.
[s] Isai. 30. 15.
[t] ver. 21. 26.
[u] ver. 8. ch. 7. 3.
[x] ver. 4.
[y] ver. 4.
[z] ch. 13. 21. & 23. 20. & 32. 34. Num. 20. 16. Isai. 63. 9.
[a] See Isai. 8. 14. 2 Cor. 4. 3.
[b] ver. 16.
[c] Ps. 66. 6.
[d] ch. 15. 8. Josh. 3. 16. & 4. 23. Neh. 9. 11. Ps. 74. 13. & 106. 9. & 114. 3.
[e] ver. 29. Num. 33. 8. Ps. 66. 6. & 78. 13. Isai. 63. 13. 1 Cor. 10. 1. Heb. 11. 29.
[f] Hab. 3. 10.
[g] See Ps. 77. 17, &c.
[h] ver. 14.
[i] ver. 16.

1 Or, *for whereas ye have seen the Egyptians to day, &c.*

2 Or, *and made them to go heavily.*

---

13. *for the Egyptians whom,* &c.] The true sense is, ye shall never see the Egyptians in the same way, under the same circumstances.

15. *Wherefore criest thou unto me?*] Moses does not speak of his intercession, and we only know of it from this answer to his prayer.

19. *the angel of God*] Cp. marg. reff. and see iii. 2.

21. *a strong east wind*] The agency by which the object effected was natural (cp. xv. 8 note): and the conditions of the narrative are satisfied by the hypothesis, that the passage took place near Suez.

the waters were divided] *i.e.* there was a complete separation between the water of the gulf and the water to the north of Kolsum.

22. *were a wall unto them*] Cp. Nahum iii. 8. The waters served the purpose of an intrenchment and wall; the people could not be attacked on either flank during the transit; to the north was the water covering the whole district; to the south was the Red Sea.

24. *in the morning watch*] At sunrise, a little before 6 A.M. in April.

troubled] By a sudden panic.

26. *that the waters may come*] A sudden cessation of the wind, possibly coinciding with a spring tide (it was full moon) would immediately convert the low flat sand-banks first into a quicksand, and then into a mass of waters, in a time far less than would suffice for the escape of a single chariot, or horseman loaded with heavy corslet.

27. *overthrew the Egyptians*] Better as in the margin, **The Lord shook them off,** hurled them from their chariots into the sea.

the sea [k]returned to his strength when the morning appeared;
and the Egyptians fled against it; and the LORD [l] [1]overthrew
28 the Egyptians in the midst of the sea. And [m]the waters returned, and [n]covered the chariots, and the horsemen, *and* all the
host of Pharaoh that came into the sea after them; there re-
29 mained not so much as one of them. But [o]the children of Israel
walked upon dry *land* in the midst of the sea; and the waters
were a wall unto them on their right hand, and on their left.
30 ¶ Thus the LORD [p]saved Israel that day out of the hand of the
Egyptians; and Israel [q]saw the Egyptians dead upon the sea
31 shore. And Israel saw that great [2]work which the LORD did
upon the Egyptians: and the people feared the LORD, and [r]be-
lieved the LORD, and his servant Moses.

CHAP. 15. THEN sang [a]Moses and the children of Israel this
song unto the LORD, and spake, saying,

I will [b]sing unto the LORD, for he hath triumphed gloriously:
The horse and his rider hath he thrown into the sea.
2 The LORD *is* my strength and [c]song,
And he is become my salvation:
He *is* my God, and I will prepare him [d]an habitation;
My [e]father's God, and I [f]will exalt him.
3 The LORD *is* a man of [g]war:
The LORD *is* his [h]name.
4 [i]Pharaoh's chariots and his host hath he cast into the sea:

[k] Josh. 4. 18. [l] ch. 15. 1, 7. [m] Hab. 3. 8. [n] Ps. 106. 11. [o] ver. 22. Ps. 77. 20. & 78. 52, 53. [p] Ps. 106. 8. [q] Ps. 58. 10. & 59. 10. [r] ch. 4. 31. & 19. 9. John 2. 11. & 11. 45. [a] Judg. 5. 1. 2 Sam. 22. 1. Ps. 106. 12. [b] ver. 21. [c] Deut. 10. 21. Ps. 18. 2. Isai. 12. 2. Hab. 3. 18. [d] ver. 13. [e] ch. 3. 15. [f] 2 Sam. 22. 47. Ps. 99. 5. & 118. 28. Isai. 25. 1. [g] Rev. 19. 11. [h] ch. 6. 3. Ps. 83. 18. [i] ch. 14. 28.

[1] Heb. *shook off*, Deut. 11. 4. Neh. 9. 11. Ps. 78. 53. Heb. 11. 29.
[2] Heb. *hand*.

---

28. *not so much as one of them*] Escape would be impossible (*v.* 26). Pharaoh's destruction, independent of the distinct statement of the Psalmist, Ps. cxxxvi. 15, was in fact inevitable. The station of the king was in the vanguard: on every monument the Pharaoh is represented as the leader of the army. The death of the Pharaoh, and the entire loss of the chariotry and cavalry accounts for the undisturbed retreat of the Israelites through a district then subject to Egypt and easily accessible to their forces. If, as appears probable, Tothmosis II. was the Pharaoh, the first recorded expedition into the Peninsula took place 17 years after his death; and 22 years elapsed before any measures were taken to recover the lost ascendancy of Egypt in Syria. So complete, so marvellous was the deliverance: thus the Israelites were "baptized unto Moses in the cloud and in the sea" (1 Cor. x. 2). When they left Baal-Zephon they were separated finally from the idolatry of Egypt: when they passed the Red Sea their independence of its power was sealed; their life as a nation then began, a life inseparable henceforth from belief in Jehovah and His servant Moses, only to be merged in the higher life revealed by His Son.

XV. **1—18.** With the deliverance of Israel is associated the development of the national poetry, which finds its first and perfect expression in this magnificent hymn. It was sung by Moses and the people, an expression which evidently points to him as the author. That it was written at the time is an assertion expressly made in the text, and it is supported by the strongest internal evidence. In every age this song gave the tone to the poetry of Israel; especially at great critical epochs of deliverance: and in the book of Revelation (xv. 3) it is associated with the final triumph of the Church.

The division of the song into three parts is distinctly marked: 1-5, 6-10, 11-18: each begins with an ascription of praise to God; each increases in length and varied imagery unto the triumphant close.

1. *He hath triumphed gloriously*] Lit. He is gloriously glorious.

the horse and his rider] The word "rider" may include horseman, but applies properly to the charioteer.

2. *The* LORD *is my strength and song*] **My strength and song is Jah.** See Ps. lxviii. 4. The name was chosen here by Moses to draw attention to the promise ratified by the name "I am."

I will prepare Him an habitation] **I will glorify Him.** Our Authorised Version is open to serious objection, as suggesting a thought (viz. of erecting a temple) which could hardly have been in the mind of Moses at that time, and unsuited to the occasion.

3. *a man of war*] Cp. Ps. xxiv. 8. The name has on this occasion a peculiar fitness: man had no part in the victory; the battle was the Lord's.

the LORD *is his name*] "Jah is His name." See *v.* 2.

4. *hath He cast*] "Hurled," as from a sling. See xiv. 27.

[k]His chosen captains also are drowned in the Red sea.
5 [l]The depths have covered them:
[m]They sank into the bottom as a stone.
6 [n]Thy right hand, O LORD, is become glorious in power:
Thy right hand, O LORD, hath dashed in pieces the enemy.
7 And in the greatness of thine [o]excellency thou hast overthrown them that rose up against thee:
Thou sentest forth thy wrath, *which* [p]consumed them [q]as
stubble.
8 And [r]with the blast of thy nostrils the waters were gathered
together,
[s]The floods stood upright as an heap,
And the depths were congealed in the heart of the sea.
9 [t]The enemy said, I will pursue, I will overtake, I will [u]divide
the spoil;
My lust shall be satisfied upon them;
I will draw my sword, my hand shall [1]destroy them.
10 Thou didst [x]blow with thy wind, [y]the sea covered them:
They sank as lead in the mighty waters.
11 [z]Who *is* like unto thee, O LORD, among the [2]gods?
Who *is* like thee, [a]glorious in holiness, fearful *in* praises,
[b]doing wonders?
12 Thou stretchedst out [c]thy right hand,
The earth swallowed them.
13 Thou in thy mercy hast [d]led forth the people *which* thou
hast redeemed:
Thou hast guided *them* in thy strength unto [e]thy holy habitation.
14 [f]The people shall hear, *and* be afraid:
[g]Sorrow shall take hold on the inhabitants of Palestina.

[k] ch. 14. 7.
[l] ch. 14. 28.
[m] Neh. 9. 11.
[n] Ps. 118. 15, 16.
[o] Deut. 33. 26.
[p] Ps. 59. 13.
[q] Isai. 5. 24. & 47. 14.
[r] ch. 14. 21. 2 Sam. 22. 16. Job 4. 9. 2 Thess. 2. 8.
[s] Ps. 78. 13. Hab. 3. 10.
[t] Judg. 5. 30.
[u] Gen. 49. 27. Isai. 53. 12. Luke 11. 22.
[x] ch. 14. 21. Ps. 147. 18.
[y] ver. 5. ch. 14. 28.
[z] 2 Sam. 7. 22. 1 Kin. 8. 23. Ps. 71. 19. Jer. 10. 6.
[a] Isai. 6. 3.
[b] Ps. 77. 14.
[c] ver. 6.
[d] Ps. 77. 15. Is. 63. 12, 13. Jer. 2. 6.
[e] Ps. 78. 54.
[f] Num. 14. 14. Deut. 2. 25. Josh. 2. 9.
[g] Ps. 48. 6.

[1] Or, *repossess.*
[2] Or, *mighty ones?*

---

his chosen captains] See xiv. 7 note.

5. *as a stone*] The warriors in chariots are always represented on the monuments with heavy coats of mail; the corslets of "chosen captains" consisted of plates of highly tempered bronze, with sleeves reaching nearly to the elbow, covering the whole body and the thighs nearly to the knee. The wearers must have sunk at once like a stone, or as we read in *v.* 10, like lumps of lead.

7. *thy wrath*] Lit. Thy burning, *i.e.* the fire of Thy wrath, a word chosen expressly with reference to the effect.

8. The blast of God's nostrils corresponds to the natural agency, the east wind (xiv. 21), which drove the waters back: on the north the waters rose high, overhanging the sands, but kept back by the strong wind: on the south they laid in massive rollers, kept down by the same agency in the deep bed of the Red Sea.

9. *The enemy said*] The abrupt, gasping utterances;—the haste, cupidity and ferocity of the Egyptians;—the confusion and disorder of their thoughts, belong to the highest order of poetry. They enable us to realize the feelings which induced Pharaoh and his host to pursue the Israelites over the treacherous sandbanks.

10. *Thou didst blow with thy wind*] Notice the solemn majesty of these few words, in immediate contrast with the tumult and confusion of the preceding verse. In xiv. 28, we read only, "the waters returned," here we are told that it was because the wind blew. A sudden change in the direction of the wind would bring back at once the masses of water heaped up on the north.

they sank as lead] See note on *v.* 5.

11. *among the gods*] Cp. Ps. lxxxvi. 8, Deut. xxxii. 16, 17. A Hebrew just leaving the land in which Polytheism attained its highest development, with gigantic statues and temples of incomparable grandeur, might well on such an occasion dwell upon this consummation of the long series of triumphs by which the "greatness beyond compare" of Jehovah was once for all established.

13. *thy holy habitation*] Either Palestine, regarded as the land of promise, sanctified by manifestations of God to the Patriarchs, and destined to be both the home of God's people, and the place where His glory and purposes were to be perfectly revealed: or Mount Moriah.

14. *the inhabitants of Palestina*] *i.e.* the country of the Philistines. They were the first who would expect an invasion, and the

[h] Gen. 36. 40. [i] Deut. 2. 4. [k] Num. 22. 3. Hab. 3. 7. [l] Josh. 5. 1. [m] Deut. 2. 25. Josh. 2. 9. [n] 1 Sam. 25. 37. [o] ch. 19. 5. Ps. 74. 2. Isai. 43. 1. Jer. 31. 11. Tit. 2. 14. 1 Pet. 2. 9. [p] Ps. 44. 2. [q] Ps. 78. 54. [r] Ps. 10. 16. & 29. 10. & 146. 10. Isai. 57. 15. [s] ch. 14. 23. Prov. 21. 31. [t] ch. 14. 28. [u] Judg. 4. 4. 1 Sam. 10. 5. [x] Num. 26. 59. [y] 1 Sam. 18. 6. [z] Ps. 68. 11. [a] 1 Sam. 18. 7. [b] ver. 1. [c] Gen. 16. 7.

15 [h]Then [i]the dukes of Edom shall be amazed;
[k]The mighty men of Moab, trembling shall take hold upon them;
[l]All the inhabitants of Canaan shall melt away.
16 [m]Fear and dread shall fall upon them;
By the greatness of thine arm they shall be *as* still [n]as a stone;
Till thy people pass over, O LORD, till the people pass over, [o]*which* thou hast purchased.
17 Thou shalt bring them in, and [p]plant them in the mountain of thine inheritance,
In the place, O LORD, *which* thou hast made for thee to dwell in,
In the [q]sanctuary, O LORD, *which* thy hands have established.
18 [r]The LORD shall reign for ever and ever.
19 For the [s]horse of Pharaoh went in with his chariots and with
his horsemen into the sea, and [t]the LORD brought again the
waters of the sea upon them; but the children of Israel went on
20 dry *land* in the midst of the sea. ¶ And Miriam [u]the prophetess,
[x]the sister of Aaron, [y]took a timbrel in her hand; and all the
21 women went out after her [z]with timbrels and with dances. And
Miriam [a]answered them,
[b]Sing ye to the LORD, for he hath triumphed gloriously;
The horse and his rider hath he thrown into the sea.
22 ¶ So Moses brought Israel from the Red sea, and they went out
into the wilderness of [c]Shur; and they went three days in the

---

first whose district would have been invaded but for the faintheartedness of the Israelites.

15. *the dukes of Edom*] See Gen. xxxvi. 15. It denotes the chieftains, not the kings of Edom.

the mighty men of Moab] The physical strength and great stature of the Moabites are noted in other passages: see Jer. xlviii. 29, 41.

Canaan] The name in this, as in many passages of Genesis, designates the whole of Palestine: and is used of course with reference to the promise to Abraham. It was known to the Egyptians, and occurs frequently on the monuments as Pa-kanana, which applies, if not to the whole of Palestine, yet to the northern district under Lebanon, which the Phœnicians occupied and called Canaan.

17. *in the mountain of thine inheritance*] See *v.* 13.

19. *For the horse*, &c.] This verse does not belong to the hymn, but marks the transition from it to the narrative.

20. *And Miriam the prophetess*] The part here assigned to Miriam and the women of Israel is in accordance both with Egyptian and Hebrew customs. The men are represented as singing the hymn in chorus, under the guidance of Moses; at each interval Miriam and the women sang the refrain, marking the time with the timbrel, and with the measured rhythmical movements always associated with solemn festivities. Compare Judg. xi. 34, 2 Sam. vi. 5, and marg. reff. The word used in this passage for the timbrel is Egyptian, and judging from its etymology and the figures which are joined with it in the inscriptions, it was probably the round instrument.

Miriam is called a prophetess, evidently (Numbers xii. 2) because she and Aaron had received divine communications. The word is used here in its proper sense of uttering words suggested by the Spirit of God. See Genesis xx. 7. She is called the sister of Aaron, most probably to indicate her special position as co-ordinate, not with Moses the leader of the nation, but with his chief aid and instrument.

22. *So Moses*] Lit. **And Moses.** The history of the journey from the Red Sea to Sinai begins in fact with this verse, which would more conveniently have been the commencement of another chapter.

from the Red sea] The station where Moses and his people halted to celebrate their deliverance is generally admitted to be the Ayoun Musa, *i.e.* the fountains of Moses. It is the only green spot near the passage over the Red Sea. There are several wells there, which in the time of Moses were probably enclosed and kept with great care by the Egyptians, for the use of the frequent convoys to and from their ancient settlements at Sarbut el Khadem and the Wady Mughara.

the wilderness of Shur] This name belongs to the whole district between the north-eastern frontier of Egypt and Palestine. The word is undoubtedly Egyptian, and is derived probably from the word Khar,

23 wilderness, and found no water. And when they came to [d]Marah,
they could not drink of the waters of Marah, for they *were*
24 bitter: therefore the name of it was called [1]Marah. And the
people [e]murmured against Moses, saying, What shall we drink?
25 And he [f]cried unto the LORD; and the LORD shewed him a tree,
[g]*which* when he had cast into the waters, the waters were made
sweet: there he [h]made for them a statute and an ordinance,
26 and there [i]he proved them, and said, [k]If thou wilt diligently
hearken to the voice of the LORD thy God, and wilt do that
which is right in his sight, and wilt give ear to his commandments, and keep all his statutes, I will put none of these [l]dis-
eases upon thee, which I have brought upon the Egyptians: for
27 I *am* the LORD [m]that healeth thee. ¶ [n]And they came to Elim,
where *were* twelve wells of water, and threescore and ten palm
trees: and they encamped there by the waters.

CHAP. 16. AND they took [a]their journey from Elim, and all the
congregation of the children of Israel came unto the wilderness
of [b]Sin, which *is* between Elim and Sinai, on the fifteenth day
of the second month after their departing out of the land of
2 Egypt. And the whole congregation of the children of Israel
3 [c]murmured against Moses and Aaron in the wilderness: and the
children of Israel said unto them, [d]Would to God we had died
by the hand of the LORD in the land of Egypt, [e]when we sat by
the flesh pots, *and* when we did eat bread to the full; for ye
have brought us forth into this wilderness, to kill this whole
4 assembly with hunger. ¶ Then said the LORD unto Moses,
Behold, I will rain [f]bread from heaven for you; and the people
shall go out and gather [2]a certain rate every day, that I may
5 [g]prove them, whether they will walk in my law, or no. And it
shall come to pass, that on the sixth day they shall prepare *that*

[d] Num. 33. 8.
[e] ch. 16. 2.
[f] ch. 14. 10. Ps. 50. 15.
[g] See 2 Kin. 2. 21.
[h] See Josh. 24. 25.
[i] ch. 16. 4. Deut. 8. 2. Judg. 2. 22. Ps. 66. 10.
[k] Deut. 7. 12, 15.
[l] Deut. 28. 27, 60.
[m] ch. 23. 25. Ps. 41. 3, 4.
[n] Num. 33. 9.
[a] Num. 33. 10, 11.
[b] Ezek. 30. 15.
[c] ch. 15. 24. Ps. 106. 25. 1 Cor. 10. 10.
[d] Lam. 4. 9.
[e] Num. 11. 4, 5.
[f] Ps. 78. 24. & 105. 40. John 6. 31. 1 Cor. 10. 3.
[g] ch. 15. 25. Deut. 8. 2.

[1] That is, *Bitterness*, Ruth 1. 20.

[2] Heb. *the portion of a day in his day*, Prov. 30. 8. Matt. 6. 11.

which designated all the country between Egypt and Syria proper.

three days] The distance between Ayoun Musa and Huwara, the first spot where any water is found on the route, is 33 geographical miles. The whole district is a tract of sand, or rough gravel.

23. *Marah*] Now identified with the fount of Huwara. The fountain rises from a large mound, a whitish petrifaction, deposited by the water, and is considered by the Arabians to be the worst in the whole district.

25. *a tree*, &c.] The statement points to a natural agency, but the result was manifestly supernatural.

he made, &c.] The Lord then set before them the fundamental principle of implicit trust, to be shown by obedience. The healing of the water was a symbol of deliverance from physical and spiritual evils.

27. *Elim*] The valley of Gharandel, two hours' journey south of Huwara.

twelve wells] Read **springs**; the Hebrew denotes natural sources. These springs may have been perennial when a richer vegetation clothed the adjacent heights.

XVI. **1.** *the wilderness of Sin*] The desert tract, called Debbet er Ramleh, extends nearly across the peninsula from the Wady Nasb in a south-easterly direction, between the limestone district of Et Tih and the granite of Sinai. The journey from the station at Elim, or even from that on the Red Sea, could be performed in a day: at that time the route was kept in good condition by the Egyptians.

2. *murmured*] The want of food was first felt after six weeks from the time of the departure from Egypt, see *v.* 1: we have no notice previously of any deficiency of bread.

3. *by the hand of the* LORD] This evidently refers to the plagues, especially the last, in Egypt: the death which befell the Egyptians appeared to the people preferable to the sufferings of famine.

flesh pots, and...bread] These expressions prove that the servile labours to which they had been subjected did not involve privations: they were fed abundantly, either by the officials of Pharaoh, or more probably by the produce of their own fertile district.

4. *that I may prove them*] The trial consisted in the restriction to the supply of their daily wants.

5. *it shall be twice as much*] They should collect and prepare a double quantity.

[h] See ver. 22. Lev. 25. 21.
[i] See ver. 12, 13. & ch. 6. 7. Num. 16. 28, 29, 30.
[k] See ver. 10. Isai. 35. 2. & 40. 5. John 11. 4, 40.
[l] Num. 16. 11.
[m] See 1 Sam. 8. 7. Luke 10. 16. Rom. 13. 2.
[n] Num. 16. 16.
[o] ver. 7. ch. 13. 21. 1 Kin. 8. 10, 11.
[p] ver. 8.
[q] ver. 6.
[r] ver. 7.
[s] Num. 11. 31. Ps. 78. 27. & 105. 40.
[t] Num. 11. 9.
[u] Num. 11. 7. Deut. 8. 3. Neh. 9. 15. Ps. 78. 24.
[x] John 6. 31, 49, 58. 1 Cor. 10. 3.
[y] ver. 36.

which they bring in; and [h]it shall be twice as much as they
6 gather daily. ¶ And Moses and Aaron said unto all the children
of Israel, [i]At even, then ye shall know that the LORD hath brought
7 you out from the land of Egypt: and in the morning, then ye
shall see [k]the glory of the LORD; for that he heareth your murmurings against the LORD: and [l]what *are* we, that ye murmur
8 against us? And Moses said, *This shall be*, when the LORD
shall give you in the evening flesh to eat, and in the morning
bread to the full; for that the LORD heareth your murmurings
which ye murmur against him: and what *are* we? Your mur-
9 murings *are* not against us, but [m]against the LORD. And Moses
spake unto Aaron, Say unto all the congregation of the children
of Israel, [n]Come near before the LORD: for he hath heard your
10 murmurings. And it came to pass, as Aaron spake unto the
whole congregation of the children of Israel, that they looked
toward the wilderness, and, behold, the glory of the LORD [o]ap-
11 peared in the cloud. And the LORD spake unto Moses, saying,
12 [p]I have heard the murmurings of the children of Israel: speak
unto them, saying, [q]At even ye shall eat flesh, and [r]in the morning ye shall be filled with bread; and ye shall know that I *am*
13 the LORD your God. ¶ And it came to pass, that at even [s]the
quails came up, and covered the camp: and in the morning [t]the
14 dew lay round about the host. And when the dew that lay was
gone up, behold, upon the face of the wilderness *there lay* [u]a small
15 round thing, *as* small as the hoar frost on the ground. And when
the children of Israel saw *it*, they said one to another, [1]It *is*
manna: for they wist not what it *was*. And Moses said unto
them, [x]This *is* the bread which the LORD hath given you to eat.
16 This *is* the thing which the LORD hath commanded, Gather of it
every man according to his eating, [y]an omer [2]for every man,
according to the number of your [3]persons; take ye every man

[1] Or, *What is this?* or, *It is a portion.*
[2] Heb. *by the poll*, or, *head.*
[3] Heb. *souls.*

---

7. *the glory of the* LORD] the visible appearance described in *v.* 10.

10. *appeared in the cloud*] Or, "was seen in a cloud." The definite article would imply that the cloud was the same which is often mentioned in connection with the tabernacle. The people saw the cloud here spoken of beyond the camp.

13. *quails*] This bird migrates in immense numbers in spring from the south: it is nowhere more common than in the neighbourhood of the Red Sea. In this passage we read of a single flight so dense that it covered the encampment. The miracle consisted in the precise time of the arrival and its coincidence with the announcement.

15. *It is manna*] "Man" or "man-hut," *i.e.* white manna, was the name under which the substance was known to the Egyptians, and therefore to the Israelites. The manna of the Peninsula of Sinai is the sweet juice of the Tarfa, a species of tamarisk. It exudes from the trunk and branches in hot weather, and forms small round white grains. In cold weather it preserves its consistency, in hot weather it melts rapidly. It is either gathered from the twigs of the tamarisk, or from the fallen leaves underneath the tree. The colour is a greyish yellow. It begins to exude in May, and lasts about six weeks. According to Ehrenberg it is produced by the puncture of an insect. It is abundant in rainy seasons, many years it ceases altogether. The whole quantity now produced in a single year does not exceed 600 or 700 pounds. It is found in the district between the Wady Gharandel, *i.e.* Elim, and Sinai, in the Wady Sheikh, and in some other parts of the Peninsula. When therefore the Israelites saw the "small round thing," they said at once "this is manna," but with an exclamation of surprise at finding it, not under the tamarisk tree, but on the open plain, in such immense quantities, under circumstances so unlike what they could have expected: in fact they did not know what it really was, only what it resembled.

16. *an omer*] *i.e.* the tenth part of an Ephah, see *v.* 36. The exact quantity cannot be determined, since the measures varied at different times. Josephus makes the omer equal to six half-pints. The ephah was an Egyptian measure, supposed to be about a

17 for *them* which *are* in his tents. And the children of Israel did
18 so, and gathered, some more, some less. And when they did
mete *it* with an omer, [z]he that gathered much had nothing over, [z] 2 Cor. 8. 15.
and he that gathered little had no lack; they gathered every
19 man according to his eating. And Moses said, Let no man leave
20 of it till the morning. Notwithstanding they hearkened not
unto Moses; but some of them left of it until the morning, and
it bred worms, and stank: and Moses was wroth with them.
21 And they gathered it every morning, every man according to
22 his eating: and when the sun waxed hot, it melted. ¶ And it
came to pass, *that* on the sixth day they gathered twice as much
bread, two omers for one *man*: and all the rulers of the congre-
23 gation came and told Moses. And he said unto them, This *is*
that which the LORD hath said, To morrow *is* [a]the rest of the [a] Gen. 2. 3.
holy sabbath unto the LORD: bake *that* which ye will bake *to* ch. 20. 8.
day, and seethe that ye will seethe; and that which remaineth & 31. 15. & 35. 3.
24 over lay up for you to be kept until the morning. And they Lev. 23. 3.
laid it up till the morning, as Moses bade: and it did not [b]stink, [b] ver. 20.
25 neither was there any worm therein. And Moses said, Eat that
to day; for to day *is* a sabbath unto the LORD: to day ye shall
26 not find it in the field. [c]Six days ye shall gather it; but on the [c] ch. 20. 9.
seventh day, *which is* the sabbath, in it there shall be none.
27 And it came to pass, *that* there went out *some* of the people on
28 the seventh day for to gather, and they found none. And the [d] 2 Kin. 17. 14.
LORD said unto Moses, How long [d]refuse ye to keep my com- Ps. 78. 10,
29 mandments and my laws? See, for that the LORD hath given 22. & 106. 13.

---

bushel or one-third of a hin. The word omer, in this sense, occurs in no other passage. It was probably not used at a later period, belonging, like many other words, to the time of Moses. It is found in old Egyptian. See Lev. xix. 36.

17. *some more, some less*] It is evidently implied that the people were in part at least disobedient and failed in this first trial.

18. *had nothing over*] Whatever quantity each person had gathered, when he measured it in his tent, he found that he had just as many omers as he needed for the consumption of his family.

20. *it bred worms*] This result was supernatural: no such tendency to rapid decomposition is recorded of common manna.

21. *it melted*] This refers to the manna which was not gathered.

22. *twice as much bread*] See *v.* 5.

From this passage and from *v.* 5 it is inferred that the seventh day was previously known to the people as a day separate from all others, and if so, it must have been observed as an ancient and primeval institution.

23. *To-morrow*, &c.] Or, **To-morrow is a rest, a Sabbath holy to Jehovah**: *i.e.* to-morrow must be a day of rest, observed strictly as a Sabbath, or festal rest, holy to Jehovah.

bake, &c.] These directions shew that the manna thus given differed essentially from the natural product. Here and in Numbers xi. 8 it is treated in a way which shews that it had the property of corn, could be ground in a mortar, baked and boiled. Ordinary manna is used as honey, it cannot be ground, and it melts when exposed to a moderate heat, forming a substance like barley sugar, called "manna tabulata." In Persia it is boiled with water and brought to the consistency of honey. The Arabs also boil the leaves to which it adheres, and the manna thus dissolved floats on the water as a glutinous or oily substance. It is obvious that these accounts are inapplicable to the manna from heaven, which had the characteristics and nutritive properties of bread.

25. *Eat that to day*] The practical observance of the Sabbath was thus formally instituted before the giving of the Law. The people were to abstain from the ordinary work of every-day life: they were not to collect food, nor, as it would seem, even to prepare it as on other days.

27. *there went out some of the people*] This was an act of wilful disobedience. It is remarkable, being the first violation of the express command, that it was not visited by a signal chastisement: the rest and peace of the "Holy Sabbath" were not disturbed by a manifestation of wrath.

28. *How long*] The reference to *v.* 4 is obvious. The prohibition involved a trial of faith, in which as usual the people were found wanting. Every miracle formed some part, so to speak, of an educational process.

29. *abide ye every man in his place*] The

you the sabbath, therefore he giveth you on the sixth day the
bread of two days; abide ye every man in his place, let no man
30 go out of his place on the seventh day. So the people rested on
31 the seventh day. And the house of Israel called the name
thereof Manna: and [e]it *was* like coriander seed, white; and the
32 taste of it *was* like wafers *made* with honey. ¶ And Moses said,
This *is* the thing which the LORD commandeth, Fill an omer of
it to be kept for your generations; that they may see the bread
wherewith I have fed you in the wilderness, when I brought
33 you forth from the land of Egypt. And Moses said unto
Aaron, [f]Take a pot, and put an omer full of manna therein,
and lay it up before the LORD, to be kept for your generations.
34 As the LORD commanded Moses, so Aaron laid it up [g]before the
35 Testimony, to be kept. And the children of Israel did eat
manna [h]forty years, [i]until they came to a land inhabited; they
did eat manna, until they came unto the borders of the land of
36 Canaan. Now an omer *is* the tenth *part* of an ephah.
CHAP. 17. AND [a]all the congregation of the children of Israel journeyed from the wilderness of Sin, after their journeys, according to the commandment of the LORD, and pitched in Rephidim:
2 and *there was* no water for the people to drink. [b]Wherefore
the people did chide with Moses, and said, Give us water that
we may drink. And Moses said unto them, Why chide ye with
3 me? Wherefore do ye [c]tempt the LORD? And the people
thirsted there for water; and the people [d]murmured against
Moses, and said, Wherefore *is* this *that* thou hast brought us up
out of Egypt, to kill us and our children and our cattle with

[e] Num. 11. 7, 8.
[f] Heb. 9. 4.
[g] ch. 25. 16. & 40. 20. Num. 17. 10. Deut. 10. 5. 1 Kin. 8. 9.
[h] Num. 33. 38. Deut. 8. 2. Neh. 9. 20. John 6. 31.
[i] Josh. 5. 12. Neh. 9. 15.
[a] ch. 16. 1. Num. 33. 12, 14.
[b] Num. 20. 3, 4.
[c] Deut. 6. 16. Ps. 78. 18. Isai. 7. 12. Matt. 4. 7. 1 Cor. 10. 9.
[d] ch. 16. 2.

---

expression in Hebrew is peculiar and seems almost to enjoin a position of complete repose; "in his place" is lit. under himself, as the Oriental sits with his legs drawn up under him. The prohibition must however be understood with reference to its immediate object; they were not to go forth from their place in order to gather manna, which was on other days without the camp. The spirit of the law is sacred rest. The Lord gave them this Sabbath, as a blessing and privilege. It was "made for man." (Mark ii. 27.)

31. *Manna*] It was not indeed the common manna, as they then seem to have believed, but the properties which are noted in this passage are common to it and the natural product: in size, form and colour it resembled the seed of the white coriander, a small round grain of a whitish or yellowish grey.

33. *a pot*] The word here used occurs in no other passage. It corresponds in form and use to the Egyptian for a casket or vase in which oblations were presented.

34. *the Testimony*] See marg. reff.

35. *did eat manna forty years*] This does not necessarily imply that the Israelites were fed exclusively on manna, or that the supply was continuous during forty years: but that whenever it might be needed, owing to the total or partial failure of other food, it was given until they entered the promised land. They had numerous flocks and herds, which were not slaughtered (see Numbers xi. 22), but which gave them milk, cheese and of course a limited supply of flesh: nor is there any reason to suppose that during a considerable part of that time they may not have cultivated some spots of fertile ground in the wilderness. We may assume, as in most cases of miracle, that the supernatural supply was commensurate with their actual necessity. The manna was not withheld in fact until the Israelites had passed the Jordan.

XVII. **1.** *according to their journeys*] The Israelites rested at two stations before they reached Rephidim, viz. Dophkah and Alush (Numbers xxxiii. 12-14). Dophkah was in the Wady Sih, a day's journey from the Wady Nasb. The wilderness of Sin (xvi. 1) properly speaking ends here, the sandstone ceases, and is replaced by the porphyry and granite which belong to the central formation of the Sinaitic group. Alush may have been near the entrance to the Wady Sheikh.

Rephidim] [Variously placed at Feiran at the base of Mount Serbal, or at the pass of El Watiyeh.]

2. *tempt the* LORD] It is a general characteristic of the Israelites that the miracles, which met each need as it arose, failed to produce a habit of faith: but the severity of the trial, the faintness and anguish of thirst in the burning desert, must not be overlooked in appreciating their conduct.

4 thirst? And Moses [e]cried unto the LORD, saying, What shall
5 I do unto this people? they be almost ready to [f]stone me. And
the LORD said unto Moses, [g]Go on before the people, and take
with thee of the elders of Israel; and thy rod, wherewith [h]thou
6 smotest the river, take in thine hand, and go. [i]Behold, I will
stand before thee there upon the rock in Horeb; and thou shalt
smite the rock, and there shall come water out of it, that the
people may drink. And Moses did so in the sight of the elders
7 of Israel. And he called the name of the place [k][1]Massah, and
[2]Meribah, because of the chiding of the children of Israel, and
because they tempted the LORD, saying, Is the LORD among us,
8 or not? ¶ [l]Then came Amalek, and fought with Israel in
9 Rephidim. And Moses said unto [m]Joshua, Choose us out men,
and go out, fight with Amalek: to morrow I will stand on the
10 top of the hill with [n]the rod of God in mine hand. So Joshua
did as Moses had said to him, and fought with Amalek: and
11 Moses, Aaron, and Hur went up to the top of the hill. And it
came to pass, when Moses [o]held up his hand, that Israel pre-
12 vailed: and when he let down his hand, Amalek prevailed. But
Moses' hands *were* heavy; and they took a stone, and put *it*
under him, and he sat thereon; and Aaron and Hur stayed up
his hands, the one on the one side, and the other on the other
side; and his hands were steady until the going down of the sun.
13 And Joshua discomfited Amalek and his people with the edge of
14 the sword. ¶ And the LORD said unto Moses, [p]Write this *for* a

[e] ch. 14. 15.
[f] 1 Sam. 30. 6. John 8. 59. & 10. 31.
[g] Ezek. 2. 6.
[h] ch. 7. 20. Num. 20. 8.
[i] Num. 20. 10, 11. Ps. 78. 15. & 105. 41. & 114. 8. 1 Cor. 10. 4.
[k] Num. 20. 13. Ps. 81. 7. & 95. 8. Heb. 3. 8.
[l] Gen. 36. 12. Num. 24. 20. Deut. 25. 17. 1 Sam. 15. 2.
[m] Called *Jesus*, Acts 7. 45. Heb. 4. 8.
[n] ch. 4. 20.
[o] Jam. 5. 16.
[p] ch. 34. 27.

[1] That is, *Tentation*. [2] That is, *Chiding*, or, *Strife*.

---

6. *the rock in Horeb*] [a rock situate, according to Arab tradition, in Wady Feiran. Horeb was a name given to the whole desert of Sinai and subsequently attached to the mountain. Palmer].

It is questioned whether the water thus supplied ceased with the immediate occasion; see 1 Cor. x. 4, the general meaning of which appears to be that their wants were ever supplied from Him, of Whom the rock was but a symbol, and Who accompanied them in all their wanderings.

7. *Massah...Meribah*] See margin. On the importance of this lesson see our Lord's words, Matt. iv. 7.

8. *Then came Amalek*] The attack occurred about two months after the Exodus, towards the end of May or early in June, when the Bedouins leave the lower plains in order to find pasture for their flocks on the cooler heights. The approach of the Israelites to Sinai would of course attract notice, and no cause of warfare is more common than a dispute for the right of pasturage. The Amalekites were at that time the most powerful race in the Peninsula; here they took their position as the chief of the heathens. They were also the first among the heathens who attacked God's people, and as such were marked out for punishment (see marg. reff.).

9. *Joshua*] This is the first mention of the great follower and successor of Moses. He died at the age of 110, some 65 years after this transaction. His original name was Hosea, but Moses calls him by the full name, which was first given about forty years afterwards, as that by which he was to be known to succeeding generations. From this it may perhaps be inferred that this portion of Exodus was written, or revised, towards the end of the sojourn in the wilderness.

the rod of God] See iv. 20. The hill is supposed to be the height now called Feria on the north side of the plain Er Rahah; [or, Jebel Tahuneh over Feiran. Palmer].

10. *Hur*] Again mentioned with Aaron, in xxiv. 14. He was grandfather of Bezaleel, the great sculptor and artificer of the tabernacle, (xxxi. 2–5), and belonged to the tribe of Judah. (See 1 Chron. ii. 18-20.)

11. The act represents the efficacy of intercessory prayer—offered doubtless by Moses—a point of great moment to the Israelites at that time and to the Church in all ages.

12. *until the going down of the sun*] The length of this first great battle indicates the strength and obstinacy of the assailants. It was no mere raid of Bedouins, but a deliberate attack of the Amalekites, who had been probably thoroughly trained in warfare by their struggles with Egypt.

13. *with the edge of the sword*] This expression always denotes a great slaughter of the enemy.

14. *in a book*] **in the book,** *i.e.* the book which contained the history of God's dealings with His people. Moses was further

q Num. 24. 20. Deut. 25. 19. 1 Sam. 15. 3, 7. & 30. 1, 17. 2 Sam. 8. 12. Ezra 9. 14.

memorial in a book, and rehearse *it* in the ears of Joshua: for [q]I
will utterly put out the remembrance of Amalek from under
15 heaven. And Moses built an altar, and called the name of it
16 [1]Jehovah-nissi: for he said, [2]Because [3]the LORD hath sworn
that the LORD *will have* war with Amalek from generation to
generation.

a ch. 2. 16. & 3. 1. b Ps. 44. 1. & 77. 14, 15. & 78. 4. & 105. 5, 43. & 106. 2, 8. c ch. 4. 26. d Acts 7. 29. e ch. 2. 22.

CHAP. 18. WHEN [a]Jethro, the priest of Midian, Moses' father in
law, heard of all that [b]God had done for Moses, and for Israel his
people, *and* that the LORD had brought Israel out of Egypt;
2 then Jethro, Moses' father in law, took Zipporah, Moses' wife,
3 [c]after he had sent her back, and her [d]two sons; of which the
[e]name of the one *was* [4]Gershom; for he said, I have been an
4 alien in a strange land: and the name of the other *was* [5]Eliezer;
for the God of my father, *said he, was* mine help, and delivered
5 me from the sword of Pharaoh: and Jethro, Moses' father in
law, came with his sons and his wife unto Moses into the wilder-
6 ness, where he encamped at [f]the mount of God: and he said
unto Moses, I thy father in law Jethro am come unto thee, and
7 thy wife, and her two sons with her. And Moses [g]went out to
meet his father in law, and did obeisance, and [h]kissed him; and
they asked each other of *their* [6]welfare; and they came into the
8 tent. ¶ And Moses told his father in law all that the LORD had
done unto Pharaoh and to the Egyptians for Israel's sake, *and* all

f ch. 3. 1, 12. g Gen. 14. 17. & 18. 2. & 19. 1. 1 Kin. 2. 19. h Gen. 29. 13. & 33. 4.

[1] That is, *The* LORD *my banner.* See Judg. 6. 24.
[2] Or, *Because the hand* of Amalek is *against the throne of the* LORD, therefore, &c.
[3] Heb. *the hand upon the throne of the* LORD.
[4] That is, *A stranger there.*
[5] That is, *My God* is *an help.*
[6] Heb. *peace,* Gen. 43. 27. 2 Sam. 11. 7.

---

instructed to impress the command specially on the mind of Joshua, as the leader to whom the first step towards its accomplishment would be entrusted on the conquest of Canaan. The work was not actually completed until the reign of Hezekiah, 1 Chron. iv. 43.

15. *Jehovah-nissi*] See the margin, "Jehovah my banner." As a proper name the Hebrew word is rightly preserved. The meaning is evidently that the name of Jehovah is the true banner under which victory is certain; so to speak, the motto or inscription on the banners of the host. Inscriptions on the royal standard were well known. Each of the Pharaohs on his accession adopted one in addition to his official name.

16. *Because the* LORD *hath sworn*] This rendering is incorrect. Our translators regard the expression as a solemn asseveration by the throne of God. To this however the objections are insuperable; it has no parallel in Scriptural usage: God swears by Himself, not by His Throne. As the Hebrew text now stands the meaning is more satisfactorily given in the margin.

An alteration, slight in form, but considerable in meaning, has been proposed with much confidence, viz. "Nes," standard for "Kes," throne; thus connecting the name of the altar with the sentence. Conjectural emendations are not to be adopted without necessity, and the obvious a priori probability of such a reading makes it improbable that one so far more difficult should have been substituted for it. One of the surest canons of criticism militates against its reception. The text as it stands was undoubtedly that which was alone known to the Targumists, the Samaritan, the Syriac, the Latin and the Arabic translators. The LXX. appear to have had a different reading, ἐν χειρὶ κρυφαίᾳ πολεμεῖ.

XVIII. The events recorded in this chapter could not have occupied many days, fifteen only elapsed between the arrival of the Israelites in the wilderness of Sin and their final arrival at Sinai, see xvi. 1, and xix. 1. This leaves however sufficient time for the interview and transactions between Moses and Jethro.

1. Jethro was in all probability the "brother in law" of Moses (iii. 1). On the parting from Zipporah, see iv. 26.

5. *the wilderness*] *i.e.*, according to the view which seems on the whole most probable, the plain near the northern summit of Horeb, the mount of God. The valley which opens upon Er Rahah on the left of Horeb is called by the Arabs Wady Shueib, *i.e.* the vale of Hobab.

6. *and he said*, &c.] Or, according to the Greek Version, "And it was told to Moses, saying, Lo, thy father in law Jether is come."

7. *asked each other of their welfare*] Addressed each other with the customary salutation, "Peace be unto you."

the travail that had [1]come upon them by the way, and *how* the
9 LORD [i]delivered them. And Jethro rejoiced for all the goodness
which the LORD had done to Israel, whom he had delivered out
10 of the hand of the Egyptians. And Jethro said, [k]Blessed *be* the
LORD, who hath delivered you out of the hand of the Egyptians,
and out of the hand of Pharaoh, who hath delivered the people
11 from under the hand of the Egyptians. Now I know that the
LORD *is* [l]greater than all gods: [m]for in the thing wherein they
12 dealt [n]proudly *he was* above them. And Jethro, Moses' father in
law, took a burnt offering and sacrifices for God: and Aaron
came, and all the elders of Israel, to eat bread with Moses' father
13 in law [o]before God. ¶ And it came to pass on the morrow, that
Moses sat to judge the people: and the people stood by Moses
14 from the morning unto the evening. And when Moses' father
in law saw all that he did to the people, he said, What *is* this
thing that thou doest to the people? Why sittest thou thyself
alone, and all the people stand by thee from morning unto even?
15 And Moses said unto his father in law, Because [p]the people come
16 unto me to enquire of God: when they have [q]a matter, they
come unto me; and I judge between [2]one and another, and I do
17 [r]make *them* know the statutes of God, and his laws. And
Moses' father in law said unto him, The thing that thou doest *is*
18 not good. [3]Thou wilt surely wear away, both thou and this
people that *is* with thee: for this thing *is* too heavy for thee;
19 [s]thou art not able to perform it thyself alone. Hearken now
unto my voice, I will give thee counsel, and [t]God shall be with
thee: Be thou [u]for the people to God-ward, that thou mayest
20 [x]bring the causes unto God: and thou shalt [y]teach them ordinances and laws, and shalt shew them [z]the way wherein
21 they must walk, and [a]the works that they must do. Moreover
thou shalt provide out of all the people [b]able men, such as
[c]fear God, [d]men of truth, [e]hating covetousness; and place

[i] Ps. 78. 42. & 107. 2.
[k] Gen. 14. 20. 2 Sam. 18. 28. Luke 1. 68.
[l] 2 Chr. 2. 5. Ps. 95. 3. & 97. 9.
[m] ch. 14. 27.
[n] 1 Sam. 2. 3. Neh. 9. 10. Job 40. 11. Ps. 31. 23. Luke 1. 51.
[o] Deut. 12. 7. 1 Chr. 29. 22. 1 Cor. 10. 18. 21, 31.
[p] Lev. 24. 12. Num. 15. 34.
[q] ch. 24. 14. 2 Sam. 15. 3. Acts 18. 15. 1 Cor. 6. 1.
[r] Lev. 24. 15. Num. 15. 35.
[s] Num. 11. 14, 17. Deut. 1. 9.
[t] ch. 3. 12.
[u] ch. 20. 19. Deut. 5. 5.
[x] Num. 27. 5.
[y] Deut. 4. 1.
[z] Ps. 143. 8.
[a] Deut. 1. 18.
[b] ver. 25. 2 Chr. 19. 5—10.
[c] Gen. 42. 18. 2 Sam. 23. 3.
[d] Ezek. 18. 8.
[e] Deut. 16. 19.

[1] Heb. *found them*, Gen. 44. 34. Num. 20. 14.
[2] Heb. *a man and his fellow*.
[3] Heb. *fading thou wilt fade*.

---

11. *greater than all gods*] See xv. 11. The words simply indicate a conviction of the incomparable might and majesty of Jehovah.

for in...above them] *i.e.* the greatness of Jehovah was shewn in those transactions wherein the Egyptians had thought to deal haughtily and cruelly against the Israelites. Jethro refers especially to the destruction of the Egyptian host in the Red Sea.

12. *a burnt offering and sacrifices*] This verse clearly shows that Jethro was recognized as a priest of the true God, and is of great importance in its bearings upon the relation between the Israelites and their congeners, and upon the state of religion among the descendants of Abraham.

13. *from the morning unto the evening*] It may be assumed as at least probable that numerous cases of difficulty arose out of the division of the spoil of the Amalekites (xvii. 13), and causes would have accumulated during the journey from Elim.

15. *to enquire of God*] The decisions of Moses were doubtless accepted by the people as oracles. The internal prompting of the Spirit was a sufficient guidance for him, and a sufficient authority for the people.

18. *Thou wilt surely wear away*] From decay and exhaustion.

19. *counsel*] Jethro draws the distinction between the functions of the legislator and the judge.

to God-ward] Lit. "before God," standing between them and God, both as His minister or representative and also as the representative of the people, their agent, so to speak, or deputy before God.

20. *teach them*] The Hebrew word is emphatic, and signifies "enlightenment." The text gives four distinct points, (*a*) the "ordinances," or specific enactments, (*b*) "the laws," or general regulations, (*c*) "the way," the general course of duty, (*d*) "the works," each specific act.

21. *able men*] The qualifications are remarkably complete, ability, piety, truthfulness, and unselfishness. From Deut. i. 13, it appears that Moses left the selection of the persons to the people, an example followed by the Apostles; see Acts vi. 3.

rulers of thousands, &c.] The numbers appear to be conventional, corresponding

such over them, *to be* rulers of thousands, *and* rulers of hun-
22 dreds, rulers of fifties, and rulers of tens: and let them judge
the people [f]at all seasons: [g]and it shall be, *that* every great
matter they shall bring unto thee, but every small matter they
shall judge: so shall it be easier for thyself, and [h]they shall
23 bear *the burden* with thee. If thou shalt do this thing, and God
command thee *so*, then thou shalt be [i]able to endure, and all
24 this people shall also go to [k]their place in peace. ¶ So Moses
hearkened to the voice of his father in law, and did all that he
25 had said. And [l]Moses chose able men out of all Israel, and
made them heads over the people, rulers of thousands, rulers of
26 hundreds, rulers of fifties, and rulers of tens. And they [m]judged
the people at all seasons: the [n]hard causes they brought unto
27 Moses, but every small matter they judged themselves. And
Moses let his father in law depart; and [o]he went his way into
his own land.

CHAP. 19. IN the third month, when the children of Israel were gone
forth out of the land of Egypt, the same day [a]came they *into*
2 the wilderness of Sinai. For they were departed from [b]Rephi-
dim, and were come *to* the desert of Sinai, and had pitched in
the wilderness; and there Israel camped before [c]the mount.
3 And [d]Moses went up unto God, and the LORD [e]called unto him
out of the mountain, saying, Thus shalt thou say to the house of
4 Jacob, and tell the children of Israel; [f]Ye have seen what I did
unto the Egyptians, and *how* [g]I bare you on eagles' wings, and
5 brought you unto myself. Now [h]therefore, if ye will obey my
voice indeed, and keep my covenant, then [i]ye shall be a peculiar
treasure unto me above all people: for [k]all the earth *is* mine:
6 and ye shall be unto me a [l]kingdom of priests, and an [m]holy

[f] ver. 26. [g] ver. 26. Lev. 24. 11. Num. 27. 2. Deut. 17. 8. [h] Num. 11. 17. [i] ver. 18. [k] Deut. 30. 16. [l] Deut. 1. 15. Acts 6. 5. [m] ver. 22. [n] Job 29. 16. [o] Num. 10. 29, 30. [a] Num. 33. 15. [b] ch. 17. 1, 8. [c] ch. 3. 1, 12. [d] ch. 20. 21. Acts 7. 38. [e] ch. 3. 4. [f] Deut. 29. 2. [g] Isai. 63. 9. [h] Deut. 5. 2. [i] Deut. 4. 20. Ps. 135. 4. Jer. 10. 16. Mal. 3. 17. Tit. 2. 14. [k] ch. 9. 29. Job 41. 11. [l] Deut. 33. 2, 3, 4. [m] Lev. 20. 24, 26.

---

nearly, but not exactly, to the military, or civil divisions of the people: the largest division 1000 is used as an equivalent of a gens under one head, Num. i. 16, x. 4; Josh. xxii. 14.

The word "rulers," sometimes rendered "princes," is general, including all ranks of officials placed in command. The same word is used regularly on Egyptian monuments of the time of Moses.

23. *to their place*] *i.e.* to Canaan, which is thus recognised by Jethro as the appointed and true home of Israel. Cp. Num. x. 29, 30.

24. *hearkened*] Nothing can be more characteristic of Moses, who combines on all occasions distrust of himself and singular openness to impressions, with the wisdom and sound judgment which chooses the best course when pointed out.

27. *into his own land*] Midian (ii. 15).

XIX. **1, 2.** *the wilderness...the desert of Sinai*] If the mount from which the Law was delivered be the rock of Ras Safsafeh, then the spacious plain of Er Rahah would be the "desert" of Sinai (see *v.* 17).

3. *Moses went up unto God*] This seems to imply that the voice was heard by Moses as he was ascending the mount.

house of Jacob] This expression does not occur elsewhere in the Pentateuch. It has a peculiar fitness here, referring doubtless to the special promises made to the Patriarch.

4. *on eagles' wings*] Both in the Law (Deut. xxxii. 11) and in the Gospel (Matt. xxiii. 37), the Church is compared to fledgelings which the mother cherishes and protects under her wings: but in the Law that mother is an eagle, in the Gospel a hen; thus shadowing forth the diversity of administration under each Covenant: the one of power, which God manifested when He brought His people out of Egypt with a mighty hand and an outstretched arm, and led them into the promised land; the other of grace, when Christ came in humility and took the form of a servant and became obedient unto death, even the death of the Cross. Cp. also Rev. xii. 14.

5. *a peculiar treasure*] A costly possession acquired with exertion, and carefully guarded. The peculiar relation in which Israel stands, taken out of the heathen world and consecrated to God, as His slaves, subjects, and children, determines their privileges, and is the foundation of their duties. The same principle applies even in a stronger sense to the Church. See Acts xx. 28; 1 Cor. vi. 20; 1 Pet. ii. 9.

all the earth is mine] It was a point of great practical importance, to impress upon the Jews that their God was no mere national Deity. Cp. Deut. x. 14; Ps. xxiv. 1.

6. *a kingdom of priests*] Israel collectively is a royal and priestly race: a dynasty of

nation. These *are* the words which thou shalt speak unto the
7 children of Israel. ¶ And Moses came and called for the elders of
the people, and laid before their faces all these words which the
8 LORD commanded him. And [n]all the people answered together,
and said, All that the LORD hath spoken we will do. And
9 Moses returned the words of the people unto the LORD. And
the LORD said unto Moses, Lo, I come unto thee [o]in a thick
cloud, [p]that the people may hear when I speak with thee, and
[q]believe thee for ever. And Moses told the words of the people
10 unto the LORD. ¶ And the LORD said unto Moses, Go unto
the people, and [r]sanctify them to day and to morrow, and let
11 them [s]wash their clothes, and be ready against the third day: for
the third day the LORD [t]will come down in the sight of all the
12 people upon mount Sinai. And thou shalt set bounds unto the
people round about, saying, Take heed to yourselves, *that ye* go
not up into the mount, or touch the border of it: [u]whosoever
13 toucheth the mount shall be surely put to death: there shall not
an hand touch it, but he shall surely be stoned, or shot through;
whether *it be* beast or man, it shall not live: when the [1][x]trumpet
14 soundeth long, they shall come up to the mount. ¶ And Moses
went down from the mount unto the people, and [y]sanctified the
15 people; and they washed their clothes. And he said unto the
people, [z]Be ready against the third day: [a]come not at *your* wives.
16 ¶ And it came to pass on the third day in the morning, that
there were [b]thunders and lightnings, and a [c]thick cloud upon
the mount, and the [d]voice of the trumpet exceeding loud; so
17 that all the people that *was* in the camp [e]trembled. And
[f]Moses brought forth the people out of the camp to meet with
18 God; and they stood at the nether part of the mount. And
[g]mount Sinai was altogether on a smoke, because the LORD descended upon it [h]in fire: [i]and the smoke thereof ascended as
the smoke of a furnace, and [k]the whole mount quaked greatly.
19 And [l]when the voice of the trumpet sounded long, and waxed
louder and louder, [m]Moses spake, and [n]God answered him by a
20 voice. And the LORD came down upon mount Sinai, on the
top of the mount: and the LORD called Moses *up* to the top of
21 the mount; and Moses went up. And the LORD said unto
Moses, Go down, [2]charge the people, lest they break through
22 unto the LORD [o]to gaze, and many of them perish. And let the

[n] ch. 24. 3, 7. Deut. 5. 27.
[o] ver. 16. Deut. 4. 11. Ps. 18. 11. Matt. 17. 5.
[p] Deut. 4. 12, 36. John 12. 29.
[q] ch. 14. 31.
[r] Lev. 11. 44, 45.
[s] ver. 14. Gen. 35. 2. Lev. 15. 5.
[t] ver. 16, 18. ch. 34. 5. Deut. 33. 2.
[u] Heb. 12. 20.
[x] ver. 16, 19.
[y] ver. 10.
[z] ver. 11.
[a] 1 Sam. 21. 4, 5. Zech. 7. 3. 1 Cor. 7. 5.
[b] Ps. 77. 18. Heb. 12. 18. Rev. 4. 5.
[c] ver. 9. ch. 40. 34. 2 Chr. 5. 14.
[d] Rev. 1. 10.
[e] Heb. 12. 21.
[f] Deut. 4. 10.
[g] Deut. 4. 11. Judg. 5. 5. Isai. 6. 4. Hab. 3. 3.
[h] ch. 3. 2. & 24. 17. 2 Chr. 7. 1.
[i] Gen. 15. 17. Ps. 144. 5. Rev. 15. 8.
[k] Ps. 68. 8. Heb. 12. 26.
[l] ver. 13.
[m] Heb. 12. 21.
[n] Neh. 9. 13. Ps. 81. 7.
[o] See ch. 3. 5. 1 Sam. 6. 19.

[1] Or, *cornet*. [2] Heb. *contest*.

---

priests, each true member uniting in himself the attributes of a king and priest. Cp. 1 Pet. ii. 5. Rev. i. 6.

an holy nation] The holiness of Israel consisted in its special consecration to God: it was a sacred nation, sacred by adoption, by covenant, and by participation in all means of grace. Cp. Deut. vii. 6, xxvi. 19, xxviii. 9. 1 Cor. iii. 17. 1 Thess. v. 27.

8. *All that the* LORD, &c.] By this answer the people accepted the covenant. It was the preliminary condition of their complete admission into the state of a royal priesthood.

10. *sanctify them*] The injunction involves bodily purification and undoubtedly also spiritual preparation. Cp. Heb. x. 22. The washing of the clothes was an outward symbol well understood in all nations.

12. *set bounds unto the people*] The low line of alluvial mounds at the foot of the cliff of Ras Safsafeh exactly answers to the bounds which were to keep the people off from touching the mount: but the bounds here spoken of were to be set up by Moses.

13. *touch it*] Rather "touch him." The person who had touched the mount was not to be touched, since the contact would be pollution.

17. *out of the camp*] The encampment must have extended far and wide over the plain in front of the mountain. From one entrance of the plain to the other there is space for the whole host of the Israelites.

18. *a furnace*] The word in the original is Egyptian, and occurs only in the Pentateuch.

22. *the priests also*] Sacrifices had hitherto been offered by firstborn, or the heads of families. See Gen. xiv. 18 note.

priests also, which come near to the LORD, [p]sanctify themselves,
23 lest the LORD [q]break forth upon them. And Moses said unto
the LORD, The people cannot come up to mount Sinai: for thou
chargedst us, saying, [r]Set bounds about the mount, and sanctify
24 it. And the LORD said unto him, Away, get thee down, and thou
shalt come up, thou, and Aaron with thee: but let not the priests
and the people break through to come up unto the LORD, lest he
25 break forth upon them. So Moses went down unto the people,
and spake unto them.

CHAP. 20. AND God spake [a]all these words, saying,
2 [b]I *am* the LORD thy God, which have brought thee out of the
3 land of Egypt, [c]out of the house of [1]bondage. [d]Thou shalt have
no other gods before me.
4 [e]Thou shalt not make unto thee any graven image, or any

[p] Lev. 10. 3. [q] 2 Sam. 6. 7, 8. [r] ver. 12. Josh. 3. 4.

[a] Deut. 5. 22. [b] Deut. 5. 6. Ps. 81. 10. Hos. 13. 4. [c] ch. 13. 3. [d] Deut. 6. 14. 2 Kin. 17. 35. Jer. 25. 6. [e] Lev. 26. 1. Deut. 4. 16. Ps. 97. 7.

[1] Heb. *servants.*

XX. **1–17.** The Hebrew name which is rendered in our Version THE TEN COMMANDMENTS occurs in xxxiv. 28; Deut. iv. 13, x. 4. It literally means *the Ten Words*. The Ten Commandments are also called **the Law, even the Commandment** (xxiv. 12), THE WORDS OF THE COVENANT (xxxiv. 28), THE TABLES OF THE COVENANT (Deut. ix. 9), THE COVENANT (Deut. iv. 13), THE TWO TABLES (Deut. ix. 10, 17), and, most frequently, THE TESTIMONY (*e.g.* xvi. 34, xxv. 16), or THE TWO TABLES OF THE TESTIMONY (*e.g.* xxxi. 18). In the New Testament they are called simply THE COMMANDMENTS (*e.g.* Matt. xix. 17). The name DECALOGUE is found first in Clement of Alexandria, and was commonly used by the Fathers who followed him.

We thus know that the Tables were two, and that the commandments were ten, in number. But the Scriptures do not, by any direct statements, enable us to determine with precision how the Ten Commandments are severally to be made out, nor how they are to be allotted to the Two Tables. On each of these points various opinions have been held (see *v.* 12).

Of the Words of Jehovah engraven on the Tables of Stone, we have two distinct statements, one in Exodus (xx. 1–17) and one in Deuteronomy (v. 7–21), apparently of equal authority, but differing principally from each other in the Fourth, the Fifth, and the Tenth Commandments.

It has been supposed that the original Commandments were all in the same terse and simple form of expression as appears (both in Exodus and Deuteronomy) in the First, Sixth, Seventh, Eighth, and Ninth, such as would be most suitable for recollection, and that the passages in each copy in which the most important variations are found were comments added when the Books were written.

The account of the delivery of them in chap. xix. and in *vv.* 18–21 of this chap. is in accordance with their importance as the recognized basis of the Covenant between Jehovah and His ancient people (xxxiv. 27, 28; Deut. iv. 13; 1 K. viii. 21, &c.), and as the Divine testimony against the sinful tendencies in man for all ages. While it is here said that "God spake all these words," and in Deut. v. 4, that He "talked face to face," in the New Testament the giving of the Law is spoken of as having been through the ministration of Angels (Acts vii. 53; Gal. iii. 19; Heb. ii. 2). We can reconcile these contrasts of language by keeping in mind that God is a Spirit, and that He is essentially present in the agents who are performing His will.

2. *which have brought thee out of the land of Egypt, out of the house of bondage*] It has been asked, Why, on this occasion, was not THE LORD rather proclaimed as "the Creator of Heaven and Earth"? The answer is, Because the Ten Commandments were at this time addressed by Jehovah not merely to human creatures, but to the people whom He had redeemed, to those who had been in bondage, but were now free men (vi. 6, 7, xix. 5). The Commandments are expressed in absolute terms. They are not sanctioned by outward penalties, as if for slaves, but are addressed at once to the conscience, as for free men. The well-being of the nation called for the infliction of penalties, and therefore statutes were passed to punish offenders who blasphemed the name of Jehovah, who profaned the Sabbath, or who committed murder or adultery. (See Lev. xviii. 24–30 note.) But these penal statutes were not to be the ground of obedience for the true Israelite according to the Covenant. He was to know Jehovah as his Redeemer, and was to obey him as such (Cp. Rom. xiii. 5).

3. *before me*] Literally, *before my face*. The meaning is that no god should be worshipped in addition to Jehovah. Cp. *v.* 23. The polytheism which was the besetting sin of the Israelites did not in later times exclude Jehovah, but associated Him with false deities. [Cp. the original of 1 Sam. ii. 25].

4. *graven image*] Any sort of image is here intended.

likeness *of any thing* that *is* in heaven above, or that *is* in the
5 earth beneath, or that *is* in the water under the earth: [f]thou [f] ch. 23. 24.
shalt not bow down thyself to them, nor serve them: for I the 2 Kin. 17. 35.
LORD thy God *am* [g]a jealous God, [h]visiting the iniquity of the Isai. 44. 15. [g] ch. 34. 14.
fathers upon the children unto the third and fourth *generation* Deut. 4. 24.
6 of them that hate me; and [i]shewing mercy unto thousands of [h] ch. 34. 7. [i] ch. 34. 7.
them that love me, and keep my commandments. [k] ch. 23. 1.
7 [k]Thou shalt not take the name of the LORD thy God in vain; [l] Mic. 6. 11.
for the LORD [l]will not hold him guiltless that taketh his name [m] ch. 31. 13. Lev. 19. 3.
in vain. [n] ch. 23. 12.
8, 9 [m]Remember the sabbath day, to keep it holy. [n]Six days shalt Lev. 23. 3.
10 thou labour, and do all thy work: but the [o]seventh day *is* the Luke 13. 14. [o] Gen. 2. 2.
sabbath of the LORD thy God: *in it* thou shalt not do any work,

---

As the First Commandment forbids the worship of any false god, seen or unseen, it is here forbidden to worship an image of any sort, whether the figure of a false deity (Josh. xxiii. 7) or one in any way symbolical of Jehovah (see xxxii. 4). The spiritual acts of worship were symbolized in the furniture and ritual of the Tabernacle and the Altar, and for this end the forms of living things might be employed as in the case of the Cherubim (see xxv. 18 note): but the Presence of the invisible God was to be marked by no symbol of Himself, but by His words written on stones, preserved in the ark in the Holy of Holies and covered by the Mercy-seat. The ancient Persians and the earliest legislators of Rome also agreed in repudiating images of the Deity.

a jealous God] Deut. vi. 15; Josh. xxiv. 19; Is. xlii. 8, xlviii. 11; Nahum i. 2. This reason applies to the First, as well as to the Second Commandment. The truth expressed in it was declared more fully to Moses when the name of Jehovah was proclaimed to him after he had interceded for Israel on account of the golden calf (xxxiv. 6, 7; see note).

visiting the iniquity of the fathers upon the children] (Cp. xxxiv. 7; Jer. xxxii. 18). Sons and remote descendants inherit the consequences of their fathers' sins, in disease, poverty, captivity, with all the influences of bad example and evil communications. (See Lev. xxvi. 39; Lam. v. 7 sq.) The "inherited curse" seems to fall often most heavily on the least guilty persons; but such suffering must always be free from the sting of conscience; it is not like the visitation for sin on the individual by whom the sin has been committed. The suffering, or loss of advantages, entailed on the unoffending son, is a condition under which he has to carry on the struggle of life, and, like all other inevitable conditions imposed upon men, it cannot tend to his ultimate disadvantage, if he struggles well and perseveres to the end. The principle regulating the administration of justice by earthly tribunals (Deut. xxiv. 16), is carried out in spiritual matters by the Supreme Judge.

6. *unto thousands*] **unto the thousandth generation.** Jehovah's visitations of chastisement extend to the third and fourth generation, his visitations of mercy to the thousandth; that is, for ever. That this is the true rendering seems to follow from Deut. vii. 9. Cp. 2 S. vii. 15, 16.

7. Our translators make the Third Commandment bear upon any profane and idle utterance of the name of God. Others give it the sense, *Thou shalt not swear falsely by the name of Jehovah thy God.* The Hebrew word which answers to *in vain* may be rendered either way. The two abuses of the sacred name seem to be distinguished in Lev. xix. 12 (see Matt. v. 33). Our Version is probably right in giving the rendering which is more inclusive. The caution that a breach of this Commandment incurs guilt in the eyes of Jehovah is especially appropriate, in consequence of the ease with which the temptation to take God's name "in vain" besets men in their common intercourse with each other.

8. *Remember the sabbath day*] There is no distinct evidence that the Sabbath, as a formal ordinance, was recognised before the time of Moses (cp. Neh. ix. 14, Ezek. xx. 10–12, Deut. *v.* 15). The word *remember* may either be used in the sense of *keep in mind* what is here enjoined for the first time, or it may refer back to what is related in xvi. 22–26.

10. *the sabbath,* &c.] **a Sabbath to Jehovah thy God.** The proper meaning of *sabbath* is, *rest after labour.* Cp. xvi. 26.

thy stranger that is within thy gates] Not a *stranger*, as is an unknown person, but a *lodger*, or *sojourner*. In this place it denotes one who had come from another people to take up his permanent abode among the Israelites, and who might have been well known to his neighbours. That the word did not primarily refer to foreign domestic servants (though all such were included under it) is to be inferred from the term used for *gates*, signifying not the doors of a private dwelling, but the gates of a town or camp.

thou, nor thy son, nor thy daughter, thy manservant, nor thy
maidservant, nor thy cattle, [p]nor thy stranger that *is* within thy
11 gates: for [q]*in* six days the LORD made heaven and earth, the
sea, and all that in them *is*, and rested the seventh day: wherefore the LORD blessed the sabbath day, and hallowed it.
12 [r]Honour thy father and thy mother: that thy days may be
long upon the land which the LORD thy God giveth thee.
13 [s]Thou shalt not kill.
14 [t]Thou shalt not commit adultery.
15 [u]Thou shalt not steal.
16 [w]Thou shalt not bear false witness against thy neighbour.
17 [x]Thou shalt not covet thy neighbour's house, [y]thou shalt not
covet thy neighbour's wife, nor his manservant, nor his maidservant, nor his ox, nor his ass, nor any thing that *is* thy
neighbour's.
18 ¶ And [z]all the people [a]saw the thunderings, and the lightnings,
and the noise of the trumpet, and the mountain [b]smoking: and
19 when the people saw *it*, they removed, and stood afar off. And
they said unto Moses, [c]Speak thou with us, and we will hear:
20 but [d]let not God speak with us, lest we die. And Moses said
unto the people, [e]Fear not: [f]for God is come to prove you, and
21 [g]that his fear may be before your faces, that ye sin not. ¶ And
the people stood afar off, and Moses drew near unto [h]the thick
22 darkness where God *was*. ¶ And the LORD said unto Moses, Thus
thou shalt say unto the children of Israel, Ye have seen that I
23 have talked with you [i]from heaven. Ye shall not make [k]with
me gods of silver, neither shall ye make unto you gods of gold.

[p] Neh. 13. 16, 17, 18.
[q] Gen. 2. 2.
[r] ch. 23. 26. Lev. 19. 3.
[s] Deut. 5. 17.
[t] Deut. 5. 18.
[u] Lev. 19. 11. Matt. 19. 18. 1 Thess. 4. 6.
[w] ch. 23. 1.
[x] Mic. 2. 2. Acts 20. 33. Rom. 7. 7. Heb. 13. 5.
[y] Job 31. 9. Prov. 6. 29.
[z] Heb. 12. 18.
[a] Rev. 1. 10.
[b] ch. 19. 18.
[c] Gal. 3. 19. Heb. 12. 19.
[d] Deut. 5. 25.
[e] 1 Sam. 12. 20. Isai. 41. 10.
[f] Gen. 22. 1. Deut. 13. 3.
[g] Deut. 4. 10. Isai. 8. 13.
[h] ch. 19. 16. 1 Kin. 8. 12.
[i] Deut. 4. 36. Neh. 9. 13.
[k] ch. 32. 1. 2 Kin. 17. 33. Ezek. 20. 39. Dan. 5. 4, 23.

---

12. *Honour thy father and thy mother*] According to our usage, the Fifth Commandment is placed as the first in the second table; and this is necessarily involved in the common division of the Commandments into our duty towards God and our duty towards men. But the more ancient, and probably the better, division allots five Commandments to each Table (cp. Rom. xiii. 9), proceeding on the distinction that the First Table relates to the duties which arise from our filial relations, the Second to those which arise from our fraternal relations. The connexion between the first four Commandments and the Fifth exists in the truth that all faith in God centres in the filial feeling. Our parents stand between us and God in a way in which no other beings can. On the maintenance of parental authority, see xxi. 15, 17; Deut. xxi. 18–21.

that thy days may be long upon the land] Filial respect is the ground of national permanence (cp. Jer. xxxv. 18, 19; Matt. xv. 4–6; Mark vii. 10, 11). The Divine words were addressed emphatically to Israel, but they set forth a universal principle of national life (Eph. vi. 2).

13, 14. Matthew v. 21–32 is the best comment on these two verses.

15. The right of property is sanctioned in the Eighth Commandment by an external rule: its deeper meaning is involved in the Tenth Commandment.

17. As the Sixth, Seventh, and Eighth Commandments forbid us to injure our neighbour in deed, the Ninth forbids us to injure him in word, and the Tenth, in thought. No human eye can see the coveting heart; it is witnessed only by him who possesses it and by Him to Whom all things are naked and open (Luke xii. 15–21). But it is the root of all sins of word or deed against our neighbour (Jam. i. 14, 15).

18–21. Cp. Deut. v. 22–31. Aaron (xix. 24) on this occasion accompanied Moses in drawing near to the thick darkness.

22—xxiii. 33. A series of laws which we may identify with what was written by Moses in the book called the BOOK OF THE COVENANT, and read by him in the audience of the people (xxiv. 7).

The document cannot be regarded as a strictly systematic whole. Portions of it were probably traditional rules handed down from the Patriarchs, and retained by the Israëlites in Egypt.

22–26. Nothing could be more appropriate as the commencement of the Book of the Covenant than these regulations for public worship. The rules for the building of altars must have been old and accepted, and are not inconsistent with the directions for the construction of the Altar of the Court of the Tabernacle, xxvii. 1–8 (cp. Josh. xxii. 26–28).

24 An altar of earth thou shalt make unto me, and shalt sacrifice
thereon thy burnt offerings, and thy peace offerings, [l]thy sheep, [l] Lev. 1. 2.
and thine oxen: in all [m]places where I record my name I will [m] Deut. 12. 5.
25 come unto thee, and I will [n]bless thee. And [o]if thou wilt make 1 Kin. 8. 43. 2 Chr. 6. 6.
me an altar of stone, thou shalt not [1]build it of hewn stone: for Ezra 6. 12.
26 if thou lift up thy tool upon it, thou hast polluted it. Neither Neh. 1. 9. Ps. 74. 7.
shalt thou go up by steps unto mine altar, that thy nakedness be Jer. 7. 10, 12.
not discovered thereon. [n] Gen. 12. 2.
Chap. 21. NOW these *are* the judgments which thou shalt [a]set Deut. 7. 13. [o] Deut. 27. 5.
2 before them. ¶ [b]If thou buy an Hebrew servant, six years he Josh. 8. 31.
shall serve: and in the seventh he shall go out free for nothing. [a] ch. 24. 3, 4. Deut. 4. 14.
3 If he came in [2]by himself, he shall go out by himself: if he were [b] Deut. 15. 12.
4 married, then his wife shall go out with him. If his master Jer. 34. 14.
have given him a wife, and she have born him sons or daughters;
the wife and her children shall be her master's, and he shall go
5 out by himself. [c]And if the servant [3]shall plainly say, I love [c] Deut. 15.
my master, my wife, and my children; I will not go out free: 16, 17.
6 then his master shall bring him unto the [d]judges; he shall also [d] ch. 12. 12.
bring him to the door, or unto the door post; and his master & 22. 8, 28.
shall [e]bore his ear through with an aul; and he shall serve him [e] Ps. 40. 6.
7 for ever. ¶ And if a man [f]sell his daughter to be a maidservant, [f] Neh. 5. 5.
8 she shall not go out [g]as the menservants do. If she [4]please not [g] ver. 2, 3.
her master, who hath betrothed her to himself, then shall he let
her be redeemed: to sell her unto a strange nation he shall have
9 no power, seeing he hath dealt deceitfully with her. And if he
have betrothed her unto his son, he shall deal with her after the
10 manner of daughters. If he take him another *wife;* her food,
her raiment, [h]and her duty of marriage, shall he not diminish. [h] 1 Cor. 7. 5.
11 And if he do not these three unto her, then shall she go out [i] Gen. 9. 6. Lev. 24. 17.
12 free without money. ¶ [i]He that smiteth a man, so that he die, Num. 35. 30, 31. Matt. 26. 52.

[1] Heb. *build them* with *hewing.*
[2] Heb. *with his body.*
[3] Heb. *saying shall say.*
[4] Heb. *be evil in the eyes of, &c.*

XXI. 1. *judgments*] *i.e.* decisions of the Law.

2. A Hebrew might be sold as a bondman in consequence either of debt (Lev. xxv. 39) or of the commission of theft (xxii. 3). But his servitude could not be enforced for more than six full years. Cp. marg. reff.

3. If a married man became a bondman, his rights in regard to his wife were respected: but if a single bondman accepted at the hand of his master a bondwoman as his wife, the master did not lose his claim to the woman or her children, at the expiration of the husband's term of service. Such wives, it may be presumed, were always foreign slaves.

6. *for ever*] That is, most probably, till the next Jubilee, when every Hebrew was set free. See Lev. xxv. 40, 50. The custom of boring the ear as a mark of slavery appears to have been a common one in ancient times, observed in many nations.

6. *unto the judges*] Literally, *before the gods* (*elohim*). The word does not denote *judges* in a direct way, but it is to be understood as the name of God, in its ordinary plural form, God being the source of all justice. The name in this connection always has the definite article prefixed. See marg. reff. Cp. Ps. lxxxii. 1, 6; John x. 34.

7. A man might, in accordance with existing custom, sell his daughter to another man with a view to her becoming an inferior wife, or concubine. In this case, she was not "to go out," like the bondman; that is, she was not to be dismissed at the end of the sixth year. But women who were bound in any other way, would appear to have been under the same conditions as bondmen. See Deut. xv. 17.

11. *if he do not these three unto her*] The words express a choice of one of three things. The man was to give the woman, whom he had purchased from her father, her freedom, unless (i) he caused her to be redeemed by a Hebrew master (*v.* 8); or, (ii) gave her to his son, and treated her as a daughter (*v.* 9); or, (iii) in the event of his taking another wife (*v.* 10), unless he allowed her to retain her place and privileges. These rules (*vv.* 7–11) are to be regarded as mitigations of the then existing usages of concubinage.

12. The case of murder of a free man and

[k] Num. 35. 22. Deut. 19. 4. [l] 1 Sam. 24. 4, 10, 18. [m] Num. 35. 11. Deut. 19. 3. Josh. 20. 2. [n] Num. 15. 30. Deut. 19. 11. Heb. 10. 26. [o] 1 Kin. 2. 28—34. 2 Kin. 11. 15. [p] Deut. 24. 7. [q] Gen. 37. 28. [r] ch. 22. 4. [s] Lev. 20. 9. Prov. 20. 20. Matt. 15. 4. [t] 2 Sam. 3. 29. [u] Lev. 25. 45, 46. [x] ver. 30. Deut. 22. 18, 19. [y] Lev. 24. 20. Deut. 19. 21. Matt. 5. 38.

13 shall be surely put to death. And [k]if a man lie not in wait, but
God [l]deliver *him* into his hand; then [m]I will appoint thee a place
14 whither he shall flee. But if a man come [n]presumptuously upon
his neighbour, to slay him with guile; [o]thou shalt take him from
15 mine altar, that he may die. And he that smiteth his father,
16 or his mother, shall be surely put to death. ¶ And [p]he that
stealeth a man, and [q]selleth him, or if he be [r]found in his hand,
17 he shall surely be put to death. ¶ And [s]he that [1]curseth his
18 father, or his mother, shall surely be put to death. ¶ And if
men strive together, and one smite [2]another with a stone, or with
19 *his* fist, and he die not, but keepeth *his* bed: if he rise again, and
walk abroad [t]upon his staff, then shall he that smote *him* be
quit: only he shall pay *for* [3]the loss of his time, and shall cause
20 *him* to be thoroughly healed. And if a man smite his servant,
or his maid, with a rod, and he die under his hand; he shall be
21 surely [4]punished. Notwithstanding, if he continue a day or two,
22 he shall not be punished: for [u]he *is* his money. If men strive,
and hurt a woman with child, so that her fruit depart *from*
her, and yet no mischief follow: he shall be surely punished,
according as the woman's husband will lay upon him; and he
23 shall [x]pay as the judges *determine*. And if *any* mischief follow,
24 then thou shalt give life for life, [y]eye for eye, tooth for tooth,
25 hand for hand, foot for foot, burning for burning, wound for

[1] Or, *revileth*.
[2] Or, *his neighbour*.
[3] Heb. *his ceasing*.
[4] Heb. *avenged*, Gen. 4. 15, 24. Rom. 13. 4.

---

of a bondman. See *v.* 20 note. The law was afterwards expressly declared to relate also to foreigners, Lev. xxiv. 17, 21, 22; cp. marg. reff.

13, 14. There was no place of safety for the guilty murderer, not even the Altar of Jehovah. Thus all superstitious notions connected with the right of sanctuary were excluded. Adonijah and Joab (1 K. i. 50, ii. 28) appear to have vainly trusted that the vulgar feeling would protect them, if they took hold of the horns of the Altar on which atonement with blood was made (Lev. iv. 7). But for one who killed a man "at unawares," that is, without intending to do it, the Law afterwards appointed places of refuge, Num. xxxv. 6-34; Deut. iv. 41-43, xix. 2-10; Josh. xx. 2-9. It is very probable that there was some provision answering to the cities of refuge, that may have been based upon old usage, in the camp in the Wilderness.

15, 16, 17. The following offences were to be punished with death:—

Striking a parent, cp. Deut. xxvii. 16.

Cursing a parent, cp. marg. reff.

Kidnapping, whether with a view to retain the person stolen, or to sell him, cp. marg. reff.

19. *quit*] *i.e.* if one man injured another in a quarrel so as to oblige him to keep his bed, he was free from the liability to a criminal charge (such as might be based upon *v.* 12): but he was required to compensate the latter for the loss of his time, and for the cost of his healing.

20, 21. The Jewish authorities appear to be right in referring this law, like those in *vv.* 26, 27, 32, to foreign slaves (see Lev. xxv. 44-46). The protection here afforded to the life of a slave may seem to us but a slight one; but it is the very earliest trace of such protection in legislation, and it stands in strong and favourable contrast with the old laws of Greece, Rome, and other nations. If the slave survived the castigation a day or two, the master did not become amenable to the law, because the loss of the slave was accounted, under the circumstances, as a punishment.

22-25. The rule would seem to refer to a case in which the wife of a man interfered in a quarrel. This law, the *jus talionis*, is elsewhere repeated in substance, cp. marg. reff. and Gen. ix. 6. It has its root in a simple conception of justice, and is found in the laws of many ancient nations. It serves in this place as a maxim for the magistrate in awarding the amount of compensation to be paid for the infliction of personal injury. The sum was to be as nearly as possible the worth in money of the power lost by the injured person.—Our Lord quotes *v.* 24 as representing the form of the Law, in order to illustrate the distinction between the letter and the spirit (Matt. v. 38). The tendency of the teaching of the Scribes and Pharisees was to confound the obligations of the conscience with the external requirements of the Law. The Law, in its place, was still to be "holy and just and good," (Rom. vii. 12,) but its direct purpose was to protect the community, not to guide the heart of the believer, who was not to exact

26 wound, stripe for stripe. And if a man smite the eye of his
servant, or the eye of his maid, that it perish; he shall let him
27 go free for his eye's sake. And if he smite out his manservant's
tooth, or his maidservant's tooth; he shall let him go free for his
28 tooth's sake. ¶ If an ox gore a man or a woman, that they die:
then [z]the ox shall be surely stoned, and his flesh shall not be [z] Gen. 9. 5.
29 eaten; but the owner of the ox *shall be* quit. But if the ox were
wont to push with his horn in time past, and it hath been testified
to his owner, and he hath not kept him in, but that he hath
killed a man or a woman; the ox shall be stoned, and his owner
30 also shall be put to death. If there be laid on him a sum of
money, then he shall give for [a]the ransom of his life whatsoever [a] ver. 22.
31 is laid upon him. Whether he have gored a son, or have gored a Num. 35. 31.
daughter, according to this judgment shall it be done unto him.
32 If the ox shall push a manservant or a maidservant; he shall
give unto their master [b]thirty shekels of silver, and the [c]ox shall [b] See Zech.
33 be stoned. ¶ And if a man shall open a pit, or if a man shall 11. 12, 13.
34 dig a pit, and not cover it, and an ox or an ass fall therein; the Matt. 26. 15. Phil. 2. 7.
owner of the pit shall make *it* good, *and* give money unto the [c] ver. 28.
35 owner of them; and the dead *beast* shall be his. ¶ And if one
man's ox hurt another's, that he die; then they shall sell the
live ox, and divide the money of it; and the dead *ox* also they
36 shall divide. Or if it be known that the ox hath used to push in
time past, and his owner hath not kept him in; he shall surely
pay ox for ox; and the dead shall be his own.
Chap. 22. IF a man shall steal an ox, or a [1]sheep, and kill it, or [a] 2 Sam. 12.
sell it; he shall restore five oxen for an ox, and [a]four sheep for 6.
2 a sheep. If a thief be found [b]breaking up, and be smitten See Prov. 6. 31.
3 that he die, *there shall* [c]no blood *be shed* for him. If the sun Luke 19. 8.
be risen upon him, *there shall be* blood *shed* for him; *for* he [b] Matt. 24. 43.
should make full restitution; if he have nothing, then he shall [c] Num. 35.
4 be [d]sold for his theft. If the theft be certainly [e]found in his 27.
hand alive, whether it be ox, or ass, or sheep; he shall [f]restore [d] ch. 21. 2. [e] ch. 21. 16.
5 double. ¶ If a man shall cause a field or vineyard to be eaten, [f] See ver. 1, 7. Prov. 6. 31.

[1] Or, *goat*.

eye for eye, tooth for tooth, but to love his enemies, and to forgive all injuries.

26, 27. Freedom was the proper equivalent for permanent injury.

28–32. The animal was slain as a tribute to the sanctity of human life (Cp. marg. reff. and Gen. iv. 11). It was stoned, and its flesh was treated as carrion. Guilty negligence on the part of its owner was reckoned a capital offence, to be commuted for a fine.

In the case of a slave, the payment was the standard price of a slave, thirty shekels of silver. See Lev. xxv. 44–46, xxvii. 3, and the marg. reff. for the New Test. application of this fact.

33, 34. The usual mode of protecting a well in the East was probably then, as now, by building round it a low circular wall.

35, 36. The dead ox in this case, as well as in the preceding one, must have been worth no more than the price of the hide, as the flesh could not be eaten. See Lev. xvii. 1–6.

XXII. **1.** The theft of an ox appears to have been regarded as a greater crime than the theft of a sheep, because it shewed a stronger purpose in wickedness to take the larger and more powerful animal. It may have been on similar moral ground that the thief, when he had proved his persistency in crime by adding to his theft the slaughter, or sale, of the animal, was to restore four times its value in the case of a sheep (cp. marg. reff.), and five times its value in the case of an ox; but if the animal was still in his possession alive (see *v.* 4) he had to make only twofold restitution.

2–4. If a thief, in breaking into a dwelling in the night, was slain, the person who slew him did not incur the guilt of blood; but if the same occurred in daylight, the slayer was guilty in accordance with xxi. 12. The distinction may have been based on the fact that in the light of day there was a fair chance of identifying and apprehending the thief.

5. *shall put in his beast, and shall feed*] Rather, **shall let his beast go loose, and it shall feed.**

and shall put in his beast, and shall feed in another man's field;
of the best of his own field, and of the best of his own vineyard,
6 shall he make restitution. ¶ If fire break out, and catch in
thorns, so that the stacks of corn, or the standing corn, or the
field, be consumed *therewith;* he that kindled the fire shall
7 surely make restitution. ¶ If a man shall deliver unto his neighbour money or stuff to keep, and it be stolen out of the man's
8 house; [g]if the thief be found, let him pay double. If the thief
be not found, then the master of the house shall be brought
unto the [h]judges, *to see* whether he have put his hand unto his
9 neighbour's goods. For all manner of trespass, *whether it be*
for ox, for ass, for sheep, for raiment, *or* for any manner of lost
thing, which *another* challengeth to be his, the [i]cause of both
parties shall come before the judges; *and* whom the judges shall
10 condemn, he shall pay double unto his neighbour. ¶ If a man
deliver unto his neighbour an ass, or an ox, or a sheep, or any
beast, to keep; and it die, or be hurt, or driven away, no man
11 seeing *it: then* shall an [k]oath of the LORD be between them both,
that he hath not put his hand unto his neighbour's goods; and
the owner of it shall accept *thereof,* and he shall not make *it*
12 good. And [l]if it be stolen from him, he shall make resti-
13 tution unto the owner thereof. If it be torn in pieces, *then* let
him bring it *for* witness, *and* he shall not make good that which
14 was torn. And if a man borrow *ought* of his neighbour, and it
be hurt, or die, the owner thereof *being* not with it, he shall surely
15 make *it* good. *But* if the owner thereof *be* with it, he shall not
make *it* good: if it *be* an hired *thing,* it came for his hire.
16 ¶ And [m]if a man entice a maid that is not betrothed, and lie
17 with her, he shall surely endow her to be his wife. If her father
utterly refuse to give her unto him, he shall [1]pay money accord-
18 ing to the [n]dowry of virgins. ¶ [o]Thou shalt not suffer a witch
19 to live. ¶ [p]Whosoever lieth with a beast shall surely be put to
20 death. ¶ [q]He that sacrificeth unto *any* god, save unto the LORD
21 only, he shall be utterly destroyed. ¶ [r]Thou shalt neither vex a

[g] ver. 4.
[h] ch. 21. 6. & ver. 28.
[i] Deut. 25. 1. 2 Chr. 19. 10.
[k] Heb. 6. 16.
[l] Gen. 31. 39.
[m] Deut. 22. 28, 29.
[n] 1 Sam. 18. 25.
[o] Lev. 19. 26, 31. Deut. 18. 10. 11. 1 Sam. 28. 3, 9.
[p] Lev. 18. 23. & 20. 15.
[q] Num. 25. 2, 7, 8. Deut. 13. 1. & 17. 2, 3, 5.
[r] ch. 23. 9. Lev. 19. 33. & 25. 35. Deut. 10. 19. Jer. 7. 6. Zech. 7. 10. Mal. 3. 5.

[1] Heb. *weigh,* Gen. 23. 16.

---

8. It would appear that if the master of the house could clear himself of imputation, the loss of the pledged article fell upon its owner.

9. *all manner of trespass*] He who was accused, and he who had lost the stolen property, were both to appear before the judges (xviii. 25, 26).

10–13. This law appears to relate chiefly to herdsmen employed by the owners of cattle. When an animal was stolen (*v.* 12), it was presumed either that the herdsman might have prevented it, or that he could find the thief and bring him to justice (see *v.* 4). When an animal was killed by a wild beast, the keeper had to produce the mangled carcase, not only in proof of the fact, but to shew that he had, by his vigilance and courage, deprived the wild beast of its prey.

15. *it came for his hire*] The sum paid for hiring was regarded as covering the risk of accident.

16, 17. See marg. reff.

18. *Thou shalt not suffer a witch to live*] See marg. reff. and Lev. xx. 27. The witch is here named to represent the class. This is the earliest denunciation of witchcraft in the Law. In every form of witchcraft there is an appeal to a power not acting in subordination to the Divine Law. From all such notions and tendencies true worship is designed to deliver us. The practice of witchcraft was therefore an act of rebellion against Jehovah, and, as such, was a capital crime. The passages bearing on the subject in the Prophets, as well as those in the Law, carry a lesson for all ages. Isa. viii. 19, xix. 3, xliv. 25, xlvii. 12, 13; Micah v. 12, &c.

20. This was probably an old formula, the sense of which, on its ethical side, is comprised in the First and Second Commandments.

shall be utterly destroyed] The Hebrew word here used is *cherem* (*i.e. devoted*). See Lev. xxvii. 28.

21. *a stranger*] See xx. 10 note.

stranger, nor oppress him: for ye were strangers in the land of
22 Egypt. [s]Ye shall not afflict any widow, or fatherless child.
23 If thou afflict them in any wise, and they [t]cry at all unto me, I
24 will surely [u]hear their cry; and my [x]wrath shall wax hot, and I
will kill you with the sword; and [y]your wives shall be widows, and
25 your children fatherless. ¶ [z]If thou lend money to *any* of my
people *that is* poor by thee, thou shalt not be to him as an usurer,
26 neither shalt thou lay upon him usury. [a]If thou at all take thy
neighbour's raiment to pledge, thou shalt deliver it unto him by
27 that the sun goeth down: for that *is* his covering only, it *is* his
raiment for his skin: wherein shall he sleep? And it shall come
to pass, when he [b]crieth unto me, that I will hear; for I *am*
28 [c]gracious. ¶ [d]Thou shalt not revile the [1]gods, nor curse the
29 ruler of thy people. ¶ Thou shalt not delay *to offer* [2][e]the first of
thy ripe fruits, and of thy [3]liquors: [f]the firstborn of thy sons
30 shalt thou give unto me. [g]Likewise shalt thou do with thine
oxen, *and* with thy sheep: [h]seven days it shall be with his dam;
31 on the eighth day thou shalt give it me. ¶ And ye shall be [i]holy
men unto me: [k]neither shall ye eat *any* flesh *that is* torn of
beasts in the field; ye shall cast it to the dogs.

Chap. 23. THOU [a]shalt not [4]raise a false report: put not thine hand
2 with the wicked to be an [b]unrighteous witness. [c]Thou shalt
not follow a multitude to *do* evil; [d]neither shalt thou [5]speak in
3 a cause to decline after many to wrest *judgment:* neither shalt
4 thou countenance a poor man in his cause. ¶ [e]If thou meet
thine enemy's ox or his ass going astray, thou shalt surely bring
5 it back to him again. [f]If thou see the ass of him that hateth
thee lying under his burden, [6]and wouldest forbear to help him,
6 thou shalt surely help with him. ¶ [g]Thou shalt not wrest the

[s] Ps. 94. 6. Isai. 1. 17. Ezek. 22. 7. Zech. 7. 10. Jam. 1. 27.
[t] Deut. 15. Luke 18. 7.
[u] ver. 27. Job 34. 28. Jam. 5. 4.
[x] Ps. 69. 24.
[y] Ps. 109. 9. Lam. 5. 3.
[z] Neh. 5. 7.
[a] Job 22. 6.
[b] ver. 23.
[c] ch. 34. 6. 2 Chr. 30. 9.
[d] Eccles. 10. 20. Jude 8.
[e] Prov. 3. 9.
[f] ch. 13. 2.
[g] Deut. 15. 19.
[h] Lev. 22. 27.
[i] ch. 19. 6.
[k] Lev. 22. 8. Ezek. 4. 14.
[a] ver. 7.
[b] ch. 20. 16. Matt. 26. 59, 60, 61.
[c] Gen. 7. 1. Matt. 27. 24.
[d] ver. 6. 7. Ps. 72. 2.
[e] Deut. 22. 1 Matt. 5. 44. Rom. 12. 20
[f] Deut. 22. 4
[g] Deut. 27. 19. Job 31. 13, 21. Isai. 10. 1, : Mal. 3. 5.

[1] Or, *judges*, ver. 8, 9. Ps. 82. 6.
[2] Heb. *thy fulness.*
[3] Heb. *tear.*
[4] Or, *receive.*
[5] Heb. *answer.*
[6] Or, *wilt thou cease to help him?* or, *and wouldest cease to leave* thy business *for him; thou shalt surely leave* it to join *with him.*

---

22. *afflict*] A word including all cold and contemptuous treatment. See Deut. x. 18. Contrast the blessing, Deut. xiv. 29.

25. See notes on Lev. xxv. 35–43; cp. Deut. xxiii. 19.

26, 27. The law regarding pledges is expanded, Deut. xxiv. 6, 10–13.

28. *the gods*] Heb. *elohim.* See xxi. 6 note. Many take it as the name of **God** (as in Gen. i. 1), and this certainly seems best to represent the Hebrew, and to suit the context.

curse the ruler, &c.] See Acts xxiii. 5.

29, 30. The offering of Firstfruits appears to have been a custom of primitive antiquity and was connected with the earliest acts of sacrifice. See Gen. iv. 3, 4. The references to it here and in xxiii. 19 had probably been handed down from patriarchal times. The specific law relating to the firstborn of living creatures was brought out in a strong light in connection with the deliverance from Egypt (xiii. 2, 12, 13); cp. xxiii. 19, Lev. xxii. 27; Deut. xxvi. 2–11; Neh. x. 35.

the first of thy ripe fruits, and of thy liquors] See the margin. The rendering of our Bible is a paraphrase.

31. The sanctification of the nation was emphatically symbolized by strictness of diet as regards both the kind of animal, an the mode of slaughtering. See Lev. ch xi. and xvii.

XXIII. **1–3.** These four commands, a dressed to the conscience, are illustratio of the Ninth Commandment, mainly in r ference to the giving of evidence in leg causes. Cp. 1 Kings xxi. 10; Acts vi. 11.

2. This verse might be more strictly re dered, *Thou shalt not follow the many to ev neither shalt thou bear witness in a cause so to incline after the many to pervert justice.*

3. *countenance*] Rather, **show partiali to** a man's cause because he is poor ((Lev. xix. 15).

4, 5. So far was the spirit of the L from encouraging personal revenge that would not allow a man to neglect an opp tunity of saving his enemy from loss.

5. The sense appears to be :—*If thou the ass of thine enemy lying down under burden, thou shalt forbear to pass by hi thou shalt help him in loosening the girth the ass.*

6–9. Four precepts evidently addres to those in authority as judges :—

(*a*) To do justice to the poor.—Compar *v.* 6 with *v.* 3, it was the part of the ju

7 judgment of thy poor in his cause. [h]Keep thee far from a false
matter; [i]and the innocent and righteous slay thou not: for [k]I
8 will not justify the wicked. And [l]thou shalt take no gift: for
the gift blindeth [1]the wise, and perverteth the words of the
9 righteous. Also [m]thou shalt not oppress a stranger: for ye
know the [2]heart of a stranger, seeing ye were strangers in the
10 land of Egypt. ¶ And [n]six years thou shalt sow thy land, and
11 shalt gather in the fruits thereof: but the seventh *year* thou shalt
let it rest and lie still; that the poor of thy people may eat: and
what they leave the beasts of the field shall eat. In like manner
thou shalt deal with thy vineyard, *and* with thy [3]oliveyard.
12 [o]Six days thou shalt do thy work, and on the seventh day thou
shalt rest: that thine ox and thine ass may rest, and the son of
13 thy handmaid, and the stranger, may be refreshed. ¶ And in all
things that I have said unto you [p]be circumspect: and [q]make no
mention of the name of other gods, neither let it be heard out of
14 thy mouth. ¶ [r]Three times thou shalt keep a feast unto me in
15 the year. [s]Thou shalt keep the feast of unleavened bread: (thou
shalt eat unleavened bread seven days, as I commanded thee, in
the time appointed of the month Abib; for in it thou camest
16 out from Egypt: [t]and none shall appear before me empty:) [u]and
the feast of harvest, the firstfruits of thy labours, which thou

[h] ver. 1. Luke 3. 14. Eph. 4. 25.
[i] Deut. 27. 25. Ps. 94. 21. Matt. 27. 4.
[k] ch. 34. 7. Rom. 1. 18.
[l] Deut. 16. 19. Ps. 26. 10. Isai. 1. 23. Ezek. 22. 12.
[m] Deut. 10. 19. & 24. 14.
[n] Lev. 25. 3.
[o] ch. 20. 8. 9.
[p] Ps. 39. 1. 1 Tim. 4. 16.
[q] Num. 32. 38. Deut. 12. 3.
[r] Lev. 23. 4. Deut. 16. 16.
[s] Deut. 16. 4.
[t] ch. 34. 20.
[u] ch. 34. 22.

1 Heb. *the seeing.* 2 Heb. *soul.* 3 Or, *olive trees.*

---

to defend the poor against the oppression of the rich, and the part of the witness to take care lest his feelings of natural pity should tempt him to falsify evidence.

(*b*) To be cautious of inflicting capital punishment on one whose guilt was not clearly proved.—A doubtful case was rather to be left to God Himself, Who would "not justify the wicked," nor suffer him to go unpunished though he might be acquitted by an earthly tribunal. *v.* 7.

(*c*) To take no bribe or present which might in any way pervert judgment (*v.* 8); cp. Num. xvi. 15; 1 S. xii. 3; Acts xxvi. 26.

(*d*) To vindicate the rights of the stranger (*v.* 9)—rather, the **foreigner.** (xx. 10 note.) This verse is a repetition of xxii. 21, but the precept is there addressed to the people at large, while it is here addressed to the judges in reference to their official duties. The caution was perpetually necessary. Cp. Ezek. xxii. 7; Mal. iii. 5. The word rendered *heart* is more strictly *soul*, and would be better represented here by **feelings.**

10–12. This is the first mention of the Sabbatical year; the law for it is given at length in Lev. xxv. 2. Both the Sabbatical year and the weekly Sabbath are here spoken of exclusively in their relation to the poor, as bearing testimony to the equality of the people in their Covenant with Jehovah. In the first of these institutions, the proprietor of the soil gave up his rights for the year to the whole community of living creatures, not excepting the beasts: in the latter, the master gave up his claim for the day to the services of his servants and cattle.

12. *may be refreshed*] Literally, *may take breath.*

13. Cp. Deut. iv. 9; Josh. xxii. 5; Eph. v. 15.

14–17. This is the first mention of the three great Yearly Festivals. The Feast of Unleavened Bread, in its connection with the Paschal Lamb, is spoken of in chs. xii., xiii.: but the two others are here first named. The whole three are spoken of as if they were familiarly known to the people. The points that are especially enjoined are that every male Israelite should attend them at the Sanctuary (cp. xxxiv. 23), and that he should take with him an offering for Jehovah, presenting himself before his King with his tribute in his hand. That this condition belonged to all the Feasts, though it is here stated only in regard to the Passover, cannot be doubted. See Deut. xvi. 16.

15, 16. On the Feast of Unleavened Bread, or the Passover, see xii. 1-20, 43–50, xiii. 3-16, xxxiv. 18–20; Lev. xxiii. 4-14. On the Feast of the Firstfruits of Harvest, called also the Feast of Weeks, and the Feast of Pentecost, see xxxiv. 22; Lev. xxiii. 15–21. On the Feast of Ingathering, called also the Feast of Tabernacles, see Lev. xxiii. 34-36, 39–43.

16. *in the end of the year*] Cp. xxxiv. 22. The year here spoken of must have been the civil or agrarian year, which began after harvest, when the ground was prepared for sowing. Cp. Lev. xxiii. 39; Deut. xvi. 13-15. The sacred year began in spring, with the month Abib, or Nisan. See xii. 2 note, and Lev. xxv. 9.

when thou hast gathered] Rather, **when thou gatherest in.**

hast sown in the field: and [x]the feast of ingathering, *which is* in
the end of the year, when thou hast gathered in thy labours out
17 of the field. [y]Three times in the year all thy males shall appear
18 before the Lord GOD. ¶ [z]Thou shalt not offer the blood of my
sacrifice with leavened bread; neither shall the fat of my [1]sacri-
19 fice remain until the morning. [a]The first of the firstfruits of
thy land thou shalt bring into the house of the LORD thy God.
20 ¶ [b]Thou shalt not seethe a kid in his mother's milk. ¶ [c]Behold, I
send an Angel before thee, to keep thee in the way, and to bring
21 thee into the place which I have prepared. Beware of him, and
obey his voice, [d]provoke him not; for he will [e]not pardon your
22 transgressions: for [f]my name *is* in him. But if thou shalt
indeed obey his voice, and do all that I speak; then [g]I will be
an enemy unto thine enemies, and [2]an adversary unto thine
23 adversaries. [h]For mine Angel shall go before thee, and [i]bring
thee in unto the Amorites, and the Hittites, and the Perizzites,
and the Canaanites, the Hivites, and the Jebusites: and I will
24 cut them off. Thou shalt not [k]bow down to their gods, nor
serve them, [l]nor do after their works: [m]but thou shalt utterly
25 overthrow them, and quite break down their images. And ye
shall [n]serve the LORD your God, and [o]he shall bless thy bread,
and thy water; and [p]I will take sickness away from the midst of
26 thee. [q]There shall nothing cast their young, nor be barren, in
27 thy land: the number of thy days I will [r]fulfil. I will send [s]my
fear before thee, and will [t]destroy all the people to whom thou

[x] Deut. 16. 13.
[y] ch. 34. 23.
[z] Lev. 2. 11.
[a] ch. 22. 29.
[b] ch. 34. 26. Deut. 14. 21.
[c] Num. 20. 16. Ps. 91. 11.
[d] Num. 14. 11. Ps. 78. 40, 56. Eph. 4. 30.
[e] ch. 32. 34. Num. 14. 35. Josh. 24. 20. Jer. 5. 7. 1 John 5. 16.
[f] Isai. 9. 6. Jer. 23. 6. John 10. 30, 38.
[g] Gen. 12. 3.
[h] ver. 20.
[i] Josh. 24. 8, 11.
[k] ch. 20. 5.
[l] Lev. 18. 3.
[m] ch. 34. 13.
[n] 1 Sam. 7. 3.
[o] Deut. 7. 13.
[p] ch. 15. 26.
[q] Job 21. 10.
[r] Gen. 25. 8. 1 Chr. 23. 1.
[s] Gen. 35. 5.
[t] Deut. 7. 23.

[1] Or, *feast*. [2] Or, *I will afflict them that afflict thee.*

---

18. *the blood of my sacrifice*] It is generally considered that this must refer to the Paschal Lamb. See xii. 7, 11, 13, 22, 23, 27.

the fat of my sacrifice] Strictly, **the fat of my feast;** the *best part* of the feast, that is, the Paschal Lamb itself. Cp. xxxiv. 25.

19. *The first of the firstfruits of thy land*] The *best*, or *chief* of the Firstfruits, that is, the two wave loaves described Lev. xxiii. 17. As the preceding precept appears to refer to the Passover, so it is likely that this refers to Pentecost. They are called in Leviticus, "the firstfruits unto the LORD;" and it is reasonable that they should here be designated the *chief* of the Firstfruits. If, with some, we suppose the precept to relate to the offerings of Firstfruits in general, the command is a repetition of xxii. 29.

Thou shalt not seethe a kid in his mother's milk] This precept is repeated. See marg. reff. If we connect the first of the two preceding precepts with the Passover, and the second with Pentecost, it seems reasonable to connect this with the Feast of Tabernacles. The only explanation which accords with this connexion is one which refers to a superstitious custom connected with the harvest; in which a kid was seethed in its mother's milk to propitiate in some way the deities, and the milk was sprinkled on the fruit trees, fields and gardens, as a charm to improve the crops of the coming year. Others take it to be a prohibition of a custom of great antiquity among the Arabs, of preparing a gross sort of food by stewing a kid in milk, with the addition of certain ingredients of a stimulating nature: and others take it in connexion with the prohibitions to slaughter a cow and a calf, or a ewe and her lamb, on the same day (Lev. xxii. 28), or to take a bird along with her young in the nest (Deut. xxii. 6). It is thus understood as a protest against cruelty and outraging the order of nature.

20. *an Angel*] See iii. 2, 8; Josh. v. 13; Isai. lxiii. 9.

22. The rendering in the margin is better. Cf. Deut. xx. 4.

23. *I will cut them off*] The national existence of the Canaanites was indeed to be *utterly* destroyed, every trace of their idolatries was to be blotted out, no social intercourse was to be held with them while they served other gods, nor were alliances of any kind to be formed with them. (See Deut. vii.; xii. 1-4, 29-31.) But it is alike contrary to the spirit of the Divine Law, and to the facts bearing on the subject scattered in the history, to suppose that any obstacle was put in the way of well disposed individuals of the denounced nations who left their sins and were willing to join the service of Jehovah. The spiritual blessings of the Covenant were always open to those who sincerely and earnestly desired to possess them. See xx. 10; Lev. xix. 34, xxiv. 22.

27. *destroy*] Rather, **overthrow.** See *v.* 23.

shalt come, and I will make all thine enemies turn their [1]backs
28 unto thee. And [u]I will send hornets before thee, which shall
drive out the Hivite, the Canaanite, and the Hittite, from before
29 thee. [w]I will not drive them out from before thee in one year;
lest the land become desolate, and the beast of the field multiply
30 against thee. By little and little I will drive them out from
31 before thee, until thou be increased, and inherit the land. And
[x]I will set thy bounds from the Red sea even unto the sea of
the Philistines, and from the desert unto the river: for I will
[y]deliver the inhabitants of the land into your hand; and thou
32 shalt drive them out before thee. [z]Thou shalt make no cove-
33 nant with them, nor with their gods. They shall not dwell in
thy land, lest they make thee sin against me: for if thou serve
their gods, [a]it will surely be a snare unto thee.
CHAP. 24. AND he said unto Moses, Come up unto the LORD, thou,
and Aaron, [a]Nadab, and Abihu, [b]and seventy of the elders of
2 Israel; and worship ye afar of. And Moses [c]alone shall come
near the LORD: but they shall not come nigh; neither shall the
3 people go up with him. ¶ And Moses came and told the people
all the words of the LORD, and all the judgments: and all the
people answered with one voice, and said, [d]All the words which
4 the LORD hath said will we do. ¶ And Moses [e]wrote all the
words of the LORD, and rose up early in the morning, and
builded an altar under the hill, and twelve [f]pillars, according to
5 the twelve tribes of Israel. And he sent young men of the
children of Israel, which offered burnt offerings, and sacrificed
6 peace offerings of oxen unto the LORD. And Moses [g]took half
of the blood, and put *it* in basons; and half of the blood he
7 sprinkled on the altar. And he [h]took the book of the covenant,
and read in the audience of the people: and they said, [i]All that
8 the LORD hath said will we do, and be obedient. And Moses
took the blood, and sprinkled *it* on the people, and said, Behold

[u] Deut. 7. 20. Josh. 24. 12.
[w] Deut. 7. 22.
[x] Gen. 15. 18. & reff.
[y] Josh. 21. 44. Judg. 1. 4.
[z] ch. 34. 12. Deut. 7. 2.
[a] Josh. 23. 13. Judg. 2. 3. 1 Sam. 18. 21. Ps. 106. 36.
[a] ch. 28. 1. Lev. 10. 1, 2.
[b] ch. 1. 5. Num. 11. 16.
[c] ver. 13, 15.
[d] ver. 7. Deut. 5. 27. Gal. 3. 19.
[e] Deut. 31. 9.
[f] Gen. 28. 18.
[g] Heb. 9. 18.
[h] Heb. 9. 19.
[i] ver. 3.

[1] Heb. *neck*, Ps. 18. 40.

---

28. *hornets*] Cp. marg. reff. The word is used figuratively for a cause of terror and discouragement. Bees are spoken of in the like sense, Deut. i. 44; Ps. cxviii. 12.

29. *beast of the field*] *i.e.* destructive animals.

31. In *v.* 23, the limits of the Land of Canaan, strictly so called, are indicated; to this, when the Israelites were about to take possession of it, were added the regions of Gilead and Bashan on the left side of the Jordan (Num. xxxii. 33–42; Josh. xiii. 29–32). These two portions made up the Holy Land, of which the limits were recognized, with inconsiderable variations, till the final overthrow of the Jewish polity. But in this verse the utmost extent of Hebrew dominion, as it existed in the time of David and Solomon, is set forth. The kingdom then reached to Eloth and Ezion-geber on the Ælanitic Gulf of the Red Sea (1 K. ix. 26), and to Tiphsah on the "River," that is, the River Euphrates (1 K. iv. 24), having for its western boundary "the Sea of the Philistines," that is, the Mediterranean, and for its southern boundary "the desert," that is, the wildernesses of Shur and Paran (cp. Gen. xv. 18; Deut. i. 7, xi. 24; Josh. i. 4).

XXIV. **1, 2** are placed by some with great probability between verses 8 and 9.

4. *twelve pillars*] As the altar was a symbol of the Presence of Jehovah, so these twelve pillars represented the presence of the Twelve Tribes with whom He was making the Covenant.

5. *young men of the children of Israel*] See xix. 22; xxviii. 1; Lev. i. 5.

burnt offerings...peace offerings] The Burnt offerings (Lev. i.) figured the dedication of the nation to Jehovah, and the Peace offerings (Lev. iii.) their communion with Jehovah and with each other.

6. *he sprinkled*] Rather, **he cast.** See Lev. i. 5.

7. *the book of the covenant*] See xx. 22 note. The people had to repeat their assent to the Book of the Covenant before the blood was thrown upon them. Cp. 2 K. xxiii. 2, 21; 2 Chron. xxxiv. 30.

8. The blood which sealed the Covenant was the blood of Burnt offerings and Peace offerings. The Sin offering (Lev. iv.) had

[k]the blood of the covenant, which the LORD hath made with you
9 concerning all these words. ¶Then [l]went up Moses, and Aaron,
10 Nadab, and Abihu, and seventy of the elders of Israel: and
they [m]saw the God of Israel: and *there was* under his feet as it
were a paved work of a [n]sapphire stone, and as it were the [o]body
11 of heaven in *his* clearness. And upon the nobles of the children
of Israel he [p]laid not his hand: also [q]they saw God, and did
12 [r]eat and drink. ¶And the LORD said unto Moses, [s]Come up to
me into the mount, and be there: and I will give thee [t]tables of
stone, and a law, and commandments which I have written;
13 that thou mayest teach them. And Moses rose up, and [u]his
minister Joshua: and Moses [w]went up into the mount of God.
14 And he said unto the elders, Tarry ye here for us, until we come
again unto you: and, behold, Aaron and Hur *are* with you: if
any man have any matters to do, let him come unto them.
15 And Moses went up into the mount, and [x]a cloud covered the
16 mount. And [y]the glory of the LORD abode upon mount Sinai,
and the cloud covered it six days: and the seventh day he called
17 unto Moses out of the midst of the cloud. And the sight of the
glory of the LORD *was* like [z]devouring fire on the top of the
18 mount in the eyes of the children of Israel. And Moses went
into the midst of the cloud, and gat him up into the mount: and
[a]Moses was in the mount forty days and forty nights.

[k] Heb. 9. 20. 1 Pet. 1. 2.
[l] ver. 1.
[m] John 1. 18. 1 Tim. 6. 16. 1 John 4. 12.
[n] Rev. 4. 3.
[o] Matt. 17. 2.
[p] ch. 19. 21.
[q] ver. 10.
[r] Gen. 31. 54. ch. 18. 12. 1 Cor. 10. 18
[s] ver. 2, 15.
[t] ch. 31. 18. & 32. 15, 16. Deut. 5. 22.
[u] ch. 32. 17.
[w] ver. 2.
[x] ch. 19. 9. Matt. 17. 5.
[y] ch. 16. 10. Num. 14. 10.
[z] ch. 3. 2. & 19. 18. Deut. 4. 36. Heb. 12. 18,
[a] ch. 34. 28. Deut. 9. 9.

---

not yet been instituted. That more complicated view of human nature which gave to the Sin offering its meaning, had yet to be developed by the Law, which was now only receiving its ratification. The Covenant between Jehovah and His people therefore took precedence of the operation of the Law, by which came the knowledge of sin. Rom. iii. 20.

upon the people] Either upon the elders or those who stood foremost; or, upon the twelve pillars representing the Twelve Tribes, as the first half had been cast upon the altar, which witnessed to the Presence of Jehovah. The blood thus divided between the two parties to the Covenant signified the sacramental union between the Lord and His people. Cf. Ps. l. 5; Zech. ix. 11.

9. It would appear that Moses, Aaron with his two sons, and seventy of the elders (xix. 7) went a short distance up the mountain to eat the meal of the Covenant (cp. Gen. xxxi. 43–47), which must have consisted of the flesh of the Peace offerings (*v.* 5). Joshua accompanied Moses as his servant (*v.* 13).

10. *And they saw the God of Israel*] As they ate the sacrificial feast, the Presence of Jehovah was manifested to them with special distinctness. In the act of solemn worship, they perceived that He was present with them, as their Lord and their Deliverer. It is idle to speculate on the mode of this revelation. That no visible form was presented to their bodily eyes, we are expressly informed, Deut. iv. 12; see xxxiii. 20; cp. Isa. vi. 1. The latter part of this verse may be read: *under His feet, it was like a work of bright sapphire stone, and like the heaven itself in clearness.* On the sapphire, see xxviii. 18; cp. Ezek. i. 26. The pure blue of the heaven above them lent its influence to help the inner sense to realize the vision which no mortal eye could behold.

11. *he laid not his hand*] *i.e.* He did not smite them. It was believed that a mortal could not survive the sight of God (xxxiii. 20; Gen. xxxii. 30; Judg. vi. 22; xiii. 22): but these rulers of Israel were permitted to eat and drink, while they were enjoying in an extraordinary degree the sense of the Divine Presence, and took no harm.

12. Many Jews understand the *tables of stone* to denote the Ten Commandments; *a law*, the Law written in the Pentateuch; and the *commandments* (or *the commandment*), the oral or traditional law which was in after ages put into writing in the Mishna and the Gemara. But it is more probable that the Ten Commandments alone are spoken of, and that the meaning is, *the Tables of stone with the Law, even the Commandment.*

18. During this period of forty days, and the second period when the Tables were renewed, Moses neither ate bread nor drank water. Cp. marg. reff. Elijah in like manner fasted for forty days, when he visited the same spot (1 K. xix. 8). The two who met our Saviour on the Mount of Transfiguration (Matt. xvii. 3), the one representing the Law, the other representing the Prophets, thus shadowed forth in their own experience the Fast of Forty days in the wilderness of Judæa.

a ch. 35. 5, 21. Ezra 3. 5. & 7. 16. Neh. 11. 2.
b ch. 27. 20.
c ch. 30. 23.
d ch. 30. 34.
e ch. 28. 4, 6.
f ch. 28. 15.

CHAP. 25. AND the LORD spake unto Moses, saying, Speak unto
2 the children of Israel, that they [1]bring me an [2]offering: [a] of every
man that giveth it willingly with his heart ye shall take my
3 offering. And this *is* the offering which ye shall take of them;
4 gold, and silver, and brass, and blue, and purple, and scarlet,
5 and [3]fine linen, and goats' *hair*, and rams' skins dyed red, and
6 badgers' skins, and shittim wood, [b]oil for the light, [c]spices for
7 anointing oil, and for [d]sweet incense, onyx stones, and stones to
8 be set in the [e]ephod, and in the [f]breastplate. And let them

1 Heb. *take for me.* 2 Or, *heave offering.* 3 Or, *silk*, Gen. 41. 42.

XXV. XXVI. Jehovah had redeemed the Israelites from bondage. He had made a Covenant with them and had given them laws. He had promised, on condition of their obedience, to accept them as His own "peculiar treasure," as "a kingdom of priests and an holy nation" (xix. 5, 6). And now He was ready visibly to testify that He made his abode with them. He claimed to have a dwelling for Himself, which was to be in external form a tent of goats' hair (*v.* 4), to take its place among their own tents, and formed out of the same material (see xxvi. 7 note). The special mark of His Presence within the Tent was to be the Ark or chest containing the Ten Commandments on two tables of stone (xxxi. 18), symbolizing the divine Law of holiness, and covered by the Mercy seat, the type of reconciliation.—Moses was divinely taught regarding the construction and arrangement of every part of the Sanctuary. The directions which were given him are comprised in xxv. 1-xxxi. 11. The account of the performance of the work, expressed generally in the same terms, is given xxxv. 21-xl. 33.

1-9. Moses is commanded to invite the people to bring their gifts for the construction and service of the Sanctuary and for the dresses of the priests.

2. *an offering*] The word is used here in its general sense, being equivalent to *korban*, (cp. St. Mark vii. 11). On the marginal rendering "heave offering," see note on xxix. 27.

that giveth it willingly with his heart] The public service of Jehovah was to be instituted by freewill offerings, not by an enforced tax. Cp. 1 Chron. xxix. 3, 9, 14; Ezra ii. 68, 69; 2 Cor. viii. 11, 12, ix. 7. On the zeal with which the people responded to the call, see xxxv. 21-29, xxxvi. 5-7.

3. *gold, and silver, and brass*] The supply of these metals possessed by the Israelites at this time probably included what they had inherited from their forefathers, what they had obtained from the Egyptians (xii. 35), and what may have been found amongst the spoils of the Amalekites (xvii. 8-13). But with their abundant flocks and herds, it can hardly be doubted that they had carried on important traffic with the trading caravans that traversed the wilderness, some of which, most likely, in the earliest times were furnished with silver, with the gold of Ophir (or gold of Sheba, as it seems to have been indifferently called), and with the "brass" (the alloy of copper and tin, called bronze) of Phœnicia and Egypt. Cp. xxxviii. 24 note.

4. *blue, and purple, and scarlet*] *i.e.* the material dyed with these colours. The Jewish tradition has been very generally received that this material was wool. Cp. Heb. ix. 19 with Lev. xiv. 4, 49, &c. When spun and dyed by the women, it was delivered in the state of yarn; and the weaving and embroidering was left to Aholiab and his assistants, xxxv. 25, 35. The "blue" and "purple" dye are usually thought to have been obtained from shell-fish, the "scarlet" from the cochineal insect of the holm-oak.

fine linen] The fine flax or the manufactured linen, for which Egypt was famous (Ezek. xxvii. 7), and which the Egyptians were in the habit of using for dresses of state (Gen. xli. 42). It was used as the groundwork of the figured curtains of the Tabernacle as well as of the embroidered hangings of the Tent and the Court. See xxxv. 35.

5. *rams' skins dyed red*] Skins tanned and coloured like the leather now known as red morocco.

badgers' skins] Rather, leather, probably of a sky-blue colour, formed from the skins of the *tachash* (a general name for marine animals), which was well adapted as a protection against the weather.

shittim wood] The word *shittim* is the plural form of *shittah*, which occurs as the name of the growing tree, Is. xli. 19. The tree is satisfactorily identified with the *Acacia seyal*, a gnarled and thorny tree, somewhat like a solitary hawthorn in its habit and manner of growth, but much larger. It flourishes in the driest situations, and is scattered more or less numerously over the Sinaitic Peninsula. It appears to be the only good wood produced in the wilderness. No other kind of wood was employed in the Tabernacle or its furniture. In the construction of the Temple cedar and fir took its place (1 K. v. 8, vi. 18; 2 Chron. ii. 8).

6, 7. See notes to chs. xxvii., xxviii., xxx.

8. *sanctuary*] *i.e.* a hallowed place. This

make me a [g]sanctuary; that [h]I may dwell among them.
9 [i]According to all that I shew thee, *after* the pattern of the
tabernacle, and the pattern of all the instruments thereof, even
10 so shall ye make *it*. ¶ [k]And they shall make an ark *of* shittim
wood: two cubits and a half *shall be* the length thereof, and a
cubit and a half the breadth thereof, and a cubit and a half the
11 height thereof. And thou shalt overlay it with pure gold, within
and without shalt thou overlay it, and shalt make upon it a
12 crown of gold round about. And thou shalt cast four rings of
gold for it, and put *them* in the four corners thereof; and two
rings *shall be* in the one side of it, and two rings in the other side
13 of it. And thou shalt make staves *of* shittim wood, and overlay
14 them with gold. And thou shalt put the staves into the rings by
15 the sides of the ark, that the ark may be borne with them. [l]The
staves shall be in the rings of the ark: they shall not be taken
16 from it. And thou shalt put into the ark [m]the testimony which

[g] ch. 36. 1. Lev. 4. 6. & 10. 4. & 21. 12. Heb. 9. 1, 2.
[h] ch. 29. 45. 1 Kin. 6. 13. 2 Cor. 6. 16. Heb. 3. 6. Rev. 21. 3.
[i] ver. 40.
[k] ch. 37. 1. Deut. 10. 3. Heb. 9. 4.
[l] 1 Kin. 8. 8.
[m] ch. 16. 34. & 31. 18. Deut. 10. 2. & 31. 36. 1 Kin. 8. 9. 2 Kin. 11. 12. Heb. 9. 4.

---

is the most comprehensive of the words that relate to the place dedicated to Jehovah. It included the Tabernacle with its furniture, its Tent, and its Court.

that I may dwell among them] The purpose of the Sanctuary is here definitely declared by the Lord Himself. It was to be the constant witness of His Presence amongst His people. Cp. marg. reff.

9. *According to all that I shew thee*] The Tabernacle and all that pertained to it were to be in strict accordance with the ideas revealed by the Lord to Moses (cp. *v.* 40, xxvi. 30; Acts vii. 44; Heb. viii. 5). The word here translated *pattern* is also used to denote the plans for the Temple which were given by David to Solomon (1 Chron. xxviii. 11, 12, 19); it is elsewhere rendered *form, likeness, similitude,* Deut. iv. 16, 17; Ezek. viii. 3, 10.

the tabernacle] The Hebrew word signifies the "dwelling-place." It here denotes the wooden structure, containing the Holy Place and the most Holy Place, with the tent which sheltered it. See xxvi. 1 note.

10–16 (cp. xxxvii. 1–5). The ARK is uniformly designated in Exodus the ARK OF THE TESTIMONY. Elsewhere it is called THE TESTIMONY, THE ARK OF THE COVENANT (most frequently in Deuteronomy and the other books of the Old Testament), THE ARK OF THE LORD, THE ARK OF GOD, THE ARK OF THE STRENGTH OF THE LORD, and THE HOLY ARK.

The Ark of the Covenant was the central point of the Sanctuary. It was designed to contain the Testimony (*v.* 16, xl. 20; Deut. xxxi. 26), that is, the Tables of the Divine Law, the terms of the Covenant between Jehovah and His people: and it was to support the Mercy seat with its Cherubim, from between which He was to hold communion with them (*v.* 22). On this account, in these directions for the construction of the Sanctuary, it is named first of all the parts. But on the other hand, in the narrative of the work as it was actually carried out, we find that it was not made till after the Tabernacle (xxxvii. 1–9). It was suitable that the receptacle should be first provided to receive and shelter the most sacred of the contents of the Sanctuary as soon as it was completed. The order in which the works were executed seems to be given in xxxi. 7–10, and xxxv. 11–19. The completion of the Ark is recorded in xxxvii. 1–5. On its history, see the concluding note to ch. xl.

10. *an ark*] Taking the cubit at 18 inches (see Gen. vi. 15 note), the Ark of the Covenant was a box 3ft. 9in. long, 2ft. 3in. wide, and 2ft. 3in. deep.

11. *overlay it with pure gold*] Words descriptive of the common process of gilding. The Egyptians in early times were acquainted with both the art of gilding and that of covering a substance with thin plates of gold.

a crown of gold] That is, an edging or **moulding** of gold round the top of the Ark, within which the cover or Mercy seat (*v.* 17) may have fitted (cp. xxxviii. 2). There were golden mouldings, called by the same name, to the Table of Shewbread (*v.* 24, xxxvii. 11, 12), and to the Golden Altar (xxx. 3, xxxvii. 26).

12. *four corners thereof*] Rather, **its four bases**, or feet. It is not unlikely that there were low blocks, or plinths, placed under the corners to which the rings were attached (see *v.* 26), and that it is to them the word is here applied. The Ark, when it was carried, must thus have been raised above the shoulders of the bearers.

15. *they shall not be taken from it*] This direction was probably given in order that the Ark might not be touched by the hand (cp. 2 S. vi. 6).

16. *the testimony*] Literally, *something spoken again and again.* The stone Tables of the Ten Commandments are called the Testimony, or, the Tables of the Testimony, as the Ark which contained them is called the Ark of the Testimony, and the Taber-

[n] ch. 37. 6. Rom. 3. 25. Heb. 9. 5.
[o] 1 Kin. 8. 7. 1 Chr. 28. 18. Heb. 9. 5.
[p] ch. 26. 34.
[q] ver. 16.
[r] ch. 29. 42, 43. & 30. 6, 36. Lev. 16. 2. Num. 17. 4.

17 I shall give thee. ¶ And [n]thou shalt make a mercy seat *of*
pure gold: two cubits and a half *shall be* the length thereof,
18 and a cubit and a half the breadth thereof. And thou shalt
make two cherubims *of* gold, *of* beaten work shalt thou make
19 them, in the two ends of the mercy seat. And make one
cherub on the one end, and the other cherub on the other end:
even [1]of the mercy seat shall ye make the cherubims on the two
20 ends thereof. And [o]the cherubims shall stretch forth *their* wings
on high, covering the mercy seat with their wings, and their
faces *shall look* one to another; toward the mercy seat shall the
21 faces of the cherubims be. [p]And thou shalt put the mercy seat
above upon the ark; and [q]in the ark thou shalt put the testimony
22 that I shall give thee. And [r]there I will meet with thee, and I
will commune with thee from above the mercy seat, from

[1] Or, *of the* matter *of the mercy seat.*

---

nacle in which the Ark was placed, the Tabernacle of the Testimony. Taking this in connexion with the prohibitory form of the Commandments, the name must have been understood as signifying the direct testimony of Jehovah against sin in man (Deut. xxxi. 26, 27).

The Ark of the Covenant has been most generally likened to the arks, or moveable shrines, which are represented on Egyptian monuments. The Egyptian arks were carried by poles on the shoulders, and some of them had on the cover two winged figures not unlike what we conceive the golden Cherubim to have been. Thus far the similarity is striking. But there were points of great dissimilarity. Between the winged figures on the Egyptian arks there was placed the material symbol of a deity, and the arks themselves were carried about in religious processions, so as to make a show in the eyes of the people. We know not what they contained. As regards the Ark of the Covenant, the absence of any symbol of God was one of its great characteristics. It was never carried in a ceremonial procession: when it was moved from one place to another, it was closely packed up, concealed from the eyes even of the Levites who bore it. When the Tabernacle was pitched, the Ark was never exhibited, but was kept in solemn darkness. Rest, it is evident, was its appointed condition. It was occasionally moved out of its place in the Holy of Holies, but only so long as the nation was without a settled capital, and had something of the character of an army on the march. Not less was it distinguished from all other arks in the simple grandeur of its purpose: it was constructed to contain the plain text of the Ten Commandments written on stone in words that were intelligible to all.

17–22. *a mercy seat of pure gold*] (Cp. xxxvii. 6-9.) In external form, the Mercy seat was a plate of gold with the Cherubim standing on it, the whole beaten out of one solid piece of metal (xxxvii. 7); it was placed upon the Ark and so took the place of a cover. *Mercy* seat expresses well the distinct significance and recognized designation of the Hebrew name.

18–20. The Cherubim of the Mercy seat were human figures, each having two wings. They must have been of small size, proportioned to the area of the Mercy seat. Comparing the different references to form in this place, in 2 Sam. xxii. 11 (Ps. xviii. 10), in Ezek. chs. i. x. and in Rev. ch. iv., it would appear that the name *Cherub* was applied to various combinations of animal forms. Amongst the Egyptians, the Assyrians and the Greeks, as well as the Hebrews, the creatures by far most frequently introduced into these composite figures, were man, the ox, the lion, and the eagle, as being types of the most important and familiarly known classes of living material beings. Hence the Cherubim, described by Ezekiel, have been regarded as representing the whole creation engaged in the worship and service of God (cp. Rev. iv. 9–11, v. 13); and it would be in harmony with this view to suppose that the more strictly human shape of the Cherubim of the Mercy seat represented the highest form of created intelligence engaged in the devout contemplation of the divine Law of love and justice. (Cp. 1 Pet. i. 12.) It is worthy of notice that the golden Cherubim from between which Jehovah spoke (*v.* 22) to His people bore witness, by their place on the Mercy seat, to His redeeming mercy; while the Cherubim that took their stand at the gate of Eden, Gen. iii. 24, to keep the way to the tree of life, witnessed to His condemnation of sin in man.

18. *of beaten work*] *i.e.* elaborately wrought with the hammer.

19. *even of the mercy seat*] See margin. The sense appears to be that the Cherubim and the Mercy seat were to be wrought out of one mass of gold. (Cp. xxxvii. 7.)

21. *the testimony*] See *v.* 16 note. Cp. xl. 20.

[s]between the two cherubims which *are* upon the ark of the testi- [s] Num. 7. 89.
mony, of all *things* which I will give thee in commandment unto 1 Sam. 4. 4.
23 the children of Israel. ¶ [t]Thou shalt also make a table *of* shittim 2 Sam. 6. 2.
wood: two cubits *shall be* the length thereof, and a cubit the 2 Kin. 19. 15.
24 breadth thereof, and a cubit and a half the height thereof. And Ps. 80. 1. & 90. 1.
thou shalt overlay it with pure gold, and make thereto a crown Isai. 37. 16.
25 of gold round about. And thou shalt make unto it a border of [t] ch. 37. 10.
an hand breadth round about, and thou shalt make a golden 1 Kin. 7. 48.
26 crown to the border thereof round about. And thou shalt make 2 Chr. 4. 8.
for it four rings of gold, and put the rings in the four corners Heb. 9. 2.
27 that *are* on the four feet thereof. Over against the border shall
28 the rings be for places of the staves to bear the table. And thou
shalt make the staves *of* shittim wood, and overlay them with
29 gold, that the table may be borne with them. And thou shalt
make [u]the dishes thereof, and spoons thereof, and covers thereof, [u] ch. 37. 16.
and bowls thereof, [1]to cover withal: *of* pure gold shalt thou Num. 4. 7.

[1] Or, *to pour out withal.*

23–30. (Cp. xxxvii. 10–16.) The Table and the Candlestick figured on the Arch of Titus at Rome are those of the Maccabæan times, but made as nearly as possible after the ancient models reproduced under the direction of Solomon and Zerubbabel. The details and size of the figure, and the description of Josephus, appear to agree very nearly with the directions here given to Moses, and to illustrate them in several particulars. Josephus says that the Table was like the so-called Delphic tables, richly ornamented pieces of furniture in use amongst the Romans, which were sometimes, if not always, covered with gold or silver.

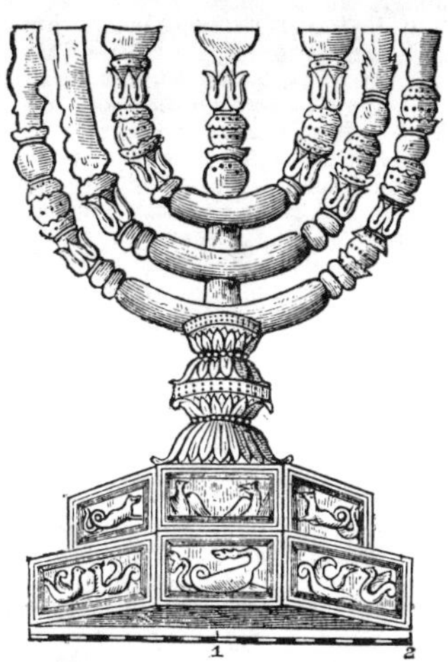

24. See *v.* 11 note. The moulding of the Table is still seen at the ends of the sculptured figure.

25. *a border*] Rather **a framing,** which reached from leg to leg so as to make the Table firm, as well as to adorn it with a second moulding of gold. Two fragments of such framing are still seen in the sculpture attached to the legs half-way down.

27. *Over against the border*] Rather, **Over against the framing;** that is, the rings were to be placed not upon the framing itself, but at the extremities of the legs answering to each corner of it.

29. *dishes*] deep vessels like *bowls,* similar to the large silver vessels (or *chargers*) which were filled with fine flour, and formed part of the offerings of the Princes of Israel (Num. vii. 13 sq.).

spoons] Rather, the small gold **cups that**

[w] Lev. 24. 5, 6.
[x] 1 Kin. 7. 49. Zech. 4. 2. Heb. 9. 2. Rev. 1. 12. & 4. 5.

30 make them. And thou shalt set upon the table [w]shewbread
31 before me alway. ¶ [x]And thou shalt make a candlestick *of* pure
gold: *of* beaten work shall the candlestick be made: his shaft,
and his branches, his bowls, his knops, and his flowers, shall be
32 of the same. And six branches shall come out of the sides of it;
three branches of the candlestick out of the one side, and three
33 branches of the candlestick out of the other side: three bowls
made like unto almonds, *with* a knop and a flower in one branch;
and three bowls made like almonds in the other branch, *with*
a knop and a flower: so in the six branches that come out of the
34 candlestick. And in the candlestick *shall be* four bowls made
35 like unto almonds, *with* their knops and their flowers. And
there shall be a knop under two branches of the same, and a knop
under two branches of the same, and a knop under two branches
of the same, according to the six branches that proceed out of
36 the candlestick. Their knops and their branches shall be of the
37 same: all it *shall be* one beaten work *of* pure gold. And thou
shalt make the seven lamps thereof: and [y]they shall [1]light the

[y] ch. 27. 21. & 30. 8. Lev. 24. 3, 4. 2 Chr. 13. 11.

[1] Or, *cause to ascend.*

---

were filled with frankincense in the offerings of the Princes (Num. vii. 14), and represented on the Table in the sculpture.

covers...bowls] Or **flagons** and **chalices,** such as were used for the rite of the Drink offering, which appears to have regularly accompanied every Meat offering (Lev. xxiii. 18; Num. vi. 15, xxviii. 14, &c.). The subject is important in its bearing upon the meaning of the Shewbread: the corrected rendering of the words tends to show that it was a true Meat offering.

to cover withal] See the margin. The first part of the verse might be better rendered:— **And thou shalt make its bowls and its incense-cups and its flagons and its chalices for pouring out** *the Drink offerings.*

30. The Shewbread Table was placed in the Holy Place on the north side (xxvi. 35). Directions for preparing the Shewbread are given in Lev. xxiv. 5-9. It consisted of twelve large cakes of unleavened bread, which were arranged on the Table in two piles, with a golden cup of frankincense on each pile. It was renewed every Sabbath day. The stale loaves were given to the priests, and the frankincense appears to have been lighted on the Altar for a memorial. The Shewbread, with all the characteristics and significance of a great national Meat offering, in which the twelve tribes were represented by the twelve cakes, was to stand before Jehovah *perpetually,* in token that He was always graciously accepting the good works of His people, for whom atonement had been made by the victims offered on the Altar in the Court of the Sanctuary. The Shewbread or bread which is set forth would be more fairly rendered "Bread of the Presence." See notes on Lev. xxiv. 5-9.

31–39. (Cp. xxxvii. 17–24.) *a candlestick of pure gold*] A lamp-stand rather than a candlestick. Its purpose was to support seven oil-lamps. Its height appears to have been about three feet, and its width two feet. The original foot was lost or stolen when the Candlestick was taken out of the Temple, and the pedestal in the sculpture was added by some Roman artist to set off the trophy.

his shaft, and his branches, his bowls, his knops, and his flowers] Or, **its base, its stem, its flower cups, its knobs, and its lilies.**

33. *three bowls made like unto almonds*] **Three cups of almond flowers.** These appear to be the cups in immediate contact with the knobs as shown in the sculpture.

a flower] **A lily;** and this rendering well agrees with the sculpture.

the candlestick] Here, and in the two following verses, the word appears to denote *the stem,* as the essential part of the Candlestick. It would seem from *vv.* 33-35 that the ornamentation of the Candlestick consisted of uniform members, each comprising a series of an almond flower, a knob and a lily; that the stem comprised four of these members; that each pair of branches was united to the stem at one of the knobs; and that each branch comprised three members. In comparing the description in the text with the sculptured figure, allowance must be made for some deviation in the sculptor's copy.

37. *seven lamps*] These lamps were probably like those used by the Egyptian and other nations, shallow covered vessels more or less of an oval form, with a mouth at one end from which the wick protruded. The Candlestick was placed on the south side of the Holy Place (xxvi. 35), with the line of lamps parallel with the wall, or, according to Josephus, somewhat obliquely. If the wick-mouths of the lamps were turned outwards, they would give light over against

38 lamps thereof, that they may [z]give light over against [1]it. And [z] Num. 8. 2.
the tongs thereof, and the snuffdishes thereof, *shall be of* pure
39 gold. *Of* a talent of pure gold shall he make it, with all these
40 vessels. And [a]look that thou make *them* after their pattern, [a] ch. 26. 30.
[2]which was shewed thee in the mount. Num. 8. 4. 1 Chr. 28.
CHAP. 26. MOREOVER [a]thou shalt make the tabernacle *with* ten 11, 19.
curtains *of* fine twined linen, and blue, and purple, and scarlet: Acts 7. 44. Heb. 8. 5.
2 *with* cherubims [3]of cunning work shalt thou make them. The [a] ch. 36. 8.
length of one curtain *shall be* eight and twenty cubits, and the
breadth of one curtain four cubits: and every one of the curtains
3 shall have one measure. The five curtains shall be coupled
together one to another; and *other* five curtains *shall be* coupled
4 one to another. And thou shalt make loops of blue upon the
edge of the one curtain from the selvedge in the coupling; and

[1] Heb. *the face of it.*
[2] Heb. *which thou wast caused to see.*
[3] Heb. *the work of a cunning workman,* or, *embroiderer.*

---

the Candlestick; that is, towards the north side [see Num. viii. 2].

Light was of necessity required in the Tabernacle, and wherever light is used in ceremonial observance, it may of course be taken in a general way as a figure of the Light of Truth; but in the Sanctuary of the covenanted people, it must plainly have been understood as expressly significant that the number of the lamps (seven) agreed with the number of the Covenant. The Covenant of Jehovah was essentially a Covenant of light.

37. *they shall light*] See margin and note on Lev. i. 9.

38. *the tongs*] Used to trim and adjust the wicks. (Cp. Is. vi. 6.)

the snuff-dishes] These were shallow vessels used to receive the burnt fragments of wick removed by the tongs. The same Hebrew word is translated, in accordance with its connection, *fire pans*, xxvii. 3, xxxviii. 3; and *censers*, Numb. iv. 14, xvi. 6.

39. *a talent of pure gold*] about 94 lbs.

XXVI. 1–37. (Cp. xxxvi. 8–33.) The Tabernacle was to comprise three main parts, the TABERNACLE (1–6), more strictly so-called, its TENT (7–13), and its COVERING (*v.* 14) (Cp. xxxv. 11, xxxix. 33, 34, xl. 19, 34; Num. iii. 25, &c.). These parts are very clearly distinguished in the Hebrew, but they are confounded in many places of the English Version [see *vv.* 7, 9, &c.]. The TABERNACLE itself was to consist of curtains of fine linen woven with coloured figures of Cherubim, and a structure of boards which was to contain the Holy Place and the Most Holy Place; the TENT was to be a true tent of goats' hair cloth to contain and shelter the Tabernacle: the COVERING was to be of red rams' skins and "tachash" skins (xxv. 5), and was spread over the goats' hair tent as an additional protection against the weather. On the external form of the Tabernacle and the arrangement of its parts, see Cuts at the end of the chap.

1. *the tabernacle*] The *Mishkān*, *i.e.* the dwelling-place; the definite article regularly accompanies the Hebrew word when the Dwelling-place of Jehovah is denoted. But in this place the word is not used in its full sense as denoting the Dwelling-place of Jehovah: it denotes only the Tabernacle-cloth (*v.* 6). The word is, in fact, employed with three distinct ranges of meaning, (1) in its strict sense, comprising the cloth of the Tabernacle with its woodwork (xxv. 9, xxvi. 30, xxxvi. 13, xl. 18, &c.); (2) in a narrower sense, for the Tabernacle-cloth only (xxvi. 1, 6, xxxv. 11, xxxix. 33, 34, &c.); (3) in a wider sense, for the Tabernacle with its Tent and Covering (xxvii. 19, xxxv. 18, &c.).

with ten curtains] Rather, **of ten breadths.** Five of these breadths were united so as to form what, in common usage, we should call a large curtain (*v.* 3). The two curtains thus formed were coupled together by the loops and taches to make the entire tabernacle-cloth (*v.* 6).

of cunning work] More properly, **of the work of the skilled weaver.** The coloured figures of Cherubim (see xxv. 4, 18) were to be worked in the loom, as in the manufacture of tapestry and carpets (see *v.* 36 note). On the different kinds of workmen employed on the textile fabrics, see xxxv. 35.

3. Each curtain formed of five breadths (see *v.* 1), was 42 feet in length and 30 feet in breadth, taking the cubit at 18 inches.

4. The meaning appears to be, *And thou shalt make loops of blue on the edge of the one breadth* (*which is*) *on the side* (*of the one curtain*) *at the coupling; and the same shalt thou do in the edge of the outside breadth of the other* (*curtain*) *at the coupling.* The "coupling" is the uniting together of the two curtains: ["selvedge" is the translation of a word signifying extremity or end].

likewise shalt thou make in the uttermost edge of *another* cur-
5 tain, in the coupling of the second. Fifty loops shalt thou make
in the one curtain, and fifty loops shalt thou make in the edge
of the curtain that *is* in the coupling of the second; that the
6 loops may take hold one of another. And thou shalt make fifty
taches of gold, and couple the curtains together with the taches:
[b] ch. 36. 14. 7 and it shall be one tabernacle. ¶ And [b] thou shalt make curtains
of goats' *hair* to be a covering upon the tabernacle: eleven cur-
8 tains shalt thou make. The length of one curtain *shall be* thirty
cubits, and the breadth of one curtain four cubits: and the eleven
9 curtains *shall be all* of one measure. And thou shalt couple five
curtains by themselves, and six curtains by themselves, and shalt
10 double the sixth curtain in the forefront of the tabernacle. And
thou shalt make fifty loops on the edge of the one curtain *that is*
outmost in the coupling, and fifty loops in the edge of the curtain
11 which coupleth the second. And thou shalt make fifty taches of
brass, and put the taches into the loops, and couple the [1] tent
12 together, that it may be one. And the remnant that remaineth
of the curtains of the tent, the half curtain that remaineth, shall
13 hang over the backside of the tabernacle. And a cubit on the
one side, and a cubit on the other side [2] of that which remaineth
in the length of the curtains of the tent, it shall hang over the
sides of the tabernacle on this side and on that side, to cover it.
[c] ch. 36. 19. 14 And [c] thou shalt make a covering for the tent *of* rams' skins
15 dyed red, and a covering above *of* badgers' skins. ¶ And thou
shalt make boards for the tabernacle *of* shittim wood standing
16 up. Ten cubits *shall be* the length of a board, and a cubit and a
17 half *shall be* the breadth of one board. Two [3] tenons *shall there
be* in one board, set in order one against another: thus shalt
18 thou make for all the boards of the tabernacle. And thou shalt
make the boards for the tabernacle, twenty boards on the south
19 side southward. And thou shalt make forty sockets of silver

[1] Or, *covering*. [2] Heb. *in the remainder*, or, *surplusage*. [3] Heb. *hands*.

5. The words "in the edge," &c. mean, *on the edge of the breadth that is at the coupling in the second (curtain)*.

6. *taches of gold*] Each *tache*, or clasp, was to unite two opposite loops.

couple the curtains] *i.e.* couple the two outside breadths mentioned in *v.* 4.

7. *a covering upon the tabernacle*] **A Tent over the Tabernacle.** The Hebrew word here used, is the regular one for a tent of skins or cloth of any sort.

9. *tabernacle*] **Tent,** not tabernacle. The passage might be rendered, *thou shalt equally divide the sixth breadth at the front of the Tent*. In this way, half a breadth would overhang at the front and half at the back.

10. Or:—*And thou shalt make fifty loops on the edge of the outside breadth of the one (curtain) at the coupling, and fifty loops on the edge of the outside breadth of the other (curtain) at the coupling.*

11. In the Tent, clasps of bronze were used to unite the loops of the two curtains; in the Tabernacle, clasps of gold, cp. *v.* 6 and *v.* 37.

couple the tent together] Not "covering," as in the margin. By "the tent" is here meant the Tent-cloth alone.

13. The measure of the entire Tabernacle-cloth was about 60 ft. by 42; that of the Tent-cloth was about 67 ft. by 45. When the latter was placed over the former, it spread beyond it at the back and front about 3 ft. (the "half-curtain," *vv.* 9, 12) and at the sides 18 inches.

16. The board would therefore be about 15 ft. long, and 27 in. broad.

18. The entire length of the structure was about 45 ft. in the clear, and its width about 15 ft.

the south side southward] Or, **the south side on the right.** As the entrance of the Tabernacle was at its east end, the south side, to a person entering it, would be on the *left* hand: but we learn from Josephus that it was usual in speaking of the Temple to identify the south with the right hand and the north with the left hand, the entrance being regarded as the face of the structure and the west end as its back.

19. *sockets*] More literally, **bases,** or foundations. Each base weighed a talent, that is, about 94 lbs. (see xxxviii. 27), and

under the twenty boards; two sockets under one board for his
two tenons, and two sockets under another board for his two
20 tenons. And for the second side of the tabernacle on the north
21 side *there shall be* twenty boards: and their forty sockets *of* silver;
two sockets under one board, and two sockets under another
22 board. And for the sides of the tabernacle westward thou shalt
23 make six boards. And two boards shalt thou make for the
24 corners of the tabernacle in the two sides. And they shall be
[1]coupled together beneath, and they shall be coupled together
above the head of it unto one ring: thus shall it be for them
25 both; they shall be for the two corners. And they shall be eight
boards, and their sockets *of* silver, sixteen sockets; two sockets
26 under one board, and two sockets under another board. And
thou shalt make bars *of* shittim wood; five for the boards of the
27 one side of the tabernacle, and five bars for the boards of the
other side of the tabernacle, and five bars for the boards of the
28 side of the tabernacle, for the two sides westward. And the
middle bar in the midst of the boards shall reach from end to
29 end. And thou shalt overlay the boards with gold, and make
their rings *of* gold *for* places for the bars: and thou shalt over-
30 lay the bars with gold. ¶ And thou shalt rear up the tabernacle
[d]according to the fashion thereof which was shewed thee in the
31 mount. ¶ And [e]thou shalt make a vail *of* blue, and purple, and
scarlet, and fine twined linen of cunning work: with cherubims
32 shall it be made: and thou shalt hang it upon four pillars of
shittim *wood* overlaid with gold: their hooks *shall be of* gold,
33 upon the four sockets of silver. And thou shalt hang up the vail
under the taches, that thou mayest bring in thither within the
vail [f]the ark of the testimony: and the vail shall divide unto you
34 between [g]the holy *place* and the most holy. And [h]thou shalt
put the mercy seat upon the ark of the testimony in the most
35 holy *place*. And [i]thou shalt set the table without the vail, and
[k]the candlestick over against the table on the side of the tabernacle toward the south: and thou shalt put the table on the
36 north side. ¶ And [l]thou shalt make an hanging for the door of
the tent, *of* blue, and purple, and scarlet, and fine twined linen,

[d] ch. 25. 9, 40 & 27. 8. Acts 7. 44. Heb. 8. 5.
[e] ch. 36. 35. Lev. 16. 2. 2 Chr. 3. 14. Matt. 27. 51. Heb. 9. 3.
[f] ch. 40. 21.
[g] Lev. 16. 2. Heb. 9. 2, 3.
[h] ch. 25. 21. & 40. 20. Heb. 9. 5.
[i] ch. 40. 22. Heb. 9. 2.
[k] ch. 40. 24.
[l] ch. 36. 37.

[1] Heb. *twinned*.

must have been a massive block. The bases formed a continuous foundation for the walls of boards, presenting a succession of sockets or mortices (each base having a single socket), into which the tenons were to fit. They served not only for ornament but also for the protection of the lower ends of the boards from the decay which would have resulted from contact with the ground.

22. *the sides of the tabernacle westward*] Rather, **the back of the Tabernacle towards the west.** See *v.* 18.

23. *in the two sides*] Rather, **at the back.**

24. The corner boards appear to have been of such width, and so placed, as to add 18 in. to the width of the structure, making up with the six boards of full width (*v.* 22) about 15 ft. in the clear (see *v.* 18). The "ring" was so formed as to receive two bars meeting "beneath" and "above" at a right angle.

27. *for the two sides westward*] **For the back towards the west.** Cp. *v.* 22.

28. *in the midst of the boards*] If we suppose the boards to have been of ordinary thickness (*v.* 16), the bar was visible and passed through an entire row of rings. In any case, it served to hold the whole wall together.

31. *vail*] Literally *separation* (see xxxv. 12 note).

33. *taches*] Not the same as the *hooks* of the preceding verse, but the clasps of the tabernacle-cloth (see *v.* 6).

34, 35. See xxv. 10–16, 23, 31.

36. *the door of the tent*] **The entrance to the Tent,** closed by the "hanging" or curtain (xxvii. 16).

wrought with needlework] **The work of the embroiderer.** The entrance curtain of the Tent and that of the Court (xxvii. 16) were to be of the same materials, but embroidered with the needle, not wrought in

37 wrought with needlework. And thou shalt make for the
[m] ch. 36. 38. hanging [m]five pillars *of* shittim *wood*, and overlay them with
gold, *and* their hooks *shall be of* gold: and thou shalt cast five
sockets of brass for them.

[a] ch. 38. 1. Ezek. 43. 13. CHAP. 27. AND thou shalt make [a]an altar *of* shittim wood, five
cubits long, and five cubits broad; the altar shall be foursquare:
2 and the height thereof *shall be* three cubits. And thou shalt make
the horns of it upon the four corners thereof: his horns shall be

---

figures in the loom (see *v.* 1, and xxxv. 35).

37. *five pillars*] These, it should be observed, belonged to the entrance of the Tent, not, in their architectural relation, to the entrance of the Tabernacle.

sockets of brass] Their bases (see *v.* 19) were of bronze (like the taches of the tent-cloth, *v.* 11), not of silver, to mark the inferiority of the Tent to the Tabernacle.

We are indebted to Mr. Fergusson for what may be regarded as a satisfactory reconstruction of the Sanctuary in all its main particulars. He holds that what sheltered the *Mishkān* was actually a Tent of ordinary form, such as common sense and practical experience would suggest as best suited for the purpose.

According to this view the five pillars at the entrance of the Tent (xxvi. 37) were graduated as they would naturally be at the entrance of any large tent of the best form, the tallest one being in the middle to support one end of a ridge-pole.

Such a ridge-pole, which must have been sixty feet in length, would have required support, and this might have been afforded by a plain pole in the middle of the structure. Over this framing of wood-work the Tent-cloth of goats' hair was strained with its cords and tent-pins in the usual way. (See cut.)

Above the Tent-cloth of goats' hair was spread the covering of red rams' skins.

The five pillars, to reach across the front of the Tent, must have stood five cubits (about 7½ ft.) apart. Their heads were united by connecting rods ("fillets" xxvii. 10) overlaid with gold (xxxvi. 38). The spaces at the sides and back may have been wholly or in part covered in for the use of the officiating priests, like the small apartments which in after times skirted three sides of the Temple. It was probably here that those portions of the sacrifices were eaten which were not to be carried out of the sacred precincts (Lev. vi. 16, 26). We may also infer that priests lodged in them. Cp. viii. 33; 1 S. iii. 2, 3.

XXVII. **1–8.** (Cp. xxxviii. 1-7.) The great Altar which stood in the Court immediately in front of the Tabernacle was commonly called the ALTAR OF BURNT-OFFERING, because on it were burnt the whole Burnt-offerings, and all those parts of the other animal sacrifices which were offered to the Lord. It was also called the BRAZEN ALTAR, because it was covered with bronze, in distinction from the Golden Altar or Altar of Incense (xxxix. 38, 39, xl. 5, 6).

2. *his horns shall be of the same*] These horns were projections pointing upwards in

3 of the same: and [b]thou shalt overlay it with brass. And thou
shalt make his pans to receive his ashes, and his shovels, and his
basons, and his fleshhooks, and his firepans: all the vessels
4 thereof thou shalt make *of* brass. And thou shalt make for it a
grate of network *of* brass; and upon the net shalt thou make
5 four brasen rings in the four corners thereof. And thou shalt
put it under the compass of the altar beneath, that the net may
6 be even to the midst of the altar. And thou shalt make staves
for the altar, staves *of* shittim wood, and overlay them with
7 brass. And the staves shall be put into the rings, and the staves
8 shall be upon the two sides of the altar, to bear it. Hollow with

[b] See Num. 16. 38.

---

the form either of a small obelisk, or of the horn of an ox. They were to be actually parts of the Altar, not merely superadded to it. On them the blood of the Sin-offering was smeared (xxix. 12; Lev. iv. 7, viii. 15, ix. 9, xvi. 18). To take hold of them appears to have been regarded as an emphatic mode of laying claim to the supposed right of Sanctuary (xxi. 14 note; 1 K. i. 50).

3. *pans*] Rather **pots** as in xxxviii. 3; 1 K. vii. 45. On the use to which these pots were put in disposing of the ashes of the Altar, see Lev. i. 16.

basons] Vessels used for receiving the blood of the victims and casting it upon the Altar (see xxiv. 6, Lev. i. 5, &c.).

fleshhooks] These were for adjusting the pieces of the victims upon the Altar (cf. 1 S. ii. 13).

firepans] The same word is rendered *snuffdishes*, xxv. 38, xxxvii. 23: *censers*, Lev. x. 1, xvi. 12; Num. iv. 14, xvi. 6, &c. These utensils appear to have been shallow metal vessels which were employed merely to carry burning embers from the Brazen Altar to the Altar of Incense.

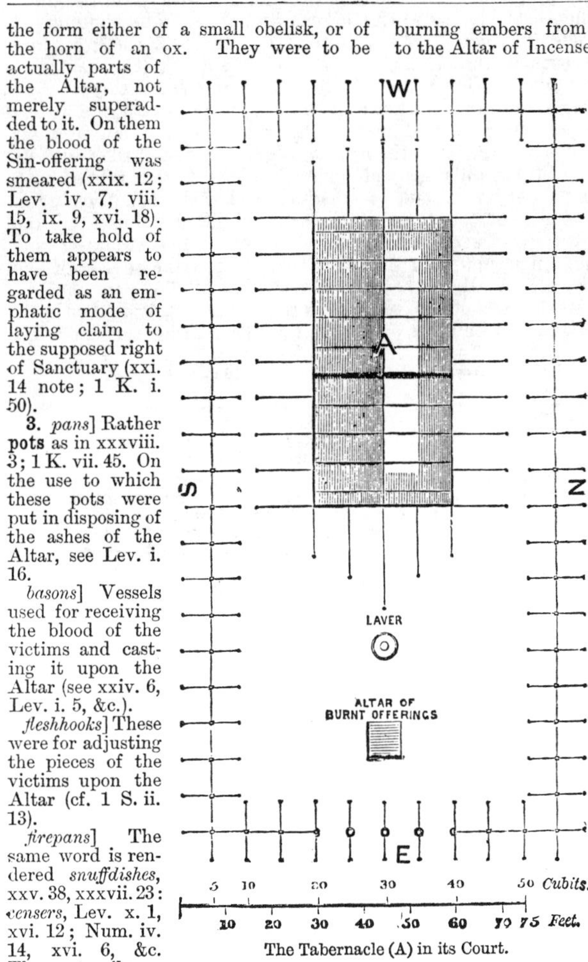

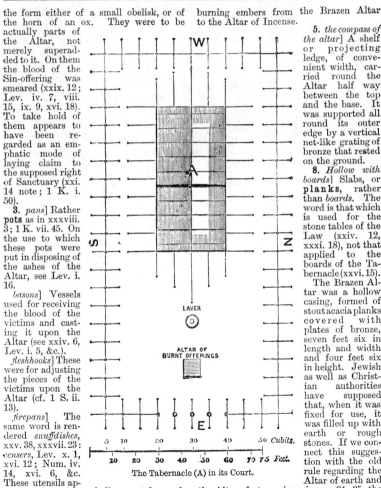

The Tabernacle (A) in its Court.

5. *the compass of the altar*] A shelf or projecting ledge, of convenient width, carried round the Altar half way between the top and the base. It was supported all round its outer edge by a vertical net-like grating of bronze that rested on the ground.

8. *Hollow with boards*] Slabs, or **planks**, rather than *boards*. The word is that which is used for the stone tables of the Law (xxiv. 12, xxxi. 18), not that applied to the boards of the Tabernacle (xxvi. 15).

The Brazen Altar was a hollow casing, formed of stout acacia planks covered with plates of bronze, seven feet six in length and width and four feet six in height. Jewish as well as Christian authorities have supposed that, when it was fixed for use, it was filled up with earth or rough stones. If we connect this suggestion with the old rule regarding the Altar of earth and the Altar of stone given in xx. 24, 25, the woodwork might in fact be regarded merely

[c] ch. 25. 40. & 26. 30.
[d] ch. 38. 9.
[e] Lev. 24. 2.

boards shalt thou make it: [c]as [1]it was shewed thee in the
9 mount, so shall they make *it*. ¶ And [d]thou shalt make the court
of the tabernacle: for the south side southward *there shall be*
hangings for the court *of* fine twined linen of an hundred cubits
10 long for one side: and the twenty pillars thereof and their
twenty sockets *shall be of* brass; the hooks of the pillars and
11 their fillets *shall be of* silver. And likewise for the north side in
length *there shall be* hangings of an hundred *cubits* long, and his
twenty pillars and their twenty sockets *of* brass; the hooks of
12 the pillars and their fillets *of* silver. And *for* the breadth of the
court on the west side *shall be* hangings of fifty cubits: their
13 pillars ten, and their sockets ten. And the breadth of the court
14 on the east side eastward *shall be* fifty cubits. The hangings of
one side *of the gate shall be* fifteen cubits: their pillars three, and
15 their sockets three. And on the other side *shall be* hangings
16 fifteen *cubits*: their pillars three, and their sockets three. And
for the gate of the court *shall be* an hanging of twenty cubits, *of*
blue, and purple, and scarlet, and fine twined linen, wrought
with needlework: *and* their pillars *shall be* four, and their sockets
17 four. All the pillars round about the court *shall be* filleted with
silver; their hooks *shall be of* silver, and their sockets *of* brass.
18 The length of the court *shall be* an hundred cubits, and the
breadth [2]fifty every where, and the height five cubits *of* fine
19 twined linen, and their sockets *of* brass. All the vessels of the
tabernacle in all the service thereof, and all the pins thereof,
20 and all the pins of the court, *shall be of* brass. ¶ And [e]thou shalt
command the children of Israel, that they bring thee pure oil

[1] Heb. *he shewed.* [2] Heb. *fifty by fifty.*

---

as the case of the Altar on which the victims were actually burned. The shelf round the sides (*v.* 5) was required as a stage for the priests to enable them to carry on their work conveniently on the top of the Altar. Hence it is said of Aaron that he *came down* from the Altar (Lev. ix. 22). According to rabbinical tradition, there was a slope of earth at the south side banked up for the priest to ascend to the stage (cp. Ex. xx. 26).

9–19. *The Court of the Tabernacle*]. (Cp. xxxviii. 9–20) See Cut at the end of ch. xxvi.

9. *the south side southward*] **The south side on the right.** See xxvi. 18.

10. *sockets*] **Bases.** See xxvi. 19.

fillets] Rather, **Connecting rods**; curtain-rods of silver connecting the heads of the pillars. The hangings were attached to the pillars by the silver hooks; but the length of the space between the pillars would render it most probable that they were also in some way fastened to these rods.

13. *the east side eastward*] **On the front side eastward.**

16. *an hanging*] An entrance curtain, which, unlike the hangings at the sides and back of the Court, could be drawn up, or aside, at pleasure. The words are rightly distinguished in our Bible in Num. iii. 26.

wrought with needlework] **The work of the embroiderer.** See xxvi. 36, xxxv. 35. On the materials, see xxv. 4.

17. *filleted with silver*] **Connected with silver rods.** See *v.* 10.

19. *All the vessels,* &c.] **All the tools of the tabernacle** *used* **in all its workmanship, and all its tent-pins, and all the tent-pins of the court, shall be of bronze.**—The working tools of the Sanctuary were most probably such things as axes, knives, hammers, &c. that were employed in making, repairing, setting up and taking down the structure. Cp. Num. iii. 36.

the tabernacle] The word is here to be taken as including both the *Mishkān* and the Tent, as in Num. i. 51, 53, &c. (see xxvi. 1 note).

the pins] Tent-pins.

20. *pure oil olive beaten*] The oil was to be of the best kind. It is called *beaten,* because it was obtained by merely bruising the olives in a mortar or mill, without the application of heat. The finest oil is now thus obtained from young fruit freshly gathered. The inferior kind is pressed from unselected fruit, under stronger pressure, and with the application of heat.

the lamp] *i.e.* the lamps of the Golden Candlestick. (See xxv. 37.)

to burn] See the margin *to ascend up.* It

olive beaten for the light, to cause the lamp [1]to burn always.
21 In the tabernacle of the congregation [f]without the vail, which
is before the testimony, [g]Aaron and his sons shall order it from
evening to morning before the LORD: [h]*it shall be* a statute
for ever unto their generations on the behalf of the children of
Israel.
CHAP. 28. AND take thou unto thee [a]Aaron thy brother, and his
sons with him, from among the children of Israel, that he may
minister unto me in the priest's office, *even* Aaron, Nadab and
2 Abihu, Eleazar and Ithamar, Aaron's sons. And [b]thou shalt
make holy garments for Aaron thy brother for glory and for
3 beauty. And [c]thou shalt speak unto all *that are* wise hearted,
[d]whom I have filled with the spirit of wisdom, that they may
make Aaron's garments to consecrate him, that he may minister
4 unto me in the priest's office. And these *are* the garments
which they shall make; [e]a breastplate, and [f]an ephod, and [g]a
robe, and [h]a broidered coat, a mitre, and a girdle: and they
shall make holy garments for Aaron thy brother, and his sons,
5 that he may minister unto me in the priest's office. And they
shall take gold, and blue, and purple, and scarlet, and fine linen.

[f] ch. 26. 31.
[g] ch. 30. 8. 1 Sam. 3. 3. 2 Chr. 13. 11.
[h] ch. 28. 43. & 29. 9, 28. Lev. 3. 17. Num. 18. 23. & 19. 21. 1 Sam. 30. 25.
[a] Num. 18. 7. Heb. 5. 1, 4.
[b] ch. 29. 5, 29 & 31. 10. Lev. 8. 7, 30. Num. 20. 26, 28.
[c] ch. 36. 1.
[d] ch. 31. 3. & 35. 30, 31.
[e] ver. 15.
[f] ver. 6.
[g] ver. 31.
[h] ver. 39.

[1] Heb. *to ascend up*.

should be observed that the word does not properly mean to burn in the sense of to consume, but is the word regularly used to express the action of fire upon what was offered to Jehovah (see Lev. i. 9).

always] *i.e.* every night "from evening till morning." Cp. xxx. 8.

21. *the tabernacle of the congregation*] More literally, **the Tent of meeting**. This is the first occurrence of this designation of the Tabernacle, and the idea connected with it is that of Jehovah meeting with either Moses, or the priests, or (in a few cases) with the people gathered into a congregation at the entrance of the Tent.

without the vail, which is before the testimony] *i.e.* the Holy Place (see xxv. 16).

XXVIII. **1-43.** (Cp. xxxix. 1-31.) Moses is now commanded to commit all that pertains to the Offerings made to the Lord in the Sanctuary to the exclusive charge of the members of a single family, who were to hold their office from generation to generation. In the patriarchal times, the external rites of worship had generally been conducted by the head of the tribe or family, in accordance with the principle involved in the dedication of the first-born (xiii. 2; Num. iii. 12, 13). Moses, as the divinely-appointed and acknowledged leader of the nation, had, on a special occasion, appointed those who were to offer sacrifice, and had himself sprinkled the consecrating blood of the victims on the people (xxiv. 5, 6, 8). On the completion of the Tabernacle, after Aaron and his sons had been called to the priesthood, he took chief part in the daily service of the Sanctuary (xl. 23-29, 31, 32) until the consecration of the family of Aaron, on which occasion he appears to have exercised the priest's office for the last time (Lev. viii. 14-29; cp. xxix. 10-26). The setting apart of the whole tribe of Levi for the entire cycle of religious services is mentioned Num. iii. 5-13, viii. 5-26, xviii. 1-32.

1. Nadab and Abihu, the two elder sons of Aaron, had accompanied their father and the seventy Elders when they went a part of the way with Moses up the mountain (xxiv. 1, 9). Soon after their consecration they were destroyed for offering "strange fire before the Lord" (Lev. x. 1, 2). Eleazar and Ithamar are here mentioned for the first time, except in the genealogy, vi. 23. Eleazar succeeded his father in the High-priesthood, and was himself succeeded by his son Phinehas (Judg. xx. 28). But Eli, the next High-priest named in the history, was of the line of Ithamar. The representatives of both families held office at the same time in the days of David. See 1 Chr. xxiv. 1-3; 2 S. viii. 17.

3. *the spirit of wisdom*] See xxxi. 3 note. What may be especially noticed in this place is, that the spirit of wisdom given by the Lord is spoken of as conferring practical skill in the most general sense.

garments to consecrate him] A solemn recognition of the significance of an appointed official dress. It expresses that the office is not created or defined by the man himself (Heb. v. 4), but that he is *invested* with it according to prescribed institution. The rite of anointing was essentially connected with investiture in the holy garments (xxix. 29, 30; xl. 12-15).—The history of all nations shews the importance of these forms.

5. With the exception of the gold, the materials were the same as those of the Tabernacle-cloth, the vail of the Tabernacle and the entrance-curtain of the Tent (xxvi.

[i] ch. 39. 2.

6 [i]And they shall make the ephod *of* gold, *of* blue, and *of* purple,
7 *of* scarlet, and fine twined linen, with cunning work. It shall
have the two shoulderpieces thereof joined at the two edges
8 thereof; and *so* it shall be joined together. And the [1]curious
girdle of the ephod, which *is* upon it, shall be of the same,
according to the work thereof; *even of* gold, *of* blue, and purple,
9 and scarlet, and fine twined linen. And thou shalt take two
onyx stones, and grave on them the names of the children of
10 Israel: six of their names on one stone, and *the other* six names
11 of the rest on the other stone, according to their birth. With
the work of an engraver in stone, *like* the engravings of a signet,
shalt thou engrave the two stones with the names of the children
of Israel: thou shalt make them to be set in ouches of gold.
12 And thou shalt put the two stones upon the shoulders of the
ephod *for* stones of memorial unto the children of Israel: and
[k]Aaron shall bear their names before the LORD upon his two
13 shoulders [l]for a memorial. And thou shalt make ouches *of*
14 gold; and two chains *of* pure gold at the ends; *of* wreathen
work shalt thou make them, and fasten the wreathen chains to
15 the ouches. ¶ And [m]thou shalt make the breastplate of judgment with cunning work; after the work of the ephod thou

[k] ver. 29. ch. 39. 7.
[l] See Josh. 4. 7. Zech. 6. 14.
[m] ch. 39. 8.

[1] Or, *embroidered.*

1, 31, 36; xxv. 4). The gold was wrought into thin flat wires which could either be woven with the woollen and linen threads, or worked with the needle. In regard to the mixture of linen and woollen threads in the High-priest's dress, see Lev. xix. 19.

6–12. *the ephod*] (xxxix. 2–7.) The Hebrew word has the same breadth of meaning as our word *vestment.* The garment was worn over the shoulders, and was the distinctive vestment of the High-priest, to which "the breast-plate of judgment" was attached (*vv.* 25–28).

cunning work] *Skilled* work, or work of a *skilled* man (xxxv. 35).

7. Cp. xxxix. 4. The Ephod consisted of two principal pieces of cloth, one for the back and the other for the front, joined together by shoulder straps (see *v.* 27 note). Below the arms, probably just above the hips, the two pieces were kept in place by a band attached to one of the pieces. On the respect in which the Ephod of the High-priest was held, see 1 S. ii. 28, xiv. 3, xxi. 9, xxiii. 6–9, xxx. 7. But an Ephod made of linen appears to have been a recognised garment not only for the common priests (1 S. xxii. 18), but also for those who were even temporarily engaged in the service of the Sanctuary (1 S. ii. 18; 2 S. vi. 14; 1 Chr. xv. 27).

8. *the curious girdle,* &c.] Rather:—*the band for fastening it, which is upon it, shall be of the same work, of one piece with it.* This band being woven on to one of the pieces of the Ephod, was passed round the body, and fastened by buttons, or strings, or some other suitable contrivance.

11. *like the engravings of a signet*] Cp. *vv.* 21, 36. These words probably refer to a peculiar way of shaping the letters, adapted for engraving on a hard substance.—Seal engraving on precious stones was practised in Egypt from very remote times.

ouches of gold] Gold settings formed not of solid pieces of metal, but of woven wire, wreathed round the stones in what is called *cloisonnée* work, a sort of filigree, often found in Egyptian ornaments. These stones, as well as those on the breastplate, were perhaps in the form of ovals, or rather ellipses, like the cartouches, containing proper names, in hieroglyphic inscriptions. The word *ouches* is used by Shakspeare, Spenser, and some of their contemporaries in the general sense of jewels.

12. *upon the shoulders*] *i.e.* upon the **shoulder-pieces** of the ephod. See *v.* 7.

upon his two shoulders] Cp. Isa. ix. 6, xxii. 22. The High-priest had to represent the Twelve Tribes in the Presence of Jehovah; and the burden of his office could not be so aptly symbolized anywhere as on his shoulders, the parts of the body fittest for carrying burdens.

13–30. Cp. xxxix. 8–21.

14. Rather, two chains of pure gold **shalt thou make of wreathen work, twisted like cords.**—They were more like cords of twisted gold wire than chains in the ordinary sense of the word. Such chains have been found in Egyptian tombs.

15. *the breastplate of judgment*] The meaning of the Hebrew word rendered *breastplate,* appears to be simply *ornament.* The term *breastplate* relates merely to its place in the dress.

shalt make it; *of* gold, *of* blue, and *of* purple, and *of* scarlet,
16 and *of* fine twined linen, shalt thou make it. Foursquare it
shall be *being* doubled; a span *shall be* the length thereof, and a
17 span *shall be* the breadth thereof. [n]And thou shalt [1]set in it
settings of stones, *even* four rows of stones: *the first* row *shall be*
a [2]sardius, a topaz, and a carbuncle: *this shall be* the first row.
18 And the second row *shall be* an emerald, a sapphire, and a
19 diamond. And the third row a ligure, an agate, and an ame-
20 thyst. And the fourth row a beryl, and an onyx, and a jasper:
21 they shall be set in gold in their [3]inclosings. And the stones
shall be with the names of the children of Israel, twelve, according to their names, *like* the engravings of a signet; every one
22 with his name shall they be according to the twelve tribes. And
thou shalt make upon the breastplate chains at the ends *of*
23 wreathen work *of* pure gold. And thou shalt make upon the
breastplate two rings of gold, and shalt put the two rings on
24 the two ends of the breastplate. And thou shalt put the two
wreathen *chains* of gold in the two rings *which are* on the ends
25 of the breastplate. And *the other* two ends of the two wreathen
chains thou shalt fasten in the two ouches, and put *them* on the
26 shoulderpieces of the ephod before it. And thou shalt make
two rings of gold, and thou shalt put them upon the two ends
of the breastplate in the border thereof, which *is* in the side of
27 the ephod inward. And two *other* rings of gold thou shalt make,
and shalt put them on the two sides of the ephod underneath,
toward the forepart thereof, over against the *other* coupling
28 thereof, above the curious girdle of the ephod. And they shall
bind the breastplate by the rings thereof unto the rings of the
ephod with a lace of blue, that *it* may be above the curious girdle
of the ephod, and that the breastplate be not loosed from the

[n] ch. 39. 10, &c.

[1] Heb. *fill in it fillings of stone.* [2] Or, *ruby.* [3] Heb. *fillings.*

---

16. *doubled*] To give it stability, or to form what was used as a bag for the Urim and Thummim: the latter appears to be the more likely.

17. *settings*] Ouches of *cloisonnée* work, like those mentioned in *v.* 11.

a sardius] *i.e. the red stone.* The Sardian stone, or **sard**, was much used by the ancients for seals; and it is perhaps the stone of all others the best for engraving.

topaz] Not the stone now called the topaz: it may have been the chrysolite, a stone of a greenish hue.

a carbuncle] More probably the **beryl**, which is a kind of emerald.

18. *an emerald*] Rather the garnet, which when cut with a convex face is termed the **carbuncle**.

a sapphire] Not the stone now called the sapphire; the lapis-lazuli is most probably meant.

a diamond] There is no trace of evidence that the ancients ever acquired the skill to engrave on the diamond, or even that they were acquainted with the stone. The "diamond" here may possibly be some variety of chalcedony, or (perhaps) rock **crystal.**

19. *a ligure*] **Amber,** which came from Liguria.

20. *a beryl*] Supposed to be a brilliant yellow stone, identified with what is now known as the Spanish topaz.

a jasper] Probably the green jasper.

22. *chains*, &c.] See *v.* 14.

23. *on the two ends of the breastplate*] The extremities spoken of here, and in the next verse, must have been the upper corners of the square. The chains attached to them (*v.* 25) suspended the Breastplate from the ouches of the shoulder-pieces (*vv.* 9, 11, 12).

27. "And two rings of gold shalt thou make and put them on **the two shoulder-pieces of the Ephod, low down in the front of it, near the joining, above the band for fastening it."** It would seem that the shoulder-pieces were continued down the front of the Ephod as far as the band (see *v.* 8); **the joining** appears to have been the meeting of the extremities of the shoulder-pieces with the band. These rings were attached to the shoulder-pieces just above this joining.

28. *the curious girdle of the ephod* **The band for fastening it** (see *v.* 8 note).

29 ephod. And Aaron shall bear the names of the children of
Israel in the breastplate of judgment upon his heart, when he
goeth in unto the holy *place*, [o]for a memorial before the LORD
30 continually. And [p]thou shalt put in the breastplate of judgment the Urim and the Thummim; and they shall be upon
Aaron's heart, when he goeth in before the LORD: and Aaron
shall bear the judgment of the children of Israel upon his heart
31 before the LORD continually. ¶ And [q]thou shalt make the robe
32 of the ephod all *of* blue. And there shall be an hole in the top
of it, in the midst thereof: it shall have a binding of woven work
round about the hole of it, as it were the hole of an habergeon,
33 that it be not rent. And *beneath* upon the [1]hem of it thou shalt
make pomegranates *of* blue, and *of* purple, and *of* scarlet,
round about the hem thereof; and bells of gold between them
34 round about: a golden bell and a pomegranate, a golden bell
and a pomegranate, upon the hem of the robe round about.
35 And it shall be upon Aaron to minister: and his sound shall be
heard when he goeth in unto the holy *place* before the LORD,
36 and when he cometh out, that he die not. ¶ And [r]thou shalt
make a plate *of* pure gold, and grave upon it, *like* the engravings

[o] ver. 12.
[p] Lev. 8. 8. Num. 27. 21. Deut. 33. 8. 1 Sam. 28. 6. Ezra 2. 63. Neh. 7. 65.
[q] ch. 39. 22.
[r] ch. 39. 30. Zech. 14. 20.

[1] Or, *skirts*.

---

29. See *v.* 12; the same names engraved on the stones of the breastplate were worn over the heart, the seat of the affections, as well as of the intellect, to symbolize the relation of love and of personal interest which the Lord requires to exist between the priest and the people.

30. *the Urim and the Thummim*] *The Light and the Truth*, or *perfection.*

From the way in which they are spoken of here and in Lev. viii. 8, compared with xxviii. 15-21, it would appear that the Urim and the Thummim were some material things, previously existing and familiarly known, that they were separate from the Breastplate itself, as well as from the gems that were set upon it, and were kept in the bag of the Breastplate (*v.* 16).

By means of them the Will of Jehovah, especially in what related to the wars in which His people were engaged, was made known. They were formally delivered by Moses to Aaron (Lev. viii. 8), and subsequently passed on to Eleazar (Num. xx. 28, xxvii. 21). They were esteemed as the crowning glory of the Tribe of Levi (Deut. xxxiii. 8). There is no instance on record of their being consulted after the time of David.

The opinion has prevailed to a great extent that the Urim and the Thummim were of Egyptian origin, and two small images of precious stone, and that the Divine Will was manifested through them by some physical effect addressed to the eye or the ear.

Others prefer the view that they were some means for casting lots. Appeals to lots were made under divine authority by the chosen people on the most solemn occasions (Lev. xvi. 8; Num. xxvi. 55; Josh. vii. 14-18, xiii. 6, xviii. 8; 1 S. xiv. 41, 42; Acts i. 26), and it must have been a truth commonly recognized by the people that though "the lot was cast into the lap, the whole disposing thereof was of the Lord" (Prov. xvi. 33).

31-35. *the robe of the ephod*] (xxxix. 22-26.) A frock or robe of the simplest form, woven without seam, wholly of blue. It was put on by being drawn over the head. It appears to have had no sleeves. It probably reached a little below the knees. It must have been visible above and below the Ephod, the variegated texture of which it must have set off as a plain blue groundwork.

32. *an habergeon*] Corselets of linen, such as appear to be here referred to, were well known amongst the Egyptians.

35. *his sound*] Its sound, *i.e.* the sound of the robe, that the people, who stood without, when they heard the sound of the bells within the Tabernacle, might have a sensible proof that the High-priest was performing the sacred rite in their behalf, though he was out of their sight.

that he die not] The bells also bore witness that the High-priest was, at the time of his ministration, duly attired in the dress of his office, and so was not incurring the sentence of death (see also *v.* 43). An infraction of the laws for the service of the Sanctuary was not merely an act of disobedience; it was a direct insult to the Presence of Jehovah from His ordained minister, and justly incurred a sentence of capital punishment. Cp. xxx. 21; Lev. viii. 35, x. 7.

36-43. Cp. xxxix. 27-31.

36. *HOLINESS TO THE LORD*] This inscription testified in express words the

37 of a signet, HOLINESS TO THE LORD. And thou shalt put
it on a blue lace, that it may be upon the mitre; upon the fore-
38 front of the mitre it shall be. And it shall be upon Aaron's
forehead, that Aaron may [s]bear the iniquity of the holy things,
which the children of Israel shall hallow in all their holy gifts;
and it shall be always upon his forehead, that they may be
39 [t]accepted before the LORD. And thou shalt embroider the coat
of fine linen, and thou shalt make the mitre *of* fine linen, and
40 thou shalt make the girdle *of* needlework. [u]And for Aaron's
sons thou shalt make coats, and thou shalt make for them girdles,
and bonnets shalt thou make for them, for glory and for beauty.
41 And thou shalt put them upon Aaron thy brother, and his sons
with him; and shalt [w]anoint them, and [1x]consecrate them, and
sanctify them, that they may minister unto me in the priest's
42 office. And thou shalt make them [y]linen breeches to cover
[2]their nakedness; from the loins even unto the thighs they shall
43 [3]reach: and they shall be upon Aaron, and upon his sons, when
they come in unto the tabernacle of the congregation, or when
they come near [z]unto the altar to minister in the holy *place*;
that they [a]bear not iniquity, and die: [b]*it shall be* a statute for
ever unto him and his seed after him.

[s] Lev. 22. 9. Num. 18. 1. Isai. 53. 11. Ezek. 4. 4, 5, 6. John 1. 29. Heb. 9. 28. 1 Pet. 2. 24.
[t] Lev. 1. 4. & 22. 27. Isai. 56. 7.
[u] ver. 4. ch. 39. 27, 28, 29, 41.
[w] ch. 29. 7. & 40. 15. Lev. 10. 7.
[x] ch. 29. 9, &c. Lev. ch. 8. Heb. 7. 28.
[y] ch. 39. 28. Lev. 6. 10.
[z] ch. 20. 26.
[a] Lev. 20. 19, 20. & 22. 9. Num. 9. 13.
[b] ch. 27. 21. Lev. 17. 7.

[1] Heb. *fill their hand.* [2] Heb. *flesh of their nakedness.* [3] Heb. *be.*

---

holiness with which the High-priest was invested in virtue of his sacred calling.

37. *a blue lace*] The plate was fastened upon a blue band or fillet, so tied round the mitre as to show the plate in front.

the mitre] A twisted band of linen (*v.* 39) coiled into a cap, to which the name *mitre,* in its original sense. closely answers, but which, in modern usage, would rather be called a *turban.*

38. *bear the iniquity of the holy things*] The Hebrew expression "to bear iniquity" is applied either to one who suffers the penalty of sin (*v.* 43; Lev. v. 1, 17, xvii. 16, xxvi. 41, &c.), or to one who takes away the sin of others (Gen. l. 17; Lev. x. 17, xvi. 22; Num. xxx. 15; 1 S. xv. 25, &c.). In several of these passages the verb is rightly rendered to *forgive.*—The iniquity which is spoken of in this place does not mean particular sins actually committed, but that condition of alienation from God in every earthly thing which makes reconciliation and consecration needful. Cp. Num. xviii. 1. It belonged to the High-priest, as the chief atoning mediator between Jehovah and His people (see on *v.* 36), to atone for the holy things that they might be "accepted before the Lord" (cp. Lev. viii. 15, xvi. 20, 33, with the notes): but the common priests also, in their proper functions, had to take their part in making atonement (Lev. iv. 20, v. 10, x. 17, xxii. 16; Num. xviii. 23, &c.).

39. *the coat of fine linen*] A long tunic, or cassock. Josephus says that it was worn next the skin, that it reached to the feet, and that it had closely fitting sleeves. The verb translated *embroider* appears rather to mean **weave in diaper work.** The tissue consisted of threads of one and the same colour diapered in checkers, or in some small figure.

the girdle of needlework] **The girdle of the work of the embroiderer** (xxvi. 1, xxxv. 35). The word translated *girdle* is different from that so rendered in *v.* 8 (see note), and is probably Egyptian. Josephus says that it was wound several times round the body, and that its ends ordinarily hung down to the feet, but were thrown over the shoulder when the priest was engaged in his work.

40. *bonnets*] **Caps** of a simple construction which seem to have been cup-shaped.

41-43. The dress of white linen was the strictly sacerdotal dress common to the whole body of priests (Ezek. xliv. 17, 18). These were "for glory and for beauty" not less than "the golden garments" (as they were called by the Jews) which formed the High-priest's dress of state (*v.* 2). The linen suit which the High-priest put on when he went into the Most Holy Place on the Day of Atonement, appears to have been regarded with peculiar respect (Cp. xxxi. 10; Lev. xvi. 4, 23), though it is nowhere stated that it was distinguished in its make or texture, except in having a girdle (*v.* 39) wholly of white linen, instead of a variegated one. The ancient Egyptian priests, like the Hebrew priests, wore nothing but white linen garments in the performance of their duties.

43. *that they bear not iniquity and die*] See *vv.* 35, 38 notes.

Chap. 29. AND this *is* the thing that thou shalt do unto them to
hallow them, to minister unto me in the priest's office: [a]Take
2 one young bullock, and two rams without blemish, and [b]un-
leavened bread, and cakes unleavened tempered with oil, and
wafers unleavened anointed with oil: *of* wheaten flour shalt
3 thou make them. And thou shalt put them into one basket, and
bring them in the basket, with the bullock and the two rams.
4 And Aaron and his sons thou shalt bring unto the door of the
tabernacle of the congregation, [c]and shalt wash them with
5 water. [d]And thou shalt take the garments, and put upon Aaron
the coat, and the robe of the ephod, and the ephod, and the
breastplate, and gird him with [e]the curious girdle of the ephod:
6 [f]and thou shalt put the mitre upon his head, and put the holy
7 crown upon the mitre. Then shalt thou take the anointing
8 [g]oil, and pour *it* upon his head, and anoint him. ¶ And [h]thou
9 shalt bring his sons, and put coats upon them. And thou shalt
gird them with girdles, Aaron and his sons, and [1]put the bonnets
on them: and [i]the priest's office shall be theirs for a perpetual
10 statute: and thou shalt [2k]consecrate Aaron and his sons. And
thou shalt cause a bullock to be brought before the tabernacle of the congregation: and [l]Aaron and his sons shall put
11 their hands upon the head of the bullock. And thou shalt kill
the bullock before the Lord, *by* the door of the tabernacle of the
12 congregation. And thou [m]shalt take of the blood of the bullock,
and put *it* upon [n]the horns of the altar with thy finger, and
13 pour all the blood beside the bottom of the altar. And [o]thou
shalt take all the fat that covereth the inwards, and [3]the caul
that is above the liver, and the two kidneys, and the fat that *is*
14 upon them, and burn *them* upon the altar. But [p]the flesh of the
bullock, and his skin, and his dung, shalt thou burn with fire
15 without the camp: it *is* a sin offering. ¶ [q]Thou shalt also take
one ram; and Aaron and his sons shall [r]put their hands upon
16 the head of the ram. And thou shalt slay the ram, and thou
shalt take his blood, and sprinkle *it* round about upon the altar.
17 And thou shalt cut the ram in pieces, and wash the inwards of
him, and his legs, and put *them* unto his pieces, and [4]unto his head.
18 And thou shalt burn the whole ram upon the altar: it *is* a burnt
offering unto the Lord: it *is* a [s]sweet savour, an offering made
19 by fire unto the Lord. ¶ [t]And thou shalt take the other ram;
and Aaron and his sons shall put their hands upon the head of the
20 ram. Then shalt thou kill the ram, and take of his blood, and put
it upon the tip of the right ear of Aaron, and upon the tip of the
right ear of his sons, and upon the thumb of their right hand, and
upon the great toe of their right foot, and sprinkle the blood upon
21 the altar round about. And thou shalt take of the blood that *is*
upon the altar, and of [u]the anointing oil, and sprinkle *it* upon
Aaron, and upon his garments, and upon his sons, and upon the
garments of his sons with him: and [w]he shall be hallowed, and
his garments, and his sons, and his sons' garments with him.
22 Also thou shalt take of the ram the fat and the rump, and the
fat that covereth the inwards, and the caul *above* the liver, and

[a] Lev. 8. 2.
[b] Lev. 2. 4. & 6. 20, 21, 22.
[c] ch. 40. 12. Lev. 8. 6. Heb. 10. 22.
[d] ch. 28. 2. Lev. 8. 7.
[e] ch. 28. 8.
[f] Lev. 8. 9.
[g] ch. 28. 41. & 30. 25. Lev. 8. 12. & 10. 7. & 21. 10. Num. 35. 25.
[h] Lev. 8. 13.
[i] Num. 18. 7.
[k] ch. 28. 41. Lev. 8. 22. Heb. 7. 28.
[l] Lev. 1. 4. & 8. 14.
[m] Lev. 8. 15.
[n] ch. 27. 2. & 30. 2.
[o] Lev. 3. 3.
[p] Lev. 4. 11, 12, 21. Heb. 13. 11.
[q] Lev. 8. 18.
[r] Lev. 1. 4—9.
[s] Gen. 8. 21.
[t] ver. 3. Lev. 8. 22.
[u] ch. 30. 25, 31. Lev. 8. 30.
[w] ver. 1. Heb. 9. 22.

[1] Heb. *bind.*
[2] Heb. *fill the hand of.*
[3] It seemeth by anatomy and the Hebrew doctors to be *the midriff.*
[4] Or, *upon.*

XXIX. 1-37. The Consecration of the Priests. See notes to Lev. viii. ix.

4. *door of the tabernacle*] **Entrance of the Tent.** See Lev. viii. 3.

the two kidneys, and the fat that *is* upon them, and the right
23 shoulder; for it *is* a ram of consecration: [x]and one loaf of [x] Lev. 8. 26.
bread, and one cake of oiled bread, and one wafer out of the
24 basket of the unleavened bread that *is* before the LORD: and
thou shalt put all in the hands of Aaron, and in the hands of his
sons; and shalt [1][y]wave them *for* a wave offering before the [y] Lev. 7. 30.
25 LORD. [z]And thou shalt receive them of their hands, and burn [z] Lev. 8. 28.
them upon the altar for a burnt offering, for a sweet savour before the LORD: it *is* an offering made by fire unto the LORD.
26 And thou shalt take [a]the breast of the ram of Aaron's consecra- [a] Lev. 8. 29.
tion, and wave it *for* a wave offering before the LORD: and [b]it [b] Ps. 99. 6.
27 shall be thy part. And thou shalt sanctify [c]the breast of the [c] Lev. 7. 31,
wave offering, and the shoulder of the heave offering, which is 34.
waved, and which is heaved up, of the ram of the consecration, Num. 18. 11, 18.
even of *that* which *is* for Aaron, and of *that* which is for his sons: Deut. 18. 3.
28 and it shall be Aaron's and his sons' [d]by a statute for ever from [d] Lev. 10. 15.
the children of Israel: for it *is* an heave offering: and [e]it shall [e] Lev. 7. 34.
be an heave offering from the children of Israel of the sacrifice
of their peace offerings, *even* their heave offering unto the LORD.
29 ¶ And the holy garments of Aaron [f]shall be his sons' after him, [f] Num. 20.
30 [g]to be anointed therein, and to be consecrated in them. *And* 26. 28.
[2][h]that son that is priest in his stead shall put them on [i]seven [g] Num. 18. 8. & 35. 25.
days, when he cometh into the tabernacle of the congregation to [h] Num. 20.
31 minister in the holy *place*. ¶ And thou shalt take the ram of 28.
the consecration, and [k]seethe his flesh in the holy place. [i] Lev. 8. 35. & 9. 1, 8.
32 And Aaron and his sons shall eat the flesh of the ram, and the [k] Lev. 8. 31.
[l]bread that *is* in the basket, *by* the door of the tabernacle of the [l] Matt. 12. 4.
33 congregation. And [m]they shall eat those things wherewith the [m] Lev. 10.
atonement was made, to consecrate *and* to sanctify them: [n]but a 14, 15, 17.
34 stranger shall not eat *thereof*, because they *are* holy. And if [n] Lev. 22. 10.
ought of the flesh of the consecrations, or of the bread, remain [o] Lev. 8. 32.
unto the morning, then [o]thou shalt burn the remainder with fire: [p] Ex. 40. 12. Lev. 8. 33, 34, 35.
35 it shall not be eaten, because it *is* holy. ¶ And thus shalt thou [q] Heb. 10. 11.
do unto Aaron, and to his sons, according to all *things* which I [r] ch. 30. 26,
have commanded thee: [p]seven days shalt thou consecrate them. 28, 29. & 40. 10.
36 And thou shalt [q]offer every day a bullock *for* a sin offering [s] ch. 40. 10.
for atonement: and thou shalt cleanse the altar, when thou hast [t] ch. 30. 29.
made an atonement for it, [r]and thou shalt anoint it, to sanctify Matt. 23. 19.
37 it. Seven days thou shalt make an atonement for the altar, and [u] Num. 28. 3.
sanctify it; [s]and it shall be an altar most holy: [t]whatsoever 1 Chr. 16. 40. 2 Chr. 2. 4. & 13. 11.
38 toucheth the altar shall be holy. ¶ Now this *is that* which thou & 31. 3. Ezra 3. 3.
shalt offer upon the altar; [u]two lambs of the first year [w]day by [w] See Dan.
39 day continually. The one lamb thou shalt offer [x]in the morning; 9. 27. & 12. 11.
40 and the other lamb thou shalt offer at even: and with the one [x] 2 Kin. 16.
lamb a tenth deal of flour mingled with the fourth part of an hin 15. Ezek. 46. 13, 14, 15.

[1] Or, *shake to and fro.* [2] Heb. he *of his sons.*

---

27. The *waving* was the more solemn process of the two: it was a movement several times repeated, while *heaving* was simply a lifting up once.

33. *a stranger*] **One of another family,** *i.e.* in this case, one not of the family of Aaron.

38–46. *The continual Burnt-offering*] The primary purpose of the national Altar is here set forth. The victim slain every morning and every evening was an acknowledgment that the life of the people belonged to Jehovah; the offering of meal was an acknowledgment that all their works rightly done were His due (see Lev. ii.); while the incense symbolized their daily prayers.

39. *at even*] See xii. 6.

40. *a tenth deal*] *i.e.* the tenth part of an Ephah; it is sometimes called an Omer (xvi. 36; see Lev. xxiii. 13). The Ephah seems to have been rather less than four gallons and a half (see Lev. xix.

[y] 1 Kin. 18. 29, 36. 2 Kin. 16. 15. Ezra 9. 4, 5. Ps. 141. 2. Dan. 9. 21. [z] ver. 38. ch. 30. 8. Num. 28. 6. Dan. 8. 11, 12, 13. [a] ch. 25. 22. & 30. 6, 36. Num. 17. 4. [b] ch. 40. 34. 1 Kin. 8. 11. 2 Chr. 5. 14. & 7. 1, 2, 3. Ezek. 43. 5. Hag. 2. 7, 9. Mal. 3. 1. [c] Lev. 21. 15. & 22. 9, 16. [d] Ex. 25. 8. Lev. 26. 12. Zech. 2. 10. John 14. 17, 23. 2 Cor. 6. 16. Rev. 21. 3. [e] ch. 20. 2. [a] ch. 37. 25. & 40. 5. [b] See ver. 7, 8, 10. Lev. 4. 7, 18.

of beaten oil; and the fourth part of an hin of wine *for* a drink
41 offering. And the other lamb thou shalt [y]offer at even, and
shalt do thereto according to the meat offering of the morning, and according to the drink offering thereof, for a sweet
42 savour, an offering made by fire unto the LORD. *This shall be*
[z]a continual burnt offering throughout your generations *at* the
door of the tabernacle of the congregation before the LORD:
43 [a]where I will meet you, to speak there unto thee. And there I
will meet with the children of Israel, and [1]*the tabernacle* [b]shall
44 be sanctified by my glory. And I will sanctify the tabernacle of
the congregation, and the altar: I will [c]sanctify also both Aaron
45 and his sons, to minister to me in the priest's office. And [d]I will
46 dwell among the children of Israel, and will be their God. And
they shall know that [e]I *am* the LORD their God, that brought
them forth out of the land of Egypt, that I may dwell among
them: I *am* the LORD their God.

CHAP. 30. AND thou shalt make [a]an altar [b]to burn incense upon:
2 *of* shittim wood shalt thou make it. A cubit *shall be* the length
thereof, and a cubit the breadth thereof; foursquare shall it be:
and two cubits *shall be* the height thereof: the horns thereof
3 *shall be* of the same. And thou shalt overlay it with pure gold,
the [2]top thereof, and the [3]sides thereof round about, and the
horns thereof; and thou shalt make unto it a crown of gold
4 round about. And two golden rings shalt thou make to it under
the crown of it, by the two [4]corners thereof, upon the two sides
of it shalt thou make *it;* and they shall be for places for the
5 staves to bear it withal. And thou shalt make the staves *of*
6 shittim wood, and overlay them with gold. And thou shalt put
it before the vail that *is* by the ark of the testimony, before the

[1] Or, Israel. [2] Heb. *roof.* [3] Heb. *walls.* [4] Heb. *ribs.*

---

36 note); and the tenth deal of flour may have weighed about 3 lbs. 2 oz.

an hin] The word appears to be Egyptian. The measure was one-sixth of an ephah. The quarter of a hin was therefore about a pint and a half. See Lev. xix. 36 note.

beaten oil] See xxvii. 20.

wine for a drink offering] The earliest mention of the Drink-offering is found in connection with Jacob's setting up the stone at Bethel (Gen. xxxv. 14). But it is here first associated with the rites of the Altar. The Law of the Drink-offering is stated Num. xv. 5 sq. Nothing whatever is expressly said in the Old Testament regarding the mode in which the wine was treated: but it would seem probable, from the prohibition that it should not be poured upon the Altar of Incense (xxx. 9), that it used to be poured on the Altar of Burnt-offering.

42. *at the door of the tabernacle*] **At the entrance of the Tent.**

43. *the* (*tabernacle*) *shall be sanctified*] The word *tabernacle* is certainly not the right one to be here supplied. What is probably meant is the spot in which Jehovah promises to meet with the assembly of His people. The verse may be rendered, **And in that place will I meet with the children of Israel, and it shall be sanctified with my glory.** See also the margin.

44, 45. The purpose of the formal consecration of the Sanctuary and of the priests who served in it was, that the whole nation which Jehovah had set free from its bondage in Egypt might be consecrated in its daily life, and dwell continually in His presence as "a kingdom of priests and an holy nation." (xix. 6.)

46. Cp. Gen. xvii. 7.

XXX. 1–10. (xxxvii. 25–28, xl. 26, 27.) *The Altar of Incense* was to be a casing of boards of shittim wood (xxv. 5), 18 inches square and three feet in height (taking the cubit as 18 inches), entirely covered with plates of gold. Four "horns" were to project upwards at the corners like those of the Altar of Burnt-offering (xxvii. 2). A *crown* or moulding of gold was to run round the top. On each of two opposite sides there was to be a gold ring through which the staves were to be put when it was moved from place to place.

4. *by the two corners thereof*] Not *corners.* See margin. The sense appears to be: *And two gold rings shalt thou make for it under its moulding; on its two sides shalt thou make them* (*i.e.* one ring on each side).

6. The place for the Altar of Incense was outside the vail, opposite to the Ark of the

[c]mercy seat that *is* over the testimony, where I will meet with
7 thee. And Aaron shall burn thereon [1][d]sweet incense every
morning: when [e]he dresseth the lamps, he shall burn incense
8 upon it. And when Aaron [2][3]lighteth the lamps [4]at even, he
shall burn incense upon it, a perpetual incense before the LORD
9 throughout your generations. Ye shall offer no [f]strange incense
thereon, nor burnt sacrifice, nor meat offering; neither shall ye
10 pour drink offering thereon. And [g]Aaron shall make an atonement upon the horns of it once in a year with the blood of the
sin offering of atonements: once in the year shall he make
atonement upon it throughout your generations: it *is* most holy
11 unto the LORD. ¶ And the LORD spake unto Moses, saying,
12 [h]When thou takest the sum of the children of Israel after [5]their
number, then shall they give every man [i]a ransom for his soul
unto the LORD, when thou numberest them; that there be no
13 [k]plague among them, when *thou* numberest them. [l]This they
shall give, every one that passeth among them that are numbered,
half a shekel after the shekel of the sanctuary: ([m]a shekel *is*
twenty gerahs:) [n]an half shekel *shall be* the offering of the LORD.
14 Every one that passeth among them that are numbered, from
twenty years old and above, shall give an offering unto the
15 LORD. The [o]rich shall not [6]give more, and the poor shall not
[7]give less than half a shekel, when *they* give an offering unto the
16 LORD, to make an [p]atonement for your souls. And thou shalt
take the atonement money of the children of Israel, and [q]shalt

[c] ch. 25. 21, 22.
[d] ver. 34. 1 Sam. 2. 28. 1 Chr. 23. 13. Luke 1. 9.
[e] ch. 27. 21.
[f] Lev. 10. 1.
[g] Lev. 16. 18. & 23. 27.
[h] ch. 38. 25. Num. 1. 2, 5. & 26. 2. 2 Sam. 24. 2.
[i] See Num. 31. 50. Job 33. 24. & 36. 18. Ps. 49. 7. Matt. 20. 28. 1 Tim. 2. 6. 1 Pet. 1. 18, 19.
[k] 2 Sam. 24. 15.
[l] Matt. 17. 24.
[m] Lev. 27. 25. Num. 3. 47. Ezek. 45. 12.
[n] ch. 38. 26.
[o] Job 34. 19. Prov. 22. 2. Eph. 6. 9. Col. 3. 25.
[p] ver. 12.
[q] ch. 38. 25.

[1] Heb. *incense of spices.*
[2] Or, *setteth up.*
[3] Heb. *causeth to ascend.*
[4] Heb. *between the two evens*, ch. 12. 6.
[5] Heb. *them that are to be numbered.*
[6] Heb. *multiply.*
[7] Heb. *diminish.*

Covenant and between the Candlestick on the south side and the Shewbread Table on the north (xl. 22–24). It appears to have been regarded as having a more intimate connection with the Holy of Holies than the other things in the Holy Place; and the mention of the Mercy-seat in this verse, if we associate with it the significance of incense as figuring the prayers of the Lord's people (Ps. cxli. 2; Rev. v. 8, viii. 3, 4), seems to furnish additional ground for an inference that the Incense Altar took precedence of the Table of Shewbread and the Candlestick.

7. *the lamps*] See xxv. 37.

7, 8. The offering of the Incense accompanied that of the morning and evening sacrifice. The two forms of offering symbolized the spirit of man reaching after communion with Jehovah, both in act and utterance. See Ps. cxli. 2.

9. By this regulation, the symbolism of the Altar of Incense was kept free from ambiguity. Atonement was made by means of the victim on the Brazen altar in the court outside; the prayers of the reconciled worshippers had their type within the Tabernacle.

10. See marg. reff.

11–16. (xxxviii. 25–28.) *The Ransom of Souls.* On comparing these words with those of Num. i. 1–3, we may perhaps infer that the first passage relates to a mere counting of the adult Israelites at the time when the money was taken from each, and that what the latter passage enjoins was a formal enrolment of them according to their genealogies and their order of military service.

a ransom for his soul] What the sincere worshipper thus paid was at once the fruit and the sign of his faith in the goodness of Jehovah, Who had redeemed him and brought him into the Covenant. Hence the payment is rightly called a *ransom* inasmuch as it involved a personal appropriation of the fact of his redemption. On the word *soul*, see Lev. xvii. 11.

that there be no plague] *i.e.* that they might not incur punishment for the neglect and contempt of spiritual privileges. Cp. xxviii. 35; 1 Cor. xi. 27–30; and the Exhortation in our Communion Service.

13. *half a shekel*] The probable weight of silver in the half-shekel would now be worth about 1*s.* 3½*d.* (Cp. Gen. xxiii. 16. See xxxviii. 24 note.) *Gerah* is, literally, a *bean*, probably the bean of the carob or locust-tree. It was used as the name of a small weight, as our word *grain* came into use from a grain of wheat.

15. Every Israelite stood in one and the same relation to Jehovah. See *vv.* 11, 12.

16. *tabernacle of the congregation*] **Tent of meeting**, here and in *vv.* 18, 20.

a memorial unto the children of Israel] The

appoint it for the service of the tabernacle of the congregation;
that it may be [r] a memorial unto the children of Israel before the
17 LORD, to make an atonement for your souls. ¶ And the LORD
spake unto Moses, saying, [s] Thou shalt also make a laver *of*
18 brass, and his foot *also of* brass, to wash *withal:* and thou shalt
[t] put it between the tabernacle of the congregation and the altar,
19 and thou shalt put water therein. For Aaron and his sons [u] shall
20 wash their hands and their feet thereat: when they go into the
tabernacle of the congregation, they shall wash with water, that
they die not; or when they come near to the altar to minister,
21 to burn offering made by fire unto the LORD: so they shall wash
their hands and their feet, that they die not: and [w] it shall be a
statute for ever to them, *even* to him and to his seed throughout
22 their generations. ¶ Moreover the LORD spake unto Moses, say-
23 ing, Take thou also unto thee [x] principal spices, of pure [y] myrrh
five hundred *shekels*, and of sweet cinnamon half so much, *even*
two hundred and fifty *shekels*, and of sweet [z] calamus two hun-
24 dred and fifty *shekels*, and of [a] cassia five hundred *shekels*, after the
25 shekel of the sanctuary, and of oil olive an [b] hin: and thou shalt
make it an oil of holy ointment, an ointment compound after the
26 art of the [1] apothecary: it shall be [c] an holy anointing oil. [d] And

[r] Num. 16. 40.
[s] ch. 38. 8. 1 Kin. 7. 38.
[t] ch. 40. 7, 30.
[u] ch. 40. 31, 32. Ps. 26. 6. Isai. 52. 11. John 13. 10. Heb. 10. 22.
[w] ch. 28. 43.
[x] Cant. 4. 14. Ezek. 27. 22.
[y] Ps. 45. 8. Prov. 7. 17.
[z] Cant. 4. 14. Jer. 6. 20.
[a] Ps. 45. 8.
[b] ch. 29. 40.
[c] Num. 35. 25. Ps. 89. 20. & 133. 2.
[d] ch. 40. 9. Lev. 8. 10. Num. 7. 1.

[1] Or, *perfumer.*

---

silver used in the Tabernacle was a memorial to remind each man of his position before the Lord, as one of the covenanted people.

17–21. (xxxviii. 8.) The bronze for the "Laver of brass" and its foot was supplied from the bronze mirrors of the women who voluntarily gave up these articles of luxury. Bronze mirrors were much used by the ancient Egyptians. No hint is given as to the form of the Laver. The Brazen Sea and the ten Lavers that served the same purpose in the Temple of Solomon, were elaborately wrought in artistic designs and are minutely described (1 K. vii. 23–29).

19. *wash their hands and their feet*] On certain solemn occasions he was required to bathe his whole person (xxix. 4; Lev. xvi. 4). The Laver must also have furnished the water for washing those parts of the victims that needed cleansing (Lev. i. 9).

20. *that they die not*] See xxviii. 35 note.

22–33. Cp. xxxvii. 29.

23. *principal spices*] *i.e.* the best spices.

pure myrrh] Is a gum which comes from the stem of a low, thorny, ragged tree, that grows in Arabia Felix and Eastern Africa, called by botanists *Balsamodendron myrrha.* The word here rendered *pure*, is literally, *freely flowing*, an epithet which is explained by the fact that the best myrrh is said to exude spontaneously from the bark, while that of inferior quality oozes out in greater quantity from incisions made in the bark.

five hundred shekels] Probably rather more than 15¼ lbs. See xxxviii. 24.

cinnamon is obtained from a tree allied to the laurel that grows in Ceylon and other islands of the Indian Ocean, known in Botany as the *Cinnamomum zeylanicum.* It is the inner rind of the tree dried in the sun. It was imported from India in very early times by the people of Ophir, and brought with other spices from the south part of Arabia by the trading caravans that visited Egypt and Syria. The mention of these spices in Exodus may be taken as the earliest notice we have connected with commerce with the remote East.

two hundred and fifty shekels] about 7 lbs. 14 oz.

sweet calamus] The **fragrant cane** (or *rush*) was probably what is now known in India as the Lemon Grass.

24. *cassia* is the inner bark of an Indian tree (*Cinnamomum cassia*), which differs from that which produces cinnamon in the shape of its leaves and some other particulars. It was probably in ancient times, as it is at present, by far less costly than cinnamon, and it may have been on this account that it was used in double quantity.

an hin] Probably about six pints. See Lev. xix. 36.

25. *an oil of holy ointment*] Rather, **a holy anointing oil.**

after the art of the apothecary] According to Jewish tradition, the essences of the spices were first extracted, and then mixed with the oil. The preparation of the Anointing Oil, as well as of the Incense, was entrusted to Bezaleel (xxxvii. 29), and the care of preserving it to Eleazar the son of Aaron (Num. iv. 16). In a later age, it was prepared by the sons of the priests (1 Chr. ix. 30).

thou shalt anoint the tabernacle of the congregation therewith,
27 and the ark of the testimony, and the table and all his vessels,
28 and the candlestick and his vessels, and the altar of incense, and
the altar of burnt offering with all his vessels, and the laver and
29 his foot. And thou shalt sanctify them, that they may be most
30 holy: [e]whatsoever toucheth them shall be holy. [f]And thou
shalt anoint Aaron and his sons, and consecrate them, that *they*
31 may minister unto me in the priest's office. And thou shalt
speak unto the children of Israel, saying, This shall be an holy
32 anointing oil unto me throughout your generations. Upon
man's flesh shall it not be poured, neither shall ye make *any*
other like it, after the composition of it: [g]it *is* holy, *and* it
33 shall be holy unto you. [h]Whosoever compoundeth *any* like it,
or whosoever putteth *any* of it upon a stranger, [i]shall even be
34 cut off from his people. ¶ And the LORD said unto Moses,
[k]Take unto thee sweet spices, stacte, and onycha, and galbanum;
these sweet spices with pure frankincense: of each shall there be
35 a like *weight:* and thou shalt make it a perfume, a confection
[l]after the art of the apothecary, [1]tempered together, pure *and*
36 holy: and thou shalt beat *some* of it very small, and put of it
before the testimony in the tabernacle of the congregation,
[m]where I will meet with thee: [n]it shall be unto you most holy.
37 And *as for* the perfume which thou shalt make, [o]ye shall not
make to yourselves according to the composition thereof: it shall
38 be unto thee holy for the LORD. [p]Whosoever shall make like
unto that, to smell thereto, shall even be cut off from his people.
CHAP. 31. AND the LORD spake unto Moses, saying, [a]See, I have
2 called by name Bezaleel the [b]son of Uri, the son of Hur, of the

[e] ch. 29. 37.
[f] ch. 29. 7, &c. Lev. 8. 12, 30.
[g] ver. 25, 37.
[h] ver. 38.
[i] Gen. 17. 14. ch. 12. 15. Lev. 7. 20, 21.
[k] ch. 25. 6.
[l] ver. 25.
[m] ch. 29. 42. Lev. 16. 2.
[n] ver. 32. ch. 29. 37. Lev. 2. 3.
[o] ver. 32.
[p] ver. 33.
[a] ch. 35. 30. & 36. 1.
[b] 1 Chr. 2. 20.

[1] Heb. *salted*, Lev. 2. 13.

32. *upon man's flesh*] *i.e.* on the persons of those who were not priests who might employ it for such anointing as was usual on festive occasions (Ps. civ. 15; Prov. xxvii. 9; Matt. vi. 17, &c.).

33. *a stranger*] See xxix. 33.

cut off from his people] See xxxi. 14.

34-38. (xxxvii. 29.) The Incense, like the Anointing Oil, consisted of four aromatic ingredients.

stacte supposed to be either the gum of the Storax-tree (*Styrax officinale*) found in Syria and the neighbouring countries, or the gum known as Benzoin, or Gum Benjamin, which is an important ingredient in the incense now used in churches and mosks, and is the produce of another storax-tree (*Styrax benzoin*) that grows in Java and Sumatra.

onycha, a perfume perhaps made from the cap of the strombus, or wing-shell, which abounds in the Red Sea.

galbanum, a gum of a yellowish brown colour, in the form of either grains or masses. It is imported from India, Persia, and Africa; but the plant from which it comes is not yet certainly known.

pure frankincense] This was the most important of the aromatic gums. Like myrrh, it was regarded by itself as a precious perfume (Cant. iii. 6; Matt. ii. 11), and it was used unmixed with other substances in some of the rites of the Law. The tree from which it is obtained is not found in Arabia, and it was most likely imported from India by the Sabæans, like Cinnamon, Cassia, and Calamus (see *v.* 23). The tree is now known as the *Boswellia serrata*, or *B. thurifera*, and grows abundantly in the highlands of India. The frankincense of commerce is a different substance, the resin of the spruce and of some other kinds of fir.

35. See *v.* 25.

tempered together] The four substances were perhaps pounded and thoroughly mixed together, and then fused into a mass. This rendering is to be preferred to that in the margin.

36. See *v.* 6.

37, 38. Cp. *vv.* 32, 33.

XXXI. **1-11.** (xxxv. 30-35.) This solemn call of Bezaleel and Aholiab is full of instruction. Their work was to be only that of handicraftsmen. Still it was Jehovah Himself Who called them by name to their tasks, and the powers which they were now called upon to exercise in their respective crafts, were declared to have been given them by the Holy Spirit. Thus is every effort of skill, every sort of well-ordered labour, when directed to a right end, brought into the very highest sphere of association.

There appears to be sufficient reason

[c] ch. 35. 31. 1 Kin. 7. 14.
[d] ch. 35. 34.
[e] ch. 28. 3. & 35. 10, 35. & 36. 1.
[f] ch. 36. 8.
[g] ch. 37. 1.
[h] ch. 37. 6.
[i] ch. 37. 10.
[k] ch. 37. 17.
[l] ch. 38. 1.
[m] ch. 38. 8.
[n] ch. 39. 1, 41. Num. 4. 5, 6, &c.
[o] ch. 30. 25, 31. & 37. 29.
[p] ch. 30. 34. & 37. 29.
[q] Lev. 19. 3, 30. & 26. 2. Ezek. 20. 12, 20. & 44. 24.
[r] ch. 20. 8. Deut. 5. 12. Ezek. 20. 12.
[s] ch. 35. 2.

3 tribe of Judah: and I have [c]filled him with the spirit of God, in
wisdom, and in understanding, and in knowledge, and in all
4 manner of workmanship, to devise cunning works, to work in
5 gold, and in silver, and in brass, and in cutting of stones, to set
them, and in carving of timber, to work in all manner of work-
6 manship. And I, behold, I have given with him [d]Aholiab, the
son of Ahisamach, of the tribe of Dan: and in the hearts of all
that are [e]wise hearted I have put wisdom, that they may make
7 all that I have commanded thee; [f]the tabernacle of the congregation, and [g]the ark of the testimony, and [h]the mercy seat that
8 *is* thereupon, and all the [1]furniture of the tabernacle, and [i]the
table and his furniture, and [k]the pure candlestick with all his
9 furniture, and the altar of incense, and [l]the altar of burnt offer-
10 ing with all his furniture, and [m]the laver and his foot, and [n]the
cloths of service, and the holy garments for Aaron the priest,
and the garments of his sons, to minister in the priest's office,
11 [o]and the anointing oil, and [p]sweet incense for the holy *place*:
according to all that I have commanded thee shall they do.
12, 13 ¶ And the LORD spake unto Moses, saying, Speak thou also
unto the children of Israel, saying, [q]Verily my sabbaths ye shall
keep: for it *is* a sign between me and you throughout your
generations; that *ye* may know that I *am* the LORD that doth
14 sanctify you. [r]Ye shall keep the sabbath therefore; for it *is*
holy unto you: every one that defileth it shall surely be put to
death: for [s]whosoever doeth *any* work therein, that soul shall

[1] Heb. *vessels*.

---

for identifying Hur, the grandfather of Bezaleel, with the Hur who assisted Aaron in supporting the hands of Moses during the battle with Amalek at Rephidim (xvii. 10), and who was associated with Aaron in the charge of the people while Moses was on the mountain (xxiv. 14). Josephus says that he was the husband of Miriam. It is thus probable that Bezaleel was related to Moses. He was the chief artificer in metal, stone, and wood; he had also to perform the apothecary's work in the composition of the Anointing Oil and the Incense (xxxvii. 29). He had precedence of all the artificers, but Aholiab appears to have had the entire charge of the textile work (xxxv. 35, xxxviii. 23).

3. *wisdom, understanding, knowledge*] Or, that "right judgment in all things" for which we specially pray on Whitsun-day; the perceptive faculty; and experience, a practical acquaintance with facts.

4. *to devise cunning works*] Rather, **to devise works of skill.** The Hebrew phrase is not the same as that rendered "cunning work" in respect to textile fabrics in xxvi. 1.

10. *and the cloths of service*] Rather, **And the garments of office**; that is, the distinguishing official garments of the High-priest. The three kinds of dress mentioned in this verse appear to be the only ones which were peculiar to the Sanctuary. They were: (1) The richly adorned state robes of the High-priest (see xxviii. 6–38, xxxix. 1 sq.). (2) The "holy garments" of white linen for the High-priest, worn on the most solemn occasion in the year (see xxviii. 39; Lev. xvi. 4. (3) The garments of white linen for all the priests, worn in their regular ministrations (see xxviii. 40, 41).

12–17. (xxxv. 2, 3.) *The Penal Law of the Sabbath.* In the Fourth Commandment the injunction to observe the Seventh Day is addressed to the conscience of the people (see xx. 8 note): in this place, the object is to declare an infraction of the Commandment to be a capital offence. The two passages stand in a relation to each other similar to that between Lev. xviii. xix. and Lev. xx. It seems likely that the penal edict was specially introduced as a caution in reference to the construction of the Tabernacle, lest the people, in their zeal to carry on the work, should be tempted to break the divine Law for the observance of the Day.

14. See Num. xv. 32–36. The distinction between the meaning of the two expressions, *to be cut off from the people*, and *to be put to death*, is here indicated. He who was cut off from the people had, by his offence, put himself out of the terms of the Covenant, and was an outlaw. On such, and on such alone, when the offence was one which affected the well-being of the nation, as it was in this case, death could be inflicted by the public authority.

15 be cut off from among his people. [t]Six days may work be — [t] ch. 20. 9.
done; but in the [u]seventh *is* the sabbath of rest, [1]holy to the LORD: — [u] Gen. 2. 2.
whosoever doeth *any* work in the sabbath day, he shall surely be — ch. 16. 23.
16 put to death. Wherefore the children of Israel shall keep the — & 20. 10.
sabbath, to observe the sabbath throughout their generations,
17 *for* a perpetual covenant. It *is* [x]a sign between me and the chil- — [x] ver. 13.
dren of Israel for ever: for [y]*in* six days the LORD made heaven — Ezek. 20. 12, 20.
and earth, and on the seventh day he rested, and was refreshed. — [y] Gen. 1. 31.
18 ¶ And he gave unto Moses, when he had made an end of com- — & 2. 2.
muning with him upon mount Sinai, [z]two tables of testimony, — [z] ch. 24. 12.
tables of stone, written with the finger of God. — Deut. 4. 13. 2 Cor. 3. 3.
CHAP. 32. AND when the people saw that Moses [a]delayed to come — [a] ch. 24. 18.
down out of the mount, the people gathered themselves together
unto Aaron, and said unto him, [b]Up, make us gods, which shall — [b] Acts 7. 40.
[c]go before us; for *as for* this Moses, the man that brought us up — [c] ch. 13. 21.
out of the land of Egypt, we wot not what is become of him.
2 And Aaron said unto them, Break off the [d]golden earrings, — [d] Judg. 8.
which *are* in the ears of your wives, of your sons, and of your — 24, 25, 26, 27.
3 daughters, and bring *them* unto me. And all the people brake — [e] ch. 20. 23.
off the golden earrings which *were* in their ears, and brought — Judg. 17. 3, 4.
4 *them* unto Aaron. [e]And he received *them* at their hand, and — 1 Kin. 12. 28.
fashioned it with a graving tool, after he had made it a molten — Neh. 9. 18. Ps. 106. 19.
calf: and they said, These *be* thy gods, O Israel, which brought — Isai. 46. 6. Acts 7. 41. Rom. 1. 23.

[1] Heb. *holiness*.

---

17. *was refreshed*] Literally, *he took breath.* Cp. xxiii. 12; 2 S. xvi. 14. The application of the word to the Creator, which occurs nowhere else, is remarkable.

18. *two tables of testimony*] See xxv. 16; xxxii. 15.

The Tables of stone which represented the Covenant between Jehovah and His people, and which, when covered with the Mercy-seat were to give the Sanctuary its significance, are now delivered to Moses in accordance with the promise in xxiv. 12.

The history of what relates to the construction of the Sanctuary is here interrupted, and is taken up again chap. xxxv. 1.

XXXII.-XXXIV. In all probability these three chapters originally formed a distinct composition. The main incidents recorded in them follow in the order of time, and are therefore in their proper place as regards historical sequence.

xxxii. **1-6.** *The Golden Calf.* The people had, to a great extent, lost the patriarchal faith, and were but imperfectly instructed in the reality of a personal unseen God. Being disappointed at the long absence of Moses, they seem to have imagined that he had deluded them, and had probably been destroyed amidst the thunders of the mountain (xxiv. 15-18). They accordingly gave way to their superstitious fears and fell back upon that form of idolatry which was most familiar to them (see *v.* 4 note). The narrative of the circumstances is more briefly given by Moses at a later period in one of his addresses to the people (Deut. ix. 8-21, 25-29, x. 1-5, 8-11). It is worthy of remark, that Josephus, in his very characteristic chapter on the giving of the Law, says nothing whatever of this act of apostacy, though he relates that Moses twice ascended the mountain.

1. *unto Aaron*] The chief authority during the absence of Moses was committed to Aaron and Hur (xxiv. 14).

make us gods] The substantive (*elohim*) is plural in form and may denote *gods.* But according to the Hebrew idiom, the meaning need not be plural, and hence the word is used as the common designation of the true God (Gen. i. 1, &c. See xxi. 6 note). It here denotes **a god**, and should be so rendered.

2. *Break off the golden earrings*] It has been very generally held from early times, that Aaron did not willingly lend himself to the mad design of the multitude; but that, overcome by their importunity, he asked them to give up such possessions as he knew they would not willingly part with, in the hope of putting a check on them. Assuming this to have been his purpose, he took a wrong measure of their fanaticism, for all the people made the sacrifice at once (*v.* 3). His weakness, in any case, was unpardonable and called for the intercession of Moses (Deut. ix. 20).

4. The sense approved by most modern critics is:—*and he received the gold at their hand and collected it in a bag and made it a molten calf.* The Israelites must have been familiar with the ox-worship of the Egyptians; perhaps many of them had witnessed the rites of Mnevis at Heliopolis, almost

5 thee up out of the land of Egypt. And when Aaron saw *it*, he
built an altar before it; and Aaron made [f]proclamation, and
6 said, To morrow *is* a feast to the LORD. And they rose up early
on the morrow, and offered burnt offerings, and brought peace
offerings; and the [g]people sat down to eat and to drink, and rose
7 up to play. ¶ And the LORD said unto Moses, [h]Go, get thee
down; for thy people, which thou broughtest out of the land
8 of Egypt, [i]have corrupted *themselves*: they have turned aside
quickly out of the way which [k]I commanded them: they have
made them a molten calf, and have worshipped it, and have
sacrificed thereunto, and said, [l]These *be* thy gods, O Israel, which
9 have brought thee up out of the land of Egypt. And the LORD
said unto Moses, [m]I have seen this people, and, behold, it *is* a
10 stiffnecked people: now therefore [n]let me alone, that [o]my wrath
may wax hot against them, and that I may consume them: and
11 [p]I will make of thee a great nation. ¶ [q]And Moses besought
[1]the LORD his God, and said, LORD, why doth thy wrath wax
hot against thy people, which thou hast brought forth out of the
land of Egypt with great power, and with a mighty hand?
12 [r]Wherefore should the Egyptians speak, and say, For mischief
did he bring them out, to slay them in the mountains, and to
consume them from the face of the earth? Turn from thy fierce
13 wrath, and [s]repent of this evil against thy people. Remember
Abraham, Isaac, and Israel, thy servants, to whom thou [t]swarest
by thine own self, and saidst unto them, [u]I will multiply your
seed as the stars of heaven, and all this land that I have spoken
of will I give unto your seed, and they shall inherit *it* for ever.
14 And the LORD [w]repented of the evil which he thought to do unto

[f] Lev. 23. 2. 2 Kin. 10. 20. 2 Chr. 30. 5.
[g] 1 Cor. 10. 7.
[h] ver. 1. ch. 33. 1. Dan. 9. 24.
[i] Gen. 6. 11. Deut. 4. 16. Judg. 2. 19. Hos. 9. 9.
[k] ch. 20. 3.
[l] 1 Kin. 12. 28.
[m] ch. 33. 3, 5. & 34. 9. Deut. 31. 27. 2 Chr. 30. 8. Isai. 48. 4. Acts 7. 51.
[n] Deut. 9. 14, 19.
[o] ch. 22. 24.
[p] Num. 14. 12.
[q] Ps. 74. 1, 2. & 106. 23.
[r] Num. 14. 13. Deut. 32. 27.
[s] ver. 14.
[t] Gen. 22. 16. Heb. 6. 13.
[u] Gen. 12. 7. & reff.
[w] Deut. 32. 26. 1 Chr. 21. 15. Ps. 106. 45. Jer. 18. 8.

[1] Heb. *the face of the* LORD.

---

on the borders of the Land of Goshen, and they could not have been unacquainted with the more famous rites of Apis at Memphis. It is expressly said that they yielded to the idolatry of Egypt while they were in bondage (Josh. xxiv. 14; Ezek. xx. 8, xxiii. 3, 8); and this is in keeping with the earliest Jewish tradition (Philo). In the next verse, Aaron appears to speak of the calf as if it was a representative of Jehovah—"To-morrow is a feast to the LORD." The Israelites did not, it should be noted, worship a living Mnevis, or Apis, having a proper name, but only the golden type of the animal. The mystical notions connected with the ox by the Egyptian priests may have possessed their minds, and, when expressed in this modified and less gross manner, may have been applied to the LORD, Who had really delivered them out of the hand of the Egyptians. Their sin then lay, not in their adopting another god, but in their pretending to worship a visible symbol of Him Whom no symbol could represent. The close connection between the calves of Jeroboam and this calf is shewn by the repetition of the formula, "which brought thee up out of the land of Egypt" (1 Kings xii. 28).

These be thy gods] **This is thy god.** See *v.* 1 note.

7-35. The faithfulness of Moses in the office that had been entrusted to him was now to be put to the test. It was to be made manifest whether he loved his own glory better than he loved the brethren who were under his charge; whether he would prefer that he should himself become the founder of a "great nation," or that the LORD's promise should be fulfilled in the whole people of Israel. This may have been especially needful for Moses, in consequence of his natural disposition. See Num. xii. 3; and cp. iii. 11.—With this trial of Moses repeated in a very similar manner (Num. xiv. 11-23), may be compared the trial of Abraham (Gen. xxii.) and of our Saviour (Matt. iv. 8-10).

8. *These be thy gods...have brought*] **This is thy god, O Israel, who has brought—**

10. *let me alone*] But Moses did not let the LORD alone; he wrestled, as Jacob had done, until, like Jacob, he obtained the blessing (Gen. xxxii. 24-29).

14. This states a fact which was not revealed to Moses till after his second intercession when he had come down from the mountain and witnessed the sin of the people (*vv.* 30-34). He was then assured that the Lord's love to His ancient people would prevail. God is said, in the language of Scripture, to "repent," when His forgiving

15 his people. ¶ And [x]Moses turned, and went down from the [x] Deut. 9. 15.
mount, and the two tables of the testimony *were* in his hand:
the tables *were* written on both their sides; on the one side and
16 on the other *were* they written. And the [y]tables *were* the work [y] ch. 31. 18.
of God, and the writing *was* the writing of God, graven upon the
17 tables. And when Joshua heard the noise of the people as they
shouted, he said unto Moses, *There is* a noise of war in the camp.
18 And he said, *It is* not the voice of *them that* shout for mastery,
neither *is it* the voice of *them that* cry for [1]being overcome: *but*
19 the noise of *them that* sing do I hear. And it came to pass, as
soon as he came nigh unto the camp, that [z]he saw the calf, and [z] Deut. 9.
the dancing: and Moses' anger waxed hot, and he cast the tables 16, 17.
20 out of his hands, and brake them beneath the mount. [a]And he [a] Deut. 9. 21.
took the calf which they had made, and burnt *it* in the fire, and
ground *it* to powder, and strawed it upon the water, and made
21 the children of Israel drink *of it.* ¶ And Moses said unto Aaron,
[b]What did this people unto thee, that thou hast brought so great [b] Gen. 20. 9.
22 a sin upon them? And Aaron said, Let not the anger of my & 26. 10.
lord wax hot: [c]thou knowest the people, that they *are set* on [c] ch. 14. 11.
23 mischief. For they said unto me, [d]Make us gods, which shall go & 15. 24.
before us: for *as for* this Moses, the man that brought us up out & 16. 2, 20,
24 of the land of Egypt, we wot not what is become of him. And 28.
I said unto them, Whosoever hath any gold, let them break *it* & 17. 2, 4.
off. So they gave *it* me: then I cast it into the fire, and there [d] ver. 1.
25 [e]came out this calf. ¶ And when Moses saw that the people [e] ver. 4.
were [f]naked; (for Aaron [g]had made them naked unto *their* [f] ch. 33. 4, 5.
26 shame among [2]their enemies:) then Moses stood in the gate of [g] 2 Chr. 28.
the camp, and said, Who *is* on the LORD'S side? *Let him come* 19.

[1] Heb. *weakness.* [2] Heb. *those that rose up against them.*

love is seen by man to blot out the letter of His judgments against sin (2 Sam. xxiv. 16; Joel ii. 13; Jonah iii. 10, &c.); or when the sin of man seems to human sight to have disappointed the purposes of grace (Gen. vi. 6; 1 Sam. xv. 35, &c.). The awakened conscience is said to "repent," when, having felt its sin, it feels also the divine forgiveness: it is at this crisis that God, according to the language of Scripture, repents towards the sinner. Thus the repentance of God made known in and through the One true Mediator reciprocates the repentance of the returning sinner, and reveals to him atonement.

17, 18. Moses does not tell Joshua of the divine communication that had been made to him respecting the apostasy of the people, but only corrects his impression by calling his attention to the kind of noise which they are making.

19. Though Moses had been prepared by the revelation on the Mount, his righteous indignation was stirred up beyond control when the abomination was before his eyes.

20. See Deut. ix. 21. What is related in this verse must have occupied some time and may have followed the rebuke of Aaron. The act was of course symbolical. The idol was brought to nothing and the people were made to swallow their own sin (cp. Mic. vii. 13, 14).

22. Aaron's reference to the character of the people, and his manner of stating what he had done (*v.* 24), are very characteristic of the deprecating language of a weak mind.

23. *make us gods*] **Make us a god.**

25. *naked*] Rather **unruly,** or *licentious.*

shame among their enemies] Cp. Ps. xliv. 13; lxxix. 4; Deut. xxviii. 37.

26–29. The tribe of Levi, Moses' own Tribe, now distinguished itself by immediately returning to its allegiance and obeying the call to fight on the side of Jehovah. We need not doubt that the 3000 who were slain were those who persisted in resisting Moses. The spirit of the narrative forbids us to conceive that the act of the Levites was anything like an indiscriminate massacre. An amnesty had first been offered to all in the words, "Who is on the LORD'S side?" Those who were forward to draw the sword were directed not to spare their closest relations or friends; but this must plainly have been with an understood qualification as regards the conduct of those who were to be slain. Had it not been so, they who were on the LORD'S side would have had to destroy each other. We need not stumble at the bold, simple way in which the statement is made.

unto me. And all the sons of Levi gathered themselves together
27 unto him. And he said unto them, Thus saith the LORD God of
Israel, Put every man his sword by his side, *and* go in and out
from gate to gate throughout the camp, and [h]slay every man his
brother, and every man his companion, and every man his
28 neighbour. And the children of Levi did according to the word
of Moses: and there fell of the people that day about three
29 thousand men. [i][1]For Moses had said, [2]Consecrate yourselves to
day to the LORD, even every man upon his son, and upon his
brother; that he may bestow upon you a blessing this day.
30 ¶ And it came to pass on the morrow, that Moses said unto the
people, [k]Ye have sinned a great sin: and now I will go up
unto the LORD; [l]peradventure I shall [m]make an atonement
31 for your sin. And Moses [n]returned unto the LORD, and said,
Oh, this people have sinned a great sin, and have [o]made them
32 gods of gold. Yet now, if thou wilt forgive their sin—; and if
not, [p]blot me, I pray thee, [q]out of thy book which thou hast
33 written. And the LORD said unto Moses, [r]Whosoever hath sinned
34 against me, him will I blot out of my book. Therefore now
go, lead the people unto *the place* of which I have spoken unto
thee: [s]behold, mine Angel shall go before thee: nevertheless [t]in
35 the day when I visit I will visit their sin upon them. ¶ And
the LORD plagued the people, because [u]they made the calf, which
Aaron made.
CHAP. 33. AND the LORD said unto Moses, Depart, *and* go up hence,
thou [a]and the people which thou hast brought up out of the land
of Egypt, unto the land which I sware unto Abraham, to Isaac,
2 and to Jacob, saying, [b]Unto thy seed will I give it: [c]and I will
send an angel before thee; [d]and I will drive out the Canaanite,

[h] Num. 25. 5. Deut. 33. 9. [i] Num. 25. 11, 12, 13. Deut. 13. 6. 1 Sam. 15. 18, 22. Prov. 21. 3. Zech. 13. 3. Matt. 10. 37. [k] 1 Sam. 12. 20, 23. Luke 15. 18. [l] 2 Sam. 16. 12. Amos 5. 15. [m] Num. 25. 13. [n] Deut. 9. 18. [o] ch. 20. 23. [p] Ps. 69. 28. [q] Ps. 56. 8. & 139. 16. [r] Lev. 23. 30. Ezek. 18. 4. [s] ch. 33. 2. Num. 20. 16. [t] Deut. 32. 35. Amos 3. 14. Rom. 2. 5. [u] 2 Sam. 12. 9. Acts 7. 41.
[a] ch. 32. 7.
[b] Gen. 12. 7. ch. 32. 13. [c] ch. 32. 34. & 34. 11. [d] Deut. 7. 22. Josh. 24. 11.

[1] Or, *And Moses said, Consecrate yourselves to-day to the* LORD, *because every* man hath been *against his son, and against his brother, &c.*

[2] Heb. *Fill your hands.*

---

29. *Consecrate yourselves to day to the* LORD, &c.] The margin contains the literal rendering. Our version gives the most probable meaning of the Hebrew, and is supported by the best authority. The Levites were to prove themselves in a special way the servants of Jehovah, in anticipation of their formal consecration as ministers of the Sanctuary (cp. Deut. x. 8), by manifesting a self-sacrificing zeal in carrying out the divine command, even upon their nearest relatives.

31. *returned unto the* LORD] *i.e.* he again ascended the Mount.

gods of gold] **a god of gold.**

32. For a similar form of expression, in which the conclusion is left to be supplied by the mind of the reader, see Dan. iii. 15; Luke xiii. 9, xix. 42; John vi. 62; Rom. ix. 22.—For the same thought, see Rom. ix. 3. It is for such as Moses and St. Paul to realize, and to dare to utter, their readiness to be wholly sacrificed for the sake of those whom God has entrusted to their love. This expresses the perfected idea of the whole Burnt-offering.

thy book] The figure is taken from the enrolment of the names of citizens. This is its first occurrence in the Scriptures. See marg. reff. and Isa. iv. 3; Dan. xii. 1; Luke x. 20; Phil. iv. 3; Rev. iii. 5, &c.

33, 34. Each offender was to suffer for his own sin. Cp. xx. 5; Ezek. xviii. 4, 20. Moses was not to be taken at his word. He was to fulfil his appointed mission of leading on the people towards the Land of Promise.

34. *mine Angel shall go before thee*] See marg. reff. and Gen. xii. 7.

in the day when I visit, &c.] Cp. Num. xiv. 22–24. But though the LORD chastised the individuals, He did not take His blessing from the nation.

XXXIII. **2, 3.** See iii. 8.

for I will not go up in the midst of thee] The Covenant on which the original promise (xxiii. 20–23) was based had been broken by the people. Jehovah now therefore declared that though His Angel should go before Moses, He would withhold His own favouring Presence. The nation should be put on a level with other nations, to lose its character as the people in special covenant with Jehovah (see on *v.* 16). Thus were the people forcibly warned that His Presence could prove a blessing to them

the Amorite, and the Hittite, and the Perizzite, the Hivite, and
3 the Jebusite: [e]unto a land flowing with milk and honey: [f]for
I will not go up in the midst of thee; for thou *art* a [g]stiffnecked
4 people: lest [h]I consume thee in the way. ¶And when the
people heard these evil tidings, [i]they mourned: [k]and no man
5 did put on him his ornaments. For the LORD had said unto
Moses, Say unto the children of Israel, [l]Ye *are* a stiffnecked
people: I will come up [m]into the midst of thee in a moment, and
consume thee: therefore now put off thy ornaments from thee,
6 that I may [n]know what to do unto thee. And the children of
Israel stripped themselves of their ornaments by the mount Horeb.
7 ¶And Moses took the tabernacle, and pitched it without the
camp, afar off from the camp, [o]and called it the Tabernacle of
the congregation. And it came to pass, *that* every one which
[p]sought the LORD went out unto the tabernacle of the congrega-
8 tion, which *was* without the camp. And it came to pass, when
Moses went out unto the tabernacle, *that* all the people rose up,
and stood every man [q]*at* his tent door, and looked after Moses,
9 until he was gone into the tabernacle. ¶And it came to pass, as
Moses entered into the tabernacle, the cloudy pillar descended,
and stood *at* the door of the tabernacle, and *the* LORD [r]talked
10 with Moses. And all the people saw the cloudy pillar stand *at*
the tabernacle door: and all the people rose up and [s]worshipped,
11 every man *in* his tent door. And [t]the LORD spake unto Moses
face to face, as a man speaketh unto his friend. And he turned
again into the camp: but [u]his servant Joshua, the son of Nun,
12 a young man, departed not out of the tabernacle. ¶And Moses
said unto the LORD, See, [x]thou sayest unto me, Bring up this
people: and thou hast not let me know whom thou wilt send
with me. Yet thou hast said, [y]I know thee by name, and thou
13 hast also found grace in my sight. Now therefore, I pray thee,
[z]if I have found grace in thy sight, [a]shew me now thy way, that
I may know thee, that I may find grace in thy sight: and con-
14 sider that this nation *is* [b]thy people. And he said, [c]My presence
15 shall go *with thee*, and I will give thee [d]rest. And he said unto
him, [e]If thy presence go not *with me*, carry us not up hence.
16 For wherein shall it be known here that I and thy people have

[e] ch. 3. 8.
[f] ver. 15, 17.
[g] ch. 32. 9. Deut. 9. 6, 13.
[h] ch. 23. 21. Num. 16. 21, 45.
[i] Num. 14. 1, 39.
[k] 2 Sam. 19. 24. 1 Kin. 21. 27. Isai. 32. 11.
[l] ver. 3.
[m] See Num. 16. 45, 46.
[n] Deut. 8. 2. Ps. 139. 23.
[o] ch. 29. 42, 43.
[p] Deut. 4. 29. 2 Sam. 21. 1.
[q] Num. 16. 27.
[r] ch. 25. 22. & 31. 18. Ps. 99. 7.
[s] ch. 4. 31.
[t] Gen. 32. 30.
[u] ch. 24. 13.
[x] ch. 32. 34.
[y] ver. 17. Gen. 18. 19. John 10. 3. 2 Tim. 2. 19.
[z] ch. 34. 9.
[a] Ps. 25. 4. & 27. 11.
[b] Deut. 9. 26, 29. Joel. 2. 17.
[c] ch. 13. 21. Isai. 63. 9.
[d] Josh. 21. 44. Ps. 95. 11.
[e] ver. 3. ch. 34. 9.

---

only on condition of their keeping their part of the covenant (*v.* 3). If they failed in this, His presence would be to them "a consuming fire" (Deut. iv. 24; cp. xxxii. 10).

5. *I will come up*, &c.] Better; **If I were to go up for one moment in the midst of thee, I should consume thee.**

that I may know, &c.] By that sign of their repentance Jehovah would decide in what way they were to be punished.

6. *by the mount Horeb*] **From mount Horeb** *onwards*. They ceased to wear their ornaments from the time they were at Mount Horeb.

7. *the tabernacle*] **The Tent.** The only word in the Old Testament which ought to be rendered *tabernacle* (*mishkān*) does not occur once in this narrative (xxvi. 1). What is here meant is a tent appointed for this temporary purpose by Moses, possibly that in which he was accustomed to dwell.

pitched it without the camp, afar off from the camp] That the people might feel that they had forfeited the Divine presence (see xxv. 8). This tent was to be a place for meeting with Jehovah, like the Tabernacle which was about to be constructed.

The Tent of meeting (as it should be called, see xxvii. 21 note, and note at end of Chap. xl.) was placed "afar off from the camp," and the mediator and his faithful servant Joshua were alone admitted to it (*v.* 11).

10. *the tabernacle door*] **The entrance of the Tent.**

The people by their act of worship gave another proof of their penitence.

11. *face to face*] See *v.* 20 note.

13. *thy way*] He desires not to be left in uncertainty, but to be assured, by Jehovah's mode of proceeding, of the reality of the promises that had been made to him.

14. *rest*] This was the common expression for the possession of the promised Land. Deut. iii. 20; Josh. i. 13, 15; cp. Heb. iv. 8.

16. *thou goest with us*] It was this which alone **distinguished** (rather than "sepa-

found grace in thy sight? [f] *Is it* not in that thou goest with us?
So [g] shall we be separated, I and thy people, from all the people
17 that *are* upon the face of the earth. ¶ And the LORD said unto
Moses, [h] I will do this thing also that thou hast spoken: for
[i] thou hast found grace in my sight, and I know thee by name.
18, 19. And he said, I beseech thee, shew me [k] thy glory. And he said,
[l] I will make all my goodness pass before thee, and I will proclaim the name of the LORD before thee; [m] and will be [n] gracious
to whom I will be gracious, and will shew mercy on whom I
20 will shew mercy. And he said, Thou canst not see my face:
21 for [o] there shall no man see me, and live. And the LORD said,
Behold, *there is* a place by me, and thou shalt stand upon a rock:
22 and it shall come to pass, while my glory passeth by, that I will
put thee [p] in a clift of the rock, and will [q] cover thee with my
23 hand while I pass by: and I will take away mine hand, and thou
shalt see my back parts: but my face shall [r] not be seen.

CHAP. 34. AND the LORD said unto Moses, [a] Hew thee two tables
of stone like unto the first: [b] and I will write upon *these* tables
the words that were in the first tables, which thou brakest.
2 And be ready in the morning, and come up in the morning unto
mount Sinai, and present thyself there to me [c] in the top of the
3 mount. And no man shall [d] come up with thee, neither let any
man be seen throughout all the mount; neither let the flocks
4 nor herds feed before that mount. ¶ And he hewed two tables
of stone like unto the first; and Moses rose up early in the
morning, and went up unto mount Sinai, as the LORD had com-
5 manded him, and took in his hand the two tables of stone. And
the LORD descended in the cloud, and stood with him there, and
6 [e] proclaimed the name of the LORD. And the LORD passed by
before him, and proclaimed, The LORD, The LORD [f] God, merciful

[f] Num. 14. 14.
[g] ch. 34. 10. Deut. 4. 7. 2 Sam. 7. 23. 1 Kin. 8. 53.
[h] Gen. 19. 21. Jam. 5. 16.
[i] ver. 12.
[k] ver. 20. 1 Tim. 6. 16.
[l] ch. 34. 5. Jer. 31. 14.
[m] Rom. 9. 15, 16, 18.
[n] Rom. 4. 4, 16.
[o] Gen. 32. 30. Deut. 5. 24. Rev. 1. 16.
[p] Isai. 2. 21.
[q] Ps. 91. 1, 4.
[r] ver. 20. John 1. 18.
[a] Deut. 10. 1.
[b] Deut. 10. 2.
[c] ch. 19. 20. & 24. 12.
[d] ch. 19. 12.
[e] ch. 33. 19. Num. 14. 17.
[f] Num. 14. 18. 2 Chr. 30. 9. Neh. 9. 17. Ps. 86. 15. & 103. 8.

---

rated") them from other nations, and which alone would render the Land of Promise a home to be desired. Cp. 2 Sam. vii. 23.

17. Cp. *v.* 13. His petition for the nation, and his own claims as a mediator, are now granted to the full.

18. *shew me thy glory*] The faithful servant of Jehovah, now assured by the success of his mediation, yearns, with the proper tendency of a devout spirit, for a more intimate communion with his Divine Master than he had yet enjoyed. He seeks for something surpassing all former revelations.

19, 20. But his request could not be granted in accordance with the conditions of human existence. The glory of the Almighty in its fulness is not to be revealed to the eye of man. Cp. Judg. vi. 22; Isai. vi. 5. A further revelation of the Divine goodness was however possible (see *vv.* 6, 7).

It was vouchsafed to St. Paul, as it had been to Moses, to have special "visions and revelations of the Lord" (2 Cor. xii. 1–4). But he had, also like Moses, to find the narrow reach of the intellect of man in the region of Godhead (1 Tim. vi. 16). However intimate may be our communion with the Holy One, we are still, as long as we are in the flesh, "to see through a glass darkly," waiting for the time when we shall see, with no figure of speech, "face to face" (1 Cor. xiii. 12). Then we know "that we shall be like Him, for we shall see Him as He is" (1 John iii. 2).

19. *will be gracious*, &c.] Jehovah declares His own will to be the ground of the grace which He is going to shew the nation. St. Paul applies these words to the election of Jacob in order to overthrow the self-righteous boasting of the Jews (Rom. ix. 15).

20. Such passages as this, being clearly in accordance with what we know of the relation of spiritual existence to the human senses, shew how we are to interpret the expressions "face to face" (*v.* 11; Deut. xxxiv. 10), "mouth to mouth" (Num. xii. 8), and others of the like kind. See xxiv. 10; Isa. vi. 1; and cp. John xiv. 9.

XXXIV. **1.** *Hew thee*] The former tables are called "the work of God;" cp. xxxii. 16.

the words] See *v.* 28.

6, 7. This was the second revelation of the name of the God of Israel to Moses. The first revelation was of Jehovah as the self-existent One, Who purposed to deliver His people with a mighty hand (iii. 14); this was of the same Jehovah as a loving Saviour Who was now forgiving their sins. The two ideas that mark these revelations are found combined, apart from their historical development, in the Second Com-

and gracious, longsuffering, and abundant in [g]goodness and
7 [h]truth, [i]keeping mercy for thousands, [k]forgiving iniquity and
transgression and sin, and [l]that will by no means clear *the*
guilty; visiting the iniquity of the fathers upon the children,
and upon the children's children, unto the third and to the fourth
8 *generation.* And Moses made haste, and [m]bowed his head toward
9 the earth, and worshipped. And he said, If now I have found
grace in thy sight, O Lord, [n]let my Lord, I pray thee, go
among us; for [o]it *is* a stiffnecked people; and pardon our iniquity
10 and our sin, and take us for [p]thine inheritance. ¶ And he said,
Behold, [q]I make a covenant: before all thy people I will [r]do
marvels, such as have not been done in all the earth, nor in any
nation: and all the people among which thou *art* shall see the
work of the LORD: for it *is* [s]a terrible thing that I will do with
11 thee. [t]Observe thou that which I command thee this day: behold, [u]I drive out before thee the Amorite, and the Canaanite,
and the Hittite, and the Perizzite, and the Hivite, and the
12 Jebusite. [x]Take heed to thyself, lest thou make a covenant
with the inhabitants of the land whither thou goest, lest it be
13 for [y]a snare in the midst of thee: but ye shall [z]destroy their
14 altars, break their [1]images, and [a]cut down their groves: for
thou shalt worship [b]no other god: for the LORD, whose [c]name
15 *is* Jealous, *is* a [d]jealous God: [e]lest thou make a covenant with
the inhabitants of the land, and they [f]go a whoring after their
gods, and do sacrifice unto their gods, and *one* [g]call thee, and
16 thou [h]eat of his sacrifice; and thou take of [i]their daughters unto

[g] Rom. 2. 4.
[h] Ps. 57. 10.
[i] ch. 20. 6.
[k] Ps. 103. 3. Dan. 9. 9. Eph. 4. 32. 1 John 1. 9.
[l] Josh. 24. 19. Nah. 1. 3.
[m] ch. 4. 31.
[n] ch. 33. 15.
[o] ch. 33. 3.
[p] Deut. 32. 9.
[q] Deut. 5. 2. & 29. 12, 14.
[r] Deut. 4. 32. Ps. 77. 14.
[s] Ps. 145. 6. Isai. 64. 3.
[t] Deut. 5. 32.
[u] ch. 33. 2.
[x] Deut. 7. 2.
[y] ch. 23. 33.
[z] Judg. 2. 2.
[a] Deut. 7. 5.
[b] ch. 20. 3, 5.
[c] So Isai. 9. 6. & 57. 15.
[d] ch. 20. 5.
[e] ver. 12.
[f] Judg. 2. 17. Jer. 3. 9. Ezek. 6. 9.
[g] 1 Cor. 10. 27.
[h] Ps. 106. 28. 1 Cor. 8. 4.
[i] Deut. 7. 3. Ezra 9. 2.

[1] Heb. *statues.*

mandment, where the Divine unity is shewn on its practical side, in its relation to human obligations (cp. *v.* 14; xx. 4). Both in the Commandment and in this passage, the Divine Love is associated with the Divine Justice; but in the former there is a transposition to serve the proper purpose of the Commandments, and the Justice stands before the Love. This is strictly the legal arrangement, brought out in the completed system of the ceremonial Law, in which the Sin-offering, in acknowledgment of the sentence of Justice against sin, was offered before the Burnt-offering and the Peace-offering. But in this place the truth appears in its essential order; the retributive Justice of Jehovah is subordinated to, rather it is made a part of, His forgiving LOVE (see xxxii. 14 note). The visitation of God, whatever form it may wear, is in all ages the working out purposes of Love towards His children. The diverse aspects of the Divine nature, to separate which is the tendency of the unregenerate mind of man and of all heathenism, are united in perfect harmony in the Lord Jehovah, of Whom the saying is true in all its length and breadth, "God is love" (1 Joh. iv. 8). It was the sense of this, in the degree to which it was now revealed to him, that caused Moses to bow his head and worship (*v.* 8). But the perfect revelation of the harmony was reserved for the fulness of time when "the Lamb slain from the foundation of the world" (Rev. xiii. 8) was made known to us in the flesh as both our Saviour and our Judge.

9. This yearning struggle after assurance is like the often-repeated utterance of the heart, when it receives a blessing beyond its hopes, "can this be real?"

10. *marvels*] Explained in the following verse. Cp. 2 Sam. vii. 23; Ps. lxxvii. 14.

12–27. The precepts contained in these verses are, for the most part, identical in substance with some of those which follow the Ten Commandments and are recorded in "the Book of the Covenant" (xx.–xxiii.; see xxiv. 7).

13. *cut down their groves*] This is the first reference to what is commonly known as grove-worship. The original word for *grove* in this connection (*ashērāh*) is different from that so rendered in Gen. xxi. 33. Our translators supposed that what the Law commands is the destruction of groves dedicated to the worship of false deities (Judg. vi. 25; 2 Kings xviii. 4); but inasmuch as the worship of *ashērāh* is found associated with that of Astarte, or *Ashtoreth* (Judg. ii. 13, x. 6; 1 S. vii. 4), it seems probable that while Astarte was the personal name of the goddess, the *ashērāh* was a symbol of her, probably in some one of her characters, wrought in wood in some conventional form.

15, 16. An expansion of *v.* 12. The unfaithfulness of the nation to its Covenant with Jehovah is here for the first time spoken of as a breach of the marriage

thy sons, and their daughters [k]go a whoring after their gods,
17 and make thy sons go a whoring after their gods. [l]Thou shalt
18 make thee no molten gods. ¶ The feast of [m]unleavened bread
shalt thou keep. Seven days thou shalt eat unleavened bread,
as I commanded thee, in the time of the month Abib: for in the
19 [n]month Abib thou camest out from Egypt. ¶ [o]All that openeth
the matrix *is* mine; and every firstling among thy cattle, *whether*
20 ox or sheep, *that is male*. But [p]the firstling of an ass thou
shalt redeem with a [1]lamb: and if thou redeem *him* not, then
shalt thou break his neck. All the firstborn of thy sons thou
21 shalt redeem. And none shall appear before me [q]empty. ¶ [r]Six
days thou shalt work, but on the seventh day thou shalt rest:
22 in earing time and in harvest thou shalt rest. ¶ [s]And thou shalt
observe the feast of weeks, of the firstfruits of wheat harvest,
23 and the feast of ingathering at the [2]year's end. [t]Thrice in
the year shall all your menchildren appear before the Lord GOD,
24 the God of Israel. For I will [u]cast out the nations before thee,
and [x]enlarge thy borders: [y]neither shall any man desire thy
land, when thou shalt go up to appear before the LORD thy God
25 thrice in the year. ¶ [z]Thou shalt not offer the blood of my
sacrifice with leaven; [a]neither shall the sacrifice of the feast of
26 the passover be left unto the morning. ¶ [b]The first of the firstfruits of thy land thou shalt bring unto the house of the LORD
thy God. ¶ [c]Thou shalt not seethe a kid in his mother's milk.
27 ¶ And the LORD said unto Moses, Write thou [d]these words:
for after the tenor of these words I have made a covenant with
28 thee and with Israel. [e]And he was there with the LORD forty
days and forty nights; he did neither eat bread, nor drink water.
And [f]he wrote upon the tables the words of the covenant, the
29 ten [3]commandments. ¶ And it came to pass, when Moses came
down from mount Sinai with the [g]two tables of testimony in
Moses' hand, when he came down from the mount, that Moses
wist not that [h]the skin of his face shone while he talked with
30 him. And when Aaron and all the children of Israel saw Moses,
behold, the skin of his face shone; and they were afraid to come
31 nigh him. And Moses called unto them; and Aaron and all the
rulers of the congregation returned unto him: and Moses talked
32 with them. And afterward all the children of Israel came nigh:
[i]and he gave them in commandment all that the LORD had

[k] Num. 25. 1, 2. 1 Kin. 11. 4.
[l] ch. 32. 8. Lev. 19. 4.
[m] ch. 12. 15.
[n] ch. 13. 4.
[o] ch. 13. 2. Ezek. 44. 30. Luke 2. 23.
[p] ch. 13. 13. Num. 18. 15.
[q] ch. 23. 15. Deut. 16. 16. 1 Sam. 9. 7.
[r] ch. 20. 9.
[s] ch. 23. 16. Deut. 16. 10.
[t] ch. 23. 14. Deut. 16. 16.
[u] ch. 33. 2. Lev. 18. 24. Deut. 7. 1. Ps. 78. 55. & 80. 8.
[x] Deut. 12. 20. & 19. 8.
[y] See Gen. 35. 5. 2 Chr. 17. 10. Prov. 16. 7. Acts 18. 10.
[z] ch. 23. 18.
[a] ch. 12. 10.
[b] ch. 23. 19. Deut. 26. 2, 10.
[c] ch. 23. 19. Deut. 14. 21.
[d] ver. 10. Deut. 4. 13. & 31. 9.
[e] ch. 24. 18. Deut. 9. 9.
[f] ver. 1. ch. 31. 18. Deut. 4. 13.
[g] ch. 32. 15.
[h] 2 Cor. 3. 7.
[i] ch. 24. 3.

[1] Or, *kid*. [2] Heb. *revolution of the year*. [3] Heb. *words*.

---

bond. The metaphor is, in any case, a natural one, but it seems to gain point, if we suppose it to convey an allusion to the abominations connected with heathen worship, such as are spoken of in Num. xxv. 1–3.

21. See xx. 9, xxiii. 12. There is here added to the Commandment a particular caution respecting those times of year when the land calls for most labour.—The old verb *to ear* (*i.e.* to plough) is genuine English.

24. *neither shall any man desire* &c.] Intended to encourage such as might fear the consequences of obeying the Divine Law in attending to their religious duties. Cp. Prov. xvi. 7.

28. *he wrote*] *i.e.* Jehovah wrote (*v.* 1).

29. *the two tables of testimony*] Cp. xxxi. 18.

the skin of his face shone] Cp. Matt. xvii. 2. The brightness of the Eternal Glory, though Moses had witnessed it only in a modified manner (xxxiii. 22, 23), was so reflected in his face, that Aaron and the people were stricken with awe, and feared to approach him until he gave them words of encouragement.

The word translated *shine* is closely connected with a word translated *horn*; and hence the Latin version and others have rendered the verb *to be horned*. From this rendering of the word has arisen the popular representation of Moses with horns on his forehead; *e.g.* in Michael Angelo's statue at Rome.

33 spoken with him in mount Sinai. And *till* Moses had done
34 speaking with them, he put [k]a vail on his face. But [l]when [k] 2 Cor. 3. 13.
Moses went in before the LORD to speak with him, he took the [l] 2 Cor. 3. 16.
vail off, until he came out. And he came out, and spake unto
35 the children of Israel *that* which he was commanded. And the
children of Israel saw the face of Moses, that the skin of Moses'
face shone: and Moses put the vail upon his face again until he
went in to speak with him.

CHAP. 35. AND Moses gathered all the congregation of the children of Israel together, and said unto them, [a]These *are* the [a] ch. 34. 32.
words which the LORD hath commanded, that *ye* should do them.
2 [b]Six days shall work be done, but on the seventh day there shall [b] ch. 20. 9.
be to you [1]an holy day, a sabbath of rest to the LORD: who- & 31. 14, 15. Lev. 23. 3.
3 soever doeth work therein shall be put to death. [c]Ye shall Num. 15.
kindle no fire throughout your habitations upon the sabbath day. 32, &c. Deut. 5. 12.
4 ¶ And Moses spake unto all the congregation of the children of Luke 13. 14.
Israel, saying, [d]This *is* the thing which the LORD commanded, [c] ch. 16. 23.
5 saying, Take ye from among you an offering unto the LORD: [d] ch. 25. 1, 2.
[e]Whosoever *is* of a willing heart, let him bring it, an offering of [e] ch. 25. 2.
6 the LORD; gold, and silver, and brass, and blue, and purple,
7 and scarlet, and fine linen, and goats' *hair*, and rams' skins
8 dyed red, and badgers' skins, and shittim wood, and oil for the
light, [f]and spices for anointing oil, and for the sweet incense, [f] ch. 25. 6.
9 and onyx stones, and stones to be set for the ephod, and for the
10 breastplate. And [g]every wise hearted among you shall come, [g] ch. 31. 6.
11 and make all that the LORD hath commanded; [h]the tabernacle, [h] ch. 26. 1,
his tent, and his covering, his taches, and his boards, his bars, 2, &c.
12 his pillars, and his sockets, [i]the ark, and the staves thereof, *with* [i] ch. 25. 10,
13 the mercy seat, and the vail of the covering, the [k]table, and &c. [k] ch. 25. 23.
14 his staves, and all his vessels, [l]and the shewbread, [m]the candle- [l] ch. 25. 30.
stick also for the light, and his furniture, and his lamps, with Lev. 24. 5, 6.
15 the oil for the light, [n]and the incense altar, and his staves, [o]and [m] ch. 25. 31, &c.
the anointing oil, and [p]the sweet incense, and the hanging [n] ch. 30. 1.
16 for the door at the entering in of the tabernacle, [q]the altar of [o] ch. 30. 23.
burnt offering, with his brasen grate, his staves, and all his [p] ch. 30. 34. [q] ch. 27. 1.
17 vessels, the laver and his foot, [r]the hangings of the court, his [r] ch. 27. 9.
pillars, and their sockets, and the hanging for the door of the
18 court, the pins of the tabernacle, and the pins of the court and

[1] Heb. *holiness*.

33–35. St. Paul refers to this passage as shewing forth the glory of the Law, though it was but a "ministration of condemnation," and was to be done away, in order to enhance the glory of the Gospel, "the ministration of the spirit," which is concealed by no vail from the eyes of believers, and is to last for ever (2 Cor. iii. 7–15).

33. *When* rather than *till* should be supplied. Moses did not wear the vail when he was speaking to the people, but when he was silent. See *v.* 35.

34. *Moses went in*] *i.e.* to the Tent of meeting.

XXXV. The narrative of what relates to the construction of the Sanctuary is now resumed from xxxi. 18.

2. See xxxi. 12.

3. This prohibition is here first distinctly expressed, but it is implied xvi. 23.

11. See xxvi. 1–37. It has been already observed (xxv. 10) that in the instructions for making the Sanctuary, the Ark of the Covenant, as the principal thing belonging to it, is mentioned first; but in the practical order of the work, as it is here arranged, the Tabernacle with its Tent and covering come first.

12. *the covering*] This is not the same as the *covering* of *v.* 11, which denotes the Covering of the Tent (see xxvi. 14): the word is used here for the entrance curtains (see xxvi. 36, xxvii. 16).

18. The word *tabernacle* (*mishkān*) is here used for the full name, **the Tabernacle of the Tent of meeting**. It denotes the entire structure.

s ch. 31. 10. & 39. 1, 41. Num. 4. 5, 6, &c.
t ver. 5, 22, 26, 29. ch. 25. 2. & 36. 2. 1 Chr. 28. 2, 9. & 29. 9. Ezra 7. 27. 2 Cor. 8. 12. & 9. 7.
u 1 Chr. 29. 8.
w ch. 28. 3. & 31. 6. & 36. 1. 2 Kin. 23. 7. Prov. 31. 19, 22, 24.
x 1 Chr. 29. 6. Ezra 2. 68.
y ch. 30. 23.
z ver. 21. 1 Chr. 29. 9.
a ch. 31. 2, &c.
b ch. 31. 6.
c ver. 31. ch. 31. 3, 6. 1 Kin. 7. 14. 2 Chr. 2. 14. Isai. 28. 26.

19 their cords, [s]the cloths of service, to do service in the holy *place*,
the holy garments for Aaron the priest, and the garments of his
20 sons, to minister in the priest's office. ¶ And all the congregation of the children of Israel departed from the presence of
21 Moses. And they came, every one [t]whose heart stirred him up,
and every one whom his spirit made willing, *and* they brought
the LORD's offering to the work of the tabernacle of the congregation, and for all his service, and for the holy garments.
22 And they came, both men and women, as many as were willing
hearted, *and* brought bracelets, and earrings, and rings, and
tablets, all jewels of gold: and every man that offered *offered* an
23 offering of gold unto the LORD. And [u]every man, with whom
was found blue, and purple, and scarlet, and fine linen, and
goats' *hair*, and red skins of rams, and badgers' skins, brought
24 *them*. Every one that did offer an offering of silver and brass
brought the LORD's offering: and every man, with whom was
found shittim wood for any work of the service, brought *it*.
25 And all the women that were [w]wise hearted did spin with their
hands, and brought that which they had spun, *both* of blue, and
26 of purple, *and* of scarlet, and of fine linen. And all the women
27 whose heart stirred them up in wisdom spun goats' *hair*. And
[x]the rulers brought onyx stones, and stones to be set, for the
28 ephod, and for the breastplate; and [y]spice, and oil for the light,
29 and for the anointing oil, and for the sweet incense. The
children of Israel brought a [z]willing offering unto the LORD,
every man and woman, whose heart made them willing to bring
for all manner of work, which the LORD had commanded to be
30 made by the hand of Moses. ¶ And Moses said unto the children
of Israel, See, [a]the LORD hath called by name Bezaleel the son
31 of Uri, the son of Hur, of the tribe of Judah; and he hath filled
him with the spirit of God, in wisdom, in understanding, and in
32 knowledge, and in all manner of workmanship; and to devise
33 curious works, to work in gold, and in silver, and in brass, and
in the cutting of stones, to set *them*, and in carving of wood, to
34 make any manner of cunning work. And he hath put in his
heart that he may teach, *both* he, and [b]Aholiab, the son of
35 Ahisamach, of the tribe of Dan. Them hath he [c]filled with
wisdom of heart, to work all manner of work, of the engraver,
and of the cunning workman, and of the embroiderer, in blue,
and in purple, in scarlet, and in fine linen, and of the weaver,

---

19. *the cloths of service to do service in the holy place*] Rather;—**the garments of office to do service in the Sanctuary,** &c. See xxxi. 10.

22. *bracelets*] Rather, **brooches.**

earrings] The Hebrew word signifies a ring, either for the nose (see Gen. xxiv. 22) or for the ear (xxxii. 2; Gen. xxxv. 4). That ear-rings, not nose-rings, are here meant is confirmed by what we know of early Hebrew and Egyptian customs.

rings] **Signet rings.**

tablets] More probably, **armlets.** It is most likely that all the articles mentioned in this verse were of gold. The indulgence of private luxury was thus given up for the honour of the LORD. Cp. xxx. 18 note.

27. The precious stones (xxviii. 9) and spices were contributed by the rulers, who were more wealthy than the other Israelites.

32–33. *curious works, cunning work*] **Works of skill.** Cp. xxx. 4.

35. *the engraver*] **The artificer,** lit. *one who cuts:* a general name for the workman, to which was added the name of the material in which he worked; thus the artificer in wood, or carpenter; the artificer in iron, or smith, &c. *Vv.* 32, 33 and xxxi. 4, 5 enumerate the branches of work committed to Bezaleel. What was under the charge of Aholiab is here for the first time clearly distinguished into the work of **the skilled weaver,** that of the embroiderer, and that of the weaver.

the cunning workman] **The skilled weaver,** literally, *the reckoner.* He might have been so called because he had nicely to count and

even of them that do any work, and of those that devise
cunning work.
Chap. 36. THEN wrought Bezaleel and Aholiab, and every [a]wise [a] ch. 28. 3. & 31. 6.
hearted man, in whom the LORD put wisdom and understand- & 35. 10, 35.
ing to know how to work all manner of work for the service of
the [b]sanctuary, according to all that the LORD had commanded. [b] ch. 25. 8.
2 ¶ And Moses called Bezaleel and Aholiab, and every wise
hearted man, in whose heart the LORD had put wisdom, *even*
every one [c]whose heart stirred him up to come unto the work to [c] ch. 35. 21, 26.
3 do it: and they received of Moses all the offering, which the 1 Chr. 29. 5.
children of Israel [d]had brought for the work of the service of [d] ch. 35. 27.
the sanctuary, to make it *withal*. And they brought yet unto
4 him free offerings every morning. And all the wise men, that
wrought all the work of the sanctuary, came every man from
5 his work which they made; and they spake unto Moses, saying,
[e]The people bring much more than enough for the service of the [e] 2 Cor. 8. 2, 3.
6 work, which the LORD commanded to make. And Moses gave
commandment, and they caused it to be proclaimed throughout
the camp, saying, Let neither man nor woman make any more
work for the offering of the sanctuary. So the people were
7 restrained from bringing. For the stuff they had was sufficient
8 for all the work to make it, and too much. ¶ [f]And every wise [f] ch. 26. 1.
hearted man among them that wrought the work of the taber-
nacle made ten curtains *of* fine twined linen, and blue, and
purple, and scarlet: *with* cherubims of cunning work made he
9 them. The length of one curtain *was* twenty and eight cubits,
and the breadth of one curtain four cubits: the curtains *were* all
10 of one size. And he coupled the five curtains one unto another:
11 and *the other* five curtains he coupled one unto another. And
he made loops of blue on the edge of one curtain from the
selvedge in the coupling: likewise he made in the uttermost
12 side of *another* curtain, in the coupling of the second. [g]Fifty [g] ch. 26. 5.
loops made he in one curtain, and fifty loops made he in the edge
of the curtain which *was* in the coupling of the second: the
13 loops held one *curtain* to another. And he made fifty taches of
gold, and coupled the curtains one unto another with the taches:
14 so it became one tabernacle. ¶ [h]And he made curtains *of* goats' [h] ch. 26. 7.
hair for the tent over the tabernacle: eleven curtains he made
15 them. The length of one curtain *was* thirty cubits, and four
cubits *was* the breadth of one curtain: the eleven curtains *were*
16 of one size. And he coupled five curtains by themselves, and
17 six curtains by themselves. And he made fifty loops upon the
uttermost edge of the curtain in the coupling, and fifty loops
made he upon the edge of the curtain which coupleth the second.
18 And he made fifty taches *of* brass to couple the tent together,
19 that it might be one. ¶ [i]And he made a covering for the tent [i] ch. 26. 14.
of rams' skins dyed red, and a covering *of* badgers' skins above

---

calculate the threads in weaving figures after the manner of tapestry or carpet. His work was chiefly used in the curtains and vail of the Tabernacle, in the Ephod and the Breastplate (xxvi. 1, 31, xxviii. 6, 15, &c.).

the embroiderer] He worked with a needle, either shaping his design in stitches of coloured thread, or in pieces of coloured cloth sewn upon the groundwork. His work was employed in the **entrance curtains** of the Tent and the court, and in the girdle of the High-priest (xxvi. 36, xxvii. 16, xxviii. 39).

the weaver] He appears to have worked in the loom in the ordinary way with materials of only a single colour. The tissues made by him were used for the Robe of the Ephod and its binding, and for the coats of the priests (xxviii. 32, xxxix. 22, 27).

These three classes of workers were men, while the spinners and dyers were women (*v.* 25).

XXXVI. See notes to ch. xxvi.

[k] ch. 26. 15. 20 *that.* ¶ [k]And he made boards for the tabernacle *of* shittim wood,
21 standing up. The length of a board *was* ten cubits, and the
22 breath of a board one cubit and a half. One board had two
tenons, equally distant one from another: thus did he make
23 for all the boards of the tabernacle. And he made boards for
the tabernacle; twenty boards for the south side southward;
24 and forty sockets of silver he made under the twenty boards:
two sockets under one board for his two tenons, and two
25 sockets under another board for his two tenons. And for the
other side of the tabernacle, *which is* toward the north corner,
26 he made twenty boards, and their forty sockets of silver; two
sockets under one board, and two sockets under another board.
27 And for the sides of the tabernacle westward he made six
28 boards. And two boards made he for the corners of the taber-
29 nacle in the two sides. And they were [1]coupled beneath, and
coupled together at the head thereof, to one ring: thus he did
30 to both of them in both the corners. And there were eight
boards; and their sockets *were* sixteen sockets of silver, [2]under
[l] ch. 26. 26. 31 every board two sockets. ¶ And he made [l]bars of shittim wood;
32 five for the boards of the one side of the tabernacle, and five
bars for the boards of the other side of the tabernacle, and five
bars for the boards of the tabernacle for the sides westward.
33 And he made the middle bar to shoot through the boards from
34 the one end to the other. And he overlaid the boards with gold,
and made their rings *of* gold *to be* places for the bars, and over-
[m] ch. 26. 31. 35 laid the bars with gold. ¶ And he made [m]a vail *of* blue, and
purple, and scarlet, and fine twined linen: *with* cherubims made
36 he it of cunning work. And he made thereunto four pillars *of*
shittim *wood*, and overlaid them with gold: their hooks *were of*
37 gold; and he cast for them four sockets of silver. ¶ And he
[n] ch. 26. 36. made an [n]hanging for the tabernacle door *of* blue, and purple,
38 and scarlet, and fine twined linen, [3]of needlework; and the five
pillars of it with their hooks: and he overlaid their chapiters and
their fillets with gold: but their five sockets *were of* brass.

[a] ch. 25. 10. **Chap. 37.** AND Bezaleel made [a]the ark *of* shittim wood: two cubits
and a half *was* the length of it, and a cubit and a half the
2 breadth of it, and a cubit and a half the height of it: and he
overlaid it with pure gold within and without, and made a
3 crown of gold to it round about. And he cast for it four rings
of gold, *to be set* by the four corners of it; even two rings upon
4 the one side of it, and two rings upon the other side of it. And
he made staves *of* shittim wood, and overlaid them with gold.
5 And he put the staves into the rings by the sides of the ark, to
[b] ch. 25. 17. 6 bear the ark. ¶ And he made the [b]mercy seat *of* pure gold: two
cubits and a half *was* the length thereof, and one cubit and a half
7 the breadth thereof. And he made two cherubims *of* gold,
beaten out of one piece made he them, on the two ends of the
8 mercy seat; one cherub [4]on the end on this side, and another
cherub [5]on the *other* end on that side: out of the mercy seat
9 made he the cherubims on the two ends thereof. And the cherubims spread out *their* wings on high, *and* covered with their
wings over the mercy seat, with their faces one to another; *even*
10 to the mercy seatward were the faces of the cherubims. ¶ And

[1] Heb. *twinned.*
[2] Heb. *two sockets, two sockets under one board.*
[3] Heb. *the work of a needleworker,* or, *embroiderer.*
[4] Or, *out of, &c.*
[5] Or, *out of, &c.*

XXXVII. See notes to ch. xxv.

he made [e]the table *of* shittim wood: two cubits *was* the length [e] ch. 25. 23.
thereof, and a cubit the breadth thereof, and a cubit and a half
11 the height thereof: and he overlaid it with pure gold, and made
12 thereunto a crown of gold round about. Also he made thereunto
a border of an handbreadth round about; and made a crown of
13 gold for the border thereof round about. And he cast for it four
rings of gold, and put the rings upon the four corners that *were*
14 in the four feet thereof. Over against the border were the rings,
15 the places for the staves to bear the table. And he made the
staves *of* shittim wood, and overlaid them with gold, to bear the
16 table. And he made the vessels which *were* upon the table, his
[d]dishes, and his spoons, and his bowls, and his covers [1]to cover [d] ch. 25. 29.
17 withal, *of* pure gold. ¶ And he made the [e]candlestick *of* pure [e] ch. 25. 31.
gold: *of* beaten work made he the candlestick; his shaft, and
his branch, his bowls, his knops, and his flowers, were of the
18 same: and six branches going out of the sides thereof; three
branches of the candlestick out of the one side thereof, and three
19 branches of the candlestick out of the other side thereof: three
bowls made after the fashion of almonds in one branch, a knop
and a flower; and three bowls made like almonds in another
branch, a knop and a flower: so throughout the six branches
20 going out of the candlestick. And in the candlestick *were* four
21 bowls made like almonds, his knops, and his flowers: and a
knop under two branches of the same, and a knop under two
branches of the same, and a knop under two branches of the
22 same, according to the six branches going out of it. Their knops
and their branches were of the same: all of it *was* one beaten
23 work *of* pure gold. And he made his seven lamps, and his
24 snuffers, and his snuffdishes, *of* pure gold. *Of* a talent of pure
25 gold made he it, and all the vessels thereof. ¶ [f]And he made [f] ch. 30. 1.
the incense altar *of* shittim wood: the length of it *was* a cubit,
and the breadth of it a cubit; *it was* foursquare; and two
cubits *was* the height of it; the horns thereof were of the same.
26 And he overlaid it with pure gold, *both* the top of it, and the
sides thereof round about, and the horns of it: also he made
27 unto it a crown of gold round about. And he made two rings of
gold for it under the crown thereof, by the two corners of it,
upon the two sides thereof, to be places for the staves to bear it
28 withal. And he made the staves *of* shittim wood, and overlaid
29 them with gold. ¶ And he made [g]the holy anointing oil, and [g] ch. 30. 23,
the pure incense of sweet spices, according to the work of the 34.
apothecary.

Chap. 38. AND [a]he made the altar of burnt offering *of* shittim [a] ch. 27. 1.
wood: five cubits *was* the length thereof, and five cubits the
breadth thereof; *it was* foursquare; and three cubits the height
2 thereof. And he made the horns thereof on the four corners
of it; the horns thereof were of the same: and he overlaid it
3 with brass. And he made all the vessels of the altar, the pots,
and the shovels, and the basons, *and* the fleshhooks, and the
4 firepans: all the vessels thereof made he *of* brass. And he made
for the altar a brasen grate of network under the compass there-
5 of beneath unto the midst of it. And he cast four rings for the
6 four ends of the grate of brass, *to be* places for the staves. And
he made the staves *of* shittim wood, and overlaid them with brass.

[1] Or, *to pour out withal.*

XXXVIII. 1-7: 9-20. See notes to ch. xxvii.

7 And he put the staves into the rings on the sides of the altar, to
8 bear it withal; he made the altar hollow with boards. ¶ And he
made [b]the laver *of* brass, and the foot of it *of* brass, of the [1]look-
ingglasses of *the women* [2]assembling, which assembled *at* the
9 door of the tabernacle of the congregation. ¶ And he made [c]the
court: on the south side southward the hangings of the court
10 *were of* fine twined linen, an hundred cubits: their pillars *were*
twenty, and their brasen sockets twenty; the hooks of the pillars
11 and their fillets *were of* silver. And for the north side *the hangings were* an hundred cubits, their pillars *were* twenty, and their
sockets of brass twenty; the hooks of the pillars and their fillets
12 *of* silver. And for the west side *were* hangings of fifty cubits,
their pillars ten, and their sockets ten; the hooks of the pillars
13 and their fillets *of* silver. And for the east side eastward fifty
14 cubits. The hangings of the one side *of the gate were* fifteen
15 cubits; their pillars three, and their sockets three. And for the
other side of the court gate, on this hand and that hand, *were*
hangings of fifteen cubits; their pillars three, and their sockets
16 three. All the hangings of the court round about *were* of fine
17 twined linen. And the sockets for the pillars *were of* brass; the
hooks of the pillars and their fillets *of* silver; and the overlaying
of their chapiters *of* silver; and all the pillars of the court *were*
18 filleted with silver. And the hanging for the gate of the court
was needlework, *of* blue, and purple, and scarlet, and fine twined
linen: and twenty cubits *was* the length, and the height in the
breadth *was* five cubits, answerable to the hangings of the court.
19 And their pillars *were* four, and their sockets *of* brass four; their
hooks *of* silver, and the overlaying of their chapiters and their
20 fillets *of* silver. And all the [d]pins of the tabernacle, and of the
21 court round about, *were of* brass. ¶ This is the sum of the
tabernacle, *even* of [e]the tabernacle of testimony, as it was counted,
according to the commandment of Moses, *for* the service of the
22 Levites, [f]by the hand of Ithamar, son to Aaron the priest. And
[g]Bezaleel the son of Uri, the son of Hur, of the tribe of Judah,
23 made all that the LORD commanded Moses. And with him *was*
Aholiab, son of Ahisamach, of the tribe of Dan, an engraver,
and a cunning workman, and an embroiderer in blue, and in
24 purple, and in scarlet, and fine linen. ¶ All the gold that was
occupied for the work in all the work of the holy *place*, even the
gold of the offering, was twenty and nine talents, and seven
hundred and thirty shekels, after [h]the shekel of the sanctuary.

[b] ch. 30. 18.
[c] ch. 27. 9.
[d] ch. 27. 19.
[e] Num. 1. 50. 53. & 9. 15. & 10. 11. & 17. 7, 8. & 18. 2. 2 Chr. 24. 6. Acts 7. 44.
[f] Num. 4. 28, 33.
[g] ch. 31. 2, 6.
[h] ch. 30. 13, 24. Lev. 5. 15. & 27. 3, 25. Num. 3. 47. & 18. 16.

[1] Or, *brasen glasses.*

[2] Heb. *assembling by troops*, as 1 Sam. 2. 22.

8. See marg. ref. The women who assembled **at the entrance of the Tent of meeting** were most probably devout women who loved the public service of religion. The giving up their mirrors for the use of the Sanctuary was a fit sacrifice for such women to make (cp. xxxv. 22 note).

21. *This is the sum*, &c.] "This is the **reckoning** of the Tabernacle, **the Tabernacle of the Testimony as it was reckoned up** according to the *commandment* of Moses, by the service of the Levites, by the hand of Ithamar," &c. The weight of the metals was taken by the Levites, under the direction of Ithamar. The Tabernacle is called the Tabernacle of the Testimony, or the depository of the Testimony, *i.e.* the tables of the Law (xxv. 16).

23. See xxxv. 35 note.

24. *of the holy place*] Rather, **of the Sanctuary**. The gold was employed not only in the Holy Place, but in the Most Holy Place and in the entrance to the Tent (xxxvi. 38).

the gold of the offering] **The gold of the wave offering.**

talents...the shekel of the sanctuary] The Shekel was the common standard of weight and value with the Hebrews: and is probably to be estimated at 220 English grains (just over half an ounce avoirdupois) and its value in silver as 2*s.* 7*d.*—The Shekel of the Sanctuary (or, *the Holy Shekel*) would seem to denote no more than an *exact* Shekel, "after the king's weight" (2 S. xiv. 26),

25 ¶ And the silver of them that were numbered of the congregation *was* an hundred talents, and a thousand seven hundred and
threescore and fifteen shekels, after the shekel of the sanctuary:
26 [i]a bekah for [1]every man, *that is*, half a shekel, after the shekel
of the sanctuary, for every one that went to be numbered, from
twenty years old and upward, for [k]six hundred thousand and
27 three thousand and five hundred and fifty *men*. And of the
hundred talents of silver were cast [l]the sockets of the sanctuary,
and the sockets of the vail; an hundred sockets of the hundred
28 talents, a talent for a socket. And of the thousand seven hundred seventy and five *shekels* he made hooks for the pillars, and
29 overlaid their chapiters, and filleted them. ¶ And the brass
of the offering *was* seventy talents, and two thousand and four
30 hundred shekels. And therewith he made the sockets to the
door of the tabernacle of the congregation, and the brasen altar,
31 and the brasen grate for it, and all the vessels of the altar, and
the sockets of the court round about, and the sockets of the court
gate, and all the pins of the tabernacle, and all the pins of the
court round about.

[i] ch. 30. 13, 15.
[k] Num. 1. 46.
[l] ch. 26. 19, 21, 25, 32.

CHAP. 39. AND of [a]the blue, and purple, and scarlet, they made
[b]cloths of service, to do service in the holy *place*, and made the
holy garments for Aaron; [c]as the LORD commanded Moses.
2 [d]And he made the ephod *of* gold, blue, and purple, and scarlet,
3 and fine twined linen. And they did beat the gold into thin
plates, and cut *it into* wires, to work *it* in the blue, and in the
purple, and in the scarlet, and in the fine linen, *with* cunning
4 work. They made shoulderpieces for it, to couple *it* together:
5 by the two edges was it coupled together. And the curious
girdle of his ephod, that *was* upon it, *was* of the same, according
to the work thereof; *of* gold, blue, and purple, and scarlet, and

[a] ch. 35. 23.
[b] ch. 31. 10. & 35. 19.
[c] ch. 28. 4.
[d] ch. 28. 6.

[1] Heb. *a poll*.

"current money with the merchant" (Gen. xxiii. 16).

In the reign of Joash, a collection similar to that here mentioned, apparently at the same rate of capitation, was made for the repairs of the Temple (2 Chr. xxiv. 9). The tax of later times, called *didrachma* (Matt. xvii. 27), was not, like this and that of Joash, a collection for a special occasion, but a yearly tax, for the support of the Temple, of a whole shekel.—See also xxx. 13.

The Talent contained 3000 shekels, as may be gathered from *vv.* 25, 26. According to the computation here adopted, the Hebrew Talent was 94$\frac{2}{7}$ lbs. avoirdupois. The Greek (Æginetan) Talent, from which the LXX. and most succeeding versions have taken the name *talent*, was 82$\frac{1}{4}$lbs. The original Hebrew word *kikkār* would denote a circular mass, and nearly the same word, *kerker*, was in use amongst the Egyptians for a mass of metal cast in the form of a massive ring with its weight stamped upon it.

26. *a bekah*] Literally, *a half:* the words "half a shekel," &c. appear to be inserted only for emphasis, to enforce the accuracy to be observed in the payment. See xxx. 13.—Respecting the capitation and the numbering of the people, see xxx. 12.

27. *sockets*] **Bases.** See marg. ref.

28. The hooks, chapiters, and fillets here spoken of belonged to the pillars of the Court. See xxvii. 10, 17.

24-29. According to the estimate of the shekel that has here been adopted, the weight of the metals mentioned in this chapter would be nearly as follows, in avoirdupois weight:—

Gold, 1 ton 4 cwt. 2 qrs. 13 lbs.
Silver 4 tons 4 cwt. 2 qrs. 20 lbs.
Bronze, 2 tons 19 cwt. 2 qrs. 11 lbs.

The value of the gold, if pure, in our money would be 175,075*l.* 13*s.*, and of the silver 38,034*l.* 15*s.* 10*d.* These quantities of the precious metals come quite within the limits of probability, if we consider the condition of the Israelites when they left Egypt (see xxv. 3 note), and the object for which the collection was made. Many have remarked that the quantities collected for the Tabernacle are insignificant when compared with the hoards of gold and silver collected in the East in recent, as well as in ancient, times.

XXXIX. See notes to ch. xxviii.

e ch. 28. 9. 6 fine twined linen; as the LORD commanded Moses. ¶ [e]And
they wrought onyx stones inclosed in ouches of gold, graven,
as signets are graven, with the names of the children of Israel.
7 And he put them on the shoulders of the ephod, *that they should*
f ch. 28. 12. *be* stones for a [f]memorial to the children of Israel; as the LORD
g ch. 28. 15. 8 commanded Moses. ¶ [g]And he made the breastplate *of* cunning
work, like the work of the ephod; *of* gold, blue, and purple, and
9 scarlet, and fine twined linen. It was foursquare; they made
the breastplate double: a span *was* the length thereof, and a span
h ch. 28. 17, &c. 10 the breadth thereof, *being* doubled. [h]And they set in it four
rows of stones: *the first* row *was* a [1]sardius, a topaz, and a car-
11 buncle: this *was* the first row. And the second row, an emerald,
12 a sapphire, and a diamond. And the third row, a ligure, an
13 agate, and an amethyst. And the fourth row, a beryl, an onyx, and
a jasper: *they were* inclosed in ouches of gold in their inclosings.
14 And the stones *were* according to the names of the children of
Israel, twelve, according to their names, *like* the engravings of
a signet, every one with his name, according to the twelve tribes.
15 And they made upon the breastplate chains at the ends, *of*
16 wreathen work *of* pure gold. And they made two ouches *of*
gold, and two gold rings; and put the two rings in the two ends
17 of the breastplate. And they put the two wreathen chains of
18 gold in the two rings on the ends of the breastplate. And the
two ends of the two wreathen chains they fastened in the two
ouches, and put them on the shoulderpieces of the ephod, before
19 it. And they made two rings of gold, and put *them* on the two
ends of the breastplate, upon the border of it, which *was* on the
20 side of the ephod inward. And they made two *other* golden rings,
and put them on the two sides of the ephod underneath, toward
the forepart of it, over against the *other* coupling thereof, above
21 the curious girdle of the ephod. And they did bind the breastplate by his rings unto the rings of the ephod with a lace of blue,
that it might be above the curious girdle of the ephod, and that
the breastplate might not be loosed from the ephod; as the LORD
i ch. 28. 31. 22 commanded Moses. ¶ [i]And he made the robe of the ephod *of*
23 woven work, all *of* blue. And *there was* an hole in the midst of
the robe, as the hole of an habergeon, *with* a band round about
24 the hole, that it should not rend. And they made upon the
hems of the robe pomegranates *of* blue, and purple, and scarlet,
k ch. 28. 33. 25 *and* twined *linen*. And they made [k]bells *of* pure gold, and put
the bells between the pomegranates upon the hem of the robe,
26 round about between the pomegranates; a bell and a pomegranate, a bell and a pomegranate, round about the hem of the
l ch. 28. 39, 40. 27 robe to minister *in*; as the LORD commanded Moses. ¶ [l]And
they made coats *of* fine linen *of* woven work for Aaron, and
m ch. 28. 4, 39. Ezek. 44. 18. 28 for his sons, [m]and a mitre *of* fine linen, and goodly bonnets *of*
n ch. 28. 42. 29 fine linen, and [n]linen breeches *of* fine twined linen, [o]and a
o ch. 28. 39. girdle *of* fine twined linen, and blue, and purple, and scarlet,
p ch. 28. 36, 37. 30 *of* needlework; as the LORD commanded Moses. ¶ [p]And they
made the plate of the holy crown *of* pure gold, and wrote upon
it a writing, *like to* the engravings of a signet, HOLINESS TO
31 THE LORD. And they tied unto it a lace of blue, to fasten *it*
on high upon the mitre; as the LORD commanded Moses.
32 ¶ Thus was all the work of the tabernacle of the tent of the con-
q ver. 42. 43. ch. 25. 40. gregation finished: and the children of Israel did [q]according to

[1] Or, *ruby*.

33 all that the LORD commanded Moses, so did they. ¶ And they
brought the tabernacle unto Moses, the tent, and all his furniture, his taches, his boards, his bars, and his pillars, and his
34 sockets, and the covering of rams' skins dyed red, and the cover-
35 ing of badgers' skins, and the vail of the covering, the ark of
36 the testimony, and the staves thereof, and the mercy seat, the
37 table, *and* all the vessels thereof, and the shewbread, the pure
candlestick, *with* the lamps thereof, *even with* the lamps to be set
38 in order, and all the vessels thereof, and the oil for light, and
the golden altar, and the anointing oil, and [1] the sweet incense,
39 and the hanging for the tabernacle door, the brasen altar, and
his grate of brass, his staves, and all his vessels, the laver and
40 his foot, the hangings of the court, his pillars, and his sockets,
and the hanging for the court gate, his cords, and his pins, and
all the vessels of the service of the tabernacle, for the tent of the
41 congregation, the cloths of service to do service in the holy *place*,
and the holy garments for Aaron the priest, and his sons' gar-
42 ments, to minister in the priest's office. According to all that
the LORD commanded Moses, so the children of Israel [r] made all [r] ch. 35. 10.
43 the work. And Moses did look upon all the work, and, behold,
they had done it as the LORD had commanded, even so had they
done it: and Moses [s] blessed them. [s] Lev. 9. 22,
CHAP. 40. AND the LORD spake unto Moses, saying, On the first 23.
2 day of the [a] first month shalt thou set up [b] the tabernacle of the Num. 6. 23. Josh. 22. 6.
3 tent of the congregation. And [c] thou shalt put therein the ark 2 Sam. 6. 18.
4 of the testimony, and cover the ark with the vail. And [d] thou 1 Kin. 8. 14. 2 Chr. 30. 27.
shalt bring in the table, and [e] set in order [2] the things that are to [a] ch. 12. 2.
be set in order upon it; [f] and thou shalt bring in the candlestick, & 13. 4.
5 and light the lamps thereof. [g] And thou shalt set the altar of [b] ver. 17. & ch. 26. 1,
gold for the incense before the ark of the testimony, and put the 30.
6 hanging of the door to the tabernacle. And thou shalt set the [c] ver. 21. ch. 26. 33.
altar of the burnt offering before the door of the tabernacle of Num. 4. 5.
7 the tent of the congregation. And [h] thou shalt set the laver [d] ver. 22. ch. 26. 35.
between the tent of the congregation and the altar, and shalt [e] ver. 23.
8 put water therein. And thou shalt set up the court round about, ch. 25. 30.
9 and hang up the hanging at the court gate. And thou shalt take Lev. 24. 5, 6. [f] ver. 24, 25.
the anointing oil, and [i] anoint the tabernacle, and all that *is* [g] ver. 26.
therein, and shalt hallow it, and all the vessels thereof: and it [h] ver. 30. ch. 30. 18.
10 shall be holy. And thou shalt anoint the altar of the burnt [i] ch. 30. 26.
offering, and all his vessels, and sanctify the altar: and [k] it shall [k] ch. 29. 36,
11 be an altar [3] most holy. And thou shalt anoint the laver and 37.
12 his foot, and sanctify it. [l] And thou shalt bring Aaron and his [l] Lev. 8. 1—
sons unto the door of the tabernacle of the congregation, and 13.
13 wash them with water. And thou shalt put upon Aaron the
holy garments, [m] and anoint him, and sanctify him; that he [m] ch. 28. 41.
14 may minister unto me in the priest's office. And thou shalt
15 bring his sons, and clothe them with coats: and thou shalt

[1] Heb. *the incense of sweet spices.* [2] Heb. *the order thereof.* [3] Heb. *holiness of holinesses.*

XL. **2.** See *v.* 17.

4. The directions given in Lev. xxiv. 5–9 are here presupposed, and must have been issued before this chapter was written.

9–10. *most holy*] In *v.* 9 the Tabernacle and its utensils are said to be rendered *holy* by the anointing; the Altar and its utensils are in *v.* 10 said to be *most holy*. The difference does not express a higher degree of holiness: it is only used as a caution. The position of the Altar exposed it to the chance of being touched by the people when they assembled in the Court, while they were not permitted to enter the Tabernacle. The Tabernacle itself, with all that belonged to it, is called *most holy* in xxx. 29.

anoint them, as thou didst anoint their father, that they may
minister unto me in the priest's office: for their anointing shall
surely be [n] an everlasting priesthood throughout their generations.
16 Thus did Moses: according to all that the LORD commanded
17 him, so did he. ¶ And it came to pass in the first month in the
second year, on the first *day* of the month, *that* the [o] tabernacle
18 was reared up. And Moses reared up the tabernacle, and fastened his sockets, and set up the boards thereof, and put in the
19 bars thereof, and reared up his pillars. And he spread abroad
the tent over the tabernacle, and put the covering of the tent
20 above upon it; as the LORD commanded Moses. And he took
and put [p] the testimony into the ark, and set the staves on the
21 ark, and put the mercy seat above upon the ark: and he brought
the ark into the tabernacle, and [q] set up the vail of the covering,
and covered the ark of the testimony; as the LORD commanded
22 Moses. [r] And he put the table in the tent of the congregation,
upon the side of the tabernacle northward, without the vail.
23 [s] And he set the bread in order upon it before the LORD; as the
24 LORD had commanded Moses. [t] And he put the candlestick in
the tent of the congregation, over against the table, on the side
25 of the tabernacle southward. And [u] he lighted the lamps before
26 the LORD; as the LORD commanded Moses. [x] And he put the
27 golden altar in the tent of the congregation before the vail: [y] and
he burnt sweet incense thereon; as the LORD commanded Moses.
28 [z] And he set up the hanging *at* the door of the tabernacle.
29 [a] And he put the altar of burnt offering *by* the door of the tabernacle of the tent of the congregation, and [b] offered upon it the
burnt offering and the meat offering; as the LORD commanded
30 Moses. [c] And he set the laver between the tent of the congrega-
31 tion and the altar, and put water there, to wash *withal*. And

[n] Num. 25. 13.
[o] ver. 1. Num. 7. 1.
[p] ch. 25. 16.
[q] ch. 26. 33. & 35. 12.
[r] ch. 26. 35.
[s] ver. 4.
[t] ch. 26. 35.
[u] ver. 4. ch. 25. 37.
[x] ver. 5. ch. 30. 6.
[y] ch. 30. 7.
[z] ver. 5. ch. 26. 36.
[a] ver. 6.
[b] ch. 29. 38, &c.
[c] ver. 7. ch. 30. 18.

---

17. *on the first day of the month*] That is, on the first of the month Nisan (xii. 2, xiii. 4), one year, wanting fourteen days, after the departure of the Israelites from Egypt. They had been nearly three months in reaching the foot of Mount Sinai (xix. 1); Moses had spent eighty days on the mountain (xxiv. 18, xxxiv. 28), and some time must be allowed for what is related in chap. xxiv., as well as for the interval between the two periods which Moses spent on the mountain (xxxiii. 1–23). The construction of the Tabernacle and its furniture would thus appear to have occupied something less than half a year.

19. The Tent-cloth was spread over the Tabernacle-cloth, and the covering of skins was put over the Tent-cloth. See xxvi. 1 note.

20. *the testimony*] *i.e.* the Tables of stone with the Ten Commandments engraved on them (xxv. 16, xxxi. 18). Nothing else is said to have been put into the Ark. These were found there by themselves in the time of Solomon (1 K. viii. 9; 2 Chr. v. 10). The Pot of Manna was "laid up before the testimony" (xvi. 34); Aaron's rod was also placed "before the testimony" (Num. xvii. 10); and the Book of the Law was put at "the side of the Ark" (Deut. xxxi. 26). The expression "before the testimony" appears to mean the space immediately in front of the Ark. Most interpreters hold that the Pot of Manna and Aaron's rod were at first placed between the Ark and the Vail, and afterwards within the Ark (Heb. ix. 4). It is very probable that the pot and the rod had been put into the Ark before it was taken by the Philistines, but that they were not sent back with the Ark and the tables. 1 Sam. iv. 11, vi. 11.

23–29. Moses performed these priestly functions (xxviii. 1 note), before the holy things with which they were performed were anointed. The things had been made expressly for the service of Jehovah, by His command, and in this fact lay their essential sanctity, of which the anointing was only the seal and symbol. Aaron and his sons, on similar ground, having had the divine call, took part in the service of the Sanctuary as soon as the work was completed (*v.* 31). But Moses took part with them, and most likely took the lead, until they were consecrated and invested (Lev. viii.) and publicly set apart for the office.

26. *before the vail*] That is, opposite to the Ark, in the middle between the Table of Shewbread on the North and the Candlestick on the South.

Moses and Aaron and his sons washed their hands and their feet
32 thereat: when they went into the tent of the congregation, and
when they came near unto the altar, they washed; [d]as the LORD
33 commanded Moses. [e]And he reared up the court round about the
tabernacle and the altar, and set up the hanging of the court
34 gate. So Moses finished the work. ¶ [f]Then a cloud covered the
tent of the congregation, and the glory of the LORD filled the
35 tabernacle. And Moses [g]was not able to enter into the tent of
the congregation, because the cloud abode thereon, and the
36 glory of the LORD filled the tabernacle. [h]And when the cloud
was taken up from over the tabernacle, the children of Israel
37 [1]went onward in all their journeys: but [i]if the cloud were not
taken up, then they journeyed not till the day that it was taken
38 up. For [k]the cloud of the LORD *was* upon the tabernacle by
day, and fire was on it by night, in the sight of all the house of
Israel, throughout all their journeys.

[d] ch. 30. 19, 20. [e] ver. 8. ch. 27. 9, 16. [f] ch. 29. 43. Lev. 16. 2. Num. 9. 15. 1 Kin. 8. 10, 11. 2 Chr. 5. 13. & 7. 2. Isai. 6. 4. Hag. 2. 7, 9. Rev. 15. 8. [g] Lev. 16. 2. 1 Kin. 8. 11. 2 Chr. 5. 14. [h] Num. 9. 17. & 10. 11. Neh. 9. 19. [i] Num. 9. 19—22. [k] ch. 13. 21. Num. 9. 15.

[1] Heb. *journeyed.*

34, 35. On the distinction between the Tent as the outer shelter and the Tabernacle as the *dwelling-place* of Jehovah, which is very clear in these verses, see xxvi. 1 note. The glory appeared as a light within and as a cloud on the outside.

35. Cp. the entrance of the High-priest into the Holy of Holies on the Day of Atonement, Lev. xvi. 2, 13. For special appearances of this glory in the Tabernacle, see Num. xiv. 10, xvi. 19, 42.

The Tabernacle, after it had accompanied the Israelites in their wanderings in the Wilderness, was most probably first set up in the Holy Land at Gilgal (Josh. iv. 19, v. 10, ix. 6, x. 6, 43). But before the death of Joshua, it was erected at Shiloh (Josh. xviii. 1, xix. 51). Here it remained as the national Sanctuary throughout the time of the Judges (Josh. xviii. 8, xxi. 2, xxii. 19; Judg. xviii. 31, xxi. 19; 1 S. i. 3, iv. 3). But its external construction was at this time somewhat changed, and *doors*, strictly so called, had taken the place of the entrance curtain (1 S. iii. 15): hence it seems to have been sometimes called *the temple* (1 S. i. 9, iii. 3), the name by which the structure of Solomon was afterwards commonly known. After the time of Eli it was removed to Nob in the canton of Benjamin, not far from Jerusalem (1 S. xxi. 1-9). From thence, in the time of David, it was removed to Gibeon (1 Chr. xvi. 39, xxi. 29; 2 Chr. i. 3; 1 K. iii. 4, ix. 2). It was brought from Gibeon to Jerusalem by Solomon (1 K. viii. 4). After this, it disappears from the narrative of Scripture. When the Temple of Solomon was built, "the Tabernacle of the Tent" had entirely performed its work; it had protected the Ark of the Covenant during the migrations of the people until they were settled in the Land, and the promise was fulfilled, that the Lord would choose out a place for Himself in which His name should be preserved and His service should be maintained (Deut. xii. 14, 21, xiv. 24).

In accordance with its dignity as the most sacred object in the Sanctuary, the original Ark of the Covenant constructed by Moses was preserved and transferred from the Tabernacle to the Temple. The Golden Altar, the Candlestick and the Shewbread table were renewed by Solomon. They were subsequently renewed by Zerubbabel, and lastly by the Maccabees (see xxv. 23.) But the Ark was preserved in the Temple until Jerusalem was taken by the forces of Nebuchadnezzar (2 Chr. xxxv. 3; Jer. iii. 16). It was never replaced in the Second Temple. According to a rabbinical tradition, its site was marked by a block of stone.

LEVITICUS.

INTRODUCTION.

1. LEVITICUS, that is, the Levitical Book, is the name by which this portion of the law of Moses has always been called by the Hellenistic Jews and the Christian Church.

Leviticus is closely connected with Exodus at its commencement, and with Numbers at its conclusion; but differs from those books in its general exclusion of historical narrative. The only historical portions are the accounts of the Consecration of the priests, with the deaths of Nadab and Abihu (chs. viii.—x.), and of the punishment of the blasphemer (xxiv. 10—23). A large portion of it is occupied with instructions for the service of the Sanctuary.

2. The authorship of Leviticus is ascribed in the main to Moses.

The book has no pretension to systematic arrangement as a whole, nor does it appear to have been originally written all at one time.[1] There are præ-Mosaic fragments, together with passages probably written by Moses on previous occasions and inserted in the places they now occupy when the Pentateuch was put together; insertions also occur of a later date which were written, or sanctioned, by the Prophets and holy men who, after the Captivity, arranged and edited the Scriptures of the Old Testament.

3. The instructions respecting the offerings for the Altar contained in Leviticus were recorded with a view to the guidance of those who were practically conversant with the service of the Tabernacle. They do not furnish a methodical statement for the information of those who are strangers to the subject. A short sketch of the ritual of the Altar, may therefore well form part of an Introduction to the study of this Book.

The whole sacrificial system of the Hebrew Law was intended for a people already brought into covenant with the living God, and every sacrifice was assumed to have a vital connexion with the spirit of the worshipper. A Hebrew sacrifice, like a Christian Sacrament, possessed the inward and spiritual grace, as well as the outward and visible sign;[2] and may have borne to each man a very different amount of meaning, according to the religious conditions of the mind. One may have come in devout obedience to the voice of the Law, with little more than

[1] The contents of Leviticus may be tabulated as follows:—(*a*) i–vii.; (*b*) viii.; (*c*) ix.; (*d*) x.; (*e*) xi.; (*f*) xii.; (*g*) xiii. xiv.; (*h*) xv.; (*i*) xvi.; (*j*) xvii.; (*k*) xviii. 1–18; (*l*) xviii. 19–30; (*m*) xix.; (*n*) xx.; (*o*) xxi.–xxii. 16; (*p*) xxii. 17–33; (*q*) xxiii.; (*r*) xxiv. 1–9; (*s*) xxiv. 10–23; (*t*) xxv.; (*u*) xxvi.; (*v*) xxvii.

[2] Ps. xl. 6; l. 8–14; Prov. xxi. 3; Is. i. 11–15; Jer. vii. 21–23; Hos. vi. 6; Mic. vi. 7, 8. Cp. 1 Sam. xv. 22; Matt. v. 23, 24.

a vague sense that his offering in some way expressed his own spiritual wants, and that the fact that he was permitted to offer it, was a sacramental pledge of God's good will and favour towards him. But to another, with clearer spiritual insight, the lessons conveyed in the symbols of the Altar must have all converged with more or less distinctness towards the Lamb slain from the foundation of the world,[3] Who was to come in the fulness of times that He might fulfil all righteousness,[4] and realize in the eyes of men the true Sin-offering, Burnt-offering, and Peace-offering.[5]

The general name for what was formally given up to the service of God was *korbān*,[6] which exactly answers to the English words, *offering* and *oblation*. Whatever offerings were brought to be sacrificed on the Altar, may be thus classed:—

Offerings for the Altar.

Animal.[7]	*Vegetable.*
1 Burnt-offerings,	1 Meat and Drink-offerings for the Altar in the Court.
2 Peace-offerings,	2 Incense and Meat-offerings for the Holy Place within the Tabernacle.
3 Sin-offerings.	

The offerings for the Altar were (1) public,[8] and (2) private sacrifices; the mode of conducting which was nearly the same. The first three chapters of Leviticus relate entirely to private voluntary offerings.

The external distinction between the three classes of animal sacrifices may be thus broadly stated:—the Burnt-offering was wholly burnt upon the Altar; the Sin-offering was in part burnt on the Altar, and in part, either given to the priests or burnt outside the camp; and the Peace-offering was shared between the Altar, the priests and the sacrificer. This formal difference is immediately connected with the distinctive meaning of each kind of sacrifice. See pp. 229, 230.

Five animals are named in the Law as suitable for sacrifice, the ox, the sheep, the goat, the dove and the pigeon. It is worthy of notice that these were all offered by Abraham in the great sacrifice of the Covenant.[9]

Three conditions met in the sacrificial quadrupeds; (1) they were clean according to the Law; (2) they were commonly used as food; and, being domesticated, (3) they formed a part of the home wealth of the sacrificers.[1]

Every animal offered in sacrifice was to be perfect, without spot or blemish;[2] and might vary in age between not less than a week and three years.[3]

The man who offered a private sacrifice led with his own hands the victim into the Court of the Sanctuary, and formally presented it to the priest in front of the Tabernacle.[4] The sacrificer then

---

[3] Rev. xiii. 8.

[4] Matt. iii. 15.

[5] 2 Cor. v. 21; Eph. v. 2; Eph. ii. 13, 14; 1 Cor. v. 7; Joh. vi. 54.

[6] Cp. Mark vii. 11. See ii. 12; xxvii. 30; Num. xviii. 12, 26; Num. vii. 3; xxxi. 50.

[7] Besides these three classes there were the peculiar offerings connected with the Paschal Lamb (Ex. xii. 3), the Scape goat (xvi. 10), and the Red Heifer (Num. xix. 2).

[8] Ex. xxix. 38–44; Num. xxviii. xxix.

[9] Gen. xv. 9.

[1] The absence of one or more of these conditions explains the exclusion of many animals, and (among vegetable offerings) of many natural productions.

[2] xxii. 18–25 and reff.

[3] xxii. 27; Ex. xxii. 30; Gen. xv. 9.

[4] See note on i. 3. Cp. i. 4; xvi. 21.

laid, or rather pressed, his hand upon its head, and according to Jewish traditions, always uttered a prayer or confession of some sort while his hand rested on the head of the victim, except in the case of Peace-offerings.

The regular place for slaughtering the animals for Burnt-offerings, Sin-offerings and Trespass-offerings, was the north side of the Altar.[5] Tradition tells us that before the sacrificer laid his hand upon the head of the victim, it was bound by a cord to one of the rings fixed for the purpose on the north side of the Altar, and that at the very instant when the words of the prayer, or confession, were ended, the fatal stroke was given. The Peace-offerings and the Paschal lambs, might, it would seem, be slain in any part of the Court.[6]

The mode of killing appears not to have differed from that of slaughtering animals for food. The throat was cut while a priest or assistant held a bowl under the neck to receive the blood.[7] The sacrificer, or his assistant, then flayed the victim and cut it into pieces,[8] probably while the priest was engaged in disposing of the blood.

In sacrificing the Burnt-offerings, the Peace-offerings and the Trespass-offerings,[9] the priests "sprinkled" or rather cast the blood about, so that the blood should be diffused over the sides of the Altar. In the Sin-offerings, the priest had to take some of the blood with his finger and put it upon the horns of the Altar of Burnt-offering, and to pour out what remained at the bottom of the Altar, if the Sin-offering was for one of the common people, or for a ruler: if the Sin-offering was for the Congregation or for the High-priest, in addition to these two processes, the High-priest himself had to bring a portion of the blood into the Sanctuary, to sprinkle it with his finger seven times before the vail, and to put some of it upon the horns of the Altar of Incense.[1]

The great Altar of the Temple was furnished with two holes at its south-west corner through which the blood ran into a drain which conveyed it to the Cedron. There was probably some arrangement of this kind for taking the blood away from the Altar in the Wilderness.

When the blood was disposed of, the skin removed, and the animal cut into pieces, the sacrificer, or his assistant, washed the entrails and feet. In the case of a Burnt-offering, all the pieces were then taken to the Altar and salted. The priest next piled the pieces on the Altar, the hind limbs being probably put at the base of the pile, then the entrails and other viscera with the fat, then the fore limbs, with the head at the top.

The parts burnt upon the Altar of the Peace-offering, the Sin-offering and the Trespass-offering, were the same in each case; and consisted of the fat, and the kidneys, and the caul above the liver.[2]

The parts of the victims which regularly fell to the priests were:—

Of the Burnt-offerings, only the hide, the whole of the flesh being consigned to the Altar: of the

---

[5] i. 11; vi. 25; vii. 2.
[6] Cp. i. 11 with iii. 2. See i. 5, &c. &c.; Ex. xxxvii. 1; Cp. 2 Chron. xxx. 17.
[7] ix. 9, xvii. 3.
[8] i. 5, 6, &c.
[9] i. 5, 11; iii. 2, 8, 13; vii. 2.

[1] See notes to ch. iv.
[2] ix. 10. See note.

Peace-offerings, the breast and the right shoulder (or leg), which might be eaten by the priests and their families in any unpolluted place. The hide appears to have been retained by the sacrificer : of the Sin-offerings and the Trespass-offerings, the whole of the flesh (except the fat portions burnt on the Altar), and probably the hide. The flesh could only be eaten within the precinct of the Tabernacle. It was distinguished from the "holy" flesh of the Peace-offerings as being "most holy."[3]

Connected with the priests' breast and shoulder is the inquiry as to the two ceremonies called *waving* and *heaving*. The shoulder, which belonged to the officiating priest, was heaved, and the breast, which was for the common stock of the priests in general, was waved before the Lord. Each process appears to have been a solemn form of dedicating a thing to the use of the Sanctuary. The term strictly rendered Heave-offering appears to be used in as wide a sense as *korbān*, for offerings in general.[4] That rendered Wave-offering is not so broadly applied. The Rabbinists say that heaving was a moving up and down, waving a moving to and fro. But, as waving appears to have been the more solemn process of the two, it was probably, in accordance with its derivation,[5] a movement several times repeated, while heaving was simply a lifting up once.

Every Burnt-offering and Peace-offering was accompanied by a Meat-offering (rather Vegetable-offering, see ch. ii. with the notes) and a Drink-offering (Ex. xxix. 43). There is no mention of this in Leviticus. The quantities of flour, oil and wine were proportioned to the importance of the victims.

The whole of the Meat-offerings and Drink-offerings, with the exception of what was burnt, or poured, on the Altar, fell to the lot of the priests. See ii. 3.

The Sin-offering and the Trespass-offering were sacrificed without either Meat-offering or Drink-offering.

4. In the earliest record of sacrifice (Gen. iv. 3—5) the name given in common to the animal and vegetable offerings is *minchāh* (*i. e.* a gift), which the Law afterwards restricted to the vegetable-offerings (ii. 1 note).

The sacrifices of Noah after the flood consisted of Burnt-offerings of clean beasts and birds offered upon an altar.[6]

The Covenant sacrifice of Abraham[7] consisted of one of each of the five animals which the Law afterwards recognized as fit for sacrifice. But the cutting in twain of the four-footed victims appears to mark it as a peculiar rite belonging to a personal covenant, and to distinguish it from the classes of sacrifices ordained by the Law.

Among the different aspects under which the offering up of Isaac (Gen. xxii.) may be viewed, there is perhaps one which most directly connects it with the history

---

[3] vi. 25, 26. ; vii. 6.

[4] Ex. xxv. 2. See also Num. v. 9; Deut. xii. 6, &c.

[5] The Hebrew verb is applied to such actions as using a saw, or other tool, Ex. xx. 25; Josh. viii. 31; Isa. x. 15, xxx. 28, &c. For instances of waving, see xxiii. 11, 17.

[6] Gen. viii. 20, 21. Cp. the language used with that of i. 9, ii. 3, 9, 13, iii. 5, &c.

[7] Gen. xv. 9-17.

of sacrifice.—Abraham had still one great lesson to learn. He did not clearly perceive that Jehovah did not require his gifts. The Law had not yet been given which would have suggested this truth to him by the *single* victim appointed for the Burnt-offering and for the Sin-offering, and by the sparing handful of the Meat-offering. To correct and enlighten him, the Lord "tempted" him to offer up, as a Burnt-offering, his most cherished possession, the centre of his hopes. The offering, had it been completed, would have been an actual gift to Jehovah, not a ceremonial act of worship: it would have been not an outward and visible sign of an inward and spiritual grace, but a stern reality in itself. Isaac was not, as regards his father's purpose, in any proper sense a symbol or representative. Nor is there any hint that would justify us in making the voluntary submission of Isaac a significant part of the transaction. The act of the patriarch in giving up his own flesh and blood was an analogue rather than a type of the sacrifice of the Great High Priest who gave up Himself as a victim. In order to instruct Abraham that the service of the Altar fulfilled its purpose in being the expression of the spiritual condition of the worshipper, the Lord Himself provided a ram which was accepted instead of the beloved son. Abraham had already made the offering of himself in his ready faith and obedience; the acceptable means for expressing this fact was appointed in the "ram caught in a thicket by his horns."

Isaac and Jacob built altars:[8] and the sacrifices offered by Jacob at Mizpah[9] appear to have been strictly Peace-offerings.

Sacrificial worship was familiarly known to the Israelites in Egypt: and the history of Jethro seems to show that it was common to the two great branches of the Semitic stock.[1]

We thus see that if we take the narrative of Scripture for our guide, the most ancient sacrifices were Burnt-offerings: and that the radical idea of sacrifice is to be sought in the Burnt-offering rather than in the Peace-offering, or in the Sin-offering. Assuming that the animal brought to the Altar represented the person of him who offered it, and noting that the flesh was spoken of not as destroyed by burning, but as sent up in the fire like incense towards heaven;[2]—the act of sacrifice intimated that the believer confessed the obligation of surrendering himself, body, soul and spirit, to the Lord of heaven and earth Who had been revealed to him. The truth expressed then in the whole Burnt-offering is the unqualified self-sacrifice of the person.

In the Peace-offerings of the patriarchal age, before the institution of a national priesthood, there is no reason to doubt that, as in the Peace-offerings of the Law, certain portions of the victim were burned upon the altar, and that the remainder of the flesh was eaten by the offerer and those who were associated with him by participation in the spirit of the sacrifice.

In the scriptural records there is no trace either of the Sin-offering, or of any special treatment of the

[8] Gen. xxvi. 25, xxxiii. 20, xxxv. 1, 7.

[9] Gen. xxxi. 54, xlvi. 1.
[1] See Ex. xviii. 12 note.
[2] See i. 9 note.

blood of victims, before the time of Moses. Not that we need imagine a single act of sacrifice to have been performed since the first transgression, without a consciousness of sin in the mind of the worshipper. Earnest devotion to a Holy God in a fallen creature must necessarily include a sense of sin and unworthiness. But the feeling which most prominently found its expression in the Burnt-offerings of Noah (for example), must have been rather, the sense of present deliverance, of thankfulness deeper than words, of complete self-surrender to the solemn bond now laid upon him in the Covenant.

The first instance of the blood of a sacrifice being noticed in any way occurs in the account of the institution of the Passover;[3] the next is in connexion with the Burnt-offerings and Peace-offerings of the Covenant of Sinai.[4]

We are left in no doubt as to the sacrificial meaning of the blood. As the material vehicle of the life of the victim, it was the symbol of the life of the offerer. In contrast with the flesh and bones it expressed in a distinct manner the immaterial principle which survives death. This is distinctly assigned as the reason for its appointed use in the rites of atonement.[5]

The Sin-offering is to be regarded as a creation of the Law. It was the voice of the Law that awakened the distinct consciousness of sin in the individual mind.[6]

In the perfected sacrificial system, the three classes of offerings are to be regarded as representing distinct aspects of divine truth connected with man's relation to Jehovah. But it is important to observe that in no sacrifice was the idea of the Burnt-offering left out.[7]

The natural order of victims in the sacrificial service of the Law was, first the Sin-offering, then the Burnt-offering, and last the Peace-offering. This answers to the spiritual process through which the worshipper had to pass. He had transgressed the Law, and he needed the atonement signified by the Sin-offering: if his offering had been made in truth and sincerity, he could then offer himself to the Lord as an accepted person, as a sweet savour, in the Burnt-offering, and in virtue of this acceptance, he could enjoy communion with the Lord and with his brethren in the Peace-offering.

The main additions made to the ritual of sacrifice by the Levitical Law consisted in the establishment of one national Altar, the institution of the national Priesthood, and all those particulars that were peculiar to the Sin-offerings and the Trespass-offerings. In these particulars, which in spite of prophetic teaching must have been difficult and obscure to the Israelite, we can now clearly trace the forecast shadows of the spotless Saviour Who was to come, to stand for the sinful race as its head, to make the offering of Himself as both priest and victim, to perfect the work of redemption by Himself, and so to enter into the presence of God for us as a sweet savour.[8]

---

[3] Ex. xii. 7, 22. 23.
[4] Ex. xxiv. 4–8. See notes.
[5] See xvii. 11 note.
[6] Rom. iii. 20, vii. 7.
[7] See iii. 5 note; Ex. xxix. 31–42.
[8] Heb. x. 19, 20, 21.

THE THIRD BOOK OF MOSES,

CALLED

LEVITICUS.

Chap. 1. AND the Lord [a]called unto Moses, and spake unto him
2 [b]out of the tabernacle of the congregation, saying, Speak
unto the children of Israel, and say unto them, [c]If any man of
you bring an offering unto the Lord, ye shall bring your offer-
3 ing of the cattle, *even* of the herd, and of the flock. ¶ If his
offering *be* a burnt sacrifice of the herd, let him offer a male
[d]without blemish: he shall offer it of his own voluntary will at
the door of the tabernacle of the congregation before the Lord.
4 [e] And he shall put his hand upon the head of the burnt offering;
and it shall be [f]accepted for him [g]to make atonement for him.
5 And he shall kill the [h]bullock before the Lord: [i]and the priests,
Aaron's sons, shall bring the blood, [k]and sprinkle the blood
round about upon the altar that *is by* the door of the tabernacle

[a] Ex. 19. 3.
[b] Ex. 40. 34.
[c] ch. 22. 18, 19.
[d] Ex. 12. 5. ch. 22. 20.
[e] Ex. 29. 10.
[f] ch. 22. 21.
[g] Num. 15. 25. Rom. 5. 11.
[h] Mic. 6. 6.
[i] 2 Chr. 35. 11. Heb. 10. 11.
[k] ch. 3. 8.

I. 1. *the* Lord] In the Hebrew text of Leviticus, Jehovah is the name by which God is usually called. Where Elohim occurs, it is generally with a possessive pronoun, so as to designate Him as the God of the chosen people (ii. 13; xi. 45; xviii. 21; xix. 12, 14, 32, &c.).

the tabernacle of the congregation] Rather, **the Tent of meeting**. See Ex. xxvii. 21 note. When Jehovah was about to give His people the law of the Ten Commandments (Ex. xix. 3) He called to Moses from the top of Mount Sinai in thunders and lightnings and a thick cloud. When He was now about to give them the laws by which their formal acts of worship were to be regulated, He called to Moses out of the Tabernacle which had just been constructed at the foot of the mountain. (Ex. xxv. 22.)

2. *speak unto the children of Israel*] It is important to observe that these first instructions (i. 2–iii. 17) are addressed expressly to the individual who felt the need of sacrifice on his own account. They were not delivered through the priests, nor had the officiating priest any choice as to what he was to do. He was only to examine the victim to see that it was perfect (xxii. 17-24), and to perform other strictly prescribed duties (vi. 8–vii. 21). The act of offering was to be voluntary on the part of the worshipper, but the mode of doing it was in every point defined by the Law. The presenting of the victim at the entrance of the Tabernacle was in fact a symbol of the free will submitting itself to the Law of the Lord. Such acts of sacrifice are to be distinguished from the public offerings, and those ordained for individuals on special occasions (see iv. 2 note), which belonged to the religious education of the nation.

offering] Heb. *korbān:* the general name for what was formally given up to the service of God (cp. Mark vii. 11), and exactly answering to the words *offering* and *oblation*.

3. *burnt*] Lit. that (offering) which ascends (as a flame).

a male without blemish] Males were required in most offerings, as the stronger sex which takes precedence of the other. But females were allowed in Peace-offerings (iii. 1, 6), and were expressly prescribed in the Sin-offerings of the common people (iv. 28, 32; v. 6).

at the door of the tabernacle of the congregation] Wherever these words occur they should be rendered, **at the entrance of the Tent of meeting.** The place denoted is that part of the court which was in front of the Tabernacle, in which stood the brazen Altar and the laver, and where alone sacrifices could be offered. See Cut to Ex. xxvi.

4. *And he shall put his hand upon the head of the burnt offering*] The usual ceremony. By it the sacrificer identified himself with his victim (iii. 2, 8; iv. 15; viii. 14; Rom. xii. 1).

to make atonement for him] This phrase belongs more especially to the Sin-offerings and the Trespass-offerings (cp. iv. 20, 26, 31, 35; v. 16, 18; vi. 7, &c.) It is not used in reference to the Peace-offerings, and but rarely in reference to the Burnt-offerings. It should be noticed that it is here introduced in close connection with the imposition of hands by the worshipper, not, as it is when it refers to the Sin-offering, with the special functions of the priest, iv. 26, 35; 2 Chr. xxix. 23.

5. *And he shall kill the bullock*] Tradition states that before the laying on of the hand, the victim was bound by a cord to a ring on the north side of the Altar; as the words of the prayer were ended, the throat was cut and the blood received into a bowl held by an assistant.

6 of the congregation. And he shall flay the burnt offering, and
7 cut it into his pieces. And the sons of Aaron the priest shall put
8 fire upon the altar, and [l]lay the wood in order upon the fire: and
the priests, Aaron's sons, shall lay the parts, the head, and the
fat, in order upon the wood that *is* on the fire which *is* upon the
9 altar: but his inwards and his legs shall he wash in water: and
the priest shall burn all on the altar, *to be* a burnt sacrifice, an
10 offering made by fire, of a [m]sweet savour unto the LORD. ¶ And
if his offering *be* of the flocks, *namely*, of the sheep, or of the
goats, for a burnt sacrifice; he shall bring it a male [n]without
11 blemish. [o]And he shall kill it on the side of the altar northward
before the LORD: and the priests, Aaron's sons, shall sprinkle
12 his blood round about upon the altar. And he shall cut it into
his pieces, with his head and his fat: and the priest shall lay
them in order on the wood that *is* on the fire which *is* upon the
13 altar: but he shall wash the inwards and the legs with water:
and the priest shall bring *it* all, and burn *it* upon the altar: it *is*
a burnt sacrifice, an offering made by fire, of a sweet savour unto
14 the LORD. ¶ And if the burnt sacrifice for his offering to the
LORD *be* of fowls, then he shall bring his offering of [p]turtledoves,

[l] Gen. 22. 9.
[m] Gen. 8. 21. Ezek. 20. 28, 41. 2 Cor. 2. 15. Eph. 5. 2. Phil. 4. 18.
[n] ver. 3. Deut. 15. 21. Mal. 1. 14.
[o] ver. 5.
[p] ch. 5. 7. & 12. 8. Luke 2. 24.

---

sprinkle the blood] Rather, **throw the blood,** so as to make the liquid cover a considerable surface. [The Christian significance of this typical action is referred to in Heb. xii. 24; 1 Pet. i. 2.]

by the door of the tabernacle] **At the entrance of the Tent.**

6. *And he shall flay*] The sacrificer, or his assistant, had to skin and cut up the victim. The hide was the perquisite of the officiating priest. (vii. 8.)

his pieces] That is, its proper pieces, the parts into which it was usual for a sacrificed animal to be divided.

7. *put fire upon the altar*] This must specifically refer to the first Burnt-offering on the newly constructed Altar. The rule was afterwards to be, "it shall never go out," (vi. 13.)

8. The parts of the victim were then salted by the priest in conformity with the rule, (ii. 13; Ezek. xliii. 24; Mark ix. 49), and placed "in order" upon the wood, *i.e.* in the same relation to each other that they had in the living animal.

9. The parts which were washed were the stomach, and bowels, and feet, divided from the carcase at the knee-joint.

the priest shall burn] The verb here translated *burn*, is applied exclusively to the burning of the incense, to the lights of the Tabernacle, and to the offerings on the Altar. The primary meaning of its root seems to be *to exhale odour*. (See the margin of xxiv. 2; Ex. xxx. 8). The word for burning in a common way is quite different, and is applied to the burning of those parts of victims which were burned without the camp (iv. 12, 21; Num. xix. 5, &c.). The importance of the distinction is great in its bearing on the meaning of the Burnt-offering. The substance of the victim was regarded not as something to be consumed, but as an offering of a sweet-smelling savour sent up in the flame to Jehovah.

10. *of the flocks*] These directions are more brief than those for the bullock. The Burnt-offering of the sheep must have been that with which the people were most familiar in the daily morning and evening service. Ex. xxix. 38-42. Sheep were preferred for sacrifice when they could be obtained, except in some special Sin-offerings in which goats were required (iv. 23, ix. 3, xvi. 5). The lamb "without blemish" is a well-known type of Christ. Heb. ix. 14; 1 Pet. i. 19.

11. *northward before the* LORD] That is, on the north side of the Altar. See also iv. 24, 29, 33, vii. 2. This was probably an arrangement of some practical convenience. On the west side of the Altar stood the laver; on the east side was the place of ashes (see *v.* 16 note); and the south side, where appears to have been the slope by which the priests went up to the Altar, must have been left clear for thoroughfare.

14. *of turtledoves, or of young pigeons*] The offering of a bird was permitted to one who was too poor to offer a quadruped. (Cp. marg. reff.) But in certain rites of purification birds were appointed for all, whatever might be their circumstances. See xv. 14, 29; Num. vi. 10. The limitation of the age of the pigeons may be accounted for by the natural habits of the birds. It would seem that the species which are most likely to have been the sacrificial dove and pigeon are the common turtle and the blue-rock pigeon, a bird like our stock-dove, and considerably larger than the turtle. The turtles come in the early part of April, but as the season advances they wholly disappear. The pigeons, on the contrary, do not leave the country; and their nests, with

15 or of young pigeons. And the priest shall bring it unto the
altar, and [1]wring off his head, and burn *it* on the altar; and the
16 blood thereof shall be wrung out at the side of the altar: and he
shall pluck away his crop with [2]his feathers, and cast it [q]beside [q] ch. 6. 10.
17 the altar on the east part, by the place of the ashes: and he shall
cleave it with the wings thereof, *but* [r]shall not divide *it* asunder: [r] Gen. 15. 10.
and the priest shall burn it upon the altar, upon the wood that *is*
upon the fire: [s]it *is* a burnt sacrifice, an offering made by fire, [s] ver. 9. 13.
of a sweet savour unto the LORD.

CHAP. 2. AND when any will offer [a]a meat offering unto the LORD, [a] ch. 6. 14.
his offering shall be *of* fine flour; and he shall pour oil upon it, & 9. 17. Num. 15. 4.
2 and put frankincense thereon: and he shall bring it to Aaron's
sons the priests: and he shall take thereout his handful of
the flour thereof, and of the oil thereof, with all the frankincense thereof; and the priest shall burn [b]the memorial of it [b] See note
upon the altar, *to be* an offering made by fire, of a sweet savour and Isai. 66. 3.
3 unto the LORD: and [c]the remnant of the meat offering *shall be* [c] ch. 7. 9.
Aaron's and his sons': [d]*it is* a thing most holy of the offerings of & 10. 12, 13. [d] Ex. 29. 37. Num. 18. 9.

[1] Or, *pinch off the head with the nail.* [2] Or, *the filth thereof.*

---

young ones in them, may be easily found at any season of the year. Hence it would appear, that when turtledoves could not be obtained, nestling pigeons were accepted as a substitute.

16. *his crop with his feathers*] The weight of authority is in favour of the marginal rendering. It is most probable that the feathers were burnt with the body, and that the wings, mentioned in *v.* 17, were not mutilated.

the place of the ashes] The ashes were daily removed from the Altar (except on certain holy days) and thrown into a heap on its eastern side. When the heap became inconveniently large, it was removed in vessels appropriated to the purpose (see Ex. xxvii. 3) to a spot without the camp. (iv. 12, vi. 11.)

II. **1.** *a meat offering*] Better translated in *v.* 4 **an oblation of a meat offering** (*korbān* [see i. 2] *minchah*). Minchah signifies literally *a gift;* and it appears to have been applied specially to what was given by an inferior to a superior (Gen. xxxii. 18–20, xliii. 11; Judg. iii. 15; 1 S. x. 27): but in the technical language of the Law, it regularly denoted the vegetable offerings as distinguished from the animal offerings. Our translators have rendered it *meat-offering,* applying the word *meat,* according to old usage, as a general term for food. Vegetable-offering or Meal-offering would be a more convenient rendering.

The meaning of the Minchah appears to be much more simple than that of the animal sacrifices. The Minchah, as a sacrifice, was something surrendered to God, which was of the greatest value to man as a means of living. It might thus seem to be merely eucharistic. But it should not be overlooked that the grain had been modified, and made useful, by man's own labour. Hence it has been supposed that the Minchah expressed a confession that all our good works are wrought in God and are due to Him.

The order in which the kinds of offering are named agrees with their development in order of time. The Burnt-offering and the Minchah answer to the first two offerings on record (Gen. iv. 3, 4; Amos v. 22).

Three kinds of Minchah are here mentioned; (1) *vv.* 1–3; (2) *vv.* 4–7; (3) *vv.* 14–16. Of each of them a small portion was burnt on the Altar "for a memorial," and the remainder was given to the priests. The offerings of flour belonged to the priests at large, but those of cakes and wafers to the officiating priests, vii. 9, 10.—Instructions to the priests are given in vi. 14–23.

1. *fine flour*] finely bolted flour of wheat. It was probably always presented in a bowl, cp. Num. vii. 13.

oil] For the purpose of anointing and as food; in both senses a symbol of divine grace.

frankincense] See Ex. xxx. 34 note.

2. Better: "And he shall bring it to Aaron's sons, the priests; **and the** (officiating) **priest shall take from it,"** &c.

memorial] The regular name not only for the portion of the Minchah which was burnt on the Altar (*vv.* 9, 16, v. 12, vi. 15; Num. v. 26), but for the frankincense which was laid upon the Shewbread (xxiv. 7). It is the word which is applied to the prayers and alms of Cornelius, Acts x. 4.

3. *a thing most holy*] Literally, *a holy of holies.* All offerings were *holy,* including the portions of the Peace-offerings which were eaten by the laity; but that was *most holy* of which every part was devoted either to the Altar, or to the use of the priests. Such were the Minchahs, the Shewbread, the incense, and the flesh of the Sin- and Trespass-offerings. Cp. the similar distinction between Places (Ex. xxvi. 33). The most

4 the LORD made by fire. ¶ And if thou bring an oblation of a meat
offering baken in the oven, *it shall be* unleavened cakes of fine
flour mingled with oil, or unleavened wafers [e] anointed with oil.
5 And if thy oblation *be* a meat offering *baken* [1] in a pan, it shall be
6 *of* fine flour unleavened, mingled with oil. Thou shalt part it in
7 pieces, and pour oil thereon: it *is* a meat offering. And if thy
oblation *be* a meat offering *baken* in the fryingpan, it shall be
8 made *of* fine flour with oil. And thou shalt bring the meat
offering that is made of these things unto the LORD: and when
it is presented unto the priest, he shall bring it unto the altar.
9 And the priest shall take from the meat offering [f] a memorial
thereof, and shall burn *it* upon the altar: *it is* an [g] offering made
10 by fire, of a sweet savour unto the LORD. And [h] that which is
left of the meat offering *shall be* Aaron's and his sons': *it is* a
11 thing most holy of the offerings of the LORD made by fire. No
meat offering, which ye shall bring unto the LORD, shall be
made with [i] leaven: for ye shall burn no leaven, nor any honey,
12 in any offering of the LORD made by fire. [k] As for the oblation
of the firstfruits, ye shall offer them unto the LORD: but they
13 shall not [2] be burnt on the altar for a sweet savour. And every
oblation of thy meat offering [l] shalt thou season with salt;
neither shalt thou suffer [m] the salt of the covenant of thy God to
be lacking from thy meat offering: [n] with all thine offerings
14 thou shalt offer salt. ¶ And if thou offer a meat offering of thy
firstfruits unto the LORD, [o] thou shalt offer for the meat offering
of thy firstfruits green ears of corn dried by the fire, *even* corn

[e] Ex. 29. 2.
[f] ver. 2.
[g] Ex. 29. 18.
[h] ver. 3.
[i] ch. 6. 17. See Matt. 16. 12. Mark 8. 15. Luke 12. 1. 1 Cor. 5. 8. Gal. 5. 9.
[k] Ex. 22. 29. ch. 23. 10, 11.
[l] Mark 9. 49. Col. 4. 6.
[m] Num. 18. 19.
[n] Ezek. 43. 24.
[o] ch. 23. 10, 14.

[1] Or, *on a flat plate*, or, *slice*.   [2] Heb. *ascend*.

---

holy food was eaten in "the holy place," that is the precinct of the Tabernacle, probably in the priests' lodgings; but the priests' portion of the Peace-offerings might be eaten by the priests and their families in any "clean place" (x. 12-14).

4–10. The four kinds of bread and the three cooking utensils which are mentioned in this section were probably such as were in common use in the daily life of the Israelites; and there appears no reason to doubt that they were such as are still used in the East. The variety of the offerings was most likely permitted to suit the different circumstances of the worshippers.

4. *oven*] This was probably a portable vessel of earthenware; in shape a cone about 3 ft. 6 in. high, and 1 ft. 6 in. in diameter. Similar jars are now used for the same purpose by the Arabs. After the vessel has been thoroughly heated by a fire lighted in the inside, the cakes are placed within it, and the top is covered up until they are sufficiently baked. Meantime the outside of the vessel is turned to account. Dough rolled out very thin is spread over it, and a sort of wafer is produced considerably thinner than a Scotch oat-cake.

5. *a pan*] Rather, as in the margin, **a flat plate**. It was probably of earthenware, like the oven.

6. *part it in pieces*] **Break**, not cut. The Bedouins are in the habit of breaking up their cakes when warm and mixing the fragments with butter when that luxury can be obtained.

7. *fryingpan*] Rather, **pan**, commonly used for boiling. It is possible that the cakes here spoken of were boiled in oil. The "pan" and the "frying pan" (*vv.* 5, 7) may have been the common cooking implements of the poorest of the people.

11, 12. *As for the oblation of the firstfruits*] Rather, **As an oblation of firstfruits.** The words refer to the leaven and honey mentioned in *v.* 11 which might be offered amongst the firstfruits and tithes (Deut. xxvi. 2, 12; cp. 2 Chr. xxxi. 5). Honey, being used to produce fermentation, and leaven (or, a small piece of fermented dough) were excluded because fermentation was an apt symbol of the working of corruption in the human heart.

13. *with all thine offerings thou shalt offer salt*] Not only every Minchah, but every animal offering was to be accompanied by salt. It was the one symbol which was never absent from the Altar of Burnt-offering, showing the imperishableness of the love of Jehovah for His people. In its unalterable nature, it is the contrary of leaven. The Arabs are said to retain in common use the expression, "a covenant of salt;" and the respect they pay to bread and salt in their rites of hospitality is well known.

14. *green ears of corn*] Rather, "**fresh** ears of corn;" that is, corn just ripe, freshly gathered. Parched corn, such as is

15 beaten out of [p]full ears. And [q]thou shalt put oil upon it, and
16 lay frankincense thereon: it *is* a meat offering. And the priest
shall burn [r]the memorial of it, *part* of the beaten corn thereof,
and *part* of the oil thereof, with all the frankincense thereof: *it*
is an offering made by fire unto the LORD.
CHAP. 3. AND if his oblation *be* a [a]sacrifice of peace offering, if he
offer *it* of the herd; whether *it be* a male or female, he shall
2 offer it [b]without blemish before the LORD. And [c]he shall lay
his hand upon the head of his offering, and kill it *at* the door of
the tabernacle of the congregation: and Aaron's sons the priests
3 shall sprinkle the blood upon the altar round about. And he
shall offer of the sacrifice of the peace offering an offering made
by fire unto the LORD; [d]the [1]fat that covereth the inwards, and
4 all the fat that *is* upon the inwards, and the two kidneys, and
the fat that *is* on them, which *is* by the flanks, and the [2]caul
5 above the liver, with the kidneys, it shall he take away. And
Aaron's sons [e]shall burn it on the altar upon the burnt sacrifice,
which *is* upon the wood that *is* on the fire: *it is* an offering made
6 by fire, of a sweet savour unto the LORD. ¶ And if his offering
for a sacrifice of peace offering unto the LORD *be* of the flock;
7 male or female, [f]he shall offer it without blemish. If he offer
a lamb for his offering, then shall he offer it before the LORD.
8 And he shall lay his hand upon the head of his offering, and kill
it before the tabernacle of the congregation: and Aaron's sons
shall sprinkle the blood thereof round about upon the altar.
9 And he shall offer of the sacrifice of the peace offering an offering made by fire unto the LORD; the fat thereof, *and* the whole
rump, it shall he take off hard by the backbone; and the fat
that covereth the inwards, and all the fat that *is* upon the in-
10 wards, and the two kidneys, and the fat that *is* upon them,
which *is* by the flanks, and the caul above the liver, with the
11 kidneys, it shall he take away. And the priest shall burn it
upon the altar: *it is* [g]the food of the offering made by fire unto
12 the LORD. ¶ And if his offering *be* a goat, then [h]he shall offer it
13 before the LORD. And he shall lay his hand upon the head of it,
and kill it before the tabernacle of the congregation: and the
sons of Aaron shall sprinkle the blood thereof upon the altar

[p] 2 Kin. 4. 42.
[q] ver. 1.
[r] ver. 2.
[a] ch. 7. 11, 29. & 22. 21.
[b] ch. 1. 3.
[c] Ex. 29. 10. ch. 1. 4, 5.
[d] Ex. 29. 13, 22. ch. 4. 8, 9.
[e] Ex. 29. 13. ch. 6. 12.
[f] ver. 1, &c.
[g] See ch. 21. 6, 8, 17, 21, 22. & 22. 25. Ezek. 44. 7. Mal. 1. 7, 12.
[h] ver. 1, 7, &c.

[1] Or, *suet.* [2] Or, *midriff over the liver,* and *over the kidneys.*

here spoken of, is a common article of food in Syria and Egypt, and was very generally eaten in ancient times.

beaten out] Not rubbed out by the hands, as described in Luke vi. 1, but bruised or crushed so as to form groats.

III. **1.** The Peace-offering (like the Burnt-offering, i. 3, and the Minchah, ii. 1) is here spoken of as if it was familiarly known before the giving of the Law. "Peace-offering" seems preferable to "thank-offering," which occurs in several places in the margin of our Bible. "Thank-offering" appears to be the right name for a subordinate class of Peace-offering.

2. *kill it at the door,* &c.] See i. 3. Tradition says that the Peace-offerings might be killed in any part of the Court.

3. "The fat that covereth the inwards" refers to the caul or transparent membrane which has upon it a network of fatty tissue: "the fat upon the inwards" refers to the small lumps of suet found upon the intestines of healthy animals.

4. *the caul above the liver*] Probably the membrane covering the upper part of the liver.

5. *upon the burnt sacrifice*] Upon the ashes of the continual Burnt-offering (Ex. xxix. 38), in accordance with vi. 12.

7. *a lamb*] **A sheep.** The word signifies a full-grown sheep, in its prime.

8. See i. 4, 5 notes.

9. *the whole rump*] **The whole fat tail:** *i.e.* the tail of the kind of sheep well known in the East, and often weighing 15lbs. and even as much as 50lbs. when the sheep has been increased by artificial fattening.

11. *burn it*] See i. 9 note.

12. See i. 10 note. Birds were not accepted as Peace-offerings, most probably because they were, by themselves, **insufficient to** make up a sacrificial meal.

14 round about. And he shall offer thereof his offering, *even* an
offering made by fire unto the LORD; the fat that covereth the
15 inwards, and all the fat that *is* upon the inwards, and the two
kidneys, and the fat that *is* upon them, which *is* by the flanks,
and the caul above the liver, with the kidneys, it shall he take
16 away. And the priest shall burn them upon the altar: *it is* the
food of the offering made by fire for a sweet savour: [i]all the fat
17 *is* the LORD'S. *It shall be* a [k]perpetual statute for your generations throughout all your dwellings, that ye eat neither [l]fat
nor [m]blood.

CHAP. 4. AND the LORD spake unto Moses, saying, Speak unto the
2 children of Israel, saying, [a]If a soul shall sin through ignorance
against any of the commandments of the LORD *concerning things*
which ought not to be done, and shall do against any of them:
3 ¶ [b]If the priest that is anointed do sin according to the sin of the
people; then let him bring for his sin, which he hath sinned, [c]a

[i] ch. 7, 23. 1 Sam. 2. 15. 2 Chr. 7. 7.
[k] ch. 6. 18. & pass.
[l] ver. 16. cp. Deut. 32. 14. Neh. 8. 10.
[m] Gen. 9. 4. ch. 7. 23, 26. Deut. 12. 16. 1 Sam. 14. 33. Ezek. 44. 7,
[a] ch. 5. 15, 17. 1 Sam. 14. 27.
[b] ch. 8. 12.
[c] ch. 9. 2.

---

16. Rather, **as food of an offering made by fire for a sweet savour, shall all the fat be for Jehovah.** Our bodily taste and smell furnish figures of the satisfaction with which the LORD accepts the appointed symbols of the true worship of the heart. All that was sent up in the fire of the Altar, including the parts of the Sin-offering (iv. 31), as well as the Burnt-offering (i. 9, &c.), was accepted for "a sweet savour:" but the word *food* may here have a peculiar fitness in its application to the Peace-offering, which served for food also to the priests and the offerer, and so symbolized communion between the LORD, His ministers, and His worshippers.

the fat is the LORD'S] The significance of this appears to consist in the fact that its proper development in the animal is, in general, a mark of perfection.

17. *blood*] See xvii. 11 note.

throughout all your dwellings] The suet was neither to be eaten in sacrificial meals in the Sanctuary, nor in ordinary meals in private houses.

IV. **1, 2.** *And the* LORD *spake...Israel*] This formula is the commencement of a distinct section of the Law.

2. *If a soul shall sin*] The Sin-offering was a new thing, instituted by the Law. The older kinds of sacrifice (ii. 1; iii. 1) when offered by individuals were purely voluntary: no special occasions were prescribed. But it was plainly commanded that he who was conscious that he had committed a sin should bring his Sin-offering. In the abridged rules for Sin-offerings in Numbers xv. 22-31, the kind of sin for which Sin-offerings were accepted is contrasted with that which cut off the perpetrator from among his people (cp. *v.* 22 with *v.* 30). The two classes are distinguished in the language of our Bible as sin through ignorance and presumptuous sin. The distinction is clearly recognized in Ps. xix. 12, 13 and Heb. x. 26, 27. It seems evident that the classification thus indicated refers immediately to the relation of the conscience to God, not to outward practices, nor, immediately, to outward actions. The presumptuous sinner, literally he who sinned "with a high hand," might or might not have committed such a crime as to incur punishment from the civil law: it was enough that he had with deliberate purpose rebelled against God (see Prov. ii. 13–15), and *ipso facto* was "cut off from among his people" and alienated from the divine covenant (see vii. 20; Ex. xxxi. 14; cp. Matt. xii. 31; 1 Joh. v. 16). But the other kind of sin, that for which the Sin-offering was appointed, was of a more complicated nature. It appears to have included the entire range of "sins, negligences and ignorances" for which we are accustomed to ask forgiveness. Sin-offerings were required not only when the conscience accused the offender of having yielded to temptation, but sometimes for what were breaches of the Law committed strictly in ignorance (*vv.* 13, 23, 28, v. 17), and sometimes on account of ceremonial pollution. They are thus to be regarded as protests against everything which is opposed to the holiness and purity of the divine Law. They were, in short, to be offered by the worshipper as a relief to the conscience whenever he felt the need of atonement.

sin through ignorance] **Sin through error;** that is, through straying from the right way. See Ps. cxix. 67; Eccles. v. 6.

3. *the priest that is anointed*] *i.e.* the High-priest. (Cp. viii. 12, xxi. 10; Ex. xxix. 7). On the anointing of the other priests see note on viii. 13.

The graduation of the Sin-offerings is remarkable. It might seem that the distinction addressed itself more pointedly to each individual according to his rank and consequent responsibility (see *v.* 32).

according to the sin of the people] Rather, **to** *bring* **guilt on the people.** The whole nation is concerned in every transgression of its representative.

young bullock without blemish unto the LORD for a sin offering.
4 And he shall bring the bullock [d]unto the door of the tabernacle
of the congregation before the LORD; and shall lay his hand
upon the bullock's head, and kill the bullock before the LORD.
5 And the priest that is anointed [e]shall take of the bullock's blood,
6 and bring it to the tabernacle of the congregation: and the
priest shall dip his finger in the blood, and sprinkle of the blood
seven times before the LORD, before the vail of the sanctuary.
7 And the priest shall [f]put *some* of the blood upon the horns of
the altar of sweet incense before the LORD, which *is* in the tabernacle of the congregation; and shall pour [g]all the blood of the
bullock at the bottom of the altar of the burnt offering, which
8 *is at* the door of the tabernacle of the congregation. And he
shall take off from it all the fat of the bullock for the sin offering; the fat that covereth the inwards, and all the fat that *is*
9 upon the inwards, and the two kidneys, and the fat that *is* upon
them, which *is* by the flanks, and the caul above the liver, with
10 the kidneys, it shall he take away, [h]as it was taken off from the
bullock of the sacrifice of peace offerings: and the priest shall
11 burn them upon the altar of the burnt offering. [i]And the skin
of the bullock, and all his flesh, with his head, and with his legs,
12 and his inwards, and his dung, even the whole bullock shall he
carry forth [1]without the camp unto a clean place, [k]where the
ashes are poured out, and [l]burn him on the wood with fire:
13 [2]where the ashes are poured out shall he be burnt. ¶ And [m]if
the whole congregation of Israel sin through ignorance, [n]and
the thing be hid from the eyes of the assembly, and they have
done *somewhat against* any of the commandments of the LORD
concerning things which should not be done, and are guilty;
14 when the sin, which they have sinned against it, is known, then
the congregation shall offer a young bullock for the sin, and
15 bring him before the tabernacle of the congregation. And the
elders of the congregation [o]shall lay their hands upon the head

[d] ch. 1. 3, 4.
[e] ch. 16. 14. Num. 19. 4.
[f] ch. 8. 15. & 9. 9. & 16. 18.
[g] ch. 5. 9.
[h] ch. 3. 3, 4, 5.
[i] Ex. 29. 14. Num. 19. 5.
[k] ch. 6. 11.
[l] Heb. 13. 11.
[m] Num. 15. 24. Josh. 7. 11.
[n] ch. 5. 2, 3, 4, 17.
[o] ch. 1. 4.

[1] Heb. *to without the camp*. [2] Heb. *at the pouring out of the ashes.*

5. The treatment of the blood was peculiar in the Sin-offerings. In the inferior Sin-offerings it was smeared on the horns of the Altar of Burnt-offering (*vv.* 25, 30, 34), while in this offering for the High-priest, and in that for the nation, the High-priest himself sprinkled the blood seven times within the Tabernacle and smeared it on the horns of the Altar of Incense (*vv.* 6, 7, 17, 18). The different modes of sprinkling appear to have marked successive degrees of consecration in advancing from the Altar of Burnt-offering to the Presence of Jehovah within the vail.

6. *before the vail of the sanctuary*] This is generally understood to mean the floor of the Holy Place in front of the vail.

7. *pour*] All the blood that was left after the sprinkling and the smearing should be disposed of in such a manner as to suit the decorum of divine service. It had no sacrificial significance.

12. *a clean place where the ashes are poured out*] See i. 16 note. It was a place free from impurities, not like those referred to in xiv. 40, 45. The flesh, though it was burned in an ordinary way, and not sent up in the fire of the Altar (see i. 9 note), was not to be confounded with carrion, but was associated with the remains of the sacrifices.—The priests could not eat the flesh of this victim or of that offered for the sin of the congregation, as they ate that of other Sin-offerings (vi. 26. Cp. x. 17, 18), because they were in these cases in the position of offerers. (xvi. 27; Heb. xiii. 11.) The same rule was observed in regard to the Meat-offering of the priests, vi. 23. It was only of the Peace-offering that the offerer himself could partake.

13. *congregation...assembly*] Each of the Hebrew words signifies the people in a collected body. It does not appear that there is any difference between them in the connexion in which they are here used.

14. *when the sin...is known*] Cp. 1 S. xiv. 31–35.

15. In this case the imposition of hands is performed by the elders in behalf of the nation. But in other respects the rites were performed by the High-priest in the same manner as in the Sin-offering for himself.

of the bullock before the LORD: and the bullock shall be killed
16 before the LORD. [p]And the priest that is anointed shall bring
17 of the bullock's blood to the tabernacle of the congregation: and
the priest shall dip his finger *in some* of the blood, and sprinkle
18 *it* seven times before the LORD, *even* before the vail. And he
shall put *some* of the blood upon the horns of the altar which *is*
before the LORD, that *is* in the tabernacle of the congregation,
and shall pour out all the blood at the bottom of the altar of the
burnt offering, which *is at* the door of the tabernacle of the con-
19 gregation. And he shall take all his fat from him, and burn *it*
20 upon the altar. And he shall do with the bullock as he did [q]with
the bullock for a sin offering, so shall he do with this: [r]and the
priest shall make an atonement for them, and it shall be forgiven
21 them. And he shall carry forth the bullock without the camp, and
burn him as he burned the first bullock: it *is* a sin offering for
22 the congregation. When a ruler hath sinned, and [s]done *somewhat*
through ignorance *against* any of the commandments of the
LORD his God *concerning things* which should not be done, and
23 is guilty; or [t]if his sin, wherein he hath sinned, come to his
knowledge; he shall bring his offering, a kid of the goats, a
24 male without blemish: and [u]he shall lay his hand upon the
head of the goat, and kill it in the place where they kill the
25 burnt offering before the LORD: it *is* a sin offering. [x]And the
priest shall take of the blood of the sin offering with his finger,
and put *it* upon the horns of the altar of burnt offering, and
shall pour out his blood at the bottom of the altar of burnt
26 offering. And he shall burn all his fat upon the altar, as [y]the
fat of the sacrifice of peace offerings: [z]and the priest shall make
an atonement for him as concerning his sin, and it shall be for-
27 given him. ¶ And [a]if [1]any one of the [2]common people sin
through ignorance, while he doeth *somewhat against* any of the
commandments of the LORD *concerning things* which ought not
28 to be done, and be guilty; or [b]if his sin, which he hath sinned,
come to his knowledge: then he shall bring his offering, a kid
of the goats, a female without blemish, for his sin which he hath
29 sinned. [c]And he shall lay his hand upon the head of the sin
offering, and slay the sin offering in the place of the burnt
30 offering. And the priest shall take of the blood thereof with his
finger, and put *it* upon the horns of the altar of burnt offering,
and shall pour out all the blood thereof at the bottom of the
31 altar. And [d]he shall take away all the fat thereof, [e]as the fat
is taken away from off the sacrifice of peace offerings; and the
priest shall burn *it* upon the altar for a [f]sweet savour unto the
LORD; [g]and the priest shall make an atonement for him, and it

[p] ver. 5. Heb. 9. 12, 13, 14.
[q] ver. 3.
[r] Num. 15. 25. Dan. 9. 24. Rom. 5. 11. Heb. 2. 17. & 10. 10, 11, 12. 1 John 1. 7. & 2. 2.
[s] ver. 2, 13.
[t] ver. 14.
[u] ver. 4, &c.
[x] ver. 30.
[y] ch. 3. 5.
[z] ver. 20. Num. 15. 28.
[a] ver. 2. Num. 15. 27.
[b] ver. 23.
[c] ver. 4, 24.
[d] ch. 3, 14.
[e] ch. 3. 3.
[f] Ex. 29. 18. ch. 1. 9.
[g] ver. 26.

[1] Heb. *any soul.* [2] Heb. *people of the land.*

---

18. *the altar...in the tabernacle*] *i.e.* the Altar of Incense (cp. *vv.* 5–7).

22. *ruler*] Either the head of a tribe (Num. i. 4–16), or the head of a division of a tribe (Num. xxxiv. 18; cp. Josh. xxii. 30).

23. *or if his sin*] Rather, **And if** his sin.

come to his knowledge] *i.e.* when he had become conscious of his sin.

a kid of the goats] **A shaggy he-goat,** in distinction from a smooth-haired he-goat. It was the regular Sin-offering at the yearly Festivals (xvi. 9, 15; Num. xxviii. 15, 22, 30), and at the consecration of the priests (ix. 3); while the smooth-haired goat appears to have been generally offered for the other sacrifices (Ps. l. 9; Isa. i. 11).

24. See i. 11.

27. *the common people*] Literally, as in the margin, "the people of the land." Cp. xx. 2, 4; 2 K. xi. 18. It was the ordinary designation of the people, as distinguished from the priests and the rulers.

28. *a kid of the goats*] **A shaggy she-goat.**

32 shall be forgiven him. And if he bring a lamb for a sin offering,
33 [h]he shall bring it a female without blemish. And he shall lay
his hand upon the head of the sin offering, and slay it for a sin
34 offering in the place where they kill the burnt offering. And
the priest shall take of the blood of the sin offering with his
finger, and put *it* upon the horns of the altar of burnt offering,
and shall pour out all the blood thereof at the bottom of the
35 altar: and he shall take away all the fat thereof, as the fat of
the lamb is taken away from the sacrifice of the peace offerings;
and the priest shall burn them upon the altar, [i]according to the
offerings made by fire unto the LORD: [k]and the priest shall make
an atonement for his sin that he hath committed, and it shall be
forgiven him.

CHAP. 5. AND if a soul sin, [a]and hear the voice of swearing, and
is a witness, whether he hath seen or known *of it:* if he do not
2 utter *it*, then he shall [b]bear his iniquity. Or [c]if a soul touch
any unclean thing, whether *it be* a carcase of an unclean beast,
or a carcase of unclean cattle, or the carcase of unclean creeping
things, and *if* it be hidden from him; he also shall be unclean,
3 and [d]guilty. Or if he touch [e]the uncleanness of man, whatsoever uncleanness *it be* that a man shall be defiled withal, and
it be hid from him; when he knoweth *of it*, then he shall be
4 guilty. Or if a soul swear, pronouncing with *his* lips [f]to do evil,
or [g]to do good, whatsoever *it be* that a man shall pronounce
with an oath, and it be hid from him; when he knoweth *of it*,
5 then he shall be guilty in one of these. And it shall be, when
he shall be guilty in one of these *things*, that he shall [h]confess
6 that he hath sinned in that *thing:* and he shall bring his trespass offering unto the LORD for his sin which he hath sinned, a
female from the flock, a lamb or a kid of the goats, for a sin
offering; and the priest shall make an atonement for him con-
7 cerning his sin. ¶ And [i]if [1]he be not able to bring a lamb, then

[h] ver. 28.
[i] ch. 3. 5.
[k] ver. 26. 31.
[a] 1 Kin. 8. 31. Matt. 26. 63.
[b] ver. 17. ch. 7. 18. & 17. 16. & 19. 8. & 20. 17. Num. 9. 13.
[c] ch. 11. 24, 28, 31, 39. Num. 19. 11, 13, 16.
[d] ver. 17.
[e] ch. 12, & 13, & 15.
[f] See 1 Sam. 25. 22. Acts 23. 12.
[g] See Mark 6. 23.
[h] ch. 16. 21. & 26. 40. Num. 5. 7. Ezra 10. 11, 12.
[i] ch. 12. 8. & 14. 21.

[1] Heb. *his hand cannot reach to the sufficiency of a lamb.*

---

32. *a lamb*] **A sheep.** See iii. 7 note. Three points are to be observed in regard to the victims for Sin-offerings.—(*a*) The common people had to offer a female, as the less valuable animal; they might present either a sheep or a goat to suit their convenience: (*b*) the rulers had always to offer a male-goat: (*c*) the goat was preferred to the sheep, unlike the victim for a Peace-offering or a Burnt-offering.

The Sin-offerings were not accompanied by Meat-offerings or Drink-offerings. See Num. xv. 3–11.

V. **1–13.** Special occasions are mentioned on which Sin-offerings are to be made with a particular confession of the offence for which atonement is sought (*v.* 5).

1. *swearing*] **Adjuration.** The case appears to be that of one who has been put upon his oath as a witness by a magistrate, and fails to utter all he has seen and heard (cp. marg. reff. and Prov. xxix. 24; Num. v. 21).

2, 3. *hid from him*] Either through forgetfulness or indifference, so that purification had been neglected. In such a case there had been a guilty negligence, and a Sin-offering was required. On the essential connection between impurity and the Sin-offering, see xii. 1.

4. *pronouncing*] **Idly speaking** (Ps. cvi. 33). The reference is to an oath to do something uttered in recklessness or passion and forgotten as soon as uttered.

6. *his trespass offering*] Rather, **as his forfeit**, that is, whatever is due for his offence. The term "Trespass-offering" is out of place here, since it has become the current designation for a distinct kind of Sin-offering mentioned in the next section (see *v.* 14 note).

a lamb or a kid of the goats] **A sheep** (iv. 32) **or a shaggy she-goat** (iv. 23).

7–10. See i. 14–16, xii. 8. In the larger offerings of the ox and the sheep, the fat which was burnt upon the Altar represented, like the Burnt-offering, the dedication of the worshipper; in this case, the same meaning was conveyed by one of the birds being treated as a distinct Burnt-offering.

7. *a lamb*] **One of the flock,** either a sheep or a goat.

for his trespass, which he hath committed] **As his forfeit for the sin he hath committed.**

he shall bring for his trespass, which he hath committed, two
[k]turtledoves, or two young pigeons, unto the LORD; one for a
8 sin offering, and the other for a burnt offering. And he shall
bring them unto the priest, who shall offer *that* which *is* for the
sin offering first, and [l]wring off his head from his neck, but
9 shall not divide *it* asunder: and he shall sprinkle of the blood
of the sin offering upon the side of the altar; and [m]the rest of
the blood shall be wrung out at the bottom of the altar: it *is* a
10 sin offering. And he shall offer the second *for* a burnt offering,
according to the [1][n]manner: [o]and the priest shall make an atonement
for him for his sin which he hath sinned, and it shall be
11 forgiven him. ¶ But if he be not able to bring two turtledoves,
or two young pigeons, then he that sinned shall bring for his
offering the tenth part of an ephah of fine flour for a sin offering;
[p]he shall put no oil upon it, neither shall he put *any*
12 frankincense thereon: for it *is* a sin offering. Then shall he
bring it to the priest, and the priest shall take his handful of it,
[q]*even* a memorial thereof, and burn *it* on the altar, [r]according to
the offerings made by fire unto the LORD: it *is* a sin offering.
13 [s]And the priest shall make an atonement for him as touching his
sin that he hath sinned in one of these, and it shall be forgiven
him: and [t]*the remnant* shall be the priest's, as a meat offering.
14, 15 ¶ And the LORD spake unto Moses, saying, [u]If a soul commit
a trespass, and sin through ignorance, in the holy things
of the LORD; then [x]he shall bring for his trespass unto the LORD
a ram without blemish out of the flocks, with thy estimation by
shekels of silver, after [y]the shekel of the sanctuary, for a tres-
16 pass offering: and he shall make amends for the harm that he
hath done in the holy thing, and [z]shall add the fifth part thereto,
and give it unto the priest: [a]and the priest shall make an atonement
for him with the ram of the trespass offering, and it shall
17 be forgiven him. ¶ And if a [b]soul sin, and commit any of these
things which are forbidden to be done by the commandments of
the LORD; [c]though he wist *it* not, yet is he [d]guilty, and shall
18 bear his iniquity. [e]And he shall bring a ram without blemish

[k] ch. 1. 14.
[l] ch. 1. 15.
[m] ch. 4. 7, 18, 30, 34.
[n] ch. 1. 14.
[o] ch. 4. 26.
[p] Num. 5. 15.
[q] ch. 2. 2.
[r] ch. 4. 35.
[s] ch. 4. 26.
[t] ch. 2. 3.
[u] ch. 22. 14.
[x] Ezra 10. 19.
[y] Ex. 30. 13. ch. 27. 25.
[z] ch. 6. 5. & 22. 14. & 27. 13, 15, 27, 31. Num. 5. 7.
[a] ch. 4. 26.
[b] ch. 4. 2.
[c] ver. 15. ch. 4. 2, 13, 22, 27. Ps. 19. 12. Luke 12. 48.
[d] ver. 1, 2.
[e] ver. 15.

[1] Or, *ordinance*.

---

11. *tenth part of an ephah*] *i.e.* "the tenth deal;" probably less than half a gallon. See xix. 36 note. This Sin-offering of meal was distinguished from the ordinary Minchah (ii. 1) by the absence of oil and frankincense.

14.–vi. 7. The Trespass-offerings as they are described in this section and in vii. 1–7, are clearly distinguished from the ordinary Sin-offerings in these particulars:—

(1) They were offered on account of offences which involved an injury to some person (it might be the LORD Himself) in respect to property. See *v.* 16, vi. 4, 5.

(2) They were always accompanied by a pecuniary fine equal to the value of the injury done, with the addition of one-fifth. Cp. Num. v. 5–8.

(3) The treatment of the blood was more simple. Cp. iv. 5.

(4) The victim was a ram, instead of a female sheep or goat.

(5) There was no such graduation of offerings to suit the rank or circumstances of the worshipper as is set forth in iv. 3, 32, &c.

15. *commit a trespass*] Rather, here and in vi. 2, **perpetrate a wrong.** The word is different from that rendered trespass elsewhere in these chapters.

through ignorance] **Through inadvertence.** See iv. 2 note.

in the holy things of the LORD] The reference is to a failure in the payment of firstfruits, tithes or fees of any kind connected with the public service of religion by which the Sanctuary suffered loss; cf. Num. v. 6–8.

shekel of the sanctuary] See Exod. xxxviii. 24 note.

17. *though he wist it not*] Ignorance of the Law, or even of the consequences of the act at the time it was committed, was not to excuse him from the obligation to offer the sacrifice.

out of the flock, with thy estimation, for a trespass offering,
unto the priest: [f]and the priest shall make an atonement for
him concerning his ignorance wherein he erred and wist *it* not,
19 and it shall be forgiven him. It *is* a trespass offering: [g]he hath
certainly trespassed against the LORD.
CHAP. 6. AND the LORD spake unto Moses, saying, If a soul
2 sin, and [a]commit a trespass against the LORD, and [b]lie unto
his neighbour in that [c]which was delivered him to keep, or in
[1][2]fellowship, or in a thing taken away by violence, or hath [d]de-
3 ceived his neighbour; or [e]have found that which was lost, and
lieth concerning it, and [f]sweareth falsely; in any of all these
4 that a man doeth, sinning therein: then it shall be, because he
hath sinned, and is guilty, that he shall restore that which he
took violently away, or the thing which he hath deceitfully
gotten, or that which was delivered him to keep, or the lost
5 thing which he found, or all that about which he hath sworn
falsely; he shall even [g]restore it in the principal, and shall add
the fifth part more thereto, *and* give it unto him to whom it
6 appertaineth, [3][4]in the day of his trespass offering. And he shall
bring his trespass offering unto the LORD, [h]a ram without
blemish out of the flock, with thy estimation, for a trespass
7 offering, unto the priest: [i]and the priest shall make an atonement for him before the LORD: and it shall be forgiven him for
8 anything of all that he hath done in trespassing therein. ¶ And
9 the LORD spake unto Moses, saying, Command Aaron and his
sons, saying, This *is* the law of the burnt offering: It *is* the
burnt offering, [5]because of the burning upon the altar all night
unto the morning, and the fire of the altar shall be burning in it.
10 [k]And the priest shall put on his linen garment, and his linen
breeches shall he put upon his flesh, and take up the ashes
which the fire hath consumed with the burnt offering on the
11 altar, and he shall put them [l]beside the altar. And [m]he shall
put off his garments, and put on other garments, and carry forth
12 the ashes without the camp [n]unto a clean place. And the fire
upon the altar shall be burning in it; it shall not be put out:
and the priest shall burn wood on it every morning, and lay the
burnt offering in order upon it; and he shall burn thereon [o]the
13 fat of the peace offerings. The fire shall ever be burning upon
14 the altar; it shall never go out. ¶ [p]And this *is* the law of the
meat offering: the sons of Aaron shall offer it before the LORD,
15 before the altar. And he shall take of it his handful, of the
flour of the meat offering, and of the oil thereof, and all the
frankincense which *is* upon the meat offering, and shall burn *it*
upon the altar *for* a sweet savour, *even* the [q]memorial of it, unto

[f] ver. 16.
[g] Ezra 10. 2.
[a] Num. 5. 6.
[b] ch. 19. 11. Acts 5. 4. Col. 3. 9.
[c] Ex. 22. 7, 10.
[d] Prov. 24. 28. & 26. 19.
[e] Deut. 22. 1, 2, 3.
[f] Ex. 22. 11. ch. 19. 12. Jer. 7. 9. Zech. 5. 4.
[g] ch. 5. 16. Num. 5. 7. 2 Sam. 12. 6. Luke 19. 8.
[h] ch. 5. 15.
[i] ch. 4. 26.
[k] Ex. 28. 39, 40, 41, 43. ch. 16. 4. Ezek. 44. 17, 18.
[l] ch. 1. 16.
[m] Ezek. 44. 19.
[n] ch. 4. 12.
[o] ch. 3. 3, 9, 14.
[p] ch. 2. 1. Num. 15. 4.
[q] ch. 2. 2, 9.

[1] Or, *in dealing*.
[2] Heb. *putting of the hand*.
[3] Or, *in the day of his being found guilty*.
[4] Heb. *in the day of his trespass*.
[5] Or, *for the burning*.

VI. **1.** In the Hebrew Bible *vv.* 1–7 form part of Ch. v. It is evident that they ought to do so.

5. *in the day of his trespass offering*] The restitution was thus to be associated with the religious act by which the offender testified his penitence.

9. Rather, "**This, the Burnt-offering, shall be upon the fire on the Altar** all night unto the morning." See Ex. xxix. 38–46, with the notes.

10. *Ashes...with the burnt-offering*] Rather, **the ashes to which the fire hath consumed the Burnt-offering.**

13. *The fire shall ever be burning*] This was a symbol of the never-ceasing worship which Jehovah required of His people. It was essentially connected with their acts of sacrifice.

14–18. See ii. 1–10; Ex. xxix. 40, 41.

[r] ch. 2. 3. Ezek. 44. 29. [s] ver. 26. ch. 10. 12, 13. Num. 18. 10. [t] ch. 2. 11. [u] Num. 18. 9, 10. [x] Ex. 29. 37. ver. 25. ch. 2. 3. & 7. 1. [y] ver. 29. Num. 18. 10. [z] ch. 3. 17. [a] Ex. 29. 37. ch. 22. 3, 4, 5, 6, 7. [b] Ex. 29. 2. [c] Ex. 16. 36. [d] ch. 4. 3. [e] Ex. 29. 25. [f] ch. 4. 2. [g] ch. 1. 3, 5, 11. & 4. 24, 29, 33. [h] ver. 17. ch. 21. 22. [i] ch. 10. 17, 18. Num. 18. 9, 10. Ezek. 44. 28, 29. [k] ver. 16. [l] Ex. 29. 37. & 30. 29. [m] ch. 11. 33. & 15, 12. [n] ver. 18. Num. 18. 10. [o] ver. 25. [p] ch. 4. 7, 11, 12, 18, 21. & 10. 18. & 16. 27. Heb. 13. 11. [a] ch. 5, & 6. 1—7. [b] ch. 6. 17, 25. & 21. 22. [c] ch. 1. 11.

16 the LORD. And [r]the remainder thereof shall Aaron and his
sons eat: [s]with unleavened bread shall it be eaten in the holy
place; in the court of the tabernacle of the congregation they
17 shall eat it. [t]It shall not be baken with leaven. [u]I have given
it *unto them for* their portion of my offerings made by fire; [x]it *is*
most holy, as *is* the sin offering, and as the trespass offering.
18 [y]All the males among the children of Aaron shall eat of it. [z]*It
shall be* a statute for ever in your generations concerning the
offerings of the LORD made by fire: [a]every one that toucheth
19 them shall be holy. ¶ And the LORD spake unto Moses, saying,
20 [b]This *is* the offering of Aaron and of his sons, which they shall
offer unto the LORD in the day when he is anointed; the tenth
part of an [c]ephah of fine flour for a meat offering perpetual,
21 half of it in the morning, and half thereof at night. In a pan it
shall be made with oil; *and when it is* baken, thou shalt bring it
in: *and* the baken pieces of the meat offering shalt thou offer
22 *for* a sweet savour unto the LORD. And the priest of his sons
[d]that is anointed in his stead shall offer it: *it is* a statute for
23 ever unto the LORD; [e]it shall be wholly burnt. For every meat
offering for the priest shall be wholly burnt: it shall not be
24, 25 eaten. ¶ And the LORD spake unto Moses, saying, Speak unto
Aaron and to his sons, saying, [f]This *is* the law of the sin offering: [g]In the place where the burnt offering is killed shall the
26 sin offering be killed before the LORD: [h]it *is* most holy. [i]The
priest that offereth it for sin shall eat it: [k]in the holy place shall
it be eaten, in the court of the tabernacle of the congregation.
27 [l]Whatsoever shall touch the flesh thereof shall be holy: and
when there is sprinkled of the blood thereof upon any garment,
thou shalt wash that whereon it was sprinkled in the holy place.
28 But the earthen vessel wherein it is sodden [m]shall be broken:
and if it be sodden in a brazen pot, it shall be both scoured, and
29 rinsed in water. [n]All the males among the priests shall eat
30 thereof: [o]it *is* most holy. [p]And no sin offering, whereof *any*
of the blood is brought into the tabernacle of the congregation
to reconcile *withal* in the holy *place*, shall be eaten: it shall
be burnt in the fire.

CHAP. 7. LIKEWISE [a]this *is* the law of the trespass offering: [b]it *is*
2 most holy. [c]In the place where they kill the burnt offering shall

---

16. *with unleavened bread shall it be eaten*] This should be, **it** (the remainder) **shall be eaten unleavened.**

20. See iv. 3. Aaron's sons here spoken of (as in *v.* 22) must be the succession of High-priests who succeeded him. The day of this offering was probably the eighth day of the ceremony of consecration (viii. 35, ix. 1), when the High-priest appears to have entered upon the duties of his office.

a meat offering perpetual] Jewish tradition is in favour of these words implying that this Minchah was offered by the High-priest as a daily rite from the time of his consecration.

21. *In a pan*] See ii. 5 note.

22. *it shall be wholly burnt*] Literally, *it shall ascend in fire as a whole Burnt-offering.*

23. *not be eaten*] Cp. *v.* 30, iv. 12 note.

25. *the place where,* &c.] See i. 11.

it is most holy] See ii. 3. The key to the peculiar sanctity of the flesh of the Sin-offering, as set forth in *vv.* 26–30, must, it would seem, be found in the words of Moses to the priests (x. 17). The flesh of the victim, which represented the sinner for whom atonement was now made, was to be solemnly, and most exclusively, appropriated by those who were appointed to mediate between the sinner and the Lord. The far-reaching symbolism of the act met its perfect fulfilment in the One Mediator Who took our nature upon Himself. (Phil. ii. 7).

28. *the earthen vessel*] Unglazed pottery would absorb some of the juices of the meat: and a vessel made holy could not be put to any other purpose.

30. *to reconcile withal*] generally rendered "to make atonement for."

the holy place] The outer apartment of the Tabernacle. See x. 18 note.

they kill the trespass offering: and the blood thereof shall he
3 sprinkle round about upon the altar. And he shall offer of it [d]all [d] Ex. 29. 13.
the fat thereof; the rump, and the fat that covereth the inwards, ch. 3. 4, 9,
4 and the two kidneys, and the fat that *is* on them, which *is* by 10, 14, 15, 16. & 4. 8, 9.
the flanks, and the caul *that is* above the liver, with the kidneys,
5 it shall he take away: and the priest shall burn them upon the
altar *for* an offering made by fire unto the LORD: it *is* a trespass
6 offering. [e]Every male among the priests shall eat thereof: it [e] ch. 6. 16,
7 shall be eaten in the holy place: [f]it *is* most holy. As the 17, 18.
sin offering *is*, so *is* [g]the trespass offering: *there is* one law for Num. 18.
them: the priest that maketh atonement therewith shall have 9, 10. [f] ch. 2. 3.
8 *it*. And the priest that offereth any man's burnt offering, *even* [g] ch. 6. 25, 26.
the priest shall have to himself the skin of the burnt offering & 14. 13.
9 which he hath offered. And [h]all the meat offering that is baken [h] ch. 2. 3, 10.
in the oven, and all that is dressed in the fryingpan, and [1]in the Num. 18. 9.
10 pan, shall be the priest's that offereth it. And every meat offer- Ezek. 44, 29.
ing, mingled with oil, and dry, shall all the sons of Aaron have,
11 one *as much* as another. ¶ And [i]this *is* the law of the sacrifice of [i] ch. 3. 1.
12 peace offerings, which he shall offer unto the LORD. If he offer & 22. 18, 21.
it for a thanksgiving, then he shall offer with the sacrifice of
thanksgiving unleavened cakes mingled with oil, and unleavened
wafers [k]anointed with oil, and cakes mingled with oil, of fine [k] ch. 2. 4.
13 flour, fried. Besides the cakes, he shall offer *for* his offering Num. 6. 15.
[l]leavened bread with the sacrifice of thanksgiving of his peace [l] Amos 4. 5.
14 offerings. And of it he shall offer one out of the whole oblation
for an heave offering unto the LORD, [m]*and* it shall be the priest's [m] Num. 18.
15 that sprinkleth the blood of the peace offerings. [n]And the flesh 8, 11, 19.
of the sacrifice of his peace offerings for thanksgiving shall [n] ch. 22, 30.
be eaten the same day that it is offered; he shall not leave any
16 of it until the morning. But [o]if the sacrifice of his offering *be* a [o] ch. 19. 6,
vow, or a voluntary offering, it shall be eaten the same day that 7, 8.
he offereth his sacrifice: and on the morrow also the remainder
17 of it shall be eaten: but the remainder of the flesh of the sacri-
18 fice on the third day shall be burnt with fire. And if *any* of the
flesh of the sacrifice of his peace offerings be eaten at all on the

[1] Or, *on the flat plate*, or, *slice*.

VII. **1–7.** See v. 14 note. In *v.* 2 "sprinkle" should rather be **cast** (i. 5). All the details regarding the parts put on the Altar are repeated for each kind of sacrifice, because the matter was one of paramount importance.

8. *the skin of the burnt offering*] It is most likely that the skins of the Sin-offering and the Trespass-offering also fell to the lot of the officiating priest.

9, 10. See marg. reff.

11, &c. See iii. 1–17. What is here added, relates to the accompanying Minchah (ii. 1), the classification of Peace-offerings into (1) Thank-offerings, (2) Vow-offerings and (3) Voluntary-offerings, and the conditions to be observed by the worshipper in eating the flesh.

12. *for a thanksgiving*] *i.e.*, a Thank-offering for mercies received.

13. *for his offering*] The leavened bread was a distinct offering.

14. *out of the whole oblation*] Rather, **out of each offering.** That is, one loaf or cake out of each kind of Meat-offering was to be a heave-offering (*v.* 32) for the officiating priest. According to Jewish tradition, there were to be ten cakes of each kind of bread in every Thank-offering. The other cakes were returned to the sacrificer.

16. The Vow-offering appears to have been a Peace-offering vowed upon a certain condition; the Voluntary-offering, one offered as the simple tribute of a devout heart rejoicing in peace with God and man offered on no external occasion (cp. xxii. 17–25).

18, 19. It was proper that the sacrificial meat should not be polluted by any approach to putrefaction. But the exclusion of a mean-spirited economy may further have furnished the ground for the distinction between the Thank-offerings and the others. The most liberal distribution of the meat of the offering, particularly amongst the poor who were invited to par-

third day, it shall not be accepted, neither shall it be [p]imputed
unto him that offereth it: it shall be an [q]abomination, and the
19 soul that eateth of it shall bear his iniquity. And the flesh that
toucheth any unclean *thing* shall not be eaten; it shall be burnt
with fire: and as for the flesh, all that be clean shall eat thereof.
20 But the soul that eateth *of* the flesh of the sacrifice of peace
offerings, that *pertain* unto the LORD, [r]having his uncleanness
upon him, even that soul [s]shall be cut off from his people.
21 Moreover the soul that shall touch any unclean *thing*, *as* [t]the
uncleanness of man, or *any* [u]unclean beast, or any [w]abominable
unclean *thing*, and eat of the flesh of the sacrifice of peace offerings, which *pertain* unto the LORD, even that soul [x]shall be cut
22 off from his people. ¶ And the LORD spake unto Moses, saying,
23 Speak unto the children of Israel, saying, [y]Ye shall eat no
24 manner of fat, of ox, or of sheep, or of goat. And the fat of the
[1]beast that dieth of itself, and the fat of that which is torn with
beasts, may be used in any other use: but ye shall in no wise eat
25 of it. For whosoever eateth the fat of the beast, of which men
offer an offering made by fire unto the LORD, even the soul that
26 eateth *it* shall be cut off from his people. [z]Moreover ye shall
eat no manner of blood, *whether it be* of fowl or of beast, in any of
27 your dwellings. Whatsoever soul *it be* that eateth any manner
28 of blood, even that soul shall be cut off from his people. ¶ And
29 the LORD spake unto Moses, saying, Speak unto the children of
Israel, saying, [a]He that offereth the sacrifice of his peace offerings unto the LORD shall bring his oblation unto the LORD of
30 the sacrifice of his peace offerings. [b]His own hands shall bring
the offerings of the LORD made by fire, the fat with the breast,
it shall he bring, that [c]the breast may be waved *for* a wave
31 offering before the LORD. [d]And the priest shall burn the fat
upon the altar: [e]but the breast shall be Aaron's and his sons'.
32 And [f]the right shoulder shall ye give unto the priest *for* an
33 heave offering of the sacrifices of your peace offerings. He
among the sons of Aaron, that offereth the blood of the peace
offerings, and the fat, shall have the right shoulder for *his* part.
34 For [g]the wave breast and the heave shoulder have I taken of the
children of Israel from off the sacrifices of their peace offerings,
and have given them unto Aaron the priest and unto his sons
35 by a statute for ever from among the children of Israel. This *is*
the portion of the anointing of Aaron, and of the anointing of his
sons, out of the offerings of the LORD made by fire, in the day
when he presented them to minister unto the LORD in the priest's
36 office; which the LORD commanded to be given them of the
children of Israel, [h]in the day that he anointed them, *by* a

[p] Num. 18. 27.
[q] ch. 11. 10, 11, 41. & 19. 7.
[r] ch. 15. 3.
[s] Gen. 17. 14.
[t] ch. 12, & 13, & 15.
[u] ch. 11. 24, 28.
[w] Ezek. 4. 14.
[x] ver. 20.
[y] ch. 3. 17.
[z] Gen. 9. 4. ch. 3. 17. & 17. 10—14.
[a] ch. 3. 1.
[b] ch. 3. 3, 4, 9, 14.
[c] Ex. 29. 24, 27. ch. 8. 27. & 9. 21. Num. 6. 20.
[d] ch. 3. 5. 11. 16.
[e] ver. 34.
[f] ver. 34. ch. 9. 21. Num. 6. 20.
[g] Ex. 29. 28. ch. 10. 14, 15. Num. 18. 18, 19. Deut. 18. 3.
[h] Ex. 40. 13, 15. ch. 8. 12, 30.

[1] Heb. *carcase*, ch. 17. 15. Deut. 14. 21. Ezek. 4. 14. & 44. 31.

---

take, would plainly be becoming when the sacrifice was intended especially to express gratitude for mercies received.

21. *unclean beast*] That is, carrion of any kind. See ch. xi.

shall be cut off] See Ex. xxxi. 14 note.

23. This is emphatically addressed to the people. They were not to eat in their own meal what belonged to the Altar of Jehovah, nor what was the perquisite of the priests. See *vv.* 33–36.

24. Cp. xi. 39.

26. *no manner of blood*] See xvii. 10–15.

30–32. *wave-offering...heave-offering*] The latter appears to be used (like *korban*, i. 2) for offerings in general. *Waving* (a moving to and fro, repeated several times) or *heaving* (a lifting up once) the offering was a solemn form of dedicating a thing to the use of the Sanctuary.

35. *the portion of the anointing*, &c.] Rather, **the appointed share of Aaron and of his sons.**

37 statute for ever throughout their generations. ¶ This *is* the law
[i]of the burnt offering, [k]of the meat offering, [l]and of the sin — [i] ch. 6. 9.
offering, [m]and of the trespass offering, [n]and of the consecrations, — [k] ch. 6. 14. [l] ch. 6. 25.
38 and [o]of the sacrifice of the peace offerings; which the LORD — [m] ver. 1.
commanded Moses in mount Sinai, in the day that he commanded — [n] Ex. 29. 1.
the children of Israel [p]to offer their oblations unto the LORD, in — ch. 6. 20. [o] ver. 11.
the wilderness of Sinai. — [p] ch. 1. 2.

CHAP. 8. AND the LORD spake unto Moses, saying, [a]Take Aaron — [a] Ex. 29. 1,
2 and his sons with him, and [b]the garments, and [c]the anointing — 2, 3. [b] Ex. 28. 2, 4.
oil, and a bullock for the sin offering, and two rams, and a — [c] Ex. 30. 24,
3 basket of unleavened bread; and gather thou all the congrega- — 25.
tion together unto the door of the tabernacle of the congregation.
4 And Moses did as the LORD commanded him; and the assembly
was gathered together unto the door of the tabernacle of the
5 congregation. ¶ And Moses said unto the congregation, [d]This *is* — [d] Ex. 29. 4.
6 the thing which the LORD commanded to be done. And Moses
brought Aaron and his sons, [e]and washed them with water. — [e] Ex. 29. 4.
7 [f]And he put upon him the [g]coat, and girded him with the girdle, — [f] Ex. 29. 5.
and clothed him with the robe, and put the ephod upon him, and — [g] Ex. 28. 4.
he girded him with the curious girdle of the ephod, and bound *it*
8 unto him therewith. And he put the breastplate upon him:
also he [h]put in the breastplate the Urim and the Thummim. — [h] Ex. 28. 30.
9 [i]And he put the mitre upon his head; also upon the mitre, *even* — [i] Ex. 29. 6.
upon his forefront, did he put the golden plate, the holy crown;
10 as the LORD [k]commanded Moses. ¶ [l]And Moses took the — [k] Ex. 28. 37, &c.
anointing oil, and anointed the tabernacle and all that *was* — [l] Ex. 30. 26, 27, 28, 29.

---

37. *of the consecrations*] That is, of the sacrifices which were to be offered in the Consecration of the priests. See marg. reff.

38. *wilderness of Sinai*] Cp. Ex. xix. 1.

Chs. viii. ix. x. THE SERVICE OF THE SANCTUARY INAUGURATED. This is the only historical portion of the Book of Leviticus, with the exception of xxiv. 10–23.

VIII. **2.** *A bullock—two rams—a basket*] cp. Ex. xxix. 1–3. This shews the coherence of this part of Leviticus with the latter part of Exodus. The basket of unleavened bread used on this occasion appears to have contained (1) cakes or loaves of the ordinary unleavened bread; (2) cakes of oiled bread, rather, **oil bread** (see ii. 1, 4); and (3) oiled wafers (see ii. 4, 6). Rabbinical tradition says that there were six cakes of each sort.

3. *gather*, &c.] Rather, **gather all the assembly together towards the entrance of the Tent of meeting.** See iv. 13. The whole body of the people were summoned on this occasion, and the elders probably occupied the first places. The elders are specially called together in an unequivocal manner to receive directions to provide the first sacrifices for the nation to be offered by the newly consecrated priests (ix. 1), and the body of the people afterwards assemble as they do here (ix. 5).—The spot designated was the portion of the Court in front of the Tabernacle (see i. 3 note). Towards this space the people were commanded to assemble to witness the great national ceremony of the Consecration of the priesthood, the solemn setting apart of one of their families, the members of which were henceforth to stand as mediators between them and Jehovah in carrying out the precepts of the ceremonial law. Those who could do so, may have come into the Court, and a great number of others may have occupied the heights which overlooked the enclosure of the Court. As the series of ceremonies was repeated every day during a week (*v.* 33), it is natural to suppose that some of the people attended on one day and some on another.

6. *washed them with water*] Moses caused them to bathe entirely (cp. xvi. 4), not merely to wash their hands and feet, as they were to do in their daily ministrations. See marg. ref. This bathing, which the High-priest had also to go through on the Day of Atonement, was symbolical of the spiritual cleansing required of all (2 Cor. vii. 1), but especially of those who had to draw near to God to make reconciliation for the sins of the people (Heb. vii. 26; Matt. iii. 15).

7–9. See notes on Exod. xxviii.

9. *the holy crown*] The golden plate of the mitre was so called as the distinctive badge of the High-priest's consecration. See xxi. 12.

10. Moses first anointed with the holy oil (Ex. xxx. 25) the Tabernacle and all therein, that is, the Ark of the Covenant,

11 therein, and sanctified them. And he sprinkled thereof upon the
altar seven times, and anointed the altar and all his vessels, both
12 the laver and his foot, to sanctify them. And he [m]poured of the
anointing oil upon Aaron's head, and anointed him, to sanctify
13 him. [n]And Moses brought Aaron's sons, and put coats upon
them, and girded them with girdles, and [1]put bonnets upon
14 them; as the LORD commanded Moses. ¶ [o]And he brought the
bullock for the sin offering: and Aaron and his sons [p]laid their
15 hands upon the head of the bullock for the sin offering. And
he slew *it*; [q]and Moses took the blood, and put *it* upon the horns
of the altar round about with his finger, and purified the altar,
and poured the blood at the bottom of the altar, and sanctified
16 it, to make reconciliation upon it. [r]And he took all the fat that
was upon the inwards, and the caul *above* the liver, and the two
17 kidneys, and their fat, and Moses burnt *it* upon the altar. But
the bullock, and his hide, his flesh, and his dung, he burnt with
fire without the camp; as the LORD [s]commanded Moses.

[m] Ex. 29. 7. & 30. 30. ch. 21. 10, 12. Ps. 133. 2.
[n] Ex. 29. 8, 9.
[o] Ex. 29. 10. Ezek. 43. 19.
[p] ch. 4. 4.
[q] Ex. 29. 12, 36. ch. 4. 7. Ezek. 43. 20, 26. Heb. 9. 22.
[r] Ex. 29. 13. ch. 4. 8.
[s] Ex. 29. 14. ch. 4. 11, 12.

[1] Heb. *bound*.

---

the Table of Shewbread, the Candlestick and the Golden Altar, with all the articles that belonged to them.

11. *sprinkled...the altar seven times*] The Altar of Burnt-offering was distinguished by this sevenfold sprinkling with the holy oil. The number of the Covenant was thus brought into connection with those acts of sacrifice by which the Covenant between Jehovah and the worshipper was formally renewed and confirmed.

12. As investing the priest with official garments was a recognition before men of the official position of the person (see Ex. xxviii. 3 note), so the anointing him with oil was an acknowledgment that all fitness for his office, all the powers with which he would rightly fulfil its duties, must come from the Lord.

So, again, with the sanctification of the Holy things. Each of them was intended by divine wisdom to convey a spiritual meaning to the mind of man. They were means of grace to the devout worshipper. The oil poured upon them was a recognition of this fact, and at the same time it made them holy and set them apart from all profane and ordinary uses. On kindred grounds, though to express another idea, the Altar was to be sanctified also by blood. See *v.* 15 note.

13. *Aaron's sons*] The common priests. Nothing is said here, or in Ex. xxix. 7–9, of the anointing of the common priests, though it is expressly commanded in Ex. xxviii. 41, xl. 15, and is evidently implied as a fact in vii. 36, x. 7, Num. iii. 3. It would seem that the anointing of the common priests consisted in some rite common to them and the High-priest (Ex. xl. 15), and this was the sprinkling mentioned in *v.* 30. Cp. further x. 7 with xxi. 12.

14–36. Moses as the mediator of the Covenant of the Law (Gal. iii. 19, Heb. viii. 6) was called to perform the priestly functions, in consecrating those on whom henceforth those functions were to devolve, and in inaugurating the legal order of sacrifices. See Ex. xl. 23 note. The Sin-offering was now offered for the first time. The succession in which the sacrifices followed each other on this occasion, first the Sin-offering, then the Burnt-offering, and lastly the Peace-offering, has its ground in the meaning of each sacrifice, and became the established custom in later ages. The worshipper passed through a spiritual process. He had transgressed the Law, and he needed the atonement signified by the Sin-offering: if his offering had been made in truth and sincerity, he could then offer himself as an accepted person, as a sweet savour, in the Burnt-offering; and in consequence, he could enjoy communion with the Lord and with his brethren in the Peace-offering.

14–17. See marg. reff. The flesh of the Sin-offering could not be eaten by any but a legally consecrated priest (vi. 25 note). Moses therefore could not eat of it himself, though he was, for the occasion, performing the duties of a priest. Those whom he was consecrating could not eat it, not only because they were not yet duly installed, but because the sacrifice was offered on their behalf, and the body of the victim stood to them in the same relation as that of the regular Sin-offering afterwards stood to the High-priest.

15. *purified the altar...sanctified it, to make reconciliation upon it*] The Altar had been sanctified by the anointing oil (*v.* 11) like the priests who were to officiate at it; it was now, like them, sanctified by blood, in acknowledgment of the alienation of all nature, in itself, from God, and the need of a reconciliation to Him of all things by blood. Col. i. 20; Heb. ix. 21, 22. See xvii. 11; Ex. xxviii. 38.

18 ¶ [t]And he brought the ram for the burnt offering: and Aaron [t] Ex. 29. 15.
19 and his sons laid their hands upon the head of the ram. And
he killed *it;* and Moses sprinkled the blood upon the altar
20 round about. And he cut the ram into pieces; and Moses burnt
21 the head, and the pieces, and the fat. And he washed the inwards and the legs in water; and Moses burnt the whole ram
upon the altar: it *was* a burnt sacrifice for a sweet savour, *and*
an offering made by fire unto the LORD; [u]as the LORD com- [u] Ex. 29. 18.
22 manded Moses. ¶ And [w]he brought the other ram, the ram of [w] Ex. 29. 19, 31.
consecration: and Aaron and his sons laid their hands upon the
23 head of the ram. And he slew *it;* and Moses took of the blood
of it, and put *it* upon the tip of Aaron's right ear, and upon the
thumb of his right hand, and upon the great toe of his right foot.
24 And he brought Aaron's sons, and Moses put of the blood upon
the tip of their right ear, and upon the thumbs of their right
hands, and upon the great toes of their right feet: and Moses
25 sprinkled the blood upon the altar round about. [x]And he took
the fat, and the rump, and all the fat that *was* upon the inwards, [x] Ex. 29. 22.
and the caul *above* the liver, and the two kidneys, and their fat,
26 and the right shoulder: [y]and out of the basket of unleavened [y] Ex. 29. 23.
bread, that *was* before the LORD, he took one unleavened cake,
and a cake of oiled bread, and one wafer, and put *them* on
27 the fat, and upon the right shoulder: and he put all [z]upon [z] Ex. 29. 24, &c.
Aaron's hands, and upon his sons' hands, and waved them *for* a
28 wave offering before the LORD. [a]And Moses took them from [a] Ex. 29. 25.
off their hands, and burnt *them* on the altar upon the burnt
offering: they *were* consecrations for a sweet savour: it *is* an
29 offering made by fire unto the LORD. And Moses took the breast,
and waved it *for* a wave offering before the LORD: *for* of the
ram of consecration it was Moses' [b]part; as the LORD commanded [b] Ex. 29. 26.

18-21. Atonement having been made, Aaron and his sons were now permitted, by the laying on of their hands, to make themselves one with the victim, which was to be sent up to Jehovah as "a burnt sacrifice for a sweet savour, an offering made by fire unto the Lord." All was done strictly according to the ritual (i. 3-9), except that Moses performed the duties of the priest.

22. *the ram of consecration*] The sacrifice of this ram was by far the most peculiar part of the whole ceremony. The words may be literally rendered *the ram of the fillings*, and the name has been supposed to have reference to the ceremony in which Moses filled the hands of the priests; see *v.* 27. The offering was in the highest sense *the sacrifice of completion* or *fulfilling*, as being the central point of the consecrating rite. The final perfection of the creature is Consecration to the LORD.

23, 24. Before **casting forth the blood round the Altar** in the usual manner, Moses took a portion of the blood and put some of it on the right extremities of each of the priests. This, being performed with the blood of the Peace-offering, has been supposed to figure the readiness of the priest who is at peace with Jehovah to hear with the ear and obey the divine word, to perform with the hand the sacred duties of his office, and to walk with the feet in the way of holiness.

25-28. In the rite of filling the hands of the priests, Moses took the portions of the victim which usually belonged to the Altar, with the right shoulder (or leg); he placed upon them one cake of each of the three kinds of unleavened bread contained in the basket (see *v.* 2 note), and then put the whole first upon the hands of Aaron and in succession upon the hands of his sons: in each case, according to Jewish tradition, he put his own hands under the hands of the priest, moving them backwards and forwards, so as to wave the mass to and fro.

In this remarkable ceremony the gifts of the people appear to have been made over to the priests, as if in trust, for the service of the Altar. The articles were presented to Jehovah and solemnly waved in the hands of the priests, but not by their own act and deed. The mediator of the Law, who was expressly commissioned on this occasion, was the agent in the process.

25. *the rump*] See iii. 9 note.

29. The heave-shoulder was the ordinary perquisite of the officiating priest, but the wave-breast appears to have been awarded to Moses as the servant of Jehovah now especially appointed for the priestly service.

30 Moses. ¶ And [c]Moses took of the anointing oil, and of the blood
which *was* upon the altar, and sprinkled *it* upon Aaron, *and* upon
his garments, and upon his sons, and upon his sons' garments
with him; and sanctified Aaron, *and* his garments, and his sons,
31 and his sons' garments with him. ¶ And Moses said unto Aaron
and to his sons, [d]Boil the flesh *at* the door of the tabernacle of
the congregation: and there eat it with the bread that *is* in the
basket of consecrations, as I commanded, saying, Aaron and his
32 sons shall eat it. [e]And that which remaineth of the flesh and of
33 the bread shall ye burn with fire. And ye shall not go out of
the door of the tabernacle of the congregation *in* seven days,
until the days of your consecration be at an end: for [f]seven days
34 shall he consecrate you. [g]As he hath done this day, *so* the
LORD hath commanded to do, to make an atonement for you.
35 Therefore shall ye abide *at* the door of the tabernacle of the congregation day and night seven days, and [h]keep the charge of the
36 LORD, that ye die not: for so I am commanded. So Aaron and
his sons did all things which the LORD commanded by the hand
of Moses.

CHAP. 9. AND [a]it came to pass on the eighth day, *that* Moses called
2 Aaron and his sons, and the elders of Israel; and he said unto
Aaron, [b]Take thee a young calf for a sin offering, [c]and a ram
for a burnt offering, without blemish, and offer *them* before the
3 LORD. And unto the children of Israel thou shalt speak, saying,
[d]Take ye a kid of the goats for a sin offering; and a calf and a
lamb, *both* of the first year, without blemish, for a burnt offering;
4 also a bullock and a ram for peace offerings, to sacrifice before
the LORD; and [e]a meat offering mingled with oil: for [f]to day
5 the LORD will appear unto you. ¶ And they brought *that* which
Moses commanded before the tabernacle of the congregation:
and all the congregation drew near and stood before the LORD.
6 And Moses said, This *is* the thing which the LORD commanded
that ye should do: and [g]the glory of the LORD shall appear unto
7 you. ¶ And Moses said unto Aaron, Go unto the altar, and

[c] Ex. 29. 21. & 30. 30. Num. 3. 3.
[d] Ex. 29. 31. 32.
[e] Ex. 29. 34.
[f] Ex. 29. 30, 35. Ezek. 43. 25, 26.
[g] Heb. 7. 16.
[h] Num. 3. 7. & 9. 19. Deut. 11. 1. 1 Kin. 2. 3.
[a] Ezek. 43. 27.
[b] Ex. 29. 1. ch. 4. 3. & 8. 14.
[c] ch. 8. 18.
[d] ch. 4. 23. Ezra 6. 17. & 10. 19.
[e] ch. 2. 4.
[f] ver. 6, 23. Ex. 29. 43.
[g] ver. 23. Ex. 24. 16.

---

30. The sprinkling was on their garments as well as their persons, because it belonged to them in reference to the office with which they had been formally invested by putting on the garments. (See Ex. xxviii. 3 note). The union of the two symbols of the atoning blood and the inspiring unction appears to be a fit conclusion of the entire rite.

33–36. The rites of Consecration were to last a whole week, and thus, like the longer of the annual festivals, were connected in an emphatic manner with the sabbatical number of the Covenant. During this period the priests were not to leave the Holy precinct for the sake of any worldly business; and the whole series of ceremonies, including the sacrifice of the Ram of Consecration, was to be gone through on each day. Cp. marg. reff.

33. Rather, **ye shall not go away from the entrance of the Tent.** With this agree Cranmer, the Geneva Bible, &c. The meaning is evidently that they were not to go out of the court, as is more clearly expressed in *v.* 35.

35. *that ye die not*] See Ex. xxviii. 35 note.

IX. **1–6.** *on the eighth day*] *i.e.*, on the first day after the week of Consecration.

2. *a young calf*] **A bull calf,** which might have been what we should call a yearling ox.

3. *a kid of the goats*] **A shaggy he-goat.** See iv. 23 note.

6. *the glory of the* LORD] Cp. Ex. xvi. 7.

7. It is to be remarked that Aaron offers no Peace-offering for himself. It was enough that he should participate in the Peace-offerings of the Consecration (viii. 31), and in the two Peace-offerings about to be sacrificed for the people.

His Sin-offering was probably regarded not so much as a sacrifice for his own actual sins as a typical acknowledgment of his sinful nature and of his future duty to offer for his own sins and those of the people. See marg. reff. "The law maketh men High-priests which have infirmity; but the word of the oath, which was since the law, maketh the Son, Who is consecrated (in the margin, *perfected*, see viii. 22 note) for evermore." Heb. vii. 28.

[h]offer thy sin offering, and thy burnt offering, and make an
atonement for thyself, and for the people: and [i]offer the offering
of the people, and make an atonement for them; as the LORD
8 commanded. Aaron therefore went unto the altar, and slew the
9 calf of the sin offering, which *was* for himself. [k]And the sons
of Aaron brought the blood unto him: and he dipped his finger
in the blood, and [l]put *it* upon the horns of the altar, and poured
10 out the blood at the bottom of the altar: [m]but the fat, and the
kidneys, and the caul above the liver of the sin offering, he
11 burnt upon the altar; [n]as the LORD commanded Moses. [o]And
the flesh and the hide he burnt with fire without the camp.
12 And he slew the burnt offering; and Aaron's sons presented
unto him the blood, [p]which he sprinkled round about upon the
13 altar. [q]And they presented the burnt offering unto him, with
the pieces thereof, and the head: and he burnt *them* upon the
14 altar. [r]And he did wash the inwards and the legs, and burnt
15 *them* upon the burnt offering on the altar. ¶ [s]And he brought
the people's offering, and took the goat, which *was* the sin offering for the people, and slew it, and offered it for sin, as the first.
16 And he brought the burnt offering, and offered it [t]according to
17 the [1]manner. And he brought [u]the meat offering, and [2]took an
handful thereof, and burnt *it* upon the altar, [x]beside the burnt
18 sacrifice of the morning. He slew also the bullock and the ram
for [y]a sacrifice of peace offerings, which *was* for the people: and
Aaron's sons presented unto him the blood, which he sprinkled
19 upon the altar round about, and the fat of the bullock and of
the ram, the rump, and that which covereth *the inwards*, and
20 the kidneys, and the caul *above* the liver: and they put the fat
21 upon the breasts, [z]and he burnt the fat upon the altar: and the
breasts and the right shoulder Aaron waved [a]*for* a wave offering
22 before the LORD; as Moses commanded. ¶ And Aaron lifted
up his hand toward the people, and [b]blessed them, and came
down from offering of the sin offering, and the burnt offering,
23 and peace offerings. And Moses and Aaron went into the

[h] ch. 4. 3.
[i] 1 Sam. 3. 14. Heb. 5. 3. & 7. 27. & 9. 7. ch. 4. 16, 20. Heb. 5. 1.
[k] ch. 8. 15.
[l] See ch. 4. 7.
[m] ch. 8. 16.
[n] ch. 4. 8.
[o] ch. 4. 11. & 8. 17.
[p] ch. 1. 5. & 8. 19.
[q] ch. 8. 20.
[r] ch. 8. 21.
[s] ver. 3. Isai. 53. 10. Heb. 2. 17. & 5. 3.
[t] ch. 1. 3, 10.
[u] ver. 4. ch. 2. 1, 2.
[x] Ex. 29. 38.
[y] ch. 3. 1, &c.
[z] ch. 3. 5, 16.
[a] Ex. 29. 24. ch. 7. 30.
[b] Num. 6. 23. Deut. 21. 5. Luke 24. 50.

[1] Or, *ordinance*. [2] Heb. *filled his hand out of it.*

---

9. Aaron did not act according to the ordinary Law (iv. 5, 6, 7, 16, 17, 18), but as Moses had done in the Sin-offering of the Consecration ceremony (viii. 15; cp. also iv. 25, 30, 34). The probable reason of this was that he had not yet been formally introduced as the High-priest into the Holy Place of the Tabernacle.

brought the blood] They most likely held the basons in which the blood was received as it ran from the victim, and then handed them to their father. See i. 5.

15–21. In this first complete series of offerings made by the High-priest, the sacrifices take their appointed order; first, the Sin-offering to make atonement; then the Burnt-offering, to signify the surrender of the body, soul and spirit to Jehovah in heaven; and lastly the Peace-offering, to show forth the communion vouchsafed to those who are justified and sanctified. See viii. 14 note.

22. Aaron having completed the offerings, before he came down from the stage surrounding the Altar on which the priests used to stand to officiate (see Exod. xxvii. 8), turned toward the people, and blessed them; probably using the form which became the established one for the priests (Num. vi. 24–26), and which is still maintained in the synagogues.

23. Aaron, having now gone through the cycle of priestly duties connected with the Brazen Altar, accompanies Moses into the **Tent of Meeting**. It was reasonable that Moses, as the divinely appointed leader of the nation, should induct Aaron into the Tabernacle.

blessed the people] This joint blessing of the mediator of the Law and the High-priest was the solemn conclusion of the Consecration and Inauguration. (Cp. 2 Chr. vi. 3–11.) According to one tradition the form used by Moses and Aaron resembled Ps. xc. 17. But another form is given in the Targum of Palestine, "May your offerings be accepted, and may the Lord dwell among you and forgive you your sins."

[c] ver. 6. Num. 14. 10. [d] Judg. 6. 21. [e] 2 Chr. 7. 3. Ezra 3. 11. [a] ch. 16. 1. 1 Chr. 24. 2. [b] Num. 16. 18. [c] Ex. 30. 9. [d] ch. 9. 24. Num. 16. 35. 2 Sam. 6. 7. [e] Isai. 52. 11. Ezek. 20. 41. & 42. 13. [f] Isai. 49. 3. Ezek. 28. 22. John 13. 31. 2 Thes. 1. 10. [g] Ps. 39. 9. [h] Num. 3. 19. [i] Luke 7. 12. Acts 5. 6.

tabernacle of the congregation, and came out, and blessed the
people: [c]and the glory of the LORD appeared unto all the people.
24 And [d]there came a fire out from before the LORD, and consumed
upon the altar the burnt offering and the fat: *which* when all
the people saw, [e]they shouted, and fell on their faces.
CHAP. 10. AND [a]Nadab and Abihu, the sons of Aaron, [b]took
either of them his censer, and put fire therein, and put incense
thereon, and offered [c]strange fire before the LORD, which he
2 commanded them not. And there [d]went out fire from the LORD,
3 and devoured them, and they died before the LORD. Then Moses
said unto Aaron, This *is it* that the LORD spake, saying, I will
be sanctified in them [e]that come nigh me, and before all the
4 people I will be [f]glorified. [g]And Aaron held his peace. And
Moses called Mishael and Elzaphan, the sons of [h]Uzziel the
uncle of Aaron, and said unto them, Come near, [i]carry your
5 brethren from before the sanctuary out of the camp. So they
went near, and carried them in their coats out of the camp; as
6 Moses had said. And Moses said unto Aaron, and unto Eleazar

---

24. The very ancient Jewish tradition has been widely adopted that the sacred fire of the Altar originated in this divine act, and that it was afterwards preserved on the Altar of the Tabernacle until the dedication of the Temple, when fire again "came down from heaven." (2 Chr. vii. 1.) But according to the sacred narrative the Altar-fire had been lighted in a natural way before this occasion. (Cp. viii. 16, ix. 10, 13, &c.; Ex. xl. 29.) It would therefore seem that the fire which "came out from before the Lord" manifested itself, according to the words of *v.* 24, not in kindling the fuel on the Altar, but in the sudden consuming of the victim. For the like testimony to the acceptance of a sacrifice, see Judg. xiii. 19, 20; 1 K. xviii. 38; 1 Chr. xxi. 26, and probably Gen. iv. 4. The phrase *to turn a sacrifice to ashes*, became equivalent to *accepting it* (Ps. xx. 3, see margin). The fire of the altar was maintained in accordance with vi. 13.

X. The events recorded in this chapter must have occurred immediately after the offering of the sacrifices of inauguration, in the evening of the same day. See *v.* 19.

1. *Nadab and Abihu*] The two elder sons of Aaron (Ex. vi. 23; Num. iii. 2), who were amongst those invited to accompany Moses when he was going up Mount Sinai, but who were "to worship afar off," and not "come near the Lord." Ex. xxiv. 1, 2.

censer] See Ex. xxv. 38 note.

strange fire] The point of their offence is evidently expressed in this term. This may very probably mean that the incense was lighted at an unauthorized time. And we may reasonably unite with this the supposition that they were intoxicated (cp. *v.* 9), as well as another conjecture, that they made their offering of incense an accompaniment to the exultation of the people on the manifestation of the glory of the Lord (ix. 24). As they perished not within the Tabernacle, but in front of it, it seems likely that they may have been making an ostentatious and irreverent display of their ministration to accompany the shouts of the people on their way towards the Tabernacle. The offence for which they were immediately visited with outward punishment was thus a flagrant outrage on the solemn order of the divine service, while the cause of their offence may have been their guilty excess.

2. The fire which had just before sanctified the ministry of Aaron as well pleasing to God, now brought to destruction his two eldest sons because they did not sanctify Jehovah in their hearts, but dared to perform a self-willed act of worship; just as the same Gospel is to one a savour of life unto life, and to another a savour of death unto death (2 Cor. ii. 16).

3. Rather, **I will sanctify myself in them that come near to me** (*i.e.* the priests), **and I will glorify myself before all the people.** The words used by Moses on this occasion are not found elsewhere in the Pentateuch. But the sense is implied in such passages as Exod. xix. 22, xxviii. 41, xxix. 1, 44.

Aaron's silence (cp. Psalm xxxix. 9) on this occasion may be compared with his reasonable and natural expostulation with Moses when his surviving sons were rebuked for not having eaten the flesh of the Sin-offering (*v.* 19).

4. The first cousins of Aaron (Ex. vi. 22) are selected by Moses to convey the bodies of Nadab and Abihu out of the camp and bury them, probably because they were the nearest relations who were not priests. See Num. ix. 6.

5. *coats*] See Ex. xxviii. 39. Life had been extinguished as if by a flash of lightning, but neither the bodies nor the dresses were destroyed.

6, 7. Aaron and his two surviving sons are forbidden to show the accustomed signs of

and unto Ithamar, his sons, [k]Uncover not your heads, neither
rend your clothes; lest ye die, and lest [l]wrath come upon all
the people: but let your brethren, the whole house of Israel,
7 bewail the burning which the LORD hath kindled. [m]And ye
shall not go out from the door of the tabernacle of the congregation, lest ye die: [n]for the anointing oil of the LORD *is* upon
8 you. And they did according to the word of Moses. ¶ And the
9 LORD spake unto Aaron, saying, [o]Do not drink wine nor strong
drink, thou, nor thy sons with thee, when ye go into the tabernacle of the congregation, lest ye die: *it shall be* a statute for
10 ever throughout your generations: and that ye may [p]put difference between holy and unholy, and between unclean and
11 clean; [q]and that ye may teach the children of Israel all the
statutes which the LORD hath spoken unto them by the hand of
12 Moses. ¶ And Moses spake unto Aaron, and unto Eleazar and
unto Ithamar, his sons that were left, Take [r]the meat offering
that remaineth of the offerings of the LORD made by fire, and
13 eat it without leaven beside the altar: for [s]it *is* most holy: and
ye shall eat it in the holy place, because it *is* thy due, and thy
sons' due, of the sacrifices of the LORD made by fire: for [t]so I
14 am commanded. And [u]the wave breast and heave shoulder
shall ye eat in a clean place; thou, and thy sons, and thy
daughters with thee: for *they be* thy due, and thy sons' due,
which are given out of the sacrifices of peace offerings of the
15 children of Israel. [x]The heave shoulder and the wave breast
shall they bring with the offerings made by fire of the fat, to

[k] Ex. 33. 5. & 21. 1, 10. Num. 6. 6. Deut. 33. 9. Ezek. 24. 16.
[l] Num. 16. 22, 46. Josh. 7. 1. 2 Sam. 24. 1.
[m] ch. 21. 12.
[n] Ex. 28. 41.
[o] Ezek. 44. 21. Luke 1. 15. 1 Tim. 3. 3. Tit. 1. 7.
[p] ch. 11. 47. Jer. 15. 19. Ezek. 22. 26. & 44. 23.
[q] Deut. 24. 8. Neh. 8. 2. Jer. 18. 18. Mal. 2. 7.
[r] Ex. 29. 2. ch. 6. 16. Num. 18. 9.
[s] ch. 21. 22.
[t] ch. 2. 3. & 6. 16.
[u] Ex. 29. 24. ch. 7. 31, 34. Num. 18. 11.
[x] ch. 7. 29.

---

mourning, or to leave the Court of the Tabernacle in order to attend the funeral, because, from their office, they were especially concerned as consecrated priests in outwardly maintaining the honour of Jehovah. They were to bear visible testimony to the righteousness of the punishment of Nadab and Abihu. The people, on the other hand, as not formally standing so near to Jehovah, were permitted to "bewail" as an acknowledgment that the nation had a share in the sin of its priests. (Cp. 1 Cor. xii. 26.)

6. *Uncover not your heads*] Or, *set free—let go loose*. It was a custom to let the hair grow long and fall loosely over the head and face (xiii. 45; 2 Sam. xv. 30, xix. 4); and the substance of the command would thus be that they should not let the hair go dishevelled.—Rending the clothes in front so as to lay open the breast was one of the commonest manifestations of grief (see Gen. xxxvii. 29, xliv. 13; 2 S. i. 11; Job i. 20; Joel ii. 13, &c.). The garments as well as the persons of the priests were consecrated; this appears to be the reason of the prohibition of these ordinary signs of mourning. Cp. xx. 10.

lest ye die] See Exod. xxviii. 35 note.

7. *the anointing oil...is upon you*] See viii. 12, 30. The holy oil, as the symbol of the Holy Spirit, the Spirit of Life and immortality and joy, was the sign of the priests being brought near to Jehovah. It was therefore by its meaning connected both with the general law which forbade the High-priest ever to put on signs of mourning on account of death (xxi. 10-12), and with the special reason for the prohibition on this occasion.

9-11. When the priest was on duty he was to abstain from wine and strong drink, lest he should commit excess (see *v.* 1), and so become disqualified for carrying out the precepts of the ceremonial Law.

9. *strong drink*] The Hebrew word is employed here to denote strong drinks of any kind except wine made from the grape.

10. *unholy...unclean*] Common, as not consecrated; and what would occasion defilement by being touched or eaten. Cp. Acts x. 14.

11. That is, "that you may, by your example in your ministrations, preserve the minds of the Israelites from confusion in regard to the distinctions made by the divine Law."

12-15. The argument is, that as such meals were appointed in honour of Jehovah Himself, they ought to be conducted with due reverence and discretion.

12. *beside the altar*] What is called "the holy place" in *vv.* 13, 17: it should be rather, **a holy place,** any part of the Holy precinct, as distinguished from a merely "clean place" (*v.* 14), either within or without the court of the Tabernacle.

14. *wave breast and heave shoulder*] See vii. 30 note.

wave *it for* a wave offering before the LORD; and it shall be
thine, and thy sons' with thee, by a statute for ever; as the
[y] ch. 9. 3, 15. 16 LORD hath commanded. ¶ And Moses diligently sought [y]the
goat of the sin offering, and, behold, it was burnt: and he was
angry with Eleazar and Ithamar, the sons of Aaron *which were*
[z] ch. 6. 26, 29. 17 left *alive*, saying, [z]Wherefore have ye not eaten the sin offering
in the holy place, seeing it *is* most holy, and *God* hath given it
you to bear the iniquity of the congregation, to make atonement
[a] ch. 6. 30. 18 for them before the LORD? Behold, [a]the blood of it was not
brought in within the holy *place:* ye should indeed have eaten
[b] ch. 6. 26. 19 it in the holy *place*, [b]as I commanded. And Aaron said unto
[c] ch. 9. 8, 12. Moses, Behold, [c]this day have they offered their sin offering and
their burnt offering before the LORD; and such things have
[d] Jer. 6. 20. & 14. 12. Hos. 9. 4. Mal. 1. 10, 13. befallen me: and *if* I had eaten the sin offering to day, [d]should
20 it have been accepted in the sight of the LORD? And when
Moses heard *that*, he was content.

CHAP. 11. AND the LORD spake unto Moses and to Aaron, saying
[a] Deut. 14. 4. Acts 10. 12, 14. 2 unto them, Speak unto the children of Israel, saying, [a]These
are the beasts which ye shall eat among all the beasts that *are*
3 on the earth. Whatsoever parteth the hoof, and is clovenfooted,
and cheweth the cud, among the beasts, that shall ye eat.
4 Nevertheless these shall ye not eat of them that chew the cud,
or of them that divide the hoof; *as* the camel, because he cheweth
5 the cud, but divideth not the hoof; he *is* unclean unto you. And
the coney, because he cheweth the cud, but divideth not the

---

16. The Law on the point in question was clear. See ii. 3, iv. 5, 16 notes. But on this occasion, though the Sin-offering which had been offered by Aaron was for the people (ix. 15), its blood was not carried into the Tabernacle. The priests might therefore have too readily supposed that their eating the flesh, or burning it, was a matter of indifference. Hence Moses explains that the appropriation of the flesh by the priests is an essential part of the act of atonement (*v.* 17).

it was burnt] It was consumed by fire in an ordinary way, not in the fire of the Altar. See i. 9.

17. *to bear the iniquity*] See Ex. xxviii. 38 note.

18. "The holy *place*," as it is called in our version, within the Tabernacle (see Ex. xxvi. 33, xxviii. 29, &c.) into which the blood was carried, is regularly called in Hebrew, simply, "the Holy" (as the innermost chamber is called "the Holy of Holies"), the adjective being used substantively; while the precinct in which the flesh of the Sin-offering was eaten is generally called in full the Holy Place, the substantive being expressed (*v.* 13).

19. That is: "Behold this very day, in which we have done our part in sacrificing Sin-offerings and Burnt-offerings to the Lord, this great calamity has befallen me. Could it have been well-pleasing to the Lord if those who have been so humbled as I and my sons have been by the sin of our relations and the divine judgment, had feasted on the most Holy flesh of the Sin-offering?"

XI. **1.** Jehovah speaks to Moses and Aaron conjointly. (Cp. xiii. 1, xv. 1.) The High-priest, in regard to the legal purifications, is treated as co-ordinate with the legislator.

2. Rather, "These are the **animals which ye may eat out of** all the beasts;" that is, out of the larger creatures, the quadrupeds, as distinguished from birds and reptiles. See Gen. i. 24. Of quadrupeds, those only might be eaten which completely divided the hoof and chew the cud (*vv.* 3–8).

3. *parteth*, &c.] Rather, **is clovenfooted and completely separates the hoofs.**

4. *divideth not the hoof*] The toes of the camel are divided above, but they are united below in a sort of cushion or pad resting upon the hard bottom of the foot, which is "like the sole of a shoe." The Moslems eat the flesh of the camel, but it is said not to be wholesome.

5. *the coney*] The old English name for a rabbit. The animal meant is the Hyrax Syriacus. It bears some resemblance to the guinea-pig or the marmot, and in its general appearance and habits (Prov. xxx. 26, Ps. civ. 18), it might easily be taken for a rodent. But Cuvier discovered that it is, in its anatomy, a true pachyderm, allied to the rhinoceros and the tapir, inferior to them as it is in size.

he cheweth the cud] The Hyrax has the same habit as the hare, the rabbit, the guinea-pig, and some other rodents, of

6 hoof; he *is* unclean unto you. And the hare, because he cheweth
the cud, but divideth not the hoof; he *is* unclean unto you.
7 And the swine, though he divide the hoof, and be clovenfooted,
8 yet he cheweth not the cud; [b]he *is* unclean to you. Of their
flesh shall ye not eat, and their carcase shall ye not touch;
9 [c]they *are* unclean to you. ¶ [d]These shall ye eat of all that *are*
in the waters: whatsoever hath fins and scales in the waters,
10 in the seas, and in the rivers, them shall ye eat. And all that
have not fins and scales in the seas, and in the rivers, of all
that move in the waters, and of any living thing which *is* in
11 the waters, they *shall be* an [e]abomination unto you: they shall
be even an abomination unto you; ye shall not eat of their
12 flesh, but ye shall have their carcases in abomination. Whatsoever hath no fins nor scales in the waters, that *shall be* an
13 abomination unto you. ¶ [f]And these *are they which* ye shall
have in abomination among the fowls; they shall not be eaten,
they *are* an abomination: the eagle, and the ossifrage, and the
14, 15 ospray, and the vulture, and the kite after his kind; every
16 raven after his kind; and the owl, and the night hawk, and the
17 cuckow, and the hawk after his kind, and the little owl, and the
18 cormorant, and the great owl, and the swan, and the pelican,
19 and the gier eagle, and the stork, the heron after her kind, and
20 the lapwing, and the bat. ¶ All fowls that creep, going upon *all*
21 four, *shall be* an abomination unto you. Yet these may ye eat
of every flying creeping thing that goeth upon *all* four, which

[b] Isai. 65. 4. & 66. 3. 17.
[c] Isai. 52. 11. See Matt. 15. 11, 20. Mark 7, 2, 15, 18. Acts 10. 14, 15. & 15. 29. Rom. 14. 14, 17. 1 Cor. 8. 8. Col. 2. 16, 21. Heb. 9. 10.
[d] Deut. 14. 9.
[e] ch. 7. 18. Deut. 14. 3.
[f] Deut. 14. 12.

---

moving its jaws when it is at rest as if it were masticating. The rodents were familiarly spoken of as ruminating animals, just as the bat was reckoned amongst birds because it flies (see *v.* 19), and as whales and their congeners are spoken of as fish, when there is no occasion for scientific accuracy.

7. *he divide the hoof*, &c.] **It is cloven-footed and completely,** &c. See *v.* 3 note. Of all the quadrupeds of which the Law forbids the flesh to be eaten, the pig seems to have been regarded as the most unclean. Cp. marg. reff. Several other nations have agreed with the Hebrews in this respect: the reason being that its flesh is unwholesome, especially in warm climates.

9. Any fish, either from salt water or fresh, might be eaten if it had both scales and fins, but no other creature that lives in the waters. Shellfish of all kinds, whether mollusks or crustaceans, and cetaceous animals, were therefore prohibited, as well as fish which appear to have no scales, like the eel; probably because they were considered unwholesome, and (under certain circumstances) found to be so.

13–19. As far as they can be identified, the birds here mentioned are such as live upon animal food. They were those which the Israelites might have been tempted to eat, either from their being easy to obtain, or from the example of other nations, and which served as types of the entire range of prohibited kinds.

13. *the eagle*] Rather, **the great vulture,** which the Egyptians are known to have ranked as the first amongst birds. Cp. 2 S. i. 23; Ps. ciii. 5; Prov. xxiii. 5, &c.

The *ossifrage*, or bone-breaker, was the lammer-geyer, and the *ospray* (a corruption of *ossifrage*) the sea-eagle.

14. *the vulture*] Rather, the (black) kite (Isai. xxxiv. 15): *the kite*, rather the red kite, remarkable for its piercing sight (Job xxviii. 7).

15. *every raven after his kind*] *i.e.* the whole family of corvidæ.

16. *and the owl*, &c.] Rather, "and the ostrich, and the owl, and the gull, and the hawk," &c.

18. *the swan*] More probably the ibis, the sacred bird of the Egyptians. *The gier eagle* is most likely the Egyptian vulture, a bird of unprepossessing appearance and disgusting habits, but fostered by the Egyptians as a useful scavenger.

19. *the heron...the lapwing*] Rather, the great plover—the hoopoe, so called from its peculiar cry.

20. Rather, **"All creeping things which have wings,"** &c. The word rendered creeping things may be regarded as coextensive with our word *vermin.* It is derived from a verb which signifies not only to creep, but to teem, or bring forth abundantly (Gen. i. 21, viii. 17; Exod. viii. 3; Ps. cv. 30), and so easily came to denote creatures which are apt to abound, to the annoyance of mankind.

21. *legs above their feet, to leap withal upon the earth*] The families of the Saltatoria, of which the common cricket, the common grasshopper, and the migratory locust, may be taken as types.

[g] Matt. 3. 4. Mark 1. 6.

22 have legs above their feet, to leap withal upon the earth; *even*
these of them ye may eat; [g]the locust after his kind, and the
bald locust after his kind, and the beetle after his kind, and the
23 grasshopper after his kind. But all *other* flying creeping things,
24 which have four feet, *shall be* an abomination unto you. And
for these ye shall be unclean: whosoever toucheth the carcase
25 of them shall be unclean until the even. And whosoever beareth
ought of the carcase of them [h]shall wash his clothes, and be
26 unclean until the even. ¶ *The carcases* of every beast which
divideth the hoof, and *is* not clovenfooted, nor cheweth the cud,
are unclean unto you: every one that toucheth them shall be
27 unclean. And whatsoever goeth upon his paws, among all
manner of beasts that go on *all* four, those *are* unclean unto
you: whoso toucheth their carcase shall be unclean until the
28 even. And he that beareth the carcase of them shall wash his
clothes, and be unclean until the even: they *are* unclean unto
29 you. ¶ These also *shall be* unclean unto you among the creeping things that creep upon the earth; the weasel, and [i]the
30 mouse, and the tortoise after his kind, and the ferret, and the
31 chameleon, and the lizard, and the snail and the mole. These
are unclean to you among all that creep: whosoever doth touch
32 them, when they be dead, shall be unclean until the even. And
upon whatsoever *any* of them, when they are dead, doth fall, it
shall be unclean; whether *it be* any vessel of wood, or raiment,
or skin, or sack, whatsoever vessel *it be*, wherein *any* work is
done, [k]it must be put into water, and it shall be unclean until
33 the even; so it shall be cleansed. And every earthen vessel,
whereinto *any* of them falleth, whatsoever *is* in it shall be
34 unclean; and [l]ye shall break it. Of all meat which may be
eaten, *that* on which *such* water cometh shall be unclean: and all
drink that may be drunk in every *such* vessel shall be unclean.
35 And every *thing* whereupon *any part* of their carcase falleth
shall be unclean; *whether it be* oven, or ranges for pots, they
shall be broken down: *for* they *are* unclean, and shall be unclean
36 unto you. Nevertheless a fountain or pit, [1]*wherein there is*
plenty of water, shall be clean: but that which toucheth their
37 carcase shall be unclean. And if *any part* of their carcase fall
38 upon any sowing seed which is to be sown, it *shall be* clean. But
if *any* water be put upon the seed, and *any part* of their carcase
39 fall thereon, it *shall be* unclean unto you. ¶ And if any beast,
of which ye may eat, die; he that toucheth the carcase thereof
40 shall be unclean until the even. And [m]he that eateth of the
carcase of it shall wash his clothes, and be unclean until the

[h] ch. 14. 8. & 15. 5. Num. 19. 10, 22. & 31. 24.

[i] Isai. 66. 17.

[k] ch. 15. 12.

[l] ch. 6. 28. & 15. 12.

[m] ch. 17. 15. & 22. 8. Deut. 14. 21. Ezek. 4. 14. & 44. 31.

[1] Heb. *a gathering together of waters.*

---

22. In the uncertainty of identifying these four creatures, it has been suggested that some of the names may belong to locusts in an imperfect state of development. Most modern versions have taken a safer course than our translators, by retaining the Hebrew names.

24–28. *unclean*] If the due purification was omitted at the time, through negligence or forgetfulness, a Sin-offering was required. See v. 2.

29, 30. The identification of "the creeping things" here named is not always certain. They are most likely those which were occasionally eaten. For the *tortoise* read the great lizard, for the *ferret* the gecko (one of the lizard tribe), for the *chameleon* the frog or the Nile lizard: by the word rendered *snail* is probably meant another kind of lizard, and by the *mole* the chameleon.

33. *earthen vessel*] See marg. reff.

35. See ii. 4. The word rendered "ranges for pots" has been conjectured to mean either an excavated fireplace, fitted to receive a pair of ovens, or a support like a pair of andirons.

even: he also that beareth the carcase of it shall wash his
41 clothes, and be unclean until the even. ¶ And every creeping
thing that creepeth upon the earth *shall be* an abomination; it
42 shall not be eaten. Whatsoever goeth upon the belly, and
whatsoever goeth upon *all* four, or whatsoever [1]hath more feet
among all creeping things that creep upon the earth, them ye
43 shall not eat; for they *are* an abomination. [n]Ye shall not make [n] ch. 20. 25.
your [2]selves abominable with any creeping thing that creepeth,
neither shall ye make yourselves unclean with them, that ye
44 should be defiled thereby. For I *am* the LORD your God: ye
shall therefore sanctify yourselves, and [o]ye shall be holy; for I [o] Ex. 19. 6. ch. 19. 2.
am holy: neither shall ye defile yourselves with any manner of & 20. 7, 26.
45 creeping thing that creepeth upon the earth. [p]For I *am* the 1 Thess. 4. 7.
LORD that bringeth you up out of the land of Egypt, to be your 1 Pet. 1. 15, 16.
46 God: [q]ye shall therefore be holy, for I *am* holy. This *is* the law [p] Ex. 6. 7.
of the beasts, and of the fowl, and of every living creature that [q] ver. 44.
moveth in the waters, and of every creature that creepeth upon
47 the earth: [r]to make a difference between the unclean and the [r] ch. 10. 10.
clean, and between the beast that may be eaten and the beast
that may not be eaten.

CHAP. 12. AND the LORD spake unto Moses, saying, Speak unto
2 the children of Israel, saying, If a [a]woman have conceived seed, [a] ch. 15. 19.
and born a man child: then [b]she shall be unclean seven days; [b] Luke 2. 22.
[c]according to the days of the separation for her infirmity shall [c] ch. 15. 19.
3 she be unclean. And in the [d]eighth day the flesh of his fore- [d] Gen. 17. 12.
4 skin shall be circumcised. And she shall then continue in the Luke 1. 59.
blood of her purifying three and thirty days; she shall touch no & 2. 21.
hallowed thing, nor come into the sanctuary, until the days of John 7. 22, 23.
5 her purifying be fulfilled. But if she bear a maid child, then
she shall be unclean two weeks, as in her separation: and she

[1] Heb. *doth multiply feet.* [2] Heb. *souls.*

---

42. *Whatsoever goeth upon the belly*] *i.e.* all footless reptiles, and mollusks, snakes of all kinds, snails, slugs, and worms. *Whatsoever goeth upon all four; i.e.* "creeping things," or vermin; such as the weasel, the mouse or the lizard. *Whatsoever hath more feet; i.e.* all insects, except the locust family (*v.* 22 note), myriapods, spiders, and caterpillars.

44-47. These verses set forth the spiritual ground on which the distinction between clean and unclean is based. Cp. marg. reff. and x. 10, xx. 25, 26; 1 Peter i. 15, 16.

The basis of the obligation to maintain the distinction was the call of the Hebrews to be the peculiar people of Jehovah. It was to be something in their daily life to remind them of the Covenant which distinguished them from the nations of the world. By Jesus Christ it was revealed (Matt. xv. 11) to the elect people that they were no longer to be tied by the letter of the Law in regard to their food, but were to be left to the exercise of a regenerated judgment. They were to learn that the kingdom of God is not eating, or abstaining from, meats and drinks; but righteousness, and truth, and peace, and joy in the Holy Ghost (Rom. xiv. 17. Cp. Acts x. 15; 1 Tim. iv. 4).

XII.—XV. CEREMONIAL PURIFICATIONS. The Purifications of the Law fall under three heads; (i) those for defilement arising from secretions; (ii) those for the Leprosy; (iii) those for pollution from corpses. The first and second classes are described in these chapters; the last, as relates to human corpses, in Num. xix. 11, &c., and as relates to the bodies of dead animals, in xi. 24-28, 31-40.

XII. This chapter would more naturally follow the fifteenth. See Note to xv. 1.

3. On circumcision, see Gen. xvii. 5 note.

4. The Levitical law ascribed impurity exclusively to the Mother, in no degree to the Child.

5. Some have thought that this doubling of each of the two periods was intended to remind the people of the fact that woman represents the lower side of human nature, and was the first to fall into temptation. 1 Tim. ii. 13-15; 1 Pet. iii. 7. The ancients had a notion that the mother suffers for a longer time after the birth of a girl than after the birth of a boy. The period required for the restoration of her health in

shall continue in the blood of her purifying threescore and six
[e] Luke 2. 22. 6 days. ¶ And [e] when the days of her purifying are fulfilled, for a
son, or for a daughter, she shall bring a lamb [1] of the first year
for a burnt offering, and a young pigeon, or a turtle dove, for a
sin offering, unto the door of the tabernacle of the congregation,
7 unto the priest: who shall offer it before the LORD, and make
an atonement for her; and she shall be cleansed from the issue
of her blood. This *is* the law for her that hath born a male or a
[f] ch. 5. 7. Luke 2. 24. 8 female. [f] And if [2] she be not able to bring a lamb, then she shall
bring two turtles, or two young pigeons; the one for the burnt
[g] ch. 4. 26. offering, and the other for a sin offering: [g] and the priest shall
make an atonement for her, and she shall be clean.

CHAP. 13. AND the LORD spake unto Moses and Aaron, saying,
[a] Deut. 28. 27. Isai. 3. 17. 2 When a man shall have in the skin of his flesh a [3] rising, [a] a scab,

[1] Heb. *a son of his year.* [2] Heb. *her hand find not sufficiency of.* [3] Or, *swelling.*

the one case was thirty days, and in the other, it was forty or forty-two days. This notion may have been connected with a general custom of observing the distinction as early as the time of Moses.

6–8. The sacrificial act expressed an acknowledgment of sin and a dedication of herself to Jehovah. See viii. 14.

6. *of the first year*] Literally, as in the margin, *a son of his year.* This expression is supposed to mean one less than a year old, while *the son of a year* is one that has just completed its first year.

8. *a lamb*] Rather, **one of the flock;** either a sheep or a goat; it is not the same word as in *v.* 6.

two turtles, or two young pigeons] See on i. 14. The Virgin Mary availed herself of the liberty which the Law allowed to the poor, and offered the inferior Burnt-offering (Luke ii. 24).

XIII., XIV. THE LAWS RELATING TO LEPROSY. The Leprosy is the most terrible of all the disorders to which the body of man is subject. There is no disease in which hope of recovery is so nearly extinguished. From a commencement slight in appearance, with but little pain or inconvenience, often in its earlier stage insidiously disappearing and reappearing, it goes on in its strong but sluggish course, generally in defiance of the efforts of medical skill, until it reduces the patient to a mutilated cripple with dulled or obliterated senses, the voice turned to a croak, and with features of ghastly deformity. When it reaches some vital part it generally occasions what seem like the symptoms of a distinct disease (most often Dysentery), and so puts an end to the life of the sufferer.

It was an all but universal impression that the Leprosy, above all other diseases, came upon man as an irresistible stroke of superhuman power, either in the way of punishment for personal sin or of an affliction with some definite purpose. This natural suggestion was confirmed and realized upon several occasions in the history of the Israelites. A stroke of Leprosy was the mark of the divine displeasure at the slow faith of Moses (Ex. iv. 6), at the contumacy of Miriam (Num. xii. 10), at the dishonesty of Gehazi (2 K. v. 27), and at the impious presumption of Uzziah (2 Chr. xxvi. 19, 20). One of the denunciations against Joab, on account of the death of Abner, was that his children should be lepers (2 S. iii. 29).

It is now considered by all the best authorities that the Hebrew word for the disease does not denote the disease which is more properly called the Leprosy (see xiii. 12), but that which is known to physicians as the Elephantiasis: the origin of which is ascribed to an animal poison generated in or received into the blood, and accumulated therein probably by a process analogous to fermentation. This poison primarily affects either the skin, or the nerves and nervous centres. In this way, two forms of Elephantiasis are distinguished, the *Tuberculated*, and the *Anæsthetic* or *Non-tuberculated*, of which the former is the more common.

Medical skill appears to have been more completely foiled by Elephantiasis than by any other malady. The Anæsthetic form alone seems to be in some degree amenable to remedies and regimen.

The question whether Elephantiasis is contagious or not, is the one of most peculiar interest in connection with the Levitical law. Many facts tend to prove that, as a rule, it was not; but that under certain circumstances (*e.g.* when the ulcers are running) contagion might be developed.

2. *the skin of his flesh*] An expression found nowhere but in this chapter. It probably denotes the cuticle or scarf skin, as distinguished from the cutis or true skin.

rising—scab—bright spot] The Hebrew words are the technical names applied to the common external signs of incipient Elephantiasis.

like the plague of leprosy] **Like a stroke of Leprosy.**

or bright spot, and it be in the skin of his flesh *like* the plague of
leprosy; [b]then he shall be brought unto Aaron the priest, or
3 unto one of his sons the priests: and the priest shall look on the
plague in the skin of the flesh: and *when* the hair in the plague
is turned white, and the plague in sight *be* deeper than the skin
of his flesh, it *is* a plague of leprosy: and the priest shall look on
4 him, and pronounce him unclean. If the bright spot *be* white
in the skin of his flesh, and in sight *be* not deeper than the skin,
and the hair thereof be not turned white; then the priest shall
5 shut up *him that hath* the plague seven days: and the priest
shall look on him the seventh day: and, behold, *if* the plague in
his sight be at a stay, *and* the plague spread not in the skin;
6 then the priest shall shut him up seven days more: and the
priest shall look on him again the seventh day: and, behold, *if*
the plague *be* somewhat dark, *and* the plague spread not in the
skin, the priest shall pronounce him clean: it *is but* a scab:
7 and he [c]shall wash his clothes, and be clean. But if the scab
spread much abroad in the skin, after that he hath been seen of
the priest for his cleansing, he shall be seen of the priest again:
8 and *if* the priest see that, behold, the scab spreadeth in the skin,
then the priest shall pronounce him unclean: it *is* a leprosy.
9 ¶ When the plague of leprosy is in a man, then he shall be
10 brought unto the priest; [d]and the priest shall see *him*: and,
behold, *if* the rising *be* white in the skin, and it have turned the
11 hair white, and *there be* [1]quick raw flesh in the rising; it *is* an
old leprosy in the skin of his flesh, and the priest shall pronounce
him unclean, and shall not shut him up: for he *is* unclean.
12 And if a leprosy break out abroad in the skin, and the leprosy
cover all the skin of *him that hath* the plague from his head even
13 to his foot, wheresoever the priest looketh; then the priest shall

[b] Deut. 17. 8, 9. & 24. 8. Luke 17. 14.

[c] ch. 11. 25. & 14. 8.

[d] Num. 12. 10, 12. 2 Kin. 5. 27. 2 Chr. 26. 20.

[1] Heb. *the quickening of living flesh.*

---

3. *the hair in the plague is turned white*] The sparing growth of very fine whitish hair on leprous spots in the place of the natural hair, appears to have been always regarded as a characteristic symptom.

the plague in sight be deeper than the skin of his flesh] Rather, **The stroke appears to be deeper than the scarf skin.** The 'bright spot' changed to a brownish colour with a metallic or oily lustre, and with a clearly-defined edge. This symptom, along with the whitish hair, at once decided the case to be one of Leprosy.

5. *and the plague spread not*] Rather, **advance not,** so as to shew that the disease is under the cuticle and assuming the symptoms of *v.* 3.

6. *somewhat dark*] Rather, **somewhat dim**: that is, if the spot is dying away.

7. *seen of the priest for his cleansing*] The purport of these words is doubtful. They probably mean "seen by the priest and pronounced clean," and refer to the visit of the suspected leper to the priest at the end of the second week. But some have taken the words to mean "seen by the priest with a view to be pronounced clean," and regard the sentence of the priest as provisional, holding good only till the symptoms may appear to resume their progress. Cp. *v.* 35.

10. *if the rising be white*] Or, **If there be a white rising.** The term very probably denotes the white Bulla or patch of Anæsthetic Elephantiasis when it has re-appeared.

quick raw flesh in the rising] The margin gives the literal rendering. The symptom here noted exhibits a more advanced stage of the disease. The expression might denote an ulcer or open sore with "proud flesh" appearing in it.

12-17. The disease here indicated appears to be that now known as Lepra vulgaris, the common White Leprosy, or Dry Tetter. It first shews itself in reddish pimples, the surface of which becomes white and scaly, spreading in a circular form till they meet each other and cover large patches of the body. It scarcely affects the general health, and for the most part disappears of itself, though it often lasts for years.

from his head even to his foot, wheresoever the priest looketh] The first appearance of the Lepra vulgaris may take place in any part of the body, especially however at the larger joints of the limbs; but the spots of Elephantiasis are almost always first seen on those parts which are habitually exposed, the face, ears and hands.

consider: and, behold, *if* the leprosy have covered all his flesh,
he shall pronounce *him* clean *that hath* the plague: it is all
14 turned white: he *is* clean. But when raw flesh appeareth in
15 him, he shall be unclean. And the priest shall see the raw flesh,
and pronounce him to be unclean: *for* the raw flesh *is* unclean:
16 it *is* a leprosy. Or if the raw flesh turn again, and be changed
17 unto white, he shall come unto the priest; and the priest shall
see him: and, behold, *if* the plague be turned into white; then
the priest shall pronounce *him* clean *that hath* the plague: he *is*
18 clean. ¶ The flesh also, in which, *even* in the skin thereof, was
19 a [e]boil, and is healed, and in the place of the boil there be a
white rising, or a bright spot, white, and somewhat reddish, and
20 it be shewed to the priest; and if, when the priest seeth it,
behold, it *be* in sight lower than the skin, and the hair thereof be
turned white; the priest shall pronounce him unclean: it *is* a
21 plague of leprosy broken out of the boil. But if the priest look
on it, and, behold, *there be* no white hairs therein, and *if* it *be*
not lower than the skin, but *be* somewhat dark; then the priest
22 shall shut him up seven days: and if it spread much abroad in
the skin, then the priest shall pronounce him unclean: it *is* a
23 plague. But if the bright spot stay in his place, *and* spread not,
it *is* a burning boil; and the priest shall pronounce him clean.
24 ¶ Or if there be *any* flesh, in the skin whereof *there is* [1]a hot
burning, and the quick *flesh* that burneth have a white bright
25 spot, somewhat reddish, or white; then the priest shall look
upon it: and, behold, *if* the hair in the bright spot be turned
white, and it *be in* sight deeper than the skin; it *is* a leprosy
broken out of the burning: wherefore the priest shall pronounce
26 him unclean: it *is* the plague of leprosy. But if the priest look
on it, and, behold, *there be* no white hair in the bright spot, and
it *be* no lower than the *other* skin, but *be* somewhat dark; then
27 the priest shall shut him up seven days: and the priest shall look
upon him the seventh day: *and* if it be spread much abroad in
the skin, then the priest shall pronounce him unclean: it *is* the
28 plague of leprosy. And if the bright spot stay in his place, *and*
spread not in the skin, but it *be* somewhat dark; it *is* a rising of
the burning, and the priest shall pronounce him clean: for it *is*
29 an inflammation of the burning. ¶ If a man or woman have a
30 plague upon the head or the beard; then the priest shall see the
plague: and, behold, if it *be* in sight deeper than the skin; *and*
there be in it a yellow thin hair; then the priest shall pronounce
him unclean: it *is* a dry scall, *even* a leprosy upon the head or
31 beard. And if the priest look on the plague of the scall, and,

[e] Ex. 9. 9.

[1] Heb. *a burning of fire.*

14. *raw flesh*] See *v.* 10.

18. *boil*] Probably ulcer. In Job ii. 7, and Deut. xxviii. 27, 35, it would seem highly probable that the word expresses the ulcers of Elephantiasis.

20, 21. *lower than the skin*] Rather, **reaching below the scarf skin.**

23. *a burning boil*] Rather, **the scar of the ulcer**; literally, *the burn of the ulcer.*

24. The sense of this verse is:—*Or if there be flesh of which the skin has been affected by severe inflammation, and the sore of the inflammation has become a glossy spot, somewhat reddish or white.*

28. *And if the glossy spot continues unchanged and makes no advance in the skin, and is rather indistinct* (see on *v.* 6), *it is the mark of the inflammation, and the priest shall pronounce him clean, for it is the* (*mere*) *hurt of inflammation.*

30. *scall*] As this is the name for another disease not allied to the Leprosy, it would have been better to retain the original word (*nethek*). It is a true Elephantiasis, and is recognised by modern writers under the name of the Fox mange.

31. *there is no black hair in it*] More probably, **there is no yellow hair in it.**

behold, it *be* not in sight deeper than the skin, and *that there is*
no black hair in it; then the priest shall shut up *him that hath*
32 the plague of the scall seven days: and in the seventh day the
priest shall look on the plague: and, behold, *if* the scall spread
not, and there be in it no yellow hair, and the scall *be* not in sight
33 deeper than the skin; he shall be shaven, but the scall shall he
not shave; and the priest shall shut up *him that hath* the scall
34 seven days more: and in the seventh day the priest shall look
on the scall: and, behold, *if* the scall be not spread in the skin,
nor *be* in sight deeper than the skin; then the priest shall pronounce him clean: and he shall wash his clothes, and be clean.
35 But if the scall spread much in the skin after his cleansing; then
36 the priest shall look on him: and, behold, if the scall be spread
in the skin, the priest shall not seek for yellow hair; he *is*
37 unclean. But if the scall be in his sight at a stay, and *that*
there is black hair grown up therein; the scall is healed, he *is*
38 clean: and the priest shall pronounce him clean. ¶ If a man
also or a woman have in the skin of their flesh bright spots, *even*
39 white bright spots; then the priest shall look: and, behold, *if* the
bright spots in the skin of their flesh *be* darkish white; it *is*
40 a freckled spot *that* groweth in the skin; he *is* clean. And the
man whose [1] hair is fallen off his head, he *is* bald; *yet is* he clean.
41 And he that hath his hair fallen off from the part of his head
42 toward his face, he *is* forehead bald: *yet is* he clean. And if
there be in the bald head, or bald forehead, a white reddish sore;
it *is* a leprosy sprung up in his bald head, or his bald forehead.
43 Then the priest shall look upon it: and, behold, *if* the rising of
the sore *be* white reddish in his bald head, or in his bald fore-
44 head, as the leprosy appeareth in the skin of the flesh; he is a
leprous man, he *is* unclean: the priest shall pronounce him
45 utterly unclean; his plague *is* in his head. ¶ And the leper in
whom the plague *is*, his clothes shall be rent, and his head bare,
and he shall [f] put a covering upon his upper lip, and shall cry, [f] Ezek. 24. 17, 22. Mic. 3. 7.
46 [g] Unclean, unclean. All the days wherein the plague *shall be* in
him he shall be defiled; he *is* unclean: he shall dwell alone; [g] Lam. 4. 15.

[1] Heb. *head is pilled.*

---

37. *be in his sight at a stay*] Or, **Does not alter in appearance.**

39. *freckled spot*] If *v.* 12 refers to the Lepra vulgaris, the Hebrew *bōhak* here may denote some kind of Eczema, a skin disease of a somewhat similar external character.

Verses 38, 39 would seem more in their natural place between *vv.* 17, 18.

42. *sore*] Rather, **stroke.** It is the same word which elsewhere in this and the next chapter is rendered plague.

45. The leper was to carry about with him the usual signs of mourning for the dead. Cp. x. 6 and marg. reff.

The leper was a living parable in the world of the sin of which death was the wages; not the less so because his suffering might have been in no degree due to his own personal deserts: he bore about with him at once the deadly fruit and the symbol of the sin of his race. Ex. xx. 5. As his body slowly perished, first the skin, then the flesh, then the bone, fell to pieces while yet the animal life survived; he was a terrible picture of the gradual corruption of the spirit wrought by sin.

his head bare] Rather, "his head **neglected.**" See x. 6 note.

Unclean, unclean] Cp. marg. ref.

46. *dwell alone*] More properly, **dwell apart**; that is, separated from the people.

Though thus excluded from general intercourse with society, it is not likely that lepers ceased to be objects of sympathy and kindness, such as they now are in those Christian and Moslem countries in which the Leprosy prevails. That they associated together in the Holy Land, as they do at present, is evident from 2 K. vii. 3; Luke xvii. 12. It has been conjectured that a habitation was provided for them outside Jerusalem, on the hill Gareb (Bezetha), which is mentioned only in Jer. xxxi. 39.

without the camp] Cp. marg. reff. A leper polluted everything in the house which he

[h] Num. 5. 2. & 12. 14. 2 Kin. 7. 3. & 15. 5. 2 Chr. 26. 21. Luke 17. 12.

47 [h]without the camp *shall* his habitation *be*. ¶ The garment also
that the plague of leprosy is in, *whether it be* a woollen garment,
48 or a linen garment; whether *it be* in the warp, or woof; of linen,
or of woollen; whether in a skin, or in any [1]thing made of skin;
49 and if the plague be greenish or reddish in the garment, or in
the skin, either in the warp, or in the woof, or in any [2]thing
of skin; it *is* a plague of leprosy, and shall be shewed unto the
50 priest: and the priest shall look upon the plague, and shut up *it*
51 *that hath* the plague seven days: and he shall look on the plague
on the seventh day: if the plague be spread in the garment,
either in the warp, or in the woof, or in a skin, *or* in any work
that is made of skin; the plague *is* [i]a fretting leprosy; it *is*
52 unclean. He shall therefore burn that garment, whether warp
or woof, in woollen or in linen, or anything of skin, wherein the
plague is: for it *is* a fretting leprosy; it shall be burnt in the
53 fire. ¶ And if the priest shall look, and, behold, the plague be
not spread in the garment, either in the warp, or in the woof, or
54 in anything of skin; then the priest shall command that they
wash *the thing* wherein the plague *is*, and he shall shut it up
55 seven days more: and the priest shall look on the plague, after
that it is washed: and, behold, *if* the plague have not changed
his colour, and the plague be not spread; it *is* unclean; thou
shalt burn it in the fire; it *is* fret inward, [3]*whether* it *be* bare
56 within or without. And if the priest look, and, behold, the
plague *be* somewhat dark after the washing of it; then he shall
rend it out of the garment, or out of the skin, or out of the warp,
57 or out of the woof: and if it appear still in the garment, either
in the warp, or in the woof, or in any thing of skin; it *is* a
spreading *plague*: thou shalt burn that wherein the plague *is*
58 with fire. And the garment, either warp, or woof, or whatsoever
thing of skin *it be*, which thou shalt wash, if the plague be
departed from them, then it shall be washed the second time, and
59 shall be clean. This *is* the law of the plague of leprosy in
a garment of woollen or linen, either in the warp, or woof, or any
thing of skins, to pronounce it clean, or to pronounce it unclean.

[i] ch. 14. 44.

[a] Matt. 8. 2, 4. Mark 1. 40, 44. Luke 5. 12, 14. & 17. 14.

CHAP. 14. AND the LORD spake unto Moses, saying, This shall be
2 the law of the leper in the day of his cleansing: He [a]shall be

[1] Heb. *work of*.
[2] Heb. *vessel*, or, *instrument*.
[3] Heb. whether *it* be *bald in the head thereof, or in the forehead thereof*.

---

entered. A separate space used to be provided for lepers in the Synagogues.

47. *The garment*] Rather, **The clothing**, referring to the ordinary dress of the Israelites in the wilderness; viz., a linen tunic with a fringe (Num. xv. 38) and a woollen cloak or blanket thrown on in colder weather.

47–49. Rather, *And the clothing in which there is a stroke of Leprosy, whether the stroke is in clothing of wool or in clothing of linen; or in yarn for warp or in yarn for woof, either for linen clothing or for woollen clothing; or in a skin of leather or in any article made of leather.*

51. *a fretting leprosy*] *i.e.* a malignant or corroding Leprosy. What was the nature of the Leprosy in clothing, which produced greenish or reddish spots, cannot be precisely determined. It was most likely destructive mildew, perhaps of more than one kind.

56. *somewhat dark*] Rather, **somewhat faint.** Cp. *v.* 6.

57, 58, 59. *either* in these verses, should be **or.** See *vv.* 47, 49.

It should be noticed that no religious or symbolical rite is prescribed for Leprosy in clothing. The priest had only to decide whether the process of decay was at work in the article presented to him and to pronounce accordingly. Compare the Leprosy in houses, xiv. 33–53.

XIV. **1.** The Leper was excluded not only from the Sanctuary but from the camp. The ceremony of restoration which he had to undergo was therefore twofold. The first part, performed outside the camp,

3 brought unto the priest: and the priest shall go forth out of the
camp; and the priest shall look, and, behold, *if* the plague of
4 leprosy be healed in the leper; then shall the priest command to
take for him that is to be cleansed two [1]birds alive *and* clean,
5 and [b]cedar wood, and [c]scarlet, and [d]hyssop: and the priest shall
command that one of the birds be killed in an earthen vessel over
6 running water: as for the living bird, he shall take it, and the
cedar wood, and the scarlet, and the hyssop, and shall dip them
and the living bird in the blood of the bird *that was* killed over
7 the running water: and he shall [e]sprinkle upon him that is to
be cleansed from the leprosy [f]seven times, and shall pronounce
him clean, and shall let the living bird loose [2]into the open field.
8 ¶ And he that is to be cleansed [g]shall wash his clothes, and
shave off all his hair, [h]and wash himself in water, that he may
be clean: and after that he shall come into the camp, and
9 [i]shall tarry abroad out of his tent seven days. But it shall be
on the seventh day, that he shall shave all his hair off his head
and his beard and his eyebrows, even all his hair he shall shave
off: and he shall wash his clothes, also he shall wash his flesh in
10 water, and he shall be clean. ¶ And on the eighth day [k]he shall
take two he lambs without blemish, and one ewe lamb [3]of the

[b] Num. 19. 6.
[c] Heb. 9. 19.
[d] Ps. 51. 7.
[e] Heb. 9. 13.
[f] 2 Kin. 5. 10, 14.
[g] ch. 13. 6.
[h] ch. 11. 25.
[i] Num. 12. 15.
[k] Matt. 8. 4. Mark 1. 44. Luke 5. 14.

[1] Or, *sparrows*.
[2] Heb. *upon the face of the field*.
[3] Heb. *the daughter of her year*.

entitled him to come within and to mix with his brethren, 3–9. The second part, performed in the Court of the Tabernacle and separated from the first by an interval of seven days, restored him to all the privileges of the Covenant with Jehovah, 10–32.

4. These birds were provided by the priest for the man. They were not, like the offerings for the Altar, brought by the man himself (cp. *v.* 4 with *v.* 10), they were not presented nor brought near the Sanctuary, nor was any portion of them offered on the Altar.

cedar wood, and scarlet, and hyssop] These three substances were used as the common materials in rites of purification (cp. Ex. xii. 22; Num. xix. 8; Ps. li. 7; Heb. ix. 19): the *cedar*, or juniper, the resin or turpentine of which was a preservative against decay, and employed in medicines for Elephantiasis and other skin diseases: the *scarlet*, a "tongue," or band, of twice-dyed scarlet wool, with which the living bird, the hyssop, and the cedar wood were tied together when they were dipped into the blood and water: the colour expressing the rosiness associated with health and vital energy: and the *hyssop* (see Ex. xii. 22), probably the Caper plant, whose cleansing virtues as a medicine, and use in the treatment of ulcers and diseases of the skin allied to Leprosy, were known to the ancients. It has been conjectured that the scarlet band was used to tie the hyssop upon the cedar, so as to make a sort of brush, such as would be convenient for sprinkling.

5. *running water*] Literally, living water, *i.e.* water fresh from the spring (Gen. xxvi. 19; Num. xix. 17).

7. *seven times*] The seal of the Covenant, expressed in the number seven (cp. *v.* 9), was renewed in sprinkling him who, during his Leprosy, had lived as an outcast. The details of a restoration to health and freedom appear to be well expressed in the whole ceremony. Each of the birds represented the Leper. They were to be of a clean kind, because they stood for one of the chosen race. The death-like state of the Leper during his exclusion from the camp was expressed by killing one of the birds. The living bird was identified with the slain one by being dipped in his blood mixed with the spring water that figured the process of purification, while the cured Leper was identified with the rite by having the same water and blood sprinkled over him. The bird then liberated was a sign that the Leper left behind him all the symbols of the death disease and of the remedies associated with it, and was free to enjoy health and social freedom with his kind. Cp. Col. ii. 12.

9. The best of all types of the healing of the Spirit, was the healing of the Leper. In his formal cleansing, consecration, and atonement by sacrifice (see notes on xiv. 9–20), the ministers of the Sanctuary bore public witness that he was restored to the blessing of communion with his brethren and with Jehovah. Hence when the Son of God proved His divine mission by healing the lepers (Matt. xi. 5), He did not excuse them from going to the priest to "offer for the cleansing those things which Moses commanded" (Mark i. 44; Luke v. 14) "for a testimony to the people" (Matt. viii. 4).

10, 11. Two **young rams** from one to three years old (not lambs), a ewe lamb in

first year without blemish, and three tenth deals of fine flour *for*
11 [l]a meat offering, mingled with oil, and one log of oil. And the
priest that maketh *him* clean shall present the man that is to be
made clean, and those things, before the LORD, *at* the door of the
12 tabernacle of the congregation: and the priest shall take one he
lamb, and [m]offer him for a trespass offering, and the log of oil,
13 and [n]wave them *for* a wave offering before the LORD: and he
shall slay the lamb [o]in the place where he shall kill the sin
offering and the burnt offering, in the holy place: for [p]as the
sin offering *is* the priest's, *so is* the trespass offering: [q]it *is* most
14 holy: and the priest shall take *some* of the blood of the trespass
offering, and the priest shall put *it* [r]upon the tip of the right ear
of him that is to be cleansed, and upon the thumb of his right
15 hand, and upon the great toe of his right foot: and the priest
shall take *some* of the log of oil, and pour *it* into the palm of his
16 own left hand: and the priest shall dip his right finger in the
oil that *is* in his left hand, and shall sprinkle of the oil with his
17 finger seven times before the LORD: and of the rest of the oil
that *is* in his hand shall the priest put upon the tip of the right
ear of him that is to be cleansed, and upon the thumb of his
right hand, and upon the great toe of his right foot, upon the
18 blood of the trespass offering: and the remnant of the oil that
is in the priest's hand he shall pour upon the head of him that
is to be cleansed: [s]and the priest shall make an atonement
19 for him before the LORD. And the priest shall offer [t]the sin
offering, and make an atonement for him that is to be cleansed
from his uncleanness; and afterward he shall kill the burnt
20 offering: and the priest shall offer the burnt offering and the
meat offering upon the altar: and the priest shall make an
21 atonement for him, and he shall be clean. ¶And [u]if he *be*
poor, and [1]cannot get so much; then he shall take one lamb *for*
a trespass offering [2]to be waved, to make an atonement for him,
and one tenth deal of fine flour mingled with oil for a meat
22 offering, and a log of oil; [w]and two turtledoves, or two young
pigeons, such as he is able to get; and the one shall be a sin
23 offering, and the other a burnt offering. [x]And he shall bring

[l] ch. 2. 1. Num. 15. 4, 9.
[m] ch. 5. 2, 18. & 6. 6, 7.
[n] Ex. 29. 24.
[o] Ex. 29. 11. ch. 1. 5, 11. & 4. 4, 24.
[p] ch. 7. 7.
[q] ch. 2. 3. & 7. 6. & 21. 22.
[r] Ex. 29. 20. ch. 8. 23.
[s] ch. 4. 26.
[t] ch. 5. 1, 6. & 12. 7.
[u] ch. 5. 7. & 12. 8.
[w] ch. 12. 8. & 15. 14, 15.
[x] ver. 10, 11.

[1] Heb. *his hand reach not.* [2] Heb. *for a waving.*

---

her first year (see xii. 6), three tenth parts of an ephah (something over ten pints and a half) of fine flour mingled with oil, and a log (about half a pint; see xix. 35) of oil. The priest presented both the man and his offerings to Jehovah **at the entrance of the Tent of meeting.** See i. 3.

12. This Trespass-offering, with its blood and the oil, must be regarded as the main feature in the ceremony: no alteration being permitted even in the case of the poor (*vv.* 21–23). There appears to be no other case in which an entire victim was waved (see vii. 30) before Jehovah. The Levites are spoken of as "a wave offering," Num. viii. 11–15 (see margin). The man in this case, represented by his Trespass-offering, was dedicated as a Wave-offering in like manner.

13. *it is most holy*] See vi. 25 note.

14. In the same way, and with the same significance as in viii. 23. It is said that a portion of the blood was caught by the priest in the palm of his hand as it ran from the victim.

16. The sevenfold sprinkling of the oil before the Sanctuary, in addition to the waving of it, seems to have been intended to consecrate it to represent the spiritual gift consequent upon the Covenant, the sealing of which had been figured by the sacramental blood of the offering.

17, 19. *him that is to be cleansed*] **Of him that has been cleansed.** The significance of the act is similar to that in viii. 11, 15.

19, 20. The cleansed Leper was now in a position to avail himself of the accustomed law of sacrifice as one completely restored. The ewe lamb was now offered in his behalf as a Sin-offering, one of the young rams as a Burnt-offering, and the fine flour mingled with oil as a Meat-offering.

them on the eighth day for his cleansing unto the priest, unto
the door of the tabernacle of the congregation, before the LORD.
24 [y]And the priest shall take the lamb of the trespass offering, and
the log of oil, and the priest shall wave them *for* a wave offering
25 before the LORD: and he shall kill the lamb of the trespass
offering, [z]and the priest shall take *some* of the blood of the trespass offering, and put *it* upon the tip of the right ear of him that
is to be cleansed, and upon the thumb of his right hand, and
26 upon the great toe of his right foot: and the priest shall pour of
27 the oil into the palm of his own left hand: and the priest shall
sprinkle with his right finger *some* of the oil that *is* in his left
28 hand seven times before the LORD: and the priest shall put of
the oil that *is* in his hand upon the tip of the right ear of him
that is to be cleansed, and upon the thumb of his right hand,
and upon the great toe of his right foot, upon the place of the
29 blood of the trespass offering: and the rest of the oil that *is* in
the priest's hand he shall put upon the head of him that is to be
30 cleansed, to make an atonement for him before the LORD. And
he shall offer the one of [a]the turtledoves, or of the young
31 pigeons, such as he can get; *even* such as he is able to get, the
one *for* a sin offering, and the other *for* a burnt offering, with the
meat offering: and the priest shall make an atonement for him
32 that is to be cleansed before the LORD. This *is* the law *of him*
in whom *is* the plague of leprosy, whose hand is not able to get
33 [b]*that which pertaineth* to his cleansing. ¶ And the LORD spake
34 unto Moses and unto Aaron, saying, [c]When ye be come into the
land of Canaan, which I give to you for a possession, and I put the
35 plague of leprosy in a house of the land of your possession; and
he that owneth the house shall come and tell the priest, saying,
36 It seemeth to me *there is* as it were [d]a plague in the house: then
the priest shall command that they [1]empty the house, before the
priest go *into it* to see the plague, that all that *is* in the house
be not made unclean: and afterward the priest shall go in to see
37 the house: and he shall look on the plague, and, behold, *if* the
plague *be* in the walls of the house with hollow strakes, greenish
38 or reddish, which in sight *are* lower than the wall; then the
priest shall go out of the house to the door of the house, and
39 shut up the house seven days: and the priest shall come again
the seventh day, and shall look: and, behold, *if* the plague be
40 spread in the walls of the house; then the priest shall command
that they take away the stones in which the plague *is*, and they
41 shall cast them into an unclean place without the city: and he
shall cause the house to be scraped within round about, and they
shall pour out the dust that they scrape off without the city into
42 an unclean place: and they shall take other stones, and put *them*
in the place of those stones; and he shall take other morter, and

[y] ver. 12.
[z] ver. 14.
[a] ver. 22. ch. 15. 15.
[b] ver. 10.
[c] Gen. 17. 8. Num. 32. 22. Deut. 7. 1. & 32. 49.
[d] Ps. 91. 10. Prov. 3. 33. Zech. 5. 4.

[1] Or, *prepare*.

33–53. This section is separated from that on Leprosy in clothing (xiii. 47–59) with which it would seem to be naturally connected, and is placed last of all the laws concerning Leprosy, probably on account of its being wholly prospective. While the Israelites were in the Wilderness, the materials of their dwellings were of nearly the same nature as those of their clothing, and would be liable to the same sort of decay. They were therefore included under the same law.

I put the plague] Jehovah here speaks as the Lord of all created things, determining their decay and destruction as well as their production. Cf. Isai. xlv. 6, 7; Jonah iv. 7; Matt. xxi. 20.

37. *hollow strakes*, &c.] Rather, **depressed spots of dark green or dark red, appearing beneath** (the surface of) **the wall.**

43 shall plaister the house. And if the plague come again, and
break out in the house, after that he hath taken away the stones,
and after he hath scraped the house, and after it is plaistered;
44 then the priest shall come and look, and, behold, *if* the plague
be spread in the house, it *is* [e]a fretting leprosy in the house: it
45 *is* unclean. And he shall break down the house, the stones of it,
and the timber thereof, and all the morter of the house; and he
shall carry *them* forth out of the city into an unclean place.
46 Moreover he that goeth into the house all the while that it is
47 shut up shall be unclean until the even. And he that lieth in
the house shall wash his clothes; and he that eateth in the house
48 shall wash his clothes. And if the priest [1]shall come in, and
look *upon it*, and, behold, the plague hath not spread in the
house, after the house was plaistered: then the priest shall
49 pronounce the house clean, because the plague is healed. And
[f]he shall take to cleanse the house two birds, and cedar wood,
50 and scarlet, and hyssop: and he shall kill the one of the birds in
51 an earthen vessel over running water: and he shall take the
cedar wood, and the hyssop, and the scarlet, and the living bird,
and dip them in the blood of the slain bird, and in the running
52 water, and sprinkle the house seven times: and he shall cleanse
the house with the blood of the bird, and with the running water,
and with the living bird, and with the cedar wood, and with the
53 hyssop, and with the scarlet: but he shall let go the living bird
out of the city into the open fields, and [g]make an atonement for
54 the house: and it shall be clean. ¶ This *is* the law for all manner
55 of plague of leprosy, and [h]scall, and for the [i]leprosy of a garment,
56 [k]and of a house, and [l]for a rising, and for a scab, and for a bright
57 spot: to [m]teach [2]when *it is* unclean, and when *it is* clean: this
is the law of leprosy.

Chap. 15. AND the Lord spake unto Moses and to Aaron, saying,
2 Speak unto the children of Israel, and say unto them, [a]When
any man hath a [3]running issue out of his flesh, *because of* his
3 issue he *is* unclean. And this shall be his uncleanness in his
issue: whether his flesh run with his issue, or his flesh be stopped
4 from his issue, it *is* his uncleanness. Every bed, whereon he lieth
that hath the issue, is unclean: and every [4]thing, whereon he
5 sitteth, shall be unclean. And whosoever toucheth his bed shall
wash his clothes, [b]and bathe *himself* in water, and be unclean
6 until the even. And he that sitteth on *any* thing whereon he sat
that hath the issue shall wash his clothes, and bathe *himself* in
7 water, and be unclean until the even. And he that toucheth the
flesh of him that hath the issue shall wash his clothes, and bathe
8 *himself* in water, and be unclean until the even. And if he that
hath the issue spit upon him that is clean; then he shall wash

[e] ch. 13. 51. Zech. 5. 4.
[f] ver. 4.
[g] ver. 20.
[h] ch. 13. 30.
[i] ch. 13. 47.
[k] ver. 34.
[l] ch. 13. 2.
[m] Deut. 24. 8. Ezek. 44. 23.
[a] ch. 22. 4. Num. 5. 2. 2 Sam. 3. 29. Matt. 9. 20. Mark 5. 25. Luke 8. 43.
[b] ch. 11. 25. & 17. 15.

[1] Heb. *in coming in shall come in, &c.*
[2] Heb. *in the day of the unclean, and in the day of the clean.*
[3] Or, *running of the reins.*
[4] Heb. *vessel.*

---

49. *cleanse the house*] Strictly, *purge the house from sin.* The same word is used in *v.* 52; and in *v.* 53 it is said, "and make an atonement for it." Such language is used figuratively when it is applied to things, not to persons. The Leprosy in houses, the Leprosy in clothing, and the terrible disease in the human body, were representative forms of decay which taught the lesson that all created things, in their own nature, are passing away, and are only maintained for their destined uses during an appointed period, by the power of Jehovah.

XV. This chapter would seem to take its place more naturally before the twelfth, with the subject of which it is immediately connected. Cp. especially xii. 2 with xv. 19. It stands here between two chapters, with neither of which has it any close connection.

his clothes, and bathe *himself* in water, and be unclean until
9 the even. And what saddle soever he rideth upon that hath the
10 issue shall be unclean. And whosoever toucheth any thing that
was under him shall be unclean until the even: and he that
beareth *any of* those things shall wash his clothes, and bathe
11 *himself* in water, and be unclean until the even. And whomsoever he toucheth that hath the issue, and hath not rinsed his
hands in water, he shall wash his clothes, and bathe *himself* in
12 water, and be unclean until the even. And the [c]vessel of earth, [c] ch. 6. 28.
that he toucheth which hath the issue, shall be broken: and & 11. 32, 33.
13 every vessel of wood shall be rinsed in water. And when he that
hath an issue is cleansed of his issue; then [d]he shall number to [d] ver. 28.
himself seven days for his cleansing, and wash his clothes, and ch. 14. 8.
14 bathe his flesh in running water, and shall be clean. And on
the eighth day he shall take to him [e]two turtledoves, or two [e] ch. 14. 22,
young pigeons, and come before the LORD unto the door of the 23.
tabernacle of the congregation, and give them unto the priest:
15 and the priest shall offer them, [f]the one *for* a sin offering, and [f] ch. 14. 30,
the other *for* a burnt offering; [g]and the priest shall make an 31. [g] ch. 14. 19,
16 atonement for him before the LORD for his issue. ¶ And [h]if any 31.
man's seed of copulation go out from him, then he shall wash all [h] ch. 22. 4.
17 his flesh in water, and be unclean until the even. And every Deut. 23. 10.
garment, and every skin, whereon is the seed of copulation,
18 shall be washed with water, and be unclean until the even. The
woman also with whom man shall lie *with* seed of copulation,
they shall *both* bathe *themselves* in water, and [i]be unclean until [i] 1 Sam.21.4.
19 the even. ¶ And [k]if a woman have an issue, *and* her issue in her [k] ch. 12. 2.
flesh be blood, she shall be [1]put apart seven days: and whosoever
20 toucheth her shall be unclean until the even. And every thing
that she lieth upon in her separation shall be unclean: every
21 thing also that she sitteth upon shall be unclean. And whosoever toucheth her bed shall wash his clothes, and bathe *himself*
22 in water, and be unclean until the even. And whosoever toucheth any thing that she sat upon shall wash his clothes, and
23 bathe *himself* in water, and be unclean until the even. And if
it *be* on *her* bed, or on anything whereon she sitteth, when he
24 toucheth it, he shall be unclean until the even. And [l]if any man [l] See ch. 20.
lie with her at all, and her flowers be upon him, he shall be un- 18.
clean seven days; and all the bed whereon he lieth shall be unclean.
25 ¶ And if [m]a woman have an issue of her blood many days out [m] Matt. 9.
of the time of her separation, or if it run beyond the time of her 20.
separation; all the days of the issue of her uncleanness shall be Mark 5. 25.
26 as the days of her separation: she *shall be* unclean. Every bed Luke 8. 43.
whereon she lieth all the days of her issue shall be unto her as
the bed of her separation: and whatsoever she sitteth upon
27 shall be unclean, as the uncleanness of her separation. And
whosoever toucheth those things shall be unclean, and shall wash
his clothes, and bathe *himself* in water, and be unclean until the
28 even. But [n]if she be cleansed of her issue, then she shall num- [n] ver. 13.

[1] Heb. *in her separation.*

---

13. The mere cessation of the issue does not make him clean: he must wait seven days, &c., preparatory to his offering sacrifice.

16–18. Most of the ancient religions made a similar recognition of impurity and of the need of purification.

17. *every garment*] Cp. Jude, *v.* 23.

24. This must refer to an unexpected occurrence. Intercourse during the acknowledged period was a heavy crime, and was to be punished by "cutting off" (xviii. 19, xx. 18; Ezek. xviii. 6).

ber to herself seven days, and after that she shall be clean.
29 And on the eighth day she shall take unto her two turtles, or
two young pigeons, and bring them unto the priest, to the door
30 of the tabernacle of the congregation. And the priest shall offer
the one *for* a sin offering, and the other *for* a burnt offering;
and the priest shall make an atonement for her before the LORD
31 for the issue of her uncleanness. ¶ Thus shall ye [o]separate the
children of Israel from their uncleanness; that they die not in
their uncleanness, when they [p]defile my tabernacle that *is* among
32 them. ¶ [q]This *is* the law of him that hath an issue, [r]and *of him*
33 whose seed goeth from him, and is defiled therewith; [s]and of her
that is sick of her flowers, and of him that hath an issue, of the
man, [t]and of the woman, [u]and of him that lieth with her that is
unclean.

CHAP. 16. AND the LORD spake unto Moses after [a]the death of the
two sons of Aaron, when they offered before the LORD, and died;
2 and the LORD said unto Moses, Speak unto Aaron thy brother,
that he [b]come not at all times into the holy *place* within the vail
before the mercy seat, which *is* upon the ark; that he die not:
3 for [c]I will appear in the cloud upon the mercy seat. Thus shall
Aaron [d]come into the holy *place*: [e]with a young bullock for a
4 sin offering, and a ram for a burnt offering. He shall put on
[f]the holy linen coat, and he shall have the linen breeches upon
his flesh, and shall be girded with a linen girdle, and with the
linen mitre shall he be attired: these *are* holy garments; there-
5 fore [g]shall he wash his flesh in water, and *so* put them on. And
he shall take of [h]the congregation of the children of Israel two

[o] ch. 11. 47. Deut. 24. 8. Ezek. 44. 23.
[p] Num. 5. 3. & 19. 13, 20. Ezek. 5. 11. & 23. 38.
[q] ver. 2.
[r] ver. 16.
[s] ver. 19.
[t] ver. 25.
[u] ver. 24.
[a] ch. 10. 1, 2.
[b] Ex. 30, 10. ch. 23. 27. Heb. 9. 7.
[c] Ex. 25, 22. 1 Kin. 8. 10.
[d] Heb. 9. 7.
[e] ch. 4. 3.
[f] Ex. 28. 39, 42, 43. ch. 6. 10. Ezek. 44. 17. 18.
[g] Ex. 30. 20. ch. 8. 6, 7.
[h] See ch. 4. 14. Num. 29. 11. 2 Chr. 29. 21. Ezra 6. 17. Ezek. 45. 22, 23.

31–33. This solemn admonition is addressed to Moses and Aaron, see *v.* 1.

31. *my tabernacle*] Strictly, *my dwelling-place* (*mishkān*), as in viii. 10, xvii. 4, xxvi. 11. The word rendered "tabernacle" elsewhere in Leviticus, is properly **Tent.** See Ex. xxvi. 1 note.

XVI. **1–34.** The Day of Atonement, or, as it is in the Hebrew, the Day of Atonements, is called by the Rabbins the Day, and by St. Luke (probably) "the Fast." See Acts xxvii. 9. Cp. with this chap. xxiii. 26–32.

1. The reference to the death of Nadab and Abihu is a notice of the occasion on which the instructions were given, well calculated to add point and emphasis to the solemn admonition to the High priest in the second verse. The death of his sons (x. 2), for drawing nigh to Jehovah in an unauthorised manner, was to serve as a warning to Aaron himself never to transgress in this respect.

2. *the holy place within the vail*] See Ex. xxvi. 33, 34; Heb. ix. 3.

the cloud] Cp. Ex. xvi. 10 note.

the mercy seat] See Ex. xxv. 17 note.

3. *holy place*] This name here denotes **the Sanctuary,** the whole sacred enclosure, the Court of the Tabernacle. The offerings were for Aaron and his sons, supplied by himself.

4. The High priest when he changed his dress on this day was required **to bathe himself.** In his "golden garments" he had, on this day, and for the previous week, to offer the regular daily sacrifices, and to perform the other sacerdotal duties of the Sanctuary, which were usually performed by a common priest.—The dress of white linen, which he now put on, appears to have been like the ordinary dress of the common priests, except in the substitution of a linen mitre for the bonnet (or **cap**), and of a plain linen girdle for the variegated one (Ex. xxviii. 40–43 notes). In preparing to enter the Holy of Holies, he attired himself in spotless white as a token of the holiness without which none, in a spiritual sense, can enter the divine Presence. He thus became a more distinct foreshadow of the greater High Priest (Heb. vii. 26, vi. 19, 20). This significance belonged to the High priest only in his official capacity as mediator: in his own person he had infirmity, and was required "to offer up sacrifice, *first* for his own sins, and then for the people's." Heb. vii. 27. See on ix. 7–14. On the same ground it was that, although as a mediator he had to enter the Most Holy place, as sinful man he needed the cloud of incense as a vail to come between him and the holiness of Jehovah. See *v.* 13.

5. *take of the congregation*] *i.e.* they were to be supplied at the public cost.

two kids of the goats] This should be, **two shaggy he-goats** (iv. 23 note), of the same colour, size, and value.

kids of the goats for a sin offering, and one ram for a burnt
6 offering. And Aaron shall offer his bullock of the sin offering,
which *is* for himself, and [i]make an atonement for himself, and
7 for his house. And he shall take the two goats, and present
them before the LORD *at* the door of the tabernacle of the con-
8 gregation. And Aaron shall cast lots upon the two goats; one
9 lot for the LORD, and the other lot for the [1]scapegoat. And
Aaron shall bring the goat upon which the LORD's lot [2]fell, and
10 offer him *for* a sin offering. But the goat, on which the lot fell
to be the scapegoat, shall be presented alive before the LORD, to
make [k]an atonement with him, *and* to let him go for a scape-
11 goat into the wilderness. ¶ And Aaron shall bring the bullock
of the sin offering, which *is* for himself, and shall make an
atonement for himself, and for his house, and shall kill the bul-
12 lock of the sin offering which *is* for himself: and he shall take
[l]a censer full of burning coals of fire from off the altar before the
LORD, and his hands full of [m]sweet incense beaten small, and
13 bring *it* within the vail: [n]and he shall put the incense upon the
fire before the LORD, that the cloud of the incense may cover the
14 [o]mercy seat that *is* upon the testimony, that he die not: and [p]he
shall take of the blood of the bullock, and [q]sprinkle *it* with his
finger upon the mercy seat eastward; and before the mercy seat
shall he sprinkle of the blood with his finger seven times.

[i] ch. 9, 7. Heb. 5. 2. & 7. 27, 28.
[k] 1 John 2. 2.
[l] ch. 10. 1. Num. 16. 18. 46. Rev. 8. 5.
[m] Ex. 30. 34.
[n] Ex. 30. 1. Num. 16. 7. Rev. 8. 3, 4.
[o] Ex. 25, 21.
[p] ch. 4. 5. Heb. 9. 13, 25. & 10. 4.
[q] ch. 4. 6.

[1] Heb. *Azazel.* [2] Heb. *went up.*

---

6. *shall offer*] Rather, **shall present**, as in *vv.* 7, 10, &c. The word expresses the formal act of placing the victims in front of the entrance of the Tabernacle.

for himself, and for his house] *i.e.* for himself as the High priest and all the common priests. Cp. ix. 7-14 note.

8. The two goats formed a single Sin-offering, *v.* 5. To bring out the meaning of the sacrifice it was necessary that the act of a living being should be performed after death. See *v.* 22 note. As this could not possibly be visibly set forth with a single victim, two were employed, as in the case of the birds in the rite for the healed leper (xiv. 4–6).

for the scapegoat] Rather, **for Azazel**. The word occurs nowhere else in the Old Testament but in this chapter, and is probably derived from a root in use in Arabic, but not in Hebrew, signifying *to remove*, or *to separate*.

Azazel is the pre-Mosaic name of an evil personal being placed in opposition to Jehovah. Each goat, having been presented to Jehovah before the lots were cast, stood in a sacrificial relation to Him. The casting of lots was an appeal to the decision of Jehovah (cp. Josh. vii. 16, 17, xiv. 2; Prov. xvi. 33; Acts i. 26, &c.); it was therefore His act to choose one of the goats for His service in the way of ordinary sacrifice, the other for His service in carrying off the sins to Azazel (see note on *v.* 22). By this expressive outward sign the sins were sent back to the author of sin himself, "the entirely separate one," who was banished from the realm of grace.

The goat itself did not lose the sacred character with which it had been endued in being presented before Jehovah. It was, as much as the slain goat, a figure of Him Who bore our griefs and carried our sorrows, on Whom the Lord laid the iniquity of us all (Is. liii. 4, 6), that we might become a sanctified Church to be presented unto Himself, not having spot or wrinkle or any such thing (Eph. v. 26, 27).

10. *on which the lot fell to be the scapegoat*] Rather, **on which the lot 'for Azazel' fell.**

an atonement with him] The goat "for Azazel" was to be considered as taking his part along with the other goat in the great symbol of atonement.

for a scapegoat into the wilderness] Rather, "**to Azazel,** into the Wilderness."

11-25. It is important, in reference to the meaning of the Day of Atonement, to observe the order of the rites as they are described in these verses.

12. *a censer*] See Ex. xxv. 38 note.

the altar before the LORD] *i.e.* the Altar of Burnt-offering on which the fire was always burning.

14. The High priest must have come out from the Most Holy place to fetch the blood, leaving the censer smoking within, and then have entered again within the vail. He sprinkled the blood seven times upon the Mercy seat, **on its east side** (not "eastward"), and then seven times upon the floor in front of it. If the Mercy seat may be regarded as an Altar, the holiest one of the three, on this one occasion in the year atonement was thus made for it, as for the other Altars, with sacrificial blood.

15 ¶ [r]Then shall he kill the goat of the sin offering, that *is* for the
people, and bring his blood [s]within the vail, and do with that
blood as he did with the blood of the bullock, and sprinkle it
16 upon the mercy seat, and before the mercy seat: and he shall
[t]make an atonement for the holy *place*, because of the uncleanness of the children of Israel, and because of their transgressions
in all their sins: and so shall he do for the tabernacle of the
congregation, that [1]remaineth among them in the midst of their
17 uncleanness. [u]And there shall be no man in the tabernacle of
the congregation when he goeth in to make an atonement in the
holy *place*, until he come out, and have made an atonement for
himself, and for his household, and for all the congregation of
18 Israel. And he shall go out unto the altar that *is* before the
LORD, and [x]make an atonement for it; and shall take of the
blood of the bullock, and of the blood of the goat, and put *it*
19 upon the horns of the altar round about. And he shall sprinkle
of the blood upon it with his finger seven times, and cleanse it,
and [y]hallow it from the uncleanness of the children of Israel.
20 ¶ And when he hath made an end of [z]reconciling the holy *place*,
and the tabernacle of the congregation, and the altar, he shall
21 bring the live goat: and Aaron shall lay both his hands upon
the head of the live goat, and confess over him all the iniquities
of the children of Israel, and all their transgressions in all their
sins, [a]putting them upon the head of the goat, and shall send
22 *him* away by the hand of [2]a fit man into the wilderness: and
the goat shall [b]bear upon him all their iniquities unto a land
[3]not inhabited: and he shall let go the goat in the wilderness.

[r] Heb. 2. 17. & 5. 2. & 9. 7. 28.
[s] ver. 2. Heb. 6. 19.
[t] See Ex. 29. 36. Ezek. 45. 18. Heb. 9. 22.
[u] See Ex. 34. 3. Luke 1. 10.
[x] Ex. 30. 10. ch. 4. 7, 18.
[y] Ezek. 43. 20.
[z] ver. 16. Ezek. 45. 20.
[a] Isai. 53. 6.
[b] Isai. 53. 11, 12. John 1. 29. Heb. 9. 28. 1 Pet. 2. 24.

[1] Heb. *dwelleth.* [2] Heb. *a man of opportunity.* [3] Heb. *of separation.*

---

15. Having completed the atonement in the Holy of Holies on behalf of the priests, the High priest had now to do the same thing on behalf of the people.

16. *the "holy place"*] Here the place within the vail, the Holy of Holies.

tabernacle of the congregation] **Tent of meeting.** Atonement was now to be made for the Tabernacle as a whole. The sense is very briefly expressed, but there seems to be no room to doubt that the High priest was to sprinkle the blood of each of the victims before the Altar of Incense, as he had done before the mercy seat within the vail; and also to touch with blood the horns of the Altar of Incense (Ex. xxx. 10).

that remaineth among them in the midst of their uncleanness] Cp. *v.* 19. The most sacred earthly things which came into contact with the nature of man needed from time to time to be cleansed and sanctified by the blood of the Sin-offerings which had been taken into the Presence of Jehovah. See Ex. xxviii. 38 note.

18. The order of the ceremony required that atonement should first be made for the Most Holy Place with the Mercy seat, then for the Holy Place with the Golden Altar, and then for the Altar in the Court. See *vv.* 20, 33. The horns of the Brazen altar were touched with the blood, as they were in the ordinary Sin-offerings. iv. 25, 30, 34.

of the blood of the bullock, and of the blood of the goat] Some of the blood of the two victims was mingled together in a basin.

21. *confess over him*] The form of confession used on this occasion in later times was:—"O Lord, Thy people, the house of Israel, have transgressed, they have rebelled, they have sinned before Thee. I beseech Thee now absolve their transgressions, their rebellion, and their sin that they have sinned against Thee, as it is written in the law of Moses Thy servant, that on this day he shall make atonement for you to cleanse you from all your sins, and ye shall be clean."

a fit man] Literally, *a timely man*, or *a man at hand.* Tradition says that the man was appointed for this work the year before.

22. *unto a land not inhabited*] **Unto a place cut off**, or (as in the margin) a place "of separation."

It is evident that the one signification of the ceremony of this goat was the complete removal of the sins which were confessed over him. No symbol could so plainly set forth the completeness of Jehovah's acceptance of the penitent, as a Sin-offering in which a life was given up for the Altar, and yet a living being survived to carry away all sin and uncleanness.

23 ¶ And Aaron shall come into the tabernacle of the congregation,
[c]and shall put off the linen garments, which he put on when he
24 went into the holy *place*, and shall leave them there: and he
shall wash his flesh with water in the holy place, and put on his
garments, and come forth, [d]and offer his burnt offering, and the
burnt offering of the people, and make an atonement for himself,
25 and for the people. And [e]the fat of the sin offering shall he
26 burn upon the altar. ¶ And he that let go the goat for the
scapegoat shall wash his clothes, [f]and bathe his flesh in water,
27 and afterward come into the camp. [g]And the bullock *for* the
sin offering, and the goat *for* the sin offering, whose blood was
brought in to make atonement in the holy *place*, shall *one* carry
forth without the camp; and they shall burn in the fire their
28 skins, and their flesh, and their dung. And he that burneth them
shall wash his clothes, and bathe his flesh in water, and after-
29 ward he shall come into the camp. ¶ And *this* shall be a statute
for ever unto you: *that* [h]in the seventh month, on the tenth *day*
of the month, ye shall afflict your souls, and do no work at
all, *whether it be* one of your own country, or a stranger that
30 sojourneth among you: for on that day shall *the priest* make an
atonement for you, to [i]cleanse you, *that* ye may be clean from
31 all your sins before the LORD. [k]It *shall be* a sabbath of rest
unto you, and ye shall afflict your souls, by a statute for ever.
32 [l]And the priest, whom he shall anoint, and whom he shall
[1] [m]consecrate to minister in the priest's office in his father's stead,
shall make the atonement, and [n]shall put on the linen clothes,
33 *even* the holy garments: and [o]he shall make an atonement for
the holy sanctuary, and he shall make an atonement for the

[c] Ezek. 42. 14. & 44. 19.
[d] ver. 3, 5.
[e] ch. 4. 10.
[f] ch. 15. 5.
[g] ch. 4. 12, 21. & 6. 30. Heb. 13. 11.
[h] Ex. 30. 10. ch. 23. 27. Num. 29. 7. Isai. 58. 3. Dan. 10. 3.
[i] Ps. 51. 2. Jer. 33. 8. Eph. 5. 26. Heb. 9. 13, 14. 1 John 1. 7.
[k] ch. 23. 32.
[l] ch. 4. 3, 5.
[m] Ex. 29. 29. Num. 20. 26, 28.
[n] ver. 4.
[o] ver. 6, 16, 17, 18, 24.

[1] Heb. *fill his hand.*

26–28. Both he who led away the goat, and he who burned the parts of the Sin-offerings had to purify themselves. They who went out of the camp during a religious solemnity incurred uncleanness; hence the need of purification.

27. *shall burn in the fire*] *i.e.*, **consume in the fire,** not burn sacrificially. See i. 9.

29. *seventh month, on the tenth day*] The month Ethanim or Tisri, as being the seventh in the Sacred year, has been called the Sabbatical month. On the first day was celebrated the Feast of Trumpets (xxiii. 24), the tenth day was the Day of Atonement, and on the fourteenth day the Feast of Tabernacles commenced (xxiii. 24 note, Ex. xxiii. 16).

afflict your souls] The old term for fasting; but its meaning evidently embraces, not only abstinence from food, but that penitence and humiliation which give scope and purpose to the outward act of fasting. The Day of Atonement was the only public fast commanded by the Law of Moses. See further directions in xxiii. 27–32. On fasts observed in later times, see Zech. viii. 19, and marg. reff.

a stranger that sojourneth among you] Rather, **the foreigner who dwelleth among you.** See Ex. xx. 10 note. The meaning is, one of foreign blood, who dwelt with the Israelites, had abjured false gods, and had become familiarly known to his neighbours, *e.g.* the Kenites (Judg. iv. 11, &c.); the Gibeonites (Josh. ix.); and a considerable portion of the "mixed multitude" (cp. Ex. xii. 38, 48). As the foreigner had the blessing and protection of the Law he was bound to obey its statutes.

33, 34. A summary of what was done on the Day of Atonement.

The Day was intended as an occasion for expressing more completely than could be done in the ordinary sacrifices the spiritual truth of atonement, with a fuller acknowledgment of the sinfulness and weakness of man and of the corruptible nature of all earthly things, even of those most solemnly consecrated and devoted to the service of God. It belonged to its observances especially to set forth, by the entrance of the High priest into the Holy of Holies, that atonement could only be effected before the throne of Jehovah Himself (cp. Matt. ix. 6; Mark ii. 7-10; Heb. iv. 16, &c.); and, by he goat sent into the Wilderness, that the sins atoned for were not only forgiven, but carried wholly away. See *v.* 22 note. The rites were a solemn gathering up of all other rites of atonement, so as to make them point more expressively to the

tabernacle of the congregation, and for the altar, and he shall
make an atonement for the priests, and for all the people of the
34 congregation. [p]And this shall be an everlasting statute unto
you, to make an atonement for the children of Israel for all
their sins [q]once a year. And he did as the LORD commanded
Moses.

CHAP. 17. AND the LORD spake unto Moses, saying, Speak unto
2 Aaron, and unto his sons, and unto all the children of Israel,
and say unto them; This *is* the thing which the LORD hath com-
3 manded, saying, What man soever *there be* of the house of Israel,
[a]that killeth an ox, or lamb, or goat, in the camp, or that
4 killeth *it* out of the camp, [b]and bringeth it not unto the door of
the tabernacle of the congregation, to offer an offering unto the
LORD before the tabernacle of the LORD; blood shall be [c]im-
puted unto that man; he hath shed blood; and that man [d]shall
5 be cut off from among his people: to the end that the children
of Israel may bring their sacrifices, [e]which they offer in the open
field, even that they may bring them unto the LORD, unto the
door of the tabernacle of the congregation, unto the priest, and
6 offer them *for* peace offerings unto the LORD. And the priest
[f]shall sprinkle the blood upon the altar of the LORD *at* the door
of the tabernacle of the congregation, and [g]burn the fat for a
7 sweet savour unto the LORD. And they shall no more offer
their sacrifices [h]unto devils, after whom they [i]have gone a
whoring. This shall be a statute for ever unto them throughout
8 their generations. ¶ And thou shalt say unto them, Whatsoever
man *there be* of the house of Israel, or of the strangers which

[p] ch. 23, 31. Num. 29. 7.
[q] Ex. 30. 10. Heb. 9. 7.
[a] See Deut. 12. 5, 15, 21.
[b] Deut. 12. 5, 6, 13, 14.
[c] Rom. 5. 13.
[d] Gen. 17. 14.
[e] Gen. 21. 33. & 22. 2. & 31. 54. Deut. 12. 2. 1 Kin. 14. 23. 2 Kin. 16. 4. & 17. 10. 2 Chr. 28. 4. Ezek. 20. 38. & 22. 9.
[f] ch. 3. 2.
[g] Ex. 29. 18. ch. 3. 5, 11. Num. 18. 17.
[h] Deut. 32. 17. Ps. 106. 37. 1 Cor. 10. 20. Rev. 9. 20.
[i] Ex. 34. 15. ch. 20. 5. Deut. 31. 16. Ezek. 23. 8.

---

revelation to come of God's gracious purpose to man in sending His Son to be delivered for our offences, and to rise again for our justification; to be our great High Priest for ever after the order of Melchisedec, and to enter for us within the vail (Rom. iv. 25; Heb. vi. 20). The Day of Atonement expanded the meaning of every Sin-offering, in the same way as the services for Good Friday and Ash Wednesday expand the meaning of our Litany days throughout the year, and Easter Day, that of our Sundays.

XVII. This chapter, in its immediate bearing on the daily life of the Israelites, stands as the first of four (xvii.–xx.) which set forth practical duties, directing the Israelites to walk, not in the way of the heathen, but according to the ordinances of Jehovah.

3–7. Every domesticated animal that was slain for food was a sort of Peace-offering (*v.* 5). This law could only be kept as long as the children of Israel dwelt in their camp in the Wilderness. The restriction was removed before they settled in the Holy Land, where their numbers and diffusion over the country would have rendered its strict observance impossible. See Deut. xii. 15, 16, 20–24.

4. *blood shall be imputed unto that man*] *i.e.* he has incurred guilt in shedding blood in an unlawful manner.

cut off] See Ex. xxxi. 14 note.

5. Rather, **May bring their beasts for slaughter, which they (now) slaughter in the open field, even that they may bring them before Jehovah to the entrance of the Tent of meeting unto the priests, and slaughter them as Peace-offerings to Jehovah.**

7. *devils*] The word in the original is the "shaggy goat" of iv. 23. But it is sometimes employed, as here, to denote an object of heathen worship or a demon dwelling in the deserts (2 Chr. xi. 15; Isai. xiii. 21, xxxiv. 14). The worship of the goat, accompanied by the foulest rites, prevailed in Lower Egypt; and the Israelites may have been led into this snare while they dwelt in Egypt.

This law for the slaughtering of animals was not merely to exclude idolatry from the chosen nation. It had a more positive and permanent purpose. It bore witness to the sanctity of life; it served to remind the people of the solemnity of the grant of the lives of all inferior creatures made to Noah (Gen. ix. 2, 3); it purged and directed towards Jehovah the feelings in respect to animal food which seem to be common to man's nature; and it connected a habit of thanksgiving with the maintenance of our human life by means of daily food. 1 Tim. iv. 3–5. Having acknowledged that the animal belonged to Jehovah the devout Hebrew received back its flesh as Jehovah's gift.

8. *the strangers which sojourn*] **The foreigners who dwell.** See xvi. 29 note.

sojourn among you, [k]that offereth a burnt offering or sacrifice,
9 and [l]bringeth it not unto the door of the tabernacle of the congregation, to offer it unto the LORD; even that man shall be cut
10 off from among his people. ¶ [m]And whatsoever man *there be* of
the house of Israel, or of the strangers that sojourn among you,
that eateth any manner of blood; [n]I will even set my face against
that soul that eateth blood, and will cut him off from among his
11 people. [o]For the life of the flesh *is* in the blood: and I have
given it to you upon the altar [p]to make an atonement for your
souls: for [q]it *is* the blood *that* maketh an atonement for the soul.
12 Therefore I said unto the children of Israel, No soul of you shall
eat blood, neither shall any stranger that sojourneth among you
13 eat blood. ¶ And whatsoever man *there be* of the children of
Israel, or of the strangers that sojourn among you, [1]which
[r]hunteth and catcheth any beast or fowl that may be eaten; he
shall even [s]pour out the blood thereof, and [t]cover it with dust.
14 [u]For *it is* the life of all flesh; the blood of it *is* for the life
thereof: therefore I said unto the children of Israel, Ye shall
eat the blood of no manner of flesh: for the life of all flesh *is*
15 the blood thereof: whosoever eateth it shall be cut off. ¶ [x]And
every soul that eateth [2]that which died *of itself*, or that which

[k] ch. 1. 2, 3.
[l] ver. 4.
[m] Gen. 9. 4. ch. 3. 17. Deut. 12. 16. 1 Sam. 14. 33. Ezek. 44.
[n] ch. 20. 3. Jer. 44, 11. Ezek. 14. 8.
[o] ver. 14.
[p] Matt. 26. 28. Rom. 3. 25. Eph. 1. 7. Col. 1. 14. Heb. 13. 12. 1 Pet. 1. 2. 1 John 1. 7. Rev. 1. 5.
[q] Heb. 9. 22.
[r] ch. 7. 26.
[s] Deut. 12. 24.
[t] Ezek. 24. 7.
[u] ver. 11. 12.
[x] Ex. 22. 31. ch. 22. 8. Deut. 14. 21.

[1] Heb. *that hunteth any hunting*.
[2] Heb. *a carcase*.

or sacrifice] *i.e.*, a slaughtered offering of any kind, generally a Peace-offering.

10–14. The prohibition to eat blood is repeated in seven places in the Pentateuch, but in this passage two distinct grounds are given for the prohibition: first, its own nature as the vital fluid; secondly, its consecration in sacrificial worship.

11. Rather, **For the soul of the flesh is in the blood; and I have ordained it for you upon the Altar, to make atonement for your souls; for the blood it is which makes atonement by means of the soul.** In the Old Testament there are three words relating to the constitution of man; (*a*) "life" as opposed to death (Gen. i. 20; Deut. xxx. 15); (*b*) the "soul" as distinguished from the body; the individual life either in man or beast, whether united to the body during life, or separated from the body after death (cp. Gen. ii. 7); (*c*) the "spirit" as opposed to the flesh (Rom. viii. 6), and as distinguished from the life of the flesh; the highest element in man; that which, in its true condition, holds communion with God. The soul has its abode in the blood as long as life lasts. In *v.* 14, the soul is identified with the blood, as it is in Genesis ix. 4; Deut. xii. 23. That the blood is rightly thus distinguished from all other constituents of the body is acknowledged by the highest authorities in physiology.

"It is the fountain of life (says Harvey), the first to live, and the last to die, and the primary seat of the animal soul; it lives and is nourished of itself, and by no other part of the human body." John Hunter inferred that it is the seat of life, because all the parts of the frame are formed and nourished from it. "And if (says he) it has not life previous to this operation, it must then acquire it in the act of forming: for we all give our assent to the existence of life in the parts when once formed." Milne Edwards observes that, "if an animal be bled till it falls into a state of syncope, and the further loss of blood is not prevented, all muscular motion quickly ceases, respiration is suspended, the heart pauses from its action, life is no longer manifested by any outward sign, and death soon becomes inevitable; but if, in this state, the blood of another animal of the same species be injected into the veins of the one to all appearance dead, we see with amazement this inanimate body return to life, gaining accessions of vitality with each new quantity of blood that is introduced, by-and-bye beginning to breathe freely, moving with ease, and finally walking as it was wont to do, and recovering completely." More or less distinct traces of the recognition of blood as the vehicle of life are found in Greek and Roman writers. The knowledge of the ancients on the subject may indeed have been based on the mere observation that an animal loses its life when it loses its blood: but it may deepen our sense of the wisdom and significance of the Law of Moses to know that the fact which it sets forth so distinctly and consistently, and in such pregnant connection, is so clearly recognized by modern scientific research.

14. Rather, **For the soul of all flesh is its blood with its soul** (*i.e.* its blood and soul together): **therefore spake I to the children of Israel, Ye shall not eat the blood of any flesh, for the soul of all flesh is its blood,** &c.

was torn *with beasts, whether it be* one of your own country,
or a stranger, [y]he shall both wash his clothes, [z]and bathe *himself*
in water, and be unclean until the even: then shall he be clean.
16 But if he wash *them* not, nor bathe his flesh; then [a]he shall bear
his iniquity.
CHAP. 18. AND the LORD spake unto Moses, saying, Speak unto
2 the children of Israel, and say unto them, [a]I am the LORD your
3 God. [b]After the doings of the land of Egypt, wherein ye dwelt,
shall ye not do: and [c]after the doings of the land of Canaan,
whither I bring you, shall ye not do: neither shall ye walk in
4 their ordinances. [d]Ye shall do my judgments, and keep mine
5 ordinances, to walk therein: I *am* the LORD your God. Ye
shall therefore keep my statutes, and my judgments: [e]which
6 if a man do, he shall live in them: [f]I *am* the LORD. ¶ None
of you shall approach to any that is [1]near of kin to him, to
7 uncover *their* nakedness: I *am* the LORD. [g]The nakedness of
thy father, or the nakedness of thy mother, shalt thou not uncover: she *is* thy mother; thou shalt not uncover her naked-
8 ness. [h]The nakedness of thy father's wife shalt thou not un-
9 cover: it *is* thy father's nakedness. [i]The nakedness of thy
sister, the daughter of thy father, or daughter of thy mother,
whether she be born at home, or born abroad, *even* their naked-
10 ness thou shalt not uncover. The nakedness of thy son's daughter, or of thy daughter's daughter, *even* their nakedness thou
11 shalt not uncover: for their's *is* thine own nakedness. The
nakedness of thy father's wife's daughter, begotten of thy father,
12 she *is* thy sister, thou shalt not uncover her nakedness. [k]Thou
shalt not uncover the nakedness of thy father's sister: she *is* thy
13 father's near kinswoman. Thou shalt not uncover the nakedness of thy mother's sister: for she *is* thy mother's near kins-
14 woman. [l]Thou shalt not uncover the nakedness of thy father's
brother, thou shalt not approach to his wife: she *is* thine aunt.
15 [m]Thou shalt not uncover the nakedness of thy daughter in law:
she *is* thy son's wife; thou shalt not uncover her nakedness.

[y] ch. 11. 25. [z] ch. 15. 5. [a] ch. 5. 1. Num. 19. 20.
[a] ver. 4. Ex. 6. 7. ch. 11. 44. Ezek. 20. 5.
[b] Ezek. 20. 7, 8.
[c] Ex. 23. 24. ch. 20. 23. Deut. 12. 4.
[d] Deut. 4. 1, 2.
[e] Ezek. 20. 11, 13, 21. Luke 10. 28. Rom. 10. 5. Gal. 3. 12.
[f] Ex. 6. 2, 6, 29. Mal. 3. 6.
[g] ch. 20. 11.
[h] Gen. 49. 4. Deut. 22. 30. Ezek. 22. 10. Amos 2. 7. 1 Cor. 5. 1.
[i] ch. 20. 17. 2 Sam. 13. 12.
[k] ch. 20. 19.
[l] ch. 20. 20.
[m] Gen. 38. 18, 26. ch. 20. 12. Ezek. 22. 11.

[1] Heb. *remainder of his flesh.*

---

15. This law appears to be grounded on the fact that the body of an animal killed by a wild beast, or which has died of itself, still retains a great portion of its blood. The importance ascribed to this law in later times may be seen in 1 S. xiv. 32–35; Ezek. iv. 14, xliv. 31, and still more in the Apostolic decision regarding "things strangled," which are pointedly connected with blood (Acts xv. 20).

XVIII. **2.** *I am the* LORD *your God*] The frequent repetition of this formula in these parts of the Law may be intended to keep the Israelites in mind of their Covenant with Jehovah in connection with the common affairs of life, in which they might be tempted to look at legal restrictions in a mere secular light.

3. See *vv.* 24 30 note.

5. If a man keeps the *statutes* (*i.e.* the ordinances of *v.* 4) and *judgments* of the Divine Law, he shall not be "cut off from his people" (cp. *v.* 29), he shall gain true life, the life which connects him with Jehovah through his obedience. See marg. reff. and Luke x. 28; Rom. x. 5; Gal. iii. 12.

6. *near of kin*] See margin. The term was evidently used to denote those only who came within certain limits of consanguinity, together with those who by affinity were regarded in the same relationship.

to uncover their nakedness] *i.e.* to have intercourse. The immediate object of this law was to forbid incest.

7. *or*] It might be rendered *and*, or rather, **even**; that is, which belongs to both parents as being "one flesh" (Gen. ii. 24; cp. *vv.* 8, 14). These prohibitions are addressed to men.

8. Cp. the case of Reuben, Gen. xlix. 3, 4. See 1 Cor. v. 1.

9. *thy sister*] What was here spoken of was the distinguishing offence of the Egyptians.

12. *thy father's sister*] The instance of Amram and Jochebed (Ex. vi. 20) seems to shew that marriage with an aunt was not considered wrong by the Israelites when they were in Egypt.

16 [n]Thou shalt not uncover the nakedness of thy brother's wife: it
17 *is* thy brother's nakedness. [o]Thou shalt not uncover the nakedness of a woman and her daughter, neither shalt thou take her
son's daughter, or her daughter's daughter, to uncover her naked-
18 ness; *for* they *are* her near kinswomen: it *is* wickedness. Neither shalt thou take [1]a wife to her sister, [p]to vex *her*, to uncover
19 her nakedness, beside the other in her life *time*. [q]Also thou
shalt not approach unto a woman to uncover her nakedness, as
20 long as she is put apart for her uncleanness. Moreover [r]thou
shalt not lie carnally with thy neighbour's wife, to defile thyself
21 with her. And thou shalt not let any of thy seed [s]pass through
the fire to Molech, neither shalt thou [u]profane the name of thy
22 God: I *am* the LORD. [x]Thou shalt not lie with mankind, as
23 with womankind: it *is* abomination. [y]Neither shalt thou lie
with any beast to defile thyself therewith: neither shall any
woman stand before a beast to lie down thereto; it *is* [z]con-
24 fusion. ¶[a]Defile not ye yourselves in any of these things: [b]for
in all these the nations are defiled which I cast out before you:
25 and[c] the land is defiled: therefore I do [d]visit the iniquity
thereof upon it, and the land itself [e]vomiteth out her inhabitants.
26 [f]Ye shall therefore keep my statutes and my judgments, and
shall not commit *any* of these abominations; *neither* any of your
27 own nation, nor any stranger that sojourneth among you: (for
all these abominations have the men of the land done, which *were*
28 before you, and the land is defiled;) that [g]the land spue not you
out also, when ye defile it, as it spued out the nations that *were*
29 before you. For whosoever shall commit any of these abominations, even the souls that commit *them* shall be cut off from
30 among their people. Therefore shall ye keep mine ordinance,
[h]that *ye* commit not *any one* of these abominable customs,
which were committed before you, and that ye [i]defile not yourselves therein: [k]I *am* the LORD your God.

CHAP. 19. AND the LORD spake unto Moses, saying, Speak unto all
2 the congregation of the children of Israel, and say unto them,

[n] ch. 20. 21.
[o] ch. 20. 14.
[p] 1 Sam. 1. 6.
[q] ch. 20. 18. Ezek. 18. 6.
[r] ch. 20. 10. Deut. 5. 18. Prov. 6. 29. Mal. 3. 5. Matt. 5. 27. Heb. 13. 4.
[s] 2 Kin. 16. 3. Jer. 19. 5. Ezek. 20. 31. & 23. 37.
[u] ch. 19. 12. Ezek. 36. 20. Mal. 1. 12.
[x] ch. 20. 13. Rom. 1. 27. 1 Cor. 6. 9. 1 Tim. 1. 10.
[y] ch. 20. 15. Ex. 22. 19.
[z] ch. 20. 12.
[a] ver. 30. Mark 7. 21. 1 Cor. 3. 17.
[b] ch. 20. 23. Deut. 18. 12.
[c] Num. 35. 34. Jer. 2. 7. Ezek. 36. 17.
[d] Ps. 89. 32. Isai. 26. 21. Jer. 5. 9, 29. Hos. 2. 13.
[e] ver. 28.
[f] ver. 5. 30.
[g] ch. 20. 22. Jer. 9. 19. Ezek. 36. 13.
[h] ch. 20. 23. Deut. 18. 9.
[i] ver. 24.
[k] ver. 2. 4.

[1] Or, one *wife to another*, Ex. 26. 3.

---

16. *thy brother's wife*] That is, if she had children. See Deut. xxv. 5. The law here expressed was broken by Antipas in his connexion with Herodias (Matt. xiv. 3, 4).

18. *to vex her*] Literally, to *bind* or *pack together*. The Jewish commentators illustrate this by the example of Leah and Rachel (Gen. xxix. 30).

21. *Molech*] See on xx. 2–5.

24–30. The land designed and consecrated for His people by Jehovah (xxv. 23) is here impersonated, and represented as vomiting forth its present inhabitants, in consequence of their indulgence in the abominations that have been mentioned. The iniquity of the Canaanites was now full. See Gen. xv. 16; cp. Isaiah xxiv. 1–6. The Israelites in this place, and throughout the chapter, are exhorted to a pure and holy life, on the ground that Jehovah, the Holy One, is their God and that they are His people. Cp. xix. 2. It is upon this high sanction that they are peremptorily forbidden to defile themselves with the pollutions of the heathen. The only punishment here pronounced upon individual transgressors is, that they shall "bear their iniquity" and be "cut off from among their people." We must understand this latter phrase as expressing an *ipso facto* excommunication or outlawry, the divine Law pronouncing on the offender an immediate forfeiture of the privileges which belonged to him as one of the people in Covenant with Jehovah. See Ex. xxxi. 14 note. The course which the Law here takes seems to be first to appeal to the conscience of the individual man on the ground of his relation to Jehovah, and then (ch. xx.) to enact such penalties as the order of the state required, and as represented the collective conscience of the nation put into operation.

XIX. **2.** *Ye shall be holy*, &c.] These words express the keynote to the whole book of Leviticus, being addressed to the whole nation. There does not appear to be any systematic arrangement in the laws which follow. They were intended as guards to the sanctity of the elect people, enforcing common duties by immediate ap-

[a] ch. 11. 44. 1 Pet. 1. 16. [b] Ex. 20. 12. [c] Ex. 20. 8. [d] Ex. 20. 4. 1 John 5. 21. [e] Ex. 34. 17. Deut. 27. 15. [f] ch. 7. 16. [g] ch. 23. 22. Ruth 2. 15. [h] Ex. 20. 15. [i] ch. 6. 2. Eph. 4. 25. [k] Ex. 20. 7. Matt. 5. 33. Jas. 5. 12. [l] ch. 18. 21. [m] Mark 10. 19. 1 Thes. 4. 6. [n] Deut. 24. 14, 15. James 5. 4. [o] Rom. 14. 13. [p] Eccles. 5. 7. 1 Pet. 2. 17. [q] Ex. 23. 2, 3. Deut. 1. 17. Prov. 24. 23. James 2. 9. [r] Ex. 23. 1. Ps. 15. 3. Prov. 11. 13. Ezek. 22. 9. [s] Ex. 23. 1. 1 Kin. 21. 13. [t] 1 John 2. 9. [u] Luke 17. 3. Gal. 6. 1. 2 Tim. 4. 2. [x] Prov. 20, 22. Rom. 12. 17. Eph. 4. 31. Jam. 5. 9. [y] Matt. 5. 43. Rom. 13. 9. Gal. 5. 14.

3 [a]Ye shall be holy: for I the LORD your God *am* holy. [b]Ye
shall fear every man his mother, and his father, and [c]keep my
4 sabbaths: I *am* the LORD your God. [d]Turn ye not unto idols,
[e]nor make to yourselves molten gods: I *am* the LORD your God.
5 And [f]if ye offer a sacrifice of peace offerings unto the LORD, ye
6 shall offer it at your own will. It shall be eaten the same day ye
offer it, and on the morrow: and if ought remain until the third
7 day, it shall be burnt in the fire. And if it be eaten at all on the
8 third day, it *is* abominable; it shall not be accepted. Therefore
every one that eateth it shall bear his iniquity, because he hath
profaned the hallowed thing of the LORD: and that soul shall
9 be cut off from among his people. ¶ And [g]when ye reap the
harvest of your land, thou shalt not wholly reap the corners
of thy field, neither shalt thou gather the gleanings of thy
10 harvest. And thou shalt not glean thy vineyard, neither shalt
thou gather *every* grape of thy vineyard; thou shalt leave them
11 for the poor and stranger: I *am* the LORD your God. [h]Ye shall
12 not steal, neither deal falsely, [i]neither lie one to another. And
ye shall not [k]swear by my name falsely, [l]neither shalt thou pro-
13 fane the name of thy God: I *am* the LORD. [m]Thou shalt not
defraud thy neighbour, neither rob *him:* [n]the wages of him
that is hired shall not abide with thee all night until the morn-
14 ing. Thou shalt not curse the deaf, [o]nor put a stumblingblock
15 before the blind, but shalt [p]fear thy God: I *am* the LORD. [q]Ye
shall do no unrighteousness in judgment: thou shalt not respect
the person of the poor, nor honour the person of the mighty:
16 *but* in righteousness shalt thou judge thy neighbour. [r]Thou
shalt not go up and down *as* a talebearer among thy people:
neither shalt thou [s]stand against the blood of thy neighbour: I
17 *am* the LORD. [t]Thou shalt not hate thy brother in thine heart:
[u]thou shalt in any wise rebuke thy neighbour, [1]and not suffer
18 sin upon him. [x]Thou shalt not avenge, nor bear any grudge
against the children of thy people, [y]but thou shalt love thy
19 neighbour as thyself: I *am* the LORD. Ye shall keep my

[1] Or, *that thou bear not sin for him:* See Rom. 1. 32. 1 Cor. 5. 2. 1 Tim. 5. 22. 2 John 11.

---

peal to the highest authority. Cp. xviii. 24–30 note.

3. Cp. Ex. xx. 8, 12, xxxi. 13, 14. The two laws repeated here are the only laws in the Decalogue which assume a positive shape, all the others being introduced by the formula, "Thou shalt not."—These express two great central points, the first belonging to natural law and the second to positive law, in the maintenance of the well-being of the social body of which Jehovah was the acknowledged king.

5. Rather, **ye shall offer it that you may be accepted.**

9, 10. See Deut. xxiv. 19-21. "Grape" signifies **fallen fruit** of any kind; and "vineyard" **a fruit garden** of any kind. Cp. Deut. xxiii. 24.

The poor is the poor Israelite—*the stranger* is properly **the foreigner,** who could possess no land of his own in the land of Israel.

11-13. *v.* 11 forbids injuries perpetrated by craft; *v.* 13, those perpetrated by violence or power, the conversion of might into right. In *v.* 13 "defraud" should rather be, **oppress.**

14. The meaning appears to be, *Thou shalt not utter curses to the deaf because he cannot hear thee, neither shalt thou put a stumbling-block in the way of the blind because he cannot see thee* (cp. Deut. xxvii. 18), *but thou shalt remember that though the weak and poor cannot resist, nor the deaf hear, nor the blind see, God is strong, and sees and hears all that thou doest.* Cp. Job xxix. 15.

16. *stand against the blood of thy neighbour*] Either, to put his life in danger by standing up as his accuser (cp. Matt. xxvi. 60); or, to stand by idly when thy neighbour's life is in danger.—Whichever interpretation we adopt, the clause prohibits that which might interfere with the course of justice.

17. *not suffer sin upon him*] Rather, **not bear sin on his account;** that is, either by bearing secret ill-will (Ephes. iv. 26), or by encouraging him to sin in withholding due rebuke (Rom. i. 32).

statutes. ¶ Thou shalt not let thy cattle gender with a diverse
kind: [z]thou shalt not sow thy field with mingled seed: [a]neither
shall a garment mingled of linen and woollen come upon thee.
20 And whosoever lieth carnally with a woman, that *is* a bond-
maid, [1 2]betrothed to an husband, and not at all redeemed, nor
freedom given her; [3 4]she shall be scourged; they shall not be
21 put to death, because she was not free. And [b]he shall bring his
trespass offering unto the LORD, unto the door of the tabernacle
22 of the congregation, *even* a ram for a trespass offering. And
the priest shall make an atonement for him with the ram of
the trespass offering before the LORD for his sin which he hath
done: and the sin which he hath done shall be forgiven him.
23 ¶ And when ye shall come into the land, and shall have planted
all manner of trees for food, then ye shall count the fruit thereof
as uncircumcised: three years shall it be as uncircumcised unto
24 you: it shall not be eaten of. But in the fourth year all the
25 fruit thereof shall be [5]holy [c]to praise the LORD *withal*. And in
the fifth year shall ye eat of the fruit thereof, that it may yield
26 unto you the increase thereof: I *am* the LORD your God. ¶ [d]Ye
shall not eat *any thing* with the blood: [e]neither shall ye use
27 enchantment, nor observe times. [f]Ye shall not round the
corners of your heads, neither shalt thou mar the corners of thy
28 beard. Ye shall not [g]make any cuttings in your flesh for the
29 dead, nor print any marks upon you: I *am* the LORD. [h]Do not

[z] Deut. 22. 9, 10.
[a] Deut. 22. 11.
[b] ch. 5. 15.
[c] Deut. 12. 17, 18. Prov. 3. 9.
[d] ch. 17. 10. Deut. 12. 23.
[e] Deut. 18. 10, 11, 14. 1 Sam. 15. 23. 2 Kin. 17. 17. 2 Chr. 33 6. Mal. 3. 5.
[f] ch. 21. 5. Isai. 15. 2. Jer. 9. 26.
[g] ch. 21. 5. Deut. 14. 1. Jer. 16. 6. & 48. 37.
[h] Deut. 23. 17.

1 Or, *abused by any*.
2 Heb. *reproached by*, or, *for man*.
3 Or, *they*.
4 Heb. *there shall be a scourging*.
5 Heb. *holiness of praises to the* LORD.

---

19. *linen and woollen*] The original word is found only here and in Deut. xxii. 11, where it is rendered "of divers sorts." It may denote such tissues as linsey woolsey.

20. *betrothed to an husband*] Rather, **who has been betrothed to a man.** The reference appears to be to a bondwoman who has been betrothed to a fellow-servant by her master. Death was the punishment for unfaithfulness in a betrothed woman in other cases. Cp. Deut. xxii. 23, 24.

she shall be scourged] Or, **They shall be chastised** (see margin). The Trespass-offering was especially due from the man as having not only sinned with the woman, but inflicted an injury on the rights of the master.

23. *fruit...uncircumcised*] *i.e.* unfit for presentation to Jehovah. In regard to its spiritual lesson, this law may be compared with the dedication of the first-born of beasts to Jehovah (Ex. xiii. 12, xxxiv. 19). Its meaning in a moral point of view was plain, and tended to illustrate the spirit of the whole Law.

26-28. Certain heathen customs, several of them connected with magic, are here grouped together. The prohibition to eat anything *with the blood* may indeed refer to the eating of meat which had not been properly bled in slaughtering (vii. 26, xvii. 10, &c.): but it is not improbable that there may be a special reference to some sort of magical or idolatrous rites. Cp. Ezek. xxxiii. 25.

26. *observe times*] It is not clear whether the original word refers to the fancied distinction between lucky and unlucky days, to some mode of drawing omens from the clouds, or to the exercise of "the evil eye."

27. *round the corners of your heads*] This may allude to such a custom as that of the Arabs described by Herodotus. They used to shew honour to their deity Orotal by cutting the hair away from the temples in a circular form. Cp. marg. reff.

mar the corners of thy beard] It has been conjectured that this also relates to a custom which existed amongst the Arabs, but we are not informed that it had any idolatrous or magical association. As the same, or very similar customs, are mentioned in xxi. 5, and in Deut. xiv. 1, as well as here, it would appear that they may have been signs of mourning.

28. *cuttings in your flesh for the dead*] Cp. marg. reff. Amongst the excitable races of the East this custom appears to have been very common.

print any marks] Tattooing was probably practised in ancient Egypt, as it is now by the lower classes of the modern Egyptians, and was connected with superstitious notions. Any voluntary disfigurement of the person was in itself an outrage upon God's workmanship, and might well form the subject of a law.

[1]prostitute thy daughter, to cause her to be a whore; lest the
land fall to whoredom, and the land become full of wickedness.
30 [i]Ye shall keep my sabbaths, and [k]reverence my sanctuary: I *am*
31 the LORD. [l]Regard not them that have familiar spirits, neither
seek after wizards, to be defiled by them: I *am* the LORD your
32 God. [m]Thou shalt rise up before the hoary head, and honour
the face of the old man, and [n]fear thy God: I *am* the LORD.
33 And [o]if a stranger sojourn with thee in your land, ye shall not
34 [2]vex him. [p]*But* the stranger that dwelleth with you shall be
unto you as one born among you, and [q]thou shalt love him as
thyself; for ye were strangers in the land of Egypt: I *am* the
35 LORD your God. [r]Ye shall do no unrighteousness in judgment,
36 in meteyard, in weight, or in measure. [s]Just balances, just
[3]weights, a just ephah, and a just hin, shall ye have: I *am* the
LORD your God, which brought you out of the land of Egypt.
37 [t]Therefore shall ye observe all my statutes, and all my judgments,
and do them: I *am* the LORD.
CHAP. 20. AND the LORD spake unto Moses, saying, [a]Again, thou
2 shalt say to the children of Israel, [b]Whosoever *he be* of the children of Israel, or of the strangers that sojourn in Israel, that
giveth *any* of his seed unto Molech; he shall surely be put to
3 death: the people of the land shall stone him with stones. And
[c]I will set my face against that man, and will cut him off from
among his people; because he hath given of his seed unto Molech,

[i] ver. 3. ch. 26. 2.
[k] Eccles. 5. 1.
[l] Ex. 22. 18. ch. 20. 6. Deut. 18. 10. 1 Chr. 10. 13. Isai. 8. 19. Acts 16. 16.
[m] Prov. 20. 29. 1 Tim. 5. 1.
[n] ver. 14.
[o] Ex. 22. 21.
[p] Ex. 12. 48.
[q] Deut. 10. 19.
[r] ver. 15.
[s] Deut. 25. 13, 15. Prov. 11. 1.
[t] ch. 18. 4. Deut. 4. 5. & 5. 1. & 6. 25.
[a] ch. 18. 2.
[b] Deut. 12. 31. 2 Kin. 17. 17. 2 Chr. 33. 6. Jer. 7. 31. Ezek. 20. 26, 31.
[c] ch. 17. 10.

[1] Heb. *profane*. [2] Or, *oppress*. [3] Heb. *stones*.

---

31. The devotion of faith, which would manifest itself in obedience to the commandment to keep God's Sabbaths and to reverence His Sanctuary (*v.* 30), is the true preservative against the superstition which is forbidden in this verse. The people whose God was Jehovah were not to indulge those wayward feelings of their human nature which are gratified in magical arts and pretensions. Cp. Isa. viii. 19.

familiar spirits] Literally, *bottles*. This application of the word is supposed to have been suggested by the tricks of ventriloquists, within whose bodies (as vessels or bottles) it was fancied that spirits used to speak. In other cases the word is used for the familiar spirit which a man pretended to employ in order to consult, or to raise, the spirits of the dead. See 1 S. xxviii. 7, 8.

wizard] A word equivalent to *a knowing man*, or, *a cunning man*.

32. The outward respect due to old age is here immediately connected with the fear of God. Cp. marg. reff.

33, 34. *the stranger*] **The foreigner.** See xvi. 29 note; Ex. xxiii. 9.

35, 36. The ephah is here taken as the standard of dry measure, and the hin (see Ex. xxix. 40 note) as the standard of liquid measure. Of the two very different estimates of the capacities of these measures, the more probable is that the ephah did not hold quite four gallons and a half, and the hin not quite six pints. The log was a twelfth part of the hin (xiv. 10).

36. *I am the* LORD *your God*, &c.] A full stop should precede these words. They introduce the formal conclusion to the whole string of precepts in this chapter, which are all enforced upon the ground of the election of the nation by Jehovah Who had delivered them from the bondage of Egypt.

XX. The crimes which are condemned in chapters xviii., xix. on purely spiritual ground, have here special punishments allotted to them as offences against the well-being of the nation.

2–5. Molech, literally, *the King*, called also Moloch, Milcom, and Malcham, was known in later times as "the abomination of the Ammonites" (1 Kings xi. 5). He appears to have been the fire-god of the eastern nations; related to, and sometimes made identical with, Baal, the sun-god. The nature of the rite and of the impious custom called passing children through the fire to Molech is very doubtful. The practices appear to have been essentially connected with magical arts, probably also with unlawful lusts, and with some particular form of profane swearing. The rite in the time of Moses belonged to the region rather of magic than of definite idolatrous worship, and may have been practised as a lustral charm, or fire-baptism, for the children of incest and adultery.

2. *stone him with stones*] The commonest form of capital punishment. It was probably preferred as being the one in which the execution was the act of the whole congregation.

3. *defile my sanctuary*] *i.e.* pollute the people as identified with their Sanctuary.

4 to [d]defile my sanctuary, and [e]to profane my holy name And if
the people of the land do any ways hide their eyes from the man,
when he giveth of his seed unto Molech, and [f]kill him not:
5 then [g]I will set my face against that man, and [h]against his
family, and will cut him off, and all that [i]go a whoring after
him, to commit whoredom with Molech, from among their people.
6 And [k]the soul that turneth after such as have familiar spirits,
and after wizards, to go a whoring after them, I will even set
my face against that soul, and will cut him off from among his
7 people. ¶ [l]Sanctify yourselves therefore, and be ye holy: for I
8 *am* the LORD your God. [m]And ye shall keep my statutes, and
9 do them: [n]I *am* the LORD which sanctify you. [o]For every one
that curseth his father or his mother shall be surely put to
death: he hath cursed his father or his mother; [p]his blood *shall*
10 *be* upon him. And [q]the man that committeth adultery with
another man's wife, *even he* that committeth adultery with his
neighbour's wife, the adulterer and the adulteress shall surely be
11 put to death. [r]And the man that lieth with his father's wife
hath uncovered his father's nakedness: both of them shall surely
12 be put to death; their blood *shall be* upon them. [s]And if a man
lie with his daughter in law, both of them shall surely be put to
death: [t]they have wrought confusion; their blood *shall be* upon
13 them. [u]If a man also lie with mankind, as he lieth with a
woman, both of them have committed an abomination: they
shall surely be put to death; their blood *shall be* upon them.
14 [x]And if a man take a wife and her mother, it *is* wickedness:
they shall be burnt with fire, both he and they; that there be
15 no wickedness among you. [y]And if a man lie with a beast, he
16 shall surely be put to death: and ye shall slay the beast. And
if a woman approach unto any beast, and lie down thereto,
thou shalt kill the woman, and the beast: they shall surely be
17 put to death; their blood *shall be* upon them. [z]And if a man
shall take his sister, his father's daughter, or his mother's
daughter, and see her nakedness, and she see his nakedness; it
is a wicked thing; and they shall be cut off in the sight of their
people: he hath uncovered his sister's nakedness; he shall bear
18 his iniquity. [a]And if a man shall lie with a woman having her
sickness, and shall uncover her nakedness; he hath [1]discovered
her fountain, and she hath uncovered the fountain of her blood:
and both of them shall be cut off from among their people.
19 [b]And thou shalt not uncover the nakedness of thy mother's
sister, nor of thy father's sister: [c]for he uncovereth his near
20 kin: they shall bear their iniquity. [d]And if a man shall lie
with his uncle's wife, he hath uncovered his uncle's nakedness:
21 they shall bear their sin; they shall die childless. [e]And if a
man shall take his brother's wife, it *is* [2]an unclean thing: he
hath uncovered his brother's nakedness; they shall be childless.
22 ¶ Ye shall therefore keep all my [f]statutes, and all my judg-

[d] Ezek. 5. 11. & 23. 38, 39.
[e] ch. 18. 21.
[f] Deut. 17. 2, 3, 5.
[g] ch. 17. 10.
[h] Ex. 20. 5.
[i] ch. 17. 7.
[k] ch. 19. 31.
[l] ch. 11. 44. & 19. 2. 1 Pet. 1. 16.
[m] ch. 19. 37.
[n] Ex. 31. 13. ch. 21. 8. Ezek. 37. 28.
[o] Ex. 21. 17. Matt. 15. 4.
[p] ver. 11. 2 Sam. 1. 16.
[q] ch. 18. 20. Deut. 22. 22. John 8. 4.
[r] ch. 18. 8. Deut. 27. 23.
[s] ch. 18. 15.
[t] ch. 18. 23.
[u] ch. 18. 22. See Gen. 19. 5. Judg. 19. 22.
[x] ch. 18. 17. Deut. 27. 23.
[y] ch. 18. 23. Deut. 27. 21.
[z] ch. 18. 9. Deut. 27. 22. See Gen. 20. 12.
[a] ch. 18. 19.
[b] ch. 18. 12.
[c] ch. 18. 6.
[d] ch. 18. 14.
[e] ch. 18. 16
[f] ch. 18. 26. & 19. 37.

[1] Heb. *made naked.* [2] Heb. *a separation.*

---

14. The burning under the sentence of the Law took place after the death of the criminal by stoning, or strangling. Josh. vii. 25.

17. *cut off*, &c.] See Ex. xxxi. 14 note. The more full expression here used probably refers to some special form of public excommunication, accompanied, it may be, by expulsion from the camp.

20. *they shall die childless*] Either the offspring should not be regarded as lawfully theirs, nor be entitled to any hereditary privileges, or they should have no blessing in their children.

22-26. The ground is here again stated on which all these laws of holiness should be obeyed. See xviii. 24-30 note.

ments, and do them: that the land, whither I bring you to dwell
23 therein, [g]spue you not out. [h]And ye shall not walk in the
manners of the nation, which I cast out before you: for they
committed all these things, and [i]therefore I abhorred them.
24 But [k]I have said unto you, Ye shall inherit their land, and I
will give it unto you to possess it, a land that floweth with milk
and honey: I *am* the LORD your God, [l]which have separated
25 you from *other* people. ¶ [m]Ye shall therefore put difference between clean beasts and unclean, and between unclean fowls and
clean: [n]and ye shall not make your souls abominable by beast,
or by fowl, or by any manner of living thing that [1]creepeth on
26 the ground, which I have separated from you as unclean. And
ye shall be holy unto me: [o]for I the LORD *am* holy, and [p]have
27 severed you from *other* people, that ye should be mine. ¶ [q]A man
also or woman that hath a familiar spirit, or that is a wizard,
shall surely be put to death: they shall stone them with stones:
[r]their blood *shall be* upon them.

CHAP. 21. AND the LORD said unto Moses, Speak unto the priests
the sons of Aaron, and say unto them, [a]There shall none be
2 defiled for the dead among his people: but for his kin, that is
near unto him, *that is*, for his mother, and for his father, and
3 for his son, and for his daughter, and for his brother, and for
his sister a virgin, that is nigh unto him, which hath had no
4 husband; for her may he be defiled. *But* [2]he shall not defile
himself, *being* a chief man among his people, to profane himself.
5 [b]They shall not make baldness upon their head, neither shall
they shave off the corner of their beard, nor make any cuttings
6 in their flesh. They shall be holy unto their God, and [c]not profane the name of their God: for the offerings of the LORD made
by fire, *and* [d]the bread of their God, they do offer: therefore
7 they shall be holy. ¶ [e]They shall not take a wife *that is* a whore,
or profane; neither shall they take a woman [f]put away from
8 her husband: for he *is* holy unto his God. Thou shalt sanctify

[g] ch. 18. 25.
[h] ch. 18. 3.
[i] ch. 18. 27. Deut. 9. 5.
[k] Ex. 3. 17. & 6. 8.
[l] ver. 26. Ex. 19. 5. Deut. 7. 6. 1 Kin. 8. 53.
[m] ch 11. 47. Deut. 14. 4.
[n] ch. 11. 43.
[o] ver. 7. ch. 19. 2. 1 Pet. 1. 16.
[p] ver. 24. Tit. 2. 14.
[q] Ex. 22. 18. ch. 19. 31. Deut. 18. 10, 11. 1 Sam. 28. 7, 8.
[r] ver. 9.
[a] Ezek. 44. 25.
[b] ch. 19. 27. Deut. 14. 1. Ezek. 44. 20.
[c] ch. 18. 21. & 19. 12.
[d] See ch. 3. 11.
[e] Ezek. 44. 22.
[f] See Deut. 24. 1, 2.

[1] Or, *moveth.*
[2] Or, *being an husband among his people, he shall not defile himself* for his wife, &c. See Ezek. 24. 16, 17.

---

24. Cp. marg. reff.

25, 26. The distinction between clean and unclean for the whole people, and not for any mere section of it, was one great typical mark of "the kingdom of priests, the holy nation." See xi. 42 note.

25. *any manner of living thing that creepeth*] Rather, **any creeping thing**; that is, any vermin. See xi. 20–23. The reference in this verse is to dead animals, not to the creatures when alive.

XXI. **4.** The sense seems to be that, owing to his position in the nation, the priest is not to defile himself in any cases except those named in *vv.* 2–3. The LXX. appear to have followed a different reading of the text which would mean, *he shall not defile himself for a moment.* The explanation in the margin of our version is hardly in keeping with the prohibition to Ezekiel on a special occasion. See Ezek. xxiv. 16.

5. These prohibitions given to the people at large (cp. marg. reff.) had a special fitness for the Hebrew priests. They were the instruments of the divine will for averting death, all their sacrifices were a type of the death of Christ, which swallowed up death in victory (1 Cor. xv. 54–57), and it would therefore have been unsuitable that they should have the same freedom as other people to become mourners.

6. The word here and in *v.* 8 rendered *bread*, is the same as is rendered *food* in iii. 11, 16, &c., and *meat* in xxii. 11. The reader of the English Bible should keep in view that *bread*, *meat*, and *food*, were nearly equivalent terms when our translation was made, and represent no distinctions that exist in the Hebrew.

7. *profane*] A woman who has been seduced, or one of illegitimate birth.—A somewhat stricter rule for the priests' marriages was revealed to the prophet in later times, Ezek. xliv. 22.

8. The people of Israel are now addressed. They are commanded to regard the priests, who perform for them the service of the Altar, as holy in respect of their office.

him therefore; for he offereth the bread of thy God: he shall be
holy unto thee: [g]for I the LORD, which sanctify you, *am* holy.
9 [h]And the daughter of any priest, if she profane herself by play-
ing the whore, she profaneth her father: she shall be burnt
10 with fire. ¶ [i]And *he that is* the high priest among his brethren,
upon whose head the anointing oil was poured, and [k]that is consecrated to put on the garments, [l]shall not uncover his head,
11 nor rend his clothes; neither shall he [m]go in to any dead body,
12 nor defile himself for his father, or for his mother; [n]neither
shall he go out of the sanctuary, nor profane the sanctuary of
his God; for [o]the crown of the anointing oil of his God *is* upon
13 him: I *am* the LORD. And [p]he shall take a wife in her vir-
14 ginity. A widow, or a divorced woman, or profane, *or* an harlot,
these shall he not take: but he shall take a virgin of his own
15 people to wife. Neither shall he profane his seed among his
16 people: for [q]I the LORD do sanctify him. ¶ And the LORD
17 spake unto Moses, saying, Speak unto Aaron, saying, Whosoever *he be* of thy seed in their generations that hath *any* blemish,
18 let him not [r]approach to offer the [1]bread of his God. For whatsoever man *he be* that hath a blemish, he shall not approach: a
blind man, or a lame, or he that hath a flat nose, or any thing
19 [s]superfluous, or a man that is brokenfooted, or brokenhanded,
20 or crookbackt, or [2]a dwarf, or that hath a blemish in his eye, or
21 be scurvy, or scabbed, or [t]hath his stones broken: no man that
hath a blemish of the seed of Aaron the priest shall come nigh
to [u]offer the offerings of the LORD made by fire: he hath a
blemish; he shall not come nigh to offer the bread of his God.
22 He shall eat the bread of his God, *both* of the [x]most holy, and of
23 the [y]holy. Only he shall not go in unto the vail, nor come nigh
unto the altar, because he hath a blemish; that [z]he profane not
24 my sanctuaries: for I the LORD do sanctify them. And Moses
told *it* unto Aaron, and to his sons, and unto all the children
of Israel.

CHAP. 22. AND the LORD spake unto Moses, saying, Speak unto
2 Aaron and to his sons, that they [a]separate themselves from the
holy things of the children of Israel, and that they [b]profane not
my holy name *in those things* which they [c]hallow unto me: I

[g] ch. 20. 7.
[h] Gen. 38. 24.
[i] Ex. 29. 29. ch. 16. 32. Num. 35. 25.
[k] Ex. 28. 2. ch. 16. 32.
[l] ch. 10. 6.
[m] Num. 19. 14.
[n] ch. 10. 7.
[o] Ex. 28. 36. ch. 8. 9, 12.
[p] ver. 7. Ezek. 44. 22.
[q] ver. 8.
[r] ch. 10. 3. Num. 16. 5. Ps. 65. 4.
[s] ch. 22. 23.
[t] Deut. 23. 1.
[u] ver. 6.
[x] ch. 2. 3, 10. & 6. 17, 29. Num. 18. 9.
[y] ch. 22. 10, 11, 12. Num. 18. 19.
[z] ver. 12.
[a] Num. 6. 3.
[b] ch. 18. 21.
[c] Ex. 28. 38. Num. 18. 32. Deut. 15. 19.

[1] Or, *food*, ch. 3. 11.
[2] Or, *too slender*.

---

9. *burnt with fire*] See xx. 14 note.

10. It was the distinguishing mark of the anointing of the High priest, that the holy oil was poured on his head like a crown (cp. viii. 12).

uncover his head] Rather, **let his hair be dishevelled.** See on x. 6.

12. *go out of the sanctuary*] *i.e.* not for the purpose to which reference is here made. The words do not mean, as some have imagined, that his abode was confined to the Sanctuary.

15. *profane his seed*] *i.e.* by a marriage which was not in keeping with the holiness of his office.

16–24. He was not treated as an outcast, but enjoyed his privileges as a son of Aaron, except in regard to active duties.

20. *a dwarf*] One who is small and wasted, either short, as in the text, or slender, as in the margin. It is hardly likely that dwarfishness would be overlooked in this enumeration. So most critical authorities.

scurvy or scabbed] These words most probably include all affected with any skin disease.

22. See ii. 3, vi. 25 note.

23. *sanctuaries*] The Places peculiarly Holy, including the Most Holy Place, the Holy Place, and the Altar.

This law is of course to be regarded as one development of the great principle that all which is devoted to the service of God should be as perfect as possible of its kind.

XXII. **2.** "Speak...that they **so abstain from touching** the holy things (*i.e.* the sacrificial food of all kinds) of the children of Israel **which they consecrate unto me**, that they profane not my holy name." This law related to the daily life and the ordinary food of the priests.

3 *am* the LORD. Say unto them, Whosoever *he be* of all your seed
among your generations, that goeth unto the holy things, which
the children of Israel hallow unto the LORD, [d]having his uncleanness upon him, that soul shall be cut off from my presence:
4 I *am* the LORD. What man soever of the seed of Aaron *is* a
leper, or hath [e]a [1]running issue; he shall not eat of the holy
things, [f]until he be clean. And [g]whoso toucheth any thing *that*
is unclean *by* the dead, or [h]a man whose seed goeth from him;
5 or [i]whosoever toucheth any creeping thing, whereby he may be
made unclean, or [k]a man of whom he may take uncleanness,
6 whatsoever uncleanness he hath; the soul which hath touched
any such shall be unclean until even, and shall not eat of the
7 holy things, unless he [l]wash his flesh with water. And when the
sun is down, he shall be clean, and shall afterward eat of the
8 holy things; because [m]it *is* his food. [n]That which dieth of itself, or is torn *with beasts*, he shall not eat to defile himself
9 therewith: I *am* the LORD. They shall therefore keep mine
ordinance, [o]lest they bear sin for it, and die therefore, if they
10 profane it: I the LORD do sanctify them. ¶ [p]There shall no
stranger eat *of* the holy thing: a sojourner of the priest, or an
11 hired servant, shall not eat *of* the holy thing. But if the priest
buy *any* soul [2]with his money, he shall eat of it, and he that is
12 born in his house: [q]they shall eat of his meat. If the priest's
daughter also be *married* unto [3]a stranger, she may not eat of
13 an offering of the holy things. But if the priest's daughter be
a widow, or divorced, and have no child, and is [r]returned unto
her father's house, [s]as in her youth, she shall eat of her father's
14 meat: but there shall no stranger eat thereof. [t]And if a man eat
of the holy thing unwittingly, then he shall put the fifth *part*
thereof unto it, and shall give *it* unto the priest with the holy
15 thing. And [u]they shall not profane the holy things of the
16 children of Israel, which they offer unto the LORD; or [4]suffer
them [x]to bear the iniquity of trespass, when they eat their holy
17 things: for I the LORD do sanctify them. ¶ And the LORD
18 spake unto Moses, saying, Speak unto Aaron, and to his sons,
and unto all the children of Israel, and say unto them, [y]Whatso-
ever *he be* of the house of Israel, or of the strangers in Israel,
that will offer his oblation for all his vows, and for all his freewill offerings, which they will offer unto the LORD for a burnt
19 offering; [z]*ye shall offer* at your own will a male without blemish,

[d] ch. 7. 20.
[e] ch. 15. 2.
[f] ch. 14. 2. & 15. 13.
[g] Num. 19. 11, 22.
[h] ch. 15. 16.
[i] ch. 11. 24, 43, 44.
[k] ch. 15. 7, 19.
[l] ch. 15. 5. Heb. 10. 22.
[m] ch. 21. 22. Num. 18. 11, 13.
[n] ch. 17. 15.
[o] Ex. 28. 43. Num. 18. 22, 32.
[p] See 1 Sam. 21. 6.
[q] Num. 18. 11, 13.
[r] Gen. 38. 11.
[s] ch. 10. 14. Num. 18. 11, 19.
[t] ch. 5. 15, 16.
[u] Num. 18. 32.
[x] ver. 9.
[y] ch. 1. 2, 3, 10. Num. 15. 14.
[z] ch. 1. 3.

[1] Heb. *running of the reins.*
[2] Heb. *with the purchase of his money.*
[3] Heb. *a man a stranger.*
[4] Or, *lade themselves with the iniquity of trespass in their eating.*

---

3. *cut off from my presence*] *i.e.* excluded from the Sanctuary. See xx. 17.

4. See xv. 13–16.

5. *creeping things*] *i.e.* dead vermin. Cp. xi. 29.

6. *the soul*] Rather, **the person.** Compare the use of the word *body* in the Prayer Book version of Ps. liii. 1, and in the compounds *somebody, nobody.*

8. The pollution in the priests would be an aggravated one, inasmuch as they would have to forego their sacred functions. Cp. Ezek. iv. 14, xliv. 31. The general prohibition occurs in xi. 39, xvii. 15; Ex. xxii. 31.

10. *stranger*] **One of another family.** See Ex. xxix. 33 note.

11. This shows how completely a purchased bondsman was incorporated into the household. See Ex. xxi. 2, 20, 21 notes.

12. *a stranger*] **One of another family.**

14. *unwittingly*] **Inadvertently,** or "through ignorance." Cp. iv. 2 note.

15, 16. These verses are rather difficult. Their meaning appears to be:—*The holy things of the children of Israel which are heaved before Jehovah* (see vii. 30) *shall not be profaned; and they shall incur a sin of trespass who eat of their holy things* (*so as to profane them*).

19. *Ye shall offer at your own will a male*] Rather, **That it may be accepted** (so *v.* 29) **for you it shall be a male.** See

20 of the beeves, of the sheep, or of the goats. [a] *But* whatsoever hath
a blemish, *that* shall ye not offer: for it shall not be acceptable
21 for you. And [b] whosoever offereth a sacrifice of peace offerings
unto the LORD [c] to accomplish *his* vow, or a freewill offering in
beeves, or [1] sheep, it shall be perfect to be accepted; there shall
22 be no blemish therein. [d] Blind, or broken, or maimed, or having
a wen, or scurvy, or scabbed, ye shall not offer these unto the
LORD, nor make [e] an offering by fire of them upon the altar unto
23 the LORD. Either a bullock or a [2] lamb that hath anything [f] superfluous or lacking in his parts, that mayest thou offer *for* a free-
24 will offering; but for a vow it shall not be accepted. Ye shall
not offer unto the LORD that which is bruised, or crushed, or
broken, or cut; neither shall ye make *any offering thereof* in
25 your land. Neither [g] from a stranger's hand shall ye offer
[h] the bread of your God of any of these; because their [i] corruption *is* in them, *and* blemishes *be* in them: they shall not be
26 accepted for you. ¶ And the LORD spake unto Moses, saying,
27 [k] When a bullock, or a sheep, or a goat, is brought forth, then it
shall be seven days under the dam; and from the eighth day
and thenceforth it shall be accepted for an offering made by
28 fire unto the LORD. And *whether it be* cow or [3] ewe, ye shall not
29 kill it [l] and her young both in one day. And when ye will
[m] offer a sacrifice of thanksgiving unto the LORD, offer *it* at your
30 own will. On the same day it shall be eaten up; ye shall leave
31 [n] none of it until the morrow: I *am* the LORD. ¶ [o] Therefore
shall ye keep my commandments, and do them: I *am* the LORD.
32 [p] Neither shall ye profane my holy name; but [q] I will be
hallowed among the children of Israel: I *am* the LORD which
33 [r] hallow you, [s] that brought you out of the land of Egypt, to be
your God: I *am* the LORD.

CHAP. 23. AND the LORD spake unto Moses, saying, Speak unto
2 the children of Israel, and say unto them, *Concerning* [a] the feasts
of the LORD, which ye shall [b] proclaim *to be* holy convocations,

[1] Or, *goats*. [2] Or, *kid*. [3] Or, *she goat*.

[a] Deut. 17. 1. Mal. 1. 8. Eph. 5. 27. Heb. 9. 14. 1 Pet. 1. 19.
[b] ch. 3. 1, 6.
[c] ch. 7. 16. Num. 15. 3, 8. Deut. 23. 21, 23. Ps. 61. 8. & 65. 1. Eccles. 5. 4, 5.
[d] ver. 20. Mal. 1. 8.
[e] ch. 1. 9, 13. & 3. 3, 5.
[f] ch. 21. 18.
[g] Num. 15. 15, 16.
[h] ch. 21. 6, 17.
[i] Mal. 1. 14.
[k] Ex. 22. 30.
[l] Deut. 22. 6.
[m] ch. 7. 12. Ps. 107. 22. & 116. 17. Amos 4. 5.
[n] ch. 7. 15.
[o] ch. 19. 37. Num. 15. 40. Deut. 4. 40.
[p] ch. 18. 21.
[q] ch. 10. 3. Matt. 6. 9. Luke 11. 2.
[r] ch. 20. 8.
[s] Ex. 6. 7. Num. 15. 41.
[a] ver. 4. 37.
[b] Ex. 32. 5. 2 Kin. 10. 20. Ps. 81. 3.

---

i. 3. It is the same phrase as in *vv.* 20, 21, 27.

22, 23. Cp. xxi. 19; Deut. xv. 21.

24. The literal meaning of the passage in italics is, **and this shall ye not do in your land.** It appears to have been understood by the Jews as a prohibition of the mutilation of animals.

25. *a stranger's hand*] The word here rendered *stranger*, is not the same as that in *vv.* 10, 18: it means literally, *the son of the unknown*, and probably refers to one dwelling in another land who desired to show respect to the God of Israel. See 1 Kings viii. 41.

27. No victim was to be offered in sacrifice until it was a week old. The meaning of this law appears to be that the animal should realise a distinct existence in becoming less dependent on its mother, and able to provide for its own wants.

28. A law intended to remind the Israelites of the sacredness of the relation between the parent and its offspring. Cp. Ex. xxiii. 19 note.

XXIII. **1.** The specified times for public worship according to the Law were; (1) The daily Morning and Evening sacrifices, sometimes called "the continual Burnt-offering." (2) The weekly Sabbath. (3) The day of the New Moon. (4) The "set feasts" (Num. xxix. 39) or appointed times of annual observance, of which there were five, the Passover, the Day of Pentecost, the Feast of Trumpets, the Day of Atonement, and the Feast of Tabernacles. For each of these occasions special sacrifices were appointed (Num. xxviii., xxix.).

2. *the feasts*] Literally, **the appointed times.** So in *vv.* 4, 37, &c. This section (1–38) sets forth for practical guidance the relation in which **the appointed times** of the LORD, weekly as well as annual, stood to the ordinary occupations of the people.

holy convocations] Days of sabbatical rest for the whole people; they owed their name to gatherings for religious edification, which, in later times, were probably held in every town and village in the Holy Land. There were in the course of the year, be-

3 *even* these *are* my feasts. [c]Six days shall work be done: but the
seventh day *is* the sabbath of rest, an holy convocation; ye shall
do no work *therein:* it *is* the sabbath of the LORD in all your
4 dwellings. [d]These *are* the feasts of the LORD, *even* holy convo-
5 cations, which ye shall proclaim in their seasons. [e]In the fourteenth *day* of the first month at even *is* the LORD'S passover.
6 And on the fifteenth day of the same month *is* the feast of
unleavened bread unto the LORD: seven days ye must eat un-
7 leavened bread. [f]In the first day ye shall have an holy convo-
8 cation: ye shall do no servile work therein. But ye shall offer
an offering made by fire unto the LORD seven days: in the
seventh day *is* an holy convocation: ye shall do no servile work
9, 10 *therein.* ¶ And the LORD spake unto Moses, saying, Speak
unto the children of Israel, and say unto them, [g]When ye be come
into the land which I give unto you, and shall reap the harvest
thereof, then ye shall bring a [1][2]sheaf of [h]the firstfruits of your
11 harvest unto the priest: and he shall [i]wave the sheaf before the
LORD, to be accepted for you: on the morrow after the sabbath
12 the priest shall wave it. And ye shall offer that day when ye
wave the sheaf an he lamb without blemish of the first year for
13 a burnt offering unto the LORD. [k]And the meat offering thereof
shall be two tenth deals of fine flour mingled with oil, an offering

[c] Ex. 20. 9. ch. 19. 3. Deut. 5. 13. Luke 13. 14.
[d] ver. 2, 37. Ex. 23. 14.
[e] Num. 9. 2. Deut. 16. 1–8. Josh. 5. 10.
[f] Ex. 12. 16. Num. 28. 18, 25.
[g] Ex. 23. 16. & 34. 22, 26. Num. 15. 2. & 28. 26. Deut. 16. 9. Josh. 3. 15.
[h] Rom. 11. 16. 1 Cor. 15. 20. James 1. 18. Rev. 14. 4.
[i] Ex. 29. 24.
[k] ch. 2. 14, 15, 16.

[1] Or, *handful*. [2] Heb. *omer*.

---

sides the weekly Sabbaths, seven days of Holy Convocation (Ex. xii. 16; Num. xxviii. 18, 25, 26, xxix. 1, 12, 35), with a distinction between them as regards strictness of observance (cp. *vv.* 3, 28 with *v.* 7).

3. The seventh day had been consecrated as **the Sabbath of Jehovah**, figuring His own rest; it was the acknowledged sign of the Covenant between God and His people. See Ex. xx. 1-11 notes. As such it properly held its place at the head of the days of Holy Convocation.

4. The recurrence of the Sabbatical number in the five annual days of Holy Convocation should be noticed.

5–8. In these verses, the Passover, or Paschal Supper, and the feast of Unleavened Bread, are plainly spoken of as distinct feasts. See Ex. xii. 6, 15, 17; Num. xxviii. 16, 17.

5. See Exod. xii. 6. According to the Hebrew mode of reckoning, the 15th day of the month began on the evening of the 14th. The day of Holy Convocation with which the feast of Unleavened bread commenced (*v.* 7) was the 15th, and that with which it terminated was the 21st. Cp. Num. xxviii. 16, 17.

6. *feast*] The three festivals (often called the Great Festivals), Passover, Pentecost and Tabernacles, to which the name *chag*, i.e. a *feast* or *rejoicing*, properly belongs (*vv.* 6, 34, 39, 41), were distinguished by the attendance of the male Israelites at the national Sanctuary (cp. Ex. xxiii. 17, xxxiv. 23; Deut. xvi. 16). In later times they were called by the rabbins "pilgrimage feasts." It is worthy of note that the Hebrew word is identical with the Arabic *haj*, the name of the pilgrimage to Mecca, from which comes the well-known word for a pilgrim, *haji*.

7. *no servile work*] Literally, no work of labour, no work that belongs to one's worldly calling, such as labour in agriculture or handicraft. The preparation of food was permitted (Ex. xii. 16), a licence not granted on the weekly Sabbath, or on the Day of Atonement (*vv.* 28, 30; Ex. xx. 10, xxxv. 3).

8. The sacrifices here meant are named in Num. xxviii. 19–24.

9–22. These verses contain a distinct command regarding the religious services immediately connected with the grain harvest, given by anticipation against the time when the people were to possess the Promised Land.

10. *sheaf*] The original word, *ōmer*, means either a sheaf (Deut. xxiv. 19; Ruth ii. 7), or a measure (Ex. xvi. 16). Our version is probably right in this place. The offering which was waved (vii. 30) was most likely a small sheaf of barley, the grain which is first ripe. The first fruits of the wheat harvest were offered seven weeks later in the loaves of Pentecost. See *vv.* 15–17. The two offerings thus figure the very commencement and the completion of the grain harvest; cp. Ruth i. 22, ii. 23.

11. *on the morrow after the sabbath*] It is most probable that these words denote the 16th of Abib, the day after the first day of Holy Convocation (see *vv.* 5–8 note), and that this was called *the Sabbath of the Passover*, or, *the Sabbath of Unleavened bread*.

13. *two tenth deals*] Two omers, or tenth parts of an ephah, about a gallon and three

made by fire unto the LORD *for* a sweet savour: and the drink
14 offering thereof *shall be* of wine, the fourth *part* of an hin. And
ye shall eat neither bread, nor parched corn, nor green ears,
until the selfsame day that ye have brought an offering unto
your God: *it shall be* a statute for ever throughout your gene-
15 rations in all your dwellings. And [l]ye shall count unto you — l Ex. 34. 22.
from the morrow after the sabbath, from the day that ye — ch. 25. 8.
brought the sheaf of the wave offering; seven sabbaths shall be — Deut. 16. 9.
16 complete: even unto the morrow after the seventh sabbath shall
ye number [m]fifty days; and ye shall offer [n]a new meat offering — m Acts 2. 1.
17 unto the LORD. Ye shall bring out of your habitations two — n Num. 28.
wave loaves of two tenth deals: they shall be of fine flour; they — 26.
shall be baken with leaven: *they are* [o]the firstfruits unto the — o Ex. 22. 29.
18 LORD. And ye shall offer with the bread seven lambs without — Num. 15.
blemish of the first year, and one young bullock, and two rams: — 17—21.
they shall be *for* a burnt offering unto the LORD, with their — Deut. 26. 1.
meat offering, and their drink offerings, *even* an offering made
19 by fire, of sweet savour unto the LORD. Then ye shall sacrifice
[p]one kid of the goats for a sin offering, and two lambs of the — p ch. 4. 23,
20 first year for a sacrifice of [q]peace offerings. And the priest shall — 28.
wave them with the bread of the firstfruits *for* a wave offering — Num. 28. 30. q ch. 3. 1.
before the LORD, with the two lambs: [r]they shall be holy to the — r Num. 18.
21 LORD for the priest. And ye shall proclaim on the selfsame — 12.
day, *that* it may be an holy convocation unto you: ye shall do — Deut. 18. 4.
no servile work *therein*: *it shall be* a statute for ever in all your

---

quarters. See xix. 36 note. The double quantity (contrast Ex. xxix. 40; Num. xv. 4, xxviii. 19-21), implying greater liberality, was appropriate in a harvest feast.

drink offering] This and *vv.* 18, 37 are the only places in the book of Leviticus in which Drink-offerings are mentioned. See Ex. xxix. 40 note.

14. *bread...parched corn...green ears*] These are the three forms in which grain was commonly eaten. The old name *Abib* signified "the month of green ears." See Josh. v. 11.

15. *the morrow after the sabbath*] See *v.* 11 note.

seven sabbaths] More properly, **seven weeks** (cp. Deut. xvi. 9). The word Sabbath, in the language of the New Testament as well as the Old, is used for *week* (xxv. 8; Matt. xxviii. 1; Luke xviii. 12, &c.).

16. The morrow after the seventh week was the fiftieth day after the conclusion of a week of weeks. The day is called in the Old Testament, "the feast of harvest" (Ex. xxiii. 16), "the feast of weeks," "the feast of the first fruits of wheat harvest" (Ex. xxxiv. 22; Deut. xvi. 10), and "the day of the first fruits" (Num. xxviii. 26). The word "Pentecost" used in the heading of this chapter in English Bibles is found only in the Apocrypha and the New Testament, Tobit ii. 1; 2 Macc. xii. 32; Acts ii. 1, xx. 16; 1 Cor. xvi. 8.

17. *habitations*] Not strictly houses, but places of abode in a general sense. It seems here to denote the land in which the Israelites were to dwell so as to express that the flour was to be of home growth. The two loaves were to be merely waved before Jehovah and then to become the property of the priests. No bread containing leaven could be offered on the Altar (ii. 11 note). The object of this offering seems to have been to present to the Lord the best produce of the earth in the actual condition in which it is most useful for the support of human life. It thus represented in the fittest manner the thanksgiving which was proper for the season. The loaves appear to be distinctively called "the first fruits **for Jehovah**," and references to them are found in Rom. xi. 16; 1 Cor. xv. 20, 23; James i. 18; Rev. xiv. 4, &c. As these loaves offered before Jehovah sanctified the harvest of the year, so has "Christ the first fruits" sanctified the Church, which, in its union with Him as the First fruits, becomes also the sanctifier of the world. See the services for Whitsuntide.

18. More properly, **seven sheep of a year old** (to be distinguished from the lamb in *v.* 12), and **a young bull** which might be from one to three years old. Cp. Num. xxviii. 26, 27.

19. Properly, **a shaggy he-goat** (iv. 23) and **two sheep of a year old.**

20. When living creatures were *waved* (vii. 30) before Jehovah, it is said that they were led to and fro before the Tabernacle according to an established form.

21. *the selfsame day*] The Feast of Weeks was distinguished from the two other great annual Feasts by its consisting, according to

22 dwellings throughout your generations. And [s]when ye reap the
harvest of your land, thou shalt not make clean riddance of the
corners of thy field when thou reapest, [t]neither shalt thou gather
any gleaning of thy harvest: thou shalt leave them unto the
23 poor, and to the stranger: I *am* the LORD your God. ¶ And
24 the LORD spake unto Moses, saying, Speak unto the children of
Israel, saying, In the [u]seventh month, in the first *day* of the
month, shall ye have a sabbath, [x]a memorial of blowing of
25 trumpets, an holy convocation. Ye shall do no servile work
therein: but ye shall offer an offering made by fire unto the
26, 27 LORD. ¶ And the LORD spake unto Moses, saying, [y]Also on
the tenth *day* of this seventh month *there shall be* a day of atonement:
it shall be an holy convocation unto you; and ye shall
afflict your souls, and offer an offering made by fire unto the
28 LORD. And ye shall do no work in that same day: for it *is* a
day of atonement, to make an atonement for you before the
29 LORD your God. For whatsoever soul *it be* that shall not be
afflicted in that same day, [z]he shall be cut off from among his
30 people. And whatsoever soul *it be* that doeth any work in that
same day, [a]the same soul will I destroy from among his people.
31 Ye shall do no manner of work: *it shall be* a statute for ever
32 throughout your generations in all your dwellings. It *shall be*
unto you a sabbath of rest, and ye shall afflict your souls: in the
ninth *day* of the month at even, from even unto even, shall ye
33 [1]celebrate your sabbath. ¶ And the LORD spake unto Moses,
34 saying, Speak unto the children of Israel, saying, [b]The fifteenth
day of this seventh month *shall be* the feast of tabernacles *for*
35 seven days unto the LORD. On the first day *shall be* an holy

[s] ch. 19. 9.
[t] Deut. 24. 19.
[u] Num. 29. 1.
[x] ch. 25. 9.
[y] ch. 16. 30. Num. 29. 7.
[z] Gen. 17. 14.
[a] ch. 20. 3, 5, 6.
[b] Ex. 23. 16. Num. 29. 12. Deut. 16. 13. Ezra 3. 4. Neh. 8. 14. Zech. 14. 16. John 7. 2.

[1] Heb. *rest.*

---

the Law, of only a single day. But in later times it is said that during the following six days the Israelites used to bring their offerings to the Temple, and to give the week something of a festal character in the suspension of mourning for the dead.

22. The repetition of the Law (see marg. ref.) is appropriately connected with the thanksgiving for the completed grain harvest.

24. *a sabbath*] Here and in *v.* 39 a word which should rather be rendered **a sabbatical rest.**

blowing of trumpets] Here and in Num. xxix. 1, literally *shouting*. There is no mention of trumpets in the Hebrew text of the Law in connection with the day. There is however no reason to doubt the tradition that the day was distinguished by a general blowing of trumpets throughout the land, and that the kind of trumpet generally used for the purpose was the curved horn of an animal or a cornet of metal, such as was used at Sinai (Ex. xix. 16), and on the Day of Jubilee (xxv. 9). It must have differed in this respect from the ordinary festival of the New moon when the long straight trumpet of the temple alone was blown (Num. x. 2; Ex. xxv. 23, see cut).

seventh month] Called by the Jews in later times Tisri, but in the Old Testament Ethanim, 1 K. viii. 2. According to the uniform voice of tradition "the first day" of this month was the first day of the Civil year in use before the Exodus, and was observed as the festival of the New year. Some have viewed it as a commemoration of the Creation of the world (Job xxxviii. 7): others, as the anniversary of the giving of the Law.

27. *Also*] **Surely.** On the peculiar rites of the Day, the tenth of Tisri, that is from the evening of the ninth day of the month to that of the tenth (*v.* 32), see ch. xvi.

34. *seven days*] Like the Passover, the feast of Tabernacles commenced at the Full moon, on the fifteenth of the month, and lasted for seven days. The week of the feast was followed by an eighth day, forming strictly no part of it (*v.* 36, Num. xxix. 35; Neh. viii. 18), which was a day of Holy Convocation, and appears to have been generally distinguished by the word translated "solemn assembly" (Deut. xvi. 8; 2 Kings x. 20; Is. i. 13; Joel i. 14, ii. 15). From its derivation the word in the original appears strictly to denote a *closing festival*, and this rendering would apply with the most perfect fitness to the day after the week of the Feast of Tabernacles, as the conclusion of the series of yearly festivals.

36 convocation: ye shall do no servile work *therein*. Seven days
ye shall offer an offering made by fire unto the LORD: [c] on the
eighth day shall be an holy convocation unto you; and ye shall
offer an offering made by fire unto the LORD: it *is* a [1] [d] solemn
37 assembly; *and* ye shall do no servile work *therein*. [e] These *are*
the feasts of the LORD, which ye shall proclaim *to be* holy convocations, to offer an offering made by fire unto the LORD, a
burnt offering, and a meat offering, a sacrifice, and drink offer-
38 ings, every thing upon his day: [f] beside the sabbaths of the
LORD, and beside your gifts, and beside all your vows, and beside all your freewill offerings, which ye give unto the LORD.
39 Also in the fifteenth day of the seventh month, when ye have
[g] gathered in the fruit of the land, ye shall keep a feast unto the
LORD seven days: on the first day *shall be* a sabbath, and on the
40 eighth day *shall be* a sabbath. And [h] ye shall take you on the
first day the [2] boughs of goodly trees, branches of palm trees, and
the boughs of thick trees, and willows of the brook; [i] and ye
41 shall rejoice before the LORD your God seven days. [k] And ye
shall keep it a feast unto the LORD seven days in the year. *It
shall be* a statute for ever in your generations: ye shall celebrate
42 it in the seventh month. [l] Ye shall dwell in booths seven days;
43 all that are Israelites born shall dwell in booths: [m] that your
generations may know that I made the children of Israel to
dwell in booths, when I brought them out of the land of Egypt:
44 I *am* the LORD your God. And Moses [n] declared unto the
children of Israel the feasts of the LORD.

CHAP. 24. AND the LORD spake unto Moses, saying, [a] Command
2 the children of Israel, that they bring unto thee pure oil olive

[c] Num. 29. 35. Neh. 8. 18. John 7. 37.
[d] Deut. 16. 8. 2 Chr. 7. 9. Neh. 8. 18. Joel 1. 14. & 2. 15.
[e] ver. 2, 4.
[f] Num. 29. 39.
[g] Ex. 23. 16. Deut. 16. 13.
[h] Neh. 8. 15.
[i] Deut. 16. 14, 15.
[k] Num. 29. 12. Neh. 8. 18.
[l] Neh. 8. 14, 15, 16.
[m] Deut. 31. 13. Ps. 78. 5, 6.
[n] ver. 2.
[a] Ex. 27. 20, 21.

[1] Heb. day of *restraint*.
[2] Heb. *fruit*.

36. *an offering made by fire*] See *v.* 8. The succession of sacrifices prescribed in Num. xxix. 12-38, which forms such a marked feature in the Feast of Tabernacles, tends to show the distinctness of the "solemn assembly" from the festal week.

37, 38. The meaning appears to be; *these are the yearly appointed times on which ye shall hold holy convocations and offer to Jehovah sacrifices, in addition to the Sabbath offerings* (Num. xxviii. 9, 10) *and to all your voluntary offerings*. Cp. Num. xxix. 39.

39. *Also*] **Surely**. The mode in which the Feast of Tabernacles is here reintroduced, after the mention of it in *vv.* 34-36, may suggest that this passage originally formed a distinct document.

the fruit of the land] *i.e.* the produce, including the grain, the olives, the vintage and the fruits of all kinds. The time of year so indicated would answer in the Holy Land to the beginning of October. See Ex. xxiii. 16 note.

40. *the boughs of goodly trees*] Or, the fruit (see margin) of the citron trees. It is said that every Israelite at the Feast of Tabernacles carried in one hand a bundle of branches and in the other a citron. The branches seem to have comprised the boughs of palm-trees, "thick trees" and willows here named. See note to *v.* 42; Neh. viii. 15, 16.

42. *booths*] According to Jewish tradition, what were used at the Feast of Tabernacles were strictly *tabernacula*, structures of boards, with a covering of boughs.

The "booth" in which the Israelite kept the Feast, and the "tent" which was his ordinary abode in the wilderness, had this in common—they were temporary places of sojourn, they belonged to camp-life. The seven days of abode in the booths of the festival was thus a fair symbol of the forty years of abode in tents in the Wilderness. The Feast might well become the appointed memorial of this period of their history for the ages to come.

all that are Israelites born] The omission of the foreigners in this command is remarkable. Perhaps the intention was that on this joyous occasion they were to be hospitably entertained as guests. Cp. Deut. xvi. 14.

44. *feasts*] **Appointed times**. See *v.* 2 note.

XXIV. **1-9.** The oil for the lamps of the Tabernacle and the meal for the Shewbread were to be offerings from the Congregation, like the meal for the Pentecostal loaves, (xxiii. 17). It appears that the responsibility of keeping up the lights rested on the High-priest, but the actual service might be performed, on ordinary occasions, by the common priests. Cp. marg. reff.

beaten for the light, [1]to cause the lamps to burn continually.
3 Without the vail of the testimony, in the tabernacle of the congregation, shall Aaron order it from the evening unto the morning before the LORD continually: *it shall be* a statute for ever in
4 your generations. He shall order the lamps upon [b]the pure
5 candlestick before the LORD continually. ¶ And thou shalt take
fine flour, and bake twelve [c]cakes thereof: two tenth deals shall
6 be in one cake. And thou shalt set them in two rows, six
7 on a row, [d]upon the pure table before the LORD. And thou
shalt put pure frankincense upon *each* row, that it may be on
the bread for a memorial, *even* an offering made by fire unto the
8 LORD. [e]Every sabbath he shall set it in order before the LORD
continually, *being taken* from the children of Israel by an ever-
9 lasting covenant. And [f]it shall be Aaron's and his sons'; [g]and
they shall eat it in the holy place: for it *is* most holy unto him
of the offerings of the LORD made by fire by a perpetual statute.
10 ¶ And the son of an Israelitish woman, whose father *was* an
Egyptian, went out among the children of Israel: and this son
of the Israelitish *woman* and a man of Israel strove together in
11 the camp; and the Israelitish woman's son [h]blasphemed the
name *of the LORD*, and [i]cursed. And they [k]brought him unto
Moses: (and his mother's name *was* Shelomith, the daughter of
12 Dibri, of the tribe of Dan:) and they [l]put him in ward, [2][m]that
13 the mind of the LORD might be shewed them. And the LORD
14 spake unto Moses, saying, Bring forth him that hath cursed
without the camp; and let all that heard *him* [n]lay their hands
15 upon his head, and let all the congregation stone him. And
thou shalt speak unto the children of Israel, saying, Whosoever
16 curseth his God [o]shall bear his sin. And he that [p]blasphemeth
the name of the LORD, he shall surely be put to death, *and* all
the congregation shall certainly stone him: as well the stranger,

[b] Ex. 31. 8. & 39. 37.
[c] Ex. 25. 30.
[d] 1 Kin. 7. 48. 2 Chr. 4. 19. Heb. 9. 2.
[e] Num. 4. 7. 2 Chr. 2. 4.
[f] Mark 2. 26. Luke 6. 4.
[g] Ex. 29. 33. ch. 8. 31. & 21. 22.
[h] ver. 16.
[i] Job 1. 5. Isai. 8. 21.
[k] Ex. 18. 22.
[l] Num. 15. 34.
[m] Ex. 18. 15. Num. 27. 5.
[n] Deut. 13. 9. & 17. 7.
[o] ch. 5. 1. & 20. 17. Num. 9. 13.
[p] 1 Kin. 21. 10, 13. Ps. 74. 10. Matt. 12. 31. Mark 3. 28. Jam. 2. 7.

[1] Heb. *to cause to ascend.*
[2] Heb. *to expound unto them according to the mouth of the* LORD.

---

5. Each cake or loaf of unleavened bread (ii. 11) was to contain about six pounds and a quarter (see Ex. xxix. 40 note) of fine flour. The material was the same, both in quality and in quantity, with that of each one of the wave-loaves of Pentecost (xxiii. 17). In the service of the Temple the preparation and arrangement of the cakes was committed to the Levites (1 Chr. ix. 32, xxiii. 29; 2 Chr. xiii. 11).

6. *two rows, six on a row*] Rather, **two piles, six in a pile.** On the Table, see Ex. xxv. 23-30.

7. The frankincense as a memorial (like the handful of the Meat-offering, ii. 2), was most likely cast upon the Altar-fire as "an offering made by fire unto the Lord," when the bread was removed from the Table on the Sabbath-day (*v.* 8; 1 S. xxi. 6). The frankincense was put into small gold cups, one of which was placed upon each pile of bread. (See Ex. xxv. 23-30 note.)

8. *being taken from the children of Israel*] Each cake represented the offering of a Tribe.

9. See ii. 3 note. It could have been only by a stretch of the law that Ahimelech gave a portion of the Shewbread to David and his men, on the ground that they were free from ceremonial defilement. 1 Sam. xxi. 4-6; Matt. xii. 4.

The Shewbread was a true Meat-offering (see Ex. xxv. 29). The peculiar form in which it was offered, especially in its being brought into the Tabernacle and in its consisting of twelve loaves, distinguish it as an offering made on behalf of the nation.

12. The offender may already have been pronounced guilty by the rulers (see Ex. xviii. 21, 22), and the case was referred to Moses in order that the punishment might be awarded by the divine decree. No law had as yet been enacted against blasphemy except by implication. See Ex. xxi. 17, xxii. 28.

14. *lay their hands upon his head*] As a protest against the impiety of the criminal, symbolically laying the guilt upon his head. Cp. the washing of hands, Deut. xxi. 6; Matt. xxvii. 24.

let all the congregation stone him] See xx. 2 note.

16. *stranger*] *i.e.* **foreigner.** See xvi. 29 note.

as he that is born in the land, when he blasphemeth the name
17 *of the* LORD, shall be put to death. ¶ [q]And he that [1]killeth
18 any man shall surely be put to death. [r]And he that killeth a
19 beast shall make it good; [2]beast for beast. And if a man cause
a blemish in his neighbour; as [s]he hath done, so shall it be done
20 to him; breach for breach, eye for eye, tooth for tooth: as he
hath caused a blemish in a man, so shall it be done to him *again*.
21 [t]And he that killeth a beast, he shall restore it: [u]and he that
22 killeth a man, he shall be put to death. Ye shall have [x]one
manner of law, as well for the stranger, as for one of your own
23 country: for I *am* the LORD your God. ¶ And Moses spake
to the children of Israel, [y]that they should bring forth him that
had cursed out of the camp, and stone him with stones. And
the children of Israel did as the LORD commanded Moses.

CHAP. 25. AND the LORD spake unto Moses in mount Sinai, saying,
2 Speak unto the children of Israel, and say unto them, When ye
come into the land which I give you, then shall the land [3]keep
3 [a]a sabbath unto the LORD. Six years thou shalt sow thy field,
and six years thou shalt prune thy vineyard, and gather in the
4 fruit thereof; but in the seventh year shall be a sabbath of rest
unto the land, a sabbath for the LORD: thou shalt neither sow
5 thy field, nor prune thy vineyard. [b]That which groweth of its
own accord of thy harvest thou shalt not reap, neither gather
the grapes [4]of thy vine undressed: *for* it is a year of rest unto
6 the land. And the sabbath of the land shall be meat for you;
for thee, and for thy servant, and for thy maid, and for thy hired
7 servant, and for thy stranger that sojourneth with thee, and for
thy cattle, and for the beast that *are* in thy land, shall all the
8 increase thereof be meat. ¶ And thou shalt number seven sab-

[q] Ex. 21. 12. Num. 35. 31. Deut. 19. 11, 12.
[r] ver. 21.
[s] Ex. 21. 24. Deut. 19. 21. Matt. 5. 38. & 7. 2.
[t] ver. 18.
[u] ver. 17.
[x] Ex. 12. 49. ch. 19. 34. Num. 15. 16.
[y] ver. 14.
[a] Ex. 23. 10. See ch. 26. 34, 35. 2 Chr. 36. 21.
[b] 2 Kin. 19. 29.

[1] Heb. *smiteth the life of a man.*
[2] Heb. *life for life.*
[3] Heb. *rest.*
[4] Heb *of thy separation.*

XXV. The Sabbatical year and the year of Jubilee belong to that great Sabbatical system which runs through the religious observances of the Law, but rest upon moral rather than upon formally religious ground. It is not therefore without reason that they are here set apart from the set times which fell strictly within the sphere of religious observances.

3. *vineyard*] Rather, **fruit-garden.** The Hebrew word is a general one for a plantation of fruit-trees.

4. *a sabbath of rest*] See xxiii. 3 note. The express prohibition of sowing and reaping, and of pruning and gathering, affords a presumption in favour of the Sabbatical year beginning, like the year of Jubilee (*v.* 9), in the first month of the Civil year (xxiii. 24), the seventh of the Sacred year, when the land was cleared of the crops of the preceding year.

The great material advantage of the institution must have been the increased fertility of the soil from its lying fallow one year out of seven, at a time when neither the rotation of crops nor the art of manuring were understood. It must also have kept up a salutary habit of economy in the storing of corn. Cp. Gen. xli. 48-56. Its great spiritual lesson was that there was no such thing as absolute ownership in the land vested in any man, that the soil was the property of Jehovah, that it was to be held in trust for Him, and not to be abused by overworking, but to be made the most of for the good of every creature which dwelt upon it.

5. *vine undressed*] That is, *unpruned;* lit. *Nazarite vine,* the figure being taken from the unshorn locks of the Nazarite. (Num. vi. 5.)

6. *the sabbath of the land shall be meat for you*] That is, the produce of the untilled land (its "increase," *v.* 7) shall be food for the whole of you in common, rich and poor without distinction (Ex. xxiii. 11).

8-13. The Land was to be divided by lot among the families of the Israelites when the possession of it was obtained. Num. xxvi. 52-56, xxxiii. 54, &c. At the end of every seventh sabbatical cycle of years, in the year of Jubilee, each field or estate that might have been alienated was to be restored to the family to which it had been originally allotted.

8. *seven sabbaths of years*] **seven weeks of years.**

baths of years unto thee, seven times seven years; and the space
of the seven sabbaths of years shall be unto thee forty and nine
9 years. Then shalt thou cause the trumpet [1]of the jubile to sound
on the tenth *day* of the seventh month, [c]in the day of atonement
10 shall ye make the trumpet sound throughout all your land. And
ye shall hallow the fiftieth year, and [d]proclaim liberty throughout *all* the land unto all the inhabitants thereof: it shall be a
jubile unto you; [e]and ye shall return every man unto his posses-
11 sion, and ye shall return every man unto his family. A jubile
shall that fiftieth year be unto you: [f]ye shall not sow, neither
reap that which groweth of itself in it, nor gather *the grapes* in it
12 of thy vine undressed. For it *is* the jubile; it shall be holy
unto you: [g]ye shall eat the increase thereof out of the field.
13 [h]In the year of this jubile ye shall return every man unto his
14 possession. And if thou sell ought unto thy neighbour, or
buyest *ought* of thy neighbour's hand, [i]ye shall not oppress one
15 another: [k]according to the number of years after the jubile thou
shalt buy of thy neighbour, *and* according unto the number of
16 years of the fruits he shall sell unto thee: according to the multitude of years thou shalt increase the price thereof, and according to the fewness of years thou shalt diminish the price of it:
for *according* to the number *of the years* of the fruits doth he sell
17 unto thee. ¶ [l]Ye shall not therefore oppress one another; [m]but
18 thou shalt fear thy God: for I *am* the LORD your God. [n]Where-
fore ye shall do my statutes, and keep my judgments, and do
19 them; [o]and ye shall dwell in the land in safety. And the land
shall yield her fruit, and [p]ye shall eat your fill, and dwell
20 therein in safety. ¶ And if ye shall say, [q]What shall we eat
the seventh year? Behold, [r]we shall not sow, nor gather in our
21 increase: then I will [s]command my blessing upon you in the
22 sixth year, and it shall bring forth fruit for three years. [t]And
ye shall sow the eighth year, and eat *yet* of [u]old fruit until the
ninth year; until her fruits come in ye shall eat *of* the old *store*.
23 ¶ The land shall not be sold [2] [3] for ever: for [x]the land *is* mine;

[c] ch. 23. 24. [d] Isai. 61. 2. & 63. 4. Jer. 34. 8. Luke 4. 19. [e] ver. 13. Num. 36. 4. [f] ver. 5. [g] ver. 6, 7. [h] ver. 10. ch. 27. 24. Num. 36. 4. [i] ver. 17. ch. 19. 13. Mic. 2. 2. 1 Cor. 6. 8. [k] ch. 27. 18. 23. [l] ver. 14. [m] ver. 43. ch. 19. 14. [n] ch. 19. 37. [o] Ps. 4. 8. Prov. 1. 33. Jer. 23. 6. [p] ch. 26. 5. Ez. 34. 25. [q] Matt. 6. 25, 31. [r] ver. 4, 5. [s] See Ex. 16. 29. Deut. 28. 8. [t] 2 Kin. 19. 29. [u] Josh. 5. 11, 12. [x] Deut. 32. 43. 2 Chr. 7. 20. Ps. 85. 1. Joel 2. 18.

[1] Heb. *loud of sound.* [2] Or, *to be quite cut off.* [3] Heb. *for cutting off.*

---

9. *cause the trumpet of the jubile to sound*] Rather, **cause the sound of the cornet to go through** (the land). The word *jubile* does not occur in this verse in the Hebrew. The trumpet is the *shophār*, *i.e.* the cornet (rendered "shawm" in the Prayer-Book version of Ps. xcviii. 7), either the horn of some animal or a tube of metal shaped like one. As the sound of the cornet (see *v.* 10 note) was the signal of the descent of Jehovah when He came down upon Sinai to take Israel into Covenant with Himself (Ex. xix. 13, 16, 19, xx. 18), so the same sound announced, at the close of the great Day of Atonement, after the Evening sacrifice, the year which restored each Israelite to the freedom and the blessings of the Covenant.

10. *the fiftieth year*] The Jubilee probably coincided with each seventh Sabbatical year, and was called the fiftieth, as being the last of a series of which the first was the preceding Jubilee.

a jubile] Commonly spelt *jubilee*. The original word first occurs in Ex. xix. 13, where it is rendered "trumpet," marg. "cornet." It most probably denotes the sound of the cornet, not the cornet itself, and is derived from a root, signifying to flow abundantly, which by a familiar metaphor might be applied to sound.

14. *sell ought*] *i.e.*, any piece of ground.

oppress one another] Rather, **overreach one another.** (Cp. 1 Sam. xii. 3, 4).

15, 16. *the number of years of the fruits*] *i.e.* according to the number of harvests. The average value of a yearly crop might of course be estimated, and the Sabbatical years were to be deducted from the series.

18, 19. *in safety*] *i.e.*, secure from famine, (xxvi. 5; Deut. xii. 10).

23, 24. These verses express the principle on which the law of Jubilee, as it regards the land, was based. The land belonged to Jehovah, and it was He Who allotted it amongst the families of Israel for their use. No estate could therefore be alienated in

24 for ye *are* [y]strangers and sojourners with me. And in all the
land of your possession ye shall grant a redemption for the land.
25 [z]If thy brother be waxen poor, and hath sold away *some* of his
possession, and if [a]any of his kin come to redeem it, then shall
26 he redeem that which his brother sold. And if the man have none
27 to redeem it, and [1]himself be able to redeem it; then [b]let him
count the years of the sale thereof, and restore the overplus unto
the man to whom he sold it; that he may return unto his posses-
28 sion. But if he be not able to restore *it* to him, then that which
is sold shall remain in the hand of him that hath bought it until
the year of jubile: [c]and in the jubile it shall go out, and he shall
29 return unto his possession. ¶ And if a man sell a dwelling house
in a walled city, then he may redeem it within a whole year after
30 it is sold; *within* a full year may he redeem it. And if it be not
redeemed within the space of a full year, then the house that *is*
in the walled city shall be established for ever to him that
bought it throughout his generations: it shall not go out in the
31 jubile. But the houses of the villages which have no wall round
about them shall be counted as the fields of the country: [2]they
32 may be redeemed, and they shall go out in the jubile. ¶ Notwithstanding [d]the cities of the Levites, *and* the houses of the
cities of their possession, may the Levites redeem at any time.
33 And if [3]a man purchase of the Levites, then the house that was
sold, and the city of his possession, [e]shall go out in *the year of*
jubile: for the houses of the cities of the Levites *are* their pos-
34 session among the children of Israel. But [f]the field of the
suburbs of their cities may not be sold; for it *is* their perpetual
35 possession. ¶ And if thy brother be waxen poor, and [4]fallen in
decay with thee; then thou shalt [5][g]relieve him: *yea, though he*
36 *be* a stranger, or a sojourner; that he may live with thee. [h]Take
thou no usury of him, or increase: but [i]fear thy God; that thy
37 brother may live with thee. Thou shalt not give him thy money
38 upon usury, nor lend him thy victuals for increase. [k]I *am* the
LORD your God, which brought you forth out of the land of

[y] 1 Chr. 29. 15. Ps. 39. 12. & 119. 19. 1 Pet. 2. 11.
[z] Ruth 2. 20. & 4. 4, 6.
[a] See Ruth 3. 2, 9, 12. Jer. 32. 7.
[b] ver. 50. 51, 52.
[c] ver. 13.
[d] See Num. 35. 2. Josh. 21. 2, &c.
[e] ver. 28.
[f] See Acts 4. 36, 37.
[g] Deut. 15. 7, 8. Ps. 37. 26. Prov. 14. 31. Luke 6. 35. Acts 11. 29. Rom. 12. 10. 1 John 3. 17.
[h] Ex. 22. 25. Deut. 23. 19. Neh. 5. 7. Ps. 15. 5. Prov. 28. 8. Ez. 18. 8.
[i] ver. 17. Neh. 5. 9.
[k] ch. 22. 32, 33.

[1] Heb. *his hand hath attained and found sufficiency*, ch. 5. 7.
[2] Heb. *Redemption belongeth unto it.*
[3] Or, one *of the Levites redeem* them.
[4] Heb. *his hand faileth.*
[5] Heb. *strengthen.*

perpetuity, by any human authority, from the family to whose lot it might fall.

24. *grant a redemption for the land*] *i.e.* grant power to recover the land to the original holder who had parted with it.

25. *If thy brother be waxen poor*] The Israelites never parted with their land except under the pressure of poverty. Cp. the answer of Naboth, 1 K. xxi. 3.

28. *it shall go out*] *i.e.* it shall be set free.

30. *not go out*] Because most of the houses in cities were occupied by artificers and traders whose wealth did not consist in lands.

32, 33. Rather, **And concerning the cities of the Levites, the houses in the cities of their possession,** &c. **If one of the Levites redeems a house in the city,** &c. The meaning appears to be, if a Levite redeemed a house which had been sold to a person of a different tribe by another Levite, it was to revert in the Jubilee to the latter Levite as its original possessor. The purchaser of a Levite's house was in fact only in the condition of a tenant at will, while the fields attached to the Levitical cities could never be alienated, even for a time.

For the application of the law of Jubilee to lands dedicated to the service of the Sanctuary, see xxvii. 16–25.

35. Rather, **And if thy brother** (an Israelite) **becomes poor and falls into decay with thee, thou shalt assist him and let him live with thee like a resident foreigner.** He was not to be regarded as an outcast, but was to be treated with the same respect and consideration as a resident foreigner who, like him, could possess no land, but could accumulate property and live in comfort as a free man. See xvi. 29 note.

37. *lend him thy victuals for increase*] *i.e.* supply him with food for thy own profit.

38. Here, and in *vv.* 42, 55, is expressed

[l] Ex. 21. 2. Deut. 15. 12. 1 Kin. 9. 22. 2 Kin. 4. 1. Neh. 5. 5. Jer. 34. 14.
[m] Ex. 21. 3.
[n] ver. 28.
[o] ver. 55. Rom. 6. 22. 1 Cor. 7. 23.
[p] Eph. 6. 9. Col. 4. 1.
[q] ver. 46. Ex. 1. 13.
[r] ver. 17. Ex. 1. 17, 21. Deut. 25. 18. Mal. 3. 5.
[s] Isai. 56. 3, 6.
[t] Isai. 14. 2.
[u] ver. 43.
[x] ver. 25, 35.
[y] Neh. 5. 5.
[z] ver. 26.
[a] Job 7. 1. Isai. 16. 14. & 21. 16.

Egypt, to give you the land of Canaan, *and* to be your God.
39 ¶ And [l]if thy brother *that dwelleth* by thee be waxen poor, and
be sold unto thee; thou shalt not [1]compel him to serve as a
40 bondservant: *but* as an hired servant, *and* as a sojourner, he
shall be with thee, *and* shall serve thee unto the year of jubile:
41 and *then* shall he depart from thee, *both* he and his children
[m]with him, and shall return unto his own family, and [n]unto
42 the possession of his fathers shall he return. For they *are* [o]my
servants, which I brought forth out of the land of Egypt: they
43 shall not be sold [2]as bondmen. [p]Thou shalt not rule over him
44 [q]with rigour; but [r]shalt fear thy God. Both thy bondmen,
and thy bondmaids, which thou shalt have, *shall be* of the heathen that are round about you; of them shall ye buy bondmen
45 and bondmaids. Moreover of [s]the children of the strangers that
do sojourn among you, of them shall ye buy, and of their families that *are* with you, which they begat in your land: and they
46 shall be your possession. And [t]ye shall take them as an inheritance for your children after you, to inherit *them for* a possession; [3]they shall be your bondmen for ever: but over your
brethren the children of Israel, [u]ye shall not rule one over an-
47 other with rigour. ¶ And if a sojourner or stranger [4]wax rich
by thee, and [x]thy brother *that dwelleth* by him wax poor, and sell
himself unto the stranger *or* sojourner by thee, or to the stock of
48 the stranger's family: after that he is sold he may be redeemed
49 again; one of his brethren may [y]redeem him: either his uncle,
or his uncle's son, may redeem him, or *any* that is nigh of kin
unto him of his family may redeem him; or if [z]he be able, he
50 may redeem himself. And he shall reckon with him that bought
him from the year that he was sold to him unto the year of
jubile: and the price of his sale shall be according unto the
number of years, [a]according to the time of an hired servant shall
51 it be with him. If *there be* yet many years *behind*, according unto
them he shall give again the price of his redemption out of the
52 money that he was bought for. And if there remain but few
years unto the year of jubile, then he shall count with him, *and*
according unto his years shall he give him again the price of his
53 redemption. *And* as a yearly hired servant shall he be with

[1] Heb. *serve thyself with him with the service, &c.* ver. 46. Ex. 1. 14. Jer. 25. 14. & 27. 7. & 30. 8.
[2] Heb. *with the sale of a bondman.*
[3] Heb. *ye shall serve yourselves with them,* ver. 39.
[4] Heb. *his hand obtain, &c.* ver. 26.

---

the principle which was to limit and modify the servitude of Hebrew servants.

39, 40. The law here appears harmoniously to supplement the earlier one in Ex. xxi. 1–6. It was another check applied periodically to the tyranny of the rich. Cp. Jer. xxxiv. 8–17.

43. *fear thy God*] Jehovah was the Lord and Master of His people. To treat a Hebrew as a slave was therefore to interfere with the rights of Jehovah. Cp. Rom. xiv. 4.

44–46. Property in foreign slaves is here distinctly permitted. It was a patriarchal custom (Gen. xvii. 12). Such slaves might be captives taken in war (Num. xxxi. 6 seq.; Deut. xx. 14), or those consigned to slavery for their crimes, or those purchased of foreign slave-dealers. The price of a slave is supposed to have varied from thirty to fifty shekels. See notes to xxvii. 3, 4; Ex. xxi. 32; Zech. xi. 12, 13; Matt. xxvi. 15. It was the object of Moses, not at once to do away with slavery, but to discourage and to mitigate it. The Law would not suffer it to be forgotten that the slave was a man, and protected him in every way that was possible at the time against the injustice or cruelty of his master. See notes on Ex. xxi.

46. *your bondmen for ever*] *i.e.* they were not necessarily to be released in the Sabbatical year nor at the Jubilee.

47–54. *a sojourner or stranger*] Rather, **a foreigner who has settled among you.** See notes to Lev. xvi. 29; Ex. xx. 10.

him: *and the other* shall not rule with rigour over him in thy
54 sight. And if he be not redeemed [1]in these *years*, then [b]he
shall go out in the year of jubile, *both* he, and his children with
55 him. For [c]unto me the children of Israel *are* servants; they
are my servants whom I brought forth out of the land of Egypt:
I *am* the LORD your God.
CHAP. 26. YE shall make you [a]no idols nor graven image, neither
rear you up a [2]standing image, neither shall ye set up *any*
[3][4]image of stone in your land, to bow down unto it: for I *am*
2 the LORD your God. [b]Ye shall keep my sabbaths, and reve-
3 rence my sanctuary: I *am* the LORD. ¶ [c]If ye walk in my
4 statutes, and keep my commandments, and do them; [d]then I
will give you rain in due season, [e]and the land shall yield her
5 increase, and the trees of the field shall yield their fruit. And
[f]your threshing shall reach unto the vintage, and the vintage
shall reach unto the sowing time: and [g]ye shall eat your bread
6 to the full, and [h]dwell in your land safely. And [i]I will give
peace in the land, and [k]ye shall lie down, and none shall make
you afraid: and I will [5]rid [l]evil beasts out of the land, neither
7 shall [m]the sword go through your land. And ye shall chase
8 your enemies, and they shall fall before you by the sword. And
[n]five of you shall chase an hundred, and an hundred of you

[b] ver. 41.
[c] ver. 42.
[a] Ex. 20. 4, 5. Deut. 5. 8. Ps. 97. 7.
[b] ch. 19. 30.
[c] Deut. 11. 13, 14, 15.
[d] Isai. 30. 23.
[e] Ps. 67. 6. Zech. 8. 12.
[f] Amos 9. 13.
[g] ch. 25. 19.
[h] ch. 25. 18. Ez. 34. 25.
[i] 1 Chr. 22. 9. Ps. 29. 11. Isai. 45. 7. Hag. 2. 9.
[k] Ps. 3. 5. Isai. 35. 9. Jer. 30. 10. Ez. 34. 25. Hos. 2. 18. Zeph. 3. 13.
[l] 2 Kin. 17. 25. Ez. 5. 17.
[m] Ez. 14. 17.
[n] Josh. 23. 10.

[1] Or, *by these* means.
[2] Or, *pillar.*
[3] Or, *figured stone.*
[4] Heb. *a stone of picture.*
[5] Heb. *cause to cease.*

---

54. *in these years*] More properly, **by one of these means.** The extreme period of servitude in this case was six years, as when the master was a Hebrew (Ex. xxi. 2).

Looking at the law of the Jubilee from a simply practical point of view, its operation must have tended to remedy those evils which are always growing up in the ordinary conditions of human society. It prevented the permanent accumulation of land in the hands of a few, and periodically raised those whom fault or misfortune had sunk into poverty to a position of competency. It must also have tended to keep alive family feeling, and helped to preserve the family genealogies.

But in its more special character, as a law given by Jehovah to His peculiar people, it was a standing lesson to those who would rightly regard it, on the terms upon which the enjoyment of the Land of Promise had been conferred upon them. All the land belonged to Jehovah as its supreme Lord, every Israelite as His vassal belonged to Him. The voice of the Jubilee horns, twice in every century, proclaimed the equitable and beneficent social order appointed for the people; they sounded that acceptable year of Jehovah which was to bring comfort to all that mourned, in which the slavery of sin was to be abolished, and the true liberty of God's children was to be proclaimed (Luke ii. 25; Isai. lxi. 2; Luke iv. 19; Acts iii. 21; Rom. viii. 19–23; 1 Pet. i. 3, 4).

XXVI. **1.** *idols*] Literally, *things of nought.* Heb. *eleelim.* There appears to have been a play on the similarity in sound of this word to *Elohim* (God). Cp. 1 Cor. viii. 4.

standing image] Either an upright statue, or a pillar, such as an obelisk or a Celtic menhir, set up for an idolatrous purpose (cp. Ex. xxxiv. 13 note). The public worship of Jehovah required, first, the exclusion of all visible symbols of deity as well as of all idolatrous objects, and next (*v.* 2), the keeping holy the times and the Place appointed by the Law for His formal service. The word Sabbaths must here include the whole of the set times. See xxiii. 3 note.

3–45. As "the Book of the Covenant" (Ex. xx. 22–xxiii. 33) concludes with promises and warnings (Ex. xxiii. 20–33), so does this collection of laws contained in the Book of Leviticus. But the former passage relates to the conquest of the Land of Promise, this one to the subsequent history of the nation. The longer similar passage in Deuteronomy (xxvii.–xxx.) is marked by broader and deeper promises and denunciations having immediate reference not only to outward consequences, but to the spiritual death incurred by transgressing the Divine will.

4. *rain in due season*] The periodical rains, on which the fertility of the Holy Land so much depends, are here spoken of. There are two wet seasons, called in Scripture the former and the latter rain (Deut. xi. 14; Jer. v. 24; Joel ii. 23; Hos. vi. 3; Jam. v. 7). The former or Autumn rain falls in heavy showers in November and December. In March the latter or Spring rain comes on, which is precarious in quantity and duration, and rarely lasts more than two days.

5. Cp. marg. reff.; Joel ii. 19; Job xi. 18.

8. *five of you shall chase*] A proverbial

shall put ten thousand to flight: and your enemies shall fall
9 before you by the sword. For I will [o]have respect unto you,
and [p]make you fruitful, and multiply you, and establish my
10 covenant with you. And ye shall eat [q]old store, and bring
11 forth the old because of the new. [r]And I will set my tabernacle
12 among you: and my soul shall not [s]abhor you. [t]And I will
walk among you, and [u]will be your God, and ye shall be my
13 people. [w]I *am* the LORD your God, which brought you forth
out of the land of Egypt, that ye should not be their bondmen;
[x]and I have broken the bands of your yoke, and made you go
14 upright. ¶ [y]But if ye will not hearken unto me, and will not do
15 all these commandments; and if ye shall [z]despise my statutes,
or if your soul abhor my judgments, so that ye will not do all
16 my commandments, *but* that ye break my covenant: I also will
do this unto you; I will even appoint [1]over you [a]terror, [b]con-
sumption, and the burning ague, that shall [c]consume the eyes,
and cause sorrow of heart: and [d]ye shall sow your seed in vain,
17 for your enemies shall eat it. And [e]I will set my face against
you, and [f]ye shall be slain before your enemies: [g]they that hate
you shall reign over you; and [h]ye shall flee when none pur-
18 sueth you. And if ye will not yet for all this hearken unto
19 me, then I will punish you [i]seven times more for your sins. And
I will [k]break the pride of your power; and I [l]will make your
20 heaven as iron, and your earth as brass: and your [m]strength
shall be spent in vain: for [n]your land shall not yield her increase, neither shall the trees of the land yield their fruits.
21 And if ye walk [2]contrary unto me, and will not hearken unto
me; I will bring seven times more plagues upon you according
22 to your sins. [o]I will also send wild beasts among you, which
shall rob you of your children, and destroy your cattle, and make
you few in number; and [p]your *high* ways shall be desolate.
23 And if ye [q]will not be reformed by me by these things, but will

[o] 2 Kin. 13. 23.
[p] Neh. 9. 23. Ps. 107. 38.
[q] ch. 25. 22.
[r] Josh. 22. 19. Rev. 21. 3.
[s] ch. 20. 23.
[t] 2 Cor. 6. 16.
[u] Jer. 7. 23. Ez. 11. 20.
[w] ch. 25. 38.
[x] Jer. 2. 20. Ez. 34. 27.
[y] Lam. 2. 17. Mal. 2. 2.
[z] ver. 43. 2 Kin. 17. 15.
[a] Deut. 28. 65.
[b] Deut. 28. 22.
[c] 1 Sam. 2. 33.
[d] Jer. 5. 17. Mic. 6. 15.
[e] ch. 17. 10.
[f] Judg. 2. 14. Jer. 19. 7.
[g] Ps. 106. 41.
[h] Ps. 53. 5. Prov. 28. 1.
[i] 1 Sam. 2. 5.
[k] Isai. 25. 11. Ez. 7. 24.
[l] Deut. 28. 23.
[m] Ps. 127. 1. Isai. 49. 4.
[n] Hag. 1. 10.
[o] 2 Kin. 17. 25.
[p] 2 Chr. 15. 5. Lam. 1. 4. Zech. 7. 14.
[q] Amos 4. 6.

[1] Heb. *upon you.* [2] Or, *at all adventures with me*, and so ver. 24.

---

mode of expression for superiority in warlike prowess (Deut. xxxii. 30; Isai. xxx. 17).

9. *establish my covenant*] All material blessings were to be regarded in the light of seals of the "everlasting covenant." Cp. Gen. xvii. 4–8; Neh. ix. 23.

10. *bring forth the old because of the new*] Rather, **clear away the old before the new**; that is, in order to make room for the latter. Cp. marg. ref.

16. THE FIRST WARNING for disobedience is disease. "Terror" (lit. trembling) is rendered *trouble* in Ps. lxxviii. 33; Isai. lxv. 23. It seems here to denote that terrible affliction, an anxious temperament, the mental state ever at war with Faith and Hope. This might well be placed at the head of the visitations on a backslider who had broken the Covenant with his God. Cp. Deut. xxxii. 25; Jer. xv. 8; Prov. xxviii. 1; Job xxiv. 17; Ps. xxiii. 4.

consumption, and the burning ague] Cp. marg. ref. The first of the words in the original comes from a root signifying *to waste away;* the latter (better, fever), from one signifying *to kindle a fire.* Consumption is common in Egypt and some parts of Asia Minor, but it is more rare in Syria. Fevers of different kinds are the commonest of all diseases in Syria and all the neighbouring countries. The opposite promise to the threat is given in Ex. xv. 26, xxiii. 25.

18. *for all this*] *i.e.* for all the afflictions in *vv.* 16, 17.

seven times] The sabbatical number is here proverbially used to remind the people of the Covenant. Cp. Gen. iv. 15, 24; Ps. cxix. 164; Prov. xxiv. 16; Luke xvii. 4.

19, 20. THE SECOND WARNING is utter sterility of the soil. Cp. Deut. xi. 17, xxviii. 18; Ezek. xxxiii. 28, xxxvi. 34, 35.

21, 22. THE THIRD WARNING is the multiplication of destructive animals, &c. Cp. Deut. xxxii. 24; Ezek. v. 17, xiv. 15; Judg. v. 6, 7; Isai. xxxiii. 8.

23–26. THE FOURTH WARNING. Jehovah now places Himself as it were in a hostile position towards His people who "will not be reformed" (rather, brought unto God: Jer. ii. 30). He will avenge the outraged cause of His Covenant, by the sword, pestilence, famine, and captivity.

24 walk contrary unto me; [r]then will I also walk contrary unto
25 you, and will punish you yet seven times for your sins. And [s]I
will bring a sword upon you, that shall avenge the quarrel of
my covenant: and when ye are gathered together within your
cities, [t]I will send the pestilence among you; and ye shall be
26 delivered into the hand of the enemy. [u]*And* when I have
broken the staff of your bread, ten women shall bake your
bread in one oven, and they shall deliver *you* your bread again
27 by weight: and [x]ye shall eat, and not be satisfied. And [y]if ye
will not for all this hearken unto me, but walk contrary unto
28 me; then I will walk contrary unto you also [z]in fury; and I,
29 even I, will chastise you seven times for your sins. [a]And ye
shall eat the flesh of your sons, and the flesh of your daughters
30 shall ye eat. And [b]I will destroy your high places, and cut
down your images, and [c]cast your carcases upon the carcases of
31 your idols, and my soul shall [d]abhor you. [e]And I will make
your cities waste, and [f]bring your sanctuaries unto desolation,
32 and I will not smell the savour of your sweet odours. [g]And I
will bring the land into desolation: and your enemies which
33 dwell therein shall be [h]astonished at it. And [i]I will scatter you
among the heathen, and will draw out a sword after you: and
34 your land shall be desolate, and your cities waste. ¶ [k]Then
shall the land enjoy her sabbaths, as long as it lieth desolate,
and ye *be* in your enemies' land; *even* then shall the land rest,
35 and enjoy her sabbaths. As long as it lieth desolate it shall
rest; because it did not rest in your [l]sabbaths, when ye dwelt

[r] 2 Sam. 22. 27. Ps. 18. 26.
[s] Ez. 5. 17. & pass.
[t] Num. 14. 12. Jer. 14. 12. Amos 4. 10.
[u] Ps. 105. 16.
[x] Isai. 9. 20.
[y] ver. 21. 24.
[z] Isai. 59. 18. Jer. 21. 5. Ez. 5. 13.
[a] Deut. 28. 53.
[b] Isai. 27. 9.
[c] 2 Kin. 23. 20.
[d] Ps. 78. 59.
[e] Neh. 2. 3.
[f] Lam. 1. 10.
[g] Jer. 9. 11.
[h] 1 Kin. 9. 8.
[i] Deut. 4. 27. & 28. 64.
[k] 2 Chr. 36. 21.
[l] ch. 25. 2.

---

26. Omit "*and.*"—"To break the staff of bread," was a proverbial expression for cutting off the supply of bread, the staff of life (Ps. cv. 16; Ezek. iv. 16, v. 16, xiv. 13, cp. Isai. iii. 1). The supply was to be so reduced that one oven would suffice for baking the bread made by ten women for ten families, and when made it was to be dealt out in sparing rations by weight. See 2 K. vi. 25; Jer. xiv. 18; Lam. iv. 9; Ezek. v. 12; Hos. iv. 10; Mic. vi. 14; Hagg. i. 6.

27–33. THE FIFTH WARNING. For *v.* 29 see 2 K. vi. 28, 29; Jer. xix. 8, 9; Lam. ii. 20, iv. 10; Ezek. v. 10: for *v.* 30 see 2 Chr. xxxiv. 3; Ezek. vi. 4; Jer. xiv. 19: for *v.* 31 see 2 K. xxv. 9; Ps. lxxiv. 6, 7: for *vv.* 32, 33 see Deut. xxviii. 37; Ps. xliv. 11; Jer. ix. 16, xviii. 16; Ezek. v. 1–17; Jer. iv. 7; Ezek. ix. 6, xii. 15; Zech. vii. 14.

30. *high places*] There is no doubt that the word here denotes elevated spots dedicated to false worship (see Deut. xii. 2), and especially, it would seem, to that of Baal (Num. xxii. 41; Josh. xiii. 17). Such spots were however employed and approved for the worship of Jehovah, not only before the building of the Temple, but afterwards (Jud. vi. 25, 26, xiii. 16–23; 1 S. vii. 10, xvi. 5; 1 K. iii. 2, xviii. 30; 2 K. xii. 3; 1 Chr. xxi. 26, &c.). The three altars built by Abraham at Shechem, between Bethel and Ai, and at Mamre, appear to have been on heights, and so was the Temple.

The high places in the Holy Land may thus have been divided into those dedicated to the worship of Jehovah, and those which had been dedicated to idols. And it would seem as if there was a constant struggle going on. The high places polluted by idol worship were of course to be wholly condemned. They were probably resorted to only to gratify a degraded superstition. See xix. 31, xx. 2–5. The others might have been innocently used for prayer and religious teaching. But the temptation appears to have been too great for the temper of the people. They offered sacrifice and burnt incense on them; and hence thorough reformers of the national religion, such as Hezekiah and Josiah, removed the high places altogether (2 K. xviii. 4, xxiii. 5).

your images] The original word is rendered in the margin of our Bible *sun images* (2 Chr. xiv. 5; Isai. xvii. 8; Ezek. vi. 4, &c.). Phœnician inscriptions prove that the word was commonly applied to images of Baal and Astarte, the god of the sun and the goddess of the moon. This exactly explains 2 Chr. xxxiv. 4 sq.

idols] The Heb. word here literally means things which could be rolled about, such as a block of wood or a lump of dirt. It was no doubt a name given in derision. Cp. Isai. xl. 20, xliv. 19; 2 K. i. 2.

31. *sanctuaries*] The Holy Places in the Tabernacle and the Temple (Ps. lxviii. 35. Cp. Ps. lxxiv. 7).

I will not smell the savour, &c.] See i. 9.

35. More literally: **All the days of its**

36 upon it. ¶ And upon them that are left *alive* of you [m]I will
send a faintness into their hearts in the lands of their enemies;
and [n]the sound of a [1]shaken leaf shall chase them; and they
shall flee, as fleeing from a sword; and they shall fall when
37 none pursueth. And [o]they shall fall one upon another, as it
were before a sword, when none pursueth: and [p]ye shall have
38 no power to stand before your enemies. And ye shall perish
among the heathen, and the land of your enemies shall eat you
39 up. And they that are left of you [q]shall pine away in their
iniquity in your enemies' lands; and also in the iniquities of
40 their fathers shall they pine away with them. ¶ [r]If they shall
confess their iniquity, and the iniquity of their fathers, with
their trespass which they trespassed against me, and that also
41 they have walked contrary unto me; and *that* I also have walked
contrary unto them, and have brought them into the land of
their enemies; if then their [s]uncircumcised hearts be [t]humbled,
42 and they then accept of the punishment of their iniquity: then
will I [u]remember my covenant with Jacob, and also my covenant
with Isaac, and also my covenant with Abraham will I re-
43 member; and I will [x]remember the land. ¶ [y]The land also
shall be left of them, and shall enjoy her sabbaths, while she
lieth desolate without them: and they shall accept of the punishment of their iniquity: because, even because they [z]despised
my judgments, and because their soul abhorred my statutes.
44 And yet for all that, when they be in the land of their enemies,
[a]I will not cast them away, neither will I abhor them, to destroy
them utterly, and to break my covenant with them: for I *am*
45 the LORD their God. But I will [b]for their sakes remember the
covenant of their ancestors, [c]whom I brought forth out of the
land of Egypt [d]in the sight of the heathen, that I might be their
46 God: I *am* the LORD. ¶ [e]These *are* the statutes and judgments
and laws, which the LORD made between him and the children
of Israel [f]in mount Sinai by the hand of Moses.

[m] Ez. 21. 7.
[n] Job 15. 21. Prov. 28. 1.
[o] Isai. 10. 4. 1 Sam. 14. 15, 16.
[p] Josh. 7. 12.
[q] Deut. 4. 27. Neh. 1. 8. Jer. 3. 25. Ez. 4. 17. Hos. 5. 15. Zech. 10. 9.
[r] Num. 5. 7. 1 Kin. 8. 33. Neh. 9. 2. Prov. 28. 13. Dan. 9. 3, 4. Luke 15. 18. 1 John 1. 9.
[s] Ez. 44. 7.
[t] 1 Kin. 21. 29. 2 Chr. 12. 6.
[u] Ex. 2. 24. Ps. 106. 45. Ez. 16. 60.
[x] Ps. 136. 23.
[y] ver. 34, 35.
[z] ver. 15.
[a] Deut. 4. 31. 2 Kin. 13. 23. Rom. 11. 2.
[b] Rom. 11. 28.
[c] ch. 22. 33.
[d] Ps. 98. 2. Ez. 20. 9.
[e] ch. 27. 34. Deut. 6. 1. John 1. 17.
[f] ch. 25. 1.

[1] Heb. *driven*.

---

desolation shall it rest that time which it rested not in your Sabbaths while ye dwelt upon it. That is, the periods of rest of which the land had been deprived would be made up to it. Cp. 2 Chr. xxxvi. 20, 21.

38. *the land of your enemies shall eat you up*] Cp. Num. xiii. 32; Ezek. xxxvi. 13.

39. *iniquity*] The meaning here is, **in the punishment of their iniquity**, and, in the next clause, **in the punishment of the iniquity** (as in *vv.* 41, 43) **of their fathers.** In the next verse the same Heb. word is properly represented by "iniquity." Our translators have in several places put one of the English words in the text and the other in the margin (Gen. iv. 13, xix. 15; 2 K. vii. 9; Ps. lxix. 27, &c.). The language of Scripture does not make that trenchant division between *sin* and *punishment* which we are accustomed to do. Sin is its own punishment, having in itself, from its very commencement, the germ of death. "Sin, when it is finished, bringeth forth death" (Jam. i. 15; Rom. ii. 5, v. 12).

40. *trespass*] The Hebrew word signifies an injury inflicted on the rights of a person, as distinguished from a sin or iniquity regarded as an outrage of the Divine law. Every wrong act is of course both a sin and a trespass against God. In this place Jehovah takes the breach of the Covenant as a personal trespass.

41. *uncircumcised hearts*] The outward sign of the Covenant might be preserved, but the answering grace in the heart would be wanting (Acts vii. 51; Rom. ii. 28, 29; Jer. vi. 10, ix. 26; cp. Col. ii. 11).

accept of the punishment of their iniquity] Literally, *enjoy their iniquity.* The word here and in *v.* 43 rendered "accept" in this phrase, is the same as is rendered "enjoy" in the expression "the land shall enjoy her sabbaths" (*v.* 34). The antithesis in *v.* 43 is this: *The land shall enjoy her sabbaths—and they shall enjoy the punishment of their iniquity.* The meaning is, that the land being desolate shall have the blessing of rest, and they having repented shall have the blessing of chastisement. The feelings of a devout

Chap. 27. AND the Lord spake unto Moses, saying, Speak unto
2 the children of Israel, and say unto them, [a]When a man shall — [a] Num. 6. 2.
make a singular vow, the persons *shall be* for the Lord by thy — See Judg. 11. 30, 31, 39.
3 estimation. And thy estimation shall be of the male from — 1 Sam. 1. 11, 28.
twenty years old even unto sixty years old, even thy estimation
shall be fifty shekels of silver, [b]after the shekel of the sanctuary. — [b] Ex. 30. 13.
4 And if it *be* a female, then thy estimation shall be thirty shekels,
5 And if *it be* from five years old even unto twenty years old, then
thy estimation shall be of the male twenty shekels, and for the
6 female ten shekels. And if *it be* from a month old even unto
five years old, then thy estimation shall be of the male five
shekels of silver, and for the female thy estimation *shall be* three
7 shekels of silver. And if *it be* from sixty years old and above; if
it be a male, then thy estimation shall be fifteen shekels, and for
8 the female ten shekels. But if he be poorer than thy estimation, then he shall present himself before the priest, and the
priest shall value him; according to his ability that vowed shall
9 the priest value him. And if *it be* a beast, whereof men bring
an offering unto the Lord, all that *any man* giveth of such unto
10 the Lord shall be holy. He shall not alter it, nor change it, a
good for a bad, or a bad for a good: and if he shall at all change
beast for beast, then it and the exchange thereof shall be holy.
11 And if *it be* any unclean beast, of which they do not offer a
sacrifice unto the Lord, then he shall present the beast before
12 the priest: and the priest shall value it, whether it be good or
13 bad: [1]as thou valuest it, *who art* the priest, so shall it be. [c]But — [c] ver. 15, 19.
if he will at all redeem it, then he shall add a fifth *part* thereof
14 unto thy estimation. ¶ And when a man shall sanctify his
house *to be* holy unto the Lord, then the priest shall estimate
it, whether it be good or bad: as the priest shall estimate it,
15 so shall it stand. [d]And if he that sanctified it will redeem his — [d] ver. 13.
house, then he shall add the fifth *part* of the money of thy esti-
16 mation unto it, and it shall be his. And if a man shall sanctify

[1] Heb. *according to thy estimation, O priest, &c.*

---

captive Israelite are beautifully expressed in Tobit xiii. 1–18.

XXVII. Dues. The position which this chapter holds after the formal conclusion, xxvi. 46, suggests that it is of a supplementary character. There seems, however, no reason to doubt its Mosaic origin.

2–3. Rather, **When a man makes a special vow which concerns thy valuation of persons to Jehovah, if thy estimation shall be of the male,** &c. The expression "thy estimation" is addressed either to Moses or to the priest (*v.* 12): it denoted a legal valuation. The vow of a person was perhaps most frequently made in cases of illness or danger, under the impulse of religious feeling, either in the way of thankfulness for blessings received, or of supplication for something desired. A man might dedicate himself, his wife, his child, or his bondservant. This might have been an old custom; but the Law ordained that he who had taken such a vow should pay a sum of money to the Sanctuary, determined according to the age and sex of the person.

3–7. The relative values of the persons appear to be regulated according to an estimate of the probable value of their future work:—

	Male.	Female.
From a month to five years	5	3 shekels.
From five years to twenty	20	10 ,,
From forty years to sixty	50	30 ,,
Sixty years and more	15	10 ,,

As regards the shekel of the Sanctuary, see Ex. xxxviii. 24 note.

8. *if he be poorer than thy estimation*] **Too poor (to pay) thy valuation.** Cp. v. 7, 11.

14. *sanctify*] *i.e.* vow to devote. This law relates to houses in the country (xxv. 31), which were under the same general law as the land itself, with a right of redemption for the inheritor till the next Jubilee. See *vv.* 17–19. For houses in walled towns the right of redemption lasted for only one year, (xxv. 29).

16. *some part of a field of his possession*] Rather, **a part of the land of his inheritance.**

unto the LORD *some part* of a field of his possession, then thy
estimation shall be according to the seed thereof: [1]an homer of
17 barley seed *shall be valued* at fifty shekels of silver. If he sanctify his field from the year of jubile, according to thy estimation
18 it shall stand. But if he sanctify his field after the jubile, then
the priest shall [e]reckon unto him the money according to the
years that remain, even unto the year of the jubile, and it shall
19 be abated from thy estimation. [f]And if he that sanctified the
field will in any wise redeem it, then he shall add the fifth *part*
of the money of thy estimation unto it, and it shall be assured
20 to him. And if he will not redeem the field, or if he have sold
the field to another man, it shall not be redeemed any more.
21 But the field, [g]when it goeth out in the jubile, shall be holy
unto the LORD, as a field [h]devoted; [i]the possession thereof shall
22 be the priest's. And if *a man* sanctify unto the LORD a field
which he hath bought, which *is* not of the fields of [k]his pos-
23 session; [l]then the priest shall reckon unto him the worth of thy
estimation, *even* unto the year of the jubile: and he shall give
thine estimation in that day, *as* a holy thing unto the LORD.
24 [m]In the year of the jubile the field shall return unto him of
whom it was bought, *even* to him to whom the possession of the
25 land *did belong*. And all thy estimations shall be according to
the shekel of the sanctuary: [n]twenty gerahs shall be the shekel.
26 ¶ Only the [2][o]firstling of the beasts, which should be the LORD's
firstling, no man shall sanctify it; whether *it be* ox, or sheep: it
27 *is* the LORD's. And if *it be* of an unclean beast, then he shall
redeem *it* according to thine estimation, [p]and shall add a fifth
part of it thereto: or if it be not redeemed, then it shall be sold
28 according to thy estimation. ¶ [q]Notwithstanding no devoted
thing, that a man shall devote unto the LORD of all that he hath,

[e] ch. 25. 15, 16.
[f] ver. 13.
[g] ch. 25. 10, 28, 31.
[h] ver. 28.
[i] Num. 18. 14. Ez. 44. 29.
[k] ch. 25. 10, 25.
[l] ver. 18.
[m] ch. 25. 28.
[n] Ex. 30. 13. Num. 3. 47. & 18. 16. Ez. 45. 12.
[o] Ex. 13. 2, 12. & 22. 30. Num. 18. 17. Deut. 15. 19.
[p] ver. 11, 12, 13.
[q] ver. 21.

[1] Or, the land of *an homer, &c.*

[2] Heb. *firstborn, &c.*

---

the seed thereof] *i.e.* the quantity of seed required to sow it properly. Thus the value of about 5½ bushels (an homer) was about 6*l.* 9*s.* 2*d.* (50 shekels. See Ex. xxxviii. 24.)

21. *devoted*] See *v.* 28 note.

25. On the shekel and the gerah, see Ex. xxx. 13, xxxviii. 24 notes.

28. *devoted thing*] The primary meaning of the Heb. word (*chĕrem*) is something cut off, or shut up. Its specific meaning in the Law is, that which is cut off from common use and given up in some sense to Jehovah, without the right of recal or commutation. It is applied to a field wholly appropriated to the Sanctuary (*v.* 21), and to whatever was doomed to destruction (1 S. xv. 21; 1 K. xx. 42). Our translators have often rendered the word by "cursed," or "a curse," which in some places may convey the right sense, but it should be remembered that the terms are not identical in their compass of meaning (Deut. vii. 26; Josh. vi. 17, 18, vii. 1; Isai. xxxiv. 5, xliii. 28, &c. Cp. Gal. iii. 13).

of man and beast] This passage does not permit human sacrifices. Man is elsewhere clearly recognised as one of the creatures which were not to be offered in sacrifice (Ex. xiii. 13, xxxiv. 20; Num. xviii. 15).

Therefore the application of the word *chĕrem* to man is made exclusively in reference to one rightly doomed to death and, in that sense alone, given up to Jehovah. The man who, in a right spirit, either carries out a sentence of just doom on an offender, or who, with a single eye to duty, slays an enemy in battle, must regard himself as God's servant rendering up a life to the claim of the Divine justice (cp. Rom. xiii. 4). It was in this way that Israel was required to destroy the Canaanites at Hormah (Num. xxi. 2, 3; cp. Deut. xiii. 12-18), and that Samuel hewed Agag in pieces before the Lord (1 S. xv. 33). In all such instances, a moral obligation rests upon him whose office it is to take the life: he has to look upon the object of his stroke as under a ban to the Lord (cp. Deut. xx. 4; Gal. iii. 13). There can therefore be neither redemption nor commutation.

It is evident that the righteousness of this law is not involved in the sin of rash or foolish vows, such as Saul's (1 S. xiv. 24) or Jephthah's (Judg. xi. 30).

And it seems hardly needful to add that sacrifice, as it is represented both in the Law and in the usage of the Patriarchs, is something very different from consecration

both of man and beast, and of the field of his possession, shall be
sold or redeemed: every devoted thing *is* most holy unto the
29 LORD. [r]None devoted, which shall be devoted of men, shall be
30 redeemed; *but* shall surely be put to death. And [s]all the
tithe of the land, *whether* of the seed of the land, *or* of the fruit
31 of the tree, *is* the LORD'S: *it is* holy unto the LORD. [t]And if a
man will at all redeem *ought* of his tithes, he shall add thereto
32 the fith *part* thereof. And concerning the tithe of the herd, or
of the flock, *even* of whatsoever [u]passeth under the rod, the
33 tenth shall be holy unto the LORD. He shall not search whether
it be good or bad, [x]neither shall he change it: and if he change
it at all, then both it and the change thereof shall be holy; it
34 shall not be redeemed. ¶ [y]These *are* the commandments, which
the LORD commanded Moses for the children of Israel in mount
Sinai.

r Num. 21. 2, 3.
s Gen. 28. 22. Num. 18. 21, 24. 2 Chr. 31. 5, 6, 12. Neh. 13. 12. Mal. 3. 8.
t ver. 13.
u See Jer. 33. 13. Ez. 20. 37. Mic. 7. 14.
x ver. 10.
y ch. 26. 46.

---

under a ban, though a thing to be sacrificed might come under the designation of *chērem* in its wider sense. The sacrifice was always the offering up of the innocent life of a creature chosen, approved, and without spot or blemish.

32. *whatsoever passeth under the rod*] According to rabbinical tradition, the animals to be tithed were enclosed in a pen, and as they went out one by one at the opening, every tenth animal was touched with a rod dipped in vermilion. Cp. marg. reff.

For a more full explanation of what relates to tithes, see marg. reff. and Gen. xiv. 20; Deut. xiv. 22, 28.

NUMBERS.

INTRODUCTION.

THE title commonly given to this Book is evidently suggested by the two numberings of the people recorded in chapters i. and xxvi.

The book narrates the history of the Israelites during their sojourn in the wilderness from the completion of the law-giving at Sinai, Lev. xxvii. 34, to their mustering in the plains of Moab for actual entry into the Land of Promise.[1]

The incidents are generally given in their chronological order, except in the third part. The five chapters comprised in this part appear to deal with a long period, from which only isolated episodes are given; and of these the dates can only be conjectured.

Between the two dates "the first day of the second month of the second year after they were come out of Egypt" (i. 1), and the death of Aaron (xxxiii. 38), intervene no less than thirty-eight years and three months (cp. Deut. ii. 14), the long and dreary period of tarrying in the wilderness till the disobedient generation had wasted away.[2]

From the death of Aaron to the date given in the opening verses of Deuteronomy (i. 1–3), occurred a space of exactly six months, in which all the events narrated in the fourth part of the Book of Numbers, from xx. 1 to the end, would seem to have occurred, with the probable exception of the defeat of the king of Arad (xxi. 1–3).

As regards the authorship and date of composition, the notes of time, the tenor of the contents, no less than the direct assertions of the text itself, lead to the conclusion that Moses is properly spoken of as the writer of the Book of Numbers. It is in substance his work; though many portions of it were probably committed to writing many years before the whole was completed; and the concluding chapters were not written until towards the close of the fortieth year after the Exodus.

---

[1] Its contents may be divided into four parts: (*a*) i.—x. 10; (*b*) x. 11—xiv; (*c*) xv.—xix.; (*d*) xx.—xxxvi.

[2] On the history of these years, see notes on xx. 1, and xxxiii. 19.

THE FOURTH BOOK OF MOSES,

CALLED

NUMBERS.

a Ex. 19. 1. ch. 10. 11, 12. b Ex. 25. 22. c Ex. 30. 12. & 38. 26. ch. 26. 2, 63, 64. 2 Sam. 24. 2. 1 Chr. 21. 2.

CHAP. 1. AND the LORD spake unto Moses [a]in the wilderness of
Sinai, [b]in the tabernacle of the congregation, on the first *day* of
the second month, in the second year after they were come out
2 of the land of Egypt, saying, [c]Take ye the sum of all the congregation of the children of Israel, after their families, by the
house of their fathers, with the number of *their* names, every
3 male by their polls; from twenty years old and upward, all that
are able to go forth to war in Israel: thou and Aaron shall
4 number them by their armies. And with you there shall be
a man of every tribe; every one head of the house of his fathers.
5 ¶ And these *are* the names of the men that shall stand with
6 you: of *the tribe of* Reuben; Elizur the son of Shedeur. Of
7 Simeon; Shelumiel the son of Zurishaddai. Of Judah; Nah-
8 shon the son of Amminadab. Of Issachar; Nethaneel the son
9, 10 of Zuar. Of Zebulun; Eliab the son of Helon. Of the children
of Joseph: of Ephraim; Elishama the son of Ammihud: of
11 Manasseh; Gamaliel the son of Pedahzur. Of Benjamin; Abidan
12 the son of Gideoni. Of Dan; Ahiezer the son of Ammishaddai.
13, 14 Of Asher; Pagiel the son of Ocran. Of Gad; Eliasaph the
15, 16 son of [d]Deuel. Of Naphtali; Ahira the son of Enan. [e]These
were the renowned of the congregation, princes of the tribes
17 of their fathers, [f]heads of thousands in Israel. ¶ And Moses
and Aaron took these men which are expressed by *their* names:
18 and they assembled all the congregation together on the first
day of the second month, and they declared their pedigrees after
their families, by the house of their fathers, according to the
number of the names, from twenty years old and upward, by
19 their polls. As the LORD commanded Moses, so he numbered
20 them in the wilderness of Sinai. ¶ And the children of Reuben,
Israel's eldest son, by their generations, after their families, by

d ch. 2. 14, he is called *Reuel*. e ch. 7. 2. 1 Chr. 27. 16. f Ex. 18. 21, 25.

I. **1-4.** A month had passed away since the setting up of the tabernacle (Ex. xl. 2, 17): and the Sinaitic legislation was now complete (cp. Lev. xxvii. 34).

A census ("sum") was commanded, to be based not upon any fresh registration of individuals, but upon that which had accompanied the previous collection of the offerings. Cp. Ex. xxx. 11, &c.; xxxviii. 25-28. The offerings had been probably tendered by the people in groups, and if certificates of registration were furnished to such groups, the new census might be easily carried out by means of these documents, and got through (*v.* 18) in a single day. The present registration enrolled persons "after their families, by the house of their fathers;" and was superintended not by the Levites (see Ex. xxxviii. 21 and note), but by (*v.* 4) an assessor for each tribe to act in the business with Moses and Aaron. The purpose now in view was not religious only. The census now taken would serve as a basis for various civil and military arrangements.

5-16. The princes of the tribes, selected (*v.* 4) under divine direction, were for the most part the same persons as those chosen a few months previously at the counsel of Jethro (Ex. xviii. 21-26). Nahshon, prince of Judah, is mentioned in Ex. vi. 23, and Elishama, in 1 Chr. vii. 26, 27. The peers of men like these were no doubt entitled, amongst their fellows, to the epithet "renowned," *v.* 16.

20-46. The enrolment, being taken principally for military purposes (cp. *vv.* 3, 20), would naturally be arranged by hundreds, fifties, &c. (cf. 2 K. i. 9, 11, 13). In eleven tribes the number enrolled consists of complete hundreds. The difference, in this respect, observable in the case of the tribe of Gad here (*v.* 25), and of the tribe of Reuben at the later census (xxvi. 7), is probably to be accounted for by the pastoral, and consequently nomadic, habits of these tribes,

the house of their fathers, according to the number of the names,
by their polls, every male from twenty years old and upward,
21 all that were able to go forth to war; those that were numbered
of them, *even* of the tribe of Reuben, *were* forty and six thousand
22 and five hundred. ¶ Of the children of Simeon, by their generations, after their families, by the house of their fathers, those
that were numbered of them, according to the number of the
names, by their polls, every male from twenty years old and
23 upward, all that were able to go forth to war; those that were
numbered of them, *even* of the tribe of Simeon, *were* fifty and
24 nine thousand and three hundred. ¶ Of the children of Gad, by
their generations, after their families, by the house of their
fathers, according to the number of the names, from twenty
years old and upward, all that were able to go forth to war;
25 those that were numbered of them, *even* of the tribe of Gad, *were*
26 forty and five thousand six hundred and fifty. ¶ Of the children
of Judah, by their generations, after their families, by the house
of their fathers, according to the number of the names, from
twenty years old and upward, all that were able to go forth to
27 war; those that were numbered of them, *even* of the tribe of
Judah, *were* threescore and fourteen thousand and six hundred.
28 ¶ Of the children of Issachar, by their generations, after their
families, by the house of their fathers, according to the number
of the names, from twenty years old and upward, all that were
29 able to go forth to war; those that were numbered of them,
even of the tribe of Issachar, *were* fifty and four thousand and
30 four hundred. ¶ Of the children of Zebulun, by their generations, after their families, by the house of their fathers, according to the number of the names, from twenty years old and
31 upward, all that were able to go forth to war; those that were
numbered of them, *even* of the tribe of Zebulun, *were* fifty and
32 seven thousand and four hundred. ¶ Of the children of Joseph,
namely, of the children of Ephraim, by their generations, after
their families, by the house of their fathers, according to the
number of the names, from twenty years old and upward, all
33 that were able to go forth to war; those that were numbered of
them, *even* of the tribe of Ephraim, *were* forty thousand and five
34 hundred. ¶ Of the children of Manasseh, by their generations,
after their families, by the house of their fathers, according to
the number of the names, from twenty years old and upward, all
35 that were able to go forth to war; those that were numbered of
them, *even* of the tribe of Manasseh, *were* thirty and two thou-
36 sand and two hundred. ¶ Of the children of Benjamin, by their
generations, after their families, by the house of their fathers,
according to the number of the names, from twenty years old
37 and upward, all that were able to go forth to war; those that
were numbered of them, *even* of the tribe of Benjamin, *were*
38 thirty and five thousand and four hundred. ¶ Of the children of Dan, by their generations, after their families, by
the house of their fathers, according to the number of the
names, from twenty years old and upward, all that were able
39 to go forth to war; those that were numbered of them, *even* of
the tribe of Dan, *were* threescore and two thousand and seven

---

which rendered it difficult to bring all their members together at once for a census. Judah already takes precedence of his brethren in point of numbers (cp. Gen. xlix. 8 note), and Ephraim of Manasseh (cp. Gen. xlviii. 19, 20).

40 hundred. ¶ Of the children of Asher, by their generations,
after their families, by the house of their fathers, according to
the number of the names, from twenty years old and upward,
41 all that were able to go forth to war; those that were numbered
of them, *even* of the tribe of Asher, *were* forty and one thousand
42 and five hundred. ¶ Of the children of Naphtali, throughout
their generations, after their families, by the house of their
fathers, according to the number of the names, from twenty
years old and upward, all that were able to go forth to war;
43 those that were numbered of them, *even* of the tribe of Naphtali,
44 *were* fifty and three thousand and four hundred. ¶ [g]These *are*
those that were numbered, which Moses and Aaron numbered,
and the princes of Israel, *being* twelve men: each one was for
45 the house of his fathers. So were all those that were numbered
of the children of Israel, by the house of their fathers, from
twenty years old and upward, all that were able to go forth to
46 war in Israel; even all they that were numbered were [h]six hundred thousand and three thousand and five hundred and fifty.
47 But [i]the Levites after the tribe of their fathers were not num-
48 bered among them. For the LORD had spoken unto Moses, say-
49 ing, [k]Only thou shalt not number the tribe of Levi, neither
50 take the sum of them among the children of Israel: [l]but thou
shalt appoint the Levites over the tabernacle of testimony, and
over all the vessels thereof, and over all things that *belong* to
it: they shall bear the tabernacle, and all the vessels thereof;
and they shall minister unto it, [m]and shall encamp round about
51 the tabernacle. [n]And when the tabernacle setteth forward, the
Levites shall take it down: and when the tabernacle is to be
pitched, the Levites shall set it up: [o]and the stranger that com-
52 eth nigh shall be put to death. And the children of Israel shall
pitch their tents, [p]every man by his own camp, and every man
53 by his own standard, throughout their hosts. [q]But the Levites
shall pitch round about the tabernacle of testimony, that there
be no [r]wrath upon the congregation of the children of Israel:
[s]and the Levites shall keep the charge of the tabernacle of testi-
54 mony. ¶ And the children of Israel did according to all that
the LORD commanded Moses, so did they.

CHAP. 2. AND the LORD spake unto Moses and unto Aaron, saying,
2 [a]Every man of the children of Israel shall pitch by his own
standard, with the ensign of their father's house: [1][b]far off
about the tabernacle of the congregation shall they pitch.

[g] ch. 26. 64.
[h] Ex. 38. 26. See Exod. 12. 37. ch. 2. 32. & 26. 51.
[i] ch. 2. 33. See ch. 3. & 4. & 26. 57. 1 Chr. 6. & 21. 6.
[k] ch. 2. 33. & 26. 62.
[l] Ex. 38. 21. ch. 3. 7, 8. & 4. 15, 25, 26. 27, 33.
[m] ch. 3. 23, 29, 35, 38.
[n] ch. 10. 17, 21.
[o] ch. 3. 10, 38. & 18. 22.
[p] ch. 2. 2, 34.
[q] ver. 50.
[r] Lev. 10. 6. ch. 8. 19. & 16. 46. & 18. 5. 1 Sam. 6. 19.
[s] ch. 3. 7, 8. & 8. 24, 25, 26. & 18. 3, 4, 5. & 31. 30, 47. 1 Chr. 23. 32. 2 Chr. 13. 11.
[a] ch. 1. 52.
[b] Josh. 3. 4.

[1] Heb. *over against.*

47-54. When a census of the tribe of Levi takes place (iii. 15, xxvi. 62), *all* the males are counted from a month old and upward, and not, as in the other tribes, those only who were of age for service in the field.

48. *had spoken*] Render **spake.** The formal appointment is only now made, in reward for their zeal (Ex. xxxii. 26–29), though reference to their future office appears previously in Lev. xxv. 32 sqq., and they had already acted as assistants to the priests (cp. Ex. xxxviii. 21).

II. **2.** *standard...ensign*] The "standard" marked the division, or camp (cf. *vv.* 9, 16, 24, 31); the "ensign" the family. There would thus be four "standards" only, one for each "camp" of three tribes. The "standard" was probably a solid figure or emblem mounted on a pole, such as the Egyptians used. Tradition appropriates the four cherubic forms (Ezek. i. 5–12; Rev. iv. 7 sqq.), the lion, man, ox, and eagle, to the camps of Judah, Reuben, Ephraim, and Dan respectively; and this, as to the first, has a certain support from Gen. xlix. 9 (cp. Rev. v. 5), and as to the third, from Deut. xxxiii. 17.

far off] See margin, **over against**; *i.e.* facing the tabernacle on every side. The distance was perhaps 2000 cubits or rather more than $\frac{1}{4}$ mile: cp. Josh. iii. 4.

3 ¶ And on the east side toward the rising of the sun shall they of
the standard of the camp of Judah pitch throughout their
armies: and [c]Nahshon the son of Amminadab *shall be* captain of [c] ch. 10. 14.
4 the children of Judah. And his host, and those that were num- Ruth 4. 20. 1 Chr. 2. 10.
bered of them, *were* threescore and fourteen thousand and six Matt. 1. 4.
5 hundred. And those that do pitch next unto him *shall be* the Luke 3. 32,
tribe of Issachar: and Nethaneel the son of Zuar *shall be* captain 33.
6 of the children of Issachar. And his host, and those that were
numbered thereof, *were* fifty and four thousand and four hun-
7 dred. *Then* the tribe of Zebulun: and Eliab the son of Helon
8 *shall be* captain of the children of Zebulun. And his host, and
those that were numbered thereof, *were* fifty and seven thousand
9 and four hundred. All that were numbered in the camp of
Judah *were* an hundred thousand and fourscore thousand and six
thousand and four hundred, throughout their armies. [d]These [d] ch. 10. 14.
10 shall first set forth. ¶ On the south side *shall be* the standard of
the camp of Reuben according to their armies: and the captain
11 of the children of Reuben *shall be* Elizur the son of Shedeur. And
his host, and those that were numbered thereof, *were* forty and
12 six thousand and five hundred. And those which pitch by him
shall be the tribe of Simeon: and the captain of the children of
13 Simeon *shall be* Shelumiel the son of Zurishaddai. And his host,
and those that were numbered of them, *were* fifty and nine thou-
14 sand and three hundred. Then the tribe of Gad: and the captain
15 of the sons of Gad *shall be* Eliasaph the son of [1]Reuel. And his
host, and those that were numbered of them, *were* forty and five
16 thousand and six hundred and fifty. All that were numbered in
the camp of Reuben *were* an hundred thousand and fifty and one
thousand and four hundred and fifty, throughout their armies.
17 [e]And they shall set forth in the second rank. ¶ [f]Then the taber- [e] ch. 10. 18.
nacle of the congregation shall set forward with the camp of the [f] ch. 10. 17,
Levites in the midst of the camp: as they encamp, so shall they 21.
18 set forward, every man in his place by their standards. ¶ On
the west side *shall be* the standard of the camp of Ephraim
according to their armies: and the captain of the sons of Ephraim

[1] *Deuel*, ch. 1. 14. & 7. 42, 47, & 10. 20.

14. *Reuel*] Doubtless an error of transcription for Deuel (i. 14).

3-32. The following plan shows the general arrangement of the camp, which would vary in different places according to local exigencies. The area of the camp might be about three square miles.

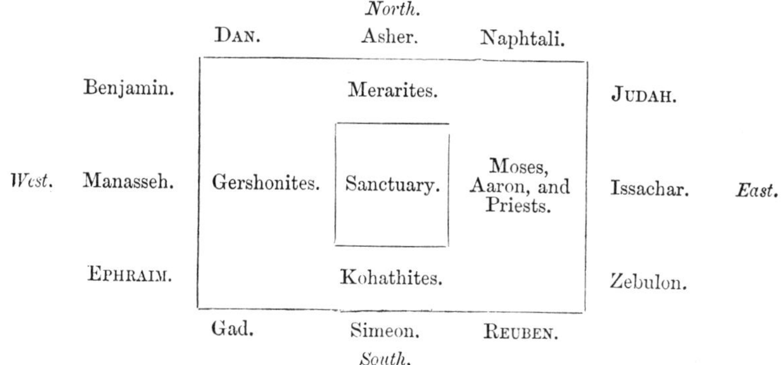

19 *shall be* Elishama the son of Ammihud. And his host, and those
that were numbered of them, *were* forty thousand and five hun-
20 dred. And by him *shall be* the tribe of Manasseh: and the
captain of the children of Manasseh *shall be* Gamaliel the son of
21 Pedahzur. And his host, and those that were numbered of them,
22 *were* thirty and two thousand and two hundred. Then the tribe
of Benjamin: and the captain of the sons of Benjamin *shall be*
23 Abidan the son of Gideoni. And his host, and those that were
numbered of them, *were* thirty and five thousand and four hun-
24 dred. All that were numbered of the camp of Ephraim *were* an
hundred thousand and eight thousand and an hundred, throughout their armies. [g]And they shall go forward in the third rank.
25 ¶ The standard of the camp of Dan *shall be* on the north side by
their armies: and the captain of the children of Dan *shall be*
26 Ahiezer the son of Ammishaddai. And his host, and those that
were numbered of them, *were* threescore and two thousand and
27 seven hundred. And those that encamp by him *shall be* the
tribe of Asher: and the captain of the children of Asher *shall be*
28 Pagiel the son of Ocran. And his host, and those that were
numbered of them, *were* forty and one thousand and five hun-
29 dred. Then the tribe of Naphtali: and the captain of the
30 children of Naphtali *shall be* Ahira the son of Enan. And his
host, and those that were numbered of them, *were* fifty and three
31 thousand and four hundred. All they that were numbered in
the camp of Dan *were* an hundred thousand and fifty and seven
thousand and six hundred. [h]They shall go hindmost with their
32 standards. ¶ These *are* those which were numbered of the children of Israel by the house of their fathers: [i]all those that were
numbered of the camps throughout their hosts *were* six hundred
33 thousand and three thousand and five hundred and fifty. But
[k]the Levites were not numbered among the children of Israel;
34 as the LORD commanded Moses. And the children of Israel did
according to all that the LORD commanded Moses: [l]so they
pitched by their standards, and so they set forward, every one
after their families, according to the house of their fathers.

CHAP. 3. THESE also *are* the generations of Aaron and Moses in
2 the day *that* the LORD spake with Moses in mount Sinai. And
these *are* the names of the sons of Aaron; Nadab the [a]firstborn,
3 and Abihu, Eleazar, and Ithamar. These *are* the names of the
sons of Aaron, [b]the priests which were anointed, [1]whom he con-
4 secrated to minister in the priest's office. [c]And Nadab and Abihu

[g] ch. 10. 22.
[h] ch. 10. 25.
[i] Ex. 38. 26. ch. 1. 46. & 11. 21.
[k] ch. 1. 47.
[l] ch. 24. 2, 5, 6.
[a] Ex. 6. 23.
[b] Ex. 28. 41. Lev. 8.
[c] Lev. 10. 1. ch. 26. 61. 1 Chr. 24. 2.

[1] Heb. *whose hand he filled.*

32–34. Such was the ideal form of the encampment in the wilderness: a form reproduced in the square court with which the Temple was eventually surrounded, and in the vision of the heavenly city as seen by Ezekiel (xlviii. 20), and by St. John (Rev. xxi. 16; cp. Rev. xx. 9). Thus the camp of God's earthly people was divinely ordered so as to set forth the completeness of His Church; and to illustrate by its whole arrangement, which was determined by the Tabernacle in the centre, both the dependance of all on God, and the access which all enjoyed to God.

III. 1. The "generations" (see Gen. ii. 4) now given, though entitled those of Aaron and Moses (Aaron standing first as the elder brother), are those of Aaron only. The personal dignity of Moses, though it gave him rank as at the head of his tribe, was not hereditary. He had, and desired to have (xiv. 12; Ex. xxxii. 10), no successor in his office but the distant Prophet like unto himself (Deut. xviii. 18). Aaron was the ancestor of a regular succession of priests.

3. *whom he consecrated*] *i.e.* whom Moses consecrated, or literally as marg., whose "hand he filled," by conferring their office upon them (Lev. viii. 1 seq.).

died before the LORD, when they offered strange fire before the
LORD, in the wilderness of Sinai, and they had no children: and
Eleazar and Ithamar ministered in the priest's office in the sight
5 of Aaron their father. ¶ And the LORD spake unto Moses, say-
6 ing, [d]Bring the tribe of Levi near, and present them before
7 Aaron the priest, that they may minister unto him. And they
shall keep his charge, and the charge of the whole congregation
before the tabernacle of the congregation, to do [e]the service of
8 the tabernacle. And they shall keep all the instruments of the
tabernacle of the congregation, and the charge of the children of
9 Israel, to do the service of the tabernacle. And [f]thou shalt give
the Levites unto Aaron and to his sons: they *are* wholly given
10 unto him out of the children of Israel. And thou shalt appoint
Aaron and his sons, [g]and they shall wait on their priest's office:
[h]and the stranger that cometh nigh shall be put to death.
11, 12 ¶ And the LORD spake unto Moses, saying, And I, behold, [i]I
have taken the Levites from among the children of Israel instead
of all the firstborn that openeth the matrix among the children
13 of Israel: therefore the Levites shall be mine; because [k]all the
firstborn *are* mine; [l]*for* on the day that I smote all the firstborn in the land of Egypt I hallowed unto me all the firstborn
in Israel, both man and beast: mine shall they be: I *am* the
14 LORD. ¶ And the LORD spake unto Moses in the wilderness of
15 Sinai, saying, Number the children of Levi after the house of
their fathers, by their families: [m]every male from a month old
16 and upward shalt thou number them. And Moses numbered
them according to the [1]word of the LORD, as he was commanded.
17 [n]And these were the sons of Levi by their names; Gershon, and
18 Kohath, and Merari. And these *are* the names of the sons of
19 Gershon by their families; [o]Libni, and Shimei. And the sons
of Kohath by their families; [p]Amram, and Izehar, Hebron,
20 and Uzziel. [q]And the sons of Merari by their families; Mahli,
and Mushi. These *are* the families of the Levites according to
21 the house of their fathers. ¶ Of Gershon *was* the family of the
Libnites, and the family of the Shimites: these *are* the families
22 of the Gershonites. Those that were numbered of them, according to the number of all the males, from a month old and
upward, *even* those that were numbered of them *were* seven thou-
23 sand and five hundred. [r]The families of the Gershonites shall
24 pitch behind the tabernacle westward. And the chief of the
house of the father of the Gershonites *shall be* Eliasaph the son of
25 Lael. And [s]the charge of the sons of Gershon in the tabernacle
of the congregation *shall be* [t]the tabernacle, and [u]the tent, [x]the
covering thereof, and [y]the hanging for the door of the tabernacle
26 of the congregation, and [z]the hangings of the court, and [a]the
curtain for the door of the court, which *is* by the tabernacle, and
by the altar round about, and [b]the cords of it for all the service
27 thereof. ¶ [c]And of Kohath *was* the family of the Amramites,
and the family of the Izeharites, and the family of the Hebronites,

[d] ch. 8. 6. & 18. 2.
[e] See ch. 1. 50. & 8. 11, 15, 24, 26.
[f] ch. 8. 19. & 18. 6.
[g] ch. 18. 7.
[h] ver. 38. ch. 1. 51. & 16. 40.
[i] ver. 41. ch. 8. 16. & 18. 6.
[k] Ex. 13. 2 Lev. 27. 26 ch. 8. 16. Luke 2. 23
[l] Ex. 13. 15. ch. 8. 17.
[m] ver. 39. ch. 26. 62.
[n] Gen. 46 11. Ex. 6. 16. ch. 26. 57. 1 Chr. 6. 16. & 23. 6.
[o] Ex. 6. 1
[p] Ex. 6. 1
[q] Ex. 6. 1
[r] ch. 1. 5
[s] ch. 4. 25, 26.
[t] Ex. 25.
[u] Ex. 26
[x] Ex. 26 14.
[y] Ex. 26
[z] Ex. 27
[a] Ex. 27
[b] Ex. 35
[c] 1 Chr. 23.

[1] Heb. *mouth*.

---

7. *keep his charge*] i.e. so assist him that the obligations incumbent on him and on the congregation may be fulfilled.

13. The concluding words are better expressed thus: "Mine shall they be, Mine, the Lord's." On the subject of the firstborn see notes on *vv.* 43-51.

26. *the cords...the service thereof*] i.e the Tabernacle, not of the hangings of Court; for these, with their cords and o fittings, belonged to the charge of the rarites (*vv.* 36, 37). The Tabernacle under the care of the Gershonites.

27-32. Of the Levites, the Kohath

and the family of the Uzzielites: these *are* the families of the
28 Kohathites. In the number of all the males, from a month
old and upward, *were* eight thousand and six hundred, keeping
29 the charge of the sanctuary. [d]The families of the sons of Kohath
30 shall pitch on the side of the tabernacle southward. And the
chief of the house of the father of the families of the Kohathites
31 *shall be* Elizaphan the son of Uzziel. And [e]their charge *shall*
be [f]the ark, and [g]the table, a d [h]the candlestick, and [i]the
altars, and the vessels of the sanctuary wherewith they minister,
32 and [k]the hanging, and all the service thereof. And Eleazar the
son of Aaron the priest *shall be* chief over the chief of the Levites, *and have* the oversight of them that keep the charge of the
33 sanctuary. ¶ Of Merari *was* the family of the Mahlites, and the
34 family of the Mushites: these *are* the families of Merari. And
those that were numbered of them, according to the number of
all the males, from a month old and upward, *were* six thousand
35 and two hundred. And the chief of the house of the father of
the families of Merari *was* Zuriel the son of Abihail: [l]*these* shall
36 pitch on the side of the tabernacle northward. And [1m]*under*
the custody and charge of the sons of Merari *shall be* the boards
of the tabernacle, and the bars thereof, and the pillars thereof,
and the sockets thereof, and all the vessels thereof, and all that
37 serveth thereto, and the pillars of the court round about, and
38 their sockets, and their pins, and their cords. ¶ [n]But those that
encamp before the tabernacle toward the east, *even* before the
tabernacle of the congregation eastward, *shall be* Moses, and
Aaron and his sons, [o]keeping the charge of the sanctuary [p]for
the charge of the children of Israel; and [q]the stranger that
39 cometh nigh shall be put to death. [r]All that were numbered of
the Levites, which Moses and Aaron numbered at the commandment of the LORD, throughout their families, all the males from
40 a month old and upward, *were* twenty and two thousand. ¶ And
the LORD said unto Moses, [s]Number all the firstborn of the
males of the children of Israel from a month old and upward,
41 and take the number of their names. [t]And thou shalt take the
Levites for me (I *am* the LORD) instead of all the firstborn
among the children of Israel; and the cattle of the Levites
instead of all the firstlings among the cattle of the children of
42 Israel. And Moses numbered, as the LORD commanded him, all
43 the firstborn among the children of Israel. And all the firstborn
males by the number of names, from a month old and upward,

[d] ch. 1. 53. [e] ch. 4. 15. [f] Ex. 25. 10. [g] Ex. 25. 23. [h] Ex. 25. 31. [i] Ex. 27. 1. & 30. 1. [k] Ex. 26. 32. [l] ch. 1. 53. [m] ch. 4. 31, 32. [n] ch. 1. 53. [o] ch. 18. 5. [p] ver. 7, 8. [q] ver. 10. [r] See ch. 26. 62. [s] ver. 15. [t] ver. 12. 45.

[1] Heb. *the office of the charge.*

the kinsmen of Moses and Aaron, and the most numerous, have the most important charge confided to them, viz. that of the Ark, the Altars, and the more especially sacred furniture generally.

39. *twenty and two thousand*] A number on which the commutation with the First-born of the Twelve tribes depends (*vv.* 43–46). The actual total of the male Levites is 22,300 (cp. *vv.* 22, 28, 34): and the extra 300 are considered by some to represent those who, being first-born themselves in the tribe of Levi, could not be available to redeem the first-born in other tribes. Others consider the difference due to an error in the Hebrew text.

The tribe of Levi is shown by this census to have been by far the smallest of the tribes.

43. This result, when compared with the number of male adults (603, 550, cp. ii. 32), is small, the usual proportion of first-born sons to a total male population being about one in four: and the explanation offered is that the law of Ex. xiii. 1, 2, prescribed a dedication of those only who should be first-born *thenceforward*.

On the other hand, the number is very large to be born amongst two millions of persons in a single year; and it must be admitted, that some unusual causes must have been concerned. Such, not to mention the

of those that were numbered of them, were twenty and two thousand two hundred and threescore and thirteen. ¶ And the LORD
44 spake unto Moses, saying, [u]Take the Levites instead of all the [u] ver. 12. 41.
45 firstborn among the children of Israel, and the cattle of the
Levites instead of their cattle; and the Levites shall be mine: I
46 *am* the LORD. And for those that are to be [x]redeemed of the [x] Ex. 13. 13. ch. 18. 15.
two hundred and threescore and thirteen of the firstborn of the
47 children of Israel, [y]which are more than the Levites; thou shalt [y] ver. 39. 43.
even take [z]five shekels apiece by the poll, after the shekel of the [z] Lev. 27. 6. ch. 18. 16.
sanctuary shalt thou take *them*: ([a]the shekel *is* twenty gerahs:) [a] Ex. 30. 13.
48 and thou shalt give the money, wherewith the odd number of Lev. 27. 25.
49 them is to be redeemed, unto Aaron and to his sons. And Moses ch. 18. 16. Ez. 45. 12.
took the redemption money of them that were over and above
50 them that were redeemed by the Levites: of the firstborn of the
children of Israel took he the money; [b]a thousand three hun- [b] ver. 46, 47.
dred and threescore and five *shekels*, after the shekel of the
51 sanctuary: and Moses [c]gave the money of them that were [c] ver. 48.
redeemed unto Aaron and to his sons, according to the word of
the LORD, as the LORD commanded Moses.

CHAP. 4. AND the LORD spake unto Moses and unto Aaron, say-
2 ing, Take the sum of the sons of Kohath from among the sons
3 of Levi, after their families, by the house of their fathers, [a]from [a] See ch. 8. 24.
thirty years old and upward even until fifty years old, all that 1 Chr. 23. 3,
enter into the host, to do the work in the tabernacle of the con- 24, 27.
4 gregation. [b]This *shall be* the service of the sons of Kohath in [b] ver. 15.
the tabernacle of the congregation, *about* [c]the most holy things: [c] ver. 19.
5 and when the camp setteth forward, Aaron shall come, and his
sons, and they shall take down [d]the covering vail, and cover the [d] Ex. 26. 31.
6 [e]ark of testimony with it: and shall put thereon the covering of [e] Ex. 25. 10,
badgers' skins, and shall spread over *it* a cloth wholly of blue, 16.
7 and shall put in [f]the staves thereof. And upon the [g]table of [f] Ex. 25. 13.
shewbread they shall spread a cloth of blue, and put thereon [g] Ex. 25. 23, 29, 30.
the dishes, and the spoons, and the bowls, and covers to [1]cover Lev. 24. 6, 8.
8 withal: and the continual bread shall be thereon: and they
shall spread upon them a cloth of scarlet, and cover the same
with a covering of badgers' skins, and shall put in the staves
9 thereof. And they shall take a cloth of blue, and cover the

[1] Or, *pour out withal.*

Divine Blessing, may be found in the sudden development of national energies which would immediately ensue on the Exodus. Before that event, the miserable estate of the people, and especially the inhuman order for the destruction of their first-born, would check very seriously the ratio of marriages and births; and this ratio would naturally, when the check was removed, exhibit a sudden and striking increase.

44–51. This redemption money (see marg. reff.) would perhaps be exacted from the parents of the *youngest* children of the 22,273 (*v.* 43). The cattle of the Levites was doubtless taken in the gross as an equivalent for the first-born cattle of the other tribes, which of course, no less than the first-born of men, belonged to the Lord; and in future would have to be redeemed (xviii. 15; Deut. xv. 19).

IV. **4.** *about the most holy things*] Omit "about." The sense is, "this is the charge of the sons of Kohath, the most holy things:" *i.e.* the Ark of the Covenant, the Table of Shewbread, the Candlestick, and the Golden Altar, together with the furniture pertaining thereto. It appears, from a comparison of *vv.* 16, 28, and 33, that the ministry of the Kohathites was superintended by Eleazar, the elder of the two surviving sons of Aaron; and that of the two other families by Ithamar.

6. *wholly of blue*] Cp. Ex. xxv. 4 note. The third and external covering of the Ark only was to be of this colour. The Table of Shewbread had (*v.* 8) an outer wrapping of scarlet; the Altar (*v.* 13) one of purple.

put in the staves] Probably, "put the staves in order." These were never taken out of the golden rings by which the Ark was to be borne (see Ex. xxv. 14, 15), but would need adjustment.

[h]candlestick of the light, [i]and his lamps, and his tongs, and
his snuffdishes, and all the oil vessels thereof, wherewith they
10 minister unto it: and they shall put it and all the vessels
thereof within a covering of badgers' skins, and shall put *it* upon
11 a bar. And upon [k]the golden altar they shall spread a cloth of
blue, and cover it with a covering of badgers' skins, and shall
12 put to the staves thereof: and they shall take all the instruments of ministry, wherewith they minister in the sanctuary,
and put *them* in a cloth of blue, and cover them with a covering
13 of badgers' skins, and shall put *them* on a bar: and they shall
take away the ashes from the altar, and spread a purple cloth
14 thereon: and they shall put upon it all the vessels thereof,
wherewith they minister about it, *even* the censers, the fleshhooks, and the shovels, and the [1]basons, all the vessels of the
altar; and they shall spread upon it a covering of badgers' skins,
15 and put to the staves of it. And when Aaron and his sons have
made an end of covering the sanctuary, and all the vessels of the
sanctuary, as the camp is to set forward; after that, [l]the sons
of Kohath shall come to bear *it:* [m]but they shall not touch *any*
holy thing, lest they die. [n]These *things are* the burden of the
16 sons of Kohath in the tabernacle of the congregation. ¶ And to
the office of Eleazar the son of Aaron the priest *pertaineth* [o]the
oil for the light, and the [p]sweet incense, and [q]the daily meat
offering, and the [r]anointing oil, *and* the oversight of all the
tabernacle, and of all that therein *is*, in the sanctuary, and in
17 the vessels thereof. ¶ And the LORD spake unto Moses and
18 unto Aaron, saying, Cut ye not off the tribe of the families of
19 the Kohathites from among the Levites: but thus do unto them,
that they may live, and not die, when they approach unto [s]the
most holy things: Aaron and his sons shall go in, and appoint
20 them every one to his service and to his burden: [t]but they
shall not go in to see when the holy things are covered, lest they
21, 22 die. ¶ And the LORD spake unto Moses, saying, Take also
the sum of the sons of Gershon, throughout the houses of their
23 fathers, by their families; [u]from thirty years old and upward
until fifty years old shalt thou number them; all that enter in
[2]to perform the service, to do the work in the tabernacle of the
24 congregation. This *is* the service of the families of the Ger-
25 shonites, to serve, and for [3]burdens: and [x]they shall bear the
curtains of the tabernacle, and the tabernacle of the congregation, his covering, and the covering of the badgers' skins that
is above upon it, and the hanging for the door of the tabernacle
26 of the congregation, and the hangings of the court, and the
hanging for the door of the gate of the court, which *is* by the
tabernacle and by the altar round about, and their cords, and all
the instruments of their service, and all that is made for them:
27 so shall they serve. At the [4]appointment of Aaron and his sons
shall be all the service of the sons of the Gershonites, in all their

[h] Ex. 25. 31.
[i] Ex. 25. 37, 38.
[k] Ex. 30. 1, 3.
[l] ch. 7. 9. & 10. 21. Deut. 31. 9. 2 Sam. 6. 13. 1 Chr. 15. 2, 15.
[m] 2 Sam. 6. 6, 7. 1 Chr. 13. 9, 10.
[n] ch. 3. 31.
[o] Ex. 25. 6. Lev. 24. 2.
[p] Ex. 30. 34.
[q] Ex. 29. 40.
[r] Ex. 30. 23.
[s] ver. 4.
[t] See Ex. 19. 21. 1 Sam. 6. 19.
[u] ver. 3.
[x] ch. 3. 25, 26.

[1] Or, *bowls.*
[2] Heb. *to war the warfare.*
[3] Or, *carriage.*
[4] Heb. *mouth.*

---

20. *to see when the holy things are covered*] Render: **to see the holy things for an instant.** The expression means literally "as a gulp," *i.e.* for the instant it takes to swallow.

23. *enter in to perform the service*] Lit. as in marg. "to war the warfare," or, as the same phrase in part is rendered, *v.* 3, "enter into the host to do the work." The language is military. The service of God is a sacred warfare (viii. 24, 25 marg. reading).

burdens, and in all their service: and ye shall appoint unto
28 them in charge all their burdens. This *is* the service of the
families of the sons of Gershon in the tabernacle of the congregation: and their charge *shall be* under the hand of Ithamar
29 the son of Aaron the priest. ¶ As for the sons of Merari, thou
shalt number them after their families, by the house of their
30 fathers; [y]from thirty years old and upward even unto fifty years — [y] ver. 3.
old shalt thou number them, every one that entereth into the
[1]service, to do the work of the tabernacle of the congregation.
31 And [z]this *is* the charge of their burden, according to all their — [z] ch. 3. 36, 37.
service in the tabernacle of the congregation; [a]the boards of — [a] Ex. 26. 15.
the tabernacle, and the bars thereof, and the pillars thereof, and
32 sockets thereof, and the pillars of the court round about, and
their sockets and their pins, and their cords, with all their
instruments, and with all their service: and by name ye shall
33 [b]reckon the instruments of the charge of their burden. This *is* — [b] Ex. 38. 21.
the service of the families of the sons of Merari, according to all
their service, in the tabernacle of the congregation, under the
34 hand of Ithamar the son of Aaron the priest. ¶ [c]And Moses and — [c] ver. 2.
Aaron and the chief of the congregation numbered the sons of
the Kohathites after their families, and after the house of their
35 fathers, from thirty years old and upward even unto fifty years
old, every one that entereth into the service, for the work in the
36 tabernacle of the congregation: and those that were numbered
of them by their families were two thousand seven hundred and
37 fifty. These *were* they that were numbered of the families of the
Kohathites, all that might do service in the tabernacle of the congregation, which Moses and Aaron did number according to the
38 commandment of the LORD by the hand of Moses. ¶ And those
that were numbered of the sons of Gershon, throughout their
39 families, and by the house of their fathers, from thirty years
old and upward even unto fifty years old, every one that entereth
into the service, for the work in the tabernacle of the congre-
40 gation, even those that were numbered of them, throughout their
families, by the house of their fathers, were two thousand and
41 six hundred and thirty. [d]These *are* they that were numbered — [d] ver. 22.
of the families of the sons of Gershon, of all that might do service in the tabernacle of the congregation, whom Moses and
Aaron did number according to the commandment of the LORD.
42 ¶ And those that were numbered of the families of the sons of
Merari, throughout their families, by the house of their fathers,
43 from thirty years old and upward even unto fifty years old,
every one that entereth into the service, for the work in the taber-
44 nacle of the congregation, even those that were numbered of
them after their families, were three thousand and two hundred.
45 These *be* those that were numbered of the families of the sons of
Merari, whom Moses and Aaron numbered [e]according to the — [e] ver. 29.

[1] Heb. *warfare*.

28, 33. The Gershonites and Merarites are superintended by Ithamar, Aaron's younger son, who had already had the oversight of the Tabernacle in its construction (Ex. xxxviii. 21). Thus readily do the permanent offices of the leaders of the Israelite community spring out of the duties which, under the emergencies of the first year of the Exodus, they had been led, from time to time, to undertake.

32. *by name ye shall reckon the instruments*] Or, assign them to their bearers singly, and "by name." These "instruments" comprised the heavier parts of the Tabernacle; and the order seems intended to prevent individual Merarites choosing their own burden, and so throwing more than the proper share on others.

46 word of the LORD by the hand of Moses. ¶ All those that were
numbered of the Levites, whom Moses and Aaron and the chief
of Israel numbered, after their families, and after the house of
47 their fathers, [f]from thirty years old and upward even unto fifty
years old, every one that came to do the service of the ministry,
and the service of the burden in the tabernacle of the congre-
48 gation, even those that were numbered of them, were eight
49 thousand and five hundred and fourscore. According to the
commandment of the LORD they were numbered by the hand of
Moses, [g]every one according to his service, and according to his
burden: thus were they numbered of him, [h]as the LORD commanded Moses.

CHAP. 5. AND the LORD spake unto Moses, saying, Command the
2 children of Israel, that they put out of the camp every [a]leper,
and every one that hath an [b]issue, and whosoever is defiled by
3 the [c]dead: both male and female shall ye put out, without the
camp shall ye put them; that they defile not their camps, [d]in
4 the midst whereof I dwell. And the children of Israel did so,
and put them out without the camp: as the LORD spake unto
5 Moses, so did the children of Israel. ¶ And the LORD spake
6 unto Moses, saying, Speak unto the children of Israel, [e]When a
man or woman shall commit any sin that men commit, to do a
7 trespass against the LORD, and that person be guilty; [f]then they
shall confess their sin which they have done: and he shall recompense his trespass [g]with the principal thereof, and add unto it
the fifth *part* thereof, and give *it* unto *him* against whom he hath
8 trespassed. But if the man have no kinsman to recompense the
trespass unto, let the trespass be recompensed unto the LORD,
even to the priest; beside [h]the ram of the atonement, whereby an
9 atonement shall be made for him. And every [1][i]offering of all
the holy things of the children of Israel, which they bring unto
10 the priest, shall be his. And every man's hallowed things shall
be his: whatsoever any man giveth the priest, it shall be [k]his.
11, 12 ¶ And the LORD spake unto Moses, saying, Speak unto the
children of Israel, and say unto them, If any man's wife go
13 aside, and commit a trespass against him, and a man [l]lie with her
carnally, and it be hid from the eyes of her husband, and be kept

[f] ver. 3, 23, 30.
[g] ver. 15, 24, 31.
[h] ver. 1. 21.
[a] Lev. 13. 3, 46. & ch. 12. 14.
[b] Lev. 15. 2.
[c] Lev. 21. 1. ch. 9. 6, 10. & 19. 11, 13. & 31. 19.
[d] Lev. 26. 11, 12. 2 Cor. 6. 16.
[e] Lev. 6. 2, 3.
[f] Lev. 5. 5. & 26. 40. Josh. 7. 19.
[g] Lev. 6. 5.
[h] Lev. 6. 6, 7. & 7. 7.
[i] Ex. 29. 28. Lev. 6. 17, 18, 26. & 7. 6, 7, 9, 10, 14. ch. 18. 8, 9, 19. Deut. 18. 3, 4. Ez. 44. 29, 30.
[k] Lev. 10. 13.
[l] Lev. 18. 20.

[1] Or, *heave offering*.

V. The general purpose of the directions given in this and the next chapter is to attest and to vindicate, by modes in harmony with the spirit of the theocratical law, the sanctity of the people of God. Thus the congregation of Israel was made to typify the Church of God, within which, in its perfection, nothing that offends can be allowed to remain (cp. St. Matt. viii. 22; Rev. xxi. 27).

1–4. Cp. marg. reff. The precepts of Lev. xiii. and xv. are now first fully carried out. They could hardly have been so earlier, during the hurry and confusion which must have attended the march out of Egypt, and the encampments which next followed.

5–10. The Law of restitution: a passage supplementary to Lev. v. 5, &c., vi. 5, &c.

7. *recompense his trespass*] *i.e.* make restitution to the person whom he has injured.

8. *whereby an atonement shall be made for him*] Lit. "which shall clear him of guilt as to it," *i.e.* as to the trespass.

10. *And every man's hallowed things shall be his*] *i.e.* the priest's. The heave offerings (*v.* 9) and dedicatory offerings (*e.g.* first-fruits) were to be the perquisite of the officiating priests.

11–31. The trial of jealousy. As the crime of adultery is peculiarly defiling and destructive of the very foundations of social order, the whole subject is dealt with at a length proportionate to its importance. The process prescribed has lately been strikingly illustrated from an Egyptian "Romance," which refers to the time of Rameses the Great, and may therefore well serve to illustrate the manners and customs of the Mosaic times. This mode of trial, like several other ordinances, was adopted by Moses from existing and probably very ancient and widely spread institutions.

close, and she be defiled, and *there be* no witness against her,
14 neither she be taken *with the manner;* and the spirit of jealousy
come upon him, and he be jealous of his wife, and she be defiled:
or if the spirit of jealousy come upon him, and he be jealous of
15 his wife, and she be not defiled: then shall the man bring his
wife unto the priest, and he shall bring her offering for her, the
tenth *part* of an ephah of barley meal; he shall pour no oil upon
it, nor put frankincense thereon; for it *is* an offering of jealousy,
an offering of memorial, [m]bringing iniquity to remembrance. [m] 1 Kin. 17.
16 And the priest shall bring her near, and set her before the 18.
17 LORD: and the priest shall take holy water in an earthen vessel; Ez. 29. 16.
and of the dust that is in the floor of the tabernacle the priest
18 shall take, and put *it* into the water: and the priest shall set
the woman before the LORD, and uncover the woman's head, and
put the offering of memorial in her hands, which *is* the jealousy
offering: and the priest shall have in his hand the bitter water
19 that causeth the curse: and the priest shall charge her by an
oath, and say unto the woman, If no man have lain with thee,
and if thou hast not gone aside to uncleanness [1,2]*with another*
instead of thy husband, be thou free from this bitter water that
20 causeth the curse: but if thou hast gone aside *to another* instead
of thy husband, and if thou be defiled, and some man have lain
21 with thee beside thine husband: then the priest shall [n]charge [n] Josh. 6. 26.
the woman with an oath of cursing, and the priest shall say unto 1 Sam. 14. 24. Neh. 10. 29.
the woman, [o]The LORD make thee a curse and an oath among [o] Jer. 29. 22.
thy people, when the LORD doth make thy thigh to [3]rot, and thy
22 belly to swell; and this water that causeth the curse [p]shall go [p] Ps. 109. 18.
into thy bowels to make *thy* belly to swell, and *thy* thigh to
23 rot: [q]And the woman shall say, Amen, amen. And the priest [q] Deut. 27.
shall write these curses in a book, and he shall blot *them* out 15.
24 with the bitter water: and he shall cause the woman to drink
the bitter water that causeth the curse: and the water that
causeth the curse shall enter into her, *and become* bitter.
25 Then the priest shall take the jealousy offering out of the
woman's hand, and shall [r]wave the offering before the LORD, and [r] Lev. 8. 27.
26 offer it upon the altar: [s]and the priest shall take an handful of [s] Lev. 2. 2, 9.
the offering, *even* the memorial thereof, and burn *it* upon the
altar, and afterward shall cause the woman to drink the water.
27 And when he hath made her to drink the water, then it shall come

[1] Or, being *in the power of thy husband*, Rom. 7. 2.
[2] Heb. *under thy husband.*
[3] Heb. *fall.*

---

15. The offering was to be of the cheapest and coarsest kind, barley (cp. 2 K. vii. 1, 16, 18), representing the abased condition of the suspected woman. It was, like the sin-offering (Lev. v. 11), to be made without oil and frankincense, the symbols of grace and acceptableness. The woman herself stood with head uncovered (*v.* 18), in token of her shame.

17. *the dust that is in the floor of the tabernacle*] To set forth the fact that the water was indued with extraordinary power by Him Who dwelt in the Tabernacle. Dust is an emblem of a state of condemnation (Gen. iii. 14; Micah vii. 17).

19. *gone aside,* &c.] Literally, "gone astray from" **thy husband by uncleanness**; cp. Hos. iv. 12.

23. *blot them out with the bitter water*] In order to transfer the curses to the water. The action was symbolical. Travellers speak of the natives of Africa as still habitually seeking to obtain the full force of a written charm by drinking the water into which they have washed it.

24. *shall cause the woman to drink*] Thus was symbolised both her full acceptance of the hypothetical curse (cp. Ezek. iii. 1–3; Jer. xv. 16; Rev. x. 9), and its actual operation upon her if she should be guilty (cp. Ps. cix. 18).

26. *the memorial thereof*] See marg. ref. "Memorial" here is not the same as "memorial" in *v.* 15.

27. Of itself, the drink was not noxious; and could only produce the effects here de-

to pass, *that*, if she be defiled, and have done trespass against
her husband, that the water that causeth the curse shall enter
into her, *and become* bitter, and her belly shall swell, and her
thigh shall rot: and the woman [t]shall be a curse among her
28 people. And if the woman be not defiled, but be clean; then
29 she shall be free, and shall conceive seed. ¶ This *is* the law of
jealousies, when a wife goeth aside *to another* [u]instead of her
30 husband, and is defiled; or when the spirit of jealousy cometh
upon him, and he be jealous over his wife, and shall set the
woman before the LORD, and the priest shall execute upon her
31 all this law. Then shall the man be guiltless from iniquity, and
this woman [x]shall bear her iniquity.
CHAP. 6. AND the LORD spake unto Moses, saying, Speak unto the
2 children of Israel, and say unto them, When either man or
woman shall [1a]separate *themselves* to vow a vow of a Nazarite, to
3 separate *themselves* unto the LORD: [b]he shall separate *himself*
from wine and strong drink, and shall drink no vinegar of wine,
or vinegar of strong drink, neither shall he drink any liquor of
4 grapes, nor eat moist grapes, or dried. All the days of his
[2]separation shall he eat nothing that is made of the [3]vine tree,
5 from the kernels even to the husk. All the days of the vow of
his separation there shall no [c]razor come upon his head: until
the days be fulfilled, in the which he separateth *himself* unto the
LORD, he shall be holy, *and* shall let the locks of the hair of his
6 head grow. All the days that he separateth *himself* unto the
7 LORD [d]he shall come at no dead body. [e]He shall not make
himself unclean for his father, or for his mother, for his brother,
or for his sister, when they die: because the [4]consecration of his

[t] Deut. 28. 37. Ps. 83. 9, 11. Jer. 24. 9. & 29. 18, 22. & 42. 18. Zech. 8. 13.
[u] ver. 19.
[x] Lev. 20. 17, 19, 20.
[a] Lev. 27. 2. Judg. 13. 5. Acts 21. 23. Rom. 1. 1.
[b] Amos 2. 12. Luke 1. 15.
[c] Judg. 13. 5. & 16. 17. 1 Sam. 1. 11.
[d] Lev. 21. 11. ch. 19. 11, 16.
[e] Lev. 21. 1, 2, 11. ch. 9. 6.

[1] Or, *make* themselves *Nazarites.*
[2] Or, *Nazariteship.*
[3] Heb. *vine of the wine.*
[4] Heb. *separation.*

---

scribed by a special interposition of God. We do not read of any instance in which this ordeal was resorted to: a fact which may be explained either (with the Jews) as a proof of its efficacy, since the guilty could not be brought to face its terrors at all, and avoided them by confession; or more probably by the license of divorce tolerated by the law of Moses. Since a husband could put away his wife at pleasure, a jealous man would naturally prefer to take this course with a suspected wife rather than to call public attention to his own shame by having recourse to the trial of jealousy.

The trial by Red water, which bears a general resemblance to that here prescribed by Moses, is still in use amongst the tribes of Western Africa.

VI. **1–21.** The law of the Nazarite is appropriately added to other enactments which concern the sanctity of the holy nation. That sanctity found its highest expression in the Nazarite vow, which was the voluntary adoption for a time of obligations to high and strict modes of self-dedication resembling, and indeed in some particulars exceeding, those under which the priests were placed. The present enactments do not institute a new kind of observance, but only regulate one already familiar to the Israelites (*v.* 2).

2. *a Nazarite*] Strictly, *Nazirite.* This term signifies "separated," *i.e.*, as the words following show, "unto God." It became a technical term at an early date; cp. Judg. xiii. 5, 7, xvi. 17.

3. *liquor of grapes*] *i.e.* a drink made of grape-skins macerated in water.

4. *from the kernels even to the husk*] A sour drink was made from the stones of unripe grapes; and cakes were also made of the husks (Hos. iii. 1). This interdict figures that separation from the general society of men to which the Nazarite for the time was consecrated.

5. Amongst the Jews the abundance of the hair was considered to betoken physical strength and perfection (cp. 2 S. xiv. 25, 26), and baldness was regarded as a grave blemish (cp. Lev. xxi. 20 note, xiii. 40 seq.; 2 K. ii. 23; Isai. iii. 24). Thus the free growth of the hair on the head of the Nazarite represented the dedication of the man with all his strength and powers to the service of God.

7. *the consecration of his God*] *i.e.* the unshorn locks: cp. Lev. xxv. 5 note, where the vine, left during the Sabbatical year untouched by the hand of man, either for pruning or for vintage, is called simply a "Nazarite."

The third rule of the Nazarite interdicted

8 God *is* upon his head. All the days of his separation he *is* holy
9 unto the LORD. And if any man die very suddenly by him, and
he hath defiled the head of his consecration; then he shall
[f]shave his head in the day of his cleansing, on the seventh day   [f] Acts 18. 18.
10 shall he shave it. And [g]on the eighth day he shall bring two   & 21. 24. [g] Lev. 5. 7.
turtles, or two young pigeons, to the priest, to the door of the   & 14. 22.
11 tabernacle of the congregation: and the priest shall offer the one   & 15. 14, 29.
for a sin offering, and the other for a burnt offering, and make
an atonement for him, for that he sinned by the dead, and shall
12 hallow his head that same day. And he shall consecrate unto
the LORD the days of his separation, and shall bring a lamb of
the first year [h]for a trespass offering: but the days that were   [h] Lev. 5. 6.
13 before shall [1]be lost, because his separation was defiled. ¶ And
this *is* the law of the Nazarite, [i]when the days of his separation   [i] Acts 21. 26.
are fulfilled: he shall be brought unto the door of the tabernacle
14 of the congregation: and he shall offer his offering unto the
LORD, one he lamb of the first year without blemish for a burnt
offering, and one ewe lamb of the first year without blemish [k]for   [k] Lev. 4. 2,
a sin offering, and one ram without blemish [l]for peace offerings,   27, 32. [l] Lev. 3. 6.
15 and a basket of unleavened bread, [m]cakes of fine flour mingled   [m] Lev. 2. 4.
with oil, and wafers of unleavened bread [n]anointed with oil, and   [n] Ex. 29. 2.
16 their meat offering, and their [o]drink offering. And the priest   [o] ch. 15. 5,
shall bring *them* before the LORD, and shall offer his sin offering,   7, 10.
17 and his burnt offering: and he shall offer the ram *for* a sacrifice
of peace offerings unto the LORD, with the basket of unleavened
bread: the priest shall offer also his meat offering, and his drink
18 offering. [p]And the Nazarite shall shave the head of his sepa-   [p] Acts 21. 24.
ration *at* the door of the tabernacle of the congregation, and shall
take the hair of the head of his separation, and put *it* in the fire
19 which *is* under the sacrifice of the peace offerings. And the
priest shall take the [q]sodden shoulder of the ram, and one un-   [q] 1 Sam. 2.
leavened cake out of the basket, and one unleavened wafer,   15.
and [r]shall put *them* upon the hands of the Nazarite, after *the*   [r] Ex. 29. 23,
20 *hair of* his separation is shaven: and the priest shall wave them   24.

[1] Heb. *fall.*

---

him from contracting any ceremonial defilement even under circumstances which excused such defilement in others: cp. Lev. xxi. 1–3.

9–12. Prescriptions to meet the case of a sudden death taking place "by him" (*i.e.* in his presence). The days of the dedication of the Nazarite had to be recommenced.

13. *when the days of his separation are fulfilled*] Perpetual Nazariteship was probably unknown in the days of Moses; but the examples of Samson, Samuel, and John the Baptist, show that it was in later times undertaken for life. Again, Moses does not expressly require that limits should be assigned to the vow; but a rule was afterwards imposed that no Nazarite vow should be taken for less than thirty days. To permit the vow to be taken for very short periods would diminish its solemnity and estimation.

14, 15. The sin-offering (cp. marg. reff.), though named second, was in practice offered first, being intended to expiate involuntary sins committed during the period of separation. The burnt-offering (Lev. i. 10 sqq.) denoted the self-surrender on which alone all acceptableness in the Nazarite before God must rest; the peace-offerings (Lev. iii. 12 sqq.) expressed thankfulness to God by whose grace the vow had been fulfilled. The offerings, both ordinary and additional, required on the completion of the Nazarite vow involved considerable expense, and it was regarded as a pious work to provide the poor with the means of making them (cp. Acts xxi. 23 sqq.; 1 Macc. iii. 49).

18. *shave the head*] As the Nazarite had during his vow worn his hair unshorn in honour of God, so when the time was complete it was natural that the hair, the symbol of his vow, should be cut off, and offered to God at the sanctuary. The burning of the hair "in the fire under the sacrifice of the peace offering," represented the eucharistic communion with God obtained by those who realised the ideal which the Nazarite set forth (cp. marg. ref.).

for a wave offering before the LORD: [s]this *is* holy for the priest,
with the wave breast and heave shoulder: and after that the
21 Nazarite may drink wine. This *is* the law of the Nazarite who
hath vowed, *and of* his offering unto the LORD for his separation,
beside *that* that his hand shall get: according to the vow which
22 he vowed, so he must do after the law of his separation. ¶ And
23 the LORD spake unto Moses, saying, Speak unto Aaron and unto
his sons, saying, On this wise [t]ye shall bless the children of
Israel, saying unto them,
24 The LORD bless thee, and [u]keep thee:
25 The LORD [w]make his face shine upon thee, and [x]be gracious
unto thee:
26 [y]The LORD lift up his countenance upon thee, and [z]give thee
peace.
27 [a]And they shall put my name upon the children of Israel; and
[b]I will bless them.
CHAP. 7. AND it came to pass on the day that Moses had fully [a]set
up the tabernacle, and had anointed it, and sanctified it, and all
the instruments thereof, both the altar and all the vessels thereof,
2 and had anointed them, and sanctified them; that [b]the princes
of Israel, heads of the house of their fathers, who *were* the
princes of the tribes, [1]and were over them that were numbered,

[s] Ex. 29. 27, 28.
[t] Lev. 9. 22. 1 Chr. 23. 13.
[u] Ps. 121. 7. John 17. 11.
[w] Ps. 31. 16. Dan. 9. 17.
[x] Gen. 43. 29.
[y] Ps. 4. 6.
[z] John 14. 27. 2 Thes. 3. 16.
[a] Deut. 28. 10. 2 Chr. 7. 14. Isai. 43. 7. Dan. 9. 18.
[b] Ps. 115. 12.
[a] Ex. 40. 18. Lev. 8. 10, 11.
[b] ch. 1. 4.

[1] Heb. *who stood.*

---

20. *the priest shall wave them*] i.e. by placing his hands under those of the Nazarite: cp. Lev. vii. 30.

21. *beside that that his hand shall get*] The Nazarite, in addition to the offerings prescribed above, was to present free-will offerings according to his possessions or means.

22–27. The priestly blessing (cp. Ecclus. xxxvi. 17) is appointed as a solemn form to be used by the priests exclusively, and in this function their office as it were culminates (cp. Lev. ix. 22 note). God Himself provides a formula, through which from time to time, as His people by obedience place themselves in true and right relationship to Him, the authorised mediators may pronounce and communicate His special blessing to them. It was a Jewish tradition that this blessing was given at the close of the daily sacrifice.

The structure of the blessing is remarkable. It is rhythmical, consists of three distinct parts, and mounts by gradual stages to that peace which forms the last and most consummate gift which God can give His people.

From a Christian point of view, and comparing the counterpart benediction of 2 Cor. xiii. 14, it is impossible not to see shadowed forth the doctrine of the Holy Trinity (cp. Isai. vi. 3; Matt. xxviii. 19). And the three several sets of terms correspond fittingly to the office of the Three Persons in Their gracious work for the redemption of man.

24. *The* LORD *bless thee, and keep thee*] The second clause here, as in the other three verses, defines more closely the general tenor of the preceding one. The singular number, which is observed throughout, indicates that the blessing is conferred on Israel *collectively*.

25. *make his face shine*] This is an enhancement of the preceding benediction. "The face of God" imports not merely God's good will in general, but His active and special regard. With the "face" or "eye of the Lord" accordingly is connected alike the judicial visitation of the wicked (Ps. xxxiv. 16), and His mercies to the righteous (Ps. iv. 6).

26. *lift up his countenance upon thee*] i.e. specially direct His thought and care towards thee: cp. 2 K. ix. 32, and similar phrases in Gen. xliii. 29, xliv. 21. Through such loving providence alone could the peace of God in which the blessing closes be given.

27. *put my name upon the children of Israel*] i.e. pronounce My Sacred Name over them in blessing them. God will give effect to the benediction pronounced by the priests.

VII. **1.** *on the day that*] i.e. "at the time that," cp. Gen. ii. 4. The presentation of the gifts in fact occupied twelve days, as the sequel shows.

The enactments set forth in the chapters from Lev. x. to Num. vi. inclusive, were doubtless promulgated at various times between the consecration of the Tabernacle and the departure from Sinai, but are for convenience set out connectedly. The contents of the present chapter are accordingly placed after them. The order pursued throughout is justly noted as one which would naturally suggest itself to a narrator who was contemporary with the events.

3 offered: and they brought their offering before the LORD, six
covered wagons, and twelve oxen; a wagon for two of the
princes, and for each one an ox: and they brought them before
4, 5 the tabernacle. And the LORD spake unto Moses, saying, Take
it of them, that they may be to do the service of the tabernacle
of the congregation; and thou shalt give them unto the Levites,
6 to every man according to his service. And Moses took the
7 wagons and the oxen, and gave them unto the Levites. Two
wagons and four oxen [c]he gave unto the sons of Gershon, [c] ch. 4. 25.
8 according to their service: [d]and four wagons and eight oxen [d] ch. 4. 31.
he gave unto the sons of Merari, according unto their service,
9 [e]under the hand of Ithamar the son of Aaron the priest. But [e] ch. 4. 28, 33.
unto the sons of Kohath he gave none: because [f]the service of [f] ch. 4. 15.
the sanctuary belonging unto them [g]*was that* they should bear [g] ch. 4. 6, 8, 10, 12, 14.
10 upon their shoulders. ¶And the princes offered for [h]dedi- 2 Sam. 6. 13.
cating of the altar in the day that it was anointed, even the [h] See Deut. 20. 5.
11 princes offered their offering before the altar. And the LORD
said unto Moses, They shall offer their offering, each prince on 1 Kin. 8. 63.
12 his day, for the dedicating of the altar. ¶And he that offered 2 Chr. 7. 5. Ezra 6. 16.
his offering the first day was [i]Nahshon the son of Amminadab, Neh. 12. 27. Ps. 30. title.
13 of the tribe of Judah: and his offering *was* one silver charger, [i] ch. 2. 3.
the weight thereof *was* an hundred and thirty *shekels*, one silver
bowl of seventy shekels, after [k]the shekel of the sanctuary; both [k] Ex. 30. 13.
of them *were* full of fine flour mingled with oil for a [l]meat offer- [l] Lev. 2. 1.
14, 15 ing: one spoon of ten *shekels* of gold, full of [m]incense: [n]one [m] Ex. 30. 34.
young bullock, one ram, one lamb of the first year, for a burnt [n] Lev. 1. 2.
16, 17 offering: one kid of the goats for a [o]sin offering: and for [o] Lev. 4. 23.
[p]a sacrifice of peace offerings, two oxen, five rams, five he goats, [p] Lev. 3. 1.
five lambs of the first year: this *was* the offering of Nahshon the
18 son of Amminadab. ¶On the second day Nethaneel the son of
19 Zuar, prince of Issachar, did offer: he offered *for* his offering one
silver charger, the weight whereof *was* an hundred and thirty
shekels, one silver bowl of seventy shekels, after the shekel of the
sanctuary; both of them full of fine flour mingled with oil for a
20, 21 meat offering: one spoon of gold of ten *shekels*, full of incense:
one young bullock, one ram, one lamb of the first year, for a burnt
22, 23 offering: one kid of the goats for a sin offering: and for a
sacrifice of peace offerings, two oxen, five rams, five he goats,
five lambs of the first year: this *was* the offering of Nethaneel
24 the son of Zuar. ¶On the third day Eliab the son of Helon,
25 prince of the children of Zebulun, *did offer:* his offering *was*
one silver charger, the weight whereof *was* an hundred and
thirty *shekels*, one silver bowl of seventy shekels, after the shekel of the sanctuary; both of them full of fine flour mingled with
26 oil, for a meat offering: one golden spoon of ten *shekels*, full of
27 incense: one young bullock, one ram, one lamb of the first
28 year, for a burnt offering: one kid of the goats for a sin offering:

---

3. *covered wagons*] Some prefer to render "litter (Isai. lxvi. 20) wagons:" *i.e.* litters which were not on wheels, but borne by two oxen, one in front and one behind. Such conveyances would probably be more convenient than wheeled wagons in the rough country to be traversed.

7–9. To the Gershonites, who had to transport the hangings and coverings of the Tabernacle, two wagons are assigned: to the Merarites, who had the charge of the solid parts of the Tabernacle, four wagons. The furniture and vessels the Kohathites were to carry on their own shoulders. Cp. iii. 25, 26, 31, 36, 37.

12–83. The several princes make their offerings in the order assigned to the tribes (ch. ii). It was doubtless the tribes themselves which presented these gifts through their chiefs. The twelve offerings are strictly alike, and were offered on twelve separate days.

29 and for a sacrifice of peace offerings, two oxen, five rams, five he
goats, five lambs of the first year: this *was* the offering of Eliab
30 the son of Helon. ¶ On the fourth day Elizur the son of Shedeur,
31 prince of the children of Reuben, *did offer:* his offering *was* one
silver charger of the weight of an hundred and thirty *shekels*,
one silver bowl of seventy shekels, after the shekel of the sanctuary; both of them full of fine flour mingled with oil for a
32 meat offering: one golden spoon of ten *shekels*, full of incense:
33 one young bullock, one ram, one lamb of the first year, for
34 a burnt offering: one kid of the goats for a sin offering:
35 and for a sacrifice of peace offerings, two oxen, five rams, five
he goats, five lambs of the first year: this *was* the offering of
36 Elizur the son of Shedeur. ¶ On the fifth day Shelumiel the son
37 of Zurishaddai, prince of the children of Simeon, *did offer:* his
offering *was* one silver charger, the weight whereof *was* an
hundred and thirty *shekels*, one silver bowl of seventy shekels,
after the shekel of the sanctuary; both of them full of fine flour
38 mingled with oil for a meat offering: one golden spoon of ten
39 *shekels*, full of incense: one young bullock, one ram, one lamb of
40 the first year, for a burnt offering: one kid of the goats for a sin
41 offering: and for a sacrifice of peace offerings, two oxen, five
rams, five he goats, five lambs of the first year: this *was* the
42 offering of Shelumiel the son of Zurishaddai. ¶ On the sixth
day Eliasaph the son of Deuel, prince of the children of Gad,
43 *offered:* his offering *was* one silver charger of the weight of an
hundred and thirty *shekels*, a silver bowl of seventy shekels,
after the shekel of the sanctuary; both of them full of fine flour
44 mingled with oil for a meat offering: one golden spoon of ten
45 *shekels*, full of incense: one young bullock, one ram, one lamb
46 of the first year, for a burnt offering: one kid of the goats for a
47 sin offering: and for a sacrifice of peace offerings, two oxen, five
rams, five he goats, five lambs of the first year: this *was* the
48 offering of Eliasaph the son of Deuel. ¶ On the seventh day
Elishama the son of Ammihud, prince of the children of Ephraim,
49 *offered:* his offering *was* one silver charger, the weight whereof
was an hundred and thirty *shekels*, one silver bowl of seventy
shekels, after the shekel of the sanctuary; both of them full of
50 fine flour mingled with oil for a meat offering: one golden spoon
51 of ten *shekels*, full of incense: one young bullock, one ram, one
52 lamb of the first year, for a burnt offering: one kid of the goats
53 for a sin offering: and for a sacrifice of peace offerings, two oxen,
five rams, five he goats, five lambs of the first year: this *was*
54 the offering of Elishama the son of Ammihud. On the eighth
day *offered* Gamaliel the son of Pedahzur, prince of the children
55 of Manasseh: his offering *was* one silver charger of the weight
of an hundred and thirty *shekels*, one silver bowl of seventy
shekels, after the shekel of the sanctuary; both of them full of
56 fine flour mingled with oil for a meat offering: one golden spoon
57 of ten *shekels*, full of incense: one young bullock, one ram, one
58 lamb of the first year, for a burnt offering: one kid of the goats
59 for a sin offering: and for a sacrifice of peace offerings, two
oxen, five rams, five he goats, five lambs of the first year: this
60 *was* the offering of Gamaliel the son of Pedahzur. ¶ On the
ninth day Abidan the son of Gideoni, prince of the children of
61 Benjamin, *offered:* his offering *was* one silver charger, the
weight whereof *was* an hundred and thirty *shekels*, one silver
bowl of seventy shekels, after the shekel of the sanctuary;

both of them full of fine flour mingled with oil for a meat offering:
62, 63 one golden spoon of ten *shekels*, full of incense: one young
bullock, one ram, one lamb of the first year, for a burnt offering:
64, 65 one kid of the goats for a sin offering: and for a sacrifice of
peace offerings, two oxen, five rams, five he goats, five lambs
of the first year: this was the offering of Abidan the son of
66 Gideoni. ¶ On the tenth day Ahiezer the son of Ammishaddai,
67 prince of the children of Dan, *offered:* his offering *was* one silver
charger, the weight whereof *was* an hundred and thirty *shekels*,
one silver bowl of seventy shekels, after the shekel of the sanctuary; both of them full of fine flour mingled with oil for a meat
68, 69 offering: one golden spoon of ten *shekels*, full of incense: one
young bullock, one ram, one lamb of the first year, for a burnt
70, 71 offering: one kid of the goats for a sin offering: and for a
sacrifice of peace offerings, two oxen, five rams, five he goats,
five lambs of the first year: this *was* the offering of Ahiezer
72 the son of Ammishaddai. ¶ On the eleventh day Pagiel the son
73 of Ocran, prince of the children of Asher, *offered:* his offering
was one silver charger, the weight whereof *was* an hundred and
thirty *shekels*, one silver bowl of seventy shekels, after the
shekel of the sanctuary; both of them full of fine flour mingled
74 with oil for a meat offering: one golden spoon of ten *shekels*, full
75 of incense: one young bullock, one ram, one lamb of the first
76 year, for a burnt offering: one kid of the goats for a sin offer-
77 ing: and for a sacrifice of peace offerings, two oxen, five rams,
five he goats, five lambs of the first year: this *was* the offering
78 of Pagiel the son of Ocran. ¶ On the twelfth day Ahira the son
79 of Enan, prince of the children of Naphtali, *offered:* his offering
was one silver charger, the weight whereof *was* an hundred and
thirty *shekels*, one silver bowl of seventy shekels, after the shekel
of the sanctuary; both of them full of fine flour mingled with
80 oil for a meat offering: one golden spoon of ten *shekels*, full of
81 incense: one young bullock, one ram, one lamb of the first year,
82 for a burnt offering: one kid of the goats for a sin offering:
83 and for a sacrifice of peace offerings, two oxen, five rams, five
he goats, five lambs of the first year: this *was* the offering of
84 Ahira the son of Enan. ¶ This *was* the dedication of the altar,
in the day when it was anointed, by the princes of Israel: twelve
chargers of silver, twelve silver bowls, twelve spoons of gold:
85 each charger of silver *weighing* an hundred and thirty *shekels*,
each bowl seventy: all the silver vessels *weighed* two thousand
86 and four hundred *shekels*, after the shekel of the sanctuary: the
golden spoons *were* twelve, full of incense, *weighing* ten *shekels*
apiece, after the shekel of the sanctuary: all the gold of the
87 spoons *was* an hundred and twenty *shekels*. All the oxen for the
burnt offering *were* twelve bullocks, the rams twelve, the lambs
of the first year twelve, with their meat offering: and the kids
88 of the goats for sin offering twelve. And all the oxen for the
sacrifice of the peace offerings *were* twenty and four bullocks,
the rams sixty, the he goats sixty, the lambs of the first year
sixty. This *was* the dedication of the altar, after that it was
89 [q]anointed. ¶ And when Moses was gone into the tabernacle of

[q] ver. 1.

84–88. The aggregate worth, by weight, of the whole of the offerings was about 438*l.* But the real worth of such a sum, when measured by the prices of clothing and food at that time, must have been vastly greater.

89. *with him*] *i.e.* as marg. "with God," not (as some) with himself.

he heard the voice of one speaking] Rather, **he heard the voice speaking**, or **conversing**. The effect was as though Moses was

the congregation [r]to speak with [1]him, then he heard [s]the voice
of one speaking unto him from off the mercy seat that *was* upon
the ark of testimony, from between the two cherubims: and he
spake unto him.

Chap. 8. AND the LORD spake unto Moses, saying, Speak unto
2 Aaron, and say unto him, When thou [a]lightest the lamps,
the seven lamps shall give light over against the candlestick.
3 And Aaron did so; he lighted the lamps thereof over against
4 the candlestick, as the LORD commanded Moses. [b]And this work
of the candlestick *was of* beaten gold, unto the shaft thereof,
unto the flowers thereof, *was* [c]beaten work: [d]according unto
the pattern which the LORD had shewed Moses, so he made the
5, 6 candlestick. ¶ And the LORD spake unto Moses, saying, Take
the Levites from among the children of Israel, and cleanse
7 them. And thus shalt thou do unto them, to cleanse them:
Sprinkle [e]water of purifying upon them, and [2][f]let them shave
all their flesh, and let them wash their clothes, and *so* make
8 themselves clean. Then let them take a young bullock with
[g]his meat offering, *even* fine flour mingled with oil, and another
9 young bullock shalt thou take for a sin offering. [h]And thou
shalt bring the Levites before the tabernacle of the congregation:
[i]and thou shalt gather the whole assembly of the children of
10 Israel together: and thou shalt bring the Levites before the
LORD: and the children of Israel [k]shall put their hands upon
11 the Levites: and Aaron shall [3]offer the Levites before the LORD
for an [4]offering of the children of Israel, that [5]they may execute
12 the service of the LORD. [l]And the Levites shall lay their hands

[r] ch. 12. 8. Ex. 33. 9. 11.
[s] Ex. 25. 22.
[a] Ex. 25. 37. & 40. 25.
[b] Ex. 25. 31.
[c] Ex. 25. 18.
[d] Ex. 25. 40.
[e] ch. 19. 9, 17, 18.
[f] Lev. 14. 8, 9.
[g] Lev. 2. 1.
[h] See Ex. 29. 4. & 40. 12.
[i] Lev. 8. 3.
[k] Lev. 1. 4.
[l] Ex. 29. 10.

1 That is, *God.*
2 Heb. *let them cause a razor to pass over, &c.*
3 Heb. *wave.*
4 Heb. *wave offering.*
5 Heb. *they may be to execute, &c.*

---

audibly addressed by another person: how this effect was produced we are not told.

Thus was the promise of Ex. xxv. 20–22 fulfilled; and that as an immediate response on the part of God to the cheerful readiness with which the tribes had made their offerings, and supplied everything needful for the Holy Place and its service. All being now complete as God had appointed, and the camp purified from defilements, God meets Moses the mediator of the people, not as before on the peak of Sinai far away, but in the midst of them, in the dwelling-place which He henceforth vouchsafed to tenant.

VIII. **1-4.** The actual lighting of the lamps (cp. marg. reff.) was to be done to set forth symbolically the peculiar Presence which God had now (vii. 89) actually established amongst His people.

5-22. The Levites could only undertake their duties (iii., iv.) after the formal exchange of the Levites for the first-born (iii. 44–51).

The distinction between the "consecration" of the priests (Lev. viii.) and the less solemn "purification" (*v.* 21) of the Levites is marked. These rites of purification are similar to those incumbent on the priests of Egypt.

7. *water of purifying*] Lit. "sin water:" *i.e.* water to cleanse from sin; no doubt taken from the laver of the Sanctuary, which was used by the priests for purification before they went into the Tabernacle to minister (cp. v. 17; Ex. xxx. 18 seq.).

The "sprinkling" of so large a body of men could have been only general, but tokens of individual purification are specified (cp. also Lev. xiv. 8).

8. The two bullocks were "to make an atonement for the Levites," and therefore are presented in their name. These offerings are similar to those prescribed in Lev. viii. 14 sqq. at the consecration of the priests, except that the burnt-offering was on that occasion a ram. The larger victim corresponds to the larger number of the Levites.

10. *the children of Israel*] *i.e.* through the heads of their tribes, who (vii. 2) no doubt acted for their tribesmen. This act, the distinguishing feature of the ceremony, represented the transfer to the Levites of the sacred duties originally incumbent on the whole people.

11. *Offer...offering*] Cp. the margin Aaron pointed to the Levites, and then waved his hands, indicating (cp. Lev. vii. 30 note) that the offering was dedicated to God, and, again, by grant from Him, withdrawn for the use of the priests.

upon the heads of the bullocks: and thou shalt offer the one *for*
a sin offering, and the other *for* a burnt offering, unto the LORD,
13 to make an atonement for the Levites. And thou shalt set the
Levites before Aaron, and before his sons, and offer them *for* an
14 offering unto the LORD. Thus shalt thou separate the Levites
from among the children of Israel: and the Levites shall be
15 [m]mine. And after that shall the Levites go in to do the service [m] ch. 3. 45.
of the tabernacle of the congregation: and thou shalt cleanse & 16. 9.
16 them, and [n]offer them *for* an offering. For they *are* wholly given [n] ver. 11. 13.
unto me from among the children of Israel; [o]instead of such as [o] ch. 3. 12,
open every womb, *even instead of* the firstborn of all the children 45.
17 of Israel, have I taken them unto me. [p]For all the firstborn of [p] Ex. 13. 2,
the children of Israel *are* mine, *both* man and beast: on the day 12, 13, 15.
that I smote every firstborn in the land of Egypt I sanctified ch. 3. 13. Luke 2. 23.
18 them for myself. And I have taken the Levites for all the first-
19 born of the children of Israel. And [q]I have given the Levites [q] ch. 3. 9.
as [1]a gift to Aaron and to his sons from among the children of
Israel, to do the service of the children of Israel in the tabernacle of the congregation, and to make an atonement for the
children of Israel: [r]that there be no plague among the children [r] ch. 1. 53.
of Israel, when the children of Israel come nigh unto the sanc- & 16. 46. & 18. 5.
20 tuary. ¶And Moses, and Aaron, and all the congregation of 2 Chr. 26. 16.
the children of Israel, did to the Levites according unto all that
the LORD commanded Moses concerning the Levites, so did the
21 children of Israel unto them. [s]And the Levites were purified, [s] ver. 7.
and they washed their clothes; [t]and Aaron offered them *as* an [t] ver. 11, 12.
offering before the LORD; and Aaron made an atonement for
22 them to cleanse them. [u]And after that went the Levites in to [u] ver. 15.
do their service in the tabernacle of the congregation before
Aaron, and before his sons: [x]as the LORD had commanded Moses [x] ver. 5.
23 concerning the Levites, so did they unto them. ¶And the
24 LORD spake unto Moses, saying, This *is it* that *belongeth* unto the
Levites: [y]from twenty and five years old and upward they [y] See ch. 4. 3.
shall go in [2]to wait upon the service of the tabernacle of the 1 Chr. 23.
25 congregation: and from the age of fifty years they shall [3]cease 3, 24, 27.
26 waiting upon the service *thereof*, and shall serve no more: but
shall minister with their brethren in the tabernacle of the congregation, [z]to keep the charge, and shall do no service. Thus shalt [z] ch. 1. 53.
thou do unto the Levites touching their charge.

CHAP. 9. AND the LORD spake unto Moses in the wilderness of
Sinai, in the first month of the second year after they were come

[1] Heb. *given*. [2] Heb. *to war the warfare of, &c.* 1 Tim. 1. 18. [3] Heb. *return from the warfare of the service.*

---

19. *make an atonement for the children of Israel*] *i.e.* by performing those services which were due from the children of Israel; the omission of which by the children of Israel would, but for the interposition of the Levites, have called down "wrath" from God, or (i. 53) *plague*. The institution of the Levites was an extension of that mediatorial system which the people themselves, terrified at the direct manifestations to them of the Divine Presence, desired; see Deut. v. 25. Further, it is suggested to us here as an act of mercy on the part of God; yet even the priests and Levites themselves were not always sufficiently heedful and reverent. Cp. xvii. 10; Lev. x. 1 seq.; 2 Sam. vi. 6 seq.

21. *were purified*] Rather, **purified themselves**; as directed in *v.* 7.

24. *twenty and five years old and upward*] The permanent limit as distinguished from the temporary (iv. 3, 23, 30), though David found it necessary to extend the period of the Levites' service by causing it to commence at 20 years of age (1 Chron. xxiii. 24-28). This rule continued in force from the time of David downwards (cp. on 2 Chron. xxxi. 17; Ezra iii. 8).

IX. 1-5. Passover at Sinai. This, as being kept in the first month, was prior in

2 out of the land of Egypt, saying, Let the children of Israel also
3 keep [a]the passover at his appointed season. In the fourteenth
day of this month, [1]at even, ye shall keep it in his appointed
season: according to all the rites of it, and according to all the
4 ceremonies thereof, shall ye keep it. And Moses spake unto the
5 children of Israel, that they should keep the passover. And
[b]they kept the passover on the fourteenth day of the first month
at even in the wilderness of Sinai: according to all that the
6 LORD commanded Moses, so did the children of Israel. ¶ And
there were certain men, who were [c]defiled by the dead body of a
man, that they could not keep the passover on that day: [d]and
7 they came before Moses and before Aaron on that day: and
those men said unto him, We *are* defiled by the dead body of a
man: wherefore are we kept back, that we may not offer an
offering of the LORD in his appointed season among the children
8 of Israel? And Moses said unto them, Stand still, and [e]I will
9 hear what the LORD will command concerning you. And the
10 LORD spake unto Moses, saying, Speak unto the children of
Israel, saying, If any man of you or of your posterity shall be
unclean by reason of a dead body, or *be* in a journey afar off,
11 yet he shall keep the passover unto the LORD. [f]The fourteenth
day of the second month at even they shall keep it, *and* [g]eat it
12 with unleavened bread and bitter *herbs*. [h]They shall leave none
of it unto the morning, [i]nor break any bone of it: [k]according to
13 all the ordinances of the passover they shall keep it. But the
man that *is* clean, and is not in a journey, and forbeareth to
keep the passover, even the same soul [l]shall be cut off from
among his people: because he [m]brought not the offering of the
14 LORD in his appointed season, that man shall [n]bear his sin. And
if a stranger shall sojourn among you, and will keep the passover
unto the LORD; according to the ordinance of the passover, and
according to the manner thereof, so shall he do: [o]ye shall have
one ordinance, both for the stranger, and for him that was born
15 in the land. ¶ And [p]on the day that the tabernacle was reared
up the cloud covered the tabernacle, *namely*, the tent of the testi-

[a] Ex. 12. 1. Lev. 23. 5. ch. 28. 16. Deut. 16. 1, 2.
[b] Josh. 5. 10.
[c] ch. 5. 2. & 19. 11, 16. See John 18. 28.
[d] Ex. 18. 15, 19, 26. ch. 27. 2.
[e] ch. 27. 5.
[f] 2 Chr. 30. 2, 15.
[g] Ex. 12. 8.
[h] Ex. 12. 10.
[i] Ex. 12. 46. John 19. 36.
[k] Ex. 12. 43.
[l] Gen. 17. 14. Ex. 12. 15.
[m] ver. 7.
[n] ch. 5. 31.
[o] Ex. 12. 49.
[p] Ex. 40. 34. Neh. 9. 12, 19. Ps. 78. 14.

[1] Heb. *between the two evenings*, Ex. 12. 6.

---

time to the numbering of ch. i. 1 seq., and to the other events narrated in this book. It is, however, recorded here as introductory to the ordinance of *vv.* 6–14 in this chapter respecting the supplementary Passover; the observance of which was one of the last occurrences during the halt at Sinai.

5. In some details, the present Passover differed both from that kept at the Exodus itself and from all subsequent Passovers. For example, the direction of Ex. xii. 22 could not be carried out in the letter whilst the people were dwelling in tents; and may be regarded as superseded by Lev. xvii. 3–6 (cp. Deut. xvi. 5 seq.).

In other points, such as how many lambs would be wanted, how the blood of the Paschal victims could be sprinkled upon the altar in the time specified, &c., the administrators of the Law of Moses would here, as elsewhere, have, from the nature of the case, power to order what might be requisite to carry the law into effect.

6. *certain men*] Probably Mishael and Elizaphan, who buried their cousins, Nadab and Abihu, within a week of this Passover (Lev. x. 4, 5).

11. The later Jews speak of this as the "little Passover." Coming, as it did, a month after the proper Passover, it afforded ample time for a man to purify himself from legal defilement, as also to return from any but a very distant journey. Cp. Hezekiah's act (2 Chron. xxx. 1–3).

12. *according to all the ordinances*] *i.e.* those relating to the Passover-lamb, not those concerning the feast; for the Little Passover lasted, according to the Jews, only one day; nor was it held to be needful that at it leaven should be put away out of the houses.

15. *the cloud,* &c.] The phenomenon first appeared at the Exodus itself, Ex. xiii. 21, 22. The cloud did not cover the whole structure, but the "tent of the testimony," *i.e.* the enclosure which contained the "Ark of the testimony" (Ex. xxv. 16, 22), and the

mony: and [q]at even there was upon the tabernacle as it were
16 the appearance of fire, until the morning. So it was alway: the
cloud covered it *by day*, and the appearance of fire by night.
17 And when the cloud [r]was taken up from the tabernacle, then
after that the children of Israel journeyed: and in the place
where the cloud abode, there the children of Israel pitched their
18 tents. At the commandment of the LORD the children of Israel
journeyed, and at the commandment of the LORD they pitched:
[s]as long as the cloud abode upon the tabernacle they rested in
19 their tents. And when the cloud [1]tarried long upon the tabernacle many days, then the children of Israel [t]kept the charge of
20 the LORD, and journeyed not. And *so* it was, when the cloud
was a few days upon the tabernacle; according to the commandment of the LORD they abode in their tents, and according to
21 the commandment of the LORD they journeyed. And *so* it was,
when the cloud [2]abode from even unto the morning, and *that* the
cloud was taken up in the morning, then they journeyed:
whether *it was* by day or by night that the cloud was taken up,
22 they journeyed. Or *whether it were* two days, or a month, or a
year, that the cloud tarried upon the tabernacle, remaining
thereon, the children of Israel [u]abode in their tents, and jour-
23 neyed not: but when it was taken up, they journeyed. At the
commandment of the LORD they rested in the tents, and at the
commandment of the LORD they journeyed: they [w]kept the
charge of the LORD, at the commandment of the LORD by the
hand of Moses.

CHAP. 10. AND the LORD spake unto Moses, saying, Make thee
2 two trumpets of silver; of a whole piece shalt thou make them:
that thou mayest use them for the [a]calling of the assembly, and
3 for the journeying of the camps. And when [b]they shall blow
with them, all the assembly shall assemble themselves to thee at
4 the door of the tabernacle of the congregation. And if they
blow *but* with one *trumpet*, then the princes, *which are* [c]heads
of the thousands of Israel, shall gather themselves unto thee.
5 When ye blow an alarm, then [d]the camps that lie on the east
6 parts shall go forward. When ye blow an alarm the second
time, then the camps that lie [e]on the south side shall take their
7 journey: they shall blow an alarm for their journeys. But when
the congregation is to be gathered together, [f]ye shall blow, but
8 ye shall not [g]sound an alarm. [h]And the sons of Aaron, the
priests, shall blow with the trumpets; and they shall be to you

[q] Ex. 13. 21. & 40. 38.
[r] Ex. 40. 36. ch. 10. 11, 33, 34. Ps. 80. 1.
[s] 1 Cor. 10. 1.
[t] ch. 1. 53. & 3. 8.
[u] Ex. 40. 36, 37.
[w] ver. 19.
[a] Isai. 1. 13.
[b] Jer. 4. 5. Joel 2. 15.
[c] Ex. 18. 21. ch. 1. 16. & 7. 2.
[d] ch. 2. 3
[e] ch. 2. 10.
[f] ver. 3.
[g] Joel 2. 1.
[h] ch. 31. 6. Josh. 6. 4. 1 Chr. 15. 24.

[1] Heb. *prolonged*. [2] Heb. *was*.

Holy Place. The phenomenon is now again described in connexion with the journeyings which are to be narrated in the sequel of the book.

22. *a year*] Lit. "days," idiomatically a year (Lev. xxv. 29), an expression equivalent to "a full period," though not necessarily the period of a year.

X. **2.** The trumpet was a straight instrument, differing in this respect from the curved horn or cornet; and is represented, among the other spoils of the temple, on the Arch of Titus. See Ex. xxv. 23 cut. From Egyptian monuments it appears that the Jewish trumpet was copied from that used in the armies of the Pharaohs. The cornet was at first a simple ram's horn (Josh. vi. 4), and the metal instrument of later times preserved the original shape.

5, 6. *blow an alarm*] *i.e.* a long continuous peal. Cp. *v.* 7, *ye shall blow, but not sound an alarm: i.e.* blow in short, sharp notes, not in a continuous peal. A third and a fourth alarm were probably blown as signals.

8. *the sons of Aaron*] As the trumpets were emblematic of the voice of God, the priests only were to use them. At this time there were only two "sons of Aaron;" but in later times, when the number of priests was greater, more trumpets were used; we read of seven in the times of Joshua and

[i] ch. 31. 6. Josh. 6. 5. 2 Chr. 13. 14. [k] Judg. 2. 18. & 4. 3. 1 Sam. 10. 18. Ps. 106. 42. [l] Gen. 8. 1. Ps. 106. 4. [m] ch. 29. 1. Lev. 23. 24. 1 Chr. 15. 24. 2 Chr. 5. 12. Ezra 3. 10. Neh. 12. 35. Ps. 81. 3. [n] ver. 9. [o] ch. 9. 17. [p] Ex. 40. 36. ch. 2. 9, 16. [q] Ex. 19. 1. ch. 1. 1. & 9. 5. [r] Gen. 21. 21. ch. 12. 16. Deut. 1. 1. [s] ver. 5. 6. ch. 2. 34. [t] ch. 2. 3, 9. [u] ch. 1. 7. [x] ch. 1. 51. [y] ch. 4. 24, 31. & 7. 6. [z] ch. 2. 10, 16. [a] ch. 4. 4, 15. & 7. 9. [b] ch. 2. 18, 24. [c] ch. 2. 25, 31. Josh. 6. 9.

9 for an ordinance for ever throughout your generations. And [i]if
ye go to war in your land against the enemy that [k]oppresseth you,
then ye shall blow an alarm with the trumpets; and ye shall be
[l]remembered before the LORD your God, and ye shall be saved
10 from your enemies. Also [m]in the day of your gladness, and in
your solemn days, and in the beginnings of your months, ye shall
blow with the trumpets over your burnt offerings, and over the
sacrifices of your peace offerings; that they may be to you [n]for
11 a memorial before your God: I *am* the LORD your God. ¶ And
it came to pass on the twentieth *day* of the second month, in the
second year, that the cloud [o]was taken up from off the taber-
12 nacle of the testimony. And the children of Israel took [p]their
journeys out of the [q]wilderness of Sinai; and the cloud rested
13 in the [r]wilderness of Paran. And they first took their journey
[s]according to the commandment of the LORD by the hand of
14 Moses. ¶ [t]In the first *place* went the standard of the camp of
the children of Judah according to their armies: and over his
15 host *was* [u]Nahshon the son of Amminadab. And over the host
of the tribe of the children of Issachar *was* Nethaneel the son of
16 Zuar. And over the host of the tribe of the children of Zebulun
17 *was* Eliab the son of Helon. And the [x]tabernacle was taken
down; and the sons of Gershon and the sons of Merari set for-
18 ward, [y]bearing the tabernacle. ¶ And [z]the standard of the camp
of Reuben set forward according to their armies: and over his
19 host *was* Elizur the son of Shedeur. And over the host of the
tribe of the children of Simeon *was* Shelumiel the son of Zuri-
20 shaddai. And over the host of the tribe of the children of Gad
21 *was* Eliasaph the son of Deuel. And the Kohathites set forward,
bearing the [a]sanctuary: and [1]*the other* did set up the tabernacle
22 against they came. ¶ And [b]the standard of the camp of the
children of Ephraim set forward according to their armies: and
23 over his host *was* Elishama the son of Ammihud. And over the
host of the tribe of the children of Manasseh *was* Gamaliel the
24 son of Pedahzur. And over the host of the tribe of the children
25 of Benjamin *was* Abidan the son of Gideoni. ¶ And [c]the standard
of the camp of the children of Dan set forward, *which was* the

[1] That is, *the Gershonites and the Merarites:* See ver. 17. ch. 1. 51.

David (see marg. reff.); and of a hundred and twenty in that of Solomon (2 Chr. v. 12).

9. For examples of the employment of trumpets in war cp. marg. reff. and 2 Chr. xx. 28. By employment of them was signified the dependence of God's people on His aid.

10. *in the day of your gladness*] Cp. xxix. 1; Lev. xxiii. 24; 2 Chr. xxix. 27; Ezra iii. 10; Neh. xii. 35, 41; Ps. lxxxi. 3.

11. At this point commences the second great division of the book, extending to the close of chapter xiv. The remaining verses of the present chapter narrate the actual break up of the camp at Sinai and the order of the march.

12. *the wilderness of Paran*] See Gen. xiv. 6 note. The wilderness is mentioned here by anticipation. The earliest halting-places, Kibroth-hattaavah and Hazeroth, were not within its limits (xi. 35, xii. 16).

13. Rather, **And they journeyed** (or, set forth) **in the order of precedence according to** (*i.e.* established by) **the commandment of the Lord,** &c., and described in *vv.* 14–28.

14. *according to their armies*] Cp. i. 3. There were three tribal hosts in each camp; and each tribe had of course its subdivisions.

17. A more precise determination of the method of executing the order given in ii. 17. The appointed place of the Tabernacle, in the midst of the host, was represented during the march by the Ark, the holy vessels, &c. carried by the Kohathites. The actual structure of the Tabernacle was borne in advance by the Gershonites and Merarites, immediately behind the camp of Judah; so as to be set up ready against the arrival of the sacred utensils borne by the Kohathites. Cp. chs. ii., iv.

rereward of all the camps throughout their hosts: and over his
26 host *was* Ahiezer the son of Ammishaddai. And over the host of
the tribe of the children of Asher *was* Pagiel the son of Ocran.
27 And over the host of the tribe of the children of Naphtali *was*
28 Ahira the son of Enan. [1][d]Thus *were* the journeyings of the [d] ch. 2. 34.
children of Israel according to their armies, when they set for-
29 ward. ¶ And Moses said unto Hobab, the son of [e]Raguel the [e] Ex. 2. 18.
Midianite, Moses' father in law, We are journeying unto the
place of which the LORD said, [f]I will give it you: come thou [f] Gen. 12. 7.
with us, and [g]we will do thee good: for [h]the LORD hath spoken [g] Judg. 1. 16. & 4. 11.
30 good concerning Israel. And he said unto him, I will not go; [h] Gen. 32. 12.
31 but I will depart to mine own land, and to my kindred. And he Ex. 3. 8.
said, Leave us not, I pray thee; forasmuch as thou knowest how & 6. 7, 8.
we are to encamp in the wilderness, and thou mayest be to us
32 [i]instead of eyes. And it shall be, if thou go with us, yea, it [i] Job 29. 15.
shall be, that [k]what goodness the LORD shall do unto us, the [k] Judg. 1. 16.
33 same will we do unto thee. ¶ And they departed from [l]the [l] See Ex. 3. 1.
mount of the LORD three days' journey: and the ark of the
covenant of the LORD [m]went before them in the three days' [m] Deut. 1. 33.
34 journey, to search out a resting place for them. And [n]the Josh. 3. 3. Ps. 132. 8.
cloud of the LORD *was* upon them by day, when they went out Jer. 31. 2.
35 of the camp. ¶ And it came to pass, when the ark set forward, Ez. 20. 6. [n] Ex. 13. 21.
that Moses said, Neh. 9. 12.

[o]Rise up, LORD, and let thine enemies be scattered; [o] Ps. 68. 1.
And let them that hate thee flee before thee. & 132. 8.

36 And when it rested, he said,

Return, O LORD, unto the [2]many thousands of Israel.

[1] Heb. *These.* [2] Heb. *ten thousand thousands.*

---

29. *Hobab, the son of Raguel*] Or Reuel (Exod. ii. 18). Reuel was probably not identical with Jethro: and Hobab was the brother-in-law, not the father-in-law, of Moses; the Hebrew word translated in A. V. "father-in-law," signifying simply any relation by marriage (Exod. iii. 1 note). Hobab (Judges i. 16, iv. 11) eventually accompanied the Israelites and obtained a settlement with them in the land of Canaan. Hobab and Jethro may have been brethren and sons of Reuel.

31. *thou mayest be to us instead of eyes*] A proverbial expression still in use in the East. Hobab would indicate the spots where water, fuel, and pasture might be found, or warn them of the dangers from hurricanes, and point out localities infested by robbers.

33. *three days' journey*] Probably a technical expression for such a distance as could not be traversed in a single day, and therefore not without intervals of encampment and due provision: cp. Gen. xxx. 36; Exod. iii. 18, v. 3, viii. 27, xv. 22. The technical use of the phrase "Sabbath-day's journey" for another average distance, Acts i. 12, is similar.

the ark of the covenant of the LORD *went before them*] From *v.* 21 and ii. 17 it would appear that the usual place of the Ark during the march was in the midst of the host. It was evidently an exceptional case when, in Josh. iii. 3, 6, the Ark preceded the people into the bed of the Jordan. Hence the words "went before them" do not here imply local precedence. The phrase, or its equivalent, is used of a leader going out in command of his troops, xxvii. 17; Deut. xxxi. 3; 1 Sam. xviii. 16; 2 Chr. i. 10; and similarly the Ark may well be said to have gone at the head of the Israelites, when it was borne solemnly in the midst of them as the outward embodiment of the Presence Whose sovereign word was their law.

a resting place] Lit. "rest." It is commonly understood of each successive encampment; or, in particular, of the first encampment. Yet the term would hardly be here employed, did it not carry with it a higher meaning, pointing to the promised rest of Canaan, for which the Israelites were now in full march, and from the speedy enjoyment of which no sentence of exclusion as yet debarred them. Cp. marg. reff.

35, 36. Each forward movement and each rest of the Ark was made to bear a sacramental character. The one betokened the going forth of God against His enemies; the other, His gathering of His own people to Himself: the one was the pledge of victory, the other the earnest of repose.

v. 36 may be translated: "Restore" (*i.e.* to the land which their fathers sojourned in),

Chap. 11. AND [a]*when* the people [1]complained, [2]it displeased the
Lord: and the Lord heard *it;* [b]and his anger was kindled; and
the [c]fire of the Lord burnt among them, and consumed *them that*
2 *were* in the uttermost parts of the camp. And the people cried
unto Moses; and when Moses [d]prayed unto the Lord, the fire
3 [3]was quenched. And he called the name of the place [4]Taberah:
4 because the fire of the Lord burnt among them. ¶ And the
[e]mixt multitude that *was* among them [5]fell a lusting: and
the children of Israel also [6]wept again, and said, [f]Who shall
5 give us flesh to eat? [g]We remember the fish, which we did
eat in Egypt freely; the cucumbers, and the melons, and the
6 leeks, and the onions, and the garlick: but now [h]our soul *is*
dried away: *there is* nothing at all, beside this manna, *before* our
7 eyes. And [i]the manna *was* as coriander seed, and the [7]colour
8 thereof as the colour of [k]bdellium. *And* the people went about,
and gathered *it*, and ground *it* in mills, or beat *it* in a mortar,
and baked *it* in pans, and made cakes of it: and [l]the taste of it
9 was as the taste of fresh oil. And [m]when the dew fell upon the
10 camp in the night, the manna fell upon it. ¶ Then Moses heard
the people weep throughout their families, every man in the door
of his tent: and [n]the anger of the Lord was kindled greatly:
11 Moses also was displeased. [o]And Moses said unto the Lord,
Wherefore hast thou afflicted thy servant? And wherefore have I
not found favour in thy sight, that thou layest the burden of all
12 this people upon me? Have I conceived all this people? Have I
begotten them, that thou shouldest say unto me, [p]Carry them in
thy bosom, as a [q]nursing father beareth the sucking child, unto
13 the land which thou [r]swarest unto their fathers? [s]Whence
should I have flesh to give unto all this people? For they weep
14 unto me, saying, Give us flesh, that we may eat. [t]I am not able

[a] Deut. 9. 22.
[b] Ps. 78. 21.
[c] Lev. 10. 2. ch. 16. 35. 2 Kin. 1. 12. Ps. 106. 18.
[d] Jam. 5. 16.
[e] As Ex. 12. 38.
[f] Ps. 78. 18. & 106. 14. 1 Cor. 10. 6.
[g] Ex. 16. 3.
[h] ch. 21. 5.
[i] Ex. 16. 14, 31.
[k] Gen. 2. 12.
[l] Ex. 16. 31.
[m] Ex. 16. 13, 14.
[n] Ps. 78. 21.
[o] Deut. 1. 12.
[p] Isai. 40. 11.
[q] Isai. 49. 23. 1 Thes. 2. 7.
[r] Gen. 26. 3. & 50. 24. Ex. 13. 5.
[s] Matt. 15. 33. Mark 8. 4.
[t] Ex. 18. 18.

[1] Or, *were as it were complainers.*
[2] Heb. *it was evil in the ears of, &c.*
[3] Heb. *sunk.*
[4] That is, *A burning,* Deut. 9. 22.
[5] Heb. *lusted a lust.*
[6] Heb. *returned and wept.*
[7] Heb. *eye of it as the eye of.*

"O Lord, the ten thousands of the thousands of Israel." (Cp. Psalm lxxxv. 4, where the verb in the Hebrew is the same.)

XI. This and the following three chapters recount the successive rebellions of the Israelites after their departure from Sinai; culminating in that by which they brought upon themselves the sentence of personal exclusion from the Land of Promise.

1. See marginal rendering. They murmured against the privations of the march.

the fire of the Lord] Probably lightning; cp. Ps. lxxviii. 21.

in the uttermost parts] Rather, **in the end.** The fire did not reach far into the camp. It was quickly quenched at the intercession of Moses.

3. *Taberah*] *i.e.* "burning": not the name of a station, and accordingly not found in the list given in ch. xxxiii., but the name of the spot where the fire broke out. This incident might seem (cp. *v.* 34) to have occurred at the station called, from another still more terrible event which shortly followed, Kibroth-hattaavah.

4–35. Occurrences at Kibroth-hattaavah.

4. *the mixt multitude*] The word in the original resembles our "riff-raff," and denotes a mob of people scraped together. It refers here to the multitude of strangers (see Ex. xii. 38) who had followed the Israelites from Egypt.

5. The natural dainties of Egypt are set forth in this passage with the fullness and relish which bespeak personal experience.

6, 7. *there is nothing at all,* &c.] Lit. "Nought at all have we except that our eyes are unto this manna;" *i.e.* "Nought else have we to expect beside this manna." On the manna see Ex. xvi. 15 note; on bdellium see Gen. ii. 12 note.

10. The weeping was general; every family wept (cp. Zech. xii. 12), and in a manner public and unconcealed.

11–15. The complaint and remonstrance of Moses may be compared with that in 1 K. xix. 4 seq.; Jonah iv. 1–3, and contrasted with the language of Abraham (Gen. xviii. 23 seq.) The meekness of Moses (cp. xii. 3) sank under vexation into despair. His language shows us how imperfect and prone to degeneracy are the best saints on earth.

to bear all this people alone, because *it is* too heavy for me.
15 And if thou deal thus with me, [u]kill me, I pray thee, out of
hand, if I have found favour in thy sight; and let me not [x]see
16 my wretchedness. ¶ And the LORD said unto Moses, Gather
unto me [y]seventy men of the elders of Israel, whom thou
knowest to be the elders of the people, and [z]officers over them;
and bring them unto the tabernacle of the congregation, that
17 they may stand there with thee. And I will [a]come down and
talk with thee there: and [b]I will take of the spirit which *is* upon
thee, and will put *it* upon them; and they shall bear the burden
of the people with thee, that thou bear *it* not thyself alone.
18 And say thou unto the people, [c]Sanctify yourselves against
to morrow, and ye shall eat flesh: for ye have wept [d]in the ears
of the LORD, saying, Who shall give us flesh to eat: [e]for *it was*
well with us in Egypt? Therefore the LORD will give you flesh,
19 and ye shall eat. Ye shall not eat one day, nor two days,
20 nor five days, neither ten days, nor twenty days; [f]*but* even
a [1]whole month, until it come out at your nostrils, and it be
loathsome unto you: because that ye have despised the LORD
which *is* among you, and have wept before him, saying, [g]Why
21 came we forth out of Egypt? And Moses said, [h]The people,
among whom I *am*, *are* six hundred thousand footmen; and thou
hast said, I will give them flesh, that they may eat a whole
22 month. [i]Shall the flocks and the herds be slain for them, to
suffice them? Or shall all the fish of the sea be gathered together
23 for them, to suffice them? And the LORD said unto Moses,
[k]Is the LORD's hand waxed short? Thou shalt see now whether
24 [l]my word shall come to pass unto thee or not. ¶ And Moses
went out, and told the people the words of the LORD, and
[m]gathered the seventy men of the elders of the people, and set
25 them round about the tabernacle. And the LORD [n]came down
in a cloud, and spake unto him, and took of the spirit that *was*
upon him, and gave *it* unto the seventy elders: and it came to
pass, *that*, [o]when the spirit rested upon them, [p]they prophesied,
26 and did not cease. But there remained two *of the* men in the
camp, the name of the one *was* Eldad, and the name of the other

[u] See 1 Kin. 19. 4. Jonah 4. 3.
[x] Zeph. 3. 15.
[y] See Ex. 24. 1, 9.
[z] Deut. 16. 18.
[a] ver. 25. Gen. 11. 5. & 18. 21. Ex. 19. 20.
[b] 1 Sam. 10. 6. 2 Kin. 2. 15. Neh. 9. 20. Isai. 44. 3. Joel 2. 28.
[c] Ex. 19. 10.
[d] Ex. 16. 7.
[e] ver. 5. Acts 7. 39.
[f] Ps. 78. 29. & 106. 15.
[g] ch. 21. 5.
[h] Gen. 12. 2. Ex. 12. 37. & 38. 26. ch. 1. 46.
[i] See 2 Kin. 7. 2. Matt. 15. 33. Mark 8. 4. John 6. 7, 9.
[k] Isai. 50. 2. & 59. 1.
[l] ch. 23. 19. Ez. 12. 25. & 24. 14.
[m] ver. 16.
[n] ver. 17. ch. 12. 5.
[o] See 2 Kin. 2. 15.
[p] See 1 Sam. 10. 5, 6, 10. & 19. 20, 21, 23. Joel 2. 28. Acts 2. 17, 18. 1 Cor. 14. 1, &c.

[1] Heb. *month of days.*

16. *seventy men of the elders of Israel*] Seventy elders had also gone up with Moses to the Lord in the mount (Ex. xxiv. 1, 9). Seventy is accordingly the number of colleagues assigned to Moses to share his burden with him. To it, the Jews trace the origin of the Sanhedrim. Subsequent notices (xvi. 25; Josh. vii. 6, viii. 10, 33, ix. 11, xxiii. 2, xxiv. 1, 31) so connect the elders with the government of Israel as to point to the fact that the appointment now made was not a merely temporary one, though it would seem to have soon fallen into desuetude. We find no traces of it in the days of the Judges and the Kings.

elders of the people, and officers over them] In English idiom, "elders and officers of the people." Both elders and officers appear in Egypt (Ex. iii. 16, v. 6 seq.): the former had headed the nation in its efforts after freedom; the latter were the subordinate, though unwilling, agents of Egyptian tyranny. The two classes no doubt were working together; and from those who belonged to either, perhaps from those who were both elders and officers, the council of Seventy was to be selected.

17. *I will take of the spirit which is upon thee*] Render rather *separate from the spirit*, &c.; *i.e.* they shall have their portion in the same divine gift which thou hast.

25. *they prophesied*] *i.e.* under the extraordinary impulse of the Holy Ghost they uttered forth the praises of God, or declared His Will. Cp. marg. reff.

and did not cease] Rather, **and added not**, *i.e.* they prophesied at this time only and not afterwards. The sign was granted on the occasion of their appointment to accredit them in their office; it was not continued, because their proper function was to be that of governing not prophesying.

26. *of them that were written*] *i.e.* enrolled amongst the Seventy. The expression

Medad; and the spirit rested upon them; and they *were* of
them that were written, but [q]went not out unto the tabernacle:
27 and they prophesied in the camp. And there ran a young man,
and told Moses, and said, Eldad and Medad do prophesy in the
28 camp. And Joshua the son of Nun, the servant of Moses, *one*
of his young men, answered and said, My lord Moses, [r]forbid
29 them. And Moses said unto him, Enviest thou for my sake?
[s]Would God that all the LORD's people were prophets, *and* that
30 the LORD would put his spirit upon them! And Moses gat him
31 into the camp, he and the elders of Israel. ¶ And there went
forth a [t]wind from the LORD, and brought quails from the sea,
and let *them* fall by the camp, [1]as it were a day's journey on
this side, and as it were a day's journey on the other side, round
about the camp, and as it were two cubits *high* upon the face of
32 the earth. And the people stood up all that day, and all *that*
night, and all the next day, and they gathered the quails: he
that gathered least gathered ten [u]homers: and they spread *them*
33 all abroad for themselves round about the camp. And while the
[x]flesh *was* yet between their teeth, ere it was chewed, the wrath
of the LORD was kindled against the people, and the LORD smote
34 the people with a very great plague. And he called the name
of that place [2]Kibroth-hattaavah: because there they buried
35 the people that lusted. ¶ [y]*And* the people journeyed from
Kibroth-hattaavah unto Hazeroth; and [3]abode at Hazeroth.
CHAP. 12. AND Miriam and Aaron spake against Moses because of
the [4]Ethiopian woman whom he had married: for [a]he had

[q] See 1 Sam. 20. 26. Jer. 36. 5.
[r] See Mark 9. 38. Luke 9. 49. John 3. 26.
[s] 1 Cor. 14. 5.
[t] Ex. 16. 13. Ps. 78. 26, 27, 28. & 105. 40.
[u] Ex. 16. 36. Ez. 45. 11.
[x] Ps. 78. 30, 31.
[y] ch. 33. 17.
[a] Ex. 2. 21.

[1] Heb. *as it were the way of a day.*
[2] That is, *The graves of lust*, Deut. 9. 22.
[3] Heb. *they were in, &c.*
[4] Or, *Cushite.*

---

points to a regular appointment duly recorded and permanent.

29. *Enviest thou for my sake?*] (Cp. Mark ix. 38 sqq.) The other members of the Seventy had been with Moses (cp. *vv.* 16, 24, 25) when the gift of prophecy was bestowed on them. They received "of the spirit that was upon him," and exercised their office visibly through and for him. Eldad and Medad prophesying in the camp seemed to Joshua to be acting independently, and so establishing a separate centre of authority.

31. The south-east wind, which blew from the neighbouring Elanitic gulf of the Red Sea, brought the quails (Ex. xvi. 13).

two cubits high] Better, "two cubits above the face of the ground:" *i.e.* the quails, wearied with their long flight, flew about breast high, and were easily secured by the people, who spread them all abroad for themselves (*v.* 32), in order to salt and dry them. The quail habitually flies with the wind, and low.

32. *ten homers*] About 55 bushels. Cp. Lev. xxvii. 16.

33. *ere it was chewed*] Better, **ere it was consumed.** See *vv.* 19, 20. The surfeit in which the people indulged, as described in *v.* 32, disposed them to sickness. God's wrath, visiting the gluttonous through their gluttony, aggravated natural consequences into a supernatural visitation.

34, 35. [Kibroth-hattaavah has been identified by Palmer with the extensive remains, graves, &c., at Erweis El Ebeirig, and Hazeroth ("enclosures") with Ain Hadherah.]

XII. **1–15.** Miriam, as a prophetess (cp. Ex. xv. 20, 21) no less than as the sister of Moses and Aaron, took the first rank amongst the women of Israel; and Aaron may be regarded as the ecclesiastical head of the whole nation. But instead of being grateful for these high dignities they challenged the special vocation of Moses and the exclusive authority which God had assigned to him. Miriam was the instigator, from the fact that her name stands conspicuously first (*v.* 1), and that the punishment (*v.* 10) fell on her alone. She probably considered herself as supplanted, and that too by a foreigner. Aaron was misled this time by the urgency of his sister, as once before (Ex. xxxii.) by that of the people.

1. *the Ethiopian* (Heb. "Cushite," cp. Gen. ii. 13, x. 6) *woman whom he had married*] It is likely that Zipporah (Ex. ii. 21) was dead, and that Miriam in consequence expected to have greater influence than ever with Moses. Her disappointment at his second marriage would consequently be very great.

The marriage of Moses with a woman descended from Ham was not prohibited, so long as she was not of the stock of Canaan (cp. Ex. xxxiv. 11–16); but it would at any

2 [1]married an Ethiopian woman. And they said, Hath the LORD
indeed spoken only by Moses? [b]Hath he not spoken also by us?
3 And the LORD [c]heard *it*. (Now the man Moses *was* very meek,
4 above all the men which *were* upon the face of the earth.) [d]And
the LORD spake suddenly unto Moses, and unto Aaron, and
unto Miriam, Come out ye three unto the tabernacle of the con-
5 gregation. And they three came out. [e]And the LORD came
down in the pillar of the cloud, and stood *in* the door of the
tabernacle, and called Aaron and Miriam: and they both came
6 forth. And he said, Hear now my words: If there be a prophet
among you, *I* the LORD will make myself known unto him [f]in
7 a vision, *and* will speak unto him [g]in a dream. [h]My servant
8 Moses *is* not so, [i]who *is* faithful in all [k]mine house. With him
will I speak [l]mouth to mouth, even [m]apparently, and not in
dark speeches; and [n]the similitude of the LORD shall he behold:
wherefore then [o]were ye not afraid to speak against my servant
9 Moses? And the anger of the LORD was kindled against them;
10 and he departed. And the cloud departed from off the tabernacle; and, [p]behold, Miriam *became* [q]leprous, *white* as snow:
and Aaron looked upon Miriam, and, behold, *she was* leprous.
11 And Aaron said unto Moses, Alas, my lord, I beseech thee, [r]lay
not the sin upon us, wherein we have done foolishly, and
12 wherein we have sinned. Let her not be [s]as one dead, of whom
the flesh is half consumed when he cometh out of his mother's
13 womb. And Moses cried unto the LORD, saying, Heal her now,
14 O God, I beseech thee. And the LORD said unto Moses, [t]If her
father had but spit in her face, should she not be ashamed seven

[b] Ex. 15. 20. Mic. 6. 4.
[c] Gen. 29. 33. ch. 11. 1. 2 Kin. 19. 4. Isai. 37. 4. Ez. 35. 12.
[d] Ps. 76. 9.
[e] ch. 11. 25.
[f] Gen. 15. 1. Job 33. 15. Ez. 1. 1. Dan. 8. 2. Luke 1. 11, 22. Acts 10. 11.
[g] Gen. 31. 10. 1 Kin. 3. 5. Matt. 1. 20.
[h] Ps. 105. 26.
[i] Heb. 3. 2, 5.
[k] 1 Tim. 3. 15.
[l] Ex. 33. 11. Deut. 34. 10.
[m] 1 Cor. 13. 12.
[n] Ex. 33. 19.
[o] 2 Pet. 2. 10. Jude 8.
[p] Deut. 24. 9.
[q] 2 Kin. 5. 27. & 15. 5. 2 Chr. 26. 19, 20.
[r] 2 Sam. 19. 19. & 24. 10. Prov. 30. 32.
[s] Ps. 88. 4.
[t] See Heb. 12. 9.

[1] Heb. *taken*.

---

time have been offensive to that intense nationality which characterized the Jews. The Christian Fathers note in the successive marriage of Moses with a Midianite and an Ethiopian a foreshadowing of the future extension to the Gentiles of God's Covenant and its promises (cp. Ps. xlv. 9 seq.; Cant. i. 4 seq.); and in the murmuring of Miriam and Aaron a type of the discontent of the Jews because of such extension: cp. St. Luke xv. 29, 30.

2. *Hath the* LORD, *&c.*] *i.e.* Is it merely, after all, by Moses that the LORD hath spoken?

3. *the man Moses was very meek*] In this and in other passages in which Moses no less unequivocally records his own faults (cp. xx. 12 seq.; Ex. iv. 24 seq.; Deut. i. 37), there is the simplicity of one who bare witness of himself, but not to himself (cp. Matt. xi. 28, 29). The words are inserted to explain how it was that Moses took no steps to vindicate himself, and why consequently the Lord so promptly intervened.

8. *mouth to mouth*] *i.e.* without the intervention of any third person or thing: cp. marg. reff.

even apparently] Moses received the word of God direct from Him and plainly, not through the medium of dream, vision, parable, dark saying, or such like; cp. marg. reff.

the similitude of the LORD *shall he behold*] But, "No man hath seen God at any time," says St. John (i. 18: cp. 1 Tim. vi. 16, and especially Ex. xxxiii. 20 seq.). It was not therefore the Beatific Vision, the unveiled essence of the Deity, which Moses saw on the one hand. Nor was it, on the other hand, a mere emblematic representation (as in Ezek. i. 26 seq., Dan. vii. 9), or an Angel sent as a messenger. It was the Deity Himself manifesting Himself so as to be cognizable to mortal eye. The special footing on which Moses stood as regards God is here laid down in detail, because it at once demonstrates that the supremacy of Moses rested on the distinct appointment of God, and also that Miriam in contravening that supremacy had incurred the penalty proper to sins against the theocracy.

12. *as one dead*] Leprosy was nothing short of a living death, a poisoning of the springs, a corrupting of all the humours, of life; a dissolution little by little of the whole body, so that one limb after another actually decayed and fell away. Cp. notes on Lev. xiii.

13. *Heal her now, O God, I beseech thee*] Others render these words: "Oh not so; heal her now, I beseech Thee."

14. *If her father, &c.*] *i.e.* If her earthly parent had treated her with contumely (cp. Deut. xxv. 9) she would feel for a time humiliated, how much more when God has visited her thus?

days? Let her be [u]shut out from the camp seven days, and after
15 that let her be received in *again*. [x]And Miriam was shut out
from the camp seven days: and the people journeyed not till
16 Miriam was brought in *again*. ¶And afterward the people
removed from [y]Hazeroth, and pitched in the wilderness of
Paran.

CHAP. 13. AND the LORD spake unto Moses, saying, [a]Send thou
2 men, that they may search the land of Canaan, which I give
unto the children of Israel: of every tribe of their fathers shall
3 ye send a man, every one a ruler among them. And Moses by
the commandment of the LORD sent them [b]from the wilderness
of Paran: all those men *were* heads of the children of Israel.
4 And these *were* their names: of the tribe of Reuben, Shammua
5 the son of Zaccur. Of the tribe of Simeon, Shaphat the son of
6 Hori. [c]Of the tribe of Judah, [d]Caleb the son of Jephunneh.
7, 8 Of the tribe of Issachar, Igal the son of Joseph. Of the tribe
9 of Ephraim, [e]Oshea the son of Nun. Of the tribe of Benjamin,
10 Palti the son of Raphu. Of the tribe of Zebulun, Gaddiel the
11 son of Sodi. Of the tribe of Joseph, *namely*, of the tribe of
12 Manasseh, Gaddi the son of Susi. Of the tribe of Dan, Ammiel
13 the son of Gemalli. Of the tribe of Asher, Sethur the son of
14 Michael. Of the tribe of Naphtali, Nahbi the son of Vophsi.
15, 16 Of the tribe of Gad, Geuel the son of Machi. These *are* the
names of the men which Moses sent to spy out the land. And
17 Moses called [f]Oshea the son of Nun Jehoshua. ¶And Moses
sent them to spy out the land of Canaan, and said unto them,
Get you up this *way* [g]southward, and go up into [h]the mountain:
18 and see the land, what it *is*; and the people that dwelleth
19 therein, whether they *be* strong or weak, few or many; and
what the land *is* that they dwell in, whether it *be* good or bad;
and what cities *they be* that they dwell in, whether in tents, or in
20 strong holds; and what the land *is*, whether it *be* [i]fat or lean,
whether there be wood therein, or not. And [k]be ye of good
courage, and bring of the fruit of the land. ¶Now the time

[u] Lev. 13. 46. ch. 5. 2, 3.
[x] Deut. 24. 9. 2 Chr. 26. 20, 21.
[y] ch. 11. 35. & 33. 18.
[a] ch. 32. 8. Deut. 1. 22.
[b] ch. 12. 16. & 32. 8. Deut. 1. 19. & 9. 23.
[c] ch. 34. 19. 1 Chr. 4. 15.
[d] ver. 30. ch. 14. 6. 30. Josh. 14. 6, 7, 13, 14. Judg. 1. 12.
[e] ver. 16.
[f] ver. 8. Ex. 17. 9. ch. 14. 6, 30.
[g] ver. 21.
[h] Gen. 14. 10. Judg. 1. 9, 19.
[i] Neh. 9. 25, 35. Ez. 34. 14.
[k] Deut. 31. 6, 7, 23.

XIII. **1.** *And the* LORD *spake*] The mission of the spies was first suggested by the Israelites themselves. See Deut. i. 22.

2. *a ruler*] A comparison of the list with that of i. 5 seq. shows that they were not the princes of the tribes, but heads of houses or families (*v.* 4).

Of the names here given those of Joshua and Caleb alone are otherwise known to us.

16. Oshea, Hoshea, or Hosea, the name also of the last king of Israel and the first minor prophet, means "deliverance" or "salvation." To this Moses added (probably, on this occasion) a syllable containing the sacred name, Jehovah or Jah: thus intimating that salvation was from God, and by the hand of him who bore the title of "God's salvation." Jehoshua was contracted (cp. Neh. viii. 17) into Jęshua.

17. *southward*] Rather, "by the Negeb," or south-country; a well-defined tract of territory forming the southernmost and least fertile portion of the land of Canaan and of the subsequent inheritance of Judah. It extended northward from Kadesh to within a few miles of Hebron, and from the Dead Sea westward to the Mediterranean (see especially Josh. xv. 21–32).

into the mountain] The hill-country of southern and central Canaan, mostly within the borders of Judah and Ephraim. It commences a few miles south of Hebron, and extending northward to the plain of Jezreel, runs out eventually north-westward into the sea in the headland of Carmel.

19. *in tents*] *i.e.* in open unwalled villages.

20. *the time...of the firstripe grapes*] The first grapes ripen in Palestine in July and August: the vintage is gathered in September and October. This indication of date tallies with what we should have inferred from the previous narrative. For the Israelitish host had quitted Sinai on the 20th day of the second month (x. 11), or about the middle of May: since then they had spent a month at Kibroth-hattaavah and a week at Hazeroth, and had accomplished, in all, from 150 to 200 miles of march: it therefore must have been at least

21 *was* the time of the firstripe grapes. So they went up, and
searched the land [l]from the wilderness of Zin unto [m]Rehob, as
22 men come to Hamath. And they ascended by the south, and
came unto Hebron; where [n]Ahiman, Sheshai, and Talmai, [o]the
children of Anak, *were*. (Now [p]Hebron was built seven years
23 before [q]Zoan in Egypt.) [r]And they came unto the [1]brook of
Eshcol, and cut down from thence a branch with one cluster of
grapes, and they bare it between two upon a staff; and *they*
24 *brought* of the pomegranates, and of the figs. The place was
called the [2]brook [3]Eshcol, because of the cluster of grapes which
25 the children of Israel cut down from thence. And they returned
26 from searching of the land after forty days. ¶ And they went
and came to Moses, and to Aaron, and to all the congregation
of the children of Israel, [s]unto the wilderness of Paran, to
[t]Kadesh; and brought back word unto them, and unto all the
27 congregation, and shewed them the fruit of the land. And they
told him, and said, We came unto the land whither thou sentest
us, and surely it floweth with [u]milk and honey; [x]and this *is* the
28 fruit of it. Nevertheless [y]the people *be* strong that dwell in the
land, and the cities *are* walled, *and* very great: and moreover
29 we saw [z]the children of Anak there. [a]The Amalekites dwell in
the land of the south: and the Hittites, and the Jebusites, and
the Amorites, dwell in the mountains: and the Canaanites dwell
30 by the sea, and by the coast of Jordan. ¶ And [b]Caleb stilled
the people before Moses, and said, Let us go up at once, and

[l] ch. 34. 3. Josh. 15. 1.
[m] Josh. 19. 28.
[n] Josh. 11. 21, 22. & 15. 13, 14. Judg. 1. 10.
[o] ver. 33.
[p] Josh. 21. 11.
[q] Ps. 78. 12. Isai. 19. 11. & 30. 4.
[r] Deut. 1. 24, 25.
[s] ver. 3.
[t] ch. 20. 1. 16. Deut. 1. 19. Josh. 14. 6.
[u] Ex. 3. 8. & 33. 3.
[x] Deut. 1. 25.
[y] Deut. 1. 28. & 9. 1.
[z] ver. 33.
[a] Ex. 17. 8. ch. 14. 43.
[b] See ch. 14, 6, 24. Josh. 14. 7.

[1] Or, *valley*, ch. 32. 9. Judg. 16. 4.
[2] Or, *valley*.
[3] That is, *A cluster of grapes*.

---

the beginning of July, and may have been a month later, when the spies were despatched into the land of promise.

21. The wilderness of Zin was the north-eastern portion of the wilderness of Paran.

Rehob (*mod.* Khurbeh) was probably the Beth-rehob of Judg. xviii. 28, near Dan-Laish; and apparently to the north of it, since it gave its name to a Syrian kingdom (2 S. viii. 3). The southern approach to Hamath from the plain of Cœle-Syria, lay between those two ranges of Lebanon called Libanus and Antilibanus. A low screen of hills connects the northernmost points of these two ranges; and through this screen the Orontes bursts from the upper Cœle-Syrian hollow into the open plain of Hamath.

22. The progenitor of the Anakim was Arba "the father of Anak" (Josh. xv. 13), from whom the city of Hebron took its name of Kirjath-Arba. Ahiman, Sheshai, and Talmai were probably not individual warriors, but names of three tribes of the Anakim. Hence we find them still in existence half a century later, when Caleb, who now brought tidings of them, became their eventual destroyer (Josh. xv. 14).

Now Hebron, &c.] This parenthesis explains that these two cities had a common founder, and were built, or perhaps, at least in the case of Zoan (Tanis, see Ex. i. 8, ii. 5 notes) rebuilt, by the Hyksos, to which nations, once the conquerors of Egypt, the Anakim perhaps belonged. The Hyksos fortified and garrisoned Zoan as a defence of their Eastern frontier.

23. The brook of Eshcol is by some identified with the rich valley immediately to the north of Hebron; [but by others with Wady Hanein to the south of Hebron]. The valley was, in all likelihood, originally named after one of the three chiefs who were confederate with Abraham (Gen. xiv. 24); but, as often came to pass, the Israelites, wittingly or unwittingly, took up in a new and significant sense the name which they found; and to them the valley thus became the Valley of the Cluster. Bunches of grapes are found in Palestine of many pounds weight.

25. *after forty days*] They had no doubt in this time explored the whole land. It was however with the southern part that the Israelites expected to have to deal immediately: and accordingly it is that which is particularly referred to in the following verses, Hebron and its vicinity above all.

26. Kadesh is usually identified with Ain-el-Weibeh, which lies in the Arabah, about ten miles north of the place in which Mount Hor abuts on that valley, [or with Ain-Gadis in Jebel Magrah].

29. *The Amalekites*] See xiv. 25 note.

the Canaanites] *i.e.* those of the Phœnician race: the word is here used in its narrow sense: cp. Gen. x. 15–18 note.

[c] ch. 32. 9. Deut. 1. 28. Josh. 14. 8. [d] ch. 14. 36. [e] Amos 2. 9. [f] Deut. 1. 28. [g] Isai. 40. 22. [h] 1 Sam. 17. 42. [a] ch. 11. 4. [b] Ex. 16. 2. ch. 16. 41. Ps. 106. 25. [c] See ver. 28, 29. [d] Neh. 9. 17. [e] See Deut. 17. 16. Acts 7. 39. [f] ch. 16. 4. [g] ver. 24. 30, 38. [h] ch. 13. 27. Deut. 1. 25. [i] Deut. 10. 15. 1 Kin. 10. 9. Ps. 22. 8. Isai. 62. 4. [k] ch. 13. 27. [l] Deut. 9. 7. [m] Deut. 7. 18. [n] ch. 24. 8. [o] Gen. 48. 21. Ex. 33. 16. Deut. 20. 1. Josh. 1. 5. Judg. 1. 22. 2 Chr. 13. 12. Ps. 46. 7, 11. Isai. 41. 10. Amos 5. 14. Zech. 8. 23. [p] Ex. 17. 4. [q] Ex. 16. 10. Lev. 9. 23. ch. 16. 19, 42. [r] Deut. 9. 7. Ps. 95. 8. Heb. 3. 8. [s] Deut. 1. 32. Ps. 78. 22. & 106. 24. John 12. 37. Heb. 3. 18. [t] Ex. 32. 10. [u] Ex. 32. 12. Ps. 106. 23. Deut. 9. 26. Ez. 20. 9, 14.

31 possess it; for we are well able to overcome it. [c]But the men
that went up with him said, We be not able to go up against
32 the people; for they *are* stronger than we. And they [d]brought
up an evil report of the land which they had searched unto the
children of Israel, saying, The land, through which we have
gone to search it, *is* a land that eateth up the inhabitants
thereof; and [e]all the people that we saw in it *are* [1]men of a
33 great stature. And there we saw the giants, [f]the sons of Anak,
which come of the giants: and we were in our own sight [g]as
grasshoppers, and so we were [h]in their sight.

Chap. 14. AND all the congregation lifted up their voice, and cried;
2 and [a]the people wept that night. [b]And all the children of
Israel murmured against Moses and against Aaron: and the
whole congregation said unto them, Would God that we had died
in the land of Egypt! or [c]would God we had died in this wil-
3 derness! And wherefore hath the LORD brought us unto this
land, to fall by the sword, that our wives and our children
should be a prey? Were it not better for us to return into Egypt?
4 And they said one to another, [d]Let us make a captain, and [e]let
5 us return into Egypt. ¶ Then [f]Moses and Aaron fell on their
faces before all the assembly of the congregation of the children
6 of Israel. [g]And Joshua the son of Nun, and Caleb the son of
Jephunneh, *which were* of them that searched the land, rent
7 their clothes: and they spake unto all the company of the children of Israel, saying, [h]The land, which we passed through to
8 search it, *is* an exceeding good land. If the LORD [i]delight in
us, then he will bring us into this land, and give it us; [k]a land
9 which floweth with milk and honey. Only [l]rebel not ye against
the LORD, [m]neither fear ye the people of the land; for [n]they *are*
bread for us: their [2]defence is departed from them, [o]and the
10 LORD *is* with us: fear them not. [p]But all the congregation
bade stone them with stones. And [q]the glory of the LORD
appeared in the tabernacle of the congregation before all the
11 children of Israel. ¶ And the LORD said unto Moses, How long
will this people [r]provoke me? And how long will it be ere they
[s]believe me, for all the signs which I have shewed among them?
12 I will smite them with the pestilence, and disinherit them, and
[t]will make of thee a greater nation and mightier than they.
13 And [u]Moses said unto the LORD, Then the Egyptians shall
hear *it*, (for thou broughtest up this people in thy might from

[1] Heb. *men of statures.*

[2] Heb. *shadow*, Ps. 121. 5. Isai. 30. 2, 3. Jer. 48. 45.

---

32. *a land that eateth up*, &c.] *i.e.* it is a land which from its position is exposed to incessant attacks from one quarter and another, and so its occupants must be always armed and watchful.

XIV. **5.** Already Caleb had endeavoured to still the people before Moses (xiii. 30); already Moses himself (Deut. i. 29 seq.) had endeavoured to recall the people to obedience. After the failure of these efforts Moses and Aaron cast themselves down in solemn prayer before God (cp. xvi. 22); and the appearance of the glory of the LORD in the "Tabernacle of the congregation" (*v.* 10) was the immediate answer.

9. *their defence*] Lit. "their shadow," *i.e.* their shelter as from the scorching sun: an Oriental figure. Cp. marg. reff.

12. *and disinherit them*] By the proposed extinction of Israel the blessings of the Covenant would revert to their original donor.

13–17. The syntax of these verses is singularly broken. As did St. Paul when deeply moved, so Moses presses his arguments one on the other without pausing to ascertain the grammatical finish of his expressions. He speaks here as if in momentary apprehension of an outbreak of God's wrath, unless he could perhaps arrest it by crowding in every topic of deprecation and intercession that he could mention on the instant.

14 among them;) and they will tell *it* to the inhabitants of this
land: [x]*for* they have heard that thou LORD *art* among this
people, that thou LORD art seen face to face, and *that* [y]thy cloud
standeth over them, and *that* thou goest before them, by day
15 time in a pillar of a cloud, and in a pillar of fire by night. Now
if thou shalt kill *all* this people as one man, then the nations
16 which have heard the fame of thee will speak, saying, Because
the LORD was not [z]able to bring this people into the land which
he sware unto them, therefore he hath slain them in the wilder-
17 ness. And now, I beseech thee, let the power of my Lord be
18 great, according as thou hast spoken, saying, The LORD *is*
[a]longsuffering, and of great mercy, forgiving iniquity and
transgression, and by no means clearing *the guilty*, [b]visiting
the iniquity of the fathers upon the children unto the third and
19 fourth *generation*. [c]Pardon, I beseech thee, the iniquity of this
people [d]according unto the greatness of thy mercy, and [e]as thou
20 hast forgiven this people, from Egypt even [1]until now. And
21 the LORD said, I have pardoned [f]according to thy word: but *as*
truly *as* I live, [g]all the earth shall be filled with the glory of the
22 LORD. [h]Because all those men which have seen my glory, and
my miracles, which I did in Egypt and in the wilderness, and
have tempted me now [i]these ten times, and have not hearkened
23 to my voice; [k][2]surely they shall not see the land which I sware
unto their fathers, neither shall any of them that provoked me
24 see it: but my servant [l]Caleb, because he had another spirit
with him, and [m]hath followed me fully, him will I bring into
the land whereinto he went; and his seed shall possess it.
25 (Now the Amalekites and the Canaanites dwelt in the valley.)
To morrow turn you, [n]and get you into the wilderness by the
26 way of the Red sea. ¶And the LORD spake unto Moses and
27 unto Aaron, saying, [o]How long *shall I bear with* this evil congregation, which murmur against me? [p]I have heard the murmurings of the children of Israel, which they murmur against
28 me. Say unto them, [q]*As truly as* I live, saith the LORD, [r]as ye
29 have spoken in mine ears, so will I do to you: your carcases
shall fall in this wilderness; and [s]all that were numbered of

[x] Ex. 15. 14. Josh. 2. 9, 10. & 5. 1.
[y] Ex. 13. 21. & 40. 38. ch. 10. 34. Neh. 9. 12. Ps. 78. 14. & 105. 39.
[z] Deut. 9. 28. Josh. 7. 9.
[a] Ex. 34. 6, 7. Ps. 103. 8. & 145. 8. Jonah 4. 2.
[b] Ex. 20. 5. & 34. 7.
[c] Ex. 34. 9.
[d] Ps. 106. 45.
[e] Ps. 78. 38.
[f] Ps. 106. 23. Jam. 5. 16. 1 John 5. 14, 15, 16.
[g] Ps. 72. 19.
[h] Deut. 1. 35. Ps. 95. 11. & 106. 26. Heb. 3. 17.
[i] Gen. 31. 7.
[k] ch. 32. 11. Ez. 20. 15.
[l] Deut. 1. 36. Josh. 14. 6.
[m] ch. 32. 12.
[n] Deut. 1. 40.
[o] ver. 11. Ex. 16. 28. Matt. 17. 17.
[p] Ex. 16. 12.
[q] ver. 23. ch. 26. 65. & 32. 11. Deut. 1. 35. Heb. 3. 17.
[r] See ver. 2.
[s] ch. 1. 45. & 26. 64.

[1] Or, *hitherto*. [2] Heb. *If they see the land*.

21–23. Render: **But as truly as I live, and as all the earth shall be filled with the glory of the** LORD; (*v.* 22) **all those men,** &c.; (*v.* 23) **shall not see,** &c.

22. *these ten times*] Ten is the number which imports completeness. Cp. Gen. xxxi. 7. The sense is that the measure of their provocation was now full: the day of grace was at last over. Some however enumerate ten several occasions on which the people had tempted God since the Exodus.

Ps. xc., which is entitled "a Prayer of Moses," has been most appropriately regarded as a kind of dirge upon those sentenced thus awfully by God to waste away in the wilderness.

24. *my servant Caleb*] Caleb only is mentioned here as also in xiii. 30 seq. Both passages probably form part of the matter introduced at a later period into the narrative of Moses, and either by Joshua or under his superintendence. Hence the name of Joshua is omitted, and his faithfulness together with its reward are taken for granted. In *vv.* 30, 38, both names are mentioned together; and these verses in all likelihood belong to the same original composition as *vv.* 6–10.

25. Render: **And now the Amalekites and the Canaanites are dwelling** (or abiding) **in the valley: wherefore turn you,** &c. (that so ye be not smitten before them). The Amalekites were the nomad bands that roved through the open pastures of the plain (*v.* 45): the Canaanites, a term here taken in its wider sense, were the Amorites of the neighbouring cities (cp. *v.* 45 with Deut. i. 44), who probably lived in league with the Amalekites.

To morrow] Not necessarily the next day, but an idiom for "hereafter," "henceforward" (cp. marg. reading in Ex. xiii. 14; Josh. iv. 6).

by the way of the Red sea] That is, apparently, by the eastern or Elanitic gulf.

you, according to your whole number, from twenty years old
30 and upward, which have murmured against me, doubtless ye
shall not come into the land, *concerning* which I [1]sware to make
you dwell therein, [t]save Caleb the son of Jephunneh, and
31 Joshua the son of Nun. [u]But your little ones, which ye said
should be a prey, them will I bring in, and they shall know the
32 land which [x]ye have despised. But *as for* you, [y]your carcases,
33 they shall fall in this wilderness. And your children shall
[2][z]wander in the wilderness [a]forty years, and [b]bear your whore-
34 doms, until your carcases be wasted in the wilderness. [c]After
the number of the days in which ye searched the land, *even*
[d]forty days, each day for a year, shall ye bear your iniquities,
even forty years, [e]and ye shall know my [3]breach of promise.
35 [f]I the LORD have said, I will surely do it unto all [g]this evil
congregation, that are gathered together against me: in this
wilderness they shall be consumed, and there they shall die.
36 ¶ [h]And the men, which Moses sent to search the land, who
returned, and made all the congregation to murmur against him,
37 by bringing up a slander upon the land, even those men that
did bring up the evil report upon the land, [i]died by the plague
38 before the LORD. [k]But Joshua the son of Nun, and Caleb the
son of Jephunneh, *which were* of the men that went to search
39 the land, lived *still*. ¶ And Moses told these sayings unto all
40 the children of Israel: [l]and the people mourned greatly. And
they rose up early in the morning, and gat them up into the top
of the mountain, saying, Lo, [m]we *be here*, and will go up unto
the place which the LORD hath promised: for we have sinned.
41 And Moses said, Wherefore now do ye transgress [n]the com-
42 mandment of the LORD? But it shall not prosper. [o]Go not up,
for the LORD *is* not among you; that ye be not smitten before
43 your enemies. For the Amalekites and the Canaanites *are* there
before you, and ye shall fall by the sword: [p]because ye are
turned away from the LORD, therefore the LORD will not be
44 with you. ¶ [q]But they presumed to go up unto the hill top:
nevertheless the ark of the covenant of the LORD, and Moses,
45 departed not out of the camp. [r]Then the Amalekites came
down, and the Canaanites which dwelt in that hill, and smote
them, and discomfited them, *even* unto [s]Hormah.

CHAP. 15. AND the LORD spake unto Moses, saying, [a]Speak unto
2 the children of Israel, and say unto them, When ye be come into

[t] ver. 38. ch. 26. 65. & 32. 12. Deut. 1. 36, 38.
[u] Deut. 1. 39.
[x] Ps. 106. 24.
[y] 1 Cor. 10. 5. Heb. 3. 17.
[z] ch. 32. 13.
[a] See Deut. 2, 14.
[b] Ez. 23. 35.
[c] ch. 13. 25.
[d] Ps. 95. 10. Ez. 4. 6.
[e] See 1 Kin. 8. 56.
[f] ch. 23. 19.
[g] ver. 27. 29. ch. 26. 65. 1 Cor. 10. 5.
[h] ch. 13. 31.
[i] 1 Cor. 10. 10. Heb. 3. 17. Jude 5.
[k] ch. 26. 65. Josh. 14. 6.
[l] Ex. 33. 4.
[m] Deut. 1. 41.
[n] ver. 25. 2 Chr. 24. 20.
[o] Deut. 1. 42.
[p] 2 Chr. 15. 2.
[q] Deut. 1. 43.
[r] ver. 43. Deut. 1. 44.
[s] ch. 21. 3. Judg. 1. 17.
[a] ver. 18. Lev. 23. 10. Deut. 7. 1.

[1] Heb. *lifted up my hand*, Gen. 14. 22.
[2] Or, *feed*.
[3] Or, *altering of my purpose*.

---

33. *your whoredoms*] Their several rebellions had been so many acts of faithless departure from the Lord Who had taken them unto Himself. And as the children of the unchaste have generally to bear in their earthly careers much of the disgrace and the misery which forms the natural penalty of their parents' transgression; so here the children of the Israelites, although suffered to hope for an eventual entry into Canaan, were yet to endure, through many long years' wandering, the appropriate punishment of their fathers' wilfulness.

34. *my breach of promise*] In the original, a word, found elsewhere only in Job xxx. 10, and meaning "my withdrawal," "my turning away." See margin.

45. *unto Hormah*] Lit. "the Hormah:" *i.e.* "the banning," or "ban-place." Cp. xxi. 3; Josh. xii. 14. According to the view taken of Kadesh (see xiii. 26), Hormah is identified, through its earlier name, Zephath (Judg. i. 17), with es-Safâh on the south-eastern frontier of Canaan, by which the Israelites quitted the Arabah for the higher ground, [or with Sebaita, which lies further to the west, about 25 miles north of Ain Gadis].

XV. The contents of the next five chapters must apparently be referred to the long period of wandering to which (xiv. 33) the people were condemned.

2. To the Israelites of the younger generation is conveyed the hope that the nation

3 the land of your habitations, which I give unto you, and [b] will — [b] Lev. 1. 2, 3.
make an offering by fire unto the LORD, a burnt offering, or a
sacrifice [c] in [1] performing a vow, or in a freewill offering, or [d] in — [c] Lev. 7. 16.
your solemn feasts, to make a [e] sweet savour unto the LORD, of — & 22. 18, 21. [d] Lev. 23. 8.
4 the herd, or of the flock: then [f] shall he that offereth his offer- — ch. 28. 19.
ing unto the LORD bring [g] a meat offering of a tenth deal of flour — & 29. 2, 8. Deut. 16. 10.
5 mingled [h] with the fourth *part* of an hin of oil. [i] And the fourth — [e] Gen. 8. 21.
part of an hin of wine for a drink offering shalt thou prepare — Ex. 29. 18.
6 with the burnt offering or sacrifice, for one lamb. [k] Or for a ram, — [f] Lev. 2. 1. & 6. 14.
thou shalt prepare *for* a meat offering two tenth deals of flour — [g] Ex. 29. 40.
7 mingled with the third *part* of an hin of oil. And for a drink — Lev. 23. 13.
offering thou shalt offer the third *part* of an hin of wine, *for* a — [h] Lev. 14. 10. ch. 28. 5.
8 sweet savour unto the LORD. And when thou preparest a — [i] ch. 28. 7, 14.
bullock *for* a burnt offering, or *for* a sacrifice in performing a — [k] ch. 28. 12.
9 vow, or [l] peace offerings unto the LORD: then shall he bring — [l] Lev. 7. 11.
[m] with a bullock a meat offering of three tenth deals of flour — [m] ch. 28. 12,
10 mingled with half an hin of oil. And thou shalt bring for a — 14.
drink offering half an hin of wine, *for* an offering made by fire,
11 of a sweet savour unto the LORD. [n] Thus shall it be done for — [n] ch. 28.
12 one bullock, or for one ram, or for a lamb, or a kid. According
to the number that ye shall prepare, so shall ye do to every one
13 according to their number. All that are born of the country
shall do these things after this manner, in offering an offering
14 made by fire, of a sweet savour unto the LORD. And if a stranger
sojourn with you, or whosoever *be* among you in your generations, and will offer an offering made by fire, of a sweet savour
15 unto the LORD; as ye do, so he shall do. [o] One ordinance *shall* — [o] Ex. 12. 49.
be both for you of the congregation, and also for the stranger — ch. 9. 14. ver. 29.
that sojourneth *with you*, an ordinance for ever in your genera-
16 tions: as ye *are*, so shall the stranger be before the LORD. One
law and one manner shall be for you, and for the stranger that
17 sojourneth with you. ¶ And the LORD spake unto Moses, saying,
18 [p] Speak unto the children of Israel, and say unto them, When — [p] ver. 2.
19 ye come into the land whither I bring you, then it shall be, that, — Deut. 26. 1.
when ye eat of [q] the bread of the land, ye shall offer up an heave — [q] Josh. 5.
20 offering unto the LORD. [r] Ye shall offer up a cake of the first of — 11, 12. [r] Deut. 26.
your dough *for* an heave offering: as *ye do* [s] the heave offering — 2, 10.
21 of the threshingfloor, so shall ye heave it. Of the first of your — Prov. 3. 9. [s] Lev. 2. 14.
dough ye shall give unto the LORD an heave offering in your — & 23. 10.
22 generations. ¶ And [t] if ye have erred, and not observed all these — [t] Lev. 4. 2.

[1] Heb. *separating*, Lev. 27. 2.

---

should yet enter into the Land of Promise. The ordinances that follow are more likely to have been addressed to adults than to children; and we may therefore assume that at the date of their delivery the new generation was growing up, and the period of wandering drawing towards its close. During that period the Meat-offerings and Drink-offerings prescribed by the Law had been probably intermitted by reason of the scanty supply of corn and wine in the wilderness. The command therefore to provide such offerings was a pledge to Israel that it should possess the land which was to furnish the wherewithal for them.

4–12. The Meat-offering is treated in Lev. ii. The Drink-offering (Ex. xxix. 40; Lev. xxiii. 13), hitherto an ordinary accessory to the former, is now prescribed for every sacrifice.

18. The general principle which includes the ordinance of this and the three verses following is laid down in Ex. xxii. 29, xxiii. 19.

20, 21. *dough*] "Coarse meal" (Neh. x. 37; Ezek. xliv. 30).

22–31. The heavy punishments which had already overtaken the people might naturally give rise to apprehensions for the future, especially in view of the fact that on the approaching entrance into Canaan the complete observance of the Law in all its details would become imperative on them. To meet such apprehensions a distinction is

23 commandments, which the LORD hath spoken unto Moses, *even*
all that the LORD hath commanded you by the hand of Moses,
from the day that the LORD commanded *Moses*, and henceforward
24 among your generations; then it shall be, [u]if *ought* be committed by ignorance [1]without the knowledge of the congregation,
that all the congregation shall offer one young bullock for a
burnt offering, for a sweet savour unto the LORD, [x]with his meat
offering, and his drink offering, according to the [2]manner, and
25 [y]one kid of the goats for a sin offering. [z]And the priest shall
make an atonement for all the congregation of the children of
Israel, and it shall be forgiven them; for it *is* ignorance: and
they shall bring their offering, a sacrifice made by fire unto the
LORD, and their sin offering before the LORD, for their ignor-
26 ance: and it shall be forgiven all the congregation of the
children of Israel, and the stranger that sojourneth among them;
27 seeing all the people *were* in ignorance. ¶ And [a]if any soul sin
through ignorance, then he shall bring a she goat of the first
28 year for a sin offering. [b]And the priest shall make an atonement
for the soul that sinneth ignorantly, when he sinneth by ignorance before the LORD, to make an atonement for him; and it
29 shall be forgiven him. [c]Ye shall have one law for him that
[3]sinneth through ignorance, *both for* him that is born among the
children of Israel, and for the stranger that sojourneth among
30 them. ¶ [d]But the soul that doeth *ought* [4]presumptuously,
whether he be born in the land, or a stranger, the same reproacheth the LORD: and that soul shall be cut off from among
31 his people. Because he hath [e]despised the word of the LORD,
and hath broken his commandment, that soul shall utterly be
32 cut off; [f]his iniquity *shall be* upon him. ¶ And while the
children of Israel were in the wilderness, [g]they found a man that
33 gathered sticks upon the sabbath day. And they that found
him gathering sticks brought him unto Moses and Aaron, and
34 unto all the congregation. And they put him [h]in ward, because
35 it was not declared what should be done to him. And the LORD
said unto Moses, [i]The man shall be surely put to death: all the
congregation shall [k]stone him with stones without the camp.
36 And all the congregation brought him without the camp, and
stoned him with stones, and he died; as the LORD commanded
37, 38 Moses. ¶ And the LORD spake unto Moses, saying, Speak

[u] Lev. 4. 13.
[x] ver. 8, 9, 10.
[y] See Lev. 4. 23. ch. 28. 15. Ezra 6. 17. & 8. 35.
[z] Lev. 4. 20.
[a] Lev. 4. 27, 28.
[b] Lev. 4. 35.
[c] ver. 15.
[d] Deut. 17. 12. Ps. 19. 13. Heb. 10. 26. 2 Pet. 2. 10.
[e] 2 Sam. 12. 9. Prov. 13. 13.
[f] Lev. 5. 1. Ez. 18. 20.
[g] Ex. 31. 14, 15. & 35. 2, 3.
[h] Lev. 24. 12.
[i] Ex. 31. 14, 15.
[k] Lev. 24. 14. 1 Kin. 21. 13. Acts 7. 58.

[1] Heb. *from the eyes.*
[2] Or, *ordinance.*
[3] Heb. *doth.*
[4] Heb. *with an high hand.*

---

emphatically drawn between sins of ignorance (Lev. iv. 13 sqq.) and those of presumption (*vv.* 30, 31). The passage deals separately with imperfections of obedience which would be regarded as attaching to the whole nation (*vv.* 22–26), and those of individuals (*vv.* 27–30).

24. *without the knowledge of the congregation*] Lit. as marg. The words point to an error of omission which escaped notice at the time: *i.e.* to an oversight.

30. *presumptuously*] The original (cp. margin, and Ex. xiv. 8) imports something done wilfully and openly; in the case of a sin against God it implies that the act is committed ostentatiously and in bravado.

reproacheth the LORD] Rather, **revileth** or **blasphemeth** the LORD: cp. Ezek. xx. 27.

32. Moses mentions here, as is his wont (cp. Lev. xxiv. 10–16), the first open transgression and its punishment in order to exemplify the laws which he is laying down. The offence of Sabbath-breaking was one for which there could be no excuse. This law at least might be observed even in the wilderness. Transgression of it was therefore a presumptuous sin, and was punished accordingly.

34. Death had indeed been assigned as the penalty (Ex. xxxi. 14, xxxv. 2); but it had not been determined how that death was to be inflicted.

38. *that they put upon the fringe of the borders a ribband of blue*] Render **that they**

unto the children of Israel, and bid [l]them that they make them
fringes in the borders of their garments throughout their generations, and that they put upon the fringe of the borders a
39 ribband of blue: and it shall be unto you for a fringe, that ye
may look upon it, and remember all the commandments of the
LORD, and do them; and that ye [m]seek not after your own
heart and your own eyes, after which ye use [n]to go a whoring:
40 that ye may remember, and do all my commandments, and be
41 [o]holy unto your God. I *am* the LORD your God, which brought
you out of the land of Egypt, to be your God: I *am* the LORD
your God.

CHAP. 16. NOW [a]Korah, the son of Izhar, the son of Kohath, the
son of Levi, and Dathan and Abiram, the sons of Eliab, and On,
2 the son of Peleth, sons of Reuben, took *men:* and they rose up
before Moses, with certain of the children of Israel, two hundred
and fifty princes of the assembly, [b]famous in the congregation,
3 men of renown: and [c]they gathered themselves together against
Moses and against Aaron, and said unto them, [1]*Ye take* too
much upon you, seeing [d]all the congregation *are* holy, every one
of them, [e]and the LORD *is* among them: wherefore then lift
4 ye up yourselves above the congregation of the LORD? And
5 when Moses heard *it*, [f]he fell upon his face: and he spake unto
Korah and unto all his company, saying, Even to morrow the
LORD will shew who *are* his, and *who is* [g]holy; and will cause
him to come near unto him: even *him* whom he hath [h]chosen

[l] Deut. 22.12. Matt. 23. 5.
[m] See Deut. 29. 19. Job 31. 7. Jer. 9. 14. Ez. 6. 9.
[n] Ps. 73. 27. & 106. 39. Jam. 4. 4.
[o] Lev. 11. 44, 45. Rom. 12. 1. Col. 1. 22. 1 Pet. 1. 15.
[a] Ex. 6. 21. ch. 26. 9. & 27. 3. Jude 11.
[b] ch. 26. 9.
[c] Ps. 106. 16.
[d] Ex. 19. 6.
[e] Ex. 29. 45. ch. 14. 14. & 35. 34.
[f] ch. 14. 5. & 20. 6.
[g] ver. 3. Lev. 21. 6, 7, 8, 12, 15.
[h] Ex. 28. 1. ch. 17. 5. 1 Sam. 2. 28. Ps. 105. 26.

[1] Heb. It is *much for you*.

---

add to the fringes of the borders (or corners) **a thread of blue** (cp. marg. reff.) These fringes are considered to be of Egyptian origin. The ordinary outer Jewish garment was a quadrangular piece of cloth like a modern plaid, to the corners of which, in conformity with this command, a tassel was attached. Each tassel had a conspicuous thread of deep blue, this colour being doubtless symbolical of the heavenly origin of the commandments of which it was to serve as a memento. Tradition determined that the other threads should be white,—this colour being an emblem of purity (cp. Isai. i. 18). The arrangement of the threads and knots, to which the Jews attached the greatest importance, was so adjusted as to set forth symbolically the 613 precepts of which the Law was believed to consist. In our Lord's time the Pharisees enlarged their fringes (Matt. xxiii. 5) in order to obtain reputation for their piety. In later times however the Jews have worn the fringed garment (*tālīth*) of a smaller size and as an under dress. Its use is still retained, especially at morning prayer in the Synagogue.

XVI. The date of this rebellion cannot be determined, but *vv.* 13, 14 probably point to a period not much later than that of the rebellion at Kadesh.

1. Amram and Izhar were brothers (cp. Ex. vi. 18), and thus Korah, the "son," *i.e.* descendant of Izhar, was connected by distant cousinship with Moses and Aaron. Though being a Kohathite, he was of that division of the Levites which had the most honourable charge, yet as Elizaphan, who had been made "chief of the families of the Kohathites" (iii. 30), belonged to the youngest branch descended from Uzziel (iii. 27), Korah probably regarded himself as injured; and therefore took the lead in this rebellion. Of the others, On is not again mentioned. He probably withdrew from the conspiracy. Dathan, Abiram, and On were Reubenites; and were probably discontented because the birthright had been taken away from their ancestor (Gen. xlix. 3), and with it the primacy of their own tribe amongst the tribes of Israel. The Reubenites encamped near to the Kohathites (cp. ii. 25 and plan), and thus the two families were conveniently situated for taking counsel together. One pretext of the insurrection probably was to assert the rights of primogeniture,—on the part of the Reubenites against Moses, on the part of Korah against the appointment of Uzziel.

2. The "princes" appear to have belonged to the other tribes (cp. xxvii. 3).

3. *all the congregation are holy*] Cp. marg. ref. Korah's object was not to abolish the distinction between the Levites and the people, but to win priestly dignity for himself and his kinsmen (*v.* 10). This ultimate design is masked for the present in order to win support from the Reubenites by putting forward claims to spiritual equality on behalf of every Israelite.

6 will he cause to [i]come near unto him. This do; Take you
7 censers, Korah, and all his company; and put fire therein, and
put incense in them before the LORD to morrow: and it shall
be *that* the man whom the LORD doth choose, he *shall be* holy:
8 *ye take* too much upon you, ye sons of Levi. And Moses said
9 unto Korah, Hear, I pray you, ye sons of Levi: *seemeth it but* [k]a
small thing unto you, that the God of Israel hath [l]separated you
from the congregation of Israel, to bring you near to himself to
do the service of the tabernacle of the LORD, and to stand before
10 the congregation to minister unto them? And he hath brought
thee near *to him*, and all thy brethren the sons of Levi with
11 thee: and seek ye the priesthood also? For which cause *both*
thou and all thy company *are* gathered together against the
LORD: [m]and what *is* Aaron, that ye murmur against him?
12 ¶ And Moses sent to call Dathan and Abiram, the sons of Eliab:
13 which said, We will not come up: [n]*is it* a small thing that thou
hast brought us up out of a land that floweth with milk and
honey, to kill us in the wilderness, except thou [o]make thyself
14 altogether a prince over us? Moreover thou hast not brought
us into [p]a land that floweth with milk and honey, or given us
inheritance of fields and vineyards: wilt thou [1]put out the eyes
15 of these men? We will not come up. ¶ And Moses was very
wroth, and said unto the LORD, [q]Respect not thou their offering:
[r]I have not taken one ass from them, neither have I hurt one of
16 them. And Moses said unto Korah, [s]Be thou and all thy company [t]before the LORD, thou, and they, and Aaron, to morrow:
17 and take every man his censer, and put incense in them, and
bring ye before the LORD every man his censer, two hundred
and fifty censers; thou also, and Aaron, each *of you* his censer.
18 And they took every man his censer, and put fire in them, and
laid incense thereon, and stood in the door of the tabernacle of
19 the congregation with Moses and Aaron. And Korah gathered
all the congregation against them unto the door of the tabernacle of the congregation: and [u]the glory of the LORD appeared
20 unto all the congregation. ¶ And the LORD spake unto Moses
21 and unto Aaron, saying, [x]Separate yourselves from among this
22 congregation, that I may [y]consume them in a moment. And
they [z]fell upon their faces, and said, O God, [a]the God of the
spirits of all flesh, shall one man sin, and wilt thou be wroth
23 with all the congregation? And the LORD spake unto Moses,
24 saying, Speak unto the congregation, saying, Get you up from

[i] ch. 3. 10. Lev. 10. 3. & 21. 17, 18. Ez. 40. 46. & 44. 15.
[k] 1 Sam. 18. 23. Isai. 7. 13.
[l] ch. 3. 41, 45. & 8. 14. Deut. 10. 8.
[m] Ex. 16. 8. 1 Cor. 3. 5.
[n] ver. 9.
[o] Ex. 2. 14. Acts 7. 27, 35.
[p] Ex. 3. 8. Lev. 20. 24.
[q] Gen. 4. 4, 5.
[r] 1 Sam. 12. 3. Acts 20. 33. 2 Cor. 7. 2.
[s] ver. 6, 7.
[t] 1 Sam. 12. 3, 7.
[u] ver. 42. Ex. 16. 7. Lev. 9. 6. ch. 14. 10.
[x] ver. 45. See Gen. 19. 17, 22. Jer. 51. 6. Acts 2. 40. Rev. 18. 4.
[y] ver. 45. Ex. 32. 10. & 33. 5.
[z] ver. 45. ch. 14. 5.
[a] ch. 27. 16. Job 12. 10. Eccles. 12. 7. Isai. 57. 16. Zech. 12. 1. Heb. 12. 9.

[1] Heb. *bore out*.

---

9. "Seemeth" is not in the original. Render: **Is it too little for you**, *i.e.* "is it less than your dignity demands?"

11. The words of Moses in his wrath are broken. The Aaronic priesthood was of divine appointment; and thus in rejecting it, the conspirators were really rebelling against God.

13. With perverse contempt for the promises, Dathan and Abiram designate Egypt by the terms appropriated elsewhere to the land of Canaan.

14. *wilt thou put out the eyes of these men?*] *i.e.* "blind them to the fact that you keep none of your promises;" "throw dust in their eyes."

24. The tent, *the tabernacle* of Korah, as a Kohathite, stood on the south side of the Tabernacle of the Lord; and those of Dathan and Abiram, as Reubenites, in the outer line of encampment on the same side. Yet though the tents of these three were thus contiguous, they did not share the same fate. Korah and his company who dared to intrude themselves on the priestly office were destroyed by fire from the Lord at the door of the Tabernacle of the Lord (*v.* 35); the Reubenites, who had reviled Moses for the failure of the promises about the pleasant land, were suddenly engulfed whilst standing at their own tent-doors in the barren wilderness (*vv.* 31-33).

25 about the tabernacle of Korah, Dathan, and Abiram. ¶ And
Moses rose up and went unto Dathan and Abiram; and the
26 elders of Israel followed him. And he spake unto the congregation, saying, [b]Depart, I pray you, from the tents of these
wicked men, and touch nothing of their's, lest ye be consumed
27 in all their sins. So they gat up from the tabernacle of Korah,
Dathan, and Abiram, on every side: and Dathan and Abiram
came out, and stood in the door of their tents, and their wives,
28 and their sons, and their little children. And Moses said,
[c]Hereby ye shall know that the LORD hath sent me to do all
these works; for *I have* not *done them* [d]of mine own mind.
29 If these men die [1]the common death of all men, or if they be
[e]visited after the visitation of all men; *then* the LORD hath not
30 sent me. But if the LORD [2]make [f]a new thing, and the earth
open her mouth, and swallow them up, with all that *appertain*
unto them, and they [g]go down quick into the pit; then ye shall
31 understand that these men have provoked the LORD. ¶ [h]And
it came to pass, as he had made an end of speaking all these
words, that the ground clave asunder that *was* under them:
32 and the earth opened her mouth, and swallowed them up, and
their houses, and [i]all the men that *appertained* unto Korah, and
33 all *their* goods. They, and all that *appertained* to them, went
down alive into the pit, and the earth closed upon them: and
34 they perished from among the congregation. And all Israel that
were round about them fled at the cry of them: for they said,
35 Lest the earth swallow us up *also*. And there [k]came out a fire
from the LORD, and consumed [l]the two hundred and fifty men
36 that offered incense. ¶ And the LORD spake unto Moses, saying,
37 Speak unto Eleazar the son of Aaron the priest, that he take up
the censers out of the burning, and scatter thou the fire yonder;
38 for [m]they are hallowed. The censers of these [n]sinners against
their own souls, let them make them broad plates *for* a covering
of the altar: for they offered them before the LORD, therefore
they are hallowed: [o]and they shall be a sign unto the children
39 of Israel. And Eleazar the priest took the brasen censers,
wherewith they that were burnt had offered; and they were
40 made broad *plates for* a covering of the altar: *to be* a memorial
unto the children of Israel, [p]that no stranger, which *is* not of
the seed of Aaron, come near to offer incense before the LORD;
that he be not as Korah, and as his company: as the LORD said
41 to him by the hand of Moses. ¶ But on the morrow [q]all the
congregation of the children of Israel murmured against Moses
and against Aaron, saying, Ye have killed the people of the LORD.
42 And it came to pass, when the congregation was gathered
against Moses and against Aaron, that they looked toward the

[b] Gen. 19. 12, 14. Isai. 52. 11. 2 Cor. 6. 17. Rev. 18. 4.
[c] Ex. 3. 12. Deut. 18. 22. Zech. 2. 9, 11. & 4. 9. John 5. 36.
[d] ch. 24. 13. Jer. 23. 16. Ez. 13. 17. John 5. 30. & 6. 38.
[e] Ex. 20. 5. & 32. 34. Job 35. 15. Isai. 10. 3. Jer. 5. 9.
[f] Job 31. 3. Isai. 28. 21.
[g] ver. 33. Ps. 55. 15.
[h] ch. 26. 10. & 27. 3. Deut. 11. 6. Ps. 106. 17.
[i] See ver. 17. & ch. 26. 11. 1 Chr. 6. 22, 37.
[k] Lev. 10. 2. ch. 11. 1. Ps. 106. 18.
[l] ver. 17.
[m] See Lev. 27. 28.
[n] Prov. 20. 2. Hab. 2. 10.
[o] ch. 17. 10. & 26. 10. Ez. 14. 8.
[p] ch. 3. 10. 2 Chr. 26. 18.
[q] ch. 14. 2. Ps. 106. 25.

[1] Heb. *as every man dieth.*
[2] Heb. *create a creature*, Isai. 45. 7.

---

27. *stood in the door of their tents*] Apparently in contumacious defiance.

32. *all the men*, &c.] Not his sons (see xxvi. 11), but all belonging to him who had associated themselves with him in this rebellion.

35. Cp. marg. reff. The fire came out from the Sanctuary or the Altar.

37. Aaron as High-priest and as one of those that offered incense (*v.* 17), could not be defiled by going among the dead.

The censers were not to be used again for censers, nor the coals on them for kindling the incense to be offered before the Lord. Yet neither of them could fittingly be employed for common purposes. The censers therefore were beaten into plates for the Altar; the coals were scattered at a distance.

38. *these sinners against their own souls*] That is, "against their own lives." By their sin they had brought destruction upon themselves.

tabernacle of the congregation: and, behold, [r]the cloud covered
43 it, and [s]the glory of the LORD appeared. And Moses and Aaron
44 came before the tabernacle of the congregation. And the LORD
45 spake unto Moses, saying, [t]Get you up from among this congregation, that I may consume them as in a moment. And [u]they
46 fell upon their faces. And Moses said unto Aaron, Take a
censer, and put fire therein from off the altar, and put on incense,
and go quickly unto the congregation, and make an atonement
for them: [x]for there is wrath gone out from the LORD; the
47 plague is begun. And Aaron took as Moses commanded, and ran
into the midst of the congregation; and, behold, the plague was
begun among the people: and he put on incense, and made an
48 atonement for the people. And he stood between the dead and
49 the living; and the plague was stayed. Now they that died in
the plague were fourteen thousand and seven hundred, beside
50 them that died about the matter of Korah. And Aaron returned
unto Moses unto the door of the tabernacle of the congregation:
and the plague was stayed.

CHAP. 17. AND the LORD spake unto Moses, saying, Speak unto the
2 children of Israel, and take of every one of them a rod according
to the house of *their* fathers, of all their princes according to the
house of their fathers twelve rods: write thou every man's name
3 upon his rod. And thou shalt write Aaron's name upon the rod
of Levi: for one rod *shall be* for the head of the house of their
4 fathers. And thou shalt lay them up in the tabernacle of the
congregation before the testimony, [a]where I will meet with you.
5 And it shall come to pass, *that* the man's rod, [b]whom I shall
choose, shall blossom: and I will make to cease from me the
murmurings of the children of Israel, [c]whereby they murmur
6 against you. ¶ And Moses spake unto the children of Israel,
and every one of their princes gave him [1]a rod apiece, for each
prince one, according to their fathers' houses, *even* twelve rods:
7 and the rod of Aaron *was* among their rods. And Moses laid up
8 the rods before the LORD in [d]the tabernacle of witness. ¶ And
it came to pass, that on the morrow Moses went into the taber-

[r] Ex. 40. 34.
[s] ver. 19. ch. 20. 6.
[t] ver. 21. 24.
[u] ver. 22. ch. 20. 6.
[x] 5 Lev. 10. 6. ch. 1. 53. & 8. 19. & 11. 33. & 18. 5. 1 Chr. 27. 24. Ps. 106. 29.
[a] Ex. 25. 22. & 29. 42, 43. & 30. 36.
[b] ch. 16. 5.
[c] ch. 16. 11.
[d] Ex. 38. 21. ch. 18. 2. Acts 7. 44.

[1] Heb. *a rod for one prince, a rod for one prince.*

---

45. *they fell upon their faces*] In intercession for the people; cp. *v.* 22, xiv. 5.

46. *a censer*] Rather, **the censer.** *i.e.* that of the High-priest which was used by him on the Great Day of Atonement: cp. Lev. xvi. 12; Heb. ix. 4.

46–48. A striking proof of the efficacy of that very Aaronic priesthood which the rebels had presumed to reject. The incense offering which had brought down destruction when presented by unauthorised hands, now in the hand of the true priest is the medium of instant salvation to the whole people. Aaron by his acceptable ministration and his personal self-devotion foreshadows emphatically in this transaction the perfect mediation and sacrifice of Himself made by Christ.

XVII. **2.** Cp. Ezek. xxxvii. 16 sqq.

3. *thou shalt write Aaron's name upon the rod of Levi*] The Levites had taken part in the late outbreak. It was therefore necessary to vindicate the supremacy of the house of Aaron over them; and accordingly his name was written on the rod of Levi, although being the son of Kohath, the *second* son of Levi (Ex. vi. 16 seq.), he would not be the natural head of the tribe.

4. *before the testimony*] See *v.* 10 note.

6. The whole number of rods was twelve exclusive of Aaron's, as the Vulgate expressly states.

8. *yielded almonds*] "Ripened almonds," *i.e.* "brought forth ripe almonds." The name almond in Hebrew denotes the "waking-tree," the "waking-fruit;" and is applied to this tree, because it blossoms early in the season. It serves here, as in Jer. i. 11, 12, to set forth the speed and certainty with which, at God's will, His purposes are accomplished. So again the blossoming and bearing of Aaron's rod, naturally impotent when severed from the parent tree, may signify the profitableness, because of God's appointment and blessing, of the various means of grace (*e.g.* the

nacle of witness; and, behold, the rod of Aaron for the house
of Levi was budded, and brought forth buds, and bloomed
9 blossoms, and yielded almonds. And Moses brought out all the
rods from before the LORD unto all the children of Israel: and
10 they looked, and took every man his rod. ¶ And the LORD said
unto Moses, Bring [e]Aaron's rod again before the testimony, to
be kept [f]for a token against the [1]rebels; [g]and thou shalt quite
11 take away their murmurings from me, that they die not. And
12 Moses did *so:* as the LORD commanded him, so did he. ¶ And
the children of Israel spake unto Moses, saying, Behold, we die,
13 we perish, we all perish. [h]Whosoever cometh any thing near
unto the tabernacle of the LORD shall die: shall we be consumed
with dying?

CHAP. 18. AND the LORD said unto Aaron, [a]Thou and thy sons
and thy father's house with thee shall [b]bear the iniquity of the
sanctuary: and thou and thy sons with thee shall bear the
2 iniquity of your priesthood. And thy brethren also of the tribe
of Levi, the tribe of thy father, bring thou with thee, that they
may be [c]joined unto thee, and [d]minister unto thee; but [e]thou
and thy sons with thee *shall minister* before the tabernacle of
3 witness. And they shall keep thy charge, and [f]the charge of all
the tabernacle: [g]only they shall not come nigh the vessels of the
4 sanctuary and the altar, [h]that neither they, nor ye also, die. And
they shall be joined unto thee, and keep the charge of the tabernacle of the congregation, for all the service of the tabernacle:
5 [i]and a stranger shall not come nigh unto you. And ye shall
keep [k]the charge of the sanctuary, and the charge of the altar:
[l]that there be no wrath any more upon the children of Israel.
6 And I, behold, I have [m]taken your brethren the Levites from
among the children of Israel: [n]to you *they are* given *as* a gift
for the LORD, to do the service of the tabernacle of the congrega-
7 tion. Therefore [o]thou and thy sons with thee shall keep your
priest's office for every thing of the altar, and [p]within the vail;

e Heb. 9. 4.
f ch. 16. 38.
g ver. 5.
h ch. 1. 51, 53. & 18. 4, 7.
a ch. 17. 13.
b Ex. 28. 38.
c See Gen. 29. 34.
d ch. 3. 6, 7.
e ch. 3. 10.
f ch. 3. 25, 31, 36.
g ch. 16. 40.
h ch. 4. 15.
i ch. 3. 10.
k Ex. 27. 21. & 30. 7. Lev. 24. 3. ch. 8. 2.
l ch. 16. 46.
m ch. 3. 12, 45.
n ch. 3. 9. & 8. 19.
o ver. 5. ch. 3. 10.
p Heb. 9. 3, 6.

[1] Heb. *children of rebellion.*

---

priesthood, the Sacraments), which of themselves and apart from Him could have no such efficacy. Cp. Isai. iv. 2, xi. 1, liii. 2; Jer. xxxiii. 5; Zech. vi. 12.

10. *the testimony*] i.e. the Two Tables of the Law; cp. Ex. xxv. 16 note. No doubt the rod lay in front of the Tables within the Ark. In the days of Solomon (1 Kings viii. 9) there was nothing in the ark save the Two Tables. Aaron's rod was probably lost when the Ark was taken by the Philistines.

12, 13. A new section should begin with these verses. They are connected retrospectively with ch. xvi.; and form the immediate introduction to ch. xviii. The people were terror-stricken by the fate of the company of Korah and by the plague. Presumption passed by reaction into despair. Was there any approach for them to the Tabernacle of the Lord? Was there any escape from death, except by keeping aloof from His Presence? The answers are supplied by the ordinances which testified that the God of judgment was still a God of grace and of love.

XVIII. **1.** *the iniquity of the sanctuary*] *i.e.* the guilt of the offences which an erring people would be continually committing against the majesty of God, when brought into contact, through the ordinances, with the manifestations of His Presence. Cp. marg. ref.

the iniquity of your priesthood] As the priests themselves were but men, they were strengthened to bear the iniquity of their own unintentional offences, by being entrusted with the ceremonial means of taking it away (cp. Lev. xvi.). The word "bear" has, in the Old Testament, this double sense of "enduring" and "removing;" but in the person of Christ, Who atoned by His own endurance, the two are in effect one.

4. *a stranger*] *i.e.* every one not a Levite. So in *v.* 7, it denotes every one who was not a priest: cp. iii. 10, xvi. 40.

6, 7. The Lord instructs here the priests that the office which they fill, and the help which they enjoy, are gifts from Him, and are to be viewed as such.

and ye shall serve: I have given your priest's office *unto you as*
a service of gift: and the stranger that cometh nigh shall be put
8 to death. ¶ And the LORD spake unto Aaron, Behold, [q]I also
have given thee the charge of mine heave offerings of all the
hallowed things of the children of Israel; unto thee have I given
them [r]by reason of the anointing, and to thy sons, by an ordi-
9 nance for ever. This shall be thine of the most holy things,
reserved from the fire: every oblation of their's, every [s]meat
offering of their's, and every [t]sin offering of their's, and every
[u]trespass offering of their's, which they shall render unto me,
10 *shall be* most holy for thee and for thy sons. [x]In the most holy
place shalt thou eat it; every male shall eat it: it shall be holy
11 unto thee. And this *is* thine; [y]the heave offering of their gift,
with all the wave offerings of the children of Israel: I have given
them unto [z]thee, and to thy sons and to thy daughters with
thee, by a statute for ever: [a]every one that is clean in thy house
12 shall eat of it. [b]All the [1]best of the oil, and all the best of the
wine, and of the wheat, [c]the firstfruits of them which they shall
13 offer unto the LORD, them have I given thee. *And* whatsoever
is first ripe in the land, [d]which they shall bring unto the LORD,
shall be thine; [e]every one that is clean in thine house shall eat
14, 15 *of* it. [f]Every thing devoted in Israel shall be thine. Every
thing that openeth [g]the matrix in all flesh, which they bring
unto the LORD, *whether it be* of men or beasts, shall be thine:
nevertheless [h]the firstborn of man shalt thou surely redeem,
16 and the firstling of unclean beasts shalt thou redeem. And
those that are to be redeemed from a month old shalt thou redeem, [i]according to thine estimation, for the money of five
shekels, after the shekel of the sanctuary, [k]which *is* twenty
17 gerahs. [l]But the firstling of a cow, or the firstling of a sheep,
or the firstling of a goat, thou shalt not redeem; they *are* holy:
[m]thou shalt sprinkle their blood upon the altar, and shalt burn
their fat *for* an offering made by fire, for a sweet savour unto the
18 LORD. And the flesh of them shall be thine, as the [n]wave breast
19 and as the right shoulder are thine. [o]All the heave offerings of
the holy things, which the children of Israel offer unto the LORD,
have I given thee, and thy sons and thy daughters with thee,
by a statute for ever: [p]it *is* a covenant of salt for ever before
20 the LORD unto thee and to thy seed with thee. ¶ And the LORD
spake unto Aaron, Thou shalt have no inheritance in their land,
neither shalt thou have any part among them: [q]I *am* thy part
21 and thine inheritance among the children of Israel. And, behold, [r]I have given the children of Levi all the tenth in Israel

q Lev. 6. 16, 18. & 7. 6. ch. 5. 9.
r Ex. 29. 29. & 40. 13, 15.
s Lev. 2. 2, 3.
t Lev. 4. 22.
u Lev. 5. 1.
x Lev. 6. 16, 18, 26, 29. & 7. 6.
y Ex. 29. 27. Lev. 7. 30.
z Lev. 10. 14. Deut. 18. 3.
a Lev. 22. 2.
b Ex. 23. 19. Deut. 18. 4. Neh. 10. 35.
c Ex. 22. 29.
d Ex. 23. 19. & 34. 26. Lev. 2. 14. ch. 15. 19. Deut. 26. 2.
e ver. 11.
f Lev. 27. 28.
g Ex. 13. 2. Lev. 27. 26. ch. 3. 13.
h Ex. 13. 13. & 34. 20.
i Lev. 27. 2, 6. ch. 3. 47.
k Ex. 30. 13. Lev. 27. 25. ch. 3. 47. Ez. 45. 12.
l Deut. 15. 19.
m Lev. 3. 2, 5.
n Ex. 29. 26. Lev. 7. 31.
o ver. 11.
p Lev. 2. 13. 2 Chr. 13. 5.
q Deut. 10. 9. Josh. 13. 14, 33. Ps. 16. 5. Ez. 44. 28.
r Lev. 27. 30, 32. ver. 24. 26. Neh. 10. 37. & 12. 44. Heb. 7. 5.

[1] Heb. *fat*, ver. 29.

---

8. *by reason of the anointing*] See Lev. vii. 35.

10. *in the most holy place*] Rather, "among the most holy things;" as in iv. 4: *i.e.* "As the most holy of things shalt thou eat it." Accordingly only the males of the priestly families could eat of the things here specified.

15. *surely redeem...redeem*] A stronger expression is intentionally used in reference to the redemption of the first-born of man than in reference to that of unclean beasts. For the rule as to the former admitted of no exception: the owner of the latter, if unwilling to redeem, might destroy the beasts. Cp. marg. reff.

19. *a covenant of salt*] Cp. marg. ref. Covenants were ordinarily cemented in the East by the rites of hospitality; of which salt was the obvious token, entering as it does into every article of diet. It indicates perpetuity: cp. Lev. ii. 13 note.

20. *I am thy part and thine inheritance*] Cp. marg. reff.

21. Abraham paid tithes to Melchizedek: Jacob had promised the tithe of all where-

for an inheritance, for their service which they serve, *even* [s]the [s] ch. 3. 7, 8.
22 service of the tabernacle of the congregation. [t]Neither must [t] ch. 1. 51.
the children of Israel henceforth come nigh the tabernacle of the
23 congregation, [u]lest they bear sin, [1]and die. [x]But the Levites [u] Lev. 22. 9.
shall do the service of the tabernacle of the congregation, and [x] ch. 3. 7.
they shall bear their iniquity: *it shall be* a statute for ever
throughout your generations, that among the children of Israel
24 they have no inheritance. [y]But the tithes of the children of [y] ver. 21.
Israel, which they offer *as* an heave offering unto the LORD, I
have given to the Levites to inherit: therefore I have said unto
them, [z]Among the children of Israel they shall have no inheri- [z] ver. 20.
25, 26 tance. ¶ And the LORD spake unto Moses, saying, Thus speak Deut. 14. 27,
unto the Levites, and say unto them, When ye take of the 29. & 18. 1.
children of Israel the tithes which I have given you from them
for your inheritance, then ye shall offer up an heave offering of
27 it for the LORD, *even* [a]a tenth *part* of the tithe. [b]And *this* your [a] Neh. 10.
heave offering shall be reckoned unto you, as though *it were* the 38.
corn of the threshingfloor, and as the fulness of the winepress. [b] ver. 30.
28 Thus ye also shall offer an heave offering unto the LORD of all
your tithes, which ye receive of the children of Israel; and ye
shall give thereof the LORD's heave offering to Aaron the priest.
29 Out of all your gifts ye shall offer every heave offering of the
LORD, of all the [2]best thereof, *even* the hallowed part thereof out
30 of it. Therefore thou shalt say unto them, When ye have heaved
the best thereof from it, [c]then it shall be counted unto the [c] ver. 27.
Levites as the increase of the threshingfloor, and as the increase
31 of the winepress. And ye shall eat it in every place, ye and
your households: for it *is* [d]your reward for your service in the [d] Matt. 10.
32 tabernacle of the congregation. And ye shall [e]bear no sin by 10.
reason of it, when ye have heaved from it the best of it: neither Luke 10. 7.
shall ye [f]pollute the holy things of the children of Israel, lest 1 Cor. 9. 13.
ye die. 1 Tim. 5. 18.
[e] Lev. 19. 8. & 22. 16.

CHAP. 19. AND the LORD spake unto Moses and unto Aaron, saying, [f] Lev. 22. 2, 15.

[1] Heb. *to die*. [2] Heb. *fat*, ver. 12.

---

with God blessed him if he should return in peace to his father's house. But now first the Lord's tithes are assigned to the Levites for their support (cp. Lev. xxvii. 30). The payment of tithes to them is recognised in Neh. x. 37, xii. 44; Tobit i. 7.

23. *bear their iniquity*] The words probably refer to the iniquity of the people; who would, had they approached the Tabernacle have fallen, from their proneness to transgress, into overt acts of offence. Against such a result they were, through the ministrations of the Levites, mercifully protected. Cp. *v.* 1.

24. Here the tithes (and in *v.* 26 the priestly tithes) are to be dedicated to their purpose by the ceremony of heaving them to the Lord. The tithes, being solemnly set apart for sacred purposes, became virtually a heave-offering, like the gifts for the Tabernacle (Ex. xxv. 2).

27. *reckoned unto you*] Or, **by you**. The Levites were, of their tithes, to pay tithe to the priests, just as other Israelites paid tithe to the Levites.

29. *out of all your gifts*] The spirit of this law would extend to all the revenues of the Levites; of the increase of their cattle, as well as of their tithes, a tithe would be paid by them for the Lord's service.

32. *neither shall ye pollute*, &c.] Rather, **and by not polluting the holy things of the children of Israel, ye shall not die.**

XIX. The principle that death and all pertaining to it, as being the manifestation and result of sin (Gen. ii. 17), are defiling, and so lead to interruption of the living relationship between God and His people, is not now introduced for the first time, nor is it at all peculiar to the Mosaic law. It was, on the contrary, traditional amongst the Israelites from the earliest times, it is assumed in various enactments made already (cp. v. 2, ix. 6 seq.; Lev. x. 1, 7, xi. 8, 11, 24, xxi. 1 seq.), and it is traceable in various forms amongst many nations, both ancient and modern. Moses adopted, here as elsewhere, existing and ancient customs, with significant additions, as helps in the spiritual education of his people.

2 This *is* the ordinance of the law which the LORD hath commanded, saying, Speak unto the children of Israel, that they
bring thee a red heifer without spot, wherein *is* no blemish,
3 [a]*and* upon which never came yoke: and ye shall give her unto
Eleazar the priest, that he may bring her [b]forth without the
4 camp, and *one* shall slay her before his face: and Eleazar the
priest shall take of her blood with his finger, and [c]sprinkle of
her blood directly before the tabernacle of the congregation
5 seven times: and *one* shall burn the heifer in his sight; [d]her
skin, and her flesh, and her blood, with her dung, shall he burn:
6 and the priest shall take [e]cedar wood, and hyssop, and scarlet,
7 and cast *it* into the midst of the burning of the heifer. [f]Then
the priest shall wash his clothes, and he shall bathe his flesh in
water, and afterward he shall come into the camp, and the priest
8 shall be unclean until the even. And he that burneth her shall
wash his clothes in water, and bathe his flesh in water, and shall
9 be unclean until the even. And a man *that is* clean shall gather
up [g]the ashes of the heifer, and lay *them* up without the camp in
a clean place, and it shall be kept for the congregation of the
children of Israel [h]for a water of separation: it *is* a purification
10 for sin. And he that gathereth the ashes of the heifer shall
wash his clothes, and be unclean until the even: and it shall be
unto the children of Israel, and unto the stranger that sojourneth
11 among them, for a statute for ever. ¶ [i]He that toucheth the
12 dead body of any [1]man shall be unclean seven days. [k]He shall
purify himself with it on the third day, and on the seventh
day he shall be clean: but if he purify not himself the third
13 day, then the seventh day he shall not be clean. Whosoever
toucheth the dead body of any man that is dead, and purifieth

[a] Deut. 21. 3. 1 Sam. 6. 7.
[b] Lev. 4. 12, 21. & 16. 27. Heb. 13. 11.
[c] Lev. 4. 6. & 16. 14, 19. Heb. 9. 13.
[d] Ex. 29. 14. Lev. 4. 11.
[e] Lev. 14. 4, 6, 49.
[f] Lev. 11. 25. & 15. 5.
[g] Heb. 9. 13.
[h] ver. 13. 20, 21. ch. 31. 23.
[i] ver. 16. Lev. 21. 1. ch. 5. 2. Lam. 4. 14. Hag. 2. 13.
[k] ch. 31. 19.

[1] Heb. *soul of man.*

The ordinance was probably given at this time because the plague which happened (xvi. 46–50) about the matter of Korah had spread the defilement of death so widely through the camp as to seem to require some special measures of purification, more particularly as the deaths through it were in an extraordinary manner the penalty of sin.

2. *a red heifer*] Red, in order to shadow forth man's earthly body, even as the name Adam bears allusion to the red earth of which man's body was fashioned.

without spot, wherein is no blemish] As with sin-offerings generally (Lev. iv. 3).

upon which never came yoke] So here and elsewhere (see marg. reff.), in the case of female victims.

3. The work would necessarily require a priest; yet as it rendered him unclean for the day (*v.* 22), the High-priest was relieved from performing it.

without the camp] The defilement was viewed as transferred to the victim that was to be offered for its removal. Under these circumstances the victim, like the defiled persons themselves, would be removed outside the camp. The particular pollution to be remedied by this ordinance was the indirect one resulting from contact with tokens and manifestations of sin, not the direct and personal one arising from actual commission of sin. So too the sinless Antitype had to bear the reproach of associating with sinners (Luke v. 30, xv. 2). And as the red heifer was expelled from the precincts of the camp, so was the Saviour cut off in no small measure during His Life from the fellowship of the chief representatives of the Theocracy, and put to death outside Jerusalem between two thieves. Cp. Heb. xiii. 11, 12.

6. Cp. Lev. xiv. 4 note.

9. *water of separation*] In viii. 7, the water of purification from sin is the "water of purifying." So that which was to remedy a state of legal separation is here called "water of separation."

10. He that gathered the ashes became equally unclean with the others. For the defilement of the people, previously transferred to the heifer, was regarded as concentrated in the ashes.

11–22. One practical effect of attaching defilement to a dead body, and to all that touched it, &c., would be to insure early burial, and to correct a practice not uncommon in the East, of leaving the dead to be devoured by the wild beasts.

not himself, [l]defileth the tabernacle of the LORD; and that soul
shall be cut off from Israel: because [m]the water of separation
was not sprinkled upon him, he shall be unclean; [n]his unclean-
14 ness *is* yet upon him. This *is* the law, when a man dieth in a
tent: all that come into the tent, and all that *is* in the tent, shall
15 be unclean seven days. And every [o]open vessel, which hath no
16 covering bound upon it, *is* unclean. And [p]whosoever toucheth
one that is slain with a sword in the open fields, or a dead body,
or a bone of a man, or a grave, shall be unclean seven days.
17 ¶ And for an unclean *person* they shall take of the [1][q]ashes of
the burnt heifer of purification for sin, and [2]running water shall
18 be put thereto in a vessel: and a clean person shall take
[r]hyssop, and dip *it* in the water, and sprinkle *it* upon the tent,
and upon all the vessels, and upon the persons that were there,
and upon him that touched a bone, or one slain, or one dead, or
19 a grave: and the clean *person* shall sprinkle upon the unclean on the third day, and on the seventh day: [s]and on the
seventh day he shall purify himself, and wash his clothes, and
20 bathe himself in water, and shall be clean at even. But the man
that shall be unclean, and shall not purify himself, that soul
shall be cut off from among the congregation, because he hath
[t]defiled the sanctuary of the LORD: the water of separation hath
21 not been sprinkled upon him; he *is* unclean. And it shall be a
perpetual statute unto them, that he that sprinkleth the water
of separation shall wash his clothes; and he that toucheth the
22 water of separation shall be unclean until even. And [u]whatso-
ever the unclean *person* toucheth shall be unclean; and [x]the
soul that toucheth *it* shall be unclean until even.

CHAP. 20. THEN [a]came the children of Israel, *even* the whole
congregation, into the desert of Zin in the first month: and

[l] Lev. 15. 31.
[m] ch. 8. 7. ver. 9.
[n] Lev. 7. 20. & 22. 3.
[o] Lev. 11. 32. ch. 31. 20.
[p] ver. 11.
[q] ver. 9.
[r] Ps. 51. 7.
[s] Lev. 14. 9.
[t] ver. 13.
[u] Hag. 2. 13.
[x] Lev. 15. 5.
[a] ch. 33. 36.

[1] Heb. *dust*. [2] Heb. *living waters shall be given*, Gen. 26. 19.

XX. & XXI. narrate the journey of the people from Kadesh round Mount Seir to the heights of Pisgah, near the Jordan, and the various incidents connected with that journey (cp. xxxiii. 37-41). This formed the third and last stage of the progress of Israel from Sinai to Canaan, and took place in the fortieth year of the Exodus.

The incidents are apparently not narrated in a strictly chronological order (see xxi. 1). The leading purpose of ch. xx. seems to be to narrate the loss by the people of their original leaders before their entrance into the Land of Promise.

1. *even the whole congregation*] This emphatic expression (cp. xiii. 26, xiv. 1) points to a re-assembling of the people for the purpose of at last resuming the advance to the Promised Land. During the past 38 years the "congregation" had been broken up. No doubt round the Tabernacle there had continued an organised camp consisting of the Levites and others, which had been moved from time to time up and down the country (cp. xxxiii. 18-36). But the mass of the people had been scattered over the face of the wilderness of Paran, and led a nomadic life as best suited the pasturage of the cattle; trafficking in provisions with surrounding tribes (cp. Deut. ii. 26-29; Ps. lxxiv. 14); and availing themselves of the resources of a district which were in ancient times vastly greater than they now are.

These natural resources were supplemented, where needful, by miraculous aid. The whole guidance of Israel through the wilderness is constantly referred to God's special and immediately superintending care (Deut. viii. 4 seq., xxix. 5; Neh. ix. 21; Isai. lxiii. 11-14; Amos ii. 10, &c.).

Yet though God's extraordinary bounty was vouchsafed to them, it is probable that this period was, amongst the perishing generation at all events, one of great religious declension, or even apostasy. To it must no doubt be referred such passages as Ezek. xx. 15 seq.; Amos v. 25 seq.; Hosea ix. 10.

into the desert of Zin] The north-eastern part of the wilderness of Paran [or, now definitely fixed by Palmer as the south-eastern corner of the desert of Et-Tih, between Akabah and the head of Wady Garaiyeh]. The place of encampment was no doubt adjacent to the spring of Kadesh.

in the first month] *i.e.* of the fortieth year of the Exodus.

the people abode in Kadesh; and [b]Miriam died there, and was
2 buried there. ¶ [c]And there was no water for the congregation:
[d]and they gathered themselves together against Moses and
3 against Aaron. And the people [e]chode with Moses, and spake,
saying, Would God that we had died [f]when our brethren died
4 before the LORD! And [g]why have ye brought up the congregation of the LORD into this wilderness, that we and our cattle
5 should die there? And wherefore have ye made us to come up
out of Egypt, to bring us in unto this evil place? It *is* no place
of seed, or of figs, or of vines, or of pomegranates; neither *is*
6 there any water to drink. ¶ And Moses and Aaron went from
the presence of the assembly unto the door of the tabernacle of
the congregation, and [h]they fell upon their faces: and [i]the
7 glory of the LORD appeared unto them. And the LORD spake
8 unto Moses, saying, [k]Take the rod, and gather thou the assembly
together, thou, and Aaron thy brother, and speak ye unto the
rock before their eyes; and it shall give forth his water, and
[l]thou shalt bring forth to them water out of the rock: so thou
9 shalt give the congregation and their beasts drink. And
Moses took the rod [m]from before the LORD, as he commanded
10 him. And Moses and Aaron gathered the congregation together
before the rock, and he said unto them, [n]Hear now, ye rebels;
11 must we fetch you water out of this rock? And Moses lifted
up his hand, and with his rod he smote the rock twice: and
[o]the water came out abundantly, and the congregation drank,
12 and their beasts *also*. And the LORD spake unto Moses and
Aaron, Because [p]ye believed me not, to [q]sanctify me in the eyes
of the children of Israel, therefore ye shall not bring this con-
13 gregation into the land which I have given them. [r]This *is* the
water of [1]Meribah; because the children of Israel strove with
14 the LORD, and he was sanctified in them. ¶ [s]And Moses sent

[b] Ex. 15. 20. ch. 26. 59.
[c] Ex. 17. 1.
[d] ch. 16. 19, 42.
[e] Ex. 17. 2. ch. 14. 2.
[f] ch. 11. 1, 33. & 14. 37. & 16. 32, 35, 49.
[g] Ex. 17. 3.
[h] ch. 14. 5. & 16. 4, 22, 45.
[i] ch. 14. 10.
[k] Ex. 17. 5.
[l] Neh. 9. 15. Ps. 78. 15, 16. & 105. 41. & 114. 8. Isai. 43. 20. & 48. 21.
[m] ch. 17. 10.
[n] Ps. 106. 33.
[o] Ex. 17. 6. Deut. 8. 15. 1 Cor. 10. 4.
[p] ch. 27. 14. Deut. 1. 37. & 3. 26. & 32. 51.
[q] Lev. 10. 3. Ez. 20. 41. & 36. 23. 1 Pet. 3. 15.
[r] Deut. 33. 8. Ps. 95. 8.
[s] Judg. 11. 16, 17.

[1] That is, *Strife*. See Ex. 17. 7.

2–6. The language of the murmurers is noteworthy. It has the air of a traditional remonstrance handed down from the last generation. Cp. marg. reff.

8. *take the rod*] That with which the miracles in Egypt had been wrought (Ex. vii. 8 seq., 19 seq., viii. 5 seq., &c.), and which had been used on a similar occasion at Rephidim (Ex. xvii. 5 seq.). This rod, as the memorial of so many Divine interpositions, was naturally laid up in the Tabernacle, and is accordingly (*v.* 9) described now as taken by Moses "from before the Lord."

11, 12. The command (*v.* 8) was "Speak ye unto the rock." The act of smiting, and especially with two strokes, indicates violent irritation on the part of Moses; as does also his unseemly mode of addressing the people: "Hear now, ye rebels." The form too of the question, "must *we*, &c.," directs the people not, as ought to have been the case, to God as their deliverer, but to Moses and Aaron personally. In fact the faithful servant of God, worn out by the reiterated perversities of the people, breaks down; and in the actual discharge of his duty as God's representative before Israel, acts unworthily of the great function entrusted to him. Thus Moses did not "sanctify God in the eyes of the children of Israel." Aaron might have checked the intemperate words and acts of Moses, and did not. Hence God punishes both by withdrawing them from their work for Him, and handing over its accomplishment to another.

13. *the water of Meribah*] *i.e.* "Strife." The place is called "Meribah in Kadesh" (xxvii. 14), and "Meribah-Kadesh" (Deut. xxxii. 51), to distinguish it from the "Meribah" of Ex. xvii. 2 seq.

and he was sanctified in them] An allusion doubtless to the name "Kadesh" (holy), which though not now bestowed, acquired a new significance from the fact that God here vindicated His own sanctity, punishing Moses and Aaron who had trespassed against it.

14. Cp. marg. ref. It appears from comparing xx. 1 with xxxiii. 38, that the host must have remained in Kadesh some three or four months. No doubt time was required for re-organization. In order to gain the banks of Jordan by the shortest route they had to march nearly due east from Kadesh, and pass through the heart

messengers from Kadesh unto the king of Edom, [t]Thus saith
thy brother Israel, Thou knowest all the travel that hath [1]be-
15 fallen us: [u]how our fathers went down into Egypt, [w]and we
have dwelt in Egypt a long time; [x]and the Egyptians vexed us,
16 and our fathers: and [y]when we cried unto the LORD, he heard
our voice, and [z]sent an angel, and hath brought us forth out of
Egypt: and, behold, we *are* in Kadesh, a city in the uttermost
17 of thy border: [a]let us pass, I pray thee, through thy country:
we will not pass through the fields, or through the vineyards,
neither will we drink *of* the water of the wells: we will go by
the king's *high* way, we will not turn to the right hand nor to
18 the left, until we have passed thy borders. And Edom said unto
him, Thou shalt not pass by me, lest I come out against thee
19 with the sword. And the children of Israel said unto him, We
will go by the high way: and if I and my cattle drink of thy
water, [b]then I will pay for it: I will only, without *doing* any
20 thing *else*, go through on my feet. And he said, [c]Thou shalt
not go through. And Edom came out against him with much
21 people, and with a strong hand. Thus Edom [d]refused to give
Israel passage through his border: wherefore Israel [e]turned
22 away from him. ¶ And the children of Israel, *even* the whole
congregation, journeyed from [f]Kadesh, [g]and came unto mount
23 Hor. And the LORD spake unto Moses and Aaron in mount
24 Hor, by the coast of the land of Edom, saying, Aaron shall be
[h]gathered unto his people: for he shall not enter into the land
which I have given unto the children of Israel, because [i]ye re-
25 belled against my [2]word at the water of Meribah. [k]Take Aaron
26 and Eleazar his son, and bring them up unto mount Hor: and
strip Aaron of his garments, and put them upon Eleazar his son:
and Aaron shall be gathered *unto his people*, and shall die there.
27 And Moses did as the LORD commanded: and they went up
28 into mount Hor in the sight of all the congregation. [l]And
Moses stripped Aaron of his garments, and put them upon
Eleazar his son; and [m]Aaron died there in the top of the
mount: and Moses and Eleazar came down from the mount.
29 And when all the congregation saw that Aaron was dead, they
mourned for Aaron [n]thirty days, *even* all the house of Israel.
CHAP. 21. AND *when* [a]king Arad the Canaanite, which dwelt in
the south, heard tell that Israel came [b]by the way of the spies;

[t] Deut. 2. 4. Obad. 10. 12.
[u] Gen. 46. 6. Acts 7. 15.
[w] Ex. 12. 40.
[x] Ex. 1. 11. Deut. 26. 6. Acts 7. 19.
[y] Ex. 2. 23. & 3. 7.
[z] Ex. 3. 2. & 14. 19. & 23. 20. & 33. 2.
[a] See ch. 21. 22. Deut. 2. 27.
[b] Deut. 2. 6, 28.
[c] Judg. 11. 17.
[d] See Deut. 2. 27, 29.
[e] Deut. 2. 4. Judg. 11. 18.
[f] ch. 33. 37.
[g] ch. 21. 4.
[h] Gen. 25. 8. ch. 27. 13. & 31. 2.
[i] ver. 12.
[k] ch. 33. 38. Deut. 32. 50.
[l] Ex. 29. 29.
[m] ch. 33. 38. Deut. 10. 6. & 32. 50.
[n] So Deut. 34. 8.
[a] ch. 33. 40. See Judg. 1. 16.
[b] ch. 13. 21.

[1] Heb. *found us*, Ex. 18. 8.
[2] Heb. *mouth*.

---

of the Edomitish mountains. These are lofty and precipitous, traversed by two or three narrow defiles. Hence the necessity of the request in *v.* 17.

thy brother] An appeal to the Edomites to remember and renew the old kindnesses of Jacob and Esau (Gen. xxxiii. 1-17).

It appears from Judg. xi. 17 that a similar request was addressed to the Moabites.

16. *an angel*] See Gen. xii. 7; Ex. iii. 2, and notes. The term is to be understood as importing generally the supernatural guidance under which Israel was.

20. The Israelites, without awaiting at Kadesh the return of their ambassadors, commenced their eastward march. At the tidings of their approach the Edomites mustered their forces to oppose them; and on crossing the Arabah they found their ascent through the mountains barred. The notice of this is inserted here to complete the narrative; but in order of time it comes after the march described in *v.* 22.

22. *mount Hor*] The modern Jebel Harun, situated on the eastern side of the Arabah, and close to Petra. This striking mountain, rising on a dark red bare rock, to a height of near 5,000 feet above the Mediterranean, is remarkable far and near for its two summits, on one of which is still shown a small square building, crowned with a dome, called the Tomb of Aaron.

26. The priestly garments, wherewith Moses had invested Aaron (Lev. viii. 7-9), were put upon Eleazar by way of solemn transference of Aaron's office to him; cp. 1 Kings xix. 19.

XXI. **1.** *king Arad the Canaanite*] Rather,

[c] Gen. 28. 20. Judg. 11. 30.
[d] Lev. 27. 28.
[e] ch. 20. 22. & 33. 41.
[f] Judg. 11. 18.
[g] Ps. 78. 19.
[h] Ex. 16, 3. & 17. 3.
[i] ch. 11. 6.
[k] 1 Cor. 10. 9.
[l] Deut. 8. 15.
[m] Ps. 78. 34.
[n] ver. 5.
[o] Ex. 8. 8, 28. 1 Sam. 12. 19. 1 Kin. 13. 6. Acts 8. 24.

then he fought against Israel, and took *some* of them prisoners.
2 [c]And Israel vowed a vow unto the LORD, and said, If thou wilt
indeed deliver this people into my hand, then [d]I will utterly
3 destroy their cities. And the LORD hearkened to the voice of
Israel, and delivered up the Canaanites; and they utterly destroyed them and their cities: and he called the name of the
4 place [1]Hormah. ¶ And [e]they journeyed from mount Hor by
the way of the Red sea, to [f]compass the land of Edom: and the
soul of the people was much [2][3]discouraged because of the way.
5 And the people [g]spake against God, and against Moses, [h]Where-
fore have ye brought us up out of Egypt to die in the wilderness?
for *there is* no bread, neither *is there any* water; and [i]our soul
6 loatheth this light bread. And [k]the LORD sent [l]fiery serpents
among the people, and they bit the people; and much people of
7 Israel died. [m]Therefore the people came to Moses, and said,
We have sinned, for [n]we have spoken against the LORD, and
against thee; [o]pray unto the LORD, that he take away the ser-
8 pents from us. And Moses prayed for the people. And the
LORD said unto Moses, Make thee a fiery serpent, and set it

[1] That is, *Utter destruction.* [2] Or, *grieved.* [3] Heb. *shortened,* Ex. 6. 9.

"the Canaanite, the king of Arad." Arad stood on a small hill, now called Tel-Arad, 20 miles south of Hebron.

in the south] See xiii. 17, 22.

by the way of the spies] *i.e.* through the desert of Zin, the route which the spies sent out by Moses 38 years before had adopted (cp. xiii. 21).

he fought against Israel] This attack (cp. xx. 1 and note), can hardly have taken place after the death of Aaron. It was most probably made just when the camp broke up from Kadesh, and the ultimate direction of the march was not as yet pronounced. The order of the narrative in these chapters, as occasionally elsewhere in this book (cp. ix. 1, &c.), is not that of time, but of subject-matter; and the war against Arad is introduced here as the first of the series of victories gained under Moses, which the historian now takes in hand to narrate.

3. *he called the name of the place*] Render, **the name of the place was called.** The transitive verb here is, by a common Hebrew idiom, equivalent to an impersonal one.

Hormah] *i.e.* "Ban." See xiv. 45 and note. In Judges i. 17, we read that the men of Judah and Simeon "slew the Canaanites that inhabited Zephath, and utterly destroyed it;" and further, that "the name of the city was called Hormah." But it does not follow that the name "Hormah" was first bestowed in consequence of the destruction of the place in the time of the Judges, and that in Numbers its occurrence is a sign of a post-Mosaic date of composition. The text here informs us that this aggression of the king of Arad was repelled, and avenged by the capture and sack of his cities; and that the Israelites "banned" them (cp. Lev. xxvii. 28, 29). But it was not the plan of the Israelites in the time of Moses to remain in this district. They therefore marched away south-eastward; and no doubt for the time the Canaanites resumed possession, and restored the ancient name (Zephath). But Joshua again conquered the king of this district, and finally in the time of the early Judges the ban of Moses and his contemporaries was fully executed. We have therefore in the passage before us the history of the actual origin of the name "Hormah."

4. The direct route to Moab through the valleys of Edom being closed against them (xx. 20, 21), they were compelled to turn southward. Their course lay down the Arabah; until, a few hours north of Akaba (Ezion-Geber) the Wady Ithm opened to them a gap in the hostile mountains, allowed them to turn to their left, and to march northwards towards Moab (Deut. ii. 3). They were thus for some days (see xxii. 1 note) in the Arabah, a mountain plain of loose sand, gravel, and detritus of granite, which though sprinkled with low shrubs, especially near the mouths of the wadys and the courses of the winter-torrents, furnishes extremely little food or water, and is often troubled by sand-storms from the shore of the gulf. Hence "the soul of the people was much discouraged because of the way."

5. *this light bread*] *i.e.* "this vile, contemptible bread."

6. *fiery serpents*] The epithet (Deut. viii. 15, Isai. xiv. 29, xxx. 6) denotes the inflammatory effect of their bite. The peninsula of Sinai, and not least, the Arabah, abounds in mottled snakes of large size, marked with fiery red spots and wavy stripes, which belong to the most poisonous species, as the formation of the teeth clearly show.

8. *make thee a fiery serpent*] *i.e.* a serpent resembling in appearance the reptiles which

upon a pole: and it shall come to pass, that every one that is
9 bitten, when he looketh upon it, shall live. And [p]Moses made
a serpent of brass, and put it upon a pole, and it came to pass,
that if a serpent had bitten any man, when he beheld the serpent
10 of brass, he lived. ¶ And the children of Israel set forward,
11 and [q]pitched in Oboth. And they journeyed from Oboth,
and [r]pitched at [1]Ije-abarim, in the wilderness which *is* before
12 Moab, toward the sun-rising. [s]From thence they removed, and
13 pitched in the valley of Zared. From thence they removed,
and pitched on the other side of Arnon, which *is* in the wilderness
that cometh out of the coasts of the Amorites: for [t]Arnon
14 *is* the border of Moab, between Moab and the Amorites. Wherefore
it is said in the book of the wars of the LORD,

[2]What he did in the Red sea, and in the brooks of Arnon,
15 And at the stream of the brooks that goeth down to the dwelling of Ar,
[u]And [3]lieth upon the border of Moab.

16 ¶ And from thence *they went* [x]to Beer: that *is* the well whereof
the LORD spake unto Moses, Gather the people together, and I

[p] 2 Kin. 18. 4. John 3. 14, 15.
[q] ch. 33. 43.
[r] ch. 33. 44.
[s] Deut. 2. 13.
[t] ch. 22. 36. Judg. 11. 18.
[u] Deut. 2. 18, 29.
[x] Judg. 9. 21.

[1] Or, *Heaps of Abarim.* [2] Or, *Vaheb in Suphah.* [3] Heb. *leaneth.*

---

attacked the people. The resemblance was of the essence of the symbolism (cp. 1 Sam. vi. 5). As the brazen serpent represented the instrument of their chastisement, so the looking unto it at God's word denoted acknowledgment of their sin, longing for deliverance from its penalty, and faith in the means appointed by God for healing. In the serpent of brass, harmless itself, but made in the image of the creature that is accursed above others (Gen. iii. 14), the Christian Fathers rightly see a figure of Him (John iii. 14, 15) Who though "holy, harmless, undefiled, separate from sinners" (Heb. vii. 26), was yet "made sin" (2 Cor. v. 21), and "made a curse for us" (Gal. iii. 13). And the eye of faith fixed on Him beholds the manifestation at once of the deserts of sin, of its punishment imminent and deprecated, and of the method of its remission devised by God Himself.

10, 11. The earlier stations in this part of their journey were Zalmonah and Punon (xxxiii. 41, 42). Oboth was north of Punon, east of the northern part of Edom, and is pretty certainly the same as the present pilgrim halting-place el-Ahsa. Ije ("ruinous heaps") of Abarim, or Iim of Abarim, was so called to distinguish it from another Iim in south-western Canaan (Josh. xv. 29). Abarim denotes generally the whole upland country on the east of the Jordan. The Greek equivalent of the name is Peræa.

12. *the valley of Zared*] Rather, the **brook** or watercourse of Zared "the willow." It is probably the present Wady Ain Franjy.

13. The Arnon, now the Wady Môjeb, an impetuous torrent, divided the territory which remained to the Moabites from that which the Amorites had wrested from them, *v.* 26.

14. Of "the book of the wars of the LORD" nothing is known except what may be gathered from the passage before us. It was apparently a collection of sacred odes commemorative of that triumphant progress of God's people which this chapter records. From it is taken the ensuing fragment of ancient poetry relating to the passage of the Arnon, and probably also the Song of the Well, and the Ode on the Conquest of the Kingdom of Sihon (*vv.* 17, 18, 27–30).

what he did, &c.] The words which follow to the end of the next verse are a reference rather than a quotation. Contemporaries who had "the Book" at hand, could supply the context. We can only conjecture the sense of the words; which in the original are grammatically incomplete. The marg. is adopted by many, and suggests a better sense: supplying some such verb as "conquered," the words would run "He" (*i.e.* the Lord) "conquered Vaheb in Suphah, and the brooks, &c." Suphah would thus be the name of a district remarkable for its reeds and water-flags in which Vaheb was situated.

15. *to the dwelling of Ar*] Ar (cp. *v.* 28, Isai. xv. 1) was on the bank of the Arnon, lower down the stream than where the Israelites crossed. Near the spot where the upper Arnon receives the tributary Nahaliel (*v.* 19), there rises, in the midst of the meadow-land between the two torrents, a hill covered with the ruins of the ancient city (Josh. xiii. 9, 16; cp. Deut. ii. 36).

16. Beer is probably the "Well," afterwards known as Beer-elim, the "well of heroes" (Isai. xv. 8).

17 will give them water. [y]Then Israel sang this song,
[1]Spring up, O well; [2]sing ye unto it:
18 The princes digged the well,
The nobles of the people digged it,
By *the direction of* [z]the lawgiver, with their staves.

19 ¶And from the wilderness *they went* to Mattanah: and from
20 Mattanah to Nahaliel: and from Nahaliel to Bamoth: and
from Bamoth *in* the valley, that *is* in the [3]country of Moab, to
21 the top of [4]Pisgah, which looketh [a]toward [5]Jeshimon. ¶And
[b]Israel sent messengers unto Sihon king of the Amorites, saying,
22 [c]Let me pass through thy land: we will not turn into the fields,
or into the vineyards; we will not drink *of* the waters of the
well: *but* we will go along by the king's *high* way, until we be
23 past thy borders. [d]And Sihon would not suffer Israel to pass
through his border: but Sihon gathered all his people together,
and went out against Israel into the wilderness: [e]and he came to
24 Jahaz, and fought against Israel. And [f]Israel smote him with
the edge of the sword, and possessed his land from Arnon unto
Jabbok, even unto the children of Ammon: for the border of
25 the children of Ammon *was* strong. And Israel took all these
cities: and Israel dwelt in all the cities of the Amorites, in
26 Heshbon, and in all the [6]villages thereof. For Heshbon *was*
the city of Sihon the king of the Amorites, who had fought
against the former king of Moab, and taken all his land out
27 of his hand, even unto Arnon. Wherefore they that speak in
proverbs say,

Come into Heshbon,
Let the city of Sihon be built and prepared:

[y] Ex. 15. 1. Ps. 105. 2. & 106. 12.
[z] Isai. 33. 22.
[a] ch. 23. 28.
[b] Deut. 2. 26, 27. Judg. 11. 19.
[c] ch. 20. 17.
[d] Deut. 29. 7.
[e] Deut. 2. 32. Judg. 11. 20.
[f] Deut. 2. 33. & 29. 7. Josh. 12. 1, 2. & 24. 8. Neh. 9. 22. Ps. 135. 10. & 136. 19. Amos 2. 9.

[1] Heb. *Ascend.*
[2] Or, *answer.*
[3] Heb. *field.*
[4] Or, *The hill.*
[5] Or, *The wilderness.*
[6] Heb. *daughters.*

17, 18. This song, recognised by all authorities as dating from the earliest times, and suggested apparently by the fact that God in this place gave the people water not from the rock, but by commanding Moses to cause a well to be dug, bespeaks the glad zeal, the joyful faith, and the hearty co-operation amongst all ranks, which possessed the people. In after time it may well have been the water-drawing song of the maidens of Israel.

18. *by the direction of the lawgiver*] Some render, **with the lawgiver's sceptre**; *i.e.* under the direction and with the authority of Moses; cp. Gen. xlix. 10, and note.

19. *Nahaliel*] *i.e.* "brook of God;" the modern Wady Enkheileh. The Israelites must have crossed the stream not much above Ar.

Bamoth] Otherwise Bamoth-baal, "the high places of Baal" (xxii. 41): mentioned as near Dibon (Dhiban) in Josh. xiii. 17, and Isai. xv. 2. See xxxii. 34.

20. *in the country of Moab*] Rather, **in the field of Moab**: the upland pastures, or flat downs, intersected by the ravine of Wady Wâleh.

Pisgah, which looketh toward Jeshimon] Or, "toward the waste." See xxxiii. 47. Pisgah was a ridge of the Abarim mountains, westward from Heshbon. From the summit the Israelites gained their first view of the wastes of the Dead Sea and of the valley of the Jordan: and Moses again ascended it, to view, before his death, the Land of Promise. The interest attaching to the spot, and the need of a convenient name for it, has led Christians often to designate it as "Nebo," rather than as "the mountain of, or near to, Nebo;" but the latter is the more correct: Nebo denoted the town (Isai. xv. 2; Jer. xlviii. 1, 22) on the western slope of the ridge.

24. Jabbok (now Wâdy Zerka: cp. Gen. xxxii. 22) runs eastward under Rabbah of the children of Ammon, thence westward, and reaches the Jordan, 45 miles north of the Arnon. It was between Rabbah and Gerasa that it formed the Ammonite boundary.

25. *Heshbon*] Now Heshbân, a ruined city, due east of the point where the Jordan enters the Dead Sea; conspicuous from all parts of the high plateau on which it stands, but concealed, like the rest of the plateau, from the valley beneath.

27. *they that speak in proverbs*] The original word is almost equivalent to "the poets." The word supplies the title of the Book of Proverbs itself; and is used of the

28 For there is [g]a fire gone out of Heshbon, [g] Jer. 48. 45, 46.
A flame from the city of Sihon:
It hath consumed [h]Ar of Moab, [h] Deut. 2. 9, 18.
And the lords of the high places of Arnon. Isai. 15. 1.
29 Woe to thee, Moab!
Thou art undone, O people of [i]Chemosh: [i] Judg. 11. 24.
He hath given his sons that escaped, 1 Kin. 11. 7, 33.
And his daughters, into captivity
Unto Sihon king of the Amorites. 2 Kin. 23. 13.
30 We have shot at them; Jer. 48. 7, 13.
Heshbon is perished even [k]unto Dibon,
And we have laid them waste even unto Nophah, [k] Jer. 48. 18, 22.
Which *reacheth* unto [l]Medeba. [l] Isai. 15. 2.

31, 32 ¶ Thus Israel dwelt in the land of the Amorites. And Moses
sent to spy out [m]Jaazer, and they took the villages thereof, and [m] ch. 32. 1. Jer. 48. 32.
33 drove out the Amorites that *were* there. [n]And they turned and [n] Deut. 3. 1.
went up by the way of Bashan: and Og the king of Bashan & 29. 7.
went out against them, he, and all his people, to the battle [o]at [o] Josh. 13. 12.
34 Edrei. And the LORD said unto Moses, [p]Fear him not: for I [p] Deut. 3. 2.
have delivered him into thy hand, and all his people, and his [q] ver. 24.
land; and [q]thou shalt do to him as thou didst unto Sihon king Ps. 135. 10. & 136. 20.
35 of the Amorites, which dwelt at Heshbon. [r]So they smote him, [r] Deut. 3. 3.
and his sons, and all his people, until there was none left him
alive: and they possessed his land.

CHAP. 22. AND [a]the children of Israel set forward, and pitched [a] ch. 33. 48.

---

parable proper in Ezek. xvii. 2; of the prophecies of Balaam in xxiii. 7-10, xxiv. 3-9, &c.; and of a song of triumph over Babylon in Isai. xiv. 4.

29. *Chemosh*] The national God of the Moabites (cp. marg. reff.). The name probably means "Vanquisher," or "Master." The worship of Chemosh was introduced into Israel by Solomon (1 K. xi. 7; 2 K. xxiii. 13). It was no doubt to Chemosh that Mesha, king of Moab, offered up his son as a burnt-offering (2 K. iii. 26, 27).

In the first six lines (*vv.* 27, 28) the poet imagines for the Amorites a song of exultation for their victories over Moab, and for the consequent glories of Heshbon, their own capital. In the next lines (*v.* 29) he himself joins in this strain; which now becomes one of half-real, half-ironical compassion for the Moabites, whom their idol Chemosh was unable to save. But in the last lines (*v.* 30) a startling change takes place; the new and decisive triumph of the poet's own countrymen is abruptly introduced; and the boastings of the Amorites fade utterly away. Of the towns Heshbon was the northernmost, and therefore, to the advancing Israelites, the last to be reached. Medeba, now Mâdeba, was four miles south of Heshbon (cp. 1 Chr. xix. 7, 15).

32. *Jaazer*] To be identified probably with the ruins Sîr or es-Sîr, ten miles north of Heshbon. The occupation of it by the Israelites virtually completed their conquest of the Amorite kingdom; and prepared the way for the pastoral settlements in it which they not long after established (xxxii. 35).

33. In these apparently unimportant words is contained the record of the Israelitish (xxxii. 39) occupation of Gilead north of the Jabbok; a territory which, though peopled, like southern Gilead, by the Amorites (Deut. iii. 9; Josh. ii. 10, &c.), formed part of the domain of Og king of Bashan, who was himself of a different race (Deut. iii. 2; Josh. xii. 5, xiii. 11). We are not told whether they were led thither by express warrant of God, or whether their advance upon Bashan was provoked by Og and his people.

at Edrei] Now Edhra'âh, vulgarly Der'a; situate on a branch of the Jarmuk. This river formed the boundary between Gilead and Bashan.

XXII. With this chapter begins the fourth and last division of the Book, comprising fourteen chapters. In them are narrated the events which befell Israel whilst encamped in the plains of Moab, and certain instructions and arrangements are laid down by Moses with reference to their actual entry upon the promised inheritance.

1. *the plains*] Heb. *araboth;* the word is the plural of that which is used to denote the whole depressed tract along the Jordan and the Dead Sea, and onward, where it is still called the Arabah (cp. xxi. 4 note), to the Elanitic gulf.

[b] Judg. 11. 25.
[c] Ex. 15. 15.
[d] ch. 31. 8. Josh. 13. 21.
[e] Deut. 23.4. Josh. 13. 22. & 24. 9. Neh. 13. 1, 2. Mic. 6. 5. 2 Pet. 2. 15. Jude 11. Rev. 2. 14.
[f] See ch. 23. 7. Deut. 23. 4.
[g] ch. 23. 7.
[h] 1 Sam. 9. 7, 8.
[i] ver. 19.
[k] Gen. 20. 3. ver. 20.

2 in the plains of Moab on this side Jordan *by* Jericho. ¶ And
[b]Balak the son of Zippor saw all that Israel had done to the
3 Amorites. And [c]Moab was sore afraid of the people, because
they *were* many: and Moab was distressed because of the chil-
4 dren of Israel. And Moab said unto [d]the elders of Midian,
Now shall this company lick up all *that are* round about us, as
the ox licketh up the grass of the field. And Balak the son of
5 Zippor *was* king of the Moabites at that time. [e]He sent messengers therefore unto Balaam the son of Beor to [f]Pethor, which
is by the river of the land of the children of his people, to call
him, saying, Behold, there is a people come out from Egypt:
behold, they cover the [1]face of the earth, and they abide over
6 against me: come now therefore, I pray thee, [g]curse me this
people; for they *are* too mighty for me: peradventure I shall
prevail, *that* we may smite them, and *that* I may drive them out
of the land: for I wot that he whom thou blessest *is* blessed,
7 and he whom thou cursest is cursed. ¶ And the elders of Moab
and the elders of Midian departed with [h]the rewards of divination in their hand; and they came unto Balaam, and spake unto
8 him the words of Balak. And he said unto them, [i]Lodge here
this night, and I will bring you word again, as the LORD shall
speak unto me: and the princes of Moab abode with Balaam.
9 [k]And God came unto Balaam, and said, What men *are* these
10 with thee? And Balaam said unto God, Balak the son of Zippor,
11 king of Moab, hath sent unto me, *saying*, Behold, *there is* a
people come out of Egypt, which covereth the face of the earth:

[1] Heb. *eye*.

---

on this side Jordan by Jericho] Rather, **across the Jordan of Jericho,** *i.e.* that part of Jordan which skirted the territory of Jericho. This form of expression indicates the site of the camp in its relation to the well-known city of Jericho. See Deut. i. 1.

2. *Balak the son of Zippor*] The comparison of *v.* 4 with xxi. 26 suggests that Balak was not the hereditary king but a Midianite, and that a change of dynasty had taken place. His father's name, Zippor, "Bird," reminds us of those of other Midianites, *e.g.* Oreb, "Crow," Zeeb, "Wolf." Possibly the Midianitish chieftains had taken advantage of the weakness of the Moabites after the Amoritish victories to establish themselves as princes in the land.

5. Balaam the son of Beor was from the first a worshipper in some sort of the true God; and had learned some elements of pure and true religion in his home in the far East, the cradle of the ancestors of Israel. But though prophesying, doubtless even before the ambassadors of Balak came to him, in the name of the true God, yet prophecy was still to him as before a mere business, not a religion. The summons of Balak proved to be a crisis in his career: and he failed under the trial. When the gold and honours of Balak seemed to be finally lost, he became reckless and desperate; and, as if in defiance, counselled the evil stratagem by which he hoped to compass indirectly that ruin of God's people which he had been withheld from working otherwise. He thus, like Judas and Ahithophel, set in motion a train of events which involved his own destruction.

The name Balaam signifies "destroyer," or "glutton," and is in part identical with "Bela, son of Beor," the first king of Edom (Gen. xxxvi. 32). The name "Beor" ("to burn up") is that of the father, or possibly ancestor, of the prophet.

Pethor, which is by the river of the land of the children of his people] Rather, **Pethor which was . . . . . land.** Pethor (Pitru, Assyrian) was on the river Sagura (mod. Sajur) near its junction with the Euphrates.

7. *Rewards of divination*] Rightly interpreted in 2 Pet. ii. 15 as "the wages of unrighteousness."

8. Balaam must surely have known that God's blessing was on the people with whose marvellous march forth from Egypt he was acquainted (Ex. xv. 14, xviii. 1; Josh. ii. 9), and from whom he had himself probably learned much (cp. the language of xxiii. 12 with Gen. xiii. 6, and that of xxiv. 9 with Gen. xlix. 9). But his reply to the messengers next morning (*v.* 13), betrays the desire to venture to the utmost of that which God would not forbid rather than to carry out God's will in hearty sincerity.

come now, curse me them; peradventure [1]I shall be able to
12 overcome them, and drive them out. And God said unto Balaam, Thou shalt not go with them; thou shalt not curse the
13 people: for [l]they *are* blessed. And Balaam rose up in the morning, and said unto the princes of Balak, Get you into your land:
14 for the LORD refuseth to give me leave to go with you. And the princes of Moab rose up, and they went unto Balak, and
15 said, Balaam refuseth to come with us. And Balak sent yet
16 again princes, more, and more honourable than they. And they came to Balaam, and said to him, Thus saith Balak the son of Zippor, [2]Let nothing, I pray thee, hinder thee from coming
17 unto me: for I will promote thee unto very great honour, and I will do whatsoever thou sayest unto me: [m]come therefore, I
18 pray thee, curse me this people. And Balaam answered and said unto the servants of Balak, [n]If Balak would give me his house full of silver and gold, [o]I cannot go beyond the word of
19 the LORD my God, to do less or more. Now therefore, I pray you, [p]tarry ye also here this night, that I may know what the
20 LORD will say unto me more. [q]And God came unto Balaam at night, and said unto him, If the men come to call thee, rise up, *and* go with them; but [r]yet the word which I shall say unto
21 thee, that shalt thou do. And Balaam rose up in the morning,
22 and saddled his ass, and went with the princes of Moab. ¶ And God's anger was kindled because he went: [s]and the angel of the LORD stood in the way for an adversary against him. Now he was riding upon his ass, and his two servants *were* with him.
23 And [t]the ass saw the angel of the LORD standing in the way, and his sword drawn in his hand: and the ass turned aside out of the way, and went into the field: and Balaam smote the ass,
24 to turn her into the way. But the angel of the LORD stood in a path of the vineyards, a wall *being* on this side, and a wall on
25 that side. And when the ass saw the angel of the LORD, she thrust herself unto the wall, and crushed Balaam's foot against
26 the wall: and he smote her again. And the angel of the LORD went further, and stood in a narrow place, where *was* no way to
27 turn either to the right hand or to the left. And when the ass saw the angel of the LORD, she fell down under Balaam: and Balaam's anger was kindled, and he smote the ass with a staff.
28 And the [u]LORD opened the mouth of the ass, and she said unto

[l] ch. 23. 20. Rom. 11. 29.
[m] ver. 6.
[n] ch. 24. 13.
[o] 1 Kin. 22. 14. 2 Chr. 18. 13.
[p] ver. 8.
[q] ver. 9.
[r] ver. 35. ch. 23. 12, 26. & 24. 13.
[s] Ex. 4. 24.
[t] See 2 Kin. 6. 17. Dan. 10. 7. Acts 22. 9. 2 Pet. 2. 16. Jude 11.
[u] 2 Pet. 2. 16.

[1] Heb. *I shall prevail in fighting against him.*

[2] Heb. *Be not thou letted from, &c.*

15. Balak, like the ancient heathen world generally, not only believed in the efficacy of the curses and incantations of the soothsayers, but regarded their services as strictly venal. Hence, when his first offer was declined, he infers at once that he had not bid high enough.

19. *ye also*] *i.e.* as the other envoys before you. Had Balaam possessed a sincere spirit of obedience, he would have found in the first instructions (*v.* 12) a final decision upon the matter. His hypocritical importunity with God when the fresh messengers came from Balak demonstrates his aversion to God's declared will.

22. *the angel*] *i.e.* the Angel that led the Israelites through the wilderness (cp. xx. 16 and reff.), and subsequently appeared as the Captain of the LORD's host to Joshua (Josh. vi. 13). In desiring to curse Israel, Balaam was fighting against Israel's Leader. The presence of the Angel in his path was designed to open his eyes, blinded by sin, to the real character of his course of conduct.

24. *in a path of the vineyards*] *i.e.* in a path shut in by vineyard-walls on each side. The progress from the road through the open field (*v.* 23) to that walled in, and thence to the strait place, where there was no room to turn (*v.* 26), shews that Balaam was approaching a city, no doubt that which was the goal of his journey.

28. *And the* LORD *opened the mouth of the ass*] The account was perhaps given by Balaam to the Israelites after his capture in the war against Midian. Cp. xxxi. 8.

Balaam, What have I done unto thee, that thou hast smitten
29 me these three times? And Balaam said unto the ass, Because
thou hast mocked me: I would there were a sword in mine
30 hand, [x]for now would I kill thee. [y]And the ass said unto
Balaam, *Am* not I thine ass, [1]upon which thou hast ridden
[2]ever since *I was* thine unto this day? Was I ever wont to do so
31 unto thee? And he said, Nay. ¶ Then the LORD [z]opened the
eyes of Balaam, and he saw the angel of the LORD standing in
the way, and his sword drawn in his hand: and he [a]bowed down
32 his head, and [3]fell flat on his face. And the angel of the LORD
said unto him, Wherefore hast thou smitten thine ass these three
times? Behold, I went out [4]to withstand thee, because *thy* way
33 is [b]perverse before me: and the ass saw me, and turned from
me these three times: unless she had turned from me, surely
34 now also I had slain thee, and saved her alive. And Balaam
said unto the angel of the LORD, [c]I have sinned; for I knew not
that thou stoodest in the way against me: now therefore, if it
35 [5]displease thee, I will get me back again. And the angel of the
LORD said unto Balaam, Go with the men: [d]but only the word
that I shall speak unto thee, that thou shalt speak. So Balaam
36 went with the princes of Balak. ¶ And when Balak heard that
Balaam was come, [e]he went out to meet him unto a city of Moab,
[f]which *is* in the border of Arnon, which *is* in the utmost coast.
37 And Balak said unto Balaam, Did I not earnestly send unto thee
to call thee? Wherefore camest thou not unto me? Am I not
38 able indeed [g]to promote thee to honour? And Balaam said unto
Balak, Lo, I am come unto thee: have I now any power at all
to say any thing? [h]The word that God putteth in my mouth,
39 that shall I speak. And Balaam went with Balak, and they
40 came unto [6]Kirjath-huzoth. And Balak offered oxen and sheep,
and sent to Balaam, and to the princes that *were* with him.
41 And it came to pass on the morrow, that Balak took Balaam,
and brought him up into the [i]high places of Baal, that thence
he might see the utmost *part* of the people.

CHAP. 23. AND Balaam said unto Balak, [a]Build me here seven

[x] Prov. 12. 10.
[y] 2 Pet. 2. 16.
[z] See Gen. 21. 19. 2 Kin. 6. 17. Luke 24. 16, 31.
[a] Ex. 34. 8.
[b] 2 Pet. 2. 14, 15.
[c] 1 Sam. 15. 24, 30. & 26. 21. 2 Sam. 12. 13. Job 34. 31, 32.
[d] ver. 20.
[e] Gen. 14. 17.
[f] ch. 21. 13.
[g] ver. 17. ch. 24. 11.
[h] ch. 23. 26. & 24. 13. 1 Kin. 22. 14. 2 Chr. 18. 13.
[i] Deut. 12. 2.
[a] ver. 29.

[1] Heb. *who hast ridden upon me.*
[2] Or, *ever since thou* wast, &c.
[3] Or, *bowed himself.*
[4] Heb. *to be an adversary unto thee.*
[5] Heb. *be evil in thine eyes.*
[6] Or, *A city of streets.*

That which is here recorded was apparently perceived by him alone amongst human witnesses. God may have brought it about that sounds uttered by the creature after its kind became to the prophet's intelligence as though it addressed him in rational speech. Indeed to an augur, priding himself on his skill in interpreting the cries and movements of animals, no more startling warning could be given than one so real as this, yet conveyed through the medium of his own art.

32. *is perverse*] Rather, **is headlong**. Cp. St. Peter's words (2 Pet. ii. 16), "the madness of the prophet."

35. *Go with the men*] A command, not a permission merely. Balaam, no longer a faithful servant of God, was henceforth overruled in all his acts so that he might subserve the Divine purpose as an instrument.

26. *a city of Moab*] Or, **Ir-Moab**, probably the same with Ar-Moab (xxi. 15). As Balaam in his journey would avoid the districts occupied by the Israelites, he must have approached this city from the east, by the course of the Nahaliel; and in the name Balû'a, still borne by one of the upper branches of this stream, there is perhaps a reminiscence of the name of the prophet.

39. *Kirjath-huzoth*] *i.e.* "city of streets," within Balak's dominions, south of the Arnon, and identified either with the ruins of Shîhân, 4 miles west by south of the site assigned to Ar or Ir, or with Kirjathaim (Kureiyat).

41. *that thence he might see*] Rather, **and thence he saw.**

XXIII. **1.** Balaam, after the general custom of the heathen, prefaced his divinations by sacrifice. In the number of the altars regard was probably had to the number of

2 altars, and prepare me here seven oxen and seven rams. And
Balak did as Balaam had spoken; and Balak and Balaam
3 [b]offered on *every* altar a bullock and a ram. And Balaam said
unto Balak, [c]Stand by thy burnt offering, and I will go: peradventure the LORD will come [d]to meet me: and whatsoever he
sheweth me I will tell thee. And [1]he went to an high place.
4 [e]And God met Balaam: and he said unto him, I have prepared
seven altars, and I have offered upon *every* altar a bullock and a
5 ram. And the LORD [f]put a word in Balaam's mouth, and said,
6 Return unto Balak, and thus thou shalt speak. And he returned
unto him, and, lo, he stood by his burnt sacrifice, he, and all the
7 princes of Moab. And he [g]took up his parable, and said,

Balak the king of Moab hath brought me from Aram,
Out of the mountains of the east, *saying*,
[h]Come, curse me Jacob,
And come, [i]defy Israel.
8 [k]How shall I curse, whom God hath not cursed?
Or how shall I defy, *whom* the LORD hath not defied?
9 For from the top of the rocks I see him,
And from the hills I behold him:
Lo, [l]the people shall dwell alone,
And [m]shall not be reckoned among the nations.
10 [n]Who can count the dust of Jacob,
And the number of the fourth *part* of Israel?
Let [2]me die [o]the death of the righteous,
And let my last end be like his!

[b] ver. 14.
[c] ver. 15.
[d] ch. 24. 1.
[e] ver. 16.
[f] ch. 22. 35. ver. 16. Deut. 18. 18. Jer. 1. 9.
[g] ver. 18. ch. 24. 3, 15, 23. Job 27. 1. Ps. 78. 2. Ez. 17. 2. Mic. 2. 4. Hab. 2. 6.
[h] ch. 22. 6, 11, 17.
[i] 1 Sam. 17. 10.
[k] Isai. 47. 12, 13.
[l] Deut. 33. 28.
[m] Ex. 33. 16. Ezra 9. 2. Eph. 2. 14.
[n] Gen. 13. 16. & 22. 17.
[o] Ps. 116. 15.

[1] Or, *he went solitary.*
[2] Heb. *my soul*, or, *my life.*

---

the then known planets. Yet Balaam evidently intended his sacrifice as an offering to the true God.

3. Balaam apparently expected to mark some phenomenon in the sky or in nature, which he would be able, according to the rules of his art, to interpret as a portent. It was for such "auguries" (not as A. V. "enchantments" *v.* 23) that he now departed to watch; contrast xxiv. 1.

an high place] Or, "A bare place on the hill," as opposed to the high place with its grove of trees.

4. *God met Balaam*] God served His own purposes through the arts of Balaam, and manifested His will through the agencies employed to seek it, dealing thus with Balaam in an exceptional manner. To God's own people auguries were forbidden (Lev. xix. 26).

I have prepared seven altars] And therefore Balaam expected that God on His part would do what was desired by the donor; cp. xxii. 15 note.

7. *Aram*] Or, "highland." This term denotes the whole elevated region, from the north-eastern frontier of Palestine to the Euphrates and the Tigris. The country between these streams was specially designated "Aram-naharaim," or "Aram of the two rivers;" the Greeks called it Mesopotamia; and here, according to Deut. xxiii. 4, was Balaam's home. Cp. xxii. 5 note.

9. *For from the top of the rocks*, &c.] The "for" indicates the constraint under which Balaam felt himself. He had been met by God in his own way; from the cliff he had watched for the expected augury; and by the light of this he here interprets, according to the rules of his art, the destiny of Israel.

dwell alone] *i.e.* apart from others, undisturbed by their tumults, and therefore in safety and just security. Cp. the same idea in marg. ref.; Jer. xlix. 31; and Micah vii. 14. This tranquillity was realized by the Israelites so long as they clave to God as their shelter and protection. But the inward "dwelling alone" was the indispensable condition of the outward "dwelling alone," and so soon as the influence of the heathen world affected Israel internally, the external power of heathenism prevailed also. Balaam himself, when he eventually counselled tempting the people into sin, acted upon the knowledge that God's blessing and Israel's prosperity depended essentially on faithfulness to God.

10. *the fourth part of Israel*] *i.e.* each one of the four camps, into which the host of Israel was divided (see ch. ii.), seemed to swarm with innumerable multitudes. Possibly Balaam could only see one camp. Balaam bears testimony in this verse to the fulfilment of the promises in Gen. xiii. 16, xxviii. 14.

11 And Balak said unto Balaam, What hast thou done unto me?
[p]I took thee to curse mine enemies, and, behold, thou hast
12 blessed *them* altogether. And he answered and said, [q]Must I
not take heed to speak that which the LORD hath put in my
13 mouth? ¶ And Balak said unto him, Come, I pray thee, with
me unto another place, from whence thou mayest see them: thou
shalt see but the utmost part of them, and shalt not see them
14 all: and curse me them from thence. And he brought him into
the field of Zophim, to the top of [1]Pisgah, [r]and built seven
15 altars, and offered a bullock and a ram on *every* altar. And he
said unto Balak, Stand here by thy burnt offering, while I meet
16 *the LORD* yonder. And the LORD met Balaam, and [s]put a word
in his mouth, and said, Go again unto Balak, and say thus.
17 And when he came to him, behold, he stood by his burnt offering, and the princes of Moab with him. And Balak said unto
18 him, What hath the LORD spoken? And he took up his parable,
and said,

[t]Rise up, Balak, and hear;
Hearken unto me, thou son of Zippor:
19 [u]God *is* not a man, that he should lie;
Neither the son of man, that he should repent:
Hath he said, and shall he not do *it?*
Or hath he spoken, and shall he not make it good?
20 Behold, I have received *commandment* to bless:
And [x]he hath blessed; and I cannot reverse it.
21 [y]He hath not beheld iniquity in Jacob,
Neither hath he seen perverseness in Israel:
[z]The LORD his God *is* with him,
[a]And the shout of a king *is* among them.
22 [b]God brought them out of Egypt;
He hath as it were [c]the strength of an unicorn.

[p] ch. 22. 11, 17. & 24. 10.
[q] ch. 22. 38.
[r] ver. 1, 2.
[s] ch. 22. 35. ver. 5.
[t] Judg. 3. 20.
[u] 1 Sam. 15. 29. Mal. 3. 6. Rom. 11. 29. Tit. 1. 2. Jam. 1. 17.
[x] Gen. 12. 2. & 22. 17. Num. 22. 12.
[y] Rom. 4. 7.
[z] Ex. 13. 21. & 29. 45, 46. & 33. 14.
[a] Ps. 89. 15.
[b] ch. 24. 8.
[c] Deut. 33. 17. Job 39. 10.

[1] Or, *The hill.*

---

the righteous] *i.e.* the ancestors of Israel, who "died in faith, not having received the promises, but having seen them afar off" (Heb. xi. 13). With their histories Balaam was familiar, particularly with that of Abraham, "the righteous man" whom God had "raised up from the east (and) called to His foot" (Isai. xli. 2).

let my last end be like his] Render rather "last estate," for the reference is not so much to the act of death, as to all that followed upon it—to the future, in which the name and influence of the deceased person would be perpetuated.

13. Balak seems to hope that the prophet's words in *v.* 10 reflected the impression conveyed by the scene before him at the moment of the augury; and so that the sight of a mere few straggling Israelites in the utmost part of the camp might induce a different estimate of their resources and prospects.

14. *the field of Zophim*] Or, "of watchers." It lay upon the top of Pisgah, north of the former station, and nearer to the Israelitish camp; the greater part of which was, however, probably concealed from it by an intervening spur of the hill. Beyond the camp Balaam's eye would pass on to the bed of the Jordan. It was perhaps a lion coming up in his strength from the swelling of that stream (cp. Jer. xlix. 19) that furnished him with the augury he awaited, and so dictated the final similitude of his next parable.

20. *I have received commandment to bless*] Literally, "I have received to bless." The reason of his blessing lay in the augury which he acknowledged, and in the Divine overruling impulse which he could not resist, not in any "commandment" in words.

21. "Iniquity" and "perverseness" are found together again in the Hebrew of Pss. x. 7, xc. 10, and elsewhere; and import wickedness together with that tribulation which is its proper result.

the shout] The word is used (Lev. xxiii. 24 note) to describe the sound of the silver trumpets. The "shout of a king" will therefore refer to the jubilant sounds by which the Presence of the Lord as their King amongst them was celebrated by Israel.

22. *an unicorn*] **A wild bull,** the now

23 Surely *there is* no enchantment [1]against Jacob,
Neither *is there* any divination against Israel:
According to this time it shall be said of Jacob and of Israel,
[d]What hath God wrought! [d] Ps. 31. 19. & 44. 1.
24 Behold, the people shall rise up [e]as a great lion, [e] Gen. 49. 9.
And lift up himself as a young lion: [f] Gen. 49. 27.
[f]He shall not lie down until he eat *of* the prey,
And drink the blood of the slain.

25 And Balak said unto Balaam, Neither curse them at all, nor
26 bless them at all. But Balaam answered and said unto Balak,
Told not I thee, saying, [g]All that the LORD speaketh, that [g] ch. 22. 38.
27 I must do? ¶ And Balak said unto Balaam, [h]Come, I pray ver. 12. 1 Kin. 22.
thee, I will bring thee unto another place; peradventure it will 14.
28 please God that thou mayest curse me them from thence. And [h] ver. 13.
Balak brought Balaam unto the top of Peor, that looketh [i]toward [i] ch. 21. 20.
29 Jeshimon. And Balaam said unto Balak, [k]Build me here seven [k] ver. 1.
altars, and prepare me here seven bullocks and seven rams.
30 And Balak did as Balaam had said, and offered a bullock and a
ram on *every* altar.

CHAP. 24. AND when Balaam saw that it pleased the LORD to
bless Israel, he went not, as at [a]other times, [2]to seek for en- [a] ch. 23. 3, 15.
2 chantments, but he set his face toward the wilderness. And [b] ch. 2. 2,
Balaam lifted up his eyes, and he saw Israel [b]abiding *in his* &c.
tents according to their tribes; and the [c]spirit of God came upon [c] ch. 11. 25.
3 him. [d]And he took up his parable, and said, 1 Sam. 10. 10.

Balaam the son of Beor hath said, & 19. 20. 23. 2 Chr. 15. 1.
And the man [3]whose eyes are open hath said: [d] ch. 23. 7,
4 He hath said, which heard the words of God, 18.
Which saw the vision of the Almighty, [e] See 1 Sam. 19. 24.
[e]Falling *into a trance*, but having his eyes open: Ez. 1. 28.
5 How goodly are thy tents, O Jacob, Dan. 8. 18. & 10. 15, 16.
And thy tabernacles, O Israel! 2 Cor. 12. 2, 3, 4.

[1] Or, *in*.
[2] Heb. *to the meeting of enchantments*.
[3] Heb. *who had his eyes shut*, but now opened.

Rev. 1. 10, 17.

---

extinct Aurochs, formidable for its size, strength, speed, and ferocity.

23. *enchantment...divination*] More strictly "augury" and "soothsayer's token," or the omen that was superstitiously observed. "Soothsayer" is the term applied to Balaam in Josh. xiii. 22.

The verse intimates that the seer was at last, through the overruling of his own auguries, compelled to own what, had he not been blinded by avarice and ambition, he would have discerned before—that there was an indisputable interference of God on Israel's behalf, against which all arts and efforts of man must prove vain. The sense suggested by margin (*i.e.* that the soothsayer's art was not practised in Israel) would be strictly true (cp. *v.* 4 note).

according, &c.] Rather, **in due time it shall be told to Jacob**, &c. God will, through His own divinely appointed means (*e.g.* the Urim and Thummim), reveal to Israel, as occasion may require, His will and purposes.

28. The position of Peor northward from Pisgah, along the Abarim heights, is approximately determined by the extant notices of Beth-peor.

Jeshimon was **the waste**, in the great valley below, where stood Beth-jeshimoth, "the house of the wastes."

XXIV. **2.** Balaam gazed over the camp of Israel that stretched before him, and allowed the spectacle to work its own influence upon him.

3. *whose eyes are open*] *i.e.* opened in inward vision, to discern things that were hidden from ordinary beholders.

4. The "falling" of which Balaam speaks was the condition under which the inward opening of his eyes took place. It indicates the force of the Divine inspiration overpowering the seer. The faithful prophets of the Lord do not appear to have been subject to these violent illapses (Dan. viii. 17; Rev. i. 17).

In Balaam and in Saul (1 Sam. xix. 24) the word of God could only prevail by first subduing the alien will, and overpowering the bodily energies which the will ordinarily directs.

6 As the valleys are they spread forth,
As gardens by the river's side,
[f]As the trees of lign aloes [g]which the LORD hath planted,
And as cedar trees beside the waters.
7 He shall pour the water out of his buckets,
And his seed *shall be* [h]in many waters,
And his king shall be higher than [i]Agag,
And his [k]kingdom shall be exalted.
8 [l]God brought him forth out of Egypt;
He hath as it were the strength of an unicorn:
He shall [m]eat up the nations his enemies, and shall [n]break their bones,
And [o]pierce *them* through with his arrows.
9 [p]He couched, he lay down as a lion,
And as a great lion: who shall stir him up?
[q]Blessed *is* he that blesseth thee,
And cursed *is* he that curseth thee.

10 ¶ And Balak's anger was kindled against Balaam, and he [r]smote
his hands together: and Balak said unto Balaam, [s]I called thee
to curse mine enemies, and, behold, thou hast altogether blessed
11 *them* these three times. Therefore now flee thou to thy place:
[t]I thought to promote thee unto great honour; but, lo, the LORD
12 hath kept thee back from honour. And Balaam said unto
Balak, Spake I not also to thy messengers which thou sentest
13 unto me, saying, [u]If Balak would give me his house full of
silver and gold, I cannot go beyond the commandment of the
LORD, to do *either* good or bad of mine own mind; *but* what the
14 LORD saith, that will I speak? And now, behold, I go unto my
people: come *therefore, and* [x]I will advertise thee what this
15 people shall do to thy people [y]in the latter days. [z]And he took
up his parable, and said,

Balaam the son of Beor hath said,
And the man whose eyes are open hath said:
16 He hath said, which heard the words of God,
And knew the knowledge of the most High,

[f] Ps. 1. 3. Jer. 17. 8.
[g] Ps. 104. 16.
[h] Jer. 51. 13. Rev. 17. 1, 15.
[i] 1 Sam. 15. 9.
[k] 2 Sam. 5. 12. 1 Chr. 14. 2.
[l] ch. 23. 22.
[m] ch. 14. 9. & 23. 24.
[n] Ps. 2. 9. Isai. 38. 13. Jer. 50. 17.
[o] Ps. 45. 5. Jer. 50. 9.
[p] Gen. 49. 9.
[q] Gen. 12. 3. & 27. 29.
[r] Ez. 21. 14, 17. & 22. 13.
[s] ch. 23. 11. Deut. 23. 4, 5. Josh. 24. 9. Neh. 13. 2.
[t] ch. 22. 17, 37.
[u] ch. 22. 18.
[x] Mic. 6. 5. Rev. 2. 14.
[y] Gen. 49. 1. Dan. 2. 28. & 10. 14.
[z] ver. 3, 4.

---

6. *as gardens by the river's side*] Balaam's language reflects the famous artificial gardens along the banks of his own river, the Euphrates.

as the trees of lign aloes which the LORD *hath planted*] The latter words contain an apparent reference to Paradise (cp. Gen. ii. 8). The aloe, imported from China and the far distant east, furnished to the ancients one of the most fragrant and precious of spices; cp. Ps. xlv. 8; Prov. vii. 17.

as cedar trees beside the waters] *i.e.* as the noblest of trees branching forth in the fairest of situations: an image of majestic beauty, as that of the last verse was of rare fecundity.

7. Balaam's native soil was ordinarily irrigated by water fetched from the neighbouring Euphrates, and carried in buckets suspended from the two ends of a pole. Thus the metaphor would import that Israel should have his own exuberant and unfailing channels of blessing and plenty. Some take the word to be predictive of the future benefits which, through the means of Israel, were to accrue to the rest of the world.

Agag] The name, apparently hereditary (cp. 1 S. xv.) to the chieftains of Amalek, means "high." The words point to the Amalekite kingdom as highly prosperous and powerful at the time (cp. *v.* 20); but also to be far excelled by the future glories of Israel. The Amalekites never in fact recovered their crushing defeat by Saul (1 S. xv. 2 seq.), though they appear again as foes to Israel in the reign of David (1 S. xxvii. and xxx). The remnant of them was destroyed in the reign of Hezekiah (1 Chr. iv. 43).

14. *I will advertise thee*] *i.e.* "I will advise thee," words which refer to the ensuing prophecy.

16. *and knew the knowledge of the most High*] With the addition of these words, which point to the greater importance and the more distinctly predictive character of what follows, the introduction to this last parable is the same as the introduction to the preceding parable.

Which saw the vision of the Almighty,
Falling *into a trance*, but having his eyes open:
17 [a]I shall see him, but not now: — [a] Rev. 1. 7.
I shall behold him, but not nigh:
There shall come [b]a Star out of Jacob, — [b] Matt. 2. 2. Rev. 22. 16.
And [c]a Sceptre shall rise out of Israel, — [c] Gen. 49. 10. Ps. 110. 2.
And shall [1]smite the corners of Moab,
And destroy all the children of Sheth.
18 And [d]Edom shall be a possession, — [d] 2 Sam. 8. 14. Ps. 60. 8, 9, 12.
Seir also shall be a possession for his enemies;
And Israel shall do valiantly.
19 [e]Out of Jacob shall come he that shall have dominion, — [e] Gen. 49. 10.
And shall destroy him that remaineth of the city.

20 And when he looked on Amalek, he took up his parable, and
said,

Amalek *was* [2]the first of the nations;
But his latter end [3]*shall be* that he perish for ever.

[1] Or, *smite through the princes of Moab*, 2 Sam. 8. 2. Jer. 48. 45.
[2] Or, *the first of the nations that warred against Israel*, Ex. 17. 8.
[3] Or, shall be *even to destruction*, Ex. 17. 14. 1 Sam. 15. 3, 8.

---

17. Render, **I see him, though he be not now: I behold him, though he be not nigh.** Balaam here describes what is actually before him in inward vision.

him] *i.e.* the prince, represented in the succeeding words by the Star and Sceptre. The star has amongst all nations served as a symbol of regal power and splendour: and the birth and future glory of great monarchs were believed by the ancients to be heralded by the appearance of stars or comets: cp. also Is. xiv. 12; Dan. viii. 10; Rev. i. 16, 20, ii. 1, ix. 1.

the corners of Moab] Literally, "the two sides of Moab," *i.e.* the length and breadth of the land: cp. Jer. xlviii. 45.

destroy all the children of Sheth] Rather, "overthrow the sons of tumult," *i.e.* the warriors of Moab, whose valour and fierceness is frequently referred to elsewhere (cp. Ex. xv. 15; Is. xv. 4, xvi. 6, &c.) Cp. Jer. xlviii. 45.

18. *Seir*] The older name of the mountain-land, south of Moab, and east of the Arabah, which the Edomites inhabited (Gen. xxxii. 3, xxxvi. 8, 9).

19. *destroy him that remaineth of the city*] *i.e.* shall destroy those of every city that had previously escaped. The phrase tersely describes a conqueror who first defeats his enemies in battle, and then hunts out the fugitives till he has cut off all of every place (cp. 1 K. xi. 16).

The victories of David were a partial accomplishment of the predictions (*vv.* 14, 18), but did not exhaust them.

It is apparent that Edom and Moab are named by Balaam, as they are also by the prophets (cp. *e.g.* Is. xi. 14), as representatives of the heathen nations (*v.* 8) who were hostile to the Theocracy. As Jacob therefore figures as a constant type of the kingdom of Messiah in the prophets, so do Edom and Moab of the enemies of that kingdom; and in the threatened ruin of Edom and Moab is indicated the eventual destruction of all that resist the kingdom of God in its power.

The "Star" and "Sceptre" of the prophecy, like the "Sceptre" and "Lawgiver" of Gen. xlix. 10, point also naturally to a line of princes rather than to an individual; or rather are emblems of the kingdom of Israel generally. Thus the victories of David and his successors, generation after generation, over Edom and Moab, are unquestionably recurring and progressive accomplishments of what Balaam foretold; but in addition the prophecy reaches forward to some further and culminating accomplishment; and that too in "the latter days" (*v.* 14), the ordinary prophetic designation for the time of the Messiah (cp. marg. reff.).

To a Christian the connection between the Star and Sceptre of Balaam and the Star of the king of the Jews, which the wise men saw (St. Matt. ii. 2), is self-evident.

20. *when he looked*] *i.e.* in spirit, as he saw the Star (*v.* 17).

Amalek was the first of the nations] Rather, **is** pre-eminent amongst the neighbouring nations: cp. the same expression in Amos vi. 1. Hence the force of the words (*v.* 7) "higher than Agag," *i.e.* than the king of this powerful nation (cp. xiv. 45; Ex. xvii. 8). This rank, due to the warlike prowess of the tribe, Balaam contrasts with its approaching downfall and extinction.

21 And he looked on the Kenites, and took up his parable, and said,

Strong is thy dwellingplace,
And thou puttest thy nest in a rock.
22 Nevertheless [1]the Kenite shall be wasted,
[2]Until Asshur shall carry thee away captive.

23 And he took up his parable, and said,

Alas, who shall live when God doeth this!
24 And ships *shall come* from the coast of [f]Chittim,
And shall afflict Asshur, and shall afflict [g]Eber,
And he also shall perish for ever.

[f] Gen. 10. 4. Dan. 11. 30.
[g] Gen. 10. 21, 25.

[1] Heb. *Kain*, Gen. 15. 19.
[2] Or, *how long* shall it be ere *Asshur carry thee away captive?*

21. *the Kenites*] First mentioned (Gen. xv. 19) as one of the tribes whose territory was promised to Abraham. In Judg. i. 16, where we read of them as moving with the children of Judah, to establish themselves in the pastures south of Arad, Moses' father-in-law is spoken of as a Kenite (cp. Judg. iv. 11). It appears therefore, since Moses' father-in-law was a prince or priest of Midian (Ex. ii. 15 seq.), that the Kenites must have been of Midianitish extraction, and so descended from Abraham through Keturah (Gen. xxv. 2).

But it seems unlikely that the Kenites of Gen. xv. 19, who were to be dispossessed by the descendants of Abraham, were identical with those of whom Balaam speaks, and who were, because of good offices rendered at the time of the Exodus, always regarded as kinsmen and friends by Israel (cp. 1 S. xv. 6, xxvii. 10). Rather, is it probable that the Kenites of Gen. xv. 19 were a Canaanitish people, who derived their name from the city Kain, which fell eventually within the borders of the tribe of Judah (Josh. xv. 22); and that the descendants of Hobab, who appear in Judg. i. 16 as making war in this very district, possessed themselves of this city, and with it of the name Kenite also. This they would seem to have already done when Balaam uttered his prediction; and in the next verse it is, as the margin correctly indicates, not of the Kenite, but of Kain the city, that he speaks. Nor is it surprising to find them in possession of their new abode in the Promised Land, while the Israelites were yet in their tents. It may well be that this roving band of Midianites had already entered Canaan, perhaps along the shores of the Dead Sea, and by routes impracticable for the huge host of Israel, and had, as a kind of advanced guard, made a beginning of the conquest of the country.

From 1 Chr. ii. 54, 55, we learn that the Rechabites were a branch of the Kenites; and the name Salmaites, always given to the Kenites in the Targums, connects them with Salma, the son of Caleb, there mentioned. Jer. xxxv. shows how tenaciously, for many centuries, they held fast the nomadic habits of their race.

Strong is thy dwellingplace, and thou puttest thy nest in a rock] Render, **Strong** (or firm) **be thy dwelling-place, and put thou thy nest in the rock** (or cliff). In the Hebrew there is a play on the words *ken*, "nest," and *Kain*, the name of the Kenites' abode. This nest in the cliff might be the city of Hazazon-tamar or Engedi, if that be (as is likely) the "city of palm-trees," from which they went up subsequently (Judg. i. 16). But there is another site, about ten miles south of Engedi, to which Balaam's words would be more appropriate, on the summit of the cliff rising perpendicularly from the level of the western shore of the Dead Sea, where was afterwards built the city of Masada, the scene of the closing tragedy of the Jewish-Roman war. It is not likely that such a natural fortress would ever have been unoccupied, or even excluded from a place in the list of the cities of Judah. Nor is there any site in the Holy Land which a rude but warlike people might more fittingly designate as either Ken, the Nest, or Kain, the Possession.

22. Render, **For Kain shall surely not be destroyed** (lit. "be for destruction") **until Asshur**, &c. The words are not, as they appear in A. V., a prediction of evil to the Kenites, but a promise, on the contrary, of safety to be long continued to them (cp. x. 32; Jer. xxxv. 19).

23. *when God doeth this*] The eventual carrying away of the allies of Israel by Assyria presented itself to Balaam as the ruin of all peace and safety upon earth. One prediction was however yet wanting, and is next given, viz. that the conquerors of the Kenites should fare no better than the Kenites themselves.

24. *Chittim*] *i.e.* Cyprus, the nearest of the western islands, the only one visible from Palestine, and so the representative to Balaam and to Israel of all those unknown western regions across the Mediterranean Sea, from which were at length to come the conquerors of the mighty empires of the East. Cp. Isai. xxiii. 1, 12; Jer. ii. 10.

25 ¶And Balaam rose up, and went and [h]returned to his place:
and Balak also went his way.
Chap. 25. AND Israel abode in [a]Shittim, and [b]the people began
2 to commit whoredom with the daughters of Moab. And [c]they
called the people unto [d]the sacrifices of their gods: and the
3 people did eat, and [e]bowed down to their gods. And Israel
joined himself unto Baal-peor: and [f]the anger of the Lord was
4 kindled against Israel. And the Lord said unto Moses, [g]Take
all the heads of the people, and hang them up before the Lord
against the sun, [h]that the fierce anger of the Lord may be
5 turned away from Israel. And Moses said unto [i]the judges of
Israel, [k]Slay ye every one his men that were joined unto Baal-
6 peor. ¶And, behold, one of the children of Israel came and
brought unto his brethren a Midianitish woman in the sight of
Moses, and in the sight of all the congregation of the children of
Israel, [l]who *were* weeping *before* the door of the tabernacle of
7 the congregation. And [m]when Phinehas, [n]the son of Eleazar,
the son of Aaron the priest, saw *it*, he rose up from among the
8 congregation, and took a javelin in his hand; and he went after
the man of Israel into the tent, and thrust both of them through,
the man of Israel, and the woman through her belly. So [o]the
9 plague was stayed from the children of Israel. And [p]those that
10 died in the plague were twenty and four thousand. ¶And the
11 Lord spake unto Moses, saying, [q]Phinehas, the son of Eleazar,
the son of Aaron the priest, hath turned my wrath away from

[h] See ch. 31. 8.
[a] ch. 33. 49. Josh. 2. 1. Mic. 6. 5.
[b] ch. 31. 16. 1 Cor. 10. 8.
[c] Josh. 22. 17. Ps. 106. 28. Hos. 9. 10.
[d] Ex. 34. 15, 16. 1 Cor. 10. 20.
[e] Ex. 20. 5.
[f] Ps. 106. 29.
[g] Deut. 4. 3. Josh. 22. 17.
[h] ver. 11. Deut. 13. 17.
[i] Ex. 18. 21, 25.
[k] Ex. 32. 27. Deut. 13. 6, 9, 13, 15.
[l] Joel 2. 17.
[m] Ps. 106. 30.
[n] Ex. 6. 25.
[o] Ps. 106. 30.
[p] Deut. 4. 3. 1 Cor. 10. 8.
[q] Ps. 106. 30.

Eber] *i.e.* the descendants of Shem. Of these Asshur was one (cp. marg. ref.), and is here specified by name, since the Assyrians attained, in the empires of Babylon and Nineveh, to an extraordinary grandeur, and were destined to a most signal and irretrievable fall.

he also] *i.e.* the conqueror of Asshur and Eber who should come across the sea. It is not revealed whence the blow should come that should overthrow in its turn the power that prevailed over the great monarchies of the East.

25. *returned to his own place*] *i.e.* amongst the Midianites to plot by new means against the people of God, and to perish in his sin (xxxi. 8, 16; Rev. ii. 14).

XXV. The records of the neighbouring cities of the plain, and the circumstances of the origin of Moab (Gen. xix. 30 seq.) suggest that the people amongst whom Israel was now thrown were more than ordinarily licentious.

2. *and they called*] *i.e.* "the daughters of Moab called."

3. *joined himself*] *i.e.* by taking part in the sacrificial meals as described in the last verse. Cp. Ex. xxxiv. 15; 1 Cor. x. 18. The worship of Baal was attended with the grossest impurity, and indeed partly consisted in it (Hos. iv. 14, ix. 10).

Baal-peor] *i.e.* the Baal worshipped at Peor, the place mentioned in xxiii. 28 (cp. Baal-meon, xxxii. 38). [The identification of this god with Chemosh (xxi. 29) is now given up.]

4. *take*] *i.e.* assemble the chiefs of the people to thee (cp. the phrase "took men," in xvi. 1). The offenders were to be first slain by the hands of "the judges of Israel" (*v.* 5), and afterwards hung up "against the sun" (*i.e.* publicly, openly; cp. 2 Sam. xii. 12) as an aggravation of their punishment. This would be done by impaling the body or fastening it to a cross. Cp. Deut. xxi. 23 note, and 2 Sam. xxi. 9.

6. *a Midianitish woman*] Lit. "the Midianitish woman," the particular one by whom he had been enticed (cp. *v.* 15 and xxxi. 18). Her high rank proves that Zimri had not fallen in with her by mere chance, but had been deliberately singled out by the Midianites as one whom they must at any price lead astray.

weeping before the door of the tabernacle] The plague (*v.* 9) had already broken out among the people: and the more God-fearing had assembled at the door of the Tabernacle of God (cp. marg. ref.) to intercede for mercy, when Zimri committed the fresh and public outrage just described.

8. *into the tent*] The inner recess in the tent, fashioned archwise, and appropriated as the sleeping-chamber and women's apartment.

9. *twenty and four thousand*] St. Paul (1 Cor. x. 8) says "three and twenty thousand," following probably the Jewish tradition which deducted one thousand as the number slain by the hands of their brethren.

11. *hath turned my wrath away*] The signal example thus made of a leading offender by Phinehas was accepted by God as an expiation (lit. in *v.* 13 "covering;"

the children of Israel, while he was zealous [1] for my sake among
them, that I consumed not the children of Israel in [r] my jealousy.
12 Wherefore say, [s] Behold, I give unto him my covenant of peace:
13 and he shall have it, and [t] his seed after him, *even* the covenant of
[u] an everlasting priesthood; because he was [x] zealous for his God,
14 and [y] made an atonement for the children of Israel. ¶ Now the
name of the Israelite that was slain, *even* that was slain with
the Midianitish woman, *was* Zimri, the son of Salu, a prince of a
15 [2] chief house among the Simeonites. And the name of the Midianitish woman that was slain *was* Cozbi, the daughter of [z] Zur; he
16 *was* head over a people, *and* of a chief house in Midian. ¶ And
17 the LORD spake unto Moses, saying, [a] Vex the Midianites, and
18 smite them: for they vex you with their [b] wiles, wherewith they
have beguiled you in the matter of Peor, and in the matter of
Cozbi, the daughter of a prince of Midian, their sister, which was
slain in the day of the plague for Peor's sake.

CHAP. 26. AND it came to pass after the plague, that the LORD
spake unto Moses and unto Eleazar the son of Aaron the priest,
2 saying, [a] Take the sum of all the congregation of the children of
Israel, [b] from twenty years old and upward, throughout their
3 fathers' house, all that are able to go to war in Israel. And Moses
and Eleazar the priest spake with them [c] in the plains of Moab by
4 Jordan *near* Jericho, saying, *Take the sum of the people*, from
twenty years old and upward; as the LORD [d] commanded Moses
and the children of Israel, which went forth out of the land of
5 Egypt. ¶ [e] Reuben, the eldest son of Israel: the children of

[r] Ex. 20. 5. Deut. 32. 16, 21. 1 Kin. 14. 22. Ps. 78. 58. Ez. 16. 38. Zeph. 1. 18. & 3. 8.
[s] Mal. 2. 4, 5. & 3. 1.
[t] See 1 Chr. 6, 4, &c.
[u] Ex. 40. 15.
[x] Acts 22. 3. Rom. 10. 2.
[y] Heb. 2. 17.
[z] ch. 31. 8. Josh. 13. 21.
[a] ch. 31. 2.
[b] ch. 31. 16. Rev. 2. 14.

[a] Ex. 30. 12. & 38. 25. ch. 1. 2.
[b] ch. 1. 3.
[c] ver. 63. ch. 22. 1. & 31. 12. & 33. 48. & 35. 1.
[d] ch. 1. 1.
[e] Gen. 46. 8. Ex. 6. 14. 1 Chr. 5, 1.

[1] Heb. *with my zeal*: See 2 Cor. 11. 2.
[2] Heb. *house of a father*

see on the typical significance Lev. i. 4), and the exterminating wrath which had gone forth against the whole people was arrested (Ps. cvi. 30).

The act of Phinehas must be regarded as exceptional. It was an extraordinary deed of vengeance, justified by the singular atrocity of the crime which provoked it; but it does not confer the right to every man to punish summarily any gross and flagrant breach of Divine law committed in his presence. Cp. the act of Mattathias (1 Macc. ii. 24–26).

The act was its own justification. Its merit consisted in the evidence it gave that the heart of Phinehas was right before God. He was "zealous with God's zeal," and abhorred the presumptuous wickedness of Zimri, as God abhorred it. He therefore risked his own life by dealing according to their deserts with two influential and defiant evil doers; and his act, done in the face of Moses and the people, and for them, was accepted by God as a national atonement, and rewarded by the people (cp. the leadership assigned to him in xxxi. 6; Josh. xxii. 13).

12. *my covenant of peace*] Equivalent to "the Covenant of My peace." God established with Phinehas in particular that Covenant which He had made generally with all his people; and among its blessings peace is specially mentioned, because of the peace between God and the congregation which Phinehas had brought about. As an additional gift there is assigned to him and his seed for ever the office of peace-making, the legitimate function of the priesthood (cp. Eph. ii. 14); and the Covenant was thus to him a Covenant not only of peace but of life (cp. marg. ref.). Phinehas became high-priest after the death of his father Eleazar, and the office, with a short interruption from the days of Eli to those of David, when for unknown reasons it was filled by the descendants of his uncle Ithamar, was perpetuated in his line; nor indeed is it known to have departed from that line again until the typical priesthood of the sons of Aaron was merged in the actual priesthood of the Saviour of mankind.

XXVI. The mustering of the tribes described in this chapter was immediately preparatory to the war against Midian, and to the invasion of Canaan which shortly followed. With a view also to an equitable allotment of the land to be conquered (cp. *v.* 54) the numbers of the several tribes were taken according to their families.

1. *after the plague*] These words serve to show approximately the date at which the census was taken, and intimate the reason for the great decrease in numbers which was found to have taken place in certain tribes. Cp. Deut. iv. 3 and *v.* 5 note in this chapter.

5 seq. The tribes are mentioned in the same order as in the earlier census (ch. i.), except that Manasseh here precedes Ephraim; probably as being now the larger tribe.

Reuben; Hanoch, *of whom cometh* the family of the Hanochites:
6 of Pallu, the family of the Palluites: of Hezron, the family of
7 the Hezronites: of Carmi, the family of the Carmites. These
are the families of the Reubenites: and they that were numbered
of them were forty and three thousand and seven hundred and
8, 9 thirty. And the sons of Pallu; Eliab. And the sons of Eliab;
Nemuel, and Dathan, and Abiram. This *is that* Dathan and
Abiram, *which were* [f]famous in the congregation, who strove
against Moses and against Aaron in the company of Korah,
10 when they strove against the LORD: [g]and the earth opened her
mouth, and swallowed them up together with Korah, when that
company died, what time the fire devoured two hundred and
11 fifty men: [h]and they became a sign. Notwithstanding [i]the
12 children of Korah died not. ¶ The sons of Simeon after their
families: of [k]Nemuel, the family of the Nemuelites: of Jamin,
the family of the Jaminites: of [l]Jachin, the family of the Jachin-
13 ites: of [m]Zerah, the family of the Zarhites: of Shaul, the
14 family of the Shaulites. These *are* the families of the Simeonites,
15 twenty and two thousand and two hundred. ¶ The children of
Gad after their families: of [n]Zephon, the family of the Zephon-
ites: of Haggi, the family of the Haggites: of Shuni, the family
16 of the Shunites: of [1]Ozni, the family of the Oznites: of Eri, the
17 family of the Erites: of [o]Arod, the family of the Arodites: of
18 Areli, the family of the Arelites. These *are* the families of the
children of Gad according to those that were numbered of them,
19 forty thousand and five hundred. ¶ [p]The sons of Judah *were* Er
20 and Onan: and Er and Onan died in the land of Canaan. And

f ch. 16. 1, 2.
g ch. 16. 32, 35.
h ch. 16. 38. See 1 Cor. 10. 6. 2 Pet. 2. 6.
i Ex. 6. 24. 1 Chr. 6. 22.
k Gen. 46. 10. Ex. 6. 15, *Jemuel.*
l 1 Chr. 4. 24, *Jarib.*
m Gen. 46. 10, *Zohar.*
n Gen. 46.16. *Ziphion.*
o Gen. 46.16, *Arodi.*
p Gen. 38. 2, &c. & 46. 12.

[1] Or, *Ezbon*, Gen. 46. 16.

The following table shews the numbers of the tribes at each census:

	At Sinai.	In the Plains of Moab.
Reuben	46,500	43,730
Simeon	59,300	22,200
Gad	45,650	40,500
Judah	74,600	76,500
Issachar	54,400	64,300
Zebulun	57,400	60,500
Ephraim	40,500	32,500
Manasseh	32,200	52,700
Benjamin	35,400	45,600
Dan	62,700	64,400
Asher	41,500	53,400
Naphtali	53,400	45,400
	603,550	601,730

Seven of the tribes, of which three are tribes belonging to the camp of Judah, shew an increase of numbers; and five, among whom are the three belonging to the camp of Reuben, shew a decrease. The greatest increase of any one tribe is in Manasseh. The most remarkable decrease is in Simeon, which now shews less than half its former strength. To this tribe Zimri, the chief offender in the recent transgression, belonged (xxv. 14). Probably his tribesmen generally had followed his example, and had accordingly suffered most severely in the plague. In the parting blessing of Moses, uttered at no great interval from this date, the tribe of Simeon alone is omitted.

The families of all the tribes, excluding the Levites, number fifty-seven. The ancestral heads after whom these families are named correspond nearly with the grandchildren and great-grandchildren of Jacob, enumerated in Gen. xlvi. 8 seq. Both lists consist mainly of grandchildren of Jacob, both contain also the same two grandchildren of Judah, and the same two grandchildren of Asher. The document in Genesis should be regarded as a list, not of those who went down in their own persons with Jacob into Egypt, but of those whose names were transmitted to their posterity at the date of the Exodus as the heads of Israelitish houses, and who may thus be reckoned the early ancestors of the people.

10. *together with Korah*] *i.e.* they were engulphed at the same time that Korah perished; for Korah himself appears to have died amongst the two hundred and fifty incense offerers at the door of the Tabernacle, not with Dathan and Abiram (cp. xvi. 32 note).

11. *the children of Korah died not*] Cp. *v.* 58. Samuel the prophet was of this family, and Heman, "the king's seer" (1 Chr. vi. 22, 33, xxv. 5). Several of the Psalms appear from the titles to have been composed for the sons of Korah: cp. titles of Pss. xlii., xliv., xlv., &c.

[q]the sons of Judah after their families were; of Shelah, the
family of the Shelanites: of Pharez, the family of the Pharzites:
21 of Zerah, the family of the Zarhites. And the sons of Pharez
were; of Hezron, the family of the Hezronites: of Hamul, the
22 family of the Hamulites. These *are* the families of Judah according to those that were numbered of them, threescore and sixteen
23 thousand and five hundred. ¶ [r] *Of* the sons of Issachar after their
families: *of* Tola, the family of the Tolaites: of [1]Pua, the family
24 of the Punites: of [2]Jashub, the family of the Jashubites: of
25 Shimron, the family of the Shimronites. These *are* the families
of Issachar according to those that were numbered of them,
26 threescore and four thousand and three hundred. ¶ [s] *Of* the
sons of Zebulun after their families: of Sered, the family of the
Sardites: of Elon, the family of the Elonites: of Jahleel, the family
27 of the Jahleelites. These *are* the families of the Zebulunites according to those that were numbered of them, threescore thousand
28 and five hundred. ¶ [t]The sons of Joseph after their families *were*
29 Manasseh and Ephraim. Of the sons of Manasseh: of [u]Machir,
the family of the Machirites: and Machir begat Gilead: of
30 Gilead *come* the family of the Gileadites. These *are* the sons of
Gilead: *of* [x]Jeezer, the family of the Jeezerites: of Helek, the
31 family of the Helekites: and *of* Asriel, the family of the Asriel-
32 ites: and *of* Shechem, the family of the Shechemites: and *of*
Shemida, the family of the Shemidaites: and *of* Hepher, the
33 family of the Hepherites. And [y]Zelophehad the son of Hepher
had no sons, but daughters: and the names of the daughters
of Zelophehad *were* Mahlah, and Noah, Hoglah, Milcah, and
34 Tirzah. These *are* the families of Manasseh, and those that
were numbered of them, fifty and two thousand and seven hun-
35 dred. ¶ These *are* the sons of Ephraim after their families: of
Shuthelah, the family of the Shuthalhites: of [z]Becher, the
family of the Bachrites: of Tahan, the family of the Tahanites.
36 And these *are* the sons of Shuthelah: of Eran, the family of the
37 Eranites. These *are* the families of the sons of Ephraim according to those that were numbered of them, thirty and two thousand and five hundred. These *are* the sons of Joseph after their
38 families. ¶ [a]The sons of Benjamin after their families: of Bela,
the family of the Belaites: of Ashbel, the family of the Ashbel-
39 ites: of [b]Ahiram, the family of the Ahiramites: of [c]Shupham,
the family of the Shuphamites: of Hupham, the family of the
40 Huphamites. And the sons of Bela were [d]Ard and Naaman:
of Ard, the family of the Ardites: *and* of Naaman, the family of
41 the Naamites. These *are* the sons of Benjamin after their
families: and they that were numbered of them *were* forty
42 and five thousand and six hundred. ¶ [e]These *are* the sons of
Dan after their families: of [3]Shuham, the family of the Shuham-
43 ites. These *are* the families of Dan after their families. All the
families of the Shuhamites, according to those that were numbered of them, *were* threescore and four thousand and four hun-
44 dred. ¶ [f] *Of* the children of Asher after their families: of Jimna,
the family of the Jimnites: of Jesui, the family of the Jesuites:
45 of Beriah, the family of the Beriites. Of the sons of Beriah: of
Heber, the family of the Heberites: of Malchiel, the family of the
46 Malchielites. And the name of the daughter of Asher *was* Sarah.
47 These *are* the families of the sons of Asher according to

[q] 1 Chr. 2. 3.
[r] Gen. 46. 13. 1 Chr. 7. 1.
[s] Gen. 46. 14.
[t] Gen. 46. 20.
[u] Josh. 17. 1. 1 Chr. 7. 14, 15.
[x] Called, *Abiezer*, Josh. 17. 2. Judg. 6. 11, 24, 34.
[y] ch. 27. 1. & 36. 11.
[z] 1 Chr. 7. 20, *Bered*.
[a] Gen. 46. 21. 1 Chr. 7. 6.
[b] Gen. 46. 21, *Ehi*. 1 Chr. 8. 1, *Aharah*.
[c] Gen. 46. 21, *Muppim and Huppim*.
[d] 1 Chr. 8. 3, *Addar*.
[e] Gen. 46. 23.
[f] Gen. 46. 17. 1 Chr. 7. 30.

[1] Or, *Phuvah*. [2] Or, *Job*. [3] Or, *Hushim*.

those that were numbered of them; *who were* fifty and three
48 thousand and four hundred. ¶ [g] *Of* the sons of Naphtali after their
families: of Jahzeel, the family of the Jahzeelites: of Guni, the
49 family of the Gunites: of Jezer, the family of the Jezerites: of
50 [h] Shillem, the family of the Shillemites. These *are* the families
of Naphtali according to their families: and they that were
numbered of them *were* forty and five thousand and four hun-
51 dred. ¶ [i] These *were* the numbered of the children of Israel, six
hundred thousand and a thousand seven hundred and thirty.
52, 53 ¶ And the LORD spake unto Moses, saying, [k] Unto these the
land shall be divided for an inheritance according to the number
54 of names. [l] To many thou shalt [1] give the more inheritance, and
to few thou shalt [2] give the less inheritance: to every one shall
his inheritance be given according to those that were numbered
55 of him. Notwithstanding the land shall be [m] divided by lot:
according to the names of the tribes of their fathers they shall
56 inherit. According to the lot shall the possession thereof be
57 divided between many and few. ¶ [n] And these *are* they that
were numbered of the Levites after their families: of Gershon,
the family of the Gershonites: of Kohath, the family of the
58 Kohathites: of Merari, the family of the Merarites. These *are*
the families of the Levites: the family of the Libnites, the
family of the Hebronites, the family of the Mahlites, the family
of the Mushites, the family of the Korathites. And Kohath
59 begat Amram. And the name of Amram's wife *was* [o] Jochebed,
the daughter of Levi, whom *her mother* bare to Levi in Egypt:
and she bare unto Amram Aaron and Moses, and Miriam their
60 sister. [p] And unto Aaron was born Nadab, and Abihu, Eleazar,
61 and Ithamar. And [q] Nadab and Abihu died, when they offered
62 strange fire before the LORD. [r] And those that were numbered
of them were twenty and three thousand, all males from a month
old and upward: [s] for they were not numbered among the children of Israel, because there was [t] no inheritance given them
63 among the children of Israel. ¶ These *are* they that were numbered by Moses and Eleazar the priest, who numbered the children of Israel [u] in the plains of Moab by Jordan *near* Jericho.
64 But [x] among these there was not a man of them whom Moses and
Aaron the priest numbered, when they numbered the children of
65 Israel in the wilderness of Sinai. For the LORD had said of
them, They [y] shall surely die in the wilderness. And there was not
left a man of them, [z] save Caleb the son of Jephunneh, and Joshua
the son of Nun.

CHAP. 27. THEN came the daughters of [a] Zelophehad, the son
of Hepher, the son of Gilead, the son of Machir, the son of

[g] Gen. 46. 24. 1 Chr. 7. 13.
[h] 1 Chr. 7. 13, *Shallum.*
[i] See ch. 1. 46.
[k] Josh. 11. 23. & 14. 1.
[l] ch. 33. 54.
[m] ch. 33. 54. & 34. 13. Josh. 11. 23. & 14. 2.
[n] Gen. 46. 11. Ex. 6. 16, 17, 18, 19. 1 Chr. 6. 1, 16.
[o] Ex. 2. 1, 2. & 6. 20.
[p] ch. 3. 2.
[q] Lev. 10. 1, 2. ch. 3. 4. 1 Chr. 24. 2.
[r] See ch. 3. 39.
[s] ch. 1. 49.
[t] ch. 18. 20. Deut. 10. 9. Josh. 13. 14, 33. & 14. 3.
[u] ver. 3.
[x] ch. 1. Deut. 2. 14, 15.
[y] ch. 14. 28, 29. 1 Cor. 10. 5, 6.
[z] ch. 14. 30.
[a] ch. 26. 33. & 36. 1. 11. Josh. 17. 3.

[1] Heb. *multiply his inheritance.*

[2] Heb. *diminish his inheritance.*

---

51. This shews a decrease of 1820 from the number at Sinai; a decrease due to the recent plague.

56. *according to the lot,* &c.] This method was adopted not only in order to preclude jealousies and disputes, but also that the several tribes might regard the territories as determined for them by God Himself: cp. Prov. xvi. 33.

59. *whom her mother bare*] Literally, "whom she bare;" the subject is wanting, and the verb is in the feminine gender. The words "her mother" are merely conjectural. The text is probably imperfect.

62. The total number of male Levites, 23,000, shews an increase of 1,000 on the number at Sinai (iii. 39). It is doubtless to be taken as a round number; and, as before, includes the male children from a month old and upward, as well as the male adults.

64. It appears from Deut. ii. 14, 15 that the generation numbered at the former census had perished before the host crossed the brook Zered.

XXVII. **1.** Women in Israel had not, up

Manasseh, of the families of Manasseh the son of Joseph: and
these *are* the names of his daughters; Mahlah, Noah, and Hog-
2 lah, and Milcah, and Tirzah. And they stood before Moses, and
before Eleazar the priest, and before the princes and all the
congregation, *by* the door of the tabernacle of the congregation,
3 saying, Our father [b]died in the wilderness, and he was not in the
company of them that gathered themselves together against the
LORD [c]in the company of Korah; but died in his own sin, and
4 had no sons. Why should the name of our father be [1]done
away from among his family, because he hath no son? [d]Give
unto us *therefore* a possession among the brethren of our father.
5, 6 ¶ And Moses [e]brought their cause before the LORD. And the
7 LORD spake unto Moses, saying, The daughters of Zelophehad
speak right: [f]thou shalt surely give them a possession of an inheritance among their father's brethren; and thou shalt cause
8 the inheritance of their father to pass unto them. And thou shalt
speak unto the children of Israel, saying, If a man die, and have
no son, then ye shall cause his inheritance to pass unto his
9 daughter. And if he have no daughter, then ye shall give his
10 inheritance unto his brethren. And if he have no brethren, then
11 ye shall give his inheritance unto his father's brethren. And if
his father have no brethren, then ye shall give his inheritance
unto his kinsman that is next to him of his family, and he shall
possess it: and it shall be unto the children of Israel [g]a statute
12 of judgment, as the LORD commanded Moses. ¶ And the LORD
said unto Moses, [h]Get thee up into this mount Abarim, and see the
13 land which I have given unto the children of Israel. And when
thou hast seen it, thou also [i]shalt be gathered unto thy people,
14 as Aaron thy brother was gathered. For ye [k]rebelled against
my commandment in the desert of Zin, in the strife of the congregation, to sanctify me at the water before their eyes: that
is the [l]water of Meribah in Kadesh in the wilderness of Zin.
15, 16 And Moses spake unto the LORD, saying, Let the LORD, [m]the
God of the spirits of all flesh, set a man over the congregation,

[b] ch. 14. 35. & 26. 64, 65.
[c] ch. 16. 1, 2.
[d] Josh. 17. 4.
[e] Ex. 18. 15, 19.
[f] ch. 36. 2.
[g] ch. 35. 29.
[h] ch. 33. 47. Deut. 3. 27. & 32. 49. & 34. 1.
[i] ch. 20, 24, 28. & 31. 2. Deut. 10. 6.
[k] ch. 20. 12. Deut. 1. 37. & 32. 51. Ps. 106. 32.
[l] Ex. 17. 7.
[m] ch. 16. 22. Heb. 12. 9.

[1] Heb. *diminished*.

---

to the present time, enjoyed any distinct right of inheritance. Yet a father, whether sons had been born to him or not, had the power, either before or at his death, to cause part of his estate to pass to a daughter; in which case her husband married into her family rather than she into his, and the children were regarded as of the family from which the estate had come. Thus Machir, ancestor of Zelophehad, although he had a son Gilead, left also, as is probable, an inheritance to his daughter, the wife of Hezron of the tribe of Judah, by reason of which their descendants, among whom was Jair, were reckoned as belonging to the tribe of Manasseh (xxxii. 41; 1 Chr. ii. 21 seq.).

2. *by the door of the tabernacle of the congregation*] The place of solemn assembly of the elders. The daughters of Zelophehad made their suit to the princes, the heads of tribes and of families, who were making the census under the superintendence of Moses and Eleazar.

3. *but died in his own sin*] *i.e.* perished under the general sentence of exclusion from the Land of Promise passed on all the older generation, but limited to that generation alone. By virtue of the declaration in xiv. 31 the daughters of Zelophehad claim that their father's sin should not be visited upon them.

4. *give unto us*] As representing our father; that so he, through us his representatives, may enjoy a like inheritance with his brethren.

12. *mount Abarim*] See xxi. 20 note.

16. *the God of the spirits of all flesh*] An acknowledgment that man, who is but flesh (cp. Gen. vi. 3), is of himself helpless; and "lives and moves and has his being" in God (Acts xvii. 28). The words are suitably employed here to introduce an entreaty that God would not leave the congregation without a guide and leader, and in xvi. 22 as a preface to an intercession that the whole people should not suffer for the sin of a few.

17 [n]which may go out before them, and which may go in before
them, and which may lead them out, and which may bring
them in; that the congregation of the LORD be not [o]as sheep
18 which have no shepherd. And the LORD said unto Moses,
Take thee Joshua the son of Nun, a man [p]in whom *is* the spirit,
19 and [q]lay thine hand upon him; and set him before Eleazar the
priest, and before all the congregation; and [r]give him a charge
20 in their sight. And [s]thou shalt put *some* of thine honour upon
him, that all the congregation of the children of Israel [t]may be
21 obedient. [u]And he shall stand before Eleazar the priest, who
shall ask *counsel* for him [x]after the judgment of Urim before the
LORD: [y]at his word shall they go out, and at his word they shall
come in, *both* he, and all the children of Israel with him, even all
22 the congregation. ¶And Moses did as the LORD commanded
him: and he took Joshua, and set him before Eleazar the priest,
23 and before all the congregation: and he laid his hands upon him,
[z]and gave him a charge, as the LORD commanded by the hand
of Moses.

CHAP. 28. AND the LORD spake unto Moses, saying, Command
2 the children of Israel, and say unto them, My offering, *and* [a]my
bread for my sacrifices made by fire, *for* [1]a sweet savour unto
3 me, shall ye observe to offer unto me in their due season. And
thou shalt say unto them, [b]This *is* the offering made by fire
which ye shall offer unto the LORD; two lambs of the first year
4 without spot [2]day by day, *for* a continual burnt offering. The
one lamb shalt thou offer in the morning, and the other lamb
5 shalt thou offer [3]at even; and [c]a tenth *part* of an ephah of flour
for a [d]meat offering, mingled with the fourth *part* of an [e]hin of
6 beaten oil. *It is* [f]a continual burnt offering, which was ordained

[n] Deut. 31. 2. 1 Sam. 8. 20. 2 Chr. 1. 10.
[o] 1 Kin. 22. 17. Zech. 10. 2. Matt. 9. 36. Mark 6. 34.
[p] Gen. 41. 38. Judg. 3. 10. & 11. 29. 1 Sam. 16. 13, 18.
[q] Deut. 34. 9.
[r] Deut. 31. 7.
[s] 1 Sam. 10. 6. 2 Kin. 2. 15.
[t] Josh. 1. 16, 17.
[u] See Josh. 9. 14. Judg. 1. 1. & 20. 18, 23. 1 Sam. 23. 9. & 30. 7.
[x] Ex. 28. 30.
[y] Josh. 9. 14. 1 Sam. 22. 10, 13, 15.
[z] Deut. 3. 28. & 31. 7.
[a] Lev. 3. 11. & 21. 6, 8. Mal. 1. 7, 12.
[b] Ex. 29. 38.
[c] Ex. 16. 36. ch. 15. 4.
[d] Lev. 2. 1.
[e] Ex. 29. 40.
[f] Ex. 29. 42. See Amos 5. 25.

[1] Heb. *a savour of my rest.* [2] Heb. *in a day.* [3] Heb. *between the two evenings*, Ex. 12. 6.

---

18. *in whom is the spirit*] Cp. Gen. xli. 38. Joshua was endowed by God with the requisite spiritual qualifications for the office. Moses however was to lay his hands upon him, both in order to confer formal and public appointment, and also (cp. Deut. xxxiv. 9) to confirm and strengthen the spiritual gifts already bestowed. The previous reception of the inner grace did not dispense with that of the outward sign; cp. the case of Cornelius (Acts x. 44–48); and St. Paul's Baptism after his miraculous conversion (Acts ix. 18).

20. *of thine honour*] *i.e.* of thy dignity and authority (cp. xi. 17, 28). Joshua was constituted forthwith vice-leader under Moses, by way of introduction to his becoming chief after Moses' death.

21. *and he shall stand before Eleazar the priest*, &c.] Joshua was thus to be inferior to what Moses had been. For Moses had enjoyed the privilege of unrestricted direct intercourse with God: Joshua, like all future rulers of Israel, was to ask counsel mediately, through the High-priest and those means of enquiring of God wherewith the High-priest was entrusted. Such counsel Joshua seems to have omitted to seek when he concluded his hasty treaty with the Gibeonites (Joshua ix. 3 seq.).

judgment of Urim] See Ex. xxviii. 30 note.

XXVIII. The daily offering had been already commanded (Ex. xxix. 38), and no doubt additional offerings had become customary on Festivals. But no such elaborate system as is here prescribed was or could possibly have been observed in the wilderness: cp. Deut. xii. 8, 9. The regulations of this and the next chapter therefore point to the immediate prospect of that settlement in Canaan which alone could enable the Israelites to obey them. Cp. the ordinances in ch. xv.

2. *My offering, and my bread*, &c.] Or, **my offering, even my bread**, &c. Offering is here *korban* (cp. Lev. i. 2; Mark vii. 11), a term in itself of quite general import, but often especially applied, as apparently in this instance, to the Meat-offering which accompanied the sacrifices. This Meat-offering connected itself, from its very nature, with the life of the Israelites in Canaan, not with their life in the wilderness; and it was annexed to the animal sacrifices as a token that the people must dedicate to God their property and the fruits of their labour as well as their own persons. See xv. 2 note and Lev. xxi. 6.

in mount Sinai for a sweet savour, a sacrifice made by fire unto
7 the LORD. And the drink offering thereof *shall be* the fourth
part of an hin for the one lamb: [g]in the holy *place* shalt thou
cause the strong wine to be poured unto the LORD *for* a drink
8 offering. And the other lamb shalt thou offer at even: as the
meat offering of the morning, and as the drink offering thereof,
thou shalt offer *it*, a sacrifice made by fire, of a sweet savour
9 unto the LORD. ¶ And on the sabbath day two lambs of the first
year without spot, and two tenth deals of flour *for* a meat offer-
10 ing, mingled with oil, and the drink offering thereof: *this is*
[h]the burnt offering of every sabbath, beside the continual burnt
11 offering, and his drink offering. ¶ And [i]in the beginnings of
your months ye shall offer a burnt offering unto the LORD; two
young bullocks, and one ram, seven lambs of the first year with-
12 out spot; and [k]three tenth deals of flour *for* a meat offering,
mingled with oil, for one bullock; and two tenth deals of flour
13 *for* a meat offering, mingled with oil, for one ram; and a several
tenth deal of flour mingled with oil *for* a meat offering unto
one lamb; *for* a burnt offering of a sweet savour, a sacrifice
14 made by fire unto the LORD. And their drink offerings shall be
half an hin of wine unto a bullock, and the third *part* of an hin
unto a ram, and a fourth *part* of an hin unto a lamb: this *is*
the burnt offering of every month throughout the months of the
15 year. And [l]one kid of the goats for a sin offering unto the
LORD shall be offered, beside the continual burnt offering, and
16 his drink offering. ¶ [m]And in the fourteenth day of the first
17 month *is* the passover of the LORD. [n]And in the fifteenth day
of this month *is* the feast: seven days shall unleavened bread
18 be eaten. In the [o]first day *shall be* an holy convocation; ye
19 shall do no manner of servile work *therein*: but ye shall offer
a sacrifice made by fire *for* a burnt offering unto the LORD;
two young bullocks, and one ram, and seven lambs of the first
20 year: [p]they shall be unto you without blemish: and their
meat offering *shall be of* flour mingled with oil: three tenth
deals shall ye offer for a bullock, and two tenth deals for a ram;
21 a several tenth deal shalt thou offer for every lamb, through-
22 out the seven lambs: and [q]one goat *for* a sin offering, to make
23 an atonement for you. Ye shall offer these beside the burnt
offering in the morning, which *is* for a continual burnt offering.
24 After this manner ye shall offer daily, throughout the seven
days, the meat of the sacrifice made by fire, of a sweet savour

[g] Ex. 29. 42.
[h] Ez. 46. 4.
[i] ch. 10. 10. 1 Sam. 20. 5. 1 Chr. 23. 31. 2 Chr. 2. 4. Ezra 3. 5. Neh. 10. 33. Isai. 1. 13. Ez. 45. 17. & 46. 6. Hos. 2. 11. Col. 2. 16.
[k] ch. 15. 4–12.
[l] ver. 22. ch. 15. 24.
[m] Ex. 12. 6. Lev. 23. 5. ch. 9. 3. Deut. 16. 1. Ez. 45. 21.
[n] Lev. 23. 6.
[o] Ex. 12. 16. Lev. 23. 7.
[p] ver. 31. Lev. 22. 20. ch. 29. 8. Deut. 15. 21.
[q] ver. 15.

---

7. The original of the word "strong wine" (*shechar*) is a term usually employed to describe strong drink other than wine (Lev. x. 9 note). The Israelites in the wilderness had, in their lack of wine, substituted *shechar* made from barley for it. They had thus observed the spirit, though not the letter of the ordinance. The Drink-offering was either poured round the foot of the Altar; or on the Altar, and so upon the flesh of the sacrifice by which the Altar was covered (cp. Ex. xxx. 9).

9–10. The Sabbath-offering, not previously enjoined, consisted of two lambs, properly accompanied, in addition to the regular daily offering.

11–15. The New-moon offering is here also commanded for the first time. The goat as a Sin-offering, though mentioned last, would seem in fact to have been offered first (cp. the precedents in Ex. xxix.; Lev. v., viii., ix., xiv., xvi.). The Sin-offering, which (xv. 22–26) had been contemplated in cases where a sin had been committed ignorantly without the knowledge of the congregation, was henceforth not to be offered merely at discretion, as circumstances might seem to require, but to be regularly repeated, not less frequently than once a month.

16–25. The Passover offering was the same as that of the New moon, and was repeated on each of the seven days of the Festival, thus marking the importance and the solemnity of the occasion. The details of the offering had not been previously prescribed.

unto the LORD: it shall be offered beside the continual burnt
25 offering, and his drink offering. And [r]on the seventh day ye
shall have an holy convocation; ye shall do no servile work.
26 ¶ Also [s]in the day of the firstfruits, when ye bring a new meat
offering unto the LORD, after your weeks *be out*, ye shall have
27 an holy convocation; ye shall do no servile work: but ye shall
offer the burnt offering for a sweet savour unto the LORD; [t]two
28 young bullocks, one ram, seven lambs of the first year; and
their meat offering of flour mingled with oil, three tenth deals
29 unto one bullock, two tenth deals unto one ram, a several tenth
30 deal unto one lamb, throughout the seven lambs; *and* one kid
31 of the goats, to make an atonement for you. Ye shall offer
them beside the continual burnt offering, and his meat offering,
([u]they shall be unto you without blemish) and their drink
offerings.

[r] Ex. 12. 16. & 13. 6. Lev. 23. 8.
[s] Ex. 23. 16. & 34. 22. Lev. 23. 10, 15. Deut. 16. 10. Acts 2. 1.
[t] See Lev. 23. 18, 19.
[u] ver. 19.

CHAP. 29. AND in the seventh month, on the first *day* of the
month, ye shall have an holy convocation; ye shall do no servile
2 work: [a]it is a day of blowing the trumpets unto you. And ye
shall offer a burnt offering for a sweet savour unto the LORD;
one young bullock, one ram, *and* seven lambs of the first year
3 without blemish: and their meat offering *shall be of* flour mingled
with oil, three tenth deals for a bullock, *and* two tenth deals for
4 a ram, and one tenth deal for one lamb, throughout the seven
5 lambs: and one kid of the goats *for* a sin offering, to make an
6 atonement for you: beside [b]the burnt offering of the month,
and his meat offering, and [c]the daily burnt offering, and his
meat offering, and their drink offerings, [d]according unto their
manner, for a sweet savour, a sacrifice made by fire unto the
7 LORD. ¶ And [e]ye shall have on the tenth *day* of this seventh
month an holy convocation; and ye shall [f]afflict your souls: ye
8 shall not do any work *therein*: but ye shall offer a burnt offering unto the LORD *for* a sweet savour; one young bullock, one
ram, *and* seven lambs of the first year; [g]they shall be unto you
9 without blemish: and their meat offering *shall be of* flour mingled
with oil, three tenth deals to a bullock, *and* two tenth deals to
10 one ram, a several tenth deal for one lamb, throughout the
11 seven lambs: one kid of the goats *for* a sin offering; beside [h]the
sin offering of atonement, and the continual burnt offering, and
12 the meat offering of it, and their drink offerings. ¶ And [i]on
the fifteenth day of the seventh month ye shall have an holy
convocation; ye shall do no servile work, and ye shall keep a
13 feast unto the LORD seven days: and [k]ye shall offer a burnt
offering, a sacrifice made by fire, of a sweet savour unto the
LORD; thirteen young bullocks, two rams, *and* fourteen lambs
14 of the first year; they shall be without blemish: and their meat

[a] Lev. 23. 24.
[b] ch. 28. 11.
[c] ch. 28. 3.
[d] ch. 15. 11, 12.
[e] Lev. 16. 29. & 23. 27.
[f] Ps. 35. 13. Isai. 58. 5.
[g] ch. 28. 19.
[h] Lev. 16. 3, 5.
[i] Lev. 23. 34. Deut. 16. 13. Ez. 45. 25.
[k] Ezra 3. 4.

26–31. The Festival offering at the season of firstfruits was to be offered on one day only; and was the same with that of the New moon and Passover. It nearly though not entirely accords with the sacrificial offering prescribed in Lev. xxiii. 18 seq.

XXIX. **1–6.** The ordinance of the Feast of Trumpets was to be observed on the opening day of that month within which the Great Day of the Atonement and the Feast of Tabernacles fell (cp. Lev. xxiii. 23 seq.). The special offering for the day anticipated that of the Great Day of Atonement.

7–11. The offering on the Great Day of Atonement was the same with that just specified. The great ceremonies of the day are described in Lev. xvi.

12–34. Feast of Tabernacles: cp. Lev. xxiii. 33 seq. The offerings required at this feast were the largest of all. It was especially one of thankfulness to God for the gift of the fruits of the earth; and the quantity and the nature of the offerings (see *vv.* 7–11) were determined accordingly.

offering *shall be of* flour mingled with oil, three tenth deals unto
every bullock of the thirteen bullocks, two tenth deals to each
15 ram of the two rams, and a several tenth deal to each lamb of
16 the fourteen lambs: and one kid of the goats *for* a sin offering;
beside the continual burnt offering, his meat offering, and his
17 drink offering. And on the second day *ye shall offer* twelve
young bullocks, two rams, fourteen lambs of the first year with-
18 out spot: and their meat offering and their drink offerings for
the bullocks, for the rams, and for the lambs, *shall be* according
[l] ver. 3, 4, 9, 10. 19 to their number, [l]after the manner: and one kid of the goats
for a sin offering; beside the continual burnt offering, and the
ch. 15. 12. & 28. 7, 14. 20 meat offering thereof, and their drink offerings. And on the
third day eleven bullocks, two rams, fourteen lambs of the first
21 year without blemish; and their meat offering and their drink
offerings for the bullocks, for the rams, and for the lambs, *shall*
[m] ver. 18. 22 *be* according to their number, [m]after the manner: and one goat
for a sin offering; beside the continual burnt offering, and his
23 meat offering, and his drink offering. And on the fourth day
ten bullocks, two rams, *and* fourteen lambs of the first year with-
24 out blemish: their meat offering and their drink offerings for
the bullocks, for the rams, and for the lambs, *shall be* according
25 to their number, after the manner: and one kid of the goats *for*
a sin offering; beside the continual burnt offering, his meat
26 offering, and his drink offering. And on the fifth day nine
bullocks, two rams, *and* fourteen lambs of the first year without
27 spot: and their meat offering and their drink offerings for the
bullocks, for the rams, and for the lambs, *shall be* according to
28 their number, after the manner: and one goat *for* a sin offering;
beside the continual burnt offering, and his meat offering, and
29 his drink offering. And on the sixth day eight bullocks, two
30 rams, *and* fourteen lambs of the first year without blemish: and
their meat offering and their drink offerings for the bullocks,
for the rams, and for the lambs, *shall be* according to their
31 number, after the manner: and one goat *for* a sin offering; beside the continual burnt offering, his meat offering, and his
32 drink offering. And on the seventh day seven bullocks, two
33 rams, *and* fourteen lambs of the first year without blemish: and
their meat offering and their drink offerings for the bullocks,
for the rams, and for the lambs, *shall be* according to their
34 number, after the manner: and one goat *for* a sin offering;
beside the continual burnt offering, his meat offering, and his
[n] Lev. 23. 36. 35 drink offering. On the eighth day ye shall have a [n]solemn
36 assembly: ye shall do no servile work *therein:* but ye shall
offer a burnt offering, a sacrifice made by fire, of a sweet savour
unto the LORD: one bullock, one ram, seven lambs of the first
37 year without blemish: their meat offering and their drink offer-

---

32. Stress is laid on the number seven, the holy symbolical Covenant number, by way of intimation that the mercies of the harvest accrued by virtue of God's Covenant. The diminishing number of bullocks sacrificed on the preceding days of the Feast (cp. *vv.* 13, 17, &c.), is adjusted simply to obtain the coincidence before us on the seventh day; but some have thought that the gradual evanescence of the Law till the time of its absorption in the Gospel is here presignified in the Law itself.

35–38. The offerings prescribed for the closing day of the Feast of Tabernacles were the same with those appointed for the Feast of Trumpets and the Day of Atonement. The solemnities of the month thus terminated, as a whole, with the same sacrifices with which, three weeks before, they had been introduced; and the Day of Atonement, even though succeeded by the rejoicings of the Feast of Tabernacles, thus left its impress on the whole month.

ings for the bullock, for the ram, and for the lambs, *shall be*
38 according to their number, after the manner: and one goat *for* a
sin offering; beside the continual burnt offering, and his meat
39 offering, and his drink offering. ¶These *things* ye shall [1]do
unto the LORD in your [o]set feasts, beside your [p]vows, and your
freewill offerings, for your burnt offerings, and for your meat
offerings, and for your drink offerings, and for your peace offer-
40 ings. And Moses told the children of Israel according to all that
the LORD commanded Moses.
CHAP. 30. AND Moses spake unto [a]the heads of the tribes concerning the children of Israel, saying, This *is* the thing which
2 the LORD hath commanded. [b]If a man vow a vow unto the
LORD, or [c]swear an oath to bind his soul with a bond; he shall
not [2]break his word, he shall [d]do according to all that proceed-
3 eth out of his mouth. If a woman also vow a vow unto the
LORD, and bind *herself* by a bond, *being* in her father's house in
4 her youth; and her father hear her vow, and her bond wherewith she hath bound her soul, and her father shall hold his
peace at her: then all her vows shall stand, and every bond
5 wherewith she hath bound her soul shall stand. But if her
father disallow her in the day that he heareth; not any of her
vows, or of her bonds wherewith she hath bound her soul, shall
stand: and the LORD shall forgive her, because her father dis-
6 allowed her. And if she had at all an husband, when [3]she
vowed, or uttered ought out of her lips, wherewith she bound
7 her soul; and her husband heard *it*, and held his peace at her
in the day that he heard *it*: then her vows shall stand, and her
8 bonds wherewith she bound her soul shall stand. But if her
husband [e]disallowed her on the day that he heard *it*; then he
shall make her vow which she vowed, and that which she
uttered with her lips, wherewith she bound her soul, of none
9 effect: and the LORD shall forgive her. But every vow of a
widow, and of her that is divorced, wherewith they have bound

[o] Lev. 23. 2. 1 Chr. 23. 31. 2 Chr. 31. 3. Ezra 3. 5. Neh. 10. 33. Isai. 1. 14.
[p] Lev. 7. 11, 16. & 22. 21.
[a] ch. 1. 4, 16. & 7. 2.
[b] Lev. 27. 2. Deut. 23. 21. Judg. 11. 30, 35. Eccles. 5. 4.
[c] Lev. 5. 4. Matt. 14. 9. Acts 23. 14.
[d] Job 22. 27. Ps. 22. 25. Nah. 1. 15.
[e] Gen. 3. 16.

[1] Or, *offer*.
[2] Heb. *profane*, Ps. 55. 20.
[3] Heb. *her vows were upon her*, Ps. 56. 12.

XXX. The regulations respecting vows appropriately follow those given respecting sacrifices, since a large proportion of vows would always relate to the presentation of such offerings. Rules had already been given (Lev. xxvii.) for the estimation of things vowed to God. It is probable that this fresh legislation dealing specially with vows made by persons in a state of tutelage, was occasioned by some case of practical difficulty that had recently arisen; and it is addressed by Moses to "the heads of the tribes" (*v.* 1), who would in their judicial capacity have to determine questions on these subjects.

There is no provision in the chapter for annulling vows made by boys and young men; from which it has been inferred that the vows of males were in all cases and circumstances binding.

2. The "vow" was positive; the "bond" negative or restrictive. By a vow a man engaged to dedicate something to God, or to accomplish some work for Him: by a bond he debarred himself from some privilege or enjoyment. A vow involved an obligation to do: a bond, an obligation to forbear doing.

3. *being in her father's house in her youth*] It was not ordinarily till her betrothal or marriage, that the female passed (some suppose by purchase) from the power of her father to that of her husband.

5. *the* LORD *shall forgive her*] *i.e.* shall remit the obligation. (Cp. 2 K. v. 18.)

6. Rather, **And if she shall at all be an husband's, and her vows shall be upon her, or a rash utterance of her lips, wherewith she hath bound her soul,** &c. The "at all" intimates that the case of a girl betrothed but not yet actually married is here especially contemplated. After betrothal, a woman continued to reside, till the period of her marriage arrived, in her father's house; but her property was from that time forward vested in her husband, and she was so far regarded as personally his, that an act of faithlessness to him was, like adultery, punishable with death (Deut. xxii. 23, 24). Hence his right to control her vows even before he actually took her home as his wife.

10 their souls, shall stand against her. And if she vowed in her
husband's house, or bound her soul by a bond with an oath;
11 and her husband heard *it*, and held his peace at her, *and* disallowed her not: then all her vows shall stand, and every bond
12 wherewith she bound her soul shall stand. But if her husband
hath utterly made them void on the day he heard *them; then*
whatsoever proceeded out of her lips concerning her vows, or
concerning the bond of her soul, shall not stand: her husband
13 hath made them void; and the LORD shall forgive her. Every
vow, and every binding oath to afflict the soul, her husband may
14 establish it, or her husband may make it void. But if her husband altogether hold his peace at her from day to day; then he
establisheth all her vows, or all her bonds, which *are* upon her:
he confirmeth them, because he held his peace at her in the day
15 that he heard *them*. But if he shall any ways make them void
after that he hath heard *them;* then he shall bear her iniquity.
16 These *are* the statutes, which the LORD commanded Moses, between a man and his wife, between the father and his daughter,
being yet in her youth in her father's house.

CHAP. 31. AND the LORD spake unto Moses, saying, [a]Avenge the
2 children of Israel of the Midianites: afterward shalt thou [b]be
3 gathered unto thy people. And Moses spake unto the people,
saying, Arm some of yourselves unto the war, and let them go
4 against the Midianites, and avenge the LORD of Midian. [1]Of
every tribe a thousand, throughout all the tribes of Israel, shall
5 ye send to the war. So there were delivered out of the thousands of Israel, a thousand of *every* tribe, twelve thousand armed
6 for war. And Moses sent them to the war, a thousand of *every*
tribe, them and Phinehas the son of Eleazar the priest, to the
war, with the holy instruments, and [c]the trumpets to blow in
7 his hand. And they warred against the Midianites, as the LORD
8 commanded Moses; and [d]they slew all the [e]males. And they
slew the kings of Midian, beside the rest of them that were
slain; *namely*, [f]Evi, and Rekem, and Zur, and Hur, and Reba,

[1] Heb. *A thousand of a tribe, a thousand of a tribe.*

[a] ch. 25. 17.
[b] ch. 27. 13.
[c] ch. 10. 9.
[d] Deut. 20. 13. Judg. 21. 11. 1 Sam. 27. 9. 1 Kin. 11. 15, 16.
[e] See Judg. 6. 1, 2, 33.
[f] Josh. 13. 21.

XXXI. 2. *the Midianites*] The Moabites are not included. It would thus seem that it was the Midianites, and they only, who deliberately set themselves to work the corruption of Israel.

3. *Avenge the* LORD *of Midian*] The war against the Midianites was no ordinary war. It was indeed less a war than the execution of a Divine sentence against a most guilty people.

Doubtless there were many amongst the Midianites who were personally guiltless as regards Israel. But the rulers deliberately adopted the counsel of Balaam against Israel, and their behests had been but too readily obeyed by their subjects. The sin therefore was national, and the retribution could be no less so.

But the commission of the Israelites in the text must not be conceived as a general license to slay. They had no discretion to kill or to spare. They were bidden to exterminate without mercy, and brought back to their task (*v.* 14) when they shewed signs of flinching from it. They had no alternative in this and similar matters except to fulfil the commands of God; an awful but doubtless salutary manifestation, as was afterwards the slaughter of the Canaanites, of God's wrath against sin; and a type of the future extermination of sin and sinners from His kingdom.

5. *were delivered*] Or, "were told off."

6. *Phinehas*] He was marked out as the fitting director of the expedition by his conduct (cp. xxv. 7–13) in the matter of Zimri and Cozbi.

with the holy instruments, and the trumpets] Or rather, "with the holy instruments, to wit, the trumpets," for the trumpets themselves seem to be the instruments intended.

8. *And they slew...were slain*, &c.] Render: **And the kings of Midian they put to death, beside those that fell in the battle; namely**, &c. From which it would seem that beside these five, put to death after the battle, there were other Midianitish kings who perished fighting. The five chieftains here mentioned were vassals of Sihon the Amorite (Josh. xiii. 21).

five kings of Midian: [g]Balaam also the son of Beor they slew [g] Josh. 13. 22.
9 with the sword. And the children of Israel took *all* the women
of Midian captives, and their little ones, and took the spoil of all
10 their cattle, and all their flocks, and all their goods. And they
burnt all their cities wherein they dwelt, and all their goodly
11 castles, with fire. And [h]they took all the spoil, and all the prey, [h] Deut. 20. 14.
12 *both* of men and of beasts. And they brought the captives, and
the prey, and the spoil, unto Moses, and Eleazar the priest, and
unto the congregation of the children of Israel, unto the camp
13 at the plains of Moab, which *are* by Jordan *near* Jericho. ¶ And
Moses, and Eleazar the priest, and all the princes of the con-
14 gregation, went forth to meet them without the camp. And
Moses was wroth with the officers of the host, *with* the captains
over thousands, and captains over hundreds, which came from
15 the [1]battle. And Moses said unto them, Have ye saved [i]all the [i] See Deut. 20. 14. 1 Sam. 15. 3.
16 women alive? Behold, [k]these caused the children of Israel, [k] ch. 25. 2.
through the [l]counsel of Balaam, to commit trespass against the [l] ch. 24. 14. 2 Pet. 2. 15. Rev. 2. 14.
LORD in the matter of Peor, and [m]there was a plague among the [m] ch. 25. 9.
17 congregation of the LORD. Now therefore [n]kill every male [n] Judg. 21. 11.
among the little ones, and kill every woman that hath known
18 man by lying with [2]him. But all the women children, that have
not known a man by lying with him, keep alive for yourselves.
19 And [o]do ye abide without the camp seven days: whosoever hath [o] ch. 5. 2.
killed any person, and [p]whosoever hath touched any slain, [p] ch. 19. 11, &c.
purify *both* yourselves and your captives on the third day, and
20 on the seventh day. And purify all *your* raiment, and all [3]that
is made of skins, and all work of goats' *hair*, and all things
21 made of wood. ¶ And Eleazar the priest said unto the men of
war which went to the battle, This *is* the ordinance of the law
22 which the LORD commanded Moses; only the gold, and the silver,
23 the brass, the iron, the tin, and the lead, every thing that may
abide the fire, ye shall make *it* go through the fire, and it shall be
clean: nevertheless it shall be purified [q]with the water of separa- [q] ch. 19. 9, 17.
tion: and all that abideth not the fire ye shall make go through the
24 water. [r]And ye shall wash your clothes on the seventh day, and [r] Lev. 11. 25.
ye shall be clean, and afterward ye shall come into the camp.
25, 26 ¶ And the LORD spake unto Moses, saying, Take the sum of the
prey [4]that was taken, *both* of man and of beast, thou, and Eleazar
27 the priest, and the chief fathers of the congregation: and [s]divide [s] Josh. 22. 8. 1 Sam. 30. 27.
the prey into two parts; between them that took the war upon
them, who went out to battle, and between all the congregation:
28 and levy a tribute unto the LORD of the men of war which went
out to battle: [t]one soul of five hundred, *both* of the persons, and [t] See ver. 30, 47. & ch. 18. 26.

[1] Heb. *host of war.*
[2] Heb. *a male.*
[3] Heb. *instrument*, or, *vessel of skins.*
[4] Heb. *of the captivity.*

---

10. *goodly castles*] Rather, both here and in Gen. xxv. 16, **hamlets**. The word is derived from a word (*tōr*) signifying "a row" or "range" (cp. Ezek. xlvi. 23); and probably indicates those collections of rude dwellings, made of stones piled one on another and covered with tent-cloths, which are used by the Arabs to this day; and which are frequently mentioned as *douars* in narratives of the French campaigns in Algeria. These dwellings would be formed usually in a circle. See the word "Hazeroth," in xi. 35.

11. The "prey" refers to the captives and live-stock: the "spoil" to the ornaments and other effects.

16. *caused...to commit trespass*] More lit., "became to the children of Israel for a cause (or, incitement) of treachery to the Lord."

22. *brass*] Render **copper**. See Gen. iv. 22 note. The verse is curious as illustrating the variety of metals in use at this early date for domestic purposes. All these metals were common in Egypt centuries before the date of the Exodus.

29 of the beeves, and of the asses, and of the sheep: take *it* of their
half, and give *it* unto Eleazar the priest, *for* an heave offering
30 of the LORD. And of the children of Israel's half, thou shalt
take [u]one portion of fifty, of the persons, of the beeves, of the
asses, and of the [1]flocks, of all manner of beasts, and give them
unto the Levites, [x]which keep the charge of the tabernacle of
31 the LORD. And Moses and Eleazar the priest did as the LORD
32 commanded Moses. And the booty, *being* the rest of the prey
which the men of war had caught, was six hundred thousand and
33 seventy thousand and five thousand sheep, and threescore and
34 twelve thousand beeves, and threescore and one thousand asses,
35 and thirty and two thousand persons in all, of women that had
36 not known man by lying with him. And the half, *which was*
the portion of them that went out to war, was in number three
hundred thousand and seven and thirty thousand and five hun-
37 dred sheep: and the LORD's tribute of the sheep was six hundred
38 and threescore and fifteen. And the beeves *were* thirty and six
thousand; of which the LORD's tribute *was* threescore and
39 twelve. And the asses *were* thirty thousand and five hundred;
40 of which the LORD's tribute *was* threescore and one. And the
persons *were* sixteen thousand; of which the LORD's tribute *was*
41 thirty and two persons. And Moses gave the tribute, *which was*
the LORD's heave offering, unto Eleazar the priest, [y]as the LORD
42 commanded Moses. And of the children of Israel's half, which
43 Moses divided from the men that warred, (now the half *that*
pertained unto the congregation was three hundred thousand and
44 thirty thousand *and* seven thousand and five hundred sheep, and
45 thirty and six thousand beeves, and thirty thousand asses and
46, 47 five hundred, and sixteen thousand persons;) even [z]of the
children of Israel's half, Moses took one portion of fifty, *both* of
man and of beast, and gave them unto the Levites, which kept
the charge of the tabernacle of the LORD; as the LORD com-
48 manded Moses. ¶ And the officers which *were* over thousands of
the host, the captains of thousands, and captains of hundreds,
49 came near unto Moses: and they said unto Moses, Thy servants
have taken the sum of the men of war which *are* under our
50 [2]charge, and there lacketh not one man of us. We have therefore
brought an oblation for the LORD, what every man hath [3]gotten,
of jewels of gold, chains, and bracelets, rings, earrings, and

[u] See ver. 42–47.

[x] ch. 3. 7, 8, 25, 31, 36. & 18. 3, 4.

[y] See ch. 18. 8, 19.

[z] ver. 30.

[1] Or, *goats*. [2] Heb. *hand*. [3] Heb. *found*.

---

29. *an heave-offering*] Render simply **an offering**, and cp. xviii. 24. The verb from which the word here rendered "heave-offering" is derived, is rightly translated "levy" in *v.* 28.

32. Cp. *v.* 11, and render "And the prey" (*i.e.* the live prey) "in addition to the spoil which the men of war seized, &c." The "spoil" is described in *v.* 50.

The number of sheep, beeves, asses, and persons taken is given in this and following verses in round thousands. Hence the Lord's tribute (*vv.* 29, 37, 38, &c.), being the five-hundredth part of the half, comes out also in round numbers. The enormous amount both of live stock and of personal ornament was characteristic of the Midianites. When they invaded Israel in the days of the Judges, their wealth was still of the same kind (Judg. vi. 5, viii. 24 seq.). The Bedouins, notwithstanding their wild nomadic life, retain their ancestral love of finery to the present day.

49. There is no mention of any resistance on the part of the Midianites. The Israelites saw in this and in the preservation of all those engaged, proofs that the Lord had been with them in the work, and hence the free-will oblation of *v.* 50.

50. The "chains" were "armlets" (2 Sam. i. 10). The "rings" were "finger-rings," or "seal-rings;" and the "tablets" were worn suspended from the neck (Ex. xxxv. 22).

to make an atonement for our souls before the LORD] Cp. Ex. xxx. 11-16. The atonement

tablets, [a]to make an atonement for our souls before the LORD.
51 And Moses and Eleazar the priest took the gold of them, *even* all
52 wrought jewels. And all the gold of the [1]offering that they
offered up to the LORD, of the captains of thousands, and of the
captains of hundreds, was sixteen thousand seven hundred and
53 fifty shekels. (*For* [b]the men of war had taken spoil, every man
54 for himself.) And Moses and Eleazar the priest took the gold of
the captains of thousands and of hundreds, and brought it into
the tabernacle of the congregation, [c]*for* a memorial for the
children of Israel before the LORD.

CHAP. 32. NOW the children of Reuben and the children of Gad
had a very great multitude of cattle: and when they saw the
land of [a]Jazer, and the land of Gilead, that, behold, the place
2 *was* a place for cattle; the children of Gad and the children of
Reuben came and spake unto Moses, and to Eleazar the priest,
3 and unto the princes of the congregation, saying, Ataroth, and
Dibon, and Jazer, and [b]Nimrah, and Heshbon, and Elealeh, and
4 [c]Shebam, and Nebo, and [d]Beon, *even* the country [e]which the
LORD smote before the congregation of Israel, *is* a land for
5 cattle, and thy servants have cattle: wherefore, said they, if we
have found grace in thy sight, let this land be given unto thy
6 servants for a possession, *and* bring us not over Jordan. And
Moses said unto the children of Gad and to the children of
Reuben, Shall your brethren go to war, and shall ye sit here?
7 And wherefore [2]discourage ye the heart of the children of Israel
from going over into the land which the LORD hath given them?
8 Thus did your fathers, [f]when I sent them from Kadesh-barnea
9 [g]to see the land. For [h]when they went up unto the valley of
Eshcol, and saw the land, they discouraged the heart of the
children of Israel, that they should not go into the land which
10 the LORD had given them. [i]And the LORD's anger was kindled
11 the same time, and he sware, saying, Surely none of the men
that came up out of Egypt, [k]from twenty years old and upward,
shall see the land which I sware unto Abraham, unto Isaac, and
12 unto Jacob; because [l]they have not [3]wholly followed me: save
Caleb the son of Jephunneh the Kenezite, and Joshua the son of

[a] Ex. 30. 12, 16.
[b] Deut. 20. 14.
[c] Ex. 30. 16.

[a] ch. 21. 32. Josh. 13. 25. 2 Sam. 24. 5.
[b] ver. 36, *Beth-nimrah.*
[c] ver. 38, *Shibmah.*
[d] ver. 38, *Baal-meon.*
[e] ch. 21. 24, 34.
[f] ch. 13. 3, 26.
[g] Deut. 1. 22.
[h] ch. 13. 24, 31. Deut. 1. 24, 28.
[i] ch. 14. 11, 21. Deut. 1. 34.
[k] ch. 14. 28, 29. Deut. 1. 35.
[l] ch. 14. 24, 30.

[1] Heb. *heave offering.* [2] Heb. *break.* [3] Heb. *fulfilled after me.*

---

was not for any special offence committed (which would have called for a sacrifice of blood-shedding), but rather like the half-shekel given at the census in Ex. *l. c.*, was an acknowledgment of having received undeserved mercies. These, if unacknowledged, would have entailed guilt on the soul.

52. The value of the offering was about 20,000*l.*

53. This verse seems to imply that the soldiers, as distinct from the officers (cp. *v.* 49), did not make any offering from their plunder. Of course besides the gold there would be much spoil of less precious materials; see *vv.* 20, 22.

XXXII. The record of the last war to the east of the Jordan is followed by the assignment of the lands already conquered to the tribes of Reuben and Gad and to certain families of the tribe of Manasseh.

1. *Jazer*] Cp. marg. ref. This district, although included in the land of Gilead, seems to have had especial attractions for the Israelitish settlers. All travellers in Gilead, the modern Belka, bear witness to its richness as compared with the country to the west of the Jordan. Its general character is that of an upland pasture, undulating and thickly timbered. In the last respect its northern portions excel its southern; but for fertility of soil the southern province is preferred by the Arabs, in whose lips it has passed into a proverb: "Thou canst not find a country like the Belka."

3. See *vv.* 34-38 notes.

8. *your fathers*] The generation of the Exodus was now substantially extinct. Cp. xxvi. 64, 65.

Kadesh-barnea] See xiii. 26.

12. *the Kenezite*] Kenaz (Gen. xxxvi. 11) was the name of one of the "dukes of

[m] ch. 14. 24. Deut. 1. 36. Josh. 14. 8, 9. [n] ch. 14. 33, 34, 35. [o] ch. 26. 64, 65. [p] Deut. 1. 34. [q] Deut. 30. 17. Josh. 22. 16, 18. 2 Chr. 7. 19. & 15. 2. [r] Josh. 4. 12, 13. [s] Josh. 22. 4. [t] ver. 33. Josh. 12. 1. & 13. 8. [u] Deut. 3. 18. Josh. 1. 14. & 4. 12, 13. [x] Deut. 3. 20. Josh. 11. 23. [y] Josh. 22. 4. [z] Deut. 3. 12, 15, 16. Josh. 1. 15. & 13. 8, 32. & 22. 4, 9. [a] Gen. 4. 7. & 44. 16. Isai. 59. 12. [b] ver. 16, 34, &c. [c] Josh. 1. 14. [d] Josh. 4. 12. [e] Josh. 1. 13. [f] Deut. 3. 12—17. Josh. 12. 6. [g] ch. 21. 24, 33, 35.

13 Nun: [m]for they have wholly followed the LORD. And the LORD's
anger was kindled against Israel, and he made them [n]wander in
the wilderness forty years, until [o]all the generation, that had
14 done evil in the sight of the LORD, was consumed. And, behold,
ye are risen up in your fathers' stead, an increase of sinful men,
to augment yet the [p]fierce anger of the LORD toward Israel.
15 For if ye [q]turn away from after him, he will yet again leave
them in the wilderness; and ye shall destroy all this people.
16 And they came near unto him, and said, We will build sheep-
17 folds here for our cattle, and cities for our little ones: but [r]we
ourselves will go ready armed before the children of Israel, until
we have brought them unto their place: and our little ones shall
dwell in the fenced cities because of the inhabitants of the land.
18 [s]We will not return unto our houses, until the children of Israel
19 have inherited every man his inheritance. For we will not
inherit with them on yonder side Jordan, or forward; [t]because
our inheritance is fallen to us on this side Jordan eastward.
20 And [u]Moses said unto them, If ye will do this thing, if ye will
21 go armed before the LORD to war, and will go all of you armed
over Jordan before the LORD, until he hath driven out his
22 enemies from before him, and [x]the land be subdued before the
LORD: then afterward [y]ye shall return, and be guiltless before
the LORD, and before Israel; and [z]this land shall be your pos-
23 session before the LORD. But if ye will not do so, behold, ye
have sinned against the LORD: and be sure [a]your sin will find
24 you out. [b]Build you cities for your little ones, and folds for
your sheep; and do that which hath proceeded out of your mouth.
25 And the children of Gad and the children of Reuben spake
unto Moses, saying, Thy servants will do as my lord command-
26 eth. [c]Our little ones, our wives, our flocks, and all our cattle,
27 shall be there in the cities of Gilead: [d]but thy servants will pass
over, every man armed for war, before the LORD to battle, as my
28 lord saith. ¶ So [e]concerning them Moses commanded Eleazar the
priest, and Joshua the son of Nun, and the chief fathers of the
29 tribes of the children of Israel: and Moses said unto them, If the
children of Gad and the children of Reuben will pass with you
over Jordan, every man armed to battle, before the LORD, and the
land shall be subdued before you; then ye shall give them the
30 land of Gilead for a possession: but if they will not pass over with
you armed, they shall have possessions among you in the land
31 of Canaan. And the children of Gad and the children of Reuben answered, saying, As the LORD hath said unto thy servants,
32 so will we do. We will pass over armed before the LORD into
the land of Canaan, that the possession of our inheritance on this
33 side Jordan *may be* our's. ¶ And [f]Moses gave unto them, *even*
to the children of Gad, and to the children of Reuben, and unto
half the tribe of Manasseh the son of Joseph, [g]the kingdom of

---

Edom:" but Israel and Edom were of kindred origin, and the use of similar names by the two peoples is not surprising.

23. *be sure your sin will find you out*] Lit. "know ye your sin that it will find you out." Moses implies that their sin would eventually bring its own punishment along with it.

27. *before the* LORD] *i.e.* immediately in front of the sacred tokens of the Lord's Presence; cp. x. 17 note.

33. *half the tribe of Manasseh*] That is, (cp. *v.* 39; Josh. xvii. 1) the families of Machir. Moses, when assigning to the pastoral tribes the inheritance which they desired, appropriated to these Manassites specially the district they had already subdued, as a reward for their valour and exploits. Thus the whole of the conquered country was provisionally disposed of, and the forwardness and valour of the Machirites rewarded. It seems clear from *v.* 39 and Josh. xvii. 1,

Sihon king of the Amorites, and the kingdom of Og king of
Bashan, the land, with the cities thereof in the coasts, *even* the
34 cities of the country round about. And the children of Gad
35 built [h]Dibon, and Ataroth, and [i]Aroer, and Atroth, Shophan, and
36 [k]Jaazer, and Jogbehah, and [l]Beth-nimrah, and Beth-haran,
37 [m]fenced cities: and folds for sheep. And the children of
38 Reuben [n]built Heshbon, and Elealeh, and Kirjathaim, and
[o]Nebo, and [p]Baal-meon, ([q]their names being changed,) and
Shibmah: and [1]gave other names unto the cities which they
39 builded. And the children of [r]Machir the son of Manasseh
went to Gilead, and took it, and dispossessed the Amorite which
40 *was* in it. And Moses [s]gave Gilead unto Machir the son of
41 Manasseh; and he dwelt therein. And [t]Jair the son of Manasseh went and took the small towns thereof, and called them
42 [u]Havoth-jair. And Nobah went and took Kenath, and the villages thereof, and called it Nobah, after his own name.

[1] Heb. *they called by names the names of the cities.*

[h] ch. 33. 45.
[i] Deut. 2. 36.
[k] ver. 1. 3, *Jazer.*
[l] ver. 3, *Nimrah.*
[m] ver. 24.
[n] ch. 21. 27.
[o] Isai. 46. 1.
[p] ch. 22. 41.
[q] See ver. 3. Ex. 23. 13. Josh. 23. 7.
[r] Gen. 50. 23.
[s] Deut. 3. 12, 13, 16. Josh. 13. 31. & 17. 1.
[t] Deut. 3. 14. Josh. 13. 30. 1 Chr. 2. 21, 22, 23.
[u] Judg. 10. 4. 1 Kin. 4. 13.

---

that the claims of the Machirites arose simply out of their exploits.

34–36. The cities here named fall into three groups. On *Dibon*, cp. xxi. 19. The Moabite stone was discovered here in 1868. This city, occupied on the first acquisition of the territory by the Gadites, and assigned by Joshua to the Reubenites, was eventually recaptured by the Moabites, in whose hands it remained. *Ataroth, i.e.* "crowns" (? Attârûs) was seven miles north-west of Dibon. *Aroer* (Arâir) lay between Dibon and the Arnon.

Atroth, Shophan, was **Atroth-Shophan,** *i.e.* Atroth, or Ataroth of Shophan, or "of the burrow;" thus distinguished from the Ataroth named in the verse preceding from which it was probably not far distant. These four cities may be styled the Dibon settlement.

35. *Jaazer* (cp. *v.* 1) with the neighbouring *Jogbehah* (Jebeiha), seven miles to the north-east, formed the second group.

36. The third Gadite settlement lay in the valley of the Jordan, to the west of the preceding. It comprised the cities of *Beth-nimrah* (Nimrun) and *Beth-haran* (Beit-haran).

37, 38. The Reubenites established themselves more compactly than the Gadites. *Elealeh* (el-'Al) a mile to the north-east; *Nebo* (Nebbeh) probably three miles to the south-west; *Baal-meon* (Main) nearly two miles to the south; *Kirjathaim* (? Kureiyat): and *Shibmah,* more properly Sibmah, famous at a later period for its vines (cp. Isai. xvi. 8), four miles east of Heshbon;—all clustered round the old Amoritish Capital. The Reubenites probably retained at the partition all these cities with the exception of Heshbon, which, passing to the Levites, were thenceforth reckoned as within the tribe of Gad.

Neither the Reubenites nor the Gadites were "builders" in the sense of founders of the cities of which they thus took possession. They probably fortified them, for the first time or afresh, so as to render them places of safety for their families during the campaigns on the other side of the Jordan; and provided them with all conveniences for their flocks and herds.

39. *the children of Machir*] Machir, the son of Manasseh, was long since dead: even his sons had been brought up upon Joseph's knees (Gen. l. 23). But the renown acquired by his descendants raised his family almost to the dignity of a tribe; and the Machirites are in the next verse styled Machir, just as the children of Judah or of Ephraim are often spoken of as Judah or Ephraim. So in Judg. v. 14 Machir is coupled with Ephraim and Zebulun.

went] *i.e.* "had gone:" the statement is preparatory to the ensuing record of the grant to them of the land they had won.

Gilead] More strictly part of north Gilead; which, though inhabited by the Amorites, had belonged to the kingdom of Og. Gilead was the district from which had sprung the ancestress of the Machirites (cp. 1 Chron. vii. 14).

41. The exploits of Jair—he was the conqueror of Argob (Deut. iii. 14)—gave new lustre to his name; and the fame of the family is attested by the history of Jair the Israelitish judge, doubtless a descendant; perhaps also by the mention of Jairus (Luke viii. 41), the ruler of the synagogue at the neighbouring city of Capernaum.

Havoth-jair] That is, the villages, or rather groups of tents, or "kraals," of Jair. Originally they were twenty-three in number (1 Chr. ii. 22): in the days of the younger Jair, to whom they probably descended by inheritance, they either had increased to thirty, or were reckoned at that round number (Judg. x. 4).

42. *Kenath*] Now Kenawât, an important site near the southern extremity of the tract el-Lejah, and on the western slopes of the mountains of the Haurân. The name

CHAP. 33. THESE *are* the journeys of the children of Israel, which
went forth out of the land of Egypt with their armies under the
2 hand of Moses and Aaron. And Moses wrote their goings out according to their journeys by the commandment of the LORD: and
3 these *are* their journeys according to their goings out. ¶ And
they [a]departed from Rameses in [b]the first month, on the fifteenth day of the first month; on the morrow after the passover
the children of Israel went out [c]with an high hand in the sight
4 of all the Egyptians. For the Egyptians buried all *their* firstborn, [d]which the LORD had smitten among them: [e]upon their
5 gods also the LORD executed judgments. [f]And the children of
6 Israel removed from Rameses, and pitched in Succoth. And
they departed from [g]Succoth, and pitched in Etham, which *is* in
7 the edge of the wilderness. And [h]they removed from Etham,
and turned again unto Pi-hahiroth, which *is* before Baal-zephon;
8 and they pitched before Migdol. And they departed from before
Pi-hahiroth, and [i]passed through the midst of the sea into the
wilderness, and went three days' journey in the wilderness of
9 Etham, and pitched in Marah. And they removed from Marah,
and [k]came unto Elim: and in Elim *were* twelve fountains of
water, and threescore and ten palm trees; and they pitched
10 there. And they removed from Elim, and encamped by the
11 Red sea. And they removed from the Red sea, and encamped in
12 the [l]wilderness of Sin. And they took their journey out of the
13 wilderness of Sin, and encamped in Dophkah. And they de-
14 parted from Dophkah, and encamped in Alush. And they
removed from Alush, and encamped at [m]Rephidim, where was
15 no water for the people to drink. And they departed from
16 Rephidim, and pitched in the [n]wilderness of Sinai. And they
removed from the desert of Sinai, and pitched [o]at [1]Kibroth-
17 hattaavah. And they departed from Kibroth-hattaavah, and
18 [p]encamped at Hazeroth. And they departed from Hazeroth,

a Ex. 12. 37.
b Ex. 12. 2. & 13. 4.
c Ex. 14. 8.
d Ex. 12. 29.
e Ex. 12. 12. & 18. 11. Isai. 19. 1. Rev. 12. 8.
f Ex. 12. 37.
g Ex. 13. 20.
h Ex. 14. 2, 9.
i Ex. 14. 22. & 15. 22, 23.
k Ex. 15. 27.
l Ex. 16. 1.
m Ex. 17. 1. & 19. 2.
n Ex. 16. 1. & 19. 1, 2.
o ch. 11. 34.
p ch. 11. 35.

[1] That is, *The graves of lust.*

---

given to it by its conqueror, as in other cases, fell ere long into disuse, and the old name has held its ground to this day.

The notices, both Scriptural and traditional, of the conquest of north-eastern Gilead and Bashan by the Machirites, plainly intimate that it was effected by a few chiefs of great military prowess, who overran rapidly a far larger district than they could colonize. The father of Jair, however, Segub, was of the tribe of Judah (cp. xxvii. 1, and note; 1 Chr. ii. 21, 22), and it is likely that the Manassite leaders induced many of the more adventurous of this tribe, and some possibly of other tribes, to join them in their enterprize against Bashan (see Josh. xix. 34).

The Machirites did not exterminate the whole population of this district (see Josh. xiii. 15, &c). The conquest of the district east of Jordan seems never to have been so effectually accomplished as that on the other side.

During the troublous times of the Judges the eastern Manassites rendered good service to the nation; cp. Judg. v. 14. Gideon, and probably Jephthah, were of this tribe, and reflect in a later generation the warlike and adventurous spirit which Jair and Nobah exhibited in the days of Moses.

XXXIII. **1-49.** This list was written out by Moses at God's command (*v.* 2), doubtless as a memorial of God's providential care for His people throughout this long and trying period.

3-6. For these places, see marg. reff.

8. *Pi-hahiroth*] Heb. "Hahiroth," but perhaps only by an error of transcription. The omitted "pi" is however only a common Egyptian prefix.

wilderness of Etham] *i.e.* that part of the great wilderness of Shur which adjoined Etham; cp. Ex. xv. 22 note.

The list of stations up to that at Sinai agrees with the narrative of Exodus except that we have here mentioned (*v.* 10) an encampment by the Red Sea, and two others, Dophkah and Alush (*vv.* 12-14), which are there omitted. On these places see Ex. xvii. 1 note.

16, 17. See xi. 35 note.

18. *Rithmah*] The name of this station is derived from *retem*, the broom-plant, the "juniper" of the A. V. This must be the

19 and pitched in [q]Rithmah. And they departed from Rithmah,
20 and pitched at Rimmon-parez. And they departed from Rim-
21 mon-parez, and pitched in Libnah. And they removed from
22 Libnah, and pitched at Rissah. And they journeyed from
23 Rissah, and pitched in Kehelathah. And they went from Kehe-
24 lathah, and pitched in mount Shapher. And they removed from
25 mount Shapher, and encamped in Haradah. And they re-
26 moved from Haradah, and pitched in Makheloth. And they re-
27 moved from Makheloth, and encamped at Tahath. And they
28 departed from Tahath, and pitched at Tarah. And they re-
29 moved from Tarah, and pitched in Mithcah. And they went
30 from Mithcah, and pitched in Hashmonah. And they departed
31 from Hashmonah, and [r]encamped at Moseroth. And they
32 departed from Moseroth, and pitched in Bene-jaakan. And they
removed from [s]Bene-jaakan, and [t]encamped at Hor-hagidgad.
33 And they went from Hor-hagidgad, and pitched in Jotbathah.
34 And they removed from Jotbathah, and encamped at Ebronah.
35 And they departed from Ebronah, [u]and encamped at Ezion-
36 gaber. And they removed from Ezion-gaber, and pitched in the
37 [w]wilderness of Zin, which *is* Kadesh. And they removed from
[x]Kadesh, and pitched in mount Hor, in the edge of the land of
38 Edom. ¶ And [y]Aaron the priest went up into mount Hor at
the commandment of the LORD, and died there, in the fortieth
year after the children of Israel were come out of the land of
39 Egypt, in the first *day* of the fifth month. And Aaron *was* an
hundred and twenty and three years old when he died in mount
40 Hor. ¶ And [z]king Arad the Canaanite, which dwelt in the
south in the land of Canaan, heard of the coming of the children
41 of Israel. ¶ And they departed from mount [a]Hor, and pitched
42 in Zalmonah. And they departed from Zalmonah, and pitched
43 in Punon. And they departed from Punon, and [b]pitched in
44 Oboth. And [c]they departed from Oboth, and pitched in [1][d]Ije-
45 abarim, in the border of Moab. And they departed from Iim,

[q] ch. 12. 16.
[r] Deut. 10. 6.
[s] See Gen. 36. 27. Deut. 10. 6. 1 Chr. 1. 42.
[t] Deut. 10. 7.
[u] Deut. 2. 8. 1 Kin. 9. 26. & 22. 48.
[w] ch. 20. 1. & 27. 14.
[x] ch. 20. 22, 23. & 21. 4.
[y] ch. 20. 25, 28. Deut. 10. 6. & 32. 50.
[z] ch. 21. 1, &c.
[a] ch. 21. 4.
[b] ch. 21. 10.
[c] ch. 21. 11.
[d] ch. 21. 11.

[1] Or, *Heaps of Abarim.*

---

same encampment as that which is said in xiii. 26 to have been at Kadesh.

19. *Rimmon-parez*] Or rather **Rimmon-perez,** *i.e.* "Rimmon (*i.e.* the Pomegranate) of the Breach." It may have been here that the sedition of Korah occurred.

19–36. The stations named are those visited during the years of penal wandering. The determination of their positions is, in many cases, difficult, because during this period there was no definite line of march pursued. But it is probable that the Israelites during this period did not overstep the boundaries of the Wilderness of Paran (as defined in x. 12), except to pass along the adjoining valley of the Arabah; while the Tabernacle and organized camp moved about from place to place amongst them (cp. xx. 1).

Rissah, Haradah, and *Tahath* are probably the same as Rasa, Aradeh, and Elthi of the Roman tables. The position of Hashmonah (Heshmon in Josh. xv. 27) in the Azazimeh mountains points out the road followed by the children of Israel to be that which skirts the south-western extremity of Jebel Magrah.

34. *Ebronah*] *i.e,* "passage." This station apparently lay on the shore of the Elanitic gulf, at a point where the ebb of the tide left a ford across. Hence the later Targum renders the word "fords."

35. *Ezion-gaber*] "Giant's backbone." The Wâdy Ghadhyân, a valley running eastward into the Arabah some miles north of the present head of the Elanitic gulf. A salt marsh which here overspreads a portion of the Arabah may be taken as indicating the limit to which the sea anciently reached; and we may thus infer the existence here in former times of an extensive tidal haven, at the head of which the city of Ezion-geber stood. Here it was that from the time of Solomon onward the Jewish navy was constructed (1 Kings ix. 26, xxii. 49).

41–49. *Zalmonah* and *Punon* are stations on the Pilgrim's road; and the general route is fairly ascertained by a comparison of these verses with xxi. 4, &c.

46 and pitched [e]in Dibon-gad. And they removed from Dibon-
47 gad, and encamped in Almon [f]-diblathaim. And they removed
from Almon-diblathaim, [g]and pitched in the mountains of
48 Abarim, before Nebo. And they departed from the mountains
of Abarim, and [h]pitched in the plains of Moab by Jordan *near*
49 Jericho. And they pitched by Jordan, from Beth-jesimoth *even*
50 unto [1][i]Abel-shittim in the plains of Moab. ¶ And the LORD
spake unto Moses in the plains of Moab by Jordan *near* Jericho,
51 saying, Speak unto the children of Israel, and say unto them,
52 [k]When ye are passed over Jordan into the land of Canaan; [l]then
ye shall drive out all the inhabitants of the land from before
you, and destroy all their pictures, and destroy all their molten
53 images, and quite pluck down all their high places: and ye shall
dispossess *the inhabitants of* the land, and dwell therein: for I
54 have given you the land to possess it. And [m]ye shall divide the
land by lot for an inheritance among your families: *and* to the
more ye shall [2]give the more inheritance, and to the fewer ye
shall [3]give the less inheritance: every man's *inheritance* shall be
in the place where his lot falleth; according to the tribes of your
55 fathers ye shall inherit. But if ye will not drive out the inhabitants of the land from before you; then it shall come to pass,
that those which ye let remain of them *shall be* [n]pricks in your
eyes, and thorns in your sides, and shall vex you in the land
56 wherein ye dwell. Moreover it shall come to pass, *that* I shall
do unto you, as I thought to do unto them.

CHAP. 34. AND the LORD spake unto Moses, saying, Command the
2 children of Israel, and say unto them, When ye come into [a]the
land of Canaan; (this *is* the land that shall fall unto you for an
inheritance, *even* the land of Canaan with the coasts thereof:)
3 ¶ Then [b]your south quarter shall be from the wilderness of Zin
along by the coast of Edom, and your south border shall be the
4 outmost coast of [c]the salt sea eastward: and your border shall
turn from the south [d]to the ascent of Akrabbim, and pass on to
Zin: and the going forth thereof shall be from the south [e]to

[e] ch. 32. 34. [f] Jer. 48. 22. Ez. 6. 14. [g] ch. 21. 20. Deut. 32. 49. [h] ch. 22. 1. [i] ch. 25. 1. Josh. 2. 1. [k] Deut. 7. 1, 2. & 9. 1. Josh. 3. 17. [l] Ex. 23. 24, 33. & 34. 13. Deut. 7. 2, 5. & 12. 3. Josh. 11. 12. Judg. 2. 2. [m] ch. 26. 53, 54, 55. [n] Josh. 23. 13. Judg. 2. 3. Ps. 106. 34, 36. See Ex. 23, 33. Ez. 28. 24. [a] Gen. 17. 8. Deut. 1. 7. Ps. 78. 55. & 105. 11. Ez. 47. 14. [b] Josh. 15. 1. See Ez. 47. 13, &c. [c] Gen. 14. 3. Josh. 15. 2. [d] Josh. 15. 3. [e] ch. 13. 26. & 32. 8.

[1] Or, *The plains of Shittim.*
[2] Heb. *multiply his inheritance.*
[3] Heb. *diminish his inheritance.*

50–56. The expulsion of the Canaanites and the destruction of their monuments of idolatry had been already enjoined (see marg. reff.); and *v.* 54 is substantially a repetition from Ex. xxvi. 53-55. But the solemn warning of *vv.* 55, 56 is new. A call for it had been furnished by their past transgressions in the matter of Baal-peor, and by their imperfect fulfilment, at the first, of Moses' orders in the Midianitish war.

XXXIV. **2.** *the land of Canaan*] The name Canaan is here restricted to the territory west of the Jordan.

3-5. The southern boundary commenced at the Dead Sea. The broad and desolate valley by which the depressed bed of that sea is protected toward the south, is called the Ghôr. A deep narrow glen enters it at its south-west corner; it is called Wâdy-el-Fikreh, and is continued in the same south-western direction, under the name of Wady el-Marrah; a wady which loses itself among the hills belonging to "the wilderness of Zin;" and Kadesh-barnea (see xiii. 26 note), which is "in the wilderness of Zin," will be, as the text implies, the southern-most point of the southern boundary. Thence, if Kadesh be identical with the present Ain el-Weibeh, westward to the river, or brook of Egypt, now Wady el-Arîsh, is a distance of about seventy miles. In this interval were Hazar-addar and Azmon; the former being perhaps the general name of a district of *Hazerim*, or nomad hamlets (see Deut. ii. 23), of which Addar was one: and Azmon, perhaps to be identified with Kesam, the modern Kasâimeh, a group of springs situate in the north of one of the gaps in the ridge, and a short distance west of Ain el-Kudeirât.

[Others consider the boundary line to have followed the Ghôr along the Arabah to the south of the Azazimeh mountains, thence to Gadis round the south-east of that mountain, and thence to Wady el-Arîsh.]

Kadesh-barnea, and shall go on to [f]Hazar-addar, and pass on to
5 Azmon: and the border shall fetch a compass from Azmon
[g]unto the river of Egypt, and the goings out of it shall be at the
6 sea. ¶And *as for* the western border, ye shall even have
the great sea for a border: this shall be your west border.
7 ¶And this shall be your north border: from the great sea ye
8 shall point out for you [h]mount Hor: from mount Hor ye shall
point out *your border* [i]unto the entrance of Hamath; and the
9 goings forth of the border shall be to [k]Zedad: and the border
shall go on to Ziphron, and the goings out of it shall be at
10 [l]Hazar-enan: this shall be your north border. ¶And ye shall
11 point out your east border from Hazar-enan to Shepham: and
the coast shall go down from Shepham [m]to Riblah, on the east
side of Ain; and the border shall descend, and shall reach unto
12 the [1]side of the sea [n]of Chinnereth eastward: and the border
shall go down to Jordan, and the goings out of it shall be at
[o]the salt sea: this shall be your land with the coasts thereof
13 round about. ¶And Moses commanded the children of Israel,
saying, [p]This *is* the land which ye shall inherit by lot, which the
LORD commanded to give unto the nine tribes, and to the half
14 tribe: [q]for the tribe of the children of Reuben according to the
house of their fathers, and the tribe of the children of Gad
according to the house of their fathers, have received *their*
inheritance; and half the tribe of Manasseh have received
15 their inheritance: the two tribes and the half tribe have received
their inheritance on this side Jordan *near* Jericho eastward,
16 toward the sunrising. ¶And the LORD spake unto Moses,
17 saying, These *are* the names of the men which shall divide the
land unto you: [r]Eleazar the priest, and Joshua the son of Nun.
18 And ye shall take one [s]prince of every tribe, to divide the land
19 by inheritance. And the names of the men *are* these: of the
20 tribe of Judah, Caleb the son of Jephunneh. And of the tribe of

[f] See Josh. 15. 3, 4.
[g] Gen. 15. 18. Josh. 15. 4, 47. 1 Kin. 8. 65. Isai. 27. 12.
[h] ch. 33. 37.
[i] ch. 13. 21. 2 Kin. 14. 25.
[k] Ezek. 47. 15.
[l] Ezek. 47. 17.
[m] 2 Kin. 23. 33. Jer. 39. 5, 6.
[n] Deut. 3. 17. Josh. 11. 2. & 19. 35. Matt. 14. 34. Luke 5. 1.
[o] ver. 3.
[p] ver. 1. Josh. 14. 1, 2.
[q] ch. 32. 33. Josh. 14. 2, 3.
[r] Josh. 14. 1. & 19. 51.
[s] ch. 1. 4, 16.

[1] Heb. *shoulder*.

7–9. The northern border. On the "mount Hor," cp. xx. 22 note. Here the name denotes the whole western crest of Mount Lebanon, eighty miles in length, commencing east of Zidon, and terminating with the point immediately above the entrance of Hamath (cp. xiii. 21). The extreme point in the northern border of the land was the city of Zedad (Sadad), about thirty miles east of the entrance of Hamath. Hence the border turned back south-westward to Ziphron (Zifrân), about forty miles north-east of Damascus. Hazar-enan may be conjecturally identified with Ayûn ed-Dara, a fountain situate in the very heart of the great central chain of Antilibanus.

10–12. Shepham, the first point after Hazar-enan, is unknown. The name Riblah is by some read Har-bel, *i.e.* "the Mountain of Bel;" the Har-baal-Hermon of Judg. iii. 3. No more striking landmark could be set forth than the summit of Hermon, the southernmost and by far the loftiest peak of the whole Antilibanus range, rising to a height of ten thousand feet, and overtopping every other mountain in the Holy Land. Ain, *i.e.* the fountain, is understood to be the fountain of the Jordan; and it is in the plain at the south-western foot of Hermon that the two most celebrated sources of that river, those of Daphne and of Paneas, are situate.

The "sea of Chinnereth" is better known by its later name of Gennesaret, which is supposed to be only a corruption of Chinnereth. The border ran parallel to this sea, along the line of hill about ten miles further east.

16–29. Of the representatives now selected through Moses beforehand, who were all princes, *i.e.* heads of chief families, in their respective tribes (see xiii. 2), Caleb alone, of the tribe of Judah, is otherwise known to us (see xiii. 4 seq.). The order in which the tribes are named is peculiar to this passage. If they be taken in pairs, Judah and Simeon, Benjamin and Dan, Manasseh and Ephraim, Zebulun and Issachar, Asher and Naphtali, the order of the pairs agrees with the order in which the allotments in the Holy Land, taken also in couples, followed each other in the map from south to north.

21 the children of Simeon, Shemuel the son of Ammihud. Of the
22 tribe of Benjamin, Elidad the son of Chislon. And the prince of
23 the tribe of the children of Dan, Bukki the son of Jogli. The
prince of the children of Joseph, for the tribe of the children of
24 Manasseh, Hanniel the son of Ephod. And the prince of the
tribe of the children of Ephraim, Kemuel the son of Shiphtan.
25 And the prince of the tribe of the children of Zebulun, Elizaphan
26 the son of Parnach. And the prince of the tribe of the children
27 of Issachar, Paltiel the son of Azzan. And the prince of the
28 tribe of the children of Asher, Ahihud the son of Shelomi. And
the prince of the tribe of the children of Naphtali, Pedahel the
29 son of Ammihud. These *are they* whom the LORD commanded
to divide the inheritance unto the children of Israel in the land of
Canaan.

CHAP. 35. AND the LORD spake unto Moses in the plains of Moab
2 by Jordan *near* Jericho, saying, [a]Command the children of Israel,
that they give unto the Levites of the inheritance of their possession cities to dwell in; and ye shall give *also* unto the Levites
3 suburbs for the cities round about them. And the cities shall
they have to dwell in; and the suburbs of them shall be for
4 their cattle, and for their goods, and for all their beasts. And
the suburbs of the cities, which ye shall give unto the Levites,
shall reach from the wall of the city and outward a thousand
5 cubits round about. And ye shall measure from without the
city on the east side two thousand cubits, and on the south side
two thousand cubits, and on the west side two thousand cubits,
and on the north side two thousand cubits; and the city *shall be*
in the midst: this shall be to them the suburbs of the cities.
6 And among the cities which ye shall give unto the Levites *there
shall be* [b]six cities for refuge, which ye shall appoint for the
manslayer, that he may flee thither: and [1]to them ye shall add
7 forty and two cities. *So* all the cities which ye shall give to the
Levites *shall be* [c]forty and eight cities: them *shall ye give* with
8 their suburbs. And the cities which ye shall give *shall be* [d]of
the possession of the children of Israel: [e]from *them that have*
many ye shall give many; but from *them that have* few ye shall
give few: every one shall give of his cities unto the Levites
9 according to his inheritance which [2]he inheriteth. ¶ And the
10 LORD spake unto Moses, saying, Speak unto the children of

[a] Josh. 14. 3, 4. & 21. 2. See Ez. 45. 1, &c. & 48. 8, &c.
[b] ver. 13. Deut. 4. 41. Josh. 20. 2, 7, 8. & 21. 3, 13, 21, 27, 32, 36, 38.
[c] Josh. 21. 41.
[d] Josh. 21. 3.
[e] ch. 26. 54.

[1] Heb. *above them ye shall give.*
[2] Heb. *they inherit.*

XXXV. **2.** *suburbs*] Rather, "pasture-grounds," required for their large cattle, for their sheep and goats, and for all their beasts whatsoever they might be (*v.* 3).

5. *from without the city*] Omit "from." The demarcation here intended would run parallel to the wall of the city, outside which it was made. To guard against any restrictions of area, due to such causes as the irregular forms of the cities or the physical obstacles of the ground, it was ordained that the suburb should, alike on north, south, east, and west, present, at a distance of a thousand cubits (or, nearly one-third of a mile) from the wall, a front not less than two thousand cubits in length; and, by joining the extremities of these measured fronts according to the nature of the ground, a sufficient space for the Levites would be secured.

6. The Levitical cities were in an especial manner the Lord's; and therefore the places of refuge, where the manslayer might remain under the protection of a special institution devised by Divine mercy, were appropriately selected from amongst them. No doubt also the Priests and Levites would be the fittest persons to administer the law in the doubtful cases which would be sure to occur: cp. *v.* 24 note.

8. Nine cities were eventually given to the Levites from the large joint inheritance of Judah and Simeon; three were taken from the territory of Naphtali, and the other tribes gave each four apiece.

Israel, and say unto them, [f]When ye be come over Jordan into   [f] Deut. 19. 2.
11 the land of Canaan; then [g]ye shall appoint you cities to be   Josh. 20. 2.
cities of refuge for you; that the slayer may flee thither, which   [g] Ex. 21. 13.
12 killeth any person [1]at unawares. [h]And they shall be unto you   [h] Deut. 19. 6.
cities for refuge from the avenger; that the manslayer die not,   Josh. 20. 3,
13 until he stand before the congregation in judgment. And of   5, 6.
these cities which ye shall give [i]six cities shall ye have for refuge.   [i] ver. 6.
14 [k]Ye shall give three cities on this side Jordan, and three cities   [k] Deut. 4. 41.
shall ye give in the land of Canaan, *which* shall be cities of   Josh. 20. 8.
15 refuge. These six cities shall be a refuge, *both* for the children
of Israel, and [l]for the stranger, and for the sojourner among   [l] ch. 15. 16.
them: that every one that killeth any person unawares may flee
16 thither. [m]And if he smite him with an instrument of iron, so   [m] Ex. 21. 12,
that he die, he *is* a murderer: the murderer shall surely be put   14.
17 to death. And if he smite him [2]with throwing a stone, where-   Lev. 24. 17.
with he may die, and he die, he *is* a murderer: the murderer   Deut. 19. 11, 12.
18 shall surely be put to death. Or *if* he smite him with an hand
weapon of wood, wherewith he may die, and he die, he *is* a
19 murderer: the murderer shall surely be put to death. [n]The   [n] ver. 21, 24,
revenger of blood himself shall slay the murderer: when he   27.
20 meeteth him, he shall slay him. But [o]if he thrust him of hatred,   Deut. 19. 6, 12.
21 or hurl at him [p]by laying of wait, that he die; or in enmity   Josh. 20. 3, 5.
smite him with his hand, that he die: he that smote *him* shall   [o] Gen. 4. 8.
surely be put to death; *for* he *is* a murderer: the revenger of   2 Sam. 3. 27. & 20. 10.
22 blood shall slay the murderer, when he meeteth him. But if   1 Kin. 2. 31, 32.
he thrust him suddenly [q]without enmity, or have cast upon him   [p] Ex. 21. 14.
23 any thing without laying of wait, or with any stone, wherewith   Deut. 19. 11.
a man may die, seeing *him* not, and cast *it* upon him, that he   [q] Ex. 21. 13.
24 die, and *was* not his enemy, neither sought his harm: then [r]the   [r] ver. 12.
congregation shall judge between the slayer and the revenger of   Josh. 20. 6.

[1] Heb. *by error*.   [2] Heb. *with a stone of the hand*.

---

12. *the avenger*] Heb. *goel*, a term of which the original import is uncertain. The very obscurity of its etymology testifies to the antiquity of the office which it denotes. That office rested on the principle of Gen. ix. 6, "whoso sheddeth man's blood, by man shall his blood be shed." The unwritten code of the East conceded to the nearest kinsman of a murdered man the right of avenging the blood that had been shed. Such rude justice necessarily involved grave evils. It gave no opportunity to the person charged with crime of establishing his innocence; it recognised no distinction between murder, manslaughter, and accidental homicide; it perpetuated family blood-feuds, the avenger of blood being liable to be treated in his turn as a murderer by the kinsman of the man whom he had slain. These grievances could not be removed as long as there was no central government, but they might be mitigated; and to do this was the object of the institution in the text (cp. Ex. xxi. 13).

Among the Arab tribes, who are under the control of no central authority, the practice of blood-revenge subsists in full force to the present day.

12. *the congregation*] *i.e.* local court, consisting of the elders of the city (Josh. xx. 4).

16–25. The sense is: Inasmuch as to take another man's life by any means soever is murder, and exposes the murderer to the penalty of retaliation; so, if the deed be done in enmity, it is in truth very murder, and the murderer shall be slain; but if it be not done in enmity, then the congregation shall interpose to stay the avenger's hand.

19. *when he meeteth him*] Provided, of course, it were without a city of refuge.

24. The case of the innocent slayer is here contemplated. In a doubtful case there would necessarily have to be a judicial decision as to the guilt or innocence of the person who claimed the right of asylum.

25. The homicide was safe only within the walls of his city of refuge. He became a virtual exile from his home. The provisions here made serve to mark the gravity of the act of manslaughter, even when not premeditated; and the inconveniences attending on them fell, as is right and fair, upon him who committed the deed.

unto the death of the high priest] The atoning death of the Saviour cast its shadow before on the statute-book of the Law and

25 blood according to these judgments: and the congregation shall
deliver the slayer out of the hand of the revenger of blood, and the
congregation shall restore him to the city of his refuge, whither
he was fled: and [s]he shall abide in it unto the death of the high
26 priest, [t]which was anointed with the holy oil. But if the slayer
shall at any time come without the border of the city of his
27 refuge, whither he was fled; and the revenger of blood find him
without the borders of the city of his refuge, and the revenger of
28 blood kill the slayer; [1]he shall not be guilty of blood: because
he should have remained in the city of his refuge until the death
of the high priest: but after the death of the high priest the
29 slayer shall return into the land of his possession. So these
things shall be for [u]a statute of judgment unto you throughout
30 your generations in all your dwellings. ¶ Whoso killeth any
person, the murderer shall be put to death by the [x]mouth of witnesses: but one witness shall not testify against any person *to*
31 *cause him* to die. Moreover ye shall take no satisfaction for the
life of a murderer, which *is* [2]guilty of death: but he shall be
32 surely put to death. And ye shall take no satisfaction for him
that is fled to the city of his refuge, that he should come again
33 to dwell in the land, until the death of the priest. So ye shall
not pollute the land wherein ye *are*: for blood [y]it defileth the
land: and [3]the land cannot be cleansed of the blood that is shed
34 therein, but [z]by the blood of him that shed it. [a]Defile not
therefore the land which ye shall inhabit, wherein I dwell: for
[b]I the LORD dwell among the children of Israel.

CHAP. 36. AND the chief fathers of the families of the [a]children of
Gilead, the son of Machir, the son of Manasseh, of the families
of the sons of Joseph, came near, and spake before Moses, and
before the princes, the chief fathers of the children of Israel:
2 and they said, [b]The LORD commanded my lord to give the land
for an inheritance by lot to the children of Israel: and [c]my
lord was commanded by the LORD to give the inheritance of
3 Zelophehad our brother unto his daughters. And if they be
married to any of the sons of the *other* tribes of the children of

[s] Josh. 20. 6.
[t] Ex. 29. 7. Lev. 4. 3. & 21. 10.
[u] ch. 27. 11.
[x] Deut. 17. 6. & 19. 15. Matt. 18. 16. 2 Cor. 13. 1. Heb. 10. 28.
[y] Ps. 106. 38. Mic. 4. 11.
[z] Gen. 9. 6.
[a] Lev. 18. 25. Deut. 21. 23.
[b] Ex. 29. 45, 46.
[a] ch. 26. 29.
[b] ch. 26. 55. & 33. 54. Josh. 17. 3.
[c] ch. 27. 1, 7. Josh. 17. 3, 4.

[1] Heb. *no blood* shall be *to him*, Ex. 22. 2.
[2] Heb. *faulty to die.*
[3] Heb. *there can be no expiation for the land.*

---

on the annals of Jewish history. The High-priest, as the head and representative of the whole chosen family of sacerdotal mediators, as exclusively entrusted with some of the chief priestly functions, as alone privileged to make yearly atonement within the Holy of Holies, and to gain, from the mysterious Urim and Thummim, special revelations of the will of God, was, preeminently, a type of Christ. And thus the death of each successive High-priest presignified that death of Christ by which the captives were to be freed, and the remembrance of transgressions made to cease.

30. *by the mouth of witnesses*] *i.e.* two witnesses, at the least (cp. marg. reff.). The provisions of this and the following verses protect the enactments of this chapter from abuse. The cities of refuge were not intended to exempt a criminal from deserved punishment.

31. *no satisfaction*] Rather, **ransom** (see Ex. xxi. 30). The permission to demand pecuniary compensation for murders (expressly sanctioned by the Koran) undoubtedly mitigates, in practice, the system of private retaliation; but it does so by sacrificing the principle named in *vv.* 12, 33.

34. *for I the* LORD *dwell*, &c.] An emphatic protest against all enactment or relaxation of laws by men for their own private convenience.

XXXVI. **1–13.** The daughters of Zelophehad had obtained an ordinance (xxviii. 6–11) which permitted the daughters of an Israelite dying without male issue to inherit their father's property. The chiefs of the Machirites, of whom Zelophehad had been one, now obtain a supplemental enactment, directing that heiresses should marry within their own tribe.

Israel, then shall their inheritance be taken from the inheritance
of our fathers, and shall be put to the inheritance of the tribe
[1]whereunto they are received: so shall it be taken from the lot
4 of our inheritance. And when [d]the jubile of the children of — [d] Lev. 25. 10.
Israel shall be, then shall their inheritance be put unto the
inheritance of the tribe whereunto they are received: so shall
their inheritance be taken away from the inheritance of the
5 tribe of our fathers. ¶ And Moses commanded the children of
Israel according to the word of the LORD, saying, The tribe of
6 the sons of Joseph [e]hath said well. This *is* the thing which the — [e] ch. 27. 7.
LORD doth command concerning the daughters of Zelophehad,
saying, Let them [2]marry to whom they think best; [f]only to the — [f] ver. 12.
7 family of the tribe of their father shall they marry. So shall
not the inheritance of the children of Israel remove from tribe
to tribe: for every one of the children of Israel shall [3][g]keep — [g] 1 Kin. 21. 3.
8 himself to the inheritance of the tribe of his fathers. And [h]every — [h] 1 Chr. 23. 22.
daughter, that possesseth an inheritance in any tribe of the
children of Israel, shall be wife unto one of the family of the
tribe of her father, that the children of Israel may enjoy every
9 man the inheritance of his fathers. Neither shall the inheritance
remove from *one* tribe to another tribe; but every one of the
tribes of the children of Israel shall keep himself to his own
10 inheritance. Even as the LORD commanded Moses, so did the
11 daughters of Zelophehad: [i]for Mahlah, Tirzah, and Hoglah, — [i] ch. 27. 1.
and Milcah, and Noah, the daughters of Zelophehad, were mar-
12 ried unto their father's brothers' sons: *and* they were married
[4]into the families of the sons of Manasseh the son of Joseph,
and their inheritance remained in the tribe of the family of their
13 father. ¶ These *are* the commandments and the judgments,
which the LORD commanded by the hand of Moses unto the
children of Israel [k]in the plains of Moab by Jordan *near* — [k] ch. 26. 3. & 33. 50.
Jericho.

[1] Heb. *unto whom they shall be.*
[2] Heb. *be wives.*
[3] Heb. *cleave to the, &c.*
[4] Heb. to some that were *of the families.*

---

4. *be taken away*] *i.e.* be permanently taken away. The jubilee year, by not restoring the estate to the tribe to which it originally belonged, would in effect confirm the alienation.

11. *unto their father's brothers' sons*] Or more generally, "unto the sons of their kinsmen."

DEUTERONOMY.

INTRODUCTION.

THE ordinary name of the book is derived, through the LXX. and Vulgate from that sometimes employed by the Jews, "repetition of the law," and indicates correctly enough the character and contents of the book.[1]

The bulk of Deuteronomy consists of addresses spoken within the space of forty days, and beginning on the first day of the eleventh month in the fortieth year.

The speeches exhibit an unity of style and character which is strikingly consistent with such circumstances. They are pervaded by the same vein of thought, the same tone and tenor of feeling, the same peculiarities of conception and expression. They exhibit matter which is neither documentary nor traditional, but conveyed in the speaker's own words.

Their aim is strictly hortatory; their style earnest, heart-stirring, impressive, in passages sublime, but throughout rhetorical; they keep constantly in view the circumstances then present and the crisis to which the fortunes of Israel had at last been brought Moses had before him not the men to whom by God's command he delivered the law at Sinai, but the generation following which had grown up in the wilderness. Large portions of the law necessarily stood in abeyance during the years of wandering; and of his present hearers many must have been strangers to various prescribed observances and ordinances. Now however on their entry into settled homes in Canaan a thorough discharge of the various obligations laid on them by the Covenant would become imperative; and it is to this state of things that Moses addresses himself. He speaks to hearers neither wholly ignorant of the Law, nor yet fully versed in it. Much is assumed and taken for granted in his speeches; but in other matters he goes into detail, knowing that instruction in them was needed. Sometimes too opportunity is taken of promulgating regulations which are supplementary or auxiliary to those of the preceding books; some few modifications arising out of different or altered circumstances are now made; and the whole Mosaic system is completed by the addition of several enactments in chapters xii.–xxvi. of a social, civil, and

[1] The contents of Deuteronomy consist (1) of three addresses to the people delivered by Moses in the eleventh month of the fortieth year after the Exodus (chs. i.–xxx.); and (2) of certain final acts and words of Moses, viz. the solemn appointment of his successor (xxxi.), his Song (xxxii.), and Blessing (xxxiii.), which together with the account of his death (xxxiv.) form an appropriate conclusion to the book and to the whole Pentateuch. Part (2) was probably added to the rest by Joshua or some other duly authorized prophet or leader of the people, after the death of Moses.

political nature. These would have been wholly superfluous during the nomadic life of the desert; but now that the permanent organization of Israel as a nation was to be accomplished, they could not be longer deferred. Accordingly the legislator, at the command of God, completes his great work by supplying them. Thus he providés civil institutions for his people accredited by the same Divine sanctions as had been vouchsafed to their religious rites.

The preceding books displayed Moses principally in the capacity of legislator or annalist. Deuteronomy sets him before us in that of a prophet. And he not only warns and teaches with an authority and energy which the sublimest pages of the Four Greater Prophets cannot surpass, but he delivers some of the most notable and incontrovertible predictions to be found in the Old Testament. The prophecy in xviii. 18 had no doubt its partial verifications in successive ages, but its terms are satisfied in none of them. The prospect opened by it advances continually until it finds its rest in the Messiah, Who stands alone as the only complete counterpart of Moses, and as the greater than he. Chapters xxviii., xxxii. furnish other and no less manifest examples.

It is generally allowed that Deuteronomy must, in substance, have come from one hand. The book presents, the last four chapters excepted, an undeniable unity in style and treatment; it is cast, so to speak, in one mould; its literary characteristics are such that we cannot believe the composition of it to have been spread over any long period of time: and these facts are in full accord with the traditional view which ascribes the book to Moses.

Assertions as to the spuriousness[2] of Deuteronomy, though put forward very positively, appear when sifted to rest upon most insufficient arguments. The alleged anachronisms, discrepancies, and difficulties admit for the most part of easy and complete explanation; and no serious attempt has ever been made to meet the overwhelming presumption drawn from the unanimous and unwavering testimony of the ancient Jewish Church and nation that Moses is the author of this book.

Deuteronomy has in a singular manner the attestation of the Apostles and of our Lord. St. Paul, in Romans x. 8 and xv. 11 argues from it at some length, and expressly quotes it as written by Moses; St. Peter and St. Stephen (Acts iii. 22, vii. 37) refer to the promise of "a Prophet like unto" Moses, and regard it as given, as it professes to be, by Moses himself; our Lord, wielding "the sword of the Spirit which is the word of God" against the open assaults of Satan, thrice resorts to Deuteronomy for the texts with which He repels the tempter, St. Matt. iv. 4–10. To urge in reply that the inspiration of the Apostles, and

[2] The older scholars of Germany unhesitatingly affirmed that Deuteronomy was written long after the rest of the Pentateuch was extant in its present shape. The newer school sees no less certainly in Deuteronomy the primæval quarry out of which the writers concerned in the production of the preceding books drew their materials. Out of this conflict of opinions one inference may safely be drawn. The allegation so positively made that the very style of Deuteronomy betrays its late origin is arbitrary and baseless.

even the indwelling of the Spirit "without measure" in the Saviour, would not necessarily preserve them from mistakes on such subjects as the authorship of ancient writings, or to fortify such assertions by remarking that our Lord as the Son of Man was Himself ignorant of some things, is to overlook the important distinction between ignorance and error. To be conscious that much truth lies beyond the range of the intelligence is compatible with the perfection of the creature: but to be deceived by the fraud of others and to fall into error, is not so. To assert then that He Who is "the Truth" believed Deuteronomy to be the work of Moses and quoted it expressly as such, though it was in fact a forgery introduced into the world seven or eight centuries after the Exodus, is in effect, even though not in intention, to impeach the perfection and sinlessness of His nature, and seems thus to gainsay the first principles of Christianity.

THE FIFTH BOOK OF MOSES,

CALLED

DEUTERONOMY.

CHAP. 1. THESE *be* the words which Moses spake unto all Israel
[a]on this side Jordan in the wilderness, in the plain over against
[1]the Red *sea*, between Paran, and Tophel, and Laban, and
2 Hazeroth, and Dizahab. (*There are* eleven days' *journey* from
3 Horeb by the way of mount Seir [b]unto Kadesh-barnea.) And
it came to pass [c]in the fortieth year, in the eleventh month, on
the first *day* of the month, *that* Moses spake unto the children
of Israel, according unto all that the LORD had given him in
4 commandment unto them; [d]after he had slain Sihon the king
of the Amorites, which dwelt in Heshbon, and Og the king of
5 Bashan, which dwelt at Astaroth [e]in Edrei: on this side Jordan,
in the land of Moab, began Moses to declare this law, saying,
6 ¶ The LORD our God spake unto us [f]in Horeb, saying, Ye have
7 dwelt long [g]enough in this mount: turn you, and take your
journey, and go to the mount of the Amorites, and unto [2]all *the
places* nigh thereunto, in the plain, in the hills, and in the vale,
and in the south, and by the sea side, to the land of the Canaanites, and unto Lebanon, unto the great river, the river

[a] Josh. 9. 1, 10. & 22. 4. 7.
[b] Num. 13. 26. ch. 9. 23.
[c] Num. 33. 38.
[d] Num. 21. 24, 33.
[e] Josh. 13. 12.
[f] Ex. 3. 1.
[g] See Ex. 19. 1. Num. 10. 11.

[1] Or, *Zuph.*

[2] Heb. *all his neighbours.*

I. **1, 2.** These verses are prefixed as a connecting link between the contents of the preceding books and that of Deut. now to follow. The sense of the passage might be given thus: "The discourses of Moses to the people up to the eleventh month of the fortieth year" (cp. *v.* 3) "have now been recorded." The proper names which follow seem to belong to places where "words" of remarkable importance were spoken. They are by the Jewish commentators referred to the spots which witnessed the more special sins of the people, and the mention of them here is construed as a pregnant rebuke. The Book of Deut. is known amongst the Jews as "the book of reproofs."

on this side Jordan] Rather, **beyond Jordan** (as in iii. 20 and 25). The phrase was a standing designation for the district east of Jordan, and in times when Greek became commonly spoken in the country was exactly represented by the proper name Peræa.

in the wilderness, in the plain] The former term denotes the desert of Arabia generally; the latter the sterile tract ('Arabah,' Num. xxi. 4 note) which stretches along the lower Jordan to the Dead Sea, and is continued thence to the Gulf of Akaba.

over against the Red sea] Render: **over against Suph.** "Sea" is not in the original text. "Suph" is either the pass *es Sufah* near Ain-el-Weibeh (Num. xiii. 26 note), or the name of the alluvial district (Num. xxi. 14 note).

Tophel is identified with Tufileh, the Tafyle of Burckhardt, still a considerable place,—some little distance S.E. of the Dead Sea. Paran is probably "mount Paran" (xxxiii. 2); or a city of the same name near the mountain. Cp. Gen. xiv. 6.

Laban is generally identified with Libnah (Num. xxxiii. 20), and Hazeroth with Ain Hadherah (Num. xi. 34 note); but the position of Dizahab is uncertain.

2. For Kadesh see Num. xiii. 26 note; and for Horeb see Ex. iii. 1.

4. *Astaroth*] On this place cp. Gen. xiv. 5 and note.

in Edrei] These words should, to render the sense clear, come next after "slain." The battle in which Sihon and Og were defeated took place at Edrei.

5. *in the land of Moab*] This district had formerly been occupied by the Moabites, and retained its name from them: but had been conquered by the Amorites. Cp. Num. xxi. 26, xxii. 4 notes.

declare] Render, **explain** the Law already declared.

6. The first and introductory address of Moses to the people is here commenced. It extends to iv. 40, and is divided from the second discourse by the *vv.* iv. 41–49. A summary of the address is given in the chapter-headings usually found in English Bibles.

7. *to the mount of the Amorites*] *i.e.* to the mountain district occupied by the Amorites, reaching into the Negeb, and part of the territory assigned to the tribe of Judah.

8 Euphrates. Behold, I have [1]set the land before you: go in and
possess the land which the LORD sware unto your fathers,
[h]Abraham, Isaac, and Jacob, to give unto them and to their
9 seed after them. ¶ And [i]I spake unto you at that time, saying,
10 I am not able to bear you myself alone: the LORD your God
hath multiplied you, and, behold, [k]ye *are* this day as the stars
11 of heaven for multitude. ([l]The LORD God of your fathers make
you a thousand times so many more as ye *are*, and bless you,
12 [m]as he hath promised you!) [n]How can I myself alone bear
13 your cumbrance, and your burden, and your strife? [o][2]Take
you wise men, and understanding, and known among your
14 tribes, and I will make them rulers over you. And ye answered
me, and said, The thing which thou hast spoken *is* good *for us*
15 to do. So I took the chief of your tribes, wise men, and known,
[p]and [3]made them heads over you, captains over thousands, and
captains over hundreds, and captains over fifties, and captains
16 over tens, and officers among your tribes. And I charged your
judges at that time, saying, Hear *the causes* between your
brethren, and [q]judge righteously between *every* man and his
17 [r]brother, and the stranger *that is* with him. [s]Ye shall not
[4]respect persons in judgment; *but* ye shall hear the small as
well as the great; ye shall not be afraid of the face of man; for
[t]the judgment *is* God's: and the cause that is too hard for you,
18 [u]bring *it* unto me, and I will hear it. And I commanded you
19 at that time all the things which ye should do. ¶ And when we
departed from Horeb, [x]we went through all that great and terrible wilderness, which ye saw by the way of the mountain of
the Amorites, as the LORD our God commanded us; and [y]we
20 came to Kadesh-barnea. And I said unto you, Ye are come
unto the mountain of the Amorites, which the LORD our God
21 doth give unto us. Behold, the LORD thy God hath set the land
before thee: go up *and* possess *it*, as the LORD God of thy
fathers hath said unto thee; [z]fear not, neither be discouraged.
22 And ye came near unto me every one of you, and said, We
will send men before us, and they shall search us out the land,

[h] Gen. 12. 7. & reff.
[i] Ex. 18. 18. Num. 11. 14.
[k] Gen. 15. 5. ch. 10. 22. & 28. 62.
[l] 2 Sam. 24. 3.
[m] Gen. 15. 5. & 22. 17. & 26. 4. Ex. 32. 13.
[n] 1 Kin. 3. 8, 9.
[o] See Ex. 18. 21. Num. 11. 16, 17.
[p] Ex. 18. 25.
[q] ch. 16. 18. John 7. 24.
[r] Lev. 24. 22.
[s] Lev. 19. 15. ch. 16. 19. 1 Sam. 16. 7. Prov. 24. 23. James 2. 1.
[t] 2 Chr. 19. 6.
[u] Ex. 18. 22, 26.
[x] Num. 10. 12. ch. 8. 15. Jer. 2. 6.
[y] Num. 13. 26.
[z] Josh. 1. 9.

[1] Heb. *given*.
[2] Heb. *Give*.
[3] Heb. *gave*.
[4] Heb. *acknowledge faces*.

9–15. This appointment of the "captains" (cp. Ex. xviii. 21 seq.) must not be confounded with that of the elders in Num. xi. 16 seq. The former would number 78,600; the latter were seventy only.

A comparison between this passage and that in Exodus makes it obvious that Moses is only touching on certain parts of the whole history, without regard to order of time, but with a special purpose. This important arrangement for the good government of the people took place before they quitted Horeb to march direct to the Promised Land. This fact sets more clearly before us the perverseness and ingratitude of the people, to which the orator next passes; and shows, what he was anxious to impress, that the fault of the 40 years' delay rested only with themselves.

19. *that great and terrible wilderness*] Cp. viii. 15. This language is such as men would employ after having passed with toil and suffering through the worst part of it, the southern half of the Arabah (see Num. xxi. 4 note); and more especially when they had but recently rested from their marches in the plain of Shittim, the largest and richest oasis in the whole district on the Eastern bank near the mouth of the Jordan.

22, 23. The plan of sending the spies originated with the people; and, as in itself a reasonable one, it approved itself to Moses; it was submitted to God, sanctioned by Him, and carried out under special Divine direction. The orator's purpose in this chapter is to bring before the people emphatically their own responsibilities and behaviour. It is therefore important to remind them, that the sending of the spies, which led immediately to their murmuring and rebellion, was their own suggestion.

The following verses to the end of the chapter give a condensed account, the fuller one

and bring us word again by what way we must go up, and into
23 what cities we shall come. And the saying pleased me well:
24 and [a]I took twelve men of you, one of a tribe: and [b]they turned
and went up into the mountain, and came unto the valley of
25 Eshcol, and searched it out. And they took of the fruit of the
land in their hands, and brought *it* down unto us, and brought
us word again, and said, [c]*It is* a good land which the LORD our
26 God doth give us. ¶ [d]Notwithstanding ye would not go up,
but rebelled against the commandment of the LORD your God:
27 and ye murmured in your tents, and said, Because the LORD
[e]hated us, he hath brought us forth out of the land of Egypt, to
28 deliver us into the hand of the Amorites, to destroy us. Whither
shall we go up? Our brethren have [1]discouraged our heart,
saying, [f]The people *is* greater and taller than we; the cities *are*
great and walled up to heaven; and moreover we have seen the
29 sons of the [g]Anakims there. Then I said unto you, Dread not,
30 neither be afraid of them. [h]The LORD your God which goeth
before you, he shall fight for you, according to all that he did
31 for you in Egypt before your eyes; and in the wilderness, where
thou hast seen how that the LORD thy God [i]bare thee, as a man
doth bear his son, in all the way that ye went, until ye came
32 into this place. Yet in this thing [k]ye did not believe the LORD
33 your God, [l]who went in the way before you, [m]to search you out
a place to pitch your tents *in*, in fire by night, to shew you by
34 what way ye should go, and in a cloud by day. ¶ And the LORD
heard the voice of your words, and was wroth, [n]and sware, say-
35 ing, [o]Surely there shall not one of these men of this evil generation see that good land, which I sware to give unto your
36 fathers, [p]save Caleb the son of Jephunneh; he shall see it,
and to him will I give the land that he hath trodden upon, and
to his children, because [q]he hath [2]wholly followed the LORD.
37 [r]Also the LORD was angry with me for your sakes, saying, Thou
38 also shalt not go in thither. [s]*But* Joshua the son of Nun,
[t]which standeth before thee, he shall go in thither: [u]encourage
39 him: for he shall cause Israel to inherit it. [x]Moreover your
little ones, which [y]ye said should be a prey, and your children,
which in that day [z]had no knowledge between good and evil,
they shall go in thither, and unto them will I give it, and they
40 shall possess it. [a]But *as for* you, turn you, and take your
41 journey into the wilderness by the way of the Red sea. ¶ Then
ye answered and said unto me, [b]We have sinned against the
LORD, we will go up and fight, according to all that the LORD
our God commanded us. And when ye had girded on every
man his weapons of war, ye were ready to go up into the hill.
42 And the LORD said unto me, Say unto them, [c]Go not up, neither
fight; for I *am* not among you; lest ye be smitten before your

[a] Num. 13. 3.
[b] Num. 13. 22, 23, 24.
[c] Num. 13. 27.
[d] Num. 14. 1, 2, 3, 4. Ps. 106. 24.
[e] ch. 9. 28.
[f] Num. 13. 28, 31—33. ch. 9. 1, 2.
[g] Num. 13. 28.
[h] Ex. 14. 14, 25. Neh. 4. 20.
[i] Ex. 19. 4. ch. 22. 11. Isai. 46. 3. & 63. 9. Hos. 11. 3. Acts 13. 18.
[k] Ps. 106. 24. Jude 5.
[l] Ex. 13. 21. Ps. 78. 14.
[m] Num. 10. 33. Ez. 20. 6.
[n] ch. 2. 14.
[o] Num. 14. 22, 23. Ps. 95. 11.
[p] Num. 14. 24, 30. Josh. 14. 9.
[q] Num. 14. 24.
[r] ch. 3. 26. Ps. 106. 32.
[s] Num. 14. 30.
[t] Ex. 24. 13. & 33. 11. See 1 Sam. 16. 22.
[u] Num. 27. 18. 19. ch. 31. 7, 23.
[x] Num. 14. 31.
[y] Num. 14. 3.
[z] Isai. 7. 15. Rom. 9. 11.
[a] Num. 14. 25.
[b] Num. 14. 40.
[c] Num. 14. 42.

[1] Heb. *melted*, Josh. 2. 11.
[2] Heb. *fulfilled* to go *after*.

---

being in Num. xiii. and xiv., of the occurrences which led to the banishment of the people for forty years into the wilderness.

37. The sentence on Moses was not passed when the people rebelled during their first encampment at Kadesh, but some thirty-seven years later, when they had re-assembled in the same neighbourhood at Meribah (see Num. xx. 13 note). He alludes to it here as having happened not many months previously, bearing on the facts which were to his purpose in pricking the conscience of the people.

41. *ye were ready to go up into the hill*] Rather, perhaps, "ye made light of going up;" *i.e.* "ye were ready to attempt it as a trifling undertaking." *V.* 43 shows the issue of this spirit in action; cp. marg. reff.

43 enemies. So I spake unto you; and ye would not hear, but
rebelled against the commandment of the LORD, and [1][d]went
44 presumptuously up into the hill. And the Amorites, which
dwelt in that mountain, came out against you, and chased you,
45 [e]as bees do, and destroyed you in Seir, *even* unto Hormah. And
ye returned and wept before the LORD; but the LORD would
46 not hearken to your voice, nor give ear unto you. [f]So ye
abode in Kadesh many days, according unto the days that ye
abode *there*.

CHAP. 2. THEN we turned, and took our journey into the wilderness by the way of the Red sea, [a]as the LORD spake unto
2 me: and we compassed mount Seir many days. And the LORD
3 spake unto me, saying, Ye have compassed this mountain [b]long
4 enough: turn you northward. And command thou the people,
saying, [c]Ye *are* to pass through the coast of your brethren the
children of Esau, which dwell in Seir; and they shall be afraid
5 of you: take ye good heed unto yourselves therefore: meddle
not with them; for I will not give you of their land, [2]no, not so
much as a foot breadth; [d]because I have given mount Seir
6 unto Esau *for* a possession. Ye shall buy meat of them for
money, that ye may eat; and ye shall also buy water of them
7 for money, that ye may drink. For the LORD thy God hath
blessed thee in all the works of thy hand: he knoweth thy
walking through this great wilderness: [e]these forty years the
LORD thy God *hath been* with thee; thou hast lacked nothing.
8 ¶ [f]And when we passed by from our brethren the children of
Esau, which dwelt in Seir, through the way of the plain from
[g]Elath, and from Ezion-gaber, we turned and passed by the way
9 of the wilderness of Moab. And the LORD said unto me, [3]Dis-
tress not the Moabites, neither contend with them in battle: for
I will not give thee of their land *for* a possession; because I
10 have given [h]Ar unto [i]the children of Lot *for* a possession. [k]The
Emims dwelt therein in times past, a people great, and many,
11 and tall, as [l]the Anakims; which also were accounted giants,
12 as the Anakims; but the Moabites call them Emims. [m]The

[d] Num. 14. 44, 45.
[e] Ps. 118. 12.
[f] Num. 13. 25. & 20. 1. 22. Judg. 11. 17.
[a] Num. 14. 25. ch. 1. 40.
[b] See ver. 7, 14.
[c] Num. 20. 14–20.
[d] Gen 36. 8. Josh. 24. 4.
[e] ch. 8. 2, 3, 4.
[f] Judg. 11. 18.
[g] 1 Kin. 9. 26.
[h] Num. 21. 28.
[i] Gen. 19. 36, 37.
[k] Gen. 14. 5.
[l] Num. 13. 22, 33. ch. 9. 2.
[m] Gen. 14. 6. & 36. 20. ver. 22.

[1] Heb. *ye were presumptuous, and went up.*
[2] Heb. *even to the treading of the sole of the foot.*
[3] Or, *Use no hostility against Moab.*

---

44. *the Amorites*] In Num. xiv. 45, it is "the Amalekites and the Canaanites" who are said to have discomfited them. The Amorites, as the most powerful nation of Canaan, lend their name here, as in other passages (*e.g. v.* 7) to the Canaanitish tribes generally.

II. **1–3.** *V.* 1 seems to refer in general terms to the long years of wandering, the details of which were not to Moses' present purpose. The command of *vv.* 2 and 3 relates to their journey from Kadesh to Mount Hor (Num. xx. 22; xxxiii. 37), and directs their march round the south extremity of Mount Seir, so as to "compass the land of Edom" (Judg. xi. 18; Num. xxi. 4), and so northwards towards the Arnon, *i.e.*, "by the way of the wilderness of Moab," (*v.* 8). This circuitous path was followed because of the refusal of the Edomites to allow the people to pass through their territory.

4. Cp. marg. ref. Though the Edomites resisted the passage through the midst of their land, they did not, and probably could not, oppose the "passing through the coast" or along their eastern frontier.

5. *I have given mount Seir to Esau*] Though the descendants of Esau were conquered by David (2 Sam. viii. 14), yet they were not dispossessed of their land, and in the reign of Jehoshaphat they regained their independence (2 Kings viii. 20–22).

8. Elath (Akaba) is at the northern extremity of the eastern arm of the Red Sea, and gives to that arm the name of the Elanitic Gulf. The name means "trees;" and is still justified by the grove of palm-trees at Akaba.

9. The Moabites and the Ammonites (*v.* 19) being descended from Lot, the nephew of Abraham (Gen. xix. 30–38), were, like the Edomites, kinsmen of the Israelites.

10–12. For the Emims, Horims, and Anakims, see marg. reff. These verses are either parenthetic or the insertion of a later hand.

Horims also dwelt in Seir beforetime; but the children of Esau
[1]succeeded them, when they had destroyed them from before
them, and dwelt in their [2]stead; as Israel did unto the land of
13 his possession, which the LORD gave unto them. Now rise up,
said I, and get you over [n]the [3]brook Zered. And we went over
14 the brook Zered. And the space in which we came [o]from
Kadesh-barnea, until we were come over the brook Zered, *was*
thirty and eight years; [p]until all the generation of the men of
war were wasted out from among the host, [q]as the LORD sware
15 unto them. For indeed the [r]hand of the LORD was against them,
to destroy them from among the host, until they were consumed.
16 ¶ So it came to pass, when all the men of war were consumed
17 and dead from among the people, that the LORD spake unto me,
18 saying, Thou art to pass over through Ar, the coast of Moab,
19 this day: and *when* thou comest nigh over against the children
of Ammon, distress them not, nor meddle with them: for I will
not give thee of the land of the children of Ammon *any* possession; because I have given it unto [s]the children of Lot *for* a
20 possession. (That also was accounted a land of giants: giants
dwelt therein in old time; and the Ammonites call them [t]Zam-
21 zummims; [u]a people great, and many, and tall, as the Anakims;
but the LORD destroyed them before them; and they suc-
22 ceeded them, and dwelt in their stead: as he did to the children
of Esau, [x]which dwelt in Seir, when he destroyed [y]the Horims
from before them; and they succeeded them, and dwelt in their
23 stead even unto this day: and [z]the Avims which dwelt in
Hazerim, *even* unto [a]Azzah, [b]the Caphtorims, which came forth
out of Caphtor, destroyed them, and dwelt in their stead.)
24 Rise ye up, take your journey, and [c]pass over the river Arnon:
behold, I have given into thine hand Sihon the Amorite, king of
Heshbon, and his land: [4]begin to possess *it*, and contend with
25 him in battle. [d]This day will I begin to put the dread of thee
and the fear of thee upon the nations *that are* under the whole
heaven, who shall hear report of thee, and shall tremble, and be
26 in anguish because of thee. ¶ And I sent messengers out of the
wilderness of Kedemoth unto Sihon king of Heshbon [e]with words
27 of peace, saying, [f]Let me pass through thy land: I will go along
by the high way, I will neither turn unto the right hand nor to
28 the left. Thou shalt sell me meat for money, that I may eat;
and give me water for money, that I may drink: [g]only I will
29 pass through on my feet; ([h]as the children of Esau which dwell
in Seir, and the Moabites which dwell in Ar, did unto me;) until
I shall pass over Jordan into the land which the LORD our God

[n] Num. 21. 12. [o] Num. 13. 26. [p] Num. 14. 33. & 26. 64. [q] Num. 14. 35. ch. 1. 34, 35. Ez. 20. 15. [r] Ps. 78. 33. & 106. 26. [s] Gen. 19. 38. [t] Gen. 14. 5, *Zuzims.* [u] See ver. 10. [x] Gen. 36. 8. [y] Gen. 14. 6. & 36. 20—30. ver. 12. [z] Josh. 13. 3. [a] Jer. 25. 20. [b] Gen. 10. 14. Amos 9. 7. [c] Num. 21. 13, 14. Judg. 11. 18, 21. [d] Ex. 15. 14, 15. ch. 11. 25. Josh. 2. 9. [e] ch. 20. 10. [f] Num. 21. 21, 22. Judg. 11. 19. [g] Num. 20. 19. [h] See Num. 20. 18. ch. 23. 3, 4. Judg. 11. 17, 18.

[1] Heb. *inherited them.*
[2] Or, *room.*
[3] Or, *valley*, Num. 13. 23.
[4] Heb. *begin, possess.*

---

13. The words, "said I," are not in the Hebrew. The words "rise up, and get you over the brook Zered" (Num. xxi. 12 note) connect themselves with *v.* 9, and form the conclusion of what God said to Moses.

20–23. These verses, like *vv.* 10–12, are in all likelihood an addition made by a later reviser.

20. *Zamzummims*] A giant race usually identified with the Zuzims of Gen. xiv. 5.

23. *the Avims which dwelt in Hazerim, even unto Azzah*] Read **Gaza,** of which Azzah is the Hebrew form. "Hazerim" is not strictly a proper name, but means "villages," or "enclosures," probably such as are still common in the East. The Avims are no doubt identical with the Avites of Josh. xiii. 3, and were doubtless a scattered remnant of a people conquered by the Caphtorim (Gen. x. 14 note) and living in their "enclosures" in the neighbourhood of Gerar. The word, which means "ruins," seems itself expressive of their fallen state.

26. *Kedemoth*] Lit. "Easternmost parts;" the name of a town afterwards assigned to

30 giveth us. [i]But Sihon king of Heshbon would not let us pass by
him: for [k]the LORD thy God [l]hardened his spirit, and made his
heart obstinate, that he might deliver him into thy hand, as
31 *appeareth* this day. And the LORD said unto me, Behold, I
have begun to [m]give Sihon and his land before thee: begin to
32 possess, that thou mayest inherit his land. [n]Then Sihon came
33 out against us, he and all his people, to fight at Jahaz. And [o]the
LORD our God delivered him before us; and [p]we smote him,
34 and his sons, and all his people. And we took all his cities at
that time, and [q]utterly destroyed [1]the men, and the women, and
35 the little ones, of every city, we left none to remain: only the
cattle we took for a prey unto ourselves, and the spoil of the
36 cities which we took. [r]From Aroer, which *is* by the brink of the
river of Arnon, and *from* the city that *is* by the river, even unto
Gilead, there was not one city too strong for us: [s]the LORD our
37 God delivered all unto us: only unto the land of the children of
Ammon thou camest not, *nor* unto any place of the river [t]Jabbok,
nor unto the cities in the mountains, nor unto [u]whatsoever the
LORD our God forbad us.

CHAP. 3. THEN we turned, and went up the way to Bashan: and
[a]Og the king of Bashan came out against us, he and all his
2 people, to battle [b]at Edrei. And the LORD said unto me, Fear
him not: for I will deliver him, and all his people, and his land,
into thy hand; and thou shalt do unto him as thou didst unto
3 [c]Sihon king of the Amorites, which dwelt at Heshbon. So the
LORD our God delivered into our hands Og also, the king of
Bashan, and all his people: [d]and we smote him until none was
4 left to him remaining. And we took all his cities at that time,
there was not a city which we took not from them, threescore
cities, [e]all the region of Argob, the kingdom of Og in Bashan.
5 All these cities *were* fenced with high walls, gates, and bars;

[i] Num. 21. 23. [k] Josh. 11. 20. [l] Ex. 4. 21. [m] ch. 1. 8. [n] Num. 21. 23. [o] ch. 7. 2. & 20. 16. [p] Num. 21. 24. ch. 29. 7. [q] Lev. 27. 28. ch. 7. 2, 26. [r] ch. 3. 12. & 4. 48. Josh. 13. 9. [s] Ps. 44. 3. [t] Gen. 32. 22. Num. 21. 24. ch. 3. 16. [u] ver. 5, 9, 19. [a] Num. 21. 33, &c. ch. 29. 7. [b] ch. 1. 4. [c] Num. 21. 34. [d] Num. 21. 35. [e] 1 Kin. 4. 13.

[1] Heb. *every city of men, and women, and little ones.*

---

the Reubenites, and given out of that tribe to the Levites. Cp. Josh. xiii. 18; 1 Chr. vi. 79.

34. *utterly destroyed the men, and the women, and the little ones, of every city*] Render, **laid under ban** (cp. Lev. xxvii. 28 note) **every inhabited city, both women and children**: these last words being added by way of fuller explanation.

36. *Aroer, which is by the brink of the river of Arnon*] Aroer stood on the north bank of the river, and was assigned (Josh. xiii. 9, 16) to the tribe of Reuben, of which it formed the most southerly city. The valley of the Arnon is here deep, and the descent to it abrupt. In Roman times it was spanned by a viaduct the ruins of which still remain, and which was probably built on the lines of the original structure of Mesha (2 Kings iii. 5). Aroer here must not be confounded with "Aroer, which is before Rabbah" (Josh. xiii. 25). This latter place was "built," *i.e.* rebuilt, by the Gadites (Num. xxxii. 34); it belonged to that tribe, and was consequently far to the north of the Arnon. A third Aroer in the tribe of Judah is mentioned in 1 Sam. xxx. 28.

"The city that is by the river," literally, "in the midst of the river" (cp. Josh. xiii. 9, 16) is Ar Moab (cp. Num. xxi. 15 note).

III. **4.** *threescore cities*] Probably the cities of Jair in Bashan described in *v.* 14 as Bashan-havoth-jair.

all the region of Argob] The Hebrew word here rendered "region," means literally "rope" or "cable"; and though undoubtedly used elsewhere in a general topographical sense for portion or district (*e.g.* Josh. xvii. 5), has a special propriety in reference to Argob (mod. Lejah). The name Argob means "stone-heap," and is paraphrased by the Targums, Trachonitis (Luke iii. 1), or "the rough country;" titles designating the more striking features of the district. Its borders are compared to a rugged shore-line; hence its description in the text as "the girdle of the stony country," would seem peculiarly appropriate. [Others identify Argob with the east quarter of the Hauran.]

5. *gates, and bars*] Lit. "Double gates and a bar." The stone doors of Bashan, their height pointing to a race of great stature, and the numerous cities (deserted) exist to illustrate the statements of these verses.

[f] ch. 2. 24. Ps. 135. 10. & 136. 19, 20. [g] ch. 4. 48. Ps. 29. 6. [h] 1 Chr. 5. 23. [i] ch. 4. 49. [k] Josh. 13. 11. [l] Amos 2. 9. [m] Gen. 14. 5. [n] 2 Sam. 12. 26. Jer. 49. 2. Ez. 21. 20. [o] ch. 2. 36. Josh. 12. 2. [p] Num. 32. 33. Josh. 12. 6. [q] Josh. 13. 29. [r] 1 Chr. 2. 22. [s] Josh. 13. 13. 2 Sam. 3. 3. & 10. 6. [t] Num. 32. 41. [u] Num. 32. 39. [w] 2 Sam. 24. 5.

6 beside unwalled towns a great many. And we utterly destroyed
them, as we did unto Sihon king [f]of Heshbon, utterly destroying
7 the men, women, and children, of every city. But all the cattle,
8 and the spoil of the cities, we took for a prey to ourselves. And
we took at that time out of the hand of the two kings of the
Amorites the land that *was* on this side Jordan, from the river of
9 Arnon unto mount Hermon; (*which* [g]Hermon the Sidonians
10 call Sirion; and the Amorites call it [h]Shenir;) [i]all the cities of
the plain, and all Gilead, and [k]all Bashan, unto Salchah and
11 Edrei, cities of the kingdom of Og in Bashan. [l]For only Og
king of Bashan remained of the remnant of [m]giants; behold,
his bedstead *was* a bedstead of iron; *is* it not in [n]Rabbath of the
children of Ammon? Nine cubits *was* the length thereof, and
12 four cubits the breadth of it, after the cubit of a man. ¶ And
this land, *which* we possessed at that time, [o]from Aroer, which
is by the river Arnon, and half mount Gilead, and [p]the cities
13 thereof, gave I unto the Reubenites and to the Gadites. [q]And
the rest of Gilead, and all Bashan, *being* the kingdom of Og,
gave I unto the half tribe of Manasseh; all the region of Argob,
14 with all Bashan, which was called the land of giants. [r]Jair
the son of Manasseh took all the country of Argob [s]unto the
coasts of Geshuri and Maachathi; and [t]called them after his
15 own name, Bashan-havoth-jair, unto this day. [u]And I gave
16 Gilead unto Machir. And unto the Reubenites [w]and unto the
Gadites I gave from Gilead even unto the river Arnon half the

---

9. Hermon, the southern and culminating point of the range of Lebanon, was also the religious centre of primæval Syria. Its Baal sanctuaries not only existed but gave it a name before the Exodus. Hence the careful specification of the various names by which the mountain was known. The Sidonian name of it might easily have become known to Moses through the constant traffic which had gone on from the most ancient times between Sidon and Egypt.

10. *Salchah*] Cp. Josh. xii. 5; 1 Chr. v. 11, where it is named as belonging to the tribe of Gad. It lies seven hours' journey to the south-east of Bostra or Bozrah of Moab. As the eastern border city of the kingdom of Bashan it was no doubt strongly fortified.

Edrei] Cp. Num. xxi. 33 note.

11. *giants*] Or Rephaim: see marg. ref. note.

a bedstead of iron] The "iron" was probably the black basalt of the country, which not only contains a large proportion, about 20 per cent., of iron, but was actually called iron, and is still so regarded by the Arabians. Iron was indeed both known and used, principally for tools (see *e.g.* xix. 5 and cp. Gen. iv. 22 note), at the date in question by the Semitic people of Palestine and the adjoining countries; but bronze was the ordinary metal of which weapons, articles of furniture, &c., were made.

The word translated "bedstead" is derived from a root signifying "to unite" or "bind together," and so "to arch" or "cover with a vault." The word may then certainly mean "bier," and perhaps does so in this passage. Modern travellers have discovered in the territories of Og sarcophagi as well as many other articles made of the black basalt of the country.

is it not in Rabbath of the children of Ammon?] Probably after the defeat and death of Og at Edrei the remnant of his army fled into the territory of the friendly Ammonites, and carried with them the corpse of the giant king.

after the cubit of a man] *i.e.* after the usual and ordinary cubit, counted as men are wont to count. Taking 18 inches to the cubit, the bedstead or sarcophagus would thus be from thirteen to fourteen feet long.

14. These Geshurites held territory adjoining, if not included within, Bashan. They are not to be confounded with those mentioned in Josh. xiii. 2, who were neighbours of the Philistines (1 Sam. xvii. 8).

The exact position of Maachah like that of Geshur cannot be ascertained; but it was no doubt amongst the fastnesses which lay between Bashan and the kingdom of Damascus, and on the skirts of Mount Hermon.

unto this day] This expression, like our "until now," does not, as used in the Bible, necessarily imply that the time spoken of as elapsed is long. It may here denote the duration to the time then present of that which had been already some months accomplished.

16. The sense is that the Reubenites and Gadites were to possess the district from the Jabbok on the north to the Arnon on the south, including the middle part of the

valley, and the border even unto the river Jabbok, [x]*which is* the
17 border of the children of Ammon; the plain also, and Jordan,
and the coast *thereof*, from [y]Chinnereth [z]even unto the sea of
the plain, [a]*even* the salt sea, [1]under Ashdoth-pisgah eastward.
18 ¶ And I commanded you at that time, saying, The LORD your
God hath given you this land to possess it: [b]ye shall pass over
armed before your brethren the children of Israel, all *that are*
19 [2]meet for the war. But your wives, and your little ones, and
your cattle, (*for* I know that ye have much cattle,) shall abide
20 in your cities which I have given you; until the LORD have
given rest unto your brethren, as well as unto you, and *until* they
also possess the land which the LORD your God hath given them
beyond Jordan: and *then* shall ye [c]return every man unto his
21 possession, which I have given you. ¶ And [d]I commanded
Joshua at that time, saying, Thine eyes have seen all that the
LORD your God hath done unto these two kings: so shall the
22 LORD do unto all the kingdoms whither thou passest. Ye shall
not fear them: for [e]the LORD your God he shall fight for you.
23, 24 ¶ And [f]I besought the LORD at that time, saying, O Lord
GOD, thou hast begun to shew thy servant [g]thy greatness, and thy
mighty hand: for [h]what God *is there* in heaven or in earth, that
25 can do according to thy works, and according to thy might? I
pray thee, let me go over, and see [i]the good land that *is* beyond
26 Jordan, that goodly mountain, and Lebanon. But the LORD
[k]was wroth with me for your sakes, and would not hear me:
and the LORD said unto me, Let it suffice thee; speak no more
27 unto me of this matter. [l]Get thee up into the top of [3]Pisgah,
and lift up thine eyes westward, and northward, and southward,
and eastward, and behold *it* with thine eyes: for thou shalt not
28 go over this Jordan. But [m]charge Joshua, and encourage him,
and strengthen him: for he shall go over before this people, and
he shall cause them to inherit the land which thou shalt see.
29 So we abode in [n]the valley over against Beth-peor.
CHAP. 4. NOW therefore hearken, O Israel, unto [a]the statutes and
unto the judgments, which I teach you, for to do *them*, that ye
may live, and go in and possess the land which the LORD God of

[x] Num. 21. 24. Josh. 12. 2.
[y] Num. 34. 11.
[z] Num. 34. 11. ch. 4. 49.
[a] Gen. 14. 3.
[b] Num. 32. 20, &c.
[c] Josh. 22. 4.
[d] Num. 27. 18.
[e] Ex. 14. 14. ch. 1. 30. & 20. 4.
[f] See 2 Cor. 12. 8, 9.
[g] ch. 11. 2.
[h] Ex. 15. 11. 2 Sam. 7. 22. Ps. 71. 19.
[i] Ex. 3. 8. ch. 4. 22.
[k] Num. 20. 12. & 27. 14. ch. 1. 37. & 31. 2. Ps. 106. 32.
[l] Num. 27. 12.
[m] Num. 27. 18, 23. ch. 1. 38. & 31. 3, 7.
[n] ch. 4. 46. & 34. 6.
[a] Lev. 19. 37. & 20. 8. ch. 5. 1. & 8. 1. Ez. 20. 11. Rom. 10. 5.

[1] Or, *under the springs of Pisgah*, or, *the hill*.
[2] Heb. *sons of power*.
[3] Or, *The hill*.

valley of the Arnon, and the territory ("coast" or "border") thereto pertaining.

25. *that goodly mountain*] *i.e.* that mountainous district. The flat districts of the East are generally scorched, destitute of water, and therefore sterile: the hilly ones, on the contrary, are of more tempered climate, and fertilised by the streams from the high grounds. Cp. xi. 11.

The whole of this prayer of Moses is very characteristic. The longing to witness further manifestations of God's goodness and glory, and the reluctance to leave unfinished an undertaking which he had been permitted to commence, are striking traits in his character: cp. Ex. xxxii. 32 seq., xxxiii. 12, 18 seq.; Num. xiv. 12 seq.

26. *the* LORD *was wroth with me for your sakes*] Here, as in i. 37 and iv. 21, the sin of the people is stated to be the ground on which Moses' prayer is denied. In xxxii. 51, and in Num. xxvii. 14 the transgression of Moses and Aaron themselves is assigned as the cause of their punishment. The reason why one side of the transaction is put forward in this place, and the other elsewhere, is evident. *Here* Moses is addressing the people, and mentions the punishment of their leaders as a most impressive warning to them, whose principal fault it was. In ch. xxxii. and Num. xxvii., God is addressing Moses, and visits on him, as is fitting, not the sin of the people but his own.

29. Beth-peor, *i.e.* the house of Peor, no doubt derived its name from a temple of the Moabite god Peor which was there situated. It was no doubt near to Mount Peor (Num. xxiii. 28), and also to the valley of the Jordan, perhaps in the Wady Heshban.

IV. The general entreaty contained in this chapter is pointed by special mention

2 your fathers giveth you. [b]Ye shall not add unto the word which
I command you, neither shall ye diminish *ought* from it, that ye
may keep the commandments of the LORD your God which I
3 command you. Your eyes have seen what the LORD did
because of [c]Baal-peor: for all the men that followed Baal-peor,
4 the LORD thy God hath destroyed them from among you. But
ye that did cleave unto the LORD your God *are* alive every one
5 of you this day. ¶ Behold, I have taught you statutes and judgments, even as the LORD my God commanded me, that ye should
6 do so in the land whither ye go to possess it. Keep therefore
and do *them;* for this *is* [d]your wisdom and your understanding
in the sight of the nations, which shall hear all these statutes,
and say, Surely this great nation *is* a wise and understanding
7 people. For [e]what nation *is there so* great, who *hath* [f]God *so* nigh
unto them, as the LORD our God *is* in all *things that* we call upon
8 him *for?* And what nation *is there so* great, that hath statutes
and judgments *so* righteous as all this law, which I set before you
9 this day? Only take heed to thyself, and [g]keep thy soul diligently, [h]lest thou forget the things which thine eyes have seen,
and lest they depart from thy heart all the days of thy life: but
10 [i]teach them thy sons, and thy sons' sons; *specially* [k]the day that
thou stoodest before the LORD thy God in Horeb, when the
LORD said unto me, Gather me the people together, and I will
make them hear my words, that they may learn to fear me all
the days that they shall live upon the earth, and *that* they may
11 teach their children. And ye came near and stood under the
mountain; and the [l]mountain burned with fire unto the [1]midst
12 of heaven, with darkness, clouds, and thick darkness. [m]And
the LORD spake unto you out of the midst of the fire: [n]ye heard
the voice of the words, but saw no similitude; [o][2]only *ye heard* a
13 voice. [p]And he declared unto you his covenant, which he commanded you to perform, *even* [q]ten commandments; and [r]he
14 wrote them upon two tables of stone. And [s]the LORD commanded me at that time to teach you statutes and judgments,
that ye might do them in the land whither ye go over to possess
15 it. ¶ [t]Take ye therefore good heed unto yourselves; for ye saw
no manner of [u]similitude on the day *that* the LORD spake unto
16 you in Horeb out of the midst of the fire: lest ye [x]corrupt *yourselves,* and [y]make you a graven image, the similitude of any
17 figure, [z]the likeness of male or female, the likeness of any beast
that *is* on the earth, the likeness of any winged fowl that flieth

[b] ch. 12. 32. Josh. 1. 7. Prov. 30. 6. Eccles. 12. 13. Rev. 22. 18.
[c] Num. 25. 4, &c. Josh. 22. 17 Ps. 106, 28.
[d] Job 28. 28. Ps. 19. 7. & 111. 10. Prov. 1. 7.
[e] 2 Sam. 7. 23.
[f] Ps. 46. 1. & 145. 18. & 148. 14. Isai. 55. 6.
[g] Prov. 4. 23.
[h] Prov. 3. 1, 3. & 4. 21.
[i] Gen. 18. 19. ch. 6. 7. & 11. 19. Ps. 78. 5. Eph. 6. 4.
[k] Ex. 19. 9, 16. & 20. 18. Heb. 12. 18, 19.
[l] Ex. 19. 18. ch. 5. 23.
[m] ch. 5. 4.
[n] ver. 33, 36.
[o] Ex. 20. 22. 1 Kin. 19. 12.
[p] ch. 9. 9.
[q] Ex. 34. 28.
[r] Ex. 24. 12. & 31. 18.
[s] Ex. 21. 1. & ch. 22. & ch. 23.
[t] Josh. 23. 11.
[u] Isai. 40. 18.
[x] Ex. 32. 7.
[y] Ex. 20. 4. ver. 23. ch. 5, 8.
[z] Rom. 1. 23.

[1] Heb. *heart*.
[2] Heb. *save a voice*.

---

and enforcement of the fundamental principles of the whole Covenant (*vv.* 9–40), the spiritual nature of the Deity, His exclusive right to their allegiance, His abhorrence of idolatry in every form, His choice of them for His elect people. Cp. further Moses' third and last address, ch. xxvii.–xxx.

9–11. A full stop should end *v.* 9; and *v.* 10 begin, **At the time that thou stoodest,** &c. (11) **then ye came near,** &c. Moses, exhorting to heedful observance of the Law, strives to renew the impressions of that tremendous scene which attended its promulgation at Sinai.

12 seq. Hero-worship exhibited itself in the practice of setting up images of human form as household gods (Penates, cp. Gen. xxxi. 19, xxxv. 2), or as local and civic divinities: a practice forbidden by *v.* 16. Nature-worship in its baser shapes is seen in the Egyptian idolatry of animals and animal figures, and is condemned in *vv.* 17, 18: whilst its less ignoble flight, the worship of the sun, moon, and stars, is forbidden in *v.* 19. The great legislator may be regarded as taking in the passage before us a complete and comprehensive survey of the various forms of idolatrous and corrupt worship practised by the surrounding Oriental nations, and as particularly and successively forbidding them every one.

18 in the air, the likeness of any thing that creepeth on the ground,
the likeness of any fish that *is* in the waters beneath the earth:
19 and lest thou [a]lift up thine eyes unto heaven, and when thou
seest the sun, and the moon, and the stars, *even* [b]all the host of
heaven, shouldest be driven to [c]worship them, and serve them,
which the LORD thy God hath [1]divided unto all nations under
20 the whole heaven. But the LORD hath taken you, and [d]brought
you forth out of the iron furnace, *even* out of Egypt, [e]to be unto
21 him a people of inheritance, as *ye are* this day. Furthermore
[f]the LORD was angry with me for your sakes, and sware that I
should not go over Jordan, and that I should not go in unto that
good land, which the LORD thy God giveth thee *for* an inheri-
22 tance: but [g]I must die in this land, [h]I must not go over
Jordan: but ye shall go over, and possess [i]that good land.
23 Take heed unto yourselves, [k]lest ye forget the covenant of the
LORD your God, which he made with you, [l]and make you a
graven image, *or* the likeness of any *thing*, which the LORD
24 thy God hath forbidden thee. For [m]the LORD thy GOD *is*
25 a consuming fire, *even* [n]a jealous God. When thou shalt
beget children, and children's children, and ye shall have remained long in the land, and [o]shall corrupt *yourselves*, and
make a graven image, *or* the likeness of any *thing*, and [p]shall
do evil in the sight of the LORD thy God, to provoke him to
26 anger: [q]I call heaven and earth to witness against you this
day, that ye shall soon utterly perish from off the land
whereunto ye go over Jordan to possess it; ye shall not pro-
27 long *your* days upon it, but shall utterly be destroyed. And the
LORD [r]shall scatter you among the nations, and ye shall be
left few in number among the heathen, whither the LORD shall
28 lead you. And [s]there ye shall serve gods, the work of men's
hands, wood and stone, [t]which neither see, nor hear, nor eat,
29 nor smell. ¶ [u]But if from thence thou shalt seek the LORD thy
God, thou shalt find *him*, if thou seek him with all thy heart
30 and with all thy soul. When thou art in tribulation, and all
these things [2]are come upon thee, [x]*even* in the latter days, if
thou [y]turn to the LORD thy God, and shalt be obedient unto his
31 voice; (for the LORD thy God *is* [z]a merciful God;) he will not
forsake thee, neither destroy thee, nor forget the covenant of
32 thy fathers which he sware unto them. For [a]ask now of the
days that are past, which were before thee, since the day that
God created man upon the earth, and *ask* [b]from the one side of
heaven unto the other, whether there hath been *any such thing*
33 as this great thing *is*, or hath been heard like it? [c]Did *ever*
people hear the voice of God speaking out of the midst of the
34 fire, as thou hast heard, and live? Or hath God assayed to go
and take him a nation from the midst of *another* nation, [d]by
temptations, [e]by signs, and by wonders, and by war, and [f]by a
mighty hand, and [g]by a stretched out arm, [h]and by great

[a] ch. 17. 3. Job 31. 26.
[b] Gen. 2. 1. 2 Kin. 17. 16. & 21. 3.
[c] Rom. 1. 25.
[d] 1 Kin. 8. 51. Jer. 11. 4.
[e] Ex. 19. 5. ch. 9. 29.
[f] Num. 20. 12.
[g] See 2 Pet. 1. 13, 14.
[h] ch. 3. 27.
[i] ch. 3. 25.
[k] ver. 9.
[l] ver. 16. Ex. 20. 4.
[m] Ex. 24. 17. Isai. 33. 14. Heb. 12. 29.
[n] Ex. 20. 5. ch. 6. 15. Isai. 42. 8.
[o] ver. 16.
[p] 2 Kin. 17. 17, &c.
[q] ch. 30. 18. Isai. 1. 2. Mic. 6. 2.
[r] ch. 28. 62. Neh. 1. 8.
[s] 1 Sam. 26. 19. Jer. 16. 13.
[t] Ps. 115. 4. Isai. 44. 9.
[u] Lev. 26. 39, 40. ch. 30. 1. 2 Chr. 15. 4. Neh. 1. 9. Isai. 55. 6. Jer. 29. 12.
[x] Gen. 49. 1. Jer. 23. 20. Hos. 3. 5.
[y] Joel 2. 12.
[z] 2 Chr. 30. 9. Neh. 9. 31. Ps. 116. 5. Jonah 4. 2.
[a] Job 8. 8.
[b] Matt. 24. 31.
[c] Ex. 24. 11.
[d] ch. 7. 19.
[e] Ex. 7. 3.
[f] Ex. 13. 3.
[g] Ex. 6. 6.
[h] ch. 26. 8.

[1] Or, *imparted*.

[2] Heb. *have found thee*, Ex. 18. 8. ch. 31. 17.

---

19. *divided*] i.e. "whose light God has distributed to the nations for their use and benefit, and which therefore being creatures ministering to man's convenience must not be worshipped as man's lords."

25-28. Cp. with these verses Lev. xxvi. 33-40, and ch. xxviii. 64 seq.

29-40. Unwilling, as it might seem, to close his discourse with words of terror, Moses makes a last appeal to them in these verses in a different strain.

34. *temptations*] Cp. vii. 18, 19, and xxix. 2, 3; not, *i.e.* the tribulations and persecutions undergone by the Israelites, but the plagues miraculously inflicted on the Egyptians.

terrors, according to all that the LORD your God did for you in
35 Egypt before your eyes? Unto thee it was shewed, that thou
mightest know that the LORD he *is* God; [i]*there is* none else
36 beside him. [k]Out of heaven he made thee to hear his voice, that
he might instruct thee: and upon earth he shewed thee his great
fire; and thou heardest his words out of the midst of the fire.
37 And because [l]he loved thy fathers, therefore he chose their seed
after them, and [m]brought thee out in his sight with his mighty
38 power out of Egypt; [n]to drive out nations from before thee
greater and mightier than thou *art*, to bring thee in, to give thee
39 their land *for* an inheritance, as *it is* this day. Know therefore this day, and consider *it* in thine heart, that [o]the LORD he *is*
God in heaven above, and upon the earth beneath: *there is* none
40 else. [p]Thou shalt keep therefore his statutes, and his commandments, which I command thee this day, [q]that it may go well
with thee, and with thy children after thee, and that thou mayest
prolong *thy* days upon the earth, which the LORD thy God giveth
41 thee, for ever. ¶ Then Moses [r]severed three cities on this side
42 Jordan toward the sunrising; [s]that the slayer might flee thither,
which should kill his neighbour unawares, and hated him not in
times past; and that fleeing unto one of these cities he might
43 live: *namely*, [t]Bezer in the wilderness, in the plain country, of
the Reubenites; and Ramoth in Gilead, of the Gadites; and
44 Golan in Bashan, of the Manassites. ¶ And this *is* the law
45 which Moses set before the children of Israel: these *are* the
testimonies, and the statutes, and the judgments, which Moses
spake unto the children of Israel, after they came forth out of
46 Egypt, on this side Jordan, [u]in the valley over against Beth-
peor, in the land of Sihon king of the Amorites, who dwelt at
Heshbon, whom Moses and the children of Israel [x]smote, after
47 they were come forth out of Egypt: and they possessed his land,
and the land [y]of Og king of Bashan, two kings of the Amorites,

[i] ch. 32. 39. 1 Sam. 2. 2. Isai. 45. 5. Mark 12. 29, 32.
[k] Ex. 19. 9. & 24. 16. Heb. 12. 18.
[l] ch. 10. 15.
[m] Ex. 13. 3.
[n] ch. 7. 1. & 9. 1, 4, 5.
[o] ver. 35. Josh. 2. 11.
[p] Lev. 22.31.
[q] ch. 5. 16. & 6. 3, 18. Eph. 6. 3.
[r] Num. 35. 6, 14.
[s] ch. 19. 4.
[t] Josh. 20. 8.
[u] ch. 3. 29.
[x] Num. 21. 24. ch. 1. 4.
[y] Num. 21. 35. ch. 3. 3, 4.

---

37. *he chose their seed after them*] Lit. "*his* seed after *him*." Speaking of the love of God to their fathers in general, Moses has more especially in mind that one of them who was called "the Friend of God" (James ii. 23).

brought thee out in his sight] Lit. "by His face:" *i.e.* by the might of His personal Presence. Cp. Ex. xxxiii. 14, where God promises "My Presence (lit. 'My face') shall go with thee."

41–43. These verses are inserted between two distinct and complete discourses for the reason to which they themselves call attention ("*Then* Moses severed three cities," &c.); *i.e.* the fact narrated took place historically after Moses spoke the one discourse and before he delivered the other. In thus severing the three cities of refuge Moses carried out a previous command of God (see marg. reff.); and so followed up his exhortations to obedience by setting a punctual example of it, as far as opportunity was given him.

43. *in the plain country*] Lit. "in the land of the *Mishor*." The word means a level tract of land; but when used (iii. 10; Josh. xiii. 9, &c.) with the article, seems to be the proper name for the smooth downs of Moab, which reach from the Jordan eastward of Jericho far into the desert of Arabia, and which form a striking contrast alike to the rugged country west of the river, and to the higher and remarkable districts belonging to Bashan northwards.

Bezer is, with little certainty, identified with Bostra, or (1 Macc. v. 36) Bosor. Golan gave the name of Gaulonitis to a district of some extent east of the sea of Galilee and north of the Hieromax; but the exact site of the city if uncertain.

44–49. These verses would be more properly assigned to the next chapter. They are intended to serve as the announcement and introduction of the address now to be commenced. *V.* 44 gives a kind of general title to the whole of the weighty address, including in fact the central part and substance of the book, which now follows in twenty-two chapters, divided into two groups: (*a*) ch. v.–xi., (*b*) ch. xii.–xxvi. The address was delivered when they had already received the first fruits of those promises (*v.* 46), the full fruition of which was to be consequent on their fulfilment of that Covenant now again about to be rehearsed to them in its leading features.

48 which *were* on this side Jordan toward the sunrising; [z]from — [z] ch. 2. 36.
Aroer, which *is* by the bank of the river Arnon, even unto — & 3. 12.
49 mount Sion, which *is* [a]Hermon, and all the plain on this side — [a] ch. 3. 9.
Jordan eastward, even unto the sea of the plain, under the — Ps. 133. 3.
[b]springs of Pisgah. — [b] ch. 3. 17.

CHAP. 5. AND Moses called all Israel, and said unto them, Hear,
O Israel, the statutes and judgments which I speak in your ears
this day, that ye may learn them, and [1]keep, and do them.
2, 3 [a]The LORD our God made a covenant with us in Horeb. The — [a] Ex. 19. 5.
LORD [b]made not this covenant with our fathers, but with us, — ch. 4. 23.
4 *even* us, who *are* all of us here alive this day. [c]The LORD talked — [b] See Matt. 13. 17.
with you face to face in the mount out of the midst of the fire, — Heb. 8. 9.
5 ([d]I stood between the LORD and you at that time, to shew you — [c] Ex. 19. 9. ch. 34. 10.
the word of the LORD: for [e]ye were afraid by reason of the fire, — [d] Ex. 20. 21.
and went not up into the mount;) saying, — Gal. 3. 19.
6 [f]I *am* the LORD thy God, which brought thee out of the land — [e] Ex. 19. 16. [f] Ex. 20. 2,
7 of Egypt, from the house of [2]bondage. [g]Thou shalt have none — &c.
other gods before me. — Lev. 26. 1. ch. 6. 4.
8 [h]Thou shalt not make thee *any* graven image, *or* any likeness — Ps. 81. 10.
of any thing that *is* in heaven above, or that *is* in the earth — [g] Ex. 20. 3. [h] Ex. 20. 4.
9 beneath, or that *is* in the waters beneath the earth: thou shalt
not bow down thyself unto them, nor serve them: for I the
LORD thy God *am* a jealous God, [i]visiting the iniquity of the — [i] Ex. 34. 7.
fathers upon the children unto the third and fourth *generation*
10 of them that hate me, [k]and shewing mercy unto thousands of — [k] Jer. 32. 18.
them that love me and keep my commandments. — Dan. 9. 4.
11 [l]Thou shalt not take the name of the LORD thy God in vain: — [l] Ex. 20. 7.
for the LORD will not hold *him* guiltless that taketh his name — Lev. 19. 12. Matt. 5. 33.
in vain.
12 [m]Keep the sabbath day to sanctify it, as the LORD thy God — [m] Ex. 20. 8.
13 hath commanded thee. [n]Six days thou shalt labour, and do all — [n] Ex. 23. 12.
14 thy work: but the seventh day *is* the [o]sabbath of the LORD thy — & 35. 2. Ez. 20. 12.
God: *in it* thou shalt not do any work, thou, nor thy son, nor — [o] Gen. 2. 2.
thy daughter, nor thy manservant, nor thy maidservant, nor — Ex. 16. 29.
thine ox, nor thine ass, nor any of thy cattle, nor thy stranger — Heb. 4. 4.
that *is* within thy gates; that thy manservant and thy maid-
15 servant may rest as well as thou. [p]And remember that thou — [p] ch. 15. 15.
wast a servant in the land of Egypt, and *that* the LORD thy God — & 16. 12. & 24. 18. 22.
brought thee out thence [q]through a mighty hand and by a — [q] ch. 4. 34.

[1] Heb. *keep to do them.* [2] Heb. *servants.*

---

48. Sion (see marg. ref. and note) must not be confounded with Zion (cp. Ps. xlviii. 2).

V. **3.** The "fathers" are, as in iv. 37, the patriarchs, Abraham, Isaac, and Jacob. With them God did indeed make a Covenant, but not the particular Covenant now in question. The responsibilities of this later Covenant, made at Sinai by the nation as a nation, attached in their day and generation to those whom Moses was addressing.

6-21. Cp. Ex. xx. and notes.

Moses here adopts the Ten Words as a ground from which he may proceed to reprove, warn, and exhort; and repeats them, with a certain measure of freedom and adaptation. Our Lord (Mark x. 19) and St. Paul (Eph. vi. 2, 3) deal similarly with the same subject. Speaker and hearers recognised, however, a statutory and authoritative form of the laws in question, which, because it was familiar to both parties, needed not to be reproduced with verbal fidelity.

12-15. The exhortation to observe the Sabbath and allow time of rest to servants (cp. Ex. xxiii. 12) is pointed by reminding the people that they too were formerly servants themselves. The bondage in Egypt and the deliverance from it are not assigned as grounds for the institution of the Sabbath, which is of far older date (see Gen. ii. 3), but rather as suggesting motives for the religious observance of that institution. The Exodus was an entrance into rest from the toils of the house of bondage, and is thought actually to have occurred on the Sabbath-day or "rest"-day.

stretched out arm: therefore the LORD thy God commanded thee
to keep the sabbath day.
16 [r]Honour thy father and thy mother, as the LORD thy God
hath commanded thee; [s]that thy days may be prolonged, and
that it may go well with thee, in the land which the LORD thy
God giveth thee.
17 [t]Thou shalt not kill.
18 [u]Neither shalt thou commit adultery.
19 [x]Neither shalt thou steal.
20 [y]Neither shalt thou bear false witness against thy neighbour.
21 [z]Neither shalt thou desire thy neighbour's wife, neither shalt
thou covet thy neighbour's house, his field, or his manservant,
or his maidservant, his ox, or his ass, or any *thing* that *is* thy
neighbour's.
22 ¶ These words the LORD spake unto all your assembly in the
mount out of the midst of the fire, of the cloud, and of the thick
darkness, with a great voice: and he added no more. And [a]he
wrote them in two tables of stone, and delivered them unto me.
23 [b]And it came to pass, when ye heard the voice out of the midst
of the darkness, (for the mountain did burn with fire,) that ye
came near unto me, *even* all the heads of your tribes, and your
24 elders; and ye said, Behold, the LORD our God hath shewed us
his glory and his greatness, and [c]we have heard his voice out of
the midst of the fire: we have seen this day that God doth talk
25 with man, and he [d]liveth. Now therefore why should we die?
For this great fire will consume us: [e]if we [1]hear the voice of the
26 LORD our God any more, then we shall die. [f]For who *is there*
of all flesh, that hath heard the voice of the living God speaking
27 out of the midst of the fire, as we *have*, and lived? Go thou
near, and hear all that the LORD our God shall say: and [g]speak
thou unto us all that the LORD our God shall speak unto thee;
28 and we will hear *it*, and do *it*. ¶ And the LORD heard the voice
of your words, when ye spake unto me; and the LORD said unto
me, I have heard the voice of the words of this people, which
they have spoken unto thee: they [h]have well said all that they
29 have spoken. [i]O that there were such an heart in them, that
they would fear me, and [k]keep all my commandments always,

[r] Ex. 20. 12. Lev. 19. 3. ch. 27. 16. Eph. 6. 2, 3. Col. 3. 20.
[s] ch. 4. 40.
[t] Ex. 20. 13. Matt. 5. 21.
[u] Ex. 20. 14. Luke 18. 20. Jam. 2. 11.
[x] Ex. 20. 15. Rom. 13. 9.
[y] Ex. 20. 16.
[z] Ex. 20. 17. Mic. 2. 2. Hab. 2. 9. Luke 12. 15. Rom. 7. 7. & 13. 9.
[a] Ex. 24. 12. & 31. 18. ch. 4. 13.
[b] Ex. 20. 18.
[c] Ex. 19. 19.
[d] ch. 4. 33. Judg. 13. 22.
[e] ch. 18. 16.
[f] ch. 4. 33.
[g] Ex. 20. 19. Heb. 12. 19.
[h] ch. 18. 17.
[i] ch. 32. 29. Ps. 81. 12. Isai. 48. 18. Matt. 23. 37. Luke 19. 42.
[k] ch. 11. 1.

[1] Heb. *add to hear.*

---

16. The blessing of general well-being here annexed to the keeping of the Fifth Commandment, is no real addition to the promise, but only an amplification of its expression.

21. The "field" is added to the list of objects specifically forbidden in the parallel passage (Ex. xx. 17). The addition seems very natural in one who was speaking with the partition of Canaan amongst his hearers directly in view.

22. *he added no more*] *i.e.* He spoke no more with the great voice directly to the people, but addressed all other communications to them through Moses. This unique and sublime phenomenon, followed up by the inscription of the Ten Words on the Two Tables by the finger of God, marks not only the holiness of God's Law in general, but the special eminence and permanent obligation of the Ten Words themselves as compared with the rest of the Mosaic enactments. The giving of the Two Tables did not take place until Moses had been on the Mount forty days and forty nights, as appears from the fuller account of ix. 9–12.

23–33. These verses contain a much fuller narrative of the events briefly described in Ex. xx. 18–21. Here it is important to call attention to the fact that it was on the entreaties of the people that Moses had taken on him to be the channel of communication between God and them. God approved (*v.* 28) the request of the people, because it shewed a feeling of their own unworthiness to enter into direct communion with God. The terrors of Sinai had done their work; they had awakened the consciousness of sin.

[l]that it might be well with them, and with their children for
30, 31 ever! Go say to them, Get you into your tents again. But
as for thee, stand thou here by me, [m]and I will speak unto thee
all the commandments, and the statutes, and the judgments,
which thou shalt teach them, that they may do *them* in the land
32 which I give them to possess it. Ye shall observe to do therefore as the LORD your God hath commanded you: [n]ye shall not
33 turn aside to the right hand or to the left. Ye shall walk in [o]all
the ways which the LORD your God hath commanded you, that
ye may live, [p]and *that it may be* well with you, and *that* ye may
prolong *your* days in the land which ye shall possess.
CHAP. 6. NOW these *are* [a]the commandments, the statutes, and the
judgments, which the LORD your God commanded to teach you,
that ye might do *them* in the land whither ye [1]go to possess it:
2 [b]that thou mightest fear the LORD thy God, to keep all his
statutes and his commandments, which I command thee, thou,
and thy son, and thy son's son, all the days of thy life; [c]and
3 that thy days may be prolonged. Hear therefore, O Israel,
and observe to do *it;* that it may be well with thee, and that ye
may increase mightily, [d]as the LORD God of thy fathers hath
promised thee, in [e]the land that floweth with milk and honey.
4, 5 ¶ [f]Hear, O Israel: The LORD our God *is* one LORD: and [g]thou
shalt love the LORD thy God [h]with all thine heart, and with all
6 thy soul, and with all thy might. And [i]these words, which I
7 command thee this day, shall be in thine heart: and [k]thou shalt
[2]teach them diligently unto thy children, and shalt talk of them
when thou sittest in thine house, and when thou walkest by the
8 way, and when thou liest down, and when thou risest up. [l]And
thou shalt bind them for a sign upon thine hand, and they shall
9 be as frontlets between thine eyes. [m]And thou shalt write them

[l] ch. 4. 40.
[m] Gal. 3. 19.
[n] ch. 17. 20. Josh. 1. 7. Prov. 4. 27.
[o] ch. 10. 12. Jer. 7. 23. Luke 1. 6.
[p] ch. 4. 40.
[a] ch. 4. 1. & 5. 31. & 12. 1.
[b] Ex. 20. 20. ch. 10. 12,13. Ps. 111. 10. Eccles. 12. 13.
[c] ch. 4. 40. Prov. 3. 1.
[d] Gen. 15. 5. & 22. 17.
[e] Ex. 3. 8.
[f] Isai. 42. 8. Mark 12. 29. John 17. 3. 1 Cor. 8. 4.
[g] ch. 10. 12.
[h] 2 Kin. 23. 25.
[i] ch. 11. 18. Ps. 37. 31. Prov. 3. 3. Isai. 51. 7.
[k] ch. 4. 9. Ps. 78. 4. Eph. 6. 4.
[l] Ex. 13. 9. ch. 11. 18.
[m] ch. 11. 20. Isai. 57. 8.

[1] Heb. *pass over*.

[2] Heb. *whet*, or, *sharpen*.

VI. Moses proceeds to set forth more particularly and to enforce the cardinal and essential doctrines of the Decalogue, the nature and attributes of God, and the fitting mode of honouring and worshipping Him. Two objects are indicated (*vv.* 2, 3), the glory of God and the welfare of man, as the grand aims he has in view.

3. *in the land*] Better, **According as the Lord the God of thy fathers promised thee a land flowing with milk and honey.**

4. These words form the beginning of what is termed the *Shema* ("Hear") in the Jewish Services, and belong to the daily Morning and Evening office. They may be termed the Creed of the Jews.

This weighty text contains far more than a mere declaration of the unity of God as against polytheism; or of the sole authority of the Revelation He had made to Israel as against other pretended manifestations of His will and attributes. It asserts that the Lord God of Israel is absolutely God, and none other. He, and He alone, is Jehovah the absolute, uncaused God; He Who had by His election of them made Himself known to Israel.

5. As there is but One God, and that God Israel's God, so Israel must love God unreservedly and entirely. The "heart" is mentioned as the seat of the understanding; the "soul" as the centre of will and personality; the "might" as representing the outgoings and energies of all the vital powers.

The New Testament itself requires no more than this total self-surrender of man's being to his maker (Matt. xxii. 37). The Gospel differs from the Law not so much in replacing an external and carnal service of God by an inward and spiritual one, as in supplying new motives and peculiar assistances for the attainment of that Divine love which was from the first and all along enjoined as "the first and great commandment."

8, 9. By adopting and regulating customary usages (*e.g.* Egyptian) Moses provides at once a check on superstition and a means of keeping the Divine Law in memory. On the "frontlets," the "phylacteries" of the New Test. (Matt. xxiii. 5), see Ex. xiii. 16 note. On *v.* 9 and xi. 20 is based the Jewish usage of the *Mezuzah*. This word denotes properly a door-post, as it is rendered here and in Ex. xii. 7, 22, xxi. 6 &c. Amongst the Jews however it is the name given to the square piece of parchment, inscribed with *vv.* 4–9 and xi. 13–21,

10 upon the posts of thy house, and on thy gates. ¶ And it shall
be, when the LORD thy God shall have brought thee into the
land which he sware unto thy fathers, to Abraham, to Isaac,
and to Jacob, to give thee great and goodly cities, [n]which thou
11 buildedst not, and houses full of all good *things*, which thou
filledst not, and wells digged, which thou diggedst not, vineyards and olive trees, which thou plantedst not; [o]when thou
12 shalt have eaten and be full; *then* beware lest thou forget the
LORD, which brought thee forth out of the land of Egypt, from
13 the house of [1]bondage. Thou shalt [p]fear the LORD thy God,
14 and serve him, and [q]shalt swear by his name. Ye shall not [r]go
after other gods, [s]of the gods of the people which *are* round
15 about you; (for [t]the LORD thy God *is* a jealous God among you)
[u]lest the anger of the LORD thy God be kindled against thee,
16 and destroy thee from off the face of the earth. ¶ [x]Ye shall not
17 tempt the LORD your God, [y]as ye tempted *him* in Massah. Ye
shall [z]diligently keep the commandments of the LORD your God,
and his testimonies, and his statutes, which he hath commanded
18 thee. And thou [a]shalt do *that which is* right and good in the
sight of the LORD: that it may be well with thee, and that thou
mayest go in and possess the good land which the LORD sware
19 unto thy fathers, [b]to cast out all thine enemies from before
20 thee, as the LORD hath spoken. ¶ *And* [c]when thy son asketh
thee [2]in time to come, saying, What *mean* the testimonies, and
the statutes, and the judgments, which the LORD our God
21 hath commanded you? Then thou shalt say unto thy son, We
were Pharaoh's bondmen in Egypt; and the LORD brought us
22 out of Egypt [d]with a mighty hand: [e]and the LORD shewed
signs and wonders, great and [3]sore, upon Egypt, upon Pharaoh,
23 and upon all his household, before our eyes: and he brought us
out from thence, that he might bring us in, to give us the land
24 which he sware unto our fathers. And the LORD commanded
us to do all these statutes, [f]to fear the LORD our God, [g]for our
good always, that [h]he might preserve us alive, as *it is* at this
25 day. And [i]it shall be our righteousness, if we observe to do all
these commandments before the LORD our God, as he hath commanded us.

[n] Josh. 24. 13. Ps. 105. 44.
[o] ch. 8. 10.
[p] ch. 10. 12, 20. & 13. 4. Matt. 4. 10.
[q] Ps. 63. 11. Isai. 45. 23. Jer. 4. 2.
[r] ch. 8. 19. Jer. 25. 6.
[s] ch. 13. 7.
[t] Ex. 20. 5. ch. 4. 24.
[u] ch. 11. 17.
[x] Luke 4. 12.
[y] Ex. 17. 2. Num. 20. 3, 4. 1 Cor. 10. 9.
[z] ch. 11. 13. Ps. 119. 4.
[a] Ex. 15. 26. ch. 12. 28. & 13. 18.
[b] Num. 33. 52, 53.
[c] Ex. 13. 14.
[d] Ex. 3. 19. & 13. 3.
[e] Ex. 7–12. Ps. 135. 9.
[f] ver. 2.
[g] ch. 10. 13. Job 35. 7. Jer. 32. 39.
[h] ch. 8. 1. Ps. 41. 2. Luke 10. 28.
[i] Lev. 18. 5. ch. 24. 13. Rom. 10. 3,5.

[1] Heb. *bondmen*, or, *servants*.
[2] Heb. *to morrow*.
[3] Heb. *evil*.

which is rolled up in a small cylinder of wood or metal, and affixed to the right-hand post of every door in a Jewish house. The pious Jew touches the Mezuzah on each occasion of passing, or kisses his finger, and says in Hebrew Ps. cxxi. 8.

10–25. The Israelites were on the point of quitting a nomad life for a fixed and settled abode in the midst of other nations; they were exchanging a condition of comparative poverty for great and goodly cities, houses and vineyards. There was therefore before them a double danger; (1) a God-forgetting worldliness, and (2) a false tolerance of the idolatries practised by those about to become their neighbours. The former error Moses strives to guard against in the verses before us; the latter in vii. 1–11.

13. The command "to swear by His Name" is not inconsistent with the Lord's injunction (Matt. v. 34), "Swear not at all." Moses refers to legal swearing, our Lord to swearing in common conversation. It is not the purpose of Moses to encourage the practice of taking oaths, but to forbid that when taken they should be taken in any other name than that of Israel's God. The oath involves an invocation of Deity, and so a solemn recognition of Him Whose Name is made use of in it. Hence it comes peculiarly within the scope of the commandment Moses is enforcing.

25. *it shall be our righteousness*] *i.e.* God will esteem us righteous and deal with us accordingly. Moses from the very beginning made the whole "righteousness of the Law" to depend entirely on a right state of the heart, in one word, on faith.

CHAP. 7. WHEN the [a]LORD thy God shall bring thee into the
land whither thou goest to possess it, and hath cast out many
nations before thee, [b]the Hittites and the Girgashites, and the
Amorites, and the Canaanites, and the Perizzites, and the Hivites,
and the Jebusites, seven nations [c]greater and mightier than thou;
2 and when the LORD thy God shall [d]deliver them before thee;
thou shalt smite them, *and* [e]utterly destroy them; [f]thou shalt
make no covenant with them, nor shew mercy unto them:
3 [g]neither shalt thou make marriages with them; thy daughter
thou shalt not give unto his son, nor his daughter shalt thou
4 take unto thy son. For they will turn away thy son from following me, that they may serve other gods: [h]so will the anger
of the LORD be kindled against you, and destroy thee suddenly.
5 But thus shall ye deal with them; ye shall [i]destroy their altars,
and break down their [1]images, and cut down their groves, and
6 burn their graven images with fire. [k]For thou *art* an holy
people unto the LORD thy God: [l]the LORD thy God hath chosen
thee to be a special people unto himself, above all people that
7 *are* upon the face of the earth. The LORD did not set his love
upon you, nor choose you, because ye were more in number than
8 any people; for ye *were* [m]the fewest of all people: but [n]because
the LORD loved you, and because he would keep [o]the oath which
he had sworn unto your fathers, [p]hath the LORD brought you
out with a mighty hand, and redeemed you out of the house of
9 bondmen, from the hand of Pharaoh king of Egypt. Know
therefore that the LORD thy God, he *is* God, [q]the faithful God,
[r]which keepeth covenant and mercy with them that love him
10 and keep his commandments to a thousand generations; and
[s]repayeth them that hate him to their face, to destroy them: [t]he
will not be slack to him that hateth him, he will repay him to
11 his face. Thou shalt therefore keep the commandments, and
the statutes, and the judgments, which I command thee this
12 day, to do them. ¶ [u]Wherefore it shall come to pass, [2]if ye
hearken to these judgments, and keep, and do them, that the
LORD thy God shall keep unto thee [x]the covenant and the mercy
13 which he sware unto thy fathers: and he will [y]love thee, and
bless thee, and multiply thee: [z]he will also bless the fruit of thy
womb, and the fruit of thy land, thy corn, and thy wine, and
thine oil, the increase of thy kine, and the flocks of thy sheep,
14 in the land which he sware unto thy fathers to give thee. Thou
shalt be blessed above all people: [a]there shall not be male
15 or female barren among you, or among your cattle. And the
LORD will take away from thee all sickness, and will put none

[a] ch. 31. 3. Ps. 44. 2.
[b] Gen. 15. 19, &c. Ex. 33. 2.
[c] ch. 4. 38. & 9. 1.
[d] ver. 23. ch. 23. 14.
[e] Lev. 27. 28, 29. ch. 20. 16. Josh. 6. 17.
[f] Ex. 23. 32. Judg. 2. 2. Josh. 2. 14.
[g] Josh. 23. 12. 1 Kin. 11. 2. Ezra 9. 2.
[h] ch. 6. 15.
[i] Ex. 23. 24.
[k] Ex. 19. 6. ch. 14. 2. Ps. 50. 5. Jer. 2. 3.
[l] Ex. 19. 5. 1 Pet. 2. 9.
[m] ch. 10. 22.
[n] ch. 10. 15.
[o] Ex. 32. 13. Ps. 105. 8. Luke 1. 55.
[p] Ex. 13. 3.
[q] Isai. 49. 7. 1 Cor. 1. 9.
[r] Ex. 20. 6. Neh. 1. 5. Dan. 9. 4.
[s] Isai. 59. 18. Nah. 1. 2.
[t] ch. 32. 35.
[u] Lev. 26. 3.
[x] Ps. 105. 8. Luke 1. 72.
[y] John 14. 21.
[z] ch. 28. 4.
[a] Ex. 23. 26.

[1] Heb. *statues*, or, *pillars*.

[2] Heb. *because*.

VII. **1–11.** See vi. 10 note.

5. *their groves*] Render, **their idols of wood**: the reference is to the wooden trunk used as a representation of Ashtaroth; see *v.* 13 and Ex. xxxiv. 13 note.

7. *the fewest of all people*] God chose to Himself Israel, when as yet but a single family, or rather a single person, Abraham; though there were already numerous nations and powerful kingdoms in the earth. Increase (i. 10, x. 22) had taken place because of the very blessing of God spoken of in *v.* 8.

10. *repayeth them that hate him to their face*] *i.e.* punishes His enemies in their own proper persons.

13. *flocks of thy sheep*] Render rather **the ewes of thy sheep.** The phrase is peculiar to Deuteronomy. The Hebrew word for ewes is the plural form of Ashtoreth the well-known name of the "goddess of the Zidonians" (1 K. xi. 5). This goddess, called by the classical writers Astarte, and identified with Venus, represented the fruitfulness of nature.

15. There seems to be here not so much a reference to the plagues inflicted miraculously by God on Egypt (cp. Ex. xv. 26),

of the [b]evil diseases of Egypt, which thou knowest, upon thee;
16 but will lay them upon all *them* that hate thee. And [c]thou
shalt consume all the people which the LORD thy God shall
deliver thee; [d]thine eye shall have no pity upon them: neither
shalt thou serve their gods; for that *will be* [e]a snare unto thee.
17 ¶ If thou shalt say in thine heart, These nations *are* more than I;
18 how can I [f]dispossess them? [g]Thou shalt not be afraid of them:
but shalt well [h]remember what the LORD thy God did unto
19 Pharaoh, and unto all Egypt; [i]the great temptations which
thine eyes saw, and the signs, and the wonders, and the mighty
hand, and the stretched out arm, whereby the LORD thy God
brought thee out: so shall the LORD thy God do unto all the
20 people of whom thou art afraid. [k]Moreover the LORD thy God
will send the hornet among them, until they that are left, and
21 hide themselves from thee, be destroyed. Thou shalt not be
affrighted at them: for the LORD thy God *is* [l]among you, [m]a
22 mighty God and terrible. [n]And the LORD thy God will [1]put
out those nations before thee by little and little: thou mayest
not consume them at once, lest the beasts of the field increase
23 upon thee. But the LORD thy God shall deliver them [2]unto
thee, and shall destroy them with a mighty destruction, until
24 they be destroyed. And [o]he shall deliver their kings into thine
hand, and thou shalt destroy their name [p]from under heaven:
[q]there shall no man be able to stand before thee, until thou have
25 destroyed them. The graven images of their gods [r]shall ye
burn with fire: thou [s]shalt not desire the silver or gold *that is*
on them, nor take *it* unto thee, lest thou be [t]snared therein: for
26 it *is* [u]an abomination to the LORD thy God. Neither shalt thou
bring an abomination into thine house, lest thou be a cursed
thing like it: *but* thou shalt utterly detest it, and thou shalt
utterly abhor it; [x]for it *is* a cursed thing.

CHAP. 8. ALL the commandments which I command thee this day
[a]shall ye observe to do, that ye may live, and multiply, and go
in and possess the land which the LORD sware unto your fathers.
2 And thou shalt remember all the way which the LORD thy God
[b]led thee these forty years in the wilderness, to humble thee, *and*
[c]to prove thee, [d]to know what *was* in thine heart, whether thou
3 wouldest keep his commandments, or no. And he humbled
thee, and [e]suffered thee to hunger, and [f]fed thee with manna,
which thou knewest not, neither did thy fathers know; that he
might make thee know that man doth [g]not live by bread only,

[b] Ex. 9. 14. ch. 28. 27. [c] ver. 2. [d] ch. 13. 8. & 19. 13. [e] Ex. 23. 33. ch. 12. 30. Ps. 106. 36. [f] Num. 33. 53. [g] ch. 31. 6. [h] Ps. 105. 5. [i] ch. 4. 34. & 29. 3. [k] Ex. 23. 28. [l] Num. 11. 20. Josh. 3. 10. [m] ch. 10. 17. Neh. 1. 5. [n] Ex. 23. 59, 30. [o] Josh. 10. 24, 25, 42. [p] Ex. 17. 14. ch. 9. 14. [q] ch. 11. 25. Josh. 1. 5. [r] Ex. 32. 20. ch. 12. 3. 1 Chr. 14. 12. [s] Josh. 7. 1. [t] Judg. 8. 27. Zeph. 1. 3. [u] ch. 17. 1. [x] Lev. 27. 28. ch 13. 17. Josh. 6. 17.

[a] ch. 4. 1. [b] ch. 1. 3. Ps. 136. 16. [c] Ex. 16. 4. ch. 13. 3. [d] 2 Chr. 32. 31. [e] Ex. 16. 2. [f] Ex. 16. 12. [g] Matt. 4. 4. Luke 4. 4.

[1] Heb. *pluck off.* [2] Heb. *before thy face*, ver. 2.

---

as to the terrible diseases with which, above other countries, Egypt was infested. Cp. xxviii. 27, 35. It is not without significance that Egypt, which represents in Scripture the world as contrasted with the Church, should thus above other lands lie under the power of disease and death.

25. *the silver or gold that is on them*] The silver and gold with which the statues of the gods were overlaid. St. Paul is probably alluding to this command in Rom. ii. 22, and his accusation of the Jew thus shows that the prohibition of the text was very necessary.

lest thou be snared] As by the rich ephod made by Gideon: cp. marg. ref.

VIII. **3.** *but by every* word *that proceedeth out of the mouth of the* LORD] Lit. "every outgoing of the mouth of the Lord." Cp. xxix. 5, 6. The term "word" is inserted by A. V. after the LXX., which is followed by St. Matt. and St. Luke (see marg. reff.). On the means of subsistence available to the people during the wandering, see Num. xx. 1 note. The lesson was taught, that it is not nature which nourishes man, but God the Creator by and through nature: and generally that God is not tied to the particular channels ("bread only," *i.e.* the ordinary means of earthly sustenance) through which He is usually pleased to work.

but by every *word* that proceedeth out of the mouth of the LORD
4 doth man live. [h]Thy raiment waxed not old upon thee, neither
5 did thy foot swell, these forty years. [i]Thou shalt also consider
in thine heart, that, as a man chasteneth his son, *so* the LORD
6 thy God chasteneth thee. Therefore thou shalt keep the commandments of the LORD thy God, [k]to walk in his ways, and to
7 fear him. For the LORD thy God bringeth thee into a good
land, [l]a land of brooks of water, of fountains and depths that
8 spring out of valleys and hills; a land of wheat, and barley, and
vines, and fig trees, and pomegranates; a land [1]of oil olive, and
9 honey; a land wherein thou shalt eat bread without scarceness,
thou shalt not lack any *thing* in it; a land [m]whose stones *are*
10 iron, and out of whose hills thou mayest dig brass. ¶ [n]When
thou hast eaten and art full, then thou shalt bless the LORD thy
11 God for the good land which he hath given thee. Beware that
thou forget not the LORD thy God, in not keeping his commandments, and his judgments, and his statutes, which I command
12 thee this day: [o]lest *when* thou hast eaten and art full, and hast
13 built goodly houses, and dwelt *therein;* and *when* thy herds and
thy flocks multiply, and thy silver and thy gold is multiplied,
14 and all that thou hast is multiplied; [p]then thine heart be lifted
up, and thou [q]forget the LORD thy God, which brought thee
15 forth out of the land of Egypt, from the house of bondage; who
[r]led thee through that great and terrible wilderness, [s]*wherein*
were fiery serpents, and scorpions, and drought, where *there was*
no water; [t]who brought thee forth water out of the rock of
16 flint; who fed thee in the wilderness with [u]manna, which thy
fathers knew not, that he might humble thee, and that he might
17 prove thee, [x]to do thee good at thy latter end; [y]and thou say in
thine heart, My power and the might of *mine* hand hath gotten
18 me this wealth. But thou shalt remember the LORD thy God:

[h] ch. 29. 5. Neh. 9. 21.
[i] 2 Sam. 7, 14. Ps. 89. 32. Prov. 3. 12. Heb. 12. 5. Rev. 3. 19.
[k] ch. 5. 33.
[l] ch. 11. 10.
[m] ch. 33. 25.
[n] ch. 6. 11.
[o] ch. 28. 47. Prov. 30. 9. Hos. 13. 6.
[p] 1 Cor. 4. 7.
[q] Ps. 106. 21.
[r] Isai. 63. 12, 13, 14. Jer. 2. 6.
[s] Num. 21. 6. Hos. 13. 5.
[t] Num. 20. 11. Ps. 78. 15.
[u] ver. 3.
[x] Jer. 24. 5. Heb. 12. 11.
[y] ch. 9. 4. 1 Cor. 4. 7.

[1] Heb. *of olive tree of oil.*

---

4. They had clothes, it would seem, in abundance (cp. Ex. xii. 34, 35) at the beginning of the forty years; and during those years they had many sheep and oxen, and so must have had much material for clothing always at command. No doubt also they carried on a traffic in these, as in other commodities, with the Moabites and the nomadic tribes of the desert. Such ordinary supplies must not be shut out of consideration, even if they were on occasions supplemented by extraordinary providences of God, as was undoubtedly the case with their food.

7–9. See Ex. iii. 8 note, and the contrast expressed in xi. 10, 11, between Palestine and Egypt.

The physical characteristics and advantages of a country like Palestine must have been quite strange to Israel at the time Moses was speaking: cp. iii. 25 note. To have praised the fertility and excellence of the Promised Land at an earlier period would have increased the murmurings and impatience of the people at being detained in the wilderness: whereas now it encouraged them to encounter with more cheerfulness the opposition they would meet from the inhabitants of Canaan.

8. *vines*] The abundance of wine in Syria and Palestine is dwelt upon in the Egyptian records of the campaigns of Thotmosis III. In Egypt itself but little wine is produced. The production of wine has in later times gradually ceased in Palestine.

9. For *brass* read **copper** (Gen. iv. 22 note); and compare the description of mining operations in Job xxviii. 1–11. Mining does not seem to have been extensively carried on by the Jews, though it certainly was by the Canaanitish peoples displaced by them. Traces of iron and copper works have been discovered by modern travellers in Lebanon and many parts of the country; *e.g.* the district of Argob (see iii. 4 notes) contains iron-stone in abundance.

15. Render: "Who brought thee through that great and terrible wilderness, the fiery serpent and the scorpion, and the dry land where are no waters." On the fiery serpents see Num. xxi. 6 note.

16. *to do thee good at thy latter end*] This is presented as the result of God's dealings.

[z] Prov. 10. 22.
Hos. 2. 8.
[a] ch. 7. 8.
[b] ch. 4. 26. & 30. 18.
[c] Dan. 9. 11, 12.
[a] ch. 11. 31. Josh. 3. 16.
[b] ch. 4. 38.
[c] ch. 1. 28.
[d] Num. 13. 22, 28, 32.
[e] ch. 31. 3. Josh. 3. 11.
[f] ch. 4. 24. Heb. 12. 29.
[g] ch. 7. 23.
[h] Ex. 23. 31. ch. 7. 24.
[i] ch. 8. 17. Rom. 11. 6, 20. 1 Cor. 4. 4.
[k] Gen. 15. 16. Lev. 18. 24. ch. 18. 12.
[l] Titus 3. 5.
[m] Gen. 12. 7. & reff.
[n] ver. 13. Ex. 32. 9.
[o] Ex. 14. 11. Num. 11. 4. & 20. 2. ch. 31. 27.
[p] Ex. 32. 4. Ps. 106. 19.
[q] Ex. 24. 12, 15.
[r] Ex. 24. 18. & 34. 28.
[s] Ex. 31. 18.
[t] Ex. 19. 17. & 20. 1. ch. 4. 10. & 10. 4. & 18. 16.

[z]for *it is* he that giveth thee power to get wealth, [a]that he may
establish his covenant which he sware unto thy fathers, as *it is*
19 this day. ¶ And it shall be, if thou do at all forget the LORD
thy God, and walk after other gods, and serve them, and worship them, [b]I testify against you this day that ye shall surely
20 perish. As the nations which the LORD destroyeth before your
face, [c]so shall ye perish; because ye would not be obedient unto
the voice of the LORD your God.

CHAP. 9. HEAR, O Israel: Thou *art* to [a]pass over Jordan this day,
to go in to possess nations [b]greater and mightier than thyself,
2 cities great and [c]fenced up to heaven, a people great and tall,
[d]the children of the Anakims, whom thou knowest, and *of whom*
thou hast heard *say*, Who can stand before the children of Anak!
3 Understand therefore this day, that the LORD thy God *is* he
which [e]goeth over before thee; *as* a [f]consuming fire [g]he shall
destroy them, and he shall bring them down before thy face:
[h]so shalt thou drive them out, and destroy them quickly, as the
4 LORD hath said unto thee. ¶ [i]Speak not thou in thine heart,
after that the LORD thy God hath cast them out from before
thee, saying, For my righteousness the LORD hath brought me
in to possess this land: but [k]for the wickedness of these nations
5 the LORD doth drive them out from before thee. [l]Not for thy
righteousness, or for the uprightness of thine heart, dost thou
go to possess their land: but for the wickedness of these nations
the LORD thy God doth drive them out from before thee, and
that he may perform [m]the word which the LORD sware unto
6 thy fathers, Abraham, Isaac, and Jacob. Understand therefore,
that the LORD thy God giveth thee not this good land to
possess it for thy righteousness; for thou *art* [n]a stiffnecked
7 people. ¶ Remember, *and* forget not, how thou provokedst the
LORD thy God to wrath in the wilderness: [o]from the day that
thou didst depart out of the land of Egypt, until ye came unto
8 this place, ye have been rebellious against the LORD. Also [p]in
Horeb ye provoked the LORD to wrath, so that the LORD was
9 angry with you to have destroyed you. [q]When I was gone up
into the mount to receive the tables of stone, *even* the tables of
the covenant which the LORD made with you, then [r]I abode in
the mount forty days and forty nights, I neither did eat bread
10 nor drink water: [s]and the LORD delivered unto me two tables of
stone written with the finger of God; and on them *was written*
according to all the words, which the LORD spake with you
in the mount out of the midst of the fire [t]in the day of the
11 assembly. And it came to pass at the end of forty days and

---

IX. **1–29.** The lesson of this chapter is exactly that of Eph. ii. 8, "By grace are ye saved through faith; and that not of yourselves; it is the gift of God: not of works, lest any man should boast."

In referring to their several rebellions Moses here, as elsewhere, has regard not so much to the order of time as to that of subject. (Cp. i. 9–15 note.) Such reasons as convenience and fitness to his argument sufficiently explain the variations observable when the statements of this chapter are minutely compared with those of Ex. xxxii.–xxxiv. In these variations we have simply such treatment of facts as is usual and warrantable between parties personally acquainted with the matters.

3. *so shalt thou drive them out, and destroy them quickly*] This is not inconsistent with vii. 22, in which instant annihilation is not to be expected for the reasons assigned. Here Moses urges the people to trust in God's covenanted aid; since He would then make no delay in so destroying the nations attacked by them as to put them into enjoyment of the promises, and in doing so as fast as was for the well-being of Israel itself.

8. *Also in Horeb*] Rather, "even in Horeb." The time and circumstances made the apostasy at Horeb particularly inexcusable.

forty nights, *that* the LORD gave me the two tables of stone, *even*
12 the tables of the covenant. And the LORD said unto me, [u]Arise,
get thee down quickly from hence; for thy people which thou
hast brought forth out of Egypt have corrupted *themselves;* they
are [x]quickly turned aside out of the way which I commanded
13 them; they have made them a molten image. ¶ Furthermore
[y]the LORD spake unto me, saying, I have seen this people, and,
14 behold, [z]it *is* a stiffnecked people: [a]let me alone, that I may
destroy them, and [b]blot out their name from under heaven: [c]and
I will make of thee a nation mightier and greater than they.
15 [d]So I turned and came down from the mount, and [e]the mount
burned with fire: and the two tables of the covenant *were* in my
16 two hands. And [f]I looked, and, behold, ye had sinned against
the LORD your God, *and* had made you a molten calf: ye had
turned aside quickly out of the way which the LORD had
17 commanded you. And I took the two tables, and cast them
18 out of my two hands, and brake them before your eyes. And
I [g]fell down before the LORD, as at the first, forty days and
forty nights: I did neither eat bread, nor drink water, because
of all your sins which ye sinned, in doing wickedly in the sight
19 of the LORD, to provoke him to anger. [h]For I was afraid of
the anger and hot displeasure, wherewith the LORD was wroth
against you to destroy you. [i]But the LORD hearkened unto me
20 at that time also. And the LORD was very angry with Aaron to
have destroyed him: and I prayed for Aaron also the same time.
21 And [k]I took your sin, the calf which ye had made, and burnt
it with fire, and stamped it, *and* ground *it* very small, *even*
until it was as small as dust: and I cast the dust thereof into the
22 brook that descended out of the mount. And at [l]Taberah, and
at [m]Massah, and at [n]Kibroth-hattaavah, ye provoked the LORD
23 to wrath. Likewise [o]when the LORD sent you from Kadesh-
barnea, saying, Go up and possess the land which I have given
you; then ye rebelled against the commandment of the LORD
your God, and [p]ye believed him not, nor hearkened to his voice.
24 [q]Ye have been rebellious against the LORD from the day that I
25 knew you. [r]Thus I fell down before the LORD forty days and
forty nights, as I fell down *at the first;* because the LORD had
26 said he would destroy you. [s]I prayed therefore unto the LORD,
and said, O Lord GOD, destroy not thy people and thine inheritance, which thou hast redeemed through thy greatness,

[u] Ex. 32. 7.
[x] ch. 31. 29. Judg. 2. 17.
[y] Ex. 32. 9.
[z] ver. 6. ch. 10. 16. & 31. 27. 2 Kin. 17. 14.
[a] Ex. 32. 10.
[b] ch. 29. 20. Ps. 9. 5. & 109. 13.
[c] Num. 14. 12.
[d] Ex. 32. 15.
[e] Ex. 19. 18. ch. 4. 11. & 5. 23.
[f] Ex. 32. 19.
[g] Ex. 34. 28. Ps. 106. 23.
[h] Ex. 32. 10, 11.
[i] Ex. 32. 14. & 33. 17. ch. 10. 10. Ps. 106. 23.
[k] Ex. 32. 20. Isai. 31. 7.
[l] Num. 11. 1, 3, 5.
[m] Ex. 17. 7.
[n] Num. 11. 4, 34.
[o] Num. 13. 3. & 14. 1.
[p] Ps. 106. 24, 25.
[q] ch. 31. 27.
[r] ver. 18.
[s] Ex. 32. 11, &c.

---

18. *I fell down before the* LORD, *as at the first*] Moses interceded for the people before he came down from the mountain the first time (Ex. xxxii. 11–13). This intercession is only briefly alluded to in this verse. Afterwards he spent another forty days on the mountain in fasting and prayer to obtain a complete restitution of the Covenant (Ex. xxxiv. 28). It is this second forty days, and the intercession of Moses made therein (cp. Ex. xxxiv. 9), that is more particularly brought forward here and in *vv.* 25–29.

20. Israel could not even boast that its heads and representatives continued faithful. Aaron had been already designated for the High-priestly functions; but he fell away with the rest of the people. It was due therefore solely to the grace of God and the intercession of Moses that Aaron himself and his promised priesthood with him were not cut off; just as at a later time, when Aaron had actually to die for a new sin Israel owed it still to the same causes that Eleazar was substituted and the High-priesthood perpetuated (cp. x. 6; Num. xx. 24–26).

22. See marg. ref. Taberah was the name of a spot in or near the station of Kibroth-hattaavah, and accordingly is not named in the list of encampments given in Num. xxxiii. 16. The separate mention of the two is however here appropriate; for each place and each name was a memorial of an act of rebellion. The instances in this and the next verse are not given in order of occurrence. The speaker for his own purposes advances from the slighter to the more heinous proofs of guilt.

[t] Gen. 41. 57. 1 Sam. 14. 25.
[u] Ex. 32. 12. Num. 14. 16.
[x] ch. 4. 20. 1 Kin. 8. 51. Neh. 1. 10. Ps. 95. 7.
[a] Ex. 34. 1, 2.
[b] Ex. 25. 10.
[c] Ex. 25. 16, 21.
[d] Ex. 25. 5, 10. & 37. 1.
[e] Ex. 34. 4.
[f] Ex. 34. 28.
[g] Ex. 20. 1.
[h] Ex. 19. 17. ch. 9. 10. & 18. 16.
[i] Ex. 34. 29.
[k] Ex. 40. 20.
[l] 1 Kin. 8. 9.
[m] Num. 33. 31.
[n] Num. 33. 30.
[o] Num. 20. 28. & 33. 38.
[p] Num. 33. 32, 33.
[q] Num. 3. 6.
[r] Num. 4. 15.
[s] ch. 18. 5.
[t] Lev. 9. 22. Num. 6. 23. ch. 21. 5.
[u] Num. 18. 20, 24. ch. 18. 1, 2. Ez. 44. 28.
[x] Ex. 34. 28. ch. 9. 18.
[y] Ex. 32. 14. & 33. 17. ch. 9. 19.

which thou hast brought forth out of Egypt with a mighty
27 hand. Remember thy servants, Abraham, Isaac, and Jacob;
look not unto the stubbornness of this people, nor to their wicked-
28 ness, nor to their sin: lest [t]the land whence thou broughtest us
out say, [u]Because the LORD was not able to bring them into the
land which he promised them, and because he hated them, he
29 hath brought them out to slay them in the wilderness. [x]Yet
they *are* thy people and thine inheritance, which thou broughtest out by thy mighty power and by thy stretched out arm.
CHAP. 10. AT that time the LORD said unto me, [a]Hew thee two
tables of stone like unto the first, and come up unto me into the
2 mount, and [b]make thee an ark of wood. And I will write on
the tables the words that were in the first tables which thou
3 brakest, and [c]thou shalt put them in the ark. And I made an
ark *of* [d]shittim wood, and [e]hewed two tables of stone like unto
the first, and went up into the mount, having the two tables in
4 mine hand. And [f]he wrote on the tables, according to the first
writing, the ten [1]commandments, [g]which the LORD spake unto
you in the mount out of the midst of the fire [h]in the day of the
5 assembly: and the LORD gave them unto me. And I turned
myself and [i]came down from the mount, and [k]put the tables in
the ark which I had made; [l]and there they be, as the LORD
6 commanded me. ¶ And the children of Israel took their journey
from Beeroth [m]of the children of Jaakan to [n]Mosera: [o]there
Aaron died, and there he was buried; and Eleazar his son
7 ministered in the priest's office in his stead. [p]From thence they
journeyed unto Gudgodah; and from Gudgodah to Jotbath, a
8 land of rivers of waters. ¶ At that time [q]the LORD separated
the tribe of Levi, [r]to bear the ark of the covenant of the LORD,
[s]to stand before the LORD to minister unto him, and [t]to bless in
9 his name, unto this day. [u]Wherefore Levi hath no part nor inheritance with his brethren; the LORD *is* his inheritance, accord-
10 ing as the LORD thy God promised him. And [x]I stayed in the
mount, according to the [2]first time, forty days and forty nights;
and [y]the LORD hearkened unto me at that time also, *and* the

[1] Heb. *words*. [2] Or, *former days*.

X. **1–11.** These verses are closely connected with the preceding chapter, and state very briefly the results of the intercession of Moses recorded in ix. 25–29. The people are reminded that all their blessings and privileges, forfeited by apostasy as soon as bestowed, were only now their own by a new and most unmerited act of grace on the part of God, won from Him by the self-sacrificing mediation of Moses himself (*v.* 10).

1–5. The order for making the Ark and Tabernacle was evidently given before the apostasy of the people (Ex. xxv. seq.); but the tables were not put in the Ark until the completion and dedication of the Tabernacle (Ex. xl.). But here as elsewhere (cp. ix. 1 note) Moses connects transactions closely related to each other and to his purpose without regard to the order of occurrence.

6. *there Aaron died*] *i.e.* whilst the people were encamped in Mosera or Moseroth. In xxxii. 50 as well as in Num. xx. 25 seq. Mount Hor is assigned as the place of Aaron's death. It is plain then that Moserah was in the neighbourhood of Mount Hor. The appointment of Eleazar to minister in place of Aaron, is referred to as a proof of the completeness and fulness of the reconciliation effected between God and the people by Moses. Though Aaron was sentenced to die in the wilderness for his sin at Meribah, yet God provided for the perpetuation of the High-priesthood, so that the people should not suffer. Cp. ix. 20 and note.

8. *At that time*] *i.e.* that of the encampment at Sinai, as the words also import in *v.* 1. Throughout the passage the time of the important events at Sinai is kept in view; it is reverted to as each incident is brought forward by Moses, alluded to sufficiently for his purpose, and dismissed.

Moses is evidently here speaking of the election by God of the tribe of Levi at large, priests and others also, for His own service.

11 LORD would not destroy thee. [z]And the LORD said unto me,
Arise, [1]take *thy* journey before the people, that they may go in
and possess the land, which I sware unto their fathers to give unto
12 them. ¶ And now, Israel, [a]what doth the LORD thy God require
of thee, but [b]to fear the LORD thy God, [c]to walk in all his ways,
and [d]to love him, and to serve the LORD thy God with all thy
13 heart and with all thy soul, to keep the commandments of the
LORD, and his statutes, which I command thee this day [e]for thy
14 good? Behold, [f]the heaven and the heaven of heavens *is* the
15 LORD's thy God, [g]the earth *also*, with all that therein *is*. [h]Only
the LORD had a delight in thy fathers to love them, and he chose
their seed after them, *even* you above all people, as *it is* this day.
16 Circumcise therefore [i]the foreskin of your heart, and be no more
17 [k]stiffnecked. For the LORD your God *is* [l]God of gods, and
[m]Lord of lords, a great God, [n]a mighty, and a terrible, which
18 [o]regardeth not persons, nor taketh reward: [p]he doth execute
the judgment of the fatherless and widow, and loveth the
19 stranger, in giving him food and raiment. [q]Love ye therefore
20 the stranger: for ye were strangers in the land of Egypt. [r]Thou
shalt fear the LORD thy God; him shalt thou serve, and to him
21 shalt thou [s]cleave, [t]and swear by his name. [u]He *is* thy praise,
and he *is* thy God, [x]that hath done for thee these great and
22 terrible things, which thine eyes have seen. Thy fathers went
down into Egypt [y]with threescore and ten persons; and now
the LORD thy God hath made thee [z]as the stars of heaven for
multitude.

CHAP. 11. THEREFORE thou shalt [a]love the LORD thy God, and
[b]keep his charge, and his statutes, and his judgments, and his

[z] Ex. 32. 34. & 33. 1.
[a] Mic. 6. 8.
[b] ch. 6. 13.
[c] ch. 5. 33.
[d] ch. 6. 5. Matt. 22. 37.
[e] ch. 6. 24.
[f] 1 Kin. 8.27. Ps. 115. 16.
[g] Gen. 14. 19. Ex. 19. 5. Ps. 24. 1.
[h] ch. 4. 37.
[i] ch. 30. 6. Jer. 4. 4. Rom. 2. 28.
[k] ch. 9. 6, 13.
[l] Ps. 136. 2. Dan. 2. 47.
[m] Rev. 17. 14.
[n] ch. 7. 21.
[o] Job 34. 19. Acts 10. 34.
[p] Ps. 68. 5. & 146. 9.
[q] Lev. 19. 33.
[r] Matt. 4. 10.
[s] ch. 11. 22.
[t] Ps. 63. 11.
[u] Ex. 15. 2.
[x] Ps. 106. 21.
[y] Ex. 1. 5.
[z] Gen. 15. 5.
[a] ch. 10. 12.
[b] Zech. 3. 7.

[1] Heb. *go in journey*.

---

12. seq. After these emphatic warnings against self-righteousness the principal topic is resumed from ch. vi., and this division of the discourse is drawn to a conclusion in the next two chapters by a series of direct and positive exhortations to a careful fulfilment of the duties prescribed in the first two of the Ten "Words."

12. *what doth the* LORD *thy God require*, &c.] A noteworthy demand. God has in the Mosaic law positively commanded many th ngs. These however relate to external observances, which if need be can bə enforced. But love and veneration cannot be enforced, even by God himself. They must be spontaneous. Hence, even under the law of ordinances where so much was peremptorily laid down, and omnipotence was ready to compel obedience, those sentiments, which are the spirit and life of the whole, have to be, as they here are, invited and solicited.

16. On Circumcision see Gen. xvii. 10. This verse points to the spiritual import of Circumcision. Man is by nature "very far gone from original righteousness," and in a state of enmity to God; by Circumcision, as the sacrament of admission to the privileges of the chosen people, this opposition must be taken away ere man could enter into covenant with God. It was through the flesh that man first sinned; as it is also in the flesh, its functions, lusts, &c., that man's rebellion against God chiefly manifests itself still. It was fitting therefore that the symbol which should denote the removal of this estrangement from God should be wrought in the body. Moses then fitly follows up the command "to circumcise the heart," with the warning "to be no more stiffnecked." His meaning is that they should lay aside that obduracy and perverseness towards God for which he had been reproving them, which had led them into so many transgressions of the Covenant and revolts from God, and which was especially the very contrary of that love and fear of God required by the first two of the Ten Commandments. The language associated with Circumcision in the Bible distinguishes the use made of this rite in the Jewish religion from that found amongst certain heathen nations. Circumcision was practised by some of them as a religious rite, designed (*e.g.*) to appease the deity of death supposed to delight in human suffering; but not by any, the Egyptians probably excepted, at all in the Jewish sense and meaning.

The grounds on which Circumcision was imposed as essential by the Law are the same as those on which Baptism is required in the Gospel. The latter in the New Testament is strictly analogous to the former under the Old; cp. Col. ii. 11, 12.

2 commandments, alway. And know ye this day: for *I speak*
not with your children which have not known, and which have
not seen [c]the chastisement of the LORD your God, [d]his greatness,
3 [e]his mighty hand, and his stretched out arm, [f]and his miracles,
and his acts, which he did in the midst of Egypt unto Pharaoh
4 the king of Egypt, and unto all his land; and what he did unto
the army of Egypt, unto their horses, and to their chariots;
[g]how he made the water of the Red sea to overflow them as they
pursued after you, and *how* the LORD hath destroyed them unto
5 this day; and what he did unto you in the wilderness, until ye
6 came into this place; and [h]what he did unto Dathan and Abiram,
the sons of Eliab, the son of Reuben: how the earth opened her
mouth, and swallowed them up, and their households, and their
tents, and all the [1]substance that [2]*was* in their possession, in the
7 midst of all Israel: but [i]your eyes have seen all the great acts
8 of the LORD which he did. Therefore shall ye keep all the commandments which I command you this day, that ye may [k]be
strong, and go in and possess the land, whither ye go to possess
9 it; and [l]that ye may prolong *your* days in the land, [m]which
the LORD sware unto your fathers to give unto them and to their
10 seed, [n]a land that floweth with milk and honey. ¶ For the land,
whither thou goest in to possess it, *is* not as the land of Egypt,
from whence ye came out, [o]where thou sowedst thy seed, and
11 wateredst *it* with thy foot, as a garden of herbs: [p]but the land,
whither ye go to possess it, *is* a land of hills and valleys, *and*
12 drinketh water of the rain of heaven: a land which the LORD
thy God [3]careth for: [q]the eyes of the LORD thy God *are* always
upon it, from the beginning of the year even unto the end of the

[c] ch. 8. 5.
[d] ch. 5. 24.
[e] ch. 7. 19.
[f] Ps. 78. 12. & 135. 9.
[g] Ex. 14. 27. 28. & 15. 9. Ps. 106. 11.
[h] Num. 16. 31. & 27. 3. Ps. 106. 17.
[i] ch. 5. 3. & 7. 19.
[k] Josh. 1. 6, 7.
[l] ch. 4. 40. & 5. 16. Prov. 10. 27.
[m] ch. 9. 5.
[n] Ex. 3. 8.
[o] Zech. 14. 18.
[p] ch. 8. 7.
[q] 1 Kin. 9. 3.

[1] Or, *living substance which followed them.* [2] Heb. was *at their feet.* [3] Heb. *seeketh.*

XI. 2. *And know*, &c.] Render: **And own ye this day (for I have not to do with your children which have not known and which have not seen) the chastisement of the Lord, his greatness**, &c.

The "chastisement" consisted in the many mighty acts, both of punishment and mercy, through which God had guided them from Egypt to the borders of the Promised Land.

6. See margin. Literally, "every living thing at their feet." The expression does not mean their goods, which would be included in their "households and tents," but their followers (Num. xvi. 32).

10. Another motive for fidelity is added, viz. the entire dependence of the Promised Land upon God for its fertility. It was "a land flowing with milk and honey;" yet this its richness was not, as was that of Egypt, the reward of human skill and labour, but was, on the contrary, the gift of God simply and entirely; the effect of "the former and the latter rains" sent by Him. The spiritual significance of these and many other such peculiarities of the Promised Land must not be overlooked.

Egypt and Canaan are distinguished in this and the following verses, by certain of their most remarkable physical traits. Canaan as a mountainous country (cp. iii. 25 note) was well watered, but by the rains of heaven, on which it absolutely depended for its crops. Artificial irrigation could do nothing to remedy this dependence. Hence it was a land on which, so long as God's people were faithful and consequently prosperous, "the eyes of God" would always be: *i.e.* He would supply at each successive season (cp. *vv.* 14, 15) the useful conditions of productiveness. But Egypt, fit emblem here as elsewhere of the world of nature in distinction from the world of grace, though of course deriving its all ultimately from the Giver of all good things, yet directly and immediately owed its riches and plenty to human ingenuity and capital. It enjoyed no rain worth speaking of, but drew its water supply from the annual overflowing of the Nile. This only lasts about a hundred days; but is rendered available for agricultural purposes throughout the year by an elaborate and costly system of tanks, canals, forcing machines, &c. To these mechanical appliances allusion is made in *v.* 10. The inhabitants of Egypt probably watered "with the foot" in two ways, viz. by means of tread-wheels working sets of pumps, and by means of artificial channels connected with reservoirs, and opened, turned, or closed by the feet. Both methods are still in use in Egypt.

13 year. ¶And it shall come to pass, if ye shall hearken [r]dili-
gently unto my commandments which I command you this day,
[s]to love the LORD your God, and to serve him with all your heart
14 and with all your soul, that [t]I will give *you* the rain of your
land in his due season, [u]the first rain and the latter rain, that
thou mayest gather in thy corn, and thy wine, and thine oil.
15 [x]And I will [1]send grass in thy fields for thy cattle, that thou
16 mayest [y]eat and be full. Take heed to yourselves, [z]that your
heart be not deceived, and ye turn aside, and [a]serve other gods,
17 and worship them; and *then* [b]the LORD's wrath be kindled
against you, and he [c]shut up the heaven, that there be no rain,
and that the land yield not her fruit; and *lest* [d]ye perish quickly
18 from off the good land which the LORD giveth you. ¶Therefore
[e]shall ye lay up these my words in your heart and in your soul,
and [f]bind them for a sign upon your hand, that they may be as
19 frontlets between your eyes. [g]And ye shall teach them your
children, speaking of them when thou sittest in thine house, and
when thou walkest by the way, when thou liest down, and when
20 thou risest up. [h]And thou shalt write them upon the door posts of
21 thine house, and upon thy gates: that [i]your days may be multiplied, and the days of your children, in the land which the
LORD sware unto your fathers to give them, [k]as the days of
22 heaven upon the earth. ¶For if [l]ye shall diligently keep all
these commandments which I command you, to do them, to love
the LORD your God, to walk in all his ways, and [m]to cleave
23 unto him; then will the LORD [n]drive out all these nations from
before you, and ye shall [o]possess greater nations and mightier
24 than yourselves. [p]Every place whereon the soles of your feet
shall tread shall be your's: [q]from the wilderness and Lebanon,
from the river, the river Euphrates, even unto the uttermost
25 sea shall your coast be. [r]There shall no man be able to stand
before you: *for* the LORD your God shall [s]lay the fear of you
and the dread of you upon all the land that ye shall tread upon,
26 [t]as he hath said unto you. ¶[u]Behold, I set before you this day
27 a blessing and a curse; [x]a blessing, if ye obey the commandments of the LORD your God, which I command you this day:
28 and a [y]curse, if ye will not obey the commandments of the LORD
your God, but turn aside out of the way which I command you
this day, to go after other gods, which ye have not known.
29 And it shall come to pass, when the LORD thy God hath brought
thee in unto the land whither thou goest to possess it, that thou
shalt put [z]the blessing upon mount Gerizim, and the curse upon

[r] ver. 22. ch. 6. 17.
[s] ch. 10. 12.
[t] Lev. 26. 4. ch. 28. 12.
[u] Joel 2. 23. Jam. 5. 7.
[x] Ps. 104. 14.
[y] ch. 6. 11. Joel 2. 19.
[z] ch. 29. 18. Job 31. 27.
[a] ch. 8. 19. & 30. 17.
[b] ch. 6. 15.
[c] 1 Kin. 8. 35. 2 Chr. 6. 26.
[d] ch. 4. 26. & 30. 18. Josh. 23. 13, 15, 16.
[e] ch. 6. 6. & 32. 46.
[f] ch. 6. 8.
[g] ch. 4. 9, 10. & 6. 7.
[h] ch. 6. 9.
[i] ch. 4. 40. Prov. 3. 2.
[k] Ps. 72. 5. & 89. 29.
[l] ver. 13. ch. 6. 17.
[m] ch. 10. 20. & 30. 20.
[n] ch. 4. 38. & 9. 5.
[o] ch. 9. 1.
[p] Josh. 1. 3. & 14. 9.
[q] Gen. 15. 18. Ex. 23. 31. Num. 34. 3.
[r] ch. 7. 24.
[s] ch. 2. 25.
[t] Ex. 23. 27.
[u] ch. 30. 1, 15, 19.
[x] ch. 28. 2.
[y] ch. 28. 15.
[z] ch. 27. 12. Josh. 8. 33.

[1] Heb. *give*.

---

14. *the first rain and the latter rain*] The former is the proper term for the autumn rain, falling about the time of sowing, and which may be named "the former," as occurring in the early part of the Hebrew civil year, viz. in October and November. The other word is applied to the spring rain, which falls in March and April, because it fits the earth for the ingathering of harvest. Between these two wet periods, and except them, there was little or no rain in Canaan.

21. The sense is: "Keep the covenant faithfully, and so shall your own and your children's days be multiplied as long as the heaven covers the earth." The promise of Canaan to Israel was thus a *perpetual* promise, but also a *conditional* one.

29. *thou shalt put the blessing upon mount Gerizim*] Lit. thou shalt *give, i.e.* give utterance to it. On the ceremony see xxvii. 14 seq.

Mount Gerizim, barren like Ebal, was probably selected as the hill of benediction because it was the southernmost of the two, the south being the region, according to Hebrew ideas, of light, and so of life and blessing. The situation of the mountains is described more accurately in *v.* 30. The words "by the way where the sun goeth

30 mount Ebal. *Are* they not on the other side Jordan, by the way
where the sun goeth down, in the land of the Canaanites, which
dwell in the champaign over against Gilgal, [a]beside the plains of
31 Moreh? [b]For ye shall pass over Jordan to go in to possess the
land which the LORD your God giveth you, and ye shall possess
32 it, and dwell therein. And ye shall observe [c]to do all the statutes and judgments which I set before you this day.

CHAP. 12. [a]THESE *are* the statutes and judgments, which ye shall
observe to do in the land, which the LORD God of thy fathers
giveth thee to possess it, [b]all the days that ye live upon the
2 earth. [c]Ye shall utterly destroy all the places, wherein the
nations which ye shall [1]possess served their gods, [d]upon the
high mountains, and upon the hills, and under every green tree:
3 and [e]ye shall [2]overthrow their altars, and break their pillars,
and burn their groves with fire; and ye shall hew down the
graven images of their gods, and destroy the names of them out
4 of that place. [f]Ye shall not do so unto the LORD your God.
5 But unto the place which the LORD your God shall [g]choose out
of all your tribes to put his name there, *even* unto his habitation

[a] Gen. 12. 6. Judg. 7. 1. [b] ch. 9. 1. Josh. 1. 11. [c] ch. 5. 32. & 12. 32.

[a] ch. 6. 1. [b] ch. 4. 10. 1 Kin. 8. 40. [c] Ex. 34. 13. ch. 7. 5. [d] 2 Kin. 16. 4. & 17. 10, 11. Jer. 3. 6. [e] Num. 33. 52. Judg. 2. 2. [f] ver. 31. [g] ver. 11. ch. 26. 2. Josh. 9. 27. 1 Kin. 8. 29. 2 Chr. 7. 12. Ps. 78. 68.

[1] Or, *inherit*. [2] Heb. *break down*.

---

down," should run, **beyond the road of the west**; *i.e.* on the further side of the main track which ran from Syria and Damascus to Jerusalem and Egypt through the centre of Palestine. This is called "the way of the west" in contrast to the other main route from Damascus to the south which passed through the district east of Jordan. The further specifications "Gilgal" and "the plains (rather, **the oaks**, cp. Gen. xii. 6 note) of Moreh," are added to define more particularly the section of Canaanites intended.

This Gilgal is perhaps to be found in Jiljilia, a large village about twelve miles south of Gerizim.

XII. Moses now passes on to apply (xii.–xxvi.) the leading principles of the Decalogue to the ecclesiastical, civil, and social life of the people. Particulars will be noticed which are peculiar to the Law as given in Deuteronomy; and even in laws repeated from the earlier books various new circumstances and details are introduced. This is but natural. The Sinaitic legislation was nearly forty years old, and had been given under conditions of time, place, and circumstance different and distant from those now present. Yet the Sinaitic system, far from being set aside or in any way abrogated, is on the contrary throughout presupposed and assumed. Its existence and authority are taken as the starting-point for what is here prescribed, and an accurate acquaintance with it on the part of the people is taken for granted.

3. *their groves*] Render **their idols of wood**: and see vii. 5 note.

4. *i.e.* "The idolaters set up their altars and images on any high hill, and under every green tree at their pleasure, but *ye* shall not do so; the Lord Himself shall determine the spot for your worship, and there only shall ye seek Him." The religion of the Canaanites was human; its modes of worship were of man's devising. It fixed its holy places on the hills in the vain thought of being nearer heaven, or in deep groves where the silence and gloom might overawe the worshipper. But such superstitious appliances were not worthy of the true religion. God had in it revealed Himself to men, and manifested amongst them His immediate Presence and power. He would Himself assign the Sanctuary and the ritual of His own service.

5. "To put his name there" means to manifest to men His Divine Presence. The Targumists rightly refer to the Shechinah; but the expression comprehends all the various modes in which God vouchsafed to reveal Himself and His attributes to men.

The purpose of the command of the text is to secure the unity, and through unity the purity of the worship of God. That there should be one national centre for the religion of the people was obviously essential to the great ends of the whole dispensation. Corruption began as soon as the precepts of the text were relaxed or neglected: Cp. the case of Gideon, Judg. viii. 27; of Micah, Judg. xviii.; of Jeroboam, 1 K. xii. 26 seq.

The words "the place which the LORD shall choose to put His Name there" suggest Jerusalem and Solomon's Temple to our minds. But though spoken as they were by a prophet, and interpreted as they are by the Psalms (*e.g.* Ps. lxxviii. 67-69), they have a proper application to the Temple, yet they must not be referred exclusively to it. The text does not import that God would always from the first choose one and the same locality "to put His Name there," but that there would always be a locality so

6 shall ye seek, and thither thou shalt come: and [h]thither ye shall
bring your burnt offerings, and your sacrifices, and your [i]tithes,
and heave offerings of your hand, and your vows, and your
freewill offerings, and the firstlings of your herds and of your
7 flocks: and [k]there ye shall eat before the LORD your God, and
[l]ye shall rejoice in all that ye put your hand unto, ye and your
8 households, wherein the LORD thy God hath blessed thee. ¶ Ye
shall not do after all *the things* that we do here this day, [m]every
9 man whatsoever *is* right in his own eyes. For ye are not as yet
come to the rest and to the inheritance, which the LORD your
10 God giveth you. But *when* [n]ye go over Jordan, and dwell in
the land which the LORD your God giveth you to inherit, and
when he giveth you rest from all your enemies round about, so
11 that ye dwell in safety; then there shall be [o]a place which the
LORD your God shall choose to cause his name to dwell there;
thither shall ye bring all that I command you; your burnt
offerings, and your sacrifices, your tithes, and the heave offering of your hand, and all [1]your choice vows which ye vow unto
12 the LORD: and [p]ye shall rejoice before the LORD your God, ye,
and your sons, and your daughters, and your menservants,
and your maidservants, and the Levite that *is* within your
gates; forasmuch as [q]he hath no part nor inheritance with you.
13 [r]Take heed to thyself that thou offer not thy burnt offerings
14 in every place that thou seest: [s]but in the place which the LORD
shall choose in one of thy tribes, there thou shalt offer thy burnt
offerings, and there thou shalt do all that I command thee.
15 ¶ Notwithstanding [t]thou mayest kill and eat flesh in all thy

[h] Lev. 17. 3, 4.
[i] ver. 17. ch. 14. 22. & 15. 19.
[k] ch. 14. 26.
[l] ver. 12, 18. Lev. 23. 40. ch. 16. 11. & 26. 11. & 27. 7.
[m] Judg. 17. 6. & 21. 25.
[n] ch. 11. 31.
[o] ver. 5, 14, 18, 21, 26. & ch. 14. 23. & pass. Josh. 18. 1. 1 Kin. 8. 29. Ps. 78. 68.
[p] ver. 7.
[q] ch. 10. 9. & 14. 29.
[r] Lev. 17. 4.
[s] ver. 11.
[t] ver. 21.

[1] Heb. *the choice of your vows.*

chosen by Him; and that thither the people must bring their sacrifices, and not offer them at their pleasure or convenience elsewhere. Neither does the text forbid the offering of sacrifices to God at other places than the one chosen by Him "to put His Name there" on proper occasions and by proper authority (cp. xxvii. 5, 6; Judg. vi. 24, xiii. 16; 1 Kings iii. 4, xviii. 31). The text simply prohibits sacrifices at any other locality than that which should be appointed or permitted by God for the purpose.

6. Some have objected that this command cannot possibly have been ever carried out, at all events until in later days the territory which owned obedience to it was narrowed to the little kingdom of Judah. But in these and in other precepts Moses doubtless takes much for granted. He is here, as elsewhere, regulating and defining more precisely institutions which had long been in existence, as to many details of which custom superseded the necessity of specific enactment. No doubt the people well understood what Maimonides expressly tells us in reference to the matter, namely, that where immediate payment could not be made, the debt to God was to be reserved until the next great Feast, and then duly discharged. The thing specially to be observed was that no kind of sacrifice was to be offered except at the sacred spot fixed by God for its acceptance.

7. An injunction that the feasts which accompanied certain offerings (not specified) were to be also held in the same place.

8. Moses points out that heretofore they had not observed the prescribed order in their worship, because during their migratory life in the wilderness it had been impossible to do so. During their wanderings there were doubtless times when the Tabernacle was not set up for days together, and when the daily sacrifice (Num. xxviii. 3), together with many other ordinances, were necessarily omitted (cp. Josh. v. 5). This consideration must be carefully borne in mind throughout Deuteronomy. It illustrates the necessity for a repetition of very much of the Sinaitic legislation, and suggests the reason why some parts are so urgently reiterated and impressed, whilst others are left unnoticed. Moses now warns the people that as they were about to quit their unsettled mode of life, God's purpose of choosing for Himself a place to set His Name there would be executed, and the whole of the sacred ritual would consequently become obligatory. The "rest and safety" of Canaan is significantly laid down (*vv.* 10, 11) as the indispensable condition and basis for an entire fulfilment of the Law: the perfection of righteousness coinciding thus with the cessation of wanderings, dangers, and toils.

15. Whilst a stringent injunction is laid

gates, whatsoever thy soul lusteth after, according to the blessing of the LORD thy God which he hath given thee: [u]the unclean
and the clean may eat thereof, [x]as of the roebuck, and as of the
16 hart. [y]Only ye shall not eat the blood; ye shall pour it upon
17 the earth as water. Thou mayest not eat within thy gates the
tithe of thy corn, or of thy wine, or of thy oil, or the firstlings
of thy herds or of thy flock, nor any of thy vows which thou
vowest, nor thy freewill offerings, or heave offering of thine
18 hand: [z]but thou must eat them before the LORD thy God in the
place which the LORD thy God shall choose, thou, and thy son,
and thy daughter, and thy manservant, and thy maidservant,
and the Levite that *is* within thy gates: and thou shalt rejoice
before the LORD thy God in all that thou puttest thine hands
19 unto. [a]Take heed to thyself that thou forsake not the Levite
20 [1]as long as thou livest upon the earth. ¶ When the LORD thy
God shall enlarge thy border, [b]as he hath promised thee, and
thou shalt say, I will eat flesh, because thy soul longeth to eat
flesh; thou mayest eat flesh, whatsoever thy soul lusteth after.
21 If the place which the LORD thy God hath chosen to put his
name there be too far from thee, then thou shalt kill of thy
herd and of thy flock, which the LORD hath given thee, as I
have commanded thee, and thou shalt eat in thy gates what-
22 soever thy soul lusteth after. [c]Even as the roebuck and the
hart is eaten, so thou shalt eat them: the unclean and the clean
23 shall eat *of* them alike. [d]Only [2]be sure that thou eat not the
blood: [e]for the blood *is* the life; and thou mayest not eat the
24 life with the flesh. Thou shalt not eat it; thou shalt pour it
25 upon the earth as water. Thou shalt not eat it; [f]that it may
go well with thee, and with thy children after thee, [g]when thou
26 shalt do *that which is* right in the sight of the LORD. Only thy
[h]holy things which thou hast, and [i]thy vows, thou shalt take,
27 and go unto the place which the LORD shall choose: and [k]thou
shalt offer thy burnt offerings, the flesh and the blood, upon the
altar of the LORD thy God: and the blood of thy sacrifices shall
be poured out upon the altar of the LORD thy God, and thou
28 shalt eat the flesh. Observe and hear all these words which I
command thee, [l]that it may go well with thee, and with thy
children after thee for ever, when thou doest *that which is* good
29 and right in the sight of the LORD thy God. ¶ When [m]the LORD
thy God shall cut off the nations from before thee, whither thou
goest to possess them, and thou [3]succeedest them, and dwellest
30 in their land; take heed to thyself [n]that thou be not snared [4]by
following them, after that they be destroyed from before thee;
and that thou enquire not after their gods, saying, How did
31 these nations serve their gods? Even so will I do likewise. [o]Thou

[u] ver. 22.
[x] ch. 14. 5. & 15. 22.
[y] Gen. 9. 4. Lev. 7. 26. & 17. 10. ch. 15. 23.
[z] ver. 11, 12. ch. 14. 23.
[a] ch. 14. 27.
[b] Gen. 15. 18. & 28. 14. Ex. 34. 24. ch. 11. 24. & 19. 8.
[c] ver. 15.
[d] ver. 16.
[e] Gen. 9. 4. Lev. 17. 11.
[f] ch. 4. 40. Isai. 3. 10.
[g] Ex. 15. 26. ch. 13. 18. 1 Kin. 11. 38.
[h] Num. 5. 9. & 18. 19.
[i] 1 Sam. 1. 21, 22, 24.
[k] Lev. 1. 5, 9, 13. & 17. 11.
[l] ver. 25.
[m] Ex. 23. 23. ch. 19. 1. Josh. 23. 4.
[n] ch. 7. 16.
[o] ver. 4. Lev. 18. 3, 26, 30. 2 Kin. 17. 15.

[1] Heb. *all thy days.*
[2] Heb. *be strong.*
[3] Heb. *inheritest*, or, *possessest them.*
[4] Heb. *after them.*

---

down that the old rule (cp. Lev. xvii. 3, &c.) must be adhered to as regards animals slain in sacrifice, yet permission is now given to slaughter at home what was necessary for the table. The ceremonial distinctions did not apply in such cases, any more than to "the roebuck" (or gazelle) "and hart," animals allowed for food but not for sacrifice.

21. *if the place*, &c.] Rather, "*Because*, or *since*, the place will be too far from thee." The permission given in *vv.* 15, 16 is repeated, and the reason of it assigned.

30. This caution is based upon the notion generally entertained in the ancient heathen world, that each country had its own tutelary deities whom it would be perilous to neglect; cp. 1 K. xx. 23; 2 K. xvii. 26. Israel was to shun such superstitions as unworthy of the elect people of God.

shalt not do so unto the LORD thy God: for every [1]abomination
to the LORD, which he hateth, have they done unto their gods;
for [p]even their sons and their daughters they have burnt in the
32 fire to their gods. What thing soever I command you, observe
to do it: [q]thou shalt not add thereto, nor diminish from it.
CHAP. 13. IF there arise among you a prophet, or a [a]dreamer of
2 dreams, [b]and giveth thee a sign or a wonder, and [c]the sign or
the wonder come to pass, whereof he spake unto thee, saying,
Let us go after other gods, which thou hast not known, and let
3 us serve them; thou shalt not hearken unto the words of that
prophet, or that dreamer of dreams: for the LORD your God
[d]proveth you, to know whether ye love the LORD your God with
4 all your heart and with all your soul. Ye shall [e]walk after the
LORD your God, and fear him, and keep his commandments, and
obey his voice, and ye shall serve him, and [f]cleave unto him.
5 And [g]that prophet, or that dreamer of dreams, shall be put to
death; because he hath [2]spoken to turn *you* away from the
LORD your God, which brought you out of the land of Egypt,
and redeemed you out of the house of bondage, to thrust thee
out of the way which the LORD thy God commanded thee to
walk in. [h]So shalt thou put the evil away from the midst of
6 thee. ¶ [i]If thy brother, the son of thy mother, or thy son, or
thy daughter, or [k]the wife of thy bosom, or thy friend, [l]which *is*
as thine own soul, entice thee secretly, saying, Let us go and
serve other gods, which thou hast not known, thou, nor thy
7 fathers; *namely*, of the gods of the people which *are* round about
you, nigh unto thee, or far off from thee, from the *one* end of the
8 earth even unto the *other* end of the earth; thou shalt [m]not consent unto him, nor hearken unto him; neither shall thine eye
pity him, neither shalt thou spare, neither shalt thou conceal
9 him: but [n]thou shalt surely kill him; [o]thine hand shall be first
upon him to put him to death, and afterwards the hand of all
10 the people. And thou shalt stone him with stones, that he die;
because he hath sought to thrust thee away from the LORD thy
God, which brought thee out of the land of Egypt, from the
11 house of [3]bondage. And [p]all Israel shall hear, and fear, and
12 shall do no more any such wickedness as this is among you. ¶ [q]If

[p] Lev. 18. 21 & 20. 2. ch. 18. 10. Jer. 32. 35. Ez. 23. 37.
[q] ch. 4. 2. & 13. 18. Josh. 1. 7. Prov. 30. 6. Rev. 22. 18.
[a] Zech. 10. 2.
[b] Matt. 24. 24. 2 Thes. 2. 9.
[c] See ch. 18. 22. Jer. 28. 9. Matt. 7. 22.
[d] ch. 8. 2. 1 Cor. 11. 19. 2 Thes. 2. 11. Rev. 13. 14.
[e] 2 Kin. 23. 3. 2 Chr. 34. 31.
[f] ch. 10. 20.
[g] ch. 18. 20. Jer. 14. 15. Zech. 13. 3.
[h] 1 Cor. 5. 13.
[i] ch. 17. 2.
[k] See Gen. 16. 5. ch. 28. 54. Prov. 5. 20. Mic. 7. 5.
[l] 1 Sam. 18. 1, 3. & 20. 17.
[m] Prov. 1. 10.
[n] ch. 17. 5.
[o] ch. 17. 7. Acts 7. 58.
[p] ch. 17. 13. & 19. 20.
[q] Josh. 22. 11, &c. Judg. 20. 1, 2.

[1] Heb. *abomination of the.* [2] Heb. *spoken revolt against the* LORD. [3] Heb. *bondmen.*

XIII. The admonition of the closing verse of the last chapter introduces a new series of warnings intended to serve as a further safeguard against violation of these duties. The true modes and forms of worship have been laid down: the next step is to legislate against the authors and abettors of false ones.

1. *a prophet, or a dreamer of dreams*] Cp. Num. xii. 6. The "prophet" received his revelations by vision or direct oral communication (Num. xxiv. 16; 2 Sam. vii. 4; 2 Cor. xii. 2); "the dreamer of dreams" through the medium of a dream (1 K. iii. 5; Matt. ii. 13).

2. The Lord had said, "Thou shalt have none other gods but Me." A prophet is here supposed who invites the people "to go after other gods." To such a one no credit is under any circumstances to be given, even should he show signs and wonders to authenticate his doctrine. The standing rule of faith and practice had been laid down once for all; that the people were to hold fast. The prophet who propounded another rule could only be an impostor.

A different case is considered in xviii. 18, &c.

5. The context and parallel passages (cp. xvii. 7; Lev. xx. 2) indicate that there was to be a regular judicial procedure, and that the manner of the execution was to be by stoning. In this the community was to take its part in order to show its horror at the crime, and to clear itself of complicity therein.

6. The omissions in this enumeration seem to imply that no one was bound to impeach father, mother, or husband.

12. City was to keep jealous watch over

thou shalt hear *say* in one of thy cities, which the LORD thy
13 God hath given thee to dwell there, saying, *Certain* men, [1]the
children of Belial, [r]are gone out from among you, and have
[s]withdrawn the inhabitants of their city, saying, [t]Let us go and
14 serve other gods, which ye have not known; then shalt thou
enquire, and make search, and ask diligently; and, behold, *if it*
be truth, *and* the thing certain, *that* such abomination is wrought
15 among you; thou shalt surely smite the inhabitants of that city
with the edge of the sword, [u]destroying it utterly, and all that
is therein, and the cattle thereof, with the edge of the sword.
16 And thou shalt gather all the spoil of it into the midst of the
street thereof, and shalt [x]burn with fire the city, and all the
spoil thereof every whit, for the LORD thy God: and it shall be
17 [y]an heap for ever; it shall not be built again. And [z]there shall
cleave nought of the [2]cursed thing to thine hand: that the
LORD may [a]turn from the fierceness of his anger, and shew thee
mercy, and have compassion upon thee, and multiply thee, [b]as
18 he hath sworn unto thy fathers; when thou shalt hearken to
the voice of the LORD thy God, [c]to keep all his commandments
which I command thee this day, to do *that which is* right in the
eyes of the LORD thy God.
CHAP. 14. YE *are* [a]the children of the LORD your God: [b]ye shall
not cut yourselves, nor make any baldness between your eyes for
2 the dead. [c]For thou *art* an holy people unto the LORD thy God,
and the LORD hath chosen thee to be a peculiar people unto
3 himself, above all the nations that *are* upon the earth. ¶ [d]Thou
4 shalt not eat any abominable thing. [e]These *are* the beasts
5 which ye shall eat: the ox, the sheep, and the goat, the hart,
and the roebuck, and the fallow deer, and the wild goat, and the
6 [3][4]pygarg, and the wild ox, and the chamois. And every beast
that parteth the hoof, and cleaveth the cleft into two claws, *and*
7 cheweth the cud among the beasts, that ye shall eat. Nevertheless these ye shall not eat of them that chew the cud, or of them
that divide the cloven hoof; *as* the camel, and the hare, and the
coney: for they chew the cud, but divide not the hoof; *therefore*
8 they *are* unclean unto you. And the swine, because it divideth

[r] 1 John 2. 19. Jude 19.
[s] 2 Kin. 17. 21.
[t] ver. 2. 6.
[u] Ex. 22. 20. Lev. 27. 28. Josh. 6. 17.
[x] Josh. 6. 24.
[y] Josh. 8. 28. Isai. 17. 1. & 25. 2. Jer. 49. 2.
[z] ch. 7. 26. Josh. 6. 18.
[a] Josh. 6. 26.
[b] Gen. 22. 17. & 26. 4. & 28. 14.
[c] ch. 12. 25, 28, 32.
[a] Rom. 8. 16. & 9. 8, 26. Gal. 3. 26.
[b] Lev. 19. 28. & 21. 5. Jer. 16. 6. & 41. 5. & 47. 5. 1 Thes. 4. 13.
[c] Lev. 20. 26. ch. 7. 6. & 26. 18, 19.
[d] Ez. 4. 14. Acts 10. 13.
[e] Lev. 11. 2.

[1] Or, *naughty men:* See Judg. 19. 22. 1 Sam. 2. 12. & 25. 17, 25. 1 Kin. 21. 10, 13. 2 Cor. 6. 15.
[2] Or, *devoted.*
[3] Or, *bison.*
[4] Heb. *dishon.*

---

city, as man over man. The clause "which the Lord thy God hath given thee to dwell in" significantly reminds them that the real ownership of their dwellings rested in the Lord (cp. Lev. xxv. 23), and that they, the mere tenants, must not allow His property to become a centre of rebellion against His just authority.

13. In xv. 9 and in Nah. i. 11 the word Belial is rendered in our translation by the adjective "wicked." The word means *worthlessness.*

16. *every whit, for the* LORD *thy God*] Some prefer: **"as a whole offering to the Lord thy God."**

XIV. The whole life and walk of the people were to be regulated by the principle "ye are the children of the Lord your God" (*v.* 1).

1. *make any baldness between your eyes*] *i.e.* by shaving the forepart of the head and the eyebrows. The practices named in this verse were common amongst the heathen, and seem to be forbidden, not only because such wild excesses of grief (cp. 1 Kings xviii. 28) would be inconsistent in those who as children of a heavenly Father had prospects beyond this world, but also because these usages themselves arose out of idolatrous notions.

3-21. Cp. Lev. xi. The variations here, whether omissions or additions, are probably to be explained by the time and circumstances of the speaker.

5. The "pygarg" is a species of gazelle, and the "wild ox" and "chamois" are swift kinds of antelope.

the hoof, yet cheweth not the cud, it *is* unclean unto you: ye
shall not eat of their flesh, [f] nor touch their dead carcase. [f] Lev. 11. 26,
9 ¶ [g] These ye shall eat of all that *are* in the waters: all that have 27.
10 fins and scales shall ye eat: and whatsoever hath not fins and [g] Lev. 11. 9.
11 scales ye may not eat: it *is* unclean unto you. ¶ *Of* all clean
12 birds ye shall eat. [h] But these *are they* of which ye shall not eat: [h] Lev. 11. 13.
13 the eagle, and the ossifrage, and the ospray, and the glede, and
14 the kite, and the vulture after his kind, and every raven after
15 his kind, and the owl, and the night hawk, and the cuckow, and
16 the hawk after his kind, the little owl, and the great owl, and
17 the swan, and the pelican, and the gier eagle, and the cormorant,
18 and the stork, and the heron after her kind, and the lapwing,
19 and the bat. And [i] every creeping thing that flieth *is* unclean [i] Lev. 11. 20.
20 unto you: [k] they shall not be eaten. *But of* all clean fowls ye [k] See Lev.
21 may eat. [l] Ye shall not eat *of* any thing that dieth of itself: 11. 21.
thou shalt give it unto the stranger that *is* in thy gates, that he [l] Lev. 17. 15.
may eat it; or thou mayest sell it unto an alien: [m] for thou *art* Ez. 4. 14. [m] ver. 2.
an holy people unto the LORD thy God. [n] Thou shalt not [n] Ex. 23. 19.
22 seethe a kid in his mother's milk. ¶ [o] Thou shalt truly tithe all & 34. 26.
the increase of thy seed, that the field bringeth forth year by [o] Lev. 27. 30.
23 year. [p] And thou shalt eat before the LORD thy God, in the ch. 12. 6, 17.
place which he shall choose to place his name there, the tithe of Neh. 10. 37. [p] ch. 12. 5, 6,
thy corn, of thy wine, and of thine oil, and [q] the firstlings of thy 7, 17, 18.
herds and of thy flocks; that thou mayest learn to fear the LORD [q] ch. 15. 19,
24 thy God always. And if the way be too long for thee, so that 20.
thou art not able to carry it; *or* [r] if the place be too far from [r] ch. 12. 21.
thee, which the LORD thy God shall choose to set his name there,
25 when the LORD thy God hath blessed thee: then shalt thou turn
it into money, and bind up the money in thine hand, and shalt
26 go unto the place which the LORD thy God shall choose: and
thou shalt bestow that money for whatsoever thy soul lusteth
after, for oxen, or for sheep, or for wine, or for strong drink, or
for whatsoever thy soul [1] desireth: [s] and thou shalt eat there [s] ch. 12. 7,
before the LORD thy God, and thou shalt rejoice, thou, and thine 18. & 26. 11.
27 household, and [t] the Levite that *is* within thy gates; thou shalt [t] ch. 12. 12,
not forsake him; for [u] he hath no part nor inheritance with thee. 18, 19.
28 ¶ [x] At the end of three years thou shalt bring forth all the tithe [u] Num. 18. 20.
of thine increase the same year, and shalt lay *it* up within thy ch. 18. 1, 2.
[x] ch. 26. 12. Amos 4. 4.

[1] Heb. *asketh of thee.*

---

21. The prohibition is repeated from Lev. xxii. 8. The directions as to the disposal of the carcase are peculiar to Deuteronomy, and their motive is clear. To have forbidden the people either themselves to eat that which had died, or to allow any others to do so, would have involved loss of property, and consequent temptation to an infraction of the command. The permissions now for the first time granted would have been useless in the wilderness. During the forty years' wandering there could be but little opportunity of selling such carcases; whilst non-Israelites living in the camp would in such a matter be bound by the same rules as the Israelites (Lev. xvii. 15, and xxiv. 22). Further, it would seem (cp. Lev. xvii. 15) that greater stringency is here given to the requirement of abstinence from that which had died of itself. Probably on this, as on so many other points, allowance was made for the circumstances of the people. Flesh meat was no doubt often scarce in the desert. It would therefore have been a hardship to forbid entirely the use of that which had not been killed. Now however that the plenty of the Promised Land was before them, the modified toleration of this unholy food was withdrawn.

22. These words recall in general terms the command of the earlier legislation respecting tithes (cp. Lev. xxvii. 30; Num. xviii. 26), but refer more particularly to the second or Festival tithe, which was an exclusively vegetable one.

28, 29. Cp. marg. reff. The tithe thus directed in the third year to be dispensed in charity at home, was not paid in addition to that in other years bestowed on the sacred meals, but was substituted for it. The

29 gates: [y]and the Levite, (because [z]he hath no part nor inheritance with thee,) and the stranger, and the fatherless, and the
widow, which *are* within thy gates, shall come, and shall eat and
be satisfied; that [a]the LORD thy God may bless thee in all the
work of thine hand which thou doest.
CHAP. 15. AT the end of [a]*every* seven years thou shalt make a re-
2 lease. And this *is* the manner of the release: Every [1]creditor
that lendeth *ought* unto his neighbour shall release *it;* he shall
not exact *it* of his neighbour, or of his brother; because it is called
3 the LORD's release. [b]Of a foreigner thou mayest exact *it again:*
but *that* which is thine with thy brother thine hand shall release;
4 [2]save when there shall be no poor among you; [c]for the LORD
shall greatly bless thee in the land which the LORD thy God
5 giveth thee *for* an inheritance to possess it: only [d]if thou carefully hearken unto the voice of the LORD thy God, to observe to
6 do all these commandments which I command thee this day. For
the LORD thy God blesseth thee, as he promised thee: and [e]thou
shalt lend unto many nations, but thou shalt not borrow; and
[f]thou shalt reign over many nations, but they shall not reign
7 over thee. ¶ If there be among you a poor man of one of thy
brethren within any of thy gates in thy land which the LORD
thy God giveth thee, [g]thou shalt not harden thine heart, nor shut
8 thine hand from thy poor brother: [h]but thou shalt open thine
hand wide unto him, and shalt surely lend him sufficient for his
9 need, *in that* which he wanteth. Beware that there be not a
[3]thought in thy [4]wicked heart, saying, The seventh year, the
year of release, is at hand; and thine [i]eye be evil against thy
poor brother, and thou givest him nought; and [k]he cry unto the
10 LORD against thee, and [l]it be sin unto thee. Thou shalt surely
give him, and [m]thine heart shall not be grieved when thou givest
unto him: because that [n]for this thing the LORD thy God shall
bless thee in all thy works, and in all that thou puttest thine
11 hand unto. For [o]the poor shall never cease out of the land:

[y] ch. 26. 12. [z] ver. 27. ch. 12. 12. [a] ch. 15. 10. Prov. 3. 9, 10. See Mal. 3. 10. [a] Ex. 21. 2. ch. 31. 10. Jer. 34. 14. [b] See ch. 23. 20. [c] ch. 28. 8. [d] ch. 28. 1. [e] ch. 28. 12, 44. [f] ch. 28. 13. Prov. 22. 7. [g] 1 John 3. 17. [h] Lev. 25. 35. Matt. 5. 42. Luke 6. 34, 35. [i] ch. 28. 54, 56. Prov. 23. 6. & 28. 22. Matt. 20. 15. [k] ch. 24. 15. [l] Matt. 25. 41, 42. [m] 2 Cor. 9. 5, 7. [n] ch. 14. 29. & 24. 19. Ps. 41. 1. Prov. 22. 9. [o] Matt. 26. 11. Mark 14. 7. John 12. 8.

[1] Heb. *master of the lending of his hand.* [2] Or, *To the end that there be no poor among you.* [3] Heb. *word.* [4] Heb. *Belial.*

three years would count from the Sabbatical year (see next chap.), in which year there would of course be neither payment of tithe nor celebration of the Feasts at the Sanctuary. In the third and sixth years of the septennial cycle the Feasts would be superseded by the private hospitality enjoined in these verses.

XV. 1–11. The Year of Release is no doubt identical with the Sabbatical Year of the earlier legislation (Ex. xxiii. 10 seq., and Lev. xxv. 2 seq.), the command of the older legislation being here amplified. The release was probably for the year, not total and final, and had reference only to loans lent because of poverty (cp. *vv.* 4, 7). Yet even so the law was found too stringent for the avarice of the people; for it was one of those which the Rabbins "made of none effect by their traditions."

2. *because it is called the* LORD'S *release*] Render, **because proclamation has been made of the Lord's release.** The verb is impersonal, and implies (cp. xxxi. 10) that "the solemnity of the year of release" has been publicly announced.

3. The foreigner would not be bound by the restriction of the Sabbatical year, and therefore would have no claim to its special remissions and privileges. He could earn his usual income in the seventh as in other years, and therefore is not exonerated from liability to discharge a debt any more in the one than the others.

4. There is no inconsistency between this and *v.* 11. The meaning seems simply to be, "Thou must release the debt for the year, except when there be no poor person concerned, a contingency which may happen, for the Lord shall greatly bless thee." The general object of these precepts, as also of the year of Jubilee and the laws respecting inheritance, is to prevent the total ruin of a needy man, and his disappearance from the families of Israel by the sale of his patrimony.

9. Lit.: "Beware that there be not in thy heart a word which is worthlessness" (cp. xiii. 13 note).

therefore I command thee, saying, Thou shalt open thine hand
wide unto thy brother, to thy poor, and to thy needy, in thy land.
12 ¶ *And* [p]if thy brother, an Hebrew man, or an Hebrew woman, [p] Ex. 21. 2.
be sold unto thee, and serve thee six years; then in the seventh Lev. 25. 39. Jer. 34. 14.
13 year thou shalt let him go free from thee. And when thou send-
est him out free from thee, thou shalt not let him go away
14 empty: thou shalt furnish him liberally out of thy flock, and
out of thy floor, and out of thy winepress: *of that* wherewith
the LORD thy God hath [q]blessed thee thou shalt give unto him. [q] Prov. 10.
15 And [r]thou shalt remember that thou wast a bondman in the 22.
land of Egypt, and the LORD thy God redeemed thee: therefore [r] ch. 5. 15. & 16. 12.
16 I command thee this thing to day. And it shall be, [s]if he say [s] Ex. 21. 5,
unto thee, I will not go away from thee; because he loveth thee 6.
17 and thine house, because he is well with thee; then thou shalt
take an aul, and thrust *it* through his ear unto the door, and he
shall be thy servant for ever. And also unto thy maidservant
18 thou shalt do likewise. It shall not seem hard unto thee, when
thou sendest him away free from thee; for he hath been worth
[t]a double hired servant *to thee*, in serving thee six years: and [t] See Isai.
the LORD thy God shall bless thee in all that thou doest. 16. 14. & 21. 16.
19 ¶ [u]All the firstling males that come of thy herd and of thy flock [u] Ex. 34. 19.
thou shalt sanctify unto the LORD thy God: thou shalt do no Lev. 27. 26.
work with the firstling of thy bullock, nor shear the firstling of Num. 3. 13.
20 thy sheep. [x]Thou shalt eat *it* before the LORD thy God year by [x] ch. 16. 11,
year in the place which the LORD shall choose, thou and thy 14.
21 household. [y]And if there be *any* blemish therein, *as if it be* [y] Lev. 22. 20.
lame or blind, *or have* any ill blemish, thou shalt not sacrifice it ch. 17. 1.
22 unto the LORD thy God. Thou shalt eat it within thy gates:
[z]the unclean and the clean *person shall eat it* alike, as the roe- [z] ch. 12. 15, 22.
23 buck, and as the hart. [a]Only thou shalt not eat the blood [a] ch. 12. 16,
thereof; thou shalt pour it upon the ground as water. 23.
CHAP. 16. OBSERVE the [a]month of Abib, and keep the passover [a] Ex. 12. 2, &c.
unto the LORD thy God: for [b]in the month of Abib the LORD [b] Ex. 13. 4. & 34. 18.

---

14. *thou shalt furnish him liberally*] The verb in the Hebrew is remarkable. It means "thou shalt lay on his neck," "adorn his neck with thy gifts."

12–18. The commands here are repeated from Ex. xxi. 2-6, with amplifications relative to the maidservant (*v.* 12) and to the making (*vv.* 13 seq.) liberal provision for launching the freedman on an independent course of life. The release of the servant is connected with the Sabbatical principle though not with the Sabbatical year. It is noteworthy also that the prospect of a gift of this sort, the amount of which was left to the master's discretion, would be likely to encourage diligence and faithfulness during the years of servitude.

18. *he hath been worth a double hired servant to thee, in serving thee six years*] *i.e.* such a servant has earned twice as much as a common hired labourer would have done in the same time.

19–23. Cp. Ex. xiii. 11 seq. The directions of the preceding legislation (see Num. xviii. 15 seq.) are here assumed, with the injunction added, that the animals thus set apart to God (*v.* 19) were not to be used by their owners for their earthly purposes. It is further allowed that firstborn animals which had a blemish should be regarded as exceptions, and instead of being given to God might be used as food (*vv.* 21, 22). The application of the firstborn of cattle is here directed as in xii. 6, 17 and xiv. 23: they are to be consumed in the sacred Feasts at the Sanctuary.

XVI. The cardinal point on which the whole of the prescriptions in this chapter turn, is evidently the same as has been so often insisted on in the previous chapters, viz. the concentration of the religious services of the people round one common Sanctuary. The prohibition against observing the great Feasts of Passover, Pentecost, and Tabernacle, the three annual epochs in the sacred year of the Jew, at home and in private, is reiterated in a variety of words no less than six times in the first sixteen verses of this chapter (2, 6, 7, 11, 15, 16). Hence it is easy to see why nothing is here said of the other holy days.

1–8. The Feast of Passover (Ex. xii. 1–27; Num. ix. 1-14; Lev. xxiii. 1-8). A re-enforcement of this ordinance was the more

2 thy God brought thee forth out of Egypt [c]by night. Thou shalt
therefore sacrifice the passover unto the LORD thy God, of the
flock and [d]the herd, in the [e]place which the LORD shall choose to
3 place his name there. [f]Thou shalt eat no leavened bread with
it; seven days shalt thou eat unleavened bread therewith, *even*
the bread of affliction; for thou camest forth out of the land of
Egypt in haste: that thou mayest remember the day when thou
camest forth out of the land of Egypt all the days of thy life.
4 [g]And there shall be no leavened bread seen with thee in all thy
coast seven days; [h]neither shall there *any thing* of the flesh,
which thou sacrificedst the first day at even, remain all night
5 until the morning. ¶ Thou mayest not [1]sacrifice the passover
within any of thy gates, which the LORD thy God giveth thee:
6 but at the place which the LORD thy God shall choose to place
his name in, there thou shalt sacrifice the passover [i]at even, at
the going down of the sun, at the season that thou camest forth
7 out of Egypt. And thou shalt [k]roast and eat *it* [l]in the place
which the LORD thy God shall choose: and thou shalt turn in
8 the morning, and go unto thy tents. Six days thou shalt eat
unleavened bread: and [m]on the seventh day *shall be* a [2]solemn
assembly to the LORD thy God: thou shalt do no work *therein*.
9 ¶ [n]Seven weeks shalt thou number unto thee: begin to number
the seven weeks from *such time as* thou beginnest *to put* the
10 sickle to the corn. And thou shalt keep the feast of weeks
unto the LORD thy God with [3]a tribute of a freewill offering of
thine hand, which thou shalt give *unto the LORD thy God*, [o]ac-
11 cording as the LORD thy God hath blessed thee: and [p]thou shalt
rejoice before the LORD thy God, thou, and thy son, and thy
daughter, and thy manservant, and thy maidservant, and the
Levite that *is* within thy gates, and the stranger, and the fatherless, and the widow, that *are* among you, in the place which the
12 LORD thy God hath chosen to place his name there. [q]And thou
shalt remember that thou wast a bondman in Egypt: and thou
13 shalt observe and do these statutes. ¶ [r]Thou shalt observe the
feast of tabernacles seven days, after that thou hast gathered
14 in thy [4]corn and thy wine: and [s]thou shalt rejoice in thy feast,
thou, and thy son, and thy daughter, and thy manservant, and
thy maidservant, and the Levite, the stranger, and the father-
15 less, and the widow, that *are* within thy gates. [t]Seven days
shalt thou keep a solemn feast unto the LORD thy God in the

[c] Ex. 12. 29, 42.
[d] Num. 28. 19.
[e] ch. 12. 5, 26.
[f] Ex. 12. 15, 19, 39. & 13. 3, 6, 7. & 34. 18.
[g] Ex. 13. 7.
[h] Ex. 12. 10. & 34. 25.
[i] Ex. 12. 6.
[k] Ex. 12. 8, 9. 2 Chr. 35. 13.
[l] 2 Kin. 23. 23. John 2. 13, 23. & 11. 55.
[m] Ex. 12. 16. & 13. 6. Lev. 23. 8.
[n] Ex. 23. 16. & 34. 22. Lev. 23. 15. Num. 28. 26. Acts 2. 1.
[o] ver. 17. 1 Cor. 16. 2.
[p] ch. 12. 7, 12, 18. ver. 14.
[q] ch. 15. 15.
[r] Ex. 23. 16. Lev. 23. 34. Num. 29. 12.
[s] Neh. 8. 9, &c.
[t] Lev. 23. 39, 40.

[1] Or, *kill*.
[2] Heb. *restraint*, Lev. 23, 36.
[3] Or, *sufficiency*.
[4] Heb. *floor, and thy winepress*.

necessary because its observance had clearly been intermitted for thirty-nine years (see Josh. vi. 10). One Passover only had been kept in the wilderness, that recorded in Num. ix., where see notes.

2. *sacrifice the passover*] *i.e.* offer the sacrifices proper to the Feast of the Passover, which lasted seven days. Cp. a similar use of the word in a general sense in John xviii. 28. In the latter part of *v.* 4 and in the following verses Moses passes, as the context again shows, into the narrower sense of the word Passover.

7. After the Paschal Supper in the courts or neighbourhood of the Sanctuary was over, they might disperse to their several "tents" or "dwellings" (1 K. viii. 66). These would of course be within a short distance of the Sanctuary, because the other Paschal offerings were yet to be offered day by day for seven days, and the people would remain to share them; and especially to take part in the holy convocation on the first and seventh of the days.

9–12. Feast of Weeks; and *vv.* 13–17, Feast of Tabernacles. Nothing is here added to the rules given in Leviticus and Numbers except the clauses so often recurring in Deuteronomy and so characteristic of it, which restrict the public celebration of the Festivals to the Sanctuary, and enjoin that the enjoyments of them should be extended to the Levites, widows, orphans, &c.

place which the LORD shall choose: because the LORD thy God
shall bless thee in all thine increase, and in all the works of
16 thine hands, therefore thou shalt surely rejoice. ¶ [u]Three times
in a year shall all thy males appear before the LORD thy God in
the place which he shall choose; in the feast of unleavened
bread, and in the feast of weeks, and in the feast of tabernacles:
17 and [x]they shall not appear before the LORD empty: every man
shall give [1]as he is able, [y]according to the blessing of the LORD
18 thy God which he hath given thee. ¶ [z]Judges and officers shalt
thou make thee in all thy gates, which the LORD thy God giveth
thee, throughout thy tribes: and they shall judge the people
19 with just judgment. [a]Thou shalt not wrest judgment; [b]thou
shalt not respect persons, [c]neither take a gift: for a gift doth
blind the eyes of the wise, and pervert the [2]words of the right-
20 eous. [3]That which is altogether just shalt thou follow, that
thou mayest [d]live, and inherit the land which the LORD thy God
21 giveth thee. ¶ [e]Thou shalt not plant thee a grove of any trees
near unto the altar of the LORD thy God, which thou shalt make
22 thee. [f]Neither shalt thou set thee up *any* [4]image; which the
LORD thy God hateth.
CHAP. 17. THOU [a]shalt not sacrifice unto the LORD thy God *any*
bullock, or [5]sheep, wherein is blemish, *or* any evil-favouredness:
2 for that *is* an abomination unto the LORD thy God. ¶ [b]If there
be found among you, within any of thy gates which the LORD
thy God giveth thee, man or woman, that hath wrought wickedness in the sight of the LORD thy God, [c]in transgressing his
3 covenant, and hath gone and served other gods, and worshipped
them, either [d]the sun, or moon, or any of the host of heaven,
4 [e]which I have not commanded; [f]and it be told thee, and thou
hast heard *of it*, and enquired diligently, and, behold, *it be* true,
and the thing certain, *that* such abomination is wrought in
5 Israel: then shalt thou bring forth that man or that woman,
which have committed that wicked thing, unto thy gates, *even*
that man or that woman, and [g]shalt stone them with stones, till

[u] Ex. 23. 14, 17. & 34. 23.
[x] Ex. 23. 15. & 34. 20.
[y] ver. 10.
[z] ch. 1. 16. 1 Chr. 23. 4. & 26. 29. 2 Chr. 19. 5, 8.
[a] Ex. 23. 2. Lev. 19. 15.
[b] ch. 1. 17. Prov. 24. 23.
[c] Ex. 23. 8. Prov. 17. 23. Eccles. 7. 7.
[d] Ez. 18. 5, 9.
[e] Ex. 34. 13. 1 Kin. 14. 15. 2 Kin. 17. 16. 2 Chr. 33. 3.
[f] Lev. 26. 1.

[a] Mal. 1. 8, 13, 14.
[b] ch. 13. 6.
[c] Josh. 7. 11, 15. Judg. 2. 20. 2 Kin. 18. 12. Hos. 8. 1.
[d] ch. 4. 19. Job 31. 26.
[e] Jer. 7. 22, 23, 31.
[f] ch. 13. 12.
[g] Lev. 24. 14, 16. ch. 13. 10. Josh. 7. 25.

[1] Heb. *according to the gift of his hand*, 2 Cor. 8. 12.
[2] Or, *matters*.
[3] Heb. *Justice, justice*.
[4] Or, *statue*, or, *pillar*.
[5] Or, *goat*.

18–22. These verses are closely connected in subject with the following chapter, and introduce certain directions for the administration of justice and the carrying on of the civil government of the people in Canaan. During the lifetime of Moses, he himself, specially inspired and guided by God, was sufficient, with the aid of the subordinate judges (cp. Ex. xviii. 13 seq.), for the duties in question. But now that Moses was to be withdrawn, and the people would soon be scattered up and down the land of Canaan, regular and permanent provision must be made for civil and social order and good government.

21. *a grove*, &c.] Render, **Thou shalt not plant for thee any tree as an idol**: literally "as an Asherah," *i.e.* an image of Astarte or Ashtaroth, the Phœnician goddess (cp. vii. 5 note, 13). The word is rendered "grove" by A. V. also in vii. 5, xii. 3; Ex. xxxiv. 13; Judg. vi. 25, but cannot be maintained, for the word is connected with various verbs which are quite inapplicable to a grove. The wooden idol in question was the stem of a tree, stripped of its boughs, set upright in the ground, and rudely carved with emblems.

XVII. **1.** This verse belongs in subject to the last chapter. It prohibits once more (cp. xv. 21) that form of insult to God which consists in offering to Him a blemished sacrifice.

any evil-favouredness] Render **any evil thing**. The reference is to the faults or maims enumerated in Lev. xxii. 22–24.

2–7. Cp. xiii. 1 seq. Here special reference is made to the legal forms to be adopted, *vv.* 5–7. The sentence was to be carried into effect at "the gates" (cp. Gen. xix. 1 note) of the town in which the crime was committed; because, as "all the people" were to take a part, an open space would be requisite for the execution. Note the typical and prophetical aspect of the injunction; cp. Acts vii. 58; Heb. xiii. 12.

[h] Num. 35. 30. ch. 19. 15. Matt. 18. 16. John 8. 17. 2 Cor. 13. 1. 1 Tim. 5. 19. Heb. 10. 28.
[i] ch. 13. 9.
[k] ver. 12. ch. 13. 5.
[l] 2 Chr. 19. 10. Hag. 2. 11. Mal. 2. 7.
[m] See Ex. 21. 13, 20. Num. 35. 11, 16, 19. ch. 19. 4.
[n] ch. 12. 5. Ps. 122. 5.
[o] See Jer. 18. 18.
[p] ch. 19. 17.
[q] Ez. 44. 24.
[r] Num. 15. 30. Ezra 10. 8. Hos. 4. 4.
[s] ch. 18. 5.
[t] ch. 13. 5.
[u] ch. 13. 11. & 19. 20.
[x] 1 Sam. 8. 5, 19, 20.
[y] See 1 Sam. 9. 15. 1 Chr. 22. 10.
[z] Jer. 30. 21.
[a] 1 Kin. 4. 26. Ps. 20. 7.
[b] Isai. 31. 1. Ez. 17. 15.
[c] Ex. 13. 17. Num. 14. 3, 4.

6 they die. [h]At the mouth of two witnesses, or three witnesses,
shall he that is worthy of death be put to death; *but* at the
7 mouth of one witness he shall not be put to death. [i]The hands
of the witnesses shall be first upon him to put him to death, and
afterward the hands of all the people. So [k]thou shalt put the
8 evil away from among you. ¶ [l]If there arise a matter too hard
for thee in judgment, [m]between blood and blood, between plea
and plea, and between stroke and stroke, *being* matters of controversy within thy gates: then shalt thou arise, [n]and get thee
9 up into the place which the LORD thy God shall choose; and
[o]thou shalt come unto the priests the Levites, and [p]unto the
judge that shall be in those days, and enquire; [q]and they shall
10 shew thee the sentence of judgment: and thou shalt do according to the sentence, which they of that place which the LORD
shall choose shall shew thee; and thou shalt observe to do
11 according to all that they inform thee: according to the sentence
of the law which they shall teach thee, and according to the
judgment which they shall tell thee, thou shalt do: thou shalt
not decline from the sentence which they shall shew thee, *to* the
12 right hand, nor *to* the left. And [r]the man that will do presumptuously, [1]and will not hearken unto the priest [s]that standeth to minister there before the LORD thy God, or unto the
judge, even that man shall die: and [t]thou shalt put away the
13 evil from Israel. [u]And all the people shall hear, and fear, and
14 do no more presumptuously. ¶ When thou art come unto the
land which the LORD thy God giveth thee, and shalt possess it,
and shalt dwell therein, and shalt say, [x]I will set a king over
15 me, like as all the nations that *are* about me; thou shalt in any
wise set *him* king over thee, [y]whom the LORD thy God shall
choose: *one* [z]from among thy brethren shalt thou set king over
thee: thou mayest not set a stranger over thee, which *is* not thy
16 brother. But he shall not multiply [a]horses to himself, nor
cause the people [b]to return to Egypt, to the end that he should
multiply horses: forasmuch as [c]the LORD hath said unto you,

[1] Heb. *not to hearken.*

8-13. The cases in question are such as the inferior judges did not feel able to decide satisfactorily, and which accordingly they remitted to their superiors (cp. Ex. xviii. 23–27).

The Supreme Court (*v.* 9) is referred to in very general terms as sitting at the Sanctuary (*v.* 8). "The judge" would no doubt usually be a layman, and thus the court would contain both an ecclesiastical and a civil element. Jehoshaphat (2 Chr. xix. 4–11) organized his judicial system very closely upon the lines here laid down.

14. No encouragement is given to the desire, natural in an Oriental people, for monarchical government; but neither is such desire blamed, as appears from the fact that conditions are immediately laid down upon which it may be satisfied. Cp. marg. reff.

15. The king, like the judges and officers (cp. xvi. 18), is to be chosen by the people; but their choice is to be in accordance with the will of God, and to be made from amongst "their brethren." Cp. 1 S. ix. 15, x. 24, xvi. 1; 1 K. xix. 16.

thou mayest not set a stranger over thee] The Jews extended this prohibition to all offices whatsoever (cp. Jer. xxx. 21); and naturally attached the greatest importance to it: whence the significance of the question proposed to our Lord, "Is it lawful to give tribute to Cæsar?" (Matt. xxii. 17). A Gentile head for the Jewish people, which it was a principal aim of the Law to keep peculiar and distinct from others, was an anomaly.

16. The horse was not anciently used in the East for purposes of agriculture or travelling, but ordinarily for war only. He appears constantly in Scripture as the symbol and embodiment of fleshly strength and the might of the creature (cp. Ps. xx. 7, xxxiii. 16, 17, cxlvii. 10; Job xxxix. 19 seq.), and is sometimes significantly spoken of simply as "the strong one" (cp. Jer. viii. 16). The spirit of the prohibition therefore is that the king of Israel must not, like other

17 [d]Ye shall henceforth return no more that way. Neither shall
he multiply wives to himself, that [e]his heart turn not away:
neither shall he greatly multiply to himself silver and gold.
18 [f]And it shall be, when he sitteth upon the throne of his kingdom, that he shall write him a copy of this law in a book out of
19 [g]*that which is* before the priests the Levites: and [h]it shall be with
him, and he shall read therein all the days of his life: that he
may learn to fear the LORD his God, to keep all the words
20 of this law and these statutes, to do them: that his heart be
not lifted up above his brethren, and that he [i]turn not aside
from the commandment, *to* the right hand, or *to* the left: to the
end that he may prolong *his* days in his kingdom, he, and his
children, in the midst of Israel.

CHAP. 18. THE priests the Levites, *and* all the tribe of Levi, [a]shall
have no part nor inheritance with Israel: they [b]shall eat the
2 offerings of the LORD made by fire, and his inheritance. Therefore shall they have no inheritance among their brethren: the
3 LORD *is* their inheritance, as he hath said unto them. ¶And
this shall be the priest's due from the people, from them that
offer a sacrifice, whether *it be* ox or sheep; and [c]they shall give
unto the priest the shoulder, and the two cheeks, and the maw.

[d] ch. 28. 68. Hos. 11. 5. See Jer. 42. 15.
[e] See 1 Kin. 11. 3, 4.
[f] 2 Kin. 11. 12.
[g] ch. 31. 9, 26. See 2 Kin. 22. 8.
[h] Josh. 1. 8. Ps. 119. 97.
[i] ch. 5. 32. 1 Kin. 15. 5.

[a] Num. 18. 20. & 26. 62. ch. 10. 9.
[b] Num. 18. 8, 9. 1 Cor. 9. 13.
[c] Lev. 7. 30—34.

---

earthly potentates, put his trust in costly and formidable preparations for war (cp. Hos. i. 7).

Egypt was the principal source whence the nations of western Asia drew their supplies of this animal (cp. Ex. xiv. 5 seq.; 1 K. x. 28, 29; 2 K. vii. 6); but intercourse, traffic, or alliance which would "cause the people to return to Egypt" would be to reverse that great and beneficent wonderwork of God which inaugurated the Mosaic Covenant, the deliverance from the bondage of Egypt; and to bring about of set purpose that which God threatened (xxviii. 68) as the sorest punishment for Israel's sin.

17. Multiplication of wives would lead to sensuality, and so to an apostasy no less fatal in effect than downright idolatry (cp. Ex. xxxiv. 16). This rule, like the others, abridges to the ruler of Israel liberties usually enjoyed without stint by the kings of the East. The restriction was in the days of Moses unprecedented; and demanded a higher standard in the king of Israel than was looked for amongst his equals in other nations.

neither shall he greatly multiply to himself silver and gold] In this third prohibition, as in the other two, excess is forbidden. Vast accumulation of treasure could hardly be effected without oppression; nor when effected fail to produce pride and a "trust in uncertain riches" (1 Tim. vi. 17).

18. It is in striking consistency with the dignity which everywhere throughout the Mosaic legislation surrounds the chosen people of God, that even if they will be "like as all the nations about" (*v.* 14), and be governed by a king, care should nevertheless be taken that he shall be no Oriental despot. He is to be of no royal caste, but "one from among thy brethren" (*v.* 15); he is to bear himself as a kind of "primus inter pares," his heart "not being lifted up above his brethren" (*v.* 20); he is, like his subjects, to be bound by the fundamental laws and institutions of the nation, and obliged, as they were, to do his duty in his station of life with constant reference thereto. The spirit of the text is that of Matt. xxiii. 9.

a copy of this law] The whole Pentateuch, or at any rate the legal portion of the Pentateuch.

a book...before the priests the Levites] Cp. marg. ref.

XVIII. **1.** Better, "there shall not be to the priests, the Levites, yea the whole tribe of Levi, any inheritance, &c."

and his inheritance] *i.e.* God's inheritance, that which in making a grant to His people of the Promised Land with its earthly blessings He had reserved for Himself; more particularly the sacrifices and the holy gifts, such as tithes and firstfruits. These were God's portion of the substance of Israel; and as the Levites were His portion of the persons of Israel, it was fitting that the Levites should be sustained from these. On the principle here laid down, cp. 1 Cor. ix. 13, 14.

3. For *maw* read **stomach**, which was regarded as one of the richest and choicest parts. As the animal slain may be considered to consist of three principal parts, head, feet, and body, a portion of each is by the regulation in question to be given to the priest, thus representing the consecration of the whole; or, as some ancient commentators think, the dedication of the words, acts, and appetites of the worshipper to God.

The text probably refers to Peace-offerings, and animals killed for the sacrificial meals held in connection with the Peace-offerings.

[d] Ex. 22. 29. Num. 18. 12, 24.
[e] Ex. 28. 1. Num. 3. 10.
[f] ch. 10. 8. & 17. 12.
[g] Num. 35. 2, 3.
[h] ch. 12. 5.
[i] 2 Chr. 31. 2.
[k] 2 Chr. 31. 4. Neh. 12. 44, 47.
[l] Lev. 18. 26, 27, 30. ch. 12. 29.
[m] Lev. 18. 21. ch. 12. 31.
[n] Lev. 19. 26, 31. & 20. 27. Isai. 8. 19.
[o] Lev. 20. 27.
[p] 1 Sam. 28. 7.
[q] Lev. 18. 24, 25. ch. 9. 4.
[r] ver. 18. John 1. 45. Acts 3. 22. & 7. 37.

4 [d]The firstfruit *also* of thy corn, of thy wine, and of thine oil,
and the first of the fleece of thy sheep, shalt thou give him.
5 For [e]the LORD thy God hath chosen him out of all thy tribes,
[f]to stand to minister in the name of the LORD, him and his sons
6 for ever. ¶ And if a Levite come from any of thy gates out of
all Israel, where he [g]sojourned, and come with all the desire of
7 his mind [h]unto the place which the LORD shall choose; then he
shall minister in the name of the LORD his God, [i]as all his
brethren the Levites *do*, which stand there before the LORD.
8 They shall have like [k]portions to eat, beside [1]that which cometh
9 of the sale of his patrimony. ¶ When thou art come into the
land which the LORD thy God giveth thee, [l]thou shalt not learn
10 to do after the abominations of those nations. There shall not
be found among you *any one* that maketh his son or his daughter
[m]to pass through the fire, [n]*or* that useth divination, *or* an
11 observer of times, or an enchanter, or a witch, [o]or a charmer, or
a consulter with familiar spirits, or a wizard, or a [p]necromancer.
12 For all that do these things *are* an abomination unto the LORD:
and [q]because of these abominations the LORD thy God doth
13 drive them out from before thee. Thou shalt be [2]perfect with
14 the LORD thy God. For these nations, which thou shalt
[3]possess, hearkened unto observers of times, and unto diviners:
but as for thee, the LORD thy God hath not suffered thee so *to do*.
15 ¶ [r]The LORD thy God will raise up unto thee a Prophet from
the midst of thee, of thy brethren, like unto me; unto him ye

[1] Heb. *his sales by the fathers.* [2] Or, *upright,* or, *sincere,* Gen. 17. 1. [3] Or, *inherit.*

6–8. These verses presuppose that part of the Levites only will be in residence and officiating at the place of the Sanctuary, the others of course dwelling at their own homes in the Levitical cities, or "sojourning" elsewhere; cp. marg. reff. But if any Levite out of love for the service of the Sanctuary chose to resort to it when he might reside in his own home, he was to have his share in the maintenance which was provided for those ministering in the order of their course.

8. *beside that which cometh of the sale of his patrimony*] The Levites had indeed "no part nor inheritance with Israel," but they might individually possess property, and in fact often did so (cp. 1 K. ii. 26; Jer. xxxii. 7; Acts iv. 36). The Levite who desired to settle at the place of the Sanctuary would probably sell his patrimony when quitting his former home. The text directs that he should, notwithstanding any such private resources, duly enjoy his share of the perquisites provided for the ministers at the sanctuary, and as he was "waiting at the altar" should be "partaker with the altar" (1 Cor. ix. 13).

10. *to pass through the fire*] *i.e.* to Moloch; cp. Levit. xx. 2 note.

that useth divination] Cp. Num. xxiii. 23 note.

observer of times...enchanter] Cp. Lev. xix. 26 note.

witch] Rather "sorcerer," cp. Ex. vii. 11 note.

11. *a charmer*] *i.e.* one who fascinates and subdues noxious animals or men, such as the famous serpent-charmers of the East (Ps. lviii. 4, 5).

a consulter with familiar spirits...a wizard] Cp. Lev. xix. 31 note.

necromancer] Lit. "one who interrogates the dead." The purpose of the text is obviously to group together all the known words belonging to the practices in question. Cp. 2 Chr. xxxiii. 6.

13. *perfect*] As in Gen. xvii. 1; Job i. 1; Matt. v. 48. The sense is that Israel was to keep the worship of the true God wholly uncontaminated by idolatrous pollutions.

15–19. The ancient Fathers of the Church and the generality of modern commentators have regarded our Lord as the Prophet promised in these verses. It is evident from the New Testament alone that the Messianic was the accredited interpretation amongst the Jews at the beginning of the Christian era (cp. marg. reff., and John iv. 25); nor can our Lord Himself, when He declares that Moses "wrote of Him" (John v. 45–47), be supposed to have any other words more directly in view than these, the only words in which Moses, speaking in his own person, gives any prediction of the kind. But the verses seem to have a further, no less evident if subsidiary, reference to a prophetical order which should stand from time to time, as Moses had done, between God and the people; which should make known God's will to the latter; which should by its

16 shall hearken; according to all that thou desiredst of the LORD
thy God in Horeb [s]in the day of the assembly, saying, [t]Let me
not hear again the voice of the LORD my God, neither let me see
17 this great fire any more, that I die not. And the LORD said
unto me, [u]They have well *spoken that* which they have spoken.
18 [x]I will raise them up a Prophet from among their brethren,
like unto thee, and [y]will put my words in his mouth; [z]and he
19 shall speak unto them all that I shall command him. [a]And it
shall come to pass, *that* whosoever will not hearken unto my
words which he shall speak in my name, I will require *it* of him.
20 But [b]the prophet, which shall presume to speak a word in my
name, which I have not commanded him to speak, or [c]that
shall speak in the name of other gods, even that prophet shall
21 die. And if thou say in thine heart, How shall we know the
22 word which the LORD hath not spoken? [d]When a prophet
speaketh in the name of the LORD, [e]if the thing follow not, nor
come to pass, that *is* the thing which the LORD hath not spoken,
but the prophet hath spoken it [f]presumptuously: thou shalt not
be afraid of him.
CHAP. 19. WHEN the LORD thy God [a]hath cut off the nations,
whose land the LORD thy God giveth thee, and thou [1]succeedest
2 them, and dwellest in their cities, and in their houses; [b]thou
shalt separate three cities for thee in the midst of thy land,
3 which the LORD thy God giveth thee to possess it. Thou shalt
prepare thee a way, and divide the coasts of thy land, which the
LORD thy God giveth thee to inherit, into three parts, that every
4 slayer may flee thither. And [c]this *is* the case of the slayer,
which shall flee thither, that he may live: Whoso killeth his

[s] ch. 9. 10.
[t] Ex. 20. 19. Heb. 12. 19.
[u] ch. 5. 28.
[x] ver. 15. John 1. 45. Acts 3. 22. & 7. 37.
[y] Isai. 51. 16. John 17. 8.
[z] John 4. 25. & 8. 28. & 12. 49. 50.
[a] Acts 3. 23.
[b] ch. 13. 5. Jer. 14. 14. Zech. 13. 3.
[c] ch. 13. 1. Jer. 2. 8.
[d] Jer. 28. 9.
[e] See ch. 13. 2.
[f] ver. 20.
[a] ch. 12. 29.
[b] Ex. 21. 13. Num. 35. 10, 14. Josh. 20. 2.
[c] Num. 35. 15. ch. 4. 42.

[1] Heb. *inheritest*, or, *possessest*.

---

presence render it unnecessary either that God should address the people directly, as at Sinai (*v.* 16; cp. v. 25 seq.), or that the people themselves in lack of counsel should resort to the superstitions of the heathen.

In fact, in the words before us, Moses gives promise both of a prophetic order, and of the Messiah in particular as its chief; of a line of prophets culminating in one eminent individual. And in proportion as we see in our Lord the characteristics of the Prophet most perfectly exhibited, so must we regard the promise of Moses as in Him most completely accomplished.

20. Cp. marg. reff.

21. *And if thou say in thine heart, How, &c.*] The passage evidently assumes such an occasion for consulting the prophet as was usual amongst the heathen, *e.g.* an impending battle or other such crisis (cp. 1 K. xxii. 11), in which his veracity would soon be put to the test. Failure of a prediction is set forth as a sure note of its being "presumptuous." But from xiii. 2 seq. we see that the fulfilment of a prediction would not decisively accredit him who uttered it: for the prophet or dreamer of dreams who endeavoured on the strength of miracles to seduce to idolatry was to be rejected and punished. Nothing therefore *contrary* to the revealed truth of God was to be accepted under any circumstances.

XIX. This and the next two chapters contain enactments designed to protect human life, and to impress its sanctity on Israel.

1–13. In these verses the directions respecting the preparation of the roads to the cities of refuge, the provision of additional cities in case of an extension of territory, and the intervention of the elders as representing the congregation, are peculiar to Deuteronomy and supplementary to the laws on the same subject given in the earlier books (cp. marg. ref.).

1, 2. The three cities of refuge for the district east of Jordan had been already named. Moses now directs that when the territory on the west of Jordan had been conquered, a like allotment of three other cities in it should be made. This was accordingly done; cp. Josh. xx. 1 seq.

3. *Thou shalt prepare thee a way*] It was the duty of the Senate to repair the roads that led to the cities of refuge annually, and remove every obstruction. No hillock was left, no river over which there was not a bridge; and the road was at least two and thirty cubits broad. At cross-roads there were posts bearing the words *Refuge, Refuge*, to guide the fugitive in his flight. It seems as if in Isai. xl. 3 seq. the imagery were borrowed from the preparation of the ways to the cities of refuge.

5 neighbour ignorantly, whom he hated not [1]in time past; as
when a man goeth into the wood with his neighbour to hew
wood, and his hand fetcheth a stroke with the axe to cut down
the tree, and the [2]head slippeth from the [3]helve, and [4]lighteth
upon his neighbour, that he die; he shall flee unto one of those
6 cities, and live: [d]lest the avenger of the blood pursue the slayer,
while his heart is hot, and overtake him, because the way is
long, and [5]slay him; whereas he *was* not worthy of death, inas-
7 much as he hated him not [6]in time past. ¶ Wherefore I command thee, saying, Thou shalt separate three cities for thee.
8 And if the LORD thy God [e]enlarge thy coast, as he hath sworn
unto thy fathers, and give thee all the land which he promised
9 to give unto thy fathers; if thou shalt keep all these commandments to do them, which I command thee this day, to love the
LORD thy God, and to walk ever in his ways; [f]then shalt thou
10 add three cities more for thee, beside these three: that innocent
blood be not shed in thy land, which the LORD thy God giveth
11 thee *for* an inheritance, and *so* blood be upon thee. ¶ But [g]if
any man hate his neighbour, and lie in wait for him, and rise up
against him, and smite him [7]mortally that he die, and fleeth
12 into one of these cities: then the elders of his city shall send
and fetch him thence, and deliver him into the hand of the
13 avenger of blood, that he may die. [h]Thine eye shall not pity
him, [i]but thou shalt put away *the guilt of* innocent blood from
14 Israel, that it may go well with thee. ¶ [k]Thou shalt not remove
thy neighbour's landmark, which they of old time have set in
thine inheritance, which thou shalt inherit in the land that the
15 LORD thy God giveth thee to possess it. ¶ [l]One witness shall
not rise up against a man for any iniquity, or for any sin, in any
sin that he sinneth: at the mouth of two witnesses, or at the
16 mouth of three witnesses, shall the matter be established. If a
false witness [m]rise up against any man to testify against him
17 [8]*that which is* wrong; then both the men, between whom the
controversy *is*, shall stand before the LORD, [n]before the priests
18 and the judges, which shall be in those days; and the judges
shall make diligent inquisition: and, behold, *if* the witness *be* a
false witness, *and* hath testified falsely against his brother;
19 [o]then shall ye do unto him, as he had thought to have done
unto his brother: so [p]shalt thou put the evil away from among

[d] Num. 35. 12.
[e] Gen. 15. 18. ch. 12. 20.
[f] Josh. 20. 7, 8.
[g] Ex. 21. 12. Num. 35. 16, 24. ch. 27. 24. Prov. 28. 17.
[h] ch. 13. 8. & 25. 12.
[i] Num. 35. 33, 34. ch. 21. 9. 1 Kin. 2. 31.
[k] ch. 27. 17. Job 24. 2. Prov. 22. 28. Hos. 5. 10.
[l] Num. 35. 30. ch. 17. 6.
[m] Ps. 27. 12. & 35. 11.
[n] ch. 17. 9. & 21. 5.
[o] Prov. 19. 5, 9. Dan. 6. 24.
[p] ch. 13. 5. & 17. 7.

[1] Heb. *from yesterday the third day.*
[2] Heb. *iron.*
[3] Heb. *wood.*
[4] Heb. *findeth.*
[5] Heb. *smite him in life.*
[6] Heb. *from yesterday the third day.*
[7] Heb. *in life.*
[8] Or, *falling away.*

---

5. *with the axe*] Lit. "with the iron." Note the employment of iron for tools, and cp. iii. 11 note.

8, 9. Provision is here made for the anticipated enlargement of the borders of Israel to the utmost limits promised by God, from the river of Egypt to the Euphrates (Gen. xv. 18; Ex. xxiii. 31, and notes). This promise, owing to the sins of the people, did not receive its fulfilment till after David had conquered the Philistines, Syrians, &c.; and this but a transient one, for many of the conquered peoples regained independence on the dissolution of Solomon's empire.

14. As a man's life is to be held sacred, so are his means of livelihood; and in this connection a prohibition is inserted against removing a neighbour's landmark: cp. marg. reff.

16. *testify against him that which is wrong*] Marg. more literally, "a falling away." The word is used (xiii. 5) to signify apostasy or revolt; here it is no doubt to be understood in the wider sense of any departure from the Law.

17. *both the men, between whom the controversy is*] Not the accused and the false witness, but the plaintiff and defendant (cp. Ex. xxiii. 1) who were summoned before the supreme court held, as provided in chap. xvii., at the Sanctuary. The judges acted as God's representative; to lie to them was to lie to Him.

19, 21. See marg. reff.

20 you. [q]And those which remain shall hear, and fear, and shall
21 henceforth commit no more any such evil among you. [r]And
thine eye shall not pity; *but* [s]life *shall go* for life, eye for eye,
tooth for tooth, hand for hand, foot for foot.
Chap. 20. WHEN thou goest out to battle against thine enemies,
and seest [a]horses, and chariots, *and* a people more than thou, be
not afraid of them: for the LORD thy God *is* [b]with thee, which
2 brought thee up out of the land of Egypt. And it shall be,
when ye are come nigh unto the battle, that the priest shall
3 approach and speak unto the people, and shall say unto them,
Hear, O Israel, ye approach this day unto battle against your
enemies: let not your hearts [1]faint, fear not, and do not [2]tremble,
4 neither be ye terrified because of them; for the LORD your God
is he that goeth with you, [c]to fight for you against your enemies,
5 to save you. ¶ And the officers shall speak unto the people,
saying, What man *is there* that hath built a new house, and
hath not [d]dedicated it? Let him go and return to his house, lest
6 he die in the battle, and another man dedicate it. And what
man *is he* that hath planted a vineyard, and hath not *yet* [3]eaten
of it? Let him *also* go and return unto his house, lest he die in
7 the battle, and another man eat of it. [e]And what man *is there*
that hath betrothed a wife, and hath not taken her? Let him go
and return unto his house, lest he die in the battle, and another
8 man take her. And the officers shall speak further unto the
people, and they shall say, [f]What man *is there that is* fearful
and fainthearted? Let him go and return unto his house, lest his
9 brethren's heart [4]faint as well as his heart. And it shall be,
when the officers have made an end of speaking unto the people,
that they shall make captains of the armies [5]to lead the people.
10 ¶ When thou comest nigh unto a city to fight against it, [g]then
11 proclaim peace unto it. And it shall be, if it make thee answer
of peace, and open unto thee, then it shall be, *that* all the people
that is found therein shall be tributaries unto thee, and they
12 shall serve thee. And if it will make no peace with thee, but
13 will make war against thee, then thou shalt besiege it: and when
the LORD thy God hath delivered it into thine hands, [h]thou shalt
14 smite every male thereof with the edge of the sword: but the
women, and the little ones, and [i]the cattle, and all that is in the
city, *even* all the spoil thereof, shalt thou [6]take unto thyself;

[q] ch. 17. 13. & 21. 21.
[r] ver. 13.
[s] Ex. 21. 23. Lev. 24. 20. Matt. 5. 38.
[a] See Ps. 20. 7. Isai. 31. 1.
[b] Num. 23. 21. ch. 31. 6, 8. 2 Chr. 13.12. & 32. 7, 8.
[c] ch. 1. 30. & 3. 22. Josh. 23. 10.
[d] See Neh. 12. 27. Ps. 30, title.
[e] ch. 24. 5.
[f] Judg. 7. 3.
[g] 2 Sam. 20. 18, 20.
[h] Num. 31. 7.
[i] Josh. 8. 2.

[1] Heb. *be tender.*
[2] Heb. *make haste.*
[3] Heb. *made it common:* See Lev. 19. 23, 24. ch. 28. 30.
[4] Heb. *melt.*
[5] Heb. to be *in the head of the people.*
[6] Heb. *spoil.*

XX. **1.** *horses, and chariots*] The most formidable elements of an Oriental host, which the Canaanites possessed in great numbers; cp. Josh. xvii. 16; Judg. iv. 3; 1 S. xiii. 5. Israel could not match these with corresponding forces (cp. xvii. 16 notes and reff.), but, having the God of battles on its side, was not to be dismayed by them; the assumption being that the war had the sanction of God, and was consequently just.

2. *the priest*] Not the High-priest, but one appointed for the purpose, and called, according to the Rabbins, "the Anointed of the War:" hence perhaps the expression of Jer. vi. 4, &c. "prepare ye" (lit. consecrate) "war." Thus Phinehas went with the warriors to fight against Midian, (Num. xxxi. 6; cp. 1 S. iv. 4, 11; 2 Chr. xiii. 12).

5. *the officers*] See Ex. v. 6 note.

dedicated it] Cp. marg. reff. The expression is appropriate, because various ceremonies of a religious kind were customary amongst the Jews on taking possession of a new house. The immunity conferred in this verse lasted, like that in *v.* 7 (cp. xxiv. 5), for a year.

6. See marg. and reff. The fruit of newly-planted trees was set apart from common uses for four years.

9. The meaning is that the "officers" should then subdivide the levies, and appoint leaders of the smaller divisions thus constituted.

10–20. Directions intended to prevent wanton destruction of life and property in sieges.

and [k]thou shalt eat the spoil of thine enemies, which the LORD
15 thy God hath given thee. Thus shalt thou do unto all the cities
which are very far off from thee, which *are* not of the cities of
16 these nations. But [l]of the cities of these people, which the
LORD thy God doth give thee *for* an inheritance, thou shalt save
17 alive nothing that breatheth: but thou shalt utterly destroy
them; *namely*, the Hittites, and the Amorites, the Canaanites,
and the Perizzites, the Hivites, and the Jebusites; as the LORD
18 thy God hath commanded thee: that [m]they teach you not to do
after all their abominations, which they have done unto their
19 gods; so should ye [n]sin against the LORD your God. ¶ When
thou shalt besiege a city a long time, in making war against it
to take it, thou shalt not destroy the trees thereof by forcing an
axe against them: for thou mayest eat of them, and thou shalt
not cut them down ([1]for the tree of the field *is* man's *life*) [2]to
20 employ *them* in the siege: only the trees which thou knowest
that they *be* not trees for meat, thou shalt destroy and cut them
down; and thou shalt build bulwarks against the city that
maketh war with thee, until [3]it be subdued.

CHAP. 21. IF *one* be found slain in the land which the LORD thy
God giveth thee to possess it, lying in the field, *and* it be not
2 known who hath slain him: then thy elders and thy judges
shall come forth, and they shall measure unto the cities which
3 *are* round about him that is slain: and it shall be, *that* the city
which is next unto the slain man, even the elders of that city
shall take an heifer, which hath not been wrought with, *and*
4 which hath not drawn in the yoke; and the elders of that city
shall bring down the heifer unto a rough valley, which is neither
eared nor sown, and shall strike off the heifer's neck there in the
5 valley: and the priests the sons of Levi shall come near; for
[a]them the LORD thy God hath chosen to minister unto him, and
to bless in the name of the LORD; and [b]by their [4]word shall
6 every controversy and every stroke be *tried:* and all the elders
of that city, *that are* next unto the slain *man*, [c]shall wash their
7 hands over the heifer that is beheaded in the valley: and they

[k] Josh. 22. 8.
[l] Num. 21. 2, 3, 35. & 33. 52. ch. 7. 1. 2. Josh. 11. 14.
[m] ch. 7. 4. & 12. 30, 31. & 18. 9.
[n] Ex. 23. 33.
[a] ch. 10. 8. 1 Chr. 23.13.
[b] ch. 17. 8, 9.
[c] See Ps. 19. 12. & 26. 6. Matt. 27. 24.

[1] Or, *for, O man, the tree of the field* is *to be employed in the siege.*
[2] Heb. *to go from before thee.*
[3] Heb. *it come down.*
[4] Heb. *mouth.*

---

16. Forbearance, however, was not to be shown towards the Canaanitish nations, which were to be utterly exterminated (cp. vii. 1–4). The command did not apply to beasts as well as men (cp. Josh. xi. 11 and 14).

19. The parenthesis may be more literally rendered "for man is a tree of the field," *i.e.* has his life from the tree of the field, is supported in life by it (cp. xxiv. 6). The Egyptians seem invariably to have cut down the fruit-trees in war.

XXI. **2.** The elders represented the citizens at large, the judges the magistracy: priests (*v.* 5) from the nearest priestly town, were likewise to be at hand. Thus all classes would be represented at the purging away of that blood-guiltiness which until removed attached to the whole community.

3. The requirements as regards place and victim are symbolical. The heifer represented the murderer, so far at least as to die in his stead, since he himself could not be found. As bearing his guilt the heifer must therefore be one which was of full growth and strength, and had not yet been ceremonially profaned by human use. The Christian commentators find here a type of Christ and of His sacrifice for man: but the heifer was not strictly a sacrifice or Sin-offering. The transaction was rather figurative, and was so ordered as to impress the lesson of Gen. ix. 5.

4. *eared*] *i.e.* ploughed; cp. Gen. xlv. 6 note and reff. The word is derived from the Latin, and is in frequent use by English writers of the fifteenth and two following centuries.

strike off the heifer's neck] Rather, "break its neck" (cp. Ex. xiii. 13). The mode of killing the victim distinguishes this lustration from the Sin-offering, in which there would be of course shedding and sprinkling of the blood.

shall answer and say, Our hands have not shed this blood,
8 neither have our eyes seen *it*. Be merciful, O LORD, unto thy
people Israel, whom thou hast redeemed, [d]and lay not innocent
blood [1]unto thy people of Israel's charge. And the blood shall
9 be forgiven them. So [e]shalt thou put away the *guilt of* innocent
blood from among you, when thou shalt do *that which is* right in
10 the sight of the LORD. ¶ When thou goest forth to war against
thine enemies, and the LORD thy God hath delivered them into
11 thine hands, and thou hast taken them captive, and seest among
the captives a beautiful woman, and hast a desire unto her, that
12 thou wouldest have her to thy wife; then thou shalt bring her
13 home to thine house; and she shall shave her head, and [2][3]pare
her nails; and she shall put the raiment of her captivity from
off her, and shall remain in thine house, and [f]bewail her father
and her mother a full month: and after that thou shalt go in
14 unto her, and be her husband, and she shall be thy wife. And
it shall be, if thou have no delight in her, then thou shalt let
her go whither she will; but thou shalt not sell her at all for
money, thou shalt not make merchandise of her, because thou
15 hast [g]humbled her. ¶ If a man have two wives, one beloved,
[h]and another hated, and they have born him children, *both* the
beloved and the hated; and *if* the firstborn son be her's that was
16 hated: then it shall be, [i]when he maketh his sons to inherit
that which he hath, *that* he may not make the son of the beloved
firstborn before the son of the hated, *which is indeed* the first-
17 born: but he shall acknowledge the son of the hated *for* the
firstborn, [k]by giving him a double portion of all [4]that he hath:
for he *is* [l]the beginning of his strength; [m]the right of the first-
18 born *is* his. ¶ If a man have a stubborn and rebellious son, which
will not obey the voice of his father, or the voice of his mother,
and *that*, when they have chastened him, will not hearken unto
19 them: then shall his father and his mother lay hold on him, and
bring him out unto the elders of his city, and unto the gate of

[d] Jonah 1. 14.
[e] ch. 19. 13.
[f] See Ps. 45. 10.
[g] Gen. 34. 2. ch. 22. 29. Judg. 19. 24.
[h] Gen. 29. 33.
[i] 1 Chr. 5. 2. & 26. 10. 2 Chr. 11. 19, 22.
[k] See 1 Chr. 5. 1.
[l] Gen. 49. 3.
[m] Gen. 25. 31, 33.

[1] Heb. *in the midst.*
[2] Or, *suffer to grow.*
[3] Heb. *make,* or, *dress.*
[4] Heb. *that is found with him.*

10 seq. The regulations which now follow in the rest of this and throughout the next chapter bring out the sanctity of various personal rights and relations fundamental to human life and society.

10–14. The war supposed here is one against the neighbouring nations after Israel had utterly destroyed the Canaanites (cp. vii. 3), and taken possession of their land.

12. The shaving the head (a customary sign of purification, Lev. xiv. 8; Num. viii. 7), and the putting away "the garment of her captivity," were designed to signify the translation of the woman from the state of a heathen and a slave to that of a wife amongst the Covenant-people. Consistency required that she should "pare" (dress, cp. 2 S. xix. 24), not "suffer to grow," her nails; and thus, so far as possible, lay aside everything belonging to her condition as an alien.

13. *bewail her father and her mother a full month*] This is prescribed from motives of humanity, that the woman might have time and leisure to detach her affections from their natural ties, and prepare her mind for new ones.

14. *thou shalt not make merchandise of her*] Rather, **thou shalt not constrain her**: lit. "treat her with constraint," or "treat her as a slave."

15–17. Moses did not originate the rights of primogeniture (cp. Gen. xxv. 31), but recognized them, since he found them pre-existing in the general social system of the East. Paternal authority could set aside these rights on just grounds (Gen. xxvii. 33), but it is forbidden here to do so from mere partiality.

18–21. The formal accusation of parents against a child was to be received without inquiry, as being its own proof. Thus the just authority of the parents is recognized and effectually upheld (cp. Ex. xx. 12, xxi. 15, 17; Lev. xx. 9); but the extreme and irresponsible power of life and death, conceded by the law of Rome and other heathen nations, is withheld from the Israelite father. In this, as in the last law, provision is made against the abuses of a necessary authority.

20 his place; and they shall say unto the elders of his city, This
our son *is* stubborn and rebellious, he will not obey our voice;
21 *he is* a glutton, and a drunkard. And all the men of his city
shall stone him with stones, that he die: [n]so shalt thou put evil
away from among you; [o]and all Israel shall hear, and fear.
22 ¶ And if a man have committed a sin [p]worthy of death, and he
23 be to be put to death, and thou hang him on a tree: [q]his body
shall not remain all night upon the tree, but thou shalt in any
wise bury him that day; (for [r]he that is hanged *is* [1]accursed of
God;) that [s]thy land be not defiled, which the LORD thy God
giveth thee *for* an inheritance.
CHAP. 22. THOU [a]shalt not see thy brother's ox or his sheep go
astray, and hide thyself from them: thou shalt in any case bring
2 them again unto thy brother. And if thy brother *be* not nigh
unto thee, or if thou know him not, then thou shalt bring it
unto thine own house, and it shall be with thee until thy brother
3 seek after it, and thou shalt restore it to him again. In like
manner shalt thou do with his ass; and so shalt thou do with his
raiment; and with all lost thing of thy brother's, which he hath
lost, and thou hast found, shalt thou do likewise: thou mayest
4 not hide thyself. [b]Thou shalt not see thy brother's ass or his
ox fall down by the way, and hide thyself from them: thou shalt
5 surely help him to lift *them* up again. ¶ The woman shall not
wear that which pertaineth unto a man, neither shall a man put
on a woman's garment: for all that do so *are* abomination unto
6 the LORD thy God. ¶ If a bird's nest chance to be before thee
in the way in any tree, or on the ground, *whether they be* young
ones, or eggs, and the dam sitting upon the young, or upon the
7 eggs, [c]thou shalt not take the dam with the young: *but* thou
shalt in any wise let the dam go, and take the young to thee;
[d]that it may be well with thee, and *that* thou mayest prolong *thy*
8 days. ¶ When thou buildest a new house, then thou shalt make
a battlement for thy roof, that thou bring not blood upon thine

[n] ch. 13. 5. & 19. 19, 20. & 22. 21, 24.
[o] ch. 13. 11.
[p] ch. 19. 6. & 22. 26. Acts 23. 29. & 25. 11, 25. & 26. 31.
[q] Josh. 8. 29. & 10. 26, 27. John 19. 31.
[r] Gal. 3. 13.
[s] Lev. 18. 25. Num. 35. 34.
[a] Ex. 23. 4.
[b] Ex. 23. 5.
[c] Lev. 22. 28.
[d] ch. 4. 40.

[1] Heb. *the curse of God:* See Num. 25. 4. 2 Sam. 21. 6.

---

22. There were four methods of execution in use amongst the ancient Jews; stoning (Ex. xvii. 4; Deut. xiii. 10, &c.), burning (Lev. xx. 14; xxi. 9), the sword (Ex. xxxii. 27), and strangulation. The latter, though not named in Scripture, is regarded by the Rabbins as the most common, and the proper one to be adopted when no other is expressly enjoined by the Law. Suspension, whether from cross, stake, or gallows, was not used as a mode of taking life, but was sometimes added after death as an enhancement of punishment. Pharaoh's chief baker (Gen. xl. 19) was hanged after being put to death by the sword; and similarly Joshua appears (Jos. x. 26) to have dealt with the five kings who made war against Gibeon. Cp. also Num. xxv. 4.

23. *he that is hanged is accursed of God*] *i.e.* "Bury him that is hanged out of the way before evening: his hanging body defiles the land; for God's curse rests on it." The curse of God is probably regarded as lying on the malefactor because, from the fact of his being hanged, he must have been guilty of a peculiarly atrocious breach of God's Covenant. Such an offender could not remain on the face of the earth without defiling it (cp. Lev. xviii. 25, 28; Num. xxxv. 34). Therefore after the penalty of his crime had been inflicted, and he had hung for a time as a public example, the Holy Land was to be at once and entirely delivered from his presence. See Gal. iii. 13 for St. Paul's quotation of this text and his application of it.

XXII. On the general character of the contents of this chapter see xxi. 10 note.

5. *that which pertaineth unto a man*] *i.e.* not only his dress but all that specially pertains distinctively to his sex; arms, domestic and other utensils, &c.

The distinction between the sexes is natural and divinely established, and cannot be neglected without indecorum and consequent danger to purity (cp. 1 Cor. xi. 3–15).

6–8. These precepts are designed to cultivate a spirit of humanity. Cp. xxv. 4; Lev. xxii. 28; and 1 Cor. ix. 9, 10.

8. The roofs of houses in Palestine were flat and used for various purposes. Cp. Josh. ii. 6; 2 Sam. xi. 2; Acts x. 9, &c. A battlement was almost a necessary protection. It was to be, according to the

9 house, if any man fall from thence. ¶ [e]Thou shalt not sow thy
vineyard with divers seeds: lest the [1]fruit of thy seed which thou
10 hast sown, and the fruit of thy vineyard, be defiled. [f]Thou
11 shalt not plow with an ox and an ass together. [g]Thou shalt not
wear a garment of divers sorts, *as* of woollen and linen together.
12 ¶ Thou shalt make thee [h]fringes upon the four [2]quarters of thy
13 vesture, wherewith thou coverest *thyself*. ¶ If any man take a
14 wife, and [i]go in unto her, and hate her, and give occasions of
speech against her, and bring up an evil name upon her, and
say, I took this woman, and when I came to her, I found her
15 not a maid: then shall the father of the damsel, and her mother,
take and bring forth *the tokens of* the damsel's virginity unto the
16 elders of the city in the gate: and the damsel's father shall say
unto the elders, I gave my daughter unto this man to wife, and
17 he hateth her; and, lo, he hath given occasions of speech *against
her*, saying, I found not thy daughter a maid; and yet these *are
the tokens of* my daughter's virginity. And they shall spread the
18 cloth before the elders of the city. And the elders of that city
19 shall take that man and chastise him; and they shall amerce him
in an hundred *shekels* of silver, and give *them* unto the father of
the damsel, because he hath brought up an evil name upon a
virgin of Israel: and she shall be his wife; he may not put her
20 away all his days. But if this thing be true, *and the tokens of* vir-
21 ginity be not found for the damsel: then they shall bring out
the damsel to the door of her father's house, and the men of her
city shall stone her with stones that she die: because she hath
[k]wrought folly in Israel, to play the whore in her father's house:
22 [l]so shalt thou put evil away from among you. ¶ [m]If a man be
found lying with a woman married to an husband, then they
shall both of them die, *both* the man that lay with the woman,
23 and the woman: so shalt thou put away evil from Israel. ¶ If
a damsel *that is* a virgin be [n]betrothed unto an husband, and a
24 man find her in the city, and lie with her; then ye shall bring
them both out unto the gate of that city, and ye shall stone them
with stones that they die; the damsel, because she cried not,
being in the city; and the man, because he hath [o]humbled his
neighbour's wife: [p]so thou shalt put away evil from among you.
25 ¶ But if a man find a betrothed damsel in the field, and the man
[3]force her, and lie with her: then the man only that lay with
26 her shall die: but unto the damsel thou shalt do nothing; *there
is* in the damsel no sin *worthy* of death: for as when a man
riseth against his neighbour, and slayeth him, even so *is* this
27 matter: for he found her in the field, *and* the betrothed damsel
28 cried, and *there was* none to save her. ¶ [q]If a man find a damsel
that is a virgin, which is not betrothed, and lay hold on her, and
29 lie with her, and they be found; then the man that lay with her

[e] Lev. 19. 19.
[f] See 2 Cor. 6. 14, 15, 16.
[g] Lev. 19. 19.
[h] Num. 15. 38. Matt. 23. 5.
[i] Gen. 29. 21. Judg. 15. 1.
[k] Gen. 34. 7. Judg. 20. 6, 10. 2 Sam. 13. 12, 13.
[l] ch. 13. 5.
[m] Lev. 20. 10. John 8. 5.
[n] Matt. 1. 18, 19.
[o] ch. 21. 14.
[p] ver. 21, 22.
[q] Ex. 22. 16, 17.

[1] Heb. *fulness of thy seed.*
[2] Heb. *wings.*
[3] Or, *take strong hold of her,* 2 Sam. 13. 14.

Rabbins, at least two cubits (about 3 ft.) high.

9–11. Cp. marg. ref. The prohibition of *v.* 10 was also dictated by humanity. The ox and the ass being of such different size and strength, it would be cruel to the latter to yoke them together. These two animals are named as being those ordinarily employed in agriculture; cp. Isai. xxxii. 20.

12. Cp. Num. xv. 38 and note.

19. The fine was to be paid to the father, because the slander was against him principally as the head of the wife's family. If the damsel were an orphan the fine reverted to herself. The fact that the penalties attached to bearing false witness against a wife are fixed and comparatively light indicates the low estimation and position of the woman at that time.

shall give unto the damsel's father fifty *shekels* of silver, and she
shall be his wife; [r]because he hath humbled her, he may not
30 put her away all his days. [s]A man shall not take his father's
wife, nor [t]discover his father's skirt.
Chap. 23. HE that is wounded in the stones, or hath his privy
member cut off, shall not enter into the congregation of the
2 Lord. A bastard shall not enter into the congregation of the
Lord; even to his tenth generation shall he not enter into the
3 congregation of the Lord. [a]An Ammonite or Moabite shall
not enter into the congregation of the Lord; even to their tenth
generation shall they not enter into the congregation of the Lord
4 for ever: [b]because they met you not with bread and with water in
the way, when ye came forth out of Egypt; and [c]because they
hired against thee Balaam the son of Beor of Pethor of Mesopo-
5 tamia, to curse thee. Nevertheless the Lord thy God would
not hearken unto Balaam; but the Lord thy God turned the
curse into a blessing unto thee, because the Lord thy God loved
6 thee. [d]Thou shalt not seek their peace nor their [1]prosperity all
7 thy days for ever. Thou shalt not abhor an Edomite; [e]for he *is*
thy brother: thou shalt not abhor an Egyptian; because [f]thou
8 wast a stranger in his land. The children that are begotten of
them shall enter into the congregation of the Lord in their third
9 generation. ¶ When the host goeth forth against thine enemies,
10 then keep thee from every wicked thing. [g]If there be among
you any man, that is not clean by reason of uncleanness that
chanceth him by night, then shall he go abroad out of the camp,
11 he shall not come within the camp: but it shall be, when evening [2]cometh on, [h]he shall wash *himself* with water: and when
12 the sun is down, he shall come into the camp *again*. Thou shalt
have a place also without the camp, whither thou shalt go forth

[r] ver. 24.
[s] Lev. 18. 8. & 20. 11. ch. 27. 20. 1 Cor. 5. 1.
[t] See Ruth 3. 9. Ez. 16. 8.
[a] Neh. 13. 1, 2.
[b] See ch. 2. 29.
[c] Num. 22. 5, 6.
[d] Ezra 9. 12.
[e] Gen. 25. 24, 25, 26. Obad. 10. 12.
[f] Ex. 22. 21. & 23. 9. Lev. 19. 34. ch. 10. 19.
[g] Lev. 15. 16.
[h] Lev. 15. 5.

[1] Heb. *good*. [2] Heb. *turneth toward*.

XXIII. This chapter enjoins sanctity and purity in the congregation of Israel as a whole, and lays down certain rights and duties of citizenship.

1. Cp. Lev. xxi. 17-24. Such persons, exhibiting a mutilation of that human nature which was made in God's image, were rejected from the Covenant entirely. They could however be proselytes (cp. Acts viii. 27). The Old Test. itself foretells (Isai. lvi. 3-5) the removal of this ban when under the kingdom of Messiah the outward and emblematic perfection and sanctity of Israel should be fulfilled in their inner meaning by the covenanted Presence and work of the Holy Spirit in the Church.

2. *a bastard*] Probably, a child born of incest or adultery.

even to his tenth generation] i.e. (see next verse and Neh. xiii. 1), *for ever*. Ten is the number of perfection and completeness.

3-5. This law forbids only the naturalization of those against whom it is directed. It does not forbid their dwelling in the land; and seems to refer rather to the nations than to individuals. It was not understood at any rate to interdict marriage with a Moabitess; cp. Ruth i. 4, iv. 13. Ruth however and her sister were doubtless proselytes.

4. Cp. marg. ref. The Moabites and the Ammonites are to be regarded as clans of the same stock rather than as two independent nations, and as acting together. Cp. 2 Chr. xx. 1.

6. *i.e.* "thou shalt not invite them to be on terms of amity with thee (cp. xx. 10 seq.), nor make their welfare thy care": cp. Ezra ix. 12. There is no injunction to hatred or retaliation (cp. ii. 9, 19); but later history contains frequent record of hostility between Israel and these nations.

7, 8. The Edomite, as descended from Esau the twin brother of Jacob (cp. ii. 4), and the Egyptian, as of that nation which had for long shewn hospitality to Joseph and his brethren, were not to be objects of abhorrence. The oppression of the Egyptians was perhaps regarded as the act of the Pharaohs rather than the will of the people (Ex. xi. 2, 3); and at any rate was not to cancel the memory of preceding hospitality.

8. *in their third generation*] *i.e.* the great grandchildren of the Edomite or Egyptian alien: cp. the similar phrase in Ex. xx. 5.

9-14. The whole passage refers not to the encampments of the nation whilst passing from Egypt through the wilderness, but to future warlike expeditions sent out from Canaan.

13 abroad: and thou shalt have a paddle upon thy weapon; and it
shall be, when thou [1]wilt ease thyself abroad, thou shalt dig
therewith, and shalt turn back and cover that which cometh
14 from thee: for the LORD thy God [i]walketh in the midst of thy
camp, to deliver thee, and to give up thine enemies before thee;
therefore shall thy camp be holy: that he see no [2]unclean thing
15 in thee, and turn away from thee. ¶ [k]Thou shalt not deliver
unto his master the servant which is escaped from his master
16 unto thee: he shall dwell with thee, *even* among you, in that
place which he shall choose in one of thy gates, where it [3]liketh
17 him best: [l]thou shalt not oppress him. ¶ There shall be no
[4]whore [m]of the daughters of Israel, nor [n]a sodomite of the sons
18 of Israel. Thou shalt not bring the hire of a whore, or the price
of a dog, into the house of the LORD thy God for any vow: for
even both these *are* abomination unto the LORD thy God.
19 ¶ [o]Thou shalt not lend upon usury to thy brother; usury of
money, usury of victuals, usury of anything that is lent upon
20 usury: [p]unto a stranger thou mayest lend upon usury; but
unto thy brother thou shalt not lend upon usury: [q]that the
LORD thy God may bless thee in all that thou settest thine hand
21 to in the land whither thou goest to possess it. ¶ [r]When thou
shalt vow a vow unto the LORD thy God, thou shalt not slack to
pay it: for the LORD thy God will surely require it of thee;
22 and it would be sin in thee. But if thou shalt forbear to vow,
23 it shall be no sin in thee. [s]That which is gone out of thy lips
thou shalt keep and perform; *even* a freewill offering, according
as thou hast vowed unto the LORD thy God, which thou hast
24 promised with thy mouth. ¶ When thou comest into thy neighbour's vineyard, then thou mayest eat grapes thy fill at thine
25 own pleasure; but thou shalt not put *any* in thy vessel. When
thou comest into the standing corn of thy neighbour, [t]then thou
mayest pluck the ears with thine hand; but thou shalt not move
a sickle unto thy neighbour's standing corn.

CHAP. 24. WHEN a [a]man hath taken a wife, and married her, and
it come to pass that she find no favour in his eyes, because he

[i] Lev. 26. 12.
[k] 1 Sam. 30. 15.
[l] Ex. 22. 21.
[m] Lev. 19. 29. See Prov. 2. 16.
[n] Gen. 19. 5. 2 Kin. 23. 7.
[o] Ex. 22. 25. Lev. 25. 36, 37. Neh. 5. 2, 7. Ps. 15. 5. Luke 6. 34, 35.
[p] See Lev. 19. 34. & ch. 15. 3.
[q] ch. 15. 10.
[r] Num. 30. 2. Eccles. 5. 4, 5.
[s] Num. 30. 2. Ps. 66. 13, 14.
[t] Matt. 12. 1. Mark 2. 23. Luke 6. 1.
[a] Matt. 5. 31. & 19. 7. Mark 10. 4.

[1] Heb. *sittest down.*
[2] Heb. *nakedness of any thing.*
[3] Heb. *is good for him.*
[4] Or, *sodomitess.*

15, 16. The case in question is that of a slave who fled from a heathen master to the Holy Land. It is of course assumed that the refugee was not flying from justice, but only from the tyranny of his lord.

17. Cp. marg. ref. Prostitution was a common part of religious observances amongst idolatrous nations, especially in the worship of Ashtoreth or Astarte. Cp. Micah i. 7; Baruch vi. 43.

18. Another Gentile practice, connected with the one alluded to in the preceding verse, is here forbidden. The word "dog" is figurative (cp. Rev. xxii. 15), and equivalent to the "sodomite" of the verse preceding.

XXIV. In this and the next chapter certain particular rights and duties, domestic, social, and civil, are treated. The cases brought forward have often no definite connexion, and seem selected in order to illustrate the application of the great principles of the Law in certain important events and circumstances.

1–4. These four verses contain only one sentence, and should be rendered thus: **If a man hath taken a wife, &c., and given her a bill of divorcement; and** (*v.* 2) **if she has departed out of his house and become another man's wife; and** (*v.* 3) **if the latter husband hate her, then** (*v.* 4) **her former husband, &c.**

Moses neither institutes nor enjoins divorce. The exact spirit of the passage is given in our Lord's words to the Jews, "Moses because of the hardness of your hearts suffered you to put away your wives" (Matt. xix. 8). Not only does the original institution of marriage as recorded by Moses (Gen. ii. 24) set forth the perpetuity of the bond, but the verses before us plainly intimate that divorce, whilst tolerated for

hath found [1]some uncleanness in her: then let him write her a
bill of [2]divorcement, and give *it* in her hand, and send her out of
2 his house. And when she is departed out of his house, she may
3 go and be another man's *wife*. And *if* the latter husband hate
her, and write her a bill of divorcement, and giveth *it* in her
hand, and sendeth her out of his house; or if the latter husband
4 die, which took her *to be* his wife; [b]her former husband, which
sent her away, may not take her again to be his wife, after that
she is defiled; for that *is* abomination before the LORD: and
thou shalt not cause the land to sin, which the LORD thy God
5 giveth thee *for* an inheritance. ¶ [c]When a man hath taken a
new wife, he shall not go out to war, [3]neither shall he be
charged with any business: *but* he shall be free at home one
6 year, and shall [d]cheer up his wife which he hath taken. ¶ No
man shall take the nether or the upper millstone to pledge: for
7 he taketh *a man's* life to pledge. ¶ [e]If a man be found stealing
any of his brethren of the children of Israel, and maketh merchandise of him, or selleth him; then that thief shall die; [f]and
8 thou shalt put evil away from among you. ¶ Take heed in [g]the
plague of leprosy, that thou observe diligently, and do according
to all that the priests the Levites shall teach you: as I com-
9 manded them, *so* ye shall observe to do. [h]Remember what the
LORD thy God did [i]unto Miriam by the way, after that ye were
10 come forth out of Egypt. ¶ When thou dost [4]lend thy brother
any thing, thou shalt not go into his house to fetch his pledge.
11 Thou shalt stand abroad, and the man to whom thou dost lend
12 shall bring out the pledge abroad unto thee. And if the man *be*
13 poor, thou shalt not sleep with his pledge: [k]in any case thou
shalt deliver him the pledge again when the sun goeth down,
that he may sleep in his own raiment, and [l]bless thee: and [m]it
shall be righteousness unto thee before the LORD thy God.
14 ¶ Thou shalt not [n]oppress an hired servant *that is* poor and
needy, *whether he be* of thy brethren, or of thy strangers that *are*
15 in thy land within thy gates: at his day [o]thou shalt give *him*
his hire, neither shall the sun go down upon it; for he *is* poor,
and [5]setteth his heart upon it: [p]lest he cry against thee unto
16 the LORD, and it be sin unto thee. ¶ [q]The fathers shall not be
put to death for the children, neither shall the children be put
to death for the fathers: every man shall be put to death for
17 his own sin. ¶ [r]Thou shalt not pervert the judgment of the
stranger, *nor* of the fatherless; [s]nor take a widow's raiment to

Jer. 3. 1.
[c] ch. 20. 7.
[d] Prov. 5. 18.
[e] Ex. 21. 16.
[f] ch. 19. 19.
[g] Lev. 13. 2. & 14. 2.
[h] See Luke 17. 32. 1 Cor. 10. 6.
[i] Num. 12. 10.
[k] Ex. 22. 26.
[l] Job 29. 11, 13. & 31. 20. 2 Cor. 9. 13. 2 Tim. 1. 18.
[m] ch. 6. 25. Ps. 106. 31. & 112. 9. Dan. 4. 27.
[n] Mal. 3. 5.
[o] Lev. 19.13. Jer. 22. 13. James 5. 4.
[p] James 5. 4.
[q] 2 Kin. 14. 6. 2 Chr. 25. 4. Jer. 31. 29, 30. Ez. 18. 20.
[r] Ex. 22. 21, 22. Prov. 22. 22. Isai. 1. 23. Jer. 5. 28. & 22. 3. Ez. 22. 29. Zech. 7. 10. Mal. 3. 5.
[s] Ex. 22. 26.

[1] Heb. *matter of nakedness.*
[2] Heb. *cutting off.*
[3] Heb. *not any thing shall pass upon him.*
[4] Heb. *lend the loan of any thing to, &c.*
[5] Heb. *lifteth his soul unto it*, Ps. 25. 1. & 86. 4.

---

the time, contravenes the order of nature and of God. The divorced woman who marries again is "defiled" (*v.* 4), and is grouped in this particular with the adulteress (cp. Lev. xviii. 20). Our Lord then was speaking according to the spirit of the law of Moses when he declared, "Whoso marrieth her which is put away doth commit adultery" (Matt. xix. 9). He was speaking too not less according to the mind of the Prophets (cp. Mal. ii. 14-16). But Moses could not absolutely put an end to a practice which was traditional, and common to the Jews with other Oriental nations. His aim is therefore to regulate and thus to mitigate an evil which he could not extirpate.

6. Cp. Ex. xxii. 25, 26.

7. Cp. xxi. 14, and Ex. xxi. 16.

10-13. Cp. Ex. xxii. 25-27.

13. *righteousness unto thee*] Cp. vi. 25 note.

16. A caution addressed to earthly judges. Amongst other Oriental nations the family of a criminal was commonly involved in his punishment (cp. Esth. ix. 13, 14). In Israel it was not to be so; cp. marg. reff.

17-22. Cp. marg. reff. The motive assigned for these various acts of consideration is one and the same (*vv.* 18, 22).

18 pledge: but [t]thou shalt remember that thou wast a bondman in
Egypt, and the LORD thy God redeemed thee thence: therefore
19 I command thee to do this thing. ¶ [u]When thou cuttest down
thine harvest in thy field, and hast forgot a sheaf in the field,
thou shalt not go again to fetch it: it shall be for the stranger,
for the fatherless, and for the widow: that the LORD thy God
20 may [x]bless thee in all the work of thine hands. When thou
beatest thine olive tree, [1]thou shalt not go over the boughs again:
it shall be for the stranger, for the fatherless, and for the widow.
21 When thou gatherest the grapes of thy vineyard, thou shalt not
glean *it* [2]afterward: it shall be for the stranger, for the father-
22 less, and for the widow. And [y]thou shalt remember that thou
wast a bondman in the land of Egypt: therefore I command
thee to do this thing.

CHAP. 25. IF there be a [a]controversy between men, and they come
unto judgment, that *the judges* may judge them; then they [b]shall
2 justify the righteous, and condemn the wicked. And it shall be,
if the wicked man *be* [c]worthy to be beaten, that the judge shall
cause him to lie down, [d]and to be beaten before his face, accord-
3 ing to his fault, by a certain number. [e]Forty stripes he may
give him, *and* not exceed: lest, *if* he should exceed, and beat
him above these with many stripes, then thy brother should
4 [f]seem vile unto thee. ¶ [g]Thou shalt not muzzle the ox when he
5 [3]treadeth out *the corn*. ¶ [h]If brethren dwell together, and one of
them die, and have no child, the wife of the dead shall not marry
without unto a stranger: her [4]husband's brother shall go in
unto her, and take her to him to wife, and perform the duty of
6 an husband's brother unto her. And it shall be, *that* the first-

[t] ver. 22. ch. 16. 12.
[u] Lev. 19. 9, 10. & 23. 22.
[x] ch. 15. 10. Ps. 41. 1. Prov. 19. 17.
[y] ver. 18.
[a] ch. 19. 17. Ez. 44. 24.
[b] See Prov 17. 15.
[c] Luke 12. 48.
[d] Matt. 10. 17.
[e] 2 Cor. 11. 24.
[f] Job 18. 3.
[g] Prov. 12. 10. 1 Cor. 9. 9. 1 Tim. 5. 18.
[h] Matt. 22. 24. Mark 12. 19. Luke 20. 28.

[1] Heb. *thou shalt not bough it after thee.*
[2] Heb. *after thee.*
[3] Heb. *thresheth,* Hos. 10. 11.
[4] Or, *next kinsman,* Gen. 38. 8. Ruth 1. 12, 13. & 3. 9.

XXV. 1, 2. Render: (1) **If there be a controversy between men, and they come to judgment, and the judges judge them, and justify the righteous and condemn the wicked** (cp. marg. ref. and Ex. xxiii. 7; Prov. xvii. 15); (2) **then it shall be,** &c.

2. Scourging is named as a penalty in Lev. xix. 20. The beating here spoken of would be on the back with a rod or stick (cp. Prov. x. 13, xix. 29, xxvi. 3).

3. The Jews to keep within the letter of the law fixed 39 stripes as the maximum (cp. marg. ref.). Forty signifies the full measure of judgment (cp. Gen. vii. 12; Num. xiv. 33, 34); but the son of Israel was not to be lashed like a slave at the mercy of another. The judge was always to be present to see that the Law in this particular was not overpassed.

4. Cp. marg. reff. In other kinds of labour the oxen were usually muzzled. When driven to and fro over the threshing-floor in order to stamp out the grain from the chaff, they were to be allowed to partake of the fruits of their labours.

5–10. Law of levirate marriage. The law on this subject is not peculiar to the Jews, but is found (see Gen. xxxviii. 8) in all essential respects the same amongst various Oriental nations, ancient and modern. The rules in these verses, like those upon divorce, do but incorporate existing immemorial usages, and introduce various wise and politic limitations and mitigations of them. The root of the obligation here imposed upon the brother of the deceased husband lies in the primitive idea of childlessness being a great calamity (cp. Gen. xvi. 4, and note), and extinction of name and family one of the greatest that could happen (cp. ix. 14; Ps. cix. 12-15). To avert this the ordinary rules as to inter-marriage are in the case in question (cp. Lev. xviii. 16) set aside. The obligation was onerous (cp. Ruth iv. 6), and might be repugnant; and it is accordingly considerably reduced and restricted by Moses. The duty is recognized as one of affection for the memory of the deceased; it is not one which could be enforced at law. That it continued down to the Christian era is apparent from the question on this point put to Jesus by the Sadducees (see marg. reff.).

5. *no child*] Lit. "no son." The existence of a daughter would clearly suffice. The daughter would inherit the name and property of the father; cp. Num. xxvii. 1–11.

born which she beareth [i]shall succeed in the name of his brother
7 *which is* dead, that [k]his name be not put out of Israel. And if
the man like not to take his [1]brother's wife, then let his brother's
wife go up to the [l]gate unto the elders, and say, My husband's
brother refuseth to raise up unto his brother a name in Israel,
8 he will not perform the duty of my husband's brother. Then
the elders of his city shall call him, and speak unto him: and *if*
9 he stand *to it*, and say, [m]I like not to take her; then shall his
brother's wife come unto him in the presence of the elders, and
[n]loose his shoe from off his foot, and spit in his face, and shall
answer and say, So shall it be done unto that man that will not
10 [o]build up his brother's house. And his name shall be called
11 in Israel, The house of him that hath his shoe loosed. ¶ When
men strive together one with another, and the wife of the one
draweth near for to deliver her husband out of the hand of him
that smiteth him, and putteth forth her hand, and taketh him by
12 the secrets: then thou shalt cut off her hand, [p]thine eye shall
13 not pity *her*. ¶ [q]Thou shalt not have in thy bag [2]divers weights,
14 a great and a small. Thou shalt not have in thine house [3]divers
15 measures, a great and a small. *But* thou shalt have a perfect
and just weight, a perfect and just measure shalt thou have:
[r]that thy days may be lengthened in the land which the LORD
16 thy God giveth thee. For [s]all that do such things, *and* all that
do unrighteously, *are* an abomination unto the LORD thy God.
17 ¶ [t]Remember what Amalek did unto thee by the way, when ye
18 were come forth out of Egypt; how he met thee by the way, and
smote the hindmost of thee, *even* all *that were* feeble behind thee,

i Gen. 38. 9.
k Ruth 4. 10.
l Ruth 4. 1, 2.
m Ruth 4. 6.
n Ruth 4. 7.
o Ruth 4. 11.
p ch. 19. 13.
q Prov. 11. 1.
r Ex. 20. 12.
s Prov. 11. 1. 1 Thes. 4. 6.
t Ex. 17. 8.

[1] Or, *next kinsman's wife*.
[2] Heb. *a stone and a stone*.
[3] Heb. *an ephah and an ephah*.

---

9. *loose his shoe from off his foot*] In token of taking from the unwilling brother all right over the wife and property of the deceased. Planting the foot on a thing was an usual symbol of lordship and of taking possession (cp. Gen. xiii. 17; Josh. x. 24), and loosing the shoe and handing it to another in like manner signified a renunciation and transfer of right and title (cp. Ruth iv. 7, 8; Ps. lx. 8, and cviii. 9). The widow here is directed herself, as the party slighted and injured, to deprive her brother-law of his shoe, and *spit in his face* (cp. Num. xii. 14). The action was intended to aggravate the disgrace conceived to attach to the conduct of the man.

10. *The house*, &c.] Equivalent to "the house of the barefooted one." To go barefoot was a sign of the most abject condition; cp. 2 S. xv. 30.

12. This is the only mutilation prescribed by the Law of Moses, unless we except the retaliation prescribed as a punishment for the infliction on another of bodily injuries (Lev. xxiv. 19, 20). The act in question was probably not rare in the times and countries for which the Law of Moses was designed. It is of course to be understood that the act was wilful, and that the prescribed punishment would be inflicted according to the sentence of the judges.

13–19. Honesty in trade, as a duty to our neighbour, is emphatically enforced once more (cp. Lev. xix. 35, 36). It is noteworthy that St. John the Baptist puts the like duties in the forefront of his preaching (cp. Luke iii. 12 seq.); and that "the Prophets" (cp. Ezek. xlv. 10–12; Amos viii. 5; Mic. vi. 10, 11) and "the Psalms" (Prov. xvi. 11, xx. 10, 23), not less than "the Law," specially insist on them.

13. *divers weights*] *i.e.* stones of unequal weights, the lighter to sell with, the heavier to buy with. Stones were used by the Jews instead of brass or lead for their weights, as less liable to lose anything through rust or wear.

17–19. It was not after the spirit or mission of the Law to aim at overcoming inveterate opposition by love and by attempts at conversion (contrast Luke ix. 55, 56). The law taught God's hatred of sin and of rebellion against Him by enjoining the extinction of the obstinate sinner. The Amalekites were a kindred people (Gen. xxxvi. 15, 16); and living as they did in the peninsula of Sinai, they could not but have well known the mighty acts God had done for His people in Egypt and the Red Sea; yet they manifested from the first a persistent hostility to Israel (cp. Ex. xvii. 8, and note; Num. xiv. 45). They provoked therefore the sentence here pronounced, which was executed at last by Saul (1 S. xv. 3 seq.).

when thou *wast* faint and weary; and he [u]feared not God.
19 Therefore it shall be, [x]when the LORD thy God hath given thee
rest from all thine enemies round about, in the land which the
LORD thy God giveth thee *for* an inheritance to possess it, *that*
thou shalt [y]blot out the remembrance of Amalek from under
heaven; thou shalt not forget *it*.
CHAP. 26. AND it shall be, when thou *art* come in unto the land
which the LORD thy God giveth thee *for* an inheritance, and
2 possessest it, and dwellest therein; [a]that thou shalt take of the
first of all the fruit of the earth, which thou shalt bring of thy
land that the LORD thy God giveth thee, and shalt put *it* in a
basket, and shalt [b]go unto the place which the LORD thy God
3 shall choose to place his name there. And thou shalt go unto
the priest that shall be in those days, and say unto him, I
profess this day unto the LORD thy God, that I am come unto
the country which the LORD sware unto our fathers for to give
4 us. And the priest shall take the basket out of thine hand, and
5 set it down before the altar of the LORD thy God. And thou
shalt speak and say before the LORD thy God, [c]A Syrian [d]ready
to perish *was* my father, and [e]he went down into Egypt, and
sojourned there with a [f]few, and became there a nation, great,
6 mighty, and populous: and [g]the Egyptians evil entreated us,
7 and afflicted us, and laid upon us hard bondage: and [h]when we
cried unto the LORD God of our fathers, the LORD heard our
voice, and looked on our affliction, and our labour, and our
8 oppression: and [i]the LORD brought us forth out of Egypt with
a mighty hand, and with an outstretched arm, and [k]with great
9 terribleness, and with signs, and with wonders: and he hath
brought us into this place, and hath given us this land, *even* [l]a
10 land that floweth with milk and honey. And now, behold, I
have brought the firstfruits of the land, which thou, O LORD,
hast given me. And thou shalt set it before the LORD thy
11 God, and worship before the LORD thy God: and [m]thou shalt
rejoice in every good *thing* which the LORD thy God hath given
unto thee, and unto thine house, thou, and the Levite, and the
12 stranger that *is* among you. ¶ When thou hast made an end of

[u] Ps. 36. 1. Prov. 16. 6. Rom. 3. 18.
[x] 1 Sam. 15. 3.
[y] Ex. 17. 14.
[a] Ex. 23. 19. & 34. 26. Num. 18. 13. ch. 16. 10. Prov. 3. 9.
[b] ch. 12. 5.
[c] Hos. 12. 12.
[d] Gen. 43. 1, 2. & 45. 7. 11.
[e] Gen. 46. 1, 6. Acts 7. 15.
[f] Gen. 46. 27. ch. 10. 22.
[g] Ex. 1. 11, 14.
[h] Ex. 2. 23, 24, 25. & 3. 9. & 4. 31.
[i] Ex. 12. 37, 51. & 13. 3, 14, 16. ch. 5. 15.
[k] ch. 4. 34.
[l] Ex. 3. 8.
[m] ch. 12. 7, 12, 18. & 16. 11.

XXVI. Two liturgical enactments having a clear and close reference to the whole of the preceding legislation, form a most appropriate and significant conclusion to it, viz. (1) the formal acknowledgment in deed and symbol of God's faithfulness, by presentment of a basket filled with firstfruits, and in word by recitation of the solemn formula prescribed in *v.* 3 and *vv.* 5-10; and (2) the solemn declaration and profession on the part of each Israelite on the occasion of the third tithe (*v.* 12).

2. On the subject of firstfruits see notes on Lev. xxiii. 9 seq. The firstfruits here in question are to be distinguished alike from those offered in acknowledgment of the blessings of harvest (cp. Ex. xxii. 29) at the Feasts of Passover and Pentecost, and also from the offerings prescribed in Num. xviii. 8 seq. The latter consisted of *preparations* from the produce of the earth, such as oil, flour, wine, &c.; whilst those here meant are the raw produce: the former were national and public offerings, those of this chapter were private and personal. The whole of the firstfruits belonged to the officiating priest.

5. *A Syrian ready to perish was my father*] The reference is shown by the context to be to Jacob, as the ancestor in whom particularly the family of Abraham began to develop into a nation (cp. Isai. xliii. 22, 28, &c.). Jacob is called *a Syrian* (lit. Aramæan), not only because of his own long residence in Syria with Laban (Gen. xxix.–xxxi.), as our Lord was called a Nazarene because of his residence at Nazareth (Matt. ii. 23), but because he there married and had his children (cp. Hos. xii. 12); and might be said accordingly to belong to that more than to any other land.

12. See marg. ref. to Numbers and note. A strict fulfilment of the onerous and complicated tithe obligations was a leading part of the righteousness of the Pharisees: cp. Matt. xxiii. 23.

tithing all the [n]tithes of thine increase the third year, *which is*
[o]the year of tithing, and hast given *it* unto the Levite, the
stranger, the fatherless, and the widow, that they may eat
13 within thy gates, and be filled; then thou shalt say before the
LORD thy God, I have brought away the hallowed things out of
mine house, and also have given them unto the Levite, and unto
the stranger, to the fatherless, and to the widow, according to all
thy commandments which thou hast commanded me: I have not
transgressed thy commandments, [p]neither have I forgotten *them:*
14 [q]I have not eaten thereof in my mourning, neither have I taken
away *ought* thereof for *any* unclean *use*, nor given *ought* thereof
for the dead: *but* I have hearkened to the voice of the LORD my
God, *and* have done according to all that thou hast commanded
15 me. [r]Look down from thy holy habitation, from heaven, and
bless thy people Israel, and the land which thou hast given us,
as thou swarest unto our fathers, a land that floweth with milk
16 and honey. ¶ This day the LORD thy God hath commanded
thee to do these statutes and judgments: thou shalt therefore
keep and do them with all thine heart, and with all thy soul.
17 Thou hast [s]avouched the LORD this day to be thy God, and to
walk in his ways, and to keep his statutes, and his command-
18 ments, and his judgments, and to hearken unto his voice: and
[t]the LORD hath avouched thee this day to be his peculiar people,
as he hath promised thee, and that *thou* shouldest keep all his
19 commandments; and to make thee [u]high above all nations
which he hath made, in praise, and in name, and in honour;
and that thou mayest be [x]an holy people unto the LORD thy God,
as he hath spoken.

CHAP. 27. AND Moses with the elders of Israel commanded the
people, saying, Keep all the commandments which I command
2 you this day. And it shall be on the day [a]when ye shall pass
over Jordan unto the land which the LORD thy God giveth thee,
that [b]thou shalt set thee up great stones, and plaister them with
3 plaister: and thou shalt write upon them all the words of this
law, when thou art passed over, that thou mayest go in unto the

[n] Lev. 27. 30. Num. 18. 21–24.
[o] ch. 14. 28, 29.
[p] Ps. 119. 141, 153, 176.
[q] Lev. 7. 20. & 21. 1, 11. Hos. 9. 4.
[r] Isai. 63. 15. Zech. 2. 13.
[s] Ex. 20. 19.
[t] Ex. 6. 7. & 19. 5. ch. 7. 6. & 14. 2. & 28. 9.
[u] ch. 4. 7, 8. & 28. 1. Ps. 148. 14.
[x] Ex. 19. 6. ch. 7. 6. & 28. 9. 1 Pet. 2. 9.
[a] Josh. 4. 1.
[b] Josh. 8. 32.

---

14. *I have not eaten thereof in my mourning*] When the Israelite would be unclean (cp. marg. reff.).

nor given ought thereof for the dead] The reference is not so much to the superstitious custom of placing food on or in tombs as to the funeral expenses, and more especially the usual feast for the mourners (cp. Jer. xvi. 7; Ez. xxiv. 17; Hos. ix. 4; Tob. iv. 17). The dedicated things were to be employed in glad and holy feasting, not therefore for funeral banquets; for death and all associated with it was regarded as unclean.

16–19. A brief and earnest exhortation by way of conclusion to the second and longest discourse of the book.

17. *Thou hast avouched*] Lit. "made to say:" so also in the next verse. The sense is: "Thou hast given occasion to the Lord to say that He is thy God," *i.e.* by promising that He shall be so. Cp. Ex. xxiv. 7; Josh. xxiv. 14–25.

XXVII. Moses in a third discourse (xxvii.–xxx.), proceeds more specially to dwell on the sanctions of the Law. In these chapters he sets before Israel in striking and elaborate detail the blessings which would ensue upon faithfulness to the Covenant, and the curses which disobedience would involve. The xxviith chapter introduces this portion of the book by enjoining the erection of a stone monument on which the Law should be inscribed as soon as the people took possession of the promised inheritance (*vv.* 1–10); and by next prescribing the liturgical form after which the blessings and cursings should be pronounced (*vv.* 11–26).

2. The stones here named are not those of which the altar (*v.* 5) was to be built, but are to serve as a separate monument witnessing to the fact that the people took possession of the land by virtue of the Law inscribed on them and with an acknowledgment of its obligations.

3. *all the words of this law*] *i.e.* all the laws revealed from God to the people by Moses, regarded by the Jews as 613 (cp. Num. xv. 38 note). The exhibition of laws in this manner on stones, pillars, or tables, was familiar to the ancients. The laws were

land which the LORD thy God giveth thee, a land that floweth
with milk and honey; as the LORD God of thy fathers hath
4 promised thee. Therefore it shall be when ye be gone over
Jordan, *that* ye shall set up these stones, which I command you
this day, [c]in mount Ebal, and thou shalt plaister them with [c] ch. 11. 29.
5 plaister. And there shalt thou build an altar unto the LORD Josh. 8. 30.
thy God, an altar of stones: [d]thou shalt not lift up *any* iron *tool* [d] Ex. 20. 25.
6 upon them. Thou shalt build the altar of the LORD thy God of Josh. 8. 31.
whole stones: and thou shalt offer burnt offerings thereon unto
7 the LORD thy God: and thou shalt offer peace offerings, and
8 shalt eat there, and rejoice before the LORD thy God. And thou
shalt write upon the stones all the words of this law very plainly.
9 ¶ And Moses and the priests the Levites spake unto all Israel,
saying, Take heed, and hearken, O Israel; [e]this day thou art [e] ch. 26. 18.
10 become the people of the LORD thy God. Thou shalt therefore
obey the voice of the LORD thy God, and do his commandments [f] ch. 11. 29.
11 and his statutes, which I command thee this day. ¶ And Moses Josh. 8. 33. Judg. 9. 7.
12 charged the people the same day, saying, These shall stand [g] ch. 11. 29.
[f]upon mount Gerizim to bless the people, when ye are come Josh. 8. 33. [h] ch. 33. 10.
over Jordan; Simeon, and Levi, and Judah, and Issachar, and Josh. 8. 33.
13 Joseph, and Benjamin: and [g]these shall stand upon mount Ebal Dan. 9. 11.
[1]to curse; Reuben, Gad, and Asher, and Zebulun, Dan, and [i] Ex. 20. 4. Lev. 19. 4.
14 Naphtali. And [h]the Levites shall speak, and say unto all the ch. 4. 16, 23.
15 men of Israel with a loud voice, ¶ [i]Cursed *be* the man that & 5. 8. Isai. 44. 9.

[1] Heb. *for a cursing*. Hos. 13. 2.

---

probably graven in the stone ["very plainly" (*v.* 8) is by some rendered "scoop it out well"], as are for the most part the Egyptian hieroglyphics, the "plaister" being afterwards added to protect the inscription from the weather.

4. *in mount Ebal*] Cp. marg. reff. The Samaritan Pentateuch and Version read here Gerizim instead of Ebal; but the original text was probably, as nearly all modern authorities hold, altered in order to lend a show of scriptural sanction to the Samaritan temple on mount Gerizim.

The erection of the Altar, the offering thereon Burnt offerings and Peace offerings (*vv.* 6, 7), the publication of the Law in writing, form altogether a solemn renewal of the Covenant on the entrance of the people into the Promised Land, and recall the ceremonies observed on the original grant of the Covenant at Sinai (cp. Ex. xxiv. 5). And Ebal [the mount of "barrenness"], the mount of cursing, was the fitting spot on which to celebrate them. For the curses were the penalties under which the children of Israel bound themselves to keep the Law. Suitably also was the same place selected as that in which were to be set up both the monumental stones containing the Law, and the Altar at which the Covenant was to be renewed. We must note too the fact that *vv.* 15 sqq. set out verbatim the curses only, the blessings being omitted. The law because of man's sinfulness brings on him first and chiefly a curse: cp. xxxi. 16, 17; Gal. iii. 10.

11–26. Cp. Josh. viii. 32–35. The solemnity was apparently designed only for the single occasion on which it actually took place.

12, 13. The tribes appointed to stand on Gerizim to bless the people all sprang from the two wives of Jacob, Leah and Rachel. All the four tribes which sprang from the handmaids Zilpah and Bilhah are located on Ebal. But in order, as it would seem, to effect an equal division, two tribes are added to the latter from the descendants of the wives, that of Reuben, probably because he forfeited his primogeniture (Gen. xlix. 4); and of Zebulun, apparently because he was the youngest son of Leah.

The transaction presents itself as a solemn renewal of the covenant made by God with Abraham and Isaac, but more especially with Jacob and his family. Accordingly the genealogical basis of the "twelve patriarchs" (cp. Acts vii. 12; Rev. vii. 4 seq.), the sons of Jacob, is here assumed. The tribes of Ephraim and Manasseh are merged in the name of Joseph, their father; and Levi regains on this occasion his place collaterally with the others. "The Levites" of *v.* 14 are no doubt "the priests the Levites" (cp. Josh. viii. 33), in whom the ministerial character attaching to the tribe was more particularly manifested. It is noteworthy that the group of tribes which stood on Gerizim far exceeded the other in numbers and in importance, thus perhaps indicating that even by the Law the blessing should at length prevail.

15. The "Amen" attested the conviction of the utterers that the sentences to which

maketh *any* graven or molten image, an abomination unto the
LORD, the work of the hands of the craftsman, and putteth *it* in
a secret *place*. [k]And all the people shall answer and say, Amen.
16 [l]Cursed *be* he that setteth light by his father or his mother.
17 And all the people shall say, Amen. [m]Cursed *be* he that
removeth his neighbour's landmark. And all the people shall
18 say, Amen. [n]Cursed *be* he that maketh the blind to wander out
19 of the way. And all the people shall say, Amen. [o]Cursed *be*
he that perverteth the judgment of the stranger, fatherless, and
20 widow. And all the people shall say, Amen. [p]Cursed *be* he
that lieth with his father's wife; because he uncovereth his
21 father's skirt. And all the people shall say, Amen. [q]Cursed *be*
he that lieth with any manner of beast. And all the people
22 shall say, Amen. [r]Cursed *be* he that lieth with his sister, the
daughter of his father, or the daughter of his mother. And
23 all the people shall say, Amen. [s]Cursed *be* he that lieth with
his mother in law. And all the people shall say, Amen.
24 [t]Cursed *be* he that smiteth his neighbour secretly. And all the
25 people shall say, Amen. [u]Cursed *be* he that taketh reward to
slay an innocent person. And all the people shall say, Amen.
26 [x]Cursed *be* he that confirmeth not *all* the words of this law to do
them. And all the people shall say, Amen.

CHAP. 28. AND it shall come to pass, [a]if thou shalt hearken diligently unto the voice of the LORD thy God, to observe *and* to do
all his commandments which I command thee this day, that the
LORD thy God [b]will set thee on high above all nations of the
2 earth: and all these blessings shall come on thee, and [c]overtake
thee, if thou shalt hearken unto the voice of the LORD thy God.
3 [d]Blessed *shalt* thou *be* in the city, and blessed *shalt* thou *be* [e]in
4 the field. Blessed *shall be* [f]the fruit of thy body, and the fruit
of thy ground, and the fruit of thy cattle, the increase of thy
5 kine, and the flocks of thy sheep. Blessed *shall be* thy basket
6 and thy [1]store. [g]Blessed *shalt* thou *be* when thou comest in,
7 and blessed *shalt* thou *be* when thou goest out. The LORD
[h]shall cause thine enemies that rise up against thee to be smitten before thy face: they shall come out against thee one way,
8 and flee before thee seven ways. The LORD shall [i]command the
blessing upon thee in thy [2]storehouses, and in all that thou [k]set-

[k] See Num. 5. 22. Jer. 11. 5. 1 Cor. 14. 16.
[l] Ex. 20. 12. Lev. 19. 3. ch. 21. 18.
[m] ch. 19. 14. Prov. 22. 28.
[n] Lev. 19.14.
[o] Ex. 22. 21. ch. 10. 18. Mal. 3. 5.
[p] Lev. 18. 8. ch. 22. 30.
[q] Lev. 18. 23.
[r] Lev. 18. 9.
[s] Lev. 18. 17.
[t] Ex. 20. 13. Lev. 24. 17. Num. 35. 31. ch. 19. 11.
[u] Ex. 23. 7. ch. 10. 17. Ez. 22. 12.
[x] ch. 28. 15. Ps. 119. 21. Jer. 11. 3.
[a] Ex. 15. 26. Lev. 26. 3. Isai. 55. 2.
[b] ch. 26. 19.
[c] ver. 15. Zech. 1. 6.
[d] Ps. 128. 1, 4.
[e] Gen. 39. 5.
[f] ver. 11. Gen. 22. 17. ch. 7. 13. Ps. 107. 38. Prov. 10. 22. 1 Tim. 4. 8.
[g] Ps. 121. 8.
[h] Lev. 26. 7, 8. 2 Sam. 22. 38, 39, 41. Ps. 89. 23.
[i] Lev. 25. 21.
[k] ch. 15. 10.

[1] Or, *dough*, or, *kneadingtrough*.
[2] Or, *barns*, Prov. 3. 10.

they responded were true, just, and certain; so in Num. v. 22, and in our own Commination Office, which is modelled after this ordinance of Moses.

15–26. Twelve curses against transgressions of the Covenant. The first eleven are directed against special sins which are selected by way of example, the last comprehensively sums up in general terms and condemns all and every offence against God's Law. Cp. the marg. reff.

XXVIII. A comparison of this chapter with Ex. xxiii. 20–23 and Lev. xxvi. will shew how Moses here resumes and amplifies the promises and threats already set forth in the earlier records of the Law. The language rises in this chapter to the sublimest strains, especially in the latter part of it; and the prophecies respecting the dispersion and degradation of the Jewish nation in its later days are amongst the most remarkable in scripture. They are plain, precise, and circumstantial; and the fulfilment of them has been literal, complete, and undeniable.

1–14. The Blessing. The six repetitions of the word "blessed" introduce the particular forms which the blessing would take in the various relations of life.

5. The "basket" or bag was a customary means in the East for carrying about whatever might be needed for personal uses (cp. xxvi. 2; John xiii. 29).

The "store" is rather the **kneading-trough** (Ex. viii. 3, xii. 34). The blessings here promised relate, it will be observed, to private and personal life: in *v.* 7 those which are of a more public and national character are brought forward.

test thine hand unto; and he shall bless thee in the land which
9 the LORD thy God giveth thee. [l]The LORD shall establish thee
an holy people unto himself, as he hath sworn unto thee, if thou
shalt keep the commandments of the LORD thy God, and walk
10 in his ways. And all people of the earth shall see that thou
art [m]called by the name of the LORD; and they shall be [n]afraid
11 of thee. And [o]the LORD shall make thee plenteous [1]in goods,
in the fruit of thy [2]body, and in the fruit of thy cattle, and in
the fruit of thy ground, in the land which the LORD sware unto
12 thy fathers to give thee. The LORD shall open unto thee his
good treasure, the heaven [p]to give the rain unto thy land in his
season, and [q]to bless all the work of thine hand: and [r]thou
13 shalt lend unto many nations, and thou shalt not borrow. And
the LORD shall make thee [s]the head, and not the tail; and thou
shalt be above only, and thou shalt not be beneath; if that thou
hearken unto the commandments of the LORD thy God, which
14 I command thee this day, to observe and to do *them*: [t]and thou
shalt not go aside from any of the words which I command thee
this day, *to* the right hand, or *to* the left, to go after other gods
15 to serve them. ¶ But it shall come to pass, [u]if thou wilt not
hearken unto the voice of the LORD thy God, to observe to do all
his commandments and his statutes which I command thee this
day; that all these curses shall come upon thee, and [x]overtake
16 thee: Cursed *shalt* thou *be* [y]in the city, and cursed *shalt* thou *be*
17 18, in the field. Cursed *shall be* thy basket and thy store. Cursed
shall be the fruit of thy body, and the fruit of thy land, the in-
19 crease of thy kine, and the flocks of thy sheep. Cursed *shalt*
thou *be* when thou comest in, and cursed *shalt* thou *be* when thou
20 goest out. The LORD shall send upon thee [z]cursing, [a]vexation,
and [b]rebuke, in all that thou settest thine hand unto [3]for to do,
until thou be destroyed, and until thou perish quickly; because
of the wickedness of thy doings, whereby thou hast forsaken me.
21 The LORD shall make [c]the pestilence cleave unto thee, until he
have consumed thee from off the land, whither thou goest to
22 possess it. [d]The LORD shall smite thee with a consumption,
and with a fever, and with an inflammation, and with an extreme burning, and with the [4]sword, and with [e]blasting, and
with mildew; and they shall pursue thee until thou perish.
23 And [f]thy heaven that *is* over thy head shall be brass, and the
24 earth that *is* under thee *shall be* iron. The LORD shall make the
rain of thy land powder and dust: from heaven shall it come

[l] Ex. 19. 5, 6. ch. 7. 6.
[m] Num. 6. 27. 2 Chr. 7. 14. Isai. 63. 19. Dan. 9. 18.
[n] ch. 11. 25.
[o] ver. 4. ch. 30. 9. Prov. 10. 22.
[p] Lev. 26. 4. ch. 11. 14.
[q] ch. 14. 29.
[r] ch. 15. 6.
[s] Isai. 9. 14, 15.
[t] ch. 5. 32. & 11. 16.
[u] Lev. 26.14. Lam. 2. 17. Dan. 9. 11. Mal. 2. 2.
[x] ver. 2.
[y] ver. 3, &c.
[z] Mal. 2. 2.
[a] 1 Sam. 14. 20. Zech. 14. 13.
[b] Ps. 80. 16. Isai. 30. 17. & 51. 20. & 66. 15.
[c] Lev. 26. 25. Jer. 24. 10.
[d] Lev. 26. 16.
[e] Amos 4. 9.
[f] Lev. 26. 19.

[1] Or, *for good.*
[2] Heb. *belly.*
[3] Heb. *which thou wouldest do.*
[4] Or, *drought.*

---

9. The oath with which God vouchsafed to confirm His promises to the patriarchs (cp. Gen. xxii. 16; Heb. vi. 13, 14) contained by implication these gifts of holiness and eminence to Israel (cp. marg. reff.).

15–68. The curses correspond in form and number (*vv.* 15-19) to the blessings (*vv.* 3–6), and the special modes in which these threats should be executed are described in five groups of denunciations (*vv.* 20–68).

20–26. First series of judgments. The curse of God should rest on all they did, and should issue in manifold forms of disease, in famine, and in defeat in war.

20. *vexation*] Rather, **confusion**: the word in the original is used (vii. 23; 1 S. xiv. 20) for the panic and disorder with which the curse of God smites His foes.

22. "Blasting" denotes (cp. Gen. xli. 23) the result of the scorching east wind; "mildew" that of an untimely blight falling on the green ear, withering it and marring its produce.

24. When the heat is very great the atmosphere in Palestine is often filled with dust and sand; the wind is a burning sirocco, and the air comparable to the glowing heat at the mouth of a furnace.

[g] ver. 7. Lev. 26. 17. ch. 32. 30. Isai. 30. 17.
[h] Jer. 15. 4. & 24. 9. Ez. 23. 46.
[i] 1 Sam. 17. 44, 46. Ps. 79. 2. Jer. 7. 33.
[k] ver. 35.
[l] Ps. 78. 66.
[m] Jer. 4. 9.
[n] Job 5. 14. Isai. 59. 10.
[o] Job 31. 10. Jer. 8. 10.
[p] Job 31. 8. Jer. 12. 13. Amos 5. 11. Mic. 6. 15. Zeph. 1. 13.
[q] ch. 20. 6.
[r] Ps. 119. 82.
[s] ver. 51. Lev. 26. 16. Jer. 5. 17.
[t] ver. 67.
[u] ver. 27.
[x] 2 Kin. 17. 4, 6. 2 Chr. 33. 11.
[y] ch. 4. 28. ver. 64. Jer. 16. 13.
[z] 1 Kin. 9. 7, 8. Jer. 24. 9. Zech. 8. 13.
[a] Ps. 44. 14.
[b] Mic. 6. 15. Hag. 1. 6.
[c] Joel 1. 4.

25 down upon thee, until thou be destroyed. [g]The LORD shall
cause thee to be smitten before thine enemies: thou shalt go out
one way against them, and flee seven ways before them: and
26 [h]shalt be [1]removed into all the kingdoms of the earth. And
[i]thy carcase shall be meat unto all fowls of the air, and unto
the beasts of the earth, and no man shall fray *them* away.
27 The LORD will smite thee with [k]the botch of Egypt, and with
[l]the emerods, and with the scab, and with the itch, whereof
28 thou canst not be healed. The LORD shall smite thee with
29 madness, and blindness, and [m]astonishment of heart: and thou
shalt [n]grope at noonday, as the blind gropeth in darkness, and
thou shalt not prosper in thy ways: and thou shalt be only oppressed and spoiled evermore, and no man shall save *thee*.
30 [o]Thou shalt betroth a wife, and another man shall lie with her:
[p]thou shalt build an house, and thou shalt not dwell therein:
[q]thou shalt plant a vineyard, and shalt not [2]gather the grapes
31 thereof. Thine ox *shall be* slain before thine eyes, and thou
shalt not eat thereof: thine ass *shall be* violently taken away
from before thy face, and [3]shall not be restored to thee: thy
sheep *shall be* given unto thine enemies, and thou shalt have
32 none to rescue *them*. Thy sons and thy daughters *shall be* given
unto another people, and thine eyes shall look, and [r]fail *with
longing* for them all the day long: and *there shall be* no might in
33 thine hand. [s]The fruit of thy land, and all thy labours, shall a
nation which thou knowest not eat up; and thou shalt be only
34 oppressed and crushed alway: so that thou shalt be mad [t]for the
35 sight of thine eyes which thou shalt see. The LORD shall [u]smite
thee in the knees, and in the legs, with a sore botch that cannot
be healed, from the sole of thy foot unto the top of thy head.
36 The LORD shall [x]bring thee, and thy king which thou shalt set
over thee, unto a nation which neither thou nor thy fathers have
known; and [y]there shalt thou serve other gods, wood and stone.
37 And thou shalt become [z]an astonishment, a proverb, [a]and a by-
word, among all nations whither the LORD shall lead thee.
38 [b]Thou shalt carry much seed out into the field, and shalt gather
39 *but* little in; for [c]the locust shall consume it. Thou shalt plant
vineyards, and dress *them*, but shalt neither drink *of* the wine,
40 nor gather *the grapes*; for the worms shall eat them. Thou shalt
have olive trees throughout all thy coasts, but thou shalt not
anoint *thyself* with the oil; for thine olive shall cast *his fruit*.

[1] Heb. *for a removing.*
[2] Heb. *profane*, or, *use it as common meat:* as ch. 20. 6.
[3] Heb. *shall not return to thee.*

---

25. *shalt be removed*] See margin. The threat differs from that in Lev. xxvi. 33, which refers to a dispersion of the people amongst the heathen. Here it is meant that they should be tossed to and fro at the will of others, driven from one country to another without any certain settlement.

27–37. Second series of judgments on the body, mind, and outward circumstances of the sinners.

27. The "botch" (rather "boil;" see Ex. ix. 9), the "emerods" or tumours (1 S. v. 6, 9), the "scab" and "itch" represent the various forms of the loathsome skin diseases which are common in Syria and Egypt.

28. Mental maladies shall be added to those sore bodily plagues, and should (*vv.* 29–34) reduce the sufferers to powerlessness before their enemies and oppressors.

blindness] Most probably mental blindness; cp. Lam. iv. 14; Zeph. i. 17; 2 Cor. iii. 14 seq.

30–33. See marg. reff. for the fulfilment of these judgments.

38–48. Third series of judgments, affecting every kind of labour and enterprise until it had accomplished the total ruin of the nation, and its subjection to its enemies.

39. *worms*] *i.e.* the vine-weevil. Naturalists prescribed elaborate precautions against its ravages.

40. *cast*, &c.] Some prefer "shall be spoiled" or "plundered."

41 Thou shalt beget sons and daughters, but [1]thou shalt not enjoy
42 them; for [d]they shall go into captivity. All thy trees and fruit [d] Lam. 1. 5.
43 of thy land shall the locust [2]consume. The stranger that *is*
within thee shall get up above thee very high; and thou shalt
44 come down very low. [e]He shall lend to thee, and thou shalt [e] ver. 12.
not lend to him: [f]he shall be the head, and thou shalt be the tail. [f] ver. 13.
45 ¶ Moreover [g]all these curses shall come upon thee, and shall Lam. 1. 5.
pursue thee, and overtake thee, till thou be destroyed; because [g] ver. 15.
thou hearkenedst not unto the voice of the LORD thy God, to
keep his commandments and his statutes which he commanded
46 thee: and they shall be upon thee [h]for a sign and for a wonder, [h] Isai. 8. 18.
47 and upon thy seed for ever. [i]Because thou servedst not the Ez. 14. 8.
LORD thy God with joyfulness, and with gladness of heart, [k]for [i] Neh. 9. 35, 36, 37.
48 the abundance of all *things;* therefore shalt thou serve thine [k] ch. 32. 15.
enemies which the LORD shall send against thee, in hunger, and
in thirst, and in nakedness, and in want of all *things:* and he
[l]shall put a yoke of iron upon thy neck, until he have destroyed [l] Jer. 28. 14.
49 thee. [m]The LORD shall bring a nation against thee from far, [m] Jer. 5. 15.
from the end of the earth, [n]*as swift* as the eagle flieth; a nation Luke 19. 43.
50 whose tongue thou shalt not [3]understand; a nation [4]of fierce [n] Jer. 48. 40. & 49. 22.
countenance, [o]which shall not regard the person of the old, nor Lam. 4. 19.
51 shew favour to the young: and he shall [p]eat the fruit of thy Ez. 17. 3, 12.
cattle, and the fruit of thy land, until thou be destroyed: which Hos. 8. 1.
also shall not leave thee *either* corn, wine, or oil, *or* the increase [o] 2 Chr. 36. 17.
of thy kine, or flocks of thy sheep, until he have destroyed thee. Isai. 47. 6. [p] ver. 33.
52 And he shall [q]besiege thee in all thy gates, until thy high and Isai. 1. 7.
fenced walls come down, wherein thou trustedst, throughout all & 62. 8.
thy land: and he shall besiege thee in all thy gates throughout [q] 2 Kin. 25.
53 all thy land, which the LORD thy God hath given thee. And 1, 2, 4.
[r]thou shalt eat the fruit of thine own [5]body, the flesh of thy [r] Lev. 26. 29.
sons and of thy daughters, which the LORD thy God hath given 2 Kin. 6. 28,
thee, in the siege, and in the straitness, wherewith thine enemies 29. Jer. 19. 9.
54 shall distress thee: *so that* the man *that is* tender among you, Lam. 2. 20.
and very delicate, [s]his eye shall be evil toward his brother, and [s] ch. 15. 9.
toward [t]the wife of his bosom, and toward the remnant of his [t] ch. 13. 6.
55 children which he shall leave: so that he will not give to any of
them of the flesh of his children whom he shall eat: because he
hath nothing left him in the siege, and in the straitness, where-
56 with thine enemies shall distress thee in all thy gates. The
tender and delicate woman among you, which would not adven-
ture to set the sole of her foot upon the ground for delicateness
and tenderness, [u]her eye shall be evil toward the husband of [u] ver. 54.

[1] Heb. *they shall not be thine.*
[2] Or, *possess.*
[3] Heb. *hear.*
[4] Heb. *strong of face,* Prov. 7. 13. Eccles. 8. 1. Dan. 8. 23.
[5] Heb. *belly.*

43, 44. Contrast *vv.* 12 and 13.

46. *for ever*] Yet "the remnant" (Rom. ix. 27, xi. 5) would by faith and obedience become a holy seed.

49-58. Fourth series of judgments, descriptive of the calamities and horrors which should ensue when Israel should be subjugated by its foreign foes.

49. The description (cp. marg. reffs.) applies undoubtedly to the Chaldeans, and in a degree to other nations also whom God raised up as ministers of vengeance upon apostate Israel (*e.g.* the Medes). But it only needs to read this part of the denunciation, and to compare it with the narrative of Josephus, to see that its full and exact accomplishment took place in the wars of Vespasian and Titus against the Jews, as indeed the Jews themselves generally admit.

49. *the eagle*] The Roman ensign; cp. Matt. xxiv. 28; and consult throughout this passage the marg. reff.

54. *evil*] *i.e.* grudging; cp. xv. 9.

57 her bosom, and toward her son, and toward her daughter, and
toward her [1]young one that cometh out [x]from between her feet,
and toward her children which she shall bear: for she shall
eat them for want of all *things* secretly in the siege and straitness, wherewith thine enemy shall distress thee in thy gates.
58 ¶ If thou wilt not observe to do all the words of this law that
are written in this book, that thou mayest fear [y]this glorious and
59 fearful name, THE LORD THY GOD; then the LORD will
make thy plagues [z]wonderful, and the plagues of thy seed, *even*
great plagues, and of long continuance, and sore sicknesses, and
60 of long continuance. Moreover he will bring upon thee all
[a]the diseases of Egypt, which thou wast afraid of; and they shall
61 cleave unto thee. Also every sickness, and every plague, which
is not written in the book of this law, them will the LORD [2]bring
62 upon thee, until thou be destroyed. And ye [b]shall be left few in
number, whereas ye were [c]as the stars of heaven for multitude;
because thou wouldest not obey the voice of the LORD thy God.
63 And it shall come to pass, *that* as the LORD [d]rejoiced over you
to do you good, and to multiply you; so the LORD [e]will rejoice
over you to destroy you, and to bring you to nought; and ye
shall be plucked from off the land whither thou goest to possess
64 it. And the LORD [f]shall scatter thee among all people, from
the one end of the earth even unto the other; and [g]there thou
shalt serve other gods, which neither thou nor thy fathers have
65 known, *even* wood and stone. And [h]among these nations shalt
thou find no ease, neither shall the sole of thy foot have rest:
[i]but the LORD shall give thee there a trembling heart, and failing
66 of eyes, and [k]sorrow of mind: and thy life shall hang in doubt
before thee; and thou shalt fear day and night, and shalt have
67 none assurance of thy life: [l]in the morning thou shalt say,
Would God it were even! And at even thou shalt say, Would God
it were morning! For the fear of thine heart wherewith thou
shalt fear, and [m]for the sight of thine eyes which thou shalt see.
68 And the LORD [n]shall bring thee into Egypt again with ships, by
the way whereof I spake unto thee, [o]Thou shalt see it no more
again: and there ye shall be sold unto your enemies for bondmen and bondwomen, and no man shall buy *you*.

[x] Gen. 49. 10.
[y] Ex. 6. 3.
[z] Dan. 9. 12.
[a] ch. 7. 15.
[b] ch. 4. 27.
[c] ch. 10. 22. Neh. 9. 23.
[d] ch. 30. 9. Jer. 32. 41.
[e] Prov. 1. 26. Isai. 1. 24.
[f] Lev. 26. 33. ch. 4. 27. 28. Neh. 1. 8. Jer. 16. 13.
[g] ver. 36.
[h] Amos 9. 4.
[i] Lev. 26. 36.
[k] Lev. 26. 16.
[l] Job 7. 4.
[m] ver. 34.
[n] Jer. 43. 7. Hos. 8. 13. & 9. 3.
[o] ch. 17. 16.

[1] Heb. *after birth.*
[2] Heb. *cause to ascend.*

---

57. *young one*] The "afterbirth" (see margin). The Hebrew text in fact suggests an extremity of horror which the A. V. fails to exhibit. Cp. 2 K. vi. 29.

58–68. Fifth series of judgments. The uprooting of Israel from the Promised Land, and its dispersion amongst other nations. Examine the marg. reff.

58. *in this book*] *i.e.* in the book of the Law, or the Pentateuch in so far as it contains commands of God to Israel. Deuteronomy is included, but not exclusively intended. So *v.* 61; cp. xxvii. 3 and note, xxxi. 9.

66. *thy life shall hang in doubt before thee*] *i.e.* shall be hanging as it were on a thread, and that before thine own eyes. The Fathers regard this passage as suggesting in a secondary or mystical sense Christ hanging on the cross, as the life of the Jews who would not believe in Him.

68. This is the climax. As the Exodus from Egypt was as it were the birth of the nation into its Covenant relationship with God, so the return to the house of bondage is in like manner the death of it. The mode of conveyance, "in ships," is added to heighten the contrast. They crossed the sea from Egypt with a high hand, the waves being parted before them. They should go back again cooped up in slave-ships.

there ye shall be sold] Rather, "there shall ye offer yourselves, or be offered for sale." This denunciation was literally fulfilled on more than one occasion: most signally when many thousand Jews were sold into slavery and sent into Egypt by Titus; but also under Hadrian, when numbers were sold at Rachel's grave (Gen. xxxv. 19).

no man shall buy you] *i.e.* no one shall venture even to employ you as slaves, re-

Chap. 29. THESE *are* the words of the covenant, which the Lord
commanded Moses to make with the children of Israel in the
land of Moab, beside [a]the covenant which he made with them
2 in Horeb. ¶ And Moses called unto all Israel, and said unto
them, [b]Ye have seen all that the Lord did before your eyes in
the land of Egypt unto Pharaoh, and unto all his servants, and
3 unto all his land; [c]the great temptations which thine eyes have
4 seen, the signs, and those great miracles: yet [d]the Lord hath
not given you an heart to perceive, and eyes to see, and ears to
5 hear, unto this day. [e]And I have led you forty years in the
wilderness: [f]your clothes are not waxen old upon you, and
6 thy shoe is not waxen old upon thy foot. [g]Ye have not eaten
bread, neither have ye drunk wine or strong drink: that ye
7 might know that I *am* the Lord your God. And when ye
came unto this place, [h]Sihon the king of Heshbon, and Og the
king of Bashan, came out against us unto battle, and we smote
8 them: and we took their land, and [i]gave it for an inheritance
unto the Reubenites, and to the Gadites, and to the half tribe of
9 Manasseh. [k]Keep therefore the words of this covenant, and do
10 them, that ye may [l]prosper in all that ye do. ¶ Ye stand this
day all of you before the Lord your God; your captains of your
tribes, your elders, and your officers, *with* all the men of Israel,
11 your little ones, your wives, and thy stranger that *is* in thy
camp, from [m]the hewer of thy wood unto the drawer of thy
12 water: that thou shouldest [1]enter into covenant with the Lord
thy God, and [n]into his oath, which the Lord thy God maketh
13 with thee this day: that he may [o]establish thee to day for a
people unto himself, and *that* he may be unto thee a God, [p]as he
hath said unto thee, and [q]as he hath sworn unto thy fathers, to
14 Abraham, to Isaac, and to Jacob. ¶ Neither with you only [r]do
15 I make this covenant and this oath; but with *him* that standeth
here with us this day before the Lord our God, [s]and also with
16 *him* that *is* not here with us this day: (for ye know how we
have dwelt in the land of Egypt; and how we came through
17 the nations which ye passed by; and ye have seen their abominations, and their [2]idols, wood and stone, silver and gold, which
18 *were* among them:) lest there should be among you man, or
woman, or family, or tribe, [t]whose heart turneth away this day

[a] ch. 5. 2, 3.
[b] Ex. 19. 4.
[c] ch. 4. 34. & 7. 19.
[d] See Isai. 6. 9, 10. & 63. 17. John 8. 43. Acts 28. 26. Eph. 4. 18. 2 Thes. 2. 11, 12.
[e] ch. 1. 3. & 8. 2.
[f] ch. 8. 4.
[g] See Ex. 16. 12. ch. 8. 3. Ps. 78. 24.
[h] Num. 21. 23, 24, 33. ch. 2. 32. & 3. 1.
[i] Num. 32. 33. ch. 3. 12, 13.
[k] ch. 4. 6. Josh. 1. 7. 1 Kin. 2. 3.
[l] Josh. 1. 7.
[m] See Josh. 9. 21, 23, 27.
[n] Neh. 10. 29.
[o] ch. 28. 9.
[p] Ex. 6. 7.
[q] Gen. 17. 7.
[r] Jer. 31. 31, 32, 33. Heb. 8. 7, 8.
[s] 1 Cor. 7. 14.
[t] ch. 11. 16.

[1] Heb. *pass*. [2] Heb. *dungy gods*.

---

garding you as accursed of God, and to be shunned in everything.

XXIX. This and the following chapter contain the address of Moses to the people on the solemn renewal of the Covenant. Consult the marg. reff. for proof of historical statements or explanation of obscure words.

4. Ability to understand the things of God is the gift of God (cp. 1 Cor. ii. 13, 14); yet man is not guiltless if he lacks that ability. The people had it not because they had not felt their want of it, nor asked for it. Cp. 2 Cor. iii. 14, 15.

9. *that ye may prosper*] Literally, "that ye may act wisely." The connexion of the two ideas of wisdom in conduct and prosperity in circumstances is noteworthy.

11. The Covenant was national, and therefore embraced all the elements which make up the nation. The "little ones" would of course be represented by their parents or guardians; the absent (*v.* 15) by those present; nor were the servants and proselytes to be excluded (cp. Acts ii. 39). The text is fairly alleged in justification of the Church's practice of admitting little ones into Covenant with God by Baptism, and accepting promises made on their behalf by sponsors.

15. *with him that is not here with us*] *i.e.* as the Jews explain, posterity; which throughout all generations was to be taken as bound by the act and deed of those present and living.

17. *idols*] See margin, "dungy gods;" *i.e.* clods or stocks which can be rolled about (cp. Lev. xxvi. 30).

18. The word here and in xxxii. 32 rendered "gall," is in Hos. x. 4 translated

from the LORD our God, to go *and* serve the gods of these nations;
[u]lest there should be among you a root that beareth [1][2]gall and
19 wormwood; and it come to pass, when he heareth the words of
this curse, that he bless himself in his heart, saying, I shall
have peace, though I walk [w]in the [3]imagination of mine
20 heart, [x]to add [4]drunkenness to thirst: [y]the LORD will not spare
him, but then [z]the anger of the LORD and [a]his jealousy shall
smoke against that man, and all the curses that are written in
this book shall lie upon him, and the LORD [b]shall blot out his
21 name from under heaven. And the LORD [c]shall separate him
unto evil out of all the tribes of Israel, according to all the
curses of the covenant that [5]are written in this book of the law:
22 So that the generation to come of your children that shall rise
up after you, and the stranger that shall come from a far land,
shall say, when they see the plagues of that land, and the sick-
23 nesses [6]which the LORD hath laid upon it; *and that* the whole
land thereof *is* brimstone, [d]and salt, *and* burning, *that* it is not
sown, nor beareth, nor any grass groweth therein, [e]like the
overthrow of Sodom, and Gomorrah, Admah, and Zeboim, which
24 the LORD overthrew in his anger, and in his wrath: even all
nations shall say, [f]Wherefore hath the LORD done thus unto this
25 land? What *meaneth* the heat of this great anger? Then men
shall say, Because they have forsaken the covenant of the LORD
God of their fathers, which he made with them when he brought
26 them forth out of the land of Egypt: for they went and served
other gods, and worshipped them, gods whom they knew not,
27 and [7]*whom* he had not [8]given unto them: and the anger of the
LORD was kindled against this land, [g]to bring upon it all the

[u] Acts 8. 23. Heb. 12. 15.
[w] Num. 15. 39. Eccles. 11. 9.
[x] Isai. 30. 1.
[y] Ez. 14. 7, 8.
[z] Ps. 74. 1.
[a] Ps. 79. 5. Ez. 23. 25.
[b] ch. 9. 14.
[c] Matt. 24. 51.
[d] Ps. 107. 34. Jer. 17. 6.
[e] Jer. 20. 16.
[f] 1 Kin. 9. 8, 9. Jer. 22. 8, 9.
[g] Dan. 9. 11, 13, 14.

[1] Or, *a poisonful herb.*
[2] Heb. *rosh.*
[3] Or, *stubbornness,* Jer. 3. 17. & 7. 24.
[4] Heb. *the drunken to the thirsty.*
[5] Heb. *is written.*
[6] Heb. *wherewith the* LORD *hath made it sick.*
[7] Or, who *had not given to them* any portion.
[8] Heb. *divided.*

"hemlock." It is the name of a plant of intense bitterness, and of quick growth; and is therefore repeatedly used in conjunction with "wormwood" (cp. Jer. ix. 15; Lam. iii. 19; Amos vi. 12), to express figuratively the nature and effects of sin (cp. marg. reff.). The herb is probably the poppy. Hence the "water" (*i.e.* juice) "of gall" (Jer. viii. 14, xxiii. 15) would be opium. This would explain its employment in the stupefying drink given to criminals at the time of execution (cp. Ps. lxix. 21; Matt. xxvii. 34), and the use of the word as synonymous with poison (cp. xxxii. 33; Job xx. 16).

wormwood is the plant "absinthium." It is used to denote metaphorically the distress and trouble which result from sin.

"The root that beareth gall and wormwood," means in this place any person lurking amongst them who is tainted with apostasy.

19. Cp. on the thought Jer. xxiii. 17. The secret and presumptuous sinner is meant who flatters himself that all is well and will be well with him, since he follows his own devices and prospers. Cp. Ps. lxxiii. 11 seq.

to add drunkenness to thirst] The sense is probably: "Himself, drinking iniquity like water, (Job xv. 16), he corrupts and destroys others who are thirsting for it or prone to it."

The sense of the whole passage from *v.* 16 onward to *v.* 20 may be exhibited thus: "Ye have seen the abominations of idolatry amongst the heathen. Do you therefore look diligently that there be no secret idolater amongst you; a root of bitterness to all about him. Let there be no one, I say, who when he hears the curses of the Law against this sin, flatters himself, saying within himself, 'All will be well, for I walk unmolested in my own self-chosen path;' and thus acting, not only takes his own fill of sin, but destroys likewise every tempted brother within his reach; for the LORD will not spare him," &c.

23. The description is borrowed from the local features of the Dead Sea and its vicinity. The towns of the vale of Siddim were fertile and well watered (cp. Gen. xiii. 10) until devastated by the wrath of God (Gen. xix. 24, 25). The ruin of Israel and its land should be of the like sort (cp. Lev. xxvi. 31, 32; Ps. cvii. 34; Zeph. ii. 9). The desolate state of Palestine at present, and the traces of former fertility and prosperity, are attested by every traveller.

28 curses that are written in this book: and the LORD [h]rooted — [h] 1 Kin. 14.
them out of their land in anger, and in wrath, and in great — 15. 2 Chr. 7. 20.
indignation, and cast them into another land, as *it is* this day. — Ps. 52. 5.
29 The secret *things belong* unto the LORD our God: but those — Prov. 2, 22.
things which are revealed *belong* unto us and to our children for
ever, that *we* may do all the words of this law.

CHAP. 30. AND [a]it shall come to pass, when [b]all these things are — [a] Lev. 26. 40.
come upon thee, the blessing and the curse, which I have set — [b] ch. 28.
before thee, and [c]thou shalt call *them* to mind among all the — [c] ch. 4. 29.
2 nations, whither the LORD thy God hath driven thee, and shalt — 1 Kin. 8. 47.
[d]return unto the LORD thy God, and shalt obey his voice accord- — [d] Neh. 1. 9.
ing to all that I command thee this day, thou and thy children, — Isai. 55. 7.
3 with all thine heart, and with all thy soul; [e]that then the LORD — Lam. 3. 40.
thy God will turn thy captivity, and have compassion upon thee, — Joel 2. 12. [e] Ps. 106. 45.
and will return and [f]gather thee from all the nations, whither the — & 126. 1. 4. Jer. 29. 14.
4 LORD thy God hath scattered thee. [g]If *any* of thine be driven — Lam. 3. 22,
out unto the outmost *parts* of heaven, from thence will the LORD — 32.
5 thy God gather thee, and from thence will he fetch thee: and — [f] Ps. 147. 2. [g] ch. 28. 64.
the LORD thy God will bring thee into the land which thy fathers — Neh. 1. 9.
possessed, and thou shalt possess it; and he will do thee good,
6 and multiply thee above thy fathers. And [h]the LORD thy God — [h] ch. 10. 16.
will circumcise thine heart, and the heart of thy seed, to love the
LORD thy God with all thine heart, and with all thy soul, that
7 thou mayest live. And the LORD thy God will put all these
curses upon thine enemies, and on them that hate thee, which
8 persecuted thee. And thou shalt return and obey the voice of
the LORD, and do all his commandments which I command thee
9 this day. [i]And the LORD thy God will make thee plenteous in — [i] ch. 28. 11.
every work of thine hand, in the fruit of thy body, and in the
fruit of thy cattle, and in the fruit of thy land, for good: for the

---

29. *the secret things belong unto the* LORD *our God*] This verse seems to be added as a solemn admonition on the part of Moses, in order to close the series of blessings and curses which he has delivered. The sense seems to be this: "The future, when and how these good and evil things will take effect, it lies with the Lord our God to determine; it pertains not to man's sphere and duty. God's revealed will is that which we must carry out." The 17th of our Articles of Religion concludes with much the same sentiment.

XXX. The rejection of Israel and the desolation of the promised inheritance were not to be the end of God's dispensations. The closing words of the address therefore are words of comfort and promise. Cp. marg. ref. and iv. 29 seq.; 1 K. viii. 46–50.

1–10. The chastisements of God would lead the nation to repent, and thereupon God would again bless them.

3. *will turn thy captivity*] Will change or put an end to thy state of captivity or distress (cp. Ps. xiv. 7, lxxxv. 2; Jer. xxx. 18). The rendering of the Greek version is significant; "the Lord will heal thy sins."

The promises of this and the following verses had no doubt their partial fulfilment in the days of the Judges; but the fact that various important features are repeated in Jer. xxxii. 37 seq., and in Ezek. xi. 19 seq., xxxiv. 13 seq., xxxvi. 24 seq., shews us that none of these was regarded as exhausting the promises. In full analogy with the scheme of prophecy we may add that the return from the Babylonian Captivity has not exhausted their depth. The New Testament takes up the strain (*e.g.* in Rom. xi.), and foretells the restoration of Israel to the covenanted mercies of God. True these mercies shall not be, as before, confined to that nation. The "turning again of the captivity" will be when Israel is converted to Him in Whom the Law was fulfilled, and Who died "not for that nation only," but also that he might "gather together in one the children of God that were scattered abroad" (John xi. 51, 52). Then shall there be "one fold and one shepherd" (John x. 16). But whether the general conversion of the Jews shall be accompanied with any *national* restoration, any recovery of their ancient prerogatives as the chosen people; and further, whether there shall be any local replacement of them in the land of their fathers, may be regarded as of "the secret things" which belong unto God (xxix. 29); and so indeed our Lord Himself teaches us (Acts i. 6, 7).

6. *circumcise thine heart*] Cp. x. 16 note; Jer. xxxii. 39; Ez. xi. 19.

LORD will again [k]rejoice over thee for good, as he rejoiced over
10 thy fathers: if thou shalt hearken unto the voice of the LORD
thy God, to keep his commandments and his statutes which are
written in this book of the law, *and* if thou turn unto the LORD
11 thy God with all thine heart, and with all thy soul. ¶ For this
commandment which I command thee this day, [l]it *is* not hidden
12 from thee, neither *is* it far off. [m]It *is* not in heaven, that thou
shouldest say, Who shall go up for us to heaven, and bring it
13 unto us, that we may hear it, and do it? Neither *is* it beyond
the sea, that thou shouldest say, Who shall go over the sea for us,
14 and bring it unto us, that we may hear it, and do it? But the
word *is* very nigh unto thee, in thy mouth, and in thy heart, that
15 thou mayest do it. ¶ See, [n]I have set before thee this day life
16 and good, and death and evil; in that I command thee this day
to love the LORD thy God, to walk in his ways, and to keep his
commandments and his statutes and his judgments, that thou
mayest live and multiply: and the LORD thy God shall bless
17 thee in the land whither thou goest to possess it. But if thine
heart turn away, so that thou wilt not hear, but shalt be drawn
18 away, and worship other gods, and serve them; [o]I denounce
unto you this day, that ye shall surely perish, *and that* ye shall
not prolong *your* days upon the land, whither thou passest over
19 Jordan to go to possess it. [p]I call heaven and earth to record
this day against you, *that* [q]I have set before you life and death,
blessing and cursing: therefore choose life, that both thou and
20 thy seed may live: that thou mayest love the LORD thy God,
and that thou mayest obey his voice, and that thou mayest
cleave unto him: for he *is* thy [r]life, and the length of thy days:
that thou mayest dwell in the land which the LORD sware
unto thy fathers, to Abraham, to Isaac, and to Jacob, to give
them.

CHAP. 31. AND Moses went and spake these words unto all Israel.
2 And he said unto them, I [a]*am* an hundred and twenty years
old this day; I can no more [b]go out and come in: also the

[k] ch. 28. 63. Jer. 32. 41.
[l] Isai. 45. 19.
[m] Rom. 10. 6, &c.
[n] ver. 1, 19. ch. 11. 26.
[o] ch. 4. 26. & 8. 19.
[p] ch. 4. 26. & 31. 28.
[q] ver. 15.
[r] Ps. 27. 1. & 66. 9. John 11. 25.
[a] Ex. 7. 7. ch. 34. 7.
[b] Num. 27. 17. 1 Kin. 3. 7.

10–20. Ignorance of the requirements of the law cannot be pleaded (*vv.* 10–14); hence (*vv.* 15–20) life and death, good and evil, are solemnly set before the people for their own choice; and an earnest exhortation to choose the better part concludes the address.

11–14. "The righteousness which is of faith" is really and truly described in these words of the Law; and, under St. Paul's guidance (see marg. reff.) we affirm was intended so to be. For the simplicity and accessibility which Moses here attributes to the Law of God neither is nor can be experimentally found in it except through the medium of faith; even though outwardly and in the letter that Law be written out for us so "that he may run that readeth," and be set forth in its duties and its sanctions as plainly as it was before the Jews by Moses. The seeming ease of the commandment, and yet its real impossibility to the natural man, form part of the qualifications of the Law to be our schoolmaster to bring us unto Christ.

11. *not hidden from thee*] Rather, not **too hard for thee,** as in xvii. 8.

neither is it far off] Cp. Luke xvii. 21.

13. The paraphrase of this verse in the Jerusalem Targum is noteworthy, and should be compared with St. Paul's rendering in Rom. x. 7: "Neither is the law beyond the great sea, that thou shouldest say, Oh that we had one like Jonah the prophet who could descend into the depths of the sea and bring it to us!"

14. *in thy mouth, and in thy heart*] Cp. vi. 6, xi. 18–20.

20. *that thou mayest love the* LORD] Cp. vi. 5. Love stands first as the essential and only source of obedience.

he is thy life] Or, "that" (*i.e.* "to love the Lord") "is thy life;" *i.e.* the condition of thy life and of its prolongation in the Promised Land. Cp. iv. 40, xxxii. 47.

XXXI. **2.** *I am an hundred and twenty years old*] The forty years of the wandering had passed since Moses, then fourscore years old, "spake unto Pharaoh" (Ex. vii. 7. Cp. xxxiv. 7).

I can no more go out and come in] Render **I shall not longer be able to go out and**

LORD hath said unto me, [c]Thou shalt not go over this Jordan.
3 The LORD thy God, [d]he will go over before thee, *and* he will
destroy these nations from before thee, and thou shalt possess
them: *and* Joshua, he shall go over before thee, [e]as the LORD
4 hath said. [f]And the LORD shall do unto them [g]as he did to
Sihon and to Og, kings of the Amorites, and unto the land of
5 them, whom he destroyed. And [h]the LORD shall give them up
before your face, that ye may do unto them according unto all
6 the commandments which I have commanded you. [i]Be strong
and of a good courage, [k]fear not, nor be afraid of them: for the
LORD thy God, [l]he *it is* that doth go with thee; [m]he will not
7 fail thee, nor forsake thee. ¶ And Moses called unto Joshua,
and said unto him in the sight of all Israel, [n]Be strong and of a
good courage: for thou must go with this people unto the land
which the LORD hath sworn unto their fathers to give them;
8 and thou shalt cause them to inherit it. And the LORD, [o]he
it is that doth go before thee; [p]he will be with thee, he will not
fail thee, neither forsake thee: fear not, neither be dismayed.
9 ¶ And Moses wrote this law, [q]and delivered it unto the priests
the sons of Levi, [r]which bare the ark of the covenant of the
10 LORD, and unto all the elders of Israel. And Moses commanded
them, saying, At the end of *every* seven years, in the solemnity
11 of the [s]year of release, [t]in the feast of tabernacles, when all
Israel is come to [u]appear before the LORD thy God in the
place which he shall choose, [x]thou shalt read this law before
12 all Israel in their hearing. [y]Gather the people together, men,
and women, and children, and thy stranger that *is* within thy
gates, that they may hear, and that they may learn, and fear the
LORD your God, and observe to do all the words of this law:
13 and *that* their children, [z]which have not known *any thing*, [a]may
hear, and learn to fear the LORD your God, as long as ye live in
14 the land whither ye go over Jordan to possess it. ¶ And the
LORD said unto Moses, [b]Behold, thy days approach that thou
must die: call Joshua, and present yourselves in the tabernacle
of the congregation, that [c]I may give him a charge. And Moses
and Joshua went, and presented themselves in the tabernacle of
15 the congregation. And [d]the LORD appeared in the tabernacle in

[c] Num. 20. 12. & 27. 13. ch. 3. 27.
[d] ch. 9. 3.
[e] Num. 27. 21. ch. 3. 28.
[f] ch. 3. 21.
[g] Num. 21. 24, 33.
[h] ch. 7. 2.
[i] Josh. 10. 25. 1 Chr. 22. 13.
[k] ch. 1. 29. & 7. 18.
[l] ch. 20. 4.
[m] Josh. 1. 5. Heb. 13. 5.
[n] ver. 23. Josh. 1. 6.
[o] Ex. 13. 21. & 33. 14. ch. 9. 3.
[p] Josh. 1. 5. 1 Chr. 28. 20.
[q] ver. 25. ch. 17. 18.
[r] Num. 4. 15. Josh. 3. 3. 1 Chr. 15. 12, 15.
[s] ch. 15. 1.
[t] Lev. 23. 34.
[u] ch. 16. 16.
[x] Josh. 8. 34. 2 Kin. 23. 2. Neh. 8. 1.
[y] ch. 4. 10.
[z] ch. 11. 2.
[a] Ps. 78. 6.
[b] Num. 27. 13. ch. 34. 5.
[c] ver. 23.
[d] Ex. 33. 9.

---

come in: *i.e.* discharge my duties among you. There is no inconsistency with xxxiv. 7. Moses here adverts to his own age as likely to render him in future unequal to the active discharge of his office as leader of the people: the writer of the xxxivth chapter, one of Moses' contemporaries, remarks of him that up to the close of life "his eye was not dim, nor his natural force abated" (*v.* 7); *i.e.* that he was to the last, in the judgment of others, in full possession of faculties and strength.

7, 8. Moses hands over to Joshua that office as leader of the people, to which he had already been designated (i. 38; Num. xxvii. 23). He assigns also to the Levitical priests and the elders, as the ecclesiastical and civil heads of the nation, the responsibility of teaching the law and enforcing its observance (*vv.* 10–13). Both these were symbolical acts, designed to mark the responsibility of the parties concerned after the death of Moses.

11. Cp. marg. reff. It is not to be supposed that the whole of the Pentateuch was read, nor does the letter of the command require that it should be so. This reading could not be primarily designed for the information and instruction of the people, since it only took place once in seven years; but was evidently a symbolical transaction, intended, as were so many others, to impress on the people the conditions on which they held possession of their privileges and blessings.

14–23. The transaction recorded in these verses may be regarded as the solemn inauguration of Joshua to the office to which he had some time before (Num. xxvii. 22) been called, and his recognition in it by God, which were manifested by his being summoned into the Tabernacle with Moses whilst the Lord appeared in the pillar of cloud (cp. Num. xi. 25, xii. 5).

a pillar of a cloud: and the pillar of the cloud stood over the door
16 of the tabernacle. ¶ And the LORD said unto Moses, Behold,
thou shalt [1]sleep with thy fathers; and this people will [e]rise up,
and [f]go a whoring after the gods of the strangers of the land,
whither they go *to be* among them, and will [g]forsake me, and
17 [h]break my covenant which I have made with them. Then my
anger shall be kindled against them in that day, and [i]I will forsake them, and I will [k]hide my face from them, and they shall
be devoured, and many evils and troubles shall [2]befall them;
so that they will say in that day, [l]Are not these evils come upon
18 us, because our God *is* [m]not among us? And [n]I will surely hide
my face in that day for all the evils which they shall have
19 wrought, in that they are turned unto other gods. Now therefore write ye this song for you, and teach it the children of
Israel: put it in their mouths, that this song may be [o]a witness
20 for me against the children of Israel. For when I shall have
brought them into the land which I sware unto their fathers,
that floweth with milk and honey; and they shall have eaten
and filled themselves, [p]and waxen fat; [q]then will they turn
unto other gods, and serve them, and provoke me, and break my
21 covenant. And it shall come to pass, [r]when many evils and
troubles are befallen them, that this song shall testify [3]against
them as a witness; for it shall not be forgotten out of the
mouths of their seed: for [s]I know their imagination [t]which
they [4]go about, even now, before I have brought them into the
22 land which I sware. ¶ Moses therefore wrote this song the
23 same day, and taught it the children of Israel. [u]And he gave
Joshua the son of Nun a charge, and said, [x]Be strong and of a
good courage: for thou shalt bring the children of Israel into
the land which I sware unto them, and I will be with thee.
24 ¶ And it came to pass, when Moses had made an end of [y]writing
25 the words of this law in a book, until they were finished, that
Moses commanded the Levites, which bare the ark of the cove-
26 nant of the LORD, saying, Take this book of the law, [z]and put

[e] Ex. 32. 6.
[f] Ex. 34. 15. Judg. 2. 17.
[g] ch. 32. 15. Judg. 2. 12. & 10. 6, 13.
[h] Judg. 2. 20.
[i] 2 Chr. 15. 2.
[k] ch. 32. 20. Ps. 104. 29. Isai. 8. 17. & 64. 7. Ez. 39. 23.
[l] Judg. 6. 13.
[m] Num. 14. 42.
[n] ver. 17.
[o] ver. 26.
[p] ch. 32. 15. Neh. 9. 25, 26. Hos. 13. 6.
[q] ver. 16.
[r] ver. 17.
[s] Hos. 5. 3. & 13. 5, 6.
[t] Amos 5. 25, 26.
[u] ver. 14.
[x] ver. 7. Josh. 1. 6.
[y] ver. 9.
[z] See 2 Kin. 22. 8.

[1] Heb. *lie down*, 2 Sam. 7. 12.
[2] Heb. *find them*, Neh. 9. 32.
[3] Heb. *before*.
[4] Heb. *do*.

16. The future apostasy of the people is announced in the presence of Joshua that the latter might be fully aware of the danger and strive in his day to avert it. This he faithfully did (cp. Josh. xxiv. 31); but we find him in his own last address to Israel repeating (Josh. xxiii. 15, 16) the self-same prediction and warning.

19. *a witness for me against them*] *i.e.* an attestation from their own mouths at once of God's benefits, their own duties, and their deserts when they should fall away. Being in verse it would be the more easily learned and kept in memory. The use of songs for such didactic purposes was not unknown to the legislators of antiquity. Cp. also the advice of St. Paul, "teaching and admonishing one another in psalms and hymns and spiritual songs" (Col. iii. 16).

23. *he gave*] *i.e.* the Lord gave.

24–29. Moses completes the writing out of the book of the Law, and directs it to be placed by the Ark of the Covenant.

24. The "book" here spoken of would contain the whole Pentateuch up to this verse, and be "the book of Moses," called generally by the Jews "the Law" (cp. St. Matt. xxii. 40; Gal. iv. 21).

25. *the Levites, which bare the ark*] *i.e.*, as in *v.* 9, "the priests the sons of Levi." The non-priestly Levites could not so much as enter the Sanctuary or touch the Ark (cp Num. iv. 15). Though in the journeys through the wilderness the Ark was borne by the non-priestly Kohathites, yet on occasions of a more solemn and public character it was carried by the priests themselves (Josh. iii. 3 seq., iv. 9, 10, vi. 6, 12, viii. 33; 1 K. viii. 3).

26. *put it in the side of the ark*] Rather, **by the side of the ark.** The two tables of the Decalogue were *in* the Ark (1 K. viii. 9); the book of the Law was to be laid up in the Holy of Holies close by the Ark of the Covenant, probably in a chest. Cp. 2 K. xxii. 8.

it in the side of the ark of the covenant of the LORD your God,
27 that it may be there [a]for a witness against thee. [b]For I know
thy rebellion, and thy [c]stiff neck: behold, while I am yet alive
with you this day, ye have been rebellious against the LORD;
28 and how much more after my death? Gather unto me all the
elders of your tribes, and your officers, that I may speak these
words in their ears, [d]and call heaven and earth to record against
29 them. For I know that after my death ye will utterly [e]corrupt
yourselves, and turn aside from the way which I have commanded you; and [f]evil will befall you [g]in the latter days;
because ye will do evil in the sight of the LORD, to provoke him
30 to anger through the work of your hands. ¶ And Moses spake
in the ears of all the congregation of Israel the words of this
song, until they were ended.

CHAP. 32. GIVE [a]ear, O ye heavens, and I will speak;
And hear, O earth, the words of my mouth.
2 [b]My doctrine shall drop as the rain,
My speech shall distil as the dew,
[c]As the small rain upon the tender herb,
And as the showers upon the grass:
3 Because I will publish the name of the LORD:
[d]Ascribe ye greatness unto our God.
4 ¶ *He is* [e]the Rock, [f]his work *is* perfect:

[a] ver. 19.
[b] ch. 9. 24. & 32. 20.
[c] Ex. 32. 9. ch. 9. 6.
[d] ch. 30. 19. & 32. 1.
[e] ch. 32. 5. Judg. 2. 19. Hos. 9. 9.
[f] ch. 28. 15.
[g] Gen. 49. 1. ch. 4. 30.

[a] ch. 4. 26. Ps. 50. 4. Isai. 1. 2. Jer. 2. 12.
[b] Isai. 55. 10. 1 Cor. 3. 6.
[c] Ps. 72. 6. Mic. 5. 7.
[d] 1 Chr. 29. 11.
[e] 2 Sam. 22. 3. & 23. 3. Ps. 18. 2, 31, 46. Hab. 1. 12.
[f] 2 Sam. 22. 31.

---

27. *how much more after my death*] Hence *v.* 24 and the rest of the book (with the exception of the song, *v.* 19) must be regarded as a kind of appendix added after Moses' death by another hand; though the Blessing (xxxiii.) is of course to be regarded as a composition of Moses.

XXXII. **1–43.** Song of Moses.

If *vv.* 1–3 be regarded as the introduction, and *v.* 43 as the conclusion, the main contents of the song may be grouped under three heads, viz. (1) *vv.* 4–18, the faithfulness of God, the faithlessness of Israel; (2) *vv.* 19–33, the chastisement and the need of its infliction by God; (3) *vv.* 34–42, God's compassion upon the low and humbled state of His people.

The Song differs signally in diction and idiom from the preceding chapters; just as a lyrical passage is conceived in modes of thought wholly unlike those which belong to narrative or exhortation, and is uttered in different phraseology.

There are, however, in the Song numerous coincidences both in thoughts and words with other parts of the Pentateuch, and especially with Deuteronomy; while the resemblances between it and Ps. xc. "A Prayer of Moses," have been rightly regarded as important.

The Song has reference to a state of things which did not ensue until long after the days of Moses. In this it resembles other parts of Deuteronomy and the Pentateuch which no less distinctly contemplate an apostasy (*e.g.* Deut. xxviii. 15; Lev. xxvi. 14), and describe it in general terms. If once we admit the possibility that Moses might foresee the future apostasy of Israel, it is scarcely possible to conceive how such foresight could be turned to better account by him than by the writing of this Song. Exhibiting as it does God's preventing mercies, His people's faithlessness and ingratitude, God's consequent judgments, and the final and complete triumph of the Divine counsels of grace, it forms the summary of all later Old Testament prophecies, and gives as it were the framework upon which they are laid out. Here as elsewhere the Pentateuch presents itself as the foundation of the religious life of Israel in after times. The currency of the Song would be a standing protest against apostasy; a protest which might well check waverers, and warn the faithful that the revolt of others was neither unforeseen nor unprovided for by Him in Whom they trusted.

That this Ode must on every ground take the very first rank in Hebrew poetry is universally allowed.

1–3. Introduction.

1. Heaven and earth are here invoked, as elsewhere (see marg. reff.), in order to impress on the hearers the importance of what is to follow.

4. *He is the Rock, his work is perfect*] Rather, **the Rock, perfect is His work.** This epithet, repeated no less than five times in the Song (*vv.* 15, 18, 30, 31), represents those attributes of God which Moses is seeking to enforce, immutability and impregnable strength. Cp. the expression "the stone of Israel" in Gen. xlix. 24; and see 1 S. ii. 2; Ps. xviii. 2; Matt. xvi. 18; John i. 42. Zur, the original of "Rock," enters frequently into the composition of proper names of the Mosaic time, *e.g.* Num. i. 5, 6, 10, ii. 12, iii.

[g] Dan. 4. 37. Rev. 15. 3. [h] Jer. 10. 10. [i] Job 34. 10. Ps. 92. 15. [k] ch. 31. 29. [l] Matt. 17. 17. Luke 9. 41. Phil. 2. 15. [m] Ps. 116. 12. [n] Isai. 63. 16. [o] Ps. 74. 2. [p] Isai. 27. 11. & 44. 2. [q] Ex. 13. 14. Ps. 44. 1. [r] Zech. 9. 2. Acts 17. 26. [s] Gen. 11. 8. [t] Ex. 15. 16. 1 Sam. 10. 1. Ps. 78. 71. [u] ch. 8. 15. Jer. 2. 6. Hos. 13. 5. [x] Deut. 4. 36. [y] Ps. 17. 8. Prov. 7. 2. Zech. 2. 8. [z] Ex. 19. 4. ch. 1. 31. Isai. 31. 5. Hos. 11. 3.

For [g]all his ways *are* judgment:
[h]A God of truth and [i]without iniquity,
Just and right *is* he.
5 ¶ [1] [k]They have corrupted themselves, [2]their spot *is* not *the* *spot* of his children:
They are a [l]perverse and crooked generation.
6 Do ye thus [m]requite the LORD,
O foolish people and unwise?
Is not he [n]thy father *that* hath [o]bought thee?
Hath he not [p]made thee, and established thee?
7 ¶ Remember the days of old,
Consider the years of [3]many generations:
[q]Ask thy father, and he will shew thee;
Thy elders, and they will tell thee.
8 When the Most High [r]divided to the nations their inheritance,
When he [s]separated the sons of Adam,
He set the bounds of the people
According to the number of the children of Israel.
9 For [t]the LORD's portion *is* his people;
Jacob *is* the [4]lot of his inheritance.
10 He found him [u]in a desert land,
And in the waste howling wilderness;
He [5]led him about, he [x]instructed him,
He [y]kept him as the apple of his eye.
11 [z]As an eagle stirreth up her nest,
Fluttereth over her young,
Spreadeth abroad her wings, taketh them,
Beareth them on her wings:
12 *So* the LORD alone did lead him,
And *there was* no strange god with him.

1 Heb. *he hath corrupted to himself*.
2 Or, that they are *not his children*, that is *their blot*.
3 Heb. *generation and generation*.
4 Heb. *cord*.
5 Or, *compassed him about*.

35, &c. Our translators have elsewhere rendered it according to the sense "everlasting strength" (Isai. xxvi. 4), "the Mighty One" (Isai. xxx. 29); in this chapter they have rightly adhered to the letter throughout.

5. Render, "It" (*i.e.* "the perverse and crooked generation") "hath corrupted itself before Him (cp. Isai. i. 4); they are not His children, but their blemish:" *i.e.* the generation of evil-doers cannot be styled God's children, but rather the shame and disgrace of God's children. The other side of the picture is thus brought forward with a brevity and abruptness which strikingly enforces the contrast.

6. *hath bought thee*] Rather perhaps, "hath acquired thee for His own," or "possessed thee:" cp. the expression "a peculiar people," marg. "a purchased people," in 1 Pet. ii. 9.

8. That is, whilst nations were being constituted under God's providence, and the bounds of their habitation determined under His government (cp. Acts xvii. 26), He had even then in view the interests of His elect, and reserved a fitting inheritance "according to the number of the children of Israel;" *i.e.* proportionate to the wants of their population. Some texts of the Greek Version have "according to the number of the Angels of God;" following apparently not a different reading, but the Jewish notion that the nations of the earth are seventy in number (cp. Gen. x. 1 note), and that each has its own guardian Angel (cp. Ecclus. xvii. 17). This was possibly suggested by an apprehension that the literal rendering might prove invidious to the many Gentiles who would read the Greek version.

10–14. These verses set forth in figurative language the helpless and hopeless state of the nation when God took pity on it, and the love and care which He bestowed on it.

10. *in the waste howling wilderness*] Lit. "in a waste, the howling of a wilderness," *i.e.* a wilderness in which wild beasts howl. The word for "waste" is that used in Gen. i. 2, and there rendered "without form."

11. Cp. Ex. xix. 4. The "so," which the A. V. supplies in the next verse, should be inserted before "spreadeth," and omitted from *v.* 12. The sense is, "so He spread out His wings, took them up," &c.

12. *with him*] *i.e.* with God. The Lord

13 [a]He made him ride on the high places of the earth,
That he might eat the increase of the fields;
And he made him to suck [b]honey out of the rock,
And oil out of the flinty rock;
14 Butter of kine, and milk of sheep,
With fat of lambs,
And rams of the breed of Bashan, and goats,
[c]With the fat of kidneys of wheat;
And thou didst drink the pure [d]blood of the grape.
15 ¶ But [e]Jeshurun waxed fat, and [f]kicked:
[g]Thou art waxen fat, thou art grown thick, thou art covered *with fatness;*
Then he [h]forsook God *which* [i]made him,
And lightly esteemed the [k]Rock of his salvation.
16 [l]They provoked him to jealousy with strange *gods*,
With abominations provoked they him to anger.
17 [m]They sacrificed unto devils, [1]not to God;
To gods whom they knew not,
To new *gods that* came newly up,
Whom your fathers feared not.
18 [n]Of the Rock *that* begat thee thou art unmindful,
And hast [o]forgotten God that formed thee.
19 ¶ [p]And when the LORD saw *it*, he [2]abhorred *them*,
[q]Because of the provoking of his sons, and of his daughters.
20 And he said, [r]I will hide my face from them,
I will see what their end *shall be:*
For they *are* a very froward generation,
[s]Children in whom *is* no faith.
21 [t]They have moved me to jealousy with *that which is* not God;

[a] Isai. 58. 14. Ez. 36. 2.
[b] Job 29. 6. Ps. 81. 16.
[c] Ps. 81. 16.
[d] Gen. 49. 11.
[e] ch. 33. 5.
[f] 1 Sam. 2. 29.
[g] ch. 31. 20. Neh. 9. 25. Ps. 17. 10. Jer. 2. 7. Hos. 13. 6.
[h] ch. 31. 16. Isai. 1. 4.
[i] ver. 6. Isai. 51. 13.
[k] 2 Sam. 22. 47. Ps. 89. 26.
[l] 1 Kin. 14. 22. 1 Cor. 10. 22.
[m] Lev. 17. 7. Ps. 106. 37. 1 Cor. 10. 20. Rev. 9. 20.
[n] Isai. 17. 10.
[o] Jer. 2. 32.
[p] Judg. 2. 14.
[q] Isai. 1. 2.
[r] ch. 31. 17.
[s] Isai. 30. 9. Matt. 17. 17.
[t] ver. 16. Ps. 78. 58.

[1] Or, which were *not God*, ver. 21.

[2] Or, *despised*, Lam. 2. 6.

---

alone delivered Israel; Israel therefore ought to have served none other but Him.

13. *i.e.* God gave Israel possession of those commanding positions which carry with them dominion over the whole land (cp. xxxiii. 29), and enabled him to draw the richest provision out of spots naturally unproductive.

14. *breed of Bashan*] Bashan was famous for its cattle. Cp. Ps. xxii. 12; Ezek. xxxix. 18.

fat of kidneys of wheat] *i.e.* the finest and most nutritious wheat. The fat of the kidneys was regarded as being the finest and tenderest, and was therefore specified as a part of the sacrificial animals which was to be offered to the Lord: cp. Ex. xxix. 13, &c.

the pure blood of the grape] Render, **the blood of the grape, even wine**. The Hebrew word seems (cp. Isai. xxvii. 2) a poetical term for wine.

15. *Jeshurun*] This word, found again only in xxxiii. 5, 26, and Isai. xliv. 2, is not a diminutive but an appellative (containing an allusion to the root, "to be righteous"); and describes not the character which belonged to Israel in fact, but that to which Israel was called. Cp. Num. xxiii. 21. The prefixing of this epithet to the description of Israel's apostasy contained in the words next following is full of keen reproof.

16. *They provoked him to jealousy*] The language is borrowed from the matrimonial relationship, as in xxxi. 16.

17. *devils*] Render, **destroyers**. The application of the word to the false gods points to the trait so deeply graven in all heathen worship, that of regarding the deities as malignant, and needing to be propitiated by human sufferings.

not to God] Rather, "not God," *i.e.* which were not God; see margin and *v.* 21. Cp. xiii. 7, xxix. 25.

19. The anger of God at the apostasy of His people is stated in general terms in this verse; and the results of it are described, in words as of God Himself, in the next and following verses. These results consisted negatively in the withdrawal of God's favour (*v.* 20), and positively in the infliction of a righteous retribution.

daughters] The women had their full share in the sins of the people. Cp. Isai. iii. 16 seq., xxxii. 9 seq.; Jer. vii. 18, xliv. 15 seq.

20. *I will see what their end shall be*] Cp. the similar expression in Gen. xxxvii. 20.

21. God would mete out to them the same

They have provoked me to anger [u]with their vanities:
And [x]I will move them to jealousy with *those which are* not a people;
I will provoke them to anger with a foolish nation.
22 ¶ For [y]a fire is kindled in mine anger,
And [1]shall burn unto the lowest hell,
And [2]shall consume the earth with her increase,
And set on fire the foundations of the mountains.
23 I will [z]heap mischiefs upon them;
[a]I will spend mine arrows upon them.
24 *They shall be* burnt with hunger, and devoured with [3]burning heat,
And with bitter destruction:
I will also send [b]the teeth of beasts upon them,
With the poison of serpents of the dust.
25 [c]The sword without,
And terror [4]within, shall [5]destroy
Both the young man and the virgin,
The suckling *also* with the man of gray hairs.
26 [d]I said, I would scatter them into corners,
I would make the remembrance of them to cease from among men:
27 Were it not that I feared the wrath of the enemy,
Lest their adversaries [e]should behave themselves strangely,
And lest they should [f]say, [6]Our hand *is* high,
And the LORD hath not done all this.
28 For they *are* a nation void of counsel,
[g]Neither *is there any* understanding in them.
29 ¶ [h]O that they were wise, *that* they understood this,
[i]*That* they would consider their latter end!
30 How should [k]one chase a thousand,
And two put ten thousand to flight,
Except their Rock [l]had sold them,
And the LORD had shut them up?
31 For [m]their rock *is* not as our Rock,
[n]Even our enemies themselves *being* judges.

[u] 1 Sam. 12. 21. 1 Kin. 16. 13, 26. Ps. 31. 6. Jer. 8. 19. Acts 14. 15.
[x] Hos. 1. 10. Rom. 10. 19.
[y] Jer. 15. 14. & 17. 4. Lam. 4. 11.
[z] Isai. 26. 15.
[a] Ps. 7. 12, 13. Ez. 5. 16.
[b] Lev. 26. 22.
[c] Lam. 1. 20 Ez. 7. 15. 2 Cor. 7. 5.
[d] Ez. 20. 13, 14, 23.
[e] Jer. 19. 4.
[f] Ps. 140. 8.
[g] Isai. 27. 11. Jer. 4. 22.
[h] ch. 5. 29. & reff.
[i] Isai. 47. 7. Lam. 1. 9.
[k] Lev. 26. 8.
[l] Ps. 44. 12. Isai. 50. 1.
[m] 1 Sam. 2. 2.
[n] Jer. 40. 3.

[1] Or, *hath burned.*
[2] Or, *hath consumed.*
[3] Heb. *burning coals:* Hab. 3. 5.
[4] Heb. *from the chambers.*
[5] Heb. *bereave.*
[6] Or, *Our high hand, and not the* LORD, *hath done all this.*

---

measure as they had done to Him. Though chosen by the one God to be His own, they had preferred idols, which were no gods. So therefore would He prefer to His people that which was no people. As they had angered Him with their vanities, so would He provoke them by adopting in their stead those whom they counted as nothing. The terms, "not a people," and "a foolish nation," mean such a people as, not being God's, would not be accounted a people at all (cp. Eph. ii. 12; 1 Pet. ii. 10), and such a nation as is destitute of that which alone can make a really "wise and understanding people" (iv. 6), viz. the knowledge of the revealed word and will of God (cp. 1 Cor. i. 18-28).

24. *burning heat*] *i.e.* the fear of a pestilential disease. On the "four sore judgments," famine, plague, noisome beasts, the sword, cp. Lev. xxvi. 22; Jer. xv. 2; Ezek. v. 17, xiv. 21.

26, 27. Rather, **I would utterly disperse them, &c., were it not that I apprehended the provocation of the enemy,** *i.e.* that I should be provoked to wrath when the enemy ascribed the overthrow of Israel to his own prowess and not to my judgments. Cp. ix. 28, 29; Ezek. xx. 9, 14, 22.

behave themselves strangely] Rather, **misunderstand it,** *i.e.* mistake the cause of Israel's ruin.

30. The defeat of Israel would be due to the fact that God, their strength, had abandoned them because of their apostasy.

31. *our enemies*] *i.e.* the enemies of Moses and the faithful Israelites; the heathen, more specially those with whom Israel was brought into collision, whom Israel was

32 For [o]their vine [1]*is* of the vine of Sodom,
And of the fields of Gomorrah:
Their grapes *are* grapes of gall,
Their clusters *are* bitter:
33 Their wine *is* [p]the poison of dragons,
And the cruel [q]venom of asps.
34 *Is* not this [r]laid up in store with me,
And sealed up among my treasures?
35 [s]To me *belongeth* vengeance, and recompence;
Their foot shall slide in *due* time:
For [t]the day of their calamity *is* at hand,
And the things that shall come upon them make haste.
36 ¶ [u]For the LORD shall judge his people,
[x]And repent himself for his servants,
When he seeth that *their* [2]power is gone,
And [y]*there is* none shut up, or left.
37 And he shall say, [z]Where *are* their gods,
Their rock in whom they trusted,
38 Which did eat the fat of their sacrifices,
And drank the wine of their drink offerings?
Let them rise up and help you,
And be [3]your protection.
39 See now that [a]I, *even* I, *am* he, and [b]*there is* no god with me:
[c]I kill, and I make alive;
I wound, and I heal:
Neither *is there any* that can deliver out of my hand.
40 [d]For I lift up my hand to heaven,
And say, I live for ever.
41 [e]If I whet my glittering sword,
And mine hand take hold on judgment;
[f]I will render vengeance to mine enemies,
And will reward them that hate me.
42 I will make mine arrows [g]drunk with blood,
And my sword shall devour flesh;
And that with the blood of the slain and of the captives,
From the beginning of [h]revenges upon the enemy.

[o] Isai. 1. 10.
[p] Ps. 58. 4.
[q] Ps. 140. 3. Rom. 3. 13.
[r] Job 14. 17. Jer. 2. 22. Hos. 13. 12. Rom. 2. 5.
[s] Ps. 94. 1. Rom. 12. 19. Heb. 10. 30.
[t] 2 Pet. 2. 3.
[u] Ps. 135. 14.
[x] Judg. 2. 18. Ps. 106. 45. Jer. 31. 20. Joel 2. 14.
[y] 1 Kin. 14. 10. 2 Kin. 9. 8.
[z] Judg. 10. 14. Jer. 2. 28.
[a] Ps. 102. 27. Isai. 41. 4.
[b] ch. 4. 35. Isai. 45. 5.
[c] 1 Sam. 2. 6. 2 Kin. 5. 7. Job 5. 18. Ps. 68. 20. Hos. 6. 1.
[d] Ex. 6. 8. Num. 14. 30.
[e] Isai. 27. 1. Ez. 21. 9, 10, 14.
[f] Isai. 1. 24. Nah. 1. 2.
[g] Jer. 46. 10.
[h] Job 13. 24. Jer. 30. 14. Lam. 2. 5.

[1] Or, is worse *than the vine of Sodom, &c.*
[2] Heb. *hand.*
[3] Heb. *an hiding for you.*

---

commissioned to "chase," but to whom, as a punishment for faithlessness, Israel was "sold," (*v.* 30). Moses leaves the decision, whether "their rock" (*i.e.* the false gods of the heathen to which the apostate Israelites had fallen away) or "our Rock" is superior, to be determined by the unbelievers themselves. For example, see Ex. xiv. 25; Num. xxiii. and xxiv.; Josh. ii. 9 seq.; 1 S. iv. 8 and v. 7 seq.; 1 K. xx. 28. That the heathen should thus be constrained to bear witness to the supremacy of Israel's God heightened the folly of Israel's apostasy.

32. *their vine*] *i.e.* the nature and character of Israel: cp. for similar expressions Ps. lxxx. 8, 14; Jer. ii. 21; Hos. x. 1.

Sodom...Gomorrah] Here, as elsewhere, and often in the prophets, emblems of utter depravity: cp. Isai. i. 10; Jer. xxiii. 14.

gall] Cp. xxix. 18 note.

35. Rather: "Vengeance is mine and recompence, at the time when their foot slideth.

36. *repent himself for*] Rather, **have compassion upon.** The verse declares that God's judgment of His people would issue at once in the punishment of the wicked, and in the comfort of the righteous.

none shut up, or left] A proverbial phrase (cp. 1 K. xiv. 10) meaning perhaps "married and single," or "guarded and forsaken," but signifying generally "all men of all sorts."

40–42. Render: **For I lift up my hand to heaven and say, As I live for ever, if I whet,** &c. On *v.* 40, in which God is described as swearing by Himself, cp. Isai. xlv. 23; Jer. xxii. 5; Heb. vi. 17. The lifting up of the hand was a gesture used in making oath (cp. Gen. xiv. 22; Rev. x. 5).

42. *from the beginning of revenges upon the enemy*] Render, (drunk with blood) **from the head** (*i.e.* the chief) **of the princes of the enemy.**

43 [1][i]Rejoice, O ye nations, *with* his people:
For he will [k]avenge the blood of his servants,
And [l]will render vengeance to his adversaries,
And [m]will be merciful unto his land, *and* to his people.

44 ¶ And Moses came and spake all the words of this song in the
45 ears of the people, he, and [2]Hoshea the son of Nun. And
Moses made an end of speaking all these words to all Israel:
46 and he said unto them, [n]Set your hearts unto all the words
which I testify among you this day, which ye shall command
47 your children to observe to do, all the words of this law. For it
is not a vain thing for you; [o]because it *is* your life: and through
this thing ye shall prolong *your* days in the land, whither ye go
48 over Jordan to possess it. ¶ [p]And the LORD spake unto Moses
49 that selfsame day, saying, Get thee up into this [q]mountain
Abarim, *unto* mount Nebo, which *is* in the land of Moab, that *is*
over against Jericho; and behold the land of Canaan, which I
50 give unto the children of Israel for a possession: and die in the
mount whither thou goest up, and be gathered unto thy people;
as [r]Aaron thy brother died in mount Hor, and was gathered
51 unto his people: because [s]ye trespassed against me among the
children of Israel at the waters of [3]Meribah-Kadesh, in the
wilderness of Zin; because ye [t]sanctified me not in the midst of
52 the children of Israel. [u]Yet thou shalt see the land before *thee;*
but thou shalt not go thither unto the land which I give the
children of Israel.

CHAP. 33. AND this *is* [a]the blessing, wherewith Moses [b]the man

[i] Rom. 15. 10. [k] Rev. 6. 10. [l] ver. 41. [m] Ps. 85. 1. [n] ch. 6. 6. & 11. 18. Ez. 40. 4. [o] ch. 30. 19. Lev. 18. 5. Prov. 3. 2, 22. & 4. 22. Rom. 10. 5. [p] Num. 27. 12, 13. [q] Num. 33. 47, 48. ch. 34. 1. [r] Num. 20. 25, 28. & 33. 38. [s] Num. 20. 11, 12, 13. [t] See Lev. 10. 3. [u] Num. 27. 12. ch. 34. 4. [a] Gen. 49. 28. [b] Ps. 90, title.

[1] Or, *Praise his people, ye nations:* or, *Sing ye.*
[2] Or, *Joshua.*
[3] Or, *Strife at Kadesh.*

---

43. *Rejoice, O ye nations, with His people*] Some prefer the marginal rendering.

In this profound passage, there is shadowed forth the purpose of God to overrule (1) the unbelief of the Jews to the bringing in of the Gentiles; and (2) the mercy shewn to the Gentiles to the eventual restoration of the Jews (cp. Rom. xi. 25–36).

The Song closes as it began (*vv.* 1–3), with an invitation to praise. It has reached, through a long series of Divine interpositions, its grandest theme in this call to the Gentiles, now heathen no more, to rejoice over God's restored people, the Jews.

44–52. These verses were, no doubt, added by the author of the supplement to Deuteronomy. For the statements contained in them, consult the marg. reff.

XXXIII. The Blessing contains (1) an Introduction, *vv.* 1–5; (2) the Benedictions pronounced on the tribes individually, *vv.* 6–25; (3) a Conclusion, *vv.* 26–29.

It was no doubt spoken by Moses, probably on the same day and to the same assembly as the Song (xxxii. 1–43), as soon as he received the renewed notice of his approaching decease (xxxii. 48), and just before he ascended Mount Nebo. Like the Blessing of Jacob (Gen. xlix.), to which it has an intimate though independent correspondence throughout, it is the solemn farewell of the earthly head of the race. A comparison with Genesis (see the marg. reff.) will shew how the blessings uttered by Moses over the several tribes partly repeat, partly enlarge and supplement, and sometimes modify or even reverse, the predictions of the dying Jacob.

This chapter, in striking contrast with the last, is pervaded by a tone of happy augury; and the total absence of warning and reproof has been rightly noted as indicating that Moses is here speaking of the ideal Israel, of the people of God as they might and would have been but for their perverseness, rather than foretelling what would in fact be the fate and fortunes of the twelve tribes. As the Song sets forth the calamities with which God's justice will visit Israel's fall, so does the Blessing describe the glory and greatness which would from His mercy crown Israel's faithfulness. The Song and the Blessing are therefore correspondent, and mutually supplementary. The form into which the Blessing is thrown exhibits the several tribes co-operating, each according to its peculiar characteristics and circumstances, for the accomplishment of the national mission.

1. The title "the man of God" in the Old Testament is one who is favoured with direct revelations, but not necessarily an official prophet. The occurrence of the title here is no doubt a token that the Blessing was not, as was the Song, transcribed by Moses himself. Cp. xxxi. 27.

2 of God blessed the children of Israel before his death. And he
said,
[c]The LORD came from Sinai,
And rose up from Seir unto them;
He shined forth from mount Paran,
And he came with [d]ten thousands of saints:
From his right hand *went* [1]a fiery law for them.
3 Yea, [e]he loved the people;
[f]All his saints *are* in thy hand:
And they [g]sat down at thy feet;
Every one shall [h]receive of thy words.
4 [i]Moses commanded us a law,
[k]*Even* the inheritance of the congregation of Jacob.
5 And he was [l]king in [m]Jeshurun,
When the heads of the people *and* the tribes of Israel were gathered together.
6 ¶ Let Reuben live, and not die;
And let *not* his men be few.
7 ¶ And this *is the blessing* of Judah: and he said,
Hear, LORD, the voice of Judah,
And bring him unto his people:
[n]Let his hands be sufficient for him;
And be thou [o]an help *to him* from his enemies.
8 ¶ And of Levi he said,
[p]*Let* thy Thummim and thy Urim *be* with thy holy one,

[c] Ex. 19. 18. Judg. 5. 4. Hab. 3. 3.
[d] See Ps. 68. 17. Dan. 7. 10. Acts 7. 53. Heb. 2. 2. Rev. 5. 11.
[e] Ex. 19. 5. ch. 7. 7, 8. Ps. 47. 4. Hos. 11. 1. Mal. 1. 2.
[f] ch. 7. 6. 1 Sam. 2. 9. Ps. 50. 5.
[g] Luke 10. 39. Acts 22. 3.
[h] Prov. 2. 1.
[i] John 1. 17. & 7. 19.
[k] Ps. 119. 111.
[l] See Gen. 36. 31. Judg. 9. 2. & 17. 6.
[m] ch. 32. 15.
[n] Gen. 49. 8.
[o] Ps. 146. 5.
[p] Ex. 28. 30.

[1] Heb. *a fire of law.*

---

2. By "Seir" is to be understood the mountain-land of the Edomites, and by "mount Paran" the range which forms the northern boundary of the desert of Sinai (cp. Gen. xiv. 6 note). Thus the verse forms a poetical description of the vast arena upon which the glorious manifestation of the Lord in the giving of the Covenant took place.

with ten thousands of saints] Render, **from amidst ten thousands of holy ones:** lit. from myriads of holiness, *i.e.* holy Angels (cp. Zech. xiv. 5). God is represented as leaving heaven where He dwells amidst the host of the Angels (1 K. xxii. 19) and descending in majesty to earth (Mic. i. 3).

a fiery law] more lit. as in margin, with perhaps an allusion to the pillar of fire (Ex. xiii. 21). The word is much disputed.

3. *the people* are the twelve tribes, not the Gentiles; and *his saints* refer to God's chosen people just before spoken of. Cp. vii. 18, 21; Ex. xix. 6; Dan. vii. 8-21.

5. *he was king*] *i.e.* not Moses but the Lord **became king.**

6. *let not his men be few*] Lit. "a number," *i.e.* "a small number," such as could be easily counted (cp. Gen. xxxiv. 30 note). While the verse promises that the tribe shall endure and prosper, yet it is so worded as to carry with it a warning. The Reubenites, occupied with their herds and flocks, appear, soon after the days of Joshua, to have lost their early energy, till in later times its numbers, even when counted with the Gadites and the half of Manasseh, were fewer than that of the Reubenites alone at the census of Num. i. (Cp. 1 Chr. v. 18 with Num. i. 20.) No judge, prophet, or national hero arose out of this tribe.

The tribe of Simeon, which would according to the order of birth come next, is not here named. This omission is explained by reference to the words of Jacob concerning Simeon (Gen. xlix. 7). This tribe with Levi was to be "scattered in Israel." The fulfilment of this prediction was in the case of Levi so ordered as to carry with it honour and blessing; but no such reversal of punishment was granted to Simeon. Rather had this latter tribe added new sins to those which Jacob denounced (cp. Num. xxvi. 5 note). Accordingly, though very numerous at the Exodus, it had surprisingly diminished before the death of Moses (cp. Num. i. 22, 23 with Num. xxvi. 12-14); and eventually it found territory adequate for its wants within the limits of another tribe, Judah. Cp. Josh. xix. 2-9.

7. *bring him unto his people*] Moses, taking up the promise of Jacob, prays that Judah, marching forth at the head of the tribes, might ever be brought back in safety and victory; and intimates that God would grant help to accomplish this.

8. *thy holy one*] *i.e.* Levi, regarded as the representative of the whole priestly and

[q] Ex. 17. 7. Num. 20. 13. ch. 8. 2, 3. Ps. 81. 7. [r] Gen. 29. 32. 1 Chr. 17. 17. Job 37. 24. [s] Ex. 32. 26, 27, 28. [t] See Jer. 18. 18. Mal. 2. 5, 6. [u] Lev. 10. 11. ch. 17. 9. & 24. 8. Ez. 44. 23, 24. Mal. 2. 7. [x] Ex. 30. 7, 8. Num. 16. 40. 1 Sam. 2. 28. [y] Lev. 1. 9. Ps. 51, 19. Ez. 43. 27. [z] 2 Sam. 24. 23. Ps. 20. 3. Ez. 20. 40, 41. [a] Gen. 49. 25. [b] Gen. 27. 28. [c] Gen. 49. 26. [d] Hab. 3. 6. [e] Ex. 3. 2. Acts 7. 30, 35. [f] Gen. 49. 26. [g] 1 Chr. 5. 1. [h] Num. 23. 22. Ps. 2. 10.

[q]Whom thou didst prove at Massah,
And with whom thou didst strive at the waters of Meribah;
9 Who said unto his father and to his mother, I have not [r]seen him;
[s]Neither did he acknowledge his brethren, nor knew his own children:
For [t]they have observed thy word, and kept thy covenant.
10 [1][u]They shall teach Jacob thy judgments,
And Israel thy law:
[2][x]They shall put incense [3]before thee,
[y]And whole burnt sacrifice upon thine altar.
11 Bless, LORD, his substance,
And [z]accept the work of his hands:
Smite through the loins of them that rise against him,
And of them that hate him, that they rise not again.

12 ¶ *And* of Benjamin he said,
The beloved of the LORD shall dwell in safety by him;
And the LORD shall cover him all the day long,
And he shall dwell between his shoulders.

13 ¶ And of Joseph he said,
[a]Blessed of the LORD *be* his land,
For the precious things of heaven,
For [b]the dew, and for the deep that coucheth beneath,
14 And for the precious fruits *brought forth* by the sun,
And for the precious things [4]put forth by the [5]moon,
15 And for the chief things of [c]the ancient mountains,
And for the precious things [d]of the lasting hills,
16 And for the precious things of the earth and fulness thereof,
And *for* the good will of [e]him that dwelt in the bush:
Let *the blessing* [f]come upon the head of Joseph,
And upon the top of the head of him *that was* separated from his brethren.
17 His glory *is like* the [g]firstling of his bullock,
And his horns *are like* [h]the horns of [6]unicorns:

[1] Or, *Let them teach, &c.*
[2] Or, *let them put incense.*
[3] Heb. *at thy nose.*
[4] Heb. *thrust forth.*
[5] Heb. *moons.*
[6] Heb. *an unicorn.*

Levitical stock which sprang from him. The contrast between the tone of this passage and that of Gen. xlix. 5-7 is remarkable. Though the prediction of Jacob respecting the dispersion of this tribe held good, yet it was so overruled as to issue in honour and reward. The recovery of God's favour is to be traced to the faithfulness with which Moses and Aaron, who came of this tribe, served God in their high offices; and to the zeal and constancy which conspicuous persons of the tribe (*e.g.* Phinehas, Num. xxv. 11 seq.), and the whole tribe itself (cp. Ex. xxxii. 26), manifested on critical occasions in supporting the leaders of the people. The same reasons led to Levi's being selected for the special service of God in the Sanctuary (ch. x. 8 seq., and Num. viii. 5 seq.); and for the office of instructing their brethren in the knowledge of the Law. The events at Massah and Meribah, the one occurring at the beginning, the other towards the end, of the forty years' wandering, serve to represent the whole series of trials by which God proved and exercised the faith and obedience of this chosen tribe.

9. *Who said unto his father and to his mother*] Cp. Matt. x. 37; Luke xiv. 26.

11. *smite through the loins*] Rather, **smite the loins,** *i.e.* the seat of their strength.

12. *he shall dwell between his shoulders*] *i.e.* be supported by God as a son who is carried by his father (cp. i. 31). Benjamin was specially beloved of his father (Gen. xxxv. 18, xliv. 20); Moses now promises no less love to him from God Himself.

13–17. Comparing the words of Moses with those of Jacob, it will be seen that the patriarch dwells with emphasis on the severe conflicts which Joseph, *i.e.* Ephraim and Manasseh, would undergo (cp. Gen. xlix. 23, 24); while the lawgiver seems to look beyond, and to behold the two triumphant and established in their power.

17. Rather: "The first-born of his" (*i.e.* Joseph's) "bullock is his glory": the refer-

With them [i]he shall push the people together to the ends of the earth:
And [k]they *are* the ten thousands of Ephraim,
And they *are* the thousands of Manasseh.

[i] 1 Kin. 22. 11. Ps. 44. 5.
[k] Gen. 48. 19.

18 ¶ And of Zebulun he said,

[l]Rejoice, Zebulun, in thy going out;
And, Issachar, in thy tents.
19 They shall [m]call the people unto the mountain;
There [n]they shall offer sacrifices of righteousness:
For they shall suck *of* the abundance of the seas,
And *of* treasures hid in the sand.

[l] Gen. 49. 13, 14, 15.
[m] Isai. 2. 3.
[n] Ps. 4. 5.

20 ¶ And of Gad he said,

Blessed *be* he that [o]enlargeth Gad:
He dwelleth as a lion,
And teareth the arm with the crown of the head.
21 And [p]he provided the first part for himself,
Because there, *in* a portion of the lawgiver, *was he* [1]seated;
And [q]he came with the heads of the people,
He executed the justice of the LORD,
And his judgments with Israel.

[o] See Josh. 13. 10, &c.
[p] Num. 32. 16, 17, &c.
[q] Josh. 4. 12.

22 ¶ And of Dan he said,

Dan *is* a lion's whelp:
[r]He shall leap from Bashan.

23 ¶ And of Naphtali he said,

O Naphtali, [s]satisfied with favour,

[r] Josh. 19. 47. Judg. 18. 27.
[s] Gen. 49. 21.

[1] Heb. *cieled.*

---

ence being to Ephraim, who was raised by Jacob to the honours of the firstborn (Gen. xlviii. 20), and is here likened to the firstling of Joseph's oxen, *i.e.* of Joseph's offspring. The ox is a common emblem of power and strength.

18, 19. Zebulun possessed a commodious sea-shore and the fisheries of the Lake of Tiberias: and was therefore to thrive by commerce, and to rejoice in his "going out," *i.e.* in his mercantile enterprises. Issachar possessed a fertile inland district, and would therefore dwell at home and prosper in agriculture. Both tribes distinguished themselves in the contest with Jabin (cp. Judg. v. 14, 15, 18): and of Zebulun it is particularly noted that it produced the officers and tacticians who led and marshalled the host which vanquished Sisera (see Judg. v. 14, and cp. 1 Chr. xii. 33).

19. *unto the mountain*] Cp. Ex. xv. 17.

sacrifices of righteousness] Sacrifices offered in a righteous spirit, and therefore well pleasing to God (cp. Ps. iv. 5, li. 19).

treasures hid in the sand] The riches of the seas in general. It is however noteworthy that the sand of these coasts was specially valuable in the manufacture of glass; and glass was a precious thing in ancient times (cp. Job xxviii. 17). The murex from which the highly-prized purple dye was extracted, was also found here. A typical reference to the conversion of the Gentiles is strongly suggested by Isai. lx. 5, 6, 16, and lxvi. 11, 12.

20. *i.e.* Blessed be God Who shall grant to Gad a spacious territory. Cp. the blessing of Shem (Gen. ix. 26).

with the crown] Rather, **yea, the crown.** The warlike character of this tribe is shewn by their leading the van in the long campaigns of Joshua (cp. Josh. iv. 12, 13, xxii. 1-4). Cp. also 1 Chr. v. 18-22, xii. 8 seq., and the acts of Jehu, the Gadite, in 2 K. ix. x.

21. The first fruits of the conquest made by Israel were assigned to Gad and Reuben by Moses, at their own request.

because...seated] Render, **because there was the leader's portion reserved,** *i.e.* there was reserved the fitting portion for Gad as a leader in war.

and he came, &c.] *i.e.* he joined the other leaders to fulfil the commands of God respecting the conquest of Canaan (cp. Num. xxxii. 17, 21, 32; Josh. i. 14). Moses regards the promise of the Gadites to do this as already redeemed.

22. Dan shall be like a lion which leaps forth from his covert in Bashan. Cp. Song of Solomon, iv. 8.

23. *satisfied with favour*] Cp. Gen. xlix. 21 and note.

the west and the south] *i.e.* taking the

And full with the blessing of the LORD:
[t]Possess thou the west and the south.

24 ¶ And of Asher he said,

[u]*Let* Asher *be* blessed with children;
Let him be acceptable to his brethren,
And let him [x]dip his foot in oil.
25 [1]Thy shoes *shall be* [y]iron and brass;
And as thy days, *so shall* thy strength *be*.
26 ¶ *There is* [z]none like unto the God of [a]Jeshurun,
[b]*Who* rideth upon the heaven in thy help,
And in his excellency on the sky.
27 The eternal God *is thy* [c]refuge,
And underneath *are* the everlasting arms:
And [d]he shall thrust out the enemy from before thee;
And shall say, Destroy *them*.
28 [e]Israel then shall dwell in safety alone:
[f]The fountain of Jacob *shall be* upon a land of corn and wine;
Also his [g]heavens shall drop down dew.
29 [h]Happy *art* thou, O Israel:
[i]Who *is* like unto thee, O people saved by the LORD,
[k]The shield of thy help, and who *is* the sword of thy excellency!
And thine enemies [12]shall be found liars unto thee;
And [m]thou shalt tread upon their high places.

CHAP. 34. AND Moses went up from the plains of Moab [a]unto the
mountain of Nebo, to the top of [3]Pisgah, that *is* over against
Jericho. And the LORD [b]shewed him all the land of Gilead,
2 [c]unto Dan, and all Naphtali, and the land of Ephraim, and

[t] See Josh. 19. 32, &c.
[u] Gen. 49. 20.
[x] See Job 29. 6.
[y] ch. 8. 9.
[z] Ex. 15. 11. Ps. 86. 8. Jer. 10. 6.
[a] ch. 32. 15.
[b] Ps. 68. 4, 33, 34. & 104. 3. Hab. 3. 8.
[c] Ps. 90. 1.
[d] ch. 9. 3, 4.
[e] Num. 23. 9. Jer. 23. 6. & 33. 16.
[f] ch. 8. 7, 8.
[g] Gen. 27. 28. ch. 11. 11.
[h] Ps. 144. 15.
[i] 2 Sam. 7. 23.
[k] Ps. 115. 9, 10, 11.
[l] 2 Sam. 22. 45. Ps. 18. 44.
[m] ch. 32. 13.
[a] Num. 27. 12. & 33. 47. ch. 32. 49.
[b] ch. 3. 27.
[c] Gen. 14. 14.

[1] Or, Under *thy shoes* shall be *iron*.
[2] Or, *shall be subdued*.
[3] Or, *The hill*.

---

words as referring not to geographical position but to natural characteristics, "the sea and the sunny district." The possession of Naphtali included nearly the whole west coast of the Sea of Galilee, the Lake of Merom, the modern *Bahr el Huleh*, and the well-watered district near the springs of Jordan. It contained some of the grandest scenery and some of the most fertile land in Palestine. Josephus speaks of the shore of Gennesaret as "an earthly paradise;" and Porter describes it as "the garden of Palestine." The modern name for this district, "land of good tidings," is significant.

24. Rather, "Blessed above the sons" (*i.e.* of Jacob=most blessed amongst the sons of Jacob) "be Asher; let him be the favoured one of his brethren," *i.e.* the one favoured of God. The plenty with which this tribe should be blessed is described under the figure of dipping the foot in oil (cp. marg. ref.).

25. The strength and firmness of Asher is as if he were shod with iron and brass (cp. Rev. i. 15). The territory of this tribe probably contained iron and copper. Cp. marg. ref.

as thy days, so shall thy strength be] *i.e.* "thy strength" (some prefer "thy rest") "shall be continued to thee as long as thou shalt live: thou shalt never know feebleness and decay."

26. Rather, **There is none like unto God, O Jeshurun!** See marg. ref. and note.

27. *thy refuge*] Rather, "dwellingplace." Cp. Ps. xc. 1, xci. 9.

28. *the fountain of Jacob shall be upon a land of corn and wine*] The A. V. does not preserve the symmetry of the clauses. Render, "Israel shall dwell in safety; alone shall the fountain of Jacob be" (cp. Ps. lxviii. 26; Isai. xlviii. 1); "in a land," &c.

29. *be found liars unto thee*] Perhaps rather, "cringe before thee." The verb means to shew a feigned or forced obedience: see marg. reff.

tread upon their high places] *i.e.* occupy the commanding positions in their land, and so have it in subjection.

XXXIV. **1.** *Dan*] This can hardly be the Dan (Dan-Laish) of Judg. xviii. 27 seq., which was not in Gilead. It is probably a town of this name which stood in the north of Peræa; perhaps the same as Dan-jaan, 2 S. xxiv. 6, and the Dan of Gen. xiv. 14.

3 Manasseh, and all the land of Judah, [d]unto the utmost sea, and
the south, and the plain of the valley of Jericho, [e]the city of
4 palm trees, unto Zoar. And the LORD said unto him, [f]This *is*
the land which I sware unto Abraham, unto Isaac, and unto
Jacob, saying, I will give it unto thy seed: [g]I have caused thee
to see *it* with thine eyes, but thou shalt not go over thither.
5 ¶ So Moses the servant of the LORD died there in the land of
6 Moab, according to the word of the LORD. And he buried him
in a valley in the land of Moab, over against Beth-peor: but [i]no
7 man knoweth of his sepulchre unto this day. [k]And Moses *was*
an hundred and twenty years old when he died: [l]his eye was
8 not dim, nor his [1]natural force [2]abated. And the children
of Israel wept for Moses in the plains of Moab [m]thirty days:
so the days of weeping *and* mourning for Moses were ended.
9 ¶ And Joshua the son of Nun was full of the [n]spirit of wisdom;
for [o]Moses had laid his hands upon him: and the children of
Israel hearkened unto him, and did as the LORD commanded
10 Moses. ¶ And there [p]arose not a prophet since in Israel like
11 unto Moses, [q]whom the LORD knew face to face, in all [r]the
signs and the wonders, which the LORD sent him to do in the
land of Egypt to Pharaoh, and to all his servants, and to all his
12 land, and in all that mighty hand, and in all the great terror
which Moses shewed in the sight of all Israel.

[d] ch. 11. 24.
[e] Judg. 1. 16. 2 Chr. 28. 15.
[f] Gen. 12. 7.
[g] ch. 3. 27. & 32. 52.
[h] ch. 32. 50. Josh. 1. 1.
[i] See Jude 9.
[k] ch. 31. 2.
[l] See Gen. 27. 1. & 48. 10. Josh. 14. 10, 11.
[m] See Gen. 50. 3, 10. Num. 20. 29.
[n] Isai. 11. 2. Dan. 6. 3.
[o] Num. 27. 18, 23.
[p] See chap. 18. 15, 18.
[q] Ex. 33. 11. Num. 12. 6, 8. ch. 5. 4.
[r] ch. 4. 34. & 7. 19.

[1] Heb. *moisture.* [2] Heb. *fled.*

---

3. *unto Zoar*] Cp. Gen. xix. 22.

4. *I have caused thee to see it*] The sight thus afforded to Moses, like that of "all the kingdoms of the world in a moment of time" (Luke iv. 5), was no doubt supernatural.

5. *according to the word of the* LORD] It denotes that Moses died, not because his vital powers were exhausted, but by the sentence of God, and as a punishment for his sin. Cp. xxxii. 51.

6. *no man knoweth of his sepulchre*] Hardly lest the grave of Moses should become an object of superstitious honour, for the Jews were not prone to this particular form of error. Bearing in mind the appearance of Moses at the Transfiguration (Matt. xvii. 1-10), and what is said by St. Jude (*v.* 9), we may conjecture that Moses after death passed into the same state with Enoch and Elijah; and that his sepulchre could not be found because he was shortly translated from it.

9. *spirit of wisdom*] The practical wisdom of the ruler is specially meant.

10. *there arose not a prophet since in Israel*] Words like these can only have been written some time, but not necessarily a long time, after the death of Moses. They refer more particularly to the wonders wrought by the hand of Moses at the Exodus and in the desert; and do but re-echo the declaration of God Himself (Num. xii. 6 seq). They may naturally enough be attributed to one of Moses' successors, writing perhaps soon after the settlement of the people in Canaan.

JOSHUA.

INTRODUCTION.

1. This book like several others of the historical books of Scripture derives its name from its contents. It takes up the history of the chosen people at the death of Moses, and continues it in a systematic and orderly narrative, through the leadership and government of his successor. It records almost exclusively the acts of Joshua in fulfilment of the commission laid upon him from God by the hand of Moses (cp. Deut. xxxi. 7, 8), and terminates with Joshua's death and burial.

The contents group themselves into two divisions of nearly equal length. The conquest of the land is described in twelve chapters, and then in twelve other chapters the subsequent partition of it together with Joshua's last acts and words.

The victories of Joshua described in the former of these portions were accompanied by repeated and stupendous interferences of God. This miraculous element has led some commentators to treat the book as altogether unhistorical. But it must not be forgotten that the miracles of the Book of Joshua do not stand alone. They grow as it were naturally out of the Divine interpositions on behalf of Israel in the days of Moses, and are but the close of a series of extraordinary providences begun in Egypt, and described in Exodus and the books following. No less do they stand intimately associated with the future history and development of the Jewish Church and nation, and even with the wider and more remote issues of God's counsels as manifested, or to be manifested, in the Christian Church to the end of all things. Thus the conquest of Canaan by Joshua has other and vastly grander significances than its mere dimensions as a fact in history seem at first sight to suggest. It is not to be regarded simply as the invasion of a little district about as large as three average English counties by a tribe of nomads from the Arabian deserts. It was also the accomplishment by God of a purpose revealed of old; it was an essential element in the plan ordained by Him for the preservation amongst men of His Law, Will, and Word; it was designed to foreshadow in many important particulars His future dealings with mankind at large. But for the special help of God, the Israelites could not have effected the conquest at all, for they were hardly superior to the Canaanites in numbers, and were destitute of chariots and horses, and of all the more elaborate equipments for war, above all of the appliances requisite for reducing the cities (cp. Num. xiii. 28; Deut. i. 28, and ix. 1) in which Canaan abounded. God's promise was, however, pledged to their forefathers to give them this land; whatever then might be necessary to give effect to this promise it belonged to His faithfulness to accord; and the Book of Joshua consequently is an essential sequel to the Pentateuch as declaring the thorough fulfilment by God of the covenant made by Him through Moses with Israel, and thus as illustrating His inviolable faithfulness.[2]

But important as the theocratical and theological characteristics of the book are, both in themselves and as (so to say) vindicating the miraculous elements of the narrative, we must nevertheless not lose sight of the internal evidences of common and historical fact which it presents.

The invasion of Canaan by Joshua was evidently a carefully and skilfully conducted enterprise. An army marching upon Canaan from the south would find its path intercepted by range after range of heights, each, in the days of Moses and Joshua, bristling with towns and fortresses. The progress of such an army could be but slow, and at every step would be met by better organized resistance from an increasing number of enemies. When Israel, after forty years' expiation of the revolt at Kadesh, again arose at the command of God to resume the long deferred enterprise on Canaan, the host was conducted round the whole south-east corner of the land and directed upon its comparatively defenceless eastern flank above the Dead Sea. The whole of the strong military positions and fenced cities in the "south country" and the "hill country" of what was subsequently the territory of Judah were thus taken in reverse and rendered comparatively useless. It is probable, too, that the southern Canaanites in particular were at this time greatly weakened by the invasions of Thotmes III., who had taken Gaza, apparently not many years previously, and no doubt had overrun the whole adjoining district (see note on xiii. 3). No less able were the measures adopted by Joshua to execute the plan thus judiciously laid down. The passage of the Jordan, by the special help of God, at a time of year when his enemies no doubt deemed the river to be an almost insurmountable obstacle to his advance (see on iii. 15): the seizing Gilgal, to serve as his foothold in the land: the capture and destruction of Jericho: the fall of Ai:—these events enabled him to throw the forces of Israel like a wedge through the very midst of the land almost to the western sea, and in its most vulnerable part, between the fastnesses of Judah on the south and the mountain district of Ephraim on the north. The Amorites on Joshua's left, cut off from the Hittites on his right by his whole army interposing between the two, were overpowered before Gibeon. The whole south was reduced into at least temporary subjection before the larger multitudes of the north could be mustered. These in their turn shared the fate of their brethren in the south; Joshua broke their vast host to pieces on the shores of Lake Merom.

In these campaigns of Joshua it is impossible not to see the traces of strategical skill no less conspicuously than that presence of immediate and Divine suggestion and succour which the narrative asserts.

---

[2] These typical aspects and applications are well drawn out by Pearson "On the Creed," Art. ii.

2. The leading trait in the character of Joshua is courage—the courage of the warrior: this must have been already remarkable at the time of the Exodus (Ex. xvii. 9 seq.). Subsequently Joshua appears as in constant attendance on Moses (Ex. xxiv. 13; xxxii. 1; xxxiii. 11); he without doubt acquired on Sinai, and in the precincts of the Sanctuary, that unswerving faithfulness of service and unshaken confidence in God which marked his after career. He was naturally selected as one of the twelve "rulers" sent by Moses (Num. xiii. 2) to explore the land before the invasion of it was undertaken; and the bold and truthful report brought back by him and Caleb (Num. xiv. 7–9), was no less characteristic than was his undaunted bearing before the incensed people (Num. xiv. 10). These qualities pointed him out as the fitting captain over the Lord's people, who should overthrow their enemies before them and put them in possession of the promised inheritance. Accordingly, at the express command of God, he was solemnly appointed to that office and duty by Moses before his death (Num. xxvii. 16–23; Deut. xxxi. 23).

Joshua was not a prophet (Ecclus. xlvi. 1; cp. Num. xxvii. 21), but a divinely inspired leader. After the great and peculiar work of his life was accomplished, he no longer held the same exclusive place at the head of Israel as before. In making the arrangements for settling the people in their homes, and establishing the theocracy on the lines laid down in the law of Moses, he acted in conjunction with Eleazar, the high-priest, and with the heads of the tribes (cp. xiv. 1; xvii. 4; xxi. 1). This was but natural. The armies had done their work and were dispersed, or were ready to disperse, to their several inheritances; and the military authority of their general was consequently at an end. The latter years of his life were probably passed in retirement at Timnath-serah, whence he would seem to have emerged in extreme old age to meet the princes and the people in the great gathering at Shechem (xxiii., xxiv.), and to employ once more and finally his authority as the last survivor but one of a mighty generation, and as the hero of Israel's greatest triumphs, in order to engage his people more firmly and closely in their rightful allegiance to God.

The courage which was the leading feature in the character of Joshua was very distinctly and directly built upon faith (i. 5, 6). Joshua obeyed God's call unhesitatingly and to the end, but it was because he trusted wholly in the promise which accompanied it. Hence, along with his soldierly qualities, were found others seldom present in the same man. He combined justice as a magistrate with gentleness as a man (vii. 19); spirit as a ruler, with temper and discretion in dealing with the arrogant and exacting (xvii. 14 seq.); diligence and equity in disposing of the fruits of victory with a complete unselfishness as regarded himself (xix. 49–51). Perhaps conspicuous above all was his humility. From first to last his valour and his victories are referred to God as their giver. Of his own personal work in the achievements of his life there is in his last addresses scarcely one word.

3. The chronological dates presented in this book are few :—

a. Comparing iv. 19 and v. 6, if the date of the Exodus be assumed to be B.C. 1490, that of the invasion of Canaan will be B.C. 1450.

b. The duration of Joshua's wars with the Canaanites is spoken of loosely in xi. 18 as "a long time." The words of Caleb (xiv. 7 and 10: cp. Num. xiii. 17)—who was thirty-eight years old when he passed through the Red Sea, and seventy-eight when he passed through Jordan—help us to assign a period of seven years (in round numbers) for the campaigns of Joshua.

c. The duration of Joshua's rule, and consequently the number of years covered by the record of this book, is far more uncertain. He died when he was an hundred and ten (xxiv. 29). If (cp. Ex. xxxiii. 11) we suppose him to have been about the same age as Caleb, he will have been about seventy-eight years old when he invaded Canaan, and have been at the head of Israel not much less than thirty-two years altogether after the death of Moses, surviving about twenty-five years after his retirement to Timnath-serah (cp. xxiii. 1). Josephus, however, states that Joshua's rule after the death of Moses lasted for twenty-five years, and that he had previously been forty years associated with him. This would fix Joshua's age at the time of the Exodus at forty-five. On the whole, nothing more precise seems attainable now than this : that Joshua governed Israel from twenty-five to thirty years after the death of Moses, and that about the like number of years contains the events recorded in the book which bears his name.

4. No sufficient evidence exists to enable us with certainty to name the author. That he was one of "the elders that overlived Joshua" (xxiv. 31) is probable, for the book appears to have been written by one coeval with the events recorded, and, indeed, an eye-witness of them. The spirit of the narrative in the former or historical portion of the book, and the graphic yet spontaneous rendering of details, which it everywhere presents, bespeak one who saw what he describes. And the topographical information which abounds in the latter portion of the book is of such a nature, and is presented in such a form, as strongly to suggest the use of written, and apparently contemporary documents. Some parts of this information are minute and accurate (*e.g.* ch. xv.), other statements are far less definite and complete. No doubt some of these imperfections are due to disorder in the text, or to clauses having dropped out of it, but others are mainly due to the fact that the writer's knowledge was itself imperfect. These very anomalies of the writer's most valuable description of Palestine, inconvenient as they often are, seem thus to be attributable to the early date of his information. His documents were written whilst Israel was still a stranger in the land of his inheritance, and in parts of it still a foreign invader.

The hand of a writer contemporaneous with the events is indicated in several expressions, *e.g.* in v. 6, 7 ; vi. 25 ; x. 2, a notice which plainly borrows its terms from the state of things in Canaan at the time of the invasion ; and in the record of ancient Canaanitish names of cities, though disused after the Israelites occupied them, (xiv. 15; xv. 9, 15, 49 and 60.)[3]

The book cannot, in its present form at least, be ascribed to Joshua himself. The account of his death and that of Eleazar, with the few supplementary verses at the end of the book, might have been attached by another hand, as a conclusion to the historical work of Joshua, just as a like addition was made to the work of Moses. But there are up and down the book a number of historical notices, which point to a date clearly beyond the death of Joshua (cp. xv. 13–20 and Judg. i. 1-15; xv. 63, and Judg. i. 8; xv. 13–19 and Judg. xviii.).

For these reasons the opinion of the Rabbins and many moderns which names Joshua as himself the sole writer of this book, must apparently be abandoned. The evidence internal and external renders it likely that the book was composed partly from personal observation and inquiry, partly out of pre-existing and authentic documents, within a few years after the death of Joshua, and probably from materials furnished in part by Joshua himself.

5. The book of Joshua is a work complete in itself, with an organic unity and peculiar characteristics. This appears

(1) From the definiteness of the writer's purpose, and the thoroughness with which he executes it. He proposes to narrate the conquest of Canaan, and to present that conquest as a proof of God's fidelity to his Covenant. But the writer does not limit himself to the achievements of Joshua. Such additions to the main body of his story, which belongs to the lifetime and leadership of Joshua, as are contained in chs. xiii. and xv. are to be explained only by a reference to the writer's distinct and special aim.

(2) From the tokens of connexion and method apparent throughout. Not only does the first part, which records the wars (i.–xii.), evidently lead up to the second part (xiii.–xxiv.), which describes the partition of the territory when subdued, but the contents of each part taken singly are given in proper and chronological order, each transaction growing out of the one preceding.

(3) From the style and phraseology. These are marked by distinctive features, whether the book be compared with the Pentateuch or with the other and later historical books. The difference of style, words, and treatment in the historical chapters, as contrasted with the topographical chapters is only what might be expected from the diverse nature of the subjects, and from the self-evident fact that in much of the latter part of his task the author was working from pre-existing documents.

Certain discrepancies alleged to exist in the book do not seriously impair its unity and independence. The difficulties, *e.g.* in the account of the capture of Ai (ch. viii.) arise solely out of the numbers, and are far more probably due to a

[3] Passages occur which fix a *terminus ad quem*, later than which they cannot have been penned. Thus xvi. 10 (cp. 1 Kings ix. 16) must have been written before the beginning of the reign of Solomon. From xi. 8 and xix. 28, Sidon was the capital of Phœnicia; but before the time of David, if not in or about B.C. 1208, the hegemony was transferred to Tyre. xv. 63 must belong to a time previous to the taking of Jerusalem and the destruction of the Jebusites by David (2 Sam. v. 6 seq.) ix. 27 implies that the site of the temple was not yet determined: cp. Deut. xvi. 5.

mistake in the numerals (see on viii. 3), which is by no means of infrequent occurrence, than to the presence in the narrative of two or three different versions of the events which the final editor omitted to harmonize.

The contradiction said to exist between some passages which speak of the land as completely subdued by Joshua, and of the Canaanites as utterly extirpated (xi. 16, 17, and 23; xii. 7, 8, &c.), and others which allude to "very much land," as still in possession of the native inhabitants (xiii. 1 seq.; xvii. 14 seq.; xxiii. 5, &c.), is to be explained partly by the theocratic view which the writer takes of his theme; a view which leads him to regard the conquest as complete when it was so *ex parte Dei*, and when all was done that was needed to enable the Israelites to realize fully the promises (cp. xxi. 43–45); partly also by the fact that territory was undoubtedly overrun by Joshua at the first onset, which was afterwards recovered by the Canaanites, and only again and finally wrested from them at a subsequent, sometimes a long subsequent, date. That the early campaigns of Joshua were in the nature of sudden raids, overpowering for the moment, but not effectually subduing the country, has probably much truth in it.

Thus then, the Book of Joshua, though based upon pre-existing materials of various kinds,[4] and sometimes incorporating them, appears to be a separate and complete work produced as a whole from one original hand. Its relation to the Pentateuch is that of an independent treatise by a distinct author, who resumes a theme of which the first great and important portion had been finished by a predecessor. The Pentateuch is not to be looked upon as principally a historical work. It is the statute book of the Theocracy, and contains only such historical matter as illustrates the origin and import of God's Covenant with Israel. Joshua records how the temporal promises of that Covenant were accomplished; and describes how the basis was laid for the future development of the nation, under the special superintendence of God, by its settlement in Canaan. Thus regarded, this book is no more an appendage to the Pentateuch than the books of Judges and Samuel are an appendage to it. There is, assuredly, an intimate connexion amongst these writings throughout, a connexion which is expressly indicated by the connective conjunctions used in the beginning of each book (see note on i. 1). This is due to the fact that the several authors were moved to write by one and the same Spirit, and that their one purpose in successive ages was to record the dealings of God with their nation. Hence they have selected whatever declares or illustrates the divine call of Israel; God's methods in educating that people for its functions in His world; the preparations made through the chequered history of Israel for future issues bearing on the salvation of all mankind. We find at one time periods of considerable length, and events of great importance to secular history cursorily alluded to, whilst other occurrences, often of a biographical character, are dwelt upon with

[4] We have *e.g.* in x. 12 a citation from a poetical book (see note in loc.); whilst elsewhere the writer has before him documents of a geographical character.

anxious minuteness, because of their theocratic bearings. Accordingly the name "Earlier Prophets," given to this and the following books of Judges, Samuel, and Kings by the Jewish Church which has handed them down to us as canonical, is appropriate. They were written by inspired men, and treat their subject from the prophetical point of view.

The book of Joshua is repeatedly cited or referred to in the New Testament: cp. Acts vii. 45; Heb. iii. 5; iv. 8; xi. 30, 31; James ii. 25.

6. The land of Canaan was given as a free gift by God to the Israelites—they took possession of it because He bade them do so—and He no less bade them annihilate the Canaanitish nations without mercy.[5] The question then occurs in unbroken force, all palliative explanations being disallowed:—Is this merciless treatment of the Canaanites consistent with the attributes of the Deity, especially as those attributes are illustrated for us in the New Testament?

The destruction of the Canaanites is always presented in Scripture as a judgment of God sent on them because of their wickedness. They had not only fallen into total apostacy from God, but into forms of idolatry of the most degrading kind. Their false religion cannot be regarded as a mere error of judgment; cruelty the most atrocious, and unnatural crimes the most defiling were part and parcel of its observances.[6] Moreover they had proved themselves to be incorrigible. They had had not only the general warning of the Deluge, as had other nations of the earth, but the special one of the overthrow of Sodom and Gomorrah in the very midst of them. They had had also the example and instruction of Abraham and the patriarchs living for ages amongst them. Even after the miraculous providence of God had brought the Israelites out of Egypt and across the Jordan, and even when the sword was as it were hanging over their necks, it was but in one or two isolated cases that signs of repentance and recollection of God were manifested (cp. ii. 11; ix. 24). God had forborne for ages in vain (cp. Gen. xv. 16); in the days of Joshua the time for mercy had passed, and that of judgment had come. It is impossible to acknowledge God as the moral Governor of the earth, and not to admit that it may be right or even necessary for Him to remove such nations. The fact, therefore, that God is described as having not only permitted, but even enjoined and caused the extirpation of the Canaanitish nations, depraved as they were, is not inconsistent with His moral attributes. Men, as was long ago pointed out by Bishop Butler ('Anal.' ii. 3), have no right to either life or property, but what arises solely from the grant of God. When this grant is revoked they cease to have any right at all in either. And in the case before us the forfeiture decreed by God was merited, and the execution of it was therefore righteous.

God chose to inflict His righteous judgment by the hands of the Israelites, and expressly commissioned them to be His executioners. If it be objected that this is to re-

[5] Cp. Ex. xxiii. 32 seq.; xxxiv. 12 seq.; Num. xxxiii. 52 seq.; Deut. vii. 1 seq.; Josh. ix. 24.

[6] Cp. Lev. xviii. 21 seq.; Deut. xii. 30 seq.

present God as sanctioning cruelty, the answer is obvious:—it is no sanction of cruelty to direct a lawful sentence to be carried out by human agents (cp. Num. xxxi. 3). Nor would obedience to God's command in this matter make the Israelites brutal and bloodthirsty. The behaviour of the Israelites, on many occasions, proves that they shrank from a terrible duty of this sort when laid on them by God, and did it only so far as they were compelled to do it.[7]

The slaughter of the Canaanites served various important purposes besides the mere removal of them from the face of the earth. To make and keep the Jewish people as much as possible isolated, was a marked and vital principle of the Old Testament dispensation. No more effectual means could have been adopted for inspiring God's people with an abhorrence for Canaanitish sins, to which they were not a little prone, than to make them the ministers of Divine vengeance for those sins.

They learnt by experiment that God would certainly root out those who fell away in apostacy from Him. They were warned also that if they fell into the sins of the Canaanites they would themselves be the victims of those same judgments of which they had been the reluctant executioners (cp. *e.g.* Deut. xxviii. 25). And the whole was so ordered as to exhibit a type, fearful no doubt yet salutary, of what must be the fate of the impenitent and obdurate in the upshot of God's righteous government.

[7] Cp. Num. xxxi. 13 seq.; Josh. xvi. 10; xviii. 3; Judg. i. 28 and 35; 1 Sam. xv. 24).

THE BOOK

OF

JOSHUA.

Chap. 1. NOW after the death of Moses the servant of the LORD it
came to pass, that the LORD spake unto Joshua the son of Nun,
2 Moses' [a]minister, saying, [b]Moses my servant is dead; now
therefore arise, go over this Jordan, thou, and all this people,
unto the land which I do give to them, *even* to the children of
3 Israel. [c]Every place that the sole of your foot shall tread upon,
4 that have I given unto you, as I said unto Moses. [d]From
the wilderness and this Lebanon even unto the great river, the
river Euphrates, all the land of the Hittites, and unto the great
sea toward the going down of the sun, shall be your coast.
5 [e]There shall not any man be able to stand before thee all the
days of thy life: [f]as I was with Moses, *so* [g]I will be with thee:
6 [h]I will not fail thee, nor forsake thee. [i]Be strong and of a good
courage: for [1]unto this people shalt thou divide for an inheritance the land, which I sware unto their fathers to give them.
7 Only be thou strong and very courageous, that thou mayest
observe to do according to all the law, [k]which Moses my servant
commanded thee: [l]turn not from it *to* the right hand or *to* the

[a] Ex. 24. 13. Deut. 1. 38.
[b] Deut. 34. 5.
[c] Deut. 11. 24. ch. 14. 9.
[d] Gen. 15. 18. Ex. 23. 31. Num. 34. 3—12.
[e] Deut. 7. 24.
[f] Ex. 3. 12.
[g] Deut. 31. 8, 23. ver. 9, 17. ch. 3. 7. & 6. 27. Isai. 43. 2, 5.
[h] Deut. 31. 6, 8. Heb. 13. 5.
[i] Deut. 31. 7, 23.
[k] Num. 27. 23. Deut. 31. 7. ch. 11. 15.
[l] Deut. 5. 32. & 28. 14.

[1] Or, *thou shalt cause this people to inherit the land, &c.*

I. Verses 1-9 of this chapter serve as an introduction to the history of the war, and pointedly call attention to the leading thought of the whole book,—that the invasion and subjugation of Canaan were undertaken by the Israelites at God's direct command and completed in His never-failing strength.

1. *Now,* &c.] Heb.: "and, &c." The statement following is thus connected with some previous one, which is assumed to be known to the reader. So Judges, Ruth, 1 Sam., &c., are by the same means linked on to the books preceding them. The connexion here is the closer, since the book of Deuteronomy concludes, and the book of Joshua opens, by referring to the death of Moses.

Moses, the servant of the LORD] On the epithet, see marg. ref. *b.*

Moses' minister] It is impossible altogether to pass by the typical application of this verse. Moses, representing the law, is dead; Joshua, or, as that name is written in Greek, Jesus, is now bidden by God to do what Moses could not,—lead the people into the Promised Land. Joshua was "Moses' minister," just as Christ was "made under the Law;" but it was Joshua, not Moses, who wrought out the accomplishment of the blessings which the Law promised. On the name Joshua, see Exod. xvii. 9 note, and Num. xiii. 16.

saying] No doubt directly, by an immediate revelation, but not as God spake to Moses, "mouth to mouth" (Num. xii. 8). Though upon Joshua's appointment to be Moses' successor (Num. xxvii. 18 seq.), it had been directed that "counsel should be asked" for him through the medium of Eleazar "after the judgment of Urim," yet this was evidently a resource provided to meet cases of doubt and difficulty. Here there was no such case; but the appointed leader, knowing well the purpose of God, needed to be stirred up to instant execution of it; and the people too might require the encouragement of a renewed Divine command to set out at once upon the great enterprise before them (cp. *v.* 13).

4. Lebanon is spoken of as "this Lebanon," because visible from the neighbourhood in which Israel was encamped. (Cp. Deut. iii. 8, 9.) "The wilderness" of the text is the Desert of Arabia, which forms the southern, as Lebanon does the northern, limit of the Promised Land. The boundaries on the east and west are likewise indicated; and the intervening territory is described generally as "all the land of the Hittites." The Hittites are properly the inhabitants of northern Canaan and Phœnicia (see Exod. iii. 8 note), but the name appears to be used here for the Canaanites in general, as in 1 Kings x. 29. On the boundaries of the Promised Land cp. Deut. xi. 24; Gen. xv. 18.

7. *prosper*] See margin. The literal rendering should be retained here since the notion of prosperity is separately introduced by a different word in *v.* 8.

m Deut. 17. 18, 19.
n Ps. 1. 2.
o Deut. 31. 7, 8, 23. Jer. 1. 8.
p Ps. 27. 1.
q ch. 3. 2. See Deut. 9. 1. & 11. 31.
r Num. 32. 20—28. ch. 22. 2, 3, 4.
s ch. 22. 4, &c.
t ver. 5. 1 Sam. 20. 13. 1 Kin. 1. 37.
a Num. 25. 1.

8 left, that thou mayest [1]prosper whithersoever thou goest. [m]This
book of the law shall not depart out of thy mouth; but [n]thou
shalt meditate therein day and night, that thou mayest observe
to do according to all that is written therein: for then thou
shalt make thy way prosperous, and then thou shalt [2]have good
9 success. [o]Have not I commanded thee? Be strong and of a
good courage; [p]be not afraid, neither be thou dismayed: for the
10 LORD thy God *is* with thee whithersoever thou goest. ¶ Then
11 Joshua commanded the officers of the people, saying, Pass through
the host, and command the people, saying, Prepare you victuals;
for [q]within three days ye shall pass over this Jordan, to go in to
possess the land, which the LORD your God giveth you to possess
12 it. ¶ And to the Reubenites, and to the Gadites, and to half the
13 tribe of Manasseh, spake Joshua, saying, Remember [r]the word
which Moses the servant of the LORD commanded you, saying,
The LORD your God hath given you rest, and hath given you
14 this land. Your wives, your little ones, and your cattle, shall
remain in the land which Moses gave you on this side Jordan;
but ye shall pass before your brethren [3]armed, all the mighty
15 men of valour, and help them; until the LORD have given your
brethren rest, as *he hath given* you, and they also have possessed
the land which the LORD your God giveth them: [s]then ye shall
return unto the land of your possession, and enjoy it, which
Moses the LORD's servant gave you on this side Jordan toward
16 the sunrising. And they answered Joshua, saying, All that
thou commandest us we will do, and whithersoever thou sendest
17 us, we will go. According as we hearkened unto Moses in all
things, so will we hearken unto thee: only the LORD thy God
18 [t]be with thee, as he was with Moses. Whosoever *he be* that doth
rebel against thy commandment, and will not hearken unto thy
words in all that thou commandest him, he shall be put to death:
only be strong and of a good courage.

CHAP. 2. AND Joshua the son of Nun [4]sent [a]out of Shittim two
men to spy secretly, saying, Go view the land, even Jericho.

[1] Or, *do wisely*, Deut. 29. 9.
[2] Or, *do wisely*, ver. 7.
[3] Heb. *marshalled by five*: as Ex. 13. 18.
[4] Or, *had sent*.

---

10. *officers*] The "scribes." (See Ex. v. 6 note, and Deut. xvi. 18.)

11. *Prepare you victuals*] The order was probably given with the knowledge that the manna would cease when the host crossed the Jordan (Ex. xvi. 35), and possibly because amidst their preparations there might not be opportunity to gather it in sufficient quantity. Nor does it appear that manna ever formed the whole and sole sustenance of the people. (Cp. Num. xx. 1 note.)

It is the view of the majority of commentators—Jewish and Christian, ancient and modern—that the "three days" here named are identical with those of iii. 2; and that the command of Joshua in the text was not in fact given until after the return of the spies. Here, as elsewhere in the Hebrew historical books and frequently in the Gospels, the order of time is superseded by the order of thought. For the purpose of the writer was not historical merely; it was, on the contrary, mainly religious and theoretical. Intending, then, to exhibit God as accomplishing His promises to the Covenant-people, he begins by informing us that God gave the word, and set Joshua and the host actually in motion to take possession of their inheritance. Having placed this leading fact in the forefront, he returns to mention in ch. ii. certain transactions closely relevant to the early stages of Joshua's conquests, but which had in fact happened before the camp was removed from the plains of Moab and immediately after the expiration of the thirty days' mourning for Moses. (Deut. xxxiv. 8.) The order of events was probably the following:—3rd Nisan, the spies are sent out (ii. 1); 6th, the spies return (ii. 23); 7th, the camp is removed from Shittim to the bank of Jordan (iii. 1), and the command (i. 11) is issued; 10th, the river is crossed (iv. 19).

14. *armed*] Rather, "arrayed" (see Ex. xiii. 18 note).

on this side Jordan] Cp. Deut. i. 1, note.

II. **1.** *an harlot's house*] In the face of the parallel passages (*e.g.* Lev. xxi. 7: Jer. v. 7)

And they went, and [b]came into an harlot's house, named [c]Rahab, [b] Heb. 11. 31. Jam. 2. 25.
2 and [1]lodged there. ¶ And [d]it was told the king of Jericho, saying, [c] Matt. 1. 5.
Behold, there came men in hither to night of the children of [d] Ps. 127. 1.
3 Israel to search out the country. And the king of Jericho sent Prov. 21. 30.
unto Rahab, saying, Bring forth the men that are come to thee,
which are entered into thine house: for they be come to search
4 out all the country. ¶ [e]And the woman took the two men, and [e] See 2 Sam.
hid them, and said thus, There came men unto me, but I wist 17. 19, 20.
5 not whence they *were*: and it came to pass *about the time* of shut-
ting of the gate, when it was dark, that the men went out:
whither the men went, I wot not: pursue after them quickly;
6 for ye shall overtake them. But [f]she had brought them up to [f] See Ex. 1.
the roof of the house, and hid them with the stalks of flax, 17.
7 which she had laid in order upon the roof. And the men pur- 2 Sam. 17.
sued after them the way to Jordan unto the fords: and as soon 19.
as they which pursued after them were gone out, they shut the
8 gate. ¶ And before they were laid down, she came up unto
9 them upon the roof; and she said unto the men, I know that
the LORD hath given you the land, and that [g]your terror is fallen [g] Gen. 35. 5.
upon us, and that all the inhabitants of the land [2]faint because Ex. 23. 27.
10 of you. For we have heard how the LORD [h]dried up the water Deut. 2. 25. & 11. 25.
of the Red sea for you, when ye came out of Egypt; and [i]what [h] Ex. 14. 21. ch. 4. 23.
ye did unto the two kings of the Amorites, that *were* on the other [i] Num. 21.
11 side Jordan, Sihon and Og, whom ye utterly destroyed. And 24, 34, 35.
as soon as we had [k]heard *these things*, [l]our hearts did melt, [k] Ex. 15. 14, 15.
neither [3]did there remain any more courage in any man, because [l] ch. 5. 1. & 7. 5. Isai. 13. 7.

[1] Heb. *lay*. [2] Heb. *melt*, Ex. 15. 15. [3] Heb. *rose up*.

---

the rendering advocated for obvious reasons *viz.* "the house of a woman, an innkeeper," cannot be maintained. Rahab must remain an example under the Law similar to that (Luke vii. 37) under the Gospel, of "a woman that was a sinner," yet, because of her faith, not only pardoned, but exalted to the highest honour. Rahab was admitted among the people of God; she intermarried into a chief family of a chief tribe, and found a place amongst the best remembered ancestors of King David and of Christ; thus receiving the temporal blessings of the Covenant in largest measure. The spies would of course betake themselves to such a house in Jericho as they could visit without exciting suspicion; and the situation of Rahab's, upon the wall (*v.* 15), rendered it especially suitable. It appears from *v.* 4 that Rahab hid them before the King's messengers reached her house, and probably as soon as the spies had come to her house. It is therefore most likely that they met with Rahab outside of Jericho (cp. Gen. xxxviii. 14), and ascertained where in the city she dwelt, and that they might intrust themselves to her care. Rahab (*i.e.* "spacious," "wide." Cp. the name "Japheth" and Gen. ix. 27, note) is regarded by the Fathers as a type of the Christian Church, which was gathered out of converts from the whole vast circle of heathen nations.

4. *I wist not whence they were*] Rahab acted as she did from a belief in God's declared word, and a conviction that resistance to His will would be both vain and wicked (*vv.* 9–11). Thus she manifested a faith both sound and practical, and is praised accordingly (Heb. xi. 31; James ii. 25). The falsehood to which she had recourse may be excused by the pressure of circumstances and by her own antecedents, but cannot be defended.

6. *stalks of flax*] Lit. "the carded fibres of the tree." The flax in Palestine grew to more than three feet in height, with a stalk as thick as a cane. It was probably with the flax stalks, recently cut (cp. Ex. ix. 31, note) and laid out on the house roof to dry, that Rahab hid the spies.

7. The sense is, that "they pursued along the way which leads to Jordan and across the fords;" probably those described in Judg. iii. 28.

11. *the* LORD *your God, he is God*] From the rumour of God's miraculous interpositions Rahab believed, and makes the selfsame confession to which Moses endeavours to bring Israel by rehearsing similar arguments (Deut. iv. 39). Rahab had only heard of what Israel had experienced. Her faith then was ready. It is noteworthy, too, that the same reports which work faith and conversion in the harlot, cause only terror and astonishment amongst her countrymen. (Cp. St. Luke viii. 37–39.)

m Deut. 4. 39. n See 1 Sam. 20. 14, 15, 17. o See 1 Tim. 5. 8. p ver. 18. q Judg. 1. 24. Matt. 5. 7. r Acts 9. 25. s Ex. 20. 7. t ver. 12. u ch. 6. 23. x Matt. 27. 25. y Ex. 23. 31. ch. 6. 2. & 21. 44.

of you: for [m]the LORD your God, he *is* God in heaven above,
12 and in earth beneath. Now therefore, I pray you, [n]swear unto
me by the LORD, since I have shewed you kindness, that ye will
also shew kindness unto [o]my father's house, and [p]give me a true
13 token: and *that* ye will save alive my father, and my mother,
and my brethren, and my sisters, and all that they have, and
14 deliver our lives from death. ¶ And the men answered her, Our
life [1]for your's, if ye utter not this our business. And it shall
be, when the LORD hath given us the land, that [q]we will deal
15 kindly and truly with thee. Then she [r]let them down by a
cord through the window: for her house *was* upon the town wall,
16 and she dwelt upon the wall. And she said unto them, Get you
to the mountain, lest the pursuers meet you; and hide yourselves
there three days, until the pursuers be returned: and afterward
17 may ye go your way. ¶ And the men said unto her, We *will be*
[s]blameless of this thine oath which thou hast made us swear.
18 [t]Behold, *when* we come into the land, thou shalt bind this line of
scarlet thread in the window which thou didst let us down by:
[u]and thou shalt [2]bring thy father, and thy mother, and thy
19 brethren, and all thy father's household, home unto thee. And
it shall be, *that* whosoever shall go out of the doors of thy house
into the street, his blood *shall be* upon his head, and we *will be*
guiltless: and whosoever shall be with thee in the house, [x]his
20 blood *shall be* on our head, if *any* hand be upon him. And if thou
utter this our business, then we will be quit of thine oath which
21 thou hast made us to swear. And she said, According unto
your words, so *be* it. And she sent them away, and they de-
22 parted: and she bound the scarlet line in the window. And
they went, and came unto the mountain, and abode there three
days, until the pursuers were returned: and the pursuers sought
23 *them* throughout all the way, but found *them* not. So the two
men returned, and descended from the mountain, and passed
over, and came to Joshua the son of Nun, and told him all
24 *things* that befell them: and they said unto Joshua, Truly [y]the

[1] Heb. *instead of you to die.* [2] Heb. *gather.*

---

12. *a true token*] Lit. "a sign" or "pledge of truth;" something to bind them to keep their promise faithfully. The "token" was the oath which the spies take (*v.* 14).

14. *Our life for yours*] See marg. This is (see *v.* 17) a form of oath, in which God is in effect invoked to punish them with death if they did not perform their promise to save Rahab's life. Cp. the more common form of oath, 1 Sam. i. 26, &c.

15. *upon the town wall*] The town wall probably formed the back wall of the house, and the window opened therefore into the country. (Cp. St. Paul's escape, 2 Cor. xi. 33).

18. The "line" or cord was spun of threads dyed with cochineal; *i.e.*, of a deep and bright scarlet colour. The colour would catch the eye at once, and supplied an obvious token by which the house of Rahab might be distinguished. The use of scarlet in the Levitical rites, especially in those more closely connected with the idea of putting away of sin and its consequences (cp. *e.g.*, Lev. xiv. 4, 6, 51; Num. xix. 6), naturally led the Fathers, from St. Clement of Rome onwards, to see in this scarlet thread, no less than in the blood of the Passover (Ex. xii. 7, 13, &c.), an emblem of salvation by the Blood of Christ; a salvation common alike to Christ's messengers and to those whom they visit.

22. *unto the mountain*] Probably the mountains to the west and north of Jericho, called afterwards, from the belief that the forty days of our Lord's temptation were passed amongst them, the Quarantania. The spies avoided at the first the neighbourhood of the Jordan, where the pursuers sought them: and amidst the grottoes of the limestone rocks, which in later ages were the abode of numerous hermits, they could readily shelter themselves for three days.

LORD hath delivered into our hands all the land; for even all
the inhabitants of the country do [1]faint because of us.

CHAP. 3. AND Joshua rose early in the morning; and they removed [a]from Shittim, and came to Jordan, he and all the
children of Israel, and lodged there before they passed over.
2 And it came to pass [b]after three days, that the officers went
3 through the host; and they commanded the people, saying,
[c]When ye see the ark of the covenant of the LORD your God,
[d]and the priests the Levites bearing it, then ye shall remove from
4 your place, and go after it. [e]Yet there shall be a space between
you and it, about two thousand cubits by measure: come not
near unto it, that ye may know the way by which ye must go:
5 for ye have not passed *this* way [2]heretofore. And Joshua said
unto the people, [f]Sanctify yourselves: for to morrow the LORD
6 will do wonders among you. And Joshua spake unto the priests,
saying, [g]Take up the ark of the covenant, and pass over before
the people. And they took up the ark of the covenant, and
7 went before the people. ¶ And the LORD said unto Joshua, This
day will I begin to [h]magnify thee in the sight of all Israel, that
they may know that, [i]as I was with Moses, *so* I will be with
8 thee. And thou shalt command [k]the priests that bear the ark of
the covenant, saying, When ye are come to the brink of the
9 water of Jordan, [l]ye shall stand still in Jordan. And Joshua
said unto the children of Israel, Come hither, and hear the words
10 of the LORD your God. And Joshua said, Hereby ye shall know
that [m]the living God *is* among you, and *that* he will without fail
[n]drive out from before you the Canaanites, and the Hittites, and
the Hivites, and the Perizzites, and the Girgashites, and the
11 Amorites, and the Jebusites. Behold, the ark of the covenant
of [o]the Lord of all the earth passeth over before you into Jordan.
12 Now therefore [p]take you twelve men out of the tribes of Israel,
13 out of every tribe a man. And it shall come to pass, [q]as soon as

[a] ch. 2. 1.
[b] ch. 1. 10, 11.
[c] See Num. 10. 33.
[d] Deut. 31. 9, 25.
[e] Ex. 19. 12.
[f] Ex. 19. 10. Lev. 20. 7. Num. 11. 18. ch. 7. 13. 1 Sam. 16. 5. Joel 2. 16.
[g] Num. 4. 15.
[h] 1 Chr. 29. 25. 2 Chr. 1. 1.
[i] ch. 1. 5.
[k] ver. 3.
[l] ver. 17.
[m] Deut. 5. 26. 2 Kin. 19. 4. Hos. 1. 10. Matt. 16. 16. 1 Thess. 1. 9.
[n] Ex. 33. 2. Deut. 7. 1. Ps. 44. 2.
[o] ver. 13. Mic. 4. 13. Zech. 4. 14.
[p] ch. 4. 2.
[q] ver. 15, 16.

[1] Heb. *melt*, ver. 9. [2] Heb. *since yesterday, and the third day.*

III. The contents of this and the next chapter, which record the miraculous passage of Israel over Jordan, are given in four sections:—(1) iii. 1–6, describing the preliminary directions; (2) iii. 7–17, the commencement of the passage; (3) iv. 1–14, the accomplishment of it; (4) iv. 15–24, the conclusion of the passage and erection of a monument to commemorate it. A certain completeness and finish is given to each division of the narrative, and to effect this the writer more than once repeats himself, anticipates the actual order of events, and distributes into parts occurrences which in fact took place once for all.

1. "The acacia groves" (Ex. xxv. 5 note) of Shittim on both sides of Jordan line the upper terraces of the valley (cp. 2 K. vi. 4). They would be in this part at some six miles distance from the river itself.

2. These days (i. 11 note) were no doubt occupied in preparations of various kinds. The host consisted not of armed men only, but of women and children also; and many arrangements would be necessary before they actually advanced into a hostile country.

4. The ark, which was since the making of the Covenant the special shrine and seat of God's Presence, went before to show the people that God, through its medium, was their leader. They were to follow at a distance that they might the better observe and mark how the miracle was accomplished. This they would do to the greatest advantage whilst coming down the heights, the ark going on before them into the ravine.

6. *they took up*] *i.e.* on the day following. The course of events is anticipated.

7. *This day will I begin to magnify thee*] One cause why the miracle now to be narrated was wrought is here suggested. As Moses was declared to be sent immediately from God with an extraordinary commission by the miracles which he worked, more especially that of dividing the Red Sea in two parts, so was Joshua both sent and accredited in a like manner. (Cp. i. 5, and iv. 14.) Other reasons are given in *v.* 10 and v. 1.

10. *the living God*] Cp. marg. ref. The gods of the heathen are "dead idols." On the names of the seven nations, see Gen. x. 16, &c., note.

the soles of the feet of the priests that bear the ark of the LORD,
[r] ver. 11. [r]the Lord of all the earth, shall rest in the waters of Jordan,
that the waters of Jordan shall be cut off *from* the waters that
[s] Ps. 78. 13. come down from above; and they [s]shall stand upon an heap.
14 ¶And it came to pass, when the people removed from their tents,
[t] Acts 7. 45. to pass over Jordan, and the priests bearing the [t]ark of the
15 covenant before the people; and as they that bare the ark were
[u] ver. 13. come unto Jordan, and [u]the feet of the priests that bare the ark
[x] 1 Chr. 12. 15. were dipped in the brim of the water, (for [x]Jordan overfloweth
Jer. 12. 5. 16 all his banks [y]all the time of harvest,) that the waters which
[y] ch. 4. 18. came down from above stood *and* rose up upon an heap very far
[z] 1 Kin. 4. 12. & 7. 46. from the city Adam, that *is* beside [z]Zaretan: and those that
[a] Deut. 3. 17. came down [a]toward the sea of the plain, *even* [b]the salt sea,
[b] Gen. 14. 3. Num. 34. 3. failed, *and* were cut off: and the people passed over right
17 against Jericho. And the priests that bare the ark of the cove-
nant of the LORD stood firm on dry ground in the midst of
[c] See Ex. 14. 29. Jordan, [c]and all the Israelites passed over on dry ground,
until all the people were passed clean over Jordan.

CHAP. 4. AND it came to pass, when all the people were clean
[a] Deut. 27. 2. passed [a]over Jordan, that the LORD spake unto Joshua, saying,
[b] ch. 3. 12. 2 [b]Take you twelve men out of the people, out of every tribe a
3 man, and command ye them, saying, Take you hence out of the
[c] ch. 3. 13. midst of Jordan, out of the place where [c]the priests' feet stood
firm, twelve stones, and ye shall carry them over with you, and
[d] ver. 19, 20. leave them in [d]the lodging place, where ye shall lodge this

---

15. *Jordan overfloweth all his banks*] Rather "is full up to all his banks," *i.e.* "brim-full." This remark strikingly illustrates the suddenness and completeness, not less than the greatness, of the marvel. The Jordan flows at the bottom of a deep valley, which descends to the water's edge on either side in two, occasionally in three, terraces. Within the lowest of these the stream, ordinarily less than 100 feet wide in this lower part of its course, is confined. The margin is overgrown with a jungle of tamarisks and willows, which in the spring is reached by the rising waters (cp. the figure in Jer. xlix. 19; l. 44); and the river, occasionally at least, fills the ravine which forms its proper bed to the brim. Its highest rise takes place about the time when Joshua had to cross it. By the middle of April the river cannot be forded; and, if passed at all, can only be so by swimming. This, however, was a hazardous feat (cp. 1 Chr. xii. 15); and though no doubt performed by the two spies, was utterly out of the power of the mixed multitude that followed Joshua. The mere fact that the whole vast host crossed the stream of Jordan at this season, is no small proof of the miracle here recorded. No human agency then known and available could have transported them speedily and safely from bank to bank.

16. The passage should run "**rose up, an heap far away, by Adam, the city which is beside Zarthan.**"

The city of Adam is not named elsewhere, and Zarthan (mentioned here and in marg. reff.) has also disappeared. It is, however, probably connected with the modern *Kurn Sartabeh* (Horn of Sartabeh), the name given to a lofty and isolated hill some seventeen miles on the river above Jericho.

17. The miraculous passage to the Holy Land through Jordan is not less pregnant with typical meaning than that through the Red Sea (cp. 1 Cor. x. 1, 2). The solemn inauguration of Joshua to his office, and his miraculous attestation, by the same waters with which Jesus was baptized on entering on the public exercise of His ministry (cp. Matt. iii. 16, 17); the choice of twelve men, one from each tribe to be the bearers of the twelve stones, and the builders of the monument erected therewith (cp. 1 Cor. iii. 10; Rev. xxi. 14):—these were divinely ordered occurrences, not without a further bearing than their more immediate one upon Israel. Nor must in this point of view the name "Adam," the place whence flowed to the people the stream which cut them off from the promises, and the failure for the time under the rule of Joshua of the full and rapid flood which supplies the Dead Sea, be overlooked.

IV. 2. *Take you twelve men*] The order is given in the plural, because no doubt the tribes themselves were to choose their own representatives, the choice being approved by Joshua (*v.* 4). These twelve would be left with Joshua on the hither bank of the river, waiting to receive his orders after the rest of the people had made their way across (iii. 17; iv. 1).

4 night. Then Joshua called the twelve men, whom he had
prepared of the children of Israel, out of every tribe a man:
5 and Joshua said unto them, Pass over before the ark of the
LORD your God into the midst of Jordan, and take you up every
man of you a stone upon his shoulder, according unto the
6 number of the tribes of the children of Israel: that this may be
a sign among you, *that* [e]when your children ask *their fathers* [1]in
7 time to come, saying, What *mean* ye by these stones? Then ye
shall answer them, That [f]the waters of Jordan were cut off before
the ark of the covenant of the LORD; when it passed over Jordan,
the waters of Jordan were cut off: and these stones shall be for
8 [g]a memorial unto the children of Israel for ever. And the
children of Israel did so as Joshua commanded, and took up
twelve stones out of the midst of Jordan, as the LORD spake
unto Joshua, according to the number of the tribes of the
children of Israel, and carried them over with them unto the
9 place where they lodged, and laid them down there. And
Joshua set up twelve stones in the midst of Jordan, in the place
where the feet of the priests which bare the ark of the covenant
10 stood: and they are there unto this day. ¶For the priests which
bare the ark stood in the midst of Jordan, until every thing was
finished that the LORD commanded Joshua to speak unto the
people, according to all that Moses commanded Joshua: and the
11 people hasted and passed over. And it came to pass, when all
the people were clean passed over, that the ark of the LORD
12 passed over, and the priests, in the presence of the people. And
[h]the children of Reuben, and the children of Gad, and half
the tribe of Manasseh, passed over armed before the children of
13 Israel, as Moses spake unto them: about forty thousand [2]pre-
pared for war passed over before the LORD unto battle, to the
14 plains of Jericho. ¶On that day the LORD [i]magnified Joshua in
the sight of all Israel; and they feared him, as they feared
15 Moses, all the days of his life. And the LORD spake unto

[e] ver. 21. Ex. 12. 26. & 13. 14. Deut. 6. 20. Ps. 44. 1. & 78. 3, 4, 5, 6.
[f] ch. 3. 13, 16.
[g] Ex. 12. 14. Num. 16. 40.
[h] Num. 32. 20, 27, 28.
[i] ch. 3. 7.

[1] Heb. *to morrow*.
[2] Or, *ready armed*.

8. *laid them down there*] *i.e.* in Gilgal (*v.* 20). Spoken of as the doers of this, because it was done by the twelve who acted for them.

9. Another set of stones is intended than that before mentioned. The one set was erected by the command of God at the spot where they passed the night (*v.* 3); the other by Joshua on the spot where the priests' feet rested whilst they bore up the ark during the passage of the people. This spot was near, or perhaps on, the eastern brink (cp. iii. 8). These stones would therefore mark the spot at which the people crossed, as the others marked the place in which they lodged the night after the crossing; nor, as the stones would only be reached by the water in flood time, and then by the utmost edge of it, is there any reason why they could not both be seen, and continue in their place as the writer asserts they did up to the time when he wrote.

13. The plains of Jericho, consisting of the higher terrace of the Jordan valley, are almost seven miles broad. The mountains of Judæa here recede somewhat from the river, and leave a level and fertile space, which, at the time of Joshua's invasion, was principally occupied by a forest of palms. Hence the name "city of palms," Deut. xxxiv. 3.

15. The passage of the priests to the further bank had been already referred to, *v.* 11; but the writer, in observance of his general plan (cp. introductory remarks to ch. iii.), re-introduces it here as the leading feature in the concluding section of his account, and (as before) with mention of God's special direction about it. The statement that on the removal of the ark the waters of Jordan at once returned to their former level (*v.* 18), heightens the impression which is especially inculcated throughout,—that the whole transaction was extraordinary and miraculous. The details and incidents of the passage are no doubt open to manifold discussion: but all such discussion will be futile unless it proceed throughout on the admission that we have here before us the record of a distinctly supernatural interposition: cp. Introd. p. 1.

16 Joshua, saying, Command the priests that bear [k]the ark of the
17 testimony, that they come up out of Jordan. Joshua therefore
commanded the priests, saying, Come ye up out of Jordan.
18 And it came to pass, when the priests that bare the ark of the
covenant of the LORD were come up out of the midst of Jordan,
and the soles of the priests' feet were [1]lifted up unto the dry
land, that the waters of Jordan returned unto their place, [l]and
19 [2]flowed over all his banks, as *they did* before. ¶And the people
came up out of Jordan on the tenth *day* of the first month, and
20 encamped [m]in Gilgal, in the east border of Jericho. And [n]those
twelve stones, which they took out of Jordan, did Joshua pitch
21 in Gilgal. And he spake unto the children of Israel, saying,
[o]When your children shall ask their fathers [3]in time to come,
22 saying, What *mean* these stones? Then ye shall let your
children know, saying, [p]Israel came over this Jordan on dry
23 land. For the LORD your God dried up the waters of Jordan
from before you, until ye were passed over, as the LORD your
God did to the Red sea, [q]which he dried up from before us,
24 until we were gone over: [r]that all the people of the earth might
know the hand of the LORD, that it *is* [s]mighty: that ye might
[t]fear the LORD your God [4]for ever.

CHAP. 5. AND it came to pass, when all the kings of the Amorites,
which *were* on the side of Jordan westward, and all the kings of
the Canaanites, [a]which *were* by the sea, [b]heard that the LORD
had dried up the waters of Jordan from before the children of
Israel, until we were passed over, that their heart melted,
[c]neither was there spirit in them any more, because of the
2 children of Israel. ¶At that time the LORD said unto Joshua,
Make thee [5][d]sharp knives, and circumcise again the children of
3 Israel the second time. And Joshua made him sharp knives,

[k] Ex. 25. 16, 22. [l] ch. 3. 15. [m] ch. 5. 9. [n] ver. 3. [o] ver. 6. [p] ch. 3. 17. [q] Ex. 14. 21. [r] 1 Kin. 8. 42, 43. Ps. 106. 8. [s] Ex. 15. 16. 1 Chr. 29. 12. Ps. 89. 13. [t] Ex. 14. 31. Deut. 6. 2. Jer. 10. 7. [a] Num. 13. 29. [b] Ex. 15. 14. ch. 2. 9, 10. Ps. 48. 6. Ezek. 21, 7. [c] 1 Kin. 10. 5. [d] Ex. 4. 25.

1 Heb. *plucked up*.
2 Heb. *went*.
3 Heb. *to morrow*.
4 Heb. *all days*.
5 Or, *knives of flints*.

---

19. Gilgal, mentioned here by anticipation (cp. v. 9), [the modern Jiljûlieh (Conder)], was on rising ground (cp. v. 3), and, according to Josephus, nearly five miles from the river, and consequently about two from the city itself. The site of the camp was no doubt fortified by Joshua, as it constituted for some time the abiding foothold in Canaan, whence he sallied forth to subdue the country. It was also the place of safety where the ark, and no doubt also the women, children, cattle, and other property of the people were left. Hence the demolition of Jericho and Ai, strong fortresses in the neighbourhood of Gilgal, was no doubt dictated by sound policy as well as by religious obligations.

V. **1.** The Amorites were the principal of those nations which occupied the hill country of Judæa (Gen. x. 16 note); the Canaanites of those that dwelt on the coast and low lands. These words are therefore equivalent to "all the kings of the highlanders, and all the kings of the lowlanders": *i.e.* the kings of all the tribes of the country.

until we were passed over] The use of the first person has been noted here, and in verse 6 (cp. Acts xvi. 10), as suggesting the hand of one who himself shared in what he describes. But the text as read (though not written) by the Jewish authorities here, has the third person; as have some MSS., LXX., Vulg., &c.: and a change of person like this in Hebrew, even if the text stand, does not of itself warrant the inference. (Cp. Ps. lxvi. 6.)

2. *Make thee sharp knives*] Render rather as marg., and cp. marg. ref. and note. Knives of flint or stone were in fact used for circumcision, and retained for that and other sacred purposes, even after iron had become in common use. The rendering of marg. is adopted by almost all ancient versions, by most commentators, and by the Fathers generally, who naturally regarded circumcision wrought by Joshua and by means of knives of stone or rock, as symbolical of the true circumcision wrought by Christ, Who is more than once spoken of as the Rock (cp. 1 Cor. x. 4; Rom. ii. 29; Col. ii. 11). See xxi. 42.

circumcise again, &c.] *i.e.* make that which once was a circumcised people but is not so now, once more a circumcised people. (See *vv.* 4–7.)

and circumcised the children of Israel at [1]the hill of the fore-
4 skins. And this *is* the cause why Joshua did circumcise: [e]All
the people that came out of Egypt, *that were* males, *even* all the
men of war, died in the wilderness by the way, after they came
5 out of Egypt. Now all the people that came out were circumcised: but all the people *that were* born in the wilderness by the
way as they came forth out of Egypt, *them* they had not cir-
6 cumcised. For the children of Israel walked [f]forty years in the
wilderness, till all the people *that were* men of war, which came
out of Egypt, were consumed, because they obeyed not the voice
of the LORD: unto whom the LORD sware that [g]he would not
shew them the land, which the LORD sware unto their fathers
that he would give us, [h]a land that floweth with milk and honey.
7 And [i]their children, *whom* he raised up in their stead, them
Joshua circumcised: for they were uncircumcised, because they
8 had not circumcised them by the way. And it came to pass,
[2]when they had done circumcising all the people, that they

[e] Num. 14. 29. & 26. 64, 65. Deut. 2. 16.
[f] Num. 14. 33. Deut. 1. 3. & 2. 7, 14. Ps. 95. 10.
[g] Num. 14. 23. Ps. 95. 11. Heb. 3. 11.
[h] Ex. 3. 8.
[i] Num. 14. 31. Deut. 1. 39.

[1] Or, *Gibeah-haaraloth.*

[2] Heb. *when the people had made an end to be circumcised.*

---

3. *the hill of the foreskins*] *i.e.* the hill where the foreskins, the emblem of all worldly and carnal affections, were buried. (Cp. Col. ii. 11-13; iii. 1-6.)

4-7. Of the whole nation those only were already circumcised at the time of the passage of the Jordan who had been under twenty years of age at the time of the murmuring and consequent rejection at Kadesh (cp. marg. ref.). These would have been circumcised before they left Egypt, and there would still survive of them more than a quarter of a million of thirty-eight years old and upwards.

The statements of these verses are of a general kind. The "forty years" of *v.* 6 is a round number, and the statement in the latter part of *v.* 5 cannot be strictly accurate. For there must have been male children born in the wilderness during the first year after the Exodus, and these must have been circumcised before the celebration of the Passover at Sinai in the first month of the second year (cp. Num. ix. 1-5, and Ex. xii. 48). The statements of the verses are, however, sufficiently close to the facts for the purpose in hand; namely, to render a reason for the general circumcising which is here recorded.

The reason why circumcision was omitted in the wilderness, was that the sentence of Num. xiv. 28 seq. placed the whole nation for the time under a ban; and that the discontinuance of circumcision, and the consequent omission of the Passover, was a consequence and a token of that ban. The rejection was not, indeed, total, for the children of the murmurers were to enter into the rest; nor final, for when the children had borne the punishment of the fathers' sins for the appointed years, and the murmurers were dead, then it was to be removed, as now by Joshua. But for the time the Covenant was abrogated, though God's purpose to restore it was from the first made known, and confirmed by the visible marks of His favour which He still vouchsafed to bestow during the wandering.

The years of rejection were indeed exhausted before the death of Moses (cp. Deut. ii. 14): but God would not call upon the people to renew their engagement to Him until He had first given them glorious proof of His will and power to fulfil His engagements to them. So He gave them the first fruits of the promised inheritance—the kingdoms of Sihon and Og; and through a miracle planted their feet on the very soil that still remained to be conquered; and then recalled them to His Covenant. It is to be noted, too, that they were just about to go to war against foes mightier than themselves. Their only hope of success lay in the help of God. At such a crisis the need of full communion with God would be felt indeed; and the blessing and strength of it are accordingly granted.

The revival of the two great ordinances —circumcision and the Passover—after so long an intermission could not but awaken the zeal and invigorate the faith and fortitude of the people. Both as seals and as means of grace and God's good purpose towards them then, the general circumcision of the people, followed up by the solemn celebration of the Passover—the one formally restoring the Covenant and reconciling them nationally to God, the other ratifying and confirming all that circumcision intended—were at this juncture most opportune.

8. The circumcision must have taken place on the day after the passage of Jordan, *i.e.* the 11th Nisan, and the Passover was kept on the 14th of the same month. For so long at least, they who had been circumcised would be disabled from war (cp. marg. ref.), though they would not neces-

9 abode in their places in the camp, [k] till they were whole. And
the LORD said unto Joshua, This day have I rolled away [l] the
reproach of Egypt from off you. Wherefore the name of the
10 place is called [1] [m] Gilgal unto this day. ¶ And the children of
Israel encamped in Gilgal, and kept the passover [n] on the four-
11 teenth day of the month at even in the plains of Jericho. And they
did eat of the old corn of the land on the morrow after the passover, unleavened cakes, and parched *corn* in the selfsame day.
12 And [o] the manna ceased on the morrow after they had eaten of
the old corn of the land; neither had the children of Israel
manna any more; but they did eat of the fruit of the land of
13 Canaan that year. ¶ And it came to pass, when Joshua was by
Jericho, that he lifted up his eyes and looked, and, behold, there
stood [p] a man over against him [q] with his sword drawn in his
hand: and Joshua went unto him, and said unto him, *Art* thou
14 for us, or for our adversaries? And he said, Nay; but *as*
[2] captain of the host of the LORD am I now come. And Joshua
[r] fell on his face to the earth, and did worship, and said unto him,
15 What saith my lord unto his servant? And the captain of the
LORD's host said unto Joshua, [s] Loose thy shoe from off thy
foot; for the place whereon thou standest *is* holy. And Joshua
CHAP. 6. did so. (NOW Jericho [3] was straitly shut up because of
2 the children of Israel: none went out, and none came in.) And

[k] See Gen. 34. 25. [l] Gen. 34. 14. Ezek. 20. 7. & 23. 3, 8. [m] ch. 4. 19. [n] Ex. 12. 6. Num. 9. 5. [o] Ex. 16. 35. [p] Gen. 18. 2. & 32. 24. Ex. 23. 23. Zech. 1. 8. Acts. 1. 10. [q] Num. 22. 23. [r] Gen. 17. 3. [s] Ex. 3. 5. Acts 7. 33.

[1] That is, *Rolling*.
[2] Or, *prince*. See Exod. 23. 20. Dan. 10. 13, 21. & 12. 1. Rev. 12. 7. & 19. 11, 14.
[3] Heb. *did shut up, and was shut up*.

sarily be debarred from keeping the feast. The submission of the people to the rite was a proof of faith, even though we remember that the panic of the Canaanites (*v.* 1) would render any immediate attack from them unlikely, and that there must have been a large number of "men of war" who would not need to be circumcised at all (see note on *v.* 4).

9. *the reproach of Egypt*] *i.e.* "reproach proceeding from Egypt." The expression probably refers to taunts actually uttered by the Egyptians against Israel, because of their long wanderings in the desert and failures to acquire a settlement in Canaan (cp. Ex. xxxii. 12; Num. xiv. 13-16; Deut. ix. 28 and xxxii. 27). These reproaches were now to end; for they had actually entered Canaan, and the restoration of the Covenant was a pledge from God to accomplish what was begun for them.

11. *old corn of the land*] Rather "**produce of the land,**" the new corn just coming in at the time of the Passover. (So in *v.* 12.)

on the morrow after the passover] These words denote in Num. xxxiii. 3 the 15th Nisan, but must here apparently mean the 16th. For the Israelites could not lawfully eat of the new corn until the first fruits of it had been presented, and this was done on "the morrow after the Sabbath," *i.e.* the morrow after the first day of unleavened bread, which was to be observed as a Sabbath, and is therefore so called. (Cp. Lev. xxiii. 7, 11, 14.)

The term Passover, which is sometimes used for the lamb slain on the evening of the 14th Nisan, sometimes for the paschal meal, sometimes for the whole eight days' festival, here means the first great day of the eight, the Sabbath of the first holy convocation.

13. *a man*] See notes on Gen. xii. 7; xviii. 2. The appearance was that of God manifested in the Person of His Word. Hence the command of *v.* 15. That the appearance was not in a vision merely is clear from the fact that Joshua "went unto Him" and addressed Him.

14. *captain of the host of the* LORD] *i.e.* of the angelic host, the host of heaven (cp. 1 K. xxii. 19; 1 Sam. i. 3, &c.). The armed people of Israel are never called "the host of the Lord," though once spoken of in Ex. xii. 41 as "all the hosts of the Lord." The Divine Person intimates that He, the Prince (see marg. reff.) of the Angels had come to lead Israel in the coming strife, and to overthrow by heavenly might the armies and the strongholds of God's and Israel's enemies. Accordingly, the capture of Jericho and the destruction of the Canaanites generally form a fit type of a grander and more complete conquest and excision of the powers of evil which yet waits accomplishment. (Cp. with this verse Matt. xxv. 31; 2 Thess. i. 7, 8.)

VI. **1.** This verse is strictly parenthetical. It is inserted to explain the declaration commenced v. 14, and interrupted by Joshua's question and obeisance v.14, 15, but resumed in *v.* 2.

straitly shut up] See marg., *i.e.*, not only shut, but barred and bolted.

the LORD said unto Joshua, See, [a]I have given into thine hand
Jericho, and the [b]king thereof, *and* the mighty men of valour.
3 And ye shall compass the city, all *ye* men of war, *and* go round
4 about the city once. Thus shalt thou do six days. And seven
priests shall bear before the ark seven [c]trumpets of rams' horns:
and the seventh day ye shall compass the city seven times, and
5 [d]the priests shall blow with the trumpets. And it shall come to
pass, that when they make a long *blast* with the ram's horn, *and*
when ye hear the sound of the trumpet, all the people shall
shout with a great shout; and the wall of the city shall fall
down [1]flat, and the people shall ascend up every man straight
6 before him. ¶And Joshua the son of Nun called the priests,
and said unto them, Take up the ark of the covenant, and let
seven priests bear seven trumpets of rams' horns before the ark
7 of the LORD. And he said unto the people, Pass on, and
compass the city, and let him that is armed pass on before the
8 ark of the LORD. ¶And it came to pass, when Joshua had

[a] ch. 2. 9, 24. & 8. 1.
[b] Deut. 7. 24.
[c] See Judg. 7. 16, 22.
[d] Num. 10. 8.

[1] Heb. *under it.*

3–6. The command of the Lord as to the mode in which the fall of Jericho should be brought about is given in these verses in a condensed form. Further details (see *vv.* 8–10, 16, 17, &c.), were, no doubt, amongst the commands given to Joshua by the Angel.

4. *trumpets of rams' horns*] Render rather here and in verses 5, 6, 8, &c., "**trumpets of jubilee**" (cp. Lev. xxv. 10 note). The instrument is more correctly rendered "cornet" (see Lev. xxv. 9, note).

Various attempts have been made to explain the fall of Jericho by natural causes, as, *e.g.*, by the undermining of the walls, or by an earthquake, or by a sudden assault. But the narrative of this chapter does not afford the slightest warrant for any such explanations; indeed it is totally inconsistent with them. It must be taken as it stands; and so taken it intends, beyond all doubt, to narrate a miracle, or rather a series of miracles.

In the belief that a record is not necessarily unhistorical because it is miraculous, never perhaps was a miracle more needed than that which gave Jericho to Joshua. Its lofty walls and well-fenced gates made it simply impregnable to the Israelites—a nomad people, reared in the desert, destitute alike of the engines of war for assaulting a fortified town, and of skill and experience in the use of them if they had had them. Nothing but a direct interference of the Almighty could in a week's time give a city like Jericho, thoroughly on its guard and prepared (cp. ii. 9 seq. and vi. 1), to besiegers situated as were Joshua and the Israelites.

The fall of Jericho cogently taught the inhabitants of Canaan that the successes of Israel were not mere human triumphs of man against man, and that the God of Israel was not as "the gods of the countries." This lesson some of them at least learnt to their salvation, *e.g.*, Rahab and the Gibeonites. Further, ensuing close upon the miraculous passage of Jordan, it was impressed on the people, prone ever to be led by the senses, that the same God Who had delivered their fathers out of Egypt and led them through the Red Sea, was with Joshua no less effectually than He had been with Moses.

And the details of the orders given by God to Joshua (*vv.* 3–5) illustrate this last point further. The trumpets employed were not the silver trumpets used for signalling the marshalling of the host and for other warlike purposes (cp. Num. x. 2), but the curved horns employed for ushering in the Jubilee and the Sabbatical Year (LXX., σάλπιγγες ἱεραί: cp. Lev. xxiii. 24 note). The trumpets were borne by priests, and were seven in number; the processions round Jericho were to be made on seven days, and seven times on the seventh day, thus laying a stress on the sacred number seven, which was an emblem more especially of the work of God. The Ark of God also, the seat of His special Presence, was carried round the city. All these particulars were calculated to set forth symbolically, and in a mode sure to arrest the attention of the people, the fact that their triumph was wholly due to the might of the Lord, and to that Covenant which made their cause His.

7. *he said*] The reading in the Hebrew text is "they said." Joshua no doubt issued his orders through the "officers of the people" (cp. i. 10).

him that is armed] *i.e.* the warriors generally, not a division only. "The rereward" (*v.* 9) was merely a detachment, and not a substantial portion of the host; and was told off, perhaps, from the tribe of Dan (cp. marg. ref.) to close the procession and guard the ark from behind. Thus the order would be, (1) the warriors, (2) the seven priests blowing the cornets, (3) the ark, (4) the rear-guard.

spoken unto the people, that the seven priests bearing the seven
trumpets of rams' horns passed on before the LORD, and blew
with the trumpets: and the ark of the covenant of the LORD
9 followed them. And the armed men went before the priests
that blew with the trumpets, [e]and the [1]rereward came after the
10 ark, *the priests* going on, and blowing with the trumpets. And
Joshua had commanded the people, saying, Ye shall not shout,
nor [2]make any noise with your voice, neither shall *any* word
proceed out of your mouth, until the day I bid you shout; then
11 shall ye shout. So the ark of the LORD compassed the city,
going about *it* once: and they came into the camp, and lodged
12 in the camp. ¶And Joshua rose early in the morning, [f]and the
13 priests took up the ark of the LORD. And seven priests bearing
seven trumpets of rams' horns before the ark of the LORD went
on continually, and blew with the trumpets: and the armed
men went before them; but the rereward came after the ark of
the LORD, *the priests* going on, and blowing with the trumpets.
14 And the second day they compassed the city once, and returned
15 into the camp: so they did six days. And it came to pass on
the seventh day, that they rose early about the dawning of the
day, and compassed the city after the same manner seven times:
16 only on that day they compassed the city seven times. And it
came to pass at the seventh time, when the priests blew with the
trumpets, Joshua said unto the people, Shout; for the LORD
17 hath given you the city. And the city shall be [3]accursed, *even*
it, and all that *are* therein, to the LORD: only Rahab the harlot
shall live, she and all that *are* with her in the house, because
18 [g]she hid the messengers that we sent. And ye, [h]in any wise
keep *yourselves* from the accursed thing, lest ye make *yourselves*
accursed, when ye take of the accursed thing, and make the
19 camp of Israel a curse, [i]and trouble it. But all the silver, and
gold, and vessels of brass and iron, *are* [4]consecrated unto the
20 LORD: they shall come into the treasury of the LORD. ¶So
the people shouted when *the priests* blew with the trumpets: and
it came to pass, when the people heard the sound of the trumpet,
and the people shouted with a great shout, that [k]the wall fell
down [5]flat, so that the people went up into the city, every man
21 straight before him, and they took the city. And they [l]utterly
destroyed all that *was* in the city, both man and woman, young
and old, and ox, and sheep, and ass, with the edge of the sword.
22 ¶But Joshua had said unto the two men that had spied out the
country, Go into the harlot's house, and bring out thence the

[e] Num. 10. 25.
[f] Deut. 31. 25.
[g] ch. 2. 4.
[h] Deut. 7. 26. & 13. 17. ch. 7. 1, 11, 12.
[i] ch. 7, 25. 1 Kin. 18. 17. 18. Jonah 1. 12.
[k] ver 5. Heb. 11. 30.
[l] Deut. 7. 2.

[1] Heb. *gathering* host.
[2] Heb. *make your voice to be heard.*
[3] Or, *devoted,* Mic. 4. 13.
[4] Heb. *holiness.*
[5] Heb. *under it.*

---

15. *on the seventh day*] Most probably a Sabbath day. The rising early would be necessary to give time for encompassing the city seven times. Jericho appears to have been a city of considerable size and population; and each passage of the large host round it could hardly have taken less than an hour and a half. Thus, with the necessary intervals of rest, the evening would be at hand when Joshua gave the signal to shout (*v.* 16); and the work of slaughter was probably commenced just as the hours of the Sabbath were passed.

17. *accursed*] Better as in marg., "devoted" (Lev. xxvii. 28 note). In other cases the inhabitants only of the towns were slain; their cattle and property became the booty of the victors. But Jericho, as the first Canaanitish city that was captured, was devoted by Israel as first-fruits to God, as a token that Israel received all the land from Him. Every living thing was put to death (Rahab and her household excepted) as a sacrifice to God, and the indestructible goods were (*v.* 19) brought into the treasury of the Sanctuary.

23 woman, and all that she hath, [m]as ye sware unto her. And the
young men that were spies went in, and brought out Rahab,
[n]and her father, and her mother, and her brethren, and all that
she had; and they brought out all her [1]kindred, and left them
24 without the camp of Israel. And they burnt the city with fire,
and all that *was* therein: [o]only the silver, and the gold, and the
vessels of brass and of iron, they put into the treasury of the
25 house of the LORD. And Joshua saved Rahab the harlot alive,
and her father's household, and all that she had; and [p]she
dwelleth in Israel *even* unto this day; because she hid the
26 messengers, which Joshua sent to spy out Jericho. ¶And
Joshua adjured *them* at that time, saying, [q]Cursed *be* the man
before the LORD, that riseth up and buildeth this city Jericho:
he shall lay the foundation thereof in his firstborn, and in his
27 youngest *son* shall he set up the gates of it. ¶ [r]So the LORD
was with Joshua; and [s]his fame was *noised* throughout all the
country.

[m] ch. 2. 14. Heb. 11. 31.
[n] ch. 2. 13.
[o] ver. 19.
[p] See Matt. 1. 5.
[q] 1 Kin. 16. 34.
[r] ch. 1. 5.
[s] ch. 9. 1, 3.

CHAP. 7. BUT the children of Israel committed a trespass in the
accursed thing: for [a][2]Achan, the son of Carmi, the son of
[3]Zabdi, the son of Zerah, of the tribe of Judah, took of the
accursed thing: and the anger of the LORD was kindled against

[a] ch. 22. 20.

[1] Heb. *families*. [2] 1 Chr. 2. 7, *Achar*. [3] Or, *Zimri*, 1 Chr. 2. 6.

---

23. The part of the wall adjoining Rahab's house had not fallen along with the rest. Rahab and "all that she had," *i.e.*, the persons belonging to her household, were brought out and "left without the camp of Israel." These words—literally "made to rest outside the camp of Israel"—indicate that being still in their heathenism, they were separated from the camp of the Lord. This was only for a time. They desired, and eventually obtained, admission to the Covenant of the chosen people of God (*v.* 25).

25. *even unto this day*] These words are rightly noted as implying that the narrative was written not long after the occurrences which it records.

26. *adjured*] *i.e.* put an oath upon them; or, perhaps, actually caused them themselves to take an oath (cp. Matt. xxvi. 63). The words of the oath have in the original a rhythmical character which would tend to keep them on the lips and in the memory of the people.

buildeth this city] *i.e.* rebuilds the fortifications. Jericho was at once occupied by the Benjamites (xviii. 21), and the natural advantages of the situation were such that it would not be likely to be left long desolate. Joshua speaks in the text as a warrior. He lays a ban on the re-erection of those lofty walls which had bidden defiance to God's host, and been by God's signal interposition overthrown. Hiel, the Bethelite, reckless of the prophecy recorded in our text, began and completed the circumvallation of the city a second time (see marg. ref.). Hiel did not found a new city but only fortified an existing one.

he shall lay the foundation thereof in his first-born] *i.e.* when he begins this work his eldest son shall die, when he completes it his youngest shall die (see 1 K. xvi. 34 note).

This chapter read in the light of the New Testament has indications of a further import and bearing than such as concerned Joshua and the Jews. As Joshua, the leader and captain of the Jewish theocracy, is a type of Christ, so is Jericho to be taken (with all Christian expositors) as a type of the powers opposed to Christ and His cause. The times which prepare for the close of God's present dispensation are signified in the days during which the people obeyed and waited; as the number of those days, seven, the number of perfection, represents that "fullness of time," known only to God, at which His dispensation will culminate and close. Thus the circumstances which lead up to the fall of Jericho are an acted prophecy, as was that fall itself, which sets forth the overthrow of all that resists the kingdom of which Christ is the head; and particularly the day of judgment, in which that overthrow will be fully and finally accomplished. St. Paul, in describing that day, seems to borrow his imagery from this chapter (see 1 Thess. iv. 16).

VII. **1.** *committed a trespass*] (cp. Lev. v. 15 note), "acted treacherously and committed a breach of faith." This suitably describes the sin of Achan, who had purloined and hidden away that which had been dedicated to God by the ban (vi. 19).

The "trespass" was the act of one man, yet is imputed to all Israel, who also share in the penalty of it (*v.* 5). This is not to be explained as though all the people

2 the children of Israel. ¶ And Joshua sent men from Jericho to
Ai, which *is* beside Beth-aven, on the east side of Beth-el, and
spake unto them, saying, Go up and view the country. And
3 the men went up and viewed Ai. And they returned to Joshua,
and said unto him, Let not all the people go up; but let [1]about
two or three thousand men go up and smite Ai; *and* make not
4 all the people to labour thither; for they *are but* few. So there
went up thither of the people about three thousand men: [b]and
5 they fled before the men of Ai. And the men of Ai smote of
them about thirty and six men: for they chased them *from*
before the gate *even* unto Shebarim, and smote them [2]in the
going down: wherefore [c]the hearts of the people melted, and
6 became as water. ¶ And Joshua [d]rent his clothes, and fell to
the earth upon his face before the ark of the LORD until the
eventide, he and the elders of Israel, and [e]put dust upon their
7 heads. And Joshua said, Alas, O Lord GOD, [f]wherefore hast
thou at all brought this people over Jordan, to deliver us into
the hand of the Amorites, to destroy us? would to God we had
8 been content, and dwelt on the other side Jordan! O Lord,
what shall I say, when Israel turneth their [3]backs before their
9 enemies! For the Canaanites and all the inhabitants of the
land shall hear *of it*, and shall environ us round, and [g]cut off
our name from the earth: and [h]what wilt thou do unto thy
10 great name? ¶ And the LORD said unto Joshua, Get thee up;
11 wherefore [4]liest thou thus upon thy face? [i]Israel hath sinned,
and they have also transgressed my covenant which I commanded them: [k]for they have even taken of the accursed thing,
and have also stolen, and [l]dissembled also, and they have put *it*

[b] Lev. 26. 17. Deut. 28. 25.
[c] ch. 2. 9, 11. Lev. 26. 36. Ps. 22. 14.
[d] Gen. 37. 29, 34.
[e] 2 Sam. 1. 2. & 13. 19. Neh. 9. 1. Job 2. 12.
[f] Ex. 5. 22. 2 Kin. 3. 10.
[g] Ps. 83. 4.
[h] See Ex. 32. 12. Num. 14. 13.
[i] ver. 1.
[k] ch. 6. 17.
[l] See Acts 5. 1, 2.

[1] Heb. *about* 2000 *men, or about* 3000 *men.*
[2] Or, *in Morad.*
[3] Heb. *necks.*
[4] Heb. *fallest.*

participated in the covetousness which led to Achan's sin (*v.* 21). The nation as a nation was in Covenant with God, and is treated by Him not merely as a number of individuals living together for their own purposes under common institutions, but as a Divinely constituted organic whole. Hence the sin of Achan defiled the other members of the community as well as himself, and robbed the people collectively of holiness before God and acceptableness with Him. Israel had in the person of Achan broken the Covenant (*v.* 11); God therefore would no more drive out the Canaanites before them.

the accursed thing] Rather "in that which had been devoted or dedicated." Achan in diverting any of these devoted things to his own purposes, committed the sin of sacrilege, that of Ananias and Sapphira. (Acts v. 2, 3.)

Achan or *Achar*] (marg. ref.) the *n* and *r* being interchanged, perhaps for the sake of accommodating the name to the noun *achar*, "trouble" (*v.* 25). *Zabdi* is generally identified with the *Zimri* of 1 Chr. ii. 6. *Zerah* was twin brother of Pharez and son of Judah (Gen. xxxviii. 30). In this genealogy, as in others, several generations are omitted, most likely those which intervened between Zerah and Zabdi, and which covered the space between the migration of Jacob's household to Egypt and the Exodus. (Num. xxvi. 5, see note).

2. *Ai, Bethel*] See Gen. xii. 8 note. [Modern travellers place the former at Khan Haiy, in the neighbourhood of Deir Diwan.]

3. The total population of Ai was about twelve thousand (viii. 25). It could therefore hardly muster three thousand warriors.

5. *Shebarim*] Rather, perhaps, "the stone quarries." The smallness of the slaughter amongst the Israelites indicates that they fled early, probably without real conflict in battle.

6. On these signs of mourning, cp. marg. reff. and Lev. x. 6; Num. xx. 6; 1 Sam. iv. 12.

9. *what wilt thou do unto thy great name?*] *i.e.* "after the Canaanites have cut off our name what will become of Thy Name?" This bold expostulation, that of one wrestling in sore need with God in prayer, like the similar appeals of Moses in earlier emergencies (cp. marg. reff.), is based upon God's past promises and mercies. What would be said of God by the heathen if now He permitted Israel to be destroyed?

10. God's answer is given directly, and in terms of reproof. Joshua must not lie helpless before God; the cause of the calamity was to be discovered.

11. *also stolen, and dissembled also*] The anger of God and the heinousness of Israel's

12 even among their own stuff. [m]Therefore the children of Israel
could not stand before their enemies, *but* turned *their* backs
before their enemies, because [n]they were accursed: neither will
I be with you any more, except ye destroy the accursed from
13 among you. Up, [o]sanctify the people, and say, [p]Sanctify yourselves against to morrow: for thus saith the LORD God of
Israel, *There is* an accursed thing in the midst of thee, O Israel:
thou canst not stand before thine enemies, until ye take away
14 the accursed thing from among you. In the morning therefore
ye shall be brought according to your tribes: and it shall be, *that*
the tribe which [q]the LORD taketh shall come according to the
families *thereof;* and the family which the LORD shall take shall
come by households; and the household which the LORD shall
15 take shall come man by man. [r]And it shall be, *that* he that is
taken with the accursed thing shall be burnt with fire, he and
all that he hath: because he hath [s]transgressed the covenant of
16 the LORD, and because he [t]hath wrought [1]folly in Israel. ¶ So
Joshua rose up early in the morning, and brought Israel by
17 their tribes; and the tribe of Judah was taken: and he brought
the family of Judah; and he took the family of the Zarhites:
18 and he brought the family of the Zarhites man by man; and
Zabdi was taken: and he brought his household man by man;
and Achan, the son of Carmi, the son of Zabdi, the son of Zerah,
19 of the tribe of Judah, [u]was taken. And Joshua said unto
Achan, My son, [x]give, I pray thee, glory to the LORD God of
Israel, [y]and make confession unto him; and [z]tell me now what
20 thou hast done; hide *it* not from me. And Achan answered
Joshua, and said, Indeed I have sinned against the LORD God
21 of Israel, and thus and thus have I done: when I saw among
the spoils a goodly Babylonish garment, and two hundred

[m] See Num. 14. 45. Judg. 2. 14.
[n] Deut. 7. 26.
[o] Ex. 19. 10.
[p] ch. 3. 5.
[q] Prov. 16. 33.
[r] See 1 Sam. 14. 38, 39.
[s] ver. 11.
[t] Gen. 34. 7. Judg. 20. 6.
[u] 1 Sam. 14. 42.
[x] See 1 Sam. 6. 5. Jer. 13. 16. John 9. 24.
[y] Num. 5. 6, 7. 2 Chr. 30. 22. Ps. 51. 3. Dan. 9. 4.
[z] 1 Sam. 14. 43.

[1] Or, *wickedness.*

sin are marked by the accumulation of clause upon clause. As a climax they had even appropriated to their own use the consecrated property purloined from God.

12. *accursed*] Cp. vi. 17, 18.

14. *the* LORD *taketh*] *i.e.* by lot. The Hebrew word for lot suggests that small stones, probably white and black ones, were used. These were probably drawn from a chest (cp. the expressions in xviii. 11, and xix. 1). The lot was regarded as directed in its result by God (marg. ref.); and hence was used on many important occasions by the Jews and by other nations in ancient times. *E.g.* (1.), for apportionment, as of Canaan among the Twelve Tribes (Num. xxvi. 55); of the Levitical cities (Josh. xxi. 4 seq.); of spoil or captives taken in war (Joel iii. 3). (2.) For detection of the guilty, as in the case of Achan, Jonathan (1 Sam. xiv. 42), and Jonah (Jon. i. 7). (3.) For determining the persons to undertake a dangerous or warlike enterprise (Judg. xx. 10). (4.) For making appointment to important functions (Lev. xvi. 8 seq.; Acts i. 26); or for sharing the duties or privileges of an office amongst those concerned (1 Chr. xxiv. 31; Luke i. 9). The casting of lots before Haman (Esth. iii. 7) seems to have been with a view of determining the lucky day for his undertaking against the Jews. One passage (Prov. xviii. 18) perhaps points also to the employment of the lot to decide litigation.

15. *burnt with fire*] *i.e.* after he had been put to death by stoning (*v.* 25; Lev. xx. 14).

19. *give glory to the* LORD] A form of solemn adjuration by which the person addressed was called upon before God to declare the truth. The phrase assumes that the glory of God is always promoted by manifestation of the truth (cp. marg. reff.).

21. *a goodly Babylonish garment*] Literally "a robe or cloak of Shinar," the plain in which Babylon was situated (Gen. x. 10). It was a long robe such as was worn by kings on state occasions (Jonah iii. 6), and by prophets (1 K. xix. 13; Zech. xiii. 4). The Assyrians were in early times famous for the manufacture of beautiful dyed and richly embroidered robes (cp. Ezek. xxiii. 15). That such a robe should be found in a Canaanitish city is natural enough. The productions of the far East found their way through Palestine both southward towards Egypt and westward through Tyre to the countries bordering on the Mediterranean. (Cp. Ezek. xxvii. 24 and the context.)

shekels of silver, and a [1]wedge of gold of fifty shekels weight,
then I coveted them, and took them; and, behold, they *are* hid
in the earth in the midst of my tent, and the silver under it.
22 So Joshua sent messengers, and they ran unto the tent; and,
23 behold, *it was* hid in his tent, and the silver under it. And they
took them out of the midst of the tent, and brought them unto
Joshua, and unto all the children of Israel, and [2]laid them out
24 before the LORD. And Joshua, and all Israel with him, took
Achan the son of Zerah, and the silver, and the garment, and
the wedge of gold, and his sons, and his daughters, and his oxen,
and his asses, and his sheep, and his tent, and all that he had:
25 and they brought them unto [a]the valley of Achor. And Joshua
said, [b]Why hast thou troubled us? the LORD shall trouble thee
this day. [c]And all Israel stoned him with stones, and burned
26 them with fire, after they had stoned them with stones. And
they [d]raised over him a great heap of stones unto this day. So
[e]the LORD turned from the fierceness of his anger. Wherefore
the name of that place was called, [f]The valley of [3]Achor, unto
this day.

CHAP. 8. AND the LORD said unto Joshua, [a]Fear not, neither be
thou dismayed: take all the people of war with thee, and arise,
go up to Ai: see, [b]I have given into thy hand the king of Ai,
2 and his people, and his city, and his land: and thou shalt do to
Ai and her king as thou didst unto [c]Jericho and her king: only
[d]the spoil thereof, and the cattle thereof, shall ye take for a
prey unto yourselves: lay thee an ambush for the city behind it.
3 ¶ So Joshua arose, and all the people of war, to go up against
Ai: and Joshua chose out thirty thousand mighty men of
4 valour, and sent them away by night. And he commanded them,

[a] ver. 26. ch. 15. 7. [b] ch. 6. 18. 1 Chr. 2. 7. Gal. 5. 12. [c] Deut. 17. 5. [d] Lam. 3. 53. [e] Deut. 13. 17. 2 Sam. 21. 14. [f] ver. 24. Isai. 65. 10. Hos. 2. 15. [a] Deut. 1. 21. & 7. 18. & 31. 8. ch. 1. 9. [b] ch. 6. 2. [c] ch. 6. 21. [d] Deut. 20. 14.

[1] Heb. *tongue.* [2] Heb. *poured.* [3] That is, *Trouble.*

---

wedge of gold] i.e. some implement or ornament of gold shaped like a wedge or tongue. The name *lingula* was given by the Romans to a spoon and to an oblong dagger made in shape of a tongue. The weight of this "wedge" was fifty shekels, *i.e.* about twenty-five ounces (see Ex. xxxviii. 24 note). The silver was under the rest of the stolen property. The mantle would naturally be placed uppermost, and be used to cover up the others.

24. The sin had been national (*v.* 1 note), and accordingly the expiation of it was no less so. The whole nation, no doubt through its usual representatives, took part in executing the sentence. Achan had fallen by his own act under the ban (vi. 18), and consequently he and his were treated as were communities thus devoted (Deut. xiii. 15–17). It would appear too that Achan's family must have been accomplices in his sin; for the stolen spoil could hardly have been concealed in his tent without their being privy thereto.

26. *a great heap of stones*] As a memorial of Achan's sin and its punishment. (Cp. viii. 29; 2 Sam. xviii. 17.)

the valley of Achor] Cp. marg. reff. This valley formed part of the northern border of Judah (xv. 7); and must therefore have lain amongst the ridges which cross the plain to the south of Jericho. But its exact site is uncertain. [Conder identifies it with Wady Kelt.]

VIII. **1.** God rouses Joshua from his dejection (vii. 6), and bids him march against Ai with the main body. Though Ai was but a small city (cp. *v.* 25 and vii. 3), yet the discouragement of the people rendered it inexpedient to send a second time a mere detachment against it; and the people of Ai had, as appears from *v.* 17, help from Bethel, and possibly from other places also. It was fitting too that all the people should witness with their own eyes the happy consequences of having faithfully put away the sin which had separated them from God.

3. *thirty thousand men*] Comparing *vv.* 3 and 12 ("five thousand men"), there is probably a mistake in the numbers of this verse, where an early copyist may have written the sign for 30,000 instead of that for 5,000.

sent them away by night] The selected 5,000 would accordingly post themselves in the main ravine between Ai and Bethel in the night and early morning. The neighbourhood in which Ai was situated is described as "a wild entanglement of hill and

saying, Behold, [e]ye shall lie in wait against the city, *even* behind [e] Judg. 20.29.
5 the city: go not very far from the city, but be ye all ready: and
I, and all the people that *are* with me, will approach unto the
city: and it shall come to pass, when they come out against us,
6 as at the first, that [f]we will flee before them, (for they will come [f] Judg. 20.32.
out after us) till we have [1]drawn them from the city; for they
will say, They flee before us, as at the first: therefore we will flee
7 before them. Then ye shall rise up from the ambush, and seize
upon the city: for the LORD your God will deliver it into your
8 hand. And it shall be, when ye have taken the city, *that* ye shall
set the city on fire: according to the commandment of the LORD
9 shall ye do. [g]See, I have commanded you. Joshua therefore [g] 2 Sam. 13. 28.
sent them forth: and they went to lie in ambush, and abode
between Beth-el and Ai, on the west side of Ai: but Joshua
10 lodged that night among the people. ¶ And Joshua rose up
early in the morning, and numbered the people, and went up,
11 he and the elders of Israel, before the people to Ai. [h]And all [h] ver. 5.
the people, *even the people* of war that *were* with him, went up,
and drew nigh, and came before the city, and pitched on the
north side of Ai: now *there was* a valley between them and Ai.
12 And he took about five thousand men, and set them to lie in
ambush between Beth-el and Ai, on the west side [2]of the city.
13 And when they had set the people, *even* all the host that *was* on
the north of the city, and [3]their liers in wait on the west of
the city, Joshua went that night into the midst of the valley.
14 ¶ And it came to pass, when the king of Ai saw *it*, that they
hasted and rose up early, and the men of the city went out
against Israel to battle, he and all his people, at a time ap-
pointed, before the plain; but he [i]wist not that *there were* liers [i] Jugd. 20.34. Eccles. 9. 12.
15 in ambush against him behind the city. And Joshua and all
Israel [k]made as if they were beaten before them, and fled by the [k] Judg. 20. 36, &c.
16 way of the wilderness. And all the people that *were* in Ai were
called together to pursue after them: and they pursued after
17 Joshua, and were drawn away from the city. And there was
not a man left in Ai or Beth-el, that went not out after Israel:
18 and they left the city open, and pursued after Israel. And
the LORD said unto Joshua, Stretch out the spear that *is* in
thy hand toward Ai; for I will give it into thine hand. And

[1] Heb. *pulled*. [2] Or, *of Ai*. [3] Heb. *their lying in wait*, ver. 4.

---

valley;" and amidst its recesses the detachment could easily shelter itself from observation until Joshua's other measures were taken.

10. *numbered the people*] Rather, perhaps, "mustered" or "arrayed" them for their march. The distance from the camp at Gilgal to Ai is about fifteen miles. In the evening of the day after the despatch of the 5,000 liers in wait, Joshua and the host might make their appearance in the neighbourhood of the city.

12. *he took*] Rather "had taken;" the words refer to the ambuscade which Joshua had detached during the previous night.

13. Joshua went down by night into the valley where he would be seen at daylight by the men of Ai, and was accompanied no doubt by a picked body of troops. The king of Ai, in the morning, would see neither the ambush in his rear, nor the whole of the great host of Israel amongst the hills away to the north on his left; but supposing, as it appears, that the Israelites before him were a body detached as on the former occasion to assail his city, he sallied out promptly to attack them.

14. *at a time appointed*] Rather, "at the place appointed," *i.e.* some spot suitable for the drawing up of his men, which had been assigned beforehand. This was "before the plain," *i.e.* it was at the entrance of the depressed tract of land which runs down to the Jordan valley, up which lay the route of the Israelites from Gilgal to Ai.

17. *or Bethel*] See *v.* 1 note.

18. No doubt Joshua had ascended the heights, most likely those to the north of the valley, so as to separate himself from the flying Israelites on the lower ground,

Joshua stretched out the spear that *he had* in his hand toward
19 the city. And the ambush arose quickly out of their place, and
they ran as soon as he had stretched out his hand: and they
entered into the city, and took it, and hasted and set the city on
20 fire. And when the men of Ai looked behind them, they saw,
and, behold, the smoke of the city ascended up to heaven, and
they had no [1]power to flee this way or that way: and the people
21 that fled to the wilderness turned back upon the pursuers. And
when Joshua and all Israel saw that the ambush had taken the
city, and that the smoke of the city ascended, then they turned
22 again, and slew the men of Ai. And the other issued out of the
city against them; so they were in the midst of Israel, some on
this side, and some on that side: and they smote them, so that
[l] Deut. 7. 2. 23 they [l]let none of them remain or escape. And the king of Ai
24 they took alive, and brought him to Joshua. And it came to
pass, when Israel had made an end of slaying all the inhabitants
of Ai in the field, in the wilderness wherein they chased them,
and when they were all fallen on the edge of the sword, until
they were consumed, that all the Israelites returned unto Ai,
25 and smote it with the edge of the sword. And *so* it was, *that* all
that fell that day, both of men and women, *were* twelve thou-
26 sand, *even* all the men of Ai. For Joshua drew not his hand
back, wherewith he stretched out the spear, until he had utterly
[m] Num. 31. 22, 26. 27 destroyed all the inhabitants of Ai. [m]Only the cattle and the
spoil of that city Israel took for a prey unto themselves, accord-
[n] ver. 2. ing unto the word of the LORD which he [n]commanded Joshua.
[o] Deut. 13. 16. 28 And Joshua burnt Ai, and made it [o]an heap for ever, *even* a
[p] ch. 10. 26. 29 desolation unto this day. [p]And the king of Ai he hanged on a
Ps. 107. 40. & 110. 5. tree until eventide: [q]and as soon as the sun was down, Joshua
[q] ch. 10. 27. commanded that they should take his carcase down from the
tree, and cast it at the entering of the gate of the city, and
[r] ch. 7. 26. [r]raise thereon a great heap of stones, *that remaineth* unto this
& 10. 27. 30 day. ¶ Then Joshua built an altar unto the LORD God of Israel,
[s] Deut. 27. 4, 5. 31 [s]in mount Ebal, as Moses the servant of the LORD commanded

[1] Heb. *hand*.

and to be visible to the men in ambush behind the city. He now, at the command of God, gives the appointed signal to the ambush.

29. Cp. Deut. xxi. 22, 23 notes.

30-35. The account of this solemnity is very brief. An acquaintance with Deut. xxvii. is evidently pre-supposed; and the three several acts of which the solemnity consisted are only so far distinctly named as is necessary to show that the commands of Moses there given were fully carried out by Joshua.

It is difficult to escape the conviction that these verses are here out of their proper and original place. The connection between viii. 29, and ix. 1, is natural and obvious; and in ix. 3, the fraud of the Gibeonites is represented as growing out of the alarm caused by the fall of Jericho and Ai. It is, moreover, extremely unlikely that a solemnity of this nature in the very centre of the country should be undertaken by Joshua whilst the whole surrounding district was in the hands of the enemy; or that, if undertaken, it would have been carried out unmolested. "And the strangers that were conversant among them" (*v.* 35), were present at it. The distance from Gilgal in the Jordan valley to Mount Ebal is fully thirty miles, unless—as is unlikely—another Gilgal (Deut. xi. 29 note) be meant; and so vast a host, with its non-effective followers (*v.* 35), could certainly not have accomplished a march like this through a difficult country and a hostile population in less than three days. Moreover in ix. 6, x. 6, 15, 43, the Israelites are spoken of as still encamping at Gilgal.

It is on the whole likely that, for these and other reasons, this passage does not, in our present Bible, stand in its proper context; and it has been conjectured that the place from which these six verses have been transferred is the end of chapter xi. The "then" with which *v.* 30 opens in our present text may well have served to introduce the account of the solemnity on Gerizim and Ebal at the end of the record of Joshua's victories, to which indeed it forms a suitable climax.

the children of Israel, as it is written in the [t]book of the law
of Moses, an altar of whole stones, over which no man hath
lift up *any* iron: and [u]they offered thereon burnt offerings
32 unto the LORD, and sacrificed peace offerings. And [x]he wrote
there upon the stones a copy of the law of Moses, which he
33 wrote in the presence of the children of Israel. And all Israel,
and their elders, and officers, and their judges, stood on this
side the ark and on that side before the priests the Levites,
[y]which bare the ark of the covenant of the LORD, as well [z]the
stranger, as he that was born among them; half of them over
against mount Gerizim, and half of them over against mount
Ebal; [a]as Moses the servant of the LORD had commanded before,
34 that they should bless the people of Israel. And afterward
[b]he read all the words of the law, [c]the blessings and cursings,
35 according to all that is written in the book of the law. There
was not a word of all that Moses commanded, which Joshua
read not before all the congregation of Israel, [d]with the women,
and the little ones, and [e]the strangers that [1]were conversant
among them.

CHAP. 9. AND it came to pass, when all the kings which *were* on
this side Jordan, in the hills, and in the valleys, and in all the
coasts of [a]the great sea over against Lebanon, [b]the Hittite, and
the Amorite, the Canaanite, the Perizzite, the Hivite, and the
2 Jebusite, heard *thereof*; that they [c]gathered themselves together,
3 to fight with Joshua and with Israel, with one [2]accord. ¶ And
when the inhabitants of [d]Gibeon [e]heard what Joshua had done

[t] Ex. 20. 25. Deut. 27. 5, 6.
[u] Ex. 20. 24.
[x] Deut. 27. 2, 8.
[y] Deut. 31. 9, 29.
[z] Deut. 31. 12.
[a] Deut. 11. 29. & 27. 12.
[b] Neh. 8. 3.
[c] Deut. 28. 2, 15, 45. & 29. 20, 21. & 30. 19.
[d] Deut. 31. 12.
[e] ver. 33.

[a] Num. 34. 6.
[b] Ex. 3. 17. & 23. 23.
[c] Ps. 83. 3, 5.
[d] ch. 10. 2.
[e] ch. 6. 27.

[1] Heb. *walked*. [2] Heb. *mouth*.

---

32. See note marg. ref.

34. *all the words of the law*] See Deut. xxxi. 11 seq. It would seem that Joshua, on the present occasion, must have read at least all the legislative portion of the Pentateuch before the people (cp. on Deut. xxvii. 3). The terms of this verse cannot be satisfactorily explained as importing only the blessings and curses of Deut. xxvii. and xxviii.

IX. **1, 2.** The two verses serve as a general introduction to chapters ix., x., and xi. The Canaanites had recovered to some extent from their panic (*v.* 1), perhaps in consequence of the repulse of the Israelites before Ai. They resolved to make a league and to resist jointly the progress of the Israelites. The defection of Gibeon (*vv.* 3-27) determined the five kings of the Amorites, whose territories were nearest Gibeon, to take instant action against that city. Their forces were defeated by Joshua in the battle before Gibeon (x. 1 seq.). The other confederates subsequently gathered their armies together, xi. 1-5, and were defeated at the waters of Merom (xi. 6 seq.). The former of these two great battles gave Joshua possession of the southern half of Palestine west of Jordan; the latter of the northern half.

1. *in the hills*] See Num. xiii. 17 note.

the valleys] Or "the vale" (the Shephelah, Deut. i. 7), which imports the lowland country between the mountains and the sea coast.

3. Gibeon was the head of the four towns (*v.* 17) occupied by the Hivites (xi. 19). The inhabitants were Amorites (2 Sam. xxi. 2); the name Amorites being used as a general name for the Canaanitish population (Deut. i. 44 note). The Hivites seem to have had a non-monarchical form of government (cp. *vv.* 3, 11), but their city was (x. 2) in size and importance equal to those cities which the kings of the country made their capitals. Gibeon signifies "pertaining to a hill," *i.e.* built on a hill (cp. Gibeah and Geba, towns in the same neighbourhood), and describes the site, which is on two of the rounded hills peculiar to this district. It is still known as *El-Jib*, and lies about five miles north of Jerusalem by the most direct route. It stands at the head of the pass of Beth-horon, through which lies the main route from Jerusalem and the lower Jordan valley to Joppa and the sea coast. Thus from its position, no less than from the number and valour of its people (x. 2), it was one of the most important cities of southern Canaan. Gibeon fell within the lot of Benjamin (xviii. 25), and was one of the cities assigned to the priests (xxi. 17). In later times it was famous as the scene of various events (2 Sam. ii. 12-17; xx. 4-13; 1 Kings ii. 28, 29, cp. with 1 Chr. xvi. 39). It was for a long time the spot where the Tabernacle of Moses, together with the Brazen Altar of burnt offering (1 Chr. xxi. 29) and other portions of the sacred furni-

4 unto Jericho and to Ai, they did work wilily, and went and
made as if they had been ambassadors, and took old sacks upon
5 their asses, and wine bottles, old, and rent, and bound up; and
old shoes and clouted upon their feet, and old garments upon
them; and all the bread of their provision was dry *and* mouldy.
6 And they went to Joshua [f]unto the camp at Gilgal, and said
unto him, and to the men of Israel, We be come from a far
7 country: now therefore make ye a league with us. And the
men of Israel said unto the [g]Hivites, Peradventure ye dwell
8 among us; and [h]how shall we make a league with you? And
they said unto Joshua, [i]We *are* thy servants. And Joshua said
9 unto them, Who *are* ye? and from whence come ye? And they
said unto him, [k]From a very far country thy servants are come
because of the name of the LORD thy God: for we have [l]heard
10 the fame of him, and all that he did in Egypt, and [m]all that he
did to the two kings of the Amorites, that *were* beyond Jordan,
to Sihon king of Heshbon, and to Og king of Bashan, which
11 *was* at Ashtaroth. Wherefore our elders and all the inhabitants
of our country spake to us, saying, Take victuals [1]with you for
the journey, and go to meet them, and say unto them, We *are*
12 your servants: therefore now make ye a league with us. This
our bread we took hot *for* our provision out of our houses on
the day we came forth to go unto you; but now, behold, it is
13 dry, and it is mouldy: and these bottles of wine, which we
filled, *were* new; and, behold, they be rent: and these our garments and our shoes are become old by reason of the very long
14 journey. And [2]the men took of their victuals, [n]and asked not
15 *counsel* at the mouth of the LORD. And Joshua [o]made peace
with them, and made a league with them, to let them live: and
16 the princes of the congregation sware unto them. ¶ And it
came to pass at the end of three days after they had made a
league with them, that they heard that they *were* their neigh-
17 bours, and *that* they dwelt among them. And the children of
Israel journeyed, and came unto their cities on the third day.
Now their cities *were* [p]Gibeon, and Chephirah, and Beeroth, and

[f] ch. 5. 10.
[g] ch. 11. 19.
[h] Ex. 23. 32. Deut. 7. 2. & 20. 16. Judg. 2. 2.
[i] Deut. 20.11. 2 Kin. 10. 5.
[k] Deut. 20. 15.
[l] Ex. 15. 14. Josh. 2. 10.
[m] Num. 21. 24, 33.
[n] Num. 27. 21. Isai. 30. 1, 2. See Judg. 1. 1. 1 Sam. 22. 10. & 30. 8. 2 Sam. 2. 1.
[o] ch. 11. 19. 2 Sam. 21. 2.
[p] ch. 18. 25, 26, 28.

[1] Heb. *in your hand.* [2] Or, *they received the men by reason of their victuals.*

ture, were placed. It was the scene of the magnificent ceremonial with which Solomon inaugurated his reign (1 K. iii.), but no doubt lost much of its importance after the Tabernacle and its accompaniments were removed to the Temple of Solomon.

4. *they did work wilily*] Lit. "they also," or "they too, did work, &c." The "also" serves, apparently, to connect the stratagem of the Gibeonites with that employed by the Israelites before Ai. It hints that the Gibeonites resolved to meet craft with craft.

rent and bound up] *i.e.* the wine skins were torn and roughly repaired by tying up the edges of the rent. The more thorough and careful way, hardly feasible in a hasty journey, would have been to insert a patch.

6. *camp at Gilgal*] Whilst Joshua was engaged in more distant enterprises, the women, children, and property of the Israelites were left with a sufficient guard at this place, where they had been established immediately after crossing the Jordan (v. 9).

7. Cp. marg. reff.

14. The elders of Israel (*v.* 18), tasting what was offered them by the Gibeonites, pledged themselves according to the usage of Eastern nations to peace and friendship with them. They credited the story at once, instead of seeking the direction of God in the matter. The rendering of the margin is not to be preferred to that of the text.

at the mouth of the LORD] *i.e.* by the Urim and Thummim (Ex. xxviii. 30).

17. Chephirah (*Kefir*) is situated eight or nine miles west of Gibeon, and was an inhabited city in the days of Ezra and Nehemiah (Ezr. ii. 25; Neh. vii. 29).

Beeroth (*Bireh*), about eight miles north of Jerusalem. Kirjath-jearim, *i.e.* "city of woods," is identified by Robinson with the modern *Kuriet el Enab*, nine miles from Jerusalem on the road to Jaffa [and by

18 Kirjath-jearim. And the children of Israel smote them not,
[q] because the princes of the congregation had sworn unto them
by the LORD God of Israel. And all the congregation mur-
19 mured against the princes. But all the princes said unto all
the congregation, We have sworn unto them by the LORD God
20 of Israel: now therefore we may not touch them. This we will
do to them; we will even let them live, lest [r] wrath be upon us,
21 because of the oath which we sware unto them. And the princes
said unto them, Let them live; but let them be [s] hewers of wood
and drawers of water unto all the congregation; as the princes
22 had [t] promised them. ¶ And Joshua called for them, and he
spake unto them, saying, Wherefore have ye beguiled us, saying, [u] We *are* very far from you; when [x] ye dwell among us?
23 Now therefore ye *are* [y] cursed, and there shall [1] none of you be
freed from being bondmen, and [z] hewers of wood and drawers of
24 water for the house of my God. And they answered Joshua,
and said, Because it was certainly told thy servants, how that
the LORD thy God [a] commanded his servant Moses to give you
all the land, and to destroy all the inhabitants of the land from
before you, therefore [b] we were sore afraid of our lives because
25 of you, and have done this thing. And now, behold, we *are* [c] in
thine hand: as it seemeth good and right unto thee to do unto

[q] Ps. 15. 4. Eccles. 5. 2.
[r] See 2 Sam. 21. 1, 2, 6. Ezek. 17. 13, 15, 18, 19. Zech. 5. 3, 4. Mal. 3. 5.
[s] Deut. 29. 11.
[t] ver. 15.
[u] ver. 6, 9.
[x] ver. 16.
[y] Gen. 9. 25.
[z] ver. 21. 27.
[a] Ex. 23. 32. Deut. 7. 1, 2.
[b] Ex. 15. 14.
[c] Gen. 16. 6.

[1] Heb. *not to be cut off from you.*

Conder with *Sôba*]. The town was numbered amongst those belonging to Judah, and was in the northern boundary of that tribe. Beyond this city the six hundred Danites encamped on their famous expedition to Laish (Judg. xviii. 12). Kirjath-jearim was also, and probably before the Israelitish conquests exclusively, called Baalah and Kirjath-baal (xv. 9, 60), names which seem to point to its early sanctity as a special seat of Baal-worship. To this place also the ark was brought from Beth-shemesh after it was sent back by the Philistines, and here it remained for twenty years (1 Sam. vi. 20, 21, vii. 2). It was fetched thence by David and deposited in the house of Obed-edom (2 Sam. vi. 2). Hence the allusion, Ps. cxxxii. 6, where David is said to have found the ark "in the fields of the wood."

21. Render "**they shall be** hewers of wood and drawers of water:" menial duties belonging to the lowest classes only (cp. marg. ref.). The curse of Noah (Gen. ix. 25) on the children of Ham was thus fulfilled to the letter in the case of these Hivites.

22. Were the Israelites bound to respect an oath thus procured by fraud? Were they right in doing so? Bp. Sanderson ("Works," vol. iv. pp. 269, 300, Oxf. edit.), determines these questions in the affirmative; and rightly, since the oath, though unlawfully taken, was not an oath taken to do an unlawful thing, *i.e.* a thing in itself unlawful. It was the carelessness of the Israelites themselves which betrayed them into this league. It was therefore their duty when they found themselves entrapped into this unlawful covenant, to devise means by which they might respect both their own oath and God's purposes as intimated in His injunctions (Deut. vii. 2) against sparing the Canaanites. This was accomplished by granting their lives to the Gibeonites, but reducing them to a servile condition, which might be expected to disable them from influencing the Israelites to do wrong. It may be added, that had the Israelites broken their oath, taken solemnly in the Name of the Lord, they would have brought that Name into contempt amongst the heathen; and, whilst punishing perfidy in others, would have themselves, the Lord's people, incurred the reproach of perjury. The result showed that Joshua and the princes judged rightly in this matter. God gave to Israel a notable victory, crowned with special miracles, over the kings who were confederated against Gibeon, because of the treaty made with Israel (x. 4, 8, 13); and God punished as a national act of blood-guiltiness the slaughter of the Gibeonites by Saul, which was a distinct violation of the covenant here before us (cp. 2 Sam. xxi. 1). This sparing of the Gibeonites, as well as the previous sparing of Rahab and her household, must be borne in mind when the massacre of the Canaanites by Joshua and the Israelites is discussed.

24. It was mere fear which drove the Gibeonites to act as they did. They sought for union with God's people, not for its own sake, but to save their lives. Rahab's motives were higher (ii. 9 seq.). Hence she was adopted into Israel; the Gibeonites remained for ever bondsmen of Israel.

26 us, do. And so did he unto them, and delivered them out of
the hand of the children of Israel, that they slew them not.
[d] ver. 21, 23. 27 And Joshua [1]made them that day [d]hewers of wood and drawers
of water for the congregation, and for the altar of the LORD,
[e] Deut. 12. 5. even unto this day, [e]in the place which he should choose.
CHAP. 10. NOW it came to pass, when Adoni-zedec king of Jerusalem
had heard how Joshua had taken Ai, and had utterly destroyed
[a] ch. 6. 21. it; [a]as he had done to Jericho and her king, so he had done to
[b] ch. 8. 22, 26, 28. [b]Ai and her king; and [c]how the inhabitants of Gibeon had
2 made peace with Israel, and were among them; that they
[c] ch. 9. 15. [d] Ex. 15. 14, 15, 16. Deut. 11. 25. [d]feared greatly, because Gibeon *was* a great city, as one of the
[2]royal cities, and because it *was* greater than Ai, and all the
3 men thereof *were* mighty. Wherefore Adoni-zedec king of
Jerusalem sent unto Hoham king of Hebron, and unto Piram
king of Jarmuth, and unto Japhia king of Lachish, and unto
4 Debir king of Eglon, saying, Come up unto me, and help me,
[e] ver. 1. ch. 9. 15. that we may smite Gibeon: [e]for it hath made peace with Joshua
5 and with the children of Israel. Therefore the five kings of the
Amorites, the king of Jerusalem, the king of Hebron, the king
[f] ch. 9. 2. of Jarmuth, the king of Lachish, the king of Eglon, [f]gathered
themselves together, and went up, they and all their hosts, and
6 encamped before Gibeon, and made war against it. ¶ And the
[g] ch. 5. 10. & 9. 6. men of Gibeon sent unto Joshua [g]to the camp to Gilgal, saying,
Slack not thy hand from thy servants; come up to us quickly,
and save us, and help us: for all the kings of the Amorites that
7 dwell in the mountains are gathered together against us. So
[h] ch. 8. 1. Joshua ascended from Gilgal, he, and [h]all the people of war
8 with him, and all the mighty men of valour. And the LORD

[1] Heb. *gave*, or, *delivered to be*, 1 Chr. 9. 2. Ezra 8. 20.

[2] Heb. *cities of the kingdom.*

X. **1.** *Adoni-zedec*] *i.e* "Lord of righteousness" (cp. Melchizedek, "King of righteousness"); probably an official title of the Jebusite kings.

Jerusalem] *i.e.* "foundation of peace," cp. Gen. xiv. 18. The city belonged to the inheritance of Benjamin (xviii. 28), but was on the very edge of the territory of Judah (xv. 8). Hence it was the strong and warlike tribe of Judah which eventually captured the lower part of the city, most likely in the days of Joshua's later conquests (Judg. i. 8), and after the warlike strength of the Jebusites had been weakened by the defeat in the open field, recorded in this chapter. The upper town, more especially the fortified hill of Sion, remained in the hands of the Jebusites, who accordingly kept a footing in the place, along with the men of Judah and Benjamin, even after the conquest (xv. 63; Judg. i. 21); and would seem, indeed, to have so far, and no doubt gradually, regained possession of the whole, that Jerusalem was spoken of in the days of the Judges as a Jebusite city. David finally stormed "the stronghold of Zion," and called it "the City of David" (2 Sam. v. 6-9). It was, probably, only after this conquest and the adoption by David of the city as the religious and political metropolis of the whole nation, that the name Jerusalem came into use (2 Sam. v. 5) in substitution for Jebus.

3. For Hebron, see Gen. xiii. 18. Jarmuth, afterwards one of the cities of Judah (xv. 35), is probably identified with the modern *Yarmuk*. Lachish was also a city of Judah (xv. 39), and, like Jarmuth, occupied by Jews after the captivity (Neh. xi. 30). It was fortified by Rehoboam after the revolt of the Ten Tribes (2 Chr. xi. 9), and seems to have been regarded as one of the safest places of refuge (2 Kings xiv. 19). Through Lachish the idolatry of Israel was imported into Judah (Micah i. 13), and of this sin the capture of the city by Sennacherib was the punishment (2 Kings xviii. 14–17 and xix. 8). Lachish is by most authorities identified with *Um Lakis*, lying some twenty miles west of Eleutheropolis, on the road to Gaza [and by Conder with *El Hesy*].

Eglon is the modern *Ajlân*.

6. The language reflects the urgency of the crisis. Accordingly Joshua made a forced march, accompanied only by his soldiers (*v.* 7), and accomplished in a single night the distance from Gilgal to Gibeon (about fifteen miles in a direct line), which on a former occasion had been a three days' journey (ix. 17).

said unto Joshua, [i]Fear them not: for I have delivered them [i] ch. 11. 6.
into thine hand; [k]there shall not a man of them stand before Judg. 4. 14.
9 thee. Joshua therefore came unto them suddenly, *and* went up [k] ch. 1. 5.
10 from Gilgal all night. And the LORD [l]discomfited them before [l] Judg. 4. 15.
Israel, and slew them with a great slaughter at Gibeon, and
chased them along the way that goeth up [m]to Beth-horon, and
11 smote them to [n]Azekah, and unto Makkedah. And it came to [m] ch. 16. 3, 5.
pass, as they fled from before Israel, *and* were in the going down [n] ch. 15. 35.
to Beth-horon, [o]that the LORD cast down great stones from [o] Ps. 18. 13,
heaven upon them unto Azekah, and they died: *they were* more 14. & 77. 17.
which died with hailstones than *they* whom the children of Israel Isai. 30. 30. Rev. 16. 21.

---

10. *Beth-horon*] The two places of this name, the upper and the lower Beth-horon (marg. ref.), are identified with the villages *Beit-ur el Foka* (the upper) and *Beit-ur et Tahta* (the lower): *Beit-ur* being probably a corruption of Beth-horon. The name itself ("house of caves") points to the exceedingly rocky character of the district. Upper Beth-horon was between six and seven miles west of Gibeon; and "the way that goeth up to Beth-horon" must accordingly be the hilly road which leads from Gibeon to it. Between the two Beth-horons is a steep pass, "the going down to Beth-horon" (*v.* 11); and here the Amorites were crushed by the hailstones. The main road from Jerusalem and the Jordan valley to the sea-coast lay through the pass of Beth-horon; and, accordingly, both the Beth-horons were secured by Solomon with strong fortifications (2 Chr. viii. 5). It was in this pass that Judas Maccabæus routed the Syrians under Seron (1 Macc. iii. 13 seq.), and here also, according to Jewish traditions, the destruction of the host of Sennacherib took place (2 K. xix. 35).

Azekah, which has not been as yet certainly identified, was in the hill country, between the mountains around Gibeon and the plain (see marg. ref.). It was fortified by Rehoboam (2 Chr. xi. 9) and besieged by the Babylonians (Jer. xxxiv. 7) shortly before the Captivity. It was an inhabited city after the return from the exile (Neh. xi. 30).

Makkedah] The exact site of this town is uncertain. It was situated in the plain between the mountains and the line of sea-coast which the Philistines held (xv. 41), and no great way north-east of Libnah (xii. 15, 16). [Warren (Conder) identifies it with the modern *el Mughhâr*, a village on the south side of the valley of Torek.]

11. Cp. Ecclus. xlvi. 6. Frightful storms occasionally sweep over the hills of Judæa; but this was evidently a miraculous occurrence, like the hail which smote Egypt (Ex. ix. 24) and the tempest which fell on the Philistines at Ebenezer (1 Sam. vii. 10).

12-15. These four verses seem to be a fragment or extract taken from some other and independent source and inserted into the thread of the narrative after it had been completed, and inserted most probably by another hand than that of the author of the Book of Joshua.

It is probable that verse 12 and the first half of verse 13 alone belong to the Book of Jasher and are poetical, and that the rest of this passage is prose.

The writer of this fragment seems to have understood the words of the ancient song literally, and believed that an astronomical miracle really took place, by which the motion of the heavenly bodies was for some hours suspended. (Cp. also Ecclus. xlvi. 4.) So likewise believed the older Jewish authorities generally, the Christian Fathers, and many commentators ancient and modern.

It must be allowed, indeed, that some of the objections which have been urged against this view on scientific grounds are easily answered. The interference, if such there were, with the earth's motion was not an act of blind power *ab extra* and nothing more. The Agent here concerned is omnipotent and omniscient, and could, of course, as well arrest the regular consequences of such a suspension of nature's ordinary working as He could suspend that working itself. It is, however, obvious, that any such stupendous phenomenon would affect the chronological calculations of all races of men over the whole earth and do so in a similarly striking and very intelligible manner. Yet no record of any such perturbation is anywhere to be found, and no marked and unquestionable reference is made to such a miracle by any of the subsequent writers in the Old or New Testament. For reasons like these, many commentators have explained the miracle as merely optical.

The various explanations show how strongly the difficulties which arise out of the passage have been felt. Accordingly stress has been laid by recent commentators on the admitted fact that the words out of which the difficulty springs are an extract from a poetical book. They must consequently, it is argued, be taken in a popular and poetical, and not in a literal sense. Joshua feared lest the sun should set before the people had fully "avenged themselves of their enemies." In his anxiety he prayed to God, and God hearkened to him. This is boldly and strikingly expressed in the

12 slew with the sword. ¶Then spake Joshua to the LORD in the
day when the LORD delivered up the Amorites before the children
of Israel, and he said in the sight of Israel,

[p] Isai. 28. 21. Hab. 3. 11. [q] Judg. 12. 12. [r] 2 Sam. 1. 18.

[p]Sun, [1]stand thou still upon Gibeon;
And thou, Moon, in the valley of [q]Ajalon.

13 ¶And the sun stood still, and the moon stayed, until the people
had avenged themselves upon their enemies. [r]*Is* not this written
in the book of [2]Jasher? So the sun stood still in the midst of
14 heaven, and hasted not to go down about a whole day. And
there was [s]no day like that before it or after it, that the LORD
hearkened unto the voice of a man: for [t]the LORD fought for
15 Israel. [u]And Joshua returned, and all Israel with him, unto
16 the camp to Gilgal. ¶But these five kings fled, and hid them-
17 selves in a cave at Makkedah. And it was told Joshua, saying,
18 The five kings are found hid in a cave at Makkedah. And
Joshua said, Roll great stones upon the mouth of the cave, and
19 set men by it for to keep them: and stay ye not, *but* pursue
after your enemies, and [3]smite the hindmost of them; suffer
them not to enter into their cities: for the LORD your God hath
20 delivered them into your hand. And it came to pass, when
Joshua and the children of Israel had made an end of slaying
them with a very great slaughter, till they were consumed, that
21 the rest *which* remained of them entered into fenced cities. And
all the people returned to the camp to Joshua at Makkedah in

[s] See Isai. 38. 8. [t] Deut. 1. 30. ver. 42. & ch. 23. 3. [u] ver. 43.

[1] Heb. *be silent.* [2] Or, *The upright?* [3] Heb. *cut off the tail.*

words of the ancient book, which describes Joshua as praying that the day might be prolonged, or, in poetical diction, that the sun might be stayed, until the work was done. Similarly, Judg. v. 20 and Ps. xviii. 9–15 are passages which no one construes as describing actual occurrences: they set forth only internal, although most sincere and, in a spiritual sense, real and true convictions. This explanation is now adopted by theologians whose orthodoxy upon the plenary inspiration and authority of Holy Scripture is well known and undoubted.

12. *in the sight of Israel*] Literally, "before the eyes of Israel," *i.e.* in the sight or presence of Israel, so that the people were witnesses of his words. (Cp. Deut. xxxi. 7.)

Sun, stand thou still] Literally, as marg., "be silent" (cp. Lev. x. 3); or rather, perhaps, "tarry," as in 1 Sam. xiv. 9.

thou, moon] The words addressed to the moon as well as to the sun, indicate that both were visible as Joshua spoke. Below and before him, westward, was the valley of Ajalon; behind him, eastward, were the hills around Gibeon. Some hours had passed, since in the early dawn he had fallen upon the host of the enemy, and the expression "in the midst of heaven" (*v.* 13) seems to import that it was now drawing towards mid-day, though the moon was still faintly visible in the west. If the time had been near sunset, Joshua would have seen the sun, not, as he did, eastward of him, but westward, sinking in the sea.

the valley of Ajalon] *i.e.* "the valley of the gazelles." This is the modern *Merj Ibn Omeir*, described by Robinson, a broad and beautiful valley running in a westerly direction from the mountains towards the great western plain. The ancient name is still preserved in *Yalo*, a village situated on the hill which skirts the south side of the valley.

13. *Book of Jasher*] *i.e.* as marg., "of the upright" or "righteous," a poetical appellation of the Covenant-people (cp. "Jeshurun" in Deut. xxxii. 15, and note; and cp. Num. xxiii. 10 and 21; Ps. cxi. 1). This book was probably a collection of national odes celebrating the heroes of the theocracy and their achievements, and is referred to again (marg. ref.) as containing the dirge composed by David over Saul and Jonathan.

about a whole day] *i.e.* about twelve hours; the average space between sunrise and sunset.

15. Joshua's return (cp. *v.* 43) to Gilgal was not until after he had, by the storm and capture of the principal cities of south Canaan, completed the conquest of which the victory at Gibeon was only the beginning.

This verse is evidently the close of the extract from an older work, which connected the rescue of Gibeon immediately with the return to Gilgal, and omitted the encampment at Makkedah (*v.* 21), and also the details given in *vv.* 28–42.

16. The thread of the narrative, broken by the four intermediate verses, 12–15, is now resumed from *v.* 11.

21. Joshua himself remained at Makkedah with the guards set before the cave.

peace: [x] none moved his tongue against any of the children of [x] Ex. 11. 7.
22 Israel. ¶ Then said Joshua, Open the mouth of the cave, and
23 bring out those five kings unto me out of the cave. And they
did so, and brought forth those five kings unto him out of the
cave, the king of Jerusalem, the king of Hebron, the king of
24 Jarmuth, the king of Lachish, *and* the king of Eglon. And it
came to pass, when they brought out those kings unto Joshua,
that Joshua called for all the men of Israel, and said unto the
captains of the men of war which went with him, Come near,
[y] put your feet upon the necks of these kings. And they came [y] Ps. 107. 40.
25 near, and put their feet upon the necks of them. And Joshua & 110. 5.
said unto them, [z] Fear not, nor be dismayed, be strong and of & 149. 8, 9. Isai. 26. 5.
good courage: for [a] thus shall the LORD do to all your enemies Mal. 4. 3.
26 against whom ye fight. And afterward Joshua smote them, and [z] Deut. 31.
slew them, and hanged them on five trees: and they [b] were 6, 8.
27 hanging upon the trees until the evening. And it came to pass ch. 1. 9. [a] Deut. 3. 21.
at the time of the going down of the sun, *that* Joshua commanded, & 7. 19. [b] ch. 8. 29.
and they [c] took them down off the trees, and cast them into the [c] Deut. 21.
cave wherein they had been hid, and laid great stones in the 23.
28 cave's mouth, *which remain* until this very day. ¶ And that day ch. 8. 29.
Joshua took Makkedah, and smote it with the edge of the sword,
and the king thereof he utterly destroyed, them, and all the
souls that *were* therein; he let none remain: and he did to the
29 king of Makkedah [d] as he did unto the king of Jericho. ¶ Then [d] ch. 6. 21.
Joshua passed from Makkedah, and all Israel with him, unto
30 Libnah, and fought against Libnah: and the LORD delivered
it also, and the king thereof, into the hand of Israel; and he
smote it with the edge of the sword, and all the souls that *were*
therein; he let none remain in it; but did unto the king thereof
31 as he did unto the king of Jericho. ¶ And Joshua passed from
Libnah, and all Israel with him, unto Lachish, and encamped
32 against it, and fought against it: and the LORD delivered
Lachish into the hand of Israel, which took it on the second
day, and smote it with the edge of the sword, and all the souls
that *were* therein, according to all that he had done to Libnah.
33 Then Horam king of Gezer came up to help Lachish; and
Joshua smote him and his people, until he had left him none re-
34 maining. ¶ And from Lachish Joshua passed unto Eglon, and
all Israel with him; and they encamped against it, and fought
35 against it: and they took it on that day, and smote it with the
edge of the sword, and all the souls that *were* therein he utterly
destroyed that day, according to all that he had done to Lachish.
36 ¶ And Joshua went up from Eglon, and all Israel with him, unto

---

The other warriors would not return from the pursuit until the evening of the overthrow of the Amorites; and the execution of the kings and the capture of Makkedah itself belong, no doubt, to the day following (*vv.* 27, 28).

none moved his tongue] See marg. ref. and note.

24. *put your feet upon the necks of these kings*] A symbol of complete subjugation (cp. marg. reff. and 1 Cor. xv. 25).

29. *Libnah*] The word means "white" or "distinct," and undoubtedly points to some natural feature of the spot, perhaps the "Garde Blanche" of the Crusaders, a castle which stood on or near the white cliffs which bound the plain of Philistia to the east opposite to Ascalon. It was in the southern part of the hill-country of Judah (xv. 42), and was one of the cities afterwards assigned to the priests (xxi. 13).

33. Gezer lies on the southern border of the tribe of Ephraim (xvi. 3). It was considerably to the northward of Joshua's present line of operations, and does not appear to have been captured at this time. He contented himself for the present with repulsing the attack made upon him, slew Horam (cp. xii. 12), inflicting a severe defeat upon his people, and then continued to pursue his conquests over the confederated kings and their allies in south Canaan.

[e] See ch. 14. 13. & 15. 13. Judg. 1. 10.
[f] See chap. 15. 15. Judg. 1. 11.
[g] Deut. 20. 16, 17.
[h] Gen. 10.19.
[i] ch. 11. 16.
[k] ver. 14.

37 [e]Hebron; and they fought against it: and they took it, and
smote it with the edge of the sword, and the king thereof, and
all the cities thereof, and all the souls that *were* therein; he left
none remaining, according to all that he had done to Eglon; but
38 destroyed it utterly, and all the souls that *were* therein. ¶ And
Joshua returned, and all Israel with him, to [f]Debir; and fought
39 against it: and he took it, and the king thereof, and all the
cities thereof; and they smote them with the edge of the sword,
and utterly destroyed all the souls that *were* therein; he left
none remaining: as he had done to Hebron, so he did to Debir,
and to the king thereof; as he had done also to Libnah, and to
40 her king. ¶ So Joshua smote all the country of the hills, and of
the south, and of the vale, and of the springs, and all their kings:
he left none remaining, but utterly destroyed all that breathed,
41 as the LORD God of Israel [g]commanded. And Joshua smote them
from Kadesh-barnea even unto [h]Gaza, [i]and all the country of
42 Goshen, even unto Gibeon. And all these kings and their land
did Joshua take at one time, [k]because the LORD God of Israel
43 fought for Israel. And Joshua returned, and all Israel with
him, unto the camp to Gilgal.

[a] ch. 10. 3.
[b] ch. 19. 15.
[c] Num. 34. 11.
[d] ch. 17. 11. Judg. 1. 27.

CHAP. 11. AND it came to pass, when Jabin king of Hazor had
heard *those things*, that he [a]sent to Jobab king of Madon, and to
2 the king [b]of Shimron, and to the king of Achshaph, and to the
kings that *were* on the north of the mountains, and of the plains
south of [c]Chinneroth, and in the valley, and in the borders [d]of

---

37. *the king thereof*] No doubt the successor of the king slain at Makkedah (*v.* 23).

all the cities thereof] *i.e.* the smaller towns dependent upon Hebron. The expression marks Hebron as the metropolis of other subject towns.

38. *Joshua returned*] The words mark a change in the direction of the march. Joshua from Hebron turned to the south-west, and attacked Debir or Kirjath-sepher and its dependencies (xv. 15).

40. See ix. 1. "The south" was the Negeb (Num. xiii. 17). Render "the springs" "slopes." The word here means the district of undulating ground between "the vale" (or *shephelah*) last named and "the hills."

41. *from Kadesh-barnea* (Num. xiii. 26) *unto Gaza*] This limits Joshua's conquests on the west, as the other line, "all the country of Goshen unto Gibeon," does on the east. Goshen (xv. 51) has not been identified. It was in the southern part of the territory of Judah, and is, of course, quite distinct from the Goshen of Gen. xlvi. 28.

42. *at one time*] *i.e.* in one campaign or expedition, which no doubt lasted some days, or perhaps weeks (cp. xi. 18).

XI. **1.** *Jabin*] Probably the hereditary and official title of the kings of Hazor (see Judg. iv. 2). The word means literally "he shall understand," and is equivalent to "the wise" or "intelligent."

Hazor] This name, which means "enclosed" or "fortified," belonged also to two other towns in the south of Judah (cp. xv. 23, 25). The Hazor here in question, the head of the principalities of Northern Canaan (*v.* 10) overlooked the lake of Merom, and was afterwards assigned to the tribe of Naphtali (xix. 36). It doubtless was one of the strongest fortresses in the north, both by nature and art. It is mentioned in Egyptian inscriptions of an early date. Its situation in the midst of a plain, though itself on a hill, rendered it peculiarly suitable as a stronghold for people whose main reliance was on horses and chariots (*v.* 4; Judg. iv. 3). Its position on the northern frontier led to its being fortified by Solomon (1 K. ix. 15). Its people were carried away captive, with those of the other cities of Naphtali, by Tiglath-Pileser (2 K. xv. 29). By the "plain of Nasor," where (1 Macc. xi. 67) Jonathan gained a victory over the Syrians, is doubtless to be understood "the plain of Asor" (*i.e.* Hazor). Hazor is conjecturally identified with the modern *Tell Kuraibeh*.

had heard those things] *i.e.* of the defeat of the southern Canaanites at Beth-horon and of the conquest of their country.

The sites of Madon, Shimron, and of Achshaph, are unknown.

2. *on the north of the mountains*] Rather, "northwards in the mountains." The reference is to the mountain district of Galilee, called (xx. 7) "mount Naphtali."

on the plains south of Chinneroth] Literally "in the Arabah south of Chinneroth." The words describe the northern portion of the "Arabah" (see Deut. i. 1), or depressed tract, which extends along the Jordan from the lake of Gennesaret southwards.

Chinneroth] Identical with the later Gennesaret (see Num. xxxiv. 10). The lake

3 Dor on the west, *and to* the Canaanite on the east and on the
west, and *to* the Amorite, and the Hittite, and the Perizzite, and
the Jebusite in the mountains, [e] and *to* the Hivite under [f] Hermon
4 [g] in the land of Mizpeh. And they went out, they and all their
hosts with them, much people, [h] even as the sand that *is* upon
the sea shore in multitude, with horses and chariots very many.
5 And when all these kings were [1] met together, they came and
pitched together at the waters of Merom, to fight against Israel.
6 ¶ And the LORD said unto Joshua, [i] Be not afraid because of
them: for to morrow about this time will I deliver them up
all slain before Israel: thou shalt [k] hough their horses, and burn
7 their chariots with fire. So Joshua came, and all the people of
war with him, against them by the waters of Merom suddenly;
8 and they fell upon them. And the LORD delivered them into
the hand of Israel, who smote them, and chased them unto
[2] great Zidon, and unto [l] [3] [4] Misrephoth-maim, and unto the
valley of Mizpeh eastward; and they smote them, until they

[e] Judg. 3. 3.
[f] ch. 13. 11.
[g] Gen. 31. 49.
[h] Gen. 22. 17. & 32. 12. Judg. 7. 12. 1 Sam. 13. 5.
[i] ch. 10. 8.
[k] 2 Sam. 8. 4.
[l] ch. 13. 6.

[1] Heb. *assembled by appointment.*
[2] Or, *Zidon-rabbah.*
[3] Or, *Salt pits.*
[4] Heb. *Burnings.*

derived its name from a town on its banks (cp. xix. 35).

in the valley] The northern part of the same flat district mentioned in ix. 1. This "valley" is the level plain adjacent to the sea and extending from Carmel southwards.

borders of Dor] Render "**highlands of Dor.**" Dor was a royal city, and gave its name to the district around it (cp. xii. 23; 1 K. iv. 11). Its importance was derived from its having an excellent and well-sheltered haven, and from the abundance among its rocks of the shell-fish which furnished the famous Tyrian purple. The site of Dor is identified by travellers as the modern *Tantura* or *Dandora,*—a name which is itself only a corruption of the ancient Dor. It lies near the foot of Carmel some six miles north of Cæsarea.

3. *Hermon*] See Deut. iii. 9 note.

the land of Mizpeh] or *Mizpah,* "the land of the watch-tower." The locality is probably identified as a plain stretching at the foot of Hermon south-westwards, from *Hasbeya,* towards the *Bahr el Huleh.* In a land abounding in striking points of view like Palestine, the name Mizpah was naturally, like "Belle Vue" amongst ourselves, bestowed on many places. The Mizpeh here mentioned must not be confounded with the Mizpeh of Gilead (xiii. 26, and Judg. xi. 29); nor with the Mizpeh of Judah (xv. 38); nor yet with that of Moab (1 Sam. xxii. 3).

5. *waters of Merom*] *i.e.* "the upper waters," the modern *Bahr el Huleh,* the lake Semechonitis, or Samochonitis of Josephus. This lake occupies the southern half of the *Ard el Huleh,* a depressed basin some fifteen miles long and three or four broad lying between the hills of Galilee on the west and the lower spurs of Hermon on the east. The size of the lake varies with the season, and the northern side of it ends in a large swamp. The shape of the lake is triangular, the point being at the south, where the Jordan, which enters it on the north, again quits it. There is a considerable space of table-land along the south-western shore, and here probably the troops of Jabin and his confederates were encamped, preparing to move southwards when Joshua and his army fell suddenly upon them.

6. *hough their horses*] *i.e.* cut the sinews of the hinder hoofs. This sinew once severed cannot be healed, and the horses would thus be irreparably lamed. This is the first appearance of horses in the wars with the Canaanites (Deut. xvii. 16 and note).

7. *suddenly*] As before, at Gibeon (x. 9), so now Joshua anticipates his enemies. Taken by surprise, and hemmed in between the mountains and the lake, the chariots and horses would have no time to deploy and no room to act effectively; and thus, in all probability, the unwieldy host of the Canaanites fell at once into hopeless confusion.

8. One portion of the defeated host fled north-westwards towards Zidon; the other north-eastwards up the *Ard el Huleh.*

Zidon, as the metropolis of various subject towns and territories, appears (xix. 28) to have been afterwards assigned to Asher, but was not, in fact, conquered by that tribe (Judg. i. 31). It is mentioned in Egyptian papyri of great antiquity, and by Homer, and was in the most ancient times the capital of Phœnicia. In later times it was eclipsed by Tyre (cp. 2 Sam. v. 11). The prophets frequently couple Tyre and Sidon together, as does also the New Test. (Is. xxiii. 2, 4, 12; Jer. xxvii. 3; xlvii. 4; Matt. xi. 22; xv. 21, &c.).

Both the site and signification of Misrephoth-maim are uncertain. Some have thought it identical with "Zarephath which belongeth to Zidon" (1 K. xvii. 9), the Sarepta of the New Test. The name is explained by

9 left them none remaining. And Joshua did unto them [m]as
the LORD bade him: he houghed their horses, and burnt their
10 chariots with fire. ¶ And Joshua at that time turned back, and
took Hazor, and smote the king thereof with the sword: for
11 Hazor beforetime was the head of all those kingdoms. And
they smote all the souls that *were* therein with the edge of the
sword, utterly destroying *them*: there was not [1]any left to
12 breathe: and he burnt Hazor with fire. And all the cities of
those kings, and all the kings of them, did Joshua take, and
smote them with the edge of the sword, *and* he utterly destroyed
13 them, [n]as Moses the servant of the LORD commanded. But *as*
for the cities that stood still [2]in their strength, Israel burned
14 none of them, save Hazor only; *that* did Joshua burn. And all
the spoil of these cities, and the cattle, the children of Israel
took for a prey unto themselves; but every man they smote with
the edge of the sword, until they had destroyed them, neither
15 left they any to breathe. [o]As the LORD commanded Moses his
servant, so [p]did Moses command Joshua, and [q]so did Joshua;
[3]he left nothing undone of all that the LORD commanded Moses.
16 ¶ So Joshua took all that land, [r]the hills, and all the south
country, [s]and all the land of Goshen, and the valley, and the
plain, and the mountain of Israel, and the valley of the same;
17 [t]*even* from [4]the mount Halak, that goeth up to Seir, even unto
Baal-gad in the valley of Lebanon under mount Hermon: and
[u]all their kings he took, and smote them, and slew them.
18, 19 [5]Joshua made war a long time with all those kings. There was
not a city that made peace with the children of Israel, save [x]the
Hivites the inhabitants of Gibeon: all *other* they took in battle.
20 For [y]it was of the LORD to harden their hearts, that they should
come against Israel in battle, that he might destroy them
utterly, *and* that they might have no favour, but that he might
21 destroy them, [z]as the LORD commanded Moses. ¶ And at that
time came Joshua, and cut off [a]the Anakims from the mountains,

[m] ver. 6.
[n] Num. 33. 52. Deut. 7. 2. & 20. 16, 17.
[o] Ex. 34. 11, 12.
[p] Deut. 7. 2.
[q] ch. 1. 7.
[r] ch. 12. 8.
[s] ch. 10. 41.
[t] ch. 12. 7.
[u] Deut. 7. 24. ch. 12. 7.
[x] ch. 9. 3, 7.
[y] Deut. 2. 30. Judg. 14. 4. 1 Sam. 2. 25. 1 Kin. 12. 15. Rom. 9. 18.
[z] Deut. 20. 16, 17.
[a] Deut. 1. 28. ch. 15. 13.

[1] Heb. *any breath.*
[2] Heb. *on their heap.*
[3] Heb. *he removed nothing.*
[4] Or, *the smooth mountain.*
[5] Till 1445. ver. 23.

---

some (see marg.) as meaning hot-springs; by others as salt-pits; *i.e.* pits where the sea water was evaporated for the sake of its salt; and again by others as "smelting factories near the waters." Some, tracing the word to quite another root, render it "heights of waters," or copious springs.

13. Render: "**But the cities standing each on its own hill**" (cp. Jer. xxx. 18). The meaning is simply that, with the exception of Hazor, Joshua did not burn the cities, but left them standing, each on its former site. This site is spoken of as a hill, because such was the ordinary site chosen for cities in Canaan (cp. Matt. v. 14).

17. *the mount Halak*] See marg. and ref. The name serves to mark the southern limit of Joshua's conquests. It suits equally well several of the ranges near the south border of Palestine, and it is uncertain which of them is the one here indicated.

Baal-gad (xii. 7 and xiii. 5) is probably Paneas, the Cæsarea Philippi of later times. The name means "troop or city of Baal," or a place where Baal was worshipped as the giver of "good luck." Cp. Is. lxv. 11. It was probably the same as *Baal-Hermon* (Judg. iii. 3; 1 Chr. v. 23; and see Deut. iii. 9).

18. *a long time*] At least five years; according to others, seven years (see xiv. 10, and Introd. p. 4). This and the preceding chapter contain a very condensed account of the wars of Joshua, giving particulars about leading events only.

20. See marg. reff.

21. *at that time*] *i.e.* in course of the "long time" mentioned in *v.* 18.

the Anakims] See Num. xiii. 22. As it was the report of the spies respecting the Anakims which, above all, struck terror into the Israelites in the wilderness, and caused their faithless murmuring and revolt, so the sacred writer goes back here in his story to record pointedly the overthrow of this gigantic and formidable race. They had their chief settlements in the mountains around Hebron (x. 3) or Debir. See xv. 15.

Anab was a city in the mountain district

from Hebron, from Debir, from Anab, and from all the mountains of Judah, and from all the mountains of Israel: Joshua
22 destroyed them utterly with their cities. There was none of the
Anakims left in the land of the children of Israel: only in Gaza,
23 in [b]Gath, [c]and in Ashdod, there remained. ¶So Joshua took — [b] 1 Sam. 17. 4.
the whole land, [d]according to all that the LORD said unto Moses; — [c] ch. 15. 46.
and Joshua gave it for an inheritance unto Israel [e]according to — [d] Num. 34. 2, &c.
their divisions by their tribes. [f]And the land rested from war.

CHAP. 12. NOW these *are* the kings of the land, which the children — [e] Num. 26. 53. ch. 14 to 19.
of Israel smote, and possessed their land on the other side — [f] ch. 14. 15. ver. 18.
Jordan toward the rising of the sun, [a]from the river Arnon — [a] Num. 21. 24.
2 [b]unto mount Hermon, and all the plain on the east: [c]Sihon
king of the Amorites, who dwelt in Heshbon, *and* ruled from — [b] Deut. 3. 8.
Aroer, which *is* upon the bank of the river Arnon, and from the — [c] Deut. 2. 33. & 3. 6.
middle of the river, and from half Gilead, even unto the river
3 Jabbok, *which is* the border of the children of Ammon; and
[d]from the plain to the sea of Chinneroth on the east, and unto — [d] Deut. 3. 17.
the sea of the plain, *even* the salt sea on the east, [e]the way to — [e] ch. 13. 20.
Beth-jeshimoth; and from [1]the south, under [2][f]Ashdoth-pisgah: — [f] Deut. 3. 17.
4 and [g]the coast of Og king of Bashan, *which was* of [h]the remnant — [g] Num. 21. 35. Deut. 3. 4.
5 of the giants, [i]that dwelt at Ashtaroth and at Edrei, and reigned — [h] Deut. 3. 11.
in [k]mount Hermon, [l]and in Salcah, and in all Bashan, [m]unto the — [i] Deut. 1. 4.
border of the Geshurites and the Maachathites, and half Gilead, — [k] Deut. 3. 8.
6 the border of Sihon king of Heshbon. [n]Them did Moses the — [l] Deut. 3. 10.
servant of the LORD and the children of Israel smite: and — [m] Deut. 3. 14.
[o]Moses the servant of the LORD gave it *for* a possession unto the — [n] Num. 21. 24, 33.
Reubenites, and the Gadites, and the half tribe of Manasseh. — [o] Num. 32. 29, 33.
7 ¶And these *are* the kings of the country [p]which Joshua and the — [p] ch. 11. 17.
children of Israel smote on this side Jordan on the west, from
Baal-gad in the valley of Lebanon even unto the mount Halak,
that goeth up to [q]Seir; which Joshua [r]gave unto the tribes of — [q] Gen. 14. 6.
8 Israel *for* a possession according to their divisions; [s]in the — [r] ch. 11. 23.
mountains, and in the valleys, and in the plains, and in the — [s] ch. 10. 40.
springs, and in the wilderness, and in the south country; [t]the — [t] Ex. 3. 8.
Hittites, the Amorites, and the Canaanites, the Perizzites, the
9 Hivites, and the Jebusites: [u]the king of Jericho, one; [x]the king — [u] ch. 6. 2.
10 of Ai, which *is* beside Beth-el, one; [y]the king of Jerusalem, — [x] ch. 8. 29.
11 one; the king of Hebron, one; the king of Jarmuth, one; — [y] ch. 10. 23.
12 the king of Lachish, one; the king of Eglon, one; [z]the king of — [z] ch. 10. 33.

[1] Or, *Teman.* [2] Or, *The springs of Pisgah*, or, *The hill.*

---

of Judah, lying some distance south of Hebron. It still bears its ancient name.

22. *Gaza, Gath, Ashdod*] See xiii. 3 note.

23. These words import that Joshua had overcome all overt resistance. There were, however, many districts by no means thoroughly and finally subdued (xiii. 1-6).

XII. 1-6. Consult the notes to the passages referred to in the margin.

1. *all the plain on the east*] *i.e.* the Arabah or depressed tract along the east bank of Jordan, the modern El-Ghor (see Num. xxii. 1).

2. *from the middle of the river*] *i.e.* as appears from xiii. 9, 16, "from the city that is in the midst of the river;" viz., Ar Moab (see Deut. ii. 36).

3. *from the plain*] Render "**over the plain**;" for the words describe not one of the boundaries of Sihon's kingdom, but part of the territory included in it, *i.e.* the eastern portion of the Ghor, between the Sea of Tiberias and the Dead Sea.

7-24. The names of the kings are given in the order of their actual encounter with Joshua. Those enumerated in *vv.* 10-18 either belonged to the league of the southern Canaanites (x. 1 seq.), the power of which was broken in the battle of Beth-horon, or were at any rate conquered in the campaign following that battle. Those mentioned in *vv.* 19-24 were in like manner connected with the northern confederates (xi. 1 seq.), who were defeated at the Waters of Merom.

13 Gezer, one; [a]the king of Debir, one; the king of Geder, one;
14, 15 the king of Hormah, one; the king of Arad, one; [b]the king of
16 Libnah, one; the king of Adullam, one; [c]the king of Mak-
17 kedah, one; [d]the king of Beth-el, one; the king of Tappuah,
18 one; [e]the king of Hepher, one; the king of Aphek, one; the
19 king of [1]Lasharon, one; the king of Madon, one; [f]the king of
20 Hazor, one; the king of [g]Shimron-meron, one; the king of
21 Achshaph, one; the king of Taanach, one; the king of Megiddo,
22 one; [h]the king of Kedesh, one; the king of Jokneam of Carmel,
23 one; the king of Dor in the [i]coast of Dor, one; the king of [k]the
24 nations of Gilgal, one; the king of Tirzah, one: all the kings
thirty and one.

Chap. 13. NOW Joshua [a]was old *and* stricken in years; and the
Lord said unto him, Thou art old *and* stricken in years, and
2 there remaineth yet very much land [2]to be possessed. [b]This *is*
the land that yet remaineth: [c]all the borders of the Philistines,
3 and all [d]Geshuri, [e]from Sihor, which *is* before Egypt, even unto

[a] ch. 10. 38. [b] ch. 10. 29. [c] ch. 10. 28. [d] ch. 8. 17. Judg. 1. 22. [e] 1 Kin. 4. 10. [f] ch. 11. 10. [g] ch. 11. 1. [h] ch. 19. 37. [i] ch. 11. 2. [k] Isai. 9. 1.

[a] See ch. 14. 10. & 23. 1. [b] Judg. 3. 1. [c] Joel 3. 4. [d] 2 Sam. 3. 3. & 13. 37, 38. [e] Jer. 2. 18.

[1] Or, *Sharon*, Isai. 33. 9.

[2] Heb. *to possess it*, Deut. 31. 3.

13-20. The identification of several of these places is still uncertain: the same name (*e.g.* Aphek, *v.* 18) being applied to various places in various parts of Palestine. Geder, or Gedor (xv. 58), a city in the mountain district in the south of the territory of Judah, is no doubt the modern *Jedur*.

21. *Taanach*] A Levitical town (xxi. 25) in the territory of Issachar, but assigned to the Manassites (xvii. 11; cp. 1 Chr. vii. 29), is identified with *Taanuk*. It was here that Barak encountered the host of Sisera (Judg. v. 19). Megiddo was near it, and is thought to have been *el Lejjun* (the Roman Legion), [or Mujedd'a (Conder)].

22. *Kedesh*] *i.e.* Kedesh Naphtali, a city of refuge, a Levitical city, and the home of Barak (Judg. iv. 6).

Jokneam] A Levitical city in the territory of Zebulon (xix. 11); perhaps the modern *Kaimon*. *Tell Kaimon* is a conspicuous and important position, commanding the main pass across the ridge of Carmel from Phœnicia to Egypt. This famous mountain range (about fifteen miles long) no doubt received the name Carmel (the word means "a fruitful field" as opposed to "wilderness") as descriptive of its character; and thus the name became an emblem of beauty and luxuriance (Is. xxxv. 2; Cant. vii. 5, &c.). Its highest part, about four miles from Tell Kaimon, is nearly 1750 feet above the sea. Its modern name, *Jebel Mar Elias*, preserves still that association with the great deeds of Elijah, from which Carmel derives its chief Biblical interest. Mount Carmel was probably, like Lebanon, from very ancient Canaanitish times, regarded as specially sacred; and since the altar of the Lord repaired by Elijah (1 K. xviii. 30) was an old one which had been broken down, Carmel was probably no less esteemed by the Israelites also. In later times the caves which abound towards the western bluffs of the range have been frequented by Christian, Jewish, and Mussulman anchorites. The order of Carmelite or barefooted friars took its rise from the convent founded by St. Louis, which still crowns the western headland.

23. *the king of the nations*] See Gen. xiv. 1 and note. It means king of certain mixed and probably nomadic tribes, which regarded Gilgal (iv. 19) as their centre and capital.

24. *Tirzah*] This place, the capital of Jeroboam and his successors until the days of Omri (1 K. xiv. 17, xv. 21, &c.), is identified by some with *Tulluzah*, a town 3 m. N.E. of Nablous, [by others with Teiasir].

XIII. Here commences the second portion of the book, the statements of which were drawn from pre-existing documentary records (cp. xviii. 9); the whole of the history being introduced by a command of God to Joshua to proceed to allot the land amongst the tribes.

1. Joshua is bidden to allot the whole of the Promised Land amongst the Twelve Tribes in faith that God would perfect in due time that expulsion of the Canaanites which Joshua himself could not carry further (see xi. 23).

2. This and *v.* 3 name the still unconquered districts in the southern half of the land, *vv.* 4, 5, and 6 those in the north.

Geshuri] A district on the south of Philistia, the inhabitants of which are again named in 1 Sam. xxvii. 8; but are not to be confounded with the land of the Geshurites mentioned in *v.* 13, and in xii. 5.

3. Sihor is derived from a root signifying "to be black," and is suitable enough as an appellative of the Nile (Is. xxiii. 3). Here it most probably stands for "the river of

the borders of Ekron northward, *which* is counted to the Canaanite: [f]five lords of the Philistines; the Gazathites, and the
Ashdothites, the Eshkalonites, the Gittites, and the Ekronites;
4 also [g]the Avites: from the south, all the land of the Canaanites,
and [1]Mearah that *is* beside the Sidonians, [h]unto Aphek, to the
5 borders of [i]the Amorites: and the land of the Giblites, and all
Lebanon, toward the sunrising, [k]from Baal-gad under mount
6 Hermon unto the [l]entering into Hamath. All the inhabitants
of the hill country from Lebanon unto [m]Misrephoth-maim, *and*
all the Sidonians, them [n]will I drive out from before the children
of Israel: only [o]divide thou it by lot unto the Israelites for an
7 inheritance, as I have commanded thee. Now therefore divide
this land for an inheritance unto the nine tribes, and the half

[f] 1 Sam. 6. 4, 16.
[g] Deut. 2. 23.
[h] ch. 19. 30.
[i] See Judg. 1. 34.
[k] ch. 11. 17.
[l] Num. 13. 21.
[m] ch. 11. 8.
[n] See ch. 23. 13. Judg. 2. 21.
[o] ch. 14. 1.

[1] Or, *The cave.*

Egypt" (Num. xxxiv. 3 note), the modern *Wady el Arish.*

Ekron (*Akir*) lay on the northern boundary of Judah (xv. 11), and was actually conquered by the men of that tribe (Judg. i. 18), though assigned in the allotment of the land to Dan (xix. 43). It seems to have fallen again into the hands of the Philistines in the days of the Judges (1 Sam. v. 10), was reconquered by Samuel (cp. 1 Sam. vii. 14), but figures in subsequent times as a Philistine city only (cp. 1 Sam. xvii. 52; 2 K. i. 2, 16, &c.).

lords] The Hebrew word (*seren*) means "an axle," and is applied as a title peculiarly to the chiefs (cp. Judg. iii. 3 and marg. reff.) of the Philistines (Gen. x. 14).

Gaza was the most southern of the Philistine cities (cp. x. 41, xi. 22). It was allotted to the tribe of Judah (xv. 47), and was, with Askalon, taken by the warriors of that tribe (Judg. i. 18). Both cities were soon re-occupied by the Philistines, and subsequently are always mentioned as Philistine cities. Gaza lay on the direct route of the Egyptian armies in their invasions of Syria, by whom it was captured more than once. Special judgments are denounced against Gaza for the cruelty of its people towards the Jews in the time of their humiliation (Amos i. 6, 7; Zeph. ii. 4; Zech. ix. 5), and in the time of St. Jerome the ancient city was a ruin of which the foundations could hardly be traced, and the then existing town was built on another site. Gaza was in later times an episcopal see, and is now a thriving place containing some 15,000 inhabitants, a larger population than that of Jerusalem.

Ashdod (*Esdud;* Azotus, Acts viii. 40) was, like Gaza, allotted to Judah (see xv. 46, 47), but was soon regained by the Philistines, and became a principal seat of their Dagon worship. Hither the ark of God was taken after its capture by the Philistines (1 Sam. v. 1 seq.). Its name (="fortress," "castle"), no less than its history (cp. 2 Chr. xxvi. 6; Is. xx. 1; Neh. iv. 7, &c.) indicates its importance as a stronghold; it withstood for twenty-nine years the longest siege on record by the Egyptian king Psammetichus. Like Gaza, it was doomed by the Jewish prophets to desolation, and it was utterly destroyed by the Maccabees (1 Macc. x. 77–84, xi. 4). It was, however, rebuilt by the Romans, and figures in Christian times as an episcopal city.

Askelon (see Judg. i. 18), the birthplace of Herod the Great, figures as an important town and seaport in the history of the Crusades, and very massive ruins still attest the ancient strength and grandeur of the place. It is situated about midway between Gaza and Ashdod.

Gath seems to have been first taken by David (1 Chr. xviii. 1). It is not named again in the book of Joshua. It was the town of Goliath (1 Sam. xvii. 4), and is mentioned in David's elegy over Saul as a leading Philistine city (2 Sam. i. 20). It was the nearest of the Philistine cities to Jerusalem, but both the name and the city have perished; its site is conjecturally placed [by Conder] at Tell es Safi.

Avites] See Deut. ii. 23 note.

4. Read "**on the south,**" and connect the words with the verse preceding. They indicate the southern limit of the still unconquered territory in this neighbourhood, as *v.* 3 gives the northern one.

Mearah] The "cave" (see marg.) has been referred to *Mugr Jezzin* ("cave of Jezzin"), between Tyre and Sidon, or to a district characterized by deep cave-like ravines near Sidon and Dan-Laish.

5. *Giblites*] The people of Gebal (*Jebail,* 22 m. N. of Beyrout). They were "stone-squarers" (1 K. v. 18) and (ship) "caulkers" (Ezek. xxvii. 9).

6. The A. V. would exhibit the sense more clearly if the words from the beginning of *v.* 2 to the words "the Sidonians" in this verse were placed in a parenthesis, and the order of the words before us changed thus: "I will drive them out." The "them" meaning the inhabitants of the "very much land to be possessed," spoken of in *v.* 1.

8 tribe of Manasseh, with whom the Reubenites and the Gadites
have received their inheritance, [p] which Moses gave them, beyond
Jordan eastward, *even* as Moses the servant of the LORD gave
9 them; from Aroer, that *is* upon the bank of the river Arnon,
and the city that *is* in the midst of the river, [q] and all the plain
10 of Medeba unto Dibon; and [r] all the cities of Sihon king of the
Amorites, which reigned in Heshbon, unto the border of the
11 children of Ammon; [s] and Gilead, and the border of the Geshurites and Maachathites, and all mount Hermon, and all Bashan
12 unto Salcah; all the kingdom of Og, in Bashan, which reigned
in Ashtaroth and in Edrei, who remained of [t] the remnant of the
13 giants: [u] for these did Moses smite, and cast them out. Nevertheless the children of Israel expelled [x] not the Geshurites, nor
the Maachathites: but the Geshurites and the Maachathites
14 dwell among the Israelites until this day. [y] Only unto the tribe
of Levi he gave none inheritance; the sacrifices of the LORD God
of Israel made by fire *are* their inheritance, [z] as he said unto
15 them. ¶ And Moses gave unto the tribe of the children of
16 Reuben *inheritance* according to their families. And their coast
was [a] from Aroer, that *is* on the bank of the river Arnon, [b] and
the city that *is* in the midst of the river, [c] and all the plain by
17 Medeba; Heshbon, and all her cities that *are* in the plain;
18 Dibon, and [1] Bamoth-baal, and Beth-baal-meon, [d] and Jahaza,
19 and Kedemoth, and Mephaath, [e] and Kirjathaim, and [f] Sibmah,
20 and Zareth-shahar in the mount of the valley, and Beth-peor,
21 and [g] [2] Ashdoth-pisgah, and Beth-jeshimoth, [h] and all the cities
of the plain, and all the kingdom of Sihon king of the Amorites,
which reigned in Heshbon, [i] whom Moses smote [k] with the
princes of Midian, Evi, and Rekem, and Zur, and Hur, and
Reba, *which were* dukes of Sihon, dwelling in the country.
22 [l] Balaam also the son of Beor, the [3] soothsayer, did the children
of Israel slay with the sword among them that were slain by
23 them. And the border of the children of Reuben was Jordan,
and the border *thereof*. This *was* the inheritance of the children
of Reuben after their families, the cities and the villages thereof.

p Num. 32. 33. Deut. 3. 13. ch. 22. 4.
q Num. 21. 30.
r Num. 21. 24, 25.
s ch. 12. 5.
t Deut. 3. 11. ch. 12. 4.
u Num. 21. 24, 35.
x ver. 11.
y Num. 18. 20, 23, 24. ch. 14. 3, 4.
z ver. 33.
a ch. 12. 2.
b Num. 21. 28.
c Num. 21. 30.
d Num. 21. 23.
e Num. 32. 37.
f Num. 32. 38.
g Deut. 3. 17.
h Deut. 3. 10.
i Num. 21. 24.
k Num. 31. 8.
l Num. 22. 5.

[1] Or, *The high places of Baal, and house of Baal-meon:* See Num. 32. 38.
[2] Or, *Springs of Pisgah,* or, *The hill.*
[3] Or, *diviner.*

8–33. The writer appends to the command of God (1–7) a statement that the other two tribes and a half had already had their inheritance marked out for them by Moses in the land east of Jordan. The boundaries of this territory as a whole are first set forth (8–14), and afterwards the portions assigned within it to the two tribes and a half are severally described (15–33).

14. See Deut. xviii. 1–5 and notes.

15–24. Inheritance of the tribe of Reuben. This territory was the most southerly of the trans-Jordanic possessions of Israel, and adjoined Moab, which lay only on the other side of the Arnon. Hence the Reubenites became in after times much intermixed with the Moabites, who in fact eventually acquired much of the land, and several, if not all, of the cities here named as belonging to Reuben. This acquisition was probably assisted by the fact that the territory north of Arnon had formerly belonged to the Moabites, from whom it was wrested by the Amorites (see Num. xxi. 26, &c. notes). It is not likely that the Amorite conquerors had completely extirpated the Moabite inhabitants. Hence, in the days when the Reubenites became engrossed in their pastoral pursuits, and probably not very long after the days of Joshua, the Moabites easily encroached on their inheritance, and in the end probably reoccupied nearly the whole of the ancient kingdom of Sihon (cp. Deut. xxxiii. 6 note).

17–21. See marg. reff. for some of these names. Heshbon, Kedemoth, and Mephaath became eventually Levitical cities.

21. *dukes of Sihon*] Rather "vassals of Sihon," probably those "dedicated" or "appointed" with a libation.

23. *Jordan* &c.] *i.e.* the Jordan and its territory (cp. similar expressions in Num. xxxiv.

24 ¶ And Moses gave *inheritance* unto the tribe of Gad, *even* unto
25 the children of Gad according to their families. [m]And their
coast was Jazer, and all the cities of Gilead, [n]and half the land
of the children of Ammon, unto Aroer, that *is* before [o]Rabbah;
26 and from Heshbon unto Ramath-mizpeh, and Betonim; and
27 from Mahanaim unto the border of Debir; and in the valley,
[p]Beth-aram, and Beth-nimrah, [q]and Succoth, and Zaphon, the
rest of the kingdom of Sihon king of Heshbon, Jordan and *his*
border, *even* unto the edge [r]of the sea of Chinnereth on the other
28 side Jordan eastward. This *is* the inheritance of the children
29 of Gad after their families, the cities, and their villages. ¶ And
Moses gave *inheritance* unto the half tribe of Manasseh: and
this was *the possession* of the half tribe of the children of Ma-
30 nasseh by their families. And their coast was from Mahanaim,
all Bashan, all the kingdom of Og king of Bashan, and [s]all the
31 towns of Jair, which *are* in Bashan, threescore cities: and half
Gilead, and [t]Ashtaroth, and Edrei, cities of the kingdom of Og
in Bashan, *were pertaining* unto the children of Machir the son
of Manasseh, *even* to the one half of the [u]children of Machir by
32 their families. ¶ These *are the countries* which Moses did dis-
tribute for inheritance in the plains of Moab, on the other side
33 Jordan, by Jericho, eastward. [x]But unto the tribe of Levi
Moses gave not *any* inheritance: the LORD God of Israel *was*
their inheritance, [y]as he said unto them.
CHAP. 14. AND these *are the countries* which the children of Israel
inherited in the land of Canaan, [a]which Eleazar the priest, and
Joshua the son of Nun, and the heads of the fathers of the tribes
of the children of Israel, distributed for inheritance to them.
2 [b]By lot *was* their inheritance, as the LORD commanded by the

[m] Num. 32. 35.
[n] Cp. Num. 21. 26, 28, 29, with Deut. 2. 19.
[o] Deut. 3. 11. 2 Sam. 11. 1.
[p] Num. 32. 36.
[q] Gen. 33. 17. 1 Kin. 7. 46.
[r] Num. 34. 11.
[s] Num. 32. 41. 1 Chr. 2. 23.
[t] ch. 12. 4.
[u] Num. 32. 39, 40.
[x] ver. 14. ch. 18. 7.
[y] Deut. 10. 9. & 18. 1, 2.
[a] Num. 34. 17, 18.
[b] Num. 26. 55. & 33. 54.

6; Deut. iii. 16). The portion of the tribe of Reuben at its northern extremity touched the Jordan; the main part of his inheritance lay on the east of the Dead Sea.

25. *all the cities of Gilead*] *i.e.* of Gilead in the narrower sense, included in the territory of Sihon, and distinct from Bashan (Deut. iii. 10).

half the land of the children of Ammon] *i.e.* that half of the Ammonite territory which had been conquered by the Amorites. This, after the overthrow of Sihon, the Israelites took for their own. The land which the Ammonites still held in the days of Moses, the Israelites were not permitted to attack.

Rabbah was a border fortress, the principal stronghold of the Ammonites (Num. xxi. 24), and the residence of their king. It was attacked and taken by Joab (2 Sam. xi. xii.; 1 Chr. xx. 1), but appears in later times again as an Ammonitish city (Jer. xlix. 3; Ezek. xxv. 5; Amos i. 13-15). In the third century B.C. it received from Ptolemy Philadelphus the name of Philadelphia, and was in later times the seat of a Christian bishop; but has now for many centuries been in ruins, remarkable for their grandeur and extent.

26. *the border of Debir*] Rather perhaps "the border of Lidbir," which is regarded as identical with the Lo-debar of 2 Sam. ix. 4, and xvii. 27, one of the towns from which provisions were brought to David at Mahanaim (Gen. xxxii. 2).

29-33. On the conquest of Bashan, see especially Num. xxxii. 33, &c. and notes.

XIV. **2.** *By lot*] We are not told in what manner the lot was cast. Perhaps two urns were employed, one containing a description of the several districts to be allotted, the other the names of the tribes; and the portion of each tribe would then be determined by a simultaneous drawing from the two urns. Or a drawing might be made by some appointed person, or by a delegate of each tribe from one urn containing the description of the ten inheritances. The lot only determined in a general way the position in the country of the particular tribe concerned, whether north or south, &c.; the dimensions of each territory being left to be adjusted subsequently, according to the numbers and wants of the tribe to be provided for. Since the predilections and habits of two tribes and a half were consulted in the apportionment to them of the trans-Jordanic territory (Num. xxxii. 1) there is no objection to the supposition that something of the same kind may have taken place, subject to the Divine approval, in the distribution of the lands to the nine and a

3 hand of Moses, for the nine tribes, and *for* the half tribe. [c]For
Moses had given the inheritance of two tribes and an half tribe
on the other side Jordan: but unto the Levites he gave none
4 inheritance among them. For [d]the children of Joseph were two
tribes, Manasseh and Ephraim: therefore they gave no part
unto the Levites in the land, save cities to dwell *in*, with their
5 suburbs for their cattle and for their substance. [e]As the LORD
commanded Moses, so the children of Israel did, and they divided
6 the land. ¶Then the children of Judah came unto Joshua in
Gilgal: and Caleb the son of Jephunneh the [f]Kenezite said unto
him, Thou knowest [g]the thing that the LORD said unto Moses
the man of God concerning me and thee [h]in Kadesh-barnea.
7 Forty years old *was* I when Moses the servant of the LORD
[i]sent me from Kadesh-barnea to espy out the land; and I
8 brought him word again as *it was* in mine heart. Nevertheless
[k]my brethren that went up with me made the heart of the
9 people melt: but I wholly [l]followed the LORD my God. And
Moses sware on that day, saying, [m]Surely the land [n]whereon
thy feet have trodden shall be thine inheritance, and thy children's for ever, because thou hast wholly followed the LORD my
10 God. And now, behold, the LORD hath kept me alive, [o]as he
said, these forty and five years, even since the LORD spake this
word unto Moses, while *the children of* Israel [1]wandered in the
wilderness: and now, lo, I *am* this day fourscore and five years
11 old. [p]As yet I *am as* strong this day as *I was* in the day that
Moses sent me: as my strength *was* then, even so *is* my strength
12 now, for war, both [q]to go out, and to come in. Now therefore
give me this mountain, whereof the LORD spake in that day;
for thou heardest in that day how [r]the Anakims *were* there, and
that the cities *were* great *and* fenced: [s]if so be the LORD *will be*
with me, then [t]I shall be able to drive them out, as the LORD

[c] ch. 13. 8, 32, 33.
[d] Gen. 48. 5. 1 Chr. 5. 1, 2.
[e] Num. 35. 2. ch. 21. 2.
[f] Num. 32. 12.
[g] Num. 14. 24, 30. Deut. 1. 36. 38.
[h] Num. 13. 26.
[i] Num. 13. 6.
[k] Num. 13. 31, 32. Deut. 1. 28.
[l] Num. 14. 24.
[m] ch. 1. 3.
[n] See Num. 13. 22.
[o] Num. 14. 30.
[p] See Deut. 34. 7.
[q] Deut. 31. 2.
[r] Num. 13. 28, 33.
[s] Ps. 18. 32, 34. & 60. 12. Rom. 8. 31.
[t] ch. 15. 14. Judg. 1. 20.

[1] Heb. *walked*.

---

half other tribes; and the lot would thus be appealed to as finally deciding the matter and foreclosing jealousies and disputes.

It is apparent that the casting of the ten lots did not take place simultaneously. The tribe of Judah had precedence, whether by express appointment or because its lot "came up" first, does not appear. It was, as it seems, only after this tribe had settled upon its domains, that further lots were drawn for Ephraim and the half tribe of Manasseh. After this a pause, perhaps of some duration, appears to have occurred; the camp was moved from Gilgal to Shiloh; and the further casting of lots for the other seven tribes was proceeded with at the instigation of Joshua (see xviii. 10).

6. *the children of Judah*] No doubt, in particular, the kinsmen of Caleb, and perhaps other leading men of the tribe. These came before Joshua, with Caleb, in order to make it manifest that they supported his claim, to be secured in the possessions promised him by Moses before the general allotment should be made to the tribes (cp. marg. reff.).

9. *Moses sware*] *i.e.* God sware; and His promise, confirmed by an oath, was communicated, of course, through Moses.

10. *forty and five years*] The word of God to Moses was spoken after the return of the spies in the autumn of the second year after the Exodus (Num. xiii. 25); subsequently thirty-eight years elapsed before the people reached the Jordan (Num. xx. 1); after the passage of the Jordan seven more years had passed, when Caleb claimed Hebron, before the partition of the land amongst the nine tribes and a half. These seven years then correspond to the "long time" (xi. 18) during which Joshua was making war with the Canaanites. They are in the sequel of this verse added by Caleb to the years of wandering, since during them the people had no settled abodes.

12. The Anakims had in the course of Joshua's campaigns in the south been expelled from "this mountain," *i.e.* the mountain country round Hebron, but they had only withdrawn to the neighbouring cities of Philistia (xi. 22). Thence they had, as must be inferred from the text here, returned and reoccupied Hebron, probably when Joshua and the main force of the Israelites had marched northward to deal with

13 said. ¶ And Joshua [u]blessed him, [x]and gave unto
14 son of Jephunneh Hebron for an inheritance. [y]Heb
fore became the inheritance of Caleb the son of Jep
Kenezite unto this day, because that he [z]wholly f
15 LORD God of Israel. And [a]the name of Hebron
Kirjath-arba; *which Arba was* a great man among
[b]And the land had rest from war.

CHAP. 15. *THIS* then was the lot of the tribe of the ch...
Judah by their families; [a]*even* to the border of Edom the [b]wil-
derness of Zin southward *was* the uttermost part of the south
2 coast. ¶ And their south border was from the shore of the salt
3 sea, from the [1]bay that looketh southward: and it went out to
the south side [c]to [2]Maaleh-acrabbim, and passed along to Zin, [c] Num. 34. 4.
and ascended up on the south side unto Kadesh-barnea, and
passed along to Hezron, and went up to Adar, and fetched a
4 compass to Karkaa: *from thence* it passed [d]toward Azmon, and [d] Num. 34. 5.
went out unto the river of Egypt; and the goings out of that
5 coast were at the sea: this shall be your south coast. ¶ And
the east border *was* the salt sea, *even* unto the end of Jordan.
And *their* border in the north quarter *was* from the bay of the
6 sea at the uttermost part of Jordan: and the border went up to
[e]Beth-hogla, and passed along by the north of Beth-arabah; [e] Gen. 50. 10.
and the border went up [f]to the stone of Bohan the son of [f] ch. 18. 17.
7 Reuben: and the border went up toward Debir from [g]the valley [g] ch. 7. 26.
of Achor, and so northward, looking toward Gilgal, that *is* before
the going up to Adummim, which *is* on the south side of the
river: and the border passed toward the waters of En-shemesh, [h] 2 Sam. 17. 17.
8 and the goings out thereof were at [h]En-rogel: and the border 1 Kin. 1. 9.
went up [i]by the valley of the son of Hinnom unto the south side [i] ch. 18. 16. 2 Kin. 23. 10. Jer. 19. 2, 6.

[1] Heb. *tongue*. [2] Or, *The going up to Acrabbim*.

Jabin and his confederates. Caleb finally drove out this formidable race and occupied Hebron and its dependent towns and district permanently. See xv. 13 seq.

15. *a great man*] Literally the great man; *i.e.* the renowned ancestor of the tribe, regarded as the founder of its greatness (xv. 13).

XV. The inheritance of the tribe of Judah is described first by its general boundaries on all four sides (*vv.* 1–12); then reference is again made, for the sake of completeness, to the special inheritance of Caleb which lay within these boundaries (*vv.* 13–20); and lastly a list of the towns is given (*vv.* 21–63). Consult the marg. reff.

6. *the stone of Bohan*] This stone perhaps commemorated some deed of valour belonging to the wars of Joshua (cp. 1 Sam. vii. 12). The stone was erected on the slope of a hill (see marg. ref.), no doubt one of the range which bounds the Jordan valley on the west. But its exact site is wholly uncertain.

7. *the going up to Adummim*] Rather, "**the ascent** or **pass of Adummim**" (cp. *v.* 3, marg.), on the road from Jerusalem to Jericho. Its name signifies "red" and is explained by Jerome as given because of the frequent blood shed there by robbers. This road is the scene of the parable of the Good Samaritan. Possibly the name may be due to some aboriginal tribe of "red men," who held their ground in these fastnesses after the invaders had driven them from the face of the country elsewhere.

En-shemesh] *i.e.* "fountain of the sun;" no doubt that now called "the Fountain of the Apostles," about two miles from Jerusalem, and the only well on the road to Jericho.

En-rogel] *i.e.* "fountain of the fullers" near the walls of Jerusalem. It was here that Jonathan and Ahimaaz concealed themselves after the rebellion of Absalom, in order to procure tidings for David, and here Adonijah gave a feast to his adherents preparatory to making an attempt on the crown (cp. marg. reff.). It is probably the modern "Fountain of the Virgin," the only real spring near Jerusalem, from which the Pool of Siloam is supplied. Others identify it, less probably, with the "Well of Job," situated where the valleys of Kedron and Hinnom unite.

8. *the valley of the son of Hinnom*] This valley begins on the west of Jerusalem at the road to Joppa, and turning south-eastward round the foot of Mount Zion joins the deeper valley of Kedron on the south of the

of the [k]Jebusite; the same *is* Jerusalem: and the border went
up to the top of the mountain that *lieth* before the valley of
Hinnom westward, which *is* at the end [l]of the valley of the
9 giants northward: and the border was drawn from the top of
the hill unto [m]the fountain of the water of Nephtoah, and went
out to the cities of mount Ephron; and the border was drawn
10 [n]to Baalah, which *is* [o]Kirjath-jearim: and the border compassed from Baalah westward unto mount Seir, and passed along
unto the side of mount Jearim, which *is* Chesalon, on the north
side, and went down to Beth-shemesh, and passed on to [p]Tim-
11 nah: and the border went out unto the side of [q]Ekron northward: and the border was drawn to Shicron, and passed along
to mount Baalah, and went out unto Jabneel; and the goings
12 out of the border were at the sea. ¶ And the west border *was*
[r]to the great sea, and the coast *thereof*. ¶ This *is* the coast of
the children of Judah round about according to their families.
13 ¶ [s]And unto Caleb the son of Jephunneh he gave a part among
the children of Judah, according to the commandment of the
LORD to Joshua, *even* [t][1]the city of Arba the father of Anak,
14 which *city is* Hebron. And Caleb drove thence [u]the three sons
of Anak, [x]Sheshai, and Ahiman, and Talmai, the children of

...18. 28. ...g. 1. 21. ...9. 10.
[l] ch. 18. 16.
[m] ch. 18. 15.
[n] 1 Chr. 13. 6.
[o] Judg. 18. 12.
[p] ch. 19. 43. Judg. 14. 1.
[q] ch. 19. 43.
[r] ver. 47. Num. 34. 6, 7.
[s] ch. 14. 13.
[t] ch. 14. 15.
[u] Judg. 1. 10, 20.
[x] Num. 13. 22.

[1] Or, *Kirjath-arba.*

city. It was in this ravine, more particularly at Tophet in the more wild and precipitous part of it towards the east, that the later kings of Judah offered the sacrifices of children to Moloch (2 Chr. xxviii. 3, xxxiii. 6, &c.). After these places had been defiled by Josiah, Tophet and the whole valley of Hinnom were held in abomination by the Jews, and the name of the latter was used to denote the place of eternal torment (Matt. v. 22). The Greek term Gehenna (γεέννα) is in fact formed from the Hebrew *gay-hinnom*, "valley of Hinnom." Hinnom is regarded either as the name of some ancient hero, or as an appellative (= "groaning" or "moaning"), bestowed on the spot because of the cries of the victims here offered to Moloch, and of the drums with which those cries were drowned.

the valley of the giants] Rather "the plain of Rephaim." This plain, named after an ancient and gigantic tribe of the land (Gen. xiv. 5), lies south-westward of Jerusalem, and is terminated by a slight rocky ridge forming the brow of the valley of Hinnom. The valley is fertile (Isa. xvii. 5) and broad, and has been on more than one occasion the camping ground for armies operating against Jerusalem (2 Sam. v. 18, 22, xxiii. 13).

9. Nephtoah is probably the modern *Ain Lifta*, two miles and a half north-westward of Jerusalem: and Mount Ephron is conjecturally connected with the city Ephrain (2 Chr. xiii. 19) or Ophrah (xviii. 23).

10. Mount Seir is not the well-known range of Edom. The name (= "shaggy mountain") is applicable to any rugged or well-wooded hill. Here it probably denotes the range which runs south-westward from Kirjath-jearim to the Wady Surar. Mount Jearim, *i.e.* "woody mountain," is through its other name, Chesalon, identified with the modern *Kesla*.

Beth-shemesh] *i.e.* "house of the sun," called "Ir-shemesh" or "city of the sun" (xix. 41; cp. 1 K. iv. 9), a place assigned to Dan, and one of the cities which fell by lot to the Levites (xxi. 16). Beth-shemesh was the first place at which the ark rested after its return from the hands of the Philistines (1 Sam. vi. 12). It was the residence of one of Solomon's purveyors (1 K. iv. 9), and was the spot where at a later date Amaziah was defeated and slain by Jehoash (2 K. xiv. 11 seq.). It is no doubt the modern *Ain Shems*.

Timnah, called also Timnath, and Timnathah, belonged likewise to Dan, and is to be distinguished from other places of like name (Gen. xxxviii. 12; Josh. xxiv. 30). Timnah (= "portion") was evidently, like Gilgal, Ramah, Kirjath, and several other towns, of frequent use in Canaanitish topography.

11. *Jabneel*] The modern *Yebna*, about three miles from the coast and twelve miles south of Joppa. It is called Jabneh in 2 Chr. xxvi. 6, where Uzziah is recorded to have taken it from the Philistines and destroyed its fortifications. The town is repeatedly mentioned with its haven in the wars of the Maccabees (1 Macc. iv. 15; 2 Macc. xii. 8), and by Josephus under the name of Jamnia. It is described by Philo as a very populous town; and after the destruction of Jerusalem was for a long time the seat of the Sanhedrim, and was a famous school of Jewish learning. Its ruins, which are still considerable, stand on the brink of the *Wady Rubin*.

14. See marg. reff.

15 Anak. And [y]he went up thence to the inhabitants of Debir:
16 and the name of Debir before *was* Kirjath-sepher. [z]And Caleb
said, He that smiteth Kirjath-sepher, and taketh it, to him will
17 I give Achsah my daughter to wife. And [a]Othniel the [b]son of
Kenaz, the brother of Caleb, took it: and he gave him Achsah
18 his daughter to wife. [c]And it came to pass, as she came *unto him*,
that she moved him to ask of her father a field: and [d]she lighted
19 off *her* ass; and Caleb said unto her, What wouldest thou? Who
answered, Give me a [e]blessing; for thou hast given me a south
land; give me also springs of water. And he gave her the
20 upper springs, and the nether springs. ¶ This *is* the inheritance
of the tribe of the children of Judah according to their families.
21 ¶ And the uttermost cities of the tribe of the children of Judah
toward the coast of Edom southward were Kabzeel, and Eder,
22, 23 and Jagur, and Kinah, and Dimonah, and Adadah, and
24 Kedesh, and Hazor, and Ithnan, Ziph, and Telem, and Bea-
25 loth, and Hazor, Hadattah, and Kerioth, *and* Hezron, which *is*

[y] ch. 10. 38. Judg. 1. 11.
[z] Judg. 1. 12.
[a] Judg. 1. 13. & 3. 9.
[b] Num. 32. 12.
[c] Judg. 1. 14.
[d] See Gen. 24. 64. 1 Sam. 25. 23.
[e] Gen. 33. 11.

---

15. The name Debir belonged to two other places; viz., that named in *v.* 7, between Jerusalem and Jericho, and the Gadite town mentioned in xiii. 26. The Debir here meant appears [and its site has been conjecturally placed at Dhâherîyeh (Conder)] to have been situated in the mountain district south of Hebron. It was one of the towns afterwards assigned to the Levites. Its other name (*v.* 49), *Kirjath-sannah*, *i.e.* perhaps, "city of palm branches," or "city of law, or sacred learning," no less than the two given in the text, would indicate that Debir was an ancient seat of Canaanitish learning, for Debir probably is equivalent to "oracle," and Kirjath-sepher means "city of books." This plurality of names marks the importance of the town, as the inducement held out in *v.* 16, by Caleb, to secure its capture (cp. 1 Sam. xvii. 25, xviii. 17), points to its strength.

17. Othniel was probably Caleb's younger brother; the expression "son of Kenaz" being only an equivalent for the "Kenezite" (xiv. 6).

18. *a field*] In Judg. i. 14, "the field," *i.e.* the well-known field asked by Achsah and given by Caleb as a "blessing," *i.e.* as a token of goodwill, which when the Book of Judges was written had become historical. The "field" in question was doubtless in the neighbourhood of Debir, and was specially valuable because of its copious springs. Achsah's dismounting was a sign of reverence.

19. *a south land*] This term (*negeb*) which is often equivalent to a proper name (*v.* 21), importing the well-defined district which formed the south of the Promised Land (Num. xiii. 17 note), seems here used in its more general sense (Ps. cxxvi. 4), for a dry or barren land. The rendering of this passage adopted by LXX., several Versions, and Commentators, &c., "thou hast given me into a south land," *i.e.* "hast given me in marriage into a south land," is forced; the construction of the verb "to give," with two accusatives, is natural and common to many languages.

springs of water] The Hebrew word is found only here and in the parallel passage, Judg. i. 15. Hence some take it as a proper name, "Gulloth-maim," which like Beth-horon (xvi. 3, 5), was applied to two distinct but adjoining places—distinguished as "the upper" and "the lower." The tract in question was no doubt a mountain slope which had springs both on its higher and lower ground; possibly the modern *Kurmul*.

21–63. List of the towns of the tribe of Judah. These are arranged in four divisions, according to the natural features of the district; viz., those of the Negeb or south country (21–32); of "the valley," or "the plain" (*Shephelah*, 33–47); of "the mountains" (48–60); and of "the wilderness" (61, 62). Many of the identifications are still conjectural only.

21–32. The Negeb was for the most part rocky and arid, and cannot have been at any time very thickly peopled.

21. Kabzeel was the native place of Benaiah (2 Sam. xxiii. 20), who was famous as a slayer of lions. The Negeb was a principal haunt of these beasts.

24. Telem may be the Telaim of 1 Sam. xv. 4, where Saul mustered his army for the expedition against the Amalekites. It is possibly to be looked for at *El-Kuseir*, a spot where the various routes towards different parts of the Negeb converge, and which is occupied by the Arab tribe the *Dhullam*, a word identical with Telem in its consonants. Bealoth is probably the "Baalath-beer—Ramath of the south" (xix. 8), and was one of the towns afterwards assigned to the Simeonites. It is identified with the modern *Kurnub*.

25. *and Hezron which is Hazor*] In this verse are the names of two towns only, not of four. Two places bearing the common

26, 27 Hazor, Amam, and Shema, and Moladah, and Hazar-gaddah,
28 and Heshmon, and Beth-palet, and Hazar-shual, and Beer-
29, 30 sheba, and Bizjothjah, Baalah, and Iim, and Azem, and Elto-
31 lad, and Chesil, and Hormah, and [f]Ziklag, and Madmannah,
32 and Sansannah, and Lebaoth, and Shilhim, and Ain, and Rimmon: all the cities *are* twenty and nine, with their villages:
33, 34 ¶ *And* in the valley, [g]Eshtaol, and Zoreah, and Ashnah, and

[f] 1 Sam. 27. 6.
[g] ch. 19. 41.

---

topographical appellation, Hazor ("inclosure") are here mentioned and distinguished as "Hazor Hadattah" and "Kerioth-Hezron," otherwise termed Hazor, simply: the former has been identified by some with *El-Hudhera;* the latter is probably the modern *El-Kuryetein.* Kerioth, prefixed to a name, bespeaks military occupation, as Hazor points to pastoral pursuits. The place would therefore seem to be an ancient pastoral settlement which had been fortified by the Anakims, and called accordingly Kerioth; to which name the men of Judah, after they had captured it, added that of Hezron, in honour of one of their leading ancestors (cp. Gen. xlvi. 12; Ruth iv. 18). Kerioth was the home of Judas the traitor, if the ordinary derivation of Iscariot (= *ish K'rioth, i.e.* man of Kerioth) be accepted: St. Matt. x. 4.

26. Moladah is probably the modern *El-Milh,* and like Hazar-shual (*Berrishail* near Gaza) (= "inclosure of foxes") occurs (xix. 2, 3; 1 Chr. iv. 28), as a town belonging to Simeon, and (Neh. xi. 26, 27) as a place occupied by Jews after the captivity.

29–32. Baalah (xix. 3) is found in the modern *Deir-el-Belah,* near Gaza. Iim, *i.e.* "ruinous heaps" or "conical hills" (Num. xxi. 11 note) is by some connected with Azem; and the compound name, *Ije Azem,* is traced in El-Aujeh, in the country of the Azazimeh Arabs, in whose name the ancient Azem may perhaps be traced. Eltolad is connected with *Wady-el-Thoula,* in the extreme south of the Negeb. Chesil appears to be the town called Bethul (xix. 4), and probably the Bethel (1 Sam. xxx. 27) situated not far from Ziklag. The name Chesil (= "fool") was most likely bestowed by way of opprobrium (cp. the change of Bethel, house of God, into Bethaven, house of vanity, Hos. iv. 15). As Chesil signifies the group of stars known as Orion (cp. Job xxxviii. 31; Amos v. 8), probably it was the worship of the heavenly bodies in particular that was carried on here. Bethel may have been the ancient name, and the spot was perhaps the very one near Beer-sheba where Abraham planted a tamarisk tree (Gen. xxi. 33). The place is probably *El Khulasah,* the Elusa of ecclesiastical writers, situated some fifteen miles south-west of Beer-sheba. Jerome testifies to the fact, that the worship of Venus as the morning star was practised there, and Sozomen appears to be speaking of this place, when he mentions a Bethel (Βηθελία) in the territory of Gaza, populous and famous for an ancient and splendid temple. The site of Ziklag is uncertain. Madmannah and Sansannah correspond to Beth-marcaboth (= "house of chariots") and Hazar-susah (= "horse inclosure") in xix. 5 (1 Chr. iv. 31). The latter names point to two stations of passage on or near the high road between Egypt and Palestine, and are represented by the modern *Minyay* and *Wady-es-Suny,* on the caravan route south of Gaza. Shilhim or Sharuhen, (xix. 6), and Shaaraim (1 Chr. iv. 31) is traced in *Khirbet-es-Seram,* near El Aujeh. Ain and Rimmon were possibly originally two towns, but in process of time became so connected as to be treated as one name (Neh. xi. 29). The place is probably the present *Um-er-Rummamim, i.e.* "mother of pomegranates," a place about ten miles north of Beer-sheba.

32. *twenty and nine*] The A. V. gives thirty-four names. The difference is due either to the confusion by an early copyist of letters similar in form which were used as numerals; or to the separation in the A. V. of names which in the original were one (*e.g. v.* 25).

33–47. "The valley" or the Shephelah, is bounded on the south by the Negeb, on the west by the Mediterranean, on the north by the plain of Sharon, on the east by "the mountains" (*v.* 48). It is a well-defined district, of an undulating surface and highly fertile character, thickly dotted, even at the present time, with villages, which are for the most part situated on the different hills. The towns in this district, like those in the Negeb, are classed in four groups.

33–36. First group of fourteen towns; these belong to the north-eastern portion of the Shephelah. Eshtaol and Zoreah were afterwards assigned to the tribe of Dan, and inhabited by Danites (Judg. xiii. 25, xviii. 2, 8, 11). The latter place was the home of Samson (Judg. xiii. 2). It was one of the cities fortified by Rehoboam (2 Chr. xi. 10), and was re-occupied by the Jews after the captivity (Neh. xi. 29). It is probably the modern *Surah.* [Eshtaol has been identified with Eshua (Conder)]. Both places were in later times partly peopled by Judahites from Kirjath-jearim; perhaps after the departure of the colony of Danites for Dan-Laish. Zanoah is the present *Zanna,* not far from Surah. Socoh is the modern *Shuweikah.* Sharaim is perhaps to be sought in the modern *Zakariya.* Gederah ("wall"

35 Zanoah, and En-gannim, Tappuah, and Enam, Jarmuth, and
36 Adullam, Socoh, and Azekah, and Sharaim, and Adithaim, and
Gederah, [1] and Gederothaim; fourteen cities with their villages:
37, 38 Zenan, and Hadashah, and Migdal-gad, and Dilean, and
39 [h] Mizpeh, and Joktheel, Lachish, and Bozkath, and Eglon, [h] ch. 11. 3.
40, 41 and Cabbon, and Lahmam, and Kithlish, and Gederoth,
Beth-dagon, and Naamah, and Makkedah; sixteen cities with
42, 43 their villages: Libnah, and Ether, and Ashan, and Jiphtah,
44 and Ashnah, and Nezib, and Keilah, and Achzib, and Ma-
45 reshah; nine cities with their villages: Ekron, with her towns
46 and her villages: from Ekron even unto the sea, all that *lay*
47 [2] near Ashdod, with their villages: Ashdod with her towns and
her villages, Gaza with her towns and her villages, unto [i] the [i] ver. 4.
river of Egypt, and [k] the great sea, and the border *thereof*: [k] Num. 34. 6.
48, 49 ¶ And in the mountains, Shamir, and Jattir, and Socoh, and
50 Dannah, and Kirjath-sannah, which *is* Debir, and Anab,
51 and Eshtemoh, and Anim, [l] and Goshen, and Holon, and [l] ch. 10. 41. & 11. 16.
52 Giloh; eleven cities with their villages: Arab, and Dumah,
53 and Eshean, and [3] Janum, and Beth-tappuah, and Aphekah,
54 and Humtah, and [m] Kirjath-arba, which *is* Hebron, and Zior; [m] Gen. 13. 18.
55 nine cities with their villages: Maon, Carmel, and Ziph, and
56, 57 Juttah, and Jezreel, and Jokdeam, and Zanoah, Cain,
58 Gibeah, and Timnah; ten cities with their villages: Halhul,
59 Beth-zur, and Gedor, and Maarath, and Beth-anoth, and El-

[1] Or, *or*. [2] Heb. *by the place of*. [3] Or, *Janus*.

---

or "fortress") was a name borne with various terminations by several places.

37-41. Second group of towns, containing those in the middle portion of the Shephelah, and of which some only (x. 3, 10) can be identified.

42-44. Third group; towns in the south of the Shephelah. For Libnah see x. 29. Mareshah is believed to be near *Beit-jibrin*, the ancient *Eleutheropolis*.

45-47. Fourth group: the towns of the Philistine sea-coast: see xiii. 3.

48-60. This highland district extends from the Negeb on the south to Jerusalem, and is bounded by the Shephelah on the west, and the "Wilderness" (*vv.* 61, 62) on the east. The mountains, which are of limestone, rise to a height of near 3000 feet. At present, the highlands of Judah present a somewhat dreary and monotonous aspect. The peaks are for the most part barren, though crowned almost everywhere with the ruins of ancient towns, and bearing on their sides marks of former cultivation. Many of the valleys, especially towards the south, are, however, still very productive. The towns here enumerated are given in six groups.

48-51. First group: towns on the south-west. Dannah [is identified with *Idnah* (Conder)]. Jattir (*Attir*), and Eshtemoh (*Semua*) were priestly cities (xxi. 14; 1 Chr. vi. 57), and the place to which David, after routing the Amalekites, sent presents (1 Sam. xxx. 27, 28). Socoh is *Suweikeh*.

52-54. Second group of nine towns, situated somewhat to the north of the last-mentioned. Of these Dumah is perhaps the ruined village *Ed Daumeh*, in the neighbourhood of Hebron; and Beth-tappuah, *i.e.* "house of apples," *Teffuh*, a place which has still a good number of inhabitants, is conspicuous for its olive groves and vineyards, and bears on every side the traces of industry and thrift.

55-57. Third group; lying eastward of the towns named in the last two, and next to "the wilderness."

55. The four towns retain their ancient names with but little change. Maon (1 Sam. xxiii. 24, xxv. 2), the home of Nabal, is to be looked for in the conical hill, *Main*, the top of which is covered with ruins. It lies eight or nine miles south-east of Hebron. Carmel (1 Sam. xxv. 2), the modern *Kurmul*, is a little to the north of *Main*. The name belongs to more than one place (xii. 22). Ziph gave its name to "the wilderness" into which David fled from Saul (1 Sam. xxiii. 14).

58, 59. Fourth group. Towns north of the last mentioned, of which Beth-zur and Gedor are represented by *Beit-sur* and *Jedur*.

After *v.* 59 follows in the Greek version a fifth group of eleven towns, which appears to have dropped in very ancient times out of the Hebrew text, probably because some transcriber passed unawares from the word "villages" at the end of *v.* 59, to the same word at the end of the missing passage. The omitted group contains the towns of an important, well-known, and populous district

60 tekon; six cities with their villages: [n]Kirjath-baal, which *is*
Kirjath-jearim, and Rabbah; two cities with their villages:
61, 62 in the wilderness, Beth-arabah, Middin, and Secacah, and
Nibshan, and the city of Salt, and Engedi; six cities with their
63 villages. ¶ As for the Jebusites the inhabitants of Jerusalem,
[o]the children of Judah could not drive them out: [p]but the
Jebusites dwell with the children of Judah at Jerusalem unto
this day.
Chap. 16. AND the lot of the children of Joseph [1]fell from Jordan
by Jericho, unto the water of Jericho on the east, to the wilderness that goeth up from Jericho throughout mount Beth-el,
2 and goeth out from Beth-el to [a]Luz, and passeth along unto the
3 borders of Archi to Ataroth, and goeth down westward to the
coast of Japhleti, [b]unto the coast of Beth-horon the nether, and
4 to [c]Gezer: and the goings out thereof are at the sea. [d]So the
children of Joseph, Manasseh and Ephraim, took their inhe-
5 ritance. ¶ And the border of the children of Ephraim according
to their families was *thus:* even the border of their inheritance

[n] ch. 9. 17.
[o] See Judg. 1. 8. 21. 2 Sam. 5. 6.
[p] Judg. 1. 21.
[a] Gen. 28. 19. Judg. 1. 26.
[b] ch. 10. 10. 2 Chr. 8. 5.
[c] ch. 10. 33. 1 Kin. 9. 15.
[d] ch. 17. 14.

[1] Heb. *went forth* (*i.e.*, out of the urn).

lying immediately south of Jerusalem, and containing such towns as Tekoah (2 Sam. xiv. 2; Neh. iii. 5, 27; Amos i. 1); Bethlehem, the native town of David and of Christ (Gen. xxxv. 19); and Aetan, a Grecised form of Etam (2 Chr. xi. 6).

61, 62. This district, including the towns in "the wilderness," the scene of David's wanderings (1 Sam. xxiii. 24; Ps. lxiii. title), and of the preaching of the Baptist (Matt. iii. 1), and perhaps of our Lord's temptation (Matt. iv.), extended from the northern limit of Judah along the Dead Sea to the Negeb; it was bounded on the west by that part of "the mountains" or highlands of Judah, which adjoined Bethlehem and Maon. It abounds in limestone rocks, perforated by numerous caverns, and often of fantastic shapes. It is badly supplied with water, and hence is for the most part barren, though affording in many parts, now quite desolate, clear tokens of former cultivation. It contained only a thin population in the days of Joshua.

62. "The city of Salt" is not mentioned elsewhere, but was no doubt connected with "the valley of salt" (2 Sam. viii. 13). The name itself, and the mention of En-gedi (Gen. xiv. 7 note) suggest that its site must be looked for near the Dead Sea.

XVI. This and xvii. are closely connected, and assign the boundaries of "the children of Joseph," *i.e* of the kindred tribes of Ephraim and Manasseh. These two tribes, or more strictly speaking, the tribe of Ephraim and the half tribe of Manasseh, drew one lot only, no doubt, because it was all along intended that their inheritances should be adjacent. These chapters accordingly describe (1) the southern boundary of the whole territory of the children of Joseph (xvi. 1–4); (2) the limits of Ephraim in particular (xvi. 5–10) (3); those of Manasseh (xvii. 1–13); and (4) the discontent of the descendants of Joseph with their inheritance is recorded, together with Joshua's answer to their complaints (xvii. 14–18).

The territory allotted to these two powerful tribes comprises the central and, in every way, the choicest part of Canaan west of the Jordan. The hills of this district, making up what is called (xx. 7) "Mount Ephraim," are less high and far less barren than those of Judah; the water supply is much larger; and the very rich and fertile plains of Sharon and Esdraelon are left between the rocky fastnesses of Benjamin on the south and the high lands of Galilee belonging to Issachar on the north.

1. *to the wilderness*] Strike out "to," for the word is in apposition to "lot." The wilderness is (xviii. 12) "the wilderness of Bethaven."

2. *of Archi*] Read **"of the Archite,"** also a designation of David's friend Hushai (2 Sam. xv. 32; xvi. 16, &c.). The word is derived from Erech (Gen. x. 10). But whether there was in the neighbourhood of Bethel a place bearing this Babylonian name, or whether a colony from the East had settled in this spot and brought the name with them, is unknown.

Ataroth] Called (*v.* 5 and xviii. 13) Ataroth-adar (= "crowns of fame or greatness") perhaps to distinguish it from two other places bearing the same name but situated on the other side of Jordan, in the territory of Gad (Num. xxxii. 34). It is identified with Atara, near the road from Jerusalem to Nablous.

3. *of Japhleti*] Rather **"of the Japhletite."** All history of the name is lost.

5–8. From the abrupt manner in which the statements are introduced, as well as from their imperfect character, there is

on the east side was [e]Ataroth-addar, [f]unto Beth-horon the [e] ch. 18. 13.
6 upper; and the border went out toward the sea to [g]Michmethah [f] 2 Chr. 8. 5. [g] ch. 17. 7.
on the north side; and the border went about eastward unto
7 Taanath-shiloh, and passed by it on the east to Janohah; and
it went down from Janohah to Ataroth, [h]and to Naarath, and [h] 1 Chr. 7.
8 came to Jericho, and went out at Jordan. The border went out 28.
from Tappuah westward unto the [i]river Kanah; and the goings [i] ch. 17. 9.
out thereof were at the sea. This *is* the inheritance of the tribe
9 of the children of Ephraim by their families. And [k]the separate [k] ch. 17. 9.
cities for the children of Ephraim *were* among the inheritance
of the children of Manasseh, all the cities with their villages.
10 [l]And they drave not out the Canaanites that dwelt in Gezer: [l] Judg. 1. 29. See 1 Kin.
but the Canaanites dwell among the Ephraimites unto this day, 9. 16.
and serve under tribute.

CHAP. 17. THERE was also a lot for the tribe of Manasseh; for he
was the [a]firstborn of Joseph; *to wit*, for [b]Machir the firstborn [a] Gen. 41. 51.
of Manasseh, the father of Gilead: because he was a man of & 46. 20. [b] Gen. 50. 23.
2 war, therefore he had [c]Gilead and Bashan. There was also *a lot* [c] Deut. 3. 15.
for [d]the rest of the children of Manasseh by their families; [e]for [d] Num. 26. 29–32.
the children of [1]Abiezer, and for the children of Helek, [f]and for [e] 1 Chr. 7. 18.
the children of Asriel, and for the children of Shechem, [g]and for [f] Num. 26. 31.
the children of Hepher, and for the children of Shemida: these [g] Num. 26. 32.
were the male children of Manasseh the son of Joseph by their
3 families. ¶But [h]Zelophehad, the son of Hepher, the son of [h] Num. 26.
Gilead, the son of Machir, the son of Manasseh, had no sons, 33. & 27. 1.
but daughters: and these *are* the names of his daughters, & 36. 2.
4 Mahlah, and Noah, Hoglah, Milcah, and Tirzah. And they
came near before [i]Eleazar the priest, and before Joshua the son [i] ch. 14. 1.
of Nun, and before the princes, saying, [k]The LORD commanded [k] Num. 27.
Moses to give us an inheritance among our brethren. Therefore 6, 7.
according to the commandment of the LORD he gave them an
5 inheritance among the brethren of their father. And there fell
ten portions to Manasseh, beside the land of Gilead and Bashan,
6 which *were* on the other side Jordan; because the daughters of
Manasseh had an inheritance among his sons: and the rest of
7 Manasseh's sons had the land of Gilead. ¶And the coast of
Manasseh was from Asher to [l]Michmethah, that *lieth* before [l] ch. 16. 6.

[1] Num. 26. 30. *Jeezer.*

probability in the conjecture that some words have, in these verses, fallen out of the text. Few of the places are known for certain.

9. The verb "were," introduced by A.V. in this verse should be omitted; and the full stop after *v.* 8 replaced by a colon. The purport of *v.* 9 is simply to add to the inheritance of Ephraim, defined by the preceding context, "the separate cities" or more properly "single cities" which were allotted to them in addition within the borders of Manasseh. The reasons for granting these additional cities to the Ephraimites can only be conjectured. Perhaps the territory assigned to this numerous tribe proved on experiment to be too small; and therefore some towns, which are named in 1 Chr. vii. 29, were given to them from the kindred Manassites, the latter being recompensed (xvii. 11 note) at the expense of Issachar and Asher.

XVII. **1.** Manasseh, as the "first-born," was to receive not only the territory on the east of Jordan won by the valour of the Machirites, but also a portion with the other tribes on the west of Jordan, the Holy Land of Promise strictly so called. Thus, though Ephraim took precedence of Manasseh, according to the prediction of Joseph (Gen. xlviii. 20), yet Manasseh received "the double portion" which was the peculiar privilege of the first-born (Deut. xxi. 17).

2. *for the rest*, &c.] *i.e.* for those who were not settled on the east of Jordan.

5. *ten portions*] *i.e.* five for the five families descended from the male children of Gilead, and five others for the five daughters of Zelophehad, who represented the sixth family, the Hepherites.

7. *Asher*] Not the tribe so called, but a place somewhere towards the eastern end of the boundary line here drawn: perhaps

Shechem; and the border went along on the right hand unto
8 the inhabitants of En-tappuah. *Now* Manasseh had the land of
[m] ch. 16. 8. Tappuah: but [m]Tappuah on the border of Manasseh *belonged* to
[n] ch. 16. 8. 9 the children of Ephraim; and the coast descended [n]unto the
[o] ch. 16. 9. [1]river Kanah, southward of the river: [o]these cities of Ephraim
are among the cities of Manasseh: the coast of Manasseh also
was on the north side of the river, and the outgoings of it were
10 at the sea: southward *it was* Ephraim's, and northward *it was*
Manasseh's, and the sea is his border; and they met together in
[p] 1 Chr. 7. 29. 11 Asher on the north, and in Issachar on the east. [p]And Manasseh
[q] 1 Sam. 31. 10. had in Issachar and in Asher [q]Beth-shean and her towns, and
1 Kin. 4. 12. Ibleam and her towns, and the inhabitants of Dor and her
towns, and the inhabitants of Endor and her towns, and the inhabitants of Taanach and her towns, and the inhabitants of
[r] Judg. 1. 27, 28. 12 Megiddo and her towns, *even* three countries. Yet [r]the children
of Manasseh could not drive out *the inhabitants of* those cities;
13 but the Canaanites would dwell in that land. Yet it came to
pass, when the children of Israel were waxen strong, that they
[s] ch. 16. 10. put the Canaanites to [s]tribute; but did not utterly drive them
[t] ch. 16. 4. 14 out. ¶ [t]And the children of Joseph spake unto Joshua, saying,
[u] Gen. 48. 22. Why hast thou given me *but* [u]one lot and one portion to inherit,
[x] Gen. 48. 19. seeing I *am* [x]a great people, forasmuch as the LORD hath blessed
Num. 26. 34, 37. 15 me hitherto? And Joshua answered them, If thou *be* a great

[1] Or, *brook of reeds*.

Teyasir, on the road from Sichem to Beth-shean.

9. *these cities*, &c.] The text is possibly corrupt. The intention seems to be to state that the cities lying south of the river, though within the limits of Manasseh, were in fact made over to Ephraim, and were amongst the "separate cities" (xvi. 9). On the contrary, the north bank of the river, both land and towns, belonged to Manasseh exclusively.

10. *southward*] *i.e.* of the river Kanah.

Render, "**they** (*i.e.* the two kindred tribes of Ephraim and Manasseh, the northern border being treated here as common to the two) **reached unto Asher.**" (See the map.) The northern border is only indicated in general terms, perhaps because the Israelites were not yet completely masters of this part of the country, and so had not precisely determined it.

11. Perhaps Beth-shean (in Issachar) and the other five towns (in Asher) were given to the Manassites in compensation for towns in the Manassite territory allotted to the Ephraimites. (See *v.* 9. Cp. xxi. 9.) To the wall of Beth-shean, or Bethshan (*Beisan*, about 5 miles west of the Jordan), the bodies of Saul and his sons were fastened by the Philistines after the battle on Mount Gilboa. After the exile it received the Greek name of Scythopolis, perhaps because it was principally tenanted by a rude and heathen population, styled in contempt Scythians. It was a border city of Galilee, and the chief town of the Decapolis. In Christian times it was the see of a bishop, who is enumerated as present at Nicæa and other Councils of the Church.

Ibleam (Bileam, 1 Chr. vi. 70), perhaps *Jelameh*, was a Levitical town (xxi. 25 note). Near this place Ahaziah was mortally wounded by Jehu (2 K. ix. 27), and fled to Megiddo, which was no doubt not far distant.

three countries] Rather "the three hills." The district belonging to the last-mentioned three towns had a common name, derived no doubt from its natural features, and was called "the three hills." Cp. Decapolis, Tripolis, &c.

14. *seeing I am a great people*] The assertion can hardly have been warranted by facts, for at the census (Num. xxvi.) the two tribes of Manasseh and Ephraim together were not greatly more numerous than the single tribe of Judah; and now that half the Manassites were provided for on the eastern side of Jordan, the remaining children of Joseph could hardly be stronger than the Danites or the Issacharites. The children of Joseph seem therefore to exhibit here that arrogant and jealous spirit which elsewhere characterises their conduct (Judg. viii. 1, xii. 1; 2 Sam. xix. 41; 2 Chr. xxviii. 7 &c.). A glance at the map shows that their complaint was in itself unreasonable. Their territory, which measured about 55 miles by 70, was at least as large in proportion to their numbers as that of any other tribe, and moreover comprehended some of the most fertile of the whole promised land.

15. Joshua was himself of the tribe of Ephraim, but far from supporting the de-

people, *then* get thee up to the wood *country*, and cut down for
thyself there in the land of the Perizzites and of the [1]giants, if
16 mount Ephraim be too narrow for thee. And the children of
Joseph said, The hill is not enough for us: and all the Canaanites
that dwell in the land of the valley have [y]chariots of iron, *both* [y] Judg. 1. 19 & 4. 3.
they who *are* of Beth-shean and her towns, and *they* who *are* [z]of [z] ch. 19. 18.
17 the valley of Jezreel. And Joshua spake unto the house of 1 Kin. 18.
Joseph, *even* to Ephraim and to Manasseh, saying, Thou *art* a 2 Kin. 9. &
great people, and hast great power: thou shalt not have one lot 10.
18 *only*: but the mountain shall be thine; for it *is* a wood, and
thou shalt cut it down: and the outgoings of it shall be thine:
for thou shalt drive out the Canaanites, [a]though they have iron [a] Deut. 20. 1.
chariots, *and* though they *be* strong.

Chap. 18. AND the whole congregation of the children of Israel
assembled together [a]at Shiloh, and [b]set up the tabernacle of the [a] Judg. 21.
congregation there. And the land was subdued before them. 19.
2 ¶ And there remained among the children of Israel seven tribes, [b] Judg. 18. 31.
3 which had not yet received their inheritance. And Joshua said 1 Sam. 1. 24.
unto the children of Israel, [c]How long *are* ye slack to go to & 4. 3, 4.
possess the land, which the LORD God of your fathers hath given [c] Judg. 18. 9.

[1] Or, *Rephaims*, Gen. 14. 5. & 15. 20.

---

mands of his kinsmen he reproves them, and calls upon them to make good their great words by corresponding deeds of valour. He bids them clear the country of its woods and thus make room for settling their people. The "wood country" means probably the range which runs along the northern border of Manasseh, and which connects the mountains of Gilboa with Carmel. Mount Ephraim, (a name perhaps used by anticipation) called "the hill" (*v.* 16), and "the mountain of Israel" (xi. 16), is the eastern portion of the territory of Ephraim and Manasseh extending towards the Jordan. This was a hilly, though by no means barren, district.

16. The possession by the Canaanites of chariots strengthened and tipped with iron, such as were used by the Egyptians (Ex. xiv. 7), is named here by the children of Joseph as a reason why they could not possess themselves of the plains. "The valley of Jezreel" is the broad low valley which sweeps from *Zerin* between the mountains of Gilboa and the range of little Hermon eastward down to the Jordan. It was most likely in this valley that the host of the Midianites was encamped, when attacked by Gideon (Judg. vii. 1, 8). The great plain of Jezreel, called the plain of Esdraelon (Esdrelom, Judith i. 8), extends from Carmel on the west to the hills of Gilboa, little Hermon, and Tabor on the east, a distance of full sixteen miles; and its breadth between the rocky mass of southern Palestine and the bolder mountains of Galilee on the north, is about twelve miles. Its position as well as its open area make it the natural battle-field of Palestine.

17. *thou shalt not have one lot only*] *i.e.* by dispossessing the Canaanites, thou shalt double the portion of land at thy disposal. The "but" with which A. V. begins *v.* 18 should be "**for.**"

XVIII. **1.** After all overt resistance was overcome, the Tabernacle with its sacred contents was removed from its place of safety at Gilgal, in a corner of the land near the Jordan, to a central place, Shiloh, the modern *Seilun*, which is two or three miles east of the main road, and rather more than half way between Jerusalem and Nablous. Its choice as the national Sanctuary may indeed have been determined by Joshua, no doubt under Divine direction (Deut. xii. 11), because of its insignificance, in order to avoid local jealousies, as well as because of its position in the very centre of the whole land, and perhaps also because of its seclusion. Its very name (= "rest") was probably bestowed at this juncture when God had given the people rest from their enemies. The Tabernacle with its contents continued at Shiloh during the whole period of the Judges, until its capture by the Philistines. Shiloh (1 Sam. iv. 3, 4) seems to have fallen into desolation at an early date (Jer. vii. 12, xxvi. 6).

2. Two tribes and a half had already received their portions on the east of Jordan; Judah, Ephraim, and the remaining half of Manasseh had also been provided for (xv.–xvii.). Thus there remained still seven tribes out of the twelve to be settled in their homes.

3. This backwardness probably arose from the indisposition of the people to abandon the nomad life in which they had been born and bred, and to settle in fixed abodes, and perhaps also from a dislike of the exterminating warfare incidental to a complete dispossessing of the Canaanites.

4 you? Give out from among you three men for *each* tribe: and
I will send them, and they shall rise, and go through the land,
and describe it according to the inheritance of them; and they
5 shall come *again* to me. And they shall divide it into seven
parts: [d]Judah shall abide in their coast on the south, and [e]the
6 house of Joseph shall abide in their coasts on the north. Ye
shall therefore describe the land *into* seven parts, and bring *the*
description hither to me, [f]that I may cast lots for you here be-
7 fore the LORD our God. [g]But the Levites have no part among
you; for the priesthood of the LORD *is* their inheritance: [h]and
Gad, and Reuben, and half the tribe of Manasseh, have received
their inheritance beyond Jordan on the east, which Moses the
8 servant of the LORD gave them. And the men arose and went
away: and Joshua charged them that went to describe the land,
saying, Go and walk through the land, and describe it, and
come again to me, that I may here cast lots for you before the
9 LORD in Shiloh. And the men went and passed through the
land, and described it by cities into seven parts in a book, and
10 came *again* to Joshua to the host at Shiloh. And Joshua cast
lots for them in Shiloh before the LORD: and there Joshua
divided the land unto the children of Israel according to their
11 divisions. ¶ And the lot of the tribe of the children of Benjamin came up according to their families: and the coast of their
lot came forth between the children of Judah and the children
12 of Joseph. [i]And their border on the north side was from
Jordan; and the border went up to the side of Jericho on the
north side, and went up through the mountains westward; and
the goings out thereof were at the wilderness of Beth-aven.
13 And the border went over from thence toward Luz, to the side of
Luz, [k]which *is* Beth-el, southward; and the border descended to
Ataroth-adar, near the hill that *lieth* on the south side [l]of the
14 nether Beth-horon. And the border was drawn *thence*, and compassed the corner of the sea southward, from the hill that *lieth*
before Beth-horon southward; and the goings out thereof were
at [m]Kirjath-baal, which *is* Kirjath-jearim, a city of the children
15 of Judah: this *was* the west quarter. And the south quarter
was from the end of Kirjath-jearim, and the border went out on
16 the west, and went out to [n]the well of waters of Nephtoah: and
the border came down to the end of the mountain that *lieth*
before [o]the valley of the son of Hinnom, *and* which *is* in the
valley of the giants on the north, and descended to the valley of
Hinnom, to the side of Jebusi on the south, and descended to
17 [p]En-rogel, and was drawn from the north, and went forth to
En-shemesh, and went forth toward Geliloth, which *is* over
against the going up of Adummim, and descended to [q]the stone
18 of Bohan the son of Reuben, and passed along toward the side
over against [r][1]Arabah northward, and went down unto Arabah:

[d] ch. 15. 1.
[e] ch. 16. 1, 4.
[f] ch. 14. 2. ver. 10.
[g] ch. 13. 33.
[h] ch. 13. 8.
[i] See ch. 16. 1.
[k] Gen. 28. 19. Judg. 1. 23.
[l] ch. 16. 3.
[m] See ch. 15. 9.
[n] ch. 15. 9.
[o] ch. 15. 8.
[p] ch. 15. 7.
[q] ch. 15. 6.
[r] ch. 15. 6.

[1] Or, *The plain.*

---

4. *three men for each tribe*] *i.e.* twenty-one in all. Their duty would be to describe the land, especially with reference to the cities it contained (*v.* 9), that Joshua might have the means of making a first apportionment amongst the tribes according to their varying numbers.

10. *cast lots*] See xiv. 2 note.

11–28. See marg. reff. There are many indications found in this and the next chapter that the text is in great disorder, and many of the places are still unknown.

14. *and compassed the corner*, &c.] Render **"and turned on the west side southward."** The meaning is, that at lower Beth-horon the northern boundary-line of Benjamin curved round and ran southward,—Beth-horon being its extreme westerly point.

19 and the border passed along to the side of Beth-hoglah northward: and the outgoings of the border were at the north [1] bay of
the salt sea at the south end of Jordan: this *was* the south coast.
20 And Jordan was the border of it on the east side. ¶ This *was*
the inheritance of the children of Benjamin, by the coasts thereof
21 round about, according to their families. ¶ Now the cities of
the tribe of the children of Benjamin according to their families
22 were Jericho, and Beth-hoglah, and the valley of Keziz, and
23 Beth-arabah, and Zemaraim, and Beth-el, and Avim, and
24 Parah, and Ophrah, and Chephar-haammonai, and Ophni, and
25 Gaba; twelve cities with their villages: Gibeon, and Ramah,
26, 27 and Beeroth, and Mizpeh, and Chephirah, and Mozah, and
28 Rekem, and Irpeel, and Taralah, and Zelah, Eleph, and [s] Jebusi,
which *is* Jerusalem, Gibeath, *and* Kirjath; fourteen cities with
their villages. This *is* the inheritance of the children of Benjamin according to their families.

[s] ch. 15. 8.

Chap. 19. AND the second lot came forth to Simeon, *even* for the
tribe of the children of Simeon according to their families: [a] and
their inheritance was within the inheritance of the children of
2 Judah. And [b] they had in their inheritance Beer-sheba, and
3 Sheba, and Moladah, and Hazar-shual, and Balah, and Azem,
4, 5 and Eltolad, and Bethul, and Hormah, and Ziklag, and Beth-
6 marcaboth, and Hazar-susah, and Beth-lebaoth, and Sharuhen;
7 thirteen cities and their villages: Ain, Remmon, and Ether, and
8 Ashan; four cities and their villages: and all the villages that
were round about these cities to Baalath-beer, Ramath of the
south. This *is* the inheritance of the tribe of the children of
9 Simeon according to their families. Out of the portion of the
children of Judah *was* the inheritance of the children of Simeon:

[a] ver. 9.

[b] 1 Chr. 4. 28. ch. 15. 26-32, 42.

[1] Heb. *tongue*.

21. The "Valley of Keziz," or *Emek-Keziz*, is perhaps the *Wady el Kaziz*, at no great distance east of Jerusalem.

22. Zemaraim, *i.e.* "two wooded hills," is supposed to be the ruins called *Es-Sumrah*, on the road from Jerusalem to Jericho.

23. Ophrah (xv. 9 note), to be distinguished here and in 1 Sam. xiii. 17 from the Ophrah of Judg. vi. 11, is probably the Ephrain of 2 Chr. xiii. 19, and the Ephraim of John xi. 54. It is conjecturally identified with *Et-Taiyibeh*, on the road from Jerusalem to Bethel.

24. *Gaba*] This name, like Gibeah, Gibeon, &c. (ix. 3), indicates a town placed on a hill, and occurs repeatedly in various forms in the topography of Palestine. Gaba is the Gibeah of 1 Sam. xiii. 15, 16, xiv. 5, where the Hebrew has Geba, which is undoubtedly the correct reading throughout. The city was one of those assigned to the Levites (xxi. 17), and lay on the northern border of Judah. It is identified with the modern *Jeba*, lying on the side of a deep ravine opposite to Michmash (*Mukhmas*). The famous "Gibeah of Saul," or "Gibeah of Benjamin" (the Gibeath of *v.* 28) lay at no great distance south-west of Geba, on the high road from Jerusalem to Bethel, and is probably to be looked for in the lofty and isolated *Tuleil-el-Ful*.

25. *Ramah*] *i.e.* "lofty;" probably the native town and abode of Samuel (1 Sam. i. 19, xxv. 1). Its exact site is uncertain.

26. *Mizpeh*] See xi. 3. Not the Mizpeh of xv. 38, but the place where Samuel judged the people and called them together for the election of a king (1 Sam. vii. 5–16, x. 17). In the Chaldæan times it was the residence of Gedaliah (2 K. xxv. 22: Jer. xl. 14). Its site is identified with *Neby Samwil*, about five miles north-west of Jerusalem.

XIX. 1-9. The inheritance of Simeon was taken out of the portion of Judah, which proved on experience to be larger than the numbers of that tribe required. The Simeonite territory is described by its towns, of which fourteen were in the Negeb, and four others (*v.* 7) partly in the Negeb and partly in "the valley." On the narrow confines here assigned to Simeon, and its insignificant position altogether amongst the Twelve Tribes, see Deut. xxxiii. 6 note.

6. *thirteen*] Fourteen names have been given. The error is probably due to the use of letters for numbers, which has led to many similar mistakes in other places (see xv. 32).

for the part of the children of Judah was too much for them:
[c ver. 1.] [c]therefore the children of Simeon had their inheritance within
10 the inheritance of them. ¶And the third lot came up for the
children of Zebulun according to their families: and the border
[d Gen. 49. 13.] 11 of their inheritance was unto Sarid: [d]and their border went up
toward the sea, and Maralah, and reached to Dabbasheth, and
[e ch. 12. 22.] 12 reached to the river that *is* [e]before Jokneam; and turned from
Sarid eastward toward the sunrising unto the border of Chisloth-tabor,
and then goeth out to Daberath, and goeth up to Japhia,
13 and from thence passeth on along on the east to Gittah-hepher,
to Ittah-kazin, and goeth out to Remmon-[1]methoar to Neah;
14 and the border compasseth it on the north side to Hannathon:
15 and the outgoings thereof are in the valley of Jiphthah-el: and
Kattath, and Nahallal, and Shimron, and Idalah, and Beth-
16 lehem: twelve cities with their villages. This *is* the inheritance
of the children of Zebulun according to their families, these
17 cities with their villages. ¶*And* the fourth lot came out to
Issachar, for the children of Issachar according to their families.
18 And their border was toward Jezreel, and Chesulloth, and
19, 20 Shunem, and Haphraim, and Shihon, and Anaharath, and
21 Rabbith, and Kishion, and Abez, and Remeth, and En-gan-
22 nim, and En-haddah, and Beth-pazzez; and the coast reacheth to
Tabor, and Shahazimah, and Beth-shemesh; and the outgoings
of their border were at Jordan: sixteen cities with their villages.
23 This *is* the inheritance of the tribe of the children of Issachar
24 according to their families, the cities and their villages. ¶And
the fifth lot came out for the tribe of the children of Asher

[1] Or, *which is drawn.*

10. Sarid, not yet identified, was evidently a leading topographical point on the south frontier of Zebulun. The boundary passed westward until it touched the Kishon, near *Tell Kaimon* (xii. 22 note), and thence turned northward, leaving Carmel, which belonged to Asher, on its west. The territory of Zebulun accordingly would not anywhere reach to the Mediterranean, though its eastern side abutted on the sea of Galilee, and gave the tribe those "outgoings" attributed to it in the Blessing of Moses (Deut. xxxiii. 18). Daberath (*v.* 12) is probably *Deburieh*.

13. Gittah (or Gath)-hepher, the birthplace of the prophet Jonah (2 K. xiv. 25), is probably the modern village of *El-Meshhad*, where the tomb of the prophet is still shown, a short way from Nazareth, on the road to Tiberias.

Remmon-methoar to Neah] Read "**and goeth out to Remmon, which reacheth to Neah.**" (See margin.) Rimmon, a Levitical city (xxi. 35; 1 Chr. vi. 77) is probably the modern *Rummaneh*, in the plain of *El Buttauf*, about six miles north of Nazareth.

14. Hannathon, more properly Channathon, has been supposed by some to be the Cana of Galilee of the New Testament, and Jiphthah-el is probably the present *Jefat;* the *Jotapata* of Roman times, which was so long and valiantly defended by Josephus against the legions of Vespasian. The "Valley" is the *Wady Abilin;* and Bethlehem (*v.* 15) is the present miserable village of *Beit-Lahin*.

15. *twelve cities*] Only five have been mentioned, and the names in the verses preceding are apparently not names of Zebulonite cities, but merely of points in or near the boundary line. It would therefore appear that seven names have disappeared from the text, and perhaps also the definition of the western frontier.

18. Jezreel and its famous and fertile plain are the choicest part of the inheritance of Issachar (xvii. 16).

Shunem] Here the Philistines pitched before the battle of Gilboa (1 Sam. xxviii. 4). The place is also known as the home of Abishag (1 K. i. 3), and in connection with Elisha (2 K. iv. 8, viii. 1). It is identified with *Solam* [or, Sulem], a small and poor village on the slope of Little Hermon.

21. *En-gannim*] i.e. "fountain of gardens;" also a Levitical city (xxi. 29), and called Anem (1 Chr. vi. 73), the modern *Jenin*, a place on the main road from Jerusalem to Nazareth, just where it enters the plain of Jezreel. Many of the places enumerated in these verses are not known. Tabor (*v.* 22) is perhaps not the famous mountain, but the town on it of the same name (1 Chr. vi. 77), given up to the Levites. Beth-shemesh (perhaps *Bessum*) is

25 according to their families. And their border was Helkath, and
26 Hali, and Beten, and Achshaph, and Alammelech, and Amad,
and Misheal; and reacheth to Carmel westward, and to Shihor-
27 libnath; and turneth toward the sunrising to Beth-dagon, and
reacheth to Zebulun, and to the valley of Jiphthah-el toward
the north side of Beth-emek, and Neiel, and goeth out to Cabul
28 on the left hand, and Hebron, and Rehob, and Hammon, and
29 Kanah, [f] *even* unto great Zidon; and *then* the coast turneth to
Ramah, and to the strong city [1]Tyre; and the coast turneth to
Hosah; and the outgoings thereof are at the sea from the coast
30 to [g]Achzib: Ummah also, and Aphek, and Rehob: twenty and
31 two cities with their villages. This *is* the inheritance of the
tribe of the children of Asher according to their families, these
32 cities with their villages. ¶ The sixth lot came out to the
children of Naphtali, *even* for the children of Naphtali according
33 to their families. And their coast was from Heleph, from Allon
to Zaanannim, and Adami, Nekeb, and Jabneel, unto Lakum;
34 and the outgoings thereof were at Jordan: and *then* [h]the coast
turneth westward to Aznoth-tabor, and goeth out from thence
to Hukkok, and reacheth to Zebulun on the south side, and
reacheth to Asher on the west side, and to Judah upon Jordan
35 toward the sunrising. And the fenced cities *are* Ziddim, Zer,

[f] ch. 11. 8. Judg. 1. 31.

[g] Gen. 38. 5. Judg. 1. 31. Mic. 1. 14.

[h] Deut. 33. 23.

[1] Heb. *Tzor*, 2 Sam. 5. 11.

not the same as Beth-shemesh of Judah (xv. 10), nor of Naphtali (*v.* 38).

25, 26. Helkath, a Levitical town (xxi. 31), is probably *Yerka*, a village about seven or eight miles north-west of Acre, in a Wady of the same name. Alammelech was in the *Wady Melik*, which joins the Kishon from the north-east, not far from the sea.

Shihor-libnath] *i.e.* "black-white." The two words are now generally admitted to be the name of a river, probably the modern *Nahr Zerka*, or Blue River, which reaches the sea about 8 miles south of Dor, and whose name has a correspondence both to black and white. Possibly we have in the occurrence of the term Shihor here a trace of the intercourse, which was close and continuous in ancient times, between Phœnicia and Egypt (xiii. 3). Cabul (*v.* 27) still retains its ancient name;—it lies between four and five miles west of Jotapata and about ten miles south-east of Acre.

28–30. These verses refer to the northern portion of the territory of Asher, on the Phœnician frontier. Some names may have dropped out of the text, the number (*v.* 30) not tallying with the catalogue. Ramah still retains its ancient name, and lies about twelve miles south-east of Tyre. Achzib is the modern *Zib*, on the coast, eight or nine miles north of Acre.

33. *from Allon to Zaanannim*] Render **"from the oak forest at Zaanannim."** From Judg. iv. 11 it appears that this oak or oak-forest was near Kedesh.

Adami, Nekeb] Render **"Adami of the Pass."** Possibly the ancient *Deir el Ahmar* ("red cloister"), which derives its name from the colour of the soil in the neighbourhood, as perhaps Adami did. The spot lies about eight miles north-west of Baalbek.

34. *Aznoth-tabor*] This place (= "ears of Tabor") was no doubt in the neighbourhood of Mount Tabor—probably on the eastern slope; and Hukkok on the western slope.

to Judah upon Jordan] *i.e.* to the "Havoth-jair" (Num. xxxii. 41), which were on the opposite side of Jordan. Jair, from whom these towns or villages were named, traced his ancestry in the male line through Hezron to Judah (Num. xxvii. 1); and it is likely that he was assisted by large numbers of his kinsmen of that tribe in his rapid conquest of Bashan. Hence the Havoth-jair were, in all likelihood, largely colonised by Judahites, especially perhaps that portion of them nearest the Jordan. Thus that part of the river and its valley adjacent to these settlements was spoken of as "Judah upon Jordan," or more literally "Judah of the Jordan" (cp. Num. xxii. 1).

35–38. The number of the fortified cities of Naphtali is remarkable, though it does not tally with the catalogue. It was no doubt good policy to protect the northern frontier by a belt of fortresses, as the south was protected by the fenced cities of Judah. Hammath, a Levitical city (cp. xxi. 32; 1 Chr. vi. 76), is not to be confounded with the Hamath on the north-eastern frontier of the land (Num. xiii. 21). The name (from a root signifying "to be warm") probably indicates that hot springs existed here; and is perhaps rightly traced in

36 and Hammath, Rakkath, and Chinnereth, and Adamah, and
37 Ramah, and Hazor, and Kedesh, and Edrei, and En-hazor,
38 and Iron, and Migdal-el, Horem, and Beth-anath, and Beth-
39 shemesh; nineteen cities with their villages. This *is* the inheritance of the tribe of the children of Naphtali according to
40 their families, the cities and their villages. ¶ *And* the seventh
lot came out for the tribe of the children of Dan according to
41 their families. And the coast of their inheritance was Zorah,
42 and Eshtaol, and Ir-shemesh, and [i]Shaalabbin, and Ajalon, and
43, 44 Jethlah, and Elon, and Thimnathah, and Ekron, and Eltekeh,
45 and Gibbethon, and Baalath, and Jehud, and Bene-berak, and
46 Gath-rimmon, and Me-jarkon, and Rakkon, with the border
47 [1]before [2]Japho. And [k]the coast of the children of Dan went
out *too little* for them: therefore the children of Dan went up to
fight against Leshem, and took it, and smote it with the edge
of the sword, and possessed it, and dwelt therein, and called
48 Leshem, [l]Dan, after the name of Dan their father. This *is* the
inheritance of the tribe of the children of Dan according to their
49 families, these cities with their villages. ¶ When they had
made an end of dividing the land for inheritance by their coasts,
the children of Israel gave an inheritance to Joshua the son of
50 Nun among them: according to the word of the LORD they gave
him the city which he asked, *even* [m]Timnath-[n]serah in mount
51 Ephraim: and he built the city, and dwelt therein. ¶ [o]These *are*
the inheritances, which Eleazar the priest, and Joshua the son of
Nun, and the heads of the fathers of the tribes of the children
of Israel, divided for an inheritance by lot [p]in Shiloh before the
LORD, at the door of the tabernacle of the congregation. So
they made an end of dividing the country.

CHAP. 20. THE LORD also spake unto Joshua, saying, Speak to
2 the children of Israel, saying, [a]Appoint out for you cities of

[i] Judg. 1. 35.
[k] See Judg. 18.
[l] Judg. 18. 29.
[m] ch. 24. 30.
[n] 1 Chr. 7. 24.
[o] Num. 34. 17. ch. 14. 1.
[p] ch. 18. 1, 10.
[a] Ex. 21. 13. Num. 35. 6, 11, 14. Deut. 19. 2, 9.

[1] Or, *over against*. [2] Or, *Joppa*, Jonah 1. 3. Acts 9. 36.

Ammaus, near Tiberias. Rakkath was, according to the Rabbins, rebuilt by Herod and called Tiberias. The name (= "bank, shore") suits the site of Tiberias very well. Migdal-el, perhaps the Magdala of Matt. xv. 39, is now the miserable village of *El Mejdel*.

46. Japho (the modern Jaffa, or Yafa), elsewhere (see marg.) called Joppa, is often mentioned in the history of the Maccabees and was, as it still is, the leading port of access to Jerusalem both for pilgrims and for merchandise. It is a very ancient town.

47. The words "too little" are an insertion of A. V. Render rather, "**the border of the children of Dan was extended.**" The Hebrew appears to mean "the children of Dan enlarged their border because they had not room enough."

The reason of this was that the Danites, a numerous tribe (Num. xxvi. 5 note), found themselves (Judg. i. 34, 35) cooped up amongst the hills by the powerful and warlike Amorites. Hence the Danite expedition (see marg. ref.), which surprised the Sidonian inhabitants of Leshem, an unwarlike and peaceable race, exterminated them, and annexed their city and territory to the portion of Dan.

50. Nothing is said of any express command of God respecting the inheritance of Joshua. But as such special portion appears to have been promised to Caleb at the time when he and Joshua alone out of the twelve spies remained faithful (xiv. 6–9), it is probable that a like promise was made to Joshua. The name of the place is also written Timnath-heres (Judg. ii. 9), by a transposition of the letters. The Rabbinical explanation that the name Timnath-heres (*i.e.* "portion of the sun") was given because a representation of the sun was affixed to the tomb in memory of Joshua's command to the sun to stand still, appears to be an afterthought. The name Timnath-serah (= "portion that remains") was perhaps conferred on the spot in consequence of its being allotted to Joshua, the last allotment made in the whole distribution of his conquests. The site has been conjectured to be *Tibneh*, a village about five miles north-west of Lydda [or, by Conder, Kefr Hâres, nine miles south of Nablous].

3 refuge, whereof I spake unto you by the hand of Moses: that the
slayer that killeth *any* person unawares *and* unwittingly may
flee thither: and they shall be your refuge from the avenger of
4 blood. And when he that doth flee unto one of those cities shall
stand at the entering of [b]the gate of the city, and shall declare
his cause in the ears of the elders of that city, they shall take
him into the city unto them, and give him a place, that he may
5 dwell among them. [c]And if the avenger of blood pursue after
him, then they shall not deliver the slayer up into his hand;
because he smote his neighbour unwittingly, and hated him not
6 beforetime. And he shall dwell in that city, [d]until he stand
before the congregation for judgment, *and* until the death of the
high priest that shall be in those days: then shall the slayer
return, and come unto his own city, and unto his own house,
7 unto the city from whence he fled. ¶ And they [1]appointed
[e]Kedesh in Galilee in mount Naphtali, and [f]Shechem in mount
Ephraim, and [g]Kirjath-arba, which *is* Hebron, in [h]the moun-
8 tain of Judah. And on the other side Jordan by Jericho eastward, they assigned [i]Bezer in the wilderness upon the plain out
of the tribe of Reuben, and [k]Ramoth in Gilead out of the tribe
of Gad, and [l]Golan in Bashan out of the tribe of Manasseh.
9 [m]These were the cities appointed for all the children of Israel,
and for the stranger that sojourneth among them, that whosoever killeth *any* person at unawares might flee thither, and not
die by the hand of the avenger of blood, [n]until he stood before
the congregation.

Chap 21. THEN came near the heads of the fathers of the Levites
unto [a]Eleazar the priest, and unto Joshua the son of Nun, and
unto the heads of the fathers of the tribes of the children of
2 Israel; and they spake unto them at [b]Shiloh in the land of
Canaan, saying, [c]The Lord commanded by the hand of Moses
to give us cities to dwell in, with the suburbs thereof for our
3 cattle. And the children of Israel gave unto the Levites out of
their inheritance, at the commandment of the Lord, these cities
4 and their suburbs. ¶ And the lot came out for the families of
the Kohathites: and [d]the children of Aaron the priest, *which*
were of the Levites, [e]had by lot out of the tribe of Judah, and
out of the tribe of Simeon, and out of the tribe of Benjamin,

[b] Ruth 4. 1, 2.
[c] Num. 35. 12.
[d] Num. 35. 12, 25.
[e] ch. 12. 22.
[f] Gen. 12. 6.
[g] ch. 14. 15.
[h] Luke 1. 39.
[i] Deut. 4. 43. 1 Chr. 6. 78.
[k] ch. 21. 38. 1 Kin. 22. 3.
[l] ch. 21. 27.
[m] Num. 35. 15.
[n] ver. 6.
[a] ch. 14. 1. & 17. 4.
[b] ch. 18. 1.
[c] Num. 35. 2.
[d] ver. 8, 19.
[e] See ch. 21. 33.

[1] Heb. *sanctified.*

XX. 4. As soon as the manslayer presented himself at the city of refuge, the elders of the city were to hold an inquiry, and receive him provisionally into the city. Afterwards, when the avenger of blood should have tracked his victim to the city, and appear to claim him, a more formal and thorough investigation (*v.* 6) was to be made. Consult the marginal references.

XXI. A list of the Levitical cities, varying in some particulars from that given in this chapter, is also given in 1 Chr. vi. 54-81.

4. *thirteen cities*] This number is said to be too great for the single family of Aaron. But it appears (1 Chr. xxiv.) that the two surviving sons of Aaron, Eleazar and Ithamar, had together 24 sons, the heads of the priestly families. Since Aaron was 123 years old when he died (Num. xxxiii. 39), his sons' grandchildren and great grandchildren were no doubt living in the closing years of Joshua's course, and had to be provided with dwellings. They might altogether number several thousands. The "cities" of Canaan were for the most part small; as is manifest from the astonishing number of them in proportion to the area of the land, more particularly in the south, where the portion of the priests was situated. The priests or Levites would not occupy the whole of the dwellings in any city, nor all its "fields," nor necessarily and always all its "villages" (cp. *v.* 12). Non-Levites, to whom the cultivation of their land, and other secular concerns, were entrusted, no doubt resided in the Levitical cities or their precincts. It appears, further, that several of the cities here enumerated were only

5 thirteen cities. And [f]the rest of the children of Kohath *had* by
lot out of the families of the tribe of Ephraim, and out of the
tribe of Dan, and out of the half tribe of Manasseh, ten cities.
6 ¶ And [g]the children of Gershon *had* by lot out of the families of
the tribe of Issachar, and out of the tribe of Asher, and out of
the tribe of Naphtali, and out of the half tribe of Manasseh in
7 Bashan, thirteen cities. ¶ [h]The children of Merari by their
families *had* out of the tribe of Reuben, and out of the tribe of
8 Gad, and out of the tribe of Zebulun, twelve cities. ¶ [i]And
the children of Israel gave by lot unto the Levites these cities
with their suburbs, [k]as the LORD commanded by the hand of
9 Moses. ¶ And they gave out of the tribe of the children of
Judah, and out of the tribe of the children of Simeon, these
10 cities which are *here* [1]mentioned by name, [l]which the children
of Aaron, *being* of the families of the Kohathites, *who were* of the
11 children of Levi, had: for their's was the first lot. [m]And they
gave them [2]the city of Arba the father of [n]Anak, which *city is*
Hebron, [o]in the hill *country* of Judah, with the suburbs thereof
12 round about it. But [p]the fields of the city, and the villages
thereof, gave they to Caleb the son of Jephunneh for his pos-
13 session. Thus [q]they gave to the children of Aaron the priest
14 [r]Hebron with her suburbs, *to be* a city of refuge for the slayer;
[s]and Libnah with her suburbs, and [t]Jattir with her suburbs,
15 [u]and Eshtemoa with her suburbs, and [x]Holon with her suburbs,
16 [y]and Debir with her suburbs, and [z]Ain with her suburbs, [a]and
Juttah with her suburbs, *and* [b]Beth-shemesh with her suburbs;
17 nine cities out of those two tribes. And out of the tribe of
Benjamin, [c]Gibeon with her suburbs, [d]Geba with her suburbs,
18 Anathoth with her suburbs, and [e]Almon with her suburbs; four
19 cities. All the cities of the children of Aaron, the priests, *were*
20 thirteen cities with their suburbs. ¶ [f]And the families of the
children of Kohath, the Levites which remained of the children
of Kohath, even they had the cities of their lot out of the tribe
21 of Ephraim. For they gave them [g]Shechem with her suburbs
in mount Ephraim, *to be* a city of refuge for the slayer; and
22 Gezer with her suburbs, and Kibzaim with her suburbs, and
23 Beth-horon with her suburbs; four cities. And out of the tribe
of Dan, Eltekeh with her suburbs, Gibbethon with her suburbs,
24 Aijalon with her suburbs, Gath-rimmon with her suburbs; four
25 cities. And out of the half tribe of Manasseh, Tanach with her
26 suburbs, and Gath-rimmon with her suburbs; two cities. All
the cities *were* ten with their suburbs for the families of the

[f] ver. 20, &c.
[g] ver. 27, &c.
[h] ver. 34, &c.
[i] ver. 3.
[k] Num. 35. 2.
[l] ver. 4.
[m] 1 Chr. 6. 55.
[n] Gen. 13. 18.
[o] ch. 20. 7.
[p] ch. 14. 14.
[q] 1 Chr. 6. 57, &c.
[r] ch. 15. 54.
[s] ch. 10. 2.
[t] ch. 15. 48.
[u] ch. 15. 50.
[x] 1 Chr. 6. 58, *Hilen.*
[y] ch. 15. 49.
[z] 1 Chr. 6. 59, *Ashan.*
[a] ch. 15. 55.
[b] ch. 15. 10.
[c] ch. 18. 25.
[d] ch. 18. 24, *Gaba.*
[e] 1 Chr. 6. 60, *Alemeth.*
[f] ver. 5. 1 Chr. 6. 66.
[g] ch. 20. 7.

[1] Heb. *called.*

[2] Or, *Kirjath-arba,* Gen. 23. 2.

---

wrested from the Canaanites at a later date.

5. The non-priestly Kohathites had been diminished by the destruction of Korah and his company (Num. xvi.). On comparing Num. xxvi. 57 seq. with Num. iii. 27 seq., two of the families of the Kohathites seem to have disappeared altogether. Hence it is not surprising that the rest of the Kohathites were sufficiently accommodated in ten cities.

9–19. The thirteen priestly cities (see marg. reff.) were all in the tribes of Judah, Simeon, and Benjamin. Thus, as Calvin remarks, God so overruled it that the priestly families were placed round the spot which He had determined beforehand to choose as the site of His temple.

20–26. Of the cities of the non-priestly Kohathites, for Kibzaim we find Jokmeam in 1 Chr. vi. 68. This is perhaps another name for the same place, since both names may be derived from roots having a similar meaning; and for Gath-rimmon in 1 Chr. vi. 70, Bileam is given, and probably correctly; Gath-rimmon having apparently been repeated inadvertently from the preceding verse. Bileam is but another form of Ibleam (xvii. 11).

27 children of Kohath that remained. ¶ [h]And unto the children of
Gershon, of the families of the Levites, out of the *other* half
tribe of Manasseh *they gave* [i]Golan in Bashan with her suburbs,
to be a city of refuge for the slayer; and Beesh-terah with her
28 suburbs; two cities. And out of the tribe of Issachar, Kishon
29 with her suburbs, Dabareh with her suburbs, Jarmuth with her
30 suburbs, En-gannim with her suburbs; four cities. And out of
the tribe of Asher, Mishal with her suburbs, Abdon with her
31 suburbs, Helkath with her suburbs, and Rehob with her
32 suburbs; four cities. And out of the tribe of Naphtali,
[k]Kedesh in Galilee with her suburbs, *to be* a city of refuge for
the slayer; and Hammoth-dor with her suburbs, and Kartan
33 with her suburbs; three cities. All the cities of the Gershonites according to their families *were* thirteen cities with their
34 suburbs. ¶ [l]And unto the families of the children of Merari, the
rest of the Levites, out of the tribe of Zebulun, Jokneam with
35 her suburbs, and Kartah with her suburbs, Dimnah with her
36 suburbs, Nahalal with her suburbs; four cities. And out of
the tribe of Reuben, [m]Bezer with her suburbs, and Jahazah
37 with her suburbs, Kedemoth with her suburbs, and Mephaath
38 with her suburbs; four cities. And out of the tribe of Gad,
[n]Ramoth in Gilead with her suburbs, *to be* a city of refuge for
39 the slayer; and Mahanaim with her suburbs, Heshbon with her
40 suburbs, Jazer with her suburbs; four cities in all. So all the
cities for the children of Merari by their families, which were
remaining of the families of the Levites, were *by* their lot
41 twelve cities. ¶ [o]All the cities of the Levites within the possession of the children of Israel *were* forty and eight cities with
42 their suburbs. These cities were every one with their suburbs
43 round about them: thus *were* all these cities. ¶ And the LORD
gave unto Israel [p]all the land which he sware to give unto their
44 fathers; and they possessed it, and dwelt therein. [q]And the

[h] ver. 6.
[i] Deut. 4. 13.
[k] ch. 12. 22.
[l] ver. 7. See 1 Chr. 6. 77.
[m] ch. 20. 8.
[n] ch. 20. 8.
[o] Num. 35. 7.
[p] Gen. 13. 15.
[q] ch. 11. 23. & 22. 4.

27–33. Cp. xix. 18, &c. Of the cities of the Gershonites, for Beesh-terah read (**Beeshterah.**) The name is a contraction of Beth-Ashterah (= "house of Ashterah") and the city is undoubtedly the Ashtaroth or Astaroth of Og (xii. 4; Deut. i. 4; 1 Chr. vi. 71).

34-40. Merarite cities. Some of these places are not found in the list of Zebulonite cities in xix. 10-16. The text is considered corrupt.

42. After this verse, the LXX. introduces a passage (in part a repetition from xix. 49, 50), recording the grant of a special inheritance to Joshua, and also that he buried at Timnath-serah the flint-knives with which he had circumcised (v. 2 note) the people after the passage of Jordan. The latter statement, which has the authority of the LXX. only, is a Jewish legend of early date.

43–45. There is no real inconsistency between the declarations of these verses and the fact that the Israelites had not as yet possessed themselves of all the cities allotted to the various tribes (Judg. i. 21-36),—nor did at any time, subdue the whole extent of country promised to them (Num. xxxiv. 1-12). God had fulfilled all His part of the Covenant. It was no part of His purpose that the native population should be annihilated suddenly (Deut. vii. 22); but they were delivered into the hand of Israel, and their complete dispossession could have been effected at any time by that Divine aid which was never wanting when sought. At the time referred to in the text, the Canaanites were discouraged, broken in strength, holding fast in isolated spots only up and down the land in the very midst of the tribes of God's people. The conquest of Canaan was already *ex parte Dei* a perfect work; just as in the New Testament the triumph of the individual Christian and of the Christian Church in their warfare is often spoken of as accomplished in view of the Divine will that it should be so, and of Divine grace that it may be so. It was therefore only the inertness and pusillanimity of the Israelites which prevented the completion of the conquest when the allotment of Canaan was made by Joshua; as it was their subsequent backslidings which caused God to turn the tide of victory against them and even to cast them out of the land

r Deut. 7. 24. • ch. 23. 14.

LORD gave them rest round about, according to all that he sware
unto their fathers: and [r]there stood not a man of all their
enemies before them; the LORD delivered all their enemies
45 into their hand. [s]There failed not ought of any good thing
which the LORD had spoken unto the house of Israel; all came
to pass.

a Num. 32. 20. Deut. 3. 18. b ch. 1. 16, 17. c Num. 32. 33. Deut. 29. 8. ch. 13. 8. d Deut. 6. 6, 17. & 11. 22. e Deut. 10. 12. f Gen. 47. 7. Ex. 39. 43. ch. 14. 13. 2 Sam. 6. 18. Luke 24. 50. g ch. 17. 5. h Num. 31. 27. 1 Sam. 30. 24. i Num. 32. 1, 26, 29.

CHAP. 22. THEN Joshua called the Reubenites, and the Gadites,
2 and the half tribe of Manasseh, and said unto them, Ye have
kept [a]all that Moses the servant of the LORD commanded you,
3 [b]and have obeyed my voice in all that I commanded you: ye
have not left your brethren these many days unto this day, but
have kept the charge of the commandment of the LORD your
4 God. And now the LORD your God hath given rest unto your
brethren, as he promised them: therefore now return ye, and
get you unto your tents, *and* unto the land of your possession,
[c]which Moses the servant of the LORD gave you on the other
5 side Jordan. But [d]take diligent heed to do the commandment and the law, which Moses the servant of the LORD charged
you, [e]to love the LORD your God, and to walk in all his ways,
and to keep his commandments, and to cleave unto him, and to
6 serve him with all your heart and with all your soul. ¶ So
Joshua [f]blessed them, and sent them away: and they went unto
7 their tents. Now to the *one* half of the tribe of Manasseh Moses
had given *possession* in Bashan: [g]but unto the *other* half thereof
gave Joshua among their brethren on this side Jordan westward. And when Joshua sent them away also unto their tents,
8 then he blessed them, and he spake unto them, saying, Return
with much riches unto your tents, and with very much cattle,
with silver, and with gold, and with brass, and with iron, and
with very much raiment: [h]divide the spoil of your enemies with
9 your brethren. ¶ And the children of Reuben and the children of
Gad and the half tribe of Manasseh returned, and departed from
the children of Israel out of Shiloh, which *is* in the land of
Canaan, to go unto [i]the country of Gilead, to the land of their
possession, whereof they were possessed, according to the word
10 of the LORD by the hand of Moses. And when they came unto
the borders of Jordan, that *are* in the land of Canaan, the
children of Reuben and the children of Gad and the half tribe
of Manasseh built there an altar by Jordan, a great altar to see

---

promised to their forefathers and actually won in the campaigns of Joshua. See Introd., p. 6.

XXII. The events of this chap. are no doubt recorded in their proper historical order. The auxiliary forces of the trans-Jordanic tribes were not sent away immediately after the campaigns against the Canaanites were over. They set forth from Shiloh (*v.* 9), to which place the sanctuary had been removed (xviii. 1) after the conquest and the settlement of the children of Judah and of Joseph in their possessions, and after the appointment of the Levitical cities.

7, 8. The insertion of this explanation about the half tribe, and the repetition of Joshua's farewell, are examples of a marked characteristic of very ancient writers—and of Hebrew writers as much as any—that of giving a completeness and finish to each section of their story. The Jewish historian scarcely ever quotes or reminds, but repeats so much as may be necessary to make his account of the transaction in hand fully intelligible by itself. (Cp. also xiii. 14 and 33, xiv. 3, xviii. 7.) It is quite possible, however, that the particulars peculiar to *v.* 8, may be due to some other narrative of the whole event than that to which *v.* 5 belongs, and may have been interwoven by a later reviser.

9. *Gilead*] Here used in the widest sense for the whole trans-Jordanic district.

10. The two tribes and a half erected this altar in order to keep alive their claim to have the same interest as the other tribes had in the Sanctuary of God, which was established on the west side of Jordan: and in order to forestall any assertion that the

11 to. ¶ And the children of Israel [k]heard say, Behold, the
children of Reuben and the children of Gad and the half tribe of
Manasseh have built an altar over against the land of Canaan,
in the borders of Jordan, at the passage of the children of Israel.
12 And when the children of Israel heard *of it*, [l]the whole congregation of the children of Israel gathered themselves together
13 at Shiloh, to go up to war against them. And the children of
Israel [m]sent unto the children of Reuben, and to the children of
Gad, and to the half tribe of Manasseh, into the land of Gilead,
14 [n]Phinehas the son of Eleazar the priest, and with him ten
princes, of each [1]chief house a prince throughout all the tribes
of Israel; and [o]each one *was* an head of the house of their
15 fathers among the thousands of Israel. And they came unto
the children of Reuben, and to the children of Gad, and to the
half tribe of Manasseh, unto the land of Gilead, and they spake
16 with them, saying, Thus saith the whole congregation of the
LORD, What trespass *is* this that ye have committed against the
God of Israel, to turn away this day from following the LORD, in
that ye have builded you an altar, [p]that ye might rebel this day
17 against the LORD? *Is* the iniquity [q]of Peor too little for us,
from which we are not cleansed until this day, although there
18 was a plague in the congregation of the LORD, but that ye must
turn away this day from following the LORD? and it will be,
seeing ye rebel to day against the LORD, that to morrow [r]he will
19 be wroth with the whole congregation of Israel. Notwithstanding, if the land of your possession *be* unclean, *then* pass ye over
unto the land of the possession of the LORD, [s]wherein the LORD'S
tabernacle dwelleth, and take possession among us: but rebel
not against the LORD, nor rebel against us, in building you an
20 altar beside the altar of the LORD our God. [t]Did not Achan the
son of Zerah commit a trespass in the accursed thing, and wrath
fell on all the congregation of Israel? and that man perished
21 not alone in his iniquity. ¶ Then the children of Reuben and
the children of Gad and the half tribe of Manasseh answered,
22 and said unto the heads of the thousands of Israel, The LORD
[u]God of gods, the LORD God of gods, he [x]knoweth, and Israel
he shall know; if *it be* in rebellion, or if in transgression against

[k] Deut. 13. 12, &c. Judg. 20. 12.
[l] Judg. 20. 1.
[m] Deut. 13. 14. Judg. 20. 12.
[n] Ex. 6. 25. Num. 25. 7.
[o] Num. 1. 4.
[p] See Lev. 17. 8, 9. Deut. 12. 13, 14.
[q] Num. 25. 3, 4. Deut. 4. 3.
[r] Num. 16. 22.
[s] ch. 18. 1.
[t] ch. 7. 1, 5.
[u] Deut. 10. 17.
[x] 1 Kin. 8. 39. Job 10. 7. & 23. 10. Ps. 44. 21. & 139. 1, 2. Jer. 12. 3. 2 Cor. 11. 11, 31.

[1] Heb. *house of the father.*

Jordan itself was a natural barrier of exclusion between them and the Sanctuary, they built it on the west or Canaanitish bank of the Jordan and not on the east.

The word rendered "borders" is noteworthy; it means circuits, arrondissements.

12. *gathered themselves together*] The various tribes had already dispersed to their homes, and were now summoned together again.

17. *from which we are not cleansed until this day*] Phinehas, who had borne a conspicuous part in vindicating the cause of God against those who fell away to Baal-peor, means that terrible as the punishment had been, there were still those amongst them who hankered after Baal worship, and even practised it in secret. (Cp. Joshua's words, xxiv. 14–23.)

19. *unclean*] *i.e.* unholy because the Sanctuary was not in it, but on the other side of Jordan.

22. The repeated invocation of God, and that by His three names (El, Elohim, Jehovah: cp. Ps. l. 1), marks the earnestness of the protestation. The conduct of the two tribes and a half has often been noted as exemplary. They had had a grave and capital crime most unexpectedly laid to their charge, of which they were entirely innocent. Yet there is no word of reproach or recrimination in their vindication of themselves. They are contented simply to repudiate the false accusation and to explain the real motives of conduct perhaps suggested to them by a precedent set by Moses (Ex. xvii. 15).

save us not this day] The words are a direct appeal to God, exactly equivalent in effect to our form "So help me God."

23 the LORD, (save us not this day,) that we have built us an
altar to turn from following the LORD, or if to offer thereon
burnt offering or meat offering, or if to offer peace offerings
24 thereon, let the LORD himself [y]require *it;* and if we have not
rather done it for fear of *this* thing, saying, [1]In time to come
your children might speak unto our children, saying, What have
25 ye to do with the LORD God of Israel? For the LORD hath
made Jordan a border between us and you, ye children of
Reuben and children of Gad; ye have no part in the LORD: so
shall your children make our children cease from fearing the
26 LORD. Therefore we said, Let us now prepare to build us an
27 altar, not for burnt offering, nor for sacrifice: but *that* it *may*
be [z]a witness between us, and you, and our generations after us,
that we might [a]do the service of the LORD before him with our
burnt offerings, and with our sacrifices, and with our peace
offerings; that your children may not say to our children in
28 time to come, Ye have no part in the LORD. Therefore said we,
that it shall be, when they should *so* say to us or to our generations in time to come, that we may say *again*, Behold the pattern
of the altar of the LORD, which our fathers made, not for burnt
offerings, nor for sacrifices; but it *is* a witness between us
29 and you. God forbid that we should rebel against the LORD,
and turn this day from following the LORD, [b]to build an altar
for burnt offerings, for meat offerings, or for sacrifices, beside
the altar of the LORD our God that *is* before his tabernacle.
30 ¶And when Phinehas the priest, and the princes of the congregation and heads of the thousands of Israel which *were* with him,
heard the words that the children of Reuben and the children of
Gad and the children of Manasseh spake, [2]it pleased them.
31 And Phinehas the son of Eleazar the priest said unto the children
of Reuben, and to the children of Gad, and to the children of
Manasseh, This day we perceive that the LORD *is* [c]among us,
because ye have not committed this trespass against the LORD:
[3]now ye have delivered the children of Israel out of the hand of
32 the LORD. ¶And Phinehas the son of Eleazar the priest, and
the princes, returned from the children of Reuben, and from the
children of Gad, out of the land of Gilead, unto the land of
Canaan, to the children of Israel, and brought them word again.
33 And the thing pleased the children of Israel; and the children
of Israel [d]blessed God, and did not intend to go up against them
in battle, to destroy the land wherein the children of Reuben
34 and Gad dwelt. ¶And the children of Reuben and the children
of Gad called the altar [4]*Ed:* for it *shall be* a witness between us
that the LORD *is* God.

CHAP. 23. AND it came to pass a long time after that the LORD [a]had
given rest unto Israel from all their enemies round about, that

[y] Deut. 18. 19. 1 Sam. 20. 16.
[z] Gen. 31. 48. ch. 24. 27. ver. 34.
[a] Deut. 12. 5, 6, 11, 12, 17, 18, 26, 27.
[b] Deut. 12. 13, 14.
[c] Lev. 26. 11, 12. 2 Chr. 15. 2.
[d] 1 Chr. 29. 20. Neh. 8. 6. Dan. 2. 19. Luke 2. 28.
[a] ch. 21. 44. & 22. 4.

[1] Heb. *To morrow.*
[2] Heb. *it was good in their eyes.*
[3] Heb. *then.*
[4] That is, A witness: So ch. 24. 27.

34. The word *Ed* is not found after "altar" in the text of most MSS., nor is it represented in the LXX. or Vulg. The passage should probably run, "the children of Reuben and the children of Gad named the altar, that (as they said) it might be, &c." The title placed on the altar was perhaps simply a witness between them that the Lord was God (Wordsworth).

XXIII. This and the next chapter contain the last addresses of Joshua. These addresses were no doubt amongst the closing acts of Joshua's life, but were evidently given on different occasions, and are of different character and scope. In the former Joshua briefly reminds the princes of the recent benefits of God towards them and their people, declares that God had fulfilled all

2 Joshua [b]waxed old, *and* [1]stricken in age. And Joshua [c]called
for all Israel, *and* for their elders, and for their heads, and for
their judges, and for their officers, and said unto them, I am
3 old *and* stricken in age: and ye have seen all that the LORD
your God hath done unto all these nations because of you; for
4 the [d]LORD your God *is* he that hath fought for you. Behold,
[e]I have divided unto you by lot these nations that remain, to be
an inheritance for your tribes, from Jordan, with all the nations
5 that I have cut off, even unto the great sea [2]westward. And
the LORD your God, [f]he shall expel them from before you, and
drive them from out of your sight; and ye shall possess their
6 land, [g]as the LORD your God hath promised unto you. [h]Be ye
therefore very courageous to keep and to do all that is written
in the book of the law of Moses, [i]that ye turn not aside there-
7 from *to* the right hand or *to* the left; that ye [k]come not among
these nations, these that remain among you; neither [l]make
mention of the name of their gods, nor cause to swear *by them*,
8 neither serve them, nor bow yourselves unto them: [3]but [m]cleave
9 unto the LORD your God, as ye have done unto this day. [4][n]For
the LORD hath driven out from before you great nations and
strong: but *as for* you, [o]no man hath been able to stand before
10 you unto this day. [p]One man of you shall chase a thousand:
for the LORD your God, he *it is* that fighteth for you, [q]as he hath
11 promised you. ¶ [r]Take good heed therefore unto [5]yourselves,
12 that ye love the LORD your God. Else if ye do in any wise [s]go
back, and cleave unto the remnant of these nations, *even* these
that remain among you, and shall [t]make marriages with them,
13 and go in unto them, and they to you: know for a certainty that
[u]the LORD your God will no more drive out *any of* these nations
from before you; [x]but they shall be snares and traps unto you,
and scourges in your sides, and thorns in your eyes, until ye
perish from off this good land which the LORD your God hath
14 given you. ¶ And, behold, this day [y]I *am* going the way of all
the earth: and ye know in all your hearts and in all your souls,
that [z]not one thing hath failed of all the good things which the
LORD your God spake concerning you; all are come to pass unto
15 you, *and* not one thing hath failed thereof. [a]Therefore it shall
come to pass, *that* as all good things are come upon you, which
the LORD your God promised you; so shall the LORD bring upon
you [b]all evil things, until he have destroyed you from off this
16 good land which the LORD your God hath given you. When ye
have transgressed the covenant of the LORD your God, which he
commanded you, and have gone and served other gods, and
bowed yourselves to them; then shall the anger of the LORD be

[b] ch. 13. 1.
[c] Deut. 31. 28. 1 Chr. 28. 1.
[d] Ex. 14. 14.
[e] ch. 13. 2. 6.
[f] Ex. 23. 30. ch. 13. 6.
[g] Num 33. 53.
[h] ch. 1. 7.
[i] Deut. 5. 32.
[k] Deut. 7. 2. Prov. 4. 14. Eph. 5. 11.
[l] Ex. 23. 13. Ps. 16. 4. Jer. 5. 7.
[m] Deut. 10. 20. & 11. 22.
[n] Deut. 11. 23.
[o] ch. 1. 5.
[p] Lev. 26. 8. Judg. 3. 31. & 15. 15. 2 Sam. 23. 8.
[q] Ex. 14. 14.
[r] ch. 22. 5.
[s] Heb. 10. 38, 39. 2 Pet. 2. 20, 21.
[t] Deut. 7. 3.
[u] Judg. 2. 3.
[x] Deut. 7. 16. 1 Kin. 11. 4.
[y] 1 Kin. 2. 2. See Heb. 9. 27.
[z] ch. 21. 45. Luke 21. 33.
[a] Deut. 28. 63.
[b] Lev. 26. 16. Deut. 28. 15, 16, &c.

[1] Heb. *come into days.*
[2] Heb. *at the sunset.*
[3] Or, *For if ye will cleave, &c.*
[4] Or, *Then the LORD will drive.*
[5] Heb. *your souls.*

His promises, and exhorts to faithfulness on their side to God that so His mercies may not be withdrawn: in the latter he takes a wider range, rehearses the gracious dealings of God with the nation from its very origin, and upon these as his grounds, he claims for God their sincere and entire service. But he grants them the option of withdrawing from the Covenant if they so choose; and when they elect still to abide by it, it is solemnly renewed by the free consent of the whole people. Joshua's reproofs and warnings are in sum and substance identical with those with which Moses closed his career (Deut. xxxi., &c.). Cp. throughout the marg. reff.

2. *all Israel, and for their elders*] Omit "and," which is not in the Hebrew. The meaning is that Joshua summoned to him all Israel as represented by its elders, &c. (Deut. i. 15.) This gathering probably took place at the Tabernacle at Shiloh.

kindled against you, and ye shall perish quickly from off the
good land which he hath given unto you.

Chap. 24. AND Joshua gathered all the tribes of Israel to [a]Shec-
hem, and [b]called for the elders of Israel, and for their heads, and
for their judges, and for their officers; and they [c]presented them-
2 selves before God. ¶ And Joshua said unto all the people, Thus
saith the Lord God of Israel, [d]Your fathers dwelt on the other
side of the flood in old time, *even* Terah, the father of Abraham,
3 and the father of Nachor: and [e]they served other gods. And [f]I
took your father Abraham from the other side of the flood, and
led him throughout all the land of Canaan, and multiplied his
4 seed, and [g]gave him Isaac. And I gave unto Isaac [h]Jacob and
Esau: and I gave unto [i]Esau mount Seir, to possess it; [k]but
5 Jacob and his children went down into Egypt. [l]I sent Moses also
and Aaron, and [m]I plagued Egypt, according to that which I did
6 among them: and afterward I brought you out. And I [n]brought
your fathers out of Egypt: and [o]ye came unto the sea; [p]and
the Egyptians pursued after your fathers with chariots and
7 horsemen unto the Red sea. And when they [q]cried unto the
Lord, [r]he put darkness between you and the Egyptians, [s]and
brought the sea upon them, and covered them; and [t]your eyes
have seen what I have done in Egypt: and ye dwelt in the wil-
8 derness [u]a long season. And I brought you into the land of
the Amorites, which dwelt on the other side Jordan; [x]and they
fought with you: and I gave them into your hand, that ye might
possess their land; and I destroyed them from before you.
9 Then [y]Balak the son of Zippor, king of Moab, arose and warred
against Israel, and [z]sent and called Balaam the son of Beor to
10 curse you: [a]but I would not hearken unto Balaam; [b]therefore
11 he blessed you still: so I delivered you out of his hand. And
[c]ye went over Jordan, and came unto Jericho: and [d]the men
of Jericho fought against you, the Amorites, and the Perizzites,
and the Canaanites, and the Hittites, and the Girgashites, the
Hivites, and the Jebusites; and I delivered them into your
12 hand. And [e]I sent the hornet before you, which drave them
out from before you, *even* the two kings of the Amorites; *but*
13 [f]not with thy sword, nor with thy bow. And I have given you a
land for which ye did not labour, and [g]cities which ye built not,
and ye dwell in them; of the vineyards and oliveyards which ye
14 planted not do ye eat. ¶ [h]Now therefore fear the Lord, and

[a] Gen. 35. 4.
[b] ch. 23. 2.
[c] 1 Sam. 10. 19.
[d] Gen. 11. 26, 31.
[e] Gen. 31. 19.
[f] Gen. 12. 1. Acts. 7. 2, 3.
[g] Gen. 21. 2, 3.
[h] Gen. 25. 24, 25, 26.
[i] Gen. 36. 8.
[k] Gen. 46. 1, 6. Acts 7. 15.
[l] Ex. 3. 10.
[m] Ex. 7–12.
[n] Ex. 12. 37.
[o] Ex. 14. 2.
[p] Ex. 14. 9.
[q] Ex. 14. 10.
[r] Ex. 14. 20.
[s] Ex. 14. 27.
[t] Deut. 4. 34.
[u] ch. 5. 6.
[x] Num. 21. 21, 33.
[y] See Judg. 11. 25.
[z] Num. 22. 5.
[a] Deut. 23. 5.
[b] Num. 23. 11, 20.
[c] ch. 3. 14.
[d] ch. 6. 1.
[e] Ex. 23. 28. Deut. 7. 20.
[f] Ps. 44. 3, 6.
[g] Deut. 6. 10.
[h] Deut. 10. 12.

XXIV. **1.** Shechem, situated between those mountains, Ebal and Gerizim, which had already been the scene of a solemn rehearsal of the Covenant soon after the first entry of the people into the Promised Land (viii. 30–35), was a fitting scene for the solemn renewal on the part of the people of that Covenant with God which had been on His part so signally and so fully kept. The spot itself suggested the allusions to Abraham, Isaac, and Jacob, &c., in Joshua's address; and its associations could not but give peculiar force and moving effect to his appeals. This address was not made to the rulers only but to the whole nation, not of course to the tribes assembled in mass, but to their representatives.

2. *the other side of the flood*] Better "**on the other side of the river,**" *i.e.* the Euphrates. See marg. ref.

they served other gods] Possibly the "images," or teraphim, which we find their ancestor Laban calling "his gods" (see marg. ref.); and of which it would seem that there were, as Joshua spoke, some secret devotees amongst the people (*vv.* 14, 25). It is not stated that Abraham himself was an idolater, though his fathers were. Jewish tradition asserts that Abraham whilst in Ur of the Chaldees was persecuted for his abhorrence of idolatry, and hence was called away by God from his native land. The reference in the text to the original state of those who were the forefathers of the nation, is made to show that they were no better than others: God chose them not for their excellences but of His own mere motion.

serve him in [i]sincerity and in truth: and [k]put away the gods
which your fathers served on the other side of the flood, and [l]in
15 Egypt; and serve ye the LORD. And if it seem evil unto you to
serve the LORD, [m]choose you this day whom ye will serve;
whether [n]the gods which your fathers served that *were* on the
other side of the flood, or [o]the gods of the Amorites, in whose
land ye dwell: [p]but as for me and my house, we will serve the
16 LORD. And the people answered and said, God forbid that we
17 should forsake the LORD, to serve other gods; for the LORD our
God, he *it is* that brought us up and our fathers out of the land
of Egypt, from the house of bondage, and which did those great
signs in our sight, and preserved us in all the way wherein we
18 went, and among all the people through whom we passed: and
the LORD drave out from before us all the people, even the Amorites which dwelt in the land: *therefore* will we also serve the
19 LORD; for he *is* our God. And Joshua said unto the people,
[q]Ye cannot serve the LORD: for he *is* an [r]holy God; he *is* [s]a
jealous God; [t]he will not forgive your transgressions nor your
20 sins. [u]If ye forsake the LORD, and serve strange gods, [x]then
he will turn and do you hurt, and consume you, after that he
21 hath done you good. And the people said unto Joshua, Nay;
22 but we will serve the LORD. And Joshua said unto the people,
Ye *are* witnesses against yourselves that [y]ye have chosen you
23 the LORD, to serve him. And they said, *We are* witnesses. Now
therefore [z]put away, *said he*, the strange gods which *are* among
24 you, and incline your heart unto the LORD God of Israel. And
the people said unto Joshua, The LORD our God will we serve,
25 and his voice will we obey. ¶ So Joshua [a]made a covenant with
the people that day, and set them a statute and an ordinance [b]in
26 Shechem. And Joshua [c]wrote these words in the book of the
law of God, and took [d]a great stone, and [e]set it up there [f]under
27 an oak, that *was* by the sanctuary of the LORD. And Joshua
said unto all the people, Behold, this stone shall be [g]a witness
unto us; for [h]it hath heard all the words of the LORD which he
spake unto us: it shall be therefore a witness unto you, lest ye
28 deny your God. So [i]Joshua let the people depart, every man
29 unto his inheritance. ¶ [k]And it came to pass after these things,
that Joshua the son of Nun, the servant of the LORD, died, *being*
30 an hundred and ten years old. And they buried him in the
border of his inheritance in [l]Timnath-serah, which *is* in mount
31 Ephraim, on the north side of the hill of Gaash. ¶ And [m]Israel
served the LORD all the days of Joshua, and all the days of the
elders that [1]overlived Joshua, and which had [n]known all the
32 works of the LORD, that he had done for Israel. ¶ And [o]the
bones of Joseph, which the children of Israel brought up out of

[i] Gen. 17. 1. Ps. 119. 1. Eph. 6. 24.
[k] Lev. 17. 7.
[l] Ezek. 20. 7.
[m] See Ruth 1. 15. 1 Kin. 18. 21. Ezek. 20. 39. John 6. 67.
[n] ver. 14.
[o] Ex. 23. 24.
[p] Gen. 18. 19.
[q] Matt. 6. 24.
[r] Lev. 19. 2. Isai. 5. 16.
[s] Ex. 20. 5.
[t] Ex. 23. 21.
[u] 1 Chr. 28. 9. Ezra 8. 22. Isai. 1. 28. Jer. 17. 13.
[x] Isai. 63. 10. Acts 7. 42.
[y] Ps. 119. 173.
[z] Gen. 35. 2. 1 Sam. 7. 3.
[a] See Exod. 15. 25.
[b] ver. 26.
[c] Deut. 31. 24.
[d] See Judg. 9. 6.
[e] See Gen. 28. 18.
[f] Gen. 35. 4.
[g] See Gen. 31. 48, 52. ch. 22. 27.
[h] Deut. 32. 1.
[i] Judg. 2. 6.
[k] Judg. 2. 8.
[l] ch. 19. 50. Judg. 2. 9.
[m] Judg. 2. 7.
[n] See Deut. 11. 2. & 31. 13.
[o] Gen. 50. 25. Ex. 13. 19.

[1] Heb. *prolonged* their *days after Joshua*.

15. *choose*] Service of God in sincerity and truth can only result from a free and willing allegiance of the heart. This accordingly is what Joshua invites, as Moses had done before him (Deut. xxx. 15 seq.).

25. *made a covenant with the people*] i.e. he solemnly ratified and renewed the Covenant of Sinai, as Moses had done before him (Deut. xxix. 1). As no new or different Covenant was made, no sacrifices were necessary.

26. Consult the marg. reff.

that was by the sanctuary of the LORD] *i.e.* the spot where Abraham and Jacob had sacrificed and worshipped, and which might well be regarded by their posterity as a holy place or sanctuary. Perhaps the very altar of Abraham and Jacob was still remaining.

[p] Gen. 33. 19.

Egypt, buried they in Shechem, in a parcel of ground [p] which
Jacob bought of the sons of Hamor the father of Shechem for an
hundred [1] pieces of silver: and it became the inheritance of the
33 children of Joseph. ¶ And Eleazar the son of Aaron died; and
they buried him in a hill *that pertained to* [q] Phinehas his son,
which was given him in mount Ephraim.

[q] Ex. 6. 25. Judg. 20. 28.

[1] Or, *lambs*.

---

33. [Eleazar's burial-place is placed by Conder not at Tibneh but in the village of 'Awertah.]

JUDGES.

INTRODUCTION.

THE Book of Judges, like the other Historical Books of the Old Testament, takes its name from the subject to which it chiefly relates, viz., the exploits of those JUDGES[1] who ruled Israel in the times between the death of Joshua and the rise of Samuel. The rule of the Judges (Ruth i. 1) in this limited sense was a distinct Dispensation, distinct from the leadership of Moses and Joshua, distinct from the more regular supremacy of Eli, the High-Priest, and from the Prophetic Dispensation inaugurated by Samuel (1 Sam. iii. 19–21; Acts iii. 24).

The book consists of three divisions. (1) The PREFACE, which extends to iii. 6 (incl.). (2) The MAIN NARRATIVE, iii. 7–xvi. 31. (3) THE APPENDIX, containing two detached narratives, (*a*) xvii.; (*b*) xviii.–xxi. To these may be added the Book of Ruth, containing another detached narrative, which anciently was included under the title of JUDGES, to which book the first verse shows that it properly belongs.

(1) The general purpose of the Preface is to prepare the ground for the subsequent narrative; to explain how it was that the heathen nations of Canaan were still so powerful, and the Israelites so destitute of Divine aid and protection against their enemies; and to draw out the striking lessons of God's righteous judgment, which were afforded by the alternate servitudes and deliverances of the Israelites, according as they either forsook God to worship idols, or returned to Him in penitence, faith, and prayer. Throughout there is a reference to the threatenings and promises of the Books of Moses (ii. 15, 20, &c.), in order both to vindicate the power and faithfulness of Jehovah the God of Israel, and to hold out a warning to the future generations for whose instruction the Book was written. In the view which the writer was inspired to present to the Church, never was God's agency more busy in relation to the affairs of His people, than when, to a superficial observer, that agency had altogether ceased. On the other hand, the writer calls attention to the fact that those heroes, who wrought such wonderful deliverances for Israel, did it not by their own power, but were divinely commissioned, and divinely endowed with courage, strength, and victory. The writer of the Preface also directs the minds of the readers of his history to that vital doctrine, which it was one main object of the Old Testament Dispensation to keep alive in the world till the coming of Christ, viz., the Unity of God. All the calami-

---

[1] The Phœnician and Carthaginian *Suffete*, mentioned by Livy as corresponding in office to the Roman Consuls, is the same word as the Hebrew *Shophet*, Judge.

ties which he was about to narrate, were the fruit and consequence of idolatry. "Keep yourselves from idols," was the chief lesson which the history of the Judges was intended to inculcate.

The Preface consists of two very different portions; the recapitulation of events before, and up to, Joshua's death (i.–ii. 9), and the reflections on the history about to be related (ii. 10–iii. 6).

(2) The MAIN NARRATIVE contains, not consecutive annals of Israel as a united people, but a series of brilliant, striking, pictures, now of one portion of the tribes, now of another. Of some epochs minute details are given; other periods of eight or ten years, nay, even of twenty, forty, or eighty years, are disposed of in four or five words. Obviously in those histories in which we find graphic touches and accurate details, we have preserved to us narratives contemporary with the events narrated—the narratives, probably, of eye-witnesses and actors in the events themselves. The histories of Ehud, of Barak and Deborah, of Gideon, of Jephthah, and of Samson, are the product of times when the invasions of Moab, of Jabin, of Midian, of Ammon, and of the Philistines, were living realities in the minds of those who penned those histories. The compiler of the Book seems to have inserted bodily in his history the ancient narratives which were extant in his day. As the mind of the reader is led on by successive steps to the various exploits of the twelve Judges, and from them to Samuel, and from Samuel to David, and from David to David's son, it cannot fail to recognize the working of one Divine plan for man's redemption, and to understand how Judges, and Prophets, and Kings were endowed with some portion of the gifts of the Holy Spirit, preparatory to the coming into the world of Him in Whom all the fulness of the Godhead should dwell bodily, and Who should save to the uttermost all that come to God by Him.

Some curious analogies have been noted between this, the heroic age of the Israelites, and the heroic ages of Greece and other Gentile countries. Here, as there, it is in the early settlement and taking possession of their new country, and in conflicts with the old races, that the virtues and prowess of the heroes are developed. Here, as there, there is oftentimes a strange mixture of virtue and vice, a blending of great and noble qualities, of most splendid deeds with cruelty and ignorance, licentiousness and barbarism. And yet, in comparing the sacred with the heathen heroes, we find in the former a faith in God and a religious purpose, of which Heathendom affords no trace. The exploits of the sacred heroes advanced the highest interests of mankind, and were made subservient to the overthrow of abominable and impure superstitions, and to the preserving a light of true religion in the world until the coming of Christ.

(3) The APPENDIX contains a record of certain events which happened "in the days when the judges ruled," but are not connected with any exploits of the Judges. Though placed at the end of the book, the two histories both manifestly belong chronologically to the beginning of it: the reason for

the place selected is perhaps that suggested in xvii. 1 note.

Exact chronology forms no part of the plan of the book. The only guide to the chronology is to be found in the genealogies which span the period: and the evidence of these genealogies concurs in assigning an average of between seven and eight generations to the time from the entrance into Canaan to the commencement of David's reign, which would make up from 240 to 260 years. Deducting 30 years for Joshua, 30 for Samuel, and 40 for the reign of Saul (Acts xiii. 21), in all 100 years, we have from 140 to 160 years left for the events related in the Book of Judges. This is a short time, no doubt, but quite sufficient, when it is remembered that many of the *rests* and *servitudes* (iii. 8 note) therein related are not successive, but synchronize; and that no great dependence can be placed on the recurring 80, 40, and 20 years, whenever they are not in harmony with historical probability.

The narratives which have the strongest appearance of synchronizing are those of the Moabite, Ammonite, and Amalekite servitude (iii. 12–30) which lasted *eighteen* years, and was closely connected with a Philistine invasion (iii. 31); of the Ammonite servitude which lasted *eighteen* years, and was also closely connected with a Philistine invasion (x. 7, 8); and of the Midianite and Amalekite servitude which lasted seven years (vi. 1), all three of which terminated in a complete expulsion and destruction of their enemies by the three leaders Ehud, Jephthah, and Gideon, heading respectively the Benjamites, the Manassites and the northern tribes, and the tribes beyond Jordan: the conduct of the Ephraimites as related in ch. viii. 1, xii. 1, being an additional very strong feature of resemblance in the two histories of Gideon and Jephthah. The 40 years of Philistine servitude mentioned in Judg. xiii. 1, seems to have embraced the last 20 years of Eli's judgeship, and the first 20 of Samuel's, and terminated with Samuel's victory at Eben-ezer: and, if so, Samson's judgeship of 20 years also coincided in part with Samuel's. The long *rests* of 40 and 80 years spoken of as following the victories of Othniel, Barak, and Ehud, may very probably have synchronized in whole or in part. It cannot however be denied that the chronology of this book is still a matter of uncertainty.

The time of the compilation of this Book, and the *final* arrangement of its component parts in their present form and in their present connexion in the series of the Historical Books of Scripture, may with most probability be assigned to the latter times of the Jewish monarchy, included in the same plan. (The Book of Ezra, it may be observed, by the way, is a continuation, not of Kings, but of Chronicles.) There is not the slightest allusion in the Book of Judges, to the Babylonish captivity. Only Judges iii. 5, 6, as regards the Canaanite races mentioned, and the context, may be compared with Ezra ix. 1, 2. The language of the Book of Judges points to the same conclusion. It is pure and good Hebrew, untainted with Chaldaisms or Persian forms. as are the later books.

The inference to which these and other such resemblances *tends*, is that the compilation of the

Book of Judges is of about the same age as that of the Books of Samuel and Kings, if not actually the work of the same hand. But no absolute certainty can be arrived at.

The chief allusions to it in the New Testament are those in Heb. xi. 32 seq., and Acts xiii. 20. But there are frequent references to the histories contained in it in the Psalms and in the Prophets. See Psalm lxxviii. 56, &c., lxxxiii. 9–11, cvi. 34–45, &c. ; Isaiah ix. 4, x. 26; Nehem. ix. 27, &c. See also 1 Sam. xii. 9–11 ; 2 Sam. xi. 21. Other Books to which it refers are Genesis, Exodus, Leviticus, Numbers, Deuteronomy, and Joshua. See marg. reff. to i. ii. 1–3, 6–10, 15, 20–23, iv. 11, vi. 8, 13, x. 11, xi. 13–26, xiii. 5, xvi. 17, xviii. 30, xix. 23, 24, xx. 26, 27, &c.

THE BOOK
OF
JUDGES.

CHAP. 1. NOW after the death of Joshua it came to pass, that the
children of Israel [a] asked the LORD, saying, Who shall go up for [a] Num. 27.
2 us against the Canaanites first, to fight against them? And the 21. ch. 20. 18.
LORD said, [b] Judah shall go up: behold, I have delivered the [b] Gen. 49. 8.
3 land into his hand. ¶ And Judah said unto Simeon his brother,
Come up with me into my lot, that we may fight against the
Canaanites; and [c] I likewise will go with thee into thy lot. So [c] ver. 17.
4 Simeon went with him. And Judah went up; and the LORD
delivered the Canaanites and the Perizzites into their hand:
5 and they slew of them in [d] Bezek ten thousand men. And they [d] 1 Sam. 11.
found Adoni-bezek in Bezek: and they fought against him, and 8.
6 they slew the Canaanites and the Perizzites. But Adoni-
bezek fled; and they pursued after him, and caught him, and
7 cut off his thumbs, and his great toes. And Adoni-bezek said,
Threescore and ten kings, having [1] their thumbs and their great
toes cut off, [2] gathered *their meat* under my table: [e] as I have [e] Lev. 24. 19.
done, so God hath requited me. And they brought him to 1 Sam. 15. 33.
8 Jerusalem, and there he died. ¶ Now [f] the children of Judah Jam. 2. 13.
had fought against Jerusalem, and had taken it, and smitten it [f] See Josh. 15. 63.

[1] Heb. *the thumbs of their hands and of their feet.* [2] Or, *gleaned.*

I. 1. *after the death of Joshua*] But from i. 1 to ii. 9 is a consecutive narrative, *ending* with the death of Joshua. Hence the events in this chapter and in ii. 1-6 are to be taken as belonging to the lifetime of Joshua. See ii. 11 note.

asked the LORD] The phrase is only found in *Judges* and *Samuel*. It was the privilege of the civil ruler, to apply to the High Priest to consult for him the Urim and Thummim (marg. ref.). (Cp. Josh. xiv. 1, xviii. 1, 10, xix. 51). Here it was not Phinehas, as Josephus concludes from placing these events after the death of Joshua, but Eleazar, through whom the children of Israel inquired "*Who*," (or, rather) "*which tribe of us shall go up?*"

2. *And the* LORD *said*] *i.e.* answered by Urim and Thummim. *The land* was the portion which fell to Judah by lot, not the whole land of Canaan (see iii. 11). The priority given to Judah is a plain indication of Divine direction. It points to the birth of our Lord of the tribe of Judah. Judah associated Simeon with him (*v.* 3) because their lots were intermingled (Josh. xix. 1).

4. *the Canaanites and the Perizzites*] See Gen. xii. 6, xiii. 7 notes. *Bezek* may be the name of a district. It has not yet been identified.

7. *threescore and ten kings*] We may infer from this number of conquered kings, that the intestine wars of the Canaanites were among the causes which, under God's Providence, weakened their resistance to the Israelites. Adoni-Bezek's cruelty to the subject kings was the cause of his receiving (cp. marg. reff.) this chastisement. The loss of the thumb would unfit a man for handling sword or bow; the loss of the great toe would impede his speed.

8. Render "**and** *the children of Judah* **fought** *against Jerusalem*, **and took it, and smote it,**" &c. With regard to the capture of Jerusalem there is some obscurity. It is here said to have been taken, smitten with the edge of the sword, and burnt, by the children of Judah. In Josh. xii. 8, 10 the Jebusite and the king of Jerusalem are enumerated among Joshua's conquests, but without any distinct mention of the capture of the city; and in the marg. ref. we read that the Jebusites were not expelled from Jerusalem, but dwelt with the children of Judah (cp. i. 21). Further we learn from xix. 10-12 that Jerusalem was wholly a Jebusite city in the lifetime of Phinehas (xx. 28), and so it continued till the reign of David (2 Sam. v. 6-9). The conclusion is that Jerusalem was only taken once, viz. at the time here described, and that this was in the lifetime of Joshua; but that the children of Judah did not occupy it in sufficient force to prevent the return of the Jebusites, who gradually recovered complete possession.

9 with the edge of the sword, and set the city on fire. [g]And afterward the children of Judah went down to fight against the
Canaanites, that dwelt in the mountain, and in the south, and in
10 the [1]valley. And Judah went against the Canaanites that dwelt
in Hebron: (now the name of Hebron before *was* [h]Kirjath-
11 arba:) and they slew Sheshai, and Ahiman, and Talmai. [i]And
from thence he went against the inhabitants of Debir: and the
12 name of Debir before *was* Kirjath-sepher: ¶ [k]And Caleb said,
He that smiteth Kirjath-sepher, and taketh it, to him will I
13 give Achsah my daughter to wife. And Othniel the son of
Kenaz, [l]Caleb's younger brother, took it: and he gave him
14 Achsah his daughter to wife. [m]And it came to pass, when she
came *to him*, that she moved him to ask of her father a field:
and she lighted from off *her* ass; and Caleb said unto her, What
15 wilt thou? And she said unto him, [n]Give me a blessing: for
thou hast given me a south land; give me also springs of water.
And Caleb gave her the upper springs and the nether springs.
16 ¶ [o]And the children of the Kenite, Moses' father in law, went
up out [p]of the city of palm trees with the children of Judah into
the wilderness of Judah, which *lieth* in the south of [q]Arad; [r]and
17 they went and dwelt among the people. ¶ [s]And Judah went
with Simeon his brother, and they slew the Canaanites that
inhabited Zephath, and utterly destroyed it. And the name of
18 the city was called [t]Hormah. Also Judah took [u]Gaza with the
coast thereof, and Askelon with the coast thereof, and Ekron
19 with the coast thereof. And [x]the LORD was with Judah; and
[2]he drave out *the inhabitants of* the mountain; but could not
drive out the inhabitants of the valley, because they had
20 [y]chariots of iron. [z]And they gave Hebron unto Caleb, as Moses
21 said: and he expelled thence the three sons of Anak. ¶ [a]And
the children of Benjamin did not drive out the Jebusites that
inhabited Jerusalem; but the Jebusites dwell with the children
22 of Benjamin in Jerusalem unto this day. ¶ And the house of
Joseph, they also went up against Beth-el: [b]and the LORD *was*
23 with them. And the house of Joseph [c]sent to descry Beth-el.
24 (Now the name of the city before *was* [d]Luz.) And the spies

[g] Josh. 10. 36. & 11. 21. & 15. 13.
[h] Josh. 14. 15. & 15. 14.
[i] Josh. 15. 15.
[k] Josh. 15. 16, 17.
[l] ch. 3. 9.
[m] Josh. 15. 18, 19.
[n] Gen. 33. 11.
[o] ch. 4. 11. 1 Sam. 15. 6. 1 Chr. 2. 55. Jer. 35. 2.
[p] Deut. 34. 3.
[q] Num. 21. 1.
[r] Num. 10. 32.
[s] ver. 3.
[t] Josh. 19. 4.
[u] Josh. 11. 22.
[x] ver. 2.
[y] Josh. 17. 16, 18.
[z] Num. 14. 24.
[a] See Josh. 18. 28.
[b] ver. 19.
[c] Josh. 2. 1. & 7. 2.
[d] Gen. 28. 19.

[1] Or, *low country*. [2] Or, *he possessed the mountain*.

---

set the city on fire] A phrase found only at xx. 48; 2 K. viii. 12, and Ps. lxxiv. 7.

16. *the children of the Kenite*] See Num. xxiv. 21 note.

the city of palm trees] Jericho (see marg. ref.). The Rabbinical story is that Jericho, with 500 cubits square of land, was given to Hobab. The use of the phrase "city of palm trees" for "Jericho," is perhaps an indication of the influence of Joshua's curse (Josh. vi. 26). The very *name* of Jericho was blotted out. There are no palm trees at Jericho now, but Josephus mentions them repeatedly, as well as the balsam trees.

17. *Hormah*] See Num. xxi. 1 note. The destruction then vowed was now accomplished. This is another decisive indication that the events here related belong to Joshua's lifetime. This would be about six years after the vow.

18. It is remarkable that *Ashdod* is not here mentioned, as it is in Josh. xv. 46, 47, in conjunction with Gaza and Ekron; but that Askelon, which is not in the list of the cities of Judah at all, is named in its stead. (See Josh. xiii. 3 note.) It is a curious fact that when Rameses III. took Askelon it was occupied, not by Philistines, but apparently by Hebrews. Rameses began to reign B.C. 1269, and reigned 25 years. At any time between 1269 and 1244 such occupation of Askelon by Hebrews agrees with the Book of Judges.

21. This verse is nearly identical with Josh. xv. 63, except in the substitution of *Benjamin* for *Judah*. Probably the original reading *Judah* was altered in later times to *Benjamin*, because Jebus was within the border of Benjamin, and neither had the Benjamites expelled the Jebusites.

22. Bethel was within the borders of Benjamin, but was captured, as we here learn, by the house of Joseph, who probably retained it.

saw a man come forth out of the city, and they said unto him,
Shew us, we pray thee, the entrance into the city, and [e]we will
25 shew thee mercy. And when he shewed them the entrance into
the city, they smote the city with the edge of the sword; but
26 they let go the man and all his family. And the man went
into the land of the Hittites, and built a city, and called the
name thereof Luz: which *is* the name thereof unto this day.
27 ¶ [f]Neither did Manasseh drive out *the inhabitants of* Beth-shean
and her towns, nor Taanach and her towns, nor the inhabitants
of Dor and her towns, nor the inhabitants of Ibleam and her
towns, nor the inhabitants of Megiddo and her towns: but the
28 Canaanites would dwell in that land. And it came to pass, when
Israel was strong, that they put the Canaanites to tribute, and
29 did not utterly drive them out. ¶ [g]Neither did Ephraim drive
out the Canaanites that dwelt in Gezer; but the Canaanites
30 dwelt in Gezer among them. ¶ Neither did Zebulun drive out
the inhabitants of Kitron, nor the [h]inhabitants of Nahalol; but
the Canaanites dwelt among them, and became tributaries.
31 ¶ [i]Neither did Asher drive out the inhabitants of Accho, nor
the inhabitants of Zidon, nor of Ahlab, nor of Achzib, nor of
32 Helbah, nor of Aphik, nor of Rehob: but the Asherites [k]dwelt
among the Canaanites, the inhabitants of the land: for they did
33 not drive them out. ¶ [l]Neither did Naphtali drive out the
inhabitants of Beth-shemesh, nor the inhabitants of Beth-anath;
but he [m]dwelt among the Canaanites, the inhabitants of the
land: nevertheless the inhabitants of Beth-shemesh and of Beth-
34 anath [n]became tributaries unto them. ¶ And the Amorites
forced the children of Dan into the mountain: for they would
35 not suffer them to come down to the valley: but the Amorites
would dwell in mount Heres [o]in Aijalon, and in Shaalbim: yet
the hand of the house of Joseph [1]prevailed, so that they became
36 tributaries. And the coast of the Amorites *was* [p]from [2]the going
up to Akrabbim, from the rock, and upward.

Chap. 2. And an [3]angel of the Lord came up from Gilgal [a]to
Bochim, and said, I made you to go up out of Egypt, and have

[e] Josh. 2. 12, 14.
[f] Josh. 17. 11, 12, 13.
[g] Josh. 16. 10. 1 Kin. 9. 16.
[h] Josh. 19. 15.
[i] Josh. 19. 24—30.
[k] Ps. 106. 34, 35.
[l] Josh. 19. 38.
[m] ver. 32.
[n] ver. 30.
[o] Josh. 19. 42.
[p] Num. 34. 4. Josh. 15. 3.
[a] ver. 5.

[1] Heb. *was heavy.* [2] Or, *Maaleh-akrabbim.* [3] Or, *messenger.*

---

26. The site of this new Luz is not known, but "the land of the Hittites" was apparently in the north of Palestine, on the borders of Syria (Gen. x. 15 note).

31. Cp. marg. ref. *Accho*, afterwards called Ptolemais, now Akka or St. Jean d'Acre, is named here for the first time.

32. It is an evidence of the power of the Canaanite in this portion of the land that it is not said (cp. *v.* 30) that the Canaanites dwelt among the Asherites, but that the Asherites (and *v.* 33, Naphtali) "dwelt among the Canaanites;" nor are the Canaanites in Accho, Zidon, and the other Asherite cities, said to have become tributaries.

34. The Amorites are usually found in the mountain (Num. xiii. 29; Josh, x. 6). Here they dwell in the valley, of which the monuments of Rameses III. show them to have been in possession when that monarch invaded Syria. It was their great strength in this district, and their forcible detention of the territory of Dan, which led to the expedition of the Danites (xviii.). The house of Joseph lent their powerful aid in subduing them, probably in the times of the Judges.

36. *the going up to Akrabbim*] See marg. and reff.; properly "the ascent of scorpions," with which the whole region abounds.

the rock] **Petra**, the capital of Idumea, so called from the mass of precipitous rock which encloses the town, and out of which many of its buildings are excavated. The original word *Selah* is always used of the rock at Kadesh-Barnea (Num. xx. 8–11), near Petra (cp. Obad. 3). This leads us to look for "the ascent of scorpions," here coupled with *has-selah*, in the same neighbourhood.

II. **1. The** *angel of the* Lord (not *an angel*).] The phrase is used nearly sixty times to designate the Angel of God's Presence. See Gen. xii. 7 note. In all cases where "the angel of the Lord" delivers a message,

[b] Gen. 17. 7. Ex. 3. 6—8.
[c] Deut. 7. 2.
[d] Deut. 12. 3.
[e] ver. 20.
[f] Josh. 23. 13.
[g] ch. 3. 6.
[h] Ex. 23. 33. & 34. 12. Deut. 7. 16.
[i] Josh. 22. 6. & 24. 28.
[k] Josh. 24. 31.
[l] Josh. 24. 29.
[m] Josh. 24. 30.
[n] Josh. 19. 50. & 24. 30. *Timnath serah.*
[o] 1 Sam. 2. 12. 1 Chr. 28. 9. Jer. 9. 3. Gal. 4. 8. 2 Thess. 1. 8. Tit. 1. 16.

brought you unto the land which I sware unto your fathers;
2 and [b]I said, I will never break my covenant with you. And [c]ye
shall make no league with the inhabitants of this land; [d]ye shall
throw down their altars: [e]but ye have not obeyed my voice:
3 why have ye done this? Wherefore I also said, I will not drive
them out from before you; but they shall be [f]*as thorns* in your
4 sides, and [g]their gods shall be a [h]snare unto you. And it
came to pass, when the angel of the LORD spake these words
unto all the children of Israel, that the people lifted up their
5 voice, and wept. And they called the name of that place
6 [1]Bochim: and they sacrificed there unto the LORD. ¶ And
when [i]Joshua had let the people go, the children of Israel went
7 every man unto his inheritance to possess the land. [k]And the
people served the LORD all the days of Joshua, and all the days
of the elders that [2]outlived Joshua, who had seen all the great
8 works of the LORD, that he did for Israel. And [l]Joshua the
son of Nun, the servant of the LORD, died, *being* an hundred and
9 ten years old. [m]And they buried him in the border of his
inheritance in [n]Timnath-heres, in the mount of Ephraim, on the
10 north side of the hill Gaash. And also all that generation were
gathered unto their fathers: and there arose another generation
after them, which [o]knew not the LORD, nor yet the works

[1] That is, *Weepers.*

[2] Heb. *prolonged days after Joshua.*

---

he does it as if God Himself were speaking, without the intervening words "*Thus saith the Lord,*" which are used in the case of prophets. (Cp. vi. 8; Josh. xxiv. 2.)

When the host of Israel came up from Gilgal in the plain of Jericho, near the Jordan (Josh. iv. 19) to Shiloh and Shechem, in the hill country of Ephraim, the Angel who had been with them at Gilgal (Exod. xxiii. 20-23, xxxiii. 1-4; Josh. v. 10-15) accompanied them. The mention of Gilgal thus fixes the transaction to the period soon after the removal of the camp from Gilgal, and the events recorded in i. 1-36 (of which those related in *vv.* 1-29 took place before, and those in *vv.* 30-36, just after that removal). It also shows that it was the conduct of the Israelites, recorded in ch. i. as in Josh. xvi. xvii., which provoked this rebuke.

2. The two articles of the Covenant here specified (cp. marg. reff.) are those which the Israelites had at this time broken. The other important prohibition (Deut. vii. 3) is not specified by the Angel, and this is an indication that at the time the Angel spoke, intermarriages with the heathen spoken of (iii. 6) had not taken place; and this again is another evidence of the early date of this occurrence.

3. "*Wherefore I also said*"] Rather because ye have done the things mentioned in *v.* 2, "**I have now said** (*i.e.* I now protest and declare) *that I will not drive them out from before you*" (cp. xix. 29). And it was the announcement of this resolution by the Angel that caused the people to weep.

The word thorns in this verse is supplied by the A. V. from the similar passage in Joshua (see marg. ref.). Other Versions adopt a different reading of the original text, and prefer the sense "they shall be to you for adversaries" (cp. the last words of Num. xxxiii. 55).

5. *Bochim*] *i.e.* weepers. It was near Shechem, but the site is unknown. Cp. the names given to places for similar reasons in Gen. xxxv. 8, l. 11.

7. If Joshua was about 80 at the entrance into Canaan, 30 years would bring us to the close of his life. The "elders" would be all that were old enough to take part in the wars of Canaan (iii. 1, 2); and therefore, reckoning from the age of 20 to 70, a period of about 50 years may be assigned from the entrance into Canaan to the death of the elders, or 20 years after the death of Joshua.

the great works of the LORD] The overthrow of the Canaanitish nations.

8. *the servant of the* LORD] This is a title specially given to Moses (Deut. xxxiv. 5; Josh. i. 1). In later books, the phrase "the servant of God" is used (1 Chr. vi. 49; Neh. x. 29; Dan. ix. 11; Rev. xv. 3). It is applied to Joshua only here and in Josh. xxiv. 29. It is spoken of David (Ps. xviii., title), and generally of the prophets; and, like the analogous phrase, "man of God," is transferred by St. Paul to the ministers of Christ under the New Testament (2 Tim. ii. 24; Jam. i. 1).

10. *all that generation*] *i.e.* the main body of those who were grown-up men at the time of the conquest of Canaan.

11 which he had done for Israel. ¶ And the children of Israel did
12 evil in the sight of the LORD, and served Baalim: and they
[p]forsook the LORD God of their fathers, which brought them out [p] Deut. 31. 16.
of the land of Egypt, and followed [q]other gods, of the gods of [q] Deut. 6. 14.
the people that *were* round about them, and [r]bowed themselves [r] Ex. 20. 5.
13 unto them, and provoked the LORD to anger. And they forsook
14 the LORD, [s]and served Baal and Ashtaroth. ¶ [t]And the anger [s] ch. 3. 7.
of the LORD was hot against Israel, and he [u]delivered them into [t] ch. 3. 8.
the hands of spoilers that spoiled them, and [x]he sold them into [u] 2 Kin. 17. 20.
the hands of their enemies round about, so that they [y]could not [x] ch. 3. 8.
15 any longer stand before their enemies. Whithersoever they Ps. 44. 12.
went out, the hand of the LORD was against them for evil, as Isai. 50. 1.
the LORD had said, and [z]as the LORD had sworn unto them: and [y] Lev. 26. 37. Josh. 7. 12.
16 they were greatly distressed. ¶ Nevertheless [a]the LORD raised [z] Lev. 26. Deut. 28.
up judges, which [1]delivered them out of the hand of those that [a] ch. 3. 9.
17 spoiled them. And yet they would not hearken unto their 1 Sam. 12. 11.
judges, but they [b]went a whoring after other gods, and bowed Acts 13. 20.
themselves unto them: they turned quickly out of the way [b] Ex. 34. 15. Lev. 17. 7.
which their fathers walked in, obeying the commandments of
18 the LORD; *but* they did not so. And when the LORD raised
them up judges, then [c]the LORD was with the judge, and [c] Josh. 1. 5.
delivered them out of the hand of their enemies all the days of
the judge: [d]for it repented the LORD because of their groanings [d] Ps. 106. 34–45.
19 by reason of them that oppressed them and vexed them. And it
came to pass, [e]when the judge was dead, *that* they returned, and
[2]corrupted *themselves* more than their fathers, in following other [e] ch. 3. 12. & 4. 1, &c.
gods to serve them, and to bow down unto them; [3]they ceased
not from their own doings, nor from their stubborn way.
20 ¶ [f]And the anger of the LORD was hot against Israel; and he [f] ver. 14.
said, Because that this people hath [g]transgressed my covenant [g] Josh. 23. 16.
which I commanded their fathers, and have not hearkened unto

[1] Heb. *saved.* [2] Or, *were corrupt.* [3] Heb. *they let nothing fall of their.*

---

11. *and the children of Israel*] Here begins the narrative of what really did happen "after the death of Joshua," but of which ch. i. conveys no hint. Israel served the Lord all the days of Joshua (i. 7). But when Joshua was dead..."the children of Israel did evil in the sight of the Lord, and served Baalim, and forsook the God of their fathers." And then follows, from *v.* 14 to the end of the chapter, a summary of the whole contents of the Book.

did evil in the sight of the LORD] Through this Book and all the Historical Books, this is the regular phrase for falling into idolatry. It occurs seven times in Judges, as descriptive of the seven apostasies of Israel, which drew down upon them the seven servitudes under (1) Chushan-Rishathaim, (2) Eglon, (3) Jabin, (4) Midian, (5) the tyranny of Abimelech, (6) the Ammonites, (7) the Philistines. The recurrence of the phrase marks the hand of one author and of one book. For the opposite phrase, see 1 K. xv. 5, 11, &c.

The plural of Baal, *Baalim*, refers to the numerous images of Baal which they set up and worshipped, as does the plural form, *Ashtaroth* (*v.* 13), to those of the female divinity, Astarte.

12. *provoked the* LORD *to anger*] A frequent expression in connexion with idolatry, especially in Deut., in the Books of the Kings, and in Jeremiah.

14, 15. Consult the marg. reff. The phrase, *he sold them into the hands &c.*, is first found in Deut. xxxii. 30.

16. *nevertheless* (rather "and") *the* LORD *raised up judges*] This is the first introduction of the term JUDGE, which gives its name to the Book (Introd. p. 67).

18. *it repented the* LORD] Rather, "**the Lord was moved with compassion,**" or "was grieved," "*because* of their groanings." (Cp. xxi. 15.)

20. This verse is connected with *v.* 13. The intermediate verses refer to much later times; they have the appearance of being the reflections of the compiler interspersed with the original narrative. But *v.* 20 catches up the thread only to let it fall immediately. All that follows, down to the end of iii. 7, seems to be another digression, closing with words like those of ii. 13.

It does not appear how this message

21 my voice; [h]I also will not henceforth drive out any from before
22 them of the nations which Joshua left when he died: [i]that
through them I may [k]prove Israel, whether they will keep the
way of the LORD to walk therein, as their fathers did keep *it*, or
23 not. Therefore the LORD [1]left those nations, without driving
them out hastily; neither delivered he them into the hand of
Joshua.
CHAP. 3. NOW these *are* [a]the nations which the LORD left, to
prove Israel by them, *even* as many *of Israel* as had not known
2 all the wars of Canaan; only that the generations of the children
of Israel might know, to teach them war, at the least such as
3 before knew nothing thereof; *namely*, [b]five lords of the Philistines, and all the Canaanites, and the Sidonians, and the Hivites
that dwelt in mount Lebanon, from mount Baal-hermon unto
4 the entering in of Hamath. [c]And they were to prove Israel by
them, to know whether they would hearken unto the commandments of the LORD, which he commanded their fathers by the
5 hand of Moses. ¶ [d]And the children of Israel dwelt among the
Canaanites, Hittites, and Amorites, and Perizzites, and Hivites,
6 and Jebusites: and [e]they took their daughters to be their wives,
and gave their daughters to their sons, and served their gods.
7 [f]And the children of Israel did evil in the sight of the LORD, and
forgat the LORD their God, [g]and served Baalim and [h]the groves.
8 Therefore the anger of the LORD was hot against Israel, and he
[i]sold them into the hand of [k]Chushan-rishathaim king of [2]Meso-
potamia: and the children of Israel served Chushan-rishathaim

[h] Josh. 23. 13.
[i] ch. 3. 1, 4.
[k] Deut. 8. 2, 16. & 13. 3.
[a] ch. 2. 21, 22.
[b] Josh 13. 2—6.
[c] ch. 2. 22.
[d] Ps. 106. 35.
[e] Ex. 34. 16. Deut. 7. 3.
[f] ch. 2. 11.
[g] ch. 2. 13.
[h] Ex. 34. 13. ch. 6. 25.
[i] ch. 2. 14.
[k] Hab. 3. 7.

[1] Or, *suffered*.

[2] Heb. *Aram-naharaim*.

---

was given to Israel, whether by Angel, or prophet, or Urim, nor indeed is it certain whether any message was given. The words may be understood as merely explaining what passed through the Divine mind, and expressing the thoughts which regulated the Divine proceeding.

III. 1. *even as many of Israel*, &c.] These words show that the writer has especially in view the generation which came to man's estate immediately after the close of the wars with the Canaanites (Josh. xxiii. 1). Cp. ii. 10.

3. *lords*] *Seranim*, a title used exclusively of the princes of the five Philistine cities. The title is probably of Phœnician origin.

Joshua appears to have smitten and subdued the Hivites as far north as Baal-Gad, in the valley of Lebanon under Mount Hermon (Josh. xi. 17, xii. 7), but no further (Josh. xiii. 5). There was an unsubdued Hivite population to the north of Baal-hermon (probably Baal-Gad under Hermon, since it is not synonymous with Hermon; see 1 Chr. v. 23), to the entering in of Hamath: *i. e.* in the fertile valley of Cœle-Syria. Hamath is always spoken of as the extreme northern boundary of the land of Canaan. It was the gate of approach to Canaan from Babylon, and all the north (Zech. ix. 2; Jer. xxxix. 5). It formed part of the dominions of Solomon (2 Ch.r. viii. 4), and of the future inheritance of Israel, as described in vision by Ezekiel (xlvii. 16).

6. See ii. 2 note.

7. *and the groves*] Lit. *Asheroth*, images of Asherah [the goddess companion of Baal]: see Deut. xvi. 21 note.

8. Here we hold again the thread of the proper narrative, which seems as if it ought to have run thus (i. 1): Now, &c. (iii. 8), therefore (or "and") &c.

served Chushan-Rishathaim] This is the same phrase as in *v.* 14. From it is derived the expression, "the times of servitude," as distinguished from "the times of rest," in speaking of the times of the Judges. Mesopotamia, or Aram-naharaim, was the seat of Nimrod's kingdom, and Nimrod was the son of Cush (Gen. x. 8-12). Rishathaim is perhaps the name of a city, or a foreign word altered to a Hebrew form. Nothing is known from history, or the cuneiform inscriptions, of the political condition of Mesopotamia at this time, though Thotmes I. and III. in the 18th Egyptian dynasty are known to have invaded Mesopotamia. It is, however, in accordance with such an aggressive Aramean movement towards Palestine, that as early as the time of Abraham we find the kings of Shinar and of Elam invading the south of Palestine. There is also distinct evidence in the names of the Edomitish kings (Gen. xxxvi. 32, 35, 37) of an Aramean dynasty in Edom

9 eight years. ¶ And when the children of Israel [l]cried unto the — [l] ver. 15.
LORD, the LORD [m]raised up a [1]deliverer to the children of Israel, — [m] ch. 2. 16.
who delivered them, *even* [n]Othniel the son of Kenaz, Caleb's — [n] ch. 1. 13.
10 younger brother. And [o]the Spirit of the LORD [2]came upon him, — [o] See Num.
and he judged Israel, and went out to war: and the LORD — 27. 18.
delivered Chushan-rishathaim king of [3]Mesopotamia into his — 1 Sam. 11. 6.
11 hand; and his hand prevailed against Chushan-rishathaim. And — 2 Chr. 15. 1.
the land had rest forty years. And Othniel the son of Kenaz
12 died. ¶ [p]And the children of Israel did evil again in the sight
of the LORD: and the LORD strengthened [q]Eglon the king of — [p] ch. 2. 19.
Moab against Israel, because they had done evil in the sight of — [q] 1 Sam. 12, 9.
13 the LORD. And he gathered unto him the children of Ammon
and [r]Amalek, and went and smote Israel, and possessed [s]the — [r] ch. 5. 14.
14 city of palm trees. So the children of Israel [t]served Eglon the — [s] ch. 1. 16.
15 king of Moab eighteen years. ¶ But when the children of Israel — [t] Deut.28.48.
[u]cried unto the LORD, the LORD raised them up a deliverer, — [u] ver. 9. ch. 4. 3. & 6. 7.
Ehud the son of Gera, [4]a Benjamite, a man [5]lefthanded: and — & 10. 10. 1 Sam.12.10. Ps. 22. 5. & 106. 44. & 107. 13, 19.

[1] Heb. *saviour.*
[2] Heb. *was.*
[3] Heb. *Aram.*
[4] Or, *the son of Gemini.*
[5] Heb. *shut of his right hand.* ch. 20. 16.

---

about the time of the early Judges. Cp., too, Job i. 17.

9. Othniel was already distinguished in Joshua's lifetime as a brave and successful leader. See Josh. xv. 16, 17.

10. *and the Spirit of the* LORD *came upon him*] The phrase occurs frequently in this Book and in the Books of Samuel and Kings. It marks the peculiar office of the Judges. They were saviours (*v.* 9 marg. Neh. ix. 27) called and directed by the Holy Spirit, Who endued them with extraordinary wisdom, courage, and strength for the work which lay before them (cp. vi. 34, xi. 29, xiii. 25, xiv. 6. 19), and were in this respect types of Christ the "Judge of Israel" (Mic. v. 1), in Whom "the Spirit of the Lord God" was "without measure" (Isai. xi. 2, lxi. 1; Matt. xii. 18-21; Joh. i. 32; Acts xiii. 2).

11. *the land* means here, as in i. 2, not the whole land of Canaan, but the part concerned, probably the land of the tribe of Judah. *Forty years,* here and elsewhere, is (like *fourscore years, v.* 30) a round number, perhaps equivalent to a generation.

12. The "strengthening" Eglon was the special work of God, and because Israel "had done evil," &c. Samuel's comment on the event is to the same effect (1 Sam. xii. 9).

13. The children of Ammon (Beni-Ammon), almost always so spoken of from their ancestor Ben-ammi (Gen. xix. 38), seem to be under the leadership of the king of Moab, as do also the Amalekites: this is perhaps the *strengthening* spoken of in *v.* 12. In ch. vi. the combination is Midianites, Amalekites, and children of the East, or Arab tribes. In the narrative of Jephthah's judgeship, the Ammonites alone are mentioned; but with a reference to the Moabites, and as if they were one people (xi. 24). The Amalekites appear as the constant and bitter foes of the Israelites (Exod. xvii. 8 notes and reff.); and the naming a mountain in Ephraim, "*the mount of the Amalekites*" (xii. 15) is probably a memorial of this joint invasion of Moabites and Amalekites, and marks the scene either of their occupation, or of some signal victory over them.

The city of palm trees: *i.e.* Jericho (i. 16), having been utterly destroyed by Joshua, and not rebuilt till the time of Ahab (Josh. vi. 24–26; 1 K. xvi. 34), can only have existed at this time as an unwalled village,—like Jerusalem after its destruction by Nebuzaradan, till Nehemiah rebuilt its walls—and like its modern representative er-Riha, a village with a fortress for the Turkish garrison. This occupation of Jericho should be compared with the invasion in x. 9, where two out of the three tribes named, Benjamin and Ephraim, are the same as those here concerned, and where (x. 7) the Philistines are coupled with the Ammonites, just as here (*v.* 31) the Philistines are mentioned in near connexion with the Moabites. See Introd. p. 69.

15. *But when the children of Israel cried unto the* LORD, *the* LORD *raised them up a deliverer*] The very same words as are used at *v.* 9. See, too, ii. 16, 18, and Neh. ix. 27.

Ehud "the *Benjamite*" was of the family or house of Gera (2 Sam. xvi. 5), the son of Bela, Benjamin's first-born, born before Jacob's descent into Egypt (Gen. xlvi. 21), and then included among "the sons of Benjamin." The genealogy in 1 Chr. viii. 6 intimates that Ehud (apparently written Abihud in *v.* 3) became the head of a separate house.

left-handed] See marg. The phrase is thought to describe not so much a defect as

by him the children of Israel sent a present unto Eglon the king
16 of Moab. But Ehud made him a dagger which had two edges,
of a cubit length; and he did gird it under his raiment upon his
17 right thigh. And he brought the present unto Eglon king of
18 Moab: and Eglon *was* a very fat man. And when he had made
an end to offer the present, he sent away the people that bare
[a] Josh. 4. 20. 19 the present. But he himself turned again [a] from the [1] quarries
that *were* by Gilgal, and said, I have a secret errand unto thee,
O king: who said, Keep silence. And all that stood by him
20 went out from him. And Ehud came unto him; and he was
sitting in [2] a summer parlour, which he had for himself alone.
And Ehud said, I have a message from God unto thee. And he
21 arose out of *his* seat. And Ehud put forth his left hand, and
took the dagger from his right thigh, and thrust it into his belly:
22 and the haft also went in after the blade; and the fat closed
upon the blade, so that he could not draw the dagger out of his
23 belly; and [3] the dirt came out. Then Ehud went forth through
the porch, and shut the doors of the parlour upon him, and
24 locked them. When he was gone out, his servants came; and
when they saw that, behold, the doors of the parlour *were*
locked, they said, Surely he [4] covereth his feet in his summer
25 chamber. And they tarried till they were ashamed: and,
behold, he opened not the doors of the parlour; therefore they
took a key, and opened *them*: and, behold, their lord *was* fallen
26 down dead on the earth. And Ehud escaped while they tarried,
27 and passed beyond the quarries, and escaped unto Seirath. And

1 Or, *graven images.*
2 Heb. *a parlour of cooling*: See Amos 3. 15.
3 Or, *it came out at the fundament.*
4 Or, *doeth his easement.* 1 Sam. 24. 3.

---

the power to use left and right hands equally well (cp. xx. 16; 1 Chr. xii. 2).

a present] *i.e.* tribute (2 Sam. viii. 2, 6; 1 K. iv. 21; Ps. lxxii. 10). The employment of Ehud for this purpose points him out as a chief of some distinction. He would be attended by a numerous suite (*v.* 18). We may conclude that the destruction of the Benjamites (ch. xx.) had not taken place at this time.

16. *upon his right thigh*] The proper side for a left-handed man. It would give him the appearance of being unarmed. The narrative shows clearly that his action was premeditated (*v.* 21).

19. Gilgal was in the immediate neighbourhood of Jericho (ii. 1), where doubtless Eglon held his court at this time (*v.* 13).

quarries] Some take the original of this word in its common meaning of carved images or idols (see marg.).

20. Probably Ehud's first message (*v.* 19) had been delivered to the attendants, and by them carried to the king. Now Ehud is admitted to the king's presence, into the cool upper chamber.

I have a message from God unto thee] Ehud believed himself to be accomplishing the Divine mandate, and so his words were true in a certain sense. But it was also a stratagem to cause the king to rise, that the thrust might be sure. [The king rose at once, in true Oriental respect for a Divine message, or from fear (cp. Josh. ix. 24).]

22. The A.V. and margin give different explanations of the last words of this verse. Others explain it of a vestibule or chamber, through which Ehud passed into the porch where the entrance doors were. He locked the doors, took the key with him, and then retired through the midst of the attendants below [or, more probably, through the door which communicated directly with the outside].

24. *he covereth his feet*] Cp. marg. reff. The explanation of the phrase as "taking sleep" suits both passages best.

25. *a key*] Literally "an opener." Probably a wooden instrument with which they either lifted up the latch within, or drew back the wooden bar or bolt. The chief officer of Eglon's household probably had a second key (cp. Isai. xxii. 15, 20-22, xxxvii. 2).

26. *Seirath*] "The forest" or "weald," which evidently bordered on the cultivated plain near Gilgal, and extended into "the mountain or hill country of Ephraim." Once there, he was safe from pursuit (cp. 1 Sam. xiii. 6), and quickly collected a strong force of Ephraimites and probably the bordering Benjamites.

it came to pass, when he was come, that [y]he blew a trumpet in
the [z]mountain of Ephraim, and the children of Israel went down
28 with him from the mount, and he before them. And he said
unto them, Follow after me: for [a]the LORD hath delivered your
enemies the Moabites into your hand. And they went down
after him, and took [b]the fords of Jordan toward Moab, and
29 suffered not a man to pass over. And they slew of Moab at
that time about ten thousand men, all [1]lusty, and all men of
30 valour; and there escaped not a man. So Moab was subdued
that day under the hand of Israel. And [c]the land had rest
31 fourscore years. ¶And after him was [d]Shamgar the son of
Anath, which slew of the Philistines six hundred men [e]with an
ox goad: [f]and he also delivered [g]Israel.

CHAP. 4. AND [a]the children of Israel again did evil in the sight of
2 the LORD, when Ehud was dead. And the LORD [b]sold them
into the hand of Jabin king of Canaan, that reigned in [c]Hazor;
the captain of whose host *was* [d]Sisera, which dwelt in [e]Ha-
3 rosheth of the Gentiles. And the children of Israel cried unto
the LORD: for he had nine hundred [f]chariots of iron; and
twenty years [g]he mightily oppressed the children of Israel.

[y] ch. 5. 14. & 6. 34. 1 Sam. 13. 3.
[z] Josh. 17. 15.
[a] ch. 7. 9. 1 Sam. 17. 47.
[b] Josh. 2. 7. ch. 12. 5.
[c] ver. 11.
[d] ch. 5. 6, 8. 1 Sam. 13. 19, 22.
[e] 1 Sam. 17. 47, 50.
[f] ch. 2. 16.
[g] ch. 4. 1, 3. & 10. 7, 17. 1 Sam. 4. 1.

[a] ch. 2. 19.
[b] ch. 2. 14.
[c] Josh. 11. 1, 10. & 19. 36.
[d] 1 Sam. 12. 9. Ps. 83. 9.
[e] ver. 13, 16.
[f] ch. 1. 19.
[g] ch. 5. 8. Ps. 106. 42.

[1] Heb *fat*.

28. Ehud "went down" from the mountain of Ephraim into the Jordan valley beneath it, straight to the Jordan fords (Josh. ii. 7), so as to intercept all communication between the Moabites on the west side and their countrymen on the east.

30. *the land*] *i.e.* that portion of it which had suffered from the oppression of Moab, probably Benjamin and Ephraim chiefly (see *v.* 11).

In judging of the nature of Ehud's act there are many considerations which must greatly modify our judgment. Acts of violence or cunning, done in an age when human society applauded such acts, when the best men of the age thought them right, and when men were obliged to take the law into their own hands in self-defence, are very different from the same acts done in an age when the enlightened consciences of men generally condemn them, and when the law of the land and the law of nations give individuals adequate security. We can allow to Ehud faith and courage and patriotism, without being blind to those defective views of moral right which made him and his countrymen glory in an act which in the light of Christianity is a crime. It is remarkable that neither Ehud nor Jael are included in St. Paul's list in Heb. xi. 32.

31. From this verse and v. 6 we may gather that Shamgar was contemporary with Jael, and that he only procured a temporary and partial deliverance for Israel by his exploit. He may have been of the tribe of Judah.

an ox goad] An instrument of wood about eight feet long, armed with an iron spike or point at one end, with which to spur the ox at plough, and with an iron scraper at the other end with which to detach the earth from the ploughshare when it became encumbered with it. The fact of their deliverer having no better weapon enhances his faith, and the power of his Divine helper. At the same time it shows how low the men of Judah were brought at this time, being disarmed by their oppressors (v. 8), as was also the case later (1 Sam. xiii. 19).

IV. 2. See Josh. xi. 1 note. Since the events there narrated, Hazor must have been rebuilt, and have resumed its position as the metropolis of the northern Canaanites; the other cities must also have resumed their independence, and restored the fallen dynasties.

Harosheth [identified by Conder with El Harathîyeh, see *v.* 6] is marked by the addition *of the Gentiles*, as in *Galilee of the nations* (Gen. xiv. 1; Isai. ix. 1). The name *Harosheth* signifies *workmanship*, *cutting* and *carving*, whether in stone or wood (Ex. xxxi. 5), and hence might be applied to the place where such works are carried on. It has been conjectured that this being a great timber district, rich in cedars and fir-trees, and near Great Zidon (Josh. xi. 8), Jabin kept a large number of oppressed Israelites at work in hewing wood, and preparing it at Harosheth for transport to Zidon; and that these woodcutters, armed with axes and hatchets, formed the soldiers of Barak's army.

3. *oppressed*] The same word is used (Ex. iii. 9) of the oppression of Israel by the Egyptians. If they were put to task-work in hewing timber, their condition was very like that of their ancestors making bricks.

4 And Deborah, a prophetess, the wife of Lapidoth, she judged
5 Israel at that time. [h]And she dwelt under the palm tree of
Deborah between Ramah and Beth-el in mount Ephraim: and
6 the children of Israel came up to her for judgment. And she
sent and called [i]Barak the son of Abinoam out [k]of Kedesh-
naphtali, and said unto him, Hath not the LORD God of Israel
commanded, *saying*, Go and draw toward mount Tabor, and
take with thee ten thousand men of the children of Naphtali
7 and of the children of Zebulun? And [l]I will draw unto thee to
the [m]river Kishon Sisera, the captain of Jabin's army, with his
chariots and his multitude; and I will deliver him into thine
8 hand. And Barak said unto her, If thou wilt go with me, then
I will go: but if thou wilt not go with me, *then* I will not go.
9 And she said, I will surely go with thee: notwithstanding the
journey that thou takest shall not be for thine honour; for the
LORD shall [n]sell Sisera into the hand of a woman. And Debo-

[h] Gen. 35. 8.
[i] Heb. 11. 32.
[k] Josh. 12. 22.
[l] Ex. 14. 4.
[m] ch. 5. 21. 1 Kin. 18. 40. Ps. 83. 9.
[n] ch. 2. 14.

---

4. *Deborah, a prophetess*] Her name, meaning *a bee*, is the same as that of Rebekah's nurse (marg. ref.). The reason of her pre-eminence is added. She was **"a woman, a prophetess,"** like Miriam (Ex. xv. 20); Huldah (2 K. xxii. 14), &c. In *vv.* 6, 9, 14, we have examples of her prophetic powers, and in ch. v. a noble specimen of prophetic song. Though the other Judges are not called prophets, yet they all seem to have had direct communications from God, either of knowledge, or power, or both (cp. iii. 10 note).

5. *she dwelt*] Rather, **"she sat,"** viz. to judge the people (*v.* 10), but not in the usual place, "the gate" (Ruth iv. 1, 2; Prov. xxii. 22). It suited her character, and the wild unsafe times better, that she should sit under a palm-tree in the secure heights of Mount Ephraim, between Ramah and Bethel (xx. 33 note). This verse shows that the Judges exercised the civil as well as military functions of rulers (1 Sam. vii. 15–17).

6. The name *Barak* signifies *lightning*, an appropriate name for a warrior. It is found also as *Barca* or *Barcas*, among Punic proper names. Cp. Mark iii. 17. On Kedesh-Naphtali see marg. ref.

Deborah speaks of God as *Jehovah the God of Israel*, because she speaks, as it were, in the presence of the heathen enemies of Israel, and to remind the Israelites, in the day of their distress, that He was ready to perform the mercy promised to their fathers, and to remember His holy Covenant. This title, too, would recall to their memories in an instant all His past acts in Egypt, at the Red Sea, in the wilderness, and in the conquest of Canaan.

The object of "drawing (toward Mount Tabor" rather, spreading out, cp. xx. 37) was to effect a junction of the northern tribes with the tribes of Ephraim and Benjamin, who were separated from them by the plain of Esdraelon, where Sisera's chariots would naturally congregate and be most effective. Mount Tabor rises from the plain of Esdraelon, about 1,865 ft. above the sea, and its broad top of nearly a mile in circumference afforded a strong position, out of reach of Sisera's chariots. If El Harathîyeh be Harosheth, Sisera must have marched from the west. Harathîyeh is a height in the range which separates Esdraelon from the plains of Acre, under which the Kishon breaks through in its course to the sea.

7. The brook or stream Kishon (Nahr Mukutta), so called from its winding course, caused by the dead level of the plain of Esdraelon through which it flows, rises, in respect to one of its sources or feeders, in Mount Tabor, and flows nearly due west through the plain, under Mount Carmel, and into the Bay of Acre. In the early or eastern part of its course, before it is recruited by the springs on Carmel, it is nothing but a torrent, often dry, but liable to swell very suddenly and dangerously, and to overflow its banks in early spring, after rain or the melting of snow. The ground on the banks of the Kishon near Megiddo [Mujedd'a, see Josh. xii. 21 note] becomes an impassable morass under the same circumstances, and would be particularly dangerous to a large number of chariots.

8. Barak, like Gideon (vi. 15, 36–40), and Abraham (Gen. xv. 2, 3, xvii. 18), and Moses (Ex. iv. 10, 13), and Peter (Matt. xiv. 30, 31), exhibited some weakness of faith at first. But this only makes his example more profitable for our encouragement, though he himself suffered some loss by his weakness (*v.* 9).

9. Mark the unhesitating faith and courage of Deborah, and the rebuke to Barak's timidity, "the Lord shall sell Sisera into the hand of a woman" (Jael, *v.* 22). For a similar use of a weak instrument, that the excellency of the power might be of God, compare the history of Gideon and his 300, David and his sling, Shamgar and his ox-goad, Samson and the jawbone of the ass. (See 1 Cor. i. 26–31.) Barak would pro-

10 rah arose, and went with Barak to Kedesh. And Barak called
[o]Zebulun and Naphtali to Kedesh; and he went up with ten
thousand men [p]at his feet: and Deborah went up with him.
11 ¶ Now Heber [q]the Kenite, *which was* of the children of
[r]Hobab the father in law of Moses, had severed himself from
the Kenites, and pitched his tent unto the plain of Zaanaim,
12 [s]which *is* by Kedesh. ¶ And they shewed Sisera that Barak the
13 son of Abinoam was gone up to mount Tabor. And Sisera
[1]gathered together all his chariots, *even* nine hundred chariots
of iron, and all the people that *were* with him, from Harosheth
14 of the Gentiles unto the river of Kishon. ¶ And Deborah said
unto Barak, Up; for this *is* the day in which the LORD hath
delivered Sisera into thine hand: [t]is not the LORD gone out
before thee? So Barak went down from mount Tabor, and ten
15 thousand men after him. And [u]the LORD discomfited Sisera,
and all *his* chariots, and all *his* host, with the edge of the
sword before Barak; so that Sisera lighted down off *his* chariot,
16 and fled away on his feet. But Barak pursued after the chariots,
and after the host, unto Harosheth of the Gentiles: and all
the host of Sisera fell upon the edge of the sword; *and* there
17 was not [2]a man left. ¶ Howbeit Sisera fled away on his feet to
the tent of Jael the wife of Heber the Kenite: for *there was*
peace between Jabin the king of Hazor and the house of Heber
18 the Kenite. And Jael went out to meet Sisera, and said unto
him, Turn in, my lord, turn in to me; fear not. And when
he had turned in unto her into the tent, she covered him with a
19 [3]mantle. And he said unto her, Give me, I pray thee, a little
water to drink; for I am thirsty. And she opened [x]a bottle of
20 milk, and gave him drink, and covered him. Again he said
unto her, Stand in the door of the tent, and it shall be, when

[o] ch. 5. 18.
[p] See Ex. 11. 8. 1 Kin. 20. 10.
[q] ch. 1. 16.
[r] Num. 10. 29.
[s] ver. 6.
[t] Deut. 9. 3. 2 Sam. 5. 24. Ps. 68. 7. Isai. 52. 12.
[u] Ps. 83. 9, 10. See Josh. 10. 10.
[x] ch. 5. 25.

[1] Heb. *gathered by cry*, or *proclamation*.
[2] Heb. *unto one*.
[3] Or, *rug*, or *blanket*.

---

bably think *the woman* must be Deborah. The prophecy was only explained by its fulfilment. Her presence as a prophetess would give a divine sanction to Barak's attempt to raise the tribes of Zebulun and Naphtali. To Barak himself it would be a pledge of her truth and sincerity. She probably commissioned some chief to raise the tribes of Ephraim, Benjamin, and Manasseh (v. 14, cp. Ps. lxxx. 2), while she went with Barak and mustered Zebulun, Naphtali, and Issachar.

10. Rather, "**and ten thousand men went up** (to Tabor) **at his feet**;" *i.e.* as his followers ("*after him*," *v.* 14).

11. Read, "**Heber the Kenite had severed himself from the Kenites which were of the children of Hobab,**" &c., "**unto the oak** (or *terebinth tree*) **in Zaanaim**" [or Bitzaanaim, which Conder identifies with Bessûm, twelve miles S.E. of Tabor, and near Kedesh on the Sea of Galilee]. This migration of Heber the Kenite, with a portion of his tribe, from the south of Judah to the north of Naphtali, perhaps caused by Philistine oppression, had clearly taken place recently. It is mentioned here to account for the subsequent narrative, but possibly also because the news of the great muster of the Israelites at Kedesh had been carried to Sisera by some of the tribe (*v.* 12), whose tents we are here informed were in the immediate neighbourhood of Kedesh.

15. *lighted down off his chariot*] Probably his chariot stuck in the morass (note on *v.* 7); or he might leave his chariot in order to mislead his pursuers, and in hope of gaining a place of safety while they were following the track of the chariot-wheels and the bulk of the host.

16. What with the overflowing of the Kishon (v. 21), by which numbers were drowned, and the panic which had seized the defeated army, and made them an easy prey to the sword of the pursuing Israelites, Sisera's whole force was cut to pieces and broken up.

17. Sisera went, not to Heber's tent, but to Jael's, as more secure from pursuit. Women occupied a separate tent. (Gen. xviii. 6, 10, xxiv. 67.)

20. *Stand in the door*, &c.] The characteristic duplicity of the Oriental character, both in Sisera and Jael, is very forcibly depicted in this narrative. It is only by the

any man doth come and enquire of thee, and say, Is there any
21 man here? that thou shalt say, No. Then Jael Heber's wife
[y]took a nail of the tent, and [1]took an hammer in her hand, and
went softly unto him, and smote the nail into his temples, and
fastened it into the ground: for he was fast asleep and weary.
22 So he died. And, behold, as Barak pursued Sisera, Jael came
out to meet him, and said unto him, Come, and I will show
thee the man whom thou seekest. And when he came into her
tent, behold, Sisera lay dead, and the nail *was* in his temples.
23 ¶ So [z]God subdued on that day Jabin the king of Canaan before
24 the children of Israel. And the hand of the children of Israel
[2]prospered, and prevailed against Jabin the king of Canaan,
until they had destroyed Jabin king of Canaan.

Chap. 5. THEN [a]sang Deborah and Barak the son of Abinoam on
that day, saying,

2 Praise ye the LORD for the [b]avenging of Israel,
[c]When the people willingly offered themselves.
3 [d]Hear, O ye kings; give ear, O ye princes;
I, *even* I, will sing unto the LORD;
I will sing *praise* to the LORD God of Israel.
4 ¶ LORD, [e]when thou wentest out of Seir,
When thou marchedst out of the field of Edom,
[f]The earth trembled, and the heavens dropped,
The clouds also dropped water.
5 [g]The mountains [3]melted from before the LORD,
Even [h]that Sinai from before the LORD God of Israel.
6 ¶ In the days of [i]Shamgar the son of Anath,
In the days of [k]Jael, [l]the highways were unoccupied,
And the [4]travellers walked through [5]byways.

[y] ch. 5. 26.
[z] Ps. 18. 47.
[a] Ps. 18. title.
[b] Ps. 18. 47.
[c] 2 Chr. 17. 16.
[d] Deut. 32. 1, 3. Ps. 2. 10.
[e] Deut. 33. 2.
[f] 2 Sam. 22. 8. Isai. 64. 3.
[g] Deut. 4. 11. Ps. 97. 5.
[h] Ex. 19. 18.
[i] ch. 3. 31.
[k] ch. 4. 17.
[l] Lev. 26. 22. Isai. 33. 8. Lam. 1. 4.

[1] Heb. *put*.
[2] Heb. *going went and was hard*.
[3] Heb. *flowed*.
[4] Heb. *walkers of paths*.
[5] Heb. *crooked ways*.

---

light of the Gospel that the law of truth is fully revealed.

21. If we can overlook the treachery and violence which belonged to the morals of the age and country, and bear in mind Jael's ardent sympathies with the oppressed people of God, her faith in the right of Israel to possess the land in which they were now slaves, her zeal for the glory of Jehovah as against the gods of Canaan, and the heroic courage and firmness with which she executed her deadly purpose, we shall be ready to yield to her the praise which is her due. See iii. 30 note.

24. See marg. The meaning is, that Barak's great victory was the beginning of a successful resistance to Jabin, by which the Israelites recovered their independence, and finally broke the Canaanite power. Accordingly we hear no more of Canaanite domination in the Book of Judges.

V. 1. Deborah, as "a prophetess," both composed and sang this noble ode, which, for poetic spirit and lyric fire, is not surpassed by any of the sacred songs in the Bible. And, as Miriam took up the first verse of the song of Moses (Ex. xv. 21), and sang it as an antiphon, so Barak, with the chorus of men, answered the song of Deborah by singing *v.* 2, which is also exactly suited for an antiphon, summing up as it does the subject matter of the whole ode. Cp. David's example (2 Sam. vi. 15).

2. Render "**For the leading of the leaders in Israel** (the princes), **for the willingness of the people** (to follow them) **bless ye the Lord.**" See Deut. xxxii. 42 note, and cp. *vv.* 9 and 13, where the *nobles* and the *people* are again contrasted.

4. Cp. Ps. lxviii. 7–9, and Habak. iii. 3–16. The three passages relate to the same events, and mutually explain each other. The subject of them is the triumphant march of Israel, with the LORD at their head, to take possession of Canaan, and the overthrow of Sihon, Og, and the Midianites. This march commenced from Kadesh, in the immediate neighbourhood of Seir, and the victories which followed were an exact parallel to the victory of Deborah and Barak, accompanied as it had been with the storm which made Kishon to overflow his banks.

6. Words descriptive of a state of weakness and fear, so that Israel could not frequent the highways. It is a graphic description of a country occupied by an enemy.

7 *The inhabitants of* the villages ceased, they ceased in Israel,
Until that I Deborah arose,
That I arose [m] a mother in Israel.
8 They [n] chose new gods;
Then *was* war in the gates:
[o] Was there a shield or spear seen
Among forty thousand in Israel?
9 My heart *is* toward the governors of Israel,
That [p] offered themselves willingly among the people.
Bless ye the LORD.
10 ¶ [1] [q] Speak, ye [r] that ride on white asses,
[s] Ye that sit in judgment,
And walk by the way.
11 *They that are delivered* from the noise of archers in the places of drawing water,
There shall they rehearse the [2] [t] righteous acts of the LORD,
Even the righteous acts *toward the inhabitants* of his villages in Israel:
Then shall the people of the LORD go down to the gates.
12 ¶ [u] Awake, awake, Deborah:
Awake, awake, utter a song:
Arise, Barak, and [x] lead thy captivity captive, thou son of Abinoam.
13 Then he made him that remaineth [y] have dominion over the nobles among the people:
The LORD made me have dominion over the mighty.
14 ¶ [z] Out of Ephraim *was there* a root of them [a] against Amalek;
After thee, Benjamin, among thy people;
Out of [b] Machir came down governors,

[m] Is. 49. 23.
[n] Deut. 32. 16.
[o] So 1 Sam. 13. 19, 22.
[p] ver. 2.
[q] Ps. 105. 2. & 145. 5.
[r] ch. 10. 4. & 12. 14.
[s] Ps. 107. 32.
[t] 1 Sam. 12. 7. Ps. 145. 7.
[u] Ps. 57. 8.
[x] Ps. 68. 18.
[y] Ps. 49. 14.
[z] ch. 3. 27.
[a] ch. 3. 13.
[b] Num. 32. 39, 40.

[1] Or, *Meditate.*
[2] Heb. *righteousnesses of the LORD.*

7. Render the word *villages* (here and in *v.* 11) *judgment, rule,* or *judges, rulers.* The sense is "**The princes** (or magistrates) ceased in Israel," *i.e.* there was no one to do justice in the gate, or defend men from their oppressors.

8. The "*war in the gates*" describes the hostile attacks of the Canaanites, which were the punishment of the idolatry of the Israelites (cp. marg. reff.), and the reduction of Israel to an unarmed and unresisting state under the Philistine dominion. See iii. 31 note.

9. *My heart,* &c.] In this deplorable weakness of Israel how noble was the conduct of the governors who volunteered to lead the people against their oppressors. Deborah's heart was filled with admiration as she thought of their patriotic devotion, and broke out into thanksgiving to Jehovah.

10. *ye that ride on white asses,* &c.] *i.e.* nobles or magistrates. Deborah appeals to the classes mentioned in *vv.* 6, 7, to bear witness to the happy change that had followed the overthrow of Jabin.

that sit in judgment] Rather "*that sit* **on saddles,** or *horse-cloths,*" a further description of those who ride on asses.

11. The sense of the A. V. is that, whereas formerly they could not go in safety to draw water from their wells, but were shot at by the archers of the enemy, now they were delivered from such tumults; and standing round the wells in security rehearsed the righteous acts of the Lord in delivering them, and "**the righteous acts of His government in Israel.**" (See *v.* 7).

then shall the people of the LORD *go down to the gates*] Israelites, who had hid themselves in caves and deserts, could return in security to the gates of their own cities for justice, or commerce, or to dwell there, now that the Canaanite was subdued.

12. Deborah incites Barak to carry off as his prey the captive Canaanites and their sheep and cattle (their "captivity").

13. This verse is otherwise rendered: "*then a remnant of the nobles came down; the people of the* LORD *came down for me against the mighty.*" The following verses mention in detail who this "remnant" were.

14. Render "**Of Ephraim** (Deborah's own tribe) **came down those whose root is in Mount Amalek** (xii. 15); **after thee** (*O Ephraim*) *came* **Benjamin amongst thy**

And out of Zebulun they that [1]handle the pen of the writer.
15 And the princes of Issachar *were* with Deborah;
c ch. 4. 14. Even Issachar, and also [c]Barak:
He was sent on [2]foot into the valley.
[3]For the divisions of Reuben
There were great [4]thoughts of heart.
d Num. 32. 1. 16 Why abodest thou [d]among the sheepfolds,
To hear the bleatings of the flocks?
[5]For the divisions of Reuben *there were* great searchings of heart.
e See Josh. 13. 25, 31. 17 [e]Gilead abode beyond Jordan:
And why did Dan remain in ships?
f Josh. 19. 29, 31. [f]Asher continued on the sea [6]shore,
And abode in his [7]breaches.
g ch. 4. 10. 18 [g]Zebulun and Naphtali *were* a people *that* [8]jeoparded their lives
Unto the death in the high places of the field.
19 ¶ The kings came *and* fought,
Then fought the kings of Canaan
In Taanach by the waters of Megiddo:
h Ps. 44. 12. [h]They took no gain of money.
i See Josh. 10. 11. 20 [i]They fought from heaven;
Ps. 77. 17. [k]The stars in their [9]courses fought against Sisera.
k ch. 4. 15. 21 [l]The river of Kishon swept them away,
l ch. 4. 7. That ancient river, the river Kishon.
O my soul, thou hast trodden down strength.
22 Then were the horsehoofs broken

1 Heb. *draw with the pen, &c.*
2 Heb. *his feet.*
3 Or, *In the divisions, &c.*
4 Heb. *impressions.*
5 Or, *In.*
6 Or, *port.*
7 Or, *creeks.*
8 Heb. *exposed to reproach.*
9 Heb. *paths.*

---

people; **of Machir** (the west-Jordanic families of Manasseh. See Josh. xvii. 1-6) **there came down the chiefs, and of Zebulon they that handle the staff of the officer**" the military *scribe*, whose duty it was, like that of the Roman tribunes, to keep the muster roll, and superintend the recruiting of the army. (See 2 K. xxv. 19.)

15. *even Issachar*, &c.] *i.e.* "and, as well as Issachar, Barak also with the tribes of Zebulun and Naphtali, rushed down on foot from Mount Tabor into the valley to attack the iron chariots of Sisera."

For the divisions] Better: "among the brooks." Reuben ought to have followed in this catalogue of patriots, but with that abruptness for which this poem is so conspicuous, Deborah adverts to his absence instead.

16. *great searchings* (*thoughts, v.* 15) *of heart*] Deborah means to say that at first the Reubenites made magnanimous resolutions to help their brethren against Jabin. But they stayed at home, and let the opportunity slip.

17. The land of Gilead, on the east of Jordan, was divided between Gad and the half tribe of Manasseh, who are both comprehended here. Joppa was in the territory of Dan (Josh. xix. 46), and was in later times the sea-port for Jerusalem.

his breaches] Rather *havens; i.e.* the creeks and bays and river-mouths by which their coast was broken. Josh. xix. 29.

18. In contrast with the selfishness of the tribes just named, Deborah reverts with enthusiasm to the heroic prowess of Zebulun and Naphtali.

19. The Canaanite hosts are now described, led to battle by their numerous kings. (Cp. Josh. xii. 21.)

they took no gain of money] *i.e.* either they got no booty, as they expected, or, they did not fight for plunder, but for life and victory (cp. iv. 16 and *v.* 30).

20. God fought on the side of Israel, and gave them the victory. Josephus relates that, just as the battle began, a violent tempest came on with a great downfall of rain, and a hailstorm, which, driving full in the faces of the Canaanites, so blinded and benumbed them with cold, that they could neither use their bows with effect nor even hold their swords.

21. The word translated *ancient* occurs only here. The phrase probably means that Kishon was celebrated from ancient times on account of the battles fought on its banks.

By the means of the [1]pransings, the pransings of their
mighty ones.
23 ¶ Curse ye Meroz, said the angel of the LORD,
Curse ye bitterly the inhabitants thereof;
[m]Because they came not to the help [n]of the LORD, [m] ch. 21. 9. Neh. 3. 5.
To the help of the LORD against the mighty. [n] 1 Sam. 17. 47. & 18. 17.
24 ¶ Blessed above women shall [o]Jael
The wife of Heber the Kenite be, [o] ch. 4. 17.
[p]Blessed shall she be above women in the tent. [p] Luke 1. 28.
25 [q]He asked water, *and* she gave *him* milk; [q] ch. 4. 19.
She brought forth butter in a lordly dish.
26 [r]She put her hand to the nail, [r] ch. 4. 21.
And her right hand to the workmen's hammer;
And [2]with the hammer she smote Sisera, she smote off
his head,
When she had pierced and stricken through his temples.
27 [3]At her feet he bowed, he fell, he lay down:
At her feet he bowed, he fell:
Where he bowed, there he fell down [4]dead.
28 ¶ The mother of Sisera looked out at a window,
And cried through the lattice,
Why is his chariot *so* long in coming?
Why tarry the wheels of his chariots?
29 Her wise ladies answered her,
Yea, she returned [5]answer to herself,
30 [s]Have they not sped? have they *not* divided the prey; [s] Ex. 15. 9.
[6]To every man a damsel *or* two;
To Sisera a prey of divers colours,
A prey of divers colours of needlework,
Of divers colours of needlework on both sides, *meet* for
the necks of *them that take* the spoil?
31 ¶ [t]So let all thine enemies perish, O LORD: [t] Ps. 83. 9, 10.
But *let* them that love him *be* [u]as the sun [x]when he [u] 2 Sam. 23, 4.
goeth forth in his might. [x] Ps. 19. 5.
And the land had rest forty years.

1 Or, *tramplings*, or, *plungings*.
2 Heb. *she hammered*.
3 Heb. *Between*.
4 Heb. *destroyed*.
5 Heb. *her words*.
6 Heb. *to the head of a man*.

---

22. Probably an allusion to the frantic efforts of the chariot-horses to disengage themselves from the morass (iv. 15 note).

mighty ones] Applied to bulls (Ps. xxii. 12) and horses (Jer. viii. 16, xlvii. 3, l. 11); elsewhere, as probably here, to men.

23. The inhabitants of Meroz (a village 12 miles from Samaria) hung back, and gave no help in the day of battle, although it was Jehovah Who called them. Hence the curse pronounced by the Angel of the Lord.

24. The blessing here pronounced is in strong contrast with the curse of Meroz. Deborah speaks of Jael's deed by the light of her own age, which did not make manifest the evil of guile and bloodshed; the light in ours does.

25. *butter*] Rather *curdled milk*, probably a fermented and intoxicating drink. All these marks of respect and friendship would lull Sisera into security.

26. Rather "**she smote his head, and she struck and pierced through his temple.**"

28. The scene is changed to the palace of Sisera.

30. Render the latter part of the verse "**a booty of dyed garments for Sisera, a booty of dyed garments** *and* **of party-coloured cloth, a dyed garment** *and* **two party-coloured clothes for the necks of the booty,**" the spoil or booty being either captive damsels, or captive cattle on whose necks these clothes are to be placed (either as ornament or as a burden; cp. viii. 21, 26). But possibly "the necks of the booty" may mean the backs or shoulders (of men or beasts) laden with booty.

31. A most striking conclusion, in which the spiritual truth which the whole narra-

[a] ch. 2. 19.
[b] Hab. 3. 7.
[c] 1 Sam. 13. 6. Heb. 11. 38.
[d] ch. 3. 13.
[e] Gen. 29. 1. ch. 7. 12. 1 Kin. 4. 30. Job 1. 3.
[f] Lev. 26. 16. Deut. 28. 30, 33, 51. Mic. 6. 15.
[g] ch. 7. 12.
[h] ch. 3. 15. Hos. 5. 15.
[i] Ps. 44. 2, 3.
[k] 2 Kin. 17. 35, 37, 38. Jer. 10. 2.

CHAP. 6. [a]AND the children of Israel did evil in the sight of the
LORD: and the LORD delivered them into the hand [b]of Midian
2 seven years. And the hand of Midian [1]prevailed against Israel:
and because of the Midianites the children of Israel made them
[c]the dens which *are* in the mountains, and caves, and strong
3 holds. And *so* it was, when Israel had sown, that the Midianites came up, and [d]the Amalekites, [e]and the children of the
4 east, even they came up against them; and they encamped
against them, and [f]destroyed the increase of the earth, till thou
come unto Gaza, and left no sustenance for Israel, neither
5 [2]sheep, nor ox, nor ass. For they came up with their cattle and
their tents, and they came [g]as grasshoppers for multitude; *for*
both they and their camels were without number: and they
6 entered into the land to destroy it. And Israel was greatly im-
poverished because of the Midianites; and the children of Israel
7 [h]cried unto the LORD. ¶And it came to pass, when the children
8 of Israel cried unto the LORD because of the Midianites, that
the LORD sent [3]a prophet unto the children of Israel, which said
unto them, Thus saith the LORD God of Israel, I brought you
up from Egypt, and brought you forth out of the house of
9 bondage; and I delivered you out of the hand of the Egyptians,
and out of the hand of all that oppressed you, and [i]drave them
10 out from before you, and gave you their land; and I said unto
you, I *am* the LORD your God; [k]fear not the gods of the Amorites, in whose land ye dwell: but ye have not obeyed my voice.
11 ¶And there came an angel of the LORD, and sat under an oak

[1] Heb. *was strong.* [2] Or, *goat.* [3] Heb. *a man a prophet.*

---

tive is intended to convey, comes out. The enemies of the Lord will perish like the host of Sisera, and all their hopes will end, like those of Sisera's mother, in bitter disappointment and shame; but all that love our Lord Jesus Christ shall shine forth as the sun in the kingdom of their Father. Cp. Matt. xiii. 43; Dan. xii. 3.

VI. **1.** *Midian*] See Gen. xxv. 2 note. They were remarkable not only for the vast number of their cattle (*v.* 5; Num. xxxi. 32–39), but also for their great wealth in gold and other metal ornaments, showing their connexion with a gold country. (Cp. Num. xxxi. 22, 50–54, with viii. 24–26.) At this time they were allies of the Amalekites and of the Arabian tribes called collectively "the children of the East" (*v.* 3). They seem to have extended their settlements to the east of Jordan, and to have belonged to the larger section of Arabs called Ishmaelites (viii. 24).

2. The word rendered *dens* is only found in this passage. It is best explained of ravines hollowed out by torrents, which the Israelites made into hiding-places.

4. Gaza indicates the extreme point south to which they spread their devastations, crossing the Jordan near Bethshan (Scythopolis), and entering by the valley of Jezreel, and sweeping along the whole of the maritime plain or Shephelah.

5. *grasshoppers*] Rather locusts (cp. Ex. x. 4–6, 14, 15; Joel i., ii.; Ps. lxxviii. 46).

8. *a prophet*] His name is not given. (Cp. 1 K. xiii.) This message is somewhat similar to that of the Angel, ii. 1–3. The reference to Ex. xx. 2 is plain, and supposes the people to whom the prophet addresses these words to be familiar with the facts recorded in that text.

10. A similar use of the name *Amorite*, instead of the more usual name *Canaanite*, occurs in Josh. xxiv. 15, 18. Perhaps a special reason may be found for the use of *Amorite*, if the prophet was addressing those who dwelt in the mountains, where the Amorites chiefly dwelt. The idolatries of the Amorites seem, too, to have been pre-eminently abominable (see 2 K. xxi. 11; 1 K. xxi. 26). It should be observed that the prophet's language, as it traces the misery of Israel to their sins, so also intimates the necessity of repentance and of breaking off their sins—specially the sin of idolatry—as preliminary to any deliverance. In exact accordance with this view, Gideon commences his work by throwing down the altar of Baal, and building up the altar of Jehovah (*vv.* 24, 25).

11. *an oak*] "**The oak,**" indicating it as a well-known tree, still standing in the writer's days.

There was another Ophrah in Benjamin (Josh. xviii. 23). This Ophrah was in Manasseh, and was the village of Joash, the head, apparently, of the family of Abiezer, which was one of the families of Gilead,

which *wás* in Ophrah, that *pertained* unto Joash [l]the Abi-ezrite:
and his son [m]Gideon threshed wheat by the winepress, [1]to hide
12 *it* from the Midianites. And the [n]angel of the LORD appeared
unto him, and said unto him, The LORD *is* [o]with thee, thou
13 mighty man of valour. And Gideon said unto him, Oh my
LORD, if the LORD be with us, why then is all this befallen us?
and [p]where *be* all his miracles [q]which our fathers told us of,
saying, Did not the LORD bring us up from Egypt? but now
the LORD hath [r]forsaken us, and delivered us into the hands of
14 the Midianites. And the LORD looked upon him, and said, [s]Go
in this thy might, and thou shalt save Israel from the hand of
15 the Midianites: [t]have not I sent thee? And he said unto him,
Oh my LORD, wherewith shall I save Israel? behold, [u][2]my
family *is* poor in Manasseh, and I *am* the least in my father's
16 house. And the LORD said unto him, [x]Surely I will be with
17 thee, and thou shalt smite the Midianites as one man. And he
said unto him, If now I have found grace in thy sight, then
18 [y]shew me a sign that thou talkest with me. [z]Depart not hence,
I pray thee, until I come unto thee, and bring forth my [3]present,
and set *it* before thee. And he said, I will tarry until thou
19 come again. ¶ [a]And Gideon went in, and made ready [4]a kid,
and unleavened cakes of an ephah of flour: the flesh he put in
a basket, and he put the broth in a pot, and brought *it* out unto
20 him under the oak, and presented *it*. And the angel of God
said unto him, Take the flesh and the unleavened cakes, and
[b]lay *them* upon this rock, and [c]pour out the broth. And he did

[l] Josh. 17. 2. [m] Heb. 11. 32, called *Gedeon*. [n] ch. 13. 3. Luke 1. 11. [o] Josh. 1. 5. [p] So Ps. 89. 49. Isai. 59. 1. [q] Ps. 44. 1. [r] 2 Chr. 15. 2. [s] 1 Sam. 12. 11. Heb. 11. 32, 34. [t] Josh. 1. 9. ch. 4. 6. [u] See 1 Sam. 9. 21. [x] Ex. 3. 12. Josh. 1. 5. [y] Ex. 4. 1—8. ver. 36. 37. Ps. 86. 17. Isai. 7. 11. [z] Gen. 18. 3, 5. ch. 13. 15. [a] Gen. 18. 6. [b] ch. 13. 19. [c] See 1 Kin. 18. 33, 34.

[1] Heb. *to cause* it *to flee*.
[2] Heb. *my thousand* is *the meanest:* Ex. 18. 21, 25. Mic. 5. 2.
[3] Or, *meat offering*.
[4] Heb. *a kid of the goats*.

---

the son of Machir, the son of Manasseh (Num. xxvi. 30).

12. *thou mighty man of valour*] Known to God to be such, though as yet not known to be such either by himself or his countrymen (cp. Luke i. 28, 30).

13. The extreme bitterness of the national sufferings under the Midianite occupation breaks out in Gideon's language. The Angel's words, suitable to times of prosperity, seemed to be a mockery, when it was evident the Lord was not with them. (Cp. Deut. xxxi. 17.)

14. *the* LORD *looked upon him*] That gracious look conferred immediate strength (cp. Ephes. vi. 10; 2 Cor. xii. 9: John xx. 22; Acts iii. 6). The change of phrase from "the angel of the LORD" to "the LORD" is remarkable. When messages are delivered by the Angel of the Lord, the form of the message is as if God Himself were speaking (cp. ii. 1).

The sending implied a valid commission and sufficient powers. Cp. Exod. iii. 10; Isai. xliv. 26; Ezek. ii. 3; Zech. ii. 11; Mal. iii. 1; Luke x. 3; John xx. 21; and the term APOSTLE, as applied to our Lord (Heb. iii. 1) and to the Twelve.

15. Gideon now perceived that the Lord was speaking to him by His angel. He saw, however, no qualifications in himself, or in his family or tribe, for the office of saviour to his people. He therefore desires some assurance that the message he had just received was indeed from God, and not a mere dream or delusion. He asks as a sign (*v.* 18) that his mysterious visitor should tarry under the oak till he should return to Him with his gifts and offerings.

17. *a sign*] If the Angel ate of Gideon's present it would be a conclusive proof of the reality of the vision. (Cp. John xxi. 9–13; Luke xxiv. 37-43; Acts x. 41.) It would also be a token of God's goodwill to Gideon. Cp. Gen. xviii. 3.

18. *my present*] My Minchah: the word used regularly, though not exclusively, for the meat and drink offering (Lev. ii. 1 note). Its double sense of an offering to God, and of a gift to man, suits the doubt in Gideon's mind as to who his visitor might be.

19. *unleavened cakes*] As being much more quickly baked (cp. Gen. xix. 3) [and as connected with the meat offering]. *An ephah,* containing 3 *measures,* was the quantity of flour commonly used at one baking (Gen. xviii. 6; Ex. xvi. 16).

presented it] A word especially, though not exclusively, proper for offerings to God. See Amos v. 25, where the same word is rendered *offered*.

20. *pour out the broth*] Libations were a very ancient form of offering (cp. Gen. xxxv. 14). The drink offerings of wine

21 so. Then the angel of the LORD put forth the end of the staff
that *was* in his hand, and touched the flesh and the unleavened
cakes; and [d]there rose up fire out of the rock, and consumed
the flesh and the unleavened cakes. Then the angel of the LORD
22 departed out of his sight. ¶ And when Gideon [e]perceived that
he *was* an angel of the LORD, Gideon said, Alas, O Lord GOD!
[f]for because I have seen an angel of the LORD face to face.
23 And the LORD said unto him, [g]Peace *be* unto thee; fear not:
24 thou shalt not die. Then Gideon built an altar there unto the
LORD, and called it [1]Jehovah-shalom: unto this day it *is* yet [h]in
25 Ophrah of the Abi-ezrites. ¶ And it came to pass the same
night, that the LORD said unto him, Take thy father's young
bullock, [2]even the second bullock of seven years old, and throw
down the altar of Baal that thy father hath, and [i]cut down the
26 grove that *is* by it: and build an altar unto the LORD thy God
upon the top of this [3]rock, [4]in the ordered place, and take the
second bullock, and offer a burnt sacrifice with the wood of the
27 grove which thou shalt cut down. Then Gideon took ten men
of his servants, and did as the LORD had said unto him: and *so*
it was, because he feared his father's household, and the men of
the city, that he could not do *it* by day, that he did *it* by night.
28 ¶ And when the men of the city arose early in the morning, behold, the altar of Baal was cast down, and the grove was cut
down that *was* by it, and the second bullock was offered upon
29 the altar *that was* built. And they said one to another, Who
hath done this thing? And when they enquired and asked, they
30 said, Gideon the son of Joash hath done this thing. Then the
men of the city said unto Joash, Bring out thy son, that he may
die: because he hath cast down the altar of Baal, and because
31 he hath cut down the grove that *was* by it. And Joash said

[d] Lev. 9. 24. 1 Kin. 18. 38. 2 Chr. 7. 1.
[e] ch. 13. 21.
[f] Gen. 16. 13. & 32. 30. Ex. 33. 20. ch. 13. 22.
[g] Dan. 10. 19.
[h] ch. 8. 32.
[i] Ex. 34. 13. Deut. 7. 5.

[1] That is, *The LORD send peace.* Ex. 17. 15. Jer. 33. 16. Ezek. 48. 35.
[2] Or, *and.*
[3] Heb. *strong place.*
[4] Or, *in an orderly manner.*

---

under the Levitical law were *poured* upon the Altar (Ex. xxx. 9). The pouring of the broth upon the rock was evidently of the nature of a libation. It might also, like the water poured by Elijah upon his sacrifice, make the miracle of the fire that consumed the sacrifice more apparent. (Cp. 1 K. xviii. 33.)

22. *Alas, O Lord* GOD!] Cp. Josh. vii. 7.

because I have seen an angel of the LORD] Cp. marg. reff., in which the notion that it was death for mortal man to see God appears clearly. The same notion prevailed amongst the heathen.

24. Gideon's naming the altar which he built, in commemoration of the words of peace spoken by the Angel, is very similar to what we read of Abraham (Gen. xxii. 14), and of Moses (Ex. xvii. 15, when he named the altar *Jehovah-nissi*).

25. *even*] Rather, as in the margin, **and.**' Two bullocks are spoken of. The labour of both would be required for pulling down and removing the altar of Baal, and for bringing the materials for building the Altar of Jehovah.

the grove by it] Rather, "**the idol upon it,**" the Asherah, the wooden image of Astarte (iii. 7).

26. *in the ordered place*] See marg. "**Build an altar, &c., with the materials,**" "the wood *laid in order*" (cp. Gen. xxii. 9), that, viz., which he would find ready to hand in the altar of Baal which he was to throw down.

the wood of the grove] "**The** (blocks of) **wood of the idol,**" *i.e.* the image of Astarte. The command from God Himself to build an Altar, and sacrifice upon it, is analogous to Elijah's sacrifice (1 K. xviii.), and was doubtless caused by the extraordinary circumstance of the defection of the Israelites from the worship of the true God. Possibly, too, the Midianite invasion had made the worship at Shiloh impossible at this time.

27. The mention of the "men of the city" by the side of Gideon's "father's household" suggests the probability of their being a remnant of the Canaanite population, and the special patrons of Baal-worship.

31. From the boldness of Joash in defending his son, it is likely that the majority of the Abi-ezrites sided with him against "**the**

unto all that stood against him, Will ye plead for Baal? will ye
save him? he that will plead for him, let him be put to death
whilst *it is yet* morning: if he *be* a god, let him plead for him-
32 self, because *one* hath cast down his altar. Therefore on that
day he called him [1k]Jerubbaal, saying, Let Baal plead against
33 him, because he hath thrown down his altar. ¶ Then all [l]the
Midianites and the Amalekites and the children of the east were
gathered together, and went over, and pitched in [m]the valley of
34 Jezreel. But [n]the Spirit of the LORD [2]came upon Gideon, and
he [o]blew a trumpet; and Abi-ezer [3]was gathered after him.
35 And he sent messengers throughout all Manasseh; who also
was gathered after him: and he sent messengers unto Asher,
and unto Zebulun, and unto Naphtali; and they came up to
36 meet them. ¶ And Gideon said unto God, If thou wilt save
37 Israel by mine hand, as thou hast said, [p]Behold, I will put a
fleece of wool in the floor; *and* if the dew be on the fleece only,
and *it be* dry upon all the earth *beside*, then shall I know that
38 thou wilt save Israel by mine hand, as thou hast said. And it
was so: for he rose up early on the morrow, and thrust the
fleece together, and wringed the dew out of the fleece, a bowl
39 full of water. And Gideon said unto God, [q]Let not thine anger
be hot against me, and I will speak but this once: let me prove,
I pray thee, but this once with the fleece; let it now be dry only
40 upon the fleece, and upon all the ground let there be dew. And
God did so that night: for it was dry upon the fleece only, and
there was dew on all the ground.

CHAP. 7. THEN [a]Jerubbaal, who *is* Gideon, and all the people that
were with him, rose up early, and pitched beside the well of
Harod: so that the host of the Midianites were on the north

[k] 1 Sam. 12. 11. 2 Sam. 11. 21, *Jerubbesheth*; that is, *Let the shameful thing plead.* See Jer. 11. 13. Hos. 9. 10.
[l] ver. 3.
[m] Josh. 17. 16.
[n] ch. 3. 10. 1 Chr. 12. 18. 2 Chr. 24. 20.
[o] Num. 10. 3. ch. 3. 27.
[p] See Ex. 4. 3, 4, 6, 7.
[q] Gen. 18. 32.
[a] ch. 6. 32.

[1] That is, *Let Baal plead.* [2] Heb. *clothed.* [3] Heb. *was called after him.*

---

men of the city," and already felt drawn towards Gideon as their national and religious leader (*v.* 34). Joash appears as the chief magistrate of Ophrah.

Will ye plead, &c.? will ye save?] The emphasis is upon *ye*, as much as to say, What business is it of yours?

32. *he called him*] i.e. "He was called" *Jerubbaal*, as being the person against whom it was popularly said that Baal might strive. See marg.

33. A fresh invasion, and the last, of Midianites, Amalekites, and Arabs (see *v.* 3). But the Israelites, instead of hiding in dens and caves, and tamely leaving all their substance as plunder to the invaders, now rally round their leader.

34. *the Spirit of the* LORD *came upon Gideon*] See marg. The word contains a striking thought. It is different from that used in the case of Othniel (iii. 10), Jephthah (xi. 29), and Samson (xiii. 25, xiv. 6, 19).

35. His own tribe, Manasseh, and the three northern tribes of Asher, Zebulon, and Naphtali hastened to join him. Issachar was probably unable to do so, because the Midianites were encamped in the heart of their country. Asher no longer "abode in his breaches," as in the time of Jabin (v. 17), perhaps ashamed of their former backwardness, and stung by the rebuke of Deborah; perhaps, too, from feeling the Midianite yoke much more galling than that of Jabin.

36. The caution of Gideon, desirous of being assured that he really had a promise from God, does not imply doubts as to God's faithfulness or power to fulfil His promise. Of such doubts there is not a trace in Gideon's character. He is a worthy example of faith (Heb. xi. 32).

37. The threshing-floors were and still are under the open air, and usually circular. The second sign (*v.* 40), would be more convincing than the former, because it is the nature of fleeces to attract and retain moisture.

VII. **1.** *the well of Harod*] *i.e.* of trembling, evidently so called from the people who were *afraid* (*v.* 3). It is identified with great probability with *Ain Jalud*, a spacious pool at the foot of Gilboa; [by Conder, with Ain el Jem'ain (the spring of the two troops)].

Moreh was, probably, the little Hermon, the Jebel ed-Duhy of the Arabs, which encloses the plain two or three miles north of Gilboa, which shuts it in on the south.

2 side of them, by the hill of Moreh, in the valley. And the
LORD said unto Gideon, The people that *are* with thee *are* too
many for me to give the Midianites into their hands, lest Israel
[b]vaunt themselves against me, saying, Mine own hand hath
3 saved me. Now therefore, go to, proclaim in the ears of the
people, saying, [c]Whosoever *is* fearful and afraid, let him return
and depart early from mount Gilead. And there returned of
the people twenty and two thousand; and there remained ten
4 thousand. ¶ And the LORD said unto Gideon, The people *are*
yet *too* many; bring them down unto the water, and I will try
them for thee there: and it shall be, *that* of whom I say unto
thee, This shall go with thee, the same shall go with thee; and
of whomsoever I say unto thee, this shall not go with thee, the
5 same shall not go. So he brought down the people unto the
water: and the LORD said unto Gideon, Every one that lappeth
of the water with his tongue, as a dog lappeth, him shalt thou
set by himself; likewise every one that boweth down upon his
6 knees to drink. And the number of them that lapped, *putting*
their hand to their mouth, were three hundred men: but all
the rest of the people bowed down upon their knees to drink
7 water. And the LORD said unto Gideon, [d]By the three hundred
men that lapped will I save you, and deliver the Midianites
into thine hand: and let all the *other* people go every man unto
8 his place. So the people took victuals in their hand, and their
trumpets: and he sent all *the rest of* Israel every man unto his
tent, and retained those three hundred men: and the host of
9 Midian was beneath him in the valley. ¶ And it came to pass
the same [e]night, that the LORD said unto him, Arise, get thee
down unto the host; for I have delivered it into thine hand.
10 But if thou fear to go down, go thou with Phurah thy servant
11 down to the host: and thou shalt [f]hear what they say; and
afterward shall thine hands be strengthened to go down unto
the host. Then went he down with Phurah his servant unto the
12 outside of the [1]armed men that *were* in the host. And the
Midianites and the Amalekites and [g]all the children of the east
lay along in the valley like grasshoppers for multitude; and
their camels *were* without number, as the sand by the sea
13 side for multitude. And when Gideon was come, behold, *there*
was a man that told a dream unto his fellow, and said, Behold,
I dreamed a dream, and, lo, a cake of barley bread tumbled into
the host of Midian, and came unto a tent, and smote it that it

[b] Deut. 8. 17. Isai. 10. 13. 1 Cor. 1. 29. 2 Cor. 4. 7.
[c] Deut. 20. 8.
[d] 1 Sam. 14. 6.
[e] Gen. 46. 2, 3.
[f] ver. 13, 14, 15. See Gen. 24. 14. 1 Sam. 14. 9, 10.
[g] ch. 6. 5, 33, & 8, 10.

[1] Or, *ranks by five*, Ex. 13. 18.

---

3. The proclamation was in accordance with the Law (see marg. ref.). No mountain of the name of Gilead is known in this locality, and it has been conjectured that the right reading is Gilboa. Others think that this may be a form of proclamation customary in Manasseh.

4. *try*] The word used for refining metals by separating the dross from the pure ore. They who threw themselves on the ground and drank freely were the more self-indulgent; while they who, remembering the near presence of the enemy, slaked their thirst with moderation, and without being off their guard for an instant, were the true soldiers of the army of God.

8. The sense is, "And they (the three hundred) took the victuals and trumpets of the people (*all the people* of *v.* 7) into their hands," so that each of the three hundred should have a trumpet and a pitcher.

11. *the armed men*] The word is rendered *harnessed* in Ex. xiii. 18 (see note). The most probable meaning of the word is *arrayed in divisions* or *ranks*.

13. *a cake of barley bread*] *i.e.* such a cake as could hardly be eaten by men, it was so vile: a term expressive of the contempt of the Midianites for the people of Israel.

a tent] The *tent*, meaning, probably, the tent of the king of Midian, or of the captain of the host.

14 fell, and overturned it, that the tent lay along. And his fellow
answered and said, This *is* nothing else save the sword of Gideon
the son of Joash, a man of Israel: *for* into his hand hath God
15 delivered Midian, and all the host. ¶ And it was *so*, when
Gideon heard the telling of the dream, and [1]the interpretation
thereof, that he worshipped, and returned into the host of Israel,
and said, Arise; for the LORD hath delivered into your hand
16 the host of Midian. And he divided the three hundred men *into*
three companies, and he put [2]a trumpet in every man's hand,
17 with empty pitchers, and [3]lamps within the pitchers. And he
said unto them, Look on me, and do likewise: and, behold,
when I come to the outside of the camp, it shall be *that*, as I do,
18 so shall ye do. When I blow with a trumpet, I and all that *are*
with me, then blow ye the trumpets also on every side of all the
19 camp, and say, *The sword* of the LORD, and of Gideon. ¶ So
Gideon, and the hundred men that *were* with him, came unto
the outside of the camp in the beginning of the middle watch;
and they had but newly set the watch: and they blew the
20 trumpets, and brake the pitchers that *were* in their hands. And
the three companies blew the trumpets, and brake the pitchers,
and held the lamps in their left hands, and the trumpets in their
right hands to blow *withal*: and they cried, The sword of the
21 LORD, and of Gideon. And they [h]stood every man in his place
round about the camp: [i]and all the host ran, and cried, and
22 fled. And the three hundred [k]blew the trumpets, and [l]the
LORD set [m]every man's sword against his fellow, even throughout all the host: and the host fled to Beth-shittah [4]in Zererath,
23 *and* to the [5]border of Abel-meholah, unto Tabbath. ¶ And the

h Ex. 14. 13, 14.
i 2 Kin. 7. 7.
k Josh. 6. 4. See 2 Cor. 4. 7.
l Ps. 83. 9. Isai. 9. 4.
m 1 Sam. 14. 20. 2 Chr. 20. 23.

1 Heb. *the breaking thereof.*
2 Heb. *trumpets in the hand of all of them.*
3 Or, *firebrands*, or, *torches.*
4 Or, *toward.*
5 Heb. *lip.*

---

14. *This is nothing else save the sword of Gideon*] The word rendered *tumbled* in *v.* 13, is rather descriptive of a sword **brandished** (cp. Gen. iii. 24). Hence the interpretation "the sword of Gideon." Hearing this dream and the interpretation would convince Gideon that he was indeed under the guidance of God, and so assure him of God's aid; and secondly, it would show him that a panic had already fallen upon the mind of the enemy.

16. Gideon himself took the command of one company, and sent the other two under their respective captains to different sides of the camp (*vv.* 18 and 21).

19. *the middle watch*] The old Jewish division of the night was three watches of four hours each. They are alluded to in Ex. xiv. 24; 1 Sam. xi. 11; Ps. lxiii. 6, xc. 4, cxix. 148, cxxx. 6; Lam. ii. 19. After the Jews fell under the power of the Romans, they used the Roman division of four watches of three hours each (Matt. xiv. 25; Mark xiii. 35).

"The beginning" of the watch would be about eleven o'clock at night.

21. The effect to the Midianites would be, that they were surrounded by a mighty host. Their own camp being in darkness, as soon as the confusion of flight began they would mistake friends for foes, and fleers for pursuers. When once fighting had begun by the first casual mistake, the clashing of swords and the shouts of the combatants in the camp, accompanied by the continuous blowing of Gideon's trumpets outside, would make it appear that the whole of the enemy was in the camp. Suspicion of treachery on the part of their allies would also be likely to arise in the minds of Midianites, Amalekites, and Arabs. Cp. a similar scene in marg. reff.

22. *Beth-shittah*—"House of the acacias," the same trees which gave their name to *Shittim* (Num. xxxiii. 49) in the plains of Moab, and which grew plentifully also in the peninsula of Sinai (Ex. xxv. 5)—perhaps *Shuttah*, in the valley of Jezreel; or it may be another name of Scythopolis, or Beth-shan (cp. 1 K. iv. 12). *Zererath* or *Zeredath*, near Succoth (viii. 5), the same as *Zeredah* in Ephraim, the birth-place of Jeroboam (1 K. xi. 26), and *Zartanah* (1 K. iv. 12). *Abel-meholah* (field of the dance), the birth-place of Elisha (1 K. xix. 16) is in the Jordan valley, 10 miles from Scythopolis, if identified with Bethmaela: if the same as Abelmea, it lay between

men of Israel gathered themselves together out of Naphtali,
and out of Asher, and out of all Manasseh, and pursued after
24 the Midianites. And Gideon sent messengers throughout all
[n]mount Ephraim, saying, Come down against the Midianites,
and take before them the waters unto Beth-barah and Jordan.
Then all the men of Ephraim gathered themselves together, and
25 [o]took the waters unto [p]Beth-barah and Jordan. And they took
[q]two princes of the Midianites, Oreb and Zeeb; and they slew
Oreb upon [r]the rock Oreb, and Zeeb they slew at the winepress
of Zeeb, and pursued Midian, and brought the heads of Oreb
and Zeeb to Gideon on the [s]other side Jordan.
CHAP. 8. AND [a]the men of Ephraim said unto him, [1]Why hast
thou served us thus, that thou calledst us not, when thou wentest
to fight with the Midianites? And they did chide with him
2 [2]sharply. And he said unto them, What have I done now in
comparison of you? *Is* not the gleaning of the grapes of
3 Ephraim better than the vintage of Abi-ezer? [b]God hath
delivered into your hands the princes of Midian, Oreb and
Zeeb: and what was I able to do in comparison of you? Then
their [3][c]anger was abated toward him, when he had said that.
4 ¶ And Gideon came to Jordan, *and* passed over, he, and the
three hundred men that *were* with him, faint, yet pursuing
5 *them*. And he said unto the men of [d]Succoth, Give, I pray
you, loaves of bread unto the people that follow me; for
they *be* faint, and I am pursuing after Zebah and Zalmunna,
6 kings of Midian. And the princes of Succoth said, [e]*Are* the
hands of Zebah and Zalmunna now in thine hand, that [f]we
7 should give bread unto thine army? And Gideon said, Therefore when the LORD hath delivered Zebah and Zalmunna into
mine hand, [g]then I will [4]tear your flesh with the thorns of the
8 wilderness and with briers. And he went up thence [h]to Penuel,
and spake unto them likewise: and the men of Penuel answered
9 him as the men of Succoth had answered *him*. And he spake

[n] ch. 3. 27.
[o] ch. 3. 28.
[p] John 1. 28.
[q] ch. 8. 3. Ps. 83. 11.
[r] Isai. 10. 26.
[s] ch. 8. 4.
[a] See ch. 12. 1. 2 Sam. 19. 41.
[b] ch. 7. 24. Phil. 2. 3.
[c] Prov. 15. 1.
[d] Gen. 33. 17. Ps. 60. 6.
[e] See 1 Kin. 20. 11.
[f] See 1 Sam. 25. 11.
[g] ver. 16.
[h] Gen. 32. 30. 1 Kin. 12. 25.

[1] Heb. *What thing* is *this thou hast done unto us*.
[2] Heb. *strongly*.
[3] Heb. *spirit*.
[4] Heb. *thresh*.

Nablous and Scythopolis. [But see 1 K. xix. 16 note.] *Tabbath* was apparently lower down the Jordan valley, *i.e.* further south.

24. *the waters*] The streams which run from the mountain district of Ephraim into the Jordan in the district of Beth-shan, forming great pools and marshes, which the Midianites fleeing south would have to cross before they could reach the Jordan fords.

all the men of Ephraim] They had taken no previous part in the rising against Midian: nor had Gideon, of the smaller tribe of Manasseh, presumed before to summon his more powerful and arrogant brethren of the great tribe of Ephraim (see Josh. xvii. 14–18).

VIII. **1.** The success of Gideon's enterprise mortified the pride of Ephraim, as the chief tribe, seeing that they had played a subordinate part. Cp. Judg. xii. 1.

2. A civil war with the great tribe of Ephraim would soon have turned Israel's victory into mourning. Gideon therefore soothes their wounded pride by confessing that Ephraim had done more, though they had joined him so late in the day, than he had been able to effect in the whole campaign. The grape-gleaning of Ephraim wa better than the whole vintage of Abi-ezer.

5. Succoth was in the tribe of Gad which was entirely trans-Jordanic (Josh. xiii. 27); and the ruins are at Sukkot, on the east of Jordan, a little south of Beth-shan.

Give, I pray you, &c.] Gideon might fairly expect so much aid from the trans-Jordanic tribes, and from so considerable a town as Succoth (*v.* 14).

6. The number of the followers of Zebah and Zalmunna was still so formidable, and Gideon's enterprise still so doubtful, that the men of Succoth (being on the same side of the Jordan) would not risk the vengeance of the Midianites by giving supplies to Gideon's men.

8. Succoth was in the valley or Ghor of the Jordan (*v.* 5), and Penuel apparently

also unto the men of Penuel, saying, When I [i]come again in
10 peace, [k]I will break down this tower. ¶ Now Zebah and Zalmunna *were* in Karkor, and their hosts with them, about fifteen
thousand *men*, all that were left of [l]all the hosts of the children
of the east: for there fell [1]an hundred and twenty thousand men
11 that drew sword. And Gideon went up by the way of them
that dwelt in tents on the east of [m]Nobah and Jogbehah, and
12 smote the host: for the host was [n]secure. And when Zebah and
Zalmunna fled, he pursued after them, and [o]took the two kings
of Midian, Zebah and Zalmunna, and [2]discomfited all the host.
13 ¶ And Gideon the son of Joash returned from battle before the
14 sun *was up*, and caught a young man of the men of Succoth,
and enquired of him: and he [3]described unto him the princes
of Succoth, and the elders thereof, *even* threescore and seventeen
15 men. And he came unto the men of Succoth, and said, Behold
Zebah and Zalmunna, with whom ye did [p]upbraid me, saying,
Are the hands of Zebah and Zalmunna now in thine hand, that
16 we should give bread unto thy men *that are* weary? [q]And he
took the elders of the city, and thorns of the wilderness and
17 briers, and with them he [4]taught the men of Succoth. [r]And he
beat down the tower of [s]Penuel, and slew the men of the city.
18 ¶ Then said he unto Zebah and Zalmunna, What manner of
men *were they* whom ye slew at [t]Tabor? And they answered,
As thou *art*, so *were* they; each one [5]resembled the children of
19 a king. And he said, They *were* my brethren, *even* the sons of
my mother: *as* the LORD liveth, if ye had saved them alive, I

[i] 1 Kin. 22. 27.
[k] ver. 17.
[l] ch. 7. 12.
[m] Num. 32. 35, 42.
[n] ch. 18. 27. 1 Thess. 5. 3.
[o] Ps. 83. 11.
[p] ver. 6.
[q] ver. 7.
[r] ver. 9.
[s] 1 Kin. 12. 25.
[t] ch. 4. 6. Ps. 89. 12.

[1] Or, *an hundred and twenty thousand, every one drawing a sword*, ch. 20. 2, 15, 17, 25. 2 Kin. 3. 26.
[2] Heb. *terrified.*
[3] Heb. *writ.*
[4] Heb. *made to know.*
[5] Heb. *according to the form, &c.*

in the mountain. No identification of Penuel has taken place. It was south of the brook Jabbok, and on Jacob's way to Succoth. Gideon, journeying in the opposite direction to Jacob, comes from Succoth to Penuel.

10. Zebah and Zalmunna seem to have fled nearly due east to Karkor, which was probably an enclosure of some kind (perhaps a walled sheepfold, cp. Num. xxxi. 32 note). Its site is unknown; but it was near *Nobah*, in the half-tribe of Manasseh in Gilead (Num. xxxii. 40), and *Jogbehah* was in the tribe of Gad (ib. 34, 35). Gideon, perhaps taking a circuit so as to come upon them from the east, fell suddenly upon them, apparently at night, surprised them, and smote them.

13. *before the sun was up*] The translation of the words is doubtful, because of the rarity of the word rendered "sun" (*Heres;* cp. ii. 9 note). Many suppose it to be the name of a mountain pass, and render it *from the ascent of Heres.*

14. The written (see marg.) list would enable Gideon to punish the guilty and spare the innocent people. Succoth was governed by a sanhedrim or council of *seventy elders* (cp. Num. xi. 16), with perhaps seven others of superior rank called *princes.*

16. *he taught*] Thought to be a false reading, for "he threshed," as in *v.* 7 marg.

17. *the men of the city*] Perhaps the rulers; who, it is likely, had possession of the tower or citadel, and so could tyrannize over the people. Gideon slew the great men, and beat down their towers, but did not injure the inhabitants.

18. *what manner of men*] Lit. "**Where are the men?**" The sense, *what manner of men*, is merely gathered from the tenor of the answer. Gideon doubtless knew that his brethren had been killed by Zebah and Zalmunna, and the desire of avenging their death was one motive for his impetuous pursuit and attack. His question was rather a taunt, a bitter reproach to his captives, preparing them for their fate. Zebah and Zalmunna, in their answer, did not give evidence against themselves. Their hope was by a flattering answer to soothe Gideon's wrath.

19. *the sons of my mother*] A much closer relation than that of brothers by the father only. (Cp. Gen. xliii. 29; Deut. xiii. 6; Ps. lxix. 8). This is the only hint preserved of the transaction. We cannot say exactly when the slaughter of Gideon's brethren on Mount Tabor took place, whether before the outbreak of the war (vi. 33), or in the retreat and flight of the Midianites (vii. 22).

20 would not slay you. And he said unto Jether his firstborn, Up,
and slay them. But the youth drew not his sword: for he
21 feared, because he *was* yet a youth. Then Zebah and Zalmunna
said, Rise thou, and fall upon us: for as the man *is, so is* his
[u] Ps. 83. 11. strength. And Gideon arose, and [u]slew Zebah and Zalmunna,
and took away the [1]ornaments that *were* on their camels' necks.
22 ¶ Then the men of Israel said unto Gideon, Rule thou over us,
both thou, and thy son, and thy son's son also: for thou hast
23 delivered us from the hand of Midian. And Gideon said unto
them, I will not rule over you, neither shall my son rule over
[x] 1 Sam. 8. 7. & 10. 19. & 12. 12. 24 you: [x]the LORD shall rule over you. ¶ And Gideon said unto
them, I would desire a request of you, that ye would give me
every man the earrings of his prey. (For they had golden ear-
[y] Gen. 25. 13. & 37. 25, 28. 25 rings, [y]because they *were* Ishmaelites.) And they answered, We
will willingly give *them*. And they spread a garment, and did
26 cast therein every man the earrings of his prey. And the weight
of the golden earrings that he requested was a thousand and
seven hundred *shekels* of gold; beside ornaments, and [2]collars,
and purple raiment that *was* on the kings of Midian, and beside
27 the chains that *were* about their camels' necks. And Gideon
[z] ch. 17. 5. [z]made an ephod thereof, and put it in his city, *even* [a]in Ophrah:
[a] ch. 6. 24. [b] Ps. 106. 39. and all Israel [b]went thither a whoring after it: which thing
[c] Deut. 7. 16. 28 became [c]a snare unto Gideon, and to his house. ¶ Thus was
Midian subdued before the children of Israel, so that they lifted
[d] ch. 5. 31. & 1. 2. up their heads no more. [d]And the country was in quietness
29 forty years in the days of Gideon. And Jerubbaal the son of
30 Joash went and dwelt in his own house. And Gideon had
[e] ch. 9. 2, 5. [e]threescore and ten sons [3]of his body begotten: for he had many
[f] ch. 9. 1. 31 wives. [f]And his concubine that *was* in Shechem, she also bare
32 him a son, whose name he [4]called Abimelech. And Gideon the

[1] Or, *ornaments like the moon.*
[2] Or, *sweet jewels.*
[3] Heb. *going out of his thigh.*
[4] Heb. *set.*

---

20. It was Gideon's place to act the part of the "avenger of blood" (Num. xxxv. 12; Deut. xix. 6). The fierce manners of the age break out in the slaying of the captives (cp. 1 Sam. xv. 32, 33), and in Gideon's attempt to initiate his youthful son Jether in the stern work of slaying his country's enemies.

21. *the ornaments*] See marg. and cp. Isai. iii. 18. The custom of adorning the necks of their camels with gold chains and ornaments prevailed among the Arabs so late as the time of Mahomet.

24. In this desire for gold Gideon falls to the level of ordinary men, and we may see in it the first decline of his glory, leading to a sad tarnishing of the lustre of his bright name. The idolatrous honour paid to Gideon's ephod was probably a source of revenue to his house. Contrast the conduct of Abraham (Gen. xiv. 21–23), and of Elisha (2 K. v. 16, 26).

The *ear-ring* here mentioned is properly a *nose-ring* (cp. Gen. xxiv. 22 note). The custom of wearing nose-rings prevails in Eastern countries to the present day. The circumstance of Job's friends each contributing a nose-ring of gold (Job xlii. 11 note) is a remarkable parallel to the incident in Gideon's history. Rings of gold were also used as money in Egypt, as appears on several early monuments, and by the Celts.

25. *they spread*, &c.] The LXX. reads "He spread his garment."

26. If the Ishmaelite nose-rings were half a shekel in weight, then 1,700 shekels weight of gold implied that 3,400 persons wearing gold rings had been slain. The "collars" were rather "ear-drops."

27. The ephod was that particular part of the High-Priest's dress which was necessary to be worn when he inquired of God by Urim and Thummim. It seems that Gideon being now the civil ruler, desired to have an ephod of his own, kept in his own city, to be worn by the priest whenever Gideon might summon him to inquire of the Lord for him. His relations with the tribe of Ephraim probably made him unwilling to resort to Shiloh. Cp. the act of Jeroboam (1 K. xii. 28).

31. Abimelech's mother was not reckoned among the wives, being, probably, one of the Canaanite population in Shechem (ix. 28): neither was Abimelech himself reck-

son of Joash died [g]in a good old age, and was buried in the
sepulchre of Joash his father, [h]in Ophrah of the Abi-ezrites.
33 ¶ And it came to pass, [i]as soon as Gideon was dead, that the
children of Israel turned again, and [k]went a whoring after
34 Baalim, [l]and made Baal-berith their god. And the children of
Israel [m]remembered not the LORD their God, who had delivered
them out of the hands of all their enemies on every side:
35 [n]neither shewed they kindness to the house of Jerubbaal,
namely, Gideon, according to all the goodness which he had
shewed unto Israel.

CHAP. 9. AND Abimelech the son of Jerubbaal went to Shechem
unto [a]his mother's brethren, and communed with them, and with
2 all the family of the house of his mother's father, saying, Speak,
I pray you, in the ears of all the men of Shechem, [1]Whether *is*
better for you, either that all the sons of Jerubbaal, *which are*
[b]threescore and ten persons, reign over you, or that one reign
over you? remember also that I *am* [c]your bone and your flesh.
3 And his mother's brethren spake of him in the ears of all the
men of Shechem all these words: and their hearts inclined [2]to
4 follow Abimelech; for they said, He *is* our [d]brother. And they
gave him threescore and ten *pieces* of silver out of the house of
[e]Baal-berith, wherewith Abimelech hired [f]vain and light per-
5 sons, which followed him. And he went unto his father's house
[g]at Ophrah, and [h]slew his brethren the sons of Jerubbaal, *being*
threescore and ten persons, upon one stone: notwithstanding
yet Jotham the youngest son of Jerubbaal was left; for he hid
6 himself. And all the men of Shechem gathered together, and
all the house of Millo, and went, and made Abimelech king, [3]by
7 the plain of the pillar that *was* in Shechem. ¶ And when they
told *it* to Jotham, he went and stood in the top of [i]mount
Gerizim, and lifted up his voice, and cried, and said unto them,

[g] Gen. 25. 8. Job 5. 26.
[h] ver. 27.
ch. 6. 24.
[i] ch. 2. 19
[k] ch. 2. 17.
[l] ch. 9. 4, 46.
[m] Ps. 78. 11, 42. & 106. 13.
[n] ch. 9. 16. Eccles. 9. 14, 15.
[a] ch. 8. 31.
[b] ch. 8. 30.
[c] Gen. 29. 14.
[d] Gen. 29. 15.
[e] ch. 8. 33.
[f] ch. 11. 3. 2 Chr. 13. 7. Prov. 12. 11. Acts 17. 5.
[g] ch. 6. 24.
[h] 2 Kin. 11. 1, 2.
[i] Deut. 11. 29. Josh. 8. 33. John 4. 20.

[1] Heb. *What is good? whether, &c.*
[2] Heb. *after.*
[3] Or, *by the oak of the pillar:* See Josh. 24. 26.

---

oned with the seventy other sons of Jerubbaal (ix. 24. Cp. xi. 1, 2).

33. *turned again*] Doubtless Gideon himself had no doubt prepared the way for this apostacy by his unauthorised ephod. The Law of Moses, with its strict unity of priesthood and Altar, was the divinely-appointed and only effectual preservative from idolatry.

Baal-bereth] The god of covenants or sworn treaties, corresponding to the Zeus Orkius of the Greeks. The centre of this fresh apostacy was at Shechem.

IX. **1.** We are not told how soon after the death of Gideon these events happened. There must have been time for the apostacy and establishment of Baal-worship, and for the development of ill-will between Abimelech and his brethren.

2. *the men of Shechem*] Lit., "the masters." Cp. Josh. xxiv. 11; 1 Sam. xxiii. 11, 12.

3. The Ephraimite pride revolted from Abi-ezrite rulers, and inclined them to one who was a Shechemite by birth. (Cp. the same spirit in the time of David and Rehoboam, 2 Sam. xx. 1; 1 K. xii. 16.)

5. Such wholesale slaughters have always been common in Eastern monarchies, and are among the fruits of polygamy.

6. Millo must have been a fortified place close to, but separate from, Shechem, and perhaps the same as the tower of Shechem mentioned in *vv.* 46, 47. The building or enlarging of the better-known Millo at Jerusalem was one of Solomon's great works (1 K. ix. 15, 24). The population dwelling in Millo though perhaps numerically small, had great weight from possessing the stronghold. Their giving Abimelech the title of *king* indicates the strong Canaanite influence at Shechem. All the Canaanite chiefs were called *kings*, but it was a title hitherto unknown in Israel. This title had not been named by those Israelites who offered to make Gideon their hereditary *ruler* (viii. 22, 23).

the plain of the pillar, &c.] Rather "*the oak of the garrison which is in Shechem.*" The oak in question was probably called the "garrison oak," from a garrison being stationed near it.

7. *the top of Mount Gerizim*] The ancient Shechem was perhaps situated there. The population of Shechem is supposed to have been keeping some public festival outside the city when Jotham addressed them.

[k] See 2 Kin. 14. 9.
[l] ch. 8. 22, 23.
[m] Ps. 104. 15.
[n] Ps. 104. 15.
[o] Isai. 30. 2. Dan. 4. 12. Hos. 14. 7.
[p] ver. 20. Num. 21. 28. Ezek. 19. 14.
[q] 2 Kin. 14. 9. Ps. 104. 16.
[r] ch. 8. 35.
[s] ver. 5, 6.
[t] Isai. 8. 6. Phil. 3. 3.
[u] ver. 15, 56, 57.
[x] 2 Sam. 20. 14.
[y] 1 Sam. 16. 14. & 18. 9, 10. Isai. 19. 2, 14.
[z] Isai. 33. 1.
[a] 1 Kin. 2. 32. Esth. 9. 25. Ps. 7. 16. Matt. 23. 35, 36.

Hearken unto me, ye men of Shechem, that God may hearken
8 unto you. [k]The trees went forth *on a time* to anoint a king
over them; and they said unto the olive tree, [l]Reign thou over
9 us. But the olive tree said unto them, Should I leave my fatness, [m]wherewith by me they honour God and man, and [1]go to
10 be promoted over the trees? And the trees said to the fig tree,
11 Come thou, *and* reign over us. But the fig tree said unto them,
Should I forsake my sweetness, and my good fruit, and go to be
12 promoted over the trees? Then said the trees unto the vine,
13 Come thou, *and* reign over us. And the vine said unto them,
Should I leave my wine, [n]which cheereth God and man, and go
14 to be promoted over the trees? Then said all the trees unto the
15 [2]bramble, Come thou, *and* reign over us. And the bramble said
unto the trees, If in truth ye anoint me king over you, *then*
come *and* put your trust in my [o]shadow: and if not, [p]let fire
come out of the bramble, and devour the [q]cedars of Lebanon.
16 Now therefore, if ye have done truly and sincerely, in that ye
have made Abimelech king, and if ye have dealt well with Jerubbaal and his house, and have done unto him [r]according to
17 the deserving of his hands; (for my father fought for you, and
[3]adventured his life far, and delivered you out of the hand of
18 Midian: [s]and ye are risen up against my father's house this
day, and have slain his sons, threescore and ten persons, upon
one stone, and have made Abimelech, the son of his maidservant, king over the men of Shechem, because he *is* your brother;)
19 if ye then have dealt truly and sincerely with Jerubbaal and with
his house this day, *then* [t]rejoice ye in Abimelech, and let him
20 also rejoice in you: but if not, [u]let fire come out from Abimelech, and devour the men of Shechem, and the house of Millo;
and let fire come out from the men of Shechem, and from the
21 house of Millo, and devour Abimelech. And Jotham ran away,
and fled, and went to [x]Beer, and dwelt there, for fear of Abime-
22 lech his brother. ¶ When Abimelech had reigned three years
23 over Israel, then [y]God sent an evil spirit between Abimelech
and the men of Shechem; and the men of Shechem [z]dealt
24 treacherously with Abimelech; [a]that the cruelty *done* to the
threescore and ten sons of Jerubbaal might come, and their

[1] Heb. *go up and down for other trees.*
[2] Or, *thistle.*
[3] Heb. *cast his life.*

8-20. This fable and that noted in the marg.ref. are the only two of the kind found in Scripture. Somewhat different are the parables of the O. T. 2 Sam. xii. 1-4, xiv. 5-11; 1 K. xx. 39, 40.

9. *honour God and man*] Alluding to the constant use of oil in the meat-offerings (Lev. ii. 1-16), and in the holy ointment (Ex. xxx. 24, 25). In like manner, the allusion in *v.* 13 is to the drink-offerings of wine. See Lev. xxiii. 13; Num. xv. 10.

14. *the bramble*] Said to be the Rhamnus Paliurus of Linnæus, otherwise called Spina-Christi, or Christ's Thorn, a shrub with sharp thorns. The application is obvious. The noble Gideon and his worthy sons had declined the proffered kingdom. The vile, base-born Abimelech had accepted it, and his act would turn out to the mutual ruin of himself and his subjects.

15. *if in truth*] *i.e.* consistently with truth, honour, and uprightness, as explained in the interpretation in *vv.* 16 and 19.

let fire come out, &c.] The propriety of the image is strictly preserved, for even the thorns of the worthless bramble might kindle a flame which would burn the stately cedars to the ground. See Ps. lviii. 9.

16-20. These verses contain the interpretation of the fable. In them Jotham points out the base ingratitude of the people in raising Abimelech upon the ruin of Gideon's house, and foretells the retribution which would fall upon both parties.

22. *had reigned*] Rather, "**had ruled.**" It is not the phrase used in *v.* 6. It looks as if the Shechemites alone had made him *king*, and the rest of Israel had submitted to his *dominion*, without allowing his title of king.

blood be laid upon Abimelech their brother, which slew them;
and upon the men of Shechem, which [1]aided him in the killing
25 of his brethren. And the men of Shechem set liers in wait for
him in the top of the mountains, and they robbed all that came
26 along that way by them: and it was told Abimelech. And Gaal
the son of Ebed came with his brethren, and went over to
Shechem: and the men of Shechem put their confidence in him.
27 And they went out into the fields, and gathered their vineyards,
and trode *the grapes*, and made [2]merry, and went into [b]the house
of their god, and did eat and drink, and cursed Abimelech.
28 And Gaal the son of Ebed said, [c]Who *is* Abimelech, and who *is*
Shechem, that we should serve him? *is* not *he* the son of Jerubbaal? and Zebul his officer? serve the men of [d]Hamor the
29 father of Shechem: for why should we serve him? And [e]would
to God this people were under my hand! then would I remove
Abimelech. And he said to Abimelech, Increase thine army,
30 and come out. ¶ And when Zebul the ruler of the city heard
31 the words of Gaal the son of Ebed, his anger was [3]kindled. And
he sent messengers unto Abimelech [4]privily, saying, Behold,
Gaal the son of Ebed and his brethren be come to Shechem;
32 and, behold, they fortify the city against thee. Now therefore
up by night, thou and the people that *is* with thee, and lie in
33 wait in the field: and it shall be, *that* in the morning, as soon as
the sun is up, thou shalt rise early, and set upon the city: and,
behold, *when* he and the people that *is* with him come out against
thee, then mayest thou do to them [5]as thou shalt find occasion.
34 ¶ And Abimelech rose up, and all the people that *were* with him,
by night, and they laid wait against Shechem in four companies.
35 And Gaal the son of Ebed went out, and stood in the entering of
the gate of the city: and Abimelech rose up, and the people that
36 *were* with him, from lying in wait. And when Gaal saw the

[b] ver. 4.

[c] 1 Sam. 25. 10. 1 Kin. 12. 16.

[d] Gen. 34. 2, 6.

[e] 2 Sam. 15. 4.

[1] Heb. *strengthened his hands to kill.*

[2] Or, *songs:* See Isai. 16. 9, 10. Jer. 25. 30.

[3] Or, *hot.*

[4] Heb. *craftily,* or, *to Tormah.*

[5] Heb. *as thine hand shall find,* 1 Sam. 10. 7. & 25. 8. Eccles. 9. 10.

26. It does not appear who Gaal, son of Ebed, was; he may have been an officer sent by Abimelech with a force to bring the men of Shechem back to their allegiance, but who tried to turn the rebellion to his own account. He got into Shechem with a band of men, "his brethren," unopposed by Zebul, Abimelech's officer, and soon gained the confidence of the Shechemites.

27–29. Seditious and lawless acts (*vv.* 25, 26) now broke out into open rebellion. It was at an idolatrous feast in the house of Baal-berith, on occasion of the vintage, and when they were excited with wine, that the rebellion was matured. Those present began to "curse Abimelech," to speak insultingly of him, and to revile him (cp. Lev. xx. 9; 2 Sam. xix. 21; Isai. viii. 21). Gaal, the son of Ebed, who was watching the opportunity, immediately incited them to revolt from the dominion of Abimelech, offering himself to be their captain; adding a message of defiance to Abimelech, addressed, probably, to Zebul, who was present but too weak to resent it on the spot.

27. *made merry*] The word translated *merry* occurs only here and in Lev. xix. 24. Its etymology gives the sense of *praises, thanksgivings;* and its use in these two passages rather indicates that the fruits themselves which were brought to the House of God with songs of praise, and eaten or drunken with religious service, were so called. The thank-offerings would be a portion of the new wine of the vintage which they had just gathered in.

28. Shechem is another designation of Abimelech. Shechem means the son and heir of Shechem, Abimelech's mother being a Canaanite (*v.* 18).

31. *privily*] See marg. The word is probably the name of a place *in Tormah,* some think the same as *Arumah* (*v.* 41). Zebul was faithful to Abimelech, but dissembled his sentiments, from being too weak to oppose Gaal, till Abimelech came with his army (*v.* 38).

people, he said to Zebul, Behold, there come people down from
the top of the mountains. And Zebul said unto him, Thou seest
37 the shadow of the mountains as *if they were* men. And Gaal
spake again and said, See there come people down by the [1] middle
of the land, and another company come along by the plain of
38 [2] Meonenim. Then said Zebul unto him, Where *is* now thy
mouth, wherewith thou [f] saidst, Who *is* Abimelech, that we
should serve him? *is* not this the people that thou hast despised?
39 go out, I pray now, and fight with them. And Gaal went out
40 before the men of Shechem, and fought with Abimelech. And
Abimelech chased him, and he fled before him, and many were
overthrown *and* wounded, *even* unto the entering of the gate.
41 And Abimelech dwelt at Arumah: and Zebul thrust out Gaal
42 and his brethren, that they should not dwell in Shechem. ¶ And
it came to pass on the morrow, that the people went out into
43 the field; and they told Abimelech. And he took the people,
and divided them into three companies, and laid wait in the
field, and looked, and, behold, the people *were* come forth out of
44 the city; and he rose up against them, and smote them. And
Abimelech, and the company that *was* with him, rushed forward,
and stood in the entering of the gate of the city: and the two
other companies ran upon all *the people* that *were* in the fields,
45 and slew them. And Abimelech fought against the city all that
day; and [g] he took the city, and slew the people that *was* there-
46 in, and [h] beat down the city, and sowed it with salt. ¶ And
when all the men of the tower of Shechem heard *that*, they
47 entered into an hold of the house [i] of the god Berith. And it
was told Abimelech, that all the men of the tower of Shechem
48 were gathered together. And Abimelech gat him up to mount
[k] Zalmon, he and all the people that *were* with him; and Abimelech took an axe in his hand, and cut down a bough from the
trees, and took it, and laid *it* on his shoulder, and said unto the
people that *were* with him, What ye have seen [3] me do, make
49 haste, *and* do as I *have done*. And all the people likewise cut
down every man his bough, and followed Abimelech, and put
them to the hold, and set the hold on fire upon them; so that
all the men of the tower of Shechem died also, about a thousand

[f] ver. 28, 29.
[g] ver. 20.
[h] Deut. 29. 23. 1 Kin. 12. 25. 2 Kin. 3. 25.
[i] ch. 8. 33.
[k] Ps. 68. 14.

[1] Heb. *navel.*
[2] Or, *The regarders of times*, Deut. 18. 14.
[3] Heb. *I have done.*

37. *the plain of Meonenim*] Translate "**the oak of the soothsayers**" (see marg.). Some well-known oak, so called, but which is not mentioned elsewhere.

42. After Gaal's expulsion, *the people went out into the field*, either to complete the vintage, or for some other agricultural operation. "They" (Zebul and his party) sent word of this to Abimelech.

44. This verse explains the purpose of both the present and the former division of Abimelech's forces into several companies, viz. that while some of the companies attacked the men of Shechem in the field, another company, starting from their ambush, might occupy the approach to the city gate, and so cut off their retreat.

45. *sowed it with salt*] Expressing by this action his hatred, and his wish, that when utterly destroyed as a city, it might not even be a fruitful field. Salt is the emblem of barrenness (see marg. reff.).

46. *an hold of the house of the god Berith*] As combining the advantages of a *sanctuary* (cp. 1 K. ii. 28) and a fortress. The word rendered *hold* occurs elsewhere only in 1 Sam. xiii. 6, where it is rendered "*high-place.*" Its exact signification is uncertain.

48. *Zalmon*] A lofty and thickly-wooded hill, as the etymology of the name (*shady*) implies, in the immediate neighbourhood of Shechem: perhaps the same as Ebal. The setting fire to the hold, where the men of Shechem were all crowded together, with their wives and children, was the literal fulfilment of Jotham's curse in *v.* 20.

50 men and women. ¶ Then went Abimelech to Thebez, and en-
51 camped against Thebez, and took it. But there was a strong
tower within the city, and thither fled all the men and women,
and all they of the city, and shut *it* to them, and gat them up to
52 the top of the tower. And Abimelech came unto the tower, and
fought against it, and went hard unto the door of the tower to
53 burn it with fire. And a certain woman [l]cast a piece of a mill- [l] 2 Sam. 11.
54 stone upon Abimelech's head, and all to brake his scull. Then 21.
[m]he called hastily unto the young man his armourbearer, and [m] So 1 Sam.
said unto him, Draw thy sword, and slay me, that men say not 31. 4.
55 of me, A woman slew him. And his young man thrust him
through, and he died. And when the men of Israel saw that
Abimelech was dead, they departed every man unto his place.
56 ¶ [n]Thus God rendered the wickedness of Abimelech, which he [n] ver. 24.
57 did unto his father, in slaying his seventy brethren: and all the Job 31. 3.
evil of the men of Shechem did God render upon their heads: Ps. 94. 23. Prov. 5. 22.
and upon them came [o]the curse of Jotham the son of Jerubbaal. [o] ver. 20.
CHAP. 10. AND after Abimelech there [a]arose to [1 2]defend Israel [a] ch. 2. 16.
Tola the son of Puah, the son of Dodo, a man of Issachar;
2 and he dwelt in Shamir in mount Ephraim. And he judged
Israel twenty and three years, and died, and was buried in
3 Shamir. ¶ And after him arose Jair, a Gileadite, and judged
4 Israel twenty and two years. And he had thirty sons that
[b]rode on thirty ass colts, and they had thirty cities, [c]which [b] ch. 5. 10.
are called [3]Havoth-jair unto this day, which *are* in the land & 12. 14. [c] Deut. 3. 14.
5, 6 of Gilead. And Jair died, and was buried in Camon. ¶ And [d] ch. 2. 11.
[d]the children of Israel did evil again in the sight of the LORD, & 3. 7. & 4.
and [e]served Baalim, and Ashtaroth, and [f]the gods of Syria, 1. & 6. 1. & 13. 1.
and the gods of [g]Zidon, and the gods of Moab, and the gods [e] ch. 2. 13.
of the children of Ammon, and the gods of the Philistines, [f] ch. 2. 12. [g] 1 Kin. 11.
7 and forsook the LORD, and served not him. And the anger of 33.
the LORD was hot against Israel, and he [h]sold them into the Ps. 106. 36. [h] ch. 2. 14.
1 Sam. 12. 9.

[1] Or, *deliver.* [2] Heb. *save.* [3] Or, *the villages of Jair*, Num. 32. 41.

---

50. The men of Thebez (modern Tubas) had, doubtless, joined the Shechemites in their rebellion against Abimelech.

52. *went hard unto the door*, &c.] *i.e.* went close to the door. An act of manifest danger, seeing the roof was covered with persons who would be likely to throw down missiles of all sorts on the heads of their assailants. But the hatred of Abimelech, and his thirst for revenge, made him despise danger.

53. The phrase *all to* is now obsolete, and means *quite, entirely*, as in Chaucer, Spenser, and Milton.

X. **1.** *defend*] The marginal reading "**to deliver,**" is far preferable. The word is the same as in ii. 16, 18, iii. 9, 15, 31, &c., and is the technical word applied to the judges. Cp. Neh. ix. 27 (*saviours who saved them*, A.V.).

The term *there arose*, also marks Tola as one of the Judges, properly so called, raised by Divine Providence.

Tola and *Puah*] Both names of heads of houses in the tribe of Issachar (1 Chr. vii. 1; Gen. xlvi. 13).

Shamir] Not the same as that mentioned in Josh. xv. 48, which was in the hill country of Judah. Issachar would seem from this to have extended into the northern part of mount Ephraim.

2. Jair the Gileadite was probably the same person as is named in Num. xxxii. 41; Deut. iii. 14, as having given the name of *Havòth-jair* to certain villages in Bashan.

6. *the gods of Syria*] Or *Aram.* In the times of the Judges the various tribes of Aramites, or Syrians, were not compacted into one state, nor were they till after the time of Solomon. The national gods of these various Aramean tribes were probably the same; and their worship would be likely to be introduced into the trans-Jordanic tribes. It has been remarked that the Hebrew words for "to divine," "to practise magic," "idolatrous priests," and other like words, are of Syrian origin. The Syriac ritual proved very attractive to king Ahaz (2 K. xvi. 10–12). For the national gods of the Zidonians, Moabites, Ammonites, and Philistines, see 1 K. xi. 5, 7, 33; 1 Sam. v. 2–5.

7. The previous mention of the Philistines as oppressors of Israel (iii. 31) seems to be restricted to the south of Judah, when they

hands of the Philistines, and into the hands of the children of
8 Ammon. And that year they vexed and [1]oppressed the children
of Israel: eighteen years, all the children of Israel that *were* on
the other side Jordan in the land of the Amorites, which *is* in
9 Gilead. Moreover the children of Ammon passed over Jordan
to fight also against Judah, and against Benjamin, and against
10 the house of Ephraim; so that Israel was sore distressed. ¶ [i]And
the children of Israel cried unto the LORD, saying, We have
sinned against thee, both because we have forsaken our God,
11 and also served Baalim. And the LORD said unto the children
of Israel, *Did* not *I deliver you* [k]from the Egyptians, and [l]from
the Amorites, [m]from the children of Ammon, [n]and from the
12 Philistines? [o]The Zidonians also, [p]and the Amalekites, and
the Maonites, [q]did oppress you; and ye cried to me, and I
13 delivered you out of their hand. [r]Yet ye have forsaken me,
and served other gods: wherefore I will deliver you no more.
14 Go and [s]cry unto the gods which ye have chosen; let them
15 deliver you in the time of your tribulation. And the children
of Israel said unto the LORD, We have sinned: [t]do thou unto
us whatsoever [2]seemeth good unto thee; deliver us only, we
16 pray thee, this day. [u]And they put away the [3]strange gods
from among them, and served the LORD: and [x]his soul [4]was
17 grieved for the misery of Israel. ¶ Then the children of Ammon
were [5]gathered together, and encamped in Gilead. And the
children of Israel assembled themselves together, and encamped

[i] 1 Sam. 12. 10.
[k] Ex. 14. 30.
[l] Num. 21. 21, 24, 25.
[m] ch. 3. 12, 13.
[n] ch. 3. 31.
[o] ch. 5. 19.
[p] ch. 6. 33.
[q] Ps. 106. 42, 43.
[r] Deut. 32. 15. Jer. 2. 13.
[s] Deut. 32. 37, 38. 2 Kin. 3. 13. Jer. 2. 28.
[t] 1 Sam. 3. 18. 2 Sam. 15. 26.
[u] 2 Chr. 7. 14. & 15. 8. Jer. 18. 7, 8.
[x] Ps. 106. 44, 45. Isai. 63. 9.

[1] Heb. *crushed.*
[2] Heb. *is good in thine eyes.*
[3] Heb. *gods of strangers.*
[4] Heb. *was shortened.*
[5] Heb. *cried together.*

---

co-operated with Moab. They appear to have gradually increased in power till they reached their height in the time of Saul. In the present instance they were probably in alliance with the Ammonites, holding the western tribes in check, while the Ammonites subdued those on the east of Jordan.

8. *that year*] Perhaps the closing year of the oppression, when the Ammonites passed over the Jordan. For it was this crowning oppression which brought the Israelites to repentance (*vv.* 10, 15, 16), and so prepared the way for the deliverance. Possibly in the original narrative from which this portion of the Book of Judges is compiled, "that year" was defined.

the land of the Amorites] Viz. of Sihon king of the Amorites, Num. xxi. 21; Deut. i. 4; Josh. xiii. 10; Ps. cxxxv. 11.

11. (See marg. reff.). The Israelites were delivered from the *Egyptians* at the Exodus; from the *Amorites* in the victories over Sihon, and Og, and the five kings of the Amorites (Josh. x. 5); from the *children of Ammon* by Ehud; and from the *Philistines*, by the hand of Shamgar (cp. 1 Sam. xii. 9).

12. *the Zidonians*] An allusion to the time of Barak, when the Zidonians doubtless formed part of the great confederacy of Canaanites under Jabin king of Hazor. See Josh. xi. 8.

the Amalekites] In the time of Gideon (marg. ref.).

the Maonites] Probably one of the tribes of the "children of the East," who came with the Midianites and Amalekites in the time of Gideon, and may have been conspicuous for their hostility to Israel, and for the greatness of their discomfiture, though the record has not been preserved. The name is *Mehunims* in 2 Chr. xxvi. 7.

17. The historian, having related the preliminary incidents, now comes to the final issue which forms the subject matter of his narrative. On a certain occasion, as on many previous ones, the Ammonites were encamped in Gilead, with the intention of dispossessing the Israelites of the whole country, or at least as far as the river Jabbok (xi. 13), and of invading the West-Jordanic tribes. The children of Israel on the East of Jordan assembled together to resist them, and pitched their camp in Mizpeh. The narrative proceeds to detail what happened.

Mizpeh, as its name, "watch-tower" or "look-out" indicates, was situated on a height of Mount Gilead, and was, as such, a strong post. It is almost always written, "THE Mizpeh," or watch-tower. Four or five places of the name occur in Scripture.

18 in [y]Mizpeh. And the people *and* princes of Gilead said one to [y] Gen. 31. 49.
another, What man *is he* that will begin to fight against the ch. 11. 11, 29.
children of Ammon? he shall [z]be head over all the inhabitants [z] ch. 11. 8,
of Gilead. 11.
CHAP. 11. NOW [a]Jephthah the Gileadite was [b]a mighty man of [a] Heb. 11.
valour, and he *was* the son of [1]an harlot: and Gilead begat 32, called
2 Jephthah. And Gilead's wife bare him sons; and his wife's *Jephthae.*
sons grew up, and they thrust out Jephthah, and said unto him, [b] ch. 6. 12.
Thou shalt not inherit in our father's house; for thou *art* the son 2 Kin. 5. 1.
3 of a strange woman. Then Jephthah fled [2]from his brethren,
and dwelt in the land of Tob: and there were gathered [c]vain [c] ch. 9. 4.
4 men to Jephthah, and went out with him. ¶ And it came to pass 1 Sam. 22. 2.
[3]in process of time, that the children of Ammon made war
5 against Israel. And it was so, that when the children of Ammon
made war against Israel, the elders of Gilead went to fetch
6 Jephthah out of the land of Tob: and they said unto Jephthah, Come, and be our captain, that we may fight with the
7 children of Ammon. And Jephthah said unto the elders of
Gilead, [d]Did not ye hate me, and expel me out of my father's [d] Gen. 26.
house? and why are ye come unto me now when ye are in dis- 27.
8 tress? [e]And the elders of Gilead said unto Jephthah, Therefore [e] ch. 10. 18.
we [f]turn again to thee now, that thou mayest go with us, and [f] Luke 17. 4.
fight against the children of Ammon, and be [g]our head over all [g] ch. 10. 18.
9 the inhabitants of Gilead. And Jephthah said unto the elders
of Gilead, If ye bring me home again to fight against the children of Ammon, and the LORD deliver them before me, shall I
10 be your head? And the elders of Gilead said unto Jephthah,
[h]The LORD [4]be witness between us, if we do not so according to [h] Jer. 42. 5.
11 thy words. Then Jephthah went with the elders of Gilead, and
the people made him [i]head and captain over them: and Jeph- [i] ver. 8.
12 thah uttered all his words [k]before the LORD in Mizpeh. ¶ And [k] ch. 10. 17. & 20. 1. 1 Sam. 10. 17. & 11. 15.

[1] Heb. *a woman an harlot.*
[2] Heb. *from the face.*
[3] Heb. *after days.*
[4] Heb. *be the hearer between us.*

18. *and the people and princes,* &c.] The inhabitants of Gilead appear as a separate and independent community, electing their own chief, without any reference to the West-Jordanic tribes.

XI. **1.** The history of Jephthah appears to be an independent history inserted by the compiler of the Book of Judges. Verses 4 and 5 introduce the Ammonitish war without any apparent reference to x. 17, 18.

A genealogy of Manasseh (1 Chr. vii. 14–17) gives the families which sprang from Gilead, and among them mention is made of an *Aramitess* concubine as the mother of one family. Jephthah, the son of Gilead by a strange woman, fled, after his father's death, to the land of Tob (*v.* 3), presumably the land of his maternal ancestors (cp. ix. 1) and an *Aramean* settlement (2 Sam. x. 6, 8; 1 Macc. v. 13). It is difficult to conceive that Jephthah was literally the son of Gilead, if Gilead was the son of Machir, the son of Manasseh. Possibly *Gilead* here denotes the heir of Gilead, the head of the family, whose individual name has not been preserved, nor the time when he lived.

3. *the land of Tob*] To the north of Gilead, toward Damascus. The readiness with which Jephthah took to the freebooter's life gives us a lively picture of the unsettled times in which he lived.

7. This gives a wider signification to *vv.* 2, 3, and shows that Jephthah's *brethren* include his fellow tribesmen.

9. Jephthah made his own aggrandisement the condition of his delivering his country. The circumstances of his birth and long residence in a heathen land were little favourable to the formation of the highest type of character. Yet he has his record among the faithful (Heb. xi. 32).

11. *Jephthah uttered all his words before the* LORD *in Mizpeh*] This phrase designates the presence of the Tabernacle, or the Ark, or of the High Priest with Urim and Thummim (xx. 26, xxi. 2; Josh. xviii. 8; 1 Sam. xxi. 7). The High Priest waited upon Jephthah with the Ephod, and possibly the Ark, at his own house (see xx. 18 note). A trace of Jephthah's claim to unite

Jephthah sent messengers unto the king of the children of
Ammon, saying, What hast thou to do with me, that thou art
13 come against me to fight in my land? And the king of the
children of Ammon answered unto the messengers of Jephthah,
[l]Because Israel took away my land, when they came up out of
Egypt, from Arnon even unto [m]Jabbok, and unto Jordan: now
14 therefore restore those *lands* again peaceably. And Jephthah
sent messengers again unto the king of the children of Ammon:
15 and said unto him, Thus saith Jephthah, [n]Israel took not away
16 the land of Moab, nor the land of the children of Ammon: but
when Israel came up from Egypt, and [o]walked through the
17 wilderness unto the Red sea, and [p]came to Kadesh; then
[q]Israel sent messengers unto the king of Edom, saying, Let
me, I pray thee, pass through thy land: [r]but the king of Edom
would not hearken *thereto*. And in like manner they sent unto
the king of Moab: but he would not *consent*: and Israel [s]abode
18 in Kadesh. Then they went along through the wilderness, and
[t]compassed the land of Edom, and the land of Moab, and [u]came
by the east side of the land of Moab, [x]and pitched on the other
side of Arnon, but came not within the border of Moab: for
19 Arnon *was* the border of Moab. And [y]Israel sent messengers
unto Sihon king of the Amorites, the king of Heshbon; and
Israel said unto him, [z]Let us pass, we pray thee, through thy
20 land into my place. [a]But Sihon trusted not Israel to pass
through his coast: but Sihon gathered all his people together,
21 and pitched in Jahaz, and fought against Israel. And the
LORD God of Israel delivered Sihon and all his people into the
hand of Israel, and they [b]smote them: so Israel possessed all
22 the land of the Amorites, the inhabitants of that country. And
they possessed [c]all the coasts of the Amorites, from Arnon even
23 unto Jabbok, and from the wilderness even unto Jordan. So
now the LORD God of Israel hath dispossessed the Amorites
from before his people Israel, and shouldest thou possess it?
24 Wilt not thou possess that which [d]Chemosh thy god giveth thee
to possess? So whomsoever [e]the LORD our God shall drive out
25 from before us, them will we possess. And now *art* thou any
thing better than [f]Balak the son of Zippor, king of Moab?
did he ever strive against Israel, or did he ever fight against

[l] Num. 21. 24, 25, 26.
[m] Gen. 32. 22.
[n] Deut. 2. 9, 19.
[o] Num. 14. 25. Deut. 1. 40. Josh. 5. 6.
[p] Num. 13. 26. & 20. 1. Deut. 1. 46.
[q] Num. 20. 14.
[r] Num. 20. 18, 21.
[s] Num. 20. 1.
[t] Num. 21. 4. Deut. 2. 1—8.
[u] Num. 21. 11.
[x] Num. 21. 13.
[y] Num. 21. 21. Deut. 2. 26.
[z] Num. 21. 22.
[a] Num. 21. 23. Deut. 2. 32.
[b] Num. 21. 24, 25.
[c] Deut. 2. 36.
[d] Num. 21. 29. 1 Kin. 11. 7. Jer. 48. 7.
[e] Deut. 9. 4, 5. & 18. 12. Josh. 3. 10.
[f] Num. 22. 2. See Josh. 24. 9.

---

all Israel under his dominion is found in xii. 2, and breathes through his whole message to the king of the Ammonites. See *vv.* 12, 15, 23, 27.

13. *from Arnon even unto Jabbok*, &c.] The land bounded by the Arnon on the south, by the Jabbok on the north, by the Jordan on the west, and by the wilderness on the east was, of old, the kingdom of Sihon, but then the territory of Reuben and Gad.

15-28. Consult the marg. reff. If the Ark with the copy of the Law (Deut. xxxi. 26) was at Mizpeh, it would account for Jephthah's accurate knowledge of it; and this exact agreement of his message with Numbers and Deuteronomy would give additional force to the expression, *he uttered all his words before the* LORD (*v.* 11).

17. No mention is made of this embassy to Moab in the Pentateuch.

19. *into my place*] This expression implies that the trans-Jordanic possessions of Israel were not included in the land of Canaan properly speaking.

21. The title *God of Israel* has a peculiar emphasis here, and in *v.* 23, in a narrative of transactions relating to the heathen and their gods.

24. Chemosh was the national god of the Moabites (see marg. reff.); and as the territory in question was Moabitish territory before the Amorites took it from "the people of Chemosh," this may account for the mention of Chemosh here rather than of Moloch, or Milcom, the god of the Ammonites. Possibly the king of the children of Ammon at this time may have been a Moabite.

25, 26. Jephthah advances another historical argument. Balak, the king of Moab, never disputed the possession of Sihon's kingdom with Israel.

26 them, while Israel dwelt in [g]Heshbon and her towns, and in [h]Aroer and her towns, and in all the cities that *be* along by the coasts of Arnon, three hundred years? why therefore did ye
27 not recover *them* within that time? Wherefore I have not sinned against thee, but thou doest me wrong to war against me: the LORD [i]the Judge [k]be judge this day between the chil-
28 dren of Israel and the children of Ammon. Howbeit the king of the children of Ammon hearkened not unto the words of
29 Jephthah which he sent him. ¶ Then [l]the Spirit of the LORD came upon [1]Jephthah, and he passed over Gilead, and Manasseh, and passed over Mizpeh of Gilead, and from Mizpeh of Gilead
30 he passed over *unto* the children of Ammon. And Jephthah [m]vowed a vow unto the LORD, and said, If thou shalt without fail deliver the children of Ammon into mine hands, then it
31 shall be, that [2]whatsoever cometh forth of the doors of my house to meet me, when I return in peace from the children of Ammon, [n]shall surely be the LORD'S, [3][o]and I will offer it up
32 for a burnt offering. ¶ So Jephthah passed over unto the children of Ammon to fight against them; and the LORD delivered
33 them into his hands. And he smote them from Aroer, even till thou come to [p]Minnith, *even* twenty cities, and unto [4]the plain of the vineyards, with a very great slaughter. Thus the children of Ammon were subdued before the children of Israel.
34 ¶ And Jephthah came to [q]Mizpeh unto his house, and, behold, [r]his daughter came out to meet him with timbrels and with dances: and she *was his* only child; [5][6]beside her he had neither

[g] Num. 21. 25.
[h] Deut. 2. 36.
[i] Gen. 18. 25.
[k] Gen. 16. 5. & 31. 53. 1 Sam. 24. 12, 15.
[l] ch. 3. 10.
[m] Gen. 28. 20. 1 Sam. 1. 11.
[n] See Lev. 27. 2, 3, &c. 1 Sam. 1. 11, 28. & 2. 18.
[o] Ps. 66. 13.
[p] Ezek. 27. 17.
[q] ch. 10. 17. ver. 11.
[r] Ex. 15. 20. 1 Sam. 18. 6. Ps. 68. 25. Jer. 31. 4.

[1] Jephthah seems to have been Judge only of North east *Israel*.
[2] Heb. *that which cometh forth, which shall come forth.*
[3] Or, *or I will offer it, &c.*
[4] Or, *Abel.*
[5] Or, *he had not of his own either son or daughter.*
[6] Heb. *of himself.*

---

29. *Then the Spirit of the* LORD, &c.] This was the sanctification of Jephthah for his office of Judge and saviour of God's people Israel. Cp. vi. 34, xiii. 25. The declaration is one of the distinctive marks which stamp this history as a divine history.

The geography is rather obscure, but the sense seems to be that Jephthah first raised all the inhabitants of Mount Gilead; then he crossed the Jabbok into Manasseh, and raised them; then he returned at the head of his new forces to his own camp at Mizpeh to join the troops he had left there; and thence at the head of the whole army marched against the Ammonites, who occupied the southern parts of Gilead.

31. The words of this verse prove conclusively that Jephthah intended his vow to apply to human beings, not animals; for only one of his household could be expected to come forth from the door of his house to meet him. They also preclude any other meaning than that Jephthah contemplated a human sacrifice. This need not, however, surprise us, when we recollect his Syrian birth and long residence in a Syrian city, where such fierce rites were probably common. The Syrians and Phœnicians were conspicuous among the ancient heathen nations for human sacrifices, and the transfer, under such circumstances, to Jehovah of the rites with which the false gods were honoured, is just what one might expect. The circumstance of the Spirit of the Lord coming on Jephthah (*v.* 29) is no difficulty; as it by no means follows that because the Spirit of God endued him with supernatural valour and energy for vanquishing the Ammonites, He therefore also endued him with spiritual knowledge and wisdom. The Spirit of the Lord came upon Gideon, but that did not prevent his erring in the matter of the ephod (viii. 27). Cp. 1 Cor. xii. 4-11; Gal. ii. 11-14.

33. As in the conflicts with the Moabites, Canaanites, and Midianites (iii., iv., vii.), the battle was on Israelite territory, in self-defence, not in aggressive warfare.

the plain of the vineyards] Rather, *Abel-Ceramim* (cp. Abel-Meholah), identified with an *Abel* situated amongst vineyards, 7 miles from Rabbah. *Minnith* is *Maanith*, 4 miles from Heshbon, on the road to Rabbah.

34. *his daughter came out to meet him*] The precise phrase of his vow (*v.* 31). She was his *only child*, a term of especial endearment (see Jer. vi. 26; Zech. xii. 10). The same word is used of Isaac (Gen. xxii. 2, 12, 16).

35 son nor daughter. And it came to pass, when he saw her, that
he [s]rent his clothes, and said, Alas, my daughter! thou hast
brought me very low, and thou art one of them that trouble
me: for I [t]have opened my mouth unto the LORD, and [u]I can-
36 not go back. And she said unto him, My father, *if* thou hast
opened thy mouth unto the LORD, [x]do to me according to that
which hath proceeded out of thy mouth; forasmuch as [y]the
LORD hath taken vengeance for thee of thine enemies, *even* of
37 the children of Ammon. And she said unto her father, Let this
thing be done for me: let me alone two months, that I may [1]go
up and down upon the mountains, and bewail my virginity, I
38 and my fellows. And he said, Go. And he sent her away *for*
two months: and she went with her companions, and bewailed
39 her virginity upon the mountains. And it came to pass at the
end of two months, that she returned unto her father, who [z]did
with her *according* to his vow which he had vowed: and she
40 knew no man. ¶And it was a [2]custom in Israel, *that* the daughters of Israel went [3]yearly [4]to lament the daughter of Jephthah
the Gileadite four days in a year.
CHAP. 12. AND [a]the men of Ephraim [5]gathered themselves together, and went northward, and said unto Jephthah, Wherefore
passedst thou over to fight against the children of Ammon, and
didst not call us to go with thee? we will burn thine house upon
2 thee with fire. And Jephthah said unto them, I and my people
were at great strife with the children of Ammon; and when I
3 called you, ye delivered me not out of their hands. And when I
saw that ye delivered *me* not, I [b]put my life in my hands, and
passed over against the children of Ammon, and the LORD
delivered them into my hand: wherefore then are ye come up

[s] Gen. 37. 29, 34.
[t] Eccles. 5. 2—5.
[u] Num. 30. 2. Ps. 15. 4.
[x] Num. 30. 2.
[y] 2 Sam. 18. 19, 31.
[z] ver. 31. 1 Sam. 1. 22, 24. & 2. 18.
[a] See ch. 8. 1.
[b] Job 13. 14. Ps. 119. 109.

[1] Heb. *go and go down.*
[2] Or, *ordinance.*
[3] Heb. *from year to year.*
[4] Or, *to talk with*, ch. 5. 11.
[5] Heb. *were called.*

---

35. Jephthah was right in not being deterred from keeping his vow by the loss and sorrow to himself (cp. marg. reff.), just as Abraham was right in not withholding his son, his only son, from God, when commanded to offer him up as a burnt-offering. But Jephthah was wholly wrong in that conception of the character of God which led to his making the rash vow. And he would have done right not to slay his child, though the guilt of making and of breaking such a vow would have remained. Josephus well characterises the sacrifice as "neither sanctioned by the Mosaic law, nor acceptable to God."

36. The touching submission of Jephthah's daughter to an inevitable fate shows how deeply-rooted at that time was the heathen notion of the propriety of human sacrifice.

37. *bewail my virginity*] To become a wife and a mother was the end of existence to an Israelitish maiden. The premature death of Jephthah's daughter was about to frustrate this end.

40. There is no allusion extant elsewhere to this annual lamentation of the untimely fate of Jephthah's daughter. But the poetical turn of the narrative suggests that it may be taken from some ancient song (cp. the marginal note 4).

XII. **1.** Cp. the similar complaint of the Ephraimites to Gideon (viii. 1), when a civil war was only avoided by Gideon's wise and patriotic moderation. The overbearing pride of Ephraim comes out in both occurrences (see also Josh. xvii. 14-18).

we will burn thine house upon thee with fire] Cp. the fierce threat of the Philistines to Samson's wife (xiv. 15), and the yet fiercer execution (xv. 6). Burning appears as a mode of capital punishment (Gen. xxxviii. 24; Josh. vii. 25), and as a mode of desperate warfare (i. 8, xx. 48; Josh. viii. 8, 19, &c.).

2. *when I called you,* &c.] This circumstance is not related in the main narrative. It is likely to have occurred when Jephthah was first chosen leader by the Gileadites, and when Ephraim would probably ignore his pretensions.

3. *I put my life in my hands*] Cp. 1 Sam. xix. 5; xxviii. 21. The phrase expresses the utmost possible risk, knowingly incurred.

4 unto me this day, to fight against me? ¶ Then Jephthah
gathered together all the men of Gilead, and fought with
Ephraim: and the men of Gilead smote Ephraim, because they
said, Ye Gileadites [c] *are* fugitives of Ephraim among the Eph-
5 raimites, *and* among the Manassites. And the Gileadites took
the [d] passages of Jordan before the Ephraimites: and it was *so*,
that when those Ephraimites which were escaped said, Let me
go over; that the men of Gilead said unto him, *Art* thou an
6 Ephraimite? If he said, Nay; then said they unto him, Say
now [1] Shibboleth: and he said Sibboleth: for he could not frame
to pronounce *it* right. Then they took him, and slew him at the
passages of Jordan: and there fell at that time of the Ephraim-
7 ites forty and two thousand. ¶ And Jephthah judged Israel six
years. Then died Jephthah the Gileadite, and was buried in
8 *one of* the cities of Gilead. ¶ And after him [2] Ibzan of Beth-
9 lehem judged Israel. And he had thirty sons, and thirty
daughters, *whom* he sent abroad, and took in thirty daughters
from abroad for his sons. And he judged Israel seven years.
10, 11 Then died Ibzan, and was buried at Beth-lehem. ¶ And after
him [3] Elon, a Zebulonite, judged Israel; and he judged Israel
12 ten years. And Elon the Zebulonite died, and was buried in
13 Aijalon in the country of Zebulun. ¶ And after him [4] Abdon
14 the son of Hillel, a Pirathonite, judged Israel. And he had
forty sons and thirty [5] nephews, that [e] rode on threescore and ten
15 ass colts: and he judged Israel eight years. And Abdon the son
of Hillel the Pirathonite died, and was buried in Pirathon in the
land of Ephraim, [f] in the mount of the Amalekites.

CHAP. 13. AND the children of Israel [6] [a] did evil again in the sight
of the LORD; [7] and the LORD delivered them [b] into the hand of

[c] See 1 Sam. 25. 10. Ps. 78. 9.
[d] Josh. 22. 11. ch. 3. 28. & 7. 24.
[e] ch. 5. 10. & 10. 4.
[f] ch. 3. 13, 27. & 5. 14.
[a] ch. 2. 11. & 3. 7. & 4. 1. & 6. 1. & 10. 6.
[b] 1 Sam. 12. 9.

[1] Which signifieth *a stream*, or, *flood*, Ps. 69. 2, 15. Isai. 27. 12.
[2,3,4] A civil Judge also in North east *Israel*.
[5] Heb. *sons' sons*.
[6] Heb. *added to commit, &c.*
[7] This seems a partial captivity.

4. *because they said*, &c.] This passage is extremely obscure. Render:—"*The men of Gilead smote Ephraim, for they* (the Gileadites) *said*, **Ye are the fugitives of Ephraim. (Gilead lies between Ephraim and Manasseh; and Gilead took the fords of Jordan before Ephraim, and it came to pass, when the fugitives of Ephraim said Let me pass over, and the Gileadites asked him, art thou an Ephraimite, and he answered No, Then** (*the Gileadites*) **said to him** *say Shibboleth*, &c. **So they** (the Gileadites) **slew them at the fords of Jordan**"). All that is included in the parenthesis is explanatory of the brief statement "They smote them, for they said, Ye are the fugitives of Ephraim;" *i.e.* in spite of denial they ascertained that they were the fugitives of Ephraim, and so pitilessly slaughtered them when they endeavoured to return to their own country through Gilead. This part of Gilead, where the fords were, was clearly not in Manasseh, but in Gad. *Slew* (*v.* 6) implies *slaughtering* in cold blood, not killing in battle (see Jer. xxxix. 6). The word in the original text is the proper word for slaying animals for sacrifice.

6. *Shibboleth; and he said Sibboleth*] This is a curious instance of dialectic difference of pronunciation between the East and West Jordanic tribes. It is an evidence of the sound *sh* having passed into the Hebrew from the East of Jordan, possibly from the Arabians, with whom the sound is common.

forty-two thousand] The number includes the slain in battle and those killed at the fords.

8. *Ibzan of Bethlehem*] Some have fancied him the same as Boaz (Ruth ii. 1) of Bethlehem-Judah. Others, from the juxtaposition of Elon the Zebulonite (*v.* 11), understand Bethlehem in the tribe of Zebulon (Josh. xix. 15).

11. *a Zebulonite*] The tribe of Zebulon had shown its bravery, patriotism, and prowess in the time of Barak (iv. 10, v. 18).

13. *a Pirathonite*] He was, therefore, an Ephraimite (1 Chr. xxvii. 14). Its name still lingers in *Feratah*, 6 miles west of Shechem. The twenty-five years, apparently consecutive, occupied by the judgeship of Ibzan, Elon, and Abdon, seem to have been very uneventful and prosperous, since the only record of them, preserved in the annals of their country, relates to the flourishing families and peaceful magnificence of two of the number.

XIII. 1. The Philistines have been mentioned as oppressors of Israel in iii. 31, and

[c] Josh. 15. 33.
[d] ch. 2. 1. Luke 1. 11, 13, 28, 31.
[e] ver. 14. Num. 6. 2, 3. Luke 1. 15.
[f] Num. 6. 5. 1 Sam. 1. 11.
[g] Num. 6. 2.
[h] See 1 Sam. 7. 13. 2 Sam. 8. 1. 1 Chr. 18. 1.
[i] Deut. 33. 1. 1 Sam. 2. 27. & 9. 6. 1 Kin. 17. 24.
[k] Matt. 28. 3. Luke 9. 29. Acts 6. 15.
[l] ver. 17, 18.
[m] ver. 4.

2 the Philistines forty years. ¶ And there was a certain man of
[c]Zorah, of the family of the Danites, whose name *was* Manoah;
3 and his wife *was* barren, and bare not. And the [d]angel of the
LORD appeared unto the woman, and said unto her, Behold now,
thou *art* barren, and bearest not: but thou shalt conceive, and
4 bear a son. Now therefore beware, I pray thee, and [e]drink not
5 wine nor strong drink, and eat not any unclean *thing*: for, lo,
thou shalt conceive, and bear a son; and no [f]razor shall come
on his head: for the child shall be [g]a Nazarite unto God from
the womb: and he shall [h]begin to deliver Israel out of the hand
6 of the Philistines. ¶ Then the woman came and told her husband, saying, [i]A man of God came unto me, and his [k]counte-
nance *was* like the countenance of an angel of God, very terrible:
but I [l]asked him not whence he *was*, neither told he me his
7 name: but he said unto me, Behold, thou shalt conceive, and
bear a son; and now drink no wine nor strong drink, neither eat
any unclean *thing*: for the child shall be a Nazarite to God from
8 the womb to the day of his death. ¶ Then Manoah intreated the
LORD, and said, O my Lord, let the man of God which thou
didst send come again unto us, and teach us what we shall do
9 unto the child that shall be born. And God hearkened to the
voice of Manoah; and the angel of God came again unto the
woman as she sat in the field: but Manoah her husband *was* not
10 with her. And the woman made haste, and ran, and shewed her
husband, and said unto him, Behold, the man hath appeared
11 unto me, that came unto me the *other* day. And Manoah arose,
and went after his wife, and came to the man, and said unto
12 him, *Art* thou the man that spakest unto the woman? And he
said, I *am*. And Manoah said, Now let thy words come to pass.
[1]How shall we order the child, and [2][3]*how* shall we do unto him?
13 And the angel of the LORD said unto Manoah, Of all that I said
14 unto the woman let her beware. She may not eat of any *thing*
that cometh of the vine, [m]neither let her drink wine or strong

[1] Heb. *What shall be the manner of the, &c.*
[2] Or, what *shall he do?*
[3] Heb. what shall be *his work?*

---

x. 7, 11; and the Israelite worship of the gods of the Philistines is spoken of in x. 6. But this is the first time that we have any detailed history in connection with the Philistines. They continued to be the prominent enemies of Israel till the time of David.

forty years] The Philistine dominion began before the birth of Samson (*v.* 5), and was in force during Samson's twenty years' judgeship (xiv. 4; xv. 20). The forty years are, therefore, about coincident with Samson's life.

2. *Zorah*] See marg. ref.

his wife was barren] To mark more distinctly the high providential destiny of the child that was eventually born. Compare the similar circumstances of the birth of Isaac, Jacob, Samuel, and John the Baptist.

5. *a Nazarite*] See marg. ref. and note. The common Nazarite vow was for a limited time, like St. Paul's (Acts xviii. 18, xxi. 23-26). Others, like Samuel (1 Sam. i. 11), were Nazarites for life.

6. *a man of God*] The designation of a Prophet, of frequent use in the Books of Samuel and Kings (1 Sam. ii. 27, ix. 6, 7, 8, 10; 1 K. xii. 22, xiii. 1, 5, 6, 11), and applied to Timothy by St. Paul in the New Test. (1 Tim. vi. 11; 2 Tim. iii. 17).

his countenance] Rather, "**his appearance**," as the word is rendered in Dan. x. 18.

12. Translate, "**What shall be the manner** (or *ordering*) **of the child, and what shall be his work** (or *exploits*)." The original message of the Angel had given information on these two points: (1.) how the child was to be brought up, viz. as a Nazarite; (2.) what he should do, viz. begin to deliver Israel. Manoah desires to have the information repeated (cp. 1 Sam. xvii. 26, 27, 30). Accordingly, in *v.* 13 the Angel refers to, and enlarges upon, his former injunctions.

14. Cp. Num. vi. 4. In both passages the vine is described by the somewhat unusual though more accurate term, *vine of the wine*—the grape-bearing vine—to dis-

drink, nor eat any unclean *thing*: all that I commanded her let
15 her observe. ¶ And Manoah said unto the angel of the LORD, I
pray thee, [n]let us detain thee, until we shall have made ready a
16 kid [1]for thee. And the angel of the LORD said unto Manoah,
Though thou detain me, I will not eat of thy bread: and if thou
wilt offer a burnt offering, thou must offer it unto the LORD.
17 For Manoah knew not that he *was* an angel of the LORD. And
Manoah said unto the angel of the LORD, What *is* thy name,
that when thy sayings come to pass we may do thee honour?
18 And the angel of the LORD said unto him, [o]Why askest thou
19 thus after my name, seeing it *is* [2]secret? So Manoah took a kid
with a meat offering, [p]and offered *it* upon a rock unto the LORD:
and *the angel* did wondrously; and Manoah and his wife looked
20 on. For it came to pass, when the flame went up toward heaven
from off the altar, that the angel of the LORD ascended in the
flame of the altar. And Manoah and his wife looked on *it*, and
21 [q]fell on their faces to the ground. But the angel of the LORD
did no more appear to Manoah and to his wife. [r]Then Manoah
22 knew that he *was* an angel of the LORD. ¶ And Manoah said
unto his wife, [s]We shall surely die, because we have seen God.
23 But his wife said unto him, If the LORD were pleased to kill us,
he would not have received a burnt offering and a meat offering
at our hands, neither would he have shewed us all these *things*,
nor would as at this time have told us *such things* as these.
24 ¶ And the woman bare a son, and called his name [t]Samson:
25 and [u]the child grew, and the LORD blessed him. [x]And the
Spirit of the LORD began to move him at times in [3]the camp of
Dan [y]between Zorah and Esthaol.
CHAP. 14. AND Samson went down [a]to Timnath, and [b]saw a woman
2 in Timnath of the daughters of the Philistines. And he came
up, and told his father and his mother, and said, I have seen a
woman in Timnath of the daughters of the Philistines: now

[n] Gen. 18. 5
[o] Gen. 32. 29.
[p] ch. 6. 19, 20.
[q] Lev. 9. 24. Ezek. 1. 28. Matt. 17. 6.
[r] ch. 6. 22.
[s] Gen. 32. 30. ch. 6. 22.
[t] Heb. 11. 32.
[u] 1 Sam. 3. 19. Luke 1. 80. & 2. 52.
[x] ch. 3. 10. 1 Sam. 11. 6. Matt. 4. 1.
[y] Josh. 15. 33. ch. 18. 11.
[a] Gen. 38. 13.
[b] Gen. 34. 2.

[1] Heb. *before thee.* [2] Or, *wonderful*, Isa. 9. 6. [3] Heb. *Mahaneh-dan*, as ch. 18. 12.

---

tinguish it from the wild cucumber vine (2 K. iv. 39), or other plants to which the name *vine* was applied.

15. The language of Manoah, like that of Gideon (vi. 18), seems to indicate some suspicion that his visitor was more than human. The word rendered *made ready*, is also the proper word for *offering a sacrifice*, and is so used by the Angel in the next verse. By which it appears that the Angel understood Manoah to speak of offering a kid as a burnt-offering. Hence his caution, "thou must offer it unto the Lord." (Cp. Rev. xix. 10, xxii. 8; Acts x. 25, 26.)

17. *do thee honour*] If applied to a man, it would be by gifts, such for instance as Balak promised to the prophet Balaam (Num. xxii. 17), and such as were usually given to seers (1 Sam. ix. 7, 8; 2 K. v. 5, 15): if to God, it would be by sacrifices (Isai. xliii. 23).

18. *secret*] Rather, "**wonderful**," as in margin. In *v.* 19 the Angel "did wondrously," probably as the Angel that appeared to Gideon had done, bringing fire from the ock. See marg. reff. and notes.

24. *Samson*] The etymology is doubtful. Perhaps it comes from a word signifying *to minister*, in allusion to his Nazaritic consecration to the service of God.

25. *in the camp of Dan*] Rather "Mahaneh-Dan" (see marg.). The impulses of the Spirit of the Lord perhaps took the shape of burning indignation at the subjection of his brethren, and thoughts and plans for their deliverance, but especially showed themselves in feats of strength (xiv. 6, xv. 14, xvi. 30. Cp. Acts vii. 23–25).

XIV. **1.** *Timnath*] See Josh. xv. 10 and note. It was below Zorah (xiii. 2), about three miles S.W. of it.

2. *get her for me*] viz. by paying the requisite dowry (see marg. reff.) and gifts to relations. Hence the frequent mention of parents taking wives for their sons (Ex. xxxiv. 16; Neh. x. 30), because the parents of the bridegroom conducted the negotiation, and paid the dower to the parents of the bride.

[c] Gen. 21. 21. & 34. 4.
[d] Gen. 24. 3, 4.
[e] Gen. 34. 14. Ex. 34. 16. Deut. 7. 3.
[f] Josh. 11. 20. 1 Kin. 12. 15. 2 Kin. 6. 33. 2 Chr. 10. 15.
[g] ch. 13. 1. Deut. 28. 48.
[h] ch. 3. 10. & 13. 25. 1 Sam. 11. 6.
[i] 1 Kin. 10. 1. Ezek. 17. 2. Luke 14. 7.
[k] Gen. 29. 27.
[l] Gen. 45. 22. 2 Kin. 5. 22.

3 therefore [c]get her for me to wife. Then his father and his mother
said unto him, *Is there* never a woman among the daughters of
[d]thy brethren, or among all my people, that thou goest to take
a wife of the [e]uncircumcised Philistines? And Samson said
4 unto his father, Get her for me; for [1]she pleaseth me well. But
his father and his mother knew not that it *was* [f]of the LORD,
that he sought an occasion against the Philistines: for at that
5 time [g]the Philistines had dominion over Israel. ¶ Then went
Samson down, and his father and his mother, to Timnath, and
came to the vineyards of Timnath: and, behold, a young lion
6 roared [2]against him. And [h]the Spirit of the LORD came mightily
upon him, and he rent him as he would have rent a kid, and *he*
had nothing in his hand: but he told not his father or his mother
7 what he had done. And he went down, and talked with the
8 woman; and she pleased Samson well. And after a time he
returned to take her, and he turned aside to see the carcase of
the lion: and, behold, *there was* a swarm of bees and honey in
9 the carcase of the lion. And he took thereof in his hands, and
went on eating, and came to his father and mother, and he gave
them, and they did eat: but he told not them that he had taken
10 the honey out of the carcase of the lion. ¶ So his father went
down unto the woman: and Samson made there a feast; for so
11 used the young men to do. And it came to pass, when they
saw him, that they brought thirty companions to be with him.
12 ¶ And Samson said unto them, I will now [i]put forth a riddle unto
you: if ye can certainly declare it me [k]within the seven days of
the feast, and find *it* out, then I will give you thirty [3]sheets and
13 thirty [l]change of garments: but if ye cannot declare *it* me, then
shall ye give me thirty sheets and thirty change of garments.
And they said unto him, Put forth thy riddle, that we may hear
14 it. And he said unto them,

Out of the eater came forth meat,
And out of the strong came forth sweetness.

[1] Heb. *she is right in mine eyes.* [2] Heb. *in meeting him.* [3] Or, *shirts.*

---

3. *the uncircumcised Philistines*] Cp. 1 Sam. xiv. 6, xvii. 26, xxxi. 4, for a similar use of the term as one of reproach. Also Acts xi. 3.

4. His father and mother very properly opposed Samson's marriage with a heathen woman, the daughter of the oppressors of his race. But they could not prevail, because it was the secret purpose of God by these means to "seek occasion" against the Philistines; *i.e.* to make the misconduct of the father of Samson's wife, which He foresaw, the occasion of destruction to the Philistines. Cp. marg. reff. for similar statements.

8. The formal dowry and gifts having been given by Samson's father, an interval, varying according to the Oriental custom, from a few days to a full year, elapsed between the betrothal and the wedding, during which the bride lived with her friends. Then came the essential part of the marriage ceremony, viz. the removal of the bride from her father's house to that of the bridegroom or his father.

the carcase of the lion] The lion, slain by him a year or some months before, had now become a mere skeleton, fit for bees to swarm into. It was a universal notion among the ancients that bees were generated from the carcase of an ox.

10. *made a feast,* &c.] This was the wedding-feast, protracted in this instance seven days, in that of Tobias (Tob. viii. 19) fourteen days. It was an essential part of the marriage ceremony (Gen. xxix. 22; Esth. ii. 18; Matt. xxii. 2–4; Rev. xix. 7, 9).

11. *thirty companions*] These were "the children of the bride-chamber" (Matt. ix. 15; see *v.* 20). From the number of them it may be inferred that Samson's family was of some wealth and importance.

12. See marg. reff. Riddles formed one of the amusements of these protracted feasts.

sheets] Rather *linen shirts;* the *garments* which follow are the outward garments worn by the Orientals.

14, 15. *three days...on the seventh day*] Proposed alterations, such as *six days...on*

15 And they could not in three days expound the riddle. And it
came to pass on the seventh day, that they said unto Samson's
wife, [m]Entice thy husband, that he may declare unto us the [m] ch. 16. 5.
riddle, [n]lest we burn thee and thy father's house with fire: have [n] ch. 15. 6.
16 ye called us [1]to take that we have? *is it* not *so?* And Samson's
wife wept before him, and said, [o]Thou dost but hate me, and [o] ch. 16. 15.
lovest me not: thou hast put forth a riddle unto the children of
my people, and hast not told *it* me. And he said unto her, Behold, I have not told *it* my father nor my mother, and shall I
17 tell *it* thee? And she wept before him [2]the seven days, while
their feast lasted: and it came to pass on the seventh day, that
he told her, because she lay sore upon him: and she told the
18 riddle to the children of her people. And the men of the city
said unto him on the seventh day before the sun went down,
What *is* sweeter than honey?
And what *is* stronger than a lion?
And he said unto them, If ye had not plowed with my heifer,
19 ye had not found out my riddle. ¶And [p]the Spirit of the LORD [p] ch. 3. 10.
came upon him, and he went down to Ashkelon, and slew thirty & 13. 25.
men of them, and took their [3]spoil, and gave change of garments unto them which expounded the riddle. And his anger
20 was kindled, and he went up to his father's house. But Samson's
wife [q]was *given* to his companion, whom he had used as [r]his [q] ch. 15. 2.
friend. [r] John 3. 29.

CHAP. 15. BUT it came to pass within a while after, in the time of
wheat harvest, that Samson visited his wife with a kid; and he
said, I will go in to my wife into the chamber. But her father
2 would not suffer him to go in. And her father said, I verily
thought that thou hadst utterly [a]hated her; therefore I gave [a] ch. 14. 20.
her to thy companion: *is* not her younger sister fairer than she?
3 [4]take her, I pray thee, instead of her. ¶And Samson said concerning them, [5]Now shall I be more blameless than the Philis-

[1] Heb. *to possess us*, or, *to impoverish us?*
[2] Or, the rest of *the seven days, &c.*
[3] Or, *apparel.*
[4] Heb. *let her be thine.*
[5] Or, *Now shall I be blameless from the Philistines, though, &c.*

the fourth day, are unnecessary if it be remembered that the narrator passes on first to the seventh day (at *v.* 15), and then goes back at *v.* 16 and beginning of *v.* 17 to what happened on the 4th, 5th, and 6th days.

to take that we have] See marg. They affirm, that they were only invited to the wedding for the sake of plundering them by means of this riddle, and if Samson's wife was a party to plundering her own countrymen, she should suffer for it.

18. They try to give the answer in a way to make it appear that they had guessed it. Samson saw at once that she had betrayed him. He lets them know in a speech, which was of the nature of a riddle, that he had discovered the treachery.

20. *his companion*] Perhaps one of those mentioned in *v.* 11. The transaction denotes loose notions of the sanctity of marriage among the Philistines. It should be noted carefully that the practical lesson against ungodly marriages comes out most strongly in this case and that the providential purpose which out of this evil brought discomfiture to the Philistines, has nothing to do with the right or wrong of Samson's conduct.

XV. **1.** *visited his wife with a kid*] A common present (see Gen. xxxviii. 17; Luke xv. 29). From Samson's wife being still in her father's house, it would seem that she was only betrothed, not actually married, to his companion.

2. *I gave her*] In marriage. Samson had probably not heard of this before. Samson's father had paid the dowry for the elder sister; her father therefore offers her sister in her room. The fear of Samson probably also influenced him.

3. See marg. Before, when the Philistines injured him he was in covenant with the Timnathites through his marriage and by the rites of hospitality; for which reason he went off to Ashkelon to take his revenge (xiv. 19). But now the Philistines themselves had broken this bond, and so he was free to take his revenge on the spot.

4 tines, though I do them a displeasure. And Samson went and
caught three hundred foxes, and took [1]firebrands, and turned
tail to tail, and put a firebrand in the midst between two tails.
5 And when he had set the brands on fire, he let *them* go into the
standing corn of the Philistines, and burnt up both the shocks,
6 and also the standing corn, with the vineyards *and* olives. Then
the Philistines said, Who hath done this? And they answered,
Samson, the son in law of the Timnite, because he had taken his
[b] ch. 14. 15. wife, and given her to his companion. [b]And the Philistines
7 came up, and burnt her and her father with fire. ¶ And Samson
said unto them, Though ye have done this, yet will I be avenged
8 of you, and after that I will cease. And he smote them hip and
thigh with a great slaughter: and he went down and dwelt in
9 the top of the rock Etam. ¶ Then the Philistines went up, and
[c] ver. 19. 10 pitched in Judah, and spread themselves [c]in Lehi. And the
men of Judah said, Why are ye come up against us? And they
answered, To bind Samson are we come up, to do to him as he
11 hath done to us. Then three thousand men of Judah [2]went to
the top of the rock Etam, and said to Samson, Knowest thou not
[d] ch. 14. 4. that the Philistines *are* [d]rulers over us? what *is* this *that* thou
hast done unto us? And he said unto them, As they did unto
12 me, so have I done unto them. And they said unto him, We
are come down to bind thee, that we may deliver thee into the
hand of the Philistines. And Samson said unto them, Swear
13 unto me, that ye will not fall upon me yourselves. And they
spake unto him, saying, No; but we will bind thee fast, and
deliver thee into their hand: but surely we will not kill thee.

[1] Or, *torches*. [2] Heb. *went down*.

4. *foxes*] Rather, *jackals*, which are still very common in Palestine, especially about Joppa and Gaza. 1 Sam. xiii. 17 and Josh. xv. 28, xix. 3, are indications of the abundance of foxes or jackals giving names to places, especially in the country of the Philistines. It belongs to Samson's character, and agrees with the incident about the lion, that he should be an expert hunter. Ovid relates a very curious custom at Rome of letting loose foxes with lighted torches fastened to their tails in the circus at the Cerealia, in commemoration of the damage once done to the standing corn by a fox which a rustic had wrapped in hay and straw and set on fire, and which, running away, put the corn-fields in a blaze. This custom, which may have had a Phœnician origin, is a curious illustration of the narrative.

6. *burnt her and her father*] Out of revenge on Samson's nearest relations; or, as others think, as an act of justice in favour of Samson, and in hope of pacifying his anger. Burning was the punishment for adultery and kindred crimes among the Jews (Gen xxxviii. 24; Lev. xx. 14, xxi. 9). Samson's wife brought upon herself the very punishment which she sought to escape by betraying her husband (xiv. 15).

8. *hip and thigh*] A proverbial expression of doubtful origin, meaning all the *great* and *mighty*, all the choice pieces like the thigh and shoulder.

in the top of the rock] Rather, "**the cleft of the rock**." These **clefts** of the rock were the natural fortresses and hiding-places of the land. (Isai. ii. 21, lvii. 5. Cp. 1 Sam. xiii. 6; 1 K. xviii. 13.)

Etam] Not the same as the place in the territory of Simeon (1 Chr. iv. 32). Its situation is uncertain, but a site near Eleutheropolis (*Beth-jibrin*) is required; and there exist some extraordinary caverns in the soft limestone or chalky rock, fifteen or twenty feet deep, with perpendicular sides, opening into extensive excavations in the rock, about two hours from Eleutheropolis. [Conder conjectures it to be the same as Atab, a village 12 miles S.W. of Jerusalem, in the 'Arkûb or Ridge.]

9. *spread themselves*] An expression used of the Philistine mode of war (2 Sam. v. 18, 22), alluding to the compact way in which they came up the wadys, and then dispersed. Lehi is so called by anticipation (see *v*. 17).

11. The dispirited men of Judah were prepared to give up their champion, in order to conciliate their masters. This shows how hard was the task of the Judge, whose office it was to restore his countrymen to freedom and independence.

And they bound him with two new cords, and brought him up
14 from the rock. *And* when he came unto Lehi, the Philistines
shouted against him: and [e]the Spirit of the LORD came mightily [e] ch. 3. 10. & 14. 6.
upon him, and the cords that *were* upon his arms became as flax
that was burnt with fire, and his bands [1]loosed from off his
15 hands. And he found a [2]new jawbone of an ass, and put forth
his hand, and took it, and [f]slew a thousand men therewith. [f] Lev. 26. 8. Josh. 23. 10. ch. 3. 31. 2 Sam. 23. 8—12.
16 And Samson said,

With the jawbone of an ass, [3]heaps upon heaps,
With the jaw of an ass have I slain a thousand men.

17 And it came to pass, when he had made an end of speaking,
that he cast away the jawbone out of his hand, and called that
18 place [4]Ramath-lehi. ¶ And he was sore athirst, and called on
the LORD, and said, [g]Thou hast given this great deliverance into [g] Ps. 3. 7.
the hand of thy servant: and now shall I die for thirst, and fall
19 into the hand of the uncircumcised? But God clave an hollow
place that *was* in [5]the jaw, and there came water thereout; and
when he had drunk, [h]his spirit came again, and he revived: [h] Gen. 45. 27. Isai. 40. 29.
wherefore he called the name thereof [6]En-hakkore, which *is* in
20 Lehi unto this day. ¶ [7]And he judged Israel [i]in the days of the [i] ch. 13. 1.
Philistines twenty years.

Chap. 16. THEN went Samson to Gaza, and saw there [8]an harlot,
2 and went in unto her. *And it was told* the Gazites, saying,
Samson is come hither. And they [a]compassed *him* in, and laid [a] 1 Sam. 23. 26. Ps. 118. 10, 11, 12. Acts 9. 24.
wait for him all night in the gate of the city, and were [9]quiet all
the night, saying, In the morning, when it is day, we shall kill
3 him. And Samson lay till midnight, and arose at midnight,
and took the doors of the gate of the city, and the two posts, and
went away with them, [1]bar and all, and put *them* upon his

1 Heb. *were melted.*
2 Heb. *moist.*
3 Heb. *an heap, two heaps.*
4 That is, *The lifting up of the jawbone,* or, *casting away of the jawbone.*
5 Or, *Lehi.*
6 That is, *The well of him that called,* or, *cried,* Ps. 34. 6.
7 He seems to have judged South west Israel during twenty years of their servitude of the Philistines.
8 Heb. *a woman an harlot.*
9 Heb. *silent.*
1 Heb. *with the bar.*

---

14. *the cords...became as flax,* &c.] *i.e.* were as weak against his strength as half-burnt flax which yields to the least pressure.

15. *slew a thousand men therewith*] Cp. marg. reff. The Philistines, seized with a panic at seeing Samson suddenly burst his cords and rush at them, offered no resistance, but fell an easy prey to the blows of their mighty foe. Some perhaps were dashed down the cliffs in their flight.

16. There is a play upon the word, three times repeated, which means both "an ass" and also "a heap." The spirit of riddle-making (xiv. 12, 18) is apparent in this song of triumph (cp. v. 1; Ex. xv. 1; 1 Sam. xviii. 6, 7).

17. *Ramath-lehi*] Either the *height or hill of Lehi,* or, *of the jaw-bone;* or, as in margin, *the casting away of the jaw-bone,* with allusion to Samson casting it out of his hand, when he had finished his war-song.

19. *an hollow place that was in the jaw*] The right translation is, "**the hollow place which is in Lehi.**" The word translated "hollow place," means *a mortar* (Prov. xxvii. 22), and is here evidently a hollow or basin among the cliffs of Lehi, which, from its shape, was called "the mortar." A spring, on the way from Socho to Eleutheropolis, was commonly called Samson's spring in the time of St. Jerome and writers in the 7th, 12th, and 14th centuries.

XVI. **1.** *Gaza*] About 8 hours from Eleutheropolis, and one of the chief strongholds of the Philistines.

3. Instead of forcing the doors open, he tore the posts up, as it were, by the roots, with the barred doors attached to them. The word rendered "*went away with them,*" means "to pluck up the tent-pins," and hence "to remove." The present town of Gaza (Ghuzzeh) is an open town, without gates or walls, but the sites of the ancient gates still remain visible. One of these, on the south-east, is shown as the gate carried off by Samson.

A partially-isolated hill, about half-an-hour south-east of Gaza, and standing out from the chain that runs up to Hebron,

shoulders, and carried them up to the top of an hill that *is*
4 before Hebron. ¶And it came to pass afterward, that he loved a
5 woman [1] in the valley of Sorek, whose name *was* Delilah. And
the lords of the Philistines came up unto her, and said unto her,
[b]Entice him, and see wherein his great strength *lieth*, and by
what *means* we may prevail against him, that we may bind him
to [2]afflict him: and we will give thee every one of us eleven
6 hundred *pieces* of silver. ¶And Delilah said to Samson, Tell me,
I pray thee, wherein thy great strength *lieth*, and wherewith
7 thou mightest be bound to afflict thee. And Samson said unto
her, If they bind me with seven [3][4]green withs that were never
8 dried, then shall I be weak, and be as [5]another man. Then the
lords of the Philistines brought up to her seven green withs
9 which had not been dried, and she bound him with them. Now
there were men lying in wait, abiding with her in the chamber.
And she said unto him, The Philistines *be* upon thee, Samson.
And he brake the withs, as a thread of tow is broken when it
10 [6]toucheth the fire. So his strength was not known. ¶And
Delilah said unto Samson, Behold, thou hast mocked me, and
told me lies: now tell me, I pray thee, wherewith thou mightest
11 be bound. And he said unto her, If they bind me fast with new
ropes [7]that never were occupied, then shall I be weak, and be as
12 another man. Delilah therefore took new ropes, and bound him
therewith, and said unto him, The Philistines *be* upon thee,
Samson. And *there were* liers in wait abiding in the chamber.
13 And he brake them from off his arms like a thread. ¶And
Delilah said unto Samson, Hitherto thou hast mocked me, and
told me lies: tell me wherewith thou mightest be bound. And
he said unto her, If thou weavest the seven locks of my head
14 with the web. And she fastened *it* with the pin, and said unto
him, The Philistines *be* upon thee, Samson. And he awaked out
of his sleep, and went away with the pin of the beam, and with
15 the web. ¶And she said unto him, [c]How canst thou say, I
love thee, when thine heart *is* not with me? thou hast mocked
me these three times, and hast not told me wherein thy great
16 strength *lieth*. And it came to pass, when she pressed him
17 daily with her words, and urged him, *so* that his soul was
[8]vexed unto death; that he [d]told her all his heart, and said

[b] ch. 14. 15. See Prov. 2. 16—19. & 5. 3—11. & 6. 24, 25, 26. & 7. 21, 22, 23.

[c] ch. 14. 16.

[d] Mic. 7. 5.

[1] Or, *by the brook.*
[2] Or, *humble.*
[3] Or, *new cords.*
[4] Heb. *moist.*
[5] Heb. *one.*
[6] Heb. *smelleth.*
[7] Heb. *wherewith work hath not been done.*
[8] Heb. *shortened.*

---

bears the name of "Samson's Mount." But it may be doubted whether one of the hills overlooking Hebron is not rather meant.

4. A village to the north of Eleutheropolis, called Caphar-Sorek, was still existing in the time of Eusebius, near Zorah.

5. *and the lords of the Philistines*] See iii. 3 note.

his great strength lieth] Rather, "**wherein his strength is great.**"

eleven hundred pieces of silver] The greatness of the bribe offered to Delilah, 5,500 shekels of silver, nearly two talents (Ex. xxxviii. 24 note), shows the importance attached to Samson's capture.

11. *occupied*] The margin, "**wherewith work hath not been done,**" is better.

14. *and she fastened it with the pin*, &c.] The meaning of the verses seems to be that the seven long plaits, in which Samson's hair was arranged, were to be woven as a woof into the threads of a warp which stood prepared on a loom in the chamber, which loom Delilah fastened down with a pin, so as to keep it firm and immoveable. But Samson, when he awoke, tore up the pin from its socket, and went away with the loom and the pin fastened to his hair.

the beam] Rather, *the* "**loom,**" or *frame*. The beam is the wooden revolving cylinder, on which the cloth is rolled as fast as it is woven, the Hebrew word for which (1 Sam. xvii. 7; 1 Chr. xi. 23, xx. 5) is quite different from that here used.

unto her, [e]There hath not come a razor upon mine head; for I have been a Nazarite unto God from my mother's womb: if I be shaven, then my strength will go from me, and I shall become
18 weak, and be like any *other* man. ¶ And when Delilah saw that he had told her all his heart, she sent and called for the lords of the Philistines, saying, Come up this once, for he hath shewed me all his heart. Then the lords of the Philistines came up
19 unto her, and brought money in their hand. [f]And she made him sleep upon her knees; and she called for a man, and she caused him to shave off the seven locks of his head; and she
20 began to afflict him, and his strength went from him. And she said, The Philistines *be* upon thee, Samson. And he awoke out of his sleep, and said, I will go out as at other times before, and shake myself. And he wist not that the LORD [g]was departed
21 from him. But the Philistines took him, and [1]put out his eyes, and brought him down to Gaza, and bound him with fetters of
22 brass; and he did grind in the prison house. Howbeit the hair
23 of his head began to grow again [2]after he was shaven. ¶ Then the lords of the Philistines gathered them together for to offer a great sacrifice unto Dagon their god, and to rejoice: for they said, Our god hath delivered Samson our enemy into our hand.
24 And when the people saw him, they [h]praised their god: for they said, Our god hath delivered into our hands our enemy, and the
25 destroyer of our country, [3]which slew many of us. And it came to pass, when their hearts were [i]merry, that they said, Call for Samson, that he may make us sport. And they called for Samson out of the prison house; and he made [4]them sport: and
26 they set him between the pillars. And Samson said unto the lad that held him by the hand, Suffer me that I may feel the pillars whereupon the house standeth, that I may lean upon
27 them. Now the house was full of men and women; and all the

[e] Num. 6. 5. ch. 13. 5.
[f] Prov. 7. 26, 27.
[g] Num. 14. 9, 42, 43. Josh. 7. 12. 1 Sam. 16. 14. & 18. 12. & 28. 15. 16. 2 Chr. 15. 2.
[h] Dan. 5. 4.
[i] ch. 9. 27.

[1] Heb. *bored out.*
[2] Or, *as when he was shaven.*
[3] Heb. *and who multiplied our slain.*
[4] Heb. *before them.*

20. The possession of his extraordinary strength is ascribed (*e.g.* xiii. 25) to the Presence of the Spirit of the Lord. Now the Lord, or the Spirit of the Lord, had departed from him, and so his strength had gone too. The practical lesson against the presumption of self-dependence, and the all-importance of a hearty dependence upon God's Holy Spirit, must not be overlooked.

21. *put out his eyes*] Thus effectually, as they thought, preventing any future mischief on his part, while they prolonged their own triumph and revenge. (Cp. Num. xvi. 14; 2 K. xxv. 7; Jer. xxxix. 7.)

They applied to the two feet fetters of brass (2 Sam. iii. 34; Jer. lii. 11), and made him "grind"—the special task of slaves and captives (Ex. xi. 5; Isai. xlvii. 2; Lam. v. 13).

23. Dagon was the national idol of the Philistines (1 Chr. x. 10), so called from Dag, a fish. The description of Dagon, in his temple at Ashdod (1 Sam. v. 4), exactly agrees with the representations of a fish-god on the walls of Khorsabad, on slabs at Kouyunjik, and on sundry antique cylinders and gems. In these the figures vary. Some have a human form down to the waist, with that of a fish below the waist; others have a human head, arms, and legs, growing, as it were, out of a fish's body, and so arranged that the fish's head forms a kind of mitre to the man's head, while the body and fins form a kind of cloak, hanging down behind.

24. *Our God*, &c.] A portion of the Philistine triumphal song. Cp. ch. v., Ex. xv.

25. *that he may make us sport*] Rather, "**that he may play for us,**" *i.e.* dance and make music. At an idolatrous feast, dancing was always accompanied with vocal and instrumental music.

26. More literally, "**let me rest, and let me feel the pillars, that I may lean upon them.**" He feigned weariness with his dancing and singing, and asked to recover himself by leaning against the pillars. The flat roof, from the top of which, as well as under it, spectators could see what was being done on the stage in front, was mainly supported by two pillars. The lords and

lords of the Philistines *were* there; and *there were* upon the [k]roof
about three thousand men and women, that beheld while Samson
28 made sport. And Samson called unto the LORD, and said, O
Lord GOD, [l]remember me, I pray thee, and strengthen me, I
pray thee, only this once, O God, that I may be at once avenged
29 of the Philistines for my two eyes. And Samson took hold of
the two middle pillars upon which the house stood, and [1]on
which it was borne up, of the one with his right hand, and of
30 the other with his left. And Samson said, Let [2]me die with the
Philistines. And he bowed himself with *all his* might; and the
house fell upon the lords, and upon all the people that *were*
therein. So the dead which he slew at his death were more than
31 *they* which he slew in his life. ¶ Then his brethren and all the
house of his father came down, and took him, and brought *him*
up, and [m]buried him between Zorah and Eshtaol in the burying
place of Manoah his father. And he judged Israel twenty
years.

CHAP. 17. AND there was a man of mount Ephraim, whose name
2 *was* Micah. And he said unto his mother, The eleven hundred
shekels of silver that were taken from thee, about which thou
cursedst, and spakest of also in mine ears, behold, the silver *is*
with me; I took it. And his mother said, [a]Blessed *be thou* of
3 the LORD, my son. And when he had restored the eleven
hundred *shekels* of silver to his mother, his mother said, I had
wholly dedicated the silver unto the LORD from my hand for my
son, to [b]make a graven image and a molten image: now there-
4 fore I will restore it unto thee. Yet he restored the money unto
his mother; and his mother [c]took two hundred *shekels* of silver,
and gave them to the founder, who made thereof a graven image
and a molten image: and they were in the house of Micah.
5 And the man Micah had an house of gods, and made an [d]ephod,
and [e]teraphim, and [3]consecrated one of his sons, who became

[k] Deut. 22. 8.
[l] Jer. 15. 15.
[m] ch. 13. 25.
[a] Gen. 14. 19. Ruth 3. 10.
[b] See Exod. 20. 4, 23. Lev. 19. 4.
[c] Isai. 46. 6.
[d] ch. 8. 27.
[e] Gen. 31. 19, 30. Hos. 3. 4.

[1] Or, *he leaned on them.*
[2] Heb. *my soul.*
[3] Heb. *filled the hand*, Ex. 29. 9. 1 Kin. 13. 33.

---

principal persons sat *under* the roof, while the people, to the number of 3000, stood *on* the flat roof. When the pillars were removed, the weight of 3000 people brought the roof down with a fearful crash, and those above fell together with the stones and timbers upon those below, and a great slaughter was the result, Samson himself perishing under the ruins.

28. *at once avenged*] *i.e. with one final revenge.* These words do not breathe the spirit of the Gospel, but they express a sentiment, natural to the age, knowledge, and character of Samson.

31. "All the house of his father," in connection with "his brethren," must mean the whole tribe of Dan, aiding his nearer relations. The Danites, taking advantage of the consternation of the Philistines, and of the death of their lords and chief men, went down in force to Gaza, and recovered the body of their great captain and Judge, and buried him in his father's sepulchre.

XVII. See Introduction, p. 68. The only point of contact with the preceding history of Samson is, that we are still concerned with the tribe of Dan. See xviii. 1, 2, note. Josephus combines in one narrative what we read here and in i. 34, and places it, with the story in chapters xviii.-xxi., immediately after the death of Joshua.

2. *thou cursedst*] or, *adjuredst me by* God. Cp. Matt. xxvi. 63; Levit. v. 1.

3. Such a superstitious and unlawful mode of worshipping Jehovah is quite of a piece with viii. 27, xi. 31; 1 K. xii. 28, &c. It argues but slight acquaintance with the Ten Commandments, which, from the ignorance of reading and writing, were probably not familiar to the Israelites in those unsettled times. The mother intimates that the consecration of the silver was for the benefit of her son and his house, not for her own selfish advantage: and that she adheres to her original design of consecrating this silver for her son's benefit.

4. See viii. 27; Gen. xxxi. 19 notes.

6 his priest. [f]In those days *there was* no king in Israel, [g]*but*
7 every man did *that which was* right in his own eyes. ¶ And
there was a young man out of [h]Beth-lehem-judah of the family
8 of Judah, who *was* a Levite, and he sojourned there. And the
man departed out of the city from Beth-lehem-judah to sojourn
where he could find *a place:* and he came to mount Ephraim to
9 the house of Micah, [1]as he journeyed. And Micah said unto
him, Whence comest thou? And he said unto him, I *am* a
Levite of Beth-lehem-judah, and I go to sojourn where I may
10 find *a place*. And Micah said unto him, Dwell with me, [i]and be
unto me a [k]father and a priest, and I will give thee ten *shekels* of
silver by the year, and [2][3]a suit of apparel, and thy victuals. So
11 the Levite went in. And the Levite was content to dwell with
the man; and the young man was unto him as one of his sons.
12 And Micah [l]consecrated the Levite; and the young man [m]be-
13 came his priest, and was in the house of Micah. Then said
Micah, Now know I that the LORD will do me good, seeing I
have a Levite to *my* priest.

CHAP. 18. IN [a]those days *there was* no king in Israel: and in those
days [b]the tribe of the Danites sought them an inheritance to
dwell in; for unto that day *all their* inheritance had not fallen
2 unto them among the tribes of Israel. And the children of Dan
sent of their family five men from their coasts, [4]men of valour,
from [c]Zorah, and from Eshtaol, [d]to spy out the land, and to
search it; and they said unto them, Go, search the land: who
when they came to mount Ephraim, to the [e]house of Micah,
3 they lodged there. When they *were* by the house of Micah, they
knew the voice of the young man the Levite: and they turned
in thither, and said unto him, Who brought thee hither? and
4 what makest thou in this *place?* and what hast thou here? And
he said unto them, Thus and thus dealeth Micah with me, and
5 hath [f]hired me, and I am his priest. And they said unto
him, [g]Ask counsel, we pray thee, [h]of God, that we may know
6 whether our way which we go shall be prosperous. And the
priest said unto them, [i]Go in peace: before the LORD *is* your

[f] ch. 18. 1. & 19. 1. & 21. 25. Deut. 33. 5.
[g] Deut. 12. 8.
[h] See Josh. 19. 15. Ruth 1. 1. Mic. 5. 2. Matt. 2. 1.
[i] ch. 18. 19.
[k] Gen. 45. 8. Job 29. 16.
[l] ver. 5.
[m] ch. 18, 30.
[a] ch. 17. 6. & 21. 25.
[b] Josh. 19. 47.
[c] ch. 13. 25.
[d] Num. 13. 17. Josh. 2. 1.
[e] ch. 17. 1.
[f] ch. 17. 10.
[g] 1 Kin. 22. 5. Isai. 30. 1. Hos. 4. 12.
[h] See ch. 17. 5. & ver. 14.
[i] 1 Kin. 22. 6.

[1] Heb. *in making his way.*
[2] Or, *a double suit, &c.*
[3] Heb. *an order of garments.*
[4] Heb. *sons.*

---

6. *In those days*, &c.] This phrase, indicating distinctly that the writer lived after the establishment of the kingly government in Israel, is peculiar to the author of these last five chapters.

7. The Hebrew words for "*he sojourned there*" are, GER-SHOM, which words are used (xviii. 30) in the genealogy of this young Levite, whose name was "Jonathan, the son of Gershom." Hence some read here, "the son of Gershom."

8. Jonathan's state without a home gives us a vivid picture of what must have been the condition of many Levites.

10. *ten shekels*] About 25*s*. to 26*s*. (see Ex. xxxviii. 24).

13. This shows the ignorance as well as the superstition of the age (cp. 2 K. xviii. 22), and gives a picture of the lawlessness of the times. The incidental testimony to the Levitical priesthood is to be noted; but the idolatrous worship in the immediate neighbourhood of Shiloh is passing strange.

XVIII. **2.** This identity of locality with the scene of Samson's birth and death indicates that both narratives are drawn from the same source, probably the annals of the tribe of Dan.

3. It does not follow that they had known him before, and recognized his voice, though it may be so. But the Hebrew equally bears the sense that they heard the voice of the Levite; and, attracted by it, went into the chapel (*v.* 18) where Jonathan was. They were probably just starting on their journey, but were still within the court or precincts of Micah's house. Micah had evidently not told them of his house of God, and his Levite. Their questions indicate surprise.

5. The sight of the ephod and teraphim suggested the notion of enquiring of God.

6. *before the* LORD, &c.] *i.e.* He looks favourably upon it. (Cp. Ezr. viii. 21, 22.)

7 way wherein ye go. ¶ Then the five men departed, and came to
[k]Laish, and saw the people that *were* therein, [l]how they dwelt
careless, after the manner of the Zidonians, quiet and secure;
and *there was* no [1]magistrate in the land, that might put *them*
to shame in *any* thing; and they *were* far from the Zidonians,
8 and had no business with *any* man. And they came unto their
brethren to [m]Zorah and Eshtaol: and their brethren said unto
9 them, What *say* ye? And they said, [n]Arise, that we may go up
against them: for we have seen the land, and, behold, it *is* very
good: and *are* ye [o]still? be not slothful to go, *and* to enter to
10 possess the land. When ye go, ye shall come unto a people
[p]secure, and to a large land; for God hath given it into your
hands; [q]a place where *there is* no want of any thing that *is* in
11 the earth. ¶ And there went from thence of the family of the
Danites out of Zorah and out of Eshtaol, six hundred men [2]ap-
12 pointed with weapons of war. And they went up, and pitched
in [r]Kirjath-jearim, in Judah: wherefore they called that place
[s]Mahaneh-dan unto this day: behold, *it is* behind Kirjath-
13 jearim. And they passed thence unto mount Ephraim, and
14 came unto [t]the house of Micah. [u]Then answered the five men
that went to spy out the country of Laish, and said unto their
brethren, Do ye know that [x]there is in these houses an ephod,
and teraphim, and a graven image, and a molten image? now
15 therefore consider what ye have to do. And they turned thither-
ward, and came to the house of the young man the Levite, *even*
16 unto the house of Micah, and [3]saluted him. And the [y]six hundred men appointed with their weapons of war, which *were* of
17 the children of Dan, stood by the entering of the gate. And
[z]the five men that went to spy out the land went up, *and* came
in thither, *and* took [a]the graven image, and the ephod, and the
teraphim, and the molten image: and the priest stood in the
entering of the gate with the six hundred men *that were* ap-
18 pointed with weapons of war. And these went into Micah's
house, and fetched the carved image, the ephod, and the teraphim, and the molten image. Then said the priest unto them,
19 What do ye? And they said unto him, Hold thy peace, [b]lay

[k] Josh. 19. 47, called *Leshem.*
[l] ver. 27, 28.
[m] ver. 2.
[n] Num. 13. 30. Josh. 2. 23, 24.
[o] 1 Kin. 22. 3.
[p] ver. 7, 27.
[q] Deut. 8. 9.
[r] Josh. 15. 60.
[s] ch. 13. 25.
[t] ver. 2.
[u] 1 Sam. 14. 28.
[x] ch. 17. 5.
[y] ver. 11.
[z] ver. 2, 14.
[a] ch. 17. 4, 5.
[b] Job 21. 5. & 29. 9. & 40. 4. Prov. 30. 32. Mic. 7. 16.

[1] Heb. *possessor*, or, *heir of restraint.*
[2] Heb. *girded.*
[3] Heb. *asked him of peace*, Gen. 43. 27. 1 Sam. 17. 22.

---

7. *Laish*] Afterwards called *Dan* (*v.* 29). The exact site has not been identified, but it was the northern extremity of Israel, near the sources of the Jordan, and about four miles from Panium, or Cæsarea-Philippi. It is thought to have stood where the village Tell-el-Kadi now stands.

after the manner of the Zidonians] The genius of the Zidonians being mechanical and commercial, not military, their colonists were apt to neglect fortifications and similar warlike precautions. In Solomon's time the Zidonians were especially skilful in hewing timber (1 K. v. 6; 1 Chr. xxii. 4), and it is highly probable, from their proximity to Lebanon, that such was the occupation of the men of Laish.

quiet and secure, &c.] This is a very obscure and difficult passage. Translate thus: "**Quiet and secure, and none of them doing any injury in the land, possessing wealth,**" or *dominion.*

12. *Kirjath-jearim*] "City of forests," otherwise called "Kirjath-Baal" (marg. ref.), identified by Robinson with the modern *Kurit-el-Enab*, on the road from Jaffa to Jerusalem [and by Conder with Sôba].

14. *in these houses*] This agrees with what we saw at *vv.* 2 and 3 that the "house of God" and Jonathan's house were detached from Micah's. There were other houses besides (*v.* 22). The whole settlement was probably called Beth-Micah, contained in one court, and entered by one gate (*v.* 16).

17. The five went back to Micah's chapel (Micah's house, *v.* 18) and took the ephod, teraphim, &c., and brought them to the gate where the priest was talking to the six hundred men.

thine hand upon thy mouth, and go with us, [c]and be to us a [c] ch. 17. 10.
father and a priest: *is it* better for thee to be a priest unto the
house of one man, or that thou be a priest unto a tribe and a
20 family in Israel? And the priest's heart was glad, and he took
the ephod, and the teraphim, and the graven image, and went
21 in the midst of the people. So they turned and departed, and
put the little ones and the cattle and the carriage before them.
22 ¶ *And* when they were a good way from the house of Micah,
the men that *were* in the houses near to Micah's house were
23 gathered together, and overtook the children of Dan. And
they cried unto the children of Dan. And they turned their
faces, and said unto Micah, What aileth thee, [1]that thou comest
24 with such a company? And he said, Ye have taken away my
gods which I made, and the priest, and ye are gone away: and
what have I more? and what *is* this *that* ye say unto me, What
25 aileth thee? And the children of Dan said unto him, Let not
thy voice be heard among us, lest [2]angry fellows run upon thee,
26 and thou lose thy life, with the lives of thy household. And the
children of Dan went their way: and when Micah saw that they
were too strong for him, he turned and went back unto his house.
27 And they took *the things* which Micah had made, and the priest
which he had, and [d]came unto Laish, unto a people *that were* [d] ver. 7, 10.
at quiet and secure: [e]and they smote them with the edge of the Deut. 33. 22.
28 sword, and burnt the city with fire. And *there was* no deliverer, [e] Josh. 19. 47.
because it *was* [f]far from Zidon, and they had no business with [f] ver. 7.
any man; and it was in the valley that *lieth* [g]by Beth-rehob. [g] 2 Sam. 10. 6.
29 ¶ And they built a city, and dwelt therein. And [h]they called [h] Josh. 19. 47.
the name of the city [i]Dan, after the name of Dan their father, [i] Gen. 14. 14.
who was born unto Israel: howbeit the name of the city *was* ch. 20. 1. 1 Kin. 12.
30 Laish at the first. And the children of Dan set up the graven 29, 30.
image: and Jonathan, the son of Gershom, the son of Manasseh,
he and his sons were priests to the tribe of Dan [k]until the day [k] ch. 13. 1.
31 of the captivity of the land. And they set them up Micah's 1 Sam. 4. 2,
graven image, which he made, [l]all the time that the house of 3, 10, 11. Ps. 78. 60.
God was in Shiloh. [l] Josh. 18. 1. ch. 19. 18.

[1] Heb. *that thou art gathered together?*   [2] Heb. *bitter of soul*, 2 Sam. 17. 8.

---

21. *and put the little ones*, &c., *before them*] They expected a pursuit from Micah's people, and arranged their order of march accordingly.

the carriage] Rather, "*the valuables.*" Some interpret it "the heavy baggage."

22. *were gathered together*] Literally, "were called together." The men, who were all Micah's workmen, were probably in the fields with their master at the time of the robbery. When the women saw what was done they gave the alarm, and Micah called the men together as quickly as possible, and pursued the Danites and overtook them.

27. *the things which Micah had made*] Rather, from *v.* 24, "**the gods which Micah had made.**" See *v.* 31; Deut. xxvii. 15; Ex. xx. 4.

28. Rehob (as Dan afterwards) is mentioned as the northernmost point of the land of Canaan (Num. xiii. 21), and its position is defined with reference to the entering in of Hamath.

a city] Rather, "**the**" *city*. They rebuilt Laish, which they had burnt down (*v.* 29).

30. In the Hebrew text the name here rendered MANASSEH is written M^{N}SH. Without the N suspended over the line, the word may be read MOSES, whose son was Gershom (Ex. ii. 22), whose son or descendant Jonathan clearly was. The Masoretes, probably grieved that a descendant of Moses should have been implicated in idolatrous worship, adopted this expedient for disguising the fact without absolutely falsifying the text. The Vulgate has *Moses*, the Septuagint *Manasses*.

Verses 30, 31, seem to tell us that Jonathan's descendants were priests to the tribe of Dan till the captivity (2 K. xv. 29, xvii. 6); and that the graven image was in their custody till David's time, by whose

Chap. 19. AND it came to pass in those days, [a]when *there was* no
king in Israel, that there was a certain Levite sojourning on the
side of mount Ephraim, who took to him [1]a concubine out of
2 [b]Beth-lehem-judah. And his concubine played the whore
against him, and went away from him unto her father's house
to Beth-lehem-judah, and was there [2][3]four whole months.
3 ¶ And her husband arose, and went after her, to speak [4]friendly
unto her, *and* to bring her again, having his servant with him,
and a couple of asses: and she brought him into her father's
house: and when the father of the damsel saw him, he rejoiced
4 to meet him. And his father in law, the damsel's father, retained him; and he abode with him three days: so they did eat
5 and drink, and lodge there. And it came to pass on the fourth
day, when they arose early in the morning, that he rose up to
depart: and the damsel's father said unto his son in law, [5][c]Com-
fort thine heart with a morsel of bread, and afterward go your
6 way. And they sat down, and did eat and drink both of them
together: for the damsel's father had said unto the man, Be
content, I pray thee, and tarry all night, and let thine heart be
7 merry. And when the man rose up to depart, his father in law
8 urged him: therefore he lodged there again. And he arose
early in the morning on the fifth day to depart: and the damsel's father said, Comfort thine heart, I pray thee. And they
9 tarried [6]until afternoon, and they did eat both of them. And
when the man rose up to depart, he, and his concubine, and his
servant, his father in law, the damsel's father, said unto him,
Behold, now the day [7]draweth toward evening, I pray you tarry
all night: behold, [8]the day groweth to an end, lodge here, that
thine heart may be merry; and to morrow get you early on your
10 way, that thou mayest go [9]home. But the man would not tarry
that night, but he rose up and departed, and came [1]over against
[d]Jebus, which *is* Jerusalem; and *there were* with him two asses
11 saddled, his concubine also *was* with him. ¶ *And* when they *were*
by Jebus, the day was far spent; and the servant said unto his
master, Come, I pray thee, and let us turn in into this city [e]of
12 the Jebusites, and lodge in it. And his master said unto him,
We will not turn aside hither into the city of a stranger, that *is*
13 not of the children of Israel; we will pass over [f]to Gibeah. And

[a] ch. 17. 6. & 18. 1. & 21. 25.
[b] ch. 17. 7.
[c] Gen. 18. 5.
[d] Josh. 18. 28.
[e] Josh. 15. 8, 63. ch. 1. 21. 2 Sam. 5. 6.
[f] Josh. 18. 28.

[1] Heb. *a woman a concubine*, or, *a wife a concubine*.
[2] Or, *a year* and *four months*.
[3] Heb. *days four months*.
[4] Heb. *to her heart*, Gen. 34. 3.
[5] Heb. *strengthen*.
[6] Heb. *till the day declined*.
[7] Heb. *is weak*.
[8] Heb. it is *the pitching* time *of the day*.
[9] Heb. *to thy tent*.
[1] Heb. *to over against*.

order, perhaps, it was destroyed, though the idolatrous worship continued, or was revived, at Dan.

XIX. This history has no connexion whatever with the preceding. The note of time (xx. 28) shows that the date of it is in the lifetime of the first generation of settlers in Canaan.

1. *a concubine*] See marg. The name does not imply any moral reproach. A concubine was as much the man's wife as the woman so called, though she had not the same rights. See *vv.* 3, 4.

2. *played the whore against him*] Perhaps only meaning that she ran away from him, and left him; for she returned to her father's house.

9. This is a perfect picture of the manners of the time. It is probable that the father showed more than usual hospitality, in order to ensure the kind treatment of his daughter by her husband. These particulars are given to account for their journey running so far into the evening, which was the immediate cause of the horrible catastrophe which followed.

12. *city of a stranger*] This shows how completely, even in these early days, the Jebusite population had excluded both the tribes of Judah and Benjamin.

he said unto his servant, Come, and let us draw near to one of
14 these places to lodge all night, in Gibeah, or in [g]Ramah. And
they passed on and went their way; and the sun went down
upon them *when they were* by Gibeah, which *belongeth* to Benja-
15 min. And they turned aside thither, to go in *and* to lodge in
Gibeah: and when he went in, he sat him down in a street of
the city: for *there was* no man that [h]took them into his house to
16 lodging. ¶ And, behold, there came an old man from [i]his work
out of the field at even, which *was* also of mount Ephraim; and
he sojourned in Gibeah: but the men of the place *were* Benja-
17 mites. And when he had lifted up his eyes, he saw a wayfaring
man in the street of the city: and the old man said, Whither
18 goest thou? and whence comest thou? And he said unto him,
We *are* passing from Beth-lehem-judah toward the side of
mount Ephraim; from thence *am* I: and I went to Beth-lehem-
judah, but I *am now* going to [k]the house of the LORD; and
19 there *is* no man that [1]receiveth me to house. Yet there is both
straw and provender for our asses; and there is bread and wine
also for me, and for thy handmaid, and for the young man *which*
20 *is* with thy servants: *there is* no want of any thing. And the
old man said, [l]Peace *be* with thee; howsoever *let* all thy wants
21 *lie* upon me; [m]only lodge not in the street. [n]So he brought him
into his house, and gave provender unto the asses: [o]and they
22 washed their feet, and did eat and drink. ¶ *Now* as they were
making their hearts merry, behold, [p]the men of the city, certain
[q]sons of Belial, beset the house round about, *and* beat at the
door, and spake to the master of the house, the old man, saying,
[r]Bring forth the man that came into thine house, that we may
23 know him. And [s]the man, the master of the house, went out
unto them, and said unto them, Nay, my brethren, *nay*, I pray
you, do not *so* wickedly; seeing that this man is come into mine
24 house, [t]do not this folly. [u]Behold, *here is* my daughter a
maiden, and his concubine; them I will bring out now, and
[x]humble ye them, and do with them what seemeth good unto
25 you: but unto this man do not [2]so vile a thing. But the men
would not hearken to him: so the man took his concubine, and
brought her forth unto them; and they [y]knew her, and abused
her all the night until the morning: and when the day began to
26 spring, they let her go. Then came the woman in the dawning of the day, and fell down at the door of the man's house
27 where her lord *was*, till it was light. And her lord rose up in
the morning, and opened the doors of the house, and went out
to go his way: and, behold, the woman his concubine was fallen
down *at* the door of the house, and her hands *were* upon the
28 threshold. And he said unto her, Up, and let us be going. But

[g] Josh. 18. 25.
[h] Matt. 25. 43. Heb. 13. 2.
[i] Ps. 104. 23.
[k] Josh. 18. 1. ch. 18. 31. & 20. 18. 1 Sam. 1. 3, 7.
[l] Gen. 43. 23. ch. 6. 23.
[m] Gen. 19. 2.
[n] Gen. 24. 32.
[o] Gen. 18. 4. John 13. 5.
[p] Gen. 19. 4. ch. 20. 5. Hos. 9. 9.
[q] Deut. 13. 13.
[r] Gen. 19. 5. Rom. 1. 26.
[s] Gen. 19. 6.
[t] 2 Sam. 13. 12.
[u] Gen. 19. 8.
[x] Gen. 34. 2. Deut. 21. 14.
[y] Gen. 4. 1.

[1] Heb. *gathereth*, ver. 15. [2] Heb. *the matter of this folly*.

---

14. *Gibeah, which belongeth to Benjamin*] See Josh. xviii. 24 note.

15. *a street*] Probably the square or place within the gates, where courts were held, bargains made, and where the chief men and strangers congregated.

16. *which was also of Mount Ephraim*] *i.e.*, of the country of the Levite. This single giver of hospitality was himself a stranger and sojourner at Gibeah.

18. *the house of the* LORD] Probably at Shiloh (marg. reff.). The Levite was probably one of those who ministered at the Tabernacle. His two asses and servant show him to have been in good circumstances, and he had a home of his own.

23. *this man is come into mine house*] He appeals to the sacred rights of hospitality, just as Lot did (Gen. xix. 8). Both cases betray painfully the low place in the social scale occupied by woman in the old world, from which it is one of the glories of Christianity to have raised her.

[z] ch. 20. 5. [z]none answered. Then the man took her *up* upon an ass, and
29 the man rose up, and gat him unto his place. ¶ And when he
was come into his house, he took a knife, and laid hold on his
[a] ch. 20. 6. concubine, and [a]divided her, *together* with her bones, into twelve
30 pieces, and sent her into all the coasts of Israel. And it was so,
that all that saw it said, There was no such deed done nor seen
from the day that the children of Israel came up out of the land
[b] ch. 20. 7. Prov. 13. 10. of Egypt unto this day: consider of it, [b]take advice, and speak
your minds.

[a] Deut. 13. 12. Josh. 22. 12. ch. 21. 5. [b] ch. 18. 29. 1 Sam. 3. 20. [c] ch. 10. 17. & 11. 11. [d] ch. 8. 10.

Chap. 20. THEN [a]all the children of Israel went out, and the
congregation was gathered together as one man, from [b]Dan
even to Beer-sheba, with the land of Gilead, unto the Lord [c]in
2 Mizpeh. And the chief of all the people, *even* of all the tribes of
Israel, presented themselves in the assembly of the people of
3 God, four hundred thousand footmen [d]that drew sword. (Now
the children of Benjamin heard that the children of Israel were
gone up to Mizpeh.) ¶ Then said the children of Israel, Tell *us*,
4 how was this wickedness? And [1]the Levite, the husband of the
[e] ch. 19. 15. [f] ch. 19. 22. woman that was slain, answered and said, [e]I came into Gibeah
5 that *belongeth* to Benjamin, I and my concubine, to lodge. [f]And
the men of Gibeah rose against me, and beset the house round
[g] ch. 19. 25, 26. about upon me by night, *and* thought to have slain me: [g]and
[h] ch. 19. 29. 6 my concubine have they [2]forced, that she is dead. And [h]I took
my concubine, and cut her in pieces, and sent her throughout
[i] Josh. 7. 15. all the country of the inheritance of Israel: for they [i]have com-
7 mitted lewdness and folly in Israel. Behold, ye *are* all children
[k] ch. 19. 30. 8 of Israel; [k]give here your advice and counsel. ¶ And all the
people arose as one man, saying, We will not any *of us* go to
9 his tent, neither will we any *of us* turn into his house. But
now this *shall be* the thing which we will do to Gibeah; *we will*
10 *go up* by lot against it; and we will take ten men of an hundred

[1] Heb. *the man the Levite.* [2] Heb. *humbled.*

---

29. *a knife*] Rather, "**the**" *knife*. The single household implement used, not like our knives at our meals, but for slaughtering and cutting up the animals into joints for eating (Gen. xxii. 6, 10; Prov. xxx. 14).

together with her bones, &c.] Rather, *into her bones*, or *bone by bone, into twelve pieces.* The *pieces* are synonymous with the *bones* (cp. Ezek. xxiv. 4, 5). There is something truly terrible in the stern ferocity of grief and indignation which dictated this desperate effort to arouse his countrymen to avenge his wrong. Cp. 1 Sam. xi. 7.

XX. **1.** The *congregation* is the technical term for the whole community of the Israelitish people. Its occurrence here is an indication of the early date of these transactions.

from Dan to Beer-sheba] We cannot safely infer from this expression that the settlement of Dan, recorded in ch. xviii. had taken place at this time. It only proves that in the writer's time, from Dan to Beer-sheba was a proverbial expression for all Israel (cp. marg. ref.).

with the land of Gilead] Meaning all the trans-Jordanic tribes; mentioned particularly, both to show that the whole congregation of the children of Israel, in its widest meaning, took part in the council, and also because of Jabesh-Gilead (xxi. 8, 10).

unto the Lord *in Mizpeh*] The phrase *unto the Lord*, implies the presence of the Tabernacle (xi. 11 note). Mizpeh in Benjamin (Josh. xviii. 26), from its connexion with Bethel and Ramah, is probably meant here. It is the same as that which appears as a place of national assembly in 1 Sam. vii. 5, x. 17; 2 K. xxv. 23–25. It must have been near Shiloh and Gibeah, and in the north of Benjamin. The Benjamites were duly summoned with the other tribes; so that their absence was contumacious (*v.* 3).

2. *the chief*] Literally, "*the corner stones.*" (Cp. 1 Sam. xiv. 38.)

8. They bound themselves not to break up and disperse till they had punished the wickedness of Gibeah.

9. *by lot*] To determine who should go up first (*v.* 18). The shape of the ground probably made it impossible for the whole force to operate at once; and the question of spoil would have something to do with the arrangement. (Cp. 1 Sam. xxx. 22–25.)

10. In order to make it possible for the

throughout all the tribes of Israel, and an hundred of a thousand, and a thousand out of ten thousand, to fetch victual for
the people, that they may do, when they come to Gibeah of
Benjamin, according to all the folly that they have wrought in
11 Israel. So all the men of Israel were gathered against the city,
12 [1]knit together as one man. ¶ [l]And the tribes of Israel sent [l] Deut. 13. 14.
men through all the tribe of Benjamin, saying, What wicked- Josh. 22. 13,
13 ness *is* this that is done among you? Now therefore deliver *us* 16.
the men, [m]the children of Belial, which *are* in Gibeah, that we [m] Deut. 13.
may put them to death, and [n]put away evil from Israel. But 13.
the children of Benjamin would not hearken to the voice of ch. 19. 22. [n] Deut. 17.
14 their brethren the children of Israel: but the children of Ben- 12.
jamin gathered themselves together out of the cities unto Gibeah,
15 to go out to battle against the children of Israel. And the
children of Benjamin were numbered at that time out of the
cities twenty and six thousand men that drew sword, beside the
inhabitants of Gibeah, which were numbered seven hundred
16 chosen men. Among all this people *there were* seven hundred
chosen men [o]lefthanded; every one could sling stones at an [o] 1 Chr. 12. 2.
17 hair *breadth*, and not miss. And the men of Israel, beside Benjamin, were numbered four hundred thousand men that drew
18 sword: all these *were* men of war. ¶ And the children of Israel
arose, and [p]went up to the house of God, and [q]asked counsel [p] ver. 23, 26.
of God, and said, Which of us shall go up first to the battle [q] Num. 27. 21.
against the children of Benjamin? And the LORD said, Judah ch. 1. 1.
19 *shall go up* first. And the children of Israel rose up in the
20 morning, and encamped against Gibeah. And the men of
Israel went out to battle against Benjamin; and the men of
Israel put themselves in array to fight against them at Gibeah.
21 And [r]the children of Benjamin came forth out of Gibeah, and [r] Gen. 49. 27.
destroyed down to the ground of the Israelites that day twenty
22 and two thousand men. ¶ And the people the men of Israel
encouraged themselves, and set their battle again in array in
the place where they put themselves in array the first day.
23 ([s]And the children of Israel went up and wept before the LORD [s] ver. 26, 27.

[1] Heb. *fellows*.

---

force of Israel to keep the field, and do to the men of Gibeah what their wickedness deserved, every tenth man (forty thousand in all) was appointed to find provisions for the whole army.

15–17. Comparing the numbers here with those in Num. i. and xxvi., it is seen that in the case both of the Benjamites and the Israelites the numbers are diminished by about one-third, *i.e.* they appear as about two-thirds only of what they were at the last numbering in the plains of Moab. This diminution seems to indicate disturbed and harassing times. With this agrees the mention of the cities, as containing the whole Benjamite population. The inference is that the open country and unwalled villages were not safe, but that the Benjamites kept the Canaanites in subjection only by dwelling in fortified towns.

16. See iii. 15, and note. In the LXX. and Vulg. the seven hundred chosen men of Gibeah are represented as the seven hundred left-handed slingers.

18. *went up to the house of God*] It should be "**to Bethel.**" At this time the Ark was at Bethel (cp. 1 Sam. x. 3), and not at Shiloh. It is not unlikely that though Shiloh was the chief residence of the Ark (Jer. vii. 12), yet the Tabernacle, being moveable, was, either at stated times, or as occasion required, moved to where the Judge resided, or the congregation assembled (cp. 1 Sam. vii. 16). On the present occasion the Ark may have been moved to Bethel for the convenience of proximity to the great national council at Mizpeh.

21. Gibeah, being on a hill, was difficult of access to an attacking army, and gave great advantage to the defenders, who fought from higher ground, and probably defended a narrow pass, while their companions on the walls could gall the assailants with their slingstones.

until even, and asked counsel of the LORD, saying, Shall I go
up again to battle against the children of Benjamin my brother?
24 And the LORD said, Go up against him.) And the children of
Israel came near against the children of Benjamin the second
[t] ver. 21. 25 day. And [t]Benjamin went forth against them out of Gibeah
the second day, and destroyed down to the ground of the children of Israel again eighteen thousand men; all these drew the
26 sword. ¶ Then all the children of Israel, and all the people,
[u] ver. 18. [u]went up, and came unto the house of God, and wept, and sat
there before the LORD, and fasted that day until even, and
offered burnt offerings and peace offerings before the LORD.
[x] Josh. 18. 1. 1 Sam. 4. 3, 4. 27 And the children of Israel enquired of the LORD, (for [x]the ark
28 of the covenant of God *was* there in those days, [y]and Phinehas,
[y] Josh. 24. 33. the son of Eleazar, the son of Aaron, [z]stood before it in those
[z] Deut. 10. 8. & 18. 5. days,) saying, Shall I yet again go out to battle against the children of Benjamin my brother, or shall I cease? And the LORD
said, Go up; for to morrow I will deliver them into thine hand.
[a] So Josh. 8. 4. 29, 30 ¶ And Israel [a]set liers in wait round about Gibeah. And the
children of Israel went up against the children of Benjamin on
the third day, and put themselves in array against Gibeah, as
31 at other times. And the children of Benjamin went out against
the people, *and* were drawn away from the city; and they began
[1]to smite of the people, *and* kill, as at other times, in the highways, of which one goeth up to [2]the house of God, and the
32 other to Gibeah in the field, about thirty men of Israel. And
the children of Benjamin said, They *are* smitten down before us,
as at the first. But the children of Israel said, Let us flee, and
33 draw them from the city unto the highways. And all the men
of Israel rose up out of their place, and put themselves in array
at Baal-tamar: and the liers in wait of Israel came forth out of
34 their places, *even* out of the meadows of Gibeah. And there
came against Gibeah ten thousand chosen men out of all Israel,
[b] Josh. 8. 14. Isai. 47. 11. and the battle was sore: [b]but they knew not that evil *was* near
35 them. And the LORD smote Benjamin before Israel: and the
children of Israel destroyed of the Benjamites that day twenty
and five thousand and an hundred men: all these drew the
36 sword. ¶ So the children of Benjamin saw that they were

[1] Heb. *to smite of the people wounded as at, &c.* [2] Or, *Beth-el.*

---

26. *fasted until even*] The regular time for ending a fast among the Hebrews was sunset (cp. 1 Sam. xiv. 24; 2 Sam. i. 12). Such national fasts are called by the Rabbis *fasts of the congregation*, and were enjoined in times of great affliction.

On the offerings, see Lev. i., iii.

28. *Phinehas, the son of Eleazar*, &c.] A most important chronological statement, which makes it probable that these events occurred within twenty years of the death of Joshua.

to-morrow] The two former answers only bade them go up against Benjamin; now, for the first time, the promise is added, "To-morrow," &c. (cp. Josh. viii. 1).

29. The stratagem described is exactly that by which Joshua took Ai (marg. ref.).

31. *to the house of God*] "**To Bethel,**" as in the margin.

On "Gibeah in the field," see Josh. xviii. 24 note.

33. Baal-tamar is only mentioned here. It took its name from some palm-tree that grew there; perhaps the same as the "palm-tree of Deborah, between Ramah and Bethel" (iv. 5), the exact locality here indicated, since "the highway" (*v.* 31) along which the Israelites enticed the Benjamites to pursue them, leads straight to Ramah, which lay only a mile beyond the point where the two ways branch off.

the meadows of Gibeah] The word rendered *meadow* is only found here. According to its etymology, it ought to mean a *bare open place*, which is particularly unsuitable for an ambush. But by a change in the vowel-points, without any alteration in the letters, it becomes the common word for *a cavern*.

smitten: [c]for the men of Israel gave place to the Benjamites, [c] Josh. 8. 15.
because they trusted unto the liers in wait which they had set
37 beside Gibeah. [d]And the liers in wait hasted, and rushed upon [d] Josh. 8. 19.
Gibeah; and the liers in wait [1]drew *themselves* along, and smote
38 all the city with the edge of the sword. Now there was an
appointed [2]sign between the men of Israel [3]and the liers in
wait, that they should make a great [4]flame with smoke rise up
39 out of the city. And when the men of Israel retired in the
battle, Benjamin began [5]to smite *and* kill of the men of Israel
about thirty persons: for they said, Surely they are smitten
40 down before us, as *in* the first battle. But when the flame
began to arise up out of the city with a pillar of smoke, the
Benjamites [e]looked behind them, and, behold, [6]the flame of the [e] Josh. 8. 20.
41 city ascended up to heaven. And when the men of Israel turned
again, the men of Benjamin were amazed: for they saw that
42 evil [7]was come upon them. Therefore they turned *their backs*
before the men of Israel unto the way of the wilderness; but
the battle overtook them; and them which *came* out of the cities
43 they destroyed in the midst of them. *Thus* they inclosed the
Benjamites round about, *and* chased them, *and* [f]trode them [f] Jer. 51. 33.
down [8]with ease [9]over against Gibeah toward the sunrising.
44 And there fell of Benjamin eighteen thousand men; all these
45 *were* men of valour. And they turned and fled toward the wilderness unto the rock of Rimmon: and they gleaned of them in
the highways five thousand men; and pursued hard after them
46 unto Gidom, and slew two thousand men of them. So that all
which fell that day of Benjamin were twenty and five thousand
47 men that drew the sword; all these *were* men of valour. [g]But [g] ch. 21. 13.
six hundred men turned and fled to the wilderness unto the
rock Rimmon, and abode in the rock Rimmon four months.
48 And the men of Israel turned again upon the children of Benjamin, and smote them with the edge of the sword, as well the

[1] Or, *made a long* sound with the trumpet, Josh. 6. 5.
[2] Or, *time*.
[3] Heb. *with*.
[4] Heb. *elevation*.
[5] Heb. *to smite the wounded*.
[6] Heb. *the whole consumption*.
[7] Heb. *touched them*.
[8] Or, from *Menuchah, &c.*
[9] Heb. *unto over against*.

---

42. *the way of the wilderness*] *i.e.* the wilderness which extended from Jericho to the hills of Bethel.

them which came out of the cities] These must be the Benjamites (*v.* 15). Hence, "*in the midst of them*" must mean *in their own cities*, whither they severally fled for refuge, but failed to find shelter (*v.* 48). Anathoth, Alemath, Ramah, Ataroth, Geba, Michmash, Ai, Bethel, Migron, &c., would probably be the cities meant, all lying east and north of Gibeah.

43. The language and construction of this verse is poetical; it seems to be an extract from a song, and to describe, in the language of poetry, the same event which the preceding verse described in that of prose.

with ease] Or *rest* (Num. x. 33; Ps. xcv. 11). The expression is very obscure. The margin takes it as the name of a place.

45. *Rimmon*] A village named *Rummon*, situated on the summit of a conical chalky hill, still exists, and forms a remarkable object in the landscape, visible in all directions. It lies 15 miles north of Jerusalem. It is a different place from Rimmon in the south of Judah (Josh. xv. 32), and Remmon in Zebulon (Josh. xix. 13). Gidom, mentioned nowhere else, was evidently close to Rimmon.

46. In *v.* 35 the number given is 25,100. Verses 44—46 give the details of the loss on that day: 18,000, 5,000, and 2,000; in all 25,000. But as the Benjamites numbered 26,700 men (*v.* 15), and 600 escaped to the rock of Rimmon, it is clear that 1,100 are unaccounted for, partly from no account being taken of those who fell in the battles of the two first days, partly from the use of round numbers, or from some other cause. The numbers given both here and in *v.* 35 are expressly restricted to those who fell on *that* (the third) *day*.

48. They treated Benjamin as devoted to utter destruction, as Jericho had been (Josh. vi. 17, 21), and the whole tribe was all but actually extirpated. We see in the punish-

men of *every* city, as the beast, and all that [1] came to hand: also
they set on fire all the cities that [2] they came to.
[a] ch. 20. 1. CHAP. 21. NOW [a] the men of Israel had sworn in Mizpeh, saying,
There shall not any of us give his daughter unto Benjamin to
[b] ch. 20. 18, 26. 2 wife. And the people came [b] to the house of God, and abode
there till even before God, and lifted up their voices, and wept
3 sore; and said, O LORD God of Israel, why is this come to pass
in Israel, that there should be to day one tribe lacking in Israel?
4 And it came to pass on the morrow, that the people rose early,
[c] 2 Sam. 24. 25. and [c] built there an altar, and offered burnt offerings and peace
5 offerings. ¶ And the children of Israel said, Who *is there* among
all the tribes of Israel that came not up with the congregation
[d] ch. 5. 23. unto the LORD? [d] For they had made a great oath concerning
him that came not up to the LORD to Mizpeh, saying, He shall
6 surely be put to death. And the children of Israel repented
them for Benjamin their brother, and said, There is one tribe
7 cut off from Israel this day. How shall we do for wives for
them that remain, seeing we have sworn by the LORD that we
8 will not give them of our daughters to wives? ¶ And they said,
What one *is there* of the tribes of Israel that came not up to
Mizpeh to the LORD? And, behold, there came none to the
[e] 1 Sam. 11. 1. & 31. 11. 9 camp from [e] Jabesh-gilead to the assembly. For the people were
numbered, and, behold, *there were* none of the inhabitants of
10 Jabesh-gilead there. And the congregation sent thither twelve
thousand men of the valiantest, and commanded them, saying,
[f] ver. 5. & ch. 5. 23. 1 Sam. 11. 7. [f] Go and smite the inhabitants of Jabesh-gilead with the edge of
11 the sword, with the women and the children. And this *is* the
[g] Num. 31. 17. thing that ye shall do, [g] Ye shall utterly destroy every male, and
12 every woman that [3] hath lain by man. And they found among
the inhabitants of Jabesh-gilead four hundred [4] young virgins,
that had known no man by lying with any male: and they
[h] Josh. 18. 1. brought them unto the camp to [h] Shiloh, which *is* in the land of
13 Canaan. ¶ And the whole congregation sent *some* [5] to speak to
[i] ch. 20. 47. the children of Benjamin [i] that *were* in the rock Rimmon, and to
14 [6] call peaceably unto them. And Benjamin came again at that

[1] Heb. *was found.*
[2] Heb. *were found.*
[3] Heb. *knoweth the lying with man.*
[4] Heb. *young women virgins.*
[5] Heb. *and spake and called.*
[6] Or, *proclaim peace*, Deut. 20. 10.

---

ment inflicted the same ferocity which marked both the crime and the Levite's mode of requiring vengeance.

XXI. **2.** *to the house of God*] It should be, "**to Bethel.**" See xx. 18.

3. The repetition of the name of Israel is very striking in connexion with the title of Jehovah as *God of Israel.* It contains a very forcible pleading of the Covenant, and memorial of the promises. The very name "Israel" comprehended all the twelve tribes; with one of them blotted out, the remnant would not be Israel.

4. It is not certain whether the brazen Altar was at Bethel at this time, or whether it may not have been elsewhere, *e.g.*, at Shiloh with the Tabernacle. Some, however, think that the Altar here mentioned was *additional* to the brazen Altar, in consequence of the unusual number of sacrifices caused by the presence of the whole congregation (cp. 1 K. viii. 64 note).

8. *Jabesh-Gilead*] Is here mentioned for the first time. (See marg. reff.) The name of Jabesh survives only in the Wady Yabes (running down to the east bank of the Jordan), near the head of which are situated the ruins called Ed-Deir, which are identified with Jabesh-Gilead.

10. *And the congregation sent* 12,000 *men*] A thousand from each tribe; they followed the precedent of Num. xxxi. 4.

11. *Ye shall utterly destroy*] More exactly, "**Ye shall devote to utter destruction,**" or *cherem* (Lev. xxvii. 28 note).

12. *to Shiloh*] Whither, as the usual place of meeting for the national assembly, the Israelites had moved from Bethel (a distance of about 10 miles), during the expedition of the 12,000 to Jabesh-Gilead.

time; and they gave them wives which they had saved alive of
the women of Jabesh-gilead: and yet so they sufficed them not.
15 And the people [k]repented them for Benjamin, because that the [k] ver. 6.
16 LORD had made a breach in the tribes of Israel. ¶Then the
elders of the congregation said, How shall we do for wives for
them that remain, seeing the women are destroyed out of Ben-
17 jamin. And they said, *There must be* an inheritance for them
that be escaped of Benjamin, that a tribe be not destroyed out of
18 Israel. Howbeit we may not give them wives of our daughters:
[l]for the children of Israel have sworn, saying, Cursed *be* he that [l] ver. 1.
19 giveth a wife to Benjamin. Then they said, Behold, *there is* a ch. 11. 35.
feast of the LORD in Shiloh [1]yearly *in a place* which *is* on the
north side of Beth-el, [2]on the east side [3]of the highway that
goeth up from Beth-el to Shechem, and on the south of Lebonah.
20 Therefore they commanded the children of Benjamin, saying,
21 Go and lie in wait in the vineyards; and see, and, behold, if the
daughters of Shiloh come out [m]to dance in dances, then come ye [m] See
out of the vineyards, and catch you every man his wife of the Exod. 15. 20.
22 daughters of Shiloh, and go to the land of Benjamin. And it ch. 11. 34.
shall be, when their fathers or their brethren come unto us to 1 Sam. 18. 6.
complain, that we will say unto them, [4]Be favourable unto them Jer. 31. 13.
for our sakes: because we reserved not to each man his wife in
the war: for ye did not give unto them at this time, *that* ye
23 should be guilty. And the children of Benjamin did so, and
took *them* wives, according to their number, of them that
danced, whom they caught: and they went and returned unto
their inheritance, and [n]repaired the cities, and dwelt in them. [n] See ch.
24 And the children of Israel departed thence at that time, every 20. 48.
man to his tribe and to his family, and they went out from
25 thence every man to his inheritance. ¶[o]In those days *there was* [o] ch. 17. 6.
no king in Israel: [p]every man did *that which was* right in his & 18. 1.
own eyes. & 19. 1.
[p] Deut. 12. 8.
ch. 17. 6.

[1] Heb. *from year to year.*
[2] Or, *toward the sunrising.*
[3] Or, *on.*
[4] Or, *gratify us in them.*

---

18. *for the children of Israel have sworn*] See *v.* 1. Cp. Saul's rash oath (1 Sam. xiv. 24), and his breach of the oath made to the Gideonites (2 Sam. xxi. 2). For the guilt of a broken oath, see Ezek. xvii. 15-20; Ex. xx. 7.

19. The Feast was probably the Passover, or one of the three great Jewish Feasts. In these unsettled times men went up to Shiloh (Seilun) only once a year (1 Sam. i. 3) instead of thrice; only the males kept the Feasts, and therefore the virgins of Shiloh would naturally be the only maidens present, and the public festival would be a likely occasion for their festive dances. It is, however, possible that some particular feast peculiar to Shiloh is meant, like the yearly sacrifice of David's family in Bethlehem (1 Sam. xx. 29).

22. *ye did not give,* &c.] *i.e.* they had not broken the oath mentioned in *v.* 1, so as to be guilty of taking the Lord's name in vain. They did not give their daughters to Benjamin: the Benjamites had taken them by force. Such casuistry as this condemns the system of oaths, and illustrates the wisdom of our Lord's precept (Matt. v. 33-37).

23. Cp. the very similar account of the rape of the Sabine women by the Roman youths at the festival of the Consualia, as related by Livy.

25. The repetition of this characteristic phrase (cp. xvii. 6, xviii. 1, xix. 1) is probably intended to impress upon us the idea that these disorders arose from the want of a sufficient authority to suppress them. The preservation of such a story, of which the Israelites must have been ashamed, is a striking evidence of the Divine superintendence and direction as regards the Holy Scriptures.

RUTH.

INTRODUCTION.

THE Book of Ruth is historically important as giving the lineage of David through the whole period of the rule of the Judges (i. 1), *i.e.* from Salmon who fought under Joshua, to "Jesse the Bethlehemite" (1 Sam. xvi. 1); and as illustrating the ancestry of "Jesus Christ, the son of David," who "was born in Bethlehem of Judea" (Matt. i. 1, ii. 1). The care with which this narrative was preserved through so many centuries before the birth of Christ is a striking evidence of the Providence of God, that "known unto God are all His works from the beginning of the world." The genealogy with which the Book closes (iv. 18), is also an important contribution to the chronology of Scripture history. We learn from it, with great distinctness, that Salmon, one of the conquering host of Joshua, was the grandfather of Obed, who was the grandfather of king David; in other words, that four generations, or about 200 years, span the "days when the Judges ruled."

But the Book has another interest, from the charming view it gives us of the domestic life of pious Israelites even during the most troubled times. Had we only drawn our impressions from the records of violence and crime contained in the Book of Judges, we should have been ready to conclude that all the gentler virtues had fled from the land, while the children of Israel were alternately struggling for their lives and liberties with the tribes of Canaan, or yielding themselves to the seductions of Canaanite idolatry. But the Book of Ruth, lifting up the curtain which veiled the privacy of domestic life, discloses to us most beautiful views of piety, integrity, self-sacrificing affection, chastity, gentleness and charity, growing up amidst the rude scenes of war, discord, and strife.

The Book, from its contents, as anciently by its place in the Canon, belongs to the Book of Judges, and is a kind of appendix to it. In the present Hebrew Bible it is placed among the *Cethubim* or *Hagiographa*, in the group containing the Song of Solomon, Ruth, Lamentations, Ecclesiastes, and Esther; but in the Greek Septuagint and the Latin Vulgate it occupies the same place as in our English Bibles, which was its ancient place in the Hebrew Bible.

The language of the Book is generally pure Hebrew. But there are words of Chaldee form and origin,[1] and other expressions peculiar to the later Hebrew. The inference would be that the Book of Ruth was composed not before the later times of the Jewish monarchy;

[1] *E.g.*, the originals of the verbs *go, abide fast* (ii. 8), *lay thee down, thou shalt do* (iii. 4), *put, get thee down* (iii. 3), *confirm* (iv. 7); the word translated twice *for them* but meaning *therefore* (i. 13), *Mara* (i. 20).

and this inference is somewhat strengthened by the way in which the writer speaks of the custom which prevailed *in former time* in Israel (iv. 7). Other expressions, which the Book has in common with the Books of Samuel and Kings, and a certain similarity of narrative, tend to place it upon about the same level of antiquity with those Books.[2]

The Books of the Old Testament, to the contents of which reference seems to be made in the Book of Ruth, are Judges, Leviticus, Deuteronomy, Genesis, 1 and 2 Samuel, and perhaps Job. Ruth is not quoted or referred to in the New Testament, except that the generations from Hezron to David in our Lord's genealogy seem to be taken from it.

No mystical or allegorical sense can be assigned to the history; but Ruth, the Moabitess, was undoubtedly one of the first fruits of the ingathering of Gentiles into the Church of Christ, and so an evidence of God's gracious purpose in Christ, "also to the Gentiles to grant repentance unto life;" and the important evangelical lesson is as plainly taught in her case, as in that of Cornelius, "that God is no respecter of persons, but in every nation he that feareth God, and worketh righteousness, is accepted of Him." The great doctrine of Divine Grace is also forcibly taught by the admission of Ruth, the Moabitess, among the ancestry of our Lord Jesus Christ.

---

[2] *E. g.*, originals of *Such a one* (iv. 1); *the Lord do so to me, and more also* (i. 17); *the beginning of barley harvest* (i. 22); *lifted up their voice and wept* (i. 9, 14); *blessed be he of the Lord* (ii. 20).

THE BOOK
OF
RUTH.

Chap. 1. NOW it came to pass in the days when [a]the judges
[1]ruled, that there was [b]a famine in the land. And a certain
man of [c]Beth-lehem-judah went to sojourn in the country of
2 Moab, he, and his wife, and his two sons. And the name of the
man *was* Elimelech, and the name of his wife Naomi, and the
name of his two sons Mahlon and Chilion, [d]Ephrathites of Beth-
lehem-judah. And they came [e]into the country of Moab, and
3 [2]continued there. ¶ And Elimelech Naomi's husband died; and
4 she was left, and her two sons. And they took them wives of
the women of Moab; the name of the one *was* Orpah, and the
name of the other Ruth: and they dwelled there about ten
5 years. And Mahlon and Chilion died also both of them; and
6 the woman was left of her two sons and her husband. ¶ Then
she arose with her daughters in law, that she might return from
the country of Moab: for she had heard in the country of Moab
how that the Lord had [f]visited his people in [g]giving them
7 bread. Wherefore she went forth out of the place where she
was, and her two daughters in law with her; and they went on
8 the way to return unto the land of Judah. And Naomi said
unto her two daughters in law, [h]Go, return each to her mother's
house: [i]the Lord deal kindly with you, as ye have dealt with
9 [k]the dead, and with me. The Lord grant you that ye may find
[l]rest, each *of you* in the house of her husband. Then she
10 kissed them; and they lifted up their voice, and wept. And
they said unto her, Surely we will return with thee unto thy
11 people. ¶ And Naomi said, Turn again, my daughters: why
will ye go with me? *are* there yet *any more* sons in my womb,

[a] Judg. 2. 16.
[b] See Gen. 12. 10. 2 Kin. 8. 1.
[c] Judg. 17. 8.
[d] See Gen. 35. 19.
[e] Judg. 3. 30.
[f] Ex. 4. 31. Luke 1. 68.
[g] Ps. 132. 15. Matt. 6. 11.
[h] See Josh. 24. 15.
[i] 2 Tim. 1. 16, 17, 18.
[k] ver. 5. ch. 2. 20.
[l] ch. 3. 1.

[1] Heb. *judged*. [2] Heb. *were*.

I. 1. *in the days when the Judges ruled*] "**Judged.**" This note of time, like that in iv. 7, xviii. 1; Judg. xvii. 6, indicates that this book was written after the rule of the Judges had ceased. The genealogy (iv. 17-22) points to the time of David as the earliest when the book could have been written.

a famine] Caused probably by one of the hostile invasions recorded in the Book of Judges. Most of the Jewish commentators, from the mention of Bethlehem, and the resemblance of the names Boaz and Ibzan, refer this history to the judge Ibzan (Judg. xii. 8), but without probability.

the country of Moab] Here, and in *vv.* 2, 22, and iv. 3, literally "**the field**" or "**fields.**" As the same word is elsewhere used of the territory of Moab, of the Amalekites, of Edom, and of the Philistines, it would seem to be a term pointedly used with reference to a foreign country, not the country of the speaker, or writer; and to have been specially applied to Moab.

4. Marriages of Israelites with women of Ammon or Moab are nowhere in the Law expressly forbidden, as were marriages with the women of Canaan (Deut. vii. 1-3). In the days of Nehemiah the special law (Deut. xxiii. 3-6) was interpreted as forbidding them, and as excluding the children of such marriages from the congregation of Israel (Neh. xiii. 1-3). Probably the marriages of Mahlon and Chilion would be justified by necessity, living as they were in a foreign land. Ruth was the wife of the elder brother, Mahlon (iv. 10).

8. The accompanying their mother-in-law to the borders of their own land would probably be an act of Oriental courtesy. Naomi with no less courtesy presses them to return. The mention of the *mother's* house, which the separation of the women's house or tent from that of the men facilitates, is natural in her mouth, and has more tenderness in it than *father's house* would have had; it does not imply the death of their fathers (ii. 11).

11-13. See marg. reff. and notes. The

[m] Gen. 38. 11. Deut. 25. 5.
[n] Judg. 2. 15. Job 19. 21. Ps. 32. 4.
[o] Prov. 17. 17. & 18. 24.
[p] Judg. 11. 24.
[q] See Josh. 24. 15, 19. 2 Kin. 2. 2.
[r] 2 Kin. 2. 2, 4, 6.
[s] ch. 2. 11.
[t] 1 Sam. 3. 17. & 25. 22. 2 Sam. 19. 13. 2 Kin. 6. 31.
[u] Acts 21. 14.
[x] Matt. 21. 10.
[y] See Isai. 23. 7. Lam. 2. 15.
[z] Job 1. 21.
[a] Ex. 9. 31, 32. ch. 2. 23. 2 Sam. 21. 9.
[a] ch. 3. 2.
[b] ch. 4. 21.
[c] Lev. 19. 9. Deut. 24. 19.

12 [m]that they may be your husbands? Turn again, my daughters,
go *your way;* for I am too old to have an husband. If I should
say, I have hope, [1]*if* I should have an husband also to night,
13 and should also bear sons; would ye [2]tarry for them till they
were grown? would ye stay for them from having husbands?
nay, my daughters; for [3]it grieveth me much for your sakes
14 that [n]the hand of the LORD is gone out against me. And they
lifted up their voice, and wept again: and Orpah kissed her
15 mother in law; but Ruth [o]clave unto her. ¶And she said,
Behold, thy sister in law is gone back unto her people, and unto
16 [p]her gods: [q]return thou after thy sister in law. And Ruth
said, [4][r]Intreat me not to leave thee, *or* to return from following
after thee: for whither thou goest, I will go; and where thou
lodgest, I will lodge: [s]thy people *shall be* my people, and thy
17 God my God: where thou diest, will I die, and there will I be
buried: [t]the LORD do so to me, and more also, *if ought* but
18 death part thee and me. [u]When she saw that she [5]was sted-
fastly minded to go with her, then she left speaking unto her.
19 ¶So they two went until they came to Beth-lehem. And it
came to pass, when they were come to Beth-lehem, that [x]all the
city was moved about them, and they said, [y]*Is* this Naomi?
20 And she said unto them, Call me not [6]Naomi, call me [7]Mara:
21 for the Almighty hath dealt very bitterly with me. I went out
full, [z]and the LORD hath brought me home again empty: why
then call ye me Naomi, seeing the LORD hath testified against
22 me, and the Almighty hath afflicted me? ¶So Naomi returned,
and Ruth the Moabitess, her daughter in law, with her, which
returned out of the country of Moab: and they came to Beth-
lehem [a]in the beginning of barley harvest.

CHAP. 2. AND Naomi had a [a]kinsman of her husband's, a mighty
man of wealth, of the family of Elimelech; and his name *was*
2 [b][8]Boaz. And Ruth the Moabitess said unto Naomi, Let me now
go to the field, and [c]glean ears of corn after *him* in whose sight
I shall find grace. And she said unto her, Go, my daughter.

[1] Or, if *I were with an husband.*
[2] Heb. *hope.*
[3] Heb. *I have much bitterness.*
[4] Or, *Be not against me.*
[5] Heb. *strengthened herself.*
[6] That is, *Pleasant.*
[7] That is, *Bitter.*
[8] Called *Booz,* Matt. 1. 5.

Levirate law probably existed among the Moabites, and in Israel extended beyond the *brother* in the strict sense, and applied to the nearest relations, since Boaz was only the kinsman of Elimelech (iii. 12).

14. The kiss at parting as well as at meeting is the customary friendly and respectful salutation in the East. The difference between mere kindness of manner and self-sacrificing love is most vividly depicted in the words and conduct of the two women. Ruth's determination is stedfast to cast in her lot with the people of the Lord (cp. marg. reff. and Matt. xv. 22–28).

19. *and they said*] *i.e. the women of Beth-lehem said. They* in the Hebrew is feminine.

20. See marg. Similar allusions to the meaning of names are seen in Gen. xxvii. 36; Jer. xx. 3.

the Almighty] Shaddai (see Gen. xvii. 1 note). The name ALMIGHTY is almost peculiar to the Pentateuch, and to the Book of Job. It occurs twice in the Psalms, and four times in the Prophets.

21. *the* LORD *hath testified against me*] The phrase is very commonly applied to a man who gives witness concerning (usually against) another in a court of justice (Ex. xx. 16; 2 Sam. i. 16; Isai. iii. 9). Naomi in the bitterness of her spirit complains that the Lord Himself was turned against her, and was bringing her sins up for judgment.

II. **1.** *a kinsman*] More literally *an acquaintance;* here (and in the feminine, iii. 2) denoting the person with whom one is intimately acquainted, one's near *relation.* The *next kinsman* of ii. 20, &c. (*goel*), is a wholly different word.

Boaz] Commonly taken to mean, *strength is in him* (cp. 1 K. vii. 21).

3 And she went, and came, and gleaned in the field after the
reapers: and her [1]hap was to light on a part of the field *belonging*
4 unto Boaz, who *was* of the kindred of Elimelech. ¶ And, behold,
Boaz came from Beth-lehem, and said unto the reapers, [d]The
LORD *be* with you. And they answered him, The LORD bless
5 thee. Then said Boaz unto his servant that was set over the
6 reapers, Whose damsel *is* this? And the servant that was set
over the reapers answered and said, It *is* the Moabitish damsel
7 [e]that came back with Naomi out of the country of Moab: and
she said, I pray you, let me glean and gather after the reapers
among the sheaves: so she came, and hath continued even from
the morning until now, that she tarried a little in the house.
8 ¶ Then said Boaz unto Ruth, Hearest thou not, my daughter?
Go not to glean in another field, neither go from hence, but
9 abide here fast by my maidens: *let* thine eyes *be* on the field
that they do reap, and go thou after them: have I not charged
the young men that they shall not touch thee? and when thou
art athirst, go unto the vessels, and drink of *that* which the
10 young men have drawn. Then she [f]fell on her face, and bowed
herself to the ground, and said unto him, Why have I found
grace in thine eyes, that thou shouldest take knowledge of me,
11 seeing I *am* a stranger? And Boaz answered and said unto her,
It hath fully been shewed me, [g]all that thou hast done unto thy
mother in law since the death of thine husband: and *how* thou
hast left thy father and thy mother, and the land of thy nativity,
and art come unto a people which thou knewest not heretofore.
12 [h]The LORD recompense thy work, and a full reward be given
thee of the LORD God of Israel, [i]under whose wings thou art
13 come to trust. Then she said, [2k]Let me find favour in thy sight,
my lord; for that thou hast comforted me, and for that thou hast
spoken [3]friendly unto thine handmaid, [l]though I be not like
14 unto one of thine handmaidens. And Boaz said unto her, At
mealtime come thou hither, and eat of the bread, and dip thy
morsel in the vinegar. And she sat beside the reapers: and he
reached her parched *corn*, and she did eat, and [m]was sufficed,
15 and left. ¶ And when she was risen up to glean, Boaz com-

[d] Ps. 129. 7, 8. Luke 1. 28. 2 Thess. 3. 16.
[e] ch. 1. 22.
[f] 1 Sam. 25. 23.
[g] ch. 1. 14, 16, 17.
[h] 1 Sam. 24. 19.
[i] ch. 1. 16. Ps. 17. 8. & 36. 7. & 57. 1. & 63. 7.
[k] Gen. 33. 15. 1 Sam. 1. 18.
[l] 1 Sam. 25. 41.
[m] ver. 18.

[1] Heb. *hap happened.*
[2] Or, *I find favour.*
[3] Heb. *to the heart,* Gen. 34. 3. Judg. 19. 3.

---

7. *the house*] The shed or booth where they took their meals, and were sheltered from the sun in the heat of the day (see Gen. xxxiii. 17).

8. The grammatical forms of the verbs "go hence" and "abide," are peculiar and Chaldaic. They are supposed to indicate the dialect used at Bethlehem in the time of Boaz.

9. *after them*] *i.e.* after my maidens. The fields not being divided by hedges, but only by *baulks*, it would be easy for her to pass off Boaz's land without being aware of it, and so find herself among strangers where Boaz could not protect her.

10. *she fell on her face*] With Oriental reverence (cp. Gen. xxxiii. 3, and marg. ref.).

12. The similarity of expression here to Gen. xv. 1, and in *v.* 11 to Gen. xii. 1, makes it probable that Boaz had the case of Abraham in his mind.

the LORD *God of Israel*] "**Jehovah the God of Israel.**" Cp. Josh. xiv. 14, where, as here, the force of the addition, *the God of Israel*, lies in the person spoken of being a foreigner (see Judg. xi. 21 note).

14. To dip the morsel, or sop, whether it were bread or meat, in the *dish* containing the vinegar (cp. Matt. xxvi. 23; Mark xiv. 20; Ex. xxv. 29; Num. vii. 13) was, and still is, the common custom in the East.

parched or "**roasted**" *corn*] The common food of the country then (cp. 1 Sam. xvii. 17, xxv. 18; 2 Sam. xvii. 28) and now.

and left] Or "reserved" (*v.* 18). Rather, "**had some over**" (cp. Luke xv. 17). Verse 18 tells us that she took to her mother-in-law what she had over.

manded his young men, saying, Let her glean even among the
16 sheaves, and [1]reproach her not: and let fall also *some* of the
handfuls of purpose for her, and leave *them*, that she may glean
17 *them*, and rebuke her not. So she gleaned in the field until even,
and beat out that she had gleaned: and it was about an ephah of
18 barley. And she took *it* up, and went into the city: and her
mother in law saw what she had gleaned: and she brought forth,
and gave to her [n]that she had reserved after she was sufficed.
19 ¶ And her mother in law said unto her, Where hast thou gleaned
to day? and where wroughtest thou? blessed be he that did
[o]take knowledge of thee. And she shewed her mother in law
with whom she had wrought, and said, The man's name with
20 whom I wrought to day *is* Boaz. And Naomi said unto her
daughter in law, [p]Blessed *be* he of the LORD, who [q]hath not left
off his kindness to the living and to the dead. And Naomi said
unto her, The man *is* near of kin unto us, [r][2]one of our next
21 kinsmen. And Ruth the Moabitess said, He said unto me also,
Thou shalt keep fast by my young men, until they have ended
22 all my harvest. And Naomi said unto Ruth her daughter in
law, *It is* good, my daughter, that thou go out with his maidens,
23 that they [3]meet thee not in any other field. So she kept fast by
the maidens of Boaz to glean unto the end of barley harvest and
of wheat harvest; and dwelt with her mother in law.
CHAP. 3. THEN Naomi her mother in law said unto her, My
daughter, [a]shall I not seek [b]rest for thee, that it may be well
2 with thee? And now *is* not Boaz of our kindred, [c]with whose
maidens thou wast? Behold, he winnoweth barley to night in
3 the threshingfloor. Wash thyself therefore, [d]and anoint thee,
and put thy raiment upon thee, and get thee down to the floor:
but make not thyself known unto the man, until he shall have
4 done eating and drinking. And it shall be, when he lieth down,
that thou shalt mark the place where he shall lie, and thou shalt
go in, and [4]uncover his feet, and lay thee down; and he will
5 tell thee what thou shalt do. And she said unto her, All that
6 thou sayest unto me I will do. ¶ And she went down unto the
floor, and did according to all that her mother in law bade her.
7 And when Boaz had eaten and drunk, and [e]his heart was merry,

[n] ver. 14.
[o] ver. 10. Ps. 41. 1.
[p] ch. 3. 10. 2 Sam. 2. 5. Job 29. 13.
[q] Prov. 17. 17.
[r] ch. 3. 9. & 4. 6.
[a] 1 Cor. 7. 36. 1 Tim. 5. 8.
[b] ch. 1. 9.
[c] ch. 2. 8.
[d] 2 Sam. 14. 2.
[e] Judg. 19. 6, 9, 22. 2 Sam. 13. 28. Esth. 1. 10.

[1] Heb. *shame her not.*
[2] Or, *one that hath right to redeem.*
[3] Or, *fall upon thee.*
[4] Or, *lift up the clothes that are on his feet.*

---

17. *and beat out that she had gleaned*] Viz. with a stick, as the word implies (cp. Deut. xxiv. 20; Isai. xxvii. 12). This method is still commonly practised. Ruth gleaned enough to support herself and her mother-in-law for five days (Ex. xvi. 16).

20. *Blessed be he of the* LORD, &c.] We may gather from Naomi's allusion to the dead that both her husband and son had been faithful servants of Jehovah, the God of Israel. His kindness to the dead consisted in raising up (as Naomi hoped) an heir to perpetuate the name; and, in general, in His care for their widows.

one of our next kinsmen] The word here is GOEL, the *redeemer*, who had the right (1) of redeeming the inheritance of the person; (2) of marrying the widow; (3) of avenging the death. (See Levit. xxv. 25–31, 47–55; Deut. xxv. 5-10; xix. 1-13.) As these rights belonged to the next of kin, GOEL came to mean the nearest kinsman.

III. **2.** *behold, he winnoweth barley*, &c.] The simple manners of Boaz and his times are here before us. This "mighty man of wealth" assists personally in the winnowing of his barley, which lies in a great heap on the floor (*v.* 15), and sleeps in the open threshing-floor to protect his grain from depredation.

to-night] For the sake of the breeze which springs up at sunset, and greatly facilitates the cleansing of the corn tossed up across the wind.

4. *uncover his feet*] Rather, "**the place of his feet**;" the foot of his bed, as we should say. So also *vv.* 7, 8.

he went to lie down at the end of the heap of corn: and she
8 came softly, and uncovered his feet, and laid her down. And it
came to pass at midnight, that the man was afraid, and [1]turned
9 himself: and, behold, a woman lay at his feet. And he said,
Who *art* thou? And she answered, I *am* Ruth thine handmaid:
[f]spread therefore thy skirt over thine handmaid; for thou *art* [f] Ezek. 16. 8.
10 [2][g]a near kinsman. And he said, [h]Blessed *be* thou of the LORD, [g] ch. 2. 20. & ver. 12.
my daughter: *for* thou hast shewed more kindness in the latter [h] ch. 2. 20.
end than [i]at the beginning, inasmuch as thou followedst not [i] ch. 1. 8.
11 young men, whether poor or rich. And now, my daughter, fear
not; I will do to thee all that thou requirest: for all the [3]city of
12 my people doth know that thou *art* [k]a virtuous woman. And [k] Prov. 12. 4.
now it is true that I *am thy* [l]near kinsman: howbeit [m]there is a [l] ver. 9.
13 kinsman nearer than I. Tarry this night, and it shall be in the [m] ch. 4. 1.
morning, *that* if he will [n]perform unto thee the part of a kins- [n] Deut. 25. 5.
man, well; let him do the kinsman's part: but if he will not do ch. 4. 5.
the part of a kinsman to thee, then I will do the part of a kins- Matt. 22. 24.
man to thee, [o]*as* the LORD liveth: lie down until the morning. [o] Judg. 8. 19.
14 ¶ And she lay at his feet until the morning: and she rose up be- Jer. 4. 2.
fore one could know another. And he said, [p]Let it not be known [p] Rom. 12. 17.
15 that a woman came into the floor. Also he said, Bring the [4]vail & 14. 16.
that *thou hast* upon thee, and hold it. And when she held it, 1 Cor. 10. 32.
he measured six *measures* of barley, and laid *it* on her: and she 2 Cor. 8. 21.
16 went into the city. And when she came to her mother in law, 1 Thes. 5. 22.
she said, Who *art* thou, my daughter? And she told her all
17 that the man had done to her. And she said, These six *measures*
of barley gave he me; for he said to me, Go not empty unto thy
18 mother in law. Then said she, [q]Sit still, my daughter, until [q] Ps. 37. 3, 5.
thou know how the matter will fall: for the man will not be in
rest, until he have finished the thing this day.
CHAP. 4. THEN went Boaz up to the gate, and sat him down there:
and, behold, [a]the kinsman of whom Boaz spake came by; unto [a] ch. 3. 12.
whom he said, Ho, such a one! turn aside, sit down here. And
2 he turned aside, and sat down. And he took ten men of [b]the [b] 1 Kin. 21. 8.
elders of the city, and said, Sit ye down here. And they sat Prov. 31. 23.

[1] Or, *took hold on.*
[2] Or, *one that hath right to redeem.*
[3] Heb. *gate.*
[4] Or, *sheet,* or, *apron.*

---

8. *turned himself*] Rather, "**bent forward,**" so as to feel what it was which was at his feet. The same word is translated "took hold of," in Judg. xvi. 29.

9. *spread thy skirt,* &c.] The phrase indicates receiving and acknowledging her as a wife.

10. *thou hast shewed more kindness,* &c.] Lit., "**Thou hast made thy last kindness better than the first.**" Her last kindness was her willingness to accept Boaz for her husband, advanced in years as he was.

12, 13. By "kinsman," understand the *goel* (ii. 20 note).

15. *the vail*] Quite a different word from that rendered *vail,* in Gen. xxxviii. 14. It seems rather to mean a kind of loose **cloak,** worn over the ordinary dress (see marg.).

six measures] *i.e.* six seahs, in all two ephahs, twice as much as she gleaned (ii. 17), and a heavy load to carry; for which reason *he laid it on her,* probably placed it on her head. It is well known that women can carry great weights when duly poised on the head.

and she went into the city] The Hebrew has "**he went,**" viz. Boaz, where accordingly we find him (iv. 1).

16. *who art thou, my daughter?*] In the dim twilight (*v.* 14) her mother was not sure at first who the young woman was, who sought admittance into the house.

IV. 1. The gate is the place of concourse, of business, and of justice in Oriental cities (see Judg. xix. 15 note; Gen. xxxiv. 20; Deut. xvi. 18).

Ho, such a one!] Indicating that the name of the kinsman was either unknown or purposely concealed (1 Sam. xxi. 2; 2 K. vi. 8).

2. Every city was governed by elders (see Deut. xix. 12; Judg. viii. 14). For the number *ten,* cp. Ex. xviii. 25. Probably the presence of, at least, ten elders was

3 down. And he said unto the kinsman, Naomi, that is come
again out of the country of Moab, selleth a parcel of land, which
4 *was* our brother Elimelech's: and [1]I thought to advertise thee,
saying, [c]Buy *it* [d]before the inhabitants, and before the elders of
my people. If thou wilt redeem *it*, redeem *it*: but if thou wilt
not redeem *it*, *then* tell me, that I may know: [e]for *there is*
none to redeem *it* beside thee; and I *am* after thee. And he
5 said, I will redeem *it*. Then said Boaz, What day thou buyest
the field of the hand of Naomi, thou must buy *it* also of Ruth
the Moabitess, the wife of the dead, [f]to raise up the name of
6 the dead upon his inheritance. [g]And the kinsman said, I
cannot redeem *it* for myself, lest I mar mine own inheritance:
redeem thou my right to thyself; for I cannot redeem *it*.
7 [h]Now this *was the manner* in former time in Israel concerning
redeeming and concerning changing, for to confirm all things;
a man plucked off his shoe, and gave *it* to his neighbour: and
8 this *was* a testimony in Israel. Therefore the kinsman said
9 unto Boaz, Buy *it* for thee. So he drew off his shoe. ¶ And
Boaz said unto the elders, and *unto* all the people, Ye *are* witnesses this day, that I have bought all that *was* Elimelech's,
and all that *was* Chilion's and Mahlon's, of the hand of Naomi.
10 Moreover Ruth the Moabitess, the wife of Mahlon, have I purchased to be my wife, to raise up the name of the dead upon his
inheritance, [i]that the name of the dead be not cut off from
among his brethren, and from the gate of his place: ye *are* wit-
11 nesses this day. And all the people that *were* in the gate, and

[c] Jer. 32. 7.
[d] Gen. 23.18.
[e] Lev. 25. 25.
[f] Gen. 38. 8. Deut. 25. 5. ch. 3. 13. Matt. 22. 24.
[g] ch. 3. 12.
[h] Deut. 25. 7, 9.
[i] Deut. 25. 6.

[1] Heb. *I said I will reveal* in *thine ear.*

---

necessary to make a lawful public assembly, as among modern Jews *ten* are necessary to constitute a synagogue.

3. According to the law (Levit. xxv. 25-28), if any Israelite, through poverty, would sell his possession, the next of kin (the *goel*) had a right to redeem it by paying the value of the number of years remaining till the jubilee (see marg. ref.). This right Boaz advertises the *goel* of, so as to give him the option which the law secured to him of redeeming "our brother Elimelech's" land, *i.e.* our kinsman's, according to the common use of the term *brother*, for near relation (see Gen. xiii. 8, xxiv. 27; Lev. xxv. 25; Num. xxvii. 4; Judg. ix. 1).

4. See marg.; a phrase explained by the act of removing the end of the turban, or the hair, in order to whisper in the ear (see 1 Sam. ix. 15: 2 Sam. vii. 27).

5. Observe the action of the law of Levirate. Had there been no one interested but Naomi, she would have sold the land unclogged by any condition, the law of Levirate having no existence in her case. But there was a young widow upon whom the possession of the land would devolve at Naomi's death, and who already had a right of partnership in it, and the law of Levirate did apply in her case. It was, therefore, the duty of the *goel* to marry her and raise up seed to his brother, *i.e.* his kinsman. And he could not exercise his right of redeeming the land, unless he was willing at the same time to fulfil his obligations to the deceased by marrying the widow. This he was unwilling to do.

6. *I mar mine own inheritance*] The meaning of these words is doubtful. Some explain them by saying that the *goel* had a wife and children already, and would not introduce strife into his family. Others think that there was a risk (which he would not incur) of the *goel's* own name being blotted out from his inheritance (*v.* 10). Others take the word translated *mar* in a sense of *wasting* or *spending*. If he had to find the purchase-money, and support Naomi and Ruth, his own fortune would be broken down, if, as is likely, he was a man of slender means. Boaz, being "a mighty man of wealth," could afford this.

redeem thou my right, &c.] Literally, *redeem my redemption*—perform that act of redemption which properly belongs to me, but which I cannot perform.

7. *in former time in Israel*] Showing that the custom was obsolete in the writer's days. The letter of the law (see marg. ref.) was not strictly followed. It was thought sufficient for the man to pull off his own shoe and give it to the man to whom he ceded his right, in the presence of the elders of his city.

11. See marg. There is something of a poetical turn in this speech of the elders,

the elders, said, *We are* witnesses. [k]The LORD make the woman
that is come into thine house like Rachel and like Leah, which
two did [l]build the house of Israel: and [1]do thou worthily in
12 [m]Ephratah, and [2]be famous in Beth-lehem: and let thy house
be like the house of Pharez, [n]whom Tamar bare unto Judah, of
[o]the seed which the LORD shall give thee of this young woman.
13 ¶ So Boaz [p]took Ruth, and she was his wife: and when he went
in unto her, [q]the LORD gave her conception, and she bare a son.
14 And [r]the women said unto Naomi, Blessed *be* the LORD, which
hath not [3]left thee this day without a [4]kinsman, that his name
15 may be famous in Israel. And he shall be unto thee a restorer
of *thy* life, and [5]a nourisher of [6]thine old age: for thy daughter
in law, which loveth thee, which is [s]better to thee than seven
16 sons, hath born him. And Naomi took the child, and laid it in
17 her bosom, and became nurse unto it. [t]And the women her
neighbours gave it a name, saying, There is a son born to
Naomi; and they called his name Obed: he *is* the father of
18 Jesse, the father of David. ¶ Now these *are* the generations of
19 Pharez: [u]Pharez begat Hezron, and Hezron begat Ram, and
20 Ram begat Amminadab, and Amminadab begat [x]Nahshon, and
21 Nahshon begat [y][7]Salmon, and Salmon begat Boaz, and Boaz
22 begat Obed, and Obed begat Jesse, and Jesse begat [z]David.

[k] Ps. 127. 3. & 128. 3.
[l] Deut. 25. 9.
[m] Gen. 35. 16, 19.
[n] Gen. 38.29. 1 Chr. 2. 4. Matt. 1. 3.
[o] 1 Sam. 2. 20.
[p] ch. 3. 11.
[q] Gen. 29.31. & 33. 5.
[r] Luke 1. 58. Rom. 12. 15.
[s] 1 Sam. 1. 8.
[t] Luke 1. 58, 59.
[u] 1 Chr. 2. 4, &c. Matt. 1. 3.
[x] Num. 1. 7.
[y] Matt. 1. 4.
[z] 1 Chr. 2.15. Matt. 1. 6.

1 Or, *get thee riches*, or, *power*.
2 Heb. *proclaim* thy *name*.
3 Heb. *caused to cease unto thee*.
4 Or, *redeemer*.
5 Heb. *to nourish*, Gen. 45. 11. Ps. 55. 22.
6 Heb. *thy gray hairs*.
7 Or, *Salmah*.

---

and something prophetic in the blessing pronounced by them. It is unique and obscure. The Greek Version is unintelligible. Jerome seems to have had a slightly different reading, since he applies both clauses to Ruth. "May she be a pattern of virtue in Ephratah, and have a name famous in Bethlehem." The meaning of "be famous" seems to be, *Get thyself a name which shall be celebrated in Bethlehem*, as the head of a powerful and illustrious house: literally it is, *proclaim a name*, *i.e.* cause others to proclaim thy name, as in *v.* 14.

14. *without a kinsman*] *i.e.* Boaz, not the infant Obed.

17. *Obed*] *i.e. serving*, with allusion to the service of love and duty which he would render to his grandmother Naomi.

18. It is probable that there was a family-book for the house of Pharez, in which their genealogies were preserved, and important bits of history were recorded; and that the book of Ruth was compiled from it. (See Gen. ii. 4 note.)

21. *Salmon begat Boaz*] St. Matthew has preserved the additional interesting information that the mother of Boaz was Rahab (Josh. ii., vi.). It is possible that the circumstance that the mother of Boaz was a Canaanite may have made him less indisposed to marry Ruth the Moabitess. As regards the whole genealogy in *vv.* 18-22, it should be remarked that it occurs four times in Scripture, viz. here, 1 Chr. ii. 10-12; Matt. i. 3-6; and Luke iii. 32, 33, and is of course of singular importance as being the genealogy of our Lord. One or two difficulties in it still remain unsolved.